Management

8th Edition

DON HELLRIEGEL

Lowry Mays College and Graduate School of Business
Texas A&M University

SUSAN E. JACKSON

School of Management and Labor Relations
Rutgers University

JOHN W. SLOCUM, JR.

Edwin L. Cox School of Business
Southern Methodist University

South-Western College Publishing

an International Thomson Publishing company I(T)P®

Cincinnati • Albany • Boston • Detroit • Johannesburg • London • Madrid • Melbourne • Mexico City
New York • Pacific Grove • San Francisco • Scottsdale • Singapore • Tokyo • Toronto

Acquisitions Editor: John Szilagyi
Developmental Editor: Judith O'Neill
Production Editor: Sandra Gangelhoff
Marketing Manager: Sarah Woelfel
Manufacturing Coordinator: Sue Kirven
Copyeditor: Jerrold A. Moore
Production House: WordCrafters Editorial Services, Inc.
Photo Research: Feldmann & Associates
Internal Design: Ann Small/A Small Design Studio
Cover Design: Tin Box Studio, Cincinnati, Ohio
Cover Photography: Copyright 1996 Yoshiki Komai/Photonica

3 4 5 6 7 8 9 VH 6 5 4 3 2 1 0 9

Library of Congress Cataloging-in-Publication Data

Hellriegel, Don.
    Management / Don Hellriegel, Susan E. Jackson, John W. Slocum, Jr.
    — 8th ed.
        p. cm.
    Includes bibliographical references and index.
    ISBN 0-538-87672-7
    1. Management.   I. Jackson, Susan E.   II. Slocum, John W.
III. Title
HD31.H447   1999   98-23041
658.4—dc21   CIP

Printed in the United States of America.

I(T)P

International Thomson Publishing
South-Western College Publishing is an ITP Company.
The ITP trademark is used under license.

To Lois (DH), Randall (SEJ), and Gail (JWS)

Brief Contents

v

Contents

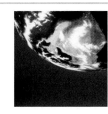

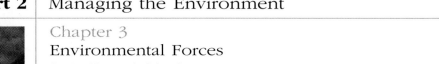

Part 2 | Managing the Environment

Chapter 3
Environmental Forces

Chapter 4

Global Considerations 110

Chapter 5

Entrepreneurs and Small-Business Owners 142

Chapter 6
Ethics and Corporate Social Responsibility   178

Part 3   Strategic Decision Making   215

Chapter 7
Planning and Strategy Formulation   216

Chapter 8
Fundamentals of Decision Making   254

Chapter 9
Planning and Decision Aids   284

Chapter 12

Human Resources Management 386

Chapter 16

Organizational Communication   538

Chapter 17

Groups and Teams in Organizations   574

Chapter 18
Organizational Cultures and Workforce Diversity 612

Part 6   Controlling and Evaluating   647

Chapter 19

Controlling in Organizations   648

Chapter 20

Information Management Technology   680

Preface

Management covers a lot of ground. Its focus ranges from understanding entire industries to making and implementing decisions to operating in foreign countries. It's leadership, corporate culture, business strategy, organization design, motivation, and ethics all rolled up into one. But, above all, it's supremely challenging and, we think, for that reason it's also great fun. We expect that students who read this book will learn a lot about management—about making a difference, about pulling together, about getting results—and have a good time doing it!

Like other aspects of business, effective management is the result of hard work. The truth is that successfully managing others is an enormously demanding task. As writers with lots of experience in both academic and professional settings, we demanded a lot from ourselves when we set out to revise *Management*. We worked hard to deliver a book that is fresh, engaging, and academically solid. We are confident that instructors and students alike will agree that we delivered.

With this edition of *Management,* we welcome Susan E. Jackson to our authorship team, who during the preparation of this text was at the Leonard N. Stern School of Business at New York University but now is at the School of Management and Labor Relations at Rutgers University.

We've taken full advantage of her special interests in the areas of developing human resources management systems, team staffing and development, workforce diversity, corporate cultures, and organizational change. Her insights and scholarship are reflected throughout the text.

As you will discover, *Management* copies no one else, yet pays homage to its past. With each succeeding edition, we've attempted to raise the bar. Although it will seem familiar and comfortable to past users in many ways, in other ways it will seem different. More than anything, though, this edition acknowledges the complexity of explaining what management is and what being managed by others is like. *Management* tells you what the most recent thinking is on various topics but quickly admits that, on many issues, definitive answers are elusive.

In terms of content and features, this book offers plenty, but, at its core, our approach is consistently constructive. We carefully developed six managerial competencies—self-management, strategic action, global awareness, teamwork, planning and administration, and communication—and have carefully woven examples of these competencies into every chapter. We chose these competencies after talking with hundreds of managers and believe that they are fundamental to managing in a variety of settings.

We were motivated by a desire to make life easier for both instructors and students by offering a wide variety of ancillary materials. In short, our ancillary package will assist teaching from the book and fully engaging students in learning about management. Details about supplements are included at the end of this preface, at South-Western's home page (www.swcollege.com), or by calling a South-Western/ITP sales representative at 1-800-423-0563.

We wrote *Management* and tailored its support package for use in introductory management classes taught anywhere in the university as well as in junior colleges. Although we recognize that other books and course packages are available for use in introductory management classes, here are four compelling reasons for using *Management.*

COMPELLING REACH

Students will really like this book. It's current and it will grab their interest through a variety of methods, including cases, the Internet, self-evaluation questionnaires, an attractive internal design, and sophisticated graphics. The examples will not only make discussions in and out of the classroom flow smoothly, but will also actually spark independent exploration. Students need to be challenged to go beyond their readings to think actively and interactively about the issues raised in them. *Management* does that.

We provide an in-depth examination of management fundamentals in lively, concise language designed for clarity and relevance. We don't beat around the bush, and we're not shy about challenging conventional management practices. Reading this book will be an engaging experience for students, and we sincerely believe that it will guide them well as they learn about management and build management competencies.

The markers of our commitment to student learning are easily identified throughout the text. Note the *Questions for Discussion* at the end of each chapter. They demand thoughtful analysis rather than mere regurgitation of material read. Exercises to Help Develop Your Managerial Competencies, Real-Time Case Analysis, and Video Cases are presented at the end of each chapter. They will help students put their learning to use in ways that guarantee that they take more away from the course than just a new and improved vocabulary and a general understanding of various management theories. In our opinion, *active learning* that requires students to approach problems intelligently and to use self-insight to gauge their responses to management issues is a tremendously powerful tool. The text compels students to actively engage in acquiring managerial competencies.

One of the most important hallmarks of pedagogy that adds value, excites students, and reinforces active learning centers on learning objectives. In *Management,* every chapter begins with a statement of *Learning Objectives,* and chapters are organized to deliver content that is responsive to each objective. Each objective is repeated in the text where content specific to that objective is covered, providing structure for self-testing and review. Every chapter ends with a *Summary* that distills that chapter's main points, and because summaries are also organized around the chapter's learning objectives, students can easily assess their mastery of learning goals.

COMPELLING FUNDAMENTALS

We fully expect to set the standard for content that merges the concerns of managers with the managerial competencies that foster excellence. No one can begin to appreciate the role of managers today or in the years ahead without a solid understanding of the competencies needed to manage. What are they? We believe there are six:

- self-management,

- strategic action,

- global awareness,

- teamwork,

- planning and administration, and

- communication.

These competencies can be learned through feedback and practice, but feedback often comes to students in bits and pieces. In *Management,* pieces of information that elsewhere are seldom related to a student's performance or to the performance of a team are linked into a meaningful whole. The payoff for students is that we've defined and clarified the competencies necessary for early successes in their careers. Throughout the book in a series of specially designed competency boxes, we present students with a variety of ways that they can assess their competencies right now and begin to develop their potential as effective managers.

Self-Management Competency. Today's successful manager knows that self-awareness is a crucial vantage point from which to view the operation of an organization and his or her role in that organization. Self-identification of strengths and developmental needs is an important first step in the process of learning to manage others. Our presentation of the self-management competency helps students identify their own strengths and developmental needs in leadership, motivation, ethics, and other areas through a series of experiential exercises and cases. Besides learning about their current strengths and developmental needs, students will gain an appreciation for the importance of continual self-assessment throughout their careers.

Strategic Action Competency. Our strategic action competency helps students learn how various managers craft distinctive strategies to guide their firms. Just as artists shape clay to form beautiful sculptures that symbolize important events, managers choose strategies that creatively link the best practices of their organizations. Developing broad strategies that can be translated into clear goals and practical action plans is one way that an organization can achieve a competitive advantage. To be sure, risk accompanies all strategic decisions; but the skillful manager acts to devise contingency plans to minimize it.

Global Awareness Competency. Effective managers must stay abreast of important global trends that have an impact on their organizations and understand the position of their organizations in global markets. Our global awareness competency challenges students to perceive the impact of global trends on an organization's plans and growth. Recognizing opportunities for global expansion and operating in foreign countries demand that students question their own leadership styles, values, and many traditional Western management practices. The main factors for successfully doing business internationally are being sensitive to key cultural differences in countries in which an organization operates and understanding the consequences of cultural differences for the organization.

Teamwork Competency. The ability to cultivate an active network of relationships and to relate well to others is the focus of our teamwork competency. Building solid relationships with others in an organization is crucial because managers must rely on others to support them in achieving organizational goals. As organizations rely more and more on teams, managers are being asked to staff teams and monitor their performance. The right combination of talents helps teams acquire the resources they need to be effective. Teamwork requires close collaboration and information sharing of unprecedented vigor. Managers can create a healthy environment by forming give-and-take relationships in which they strive to enhance understanding and mutual respect, acknowledge the needs and feelings of others, and productively manage conflict.

Planning and Administration Competency. An organization's design needs to be dynamic. What worked well in the past may no longer serve the needs of an organization or its customers. Effective managers regularly review and adjust the designs of their organizations to meet shifting internal and external needs and the changing competencies of employees. Work gets done when it is well planned, well coordinated, and well monitored. Managers need to push for setting clear and challenging goals, and, when problems arise, they need to step in to help solve them. However, tasks may be neglected when managers spend too much time dealing with trivial problems. Similarly, employees may waste time because of inadequate controls, poor guidance, and slow decision making. Through a series of examples, students will learn how effective managers use their planning and administration competency to create organizations that are increasingly responsive to customer demands while, at the same time, producing quality goods and services.

Communication Competency. The flow of information in an organization is its lifeblood. To maintain and improve the performance of an organization, information must freely flow upward, laterally, and downward. Our communication competency strengthens the foundation for successful management. It is so fundamental that managers sometimes forget its significance. Communication competency enables managers to lead others. They can't do so without being able to communicate their ideas well. Effective communication includes listening, informing others, fostering open channels, and negotiating with others. Through a series of cases and experiential exercises, students will experience the importance of sharing information with others and of developing a culture in which they and others openly share information. Mastering communication competency greatly expands a manager's influence.

COMPELLING FEATURES—EXPANDED AND ENHANCED

Every chapter of this new edition of *Management* contains features that make it more teachable, more readable, more *manageable* than ever before.

Learning Objectives and a Fully Integrated Learning System. The text and all major supplements are organized around learning objectives that form the basis of an easy-to-use integrated learning system. Every objective relates content from the text to all major supplements—*Study Guide, Test Bank,* and *Instructor's Manual*—delivering to instructors and students a fully integrated structure to teach and study from.

Chapter-Opening Previews. Every chapter opens with a current, real-world story that sets the stage for the topics to be presented in that chapter. These preview cases, which showcase organizations in the know and in the news, not only reinforce chapter concepts but also lead into the discussion and whet students' appetites for what is to come. In the preview for Chapter 1, for example, students read about Lew Platt, CEO of Hewlett-Packard, and the challenges he faces leading a high-tech organization and keeping long-standing organizational core values intact under increasingly stiff global competition. In Chapter 2, students read about how Levi Strauss, throughout its history, has striven to treat its employees and suppliers fairly. But the dilemmas it faces in its operations in Bangladesh and other foreign countries demands that the firm redouble its efforts. A sampling of other previews include

- *Kodak–Fuji Global Slugfest*, Chapter 4;

- *Can Patagonia Change the World*, Chapter 6;

- *Cirque du Soleil*, Chapter 12;

- *Katherine Hudson's View of Leadership*, Chapter 15; and

- *How FedEx Runs on Time*, Chapter 19

Dynamic Graphics. Ask any instructor or student what a management textbook should look like and you will get a consistent response: The graphics must be colorful, must reinforce chapter content, must be easy to read, and must be numerous. As you will see by quickly paging through *Management*, it more than measures up to this standard. Each figure and table is cited in the narrative and tied to the concept under discussion.

Competency Features. Every chapter in *Management* contains features set off in boxes that relate our managerial competencies to chapter content. These boxes aren't diversions unrelated to the text; rather, they provide information that is fully integrated with the text and can be easily integrated into classroom lectures. As appropriate, they challenge students to analyze and evaluate a related Web site. The boxes are for teaching, learning, and reinforcing chapter content. Questions in the *Test Bank* are provided for instructors who want to test material from this boxed material.

Let's take a look at some of these features that highlight the six managerial competencies. All condense current topics into a concise presentation. All relate to real organizations that students will immediately recognize. All strengthen our argument for the fundamental value of managerial competencies as an endlessly transferable and transformable set of knowledge and skills that managers must develop, use, and stretch if they are to excel. Many of the features draw on the Internet to aid learning.

Communication Competency

- *Black Belts Are Roaming at GE*, Chapter 1

- *Harley Hogs Ride Again*, Chapter 2

- *Training at Merrill Lynch*, Chapter 4

- *Joe Murphy at Community Grocers*, Chapter 6

- *Mark Anthony Hankins Gets Rich on Cheap Chic*, Chapter 15

- *Pizzera Uno's DSS*, Chapter 20

Planning and Administration Competency

- *Quality at KFC in Less Than Sixty Seconds*, Chapter 2

- *Continuous Improvement at Rubbermaid*, Chapter 8

- *Organizing for Effectiveness at NASA*, Chapter 10

- *Fighting Off Memory Loss*, Chapter 13

- *Goals for a Turnaround at Etec Systems*, Chapter 14

- *Holding Down Turnover at Chick-Fil-A*, Chapter 19

Strategic Action Competency

- *Chrysler: The Company That Isn't a Whole Company,* Chapter 1
- *A Turnaround at Encyclopedia Britannica,* Chapter 7
- *Starbucks Coffee,* Chapter 10
- *Continental's Blueprint for Success,* Chapter 13
- *Signicast Creates a Team-Based Learning Organization,* Chapter 17
- *Charles Schwab's Extranet,* Chapter 20

Self-Management Competency

- *Do You Have the Right Stuff to Be an Entrepreneur?* Chapter 5
- *What Are Your Managerial Values?* Chapter 6
- *How Innovative Are You?* Chapter 13
- *What's Your Leadership Style?* Chapter 15
- *Diversity Knowledge Quiz,* Chapter 18
- *Brae Landon Adapts,* Chapter 21

Global Awareness Competency

- *Peerless Clothing of Montreal,* Chapter 4
- *The Chinese Family Enterprise,* Chapter 5
- *Caux Round Table on Ethics,* Chapter 6
- *Financing Around the Globe with Citicorp,* Chapter 7
- *The Sun Never Sets at Black & Decker,* Chapter 11
- *Culture Clash at Pharmacia and Upjohn,* Chapter 18

Teamwork Competency

- *Edy's Grand Ice Cream Has It Down Cold,* Chapter 2
- *Operating Multicultural Teams in Indonesia,* Chapter 4
- *Self-Managed Teams at British Petroleum,* Chapter 12
- *Virtual Teams at IBM,* Chapter 13
- *The Power of Mary Kay Ash,* Chapter 16
- *Hughes's Nonteam/Team Approach,* Chapter 20

Key Terms. Key terms appear in boldface in the text, with definitions in the margins, making it easy for students to check their understanding of important terms and concepts. A complete glossary is included as an end-of-book appendix.

Internet Sites. In keeping with developing students' managerial competencies, Web sites in each chapter are tied to organizations featured in the text. Questions prompt students to explore, explain, describe, compare, contrast, summarize, and analyze a management practice in a real-world context online. Internet applications may be assigned as individual or team activities. They are also excellent discussion starters. An end-of-book Internet appendix containing all URLs cited in the text puts valuable online resources at the instructors' and students' fingertips and allows instructors to develop new Internet-based assignments easily and quickly.

Chapter Summaries. Every chapter ends with a *Summary* that distills that chapter's main points. Because these summaries are organized around the chapter's learning objectives, students can easily assess their mastery of learning goals.

Questions for Discussion. Every chapter includes discussion questions that require students to apply, analyze, discover, and rethink important chapter concepts. Above all, these questions build students' communication competencies because they ask for well–thought out, well-presented responses.

Exercises to Help You Develop Your Managerial Competencies. These unique sets of exercises are designed primarily to help students develop their managerial competencies. At the same time, they encourage students to make extensive use of the Internet as part of the learning process. Because the focus of these exercises is hands-on in nature, students will spend time accessing home pages, using the Web site addresses provided, and evaluating what they find. Although these applications *test and assess* each student's level of managerial competencies, their real focus is on *improving* students' competencies. Suggested answers to all exercises can be found in the *Instructor's Manual*.

Real-Time Case Analysis. At the end of each chapter is a brief but substantive case study that enables students to apply chapter concepts to a real organization's problems—to analyze, evaluate, and make recommendations. As students will discover, these cases cover a wide variety of organizations (Iams Pet Food, Microsoft, Estée Lauder, Eddie Bauer, Kinko's, Disney, and Siemens Business Communications Systems, among others), providing ample opportunities to sharpen problem-solving skills. Internet addresses are provided so that students can update the materials presented in the case and present real-time solutions to the questions posed.

Video Cases. *Prepared by Ross Stapleton-Gray, of Georgetown University's Communication, Culture, and Technology program, and President, TeleDiplomacy, Inc., a consulting firm that specializes in issues of diplomacy and international relations in the information age.* Video cases appear at the end of every chapter to add a visual dimension to case analysis. However, the real strength of these cases is their usefulness as benchmarks against which students can measure their understanding of what managers and companies do. Videos were built around various organizations (Yahoo!, Southwest Airlines, the Body Shop, UPS, and The World Gym, to name a few). The range of issues addressed in the videos and the accompanying cases should provoke interesting analyses. Each case ends with a series of on-the-Web questions designed to get students to extend their explorations into cyberspace.

COMPELLINGLY COMPREHENSIVE

Students must appreciate the full range of management tools available to them and work to develop their management competencies if they are to be effective in helping create the types of organizations that will be needed in the years ahead. We make this point in Part 1 and return to it again and again in each of the text's six parts. The accompanying figure illustrates the structure of our text and conveys our beliefs about the dynamic nature of management.

Part 1, Overview of Management, begins with a comprehensive treatment of the competencies that students must master to become successful managers. While emphasizing these competencies, we provide thorough coverage of past management principles and practices that have bearing on current management thinking and action.

In Part 2, Managing the Environment, we address the economic, demographic, cultural, competitive, technological, political, legal, global, and ethical forces that shape and influence an organization's position in the world. In response to those who have used our book, we give new emphasis to the challenges facing entrepreneurs and small-business owners.

In Part 3, Strategic Decision Making, we combine the essentials of planning and decision-making aids into one chapter, Chapter 9. This unique and comprehensive chapter vividly illustrates the key tools that influence a manager's planning and decision-making functions.

In Part 4, Organizing, we address organizational innovation and change. Students will learn how organizations manage their resources, infrastructures, and employees in changing markets and how time consuming and emotionally challenging that changing an organization is. The role each competency plays in the change process is also highlighted.

Part 5, Leading, underwent extensive revision. We added a unique chapter on organizational cultures and workforce diversity (Chapter 18) that focuses on building cultures in light of today's diverse workforces. Diversity refers to a broad range of differences among people in terms of race, gender, age, cultural heritage, lifestyle, and other factors. Building a culture that can maximize organizational functioning requires managers to understand and effectively utilize these differences.

Part 6, Controlling and Evaluating, focuses on systems of control and evaluation and their application to employees. Measuring employee work against defined standards is part of any manager's control function. Because the quality of an end product or service depends on a commitment to quality at every step in a production process, we close the book with a discussion of various operations management and management information systems that can help ensure quality. A quality revolution is sweeping organizations throughout the world. Although the desire for quality isn't new to many organizations, success in delivering it is decidedly mixed.

SUPPORT MATERIALS

We've designed a comprehensive set of support materials to guide instructors and students through not just the basics, but also the subtler issues surrounding the principles of management.

Instructor's Manual. *Prepared by Lynn Bowes-Sperry and Paula S. Daly, of James Madison University.* Available in print or on disk, the *Instructor's Manual* emphasizes our integrated learning system. Each chapter includes learning objectives, outlines annotated with additional examples and other lecture-enhancing stories and facts, cross-references to text figures (also available as transparencies) and to an expanded set of PowerPoint slides, and complete solutions to all end-of-chapter questions, activities, cases, and video cases.

Study Guide. *Prepared by Elizabeth Cameron, of Alma College.* Designed from a student's perspective, the value-laden *Study Guide* comes with all the tools necessary to maximize results on exams and in class. Chapter outlines and all exam-preparation questions are organized around the text's learning objectives so that students can isolate material that is most troublesome to them and focus on it before moving ahead. Answers, along with explicit rationales for the answers, are provided for all self-tests.

Test Bank. *Prepared by Bert Morrow, of Mississippi State University.* Also organized around the text's learning objectives, the *Test Bank* is available to instructors in print and in a computerized Windows-compatible format on disk. Tables at the beginning of each chapter classify each question according to type, difficulty level, and learning objective so that the instructor can create exams at the appropriate level, with the appropriate mix of question types. Special questions aimed at competency feature content are designated throughout. The *Test Bank* contains more than 2,900 true/false, multiple-choice, and essay questions.

Transparencies. A full set of acetate transparencies is provided free to adopters of *Management* to enhance classroom presentations. All transparencies are tied to lecture outlines presented in the *Instructor's Manual.*

PowerPoint Presentation Software. *Prepared in conjunction with the* Instructor's Manual *by Lynn Bowes-Sperry of James Madison University.* More than 200 full-color images supplement course content and extend it through slides drawn from relevant material not available in the text. Commentaries on all slides appear in the *Instructor's Manual* and provide additional background for lectures.

Videos. Our package includes twenty-one videos that bring action-based insights right into the classroom. Organizations featured include Dayton-Hudson, Tom's of Maine, Yahoo!, the World Gym (San Francisco), and Archway Cookies. These videos frame management issues in such a way that students must apply some aspect of chapter content to their analysis of the issues.

ACKNOWLEDGMENTS

We give special thanks to A. Benton Cocanougher, Dean of the Lowry Mays College and Graduate School of Business, at Texas A&M University; to Dean Al Niemi, Robin Pinkley, Head of the Organizational Behavior and Business Policy Department, Don VandeWalle, and David Lei, all of Southern Methodist University, for their personal support and encouragement; and to George Daly, Dean of the Stern School of Business, and Ari Ginsberg, Head of the Department of Management, at New York University. They created an environment that made possible completion of this project.

For their outstanding help with the many essential tasks involved in manuscript preparation and review, we express our deep gratitude to Argie Butler and Victoria Kohler of Texas A&M University and to Billie Boyd of Southern Methodist University. Their professionalism and dedication were central to the project from the very beginning to the submission of the last element.

In addition we are grateful to Ross Stapleton-Gray (Georgetown University), who wrote the video cases and their accompanying notes; and to Jerrold A. Moore, our copyeditor, whose superb skill enhanced the flow and readability of the manuscript.

Thanks also go to our excellent team of ancillary authors. They worked extremely hard to include everything necessary, exercised their creativity in developing the extras that make their ancillaries special, and contributed to the team effort of implementing the integrated learning system. They are:

Lynn Bowes-Sperry and Paula S. Daly
James Madison University
Instructor's Manual
PowerPoint Presentation Software

Bert Morrow
Mississippi State University
Test Bank

Elizabeth A. Cameron
Alma College
Study Guide

Working with all of these contributors to ensure compatibility with text material was a real pleasure.

Our colleagues and friends at Texas A&M University, Southern Methodist University, and New York University have created the environment that nurtures our continuous professional development. We thank them. We are grateful to our families for their empathy and understanding in letting us devote evenings and weekends on our authors' islands for more than a year. With the completion of this text, we look forward to having more time with our families.

Many reviewers made insightful comments on one or more of the chapters. Although there were some differences among them as to what to include, modify, or delete, their comments and suggestions resulted in substantial improvements. We are grateful to the following individuals for sharing their professional insights and suggestions.

Gemmy Allen
Mountain View College

William Bachman
Adrian College

Robert J. Bartel
King College

Lee BeLovarac
Mercyhurst College

Santanu Borah
University of North Alabama

F. R. Bosch
Snow College

Grady L. Butler
Jacksonville State University

Roosevelt D. Butler
Trenton State College

Jane Byrd
University of Mobile

S. A. Carson
Sue Bennett College

Bonnie Chavez
Santa Barbara City College

N. Christensen
Guilford College

Pam Crawford
Montana State University

Charles P. Duffy
Iona College

Kyle Dundon
Murray State College

Regina Eisenbach
California State University-San Marcos

Dan Farrell
Western Michigan University

Bonnie F. Fremgen
University of Notre Dame

Eliezer Geisler
University of Wisconsin-Whitewater

Gregory Green
Suomi College

Sandra Hanner
Meredith College

Carnella Hardin
Glendale College

Missy Hartman
Kansas Newman College

Harriet Kandelman
Barat College

Joan Keeley
Washington State University

George Kelley
Erie Community College

Mary Khalili
Oklahoma City University

Ronald A. Klocke
Mankato State University

Ray Lamanna
Berkeley College

Yet Mee Lim
Alabama State University

Thomas W. Lloyd
Westmoreland County Community College

Robert L. McChesney
McKendree College

James McHugh
St. Louis Community College

Anna McLeod
Kansas Newman College

David Meier
Thomas More College

Carl Meskimen
Sinclair Community College

Marlene Moody
Carroll College

Anthony Muiderman
Hope College

M. James Nead
Vincennes University

Lucy Newton
Berry College

Diana Page
University of West Florida

Philip Patton
Northwestern College

Monique Pelletier
San Francisco State University

Hannah H. Rothstein
Bernard Baruch College

John T. Samaras
University of Central Oklahoma

Charles H. Schneider
Molloy College

Cynthia Simerly
Lakeland Community College

Donald G. Sluti
University of Nebraska-Kearney

Robert Smith
Kent State University

Craig Tunwall
Ithaca College

Ted Valvoda
Lakeland Community College

John Wallace
Marshall University

Rod Walter
Western Illinois University

Dennis R. Williams
Pennsylvania College of Technology

Johnnie Williams
Alabama A&M University

Robert A. Zauder
Shaw University

Thomas W. Zimmerer
East Tennessee State University

Don Hellriegel
Texas A&M University

Susan E. Jackson
Rutgers—The State University of New Jersey

John W. Slocum
Southern Methodist University

About the Authors

DON HELLRIEGEL

Don Hellriegel is Professor of Management and holds the Bennett Chair in Business Administration at Texas A&M University. He currently serves as the Executive Associate Dean in the Lowry Mays College and Graduate School of Business. He received his B.S. and M.B.A. from Kent State University and his Ph.D. from the University of Washington. Dr. Hellriegel has been a member of the faculty at Texas A&M since 1975 and has served on the faculties of the Pennsylvania State University and the University of Colorado.

His research interests include interorganizational relationships, corporate venturing, effect of organizational environments, managerial cognitive styles, and organizational innovation and strategic management processes. His research has been published in a number of leading journals.

Professor Hellriegel served as Vice President and Program Chair of the Academy of Management (1986), President Elect (1987), President (1988), and Past President (1989). He served a term as Editor of the *Academy of Management Review* and served as a member of the Board of Governors of the Academy of Management (1979–1981); (1982–1989). Dr. Hellriegel has occupied many other leadership roles, among which include President, Eastern Academy of Management; Division Chair, Organization and Management Theory Division; President, Brazos County United Way; Co-Consulting Editor, West Series in Management; Head (1976–1980 and 1989–1994), Department of Management (TAMU); Interim Dean, College of Business Administration (TAMU); and Interim Executive Vice Chancellor (TAMUS).

He has consulted with a variety of groups and organizations, including—among others—3DI, Sun Ship Building, Penn Mutual Life Insurance, Texas A&M University System, Ministry of Industry and Commerce (Nation of Kuwait), Ministry of Agriculture (Nation of Dominican Republic), American Assembly of Collegiate Schools of Business, and Texas Innovation Group.

SUSAN E. JACKSON

Susan E. Jackson was Professor of Management and Organizational Behavior at the Stern School of Business, New York University during the preparation of this text. Currently, she is at the School of Management and Labor Relations at Rutgers University. She has also taught on the faculties of the University of Michigan, the University of Maryland, and Ecole des Hautes Etudes Commerciales, France. She received her B.A. in psychology and sociology from the University of Minnesota and her Ph.D. in organizational psychology from the University of California, Berkeley.

Her primary areas of expertise are the strategic management of human resources and organizational behavior; special interests include executive selection and top-management team development, workforce diversity, and the design of human resource management systems to support business imperatives. She has authored or co-authored over 100 articles and six books on these and related topics.

In addition to her university activities, Professor Jackson has held numerous positions in professional societies. In the Academy of Management, she has served as Editor of the *Academy of Management Review,* a journal devoted to the publication of scholarly reviews and theory development. She has served as President of the Academy of Management's Division of Organizational Behavior and has served as a member of the Board of Governors for the Academy of Management and currently serves as a member of the Board of Governors for the Center for Creative

Leadership. She is a Fellow of the American Psychological Association and a Fellow of the Society for Industrial and Organizational Psychology, where she served as a member of the Executive Committee for several years. Professor Jackson's consulting activities have included organizations such as General Electric, American Express, Merrill Lynch, the University of California, and the American Assembly of Collegiate Schools of Business.

JOHN W. SLOCUM, JR.

John Slocum holds the O. Paul Corley Professorship in Organizational Behavior at the Edwin L. Cox School of Business, Southern Methodist University, and is the Executive Director, Center for Global Leadership. He has also taught on the faculties of the University of Washington, the Ohio State University, the Pennsylvania State University, and the International University of Japan. He holds a B.B.A. from Westminster College, an M.B.A. from Kent State University, and a Ph.D. in organizational behavior from the University of Washington.

Professor Slocum has held a number of positions in professional societies. He was elected as a Fellow to the Academy of Management in 1976 for his outstanding contributions to the profession of management and as a Fellow to the Decision Sciences Institute in 1984 for his research in behavioral decision theory. He was awarded the Alumni Citation for Professional Accomplishment by Westminster College and both the Nicolas Salgo and the Rotunda Outstanding Teaching awards from SMU. He served as President of the Eastern Academy of Management in 1973. From 1975–1986, he served as a member of the Board of Governors, Academy of Management. From 1979–1981, he served as Editor of the *Academy of Management Journal*. In 1983–1984, he served as 39th President of the 8,500-member Academy and as Chairman of the Board of Governors of that organization. Currently, he serves as Associate Editor of *Organizational Dynamics* and Co-Editor of the *Journal of World Business*.

Professor Slocum has served as a consultant to such organizations as Mellon National Bank, ARAMARK, Corning Glass Works, Fort Worth Museum of Science and History, Pier 1, Henry C. Beck Company, Kodak, Price Waterhouse, Hershey Foods, Mack Trucks, Celanese, General Telephone and Electric, NASA, Southland Corporation, Transnational Trucks, and Brooklyn Union

PART 1

An Overview of Management

Chapter

1

Managing in a Dynamic Environment

LEARNING OBJECTIVES

AFTER STUDYING THIS CHAPTER YOU SHOULD BE ABLE TO:

1. DEFINE MANAGERS AND MANAGEMENT.

2. DESCRIBE WHAT MANAGERS DO.

3. UNDERSTAND THE COMPETENCIES USED IN MANAGERIAL WORK AND BEGIN TO PRACTICE THEM.

4. DESCRIBE THE CHANGING CONTEXT OF MANAGERIAL WORK.

Outline

Managing at Hewlett-Packard

When Lewis Platt took the reins from John Young, long-time CEO at Hewlett-Packard (HP) in 1992, many outsiders assumed that this successful high-technology company was going to maintain the status quo. Founded in 1939 by two twenty-six-year-old engineers, its first products included shock machines for weight reduction, bowling alley sensors, automatic urinal flushers, public address systems, and a variety of other products that can be loosely described as measurement instruments and radio signaling equipment. By the time Platt took over as CEO, HP had evolved into a company best known for its laser printers and sophisticated calculators. In 1997, Hewlett-Packard further expanded the range of products it offered when it unveiled a family of digital photography products. Its activities now span the globe, generating annual revenues of $38.1 billion. More than 100,000 people in forty countries are now employed by HP, all striving to achieve its basic purpose: to create information products that accelerate the advancement of knowledge and improve the effectiveness of people in industry, engineering, science, medi-cine, and education. What role has Lewis Platt played in the company's success?

Platt works in an industry where advancement means continuous product innovation and the ability to form successful partnerships with other computing and telecommunication giants, such as Hitachi, IBM, and AT&T. One key to Platt's success was that, as a three-decade veteran of HP, he had a keen understanding of this industry. Of course, both the industry and the nature of HP had changed radically over the years, so Platt always had to learn and adapt. In the midst of such rapid change, innovation was the key to success. Platt knew this and was able to formulate and communicate a strategy that would energize employees yet could not be easily copied by competitors.

Like the company's founders, he understood that managing creative and innovative employees meant that HP needed a special kind of corporate culture. Employees now refer to that special culture as "The HP Way." Built on a foundation set in place long before the existence of modern computing technology, the following are the basic values that guide how Platt and all other HP managers behave toward employees around the world.

- We have trust and respect for individuals.
- We focus on a high level of achievement and contribution.
- We conduct our business with uncompromising integrity.
- We achieve our common objectives through teamwork.
- We encourage flexibility and innovation.

Amidst all the changes, Platt communicated his belief in the original core values that guided the company's founders.[1]

* * *

To learn more about Hewlett-Packard, visit the company's home page at

www.hp.com

MANAGERS AND MANAGEMENT

1

DEFINE MANAGERS AND MANAGEMENT

Effective managers such as Lewis Platt are essential to any organization's over-all success, regardless of whether it is a global giant or a small start-up enterprise. Indeed, having talented people is so important to the success of a business that *Fortune* magazine includes "the ability to attract, develop, and keep talented people" as one of the key factors used to establish its list of Most Admired Companies. Hewlett-Packard attracted Lew Platt and kept him for more than thirty years. During that time he developed several competencies that enabled him to perform effectively in his company's top managerial job.

MANAGERIAL COMPETENCIES

Clusters of knowledge, skills, behaviors, and attitudes that a manager needs to be effective in a wide range of managerial jobs and organizations.

Managerial competencies are sets of knowledge, skills, behaviors, and attitudes that a person needs to be effective in a wide range of managerial jobs and various types of organizations.[2] Later in this chapter, we describe these competencies in more detail. For now, you simply need to know that the term ***competency*** refers to combinations of knowledge, skills, behaviors, and attitudes that contribute to personal effectiveness.

People use many types of competencies in their everyday lives, including those they need to be effective in leisure activities, in personal relationships, at school, and in other aspects of their lives. In this book we focus on managerial competencies. Throughout the book, we emphasize the competencies that you will need for jobs that include managerial responsibility. Specifically, our goal is to help you develop six key managerial competencies:

- communication,

- planning and administration,

- teamwork,

- strategic action,

- global awareness, and

- self-management.[3]

As Figure 1.1 indicates, these six competencies are essential to managerial effectiveness. Later in this chapter we describe their dimensions in detail. For now, though, an overview of what is involved in applying them is sufficient. Table 1.1 identifies several important aspects of each key managerial competency. In practice, knowing where one competency begins and another ends is difficult. You would seldom rely on one at a time, so drawing sharp distinctions between them is valuable only for purposes of identification and description. Keeping these six managerial competencies firmly in mind will help you think about how the material you are studying can improve your performance in jobs that require you to use them.

WHAT IS AN ORGANIZATION?

Effective managers must pay attention to what goes on both inside and outside their organizations. Regardless of where their attention might be focused at any particular time, managers are part and parcel of organizational settings. Profit-oriented businesses are one type of organizational setting in which managers are found, but

| Figure 1.1 | A Model of Managerial Competencies |

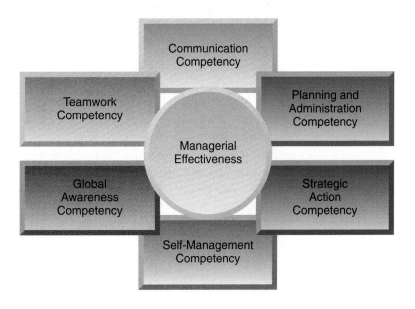

Communication Competency

- Informal communication

- Formal communication

- Negotiation

Planning and Administration Competency

- Information gathering, analysis, and problem solving

- Planning and organizing projects

- Time management

- Budgeting and financial management

Teamwork Competency

- Designing teams

- Creating a supportive environment

- Managing team dynamics

Strategic Action Competency

- Understanding the industry

- Understanding the organization

- Taking strategic actions

Global Awareness Competency

- Cultural knowledge and understanding

- Cultural openness and sensitivity

Self-Management Competency

- Integrity and ethical conduct

- Personal drive and resilience

- Balancing work and life issues

- Self-awareness and development

they aren't the only one. Undoubtedly, you could write your autobiography as a series of experiences with organizations such as hospitals, schools, museums, sports teams, stores, amusement parks, restaurants, orchestras, community groups and clubs, government agencies, and others. Some of these organizations were small, and others were large. Some were for-profit companies, and others were nonprofit organizations. Some offered products, some offered both products and services, and others offered only services. Some were well managed, and others struggled merely to survive.

ORGANIZATION

Any structured group of people brought together to achieve certain goals that the same individuals could not reach alone.

We refer to such a group of people as an ***organization*** because each has a structure and strives to achieve goals that individuals acting alone could not reach. All organizations strive to achieve specific goals, but they don't all have the same goals. For example, a goal at Southwest Airlines is to offer on-time service at the lowest prevailing price to increase its market share. A goal at Polaroid is to create innovative cameras, whereas at Minolta a goal is to produce high-quality lenses for cameras and other optical devices.

Regardless of an organization's specific goals, the job of managers is to help the organization achieve those goals. In this book, we look at managers in organizations of all types and sizes that have many different goals and many different ways of achieving their goals. Our primary purposes are to help you understand how managers accomplish their goals and to help you develop some of the managerial competencies that you will need to be effective in whatever types of organizations you find yourself. Many—indeed, most—of these competencies will be useful to you even if you never have a job with the word *manager* in the title.

WHAT IS A MANAGER?

MANAGER

A person who allocates human, material, and information resources in pursuit of an organization's goals.

We've been talking about managers for several pages, so it's time to clarify exactly what the term means. A ***manager*** is a person who plans, organizes, directs, and controls the allocation of human, material, financial, and information resources in pursuit of the organization's goals. The many different types of managers include department managers, product managers, account managers, plant managers, division managers, district managers, and task force managers. What they all have in common is responsibility for the efforts of a group of people who share a goal and access to resources that the group can use in pursuing its goal.

You don't have to be called a manager to be a manager. Some managers have unique and creative titles, such as chief knowledge officer (a person in charge of training and development) and chief information officer (a person in charge of information systems). People with the job titles of chief executive officer (CEO), president, managing director, supervisor, and coach also have the responsibility for helping a group of people achieve a common goal, so they too are managers.

Most employees contribute to organizations through their own individual work, not by directing other employees. Journalists, computer programmers, insurance agents, machine operators, newscasters, graphic designers, sales associates, stockbrokers, accountants, and lawyers are essential to achieving their organizations' goals, but many people with these job titles aren't managers.

What sets managers apart, if not their job titles? Simply put, the difference between managers and individual contributors is that *managers are evaluated on how well the people they direct do their jobs.* Consider Jennifer Laing, for example. In 1997, she left her position as chairwoman of the London office of Saatchi & Saatchi Advertising Worldwide to become chief executive of its North American operations. Her new responsibilities included supervising the accounts for brands such as Cheerios, Tide, Tylenol, and Reynolds Wrap and landing new accounts, such as Delta Air Lines. Clearly, all the work that goes into promoting these brands, which generate revenues of more than $2 billion, can't be done by one person—it takes several thousand. Laing's job is to oversee the efforts of everyone working on all the North American accounts.

An important responsibility of managers such as Laing is to ensure that their groups understand their goals and how achieving their goals is related to the success of their organizations. Saatchi & Saatchi's primary goal is to "make clients' brands famous." While achieving that goal, the company also has the goal of making its own name famous. It achieves these goals by producing excellent advertising for its current clients and by attracting new accounts.

Because managers achieve organizational goals by enabling people to do their jobs effectively and efficiently—not by performing all the tasks themselves—they must find ways to keep employees motivated. Laing describes Saatchi & Saatchi's employees as highly motivated. She gives them credit for the firm's ability to recover from the turmoil it experienced in 1995 when founders Maurice and Charles Saatchi left the firm to open their own shop. The firm's 6,200 employees then showed the "desire to prove that the next generation could not only do a good job but a better job." Laing knows that it is her job to keep their motivation high, which she plans to do by providing consistent leadership.[4]

WHAT IS MANAGEMENT?

If managers are the people responsible for making sure that an organization achieves its goals, what does the term *management* mean? In everyday usage, people often refer to management as a group of managers in an organization. For example, the CEO and other high-level executives often are referred to as top management. The managers under them may be referred to as middle management, and so on.

The term *management* can also be used to refer to the tasks that managers do. These tasks include planning, organizing, leading, and controlling the work of an organization. Business managers at General Electric (GE) plan, organize, lead, and control activities to ensure that their particular businesses are ranked either first or second against all competitors. CEO Jack Welch has a clear strategy for GE success. Part of this strategy is to improve continuously the quality of GE products and services. The following Communication Competency feature demonstrates how Welch uses communication to lead, organize, and control this activity.

In this book, we use the term **management** to refer to the tasks or activities involved in managing an organization: planning, organizing, leading, and controlling. As you will see, people in many different jobs may be expected to do some management tasks, even if that isn't their main focus. For example, quality control programs such as the one at GE involve employees throughout the entire organization in developing plans for improving quality. When GE Capital Services looks for ways to reduce errors in the bills it sends to credit card customers, managers enlist the help of billing clerks and data processors. They will be empowered to reorganize some of their work and be expected to continue to look for new ways to control quality. In other words, they will be doing some management tasks, but they won't become managers. We reserve the term *manager* for people in jobs that involve *primarily* management tasks.

SCOPE OF MANAGEMENT

There are many types of managers and many ways in which managerial jobs differ from each other. One difference is the scope of the activities being managed. The scope of activities performed by functional managers is relatively narrow, whereas the scope of activities performed by general managers is quite broad.

Functional managers supervise employees having expertise in one area, such as accounting, human resources, sales, finance, marketing, or production. For example, the head of a payroll department is a functional manager. That person doesn't determine employee salaries, as a general manager might, but makes sure that payroll checks are issued on time and in the correct amounts. Usually, functional managers have a great deal of experience and technical expertise in the areas of operation they supervise. Their success as managers is due in part to the detailed knowledge they have about the work being done by the people they supervise, the problems those people are likely to face, and the resources they need to perform well.

General managers are responsible for the operations of a more complex unit, such as a company or a division. Usually they oversee the work of functional managers. General managers must have a broad range of well-developed competencies

MANAGEMENT
Planning, organizing, leading, and controlling the people working in an organization and the ongoing set of tasks and activities they perform.

FUNCTIONAL MANAGERS
Managers who supervise employees having specialized skills in a single area of operation, such as accounting, personnel, payroll, finance, marketing, or production.

GENERAL MANAGERS
Managers responsible for the overall operations of a complex unit such as a company or a division.

Black Belts Are Roaming

Like many U.S. companies, GE has grown into a global firm that competes in every major market in the world. Among other things, it manufactures home appliances, offers financial services, and builds electrical power systems around the world. To succeed, GE's CEO Jack Welch must understand the implications of a variety of global forces. Competition has never been fiercer, especially in the manufacturing sector. Welch understands that one way to beat competitors and maximize a company's profitability is to improve quality control. To focus his managers' attention on quality control, Welch tied 40 percent of executive bonuses to implementing a quality improvement initiative. Part of Welch's plan is to train a cadre of 10,000 "Black Belts" in quality control techniques by the year 2000. After completing the training, each Black Belt goes to a plant or office to set up and organize quality improvement projects. Welch leads the way for these efforts through passionate communication. "You can't behave in a calm, rational manner; . . . you've got to be out there on the lunatic fringe. You have to tell your people that quality is critical to survival, you have to demand that everybody gets trained, you have to cheerlead, you have to have incentive bonuses, you have to say, 'We must do this.'" And you have to mean it. One way to show that you mean what you say is to invest your resources. Welch is investing hundreds of millions of dollars to carry out the training, run projects, and put in place the computer systems needed to measure quality and analyze problems. Another way to show that you mean it is to be direct. To be sure that everyone understands his message, Welch told managers that they won't have much future with the company if they don't become Black Belts and produce some results. They know he'll be true to his word.[5]

* * *

For more about General Electric, visit the company's home page at

www.ge.com

to do their jobs well. These competencies can be learned through a combination of formal training and various job assignments, or they can be learned simply in the course of trying to adapt and survive in a chosen area. Being adaptable enough to solve whatever problems he ran into along the road to success was the approach Alan Young took on the way to becoming one of the best auto dealers in Texas. Although Young's domain is small compared to Platt's at Hewlett-Packard, his job has all the complexity of that of a general manager. He oversees all marketing functions, including advertising campaigns and sales; he manages the financial side of the business; he is active in the community as a member of the Ft. Worth Chamber of Commerce and other civic organizations; and he sponsors a high school basketball tournament.[6]

WHAT MANAGERS DO

2

DESCRIBE WHAT MANAGERS DO

As we've described the various types of managers, we've given you some idea of what managers do. But these few examples don't show the whole picture by any means. Let's now consider systematically what managers do—the functions they perform and the specific tasks included in these functions.

GENERAL MANAGERIAL FUNCTIONS

The successful manager capably performs four basic managerial functions: planning, organizing, leading, and controlling. However, as you will see, the amount of time a manager spends on each function depends on the level of the particular job. After further describing each of the four general managerial functions, we consider in detail the differences among managers at various levels in organizations.

Regardless of their level, most managers perform the four general functions more or less simultaneously—rather than in a rigid, preset order—to achieve organizational goals. Figure 1.2 illustrates this point graphically. In this section we briefly examine the four functions without looking at their interrelationships. However, throughout this book we refer to those interrelationships to help explain exactly how managers do their jobs.

PLANNING

Defining goals and proposing ways to reach them.

Planning. In general, *planning* involves defining organizational goals and proposing ways to reach them. Managers plan for three reasons: (1) to establish an overall direction for the organization's future, such as increased profit, expanded market share, and social responsibility; (2) to identify and commit the organization's resources to achieving its goals; and (3) to decide which tasks must be done to reach those goals. The quality control program that Jack Welch recently began at GE is a good example of what planning involves. We discuss the planning and decision-making functions in more detail in Chapters 7–9.

Organizing. After managers have prepared plans, they must translate those relatively abstract ideas into reality. Sound organization is essential to this effort. *Organizing* is the process of creating a structure of relationships that will enable employees to carry out management's plans and meet organizational goals. By organizing effectively, managers can better coordinate human, material, and information resources. An organization's success depends largely on management's ability to utilize those resources efficiently and effectively.

ORGANIZING

The managerial function of creating a structure of relationships to enable employees to carry out management's plans and meet its goals.

Organizing involves creating a structure by setting up departments and job descriptions. For example, the U.S. Postal Service uses a different type of structure than does UPS. At the U.S. Postal Service, most employees think of themselves as production workers, and the degree of job specialization is low. Relatively little attention is paid to the marketing function. Most of the decisions are made by top managers, with mail carriers and postal clerks having little to do with decision making. Carriers and clerks are promoted to other jobs as they gain seniority.

Figure 1.2   ***Basic Managerial Functions***

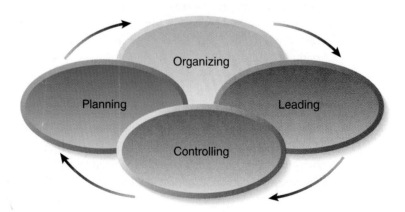

In contrast, UPS is organized into two distinct divisions: airline and ground carrier. At UPS, the degree of job specialization is high. The truck drivers don't fly planes and the pilots don't drive trucks. Parcel sorters are located in major hubs around the world and sort parcels for delivery by drivers, who have the most customer contact.

LEADING

The managerial function of communicating with and motivating others to perform the tasks necessary to achieve the organization's goals.

Leading. After management has made plans, created a structure, and hired the right personnel, someone must lead the organization. ***Leading*** involves communicating with and motivating others to perform the tasks necessary to achieve the organization's goals. Leading isn't done only after planning and organizing end; it is a crucial element of those functions. When Brian Coleman, a manager at Ford Motor Company's plant in Dagenham, England, was asked to lead his unit to produce higher quality, he understood that this task required planning, organizing, and leading simultaneously. With the goal clear in his mind, he organized a team that included several managers and a union official who then was asked to select several shop floor employees to join the team. Coleman and his team collaboratively planned how to proceed in order to reduce defects and warranty claims.[7]

CONTROLLING

The process by which a person, group, or organization consciously monitors performance and takes corrective action.

Controlling. The process by which a person, group, or organization consciously monitors performance and takes corrective action is ***controlling.*** Just as a thermostat sends signals to a heating system that the room temperature is too high or too low, so a management control system sends signals to managers that things aren't working out as planned and that corrective action is needed. Phil Knight is CEO of Nike, the global athletic apparel and shoe company based in Oregon, with annual sales of more than $9.1 billion.[8] Knight believes that Nike's success is due to its competitive spirit, ability to respond to customers' needs with diverse and genuine products, and its control procedures. In the control process at Nike and elsewhere, managers

- set standards of performance,

- measure current performance against those standards,

- take action to correct any deviations, and

- adjust the standards if necessary.

Nike establishes budgets for each shoe line, such as cross training, aerobic, walking, basketball, and football, and holds its managers responsible for meeting production and financial goals. If a shoe line can't meet its goals, the line is replaced. Knight spends a lot of time traveling globally, visiting retailers. He learns what customers want in terms of product quality, performance, and price. He uses this knowledge when setting performance standards for the firm. At the same time, he reinforces the message that a retailer in Singapore or Shanghai is just as important as one in New York City and that every consumer can count on a consistent commitment to quality. In Chapters 19–21 we present and discuss typical organizational control processes.

LEVELS OF MANAGEMENT

Now that we've exposed you to the general functions performed by managers, let's back up and talk about the work setting. As you have seen, managers work in organizations. So far, we've mostly cited examples of managers in large corporations. But managers and the need for effective management are just as important in small organizations. When Hewlett-Packard was just getting started and operated out of a garage in Palo Alto, California, it needed management to get the work done as efficiently and effectively as possible and to plan for the company's future.

In a small organization, there is usually only one level of management. As an organization grows, more levels of management are needed. When entrepreneur Ray Kroc opened his first McDonald's restaurant in Des Plaines, Illinois, on April 15, 1955, his cash register rang up sales of $366.12 for the day. In the beginning he was the only manager. As his success convinced others to join him, new locations opened, and more managers were needed. When the first McDonald's restaurant opened in Moscow with twenty-five employees, the company added yet another manager to its ranks. As McDonald's grew during its first three decades, it kept adding new managers, but they didn't replace Ray Kroc. He became president and CEO, a high-level management position he held for more than twenty-five years.

Although both Ray Kroc and the operators he hired to run local restaurants can be called managers, their jobs certainly weren't the same. The goals, tasks, and responsibilities of the first-line store manager are very different from those of the CEO. Figure 1.3 shows the three basic management levels. We define them with a broad brush here, returning to add detail later in the chapter and throughout the book.

FIRST-LINE MANAGERS

FIRST-LINE MANAGERS
Managers directly responsible for the production of goods or services.

In general, *first-line managers* are directly responsible for the production of goods or services. They may be called sales managers, section heads, or production supervisors, depending on the organization. Employees who report to them do the organization's basic production work—whether of goods or of services. For example, a first-line manager at a steel production plant supervises employees who make steel, operate and maintain machines, and write shipping orders. A sales manager at a U.S. automobile dealership supervises salespeople who sell cars to customers in the showroom. An automobile sales manager in Japan works in an office that has computers and telephones similar to a telemarketing center and supervises salespeople who go to people's homes to sell them cars.

This level of management is the link between the operations of each department and the rest of the organization. First-line managers in most companies spend little time with higher management or with people from other organizations. Most of their time is spent with the people they supervise and with other first-line managers.

Figure 1.3   *Basic Levels of Management*

First-line managers often lead hectic work lives full of pressure and having little glamour, as Richard Thibeault will tell you. Growing up in New England and working in the mills, Thibeault viewed managers as being "up there on the ladder," removed from the day-to-day grind. Now that he's manager of an Au Bon Pain bakery store, his view has changed. Working seventy-hour weeks, he begins at 3 A.M. baking muffins and making soup, working alongside his employees. The difference between them and him is that he also is worrying about how to reverse his falling sales and meet the productivity quotas mandated by headquarters. With the middle management ranks above him shrinking, he and others like him now have greater responsibility for dealing with personnel issues and meeting profit targets. "It's not the pressure out there from customers that gets me," he says, "it's the pressure from higher up." Thibeault would like to run some special sales to boost business, but the company won't let him. He would like to hire more workers to speed customer service, but he can't do that either. Many of the solutions to problems that Thibeault wants to try are being denied him. He's working in a company that expanded too rapidly and suddenly faces new competition from a wave of new coffee bars, such as Starbucks. At the same time, there seem to be fewer opportunities for advancement. For example, the ranks of store managers recently swelled from 140 to 190, but the number of district managers—the next level up—shrank from 28 to 20. No wonder nearly half the entry-level managers working in fast-food restaurants often think of quitting![9]

First-line managers spend relatively little time planning and organizing. Most of their time is spent directing the actions of employees who actually do production work or deliver services (leading) and making sure that parts arrive, settling disputes among employees, scheduling vacations and overtime, and inspecting products (controlling).

Newly appointed first-line managers have much to learn—and also to unlearn. For example, a recently promoted production worker must learn to let others do the work that she has been used to doing and to put aside thoughts about how much better and faster she did it. New first-line managers must learn to plan and schedule the work formerly laid out for them and encourage and motivate others to accomplish the work. In the process they must also learn how their group fits into the total organization. They may need to learn how to share staff services and serve on task forces with other managers to solve problems that go beyond their area of direct responsibility.

First-line managers usually need strong technical expertise to teach subordinates and supervise their day-to-day tasks. Workers usually develop technical expertise before becoming managers. Sometimes, though, a first-line manager is a recent college graduate who is responsible for the work of both hourly employees and professionals. Such a first-line manager is likely to have little hands-on experience. Lack of experience isn't a problem if the new manager is willing to learn and has the competency to communicate with diverse types of people, to coach and counsel subordinates, and to provide constructive feedback.

MIDDLE MANAGERS

MIDDLE MANAGERS
Managers who receive broad, overall strategies and policies from top managers and translate them into specific goals and plans for first-line managers to implement.

Small organizations can function successfully with only one level of management. As an organization grows, however, so do its problems. Some managers at larger organizations must focus on coordinating employee activities, determining which products or services to provide, and deciding how to market these products or services to customers. These are the problems of **middle managers,** who receive broad, general strategies and policies from top managers and translate them into specific goals and plans for first-line managers to implement. Middle managers typically have titles such as department head, plant manager, and director of finance. They are responsible for directing and coordinating the activities of first-line managers and, at times, such nonmanagerial personnel as clerks, receptionists, and staff assistants. At Au Bon Pain the middle managers are called district managers, and each is responsible for nine or ten stores like the one Richard Thibeault manages. It was Thibeault's district manager who came by the store to ask him whether he wanted to leave his urban location to run a suburban store. Knowing that his pay would be the same and that he would still be overworked, Thibeault took the new job anyway. At least the new store is less cramped and looks more inviting. Perhaps together Thibeault and the district manager can increase this store's sales. Middle managers spend much of their time planning, organizing, and leading to enable first-line managers and their subordinates to work as efficiently as possible. They also order parts, deal with customer complaints, and voice first-line managers' concerns to top management.

Many middle managers began their careers and spent several years as first-line managers. Even so, promotion from first-level to middle management is often difficult and sometimes traumatic. The heavier emphasis on managing group performance and allocating resources represent the most important differences between first-line and middle managers. The middle manager often is involved in reviewing the work plans of various groups, helping them set priorities, and negotiating and coordinating their activities. Middle managers are involved in establishing target dates for products or services to be completed; developing evaluation criteria for performance; deciding which projects should be given money, personnel, and materials; and translating top management's general goals into specific operational plans, schedules, and procedures.

Middle managers carry out top management's directives primarily by delegating authority and responsibility to their subordinates and by coordinating schedules and resources with other managers. They often spend much of their day talking on the phone, attending committee meetings, and preparing and reviewing reports. Middle managers tend to be removed from the technical aspects of work, so whatever technical expertise they may have is of less direct help to them now.

Finally, middle managers must be adept at developing their subordinates, opening lines of communication for them, and making them visible to other middle managers and to top managers. In many organizations today, developing subordinates and helping them move up in the organization is essential to being viewed as a successful manager. When middle managers fail to develop their staffs, low morale and high turnover are likely to follow.

TOP MANAGERS

TOP MANAGERS

Managers who are responsible for the overall direction and operations of an organization.

The overall direction of an organization is the responsibility of **top managers.** Linda Wachner, CEO of Warnaco, and Hiroshi Okuda, President of Toyota, are two such managers who have built hugely successful companies. Typical titles of top managers are chief executive officer, president, chairman, division president, and executive vice-president. Top managers develop goals, policies, and strategies for the entire organization. They set the goals that are handed down through the hierarchy, eventually reaching each worker. David Peterman, Au Bon Pain's senior vice-president of operations, is a top manager. Twenty years ago, he started as a first-line manager at Burger King and has since moved up through the ranks at several fast-food companies. He knows what first-line and middle managers have to go through, because he's been there himself and because he now spends much of his time visiting the company's restaurants to observe how they're doing. When he's not touring, he's in meetings with other top managers or on the phone—often in communication with his district managers.

CEOs and presidents often represent their organizations in community affairs, business deals, and government negotiations. Barbara Harding, CEO and chairman of the board of PNC bank, is especially good at this part of her job. In 1965, after graduating from high school, Harding started as a teller at PNC. By 1985, she was running the bank. Although she has no college degree, she joined the board of the Federal Reserve Bank of New York in 1991, taking part in decisions that affect national and international economic policy. Working alongside top managers such as Bob Allen, former CEO of AT&T, and former Secretary of State Cyrus Vance, she was called on to inform the board about consumer thinking and preferences. Now, as she oversees her bank's expansion throughout the northeastern United States, she also represents it in community negotiations related to opening new branches, in financial negotiations related to entering new businesses such as insurance, and in discussions with other CEOs interested in exploring possible new ventures. Yet, with all these responsibilities, she still finds time to serve on the boards of community organizations such as the Domestic Abuse and Rape Crisis Center. The key to her success, she feels, is working in a field where knowledge of the community and visibility pay off.[10]

Top managers spend most of their day (over 75 percent) planning and leading. They spend most of their leading time with key people and organizations outside their own organizations. Top managers—like middle managers—spend little time *directly* controlling the work of others.

Pressures and demands on top managers can be intense. Tightly scheduled workdays, heavy travel requirements, and workweeks of sixty or more hours are common. A true break is a luxury. Coffee is swallowed on the run, and lunch often is eaten during meetings with other managers, business associates, community representatives, or government officials. When there is some free time, eager subordinates vie for a piece of it.

A top manager spends days *and* nights working for the company. One night may be spent working late at the office, another entertaining business associates, and another traveling to or from a meeting in another city or country. On other nights the typical top manager goes home, not to relax, but to use it as a branch office. Many recreational activities and social events are arranged for business purposes. The top manager seldom stops thinking about the job. Such an approach may be necessary to get the work done, but it also creates stress in many families.

Top managers also face expanding public relations duties. They must be able to respond quickly to crises that may create image problems for their organizations. A day after tests revealed that the Bre-X Minerals Ltd. claim of a giant gold field was a fraud, founder and CEO David Walsh was the target of questions by the Royal Canadian Mounted Police, the Ontario Securities Commission, and media representatives from around the world.[11] In this case, the attention given this company, previously known only to industry experts, was brought on by the revelation of a financial debacle. For executives of other firms, such attention is routine. For example, Japanese leaders such as Toyota President Hiroshi Okuda often are visited at home by the press: "Journalists wait at my gate in the morning and in the evening to interview me," he says.[12]

SMALL-BUSINESS MANAGERS

In large organizations with several levels of management, managers at each level are responsible for different types of tasks. But in small companies, one person—usually the founder or current owner—often carries the whole load. John Burson, sole owner of a general contracting firm, illustrates this point, as described in the following Planning and Administration Competency piece.

John Burson Does It All

The Burson family has been in the construction business for two generations, so it wasn't too surprising that John Burson started his own company, which specialized in light industrial construction. Burson's own special technical expertise is the metal framing and walls used in small strip shopping centers, small apartment complexes, and light-industry build-

ings. To complete a project, he subcontracts for the services that he can't perform himself but oversees the entire construction process.

Burson, like many small-business owners, carries out the functions and tasks of all three levels of management. As CEO and president, he is responsible for creating the community relations that make his small company visible and attractive to customers. He also must establish good rapport with other contractors who will do the portion of the construction that his company doesn't do. If he uses union labor, he must be familiar with union work requirements and pay scales. If he hires employees of his own, he must understand and comply with Affirmative Action and Equal Employment Opportunity (EEO) guidelines.

As a middle manager, he must coordinate all aspects of every project

so that it is completed according to the contract and time schedule. As a first-line manager, he supervises the metal-framing and wall-building crews and may actually operate machinery or work with one of the crews.

Burson depends on new electronic devices such as cellular phones, pagers, voice mail, and fax machines to communicate from an office that is alternately in his home, in his car, and at his work site. Although he may not spend as much time communicating as the CEO of a larger company does, he shares the long workdays associated with the responsibilities of top managers. In a typical day, he will examine his company's financial performance, bid on a job, meet electronically or face to face with customers and suppliers, and even attend a meeting of a volunteer association.[13]

As John Burson's activities demonstrate, owners of small businesses don't differentiate among levels of management. As a company grows, however, the owner has to narrow the job's scope and concentrate on certain tasks. For example, an entrepreneur whose strength is in sales might focus on getting new customers to spur the growth of the business and hire other managers to handle the financing and supervise on-site work.

MANAGERIAL COMPETENCIES

3

UNDERSTAND THE COMPETENCIES USED IN MANAGERIAL WORK AND BEGIN TO PRACTICE THEM

We've talked about the various levels of management and what managers do, but you may still be wondering about what it takes to be an effective (or even a great) manager. So, let's look more closely at the competencies that managers need in order to succeed.

WHAT IT TAKES TO BE A GREAT MANAGER

At the beginning of this chapter, we defined *managerial competencies* as sets of knowledge, skills, behaviors, and attitudes that a manager needs in order to be effective in a wide range of managerial jobs and various organizational settings. We identified six specific competencies as being particularly important: communication, planning and administration, teamwork, strategic action, global awareness, and self-management.

These competencies are *transferable* from one organization to the next.[14] Managerial competencies useful to a State Farm Insurance Company sales manager responsible for increasing customer satisfaction throughout the region also would be useful if the manager later took a job at Nationwide Insurance. They would be useful to the manager of a local coffee shop interested in increasing sales during the breakfast hour and to a project manager in Paris charged with developing a new multimedia game for children. Whether you supervise the work of a small team on the shop floor or serve as CEO of a global company, honing the managerial competencies that we've identified can enhance your performance.

Regardless of when, where, or how you develop these competencies, you should be able to use them in the future in jobs that you can't yet even imagine holding—or that may not even exist today. One way to enhance your managerial competencies is by studying this book and completing the activities presented at the end of each chapter. By participating in extracurricular activities, you can develop competencies such as communication and teamwork that often can be transferred to a variety of jobs. By taking the appropriate courses and participating in international clubs and associations, you can broaden your knowledge of other countries and build your global awareness competency. By holding an office or taking responsibility for organizing a community event, such as spring cleanup day in the park, you can build your planning and administration competency.[15] Because managerial competencies can be learned through such activities, in addition to on the job, campus recruiters pay a great deal of attention to students' involvement in them, instead of just looking at grade point averages.

COMMUNICATION COMPETENCY

The term **communication competency** refers to the effective transfer and exchange of information that leads to understanding between yourself and others. Because managing involves getting work done through other people, communication competency is essential to effective managerial performance. Communication competency includes

- informal communication,

- formal communication, and

- negotiation.

Communication competency transcends the use of a particular communication medium. That is, good communication may involve having a face-to-face conversation, preparing a formal written document, participating in a global meeting via teleconferencing, giving a speech to an audience of 400 people, or using e-mail to coordinate a project team whose members work in different regions of the country.

Communication isn't something you do *to* other people; it is something you do *with* them. Usually, it is a dynamic, give-and-take process that involves receiving messages from others, as well as sending messages to others. Besides speaking and writing, it involves listening, observing body language, and picking up on the subtle cues that people sometimes use to modify the meaning of their words. Herb Kelleher, CEO of Southwest Airlines, pays attention to all these communication cues as he visits with employees on the job as well as while partying with them after hours.

Of the six managerial competencies that we've identified, communication is perhaps the most fundamental. Unless you can express yourself and understand others in written, oral, and nonverbal (e.g., facial expression and body posture) communication, you can't use the other competencies effectively to accomplish tasks through other people. Nor can you effectively manage the vast network of relationships that link you to other people inside and outside your organization.[16]

The productive employment of workers of all ages, with varying types of work experience and expertise, of both genders and varied cultural and ethnic backgrounds means that a basic level of communication competency is seldom enough these days. After all, managing effectively means getting *all* workers to contribute their best ideas and efforts in an intensely competitive global market. Day in and day out, this effort requires plenty of spontaneous, *informal communication* that is sensitive to the different backgrounds and perspectives of the people involved. Moreover, to be sure that you are understood, you need to become comfortable soliciting and accepting feedback.

Through informal communication, managers build a social network of contacts. In China, these connections are known as *guanxi*. In Japan, they're called *kankei*, and in Korea they're called *kwankye*. Whatever language you say it in, maintaining social networks is especially important to managerial work. But in a Confucian society, the web of social contacts maintained through informal communications is central to success. In fact, when business leaders in China were asked to identify the factors most important to long-term business success, *guanxi* was the only factor chosen consistently—ahead of choosing the right business location, selecting the right business strategy, and competitive pricing.[17] Through frequent informal communication, managers in all countries lay the groundwork for collaboration within and outside their organizations.

Being able to communicate in more formal situations also is important to managerial effectiveness. *Formal communications* such as newsletters often are used to inform people of relevant events and activities and to keep people up to date on the status of ongoing projects. Public speeches are another example of formal communication. Whether the audience is company executives, professional peers, shareholders, or members of the community, high-impact public presentations can be used to address stakeholder concerns and enhance the firm's reputation.

Formal communication can also take place at a more personal level, such as during conversations with suppliers and clients. Among bankers, for example, formal communication is essential to managing client relationships. T. Mark Maybell, a managing director at Merrill Lynch, is in charge of global communications for the company's investment banking group. His role as a "relationship manager" involves selling the firm's investment services to national governments and many of the world's largest corporations. Although he traveled to more than twenty-five countries during the past five years, he isn't expected to be fluent in the language of every country he visits. But he must be able to communicate, often through an interpreter, in all of these cultures. In other words, for Mark Maybell, effective communication goes hand in hand with a global perspective.[18]

Maybell's job also involves *negotiating*—sometimes at great distances. One negotiation with Denmark's telecommunications company was particularly intense, with down-to-the-wire discussions stretching over four days. Working from his hotel room, he racked up a record phone and fax bill (for someone staying at that hotel). To build consensus on goals and commitment to achieve them, good negotiators learn to seek contrary opinions and find ways to respond to the divergent views they uncover. Building consensus and commitment is useful for negotiations with bosses, peers, and subordinates, as well as with clients. Managers also must be able to negotiate to obtain resources for their subordinates and to settle disputes that arise among various stakeholders.[19]

Because managers spend so much of their time communicating, management recruiters look for people who can communicate effectively. In fact, we can't stress enough the importance of good communication. At a time when organizations increasingly expect employees to work with minimal supervision and show more initiative, competent oral, written, and electronic communication is essential. You may find yourself interviewing for your next job via videoconferencing. Hewlett-Packard (HP) took full advantage of this new recruiting technology by hosting the first ever electronic job fair in 1997. Ten colleges and universities were invited to participate. Business students sent their résumés electronically to an HP database, and the company conducted its interviews over a PC-based teleconferencing system. Other companies now using this technology include Andersen Consulting, EDS, General Mills, AT&T, IBM, Sears, Price Waterhouse, Exxon, NationsBank, and Shell Oil. After her interview with General Mills, one student, Barbara Carter, observed, "It takes a while to get used to it [videoconferencing], but it's more personal than a telephone interview."[20] For more details about communication competency, refer to Table 1.2.

PLANNING AND ADMINISTRATION COMPETENCY

Deciding the tasks that need to be done, determining how to do them, allocating resources to those tasks, and then monitoring progress to ensure that they *are* done.

PLANNING AND ADMINISTRATION COMPETENCY

Planning and administration competency involves deciding what tasks need to be done, determining how they can be done, allocating resources to enable them to be done, and then monitoring progress to ensure that they *are* done. For many people, the planning and administration competency comes to mind first when they

T a b l e 1 . 2	*Dimensions of Communication Competency*

Informal Communication

- Promotes two-way communication by soliciting feedback, listening, seeking out contrary opinions, and creating a give-and-take conversation

- Is flexible and varies approach in different situations and with others from diverse backgrounds

- Builds strong interpersonal relationships with a diverse range of people: shows genuine sensitivity to the diverse needs, opinions, and feelings of others and is tolerant of their foibles and idiosyncrasies

Formal Communication

- Informs people of relevant events and activities and keeps them up to date

- Makes persuasive, high-impact public presentations and handles questions well

- Writes clearly, concisely, and effectively, using traditional as well as electronic media

Negotiation

- Negotiates effectively on behalf of the team over roles and resources

- Comfortable with the power of the managerial role

- Skilled at developing relationships and exercising influence upward with superiors, laterally with peers, downward with subordinates, as well as externally with customers, suppliers, and other stakeholders

- Takes decisive and fair actions when handling problem subordinates

think about managers and managing. Included in this category are

- information gathering, analysis, and problem solving;
- planning and organizing projects;
- time management; and
- budgeting and financial management.

When Lew Platt of Hewlett-Packard describes what his workday is like, he puts it this way: "Basically, the whole day comes down to a series of choices." To help him hone his planning and administration competency, Platt hired a consultant to analyze his day and help him reshape his management approach. Platt instinctively knew that *information gathering, analysis,* and *problem solving* are important and that *customers* are a rich source of useful information—but they can easily eat up a whole day. The consultant helped him understand that some types of customer phone calls were something he could delegate in order to leave 20 percent of his time for meeting directly with customers.

Planning and organizing projects usually means working with employees to clarify broad objectives, discuss resource allocations, and agree to completion dates. Thus Platt spends 35 percent of his day with employees, 10 percent on the telephone, and 5 percent on paperwork. Because there are more problems and opportunities than he possibly can attend to, Platt is ruthless about *time management:* "You have to continually work to optimize your time," he says.[21]

And, of course, managers are accountable for *budgeting and managing financial resources.* Boards of directors and shareholders of public corporations hold CEOs such as Lew Platt fiscally accountable. In nonprofit and government organizations, trustees, various regulatory bodies, and elected officials oversee fiscal management. For more detail about planning and administration competency, refer to Table 1.3.

TEAMWORK COMPETENCY

Accomplishing tasks through small groups of people who are collectively responsible and whose work is interdependent requires **teamwork competency.** Managers in companies that utilize teams can become more effective by

- designing teams properly,
- creating a supportive team environment, and
- managing team dynamics appropriately.

In a recent study of 243 employers, the Hay Group, a consulting company, found that two of every three companies plan to increase their level of employee participation in teams. Improving customer service was the main reason given (84 percent), followed by improving product quality (69 percent), and improving productivity (64 percent).[22] At Southwest Airlines, effective teamwork makes it possible for ground crews to turn around a plane at the gate in record time. Regardless of their job titles, all employees work together to get passengers unloaded and reloaded. When necessary, pilots, flight attendants, and whoever else is available pitch in to ensure that a flight leaves the boarding gate on schedule.

When people think of teamwork, they often make a distinction between the team members and a team leader. We don't hold this view of teamwork. Instead, we view teamwork as a competency that involves taking the lead at times, supporting others who are taking the lead at other times, and collaborating with others in the organization on projects that don't even have a designated team leader.

TEAMWORK COMPETENCY

Accomplishing outcomes through small groups of people who are collectively responsible and whose work is interdependent.

Information Gathering, Analysis, and Problem Solving

- Monitors information and uses it to identify symptoms, underlying problems, and alternative solutions

- Makes timely decisions

- Takes calculated risks and anticipates the consequences

Planning and Organizing Projects

- Develops plans and schedules to achieve specific goals efficiently

- Assigns priorities to tasks

- Determines, obtains, and organizes necessary resources, such as materials, people, and funds

- Delegates responsibility for task completion

Time Management

- Handles several issues and projects at one time but doesn't spread self too thin

- Monitors and keeps to a schedule or negotiates changes in the schedule if needed

- Works effectively under time pressure

- Knows when to permit interruptions and when to screen them out

Budgeting and Financial Management

- Understands budgets, cash flows, financial reports, and annual reports and regularly uses such information

- Keeps accurate and complete financial records

- Creates budgetary guidelines for others and works within the guidelines given by others

We hold this view of teamwork competency because almost all managerial work involves doing all of these activities simultaneously.

Designing the team is the first step for any team project and usually is the responsibility of a manager or team leader. But in self-managed teams, the entire team participates in the design. Team design involves formulating goals to be achieved, defining tasks to be done, and identifying the staffing needed to accomplish those tasks. Team members should identify with the team's goals and feel committed to accomplishing them. Members of a well-designed team understand its tasks and how its performance will be measured; they aren't confused about which tasks are theirs and which tasks are some other team's. A well-designed team has just the right number of members. Too many members leave room for free riders; too few create too much stress and leave the team feeling incapable of successfully achieving its goals.[23]

A well-designed team is capable of high performance, but it needs a supportive environment to achieve its full potential. All members of a team should have the competencies needed to create a *supportive environment.* In a supportive environment, team members are empowered to take actions based on their best judgment, without always seeking approval first from the team leader or project manager. Support also involves eliciting contributions from members whose unique competencies are important for the team and recognizing, praising, and rewarding both minor victories and major successes. A manager having good teamwork competency respects other people and is respected and even liked by them in return. Managers who lack teamwork competency often are viewed as being rude, abrupt, and unsympathetic, making others feel inadequate and resentful. Fundamentally, creating a supportive environment involves coaching, counseling, and mentoring team members to improve their performance in the near term and prepare them for future challenges.

Conflicts and disagreements among team members are natural, which means that *managing team dynamics* is necessary for effective teamwork. During the formative years of the United States, statesman George P. Morris observed the importance of maintaining cooperative relationships while pursuing a common goal: "United we stand, divided we fall," he said. If managed well, conflict can be productive; if poorly managed, it can destroy the team.

In the health-care industry, the need to reduce administrative costs and the desire to offer a full range of specialty expertise has created a new trend: teams of physicians joining together to operate medical clinics. This new form of medical practice can be stressful for doctors who previously had individual practices. But learning to work together isn't optional, even for these highly trained professionals. As a managing director at one clinic observed, "If people can't cooperate and work as a system, they can't be efficient. They can't create processes that run smoothly. They can't get rid of variation. I think that is going to be our primary sustainable advantage . . . a medical staff that is willing to subordinate the prima donna ego kind of stuff in order for the system as a whole to succeed. I think it's a practical business strategy."[24] For more detail about teamwork competency, refer to Table 1.4.

T a b l e 1 . 4	*Dimensions of Teamwork Competency*

Designing Teams

- Formulates clear objectives that inspire team members and engender commitment

- Appropriately staffs the team, taking into account the value of diverse perspectives, technical skills needed, and development goals

- Defines responsibilities for the team as a whole and facilitates the allocation of tasks and responsibilities to individual team members, as appropriate

- Creates systems for monitoring team performance

Creating a Supportive Environment

- Creates an environment characterized by empowerment, in which effective teamwork is expected, recognized, praised, and rewarded

- Assists the team in identifying and acquiring the resources it needs to accomplish its goals

- Acts as a coach, counselor, and mentor, being patient with team members as they learn

Managing Team Dynamics

- Understands the strengths and weaknesses of team members and uses their strengths to accomplish tasks as a team

- Brings conflict and dissent into the open and uses it to enhance the quality of decisions, while at the same time facilitating cooperative behavior and keeping the group moving toward its goals

STRATEGIC ACTION COMPETENCY

Understanding the overall mission and values of the company and ensuring that your actions and those of the people you manage are aligned with them involves *strategic action competency.* Strategic action competency includes

- understanding the industry,

- understanding the organization, and

- taking strategic actions.

Today, employees at all levels and in all functional areas are being challenged to think strategically in order to perform their jobs better. They are expected to recognize that shifts in a company's strategic direction are to be expected—even anticipated. Managers and other employees *who understand the industry* can accurately anticipate strategic trends and prepare for the future needs of the organization are less likely to find themselves looking for new jobs when the organization changes direction.

One manager who has proved that he is extremely good at understanding the industry in which he works is chef and restaurateur Drew Nieporent, whose first and most famous restaurant is Montrachet. The restaurant industry and its customers are notoriously fickle, yet he has succeeded with every new restaurant he has opened in New York City, which offers some of the best cuisine in the world. Nieporent's success is due in part to his planning and administrative competency, which he uses to set up operations that run smoothly even when he isn't there to supervise. But it takes more than a smooth-running operation to earn rave reviews from food critics. Early in his career Nieporent developed keen strategic insights by observing the best in the industry, who also happened to be his bosses. "Know the industry inside and out," seems to be the best advice for any manager who is trying to develop strategic action competency.[25]

This competency also involves *understanding the organization*—not just the particular unit in which a manager works, but also understanding the organization as a system of interrelated parts. It includes comprehending how departments, functions, and divisions relate to one another and how a change in one can affect others. A manager with a well-developed strategic action competency can diagnose and assess different types of management problems and issues that might arise. Such a manager thinks in terms of relative priorities rather than ironclad goals and criteria. All managers, but especially top managers, need strategic action competency. Top managers must perceive changes in the organization's environment and be prepared to *take strategic actions.* Citicorp is widely regarded as one of the most innovative banks in the world. It pioneered the negotiable certificate of deposit, was one of the first to use automated teller machines (ATMs), has issued more credit cards than any other bank, and is the world's largest private foreign lender. It was able to do so because Walter B. Wriston, Citicorp's recently retired CEO, steered the bank toward innovative ways of thinking about and addressing the problems that the world's economy would face in the 1990s.[26] For more detail about strategic action competency, refer to Table 1.5.

GLOBAL AWARENESS COMPETENCY

Carrying out an organization's managerial work by drawing on the human, financial, information, and material resources from multiple countries and serving markets that span multiple cultures requires *global awareness competency.* Not all organizations have global markets for their products and services. Nor do they all need to set up operations in other countries in order to take advantage of labor that

---

STRATEGIC ACTION COMPETENCY
Understanding the overall mission and values of the company and ensuring that your actions and those of the people you manage are aligned with the company's mission and values.

GLOBAL AWARENESS COMPETENCY
Performing managerial work for an organization that utilizes human, financial, information, and material resources from multiple countries and serves markets that span multiple cultures.

Understanding the Industry

- Understands the history of the industry

- Stays informed of the actions of competitors and strategic partners

- Can analyze general trends in the industry and their implications for the future

- Quickly recognizes when changes in the industry create significant threats and opportunities

Understanding the Organization

- Understands and is able to balance the concerns of stakeholders

- Understands the strengths and limitations of various business strategies

- Understands the distinctive competencies of the organization

- Understands various organizational structures and the advantages and disadvantages of each

- Understands and is able to fit into the unique corporate culture of the organization

Taking Strategic Actions

- Executes specific plans that reflect cross-functional and cross-divisional knowledge

- Assigns priorities and makes decisions that are consistent with the firm's mission and strategic goals

- Recognizes the management challenges of alternative strategies and addresses them systematically

- Considers the long-term implications of actions in order to sustain and further develop the organization

- Establishes tactical and operational goals that facilitate strategy implementation

---

is cheaper or better trained. Nevertheless, over the course of your career, you probably will work for an organization that has an international component. To be prepared for such opportunities, you should begin to develop your global awareness competency, which is reflected in

- cultural knowledge and understanding, and

- cultural openness and sensitivity.[27]

In the course of growing up and being educated in a particular country or region, people naturally develop *cultural knowledge and understanding* of forces that shape their lives and the conduct of business. These forces include geography and climate, political processes and orientations, economic systems and trends, history, religion, values, beliefs, and local customs. By the time you become a manager in your home country, your own culture has become second nature to you, so you don't need to devote much time developing a general knowledge and awareness of it. However, unless you have traveled extensively, or specifically studied other cultures as part of your education, you probably have much less general knowledge and understanding of other countries, except perhaps those that share a border with your own country. Yet because business is becoming global, many managers are now expected to develop a knowledge and an understanding of at least a few other cultures, such as those where suppliers are located or those with newly emerging markets that can help sustain the company's future growth.

Simply knowing about other cultures isn't sufficient; appropriate attitudes and skills are needed to translate this knowledge into effective performance. An *open attitude* about cultural differences and a *sensitivity* to them are especially important for anyone who must operate across cultural boundaries. Openness and sensitivity involve, first and foremost, recognizing that culture makes a difference in how people think and act. You can't assume that everyone will think and act as you do, nor that everyone will automatically understand your point of view. Second, openness and sensitivity mean actively considering how another culture might differ from your own and examining how your own culture affects your behavior.

Knowledge about other cultures and an open attitude and sensitivity about cultural differences set the stage for working with people from other backgrounds. In any culture, appropriate language, social etiquette, and negotiation skills help in developing effective work relationships. Depending on your job, you may also need to learn country-specific accounting methods, hiring techniques, and so on. Because there are so many cultures and because predicting which cultures will be most important to you in the future is so difficult, you shouldn't expect to develop global awareness competency relevant to all of the world's cultures. But neither can you put off beginning to build a good foundation. For more detail about global awareness competency, refer to Table 1.6.

SELF-MANAGEMENT COMPETENCY

SELF-MANAGEMENT COMPETENCY
Taking responsibility for your life at work and beyond.

Taking responsibility for your life at work and beyond involves ***self-management competency.*** Often, when things don't go well, people tend to blame their difficulties on the situations in which they find themselves or on others. Effective managers don't fall into this trap. Self-management competency includes

- integrity and ethical conduct,

- personal drive and resilience,

T a b l e 1 . 6	*Dimensions of Global Awareness Competency*

Cultural Knowledge and Understanding

- Stays informed of political, social, and economic trends and events around the world

- Recognizes the impact of global events on the organization

- Travels regularly to gain first-hand knowledge of countries in which the organization has or is expected to have an interest

- Understands, reads, and speaks more than one language fluently

- Has a basic business vocabulary in each language relevant to own job

Cultural Openness and Sensitivity

- Understands the nature of national, ethnic, and cultural differences and is open to examining these differences honestly and objectively

- Is sensitive to cultural cues and is able to adapt quickly in novel situations

- Recognizes that there is great variation within any culture and avoids stereotyping

- Appropriately adjusts own behavior when interacting with people from various national, ethnic, and cultural backgrounds

- Understands how own cultural background affects own attitudes and behaviors

- Can empathize and see from different perspectives while still being secure in self and able to act with confidence

- balancing work/life issues, and

- self-awareness and development.

You may be thinking that self-management really doesn't require much time and effort. Dee Hock would disagree. Everyone recognizes a Visa card, but did you know that Dee Hock is the man who built this worldwide powerhouse? Since 1970, when Hock founded Visa, the company has grown from an idea to a service used by half a billion customers. It operates in 200 countries, with annual volume of roughly $1 trillion. Dee Hock was the man behind this phenomenal success story. His isn't a household name, but his success as a manager is unquestioned—which is why he is such a popular speaker at CEO gatherings. When talking to managers about how to succeed, he tells them this: "Invest at least 40 percent of your time managing yourself—your ethics, character, principles, purpose, motivation, and conduct."[28]

Just as customers expect companies to behave ethically, organizations expect their employees to *show integrity and act ethically*. When recruiting entry-level employees—who don't yet have a long record of employment nor much technical expertise—these qualities may be the most important ones that employers look for. According to a national survey of 498 small businesses employing a total of more than 5,000 people, companies seeking to hire young employees (less than twenty years old), are far more concerned with their integrity and interest in the job than with their specific technical skills and aptitudes.[29]

Personal drive and resilience are especially important when someone sets out to do something no one else has done and when that person faces setbacks and failures. As cofounder of Southwest Airlines, Herb Kelleher needed personal drive and resilience when he decided to start a new regional airline. Battling well-established national competitors, who took Kelleher to court to try to stop his new venture, wasn't easy twenty-five years ago—and it still is difficult today. Nevertheless, Kelleher's personal drive continues to help his company grow and maintain the highest net profit margins in the industry.[30]

According to a *Fortune* magazine survey of 1,792 MBA students at top-ranked U.S. and Canadian schools, building a family is a top priority for 71 percent of them. Hoping to have it all, 75 percent gave developing a career a top rating also.[31] Clearly, these future managers won't succeed unless they can find a way to *balance work and life demands*. This and other family concerns led Congress to pass and the president to sign the Family and Medical Leave Act in 1993. In addition, many leading companies have other family-friendly policies. However, self-management competency is needed to decide when and how best to take advantage of such policies. New mothers and fathers alike may feel pressure to return to work soon after the arrival of a new family member, rather than take the entire leave allowed them. But having succumbed to work pressures, many experience pangs of guilt or anxiety when they glimpse the family photo sitting on the corner of the desk. Knowing your own work and life priorities, and finding a way to juggle them all, may be the most difficult management challenge many of you will face.[32]

The dynamic work environment calls for *self-awareness and development* (as well as the ability continually to unlearn and relearn!). That includes both task-related learning and learning about yourself. On the one hand, task-related learning can directly improve your performance in your current job and prepare you to take on new jobs. Learning about yourself, on the other hand, can help you make wiser choices about which types of jobs you are likely to enjoy. With fewer opportunities for promotions and upward advancement, finding work that you enjoy doing is even more important today than in the past.[33] Taking responsibility for your own career development—by understanding the type of work you find satisfying and developing the competencies you will need—may be the best route to long-term success.

Research shows that people who take advantage of the development and training opportunities that employers offer learn much from them and advance more quickly than those who don't take advantage of them. Derailment awaits managers who fail to develop their competencies. A derailed manager is one who has moved into a position of managerial responsibility but has little chance of future advancement or gaining new responsibilities. The most common reasons for derailment are (1) problems with interpersonal relationships and inability to lead a team (weak in teamwork competency); (2) inability to learn, develop, and adapt (weak in self-management competency); (3) performance problems (weak planning and administration competency); and (4) having a narrow functional perspective (lacking strong strategic action and global awareness competencies).[34] Table 1.7 provides more detail about self-management competency.

Table 1.7	Dimensions of Self-Management Competency

Integrity and Ethical Conduct

- Has clear personal standards that serve as a foundation for maintaining a sense of integrity and ethical conduct, even in the face of strong pressure to the contrary

- Is honorable and steadfast, projects self-assurance and doesn't just tell people what they want to hear

- Willing to admit mistakes

- Accepts responsibility for own actions

Personal Drive and Resilience

- Seeks responsibility and is willing to innovate and take risks

- Ambitious and motivated to achieve objectives but doesn't put personal ambition ahead of the organization's goals

- Works hard to get things done

- Shows perseverance in the face of obstacles and bounces back from failure

Balancing Work and Life Issues

- Strikes a reasonable balance between work and other life activities so that neither aspect of living is neglected

- Takes good care of self, mentally and physically and uses constructive outlets to vent frustration and reduce tension

Self-Awareness and Development

- Has clear personal and career goals and knows own values, feelings, and areas of strengths and weaknesses

- Uses strengths to advantage while seeking to improve or compensate for weaknesses

- Accepts responsibility for continuous self-development and learning and develops plans and seeks opportunities for personal long-term growth

- Analyzes and learns from work and life experiences

- Willing to continually unlearn and relearn as changed situations call for new skills and perspectives

Headquartered in Eighty-Four, Pennsylvania, the 84 Lumber Company has nearly 400 stores in 31 states. Founded by Joseph A. Hardy, Sr., in 1956, the company has always been run as a tightly controlled family business. In a family of two sons and three daughters, it was long thought that the eldest son, Joe, Jr., would take over as president someday. So, when Joe, Sr., picked Maggie, the youngest daughter, to succeed him, it was a surprise to many. It wasn't that Maggie was unfamiliar with the busi-

ness. To the contrary, when she was only two and a half years old, she was already attending business meetings with her father. But she didn't enter the business officially until 1986, when her father put the twenty-one-year-old in charge of running a small unit south of Pittsburgh. In those early days, Maggie adopted her father's tough-as-nails style—including the liberal use of obscenities. This may have helped some men feel more comfortable working for a woman, but when a newly hired woman left an employee orientation meeting in disgust, Maggie began to reassess her approach. "I really set out to be a little Joe Hardy . . . but I overcompensated." She realizes that her chain smoking habit may damage her image and so avoids smoking during interviews. She makes a point of keeping photos of her husband and son in the office and taking a sincere interest in the family problems of her employees. As she struggles to find a style that is becoming to a female executive, she manages the company stores with a hand

as stern as her father's. However, she is moving the company in a new strategic direction. With fierce competition from rivals such as Home Depot, she has decided to replace her father's strategy of going after do-it-yourselfers with a new focus on serving building contractors. In the company's monthly newsletter, which is published on the Web, a special column spotlights building contractors. The newsletter also serves to inform contractors of operational improvements being made in response to concerns they have. For example, Maggie used her President's Column one month to describe new policies designed to ensure that building materials are delivered to a job on time, stacked in the order the materials will be used, and protected from rain and snow.[35]

* * *

To learn more about 84 Lumber Company, visit the company's home page at

www.84lumber.com

Although self-management is important for any manager, it may be especially important for managers who are considered to be different. As a woman who is president of a lumber company, whose customers usually are men but also include many women, Maggie Hardy Magerko is learning the importance of finding a management style that fits the expectations of a diverse mix of customers. Magerko's experiences are described in the Self-Management Competency feature, above.

DEVELOPING YOUR MANAGERIAL COMPETENCIES

Throughout this book, both in the text and in the exercises and cases at the end of each chapter, we present material to help you develop the six managerial competencies that we've just described. For example, you've already read about how GE's Jack Welch uses his communication competency to declare his passion for quality improvement. You've also seen how Alan Young's self-management competency helped him develop into a top-flight auto dealer. And you've learned how Maggie Hardy Magerko's self-management competency and experience as a woman who wields power in an industry dominated by men can help managers adapt to new, unfamiliar roles. Examples such as these will help you develop an understanding of how all six competencies contribute to performance in jobs that involve managerial work.

MANAGEMENT—A DYNAMIC PROCESS

4

DESCRIBE THE CHANGING
CONTEXT OF MANAGERIAL
WORK

The *process* of obtaining and organizing resources and achieving goals through other people—that is, managing—is dynamic rather than static. Struggling to manage the new realities of business competition isn't easy. People change, conditions change, technologies change, and the rules change. Managerial thought changes too. It evolves whenever new theories are presented or new practices are tried. If the theories seem to have merit or the practices appear to succeed, their use spreads to more and more organizations until, over a period of time, they become accepted ways of managing. The adoption of Japanese quality control methods by many U.S. firms is an example of evolution in management thought. In 1950, W. Edwards Deming's total quality control method was rejected by U.S. companies but was received warmly in Japan. To honor and immortalize his contributions to their industries, the Japanese created the Deming Prize, awarded annually to the Japanese company that has attained the highest level of quality. The U.S. equivalent of the Deming Prize is the coveted ***Malcolm Baldrige Quality Award.*** Congress created this award by passing the Malcolm Baldrige National Quality Improvement Act of 1987 in an attempt to create standards for measuring total quality in both small and large service and manufacturing companies. In Europe, the ***International Organization for Standardization (ISO)*** issues certification standards for excellence in quality that serve a purpose similar to that of the Deming Prize and the Baldrige Award. The primary difference is that all companies in the European Union (EU) can receive ISO certification if their products meet the specified high standards. They can then display the EC mark as a seal of approval, which can give them a competitive advantage in the marketplace.[36]

**MALCOLM BALDRIGE
QUALITY AWARD**
The award created by the Malcolm Baldrige National Quality Improvement Act of 1987 to create standards for measuring total quality in both small and large service and manufacturing companies.

**INTERNATIONAL
ORGANIZATION FOR
STANDARDIZATION (ISO)**
In Europe, an organization that issues certification standards for excellence in quality.

As you launch your career, your challenge will be to succeed in a new era that will feature change. New forms of organization will emerge. The workforce will be much different, and managers may not even see their employees on a daily basis. Technologies that are just being invented will become commonplace. Global competition will intensify. We describe many of these changes in more detail in Chapters 3–6. Here, we briefly describe and comment on the implications of this dynamic environment for first-line, middle, and top managers.

THE RESTRUCTURING OF ORGANIZATIONS

Throughout the 1990s, mergers and acquisitions have been a major source of corporate restructuring, affecting millions of workers and their families. This form of restructuring often is accompanied by downsizing. ***Downsizing*** is the process of reducing the size of a firm by laying off or retiring workers early. The primary objectives of downsizing are similar in U.S. companies and those in other countries:

DOWNSIZING
The process of reducing the size of a firm by laying off workers or retiring workers early.

- cutting costs,

- spurring decentralization and speeding up decision making,

- cutting bureaucracy and eliminating layers of hierarchy, and

- improving customer relations.

Not surprisingly, the ranks of middle managers have been especially hard hit by downsizing. According to a study by the Conference Board, about 72 percent of companies have fewer middle managers today than they did five years ago. One consequence of this trend is that today's managers supervise larger numbers of subordinates who report directly to them. In 1990, only about 20 percent of managers supervised twelve or more people and 54 percent supervised six or fewer. By 1995, 40 percent of managers supervised twelve or more people and only 15 percent supervised six or fewer.[37]

Because of downsizing, first-line managers have had to assume greater responsibility for the work of their departments. At Muratec Business Systems, which makes fax machines, specialists in quality control, human resources, and industrial engineering provide guidance and support. First-line managers participate in the production processes and other line activities and coordinate the efforts of the specialists as part of their jobs. At the same time, the workers that first-line managers supervise are less willing to put up with authoritarian management. Employees want their jobs to be more creative, challenging, fun, and satisfying and want to participate in decisions affecting their work. Thus **self-managed work teams** that bring workers and first-line managers together to make joint decisions to improve the way they do their jobs offer a solution to both supervision and employee expectation problems.[38] When you hear the word *downsizing,* you may assume that all the people "let go" have lost their jobs. However, that isn't always the case. Sometimes entire divisions of a firm are simply spun off from the main company to operate on their own as new, autonomous companies. The firm that spun them off may then become one of their most important customers or suppliers. That happened when AT&T "downsized" the old Bell Labs unit, which is now known as Lucent Technologies. Now, rather than having its research carried out in-house by Bell Labs, AT&T contracts with Lucent for the work. Lucent, in turn, is free to enter into contracts with companies other than AT&T. This method of downsizing is usually called outsourcing.

Outsourcing means letting other organizations perform a needed service and/or manufacture needed parts or products. Nike outsources the production of its shoes to low-cost plants in South Korea and China and imports the shoes for distribution in North America. These same plants also ship shoes to Europe and other parts of Asia for distribution. Thus today's managers face a new challenge: to plan, organize, lead, and control a company that may have at least some of its operating functions performed by other companies. This type of company is known as a modular corporation. The **modular corporation** is most common in three industries: apparel, auto manufacturing, and electronics.[39] The most commonly outsourced function is production. By outsourcing production, a company can switch suppliers as necessary to use the supplier best suited to a customer's needs.

Decisions about what to outsource and what to keep in-house may be one of the most important strategic decisions being made by managers today. Most experts believe that the decision to contract production to another company is a sound business decision, at least for U.S. manufacturers. It appears to hold down the unit cost of production by relieving the company of some overhead, and it frees the company to allocate scarce resources to activities for which the company holds a competitive advantage. Some well-known examples of modular companies are Dell Computer, Nike, Liz Claiborne fashions, and chip designer Cyrix. For example, the Liz Claiborne line of clothing is manufactured in Asia. The following Strategic Action Competency selection illustrates some of the new challenges created for managers of companies that outsource production, marketing, research and development, or other important activities that once were all carried out under one corporate umbrella.

As organizations downsize and outsource functions, they become flatter and smaller. Figure 1.4 illustrates the shifting size and shape of organizations. Unlike the

SELF-MANAGED WORK TEAMS
Groups formed from workers and first-line managers who make decisions together to improve the way they do their jobs.

OUTSOURCING
Letting other organizations perform a service and/or manufacture parts or a product.

MODULAR CORPORATION
A company whose operating functions are performed by other companies.

The Company That Isn't a Whole Company

Chrysler's new compact car, the Neon, is being manufactured as a modular project. The entire car is shipped to Neon assembly plants in four easy-to-assemble modules from separate suppliers. Other U.S. car manufacturers are expected to follow its lead. In the future, a car may be designed on the super CAD/CAM system at IBM's Boca Raton facility, built by suppliers in various countries, and assembled for delivery at a site closest to its targeted customer. Currently, the Neon is being made both in the United States and in Mexico for sale to customers in both countries.

This new form of company seems to be a solution to various problems in the rapidly changing business environment. But it isn't a cure-all, and, in fact, the trend may have already gone too far. Some companies that outsourced key functions such as human resource management and information technology are now reconsidering those decisions. Today's managers are being challenged to carry out the functions of planning, organizing, leading, and controlling even when the "parts" don't belong to the whole.[40]

* * *

To learn more about Chrysler, visit the company's home page at

www.chrysler.com

NETWORK FORM OF ORGANIZATION
A weblike structure that links several firms through strategic alliances.

behemoths of the past, the new, smaller firms are less like autonomous fortresses and more like nodes in a network of complex relationships. This approach, called the **network form of organization,** involves establishing strategic alliances among several entities.

In Japan, cross-ownership and alliances among firms—called *keiretsu*—have a long and successful history. Now this form of organizing is spreading to other countries. Ford, for example, has equity in both foreign and U.S. auto parts producers. It also owns 49 percent of Hertz, the car rental company that is also a major customer. Other alliances include involvement in several research consortia.[41] In the airline industry, a common type of alliance is between an airline and an airframe manufacturer. For example, Delta recently agreed to buy all its aircraft from Boeing. Boeing has a similar deal, valued at billions of dollars, with American Airlines.

Figure 1.4   **The Evolving Structure of Organizations**

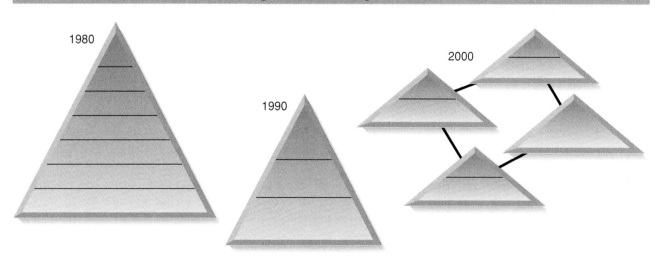

Through these agreements, Boeing guarantees that it will be able to sell specified models of its aircraft for several decades to come. The airlines, in turn, can develop a schedule for retiring old aircraft and begin to adapt their operations to the models they will be flying in the future. Thus both sides expect to reap benefits from these arrangements for many years.[42]

Network forms of organization are prevalent in high-tech industries, where they allow older, established firms to gain access to the hot new discoveries being made by scientists in universities and in small, creative organizations. For example, the U.S. biotechnology industry is characterized by networks of relationships between new biotechnology firms dedicated to research and new product development and established firms in industries that can use these new products, such as pharmaceuticals. In return for sharing technical information with the larger firms, the smaller firms gain access to their partners' resources for product testing, marketing, and distribution.[43] Big pharmaceutical firms such as Merck or Eli Lilly gain from such partnerships because the smaller firms typically develop new drugs in as little as five years, versus an eight-year average development cycle in the larger firms.[44] Biochips, which blend computer technology with biological science, are among the most exciting products being created through new network organizations. Taking advantage of a computer's ability to process massive amounts of information, biochips are being developed to scan people's genetic makeups and analyze risks associated with various genetically transmitted diseases.[45]

Being competitive increasingly requires establishing and managing strategic alliances with other firms. In a **strategic alliance,** two or more firms agree to cooperate in a venture that is expected to benefit both firms. When Eric Schmidt left Sun Microsystems to become CEO of Novell, the network software company, he knew that forming strategic partnerships with other high-tech firms was his top priority. That was the only way the firm could battle Microsoft Corporation, whose products were cutting into Novell's market share. In commenting on the qualifications of the new CEO, Wall Street analysts seemed confident that he could help Novell form strategic alliances with Oracle, Netscape, and similar companies. Schmidt added, "Of course, I'll be partnering pretty closely with Sun" (his former employer). All of these companies share one goal in common: to beat Microsoft![46]

A Changing Workforce: Older and More Diverse

At the same time that the size and shape of organizations are changing, the composition of the workforce has changed dramatically. One important change is its age distribution. A large portion of the U.S. workforce now is from the baby-boom generation (those born between 1946 and 1961), but fewer recent college graduates are entering the job market. Between 1990 and 2000, the number of people aged thirty-five to forty-seven will increase by 38 percent, and the number between forty-eight and fifty-three will increase by 67 percent. The size of the baby-boom generation created a huge workforce influx. In the late 1970s, for instance, about 3 million people entered the eighteen- to twenty-four-year-old age group each year. But, in 1990, only 1.3 million new workers were in this age group, and this number continues to shrink. One implication is that fewer employees now are expected to get more work done. For their organizations to survive, these employees must be highly productive.

Another important change is the increased diversity of the workforce. **Workforce diversity** refers to the mix of people from various backgrounds in today's labor force. More and more women are working, for example, resulting in a new gender mix that is nearly balanced instead of being male-dominated. Throughout this century, immigration patterns also have changed, resulting in more diversity in terms of

STRATEGIC ALLIANCE
Two or more firms agreeing to cooperate in a venture that is expected to benefit all the participants.

WORKFORCE DIVERSITY
A term that refers to the mix of people in terms of gender, age, race, and various ethnic backgrounds in today's labor force.

national heritage. In the 1990s, awareness of increasing workforce diversity has grown steadily. A Department of Labor report, *Workforce 2000,* initially drew attention to this issue by highlighting the changing demographics of the U.S. labor force. Then, a follow-up report by the Department of Labor's Glass Ceiling Commission showed that women and non-Caucasian men were advancing up the corporate ladder more slowly than Caucasian men were. In the Big Six accounting firms, for example, women comprise about one-quarter of the workforce, but less than 10 percent of partners are women.[47] Now, a decade after the term *workforce diversity* was coined, most Fortune 500 companies have started so-called diversity initiatives.[48] These initiatives are intended to make the workplace more hospitable for women and minorities and prevent discriminatory practices.

The ***multicultural organization,*** with a workforce that includes the full mix of cultures found in the population at large and a commitment to full utilization of its human resources, presents a significant challenge to managers. They will need to come up with creative approaches to managing people with highly diverse backgrounds. For example, the group dynamics in a team that has some members who were raised in cultures that emphasize collective behavior—found in many parts of Asia—will be much different from those of a team whose members all were raised in cultures that emphasize the role of the individual—found in Germany and the United States.[49] Different managerial approaches are needed to maximize the effectiveness of such teams. The increasing diversity of the workforce, combined with changing attitudes about differences that may have been ignored in the past (including religious traditions and life-style choices) presents both challenges and opportunities for organizations and managers.

MULTICULTURAL ORGANIZATION

An organization with a workforce that includes the full mix of cultures found in the population at large and is committed to utilizing fully their capabilities.

CHANGING TECHNOLOGY

In the United States, more than 9 million people work in the high-tech sector, developing, producing, and delivering new electronic and communications-related products. They contributed 27 percent of the growth in the U.S. gross domestic product (GDP) during the mid-1990s.[50] Rapid changes in technology are transforming all sorts of jobs. Consider the typical sales job at Caradon Everest, a British maker of replacement windows. Twenty years ago, its salespeople could make a good living in sales if they could talk and read a price list. Now, the salespeople visit customers with laptop computers in hand. Using specially designed software, they show customers how standard products can be reconfigured to fit their needs and how much those products will cost. A process that once required a week's time and assistance from technical experts now can be done on the spot. This technology has changed the job of the sales force, who can now spend more time defining customer problems and finding solutions to them, rather than selling standardized products. It also changed the jobs of area sales managers, as Richard Jones points out. Instead of spending his time trying to resolve "silly little problems" (e.g., pricing errors), he has more time to coach his sales staff on strategies for dealing more effectively with customers.[51]

New technologies are changing jobs in all types of industries. Already, hundreds of thousands of people are working full or part time at home, connected to an office by means of a computer, modem, and fax machine. Eventually millions of people will work at home instead of commuting to an office.[52] Managers will be responsible for supervising work done by people they may seldom even see. Like managers at FedEx, you may find yourself responding to employees' questions during an in-house TV talk show. Without knowing precisely what the future holds in terms of technology, we can nevertheless be certain that it will be used to reduce simple repetitive tasks, freeing people to spend more time analyzing problems and developing creative solutions.

GLOBALIZATION

During the past fifty years, technological advances in transportation and communications have spurred the growth of international commerce. As a result, many firms evolved from being purely domestic to becoming truly global. The first step in this evolution was simply to export goods for sale in one or two foreign markets. The next step was to manufacture those goods overseas because that was more efficient than shipping products thousands of miles to markets. Setting up operations close to foreign markets also helps a company better understand its customers. For example, Mercedes-Benz, the German automaker, recently opened its first foreign plant in Alabama, where it will produce its first sports utility vehicle. The company hopes that this sportier model will appeal to younger, less affluent buyers, who are the key to the company's future growth.[53]

Mercedes is just beginning to evolve into a global company; other companies started years ago. Many that succeeded with their initial foreign ventures continued to evolve to the point of becoming transnational. A transnational firm has "headquarters" in several nations, and no single national culture is dominant in the firm.[54] Customers in various countries may not even think of such firms as being foreign owned. For example, many U.S. customers don't think of Shell Oil Company as a Dutch firm.

What are the implications of globalization for managers? One is that more and more top-level employees will be sent on overseas assignments. These assignments won't be limited to top-level executives, either. Mercedes shipped 160 Alabamans to Germany, where they learned their jobs working alongside their German counterparts. In addition, seventy Germans were shipped to Alabama to help train the rest of the new U.S. employees. According to a worldwide survey of 351 companies, 43 percent of them plan to increase the number of employees sent on overseas assignments; only 13 percent plan to reduce overseas assignments in the near future. The most frequent destinations for employees are Asia and Europe. About 80 percent of companies with expatriates send their employees to these two regions. Next most popular are North, Central, and South America, which received expatriates from about 50 percent of the companies.[55]

Middle managers and the professionals they supervise often are the ones being sent on international assignments. Conversely, more and more employees are being hired from other countries. In the United States, domestic labor shortages in certain fields mean that some organizations cannot succeed unless they consider the entire world as their labor market. Similarly, the changing political and economic landscape in Europe means that workers can now more freely move across national borders to find desirable jobs. Thus many middle managers are working with a global workforce without even leaving home.

CHAPTER SUMMARY

In this chapter, we introduced several concepts that you need to understand in order to be a successful manager in the years ahead. Because the nature and scope of management are changing so rapidly, no simple prescription can be given for how to manage.

Rather, managers today and in the future need to develop six important competencies to enable them to lead dynamic organizations and tackle a variety of emerging organizational issues. You now should be able to do the following.

1. DEFINE MANAGERS AND MANAGEMENT.

Managers establish organizational goals and then direct the work of subordinates, whom they depend on to achieve those goals. Managers acquire and allocate the human and material resources without which organizations couldn't exist. Effective management is essential to the success of an organization.

2. DESCRIBE WHAT MANAGERS DO.

The managerial functions—planning, organizing, leading, and controlling—are what managers do. Managers at different levels in an organization spend their time differently, but they all spend at least some time performing each function. The three basic levels of management are first-line, middle, and top. First-line managers are directly responsible for the production of goods and services. They supervise workers and solve specific problems. Middle managers coordinate the work of several first-line managers or direct the operations of a functional department. They translate top management's goals into specific goals and programs for implementation. Top managers establish overall organizational goals and direct the activities of an entire organization or a major segment of an organization.

Managers at different levels divide their time among the managerial functions quite differently. First-line managers spend most of their time leading and controlling and the rest planning and organizing. Middle managers spend most of their time organizing and leading and the rest planning and controlling. Top managers spend most of their time planning and leading and very little time directly organizing and controlling. Managerial work also varies in scope, broadening at each higher level.

3. UNDERSTAND THE COMPETENCIES USED IN MANAGERIAL WORK AND BEGIN TO PRACTICE THEM.

To be an effective manager in a dynamic environment requires six managerial competencies: communication, teamwork, planning and administration, strategic action, global awareness, and self-management. You can develop these competencies through study, training, and experience. By doing so, you can prepare yourself for a variety of jobs in various industries and countries. You can continue practicing your managerial competencies by completing the exercises at the end of this chapter.

4. DESCRIBE THE CHANGING CONTEXT OF MANAGERIAL WORK.

Four important environmental trends are organizational restructuring, a changing workforce, changing technology, and globalization. Through downsizing and outsourcing, organizations are becoming smaller, flatter, and more dependent on strategic alliances with other firms. At the same time, the workforce is getting older and more diverse, which creates many new challenges. They include how to take advantage of the multiple perspectives that employees can bring to bear on issues and problems and how to keep employees satisfied when there is less opportunity for promotion and advancement. New technologies are rapidly changing the nature of work and the workplace. Electronic communications make it possible for people who seldom see each other to work together as a team. New technologies can also free employees from more routine and mundane tasks, giving them more time to spend on problem solving and improving relationships with customers. Globalization requires that managers stay abreast of economic, social, and political trends around the world, and understand the implications of these trends for their organizations. It also means that more employees are being sent overseas on temporary assignments.

QUESTIONS FOR DISCUSSION

1. What functions do managers usually perform today?

2. Identify three types of organizations. What are the similarities and differences in the jobs of managers at various levels in these organizations?

3. Explain the impact of workforce diversity on organizations.

4. Describe the six managerial competencies discussed in this chapter. Explain how you can use them in your life currently (e.g., in school, on the job, at home, etc.).

5. What challenges face first-line managers? Middle managers? Top managers?

6. Why are organizations restructuring themselves?

EXERCISES TO DEVELOP YOUR MANAGERIAL COMPETENCIES

1. **Self-Management Competency.** Write a short self-assessment of your managerial competencies, addressing the question: What are my strengths and weaknesses? Next, choose a relative or friend whom you can trust to be candid with you. Describe the six managerial competencies and ask that person to comment on your relative strengths and weaknesses in each. Finally, write down three things that you can begin doing immediately to improve one or more of your managerial competencies.

2. **Strategic Action Competency.** Observe a manager at a local business (e.g., a music store, an automobile dealership, or a restaurant). Explain the role of strategic action competency in this person's job. Which specific components of this competency (refer to Table 1.1) appear to be most important to this person's effectiveness? If you wanted to develop these components to prepare yourself to work at the job you observed, how would you go about it? Ask the person you observed to describe how he or she developed a strategic action competency.

3. **Communication Competency.** Select an industry or company of interest to you. Use at least two forms of communication (e.g., written, verbal, or electronic) to explore the possibility of getting a job in this industry or company. Your investigation might include (a) a visit to the human resource management or recruitment office of a company; (b) a visit to the career development office on your campus, if there is one; (c) writing a letter to a company or a professional or trade association to request information; and/or (d) exploring job announcements on the Internet. If you choose to pursue job openings on the Internet, you can begin by going to the home pages of some of the companies named in this book. A complete list of these home page addresses appears in the Internet Sources Appendix at the end of this book.

4. **Global Awareness Competency.** Where in the world, literally, would you like to work? Choose a country where you would like to work sometime but that is unfamiliar to you. Begin to learn about it by compiling some basic facts, such as: What language is spoken? What is the system of government? What is the dominant religion? Which industries are most important? Which large companies are headquartered there? Use whatever sources of information you can to complete this activity, including speaking with people who have lived in or visited the country, visiting a professor who teaches about this country, and exploring the Internet.

REAL-TIME CASE ANALYSIS

BILL GATES MANAGES A GIANT CADRE OF TECHIES

Founded in 1975 by Bill Gates and Paul Allen, Microsoft markets a variety of PC products. Perhaps most significant to the company's success was its introduction in 1981 of MS-DOS, a software operating system that now dominates the PC market. Products such as the Windows series, Microsoft Word, and Microsoft Excel are now familiar to most American PC users. Microsoft's financial success is undisputed. By the firm's twenty-first birthday, annual profits had reached nearly $3 billion. Its stock price, valued at $21 per share when it was first offered to the public in 1985, had grown 300 percent. Microsoft had become the world's largest software manufacturer, employing 20,000 people worldwide. These employees can be roughly grouped into three categories: research and development (36 percent), sales and support (46 percent), and operations (18 percent). The nearly $2 billion annual budget for R&D expenditures reflects the importance of this activity for Microsoft. The average age of its employees is about thirty-four—a figure that has inched up gradually over the years. About 80 percent of them are younger than the firm's boyish-looking forty-plus-year-old CEO, Bill Gates.

How does Gates manage these techies? He begins by hiring "smarts." "There is no way of getting around [the fact] that in terms of IQ, you've got to be elitist in picking the people to write software," Gates says. Also, he says that he prefers freshly minted college graduates because "young people are willing to learn." Of course, being smart isn't all it takes to get a job at Microsoft. Gates wants people who communicate their thoughts fluently and persuasively. He's fond of challenging his employees with tough questions—and expects quick answers. Regardless of how smart you are or how well you write programming code, if you can't win the verbal battles fought at Microsoft, you won't be there long. And, you need to be able to work as part of a team because Microsoft is structured around teams. First there is the team at the top, referred to as BOOP (Bill and the Office of the President). It includes executive vice-presidents for worldwide sales and support and worldwide products and the chief operating officer. These executives help Gates organize and structure the firm and develop the firm's strategic plans. For example, one of the first moves of the executive vice-president for worldwide products when he took the job in 1995 was to reconfigure forty product groups into five divisions. This reorganization, they hoped, would bring more uniformity to the efforts of the many individual teams working throughout the firm. Customers want products that are compatible with each other, which won't happen if every product development group goes off in its own direction when writing code. More recently, the executive vice-presidents were involved in Microsoft's decision to make a major investment in Apple Computer, a company that had long been treated as an arch rival.

Despite the size of Microsoft and this recent move toward giving teams somewhat less autonomy, Microsoft feels entrepreneurial to employees. Sandi, a mid-level group leader who joined Microsoft after ten years of experience in the industry, says that "the ideas are bottom up. It's not dictated by senior management. They have the general ideas they view as strategic for Microsoft, but the how, the why, and the what comes from the ingenuity and detail of the individual teams. . . . I'm responsible for knowing what my costs are. . . . It's very empowering, more than having the tools or getting an initiative going, to know that I'm held accountable for my business. To me, that is really motivating."

Work teams aren't the only groups at Microsoft. Smart people who communicate well and are good at teamwork come in all varieties. The Microsoft Diversity Advisory Council ensures that the company addresses their diverse concerns by offering training, resources, and support to employee groups such as Blacks at Microsoft; Chinese at Microsoft; Gay, Lesbian, and Bisexuals at Microsoft; Microsoft's Women's Group; Jews at Microsoft; Microsoft Grupo Ibero-Americano; and Native Americans at Microsoft. These groups serve employees' needs, but that isn't their only function. Sandi notes that the sense of commitment that people feel reaches beyond the company and into their communities. For example, Blacks at Microsoft hosted a one-day career development activity for local minority students. The eighty attendees were given advice and guidance about applying for college and seeking jobs. "People at Microsoft tend to reach far beyond the corporate campus to make a difference," observes Sandi. Bill Gates has built Microsoft in his own image. A product of the baby-boom generation, he will soon face a dilemma. If he remains convinced that younger, less experienced employees are vital to creativity and innovation in his firm, he will soon find himself managing an organization filled with Generation Xers and the children of his baby-boomer colleagues. But if he sticks to his current approach of hiring in his own image, he may discover that finding fresh ideas will become harder and harder.[56]

QUESTIONS

1. Will the next generation of employees find Bill Gates's management style as appealing as the earlier generation did? Should Gates stick with his current approach of hiring in his own image and not worry about the fact that the average age of his workforce is increasing, or will that put the firm in jeopardy?

2. What competencies seem most important for employees at Microsoft? Why are they important to this high-tech firm?

3. Assuming the firm continues to grow, what do you think are the most significant challenges for managers at Microsoft?

To learn more, visit Bill Gates at his Web site,

www.microsoft.com/billgates

VIDEO CASE

SOUTHWEST AIRLINES: THE FAMILY THAT FLIES TOGETHER

Southwest Airlines is a close, almost family-like organization, and bears the strong stamp of one of its "fathers," cofounder Herb Kelleher. In 1990, the family caught its breath from two decades of rapid growth and threw itself a party.

Southwest's year-and-a-half-long party for itself wasn't just that: It was a unifying theme, a public relations campaign, and, not least, a long and involved effort. Company managers needed to plan the various events (and if the party lasted eighteen months itself, a reasonable assumption is that the planning began months—if not years—before) and to direct employees responsible for implementing those plans. Time and energy spent on the anniversary meant diverting resources from carrying passengers efficiently and cheaply to their destinations, yet senior management judged that those efforts would pay off, even if the benefits were less tangible than the effect of passenger-miles on the balance sheet.

An airline is a special type of organization; in this case, management includes executive officers (e.g., the CEO and CFO) and professional officers (e.g., the company's pilots). With a sharp dividing line between worker groupings (especially where various categories of employees may belong to separate unions), making all employees feel a part of a corporate family can be a challenge. Many of the events of the year-and-a-half-long party highlighted individuals and groups among the airline's employees, at every level.

Herb Kelleher is a very hands-on CEO, from hamming it up with employees at company picnics to representing the company personally to investors and the public. For a large, public company, Southwest has an atypically charismatic and visible CEO in Kelleher. CEOs need to budget their scarce time. In opting to be so involved with the workforce and in the company's public relations, Kelleher readily delegates other executive responsibilities (e.g., discussions with major investors or negotiations with suppliers). Kelleher personally demonstrates a commitment to communication and teamwork, as he inspires the company to think of itself as family.

If Southwest is a family, the company has also cast itself as a friendly neighbor in its operating area, as a locally focused alternative to larger, impersonal airlines. From its "Lone Star" anniversary plane to the company's participation in state and local events,

Southwest attempts to blend into its customers' communities. The twentieth anniversary was as much a tribute to the State of Texas as to the airline, and the airline invited numerous state officials and celebrities to celebrate Southwest's success as a hometown business.

ON THE WEB

Companies often register a name, initials, an acronym, or a nickname to promote or capitalize on brand recognition—*www.iflyswa.com* (for "I Fly Southwest Airlines") in Southwest's case. Browsing Southwest's site reveals that, since the twentieth anniversary, the company has placed new planes in service to honor other states in its route network and has dedicated a twenty-fifth anniversary plane to its employees.

A company's Web site can be a powerful communications tool. Southwest's corporate style comes across in the choice of graphics and layout (a familiar airline gate likeness) and content from the precise (airline schedules) to the chatty. The impression is one of a company that's customer-oriented and attending to customer concerns. Included is an honest and clear explanation of why it has elected not to attempt to serve its customers via e-mail.

The Web also provides a voice for other groups, and even individuals. The Transport Workers Union of America (*www.twu.org*) represents some of Southwest's employees, and the union can use the Web to communicate quickly and easily its own information to members, the press, and the public at large. Using a Web search engine such as HotBot (*www.hotbot.com*) or AltaVista (*altavista.digital.com*), you can find media and other coverage of a company. Using HotBot and the keywords "strike" and "Southwest Airlines" leads to information about the 1997 flight attendants' contract dispute, for example.

You can find general business and financial information on publicly traded companies via the Web by using, for example, the Yahoo! finance service (*quote.yahoo.com*) and a company's stock market symbol (Southwest's is "LUV"). The Federal Aviation Administration (*www.faa.gov*) compiles statistics on all U.S. airlines, including performance measures such as the frequency of on-time arrivals and departures and safety-related incidents.

QUESTIONS

1. What sort of relations does Southwest Airlines maintain among its executives, officers, and employees? How formal is the managerial environment at Southwest?

2. How does Southwest invite employees to think of the company as more than a mere employer? What benefits do employees enjoy?

3. What special circumstances distinguish airlines from other large businesses? How might they promote, or discourage, a feeling of corporate family?

To help you answer these questions and learn more about Southwest Airlines, visit the company's home page at

www.iflyswa.com

Case contributed by Ross Stapleton-Gray, President, TeleDiplomacy, Inc., a technology and policy consultancy, and Adjunct Professor in Georgetown University's Communication, Culture, and Technology program.

Chapter

2

The Evolution of Management

LEARNING OBJECTIVES

AFTER STUDYING THIS CHAPTER, YOU SHOULD BE ABLE TO:

1 DESCRIBE THE THREE BRANCHES OF THE TRADITIONAL VIEWPOINT OF MANAGEMENT: BUREAUCRATIC, SCIENTIFIC, AND ADMINISTRATIVE.

2 STATE THE BEHAVIORAL VIEWPOINT'S CONTRIBUTION TO MANAGEMENT.

3 DESCRIBE THE SYSTEMS VIEWPOINT AND THE USE OF QUANTITATIVE TECHNIQUES TO MANAGE ORGANIZATIONS.

4 EXPLAIN THE PLACE OF THE CONTINGENCY VIEWPOINT IN MODERN MANAGEMENT.

5 DESCRIBE THE IMPACT OF THE QUALITY VIEWPOINT ON MANAGEMENT PRACTICES.

Outline

Managing at Levi Strauss

Imagine that you're a manufacturer in the garment industry and you discover that two of your sewing subcontractors in Bangladesh are using child labor, a clear violation of the law. If these kids lose their jobs, some of them may be driven to prostitution. What do you do?

For Robert Haas, CEO of Levi Strauss, the answer was simple: Take the children out of the factory; continue paying their wages on the condition that they attend school full time; and guarantee them jobs upon reaching fourteen, the local legal age for working in a factory.

The reason for this decision is that Levi Strauss has been paying attention to worker loyalty and trust throughout its history. During the Great Depression, then CEO Walter Haas kept his workers employed lay-ing new floors at the factory while waiting for business to revive. It recently stacked unsold inventory in a cafeteria in its South African plant rather than shut the plant down because of a steep decline in sales.

Throughout its history, Levi Strauss has tried to manage according to the principles laid out in its Aspirations Statement. This statement stresses teamwork, trust, diversity, recognition, ethics, openness, and empowerment. The Levi Strauss foundation does not support organizations that discriminate against atheists and gays. Managers' bonus pay, which can amount to two-thirds of their compensation, is tied explicitly to their aspirational behaviors. Their immediate boss, peers, and subordinates rate managers' performance on those aspirational behaviors. The company has promised to pay each of its 37,000 employees an extra year's salary if collectively they can meet the profitability target for 2001. This effort is requiring Strauss to double the amount of money it spends on education, showing employees how their behaviors relate to business results. Top management knows that it can't run a global organization from San Francisco, and thus the company needs an empowered workforce.[1]

* * *

To learn more about Levi Strauss, visit the company's home page at

www.levi.com

THE EVOLUTION OF MANAGEMENT THOUGHT

1

DESCRIBE THE THREE BRANCHES OF THE TRADITIONAL VIEWPOINT OF MANAGEMENT: BUREAUCRATIC, SCIENTIFIC, AND ADMINISTRATIVE

Working for a global company with plants scattered throughout the world is getting to be commonplace. In the past ten years or so, companies with complex systems, such as Levi Strauss, IBM, Colgate Palmolive, Marriott, and Nike, have challenged their employees to manage on a global scale. Managers now lead employees whom they seldom, if ever, see and who may know more about solving a problem than they do. Although new methods of managing employees are needed to keep pace with changes in today's organizations and technology, let's not discard what happened in management before the arrival of the information superhighway. The reason is that management today reflects the evolution of concepts, viewpoints, and experience gained over many decades.

During the thirty years following the Civil War, the United States emerged as a leading industrial nation. The shift from an agrarian to an urban society was abrupt and, for many Americans, meant drastic adjustment. Never before in the nation's history had so many individuals made so much money so quickly. By the end of the century a new corporate capitalism ruled by a prosperous professional class had arisen. Captains of industry freely wielded mergers and acquisitions and engaged in cutthroat competition as they created huge monopolies in the oil, meat, steel, sugar, and tobacco industries. The federal government did nothing to interfere with these monopolies. On the one hand, new technology born of the war effort offered the promise of progress and growth. On the other hand, rapid social change and a growing disparity between rich and poor caused increasing conflict and instability.

The year 1886 marked several important turning points in business and management history. Henry R. Towne (1844–1924), an engineer and cofounder of the Yale Lock Company, presented a paper titled "The Engineer as an Economist" to the American Society of Mechanical Engineers. In that paper Towne proposed that the American Society of Mechanical Engineers create an economic section to act as a clearinghouse and forum for "shop management" and "shop accounting." Shop management would deal with the subjects of organization, responsibility, reports, and the "executive management" of industrial works, mills, and factories. Shop accounting would treat the nuts and bolts of time and wage systems, cost determination and allocation, bookkeeping methods, and manufacturing accounting. The society would develop a body of literature, record members' experiences, and provide a forum for exchanging managers' ideas.

Other events in 1886 influenced the development of modern management thought and practice. During this boom period in U.S. business history, employers generally regarded labor as a commodity to be purchased as cheaply as possible and maintained at minimal expense. Thus it was also a peak period of labor unrest—during 1886 more than 600,000 employees were out of work because of strikes and lockouts. On May 4, 1886, a group of labor leaders led a demonstration in Chicago's Haymarket Square in support of an eight-hour workday. During the demonstration someone threw a bomb, killing seven bystanders. The Haymarket Affair was a setback for organized labor, because many people began to equate unionism with anarchy.

In his pioneering study of labor history in 1886, *The Labor Movement in America,* Richard T. Ely advocated a less radical approach to labor-management relations. Ely cautioned labor to work within the existing economic and political system. One union that followed Ely's advice was the American Federation of Labor (AFL), organized in 1886 by Samuel Gompers and Adolph Strasser. A conservative, "bread and butter" union, the AFL avoided politics and industrial unionism and organized skilled workers along craft lines (carpenters, plumbers, bricklayers, and other trades). Like other early unions, the AFL protected its members from unfair management practices. Gompers's goal was to increase labor's bargaining power within the existing capitalistic framework. Under his leadership, the AFL dominated the American labor scene for almost half a century.

Chicago in 1886 also was the birthplace of an aspiring mail-order business called Sears, Roebuck and Company. From its beginning Sears, founded by railroad station agent Richard W. Sears, who sold watches to farmers in his area, characterized the mass distribution system that promoted the country's economic growth. For the first time, affordable fine goods were available to both rural and urban consumers. Today, Sears offers customers some eleven different specialty catalogs, operates thousands of retail stores, and offers a wide range of insurance through Allstate. Also in 1886, the first Coca-Cola was served in Atlanta. This scarcely noticed event launched an enterprise that grew into a gigantic multinational corporation. Other companies that began in 1886 and remain in operation today include Avon Products, Cosmopolitan Magazine, Johnson & Johnson, Munsingwear, Upjohn, and Westinghouse.

Thus 1886 marked the origins of several well-known, large-scale enterprises; modern management thought and practice; and major labor unions. Even as these events were unfolding, a new symbol of optimism and opportunity took final form on an island in New York harbor: The Statue of Liberty was dedicated in October 1886.

Why are we recounting century-old events in a book that claims to teach management for the next century? One reason is that many of the principles established in the early days of management are still used today. The rules and regulations found in all organizations were originally created to protect managers from undue pressures to favor certain groups of people. Today FedEx, the IRS, and Nations-Bank, to name but a few, use rules and regulations for the same reason. A second reason is that the past is a good teacher, identifying practices that have been successful and practices that have failed. Recognizing that employees join organizations for social as well as economic reasons has led many organizations, such as Wainwright Industries and Gateway 2000, to use teams to solve problems and base employee pay on team results. A third reason is that history gives a feel for the types of problems that managers long have struggled to find solutions for. Many of these problems, such as low morale, high absenteeism, and poor workmanship, still exist in many organizations and continue to plague managers.

Looking back also underscores the fact that professional management hasn't been around all that long. In earlier, preindustrial societies, men and women paced their work according to the sun, the seasons, and the demand for what they produced. Small communities encouraged personal, often familial, relationships between employers and employees. The explosive growth of urban industry—and the factory system in particular—changed the face of the workplace forever. Workers in cities were forced to adapt to the factory's formal structure and rules and to labor long hours for employers they never saw. Many were poorly educated and needed considerable oral instruction and hands-on training in unfamiliar tasks.

The emergence of large-scale business enterprises in Canada, the United States, and Western Europe raised issues and created challenges that previously had applied only to governments. Businesses needed the equivalent of government leaders—managers—to hire and train employees and then to lead and motivate them. Managers also were needed to develop plans and design work units and, while doing so, make a profit, never a requirement for governments! In this chapter we briefly review how management viewpoints have evolved since 1886 to meet those needs.

During the past century, theorists have developed numerous responses to the same basic management question: What is the best way to manage an organization? We continue to study those responses because they still apply to the manager's job. In the following sections we discuss the five most widely accepted viewpoints of management that have evolved since about 1886: traditional (or classical), behavioral, systems, contingency, and quality. These viewpoints are based on different assumptions about the behavior of people in organizations, the key goals of an organization, the types of problems faced, and the methods that should be used to solve those problems. Figure 2.1 shows when each viewpoint emerged and began to gain popularity. As you can see, all five still influence managers' thinking. In fact, one important source of disagreement among today's managers is the emphasis that should be given to each of them. Thus a major purpose of this chapter is to show you not only how each viewpoint has contributed to the historical evolution of modern management thought, but also how each can be used effectively in different circumstances now and into the future.

The oldest and perhaps most widely accepted view of management is the *traditional* (or classical) *viewpoint.* It is split into three main branches: bureaucratic management, scientific management, and administrative management. All three emerged during roughly the same time period, the late 1890s through the early 1900s, when engineers were trying to make organizations run like well-oiled machines. The founders of these three branches came from Germany, the United States, and France, respectively.

BUREAUCRATIC MANAGEMENT

Bureaucratic management relies on rules, a set hierarchy, a clear division of labor, and detailed procedures. Max Weber (1864–1920), a German social historian,

---

TRADITIONAL VIEWPOINT
The oldest of the five principal viewpoints of management; stresses the manager's role in a strict hierarchy and focuses on efficient and consistent job performance.

BUREAUCRATIC MANAGEMENT
A system that relies on rules, a set hierarchy, a clear division of labor, and detailed rules and procedures.

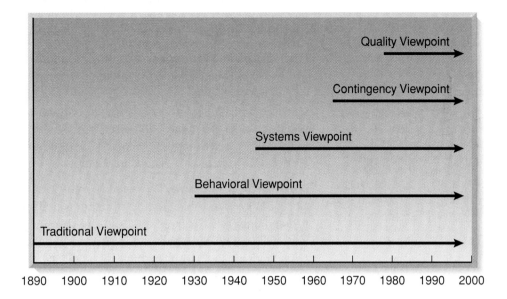

is most closely associated with bureaucratic management (so named because Weber based his work on studies of Germany's governmental bureaucracy). Although Weber was one of the first theorists to deal with the problems of organizations, he wasn't widely recognized by managers and scholars in the United States until his work was translated into English in 1947. He was concerned primarily with the broad social and economic issues facing society; his writings on bureaucracy represent only part of his total contribution to social theory.[2]

Bureaucratic management provides a blueprint of how an entire organization should operate. It prescribes seven characteristics: a formal system of rules, impersonality, division of labor, hierarchical structure, a detailed authority structure, life-long career commitment, and rationality. Together these characteristics represent a formal, somewhat rigid method of managing. Let's take a look at this method, setting aside for the moment all the negative connotations the term bureaucracy has today and focusing on the system's strengths, consistency, and predictability.

Rules. As formal guidelines for the behavior of employees while they are on the job, ***rules*** can help provide the discipline an organization needs if it is to reach its goals. Adherence to rules ensures uniformity of procedures and operations and helps maintain organizational stability, regardless of individual managers' or employees' personal desires.

Impersonality. Reliance on rules leads to treating employees impersonally. That is, all employees are evaluated according to rules and objective data, such as sales or units produced. Although the term *impersonality* can also have negative connotations, Weber believed that this approach guaranteed fairness for all employees— an impersonal superior doesn't allow subjective personal or emotional considerations to color evaluations of subordinates.

Division of Labor. The division of labor involves dividing duties into simpler, more specialized tasks. It enables the organization to use personnel and job-training resources efficiently. Managers and employees are assigned and perform duties based on specialization and personal expertise. Unskilled employees can be assigned tasks that are relatively easy to learn and do. For example, employee

RULES

Specification of a course of action that must be followed in dealing with a particular problem.

turnover at fast-food restaurants such as McDonald's, Burger King, Hardee's, and Wendy's is over 200 percent a year. Because of the narrow division of labor, most fast-food jobs can be learned quickly and require only unskilled labor. Thus high turnover in this type of business may not create serious service problems.

Hierarchical Structure. Most organizations have a pyramid-shaped hierarchical structure, as illustrated in Figure 2.2. This type of structure ranks jobs according to the amount of authority (the right to decide) given to each. Typically, authority increases at each higher level to the top of the hierarchy. Those in lower level positions are under the control and direction of those in higher level positions. According to Weber, a well-defined hierarchy helps control employee behavior by making clear exactly where each stands in relation to everyone else in the organization.

Authority Structure. A system based on rules, impersonal supervision, division of labor, and a hierarchical structure is tied together by an authority structure. It determines who has the right to make decisions of varying importance at different levels within the organization. Weber identified three types of authority structures: traditional, charismatic, and rational-legal.

- **Traditional authority** is based on custom, ancestry, gender, birth order, and the like. The divine right of kings and the magical influence of tribal witch doctors are examples of traditional authority.

- **Charismatic authority** is evident when subordinates suspend their own judgment and comply voluntarily with a leader because of special personal qualities or abilities they perceive in that individual. Charismatic leaders (e.g., Jesus, Joan of Arc, Gandhi, Martin Luther King, Jesse Jackson, and President Ronald Reagan) often head social, political, and religious movements. In contrast, business leaders seldom rely solely on charismatic authority, but some, such as Ben Cohen (cofounder of Ben & Jerry's Homemade Ice Cream Company) and Mary Kay Ash (CEO, Mary Kay Cosmetics), have used their charisma to motivate and influence subordinates.

- **Rational-legal authority** is based on established laws and rules that are applied uniformly. A superior is obeyed because of the position occupied within the organization's hierarchy. This authority depends on employees' acceptance of the organization's rules.

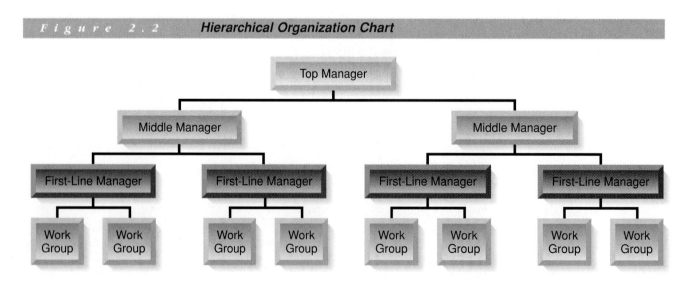

Figure 2.2   *Hierarchical Organization Chart*

Lifelong Career Commitment. In a bureaucratic management system, employment is viewed as a lifelong career commitment. That is, both the employee and the organization view themselves as being committed to each other over the working life of the employee. Traditionally, Asian organizations, such as Sanyo, Samsung, Lucky Gold Star, and Toyota, have hired key workers with the expectation—by both parties—that a permanent employment contract was being made. In general, lifelong career commitment means that job security is guaranteed as long as the employee is technically qualified and performs satisfactorily. Entrance requirements, such as level of education and experience, ensure that hiring is based on qualifications rather than connections. The organization uses job security, tenure, step-by-step salary increases, and pensions to ensure that employees satisfactorily perform assigned duties. Promotion is granted when an employee demonstrates the competencies required to handle the demands of the next higher position. Organizational level is assumed to correspond closely with expertise. Managers in bureaucratic organizations, such as the civil service, often rely on the results of written and physical tests, amount of formal education, and previous work experience in making hiring and promotion decisions.

Rationality. The last characteristic of bureaucratic management is rationality, which means using the most efficient means available. Managers in a bureaucratic management system operate logically and "scientifically," with all decisions leading directly to achieving the organization's goals. Goal-directed activities then allow the organization to use its financial and human resources efficiently. In addition, rationality allows general organizational goals to be broken into more specific goals for each part of the organization. At Celanese, for example, the overall corporate goals are to provide customers with chemicals and technical services of superior quality at a fair price and to earn enough profit to maintain the company's growth. A goal of its research and development (R&D) department is to pursue new chemical mixtures and to transform technological breakthroughs into high-quality products and services. If all departments in the company reach their individual goals, the corporation reaches its overall goals.[3]

Ranking Organizations by Bureaucratic Orientation. We can use the seven characteristics of bureaucratic management to rank organizations from low to high with respect to their bureaucratic orientation. As Figure 2.3 shows, government agencies (e.g., the Internal Revenue Service) and some private companies (e.g., United Parcel Service) rank high. Some creative and innovative companies (e.g., Dreamworks SKG and Richards Advertising) rank low.

Such rankings have to be interpreted carefully, however, because differences within organizations make precise measurement difficult. One organization may be highly bureaucratic in its division of labor but only slightly bureaucratic in its use of rules. In another organization these levels may be reversed. Are the organizations equally bureaucratic? No one can say for sure. Moreover, the degree of bureaucracy within an organization may vary considerably among departments and

Figure 2.3 **Continuum of Bureaucratic Orientation**

Low Bureaucratic Structure
• Dreamworks SKG
• Richards Advertising

Mid-Range Bureaucracy
• Coca-Cola
• Sony

High Bureaucratic Structure
• Internal Revenue Service
• UPS

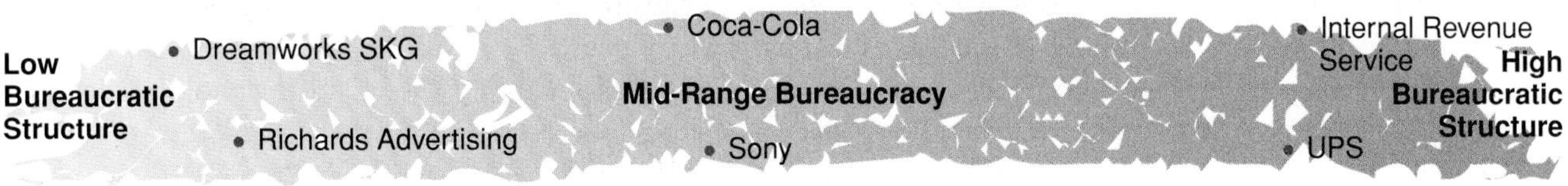

divisions. For example, Sony falls near the middle of the bureaucratic continuum, but its manufacturing plants, which produce standardized household goods (e.g., TVs, radios, clocks, and VCRs), tend to be more bureaucratic than its R&D departments, whose creativity would be stifled by too many rules.

Benefits of Bureaucracy. The expected benefits of bureaucratic management are efficiency and consistency. A bureaucracy functions best when many routine tasks need to be done. Then lower level employees can handle the bulk of the work by simply following rules and procedures. The fruits of their labor should be of standard (high) quality and produced at the rate necessary to meet organizational goals. At United Parcel Service (UPS), the use of rules and regulations for the size and weight of a package enable it to deliver more than one million packages daily throughout the world.

Costs of Bureaucracy. The same aspects of bureaucratic management that can increase one organization's efficiency can lead to great inefficiency in another. Managers at Lucent Technologies, Ernst & Young, Hospital Corporation of America, and others report that the orderliness of a bureaucracy often leads to inefficiencies that cannot be tolerated by companies operating in today's changing times. The following are five, often unanticipated, drawbacks of bureaucratic management.[4]

1. **Rigid rules and red tape.** Rigid adherence to rules and routines for their own sake is a frequent complaint of employees and customers of many organizations. Such a system leaves little room for individual freedom and creativity. This rigidity may foster low motivation, entrenched "career" employees, high turnover among the best employees, and shoddy work. A significant amount of time and money can be wasted.

2. **Protection of authority.** Managers in a bureaucratic organization may ignore issues of employee productivity while protecting and expanding their own authority. Caterpillar attacked the problem head-on. Management believed that the company couldn't afford to support a maze of corporate buck-passers, so it changed the system by focusing on customer satisfaction. Employees use their PCs to swap essential information and determine exactly what type of engine a customer wants. A computer-controlled monorail system and robots bring employees the engine, parts, and computer-generated information about what to do. This system requires 29 percent fewer people than the old system. Employees work on engines at their own pace and until they are satisfied that the job has been done right.

3. **Slow decision making.** Large, complex organizations depend heavily on timely decisions. In a highly bureaucratic organization, however, adherence to rules and procedures may take precedence over effective, timely decision making. When that happens, rules take on a life of their own. Formality and ritual delay decisions at every level until all the red tape has been cleared, petty insistence on power and status privileges has been satisfied, and any chance of blame for errors in judgment has been minimized.

4. **Incompatibility with changing technology.** Advancing technology may make bureaucratic management inappropriate. Jay Shipowitz of Ace Cashless Express believes that narrowly defined jobs based on rules and regulations generate little trust and sharing of information. There, the technology changes rapidly, and employees must be able to go directly to the person who has the information they need to do their jobs.

5. **Incompatibility with professional values.** More and more professionals are being hired by bureaucratic organizations to fill important decision-making positions. Professional values include advancing knowledge, serving clients and customers, and finding innovative solutions to problems. These values often are incompatible with the bureaucratic need for efficiency, order, and consistency. Bureaucratic authority is related to hierarchical position, but most professionals believe that authority stems from personal competence and technical knowledge. Deborah Cannon, a NationsBank vice-president, says that "I have to rely more on the professionalism and commitment of my people than on rules and regulations." NationsBank is developing a performance appraisal system that allows team members, peers, and even external customers to evaluate employees' work. They are doing so because the boss might not know enough to evaluate a particular person's contributions.

Assessing Bureaucratic Management. Not all bureaucratic organizations are inefficient and unprofitable. In fact, bureaucratic management is still widely and successfully used. This approach is most effective when (1) large amounts of standard information have to be processed and an efficient processing method has been found (as in credit card and insurance companies, the IRS, and traffic courts); (2) the needs of the customer are known and aren't likely to change (as in the registration of drivers in most states); (3) the technology is routine and stable, so employees can be easily and quickly taught how to operate machines (as at Taco Bell, McDonald's, Burger King, and in toll booths); and (4) the organization has to coordinate the activities of numerous employees in order to deliver a standardized service or product to the customer (as by the IRS, UPS, and the U.S. Postal Service).[5]

As countries and organizations move into a global arena, the challenges to the bureaucratic system are large. Many organizations in the European Union (EU), a group of fifteen European countries committed to relaxing trading barriers by forming a single European market, are battling procedures and red tape. The following Global Awareness Competency piece demonstrates some of the problems that managers face in that arena.

SCIENTIFIC MANAGEMENT

As manufacturing firms became larger and more complex in the late 1800s, not all managers could continue to be directly involved with production. Many began to spend more of their time administratively in planning, scheduling, and staffing activities. Also, managers were hard-pressed to keep up with advances in the new, machine-oriented production technology. The distancing of management from the physical production of goods created a need for operations specialists who could solve the personnel and productivity problems that accompanied rapid industrialization and threatened operating efficiency.

Frederick W. Taylor. Thus the stage was set for Frederick Winslow Taylor (1856–1915) to do his pioneering work in scientific management. Whereas bureaucratic management looks at broad organizational structures and work systems, *scientific management* focuses on individuals and their machines or tools. Its philosophy is that management practices should be based on proven fact and observation, not on hearsay or guesswork.[6] It is often practiced by Campbell Soup, Goodrich, and other manufacturers in their plants, but it is also widely used in service-based organizations, such as UPS.

Taylor, an American mechanical engineer, started out as a foreman at Midvale Steel Company in Philadelphia. He believed that increased productivity ultimately

SCIENTIFIC MANAGEMENT
Focuses on individual worker–machine relationships in manufacturing plants.

In their quest to standardize thousands of consumer products ranging from computers to condoms, EU officials have set up a variety of rules that challenge European traditions. Through flood and famine, the Dutch have worn their wooden clogs to work

for more than six centuries. The EU now says that all member organizations must apply the same safety standards—in this case steel-toed safety shoes—for employees engaged in heavy or dangerous work. The Dutch contend that the wooden shoe is an enduring and endearing symbol of their culture, much like the Eiffel Tower is to Paris. Eelke Schereon, an owner of a small shop in Noordbergum, says, "What's the matter? Our fathers and grandfathers wore these shoes. Now all of a sudden there's something wrong with them?"

Clog manufacturers say that wooden shoes have never been proven to cause an injury. On the contrary, they have evidence that clogs have protected farmers when cows stepped on their feet and have

shielded road workers whose toes might have otherwise been crushed or severed by the collapse of a steel boot plate. Clog manufacturers and the EU have hired The Netherlands Organization for Applied Scientific Research to determine whether clogs measure up to EU standards. If they pass, Dutch workers will wear clogs forever. If they fail, Dutch companies may ask workers to sign disclaimers saying that they bear all responsibility for injuries they might suffer in an accident because they will not stop wearing clogs—a clear violation of EU rules and regulations.[7]

* * *

To learn more about management practices in the European Union, visit the organization's home page at

www. eubasics.allmansland. com/general.html

depended on finding ways to make workers more efficient by using objective, scientific techniques.

When Taylor worked as a consultant to Bethlehem Steel, for example, he made a science of shoveling. Through observation and experimentation he looked for answers to questions such as the following.

1. Will a first-class worker do more work per day with a shovelful of five, ten, fifteen, twenty, thirty, or forty pounds?

2. What kinds of shovels work best with which materials?

3. How quickly can a shovel be pushed into a pile of coal and pulled out properly loaded?

4. How long does it take to swing a shovel backward and throw the load a specified horizontal distance at a specified height?

As Taylor accumulated answers to his questions, he developed views on how to increase the total amount shoveled per day. He started a program that matched workers, shovel sizes, materials, and the like for each job. By the end of the third year his program had reduced the number of shovelers needed from 600 to 140, while the average number of tons shoveled per worker per day rose from 16 to 50. Workers' earnings also increased from $1.15 to $1.88 a day.

Taylor used time-and-motion studies to analyze work flows, supervisory techniques, and worker fatigue. A ***time-and-motion study*** involves identifying and measuring a worker's physical movements when performing a task and then ana-

TIME-AND-MOTION STUDY
Identifies and measures a worker's physical movements when performing a task and then analyzes the results.

lyzing the results. Movements that slow production are dropped. One goal of a time-and-motion study is to make a job highly routine and efficient. Eliminating wasted physical effort and specifying an exact sequence of activities reduce the amount of time, money, and effort needed to make a product.

Taylor thought that there was one best way to perform any task. Like Weber, he concluded that an organization operated best with definite, predictable methods, logically determined and set down as rules. Taylor was convinced that having workers perform routine tasks that didn't require them to make decisions could increase efficiency. Performance goals expressed quantitatively (e.g., number of units produced per shift) addressed a problem that had begun to trouble managers—how to judge whether an employee had put in a fair day's work.

Advocates of scientific management stress specialization. They believe that expertise is the only source of authority and that a single foreman couldn't be an expert at all the tasks supervised. Each foreman's particular area of specialization, therefore, should become an area of authority. This solution is called *functional foremanship,* a division of labor that assigned eight foremen to each work area. Four of the foremen would handle planning, production scheduling, time-and-motion studies, and discipline. The other four would deal with machinery maintenance, machine speed, feeding material into the machine, production on the shop floor, and similar concerns.

What motivates employees to work to their capacity? Taylor believed that money was the answer. He supported the individual piecework system as the basis for pay. If workers met a certain production standard, they were to be paid at a standard wage rate. Workers who produced more than the standard were to be paid at a higher rate for all the pieces they produced, not just for those exceeding the standard. Taylor assumed that workers would be economically rational; that is, they would follow management's orders to produce more in response to financial incentives that allowed them to earn more money. Taylor argued that managers should use financial incentives if they were convinced that increases in productivity would more than offset higher employee earnings.

The Gilbreths. Frank (1868–1924) and Lillian (1878–1972) Gilbreth formed an unusual husband-and-wife engineering team who made significant contributions to scientific management. Frank used a revolutionary new tool—motion pictures—to study workers' motions. For instance, he identified eighteen individual motions that a bricklayer uses to lay bricks. By changing the bricklaying process, he reduced the eighteen motions to five, increasing a worker's overall productivity by more than 200 percent. Many of today's industrial engineers have combined Frank Gilbreth's methods with Taylor's to redesign jobs for greater efficiency.[8]

Lillian Gilbreth carried on Frank's work and raised their twelve children after his death. Concerned mainly with the human side of industrial engineering, she championed the idea that workers should have standard days, scheduled rest breaks, and normal lunch periods. Her work influenced the U.S. Congress to establish child-labor laws and develop rules for protecting workers from unsafe working conditions. Frank and Lillian Gilbreth also were the inspiration for two best selling books, *Cheaper by the Dozen* and *Belles on Their Toes,* written by their son, Frank Bunker Gilbreth.

Henry Gantt. Taylor's associate, Henry Gantt (1861–1919), focused on "control" systems for production scheduling. His Gantt charts are still widely used to plan project timelines and have been adapted for computer scheduling applications. The *Gantt chart* is a visual plan and progress report. It identifies various stages of work that must be carried out to complete a project, sets a deadline for each stage, and

FUNCTIONAL FOREMANSHIP

A division of labor that assigns a set number of foremen to each work area, with each one being responsible for the workers in his line of expertise.

GANTT CHART

A visual plan and progress report that identifies various stages of work that must be carried out in order to complete a project, sets deadlines for each stage, and documents accomplishments.

documents accomplishments. Gantt also established quota systems and bonuses for workers who exceeded their quotas.[9]

Kentucky Fried Chicken (now KFC) increased its quality through the application of scientific management ideas. It has more than 9,900 restaurants, annual sales in excess of $7.8 billion dollars, and serves more than 2.4 billion customers in 76 countries each year. The competitive pressures on all fast-food restaurants means that quick service and high quality are needed to attract and retain customers. The following Planning and Administrative Competency feature highlights how KFC managers used the principles of scientific management to improve the quality and speed of customer service.

Assessing Scientific Management. Taylor and other early proponents of scientific management would applaud the efforts of KFC, Honda, Canon, Intel, and other organizations that have successfully applied their concepts. These firms make finished products faster and cheaper than Taylor could ever have dreamed. Organizations are increasingly taking for granted his idea that managers can't expect employees to do their jobs properly without adequate skills and training. Taylor's work has led today's managers to improve their employee selection and training processes and to seek the one best way to perform each task.

Unfortunately, most proponents of scientific management misread the human side of work. When Frederick Taylor and Frank Gilbreth formulated their principles and methods, they thought that workers were motivated primarily by a desire to earn money to satisfy their economic and physical needs. They failed to recognize that workers also have social needs and that working conditions and job satisfaction often are more important than money. For example, workers have struck to protest working conditions, speedup of an assembly line, or harassment by management, even when a fair financial incentive system was in place. Managers today can't assume that workers are interested only in higher wages. Dividing jobs into their simplest tasks and setting clear rules for accomplishing those tasks won't always lead to a quality product, high morale, and an effective organization. Today's employees often want to participate in decisions that affect their performance; many want to be independent and hold jobs that give them self-fulfillment.

ADMINISTRATIVE MANAGEMENT

ADMINISTRATIVE MANAGEMENT

Focuses on the manager and basic managerial functions.

Administrative management focuses on the manager and basic managerial functions. It evolved early in this century and is most closely identified with Henri Fayol (1841–1925), a French industrialist. However, his most important writings on management weren't translated into English until 1930. Fayol credited his success as a manager to the methods he used, rather than to his personal qualities. He felt strongly that, to be successful, managers had only to understand the basic managerial functions—planning, organizing, leading, and controlling—and apply certain management principles to them. He was the first person to group managers' functions in this way.[10]

Like the other traditionalists, Fayol emphasized formal structure and processes, believing that they are necessary for the adequate performance of all important tasks. In other words, if people are to work well together, they need a clear definition of what they're trying to accomplish and how their tasks help meet organizational goals.

Fayol developed the following fourteen management principles and suggested that managers receive formal training in their application.

1. **Division of labor.** The more people specialize, the more efficiently they can perform their work.

Quality at KFC in Less Than 60 Seconds

Recognizing the importance of expectations, KFC conducts customer surveys and tracks its performance against that of its competitors (e.g., McDonald's, Wendy's, and Boston Market). From such data, senior management in KFC's south central division realized that its restaurants were in serious trouble. Profits were down by more than 50 percent, and customers ranked its outlets in the bottom half of performance for speed of service and value for money spent. As more than 50 percent of a McDonald's business is generated by the drive-through window operation, management decided to improve that operation first.

Managers formed a team of employees and trained them to use time-and-motion studies and Gantt charts and also to benchmark competitors. Through the time-and-motion studies, the KFC team found that employees took almost two minutes to complete a customer's order, whereas its competitors took less than sixty seconds. The team then proceeded to measure (1) the time a customer spent at the menu board placing the order; (2) the time required for a customer to drive from the menu board to the drive-through window, including waiting time; and (3) the time a customer waited at the window to get the order, make payment, and drive away. The timing device used had to sense the customer's car in the driveway, alert employees, and measure the time needed to serve a customer. To improve performance, the team made several recommendations: (1) all customers should be acknowledged within three seconds of arriving at the speaker, (2) customer orders should be filled within sixty seconds of arriving at the drive-through window, and (3) the total service time should average less than ninety seconds.

To implement those recommendations, the team developed administrative procedures for eliminating wasted motion by employees. These procedures included: (1) do not take more than two steps to get what is needed to fill an order; (2) do not lift anything needed to fill an order; and (3) reach up and pull down napkins, straws, cups, and other items needed to fill an order. Based on the team's recommendations, management totally reorganized drive-through service areas. This change included rearranging the placement of products, bags, boxes, cups, and salads and streamlining the movement of products from the kitchen to the packing area. High-demand items were positioned closest to the employees. The ten-piece chicken meal was priced at $11.18 so that, including tax, it totaled $12.00, eliminating a lot of effort and time on the part of the customer and cashier in counting change. From experience, KFC learned that a customer whose bill was an even-dollar amount averaged 15 to 20 seconds less at the window than a customer whose bill was an odd-dollar amount.

What were the results of all these changes? First, customer sales improved by 17.5 percent. Second, employee productivity improved by 12.3 percent. Third, most customers are now served in less than sixty seconds.[11]

* * *

To learn more about KFC, visit the company's home page at

www.kentuckyfriedchicken.com

2. **Authority.** Managers have the right, the authority, to give orders to get things done.

3. **Discipline.** Members of an organization need to respect the rules and agreements that govern it.

4. **Unity of command.** Each employee must receive instructions about a particular operation from only one person to avoid conflicting instructions and confusion.

5. **Unity of direction.** Managers should coordinate the efforts of employees working on projects, but only one should be responsible for an employee's behavior.

6. **Subordination of individual interest to the common good.** The interests of individual employees should not take precedence over the interests of the entire organization.

7. **Remuneration.** Pay for work done should be fair to both the employee and the employer.

8. **Centralization.** Managers should retain final responsibility but should also give their subordinates enough authority to do their jobs properly.

9. **Scalar chain.** A single uninterrupted line of authority (often represented by the neat boxes and lines of an organization chart) should run rank to rank from top management to the lowest level position in the company.

10. **Order.** Materials and people should be in the right place at the right time. In particular, people should be in the jobs or positions best suited to them.

11. **Equity.** Managers should be both friendly and fair to their subordinates.

12. **Stability and tenure of staff.** A high rate of employee turnover is not efficient.

13. **Initiative.** Subordinates should be given the freedom to formulate and carry out their own plans.

14. **Esprit de corps.** Promoting team spirit gives the organization a sense of unity.

Managers still use many of Fayol's principles of administrative management, but different managers seldom apply them in exactly the same way. Situations vary and so, too, does the application of these principles. At Chapparal Steel, a steel producer, the maintenance superintendent receives direction from the plant manager, the chief engineer, and the production manager—violating the unity of command principle. The maintenance superintendent has the authority to set priorities for plant maintenance—illustrating the initiative principle.

ASSESSING TRADITIONAL MANAGEMENT

Traditional management's three branches—bureaucratic, scientific, and administrative—still have their proponents, are often written about, and continue to be applied effectively. Let's summarize what they have in common and what some of their drawbacks are. Table 2.1 highlights the points discussed.

All three branches of traditional management emphasize the formal aspects of organization. Traditionalists are concerned with the formal relations among an organization's departments, tasks, and processes. Weber, Taylor, the Gilbreths, Gantt, and Fayol replaced seat-of-the-pants management practices with sound theoretical and scientific principles. Managers began to stress the division of labor, hierarchical authority, rules, and decisions that would maximize economic rewards.

Traditional management stresses the manager's role in a hierarchy. In bureaucratic management the relationship between expertise and organizational level is strong. Because of their higher position and presumed greater expertise, superiors are to be obeyed by subordinates. Administrative and scientific management's emphasis on logical processes and strict division of labor are based on similar reasoning.

Although traditionalists may recognize that people have feelings and are influenced by their friends at work, their overriding focus is on efficient and effective

Bureaucratic Management	Scientific Management	Administrative Management
Administrative Characteristics		
Rules	Training in routines and rules	Defining of management functions
Impersonality	"One best way"	Division of labor
Division of labor	Financial motivation	Hierarchy
Hierarchy		Authority
Authority structure		Equity
Lifelong career commitment		
Rationality		
Focus		
Whole organization	Employee	Manager
Benefits		
Consistency	Productivity	Clear structure
Efficiency	Efficiency	Professionalization of managerial roles
Drawbacks		
Rigidity	Overlooks social needs	Internal focus
Slowness		Overemphasizes rational behavior of managers

job performance. Taylor considered the human side of work in terms of eliminating bad feelings between workers and management and providing employees with financial incentives to increase productivity. Job security, career progression, and protection of workers from employers' whims are considered important by traditionalists. However, they do not recognize informal or social relationships among employees at work. Taylor and Frank Gilbreth focused on well-defined rules intended to ensure efficient performance, the primary standard against which employees were to be judged.

In assessing the work of the early traditional theorists, you need to keep in mind that they were influenced by the economic and societal conditions facing them at the time. The United States was becoming an industrial nation, unions were forming to protect workers' rights, and more laws were being passed to eliminate unsafe working conditions. Organizations operated in a relatively stable environment with few competitors. Much traditionalist thinking may still be found in some large organizations. For example, Fayol's principles are widely used as basic management building blocks at Kodak, Gillette, Coca-Cola, and other global corporations.

BEHAVIORAL VIEWPOINT

2

STATE THE BEHAVIORAL VIEWPOINT'S CONTRIBUTION TO MANAGEMENT

During the 1920s and 1930s, the United States and other industrialized nations experienced radical social and cultural changes. Mass production triggered a second industrial revolution. Assembly lines released a flood of inexpensive goods—cars, appliances, and clothing—into an increasingly consumer-oriented society. The overall standard of living rose, and working conditions in many industries improved.

As productivity shot up, the average workweek plunged from seventy hours to less than fifty hours in the United States. Hard-pressed to satisfy consumer demand, manufacturers eagerly tried to attract workers from the farms by making industrial employment more appealing than it was during Taylor's tenure at Midvale Steel.

During the Great Depression, the federal government began to play a more influential role in people's lives. By the time President Franklin D. Roosevelt took office in 1933, the national economy was hovering on the brink of collapse. To provide employment the government undertook temporary public works projects—constructing dams, roads, and public buildings and improving national parks. It also created agencies, such as the Social Security Administration, to assist the aged, the unemployed, and the disabled.

In one of the era's most dramatic changes, unskilled workers increased their ability to influence management decisions by forming powerful labor unions. During the 1930s Congress aided unions by enacting legislation that deterred management from restricting union activities, legalized collective bargaining, and required management to bargain with unions. As a result the labor movement grew rapidly, and the Congress of Industrial Organizations (CIO) was formed. In 1937, the autoworkers and steelworkers won their first big contracts. Eventually professionals and skilled workers, as well as unskilled laborers, formed unions to bargain for better pay, increased benefits, and improved working conditions. Following the depression and World War II, a new wave of optimism swept the U.S. economy.

Against this backdrop of change and reform, managers were forced to recognize that people have needs, cherish values, and want respect. They were now leading workers who did not appear to exhibit what the early traditional management theorists had thought was rational economic behavior. That is, workers weren't always performing up to their physiological capabilities, as Taylor had predicted rational people would do. Nor were effective managers consistently following Fayol's fourteen principles. By exploring these inconsistencies, those who favored a behavioral viewpoint of management gained recognition. The **behavioral** (human relations) **viewpoint** focuses on dealing effectively with the human aspects of organizations. Its proponents look at how managers do what they do, how managers lead subordinates and communicate with them, and why managers need to change their assumptions about people if they want to lead high-performance teams and organizations.

BEHAVIORAL VIEWPOINT
Focuses on dealing more effectively with the human aspects of organizations.

FOLLETT'S CONTRIBUTIONS

In the early decades of this century, Mary Parker Follett (1868-1933) made important contributions to the behavioral viewpoint of management. She believed that management is a flowing, continuous process, not a static one, and that if a problem has been solved, the method used to solve it probably generated new problems. She stressed (1) involvement of workers in solving problems and (2) the dynamics of management, rather than static principles. Both ideas contrasted sharply with the views of Weber, Taylor, and Fayol.[12]

Follett studied how managers did their jobs by observing them at work. Based on these observations, she concluded that coordination is vital to effective management. She developed four principles of coordination for managers to apply.

1. Coordination is best achieved when the people responsible for making a decision are in direct contact.

2. Coordination during the early stages of planning and project implementation is essential.

3. Coordination should address all the factors in a situation.

4. Coordination must be worked at continuously.

Follett believed that the people closest to the action could make the best decisions. For example, she was convinced that first-line managers are in the best position to coordinate production tasks. And by increasing communication among themselves and with workers, these managers can make better decisions regarding such tasks than managers up the hierarchy can. She also believed that first-line managers should not only plan and coordinate workers' activities, but also involve them in the process. Simply because managers told employees to do something a certain way, Follett argued, they shouldn't assume that the employees would do it. She argued further that managers at all levels should maintain good working relationships with their subordinates. One way to do so is to involve subordinates in the decision-making process whenever they will be affected by the decision. Drawing on psychology and sociology, Follett urged managers to recognize that each person is a collection of beliefs, emotions, and feelings.

Follett also believed that managers should find ways to help resolve interdepartmental conflict. Properly handled, conflict can stimulate and integrate managerial and production efforts. As part of the conflict resolution process, everyone involved should try to understand the others' views and the situations they face. At Wainwright Industries, a supplier of automobile parts to GM and others, managers resolve conflict by communicating directly with each other, with employees, and with customers.

John Mackey, president of Whole Foods, a supermarket that sells only natural foods, believes that Follett's ideas have shaped his management practices. Each Whole Foods market typically employs between 60 and 140 people and is organized into various teams to develop a sense of cooperation. Each team is responsible for doing its own work and selecting new team members. A candidate must be voted on by the team and receive a two-thirds majority to become a team member. Every four weeks, each team meets to discuss problems and make decisions.

Employees also practice self-responsibility. Mackey believes that, by placing responsibility and authority at the store and team level rather than at corporate headquarters, employees are encouraged to make decisions that affect their daily work. Mackey knows that employees will make mistakes because of their inexperience. However, the company is dedicated to learning and growing, and he believes that employees can learn from their mistakes. Recognizing that there are many different approaches to getting things done, Mackey encourages creativity and experimentation at each store and by each employee. He is convinced that only through experimentation can new information be gathered and communication increased among all employees.[13]

BARNARD'S CONTRIBUTIONS

Chester Barnard (1886–1961) studied economics at Harvard but failed to graduate because he didn't finish a laboratory course in science. He was hired by AT&T, and in 1927 he became president of New Jersey Bell. Barnard made two significant contributions to management, which are detailed in his book, *The Functions of the Executive*.[14]

Barnard viewed organizations as social systems that require employee cooperation if they are to be effective. In other words, people should continually communicate with one another. According to Barnard, managers' main roles are to communicate with employees and motivate them to work hard to help achieve the organization's goals. In his view, successful management also depends on maintaining good relations with people outside the organization with whom managers deal regularly. He stressed the dependence of the organization on investors, suppliers, customers, and other outside interests. Barnard stressed the idea that managers have to examine the organization's external environment and adjust its internal structure to balance the two.

Another of Barnard's significant contributions is the **acceptance theory of authority.** This *buy-in* theory holds that employees have free wills and thus will choose whether to follow management's orders. That is, employees will follow orders if they (1) understand what is required, (2) believe that the orders are consistent with organizational goals, and (3) see positive benefits to themselves in carrying out the orders.

THE HAWTHORNE CONTRIBUTIONS

The strongest support for the behavioral viewpoint emerged from studies carried out between 1924 and 1933 at Western Electric Company's Hawthorne plant in Chicago. The Hawthorne Illumination Tests, begun in November 1924 and conducted in three departments of the plant, initially were developed and directed by Hawthorne's engineers. They divided employees into two groups: a test group, whom they subjected to deliberate changes in lighting, and a control group, for whom lighting remained constant throughout the experiment. When lighting conditions for the test group were improved, the group's productivity increased, as expected. The engineers were mystified, though, by a similar jump in productivity upon reducing the test group's lighting to the point of twilight. To compound the mystery, the control group's output kept rising, even though its lighting condition didn't change. Western Electric called in Harvard professor Elton Mayo to investigate these peculiar and puzzling results.

Mayo and Harvard colleagues Fritz Roethlisberger and William Dickson devised a new experiment. They placed two groups of six women each in separate rooms. They changed various conditions for the test group and left conditions unchanged for the control group. The changes included shortening the test group's coffee breaks, allowing it to choose its own rest periods, and letting it have a say in other suggested changes. Once again, output of both the test group and the control group increased. The researchers decided that they could rule out financial incentives as a factor because they hadn't changed the payment schedule for either group.

The researchers concluded that the increases in productivity weren't caused by a physical event but by a complex emotional chain reaction. Because employees in both groups had been singled out for special attention, they had developed a group pride that motivated them to improve their performance. The sympathetic supervision they received further reinforced that motivation. These experimental results led to Mayo's first important discovery: When employees are given special attention, productivity is likely to change regardless of whether working conditions change. This phenomenon became known as the **Hawthorne effect.**

However, an important question remained unanswered: Why should a little special attention and the formation of group bonds produce such strong reactions? To find the answer Mayo interviewed employees. These interviews yielded a highly significant discovery: Informal work groups, the social environment of employees, greatly influence productivity. Many Western Electric employees found their lives inside and outside the factory dull and meaningless. Their workplace friends, chosen in part because of mutual antagonism toward "the bosses," gave meaning to their working lives. Thus peer pressure, rather than management demands, had a significant influence on employee productivity.

The writings of Mayo, Roethlisberger, and Dickson interpreted the basic conclusions that emerged from the Hawthorne studies and helped outline the behav-

ACCEPTANCE THEORY OF AUTHORITY
Holds that employees have free wills and thus will choose whether or not to follow management's orders.

HAWTHORNE EFFECT
A likely change in productivity, regardless of whether working conditions change, when employees are given special attention.

Edy's 225 employees are organized into cross-functional teams that actually make the ice cream. Each team is responsible for everything from quality and sanitation checks to meeting business goals to internal workday scheduling to maintaining discipline to training and career development. The company is successful because is relies on three behavioral foundations.

First, employees base their decisions on how they're going to meet their business goals. Edy's managers meet with employees to review performance, discuss customer feedback, provide an open discussion of issues facing the plant, and keep lines of communication open. The assumption is, if it is important for management to know, it is important for everyone to know. Second, the company has trained employees technically to understand their part of the business. Information systems provide employees with all the information they need to know to make defect-free ice cream. Third, each member of a team is responsible for career development of team members, as well as team discipline. Team members have found that counseling others about their performance and behaviors can be difficult.

A monthly incentive system, which is paid plantwide, is designed to reward performance in terms of people skills, customer delight, new products and processes, cost, and quality. Teams can be recognized for their contributions. This recognition is self-administered, and anyone can nominate a team. Team members are empowered to decide which award category their implemented improvement fits—bronze, silver, or gold. The awards range from a team gift certificate for dinner to individual cash payments.[15]

* * *

To learn more about Edy's Grand Ice Cream, visit the company's home page at

www.edys.com

ioral viewpoint of management. These theorists believed that individual work behavior rarely reflects simple cause-and-effect relationships based on scientific and economic principles, as the traditionalists believed. Instead it is determined by a complex set of factors. The informal work group develops its own set of norms to mediate between the needs of individuals and the work setting. The social system of such informal groups is maintained through symbols of prestige and power. The researchers also concluded that managers need to consider the personal context (e.g., family situation and friendships) in order to understand each employee's unique needs and sources of satisfaction. They suggested that awareness of employee feelings and encouragement of employee participation in decision making can reduce resistance to change.[16]

One organization that has utilized the behavioral viewpoint of management to improve its effectiveness is Edy's Grand Ice Cream of Fort Wayne, Indiana. To reach the highest level of customer satisfaction in this fiercely competitive industry, Edy's engages employees in contributing to the success of the company. It recognizes and rewards employees for their contributions in companywide celebrations and encourages employees to participate in a wide range of decisions. The above Teamwork Competency article illustrates how Edy's gets and keeps its employees involved.

ASSESSING THE BEHAVIORAL VIEWPOINT

The behavioral viewpoint of management goes beyond the traditionalists' mechanical view of work by stressing the importance of group dynamics, complex human motivations, and the manager's leadership style. It emphasizes the employee's social and economic needs and the influence of the organization's social setting on the quality and quantity of work produced. The following are the basic assumptions of the behavioral viewpoint.

- Employees are motivated by social needs and get a sense of identity through their associations with one another.

- Employees are more responsive to the social forces exerted by their peers than to management's financial incentives and rules.

- Employees are most likely to respond to managers who can help them satisfy their needs.

- Managers need to coordinate work with the participation of their subordinates to improve efficiency.

These assumptions don't always hold in practice, of course. Improving working conditions and managers' human relations skills won't always increase productivity. Economic aspects of work are still important to the employee, as Taylor believed. The major union contracts negotiated in recent years, for instance, focus on job security and wage incentives. And, although employees enjoy working with co-workers who are friendly, low salaries tend to lead to absenteeism and turnover. The negative effects of clumsy organizational structure, poor communication, and routine or boring tasks won't be overcome by the presence of pleasant co-workers. The human aspect of the job in the next century will be vastly more complex than could ever have been imagined by those advocating the behavioral viewpoint in the 1930s.[17]

SYSTEMS VIEWPOINT

3

DESCRIBE THE SYSTEMS VIEWPOINT AND THE USE OF QUANTITATIVE TECHNIQUES TO MANAGE ORGANIZATIONS

During World War II the British assembled a team of mathematicians, physicists, and others to solve various wartime problems. These professionals formed the first operations research (OR) group. Initially, they were responsible for analyzing the makeup, routes, and speeds of convoys and probable locations of German submarines. The team developed ingenious ways to analyze complex problems that couldn't be handled solely by intuition, straightforward mathematics, or experience. The British and Americans further developed this approach (called systems analysis) throughout the war and applied it to many problems of war production and military logistics. Later, systems analysis became an accepted tool in the Department of Defense (DoD) and the space program, as well as throughout private industry.[18]

SYSTEMS CONCEPTS

A **system** is an association of interrelated and interdependent parts. The human body is a system with organs, muscles, bones, nerves, and a consciousness that links all its parts. An organization is an internal system with many employees, teams, departments, and levels that are linked to achieve its goals. An organization also is linked externally to suppliers, customers, shareholders, and regulatory agencies. A competent systems-oriented manager makes decisions only after identifying and analyzing how other managers, departments, customers, or others might be affected by the decisions.

The **systems viewpoint** of management represents an approach to solving problems by diagnosing them within a framework of inputs, transformation

SYSTEM

An association of interrelated and interdependent parts.

SYSTEMS VIEWPOINT

Represents an approach to solving problems by diagnosing them within a framework of inputs, transformation processes, outputs, and feedback.

Figure 2.4 **Basic Systems View of Organization**

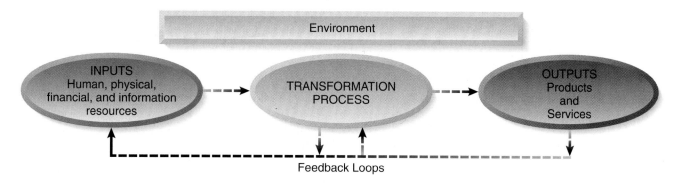

Feedback Loops

INPUTS

Physical, human, material, financial, and information resources that enter a transformation process.

TRANSFORMATION PROCESSES

The technologies used to convert inputs into outputs.

OUTPUTS

The original inputs (human, physical, material, information, and financial resources) as changed by a transformation process.

FEEDBACK

Information about a system's status and performance.

CLOSED SYSTEM

Limits interactions with environment.

OPEN SYSTEM

Interacts with the external environment.

SUBSYSTEM

A component consisting of one or more parts of a system.

processes, outputs, and feedback, as shown in Figure 2.4. The system involved may be an individual, a work group, a department, or an entire organization.

Inputs are the physical, human, material, financial, and information resources that enter a transformation process. At a university, for example, inputs include students, faculty, money, and buildings. *Transformation processes* comprise the technologies used to convert inputs into outputs. Transformation processes at a university include lectures, reading assignments, lab experiments, term papers, and tests. *Outputs* are the original inputs (human, physical, material, information, and financial resources) as changed by a transformation process. Outputs at a university include the graduating students. For a system to operate effectively, it must also provide for feedback. *Feedback* is information about a system's status and performance. One form of feedback at a university is the ability of its graduates to get jobs. In an organization, feedback may take the form of marketing surveys, financial reports, production records, performance appraisals, and the like. In the systems viewpoint, management's role is to facilitate transformation processes by planning, organizing, leading, and controlling.

SYSTEM TYPES AND LEVELS

There are two types of systems: closed and open. A *closed system* limits its interactions with its environment. Some production departments operate as closed systems, producing standardized products in an uninterrupted stream. An *open system* interacts with the external environment. Managers in Sprint's marketing department, for example, constantly try to develop new products or services to satisfy customers' telecommunications desires. They monitor what competitors are doing and then develop ways to deliver better quality and service at a lower price.

You can also think of a person, group, or organization as a *subsystem,* or a component consisting of one or more parts of a system. The subsystems at Unilever include its marketing, human resources, manufacturing, accounting, and finance departments. Lipton, a consumer soup and tea product division, is a subsystem of its parent corporation, Unilever. Even with annual sales of more than $163 billion, Unilever is still a subsystem of the United Kingdom's and the Netherlands' economic subsystems, which, in turn, are part of the world's economic system. Figure 2.5 illustrates systems and subsystems in the world economy. Note that each level or subsystem represents a successively simpler part of the overall system. Note also that one system's output is another system's input.

The following Communication Competency account reveals how Richard Teerlink used a systems viewpoint to turn around Harley-Davidson (key systems concepts are in parentheses). Over the years Harley had created the feeling of freedom

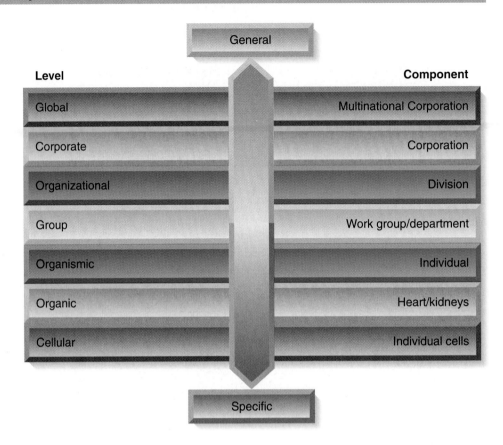

for loyal riders, but the company was increasingly losing business to Honda and other Japanese motorcycle companies because of poor quality. Teerlink changed that by using his formal communication and negotiation skills inside the company to address problems and his informal communication skills to build strong interpersonal relations with suppliers and customers. In-house, a rigorous quality control program kick-started talk at all levels of the company. With every employee involved in some form of incentive compensation, Teerlink had 5,000 people talking about how to improve the company's products.

QUANTITATIVE TECHNIQUES

While some advocates of systems analysis were suggesting that managers look at inputs, transformation processes, and outputs before making a decision, other systems advocates were developing quantitative techniques to aid in managerial decision making. Quantitative techniques have four basic characteristics, as illustrated in the Harley-Davidson feature.

1. **The primary focus is on decision making.** The solution identifies direct actions that managers can take, such as JIT to reduce inventory costs.

2. **Alternatives are based on economic criteria.** Alternative actions are presented in terms of measurable criteria, such as costs, revenues, and dealer returns.

3. **Mathematical models are used.** Situations are simulated and problems are analyzed by means of mathematical models.

Harley Hogs Ride Again

Teerlink's drive to recapture the No. 1 position for Harley-Davidson in the bike market started with talking to customers (inputs). He learned that Harley's customers aren't merely buyers of bikes; they want to feel like part of the company. They are emotionally tied to the success and failures of the company. Because of such emotional ties, Harley customers are extremely brand loyal. To help customers identify with the company, Teerlink created logos that customers could slap on anything from deodorant to throw pillows. To give customers a reason to use Harley's products and talk with managers, he also created Harley Owners Groups—HOG for short. Their members now number 375,000 and local chapters have frequent rallies, often hosted by Teerlink and his staff.

To attack quality problems, managers and employees redesigned the production (transformation) process to introduce just-in-time (JIT) inventory systems and statistical process control techniques. The JIT inventory system schedules raw materials to arrive only as needed, which produced huge inventory savings (outputs). Harley invested money in new technology, such as robots and computer-aided manufacturing techniques, to help employees improve quality. The statistical process controls enable employees to monitor quality and make corrections immediately, rather than waiting for them to show up in a dealer's showroom or out on the road. Dealer satisfaction (output) improved dramatically as customer complaints about quality dropped.

Employees created a peer review system to evaluate each others' performance instead of relying solely on first-line supervisors' evaluations (input). To communicate more clearly to all employees, Teerlink eliminated three layers of management (transformation), thereby giving employees authority to make decisions that once had been reserved for management (output). The company implemented quality circles, which became a source of bottom-up ideas for improving quality to management. As a result of these changes, Harley shipped more than 118,771 bikes in 1996 and plans to make at least 200,000 by the year 2003.[19]

* * *

To learn more about Harley-Davidson, visit the company's home page at

www.harley-davidson.com

4. **Computers are essential.** Computers are used to solve complex mathematical models that would be too costly and time-consuming to process manually, such as statistical process controls.

The range of quantitative decision-making tools available to management has expanded greatly during the past two decades. Today's managers have inventory decision models, statistical decision theory, linear programming, and many other aids for solving complex problems. Many of those tools are literally at their fingertips in the form of software that can be run on desktop computers. In the past, small businesses such as retail stores, medical offices, mom-and-pop restaurants, and farmers couldn't use systems analysis techniques. Today, many small businesses own their own computers. Ready-to-use software packages such as Microsoft Windows and Excel enable small-business owners and managers to utilize programs for accounts payable, accounts receivable, and inventory control. A medical office system can do patient scheduling and create and maintain a database for patients' medical records. In the largest companies, groups of management scientists can tackle a broad range of business problems by devising their own sophisticated mathematical models for use on mainframe, networked, and personal computers.

Gambling casinos such as Caesar's Palace, Bally's, and Harrah's in Atlantic City spend millions of dollars on complimentary services (including food, rooms, and transportation) for high rollers. To reduce the cost of these services and improve the odds that these people will play, and therefore lose, in their establishments casino managers utilize sophisticated information systems that analyze customers' favorite games, betting patterns, accommodation preferences, food and drink choices, and other habits. Similarly, Hertz uses information systems to attract customers. Available in several languages (including English, French, German, Italian, and Spanish), the Hertz destination printout for a trip specifies expressways, exits, local streets, turns, and time required. In some cities the computer prints a grid on a map to depict geographic information. A customer picking up a rental car can simply enter the destination into a computer terminal. On the spot, the computer screen gives precise directions for how to get from the customer's location to the specified destination.

ASSESSING THE SYSTEMS VIEWPOINT

Systems analysis and quantitative techniques have been used primarily to manage transformation processes and in the technical planning and decision-making aspects of management. These techniques haven't yet reached the stage where they can be used effectively to deal with the human aspects of management. Variables representing behavioral considerations and human values are difficult, if not impossible, to build into a mathematical model. Because these subjective variables must still be taken into account, judgments about people will continue to be a vital part of managerial decision making.

Research and development continues to expand the application of information systems in business, as we will explore fully in Chapter 20. In Chapter 21, we will describe the impact of systems analysis on manufacturing through the use of computer-aided design (CAD) and computer-aided manufacturing (CAM). Moreover, systems analysis is helping computer experts develop hardware, as well as software, with humanlike intelligence. These experts are trying to design computers that are capable of reasoning and processing spoken language. When machines can reason, they, like us, will be able to learn from past experience and apply what they have learned to solve new problems.

Organizations no doubt will continue to develop more sophisticated systems in order to increase productivity. Such systems will require changes in many aspects of day-to-day operations. These changes will not come without struggle and pain. Yet for organizations to survive they must install and utilize increasingly sophisticated systems to help managers make decisions.[20]

CONTINGENCY VIEWPOINT
Advocates using the other three management viewpoints independently or in a combination, as necessary to deal with various situations.

CONTINGENCY VIEWPOINT

4

EXPLAIN THE PLACE OF THE CONTINGENCY VIEWPOINT IN MODERN MANAGEMENT

The essence of the *contingency viewpoint* (sometimes called the contingency or situational approach) is that management practices should be consistent with the requirements of the external environment, technology, and capabilities of the people involved. These relationships are summarized in Figure 2.6. It was developed in the mid-1960s by managers and others who had tried unsuccessfully to apply traditional and systems concepts to actual managerial problems. For example, why did providing workers with a bonus for being on time decrease lateness at one Marriott hotel but have little impact at another? Proponents of the contingency viewpoint contend that different situations require different practices. As one manager put it, the contingency viewpoint really means that "it all depends."

Proponents of the contingency viewpoint advocate using the other three management viewpoints independently or in combination, as necessary, to deal with various situations.[21] However, this viewpoint doesn't give managers free rein to indulge their personal biases and whims. Rather, managers are expected to determine which methods are likely to be more effective than others in a given situation. Applying the contingency viewpoint requires the development and use of all six managerial competencies introduced in Chapter 1. Managers must be able to diagnose and understand a situation thoroughly—to determine which approach is most likely to succeed—before making a decision. The manager's communications competency then is essential in actually implementing the decision.

Managers who subscribe to this viewpoint use the concepts developed by traditionalists, behaviorists, and systems analysts—but go beyond them to identify the best approach for each particular situation. Because of its very nature, the contingency viewpoint can't yet offer detailed prescriptions for the *best* way to manage in *all* situations.

CONTINGENCY VARIABLES

The essence of the contingency viewpoint is that management practices should be consistent with the requirements of the external environment, the technology used to make a product or deliver a service, and the people who work for the organization.

Figure 2.6 **Contingency Viewpoint**

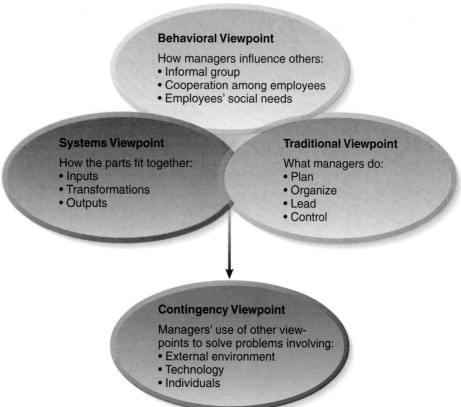

The relative importance of each contingency variable depends on the type of managerial problem being considered. For example, in designing an organization's structure a manager should consider the nature of the company's external environment and the corresponding information processing requirements. Hence the IRS's structure is different from that of United Airlines. The IRS has a fairly stable set of customers, most of whom must file their tax returns by April 15 each year. It hires many part-time people during the peak tax season to process returns and answer questions, then lays them off after the peak has passed. In contrast, United Airlines has many competitors and a constantly changing set of customers whose demands for information (about ticket costs, flight numbers, and arrival and departure times) must be processed immediately. Its continuous information processing requirements call for more reliance on full-time personnel than is necessary at the IRS.

TECHNOLOGY
The method used to transform organizational inputs into outputs.

Technology is the method used to transform organizational inputs into outputs. It is more than machinery; it also is the knowledge, tools, techniques, and actions applied to change raw materials into finished goods and services. The technologies that employees use range from simple to highly complex. A simple technology involves decision-making rules to help employees do routine jobs. For example, IRS clerks who enter tax information into computers perform routine tasks and work under such rules, requiring few (if any) independent decisions. A complex technology is one that requires employees to make numerous decisions, sometimes with limited information to guide them. A doctor treating an AIDS patient must answer many questions and make many decisions without having much guidance because the technology for treating the disease hasn't been perfected.

Joan Woodward was one of the pioneers in developing the contingency viewpoint of management. The findings of her group of researchers in England helped managers understand how one contingency variable—technology—could determine how organizations should be structured in order to become more effective. Woodward and her colleagues studied 100 English firms during the 1960s to identify the management principles followed by successful companies. They found no across-the-board application of administrative management principles; nor was a firm's success related to application of any one set of management principles. These results directly refuted the traditional viewpoint of management. Apparently, there was no "one best way"! Not satisfied with these negative results, Woodward looked for alternative explanations. She discovered that a firm's organizational characteristics and how they relate to its technology seemed to affect the likelihood of its success.[22]

Firms using mass-production (e.g., automobile manufacturers and fast-food outlets) methods are more effective operating under bureaucratic management. Numerous rules and highly formalized communication systems are needed to coordinate and control the production of standard outputs. However, firms using small-batch (e.g., home builders) and continuous-process (e.g., oil refineries and milk producers) technologies have little or no need for bureaucratic methods. Small-batch firms that followed the principles developed by the behavioral viewpoint were more effective than those that didn't. Continuous-process firms following a combination of behavioral and systems viewpoints were more effective than firms that didn't. The study's conclusion was that a firm choosing a managerial viewpoint that complements its technology is more likely to succeed than a firm choosing a design that doesn't fit its technology.

ASSESSING THE CONTINGENCY VIEWPOINT

The contingency viewpoint of management is useful because of its diagnostic approach, which clearly departs from the one-best-way approach of the traditionalists. The contingency viewpoint encourages managers to analyze and understand situational differences and to choose the solution best suited to the organization, the process, and the people involved in each situation.

Critics argue that the contingency viewpoint really is nothing new. They say that it is merely a meshing of techniques from the other viewpoints of management. The contingency viewpoint does draw heavily from the other approaches. However, it is flexible, allowing managers to apply the principles and tools from those approaches selectively and where most appropriate. It holds that a manager should rely on absolute principles from the traditional, behavioral, and systems viewpoints only after properly diagnosing the realities of the situation. Such a diagnosis looks at the nature of a situation and the means by which the manager can influence it.

QUALITY VIEWPOINT

5

DESCRIBE THE IMPACT OF THE QUALITY VIEWPOINT ON MANAGEMENT PRACTICES

QUALITY
Value conformance to established specifications or standards, excellence, or meeting and/or exceeding customers' expectations.

QUALITY VIEWPOINT
Emphasizes achieving customer satisfaction through the provision of high-quality goods and services.

TOTAL QUALITY MANAGEMENT
Organizational philosophy and strategy that makes quality a responsibility of all employees.

In the next century are new management viewpoints—beyond the contingency viewpoint—likely to emerge? The answer is yes. Today's organizations are dynamic and, whether large or small, local or global, face formidable new management challenges. Organizations feel pressure from customers and competitors to deliver high-quality products and/or services on time, reward ethical behavior of employees, and develop plans to manage highly diverse workforces effectively. Customer demand for high-quality products and services may be the dominant theme for the foreseeable future. *Quality* is defined as how well a product does what it is supposed to do—how closely and reliably it satisfies the specifications to which it is built. Managers in successful organizations are quality conscious and understand the link between high-quality goods and/or services, and competitive advantage.[23]

Recall from Chapter 1 that, for an organization to be successful, it must satisfy customer wants and needs. The *quality viewpoint* emphasizes achieving customer satisfaction through the provision of high-quality goods and services. Thus the focus of the quality viewpoint is the customer, who ultimately defines *quality* in the marketplace.[24]

Total quality management (TQM) is the continuous process of ensuring that every aspect of production builds in product quality. Quality must be stressed repeatedly so that it becomes second nature to everyone in an organization and its suppliers. Moreover, training, strategic planning, product design, management information systems, marketing, and other key activities all play a role in meeting quality goals. For example, Wainwright Industries, a mid-western parts firm and a winner of the Malcolm Baldrige National Quality Award, requires all employees to undergo fifty hours of training to learn how to use statistical and other measurement tools to ensure quality in its products.

The godfather of the quality movement was W. Edwards Deming (1900–1993).[25] Initially, U.S. managers rejected his ideas, and not until his ideas had helped rebuild Japan's industrial might after World War II were his ideas accepted in the United States. He taught eager Japanese managers how to use statistics to assess and improve quality. In 1951, Japan established the Deming Prize for corporate quality in his honor. Highly esteemed in Japan, this annual prize recognizes the company that has attained the highest level of quality that year.

In 1979, William Conway, president of Nashua Corporation, an office and computer products manufacturer, faced intense competitive pressure from the Japanese. On trips to Japan, he heard competitors praise Deming as a quality guru, and, upon his return, Conway hired Deming. Deming stressed the need for all employees to use statistics to improve quality and productivity, build trust, and work closely with customers. Deming believed that poor quality is 85 percent a management problem and 15 percent a worker problem. After implementing Deming's methods, Nashua's product quality and profits rose markedly.

In Chapter 21, we explore Deming's contributions more fully and emphasize differences between traditional quality control methods and his methods. Being aware of some of his methods is essential to an understanding of how organizations can achieve better quality. His ideas and methods include the following.

- Poor quality is unacceptable. Defective workmanship, products, and service are not to be tolerated.

- Gather statistical evidence of quality during the process, not at the end of the process. The earlier an error is caught, the less the cost to correct it.

- Rely on a few suppliers that have historically provided quality, not on sampling inspections to determine the quality of each delivery.

- Depend on training and retraining employees to use statistical methods in doing their jobs, not on slogans, to improve quality.

- Employees should feel free to report any conditions that detract from quality.

THE IMPORTANCE OF QUALITY

Producing high-quality products isn't an end in itself. Successfully offering high-quality goods and services to the customer typically results in three important benefits for the organization, as shown in Figure 2.7.[26]

Positive Company Image. A reputation for high-quality products creates a positive image for Maytag, Procter & Gamble, AT&T, Singapore Airlines, Lexus, and FedEx, among others. Such organizations gain many of the advantages of having a positive image. It helps them recruit new employees, increases sales of new products, and helps them obtain funds from various lending agencies. For example, Southwest Airlines receives 1,000 applications for each new job it advertises.

Lower Costs and Higher Market Share. Improved performance increases productivity and lowers rework time, scrap costs, and warranty costs, leading to increased profits. Improved performance features and product reliability at Wain-

---

Figure 2.7   Importance of Quality

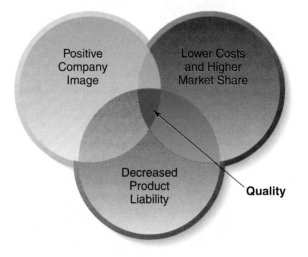

Marlow Industries Gets Smart

Raymond Marlow, CEO, thought back to 1987 when the company made thermoelectric coolers and components without thinking about standards, specifications, or quality. Employees would visually inspect the products and ship them to customers. Unfortunately, overtime costs skyrocketed as customers shipped products back for rework. The manufacturing cycle time was fifteen days, and the order-to-shipment lead time was sixteen weeks.

Today, teams of employees are responsible for their operations and for satisfying their customers. Overtime is a thing of the past because the company's strategy is to sell what it makes and not recycle. Employees, not management, control the process flow, the way components are made, and how products are assembled. They created their own statistical process control flow charts to track quality levels and designed new equipment to increase efficiency. In

the past, employees would ask management: When are you going to do something about it? Today, employees simply fix routine problems (those costing less than $300) without seeking management's approval. Employees take time to do the job right the first time, and management isn't pushing them to ship products just to meet its profitability goals.

Employees also revamped the company's approach to customer relations. Instead of having marketing representatives take calls randomly, customer service was broken down by market segment. Each marketing rep has the authority to resolve problems costing up to $20,000. Customers are called in advance to let them know when their orders have been shipped. Customers talk directly to manufacturing employees if they need an answer to a problem.

The results of these changes have been tremendous. Marlow won the Malcolm Baldrige National Quality

Award, lowered its manufacturing costs by 37 percent, reduced its order-to-shipment time to ten weeks, and cut its waste disposal costs by 57 percent.[27]

* * *

To learn more about Marlow, visit the company's home page at

www.marlow.com

wright Industries enabled the company to increase its market share and gain competitive advantage through economies of scale. Many of you have heard Ford's slogan, "Quality is Job 1," or have seen the advertisement, "The Lonely Maytag Repairman." When Ford refused to introduce its new version of the Thunderbird because it hadn't yet solved some quality problems, it suffered a short-term lag in sales. Ford overcame the lag in sales by increasing its market share by eliminating these problems.

Decreased Product Liability. Product manufacturers increasingly face costly legal suits over damages caused by faulty and/or dangerous products, ranging from asbestos to silicone breast implants to cigarettes. More and more frequently organizations that design and produce faulty products are being held liable in the courts for damages resulting from the use of such products. The current volume of litigation and proposed massive settlement with some forty states involving cigarette manufacturers—Phillip Morris, American Brands, and Liggett and Myers—is the most dramatic example. Successful TQM efforts typically result in improved products and product performance and lower product liability costs.

Decisions about quality should be an integral part of an organization's strategy—that is, how it competes in the marketplace.[26] A core strategy of quality consistently provides the best possible products in their price ranges in the marketplace. Quality therefore must be a basic component of the structure and culture of the organization. Quality isn't simply a program that can be imposed on employees by top management; it is a way of operating that permeates an organization and the thinking of everyone in it. A sign in the visitors' lounge at Marlow Industries reads: "Quality is a strategy, not a program." The previous Strategic Action Competency feature indicates how employees at Marlow Industries have designed quality into the company's operations.

INTEGRATION OF MANAGEMENT VIEWPOINTS AND COMPETENCIES

In Chapter 1, we identified six management competencies that are essential to your future success as a manager. Each of the five managerial viewpoints stresses at least one of these competencies more than others. Table 2.2 shows the relationships between these management viewpoints and these competencies.

The traditional viewpoint sought to identify management competencies that efficiently organized the work of employees. Each level of management was assigned specific goals and tasks to accomplish in an allotted time period. The structure of the organization governed relations between manager and employee. It was the manager's job to plan, organize, and lay out the task for the employee; it was the employee's job to follow the manager's instructions. Employees were thought of as "rational" people who were motivated primarily by money.

The behavioral viewpoint focused on developing two competencies: communication and teamwork. It was the manager's job to acknowledge the social and emotional needs of employees and to develop harmonious relationships in the workplace. This viewpoint stressed that employee behaviors are greatly affected by their interactions with peers. If managers communicated with employees and satisfied their workplace needs, the organization would be more effective.

The systems viewpoint stressed that managers should focus on how various inputs, transformation processes, and outputs are related to the organization's goals. The organization was viewed as a "whole," rather than simply the sum of its various departments or divisions. This wholeness requires managers to develop their communication, strategic thinking and action, and global awareness competencies. To develop these competencies, managers use quantitative models to help them understand complex organizational relationships.

The contingency viewpoint draws from each of the other viewpoints and involves a somewhat different set of competencies. Deciding whether to draw on

Table 2.2	Integration of Management Viewpoints and Competencies				
Managerial Competency	**Management Viewpoint**				
	Traditional	**Behavioral**	**Systems**	**Contingency**	**Quality**
Communication		X	X	X	X
Planning and administration	X			X	
Strategic action			X		X
Self-management					X
Global awareness			X		X
Teamwork		X		X	X

X = relatively high importance

one set of skills in a competency or on several skills across competencies is the job of the manager. How an organization is designed depends on its external environment, the skills of its employees, and the technology used to transform raw materials into finished products. The use of teams, for example, tests the manager's communication and teamwork competencies.

The quality viewpoint stresses meeting customers' expectations in terms of the value (performance and quality) of goods and services. Top management is responsible for putting the systems into place to achieve quality. One way for top management to gain the support of employees in such an effort is to design TQM practices that reward employees for meeting quality goals. The TQM philosophy requires a high level of coordination throughout the organization. One way for achieving that coordination is through teamwork. In quality conscious organizations, teamwork means sharing both responsibility and decision making. Managers delegate decision-making authority to employees, permitting them to manage themselves—but only after they have received the necessary training. Deming's philosophy of statistical quality control not only provides a method for analyzing deviations from standards, but it also provides a way to increase communication between employees.

CHAPTER SUMMARY

In this chapter we introduced several influential viewpoints and approaches that have shaped managerial thinking during the past one hundred years. Ideas from bureaucratic, scientific, and administrative management greatly influenced early managerial practices. Later, new ideas of managing stressed the human or behavioral aspects of managing. During World War II, industry and the armed forces developed sophisticated management systems to coordinate their war efforts. Then, as organizations grew and became global, none of the earlier management concepts seemed to apply totally to various situations. The contingency approach stressed that these concepts could be applied under some conditions but not under others. Today's managers are concerned primarily with the quality viewpoint of management as a way to meet consumer demand throughout the world for quality products and services.

1. **DESCRIBE THE THREE BRANCHES OF THE TRADITIONAL VIEWPOINT OF MANAGEMENT: BUREAUCRATIC, SCIENTIFIC, AND ADMINISTRATIVE.**

Max Weber developed a theory of bureaucratic management that emphasizes the need for a strict hierarchy governed by clearly defined regulations and lines of authority. His theory contains seven principles: a formal system of rules, impersonal management, division of labor, a hierarchical structure, a detailed

authority structure, lifelong career commitment, and rationality. Scientific management theorists tried to find ways to make workers more productive. Frederick Taylor thought that management's job was to make individual workers more efficient. That was to be accomplished by improving worker-machine relationships, based on time-and-motion studies. Frank and Lillian Gilbreth also studied how to make workers more efficient. Frank Gilbreth focused on the various physical motions workers used, and Lillian Gilbreth emphasized the welfare of workers. Henry Gantt thought that workers' performance could be charted and thus improved by setting deadlines. Administrative management theorists focused on principles that managers, rather than workers, could use to become more effective. Henry Fayol outlined four functions—planning, organizing, leading, and controlling—that he believed all successful managers use in their work.

2. **STATE THE BEHAVIORAL VIEWPOINT'S CONTRIBUTION TO MANAGEMENT.**

The behavioral viewpoint emphasizes employees' human and social needs. One of its first proponents, Mary Parker Follett, believed that management should coordinate the efforts of all employees to achieve organizational goals. Chester Barnard's contribution was similar to Follett's. He held, in part, that a manager doesn't have the authority to tell a worker what to do unless the worker accepts that authority. Studies conducted at the Hawthorne plant of the Western Electric Company led to the conclusion that social and human factors can be more important than physical and financial factors in influencing productivity.

3. **DESCRIBE THE SYSTEMS VIEWPOINT AND THE USE OF QUANTITATIVE TECHNIQUES TO MANAGE ORGANIZATIONS.**
The systems viewpoint looks at organizations as a series of inputs, transformation processes, and outputs. A system may either be open or closed. Systems analysis advocates that managers use quantitative techniques to solve problems.

4. **EXPLAIN THE PLACE OF THE CONTINGENCY VIEWPOINT IN MODERN MANAGEMENT.**
The contingency viewpoint, or the situational approach, encourages managers to use the concepts and methods of the traditional, behavioral, and systems viewpoints, depending on the circumstances they face at the time. The three key contingency variables that managers should consider before making a decision are the environment, technology, and people involved.

5. **DESCRIBE THE IMPACT OF THE QUALITY VIEWPOINT ON MANAGEMENT PRACTICES.**
The quality viewpoint stresses the provision of high-quality products and services at all times. One of the founders of the quality movement was W. Edwards Deming. Long after he had helped Japanese managers make statistical quality control improvements, his contributions were recognized by U.S. managers. His recommendations included planning for quality, striving for zero defects, using only a few suppliers who have demonstrated that they can deliver quality, and inspecting for quality during the process and not after.

QUESTIONS FOR DISCUSSION

1. Why should you know about the evolution of management?

2. What are some of the problems that global organizations face when they use bureaucratic principles to manage their employees?

3. Describe the principles of scientific management used by KFC to improve quality.

4. How do Barnard's management recommendations differ from Weber's?

5. What challenges face employees who are trying to implement contributions from the behavioral viewpoint in an organization?

6. What types of problems does systems analysis tackle?

7. What factors are influencing the quality movement?

8. You have been asked to address a local business group on the subject of the contingency viewpoint of management. Prepare an outline of your talk.

9. Why will the systems viewpoint be important for managers in the next century? How does this viewpoint help organizations achieve their quality goals?

EXERCISES TO DEVELOP YOUR MANAGERIAL COMPETENCIES

1. **Global Awareness Competency.** In 1991, Gillette was having financial problems. Since creating the Bic pen and introducing the first disposable razor in 1975, the company had seemed to have a strategy of selling products on price alone. Older men in the United States thought well of Gillette, remembering it as a sponsor of many sporting events. Younger men thought of the company as "cheap." In the mid-1980s, Gillette started advertising its most expensive razor, the Contour Plus, in Europe. The razor sold well and soon accounted for two-thirds of Gillette's profits. In 1988, Gillette's president merged the European and U.S. marketing

divisions into a North American Group and decided to create a world-class razor. It was a radical move for a firm long accustomed to traditional marketing operations run by individual brand managers in local markets. In 1992, Gillette created the Sensor razor and aimed a marketing campaign at shavers in both North America and Europe. Attracting shavers who used disposal razors, Gillette created advertising and promotional campaigns featuring identical television commercials (apart from language) in every market. The Sensor was a phenomenal success. What viewpoint of management did Gillette use to develop its global strategy? To learn more about Gillette's strategy and why it has been successful, visit the company's home page at

www. gillette.com

2. **Planning and Administrative Competency.** Visit a local Burger King restaurant and observe the manufacturing process. What concepts from scientific management can you identify? What particular quality principles advocated by Deming did you notice? To learn more about Burger King, visit the company's home page at

www.burgerking.com

3. **Teamwork Competency.** Select two sports teams of interest to you, a winner and loser. What specific teamwork competency did you observe in each team? What were the key differences between them? Does coaching account for all the differences?

4. **Communication Competency.** AT&T Wireless Services and GTE compete in the cellular telecommunications industry. Investigate the communication competency you would need to develop to get a job at each firm. To help you learn more about each organization's needs, visit AT&T Wireless Service's home page at

www.attws.com/jobs

and GTE's home page at

www.gte.com/business

5. **Strategic Action Competency.** Originally named American Messenger Company, United Parcel Service (UPS) was founded by James Casey in 1907. He started the firm with $100, two bicycles, one telephone, and six employees who delivered packages and telegrams. Today, UPS does more than $22 billion in annual sales and employs more than 336,000 people. The company faces many challenges from both strong domestic rivals, such as FedEx and Roadway Package Systems, and many international competitors, such as DHL. If you wanted to develop the necessary strategic action competency to get a job with UPS, how would you do it? To learn more about UPS, visit the company's home page at

www.ups.com

REAL-TIME CASE ANALYSIS

WHAT'S BEHIND GUESS?

The four Marciano brothers founded Guess? in 1981 and have watched it grow to a company having annual sales of $500 million. The company's advertising is famous, and its brand has 20 percent of the jeans' $10-billion-dollar-a-year worldwide market. Guess? became America's No.1 jeans designer and seller by creating a huge demand for $70 jeans that cost maybe $15 to make.

The brothers' success is based on management practices that might be considered unusual. Their headquarters is a 14-acre stone fortress with tinted, bulletproof windows, surrounded by armed guards and coils of razor wire. Two of the brothers have been convicted of corrupting IRS officials, getting them to launch bogus criminal tax probes of competitors.

In 1994, the brothers began fighting over the strategic direction of Guess?. One brother wanted to

go into mass marketing and sell in discount houses, such as Wal-Mart, as Jordache is doing today. Another brother wanted to keep the brand in upscale department stores. Fights over licensing deals with in-laws resulted in plots to remove the brothers from the firm. Recently, the brothers sued each other.

What would working at Guess? be like? The workday begins at 7:30 A.M., and all employees are required to punch a time clock. Tardiness starts at 7:31; security guards require employees to list the reasons they're late while one of the brothers spots violators from an office window. "It was like working in a prison," recalls Norma Fushan, a former customer relations employee. Managers also worked half-days on Saturday, a rule that they didn't learn about until the first day on the job. Skipping a Friday or Monday? You'd better have a doctor's note. On the morning of L.A.'s 1994 mega-earthquake, which damaged Guess?'s headquarters, the brothers were irritated that employees didn't show up for work.

The brothers may be responding to the competition, namely, Calvin Klein, Tommy Hilfiger, DKNY, and Ralph Lauren, by altering the consistency of their fabric's quality. "They used to buy the best, but they've become spooked since Calvin Klein started eating their lunch," says a denim salesperson who supplies the company. "Now they do a blind wash test every quarter using the cheapest wash formula. They take everybody's denim, and whoever can achieve 'the look' at the cheapest price is the one that gets the order. There's no continuity. To me, this is a recipe for disaster."

To boost profits, the company also has kept labor costs low. In 1992, it paid a $573,000 settlement to the U.S. Department of Labor for minimum-wage and overtime-pay violations. It was the first time a major clothier had been held responsible for what goes on in its independent cutting and sewing shops. The California Labor Department raided private homes where garments were being made under an illegal subcontracting sweatshop known as "homework." It again found Guess? paying wages under the table, not reporting overtime, and not withholding taxes.

The brothers hired Connie Meza to build a monitoring program, as required by the labor department.

She found evidence of "paybacks" from the contractors to Guess? managers in the form of lavish dinners, parties, and other gifts. Many of the managers didn't want Meza to crack down on them because it would slow production.

Meza found the sweatshops filthy, cramped, and overheated. Most of the workers were Latinos who were afraid to complain. Meza became disillusioned and quit. Her replacement, Marty Laal, lasted only a year and quit because the brothers didn't change their behaviors.[29]

Questions

1. What viewpoint (or viewpoints) of management is practiced at Guess? Cite specific instances to justify your answer.

2. What competencies seem lacking at Guess?

3. Assuming that the problems aren't corrected, can Guess? remain competitive? Explain the reasons for your response.

To learn more about the management practices at Guess?, visit the company's home page at

www.webgate.net/~mangear/guess.html

VIDEO CASE

WAINWRIGHT INDUSTRIES: LEADING THE FLOCK

Wainwright Industries, a supplier to the automotive industry and others, has won the U.S. Commerce Department's Malcolm Baldrige Award for its achievements in quality. Congress established the annual awards, named for President Ronald Reagan's first secretary of commerce, to promote quality awareness and publicize successful quality strategies.

Quality is the end result, but in a word, Wainwright's strategy is "communication." Managers at Wainwright have structured the company to foster communication, permit a continuous measurement of performance, and generate vital feedback. With communication comes empowerment: Employees are encouraged to observe and understand their company and to actively work to improve it.

Even as U.S. industry is deep into the information age, Wainwright can make do with decidedly "low-tech" mechanisms for communication. As an industrial shop producing for other manufacturers, the company doesn't require computers on every desktop, and communication is based on defined space (a designated meeting room), visuals (a placard for every client and flags for status), and visibility (with more glass and fewer walls).

In addition to uniforms for all of its employees, to further the feeling that all are members of a team, the company "mascot," the duck, is used as a metaphor for the opportunity—and obligation—of all employees to think like leaders. The metaphor both pushes employees to take leadership responsibility and simultaneously underscores the fact that the benefits accrue to the whole of "the flock."

Management is flexible. On the one hand, the strategies of broadening communication and erasing barriers are extremely egalitarian and make all employees (and management) feel like equals on a team. On the other hand, quality comes from clearly delineated responsibilities and recognition of leaders, wherever they might be found. An employee is responsible for each of Wainwright's customers. Regardless of the size of the contract, one individual can always be relied on to champion the customer's interests—and to keep a finger on its pulse.

Wainwright encourages employee suggestions, particularly the type that can generate small, continuous improvements. The average number of annual submissions per employee—60—is extremely high: nearly one suggestion every four days, from each of dozens of employees. But Wainwright's success in implementing its quality programs suggests that employees view the suggestion process not as an invention lottery, but as part of their continuous involvement in the production process.

Wainwright provides excellent examples of managerial competencies in communication, teamwork, and planning and administration. Even as the duck and flock were chosen to inspire employees to individual and team efforts, the metaphor of a machine itself is apt and perhaps better describes the work of the company when all its parts are "humming." Failure of any of several hundred parts—as small as a spark plug or as large as an axle—could cause a car to malfunction; all are necessary, in their separate but integrated ways. Wainwright's managers are responsible both for designing the company "machine," and observing and tweaking its operations, all the while encouraging the employees—far more than just cogs in the machine—to give feedback on themselves to gauge how well the company is doing.

Wainwright, like other Baldrige award winners, succeeds not because it focuses on its destination, but because it considers each step along the way. Even

quality, what the award honors, is, according to Wainwright, "Job 4"—after safety, and the satisfaction of both internal and external customers. Attention to those goals, in each process and all of its integral steps, generates quality as a result—an outcome that no individual need be charged with, but which follows as an inevitable consequence.

ON THE WEB

The Malcolm Baldrige award for quality is well documented on the World Wide Web (***www.quality.nist. gov***). Wainwright Industries isn't on the Web (not surprising for a business whose products are intended solely to be inputs for other businesses in heavy industry), although many other Baldrige award winners are. The Department of Commerce endeavors to share the lessons learned in determining award winners and documents their ongoing success. The "Baldrige Index" (a fictional portfolio of stocks of Baldrige Award–winning companies and parents of Baldrige award–winning subsidiaries) has regularly outperformed the Standard & Poor's stock index.

QUESTIONS

1. How are customer support relationships structured?

2. Continuous, small improvements are an effective way to be best at what a company currently does. What implications might this focus have when significant changes have to be made?

3. How might a company such as Wainwright survive the loss of a key employee?

Case contributed by Ross Stapleton-Gray, President, TeleDiplomacy, Inc., a technology and policy consultancy, and Adjunct Professor in Georgetown University's Communication, Culture, and Technology program.

PART 2

Managing the Environment

Chapter

3

Environmental Forces

LEARNING OBJECTIVES

AFTER STUDYING THIS CHAPTER YOU SHOULD BE ABLE TO:

1. DESCRIBE THE MAIN FORCES IN THE EXTERNAL BUSINESS ENVIRONMENT AND HOW THEY INFLUENCE ORGANIZATIONS.

2. UNDERSTAND THE ROLE OF THE TASK ENVIRONMENT AND ITS IMPACT ON DECISION MAKING.

3. IDENTIFY THE FIVE COMPETITIVE FORCES THAT DIRECTLY AFFECT ORGANIZATIONS IN AN INDUSTRY.

4. EXPLAIN WHY TECHNOLOGICAL FORCES HAVE BECOME INCREASINGLY IMPORTANT IN STRATEGIC PLANNING.

5. DESCRIBE THE PRINCIPAL POLITICAL STRATEGIES USED BY MANAGERS TO COPE WITH EXTERNAL POLITICAL-LEGAL FORCES.

Outline

Monsanto's Going Green

Monsanto CEO Robert Shapiro is betting billions of dollars to transform Monsanto into a biotech powerhouse capable of helping feed the planet's exploding population at the same time it works to heal a damaged environment. Monsanto recognizes the world as a closed system whose limits are already apparent. An estimated 25 billion tons of the world's topsoil are lost each year, irrigation is increasing the salinity of soil, and arable land is disappearing to development. Air is dirty, water is polluted, and animal species are disappearing. Scientists worry that the planet won't survive the expected doubling of its 5.8 billion population over the next thirty years without strong measures to save it now.

Shapiro intends to transform Monsanto into a "life-sciences" organization devoted to improving human health by seeking synergies in biotech, pharmaceutical research, and food production. Because life sciences is a fast-growing, knowledge-based industry requiring huge investments in R&D, it's selling its chemical division to focus on life sciences. This new division, with estimated annual revenues of about $7 billion, will have three major departments: agriculture, pharmaceuticals, and food products.

To change Monsanto into a life-sciences organization, Shapiro's managers will need to reinforce three managerial competencies primarily. First, they face the need to extend their global awareness competency by creating products for the world market. The company's scientists increasingly will have to focus on state-of-the-art products that have practical value around the world and that are within the economic reach of hundreds of millions of Third World people. Second, Monsanto's managers will have to channel resources into staying abreast of rapidly changing technology and pushing the scientific envelope ever further. In agriculture, for example, the company's scientists will need to continue to develop products such as disease-resistant cotton and potatoes, while management is winning governmental approval of genetically engineered seeds in various countries. Finally, Shapiro and his management team will have to develop further their strategy to compete against other organizations worldwide. In doing so they must address the concerns of environmental groups, such as Greenpeace, the Sierra Club, and the Union of Concerned Scientists, which question whether designer crops can do much to clean up pollution, and keep a close watch on herbicides and other synthetic products. Monsanto, which has traditionally relied on its successful herbicide, Roundup, and its artificial sweetener, Nutrasweet, to provide it profits must therefore carefully examine its current products, as well as the new products it brings to market, in light of these concerns.[1]

* * *

To learn more about Monsanto, visit the company's home page at

www.monsanto.com

THE BUSINESS ENVIRONMENT

1

DESCRIBE THE MAIN FORCES IN THE EXTERNAL BUSINESS ENVIRONMENT AND HOW THEY INFLUENCE ORGANIZATIONS

External changes in the business environment generate new products and create new organizations to produce and sell them. Soft contact lenses are a result of a burn-treatment material developed to provide a moist healing environment during the Vietnam War. The removal of FDA approval for silicon and dacron products for repair and replacement surgery created a market for an FDA approved surgical grafting material manufactured by Corvita, a small high-technology company.

How can managers best deal with their environments? Although there are no simple answers to this question, managers can pursue two basic approaches.

1. They can position an organization so that its own capabilities provide the best *defense* against an environmental threat. Monsanto is working with the U.S. Department of Agriculture and the Grocery Manufacturers of America to minimize the political fight over genetically engineered products.

2. They can take the *offensive* by attempting to change or take advantage of the environment. Monsanto is doing so by encouraging customers to visit its operations, including state-of-the-art greenhouses and other growing areas.

In brief, managers must develop both strong reactive (defensive) and strong proactive (offensive) strategies for taking advantage of environmental opportunities and reducing environmental threats.

We were selective in choosing the environmental forces to address in this chapter. For example, the international arena is certainly a key part of most managers' environments—today more than ever. However, we mention international forces here only briefly because we devote Chapter 4 to this topic. Also, various groups are pressing for new forms and higher levels of ethical behavior by managers and for increased social responsibility by organizations. We allude to these forces here, but cover them in detail in Chapter 6. Generally, throughout this book, we discuss environmental forces and their management whenever they are relevant to the topic being considered.

We begin this chapter by introducing the basic features of the general environment that organizations operate within: economic and political systems, demographics, and cultural forces. We then present a framework for diagnosing various types of task environments to add to your growing toolkit of managerial skills. We devote most of the chapter to three types of environmental forces that managers must monitor and diagnose because of their direct or indirect impact on organizations: competitive, technological and information technology, and political-legal.

THE GENERAL ENVIRONMENT

GENERAL ENVIRONMENT
External factors, such as inflation and demographics, that usually affect indirectly all or most organizations (also called the macroenvironment).

The **_general environment,_** sometimes called the _macroenvironment,_ includes the external factors that usually affect all or most organizations. As depicted in Figure 3.1, the general environment includes the type of economic system (capitalism, socialism, or communism) and economic conditions (expansionary and recessionary cycles and the general standard of living); type of political system (democracy, dictatorship, or monarchy); condition of the ecosystem (extent of land, water, and air pollution); demographics (age, gender, race, ethnic origin, and education level of the population); and cultural background (values, beliefs, language, and reli-

---

_F i g u r e   3 . 1_   **The General Environment and Environmental Forces Affecting Organizations**

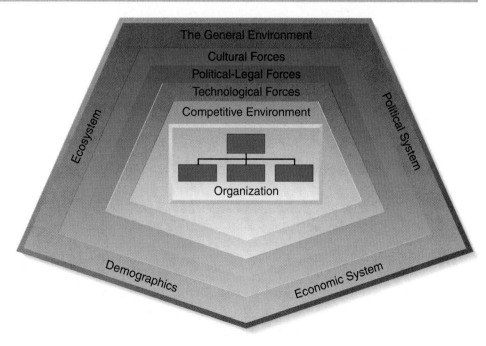

gious influences). All of these aspects of the general environment have long-range implications for managing organizations.

Although we treat each factor separately, they are linked. A prime example is the impact of the North American Free Trade Agreement (NAFTA) on the U.S., Mexican, and Canadian political systems and businesses. It removed trade barriers, incurred the wrath of organized labor, brought calls for further government subsidy of certain industries, spurred the privatization of basic Mexican industries, and stressed the need for greater ecosystem protection, among other effects. In terms of the ecosystem, U.S. and Mexican companies must now meet tighter controls regarding waste disposal and pollution emissions along the border. Overall, NAFTA created proactive (offensive) opportunities in terms of new markets for many companies (including Ford and Wal-Mart). At the same time, however, it created reactive (defensive) threats to many of the same companies in terms of having to improve their pollution abatement efforts and waste disposal practices.[2]

THE ECONOMIC SYSTEM

The United States has an economic system in which privately controlled markets based on supply and demand indicate how resources are being distributed and used within the environment. **Economics** is the discipline that focuses on understanding how a group of people or a nation produce, distribute, and consume various goods and services.[3] Important economic issues are the wages paid to labor, inflation, the taxes paid by labor and organizations, the cost of materials used in the production process, and the prices at which goods and services are sold. Free market competition, private contracts, profit incentives, technological advancement, and organized labor with collective bargaining rights are essential elements of the U.S. economic system. The government (part of the political system) acts as a watchdog over business, providing direction in antitrust, monetary policy, human rights, defense, and environmental matters. Particularly challenging economic and political conditions include the fluctuation of inflation, unemployment, tax, and interest rates and environmental and safety regulations covering both the workplace and goods produced. Government ownership of enterprises is the exception, rather than the norm. The economy is not centrally planned, as in North Korea, Cuba, and the People's Republic of China.

THE ECOSYSTEM

Political and economic conditions in the United States have led to a renewed environmentalism. A 1981 *New York Times*/CBS poll found that only 4 percent of the U.S. population agreed that "environmental improvements must be made regardless of cost." In 1997, 80 percent of the population strongly agreed. As a result, national environmental groups are becoming even more active. The Audubon Society has broadened its efforts from protection of wildlife to actively monitoring business practices that affect native plants and animals. The Audubon Society was the first to propose legal agreements that called for removal of significant amounts of phosphate from the water that had been used to refine sugar. The National Resources Defense Council has abandoned some of its earlier views—considered by some to be "fanatic and utopian"—and has displayed a greater understanding of the trade-offs that have to be made. The organization has begun to move from confrontation to collaboration as a strategy. Nonetheless, some environmental organizations, such as Wise Use, continue to press legislatures to adopt stricter laws and regulatory boards that enforce land use and waste disposal regulations to tighten their procedures.

This renewed environmentalism poses numerous challenges to business. With the passage of the U.S. Clean Air Act of 1990 and NAFTA, organizations faced more

ECONOMICS
The discipline that focuses on understanding how people of a group or nation produce, distribute, purchase, and use various goods and services.

than a choice—they faced increasingly tough requirements. However, for several years some organizations, such as Shell Oil Company, have supported increased environmental planning and action in response to the radical change in public attitudes. Managers at Monsanto and many other organizations are making environmental considerations part of their strategic action competency. They must now think long term, even though profits may suffer in the short term, not just of corporate costs but also of investments in the future of the planet. The following are a few of the actions that organizations have taken in heeding the call of renewed environmentalism.

Cut Back on Environmentally Unsafe Operations. In Japan, Mitsubishi Heavy Industries and Hitachi have cut back on operations that produced excessive nitrogen oxide and sulfur dioxide emissions. Westinghouse's $226 million deal to build two municipal trash incinerators in southern Taiwan fell apart because of local opposition to its environmentally unsafe processes.

Compensate for Environmentally Risky Endeavors. Temple-Inland, a manufacturer of corrugated containers, operates mills in both North and South America. Because trees must be cut to make paper and many species can be endangered because of the lack of forest habitat, the company has a policy of using 45 percent recycled materials in its boxes. It also maintains some forests where trees are selectively cut and other forests where all marketable timber is taken. In the latter, called plantation forests, all cut trees are replaced with seedlings; reforestation takes about 15 years. Last year, the company planted 30 million seedlings.

Avoid Confrontation with State and Federal Pollution Control Agencies. W. R. Grace failed to avoid confrontation over antipollution requirements and currently is involved in expensive restitution for asbestos-related problems and time-consuming asbestos disposal. Browning-Ferris, Waste Management, and Louisiana-Pacific abused local landfill requirements. In the future, when they bid for city, township, and county refuse collection and disposal contracts, their service plans will be examined particularly closely.

Comply Early with Government Regulations. Because compliance costs increase over time, organizations that act early will have lower costs. When they do so, they can also increase their market share, profits, and competitive advantage. In Bangkok voters swept a new governor into office last year on promises of cleaning up air and auto pollution. The Thai government, using sophisticated satellites originally designed to pinpoint missile targets, is mapping sources of pollution to make firms comply with its tighter standards. It is making organizations connect to sewer facilities, whose waste has poured directly into the canals where children bathe and housewives wash clothes and dishes.

Promote New Manufacturing Technologies. In light of the problems with the earth's ozone layer, Motorola and other microprocessor manufacturers have switched from clorofluorocarbon (CFC) chemicals, such as Freon, to a substance made from the skin of oranges, called turpene, to clean their chips. New companies will emerge to satisfy the increasing demand for turpene.

Recycle Wastes. More than 200 billion cans, bottles, plastic cartons, and paper cups are thrown away each year in developed countries. Many towns and cities have set up recycling programs to reduce the amount of waste to be disposed of and land required for disposal sites. Private companies also are involved in recycling efforts. The 3M Company is reusing solvents and other chemicals it once released into waterways and spewed into the atmosphere. Other firms with active recycling programs are SafetyKleen (solvents and motor oil), Wellman (plastics), Jefferson Smurfit (paper), and Nucor (steel). Polyfoam Packers, a Styrofoam manufacturer, has initiated a recycling process that reuses Styrofoam beads.[4]

Management Action Plans. Managers can take the following actions to respond to environmental concerns.

- Give a senior-level person well-defined environmental responsibilities. This approach makes environmental concerns a strategic issue.

- Measure everything: waste, energy use, travel in personal vehicles, and the like. Set measurable goals and target dates for environmental improvements. Monitor progress.

- Consider reformulating products in order to use less toxic chemicals in the manufacturing process and cleanup. Try to use materials that won't harm the environment when the consumer eventually discards the product.

- Consider business opportunities from recycling or disposing of products, including having customers return them when the products have reached the end of their useful lives.

- Recognize that environmental regulations are here to stay and that they are likely to become more restrictive. Environmental awareness and behavior ("green behavior") will have a lot to do with a firm's reputation in the future. Plan for the future by taking these factors into account today.

Environmental concerns have changed the way producers and consumers alike think about products, the raw materials used to make them, and the byproducts of manufacturing processes. In fact, industries have developed a whole new generation of successful products in response to the Clean Air Act and reuse and recycling regulations. For example, Louisiana-Pacific makes various wood products, including particle board, out of milling scraps.

DEMOGRAPHICS

DEMOGRAPHICS
The characteristics of
work group, organization,
specific market, or national
populations.

Demographics are the characteristics of work group, organization, specific market, or national populations, such as individuals between the ages of 18 and 25.[5] Demographics—and in particular, changes in demographics—play an important role in marketing, advertising, and human resource management. Demographic changes are having a profound influence on the health-care industry, particularly the operations of small community hospitals, such as Central Michigan Community Hospital and Plano (Texas) General Hospital. Different patient needs, ranging from OBGYN services to body-part replacements and organ transplants to treatment of Alzheimer's disease and extended geriatric care, are requiring hospitals and other health-care providers to offer an ever-widening range of services. Larger hospital systems, such as Columbia Hospital Corporation of America, have responded by buying smaller hospitals and transferring patients to other hospitals in their systems that specialize in providing certain services. Marriott and other organizations have also responded to the aging of the U.S population by opening assisted-care facilities. Let's consider a few of the broad demographic changes that have occurred in the United States recently and that are expected to continue through the beginning of the next century.

Human Resource Management Issues. During the next decade, 39 million workers will enter the U.S. labor force; one-third will be minorities. About 23 million baby-boomers will retire, the majority of whom will be white men. As a result, women and minorities will gradually represent a larger share of the labor force. The overall rate of labor force participation will barely creep upward by 2005, from 66.6 percent to 67.1 percent. The number of Hispanic workers is likely to grow by 36 percent by 2005. This growth will result from continued immigration of young adults, high birth rates, and relatively few retirees. The percentage of black workers will increase by 15 percent by 2005 and the number of Asian workers by 39 percent. Thus the workforce by 2005 will be much more diverse, which we focus on in Chapter 18. The U.S. economy has shifted from industrial production to services and information analysis. This shift means that jobs of all kinds are more likely to require some type of specialized skill. One result is that people with little education or training will continue to have a hard time finding meaningful and well-paying work and experience long spells of "labor market inactivity." Currently, home health aides, physical therapists, computer engineers and scientists, special-education teachers, child-care workers, and corrections officers—all of whom must have education and training beyond high school—are among the workers in greatest demand.[6]

Employers are likely to face new pressures from the increasingly diverse workforce. They need to recognize this trend and learn how to manage diversity. Some organizations provide training to help employees at all levels be more tolerant of language, age, race, and ethnic differences; to identify and reject racial and gender preferences in hiring and promotion; and to be responsive to the handicapped. Management no longer can impose an "Anglo male" organizational culture.[7] For example, women hold six of the fourteen executive positions at American Airlines in the Research Triangle Park, North Carolina, and nonwhite women fill 20 percent of the management positions just below the executive level [8]

One reason for slower growth is that women aren't joining the workforce as fast as they once did. The labor force participation rate of women increased more than 5 percent between 1982 and 1993, but it is projected to increase less than 3 percent between now and 2005. Most of the participation of working women will come from baby-boomers moving into their 40s and 50s, because the women of this generation are far more likely than their mothers to hold jobs. A second reason for this slowdown is that a greater proportion of women are going to college and pursuing graduate degrees.

Marketing and Advertising. Procter & Gamble, Kraft Foods, Heinz, Pillsbury, Nestlé, and other food product organizations are aware of these demographic changes. Hispanic food has become popular in Chicago, Dallas, Los Angeles, and other major cities, where a variety of restaurants—Mexican, Cuban, Salvadoran, and others—reflect large Hispanic communities. Mexican food tops the list. In the United States, 38 million households eat Mexican food, sales of which rose 60 percent between 1982 and 1990. Kraft's Velveeta cheese now comes in a spicy Mexican version, and jalapeño-flavored potato chips are sold nationally. Farmers in New Mexico report doubling their crops of chiles. Salsa is a staple in many households and now outsells ketchup. Burritos and tacos are popular substitutes for sandwiches in many college and university student centers.

Of course, efforts to target any market can have pitfalls. Borden advertised ice cream using the Mexican slang word *nieve,* which literally means "snow." The campaign worked fine in California and Texas, where there is a large Mexican-American population. But Cubans and Puerto Ricans in the East, unfamiliar with Mexican slang, thought that the company actually was selling snow because they call ice cream *helado.* Throughout the United States, the Latin community and many others recognize "snow" as being slang for cocaine.

Univision, the largest Spanish language television network, reaches an estimated 17 million Hispanics, with at least 5 million regular viewers. Formerly known as the Spanish International Network, it has been joined by a second Spanish network, Telemundo, with more than 3.3 million regular viewers.[9] In most cities, Spanish radio stations air talk shows and traffic reports in a local Spanish dialect. However, these stations are having some communication problems because of different dialects and slang terms used by a diverse Hispanic listening audience.

CULTURAL FORCES

Underlying a society and surrounding an organization are various cultural forces, which often are not as visible as other general environmental forces. **Culture** can be defined as the shared characteristics (e.g., language, religion, and heritage) and values that distinguish the members of one group of people from those of another.[10] A *value* is a basic belief about a condition that has considerable importance and meaning to individuals and is relatively stable over time. A ***value system*** comprises multiple beliefs that are compatible and supportive of one another. For example, beliefs in private enterprise and individual rights are mutually supportive. Cultural values aren't genetically transferred. People begin to learn their culture's values from the day they are born, and this learning continues throughout their lives.

Managers need to appreciate the significance of values and value systems, both their own and those of others.[11] Values can greatly affect how a manager

- **views other people and groups, thus influencing interpersonal relationships.** In Japan male managers have traditionally believed that women should defer decision-making responsibilities to men. They belonged at home where they are responsible for raising and educating the children. Until recently, similar views prevailed in many U.S. organizations. But this situation is changing rapidly. American managers and government view men and women as equals who should be recognized, consulted, and promoted because of their abilities and contributions, not their gender.

- **perceives situations and problems.** Many American managers believe that conflict and competition can be managed and used constructively to solve problems. Chinese managers believe that conflict between managers and employees should be avoided.

- **goes about solving problems.** In Korea, managers at Samsung believe that team decision making can be effective. In Germany, managers at Siemens believe that individuals should make decisions.

- **determines what is and is not ethical behavior.** One manager might believe that ethics means doing only what is absolutely required by law. Another might view ethics as going well beyond minimum legal requirements to do what is morally right.

- **leads and controls employees.** In America, many managers believe in sharing information with employees and rely on mutual trust more than rigid controls. In Mexico, most managers emphasize rules, close supervision, and a rigid chain of command.[12]

By diagnosing a culture's values, managers and employees can understand and predict others' expectations and avoid some cultural pitfalls. Otherwise, they risk inadvertently antagonizing fellow employees, customers, or other groups by breaking a sacred taboo (e.g., showing the bottom of a person's shoe to a Saudi) or

CULTURE
The shared characteristics (e.g., language, religion, and heritage) and values that distinguish one group of people from another.

VALUE SYSTEM
Multiple beliefs (values) that are compatible and supportive of one another.

ignoring a time-honored custom (e.g., preventing an employee from attending an important religious ceremony in Indonesia).

The framework of work-related values outlined here has been used in numerous studies of cultural differences among employees. It was developed by Geert Hofstede, Director of the Institute for Research on Intercultural Cooperation in the Netherlands, while he was an organizational researcher at IBM.[13] The data reported here are based on his surveys of thousands of IBM employees in fifty countries. Hofstede's project uncovered some intriguing differences among countries in terms of five value dimensions: power distance, uncertainty avoidance, individualism (versus collectivism), masculinity (versus femininity), and Confucian dynamism.[14]

The following discussion focuses primarily on Hofstede's ranking of four nations—Canada, Japan, Taiwan, and the United States—with respect to each dimension. These rankings are based on the *dominant* value orientation in each country, with a ranking of 1 for the highest and 50 for the lowest position (relative to all fifty countries in the survey) on each value dimension. Figure 3.2 shows the rankings for Canada, Japan, Taiwan, and the United States.

Power Distance. The degree to which influence and control are unequally distributed among individuals and institutions within a particular culture is the measure of its ***power distance.*** If most people in a society support an unequal distribution, the nation is ranked high. In societies ranked high (e.g., Mexico, France, Malaysia, and the Philippines), membership in a particular class or caste is crucial to an individual's opportunity for advancement. Societies ranked lower play down inequality. Individuals in the United States, Canada, Sweden, and Austria can achieve prestige, wealth, and social status, regardless of family background.

Managers operating in countries ranked low in power distance are expected to be generally supportive of equal rights and equal opportunity. For example, managers in Canada and the United States typically support participative management. In contrast, managers in Mexico, France, and India do not value the U.S. and Canadian style of participative management. Managers in the United States and Canada try not to set themselves too much apart from subordinates by appearing to be

POWER DISTANCE

Hofstede's value dimension that measures the degree to which influence and control are unequally distributed among individuals within a particular culture.

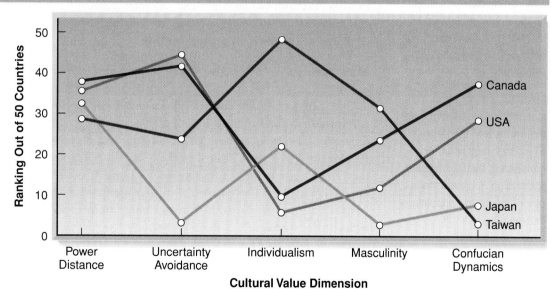

Figure 3.2   **Relative Ranking of Four Countries on Cultural Values**

Ranking Out of 50 Countries

Cultural Value Dimension: Power Distance, Uncertainty Avoidance, Individualism, Masculinity, Confucian Dynamics

Canada, USA, Japan, Taiwan

Rank Numbers: 1 = Highest; 50 = Lowest

Source: Adapted from G. Hofstede and M. H. Bond. The Confucius connection: From cultural roots to economic growth. *Organization Dynamics,* Spring 1988, pp. 12–13.

superior or unique. In countries with high power distance, however, a more autocratic management style not only is common but is expected by employees.

Uncertainty Avoidance. The degree to which members of a society attempt to avoid ambiguity, risk, and the indefiniteness of the future is the measure of its ***uncertainty avoidance.*** Individuals in cultures ranked low on this dimension generally are secure and don't expend a great deal of energy trying to avoid or minimize ambiguous situations. In cultures with high uncertainty avoidance, individuals often try to make the future more predictable by establishing procedures and rules that foster job security. In organizations, high uncertainty avoidance is often associated with built-in career stability (job security), numerous rules governing behavior, intolerance of deviant ideas and behavior, belief in absolute truths, and over-reliance on expertise.

In the United States and Canada, employees and managers ranked low on uncertainty avoidance, sharing a relatively high tolerance for uncertainty, compared with workers and managers in Japan and Taiwan. Thus Canadian and U.S. managers are more likely to be receptive to changing rules, open competition, and new ideas than workers in Japan and Taiwan.

Individualism. A combination of the degree to which society expects people to take care of themselves and their immediate families and the degree to which individuals believe they are masters of their own destiny is its measure of ***individualism.*** The opposite of individualism is ***collectivism,*** which refers to a tight social framework in which group (family, clan, organization, and nation) members focus on the common welfare and feel strong loyalty toward one another.

In the United States and Canada, employees ranked high on individualism, a result that agrees with the frequent characterization of these two countries as "I" societies rather than "we" societies. A strong sense of individualism supports and maintains a competitive market-based economic system. High individualism also is consistent with the individual merit and incentive pay systems favored in the United States and Canada. Conversely, group incentives and strong seniority systems are likely to exist in countries with low individualism (high collectivism), such as Taiwan and Japan. Managers and employees in a high-individualism culture move from organization to organization more frequently. They don't believe that their organizations are solely responsible for their welfare, nor do they expect that group decisions are better than decisions made by individuals.

Masculinity. In Hofstede's framework, ***masculinity*** is the degree to which assertiveness and the acquisition of money and material things are valued, as well as the degree of indifference to others' quality of life. The opposite of masculinity is ***femininity,*** a more nurturing, people-oriented approach to life. The masculinity dimension also reflects the division of labor among men and women in a society. Canada and the United States probably rank lower today on this dimension than they would have twenty years ago, largely because of the societal changes that have been taking place in role expectations for men and women. In recent years significant social pressures have begun to change stereotyped notions that men should be assertive and women should be nurturing or that gender roles should be clearly differentiated.

In high-masculinity cultures (e.g., Mexico, Japan, Austria, and Italy), women still do not hold many managerial jobs. Men dominate most settings, and an organization's right to influence the private lives of its employees is widely accepted. One researcher observed that Mexico, for example, rigidly defines gender-role expectations: The woman is expected to be supportive of and dependent on men—not to

UNCERTAINTY AVOIDANCE
Hofstede's value dimension that measures the degree to which individuals or societies attempt to avoid the ambiguity, risk, and indefiniteness of the future.

INDIVIDUALISM
Hofstede's value dimension that measures the extent to which a culture expects people to take care of themselves and/or individuals believe that they are masters of their own destiny (the opposite of collectivism).

COLLECTIVISM
Hofstede's value dimension that measures the tendency of group members to focus on the common welfare and feel loyalty toward one another (the opposite of individualism).

MASCULINITY
Hofstede's value dimension that measures the degree to which the acquisition of money and things is valued and a high quality of life for others is not (the opposite of femininity).

FEMININITY
Hofstede's value dimension that measures the tendency to be nurturing and people oriented (the opposite of masculinity).

do for herself, but to yield to the wishes of others, caring for their needs before her own. A common belief in Muslim countries is that women are the inferior gender and should be subordinate to men in all aspects of their lives.

Confucian Dynamism. Confucius was a civil servant in China in about 500 B.C. Known for his wisdom, he developed a pragmatic set of rules for daily life. The following key principles of *Confucian dynamics* are illustrated by references to organizational life. First, the stability of society is based on unequal relationships between people. Thus the junior manager owes the senior manager respect and obedience; the senior manager owes the junior manager protection and consideration. Second, the family is the prototype of all social organizations. Thus members of organizations should learn to promote harmony by allowing others to maintain "face," that is, dignity, self-respect, and prestige, particularly in conducting business affairs. Third, people should treat others as they would like to be treated. Thus first-line managers should encourage subordinates to acquire knowledge and skills to enable them to advance, just as these managers would like the middle managers above them to do. Finally, a person's tasks in life consist of acquiring skills and education, working hard, not spending more than necessary, being patient, and preserving the values of the society.

In high-Confucian cultures, such as Japan, Hong Kong, Taiwan, and Korea, management practices such as thrift, gift giving, good manners, and saving face are highly valued. Thrift leads to saving, which provides capital for reinvestment. Welcoming speeches by elder members of the organization and exchanges of small gifts prior to conducting business are important. Seniority is prized and is linked to the size of a person's office, pay, and other perquisites. Such practices emphasize the stability of authority relationships and respect. In the United States, Canada, and the United Kingdom, such management practices are not highly valued and/or practiced.

Applying Hofstede's Dimensions. In later chapters we use the five work-related value dimensions discussed here to address differences and similarities in cultures. Here, we briefly illustrate the application of these value dimensions to Eli Lilly and Company's recruitment and management of diverse groups of employees. Lilly is a pharmaceutical giant with more than 27,000 employees—12,700 overseas—and operations in more than ninety countries. Today, approximately 45 percent of its sales come from its overseas operations. To remain competitive, Lilly needs to promote its global presence aggressively by expanding in established markets—England, Ireland, Argentina, and France—and by venturing into new markets—Russia, China, Chile, and Japan. Fifty-five percent of Lilly's top managers have had overseas assignments for extended periods of time, ranging from twelve to eighteen months. Lilly spends more than $70 million per year to give people the overseas experience they need to develop various competencies. The following Planning and Administration Competency account highlights some of these experiences. We have noted Hofstede's cultural values in parentheses.

CONFUCIAN DYNAMICS
Hofstede's value dimension that measures a society's tendency to value people who are persistent, observe orderly relationships between people based on status, are thrifty, and have a sense of shame.

TASK ENVIRONMENT
External forces (e.g., customers or labor unions) that directly affect an organization's growth, success, and survival.

THE TASK ENVIRONMENT

2

UNDERSTAND THE ROLE OF THE TASK ENVIRONMENT AND ITS IMPACT ON DECISION MAKING

The general environment and the task environment are not separate concepts; the differences between them are matters of degree. Whereas the general environment indirectly influences all organizations in an economic system (e.g., the United States, Japan, Mexico, Canada), the *task environment* includes only those factors in the general environment that directly influence an organization's growth, success, and survival.[16] It normally includes an organization's customers or clients, competitors, suppliers, shareholders, government regulators, pressure groups,

When Eli Lilly and Company started recruiting young professionals in Japan, few top-notch Japanese graduates wanted to work for the company. They had spent decades in furious educational preparation to work for Sony or Mitsubishi. Attending Tokyo or Sophia Universities would almost guarantee them well-paying jobs in Japan's most prestigious organiza-

tions (uncertainty avoidance). Signing on with a U.S. organization would be considered a disgrace (masculinity). Therefore Lilly modified its recruiting strategy to target young professional women. In Japan's masculine culture, women are often rejected because of their gender and inability to work in Muslim countries. As a result, Lilly successfully recruited a women-dominated workforce of some of the brightest minds in Japan.

In China, which the pharmaceutical industry predicts will generate $18 billion dollars in sales annually, Lilly has to hire through a third-party state organization (high Confucian dynamism). That means hiring workers who, though fascinated by the possibilities of capitalism and TV reports about business successes in Hong Kong, have been dependent on the state (uncertainty avoidance and power distance) all their lives. Young

graduates from the University of Beijing asked, "What do you mean, eight-hour days?" In addition, U.S. organizations entering China to tap its market of 1.2 billion people have flooded the best graduates, particularly those who can speak and write English, with offers. Because workers historically have never had to leave their employer—the state—the slightest unhappiness or increase in compensation for others (through perks and expense allowances; salaries are mandated by the state) can cause such employees to go to their state employment agency to request a change of employer. Thus Lilly's managers had to learn to give incentives collectively and leave their distribution to the group.[15]

To learn more about Eli Lilly, visit the company's home page at

www.lilly.com

employees, and labor unions (if unionized). For Monsanto, the task environment includes customers, competitors, suppliers, shareholders, employees, unions, the Audubon Society and other environmental groups, and the state and federal EPAs. With so many groups putting pressure on the company, its task environment is somewhat turbulent. For hospitals, such as Central Michigan Community Hospital, the external environment includes patients; third-party payers (insurance companies); local, state, and federal government agencies; competitive hospitals; and organizations providing alternative forms of patient care.

Everyone in organizations—from the manager and checkout clerk at the local supermarket to the postmaster and mail carrier at the U.S. Postal Service—is finding that focusing on groups in the task environment is essential. Hence managers need to spend a lot of time and effort diagnosing the changing needs and expectations of these groups in order to meet them. For example, Hertz, Alamo, and other car rental agencies permit their agents to meet competitors' prices—or to take whatever other action is needed—on the spot to satisfy a customer. At Alamo, these changes have resulted in explosive growth and a 20 percent increase in sales revenues.

The task environment encompasses the competitive and technological forces shown in Figure 3.1. Although we treat political-legal forces as part of the task environment, we recognize that they can be viewed as part of the general environment, depending on the situation and the perspective of the viewer. For example, labor unions may be part of an organization's task or general environment. The United Auto Workers (UAW) is part of the task environments of Ford, General Motors, and

Chrysler and directly affects these companies. (In turn, the management of these firms directly affects the UAW.) But unions aren't part of the task environment for nonunion firms such as IBM, Hewlett-Packard, and Alamo Rent A Car. Unions indirectly affect them, however, as part of the general environment. Indirect effects might include successful union efforts to obtain legislation benefiting all workers, union and nonunion alike.

Managers must constantly evaluate the task environment as they diagnose issues and weigh decisions. The task environment has an important bearing on organizational planning, organizational structure, human resources management, and control decisions. But monitoring the complexities of the task environment can be difficult for managers because of their numerous day-to-day responsibilities. Bank of America, Qantas Airlines, Frito-Lay, and other organizations have special positions or departments (e.g., marketing research, strategic planning, and public affairs) with primary responsibility for helping managers keep track of forces in both the general and task environments. The idea for the wristwatch pager marketed in Japan by Motorola came from work teams that included representatives of major Japanese department stores. Using the same consultative process, Motorola learned that the U.S. market wouldn't be interested in such a product.

One of the unintended benefits of total quality management programs has been closer contact with suppliers. In the 1970s, for example, RCA considered Corning Glass and other glass manufacturers to be in its general environment. Today, RCA treats Corning Glass as an essential member of its task environment and listens to the inventory and logistic advice that Corning offers. Work teams at RCA now frequently include supplier and key customer representatives.

TYPES OF TASK ENVIRONMENTS

Figure 3.3 shows a simplified way to diagnose and classify the task environment of an organization. This framework has two dimensions: the simple-complex and the stable-changing.[17]

The *simple-complex dimension* identifies whether the factors in the task environment are few and similar or numerous and different. A construction firm that builds standardized low-income residential housing would have a relatively simple environment. In contrast, a firm that builds customized homes, office buildings, and shopping centers is likely to face a more complex environment. The homebuilder is affected primarily by local economic cycles, the availability of raw materials, and local building codes. However, the commercial builder must respond to the same forces as the residential builder and also deal with scheduling crews (e.g., electricians, plasterers, plumbers, and roofers) for multiple building sites, bank loan officers and bank regulators who influence lending practices, and changes in the general economy.

The *stable-changing dimension* identifies whether the factors in the task environment remain the same or vary over time. For both types of builders, the task environment may remain stable for long periods of time. But it also may change rapidly. Consider, for example, the impact of natural disasters such as the floods in North and South Dakota in 1997, the Los Angeles Earthquake of 1994, and the recent series of hurricanes along the East Coast on the building industry. These events changed the task environment radically for all builders. In particular, building materials quickly became scarce and more expensive, and local building codes were changed to minimize the loss of life and property in the future.

Governmental changes also affect the stability of the task environment. On July 1, 1997, the British handed over Hong Kong to China. As long as Hong Kong and its 6.3 million people were ruled by the British Crown, U.S. organizations relied on

	Stable	**Changing**
Simple	Factors in environment are 1. few, 2. quite similar to each other, and 3. basically the same over time. **Example:** Soft-drink distributors	Factors in environment are 1. few, 2. somewhat similar to each other, and 3. continually changing. **Example:** Fast-food outlets
Complex	Factors in environment are 1. numerous, 2. not similar to each other, and 3. basically the same over time. **Example:** Basic food products firms	Factors in environment are 1. numerous, 2. not similar to each other, and 3. continually changing. **Example:** Computer firms

the United Kingdom to protect their investments totaling more than $14 billion. Marriott, Bank of America, Sheraton, and other U.S. organizations with huge investments in Hong Kong are concerned with Beijing's replacement of Hong Kong's popularly elected legislature with appointed lawmakers. In his inaugural speech, Tung Chee Hwa, Hong Kong's new chief executive, outlined social and economic policies that would align Hong Kong with traditional Chinese values, such as dutiful allegiance to the state and discouragement of open confrontation.[18]

Four basic types of task environments—simple/stable, simple/changing, complex/stable, and complex/changing—are derived from classifying a firm's environmental factors along the simple-complex and stable-changing dimensions. Organizations having a simple/stable environment include local soft drink bottlers. They have many customers, but the services they typically provide are standardized: delivering the right number of cases of soft drinks to each customer at specified times. Most soft drink bottlers deal with national firms, such as Pepsi or Coca-Cola. Local bottlers also undertake most marketing campaigns, such as annual spring-break parties. Thus the task environment for such organizations is relatively simple and stable over time.

The simple/changing and complex/stable environments fall between the two extremes. Jiffy Lube, Q-Lube, and other quick service oil change outlets operate in a simple/changing environment. They offer limited services and have standardized and simplified procedures for servicing cars. Their customers don't expect and can't receive much personal service. However, they constantly tinker with marketing promotions to adjust to changes in consumer preferences and keep up with the competition. In contrast, Heinz, Campbell's, and other basic food products firms operate in a complex/stable environment. For example, the basic line of Campbell's soups—chicken noodle, tomato, and cream of mushroom—hasn't changed for decades. However, the production and distribution processes for getting these soups onto grocery store shelves are quite complex. They require meeting the demands of many suppliers and customers and conforming to various government regulations. Recently, the health consciousness of many consumers and the actions of consumer advocate groups have put added pressure on prepared food manufacturers to reduce the sodium, fat, and cholesterol content of their products. Thus the stability of the environment for these companies is changing.[19]

Organizations in a simple/stable environment face the least amount of uncertainty, and those in a complex/changing environment face the most. *Environmental uncertainty* refers to the ambiguity and unpredictability of some external factors. Organizations such as computer chip manufacturers (lower right-hand corner of Figure 3.3) face a *turbulent environment,* one that is complex, is constantly changing, and is both ambiguous and unpredictable.[20] In his book *Hypercompetition,* author and management consultant Richard D'Aveni concludes that revolutionary technology, globalization, radically new communication and information processing techniques, and flexible manufacturing equipment and processes require fundamental shifts in managers' thinking. Few organizations can build sustainable competitive advantages in turbulent environments.[21]

Turbulent environments aren't limited to large corporations. Consider the competitive, regulatory, and technological changes faced by doctors of optometry who run their own eye clinics and eyeglass dispensing practices. Their task environment has changed rapidly and become very complex because of competition from large retailers, such as Pearle Vision, Sears Optical, LensCrafters, and EyeMasters, among others. Their simple/stable environment has been replaced with a complex/dynamic environment, and it shows no sign of settling down. Let's look at these differences. In 1960, the environment was relatively stable: The supply of patients was ample, loan money to buy new equipment was fairly inexpensive, and regulation, beyond getting a license and observing continuing education requirements, was virtually nonexistent. The environment was fairly simple: Compliance with legal requirements and awareness of changing technology was all that was necessary to be successful.

Today, the environment is much more complex: Serious infectious diseases threaten all types of doctors and their patients; the Occupational Safety Hazards Act (OSHA) requires that doctors provide proper attire for themselves and all patient-care personnel, in addition to strict equipment and supply cleaning and disposal. Revenues come from many sources, including insurance companies and health maintenance organizations (HMOs) that pay a fixed amount for each member patient. In addition to complexity, the environment is more dynamic. Competition has increased. Advancements in contact lens and surgical procedures continually introduce new products and methods. Patients move from doctor to doctor as their insurance coverages change, often because of employment changes. Offices are equipped with fax machines and computers with modems to transmit insurance forms. Workrooms have containers with a skull and crossbones symbol on them to indicate the presence of environmentally hazardous waste.

Relatively powerless independent optometrists usually are forced to agree to the fee constraints imposed by company-purchased insurance and large retail chains. Many believe that agreeing to each new constraint is preferable to the loss of patients and income for noncompliance. Even more uncertainty faces optometrists

ENVIRONMENTAL UNCERTAINTY
The ambiguity or unpredictability of certain factors in an organization's external environment (e.g., government regulation).

TURBULENT ENVIRONMENT
An external environment that is complex, constantly changing, and both ambiguous and unpredictable.

who, thirty years ago, had a paternalistic relationship with patients and the task environment. Between 1960 and 1997, the number of optometrists in the United States more than doubled, but the U.S. population didn't increase as fast. More practicing optometrists, independent practice associations (IPAs), outpatient clinics, and large group practices have intensified the competition and changed significantly the practice of optometry.[22]

In the larger health-care scene, changes in the task environment include fewer total patient visits (both at offices and during hospital rounds), more group practices, and less real income for physicians in small general practices. Also, the technology affecting the provision of health care (new drugs, new diagnostic procedures, new specialties, and new cures) has grown and changed explosively. And, if all of this weren't enough, the constant threat of lawsuits and liability claims from patients and clients has caused malpractice insurance costs to skyrocket. Clearly, the present task environment of physicians is turbulent.

In the remainder of this chapter we address the three major forces in the task environment that organizations must continually monitor, diagnose, and manage. We begin with the innermost ring of Figure 3.1 and move outward—from competitive forces to technological forces to political-legal forces—in terms of domestic operations. In Chapter 4 we address the same forces in terms of international operations. Competitive forces have the greatest day-to-day impact on organizations. Most middle level and top managers (as well as professionals such as market researchers, planning analysts, purchasing agents, and sales representatives) spend considerable time and energy monitoring, diagnosing, and figuring out how to deal with competitive forces.

COMPETITIVE FORCES IN THE TASK ENVIRONMENT

3

IDENTIFY THE FIVE COMPETITIVE FORCES THAT DIRECTLY AFFECT ORGANIZATIONS IN AN INDUSTRY

Organizations in any industry are directly affected by at least five competitive forces: competitors, new entrants, substitute goods and services, customers, and suppliers. The combined strength of these forces affects long-term profitability, as shown in Figure 3.4.[23] Managers must therefore monitor and diagnose each one, as well as their combined strength, before making decisions about future courses of action. As we noted in Chapter 1, organizations may join together, as Lockheed Martin and Grumman Aircraft did, to create strategic partners that influence the impact of these competitive forces in an industry.

Figure 3.4 **Competitive Forces in the Task Environment**

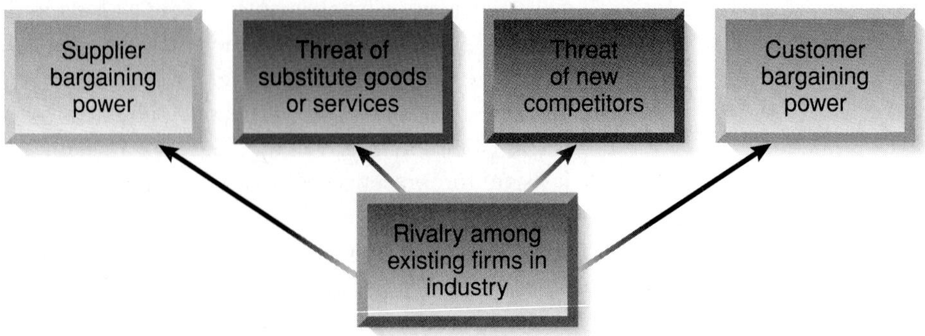

COMPETITORS

Aside from customers, competitors are the single most important day-to-day force facing organizations. Bruce D. Henderson, founder and chairman of the Boston Consulting Group, comments: "For virtually all organizations the critical environment constraint is their actions in relation to competitors. Therefore any change in the environment that affects any competitor will have consequences that require some degree of adaptation. This requires continual change and adaptation by all competitors merely to maintain relative position."[24]

Rivalry among competitors produces strategies such as price cutting, advertising promotions, enhanced customer service or warranties, and improvements in product or service quality. Competitors use these strategies to try to improve their relative positions in an industry or to respond to actions by others.[25] For example, in the airline industry when one firm cuts prices, other firms often quickly follow. All may end up worse off in the short term because lower profits or even losses may result. In the long run, though, price-cutting may increase demand for their product and leave the industry as a whole better off. Also, competition increased when numerous regional carriers began service following deregulation, but some larger airlines, such as People Express, Western Airlines, and Piedmont, couldn't compete successfully over the long term and have gone out of business or have merged with other carriers.

As organizations attempt to gain market share through advertising, claims may be made about the product and/or service that are difficult to prove. For example, Procter & Gamble recently filed a truth-in-advertising complaint with the National Advertising Review Board against Arm & Hammer baking soda toothpaste for claiming that "two out of three dentists and hygienists recommend baking soda for healthier teeth and gums." Proctor & Gamble argued that the statement had no scientific basis.

Organizations trying to create an advertising campaign for the entire European Union are running into problems when selling to children or using children in their ads. The problem is that every European country has different regulations regarding television advertising aimed at children. In the Netherlands, ads for confectionery products must not be run before 8:00 P.M. if children are targeted or children under fourteen are featured in the ad. A toothbrush must appear on the screen, either at the bottom during the entire ad or filling the entire screen for the last one and a half seconds. In Spain and Germany, war toys cannot be advertised. In France, children cannot appear in an ad unless an adult is present in the ad. However, in the United Kingdom, that same ad would not require the presence of an adult. The Greeks are trying to reinstate a 1987 law banning all toy advertising, which was struck down by the European Union in 1991 for restraining trade. In Sweden, no commercials of any kind can air before, during, or after children's programs.

NEW ENTRANTS

The threat or reality of increased competition in an industry depends on the relative ease with which new firms can compete with established firms. In an industry with low barriers to entry (e.g., the photocopy industry or the fast-food industry) competition will be fierce. The airline industry is a particularly interesting case because it has had both high and low barriers to entry during the past ten years. Economies of scale, product differentiation, capital requirements, and government regulation are four common factors that need to be diagnosed in assessing barriers to entry. Let's see how they have affected airline competition.[26]

Economies of scale refer to decreases in per unit costs as the volume of goods and services produced by a firm increases. The potential for economies of scale in

ECONOMIES OF SCALE
The decreases in per unit costs as the volume of goods and/or services produced increases.

the airline industry is substantial. For example, the Boeing 747 is a jumbo jet with relatively high fixed costs to fly (e.g., cost of the aircraft and maintenance, fuel costs, landing fees, and crew costs). Even when every passenger seat is filled and all the passengers bring extra baggage, the bottom portion of the plane contains an enormous amount of unused space. Therefore, when Singapore Airlines loads freight in addition to passengers on its Tokyo–Hong Kong flights, it takes advantage of the economies of scale made possible by the 747.

PRODUCT DIFFERENTIATION

Uniqueness in quality, price, design, brand image, or customer service that gives a product an edge over the competition.

Product differentiation is uniqueness in quality, price, design, brand image, or customer service that gives one firm's product an edge over another firm's. Its frequent flyer program is one way American Airlines tried to differentiate its service from Delta, US Airways, and other airlines. Members qualify for free tickets after flying a certain number of miles. In addition, frequent fliers receive hotel and car rental discounts and other travel related benefits. But other airlines copied American's AAdvantage Frequent Flyer Program, eliminating this aspect of product differentiation as a way to gain a competitive advantage. In addition to frequent flyer programs, Southwest Airlines offers its Friends Fly Free program and unlimited free beverages to its passengers. TWA provides more leg room between seats on its planes.[27]

CAPITAL REQUIREMENTS

The dollars needed to finance equipment, supplies, R&D, and the like.

Capital requirements are the dollars needed to finance equipment, supplies, advertising, R&D, and the like. The capital requirements for starting an airline run into the tens of millions of dollars. Recently, however, some new airlines, such as Mesa and Kiwi Airlines, have entered the marketplace by hiring an air charter service to provide passenger service. Their startup investment was only a monthly fee for service.

Government regulation is a barrier to entry if it bars or severely restricts potential new entrants to an industry. Before deregulation of the airline industry in 1978, the interstate airlines comprised a cartel regulated by the Civil Aeronautics Board (CAB), which set fares and controlled routes. From 1945 to 1975 the air carrier industry grew three times faster than the economy in general, yet no new trunk carriers entered the industry nor did any existing carriers file for bankruptcy.[28] After deregulation, fourteen new nonunion airlines emerged. With their lower labor, maintenance, and capital costs, these new airlines immediately began to compete with the eleven established trunk airlines (including American, TWA, and Delta) by cutting prices. The price wars and other forms of competition stimulated by deregulation were followed by a number of airline failures (e.g., Braniff) and mergers (e.g., People Express and New York Air into Continental). The decline in the number of domestic trunk airlines has led some politicians and consumer groups to call for reregulation of the airlines.

SUBSTITUTE GOODS AND SERVICES

SUBSTITUTE GOODS OR SERVICES

Goods or services that can easily replace other goods or services.

In a general sense, all competitors produce **substitute goods or services,** or goods or services that can easily replace another's goods or services. For example, the introduction of desktop publishing systems by IBM, Apple, and Dell enabled graphic design companies to use personal computers to design and typeset brochures, catalogs, flyers, and even books. Desktop publishing or typesetting software thus substitutes for the services of typesetting firms at a fraction of their cost. Many organizations (e.g., Amoco, Bankers Trust, and Yahoo!) commonly use fax, e-mail, and/or overnight delivery services as a substitute for long-distance telephone calls and the U.S. Postal Service. Electronic surveillance systems, such as those produced by Sensormatic, have drastically reduced the need for personnel to monitor continuously all areas of retail stores and the behavior of customers. Electronic systems thus substitute for observation by salesclerks, managers, and security guards.

CUSTOMERS

Customers for goods or services naturally try to force down prices, obtain more or higher quality products (while holding price constant), and increase competition among sellers by playing one against the other. Customer bargaining power is likely to be relatively great under the following circumstances.

- **The customer purchases a large volume relative to the supplier's total sales.** JCPenney, Kmart, and Wal-Mart have clout because their large-volume purchases account for a sizable percentage of some suppliers' total sales.

- **The product or service represents a significant expenditure by the customer.** Customers generally are motivated to cut a cost that constitutes a large portion of their total costs. An individual will spend much more time and effort to obtain a rock-bottom price on a new car than on a car wash, a cheeseburger, or a paperback book.

- **Large customers pose a threat of backward integration.** *Backward integration* is the purchase of one or more of its suppliers by a larger organization as a cost-cutting or quality enhancement strategy. McDonald's threatened to bake its own bread, grow its own potatoes, and raise its own cattle to get lower prices and better quality from suppliers.

- **Customers have readily available alternatives for the same services or products.** A consumer may not have a strong preference between Wendy's and McDonald's, a Ford truck and a Chevrolet truck, or VISA and American Express. Similarly, customers wanting to buy a new appliance can readily choose from among GE, Whirlpool, Maytag, and Electrolux.

SUPPLIERS

The bargaining power of suppliers often controls how much they can raise prices above their costs or reduce the quality of goods and services they provide before losing customers. Book publishers used to be able to dictate the net selling prices of books to merchants. However, large volume purchasers such as Barnes and Noble, Waldenbooks, and Borders Books and Music have demanded price breaks for large lots to enable them to sell at discounts to compete with Sam's, Target, and Kmart. Thus book publishers have become less able to dictate prices to such retailers.

In aircraft manufacturing, Boeing dominates the commercial aircraft market and recently merged with McDonnell Douglas to enter the military and aerospace segments of the industry in a big way. It holds 70 percent of the world market in commercial aircraft because of its reputation for quality, not because of low price. Its supplier power comes primarily from technological leadership, high quality, and excellent service. Of course, Boeing's prices probably are lower than they would be without competition from its major rival: the European Airbus Industrie consortium.

All businesses play the role of supplier and customer in their competitive environments. In these sometimes conflicting roles, they may not have equal power. For example, in its role as customer, Boeing now combines orders for similar parts for various models of jet aircraft to get prices from suppliers that are more competitive than those obtained when it bought the items separately. In its role as supplier, Boeing used to have to fill requests from commercial airline customers for 600 or more alterations to basic specifications. Now that it has an established reputation, its bargaining power with airlines is considerably greater, and customers have less of a free hand in designing their planes. As an accommodation, Boeing has a catalog from which customers may select some option packages. Barnes and Noble is a strong customer of publishing houses owing to the size of its retailer network.

However, it faces stiff competition as a supplier because customers may patronize other bookstores, department stores, discount stores, and, now, the Internet.

Copyrights and patents generally increase supplier strength over defined periods of time. The prices of movie tickets and videos of popular films are higher than they might otherwise be because of copyright protection. This protection prevents suppliers from copying and distributing a film or video without permission from and payment of a royalty to the original producer. In general, high supplier strength in unrestricted markets tends to be short-lived, as demonstrated by the personal computer industry. The PC manufacturers know that their innovations will be copied quickly. Toshiba and Texas Instrument notebook computers, for example, commanded high prices for about a year. With numerous brands of similar products now available, prices have fallen, eroding the profit margin for the manufacturers.

Supplier-Customer Alliances. Some total quality programs have increased the strength of suppliers by qualifying them as the single source supplier for a large company. Asahi Glass Company, for example, is the sole supplier to the Toyota Camry factory in Georgetown, Kentucky, as well as to Honda in Marionville, Ohio. Rohm and Haas is the sole supplier of certain resins to Ford for use in the paints and interiors of its cars. And Johnson Control's Globe Battery Company is the sole supplier of car batteries to Nissan. These companies have driven off the competition by agreeing to close collaboration with and management control by these large customers.[29] To help you understand how competitive forces shape competition in an industry, we highlight how two giants in the funeral business are competing in a $15 billion-a-year industry. After reading the following Strategic Action Competency account, you should be able to identity the forces shaping competition in this industry.

TECHNOLOGICAL FORCES AND INFORMATION TECHNOLOGY

4

EXPLAIN WHY TECHNO-
LOGICAL FORCES HAVE
BECOME INCREASINGLY
IMPORTANT IN STRATEGIC
PLANNING

TECHNOLOGY
The tools, knowledge, techniques, and actions used to transform materials, information, and other inputs into finished goods and services.

In Chapter 2 we defined **technology** as a transformation process that changes organizational inputs into outputs. Thus technology is the knowledge, tools, techniques, and actions used to transform ideas, information, and materials into finished goods and services. A technology may be as simple as making coffee at a restaurant or as complicated as driving the Pathfinder on Mars.

IMPACT OF TECHNOLOGY

Technological forces play an increasingly pivotal role in creating and changing an organization's task environment. Technological change builds on the present and helps create the future. Many new technologies are radical enough to force organizations, especially local hospitals such as Central Michigan Community Hospital, to reconsider their purposes and methods of operation or face extinction.[30] The United States and several other industrial societies have become information societies. This shift was made possible by the explosion in computer-based and telecommunication technologies. One example is the personal computer and its integration with mainframe computers and telecommunications systems to form supernets. Through them, organizations can collect, process, and transmit vast amounts of data quickly and economically. For instance, Kodak now supplies photographic dealers with a microcomputer and software system that enables them to order Kodak products directly rather than through wholesalers. The management of information technology is woven into various chapters of this book, and we devote all of Chapter 20 to this topic.

For Whom the Bell Tolls

In the death business, two firms—Service Corporation International (SCI) and The Loewen Group—aggressively compete. Presently, they have a combined 20 percent share in this industry. Traditionally, the industry has been fragmented and largely run by local families, but these two firms have been aggressively buying funeral homes. These firms envision the market for their services growing as baby-boomers start needing their services. In 1997, SCI operated more than 2,832 funeral homes, 265 cemeteries, and 331 crematoria in the United States; it also performs about 30 percent of all funerals in France. Loewen operated more than 1,000 funeral homes and 400 cemeteries across the United States and Canada. Viewed unemotionally, the funeral industry provides a service that almost everybody needs eventually and is generally recession-proof. Moreover, because customers almost never shop for prices, price competition is largely nonexistent. Both SCI and Loewen know that most family members make funeral arrangements in a daze, often picking a particular home because it happens to be close

by or has a familiar name or once buried some other member of the family. Out of grief or a desire not to seem cheap, survivors jettison the consumer instincts they would otherwise use when shopping for a new car, for example. As a result, consumers often choose expensive caskets, services, or burial vaults that increase profit margins for the funeral home.

Barriers to entry discourage new competitors from entering untapped markets. First, 85 percent of the more than 23,000 funeral homes in the United States and Canada still are locally owned and independent. Second, heritage and tradition often provide an established funeral home with the opportunity for repeat business for generations. Third, entry costs are high unless economies of scale can be achieved to lower costs. Most of SCI's and Loewen's funeral homes are in metropolitan areas. For SCI, multiple homes share the cost of its 19,800 employees, 9,300 part-time employees, a fleet of 10,500 owned and leased vehicles, five corporate aircraft, corpse preparation centers, a casket manufacturing operation, and

sixty flower shops. By cutting its costs through volume discounts and linking funeral homes in clusters that share resources, SCI often drives local owners out of the market. Fourth, prearranged sales and preneed insurance policies to healthy people result in funeral arrangements that commit family members to a course of action. Independent firms usually don't have the financial resources to provide these services.[31]

* * *

To learn more about SCI, visit the company's home page at

www.sci-corp.com

Technology's Role in Strategy. Computer-based information technologies are now essential in most organizations, which is one reason for our including technological forces as part of the task environment. Inadequate information technologies can severely limit strategic options for both manufacturing and service organizations. For example, a large bank couldn't provide online account balances to customers because of limitations in its computer software. A large, urban public library couldn't accept fines and check in a book at the same workstation, causing it to hire extra personnel. A brokerage company couldn't satisfy its clients' repeated requests for an integrated picture of its holdings because the information from its equity, bond, and commodity account management systems couldn't be easily combined. Because of weaknesses in its inventory management systems, a large truck manufacturer was losing track of cabs costing $100,000 that had been taken off the production line for rework.

Information technology creates options, including the following, that simply weren't feasible with older technologies.

- Computer-aided design linked to versatile, computer-controlled machines permits short production runs of custom designs with economies of scale approaching those of traditional large-scale manufacturing facilities.

- Consumers can shop via home pages on the Internet and "electronic shopping malls" more easily than using the Yellow Pages and telephones.

- With online, real-time financial management systems, managers can determine profit and loss positions daily, which was impossible with manual methods and earlier stages of computer technology.

- Retail banking customers can perform numerous banking functions from remote locations, including shopping centers, apartment building lobbies, corporate offices, out-of-state banks, and even their homes with personal computers.

Today, the building of an international information highway extends far beyond simple message systems and bulletin boards. Satellites, cellular towers, and fiber-optic telephone cables allow individuals and companies to exchange voice, data, and graphic messages in real time. Futurists speculate that within five to ten years everyone will have personal numbers for all the telecommunication devices they use; that wireless technology will replace twisted pair, coaxial, and fiber-optic cable; and that telephone, fax, and computing will be integrated in handheld devices. There is reason to be optimistic about these projections. In Sweden, Ericsson telephone customers already have personal cards that they can slip into such a device and receive calls anywhere in their calling areas. Malaysia, China, and other developing countries are bypassing wired systems in favor of cellular technologies. And personal communicators made by Toshiba, Sony, and others permit phone, fax, and computing with a pen input screen.[32] As a result, organizations have changed their business strategies to compete in the high-tech world. While Congress debates U.S–Chinese relations and China's human rights record, China is proving irresistibly attractive to the world's most advanced technology companies. Northern Telecom, Intel, and Philips now manufacture semiconductors in Shanghai. Sweden's Ericsson makes telephone switches in Nanjing, and IBM assembles PCs in Shenzhen. Motorola is currently completing a $560 million chip plant in Tianjin.[33] The following Global Awareness Competency feature highlights Motorola's business strategy in China. By 2000, it expects to employ more than 10,000 people there.

The information superhighway represents a change in technology for all companies. Like the computer-driven engineering technologies that revitalized manufacturing, the information superhighway has the ability to change the basic ways in which people communicate at work and home. Consider the International Cargo Management System. With this information system, Seal and other cargo carriers can send an electronic guard with cargo that will let the shipper visually inspect the product's location and condition. When the container is on land, the signal is sent via cellular carrier. When the cargo is at sea, the signal is sent via ship-to-shore radio or phone or global communication satellites. It is more than a cute gadget because theft is a major cost for shippers; more than $5 billion in losses are reported annually in the United States alone.

The information superhighway will affect every organization in the years ahead. Because it represents new technology, this element of the task environment undoubtedly will create change in the political-legal environment, as customers and managers struggle with the problems of having confidential information travel around the world and with equipment and operator safety.

GLOBAL AWARENESS COMPETENCY
Motorola Bets Big on China

Motorola's operations in China rest on two key beliefs that guide all its actions worldwide—respect for the dignity of the individual and uncompromising integrity. These beliefs help create an environment of empowerment in a culture of participation. Teamwork and continual learning are strategic goals that Motorola has established for its operations in China.

Motorola is meeting its teamwork goal by building cooperative educational relationships between its employees and customers. It established a branch of Motorola University in Beijing in 1993 to train employees, customers, suppliers, and government officials in various management and technical areas. Topics covered included the human relations principles of participative management, empowerment, motivation, organizational change, individual dignity, and ethics. Motorola founded Project Hope, a nonprofit program, to help school dropouts in poverty-stricken areas return to school and get an education. Some 300 million of China's population (about 25 percent)

are illiterate. Primary education for children is too much of a financial burden for many Chinese families, who have average annual incomes of less than RMB440 yuan (about US$50). Through Project Hope, Motorola builds schools, provides teachers, and gives financial assistance to families.

Motorola also created joint ventures with Leshan Radio Factory for the manufacture of semiconductors and Nanjing Panda Electronics to establish centers for continual learning. The managers in these plants learn how to produce personal computers by using Deming's quality control principles (see Chapter 2) and adherence to Motorola's six *sigma* quality rule—fewer than four defects per million units. All profits from these plants are plowed back into the local market. In addition to these manufacturing plants, Motorola has sales offices in six major cities and service shops and software centers in another twenty. These locations are in constant communication with each other through pagers and cellular phones. The use of cellular phones will save

billions of dollars that otherwise would be required to purchase copper wire and wooden or concrete poles and pay for countless hours of installation time.[34]

* * *

To learn more about Motorola's China operation, visit the company's home page at

www.mot.com or **www.motorola.com**

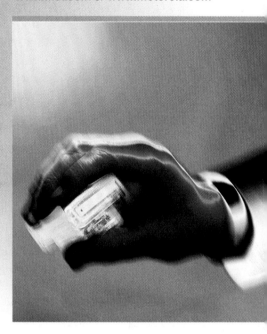

POLITICAL-LEGAL FORCES

5

DESCRIBE THE PRINCIPAL POLITICAL STRATEGIES USED BY MANAGERS TO COPE WITH EXTERNAL POLITICAL-LEGAL FORCES

Societies try to resolve conflicts over values and beliefs through their legal and political systems. For instance, in the United States and Canada the concepts of individual freedom, freedom of the press, property rights, and private enterprise are widely accepted. But these countries' legislative bodies, regulatory agencies, interest groups, and courts operate—often in conflict with one another—to define the meaning and influence the day-to-day interpretation of these values.

Many political and legal forces directly affect the way organizations operate.[35] Changes in political forces have been especially significant during the past twenty-five years and will continue to affect organizations in the future. To achieve organizational goals, managers must accurately diagnose these forces and find useful ways to anticipate, respond to, or avoid the disturbances they cause.

For many organizations (e.g., telephone companies, banks, and public utilities), government regulation is a central aspect of the task environment. Consider how two federal credit laws affect customers and creditors each time they do business in the United States.

- The *Equal Credit Opportunity Act* entitles the customer to be considered for credit without regard to race, color, age, gender, or marital status. Although the act doesn't guarantee that the customer will get credit, it does ensure that the credit grantor applies tests of credit-worthiness fairly and impartially.

- The *Truth in Lending Act* says that credit grantors must reveal the "true" cost of using credit, for instance, the annual interest rate the customer will be paying. In the case of a revolving charge account, the customer must also be told the monthly interest rate and the minimum monthly payment required.

As shown in Figure 3.5, managers can use five basic political strategies to cope with turbulence in their task environments: negotiation, lobbying, alliance, representation, and socialization. These strategies aren't mutually exclusive, are usually used in some combination, and each often contains elements of the others. Negotiation probably is the most important political strategy because each of the other four strategies involves to some degree the use of negotiation.

Negotiation is the process by which two or more individuals or groups, having both common and conflicting goals, present and discuss proposals in an attempt to reach an agreement.[36] Negotiation can take place only when the two parties believe that some form of agreement is possible and mutually beneficial. Recall the strikes in professional baseball, football, and hockey. Negotiators representing the owners and players presented various proposals in an attempt to reach an agreement. Not until both parties realized that some agreement was necessary, did they ratify new contracts.

Lobbying is an attempt to influence government decisions by providing officials with information on the anticipated effects of legislation or regulatory rulings. Congress and regulatory agencies, such as the Securities and Exchange Commission (SEC), the Federal Communications Commission (FCC), and the Interstate Commerce Commission (ICC), are the targets of continual lobbying efforts by organizations affected by their decisions. Organizations whose stability, growth, and survival are directly affected by government decisions typically use their top managers to lobby for them. Motorola, IBM, Coca-Cola, and Atlantic Richfield, among others, have lobbied Congress to maintain favored nation trade status with China after defiant student demonstrators were killed on Beijing's Tiananmen Square. These organizations agree that human rights violations have occurred in China, but its market is too attractive to be ignored. They note that a surprising number of Chinese citizens will be able to afford high-tech products by 2000.

NEGOTIATION

The process by which two or more individuals or groups having both common and conflicting goals present and discuss proposals in an attempt to reach an agreement.

LOBBYING

An attempt to influence government decisions by providing officials with information on the anticipated effects of legislation or regulatory rulings.

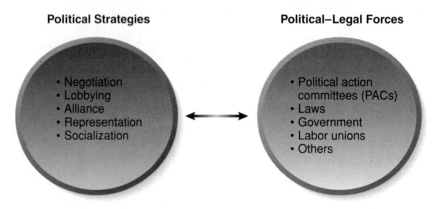

| *Figure 3.5* | ***Managerial Political Strategies*** |

Political Strategies

- Negotiation
- Lobbying
- Alliance
- Representation
- Socialization

Political–Legal Forces

- Political action committees (PACs)
- Laws
- Government
- Labor unions
- Others

Tobacco's Can of Worms

Philip Morris, the giant food, beer, and tobacco conglomerate with more than $65 billion in annual sales, paid more than $11.3 million to lobbyists. This amount includes the salaries of its own eleven-member team and twenty-three outside lobbying and law firms that press the company's views on a broad range of issues from dairy prices to trade. However, the bulk of the spending was for tobacco. R.J. Reynolds reported spending more than $1 million on outside lobbying and law firms for its tobacco interests. What did this money buy? Philip Morris donated $3.4 million to the Republican party, supported Bob Dole's charity to help the disabled, and supported the think tank created by Newt Gingrich. It also contributed more than $100,000 to help stage the Republican convention in 1996. Democrats got similar, but less, attention. The Democratic party received more than $484,000, and Philip Morris's Kraft Foods subsidiary gave the Democratic party $100,000 for its 1996 convention. Were such sums worth it?

Despite these and other huge sums contributed by the industry, in 1997 the tobacco companies negotiated a $368.5 billion settlement with the attorneys general of forty states on behalf of the states and consumers, who claimed that tobacco companies had lied to them about the dangers of smoking and second-hand smoke. In return for acknowledging such claims, the settlement would give the tobacco companies immunity from class-action lawsuits and place a limit on damage claims. In coming to terms with its roles in the health of Americans and nicotine consumption, Big Tobacco has yielded to lawmakers control over much of how they will do business in the United States. For example, Joe Camel and the Marlboro Man can no longer be used in advertising. In California, legislation is pending that would prohibit tobacco products from being advertised on billboards within 1,000 feet of playgrounds and elementary, junior high, and high schools.

International sales, which now provide the only growth market in cigarettes, are forecasted to expand rapidly. For instance, in 1996, Philip Morris earned $3.5 billion in profits from tobacco exports. However, some other countries have mounted antitobacco campaigns to prevent the kinds of health problems from developing there that the tobacco industry has (reluctantly) admitted exist in the United States.

On the one hand, Congress and the Clinton administration still regard tobacco as just another agricultural commodity (as underscored by the $2 billion subsidy approved as part of the fiscal 1998 "balanced budget" bill) and regard other countries' antitobacco policies as trade barriers. On the other hand, the Clinton administration wants more domestic concessions from the tobacco industry and insists that the FDA be given more decisive authority to regulate nicotine levels in tobacco products. Congress and the administration must approve parts of the settlement between the tobacco industry and the states. Various lobbying groups are vying over the division of the settlement money. Antitobacco congressmen are angling to win extra aid for children's health programs, cancer research, and antismoking programs overseas. Congressmen from the largest tobacco growing states are seeking economic assistance for farmers who may lose a valuable crop. Finally, Republicans are trying to trim the estimated $3.5 billion that is slated to be the lawyers' take in the settlement. Trial lawyers are usually members of the Democratic party and are among its biggest contributors.[37]

Only the largest organizations (e.g., NBC, AT&T, and Exxon) can afford to lobby for themselves. The most common form of lobbying is by associations, representing the interests of groups of individuals or organizations.[38] Approximately 4,000 national lobbying organizations maintain staffs in Washington, D.C. An additional 75,000 state and local associations and organizations occasionally lobby Washington's decision makers. Two of the largest associations representing business interests are the National Chamber of Commerce, with about 36,000 business and other organizational members, and the National Association of Manufacturers, with about

12,500 member corporations. The American Association of Retired Persons (AARP), with more than 33 million members, is the largest U.S. association representing individual interests. The AARP lobbies on behalf of U.S. citizens aged fifty and over and has a paid staff of 1,300, with headquarters in the heart of the nation's capital.[39]

During 1996 and 1997, as state, federal, consumer, and health-care provider pressure to rein in the tobacco industry escalated, tobacco companies spent more than $30 million to communicate its position and influence members of Congress. The previous article highlights how Philip Morris and R.J. Reynolds attempted to use their Communication Competency to influence members of Congress.

ALLIANCE

The uniting of two or more organizations, groups, or individuals to achieve common goals with respect to a particular issue.

An **alliance** is a unified effort involving two or more organizations, groups, or individuals to achieve common goals with respect to a particular issue.[40] Alliances, especially those created to influence government actions, typically form around issues of economic self-interest. Such issues include government policy (e.g., the control of raw materials or taxes), foreign relations (e.g., the control of foreign sales or investment in overseas plants), and labor relations (e.g., the control of industry-wide salaries and benefits, as within the construction industry or the National Football League). Alliances often are used for the following purposes:

- Oppose or support legislation, nomination of heads of regulatory agencies, and regulations issued by such agencies.

- Improve competitiveness of two or more organizations through collaboration. Corning Glass uses twenty-three joint ventures with foreign partners such as Siemens (Germany), Samsung (Korea), Asahi Chemical (Japan), and Vitro (Mexico) to penetrate and thrive in a growing number of glass markets.

- Promote particular products or services, such as oranges, computers, and electricity. For example, the Edison Electric Institute promotes both the use and conservation of electrical energy.

- Construct facilities beyond the resources of any one organization, such as new plants. General Motors and Delphi have committed $1 billion to construct a new automobile plant in Shanghai.

- Represent the interests of specific groups, such as women, the elderly, minorities, and particular industries. The National Association of Manufacturers (NAM) lobbies Congress to pass legislation favorable to its members, including restricting imports on foreign goods, such as shoes and automobiles, and trying to open new markets in foreign countries, such as the sale of rice in Japan.

An alliance both broadens and limits managerial power. When an alliance makes possible the attainment of goals that a single individual or organization would be unable to attain, it broadens managerial power. When an alliance requires a commitment to making certain decisions jointly in the future, it limits managerial power. Members of OPEC periodically negotiate production levels and the price they will charge for oil. These agreements are intended to broaden OPEC's power by generating more revenue for its members. However, to be successful in this endeavor, OPEC members must abide by the agreed production limits.

A *joint venture,* which typically involves two or more firms becoming partners to form a separate entity, is a common form of an alliance.[41] Each partner benefits from the others' competence, which allows them to achieve their goals more quickly and efficiently. For example, IBM and Toshiba have formed a joint venture to manufacture flat-panel video displays. At a jointly owned plant in Hemji, Japan, both partners equally shared in the construction of an ultramodern plant that produces flat screens used in notebook and laptop computers. IBM contributes its knowledge of the computer industry and Toshiba its advances in miniaturization.

REPRESENTATION

Membership in an outside organization for the purpose of furthering the interests of the member's organization.

Representation refers to membership in an outside organization, which is intended to serve the interests of the member's organization or group. Representation strategy often is subtle and indirect. School administrators often receive paid time off and the use of school resources to participate in voluntary community associations that might support the school system, such as the PTA, Chamber of Commerce, Elks, Kiwanis, Moose, Rotary, and United Way. A more direct form of representation, often based on some legal requirement, occurs when a specific group selects representatives to give it a voice in an organization's decisions. Union members elect officers to represent them in dealing with management.

Corporate boards of directors, the top-level policy-making groups in firms, are elected by and legally required to represent shareholders' interests. The National Association of Corporate Directors, however, suggests a much broader role for board members: They should ensure that long-term strategic goals and plans are established; that a proper management structure (organization, systems, and people) is in place to achieve these goals; and that the organization acts to maintain its integrity, reputation, and responsibility to its various constituencies. The board's responsibility to monitor and control the actions of the chief executive officer and other top officers is essential to its representing the interests of the shareholders.[42]

SOCIALIZATION

The process by which people learn the values held by an organization or the broader society.

Socialization is the process by which people learn the values held by an organization and the broader society. The assumption is that people who accept and act in accordance with these basic values are less likely to sympathize with positions that threaten the organization or the society. The so-called American business creed stresses the idea that a decentralized, privately owned, and competitive system in which price is the major regulator, should be continued and that citizens should oppose government actions that interfere with or threaten this system. Most U.S. and Canadian businesspeople subscribe to these beliefs and act on them.

Socialization includes formal and informal attempts by organizations to mold new employees to accept certain desired attitudes and ways of dealing with others and their jobs. At its headquarters in Crotonville, New York, General Electric introduces thousands of its managers to the company's values and philosophy.[43] These values include identifying and eliminating unproductive work in order to energize employees and encourage creativity and feelings of ownership at all levels. Broken Hill Proprietary of Australia uses its training facility in Yuroke, Victoria, to influence the attitudes and behaviors of new managers. Of course, top management's attempts may be offset or reinforced by the expectations of and pressures exerted by workers or other groups within the organization.

The use of socialization strategies by organizations is subject to broader cultural forces. In the United States and Canada the importance of individualism limits the extent to which organizations can use socialization strategies. Too much of what may be perceived as the "wrong kind" of socialization is likely to be met with resistance and charges of invasion of privacy or violation of individual rights.

CHAPTER SUMMARY

The purpose of this chapter was to help develop your planning and administrative, strategic thinking and action, global awareness, and communication competencies with respect to an organization's external environment. We discussed and presented examples of various reactive and proactive approaches that organizations can use in coping with general environmental forces (culture) and task environmental forces (competition, technology, and political-legal forces). Such forces create both opportunities and threats and will challenge you to use all the knowledge and skills you acquire.

1. **DESCRIBE THE MAIN FORCES IN THE EXTERNAL BUSINESS ENVIRONMENT AND HOW THEY INFLUENCE ORGANIZATIONS.**

The general environment includes the external factors that usually affect organizations, either directly or indirectly. It encompasses the economic system and current economic conditions, political system, natural resources, demographics of the population, and the ecosystem within which organizations operate. Cultural forces, primarily working through value systems, shape the viewpoints and decision-making processes of managers and employees alike. Hofstede's work-related value framework has five dimensions: power distance, uncertainty avoidance, individualism, masculinity, and Confucian dynamism.

2. **UNDERSTAND THE ROLE OF THE TASK ENVIRONMENT AND ITS IMPACT ON DECISION MAKING.**

The task environment includes all the external factors and groups—customers, competitors, technology, regulatory agencies, laws, and the like—that directly influence an organization's growth, success, and survival. Changes in the number of competitors and type of competition are increasingly common in turbulent and global task environments, requiring managers to monitor and diagnose constantly the type of task environment they face.

3. **IDENTIFY THE FIVE COMPETITIVE FORCES THAT DIRECTLY AFFECT ORGANIZATIONS IN AN INDUSTRY.**

Managers must assess and respond to five competitive forces in the task environment: competitors, new entrants, substitute goods and services, customers, and suppliers.

4. **EXPLAIN WHY TECHNOLOGICAL FORCES HAVE BECOME INCREASINGLY IMPORTANT IN STRATEGIC PLANNING.**

Technological forces in the task environment are rapidly changing the specific knowledge, tools, and techniques used to transform materials, information, and other inputs into particular goods or services. Usable technologies include four interconnecting elements: hardware, software, communications linkages, and brainware.

5. **DESCRIBE THE PRINCIPAL POLITICAL STRATEGIES USED BY MANAGERS TO COPE WITH EXTERNAL POLITICAL-LEGAL FORCES.**

Political-legal issues, which used to be in the background, now often directly influence the way organizations operate. Five political strategies that managers use in coping with political-legal forces in the task environment are negotiation, lobbying, alliances, representation, and socialization.

QUESTIONS FOR DISCUSSION

1. What are some recent (last five years) changes in the general environment that all employees should be aware of? In particular, how have these changes affected department stores such as Sears, JCPenney, Nordstrom, and Foley's?

2. How do the five cultural values presented in this chapter influence a manager's thinking about locating a plant in a foreign country, say, Mexico?

3. What are the five competitive forces in an industry? How have these forces affected competition in higher education?

4. What are some of the political tactics that managers can use to influence their environment?

   Why didn't such tactics seem to work for the U.S. tobacco industry?

5. Choose an organization that uses the new information superhighway. How could you use these new tools to assist in your selling Procter & Gamble products (e.g., Tide or Crest toothpaste) to grocers?

6. Are there any ethical considerations for companies that attempt to overcome threats from new entrants? Do these considerations vary from country to country? If so, cite two examples.

EXERCISES TO DEVELOP YOUR MANAGERIAL COMPETENCIES

1. **Planning and Administrative Competency.** In 1963, Gary Comer founded Lands' End and began filling orders out of a basement on Elstron Avenue in Chicago's tannery district. He borrowed $10,000 and a few ideas and recruited three very talented people. Together, they printed the first catalogue and built a business that has concentrated on offering (with few exceptions) cut and sewn, woven, and knit fabric products featuring natural fibers. They want products sturdy enough to withstand wear and tear, regardless of the latest fashion fad. Today, the company employs more than 7,900 people and has catalog businesses in the United States, Canada, Japan, Germany, France, and the Netherlands. These catalogues carry more than 2,100 different products. To keep current with customers' demands, Lands' End does considerable market research and planning. Visit the company's home page at

   www.landsend.com

   and find three examples of how managers' planning and administrative competencies are developed at Lands' End.

2. **Strategic Action Competency.** The movie theatre industry has become very competitive. Carmike Cinemas, SONY, AMC, and Tinsletown Theatres, among others, have been acquiring small, locally owned and operated theatres across the United States. Independent theatres and theatre chains, alike, not only face competition from each other, but also from other forms of entertainment, such as stage plays, symphonies, operas, professional sports teams, music groups' tours, TV, and video rentals and sales, to name a few. Carmike Cinemas owns movie theatres in cities and towns with populations of less than 200,000. It serves customers through standardized low-cost theatre complexes requiring few screens and unsophisticated projection technology. A single manager can run the entire theatre. Based on its strategy to be a low-cost theatre, what sources of competition does it face? Using the five competitive forces discussed in the chapter, analyze the task environment it faces. Visit the company's home page at

   www.carmike.com

   to understand how Carmike Cinemas' top managers have applied their strategic action competencies.

3. **Global Awareness Competency.** Most U.S. companies see great opportunities in international markets today. While the U.S. population is growing steadily but slowly, the population in other countries, such as India, China, Indonesia, and Vietnam, is exploding. Baskin-Robbins recently opened stores in Ho Chi Minh City after President Clinton lifted the economic embargo of Vietnam. The company chose this city because it is the country's most prosperous city and chief tourist destination. Moreover, the older residents of the city remember American ice cream from the 1960s and 1970s, when thousands of U.S. soldiers were stationed there during the Vietnam War. What global awareness competencies must Baskin-Robbins managers develop to be successful in Vietnam? What significant cultural factors do managers need to be aware of in Vietnam? To learn more about Baskin-Robbins, visit the company's home page at

   www.baskinrobbins.com

4. **Communication Competency.** Organizations use various political strategies to influence lawmakers to pass legislation favorable to their competitive positions. The dilemma some companies confront when trying to meet their social responsibilities without sacrificing corporate objectives is highlighted by Dow Corning's legal problems over the safety of the company's silicone breast-implants. In 1984, the company was sued for fraudulently misrepresenting its product and lost the case. Recently, a final settlement of $4.23 billion was reached, which almost bankrupted Dow Chemical Company and Corning, Inc. What political-legal strategies did Dow Corning use in this case? What form(s) of negotiation did Dow Corning use to influence members of the Federal Drug Administration (FDA) and Congress? How did Dow inform its shareholders about its plight? What communication competencies did John Swanson, an employee hired to create an ethics committee at Dow, employ? To learn more about Dow's political strategies, visit the company's home page at

   www.dow.com

REAL-TIME CASE ANALYSIS

THE ICE CREAM INDUSTRY SCOOP

The packaged ice cream industry includes ordinary, premium, and superpremium products. Their butterfat content and density, as well as the freshness of their ingredients and the way they were blended and treated, primarily, differentiate these products. Premium ice creams contain 12 to 16 percent butterfat and less air than regular types; a 4-ounce scoop usually has 180 calories. Superpremium ice creams generally contain 16 to 20 percent butterfat and less than 20 percent air. The caloric value of a 4-ounce scoop is about 260 calories. Producing ice cream, from mix creation to packaging and freezing, requires almost six hours. The highest quality products cost the most to make. The North American ice cream market in 1996 was roughly $4.7 billion, or more than 2.1 billion gallons. Per capita consumption of ice cream has risen from 15 quarts per year in 1970 to 23 quarts in 1996. Ninety-four percent of all households bought ice cream, and consumption is the highest among families with young children and people over 55. As you might expect, demand is seasonal, with summer sales as much as 30 percent higher than in winter. Consumption also varies by region. People in the western parts of the United States and Canada eat the most, and people in the South Atlantic States eat the least.

Gross margins in the ice cream industry average 31 percent, compared to only 20 percent for the frozen food department in grocery stores. Premium and superpremium varieties outsell other types, accounting for 46 percent of sales and 46 percent of the profits of the ice cream category as a whole. In general these ice creams generate five times more profit per square foot than the average product sold in a supermarket.

There are several major competitors in the superpremium market, including Ben & Jerry's and Haagen-Dazs. These two firms have almost 85 percent of the market. Others, such as Blue Bell, Columbo, Dannon, Edy's Grand Ice Cream, Healthy Choice, Elan, Frusen Gladje, Steve's, and Yoplait comprise the rest of the superpremium suppliers.

Although the superpremium industry had thrived for many years, a noticeable downturn started in 1996. The baby-boomers were entering middle age and becoming more health conscious. Their aversion to high-fat foods, such as superpremium ice cream, drove price competition. A variety of promotions, including discount coupons, were used to stimulate demand. Haagen-Dazs brought new flavors to the market to retain its share, but the introduction of these new flavors cannibalized its existing lines. Haagen-Dazs is owned by The Pillsbury Company, which in turn is owned by Grand Metropolitan PLC, a British food and liquor conglomerate. With Pillsbury's financial and marketing resources, Haagen-Dazs started marketing its ice cream in Europe and the Pacific Rim countries. To counter slow sales, Ben & Jerry's introduced a reduced fat, reduced calorie ice milk, but it failed because of poor quality. The company subsequently introduced a low-cholesterol frozen yogurt line that has met with some success. It also added a variety of new add-ins, such as dates, nuts, and cookies, to create new flavors for its superpremium ice cream.

Other manufacturers are trying different tactics to allure customers. For example, NITROS allows customers to select their own combinations of flavors and ingredients, satisfying their cravings at that time. This Interactive Eatery Company offers made-to-order homemade superpremium ice cream. Using television-based Internet access, the customer selects ingredients. This information is forwarded to the store closest to the customer, and the ice cream will be waiting for the customer at the store.

Mergers are taking place in this industry. DavCo Restaurants, a franchisee of Wendy's International, bought Friendly's Restaurants and Ice Cream Corporation. This merger permits Wendy's to sell superpremium ice cream in its fast-food restaurants and convenience stores, which it operates with Exxon.[44]

QUESTIONS

1. Is consumption of superpremium ice cream likely to remain at 23 quarts per person per year? What factors in the general environment could operate to reduce it? If you forecast a reduction, how will that affect competition in this industry?

2. What forces in the task environment are changing the nature of competition in this industry?

3. Visit the home pages of Ben & Jerry's (www.Benjerry.com) and Haagen-Dazs (www.haagen-dazs.com) to find out how they are using their global awareness and strategic action competencies to serve the superpremium ice cream market.

VIDEO CASE

CENTRAL MICHIGAN COMMUNITY HOSPITAL: HEALTH-CARE CONUNDRUM

Central Michigan Community Hospital has been selected as one of the 100 best hospitals in the country. But it is also a model of a business that must accept—not make—its operating environment.

Like most health service providers, the hospital's service area is relatively fixed. Moreover, its ability to attract and serve customers, and to acquire and utilize skilled labor and technology, depend on many factors that are beyond its control.

One of the most significant environmental factors is the demographics of the hospital's market. An aging U.S. population may require both more health care and different services (e.g., more geriatric specialists and fewer pediatricians). However, local conditions can dampen the effects of overall population change (e.g., if an area receives an influx of young families and individuals) or heighten them (e.g., if an area attracts large numbers of retirees).

In areas outside Michigan's large metropolitan areas, a hospital such as Central Michigan Community Hospital isn't likely to face a significant challenge from immigration. In contrast, hospitals in southern and western states face dramatic changes in the physical characteristics of the patients they receive (e.g., more elderly or a greater demand for pre- and neonatal care) and the challenge of patients whose first language is Spanish. However, various ethnic populations may cluster anywhere. For example, the Hmong, refugees from Southeast Asia who immigrated to the United States after its involvement in the war in Vietnam, form large communities in California, North Carolina, Minnesota, and Wisconsin; Vietnamese immigrant communities are common along the Gulf of Mexico.

Shortly after the 1992 election, the Clinton administration created a Health Care Task Force to come up with proposals to overhaul the nation's health-care industry. Health care constitutes a significant percentage of federal, state, and local budgets and is increasingly a household budgetary concern as Americans cope with aging parents and new—and expensive—treatments for old diseases. The initiative only modestly changed the health-care market and delivery of services, in large part because many municipalities, states, nongovernmental organizations, and other interests with a stake in its outcome lobbied extensively to influence its outcome.

Managers in the health-care industry—particularly those responsible to a community and in marginal service areas such as rural medicine—may feel whipsawed between large forces maneuvering in the "outside world," and the interests of their relatively few constituents.

Unlike many other businesses, some health services or costs may be fixed by law, regulations, or public policy. Managers of health service providers need to maintain planning and administration competencies and inspire teamwork when their organizations face challenges beyond their control. Hospital administrators and county health department directors also are often called on to demonstrate their communication competencies, as when defending budgets and helping communities recognize and combat, without panic, a contagious outbreak.

ON THE WEB

The Central Michigan Community Hospital doesn't have a Web site. However, the American Association of Retired Persons (AARP), with millions of members all aged 50 and over, does (***www.aarp.org***). The AARP has a special interest in its aging members' health and is an advocate for them on both Medicare and managed health care issues, which comprise part of hospitals' operating environments.

The *Detroit News* (***detnews.com***) and *Detroit Free Press* (***www.freep.com***) cover state issues such as the effects of population changes and state and federal legislation on health care in Michigan. The State of Michigan's primary Web site (***www.state.mi.us***) includes links to many departmental and agency Web sites, such as the one for its Department of Community Health.

The White House Web site (***www.whitehouse.gov***) provides information drawn from White House press briefings, policy statements, and other administration documents. A search of the "Virtual Library" on the phrase "health care" identifies hundreds of documents. Congressional consideration of health-care issues and legislation can be found through the "Thomas" service (***thomas.loc.gov***).

QUESTIONS

1. If a hospital were thought of as a storehouse of scarce resources, to be provided at largely externally fixed costs, why would the administrator need to be a marketer?

2. Why is the provision of medical care more difficult than selling burgers or bicycles to leave to market forces alone?

Chapter

4

Global Considerations

Outline

Kodak-Fuji Global Slugfest

For some years, Fuji and Kodak have been battling it out in overseas film markets. But in the United States the picture was quite different. Kodak and Fuji treated that market like a mutually profitable haven, with both enjoying high margins. Kodak had about 70 percent of the U.S. market as of 1998—down from over 80 percent in 1996. By pricing its film just a bit lower, Fuji gradually increased its market share at Kodak's expense.

Then during the spring of 1997, Fuji began slashing prices by as much as 25 percent. Fuji's explanation is that Costco, one of its five largest distributors in the United States, dropped Fuji for Kodak, and the company was stuck with 2.5 million rolls of film. Fuji unloaded the film at a steep discount to other distributors. For the first time in its 113-year history, Kodak can no longer take its home market for granted.

The two firms are slugging it out throughout the world for three equally important parts of the consumer photo business. The yellow and green film boxes are the most obvious part to

consumers. Fuji and Kodak also manufacture photographic paper, mostly for sale to big photo-processing laboratories and small retail developers. To ensure a market for their paper, both companies have invested heavily in the third line of business—developing—by buying up big film-processing companies across the United States. Fuji's strategic acquisition decision, including the $400 million purchase of Wal-Mart's six wholesale photo labs, gave Fuji about 15 percent of the U.S. photo-processing market.

Fuji's long-term strategy is to produce in the United States as much film and paper as it can sell there. That keeps costs down, reduces trade disputes, and makes Fuji's factories more responsive to local market demands.

Kodak has responded to Fuji's competitive threats with strategic cost-cutting and price reductions. These actions have involved significant lay-offs from Kodak's worldwide workforce—down to about 85,000 employees in 1998 from about 100,000 employees in 1995. Kodak also cut its

research expenditures by $150 million in 1998, to about $850 million. Kodak faces the erosion of prices common to many industries when supply exceeds demand. However, film photography may be on the verge of an explosion as huge markets begin developing in India, China, Russia, Brazil, and other countries. Kodak and Fuji are competing aggressively in these markets. Their long and intense rivalry includes a Kodak lawsuit against Japan's policy of limiting the U.S. company's access to the Japanese market. The case is now before the World Trade Organization, with a decision expected in 1998.[1]

* * *

To learn more about Kodak, visit the company's home page at

www.kodak.com

THE GLOBAL ECONOMY

1

STATE SEVERAL CHARAC-
TERISTICS OF THE GLOBAL
ECONOMY

The Kodak-Fuji competition illustrates the effect of several of the global forces that an increasing number of companies face—intense rivalry between competitors, pressures on prices, need for cost cutting, diversification into related lines of business, and efforts to protect markets through political and legal means.

Employees and consumers are being increasingly affected by the growing global economy. Consider, for example, these developments in the United States. Exports and imports of goods and services represent about 29 percent of the U.S. gross domestic product, up from less than 21 percent in 1992. Trade is now so important to the U.S. economy that one in five jobs depends on it. Yet a recent poll revealed that 56 percent of the population thought that expanded trade leads to a loss of U.S. jobs. When asked to identify the biggest threat to U.S. jobs, 56 percent again said that it was cheap foreign labor. This attitude reflects the fact that trade is often portrayed in the media as a war between nations in which countries that export more than they import win, whereas countries that import more than they export lose. Since 1993, U.S. exports of goods and services have soared 37 percent, accounting for much of the overall growth in the economy. However, imports have been growing more than exports, in part because the economy has expanded, which gave U.S. consumers more money to spend.[2]

The nature of trade is changing dramatically. Increasingly, trade takes place between different parts of the same corporation or through alliances (joint ventures). Asking whether a product—computer, car, or shirt—has been "Made in the USA" or "Made in Canada" has become almost meaningless. The production of components for products is increasingly scattered around the world. Sales by overseas subsidiaries of U.S. and Canadian corporations are about three times greater than the value of their exports from the home countries.[3] A second driving force is the information revolution that now permits instantaneous worldwide communication. "Information technologies are the most powerful forces ever generated to make things cost-effective," says John S. Mayo, president of AT&T Bell Laboratories (now Lucent Technologies).[4] Entrepreneurs in the industrial nations, especially the United States, are spearheading the Internet boom, building fiber-optic networks, and offering myriad new products and services on the World Wide Web. A third force is the drive for increased *openness*—both economically and politically. Governments everywhere are pursuing market-based economic policies. Multinational corporations are accelerating the exchange of innovations across open borders. Global investors are pressuring companies to open their books. Populations are demanding stronger political and economic rights.[5]

We discuss these and other forces that are driving and restraining the global economy throughout this chapter. Although any type of organization may act globally, most that do are for-profit businesses. Therefore the material covered in this chapter applies primarily to them.

Before going on, let's consider briefly the international quality standards program ISO 9000, as presented in the following Planning and Administration Competency feature. The ISO quality system helps managers and employees monitor relevant information, identify underlying quality problems, and—most important—improve quality. Some view this program as a catalyst to international trade and the global economy. It enables customers to have greater confidence in the quality of goods and services purchased from certified suppliers throughout the world.

ORGANIZING FOR INTERNATIONAL BUSINESS

2

DESCRIBE FIVE WAYS OF ORGANIZING TO ENGAGE IN INTERNATIONAL BUSINESS

The organization you will work for and your job are likely to be strongly affected by global forces. Although they are being felt around the world generally, their relative importance to specific industries and firms varies widely. Their impact depends on the level of direct international business done by an industry or firm. An ice cream manufacturer (e.g., Blue Bell Ice Cream in Texas) has minimal direct international involvement. However, a huge bank (e.g., Citicorp, headquartered in New York) is truly global in its outlook and business. For example, an automated teller machine (ATM) customer can use a Citibank machine in Hong Kong to exchange U.S. dollars for Hong Kong dollars at a favorable exchange rate. If that person is a Citibank customer, no transaction fee is charged.

Figure 4.1 shows the relative degrees of complexity (vertical axis) for firms engaged in international business and the relative degrees of their resource commitment (horizontal axis). By *resource commitment,* we mean the dedication of assets that cannot be shifted to other uses without cost. Resources can be tangible (e.g., offices and plants located abroad) or intangible (e.g., managers and employees who have the knowledge and skills—or can learn them—needed for international business). Figure 4.1 also shows how a firm might organize internationally over time, starting with hiring a commission agent to represent it in international

The ISO 9000 series of standards for quality management and quality assurance was first published in 1987 by the International Organization for Standardization (ISO), located in Geneva, Switzerland, whose members are the national standards institutes of 124 countries. More than 90 countries have adopted ISO 9000 standards for voluntary application in both the manufacturing and service sectors.

Although ISO develops and publishes standards, it does not verify that users are implementing them in conformity with the standards' requirements. ISO 9000 certificates of conformity are issued by certification bodies independently of ISO, although ISO has also published guides that form the basis of acceptable practice by such bodies. In addition, accreditation bodies, such as the U.S. Registrar Accreditation Board, have been set up in a number of countries to exercise a degree of control over certification bodies. An ISO 9000 certificate is not a product quality label but relates to a company's quality management system—what a company does to manage its processes. When an organization has its management system certified to an ISO 9000 standard, this means that an independent auditor has checked that the processes influencing quality conform to the standard's requirements. The objective is to give the organization's management and its customers confidence that the organization is in control of the way it does things and that it can meet its customers' requirements.

ISO 9000 is a set of worldwide standards that establish management requirements for obtaining quality. Meeting these standards is a challenge to managers' planning and administration competencies and, in many cases, requires their upgrading. Unlike *product* standards, these *quality* standards apply to product design, process control, inspection and testing, purchasing, after-sales service, and training. The standards are being used by many European nations to provide a framework for quality assurance—primarily through a system of internal and external audits—within the European Union (EU). The goal is to ensure that a certified firm has a quality management system in place that will enable it to meet its published quality standards. The ISO standards are general in that they apply to all functions and all industries, from banking to automobile manufacturing. This breadth of application is a source of criticism by some managers.

One example of the impact of ISO 9000 is reflected in the requirements that Siemens, the large German electronics firm, places on its suppliers. The company mandates ISO compliance in most of its contracts with suppliers, eliminating the need for Siemens to test parts received from suppliers. Not having to do so saves both Siemens and the suppliers time and money and establishes common requirements for all its suppliers, wherever they may be located.[6]

* * *

To learn more about the International Organization for Standardization, visit its home page at

www.iso.ch

ISO 9000

A set of worldwide standards that establish requirements for the management of quality.

transactions. The process can eventually lead to a firm's becoming a full-fledged multinational corporation. A firm's degree of internationalization (DOI) has three general attributes: *performance* (what goes on abroad), *resources* (what assets are abroad), and *attitudinal* (what is the international orientation of key personnel). Other DOI measures include foreign sales as a percentage of total sales, export sales as a percentage of total sales, foreign profits as a percentage of total profits, foreign assets as a percentage of total assets, and top managers' international experience.[7]

The competitive forces acting on a firm, as well as its stated goals, will influence its organization design. Let's briefly explore the five primary ways of organizing for international business—from the simplest to the most complex and from the least to the greatest resource commitment. In Chapters 10 and 11, we discuss organization design in greater detail.

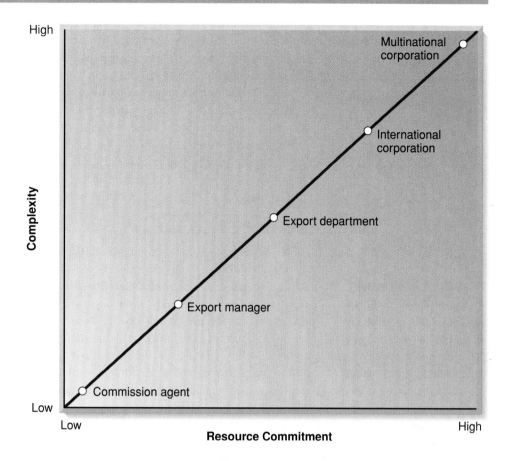

COMMISSION AGENT

A firm's first step toward international operations might be to retain one or more commission agents to handle an inquiry from a potential foreign customer or to look into the possibility of selling its goods or services abroad. A ***commission agent*** is a person or firm who represents businesses in foreign transactions in return for a negotiated percentage of each transaction's value (a commission). An agent is likely to represent more than one firm and will usually carry catalogs of their products and attempt to sell them to customers abroad. A commission agent is most likely to be a citizen of the country in which the goods or services are being sold, or at least from that region of the world. The use of commission agents is the simplest way to enter international business. The firm may not even need to create new positions or departments—a top or middle manager may simply be assigned the added responsibility of working with the agent. Hence firms with limited resources may find commission agents to be useful initially.

The use of commission agents in international trade need not be limited to small organizations. Nu Skin International is a Utah-based direct-sales company. It uses a computer network and special software to help its 300,000 independent distributors sell personal care and health products in countries where the company has a sales license.[8]

EXPORT MANAGER

As its exports increase, a firm may hire an export manager to take over from the commission agent or to work with commission agents in some countries and handle transactions directly with customers in other countries. This person is normally headquartered at the firm's home office. Much like a commission agent, an ***export manager*** actively searches out foreign markets for the firm's goods or services. Unlike most commission agents, an export manager represents only one firm. The export manager typically has a small staff—possibly only a secretary—and travels abroad extensively. A firm having a relatively small export sales volume is likely to limit itself to commission agents or an export manager.[9]

Hiring an export manager involves some new, ongoing costs. These costs include, at a minimum, the export manager's salary and benefits, office space, travel expenses, and secretarial support. Regardless of the amount of sales generated by the export manager, which may be quite small initially, these costs could easily amount to $200,000 or more per year. In contrast, commission agents receive only a percentage of the dollar value of the goods or services sold.

EXPORT DEPARTMENT

As export activities and sales increase, the export manager may have to form an export department. This unit may consist of only a few people in addition to the export manager. An ***export department*** often (1) represents the interests of foreign customers to the firm's other departments and to top management, (2) meets the increasing demand for services by foreign customers, (3) makes special arrangements for customs clearance and international shipping, (4) assists foreign customers with financing of the goods or services that they're purchasing, and (5) arranges for the collection of accounts receivable from foreign customers. An export department might also establish branches abroad to handle sales and promotional tasks.

An interest in exporting often develops in stages and may even begin quite accidentally in small firms. In the United States, both public and private agencies help businesses identify countries and customers who may be interested in their products or services. These agencies include the International Trade Administration in the U.S. Department of Commerce, U.S. Export Assistance Center, the U.S. Chamber of Commerce, and the U.S. Small Business Administration.[10] Karen Mayo, executive director of special projects for the Port of Miami and president of Mayo Communications International, comments: "What businesses must understand is that soon they will no longer have a choice about whether to go international or not, because international is coming to them. We need to start thinking global because our neighborhood is the world. And the sooner you're ready, the more likely you'll win."[11]

Some of the factors that move an organization well beyond the export department level include (1) growth in international sales and production capacity equal to 15 percent or more of domestic division growth, (2) diversification in product lines to serve a variety of customers, and (3) difficulties in coordinating between domestic and international operations.

INTERNATIONAL CORPORATION

An ***international corporation*** has significant business interests that cut across national boundaries, often focuses on importing and exporting goods or services, and operates production and marketing units in other countries. One approach is to create an international division with offices or manufacturing operations for countries—or even regions—of the world. Units might be created for the Americas (Canada, Mexico, the United States, and Central and South America), Europe (France, Germany, the United Kingdom, and others), and the Pacific Rim (Australia, Japan, Hong Kong, and others). The nature of the units would depend on market size and the scope of the international manufacturing or service operations.[12]

International units represent their country or regional interests and operate as semi-independent units. Coordination between country or regional units usually is limited, and what does occur is handled by the company's top management. Coleman, Briggs & Stratton, and the Thomson Corporation are but a few examples of international corporations.

Figure 4.2 shows a portion of Thomson's organizational structure. The company is headquartered in Toronto, Ontario, and its principal activities are specialized information and publishing, newspaper publishing, and leisure travel. The International Thomson Publishing group provides specialized information services and produces publications in various parts of the world. It is organized primarily as subsidiary companies within particular world regions or countries. South-Western College Publishing, headquartered in Cincinnati, Ohio, and the publisher of this textbook, is one of those companies. This subsidiary focuses on the U.S. markets, but any of South-Western's products may be sold through the distribution offices of International Thomson Publishing. For example, the distribution office in London serves the United Kingdom, Europe, the Middle East, and Africa.

Diversified corporations may even establish separate international divisions for each major product line. Thus top managers of those lines may have both domestic and international responsibilities. Procter & Gamble, Sara Lee, and H. J. Heinz are representative of such international corporations. Morton International, a company best known in the United States for its salt products, is an international corporation known in other countries for its automobile parts.

MULTINATIONAL CORPORATION

A ***multinational corporation*** (MNC) sells its goods and services to customers worldwide and has a global philosophy of doing business. An MNC emerges when (1) management assesses problems and opportunities in global terms; (2) one or

MULTINATIONAL CORPORATION

A firm that takes a worldwide approach to markets (customers), services, and products and has a global philosophy of doing business.

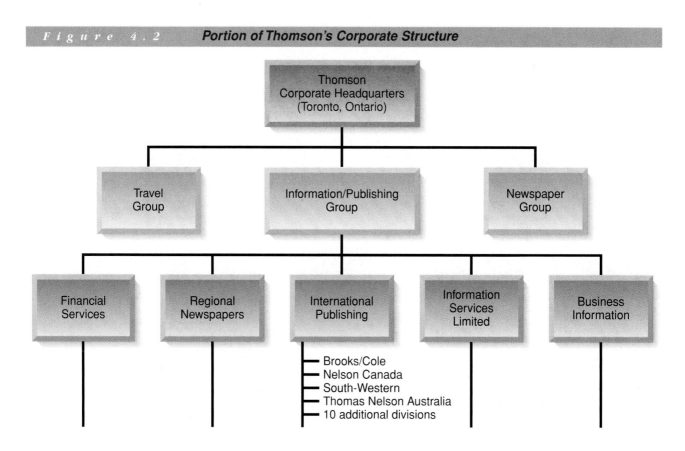

Figure 4.2   ***Portion of Thomson's Corporate Structure***

more subsidiaries operate in several countries; (3) management seeks to make sales, obtain resources, and produce goods throughout the world; (4) some of the key managers at corporate headquarters are from operations around the world, not just from the country in which the corporate headquarters is located; and (5) most of the key managers of *foreign* operations are from the countries or regions in which the operations are located. The features that most distinguish a multinational corporation from an international corporation are its integrated philosophy and view of the entire world as its market.[13] Multinational corporations include Caterpillar, IBM, and Shell.

Coca-Cola is a multinational corporation that obtains over 80 percent of its operating income from outside the United States. Its organization reflects a geographic focus. As Figure 4.3 shows, the basic functional units—marketing, operations, and bottlers—are represented in each geographic region. Coca-Cola operates in 185 markets, has more than 650,000 employees, and serves more than 5 billion customers. One of the company's core values is to "think globally, but act locally." The geographic units focus on day-to-day marketing, operations, and distribution. Corporate headquarters focuses on broad issues such as new international markets and new or improved product lines. For example, management recently created in Europe what it calls "anchor bottlers"—large dominant bottlers in local soft drink markets. The anchors distribute Coke's cola drinks, other brands that Coca-Cola owns, and brands that will make special deals to be included in Coca-Cola's marketing efforts. The company prefers to have an ownership share in as many of these anchors as possible. This strategy has proven it can work. In the Philippines, Pepsi once outsold Coca-Cola three to one. The company took over its own distribution, using an anchor bottler, and reversed that situation. Today Coca-Cola outsells Pepsi in the Philippines by a healthy three-to-one margin.[14] In Chapter 11, we explore multinational organization design in greater detail.

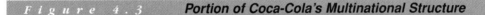

| Figure 4.3 | Portion of Coca-Cola's Multinational Structure |

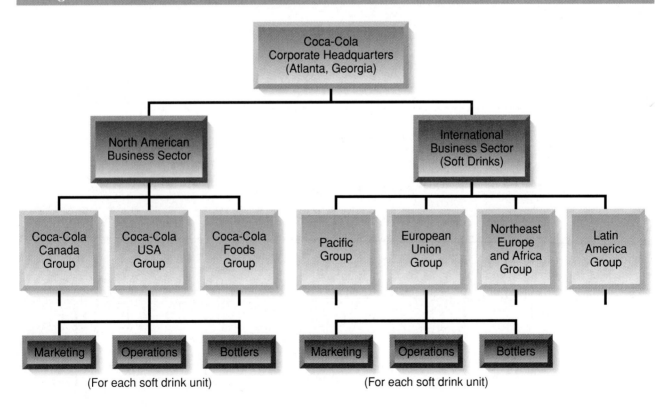

A multinational corporation often competes directly with a small number of other multinationals in each world market. It seeks to respond to local market needs while maintaining efficiency in its worldwide system. Most industries are represented by companies that are or will soon become multinationals with worldwide systems. These industries produce goods and services that vary from accounting, autos, banking, consumer electronics, and entertainment to pharmaceuticals, travel services, washing machines, and zippers. To be competitive, firms in these industries must manufacture, conduct research, raise capital, and buy supplies wherever they can gain a competitive advantage. They must stay on top of technological and market trends worldwide.[15]

Consider the potential impact of digital camera technology on Kodak and Fuji. First, there is the threat that film sales will soften as digital cameras made by Sony, Canon, Casio, and others take a bigger share of the market. Second, there is the challenge in photographic paper and processing from Canon, Epson, and Hewlett-Packard. Their latest generation ink-jet printers produce high-quality prints of digital images on plain and coated paper. Both Kodak and Fuji are working on ways to add value to digital photography—such as a service that lets customers order prints directly over the Internet. Finally, Kodak and Fuji have entered the digital camera business themselves. But they are two of nearly two dozen camera, computer, and consumer electronics companies trying to serve the same market. Kodak lost an estimated $400 million in digital imaging in 1997 and is no longer attempting to compete in all aspects of this market.[16]

STRATEGIES FOR INTERNATIONAL BUSINESS

3

EXPLAIN SIX STRATEGIES USED IN INTERNATIONAL BUSINESS

In this section, we present six strategies for conducting international business. They also range from low to high in complexity and in resource commitment, as shown in Figure 4.4. An organization may use one or more of these strategies at the same time.

EXPORTING STRATEGY

EXPORTING STRATEGY
Maintaining facilities within a home country and transferring goods and services abroad for sale in foreign markets.

The **exporting strategy** involves maintaining facilities within a home country and transferring goods and services abroad for sale in foreign markets. For many firms, it is the primary strategy of international operations. The approach used by Marianna Cooley, president of Cooley & Cooley, Ltd., to develop an exporting strategy is described in the following Strategic Action Competency piece. Cooley clearly understood changes in the firm's industry and had the ability to develop and execute plans and strategies to respond effectively to them.

COUNTER TRADE
An arrangement in which the export sales of goods and services by a producer is linked to an import purchase of other goods and services.

A variation on exporting (or importing) is **counter trade,** an arrangement by which the export sale of goods and services by a producer is linked to an import purchase of other goods and services.[17] This form of exporting is sometimes called *bartering* and may occur when the currency of the importing company can't be traded in international currency markets. The best known example of counter trade is PepsiCo's exporting of syrup and related soft drink items to Russia in exchange for vodka.

LICENSING STRATEGY

LICENSING STRATEGY
A firm (the licensor) in one country giving other domestic or foreign firms (licensees) the right to use a patent, trademark, technology, production process, or product in return for the payment of a royalty or fee.

A **licensing strategy** involves a firm (the licensor) in one country giving other domestic or foreign firms (licensees) the right to use a patent, trademark, technology, production process, or product in return for the payment of a royalty or fee. This contractual arrangement also may involve the licensor in providing manufacturing,

Cooley & Cooley, Ltd., is a Houston, Texas, manufacturer of dental products. Cooley's grandfather formed the company in 1933 to manufacture and sell Copalite. It is an easy-to-use and economical product that dentists apply between the tooth surface and a gold or silver filling.

When Cooley took over the company in 1990, Copalite was losing market share domestically and wasn't well distributed internationally. The use of plastic fillings had spread rapidly through dentistry, and Copalite had lost market share because it isn't

compatible with plastic fillings.

She concluded that one part of the solution lay abroad. Although threatened by plastic fillings in developed countries, Copalite is still very popular in developing countries. "I evaluated the business and we needed to get into export," says Cooley. She traveled to worldwide dental congresses and trade shows held in Germany, Japan, and Brazil to make direct contact with foreign Copalite distributors. These distributors act as commission agents but provide the additional services of receiving, storing, and distributing batches of Copalite shipped to them by Cooley & Cooley.

Cooley found that market advantage lies in countries where dentistry isn't as technologically advanced as it is in the United States. In those countries, Copalite can be used extensively, she says. "It's simple to apply. It's all natural and does not require a light curing gun or an electric outlet like the other products that work with plastics," explains Cooley. By following a few simple drawings, almost any

technician can use the product correctly. This ease of use is particularly helpful in China, where technicians rather than professionally trained dentists perform many of the dental procedures. Exports now comprise 80 percent of the company's sales, and annual revenue has tripled since 1990 to more than $1 million. Cooley anticipates further rapid export growth. The firm itself now operates as an *export department.*

In an effort to recapture the domestic market, Cooley and one of her staff chemists have developed a product that would be compatible with the new plastic technology. Two years in the making, the new product is called Copalite Platinum Plus and has complete Food and Drug Administration (FDA) approval. The company now offers both products for both types of markets.[18]

＊　＊　＊

To learn more about Cooley & Cooley, Ltd., visit the company's home page at

www.copalite.com

---

technical, or marketing expertise to the licensee. A simple licensing arrangement occurs when U.S. and Canadian book publishers give foreign publishers the right to translate a book into another language and then publish, market, and distribute the translated book. The licensor doesn't have to worry about making large capital investments abroad or becoming involved in the details of daily production, marketing, or management. PepsiCo and Coca-Cola have licensing agreements with bottlers/distributors in most countries.

Technological and market forces are combining to stimulate use of the licensing strategy. The reason is that licenses can be used to disseminate new technologies rapidly to new markets. In the computer industry, some firms license their technologies to users in an attempt to broaden their customer base.

FRANCHISING STRATEGY

FRANCHISING STRATEGY
A parent organization (the franchiser) granting other companies or individuals (franchisees) the right to use its trademarked name and to produce and sell its goods or services.

In a ***franchising strategy,*** a parent organization (the *franchiser*) grants other companies or individuals (*franchisees*) the right to use its trademarked name and to produce and sell its goods or services. The franchiser provides franchisees with

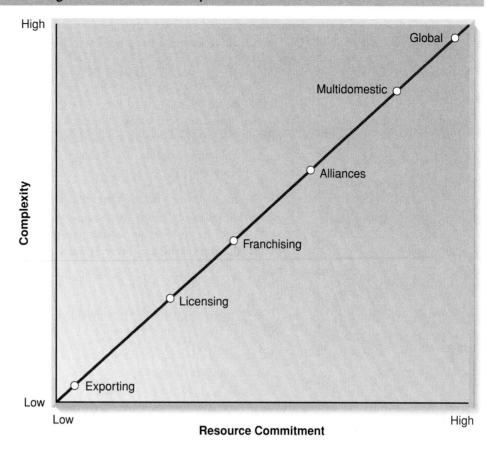

a complete assortment of materials and services for a fee. The franchiser usually is actively involved in training, monitoring, and controlling the actions of the franchisee to ensure that it conforms to the franchise agreement. Alamo Rent-A-Car, Holiday Inns, and McDonald's are but a few examples of global franchisers. The more than 3,000 franchising companies headquartered in Canada and the United States operate thousands of outlets in international markets.[19]

Wallace Doolin, president and CEO of TGI Friday's, made the following comments on its use of the franchising strategy.

> *To transplant your personal identity into a foreign setting, it usually is advisable to take on a development partner—in our case, a franchisee—who knows how to conduct business in Europe, Asia or whichever market you want to enter. A strong partner can help you negotiate government obstacles, labor unions, hiring practices and other hurdles that are unique to various parts of the world . . . . Opening businesses abroad takes two to three times longer than you would expect. Finding the right locations and securing development permits are only part of it. Training also takes longer, partly because of language barriers, but mainly because our way of doing business is literally foreign to most people outside the United States.*[20]

ALLIANCE STRATEGY

Agreeing with other companies to pool physical, financial, and human resources to achieve common goals.

ALLIANCE STRATEGY

An **_alliance strategy_** involves agreeing with other organizations to pool physical, financial, and human resources to achieve common goals. International business alliances take many forms, from straightforward marketing agreements to joint ventures (ownership) of worldwide operations. Interestingly, the first Chinese-foreign joint venture was formed in 1979. Today, thousands of Chinese-foreign joint ventures are doing business in China.

The following factors have stimulated the formation of alliances, especially joint ventures.

- The need to share and lower the costs of high-risk, technologically intensive development projects, such as computer-based information systems. Inmarsat, a joint venture with sixty-five partners from various countries, operates telecommunications satellites. The partners are simultaneously *owners* investing capital, *customers* routing calls through the satellites, and *suppliers* of technology to the venture.

- The desire to lower costs by sharing the large fixed-cost investments for manufacturing plants in some locations and in industries such as autos, steel, and appliances. To reduce manufacturing costs, Ford and Volkswagen formed a joint venture to make four-wheel-drive vehicles in Portugal.

- The desire to learn another firm's technology and special processes or to gain access to customers and distribution channels. Samsung entered into a joint venture with GE to produce microwave ovens and later became a competitor of GE's in the full line of household appliances.

- The desire to participate in the evolution of competitive activity in growing global industries. Royal Crown Company signed a joint venture agreement with Consorcio Aga. Royal Crown hopes that this bottler will help it boost sales in Mexico. In addition to licensing its brands, Royal Crown provides advertising, promotional, and technical support to Consorcio Aga.[21]

Alliances provide entry into markets that are risky because of strict political requirements or great economic uncertainty. For example, China usually doesn't permit foreign corporations to establish solely owned subsidiaries there—they must form some sort of alliance with Chinese participants. Finally, domestic partners are likely to have a deeper understanding of how to deal with great political and economic uncertainty in countries such as China and Russia.

MULTIDOMESTIC STRATEGY

MULTIDOMESTIC STRATEGY
Adjusting products, services, and practices to individual countries or regions (for example, Pacific Rim versus Western Europe versus North America).

A *multidomestic strategy* involves adjusting products, services, and practices to individual countries or regions (for example, Pacific Rim versus Western Europe versus North America). Pressures for local customizing to respond to differences in customer demand, distribution channels, host government demands, and/or employee needs drive this strategy. It is based on the assumption that the benefits of local response will outweigh the extra costs of customizing.[22] Companies that have followed a multidomestic strategy successfully include Honeywell (process controls), Alcoa (aluminum), and Campbell Foods (food products). These companies view the world as a whole of unique parts and deal with each part individually.

PROFIT CENTER
An organizational unit that is accountable for both the revenues generated by its activities and the costs of those activities.

Under a multidomestic strategy, each major overseas subsidiary usually is somewhat independent. Often each is a profit center and contributes earnings and growth according to its market opportunity. A *profit center* is an organizational unit that is accountable for both the revenues generated by its activities and the costs of those activities. Its managers are responsible for generating the revenues and minimizing the costs necessary to achieve the unit's profit goals. For example, Coca-Cola has more than 200 profit centers worldwide. The company's world headquarters maintains overall financial control and coordinates broad marketing (including product line) policies worldwide. A multidomestic strategy also means that some R&D, and even production, may be handled in the home country. But the specific marketing and transportation operations usually are delegated to managers in each nation or region.[23]

Frito-Lay uses a multidomestic strategy in tailoring its snack foods to taste preferences around the world. For example, Janjaree Thanma directs marketing research for Frito-Lay in Thailand. Interestingly, after testing 500 flavors for its chips with Thai consumers, the results showed that their preference was for American flavors, such as barbecue.[24]

GLOBAL STRATEGY

A *global strategy* stresses worldwide consistency, standardization, and low relative cost. Subsidiaries in various countries are highly interdependent in terms of goals, practices, and operations. As much as possible, top managers focus on coordination and mutual support of the firm's worldwide activities. For example, a Black & Decker subsidiary in one country might manufacture certain parts for families of products; subsidiaries in other countries do the same with regard to other parts. The subsidiaries then exchange components to complete assembly of their particular products. Profit targets vary for each subsidiary, reflecting its importance to the company's total sytem.[25]

The customers (e.g., purchasers of personal computers) of global firms have needs that are basically similar in many countries. Thus primary marketing strategies are highly transferable across national boundaries. For example, the marketing of Intel's Pentium chips to computer manufacturers in various countries has many similarities. Customers' technical standards are relatively compatible, and, for the most part, governments don't regulate computer chip production and sales practices.[26]

An increasing number of multinational corporations are using global strategies. They include Caterpillar and Komatsu (heavy construction equipment); Kodak and Fuji (film); and Texas Instruments, Intel, and Hitachi (semiconductors). As demonstrated in the following Communication Competency account, Merrill Lynch's top management, through formal and informal communication networks and media, created a relatively uniform corporate culture for relating to customers and fellow employees in implementing its global strategy.

Various needs must be addressed for a multinational's global strategy to be successful. The following are six such needs.

1. The firm needs to be a significant competitor in the world's most important regional markets—North America, Europe, and Asia.

2. Most new goods and services need to be developed for the whole world—such as Merrill Lynch's financial services and Kodak's film and related products.

3. Profit targets need to be based on product lines—such as Black & Decker's line of handheld power drills—rather than countries or regions of the world.

4. Decisions about products, capital investment, R&D, and production need to be based on global considerations—such as Kodak's and Fuji's strategic location of plants for producing film and related products in various regions worldwide.

5. Narrow-minded attitudes—such as "this isn't how we operate here"—need to be overcome. Some ways to shape work-related attitudes and values include training employees to think globally, sending them to various countries for first-hand exposure, and giving them the latest information technology. Merrill Lynch recently spent more than $800 million on 25,000 state-of-the art workstations.

Merrill Lynch

Merrill Lynch is a global financial services firm. It has two major lines of business—one as an investment bank to corporations and government and the other as a retail financial services firm to individuals. It has offices in forty countries and is rapidly establishing offices in other countries. One of Merrill Lynch's strategic initiatives is to expand its retail financial services in all of these international markets.

Chief Executive Officer David Komansky comments: "The U.S. mar-

ket is mature, and to some extent overbanked. The ability to have a truly global reach is going to be critical. We are talking about something far in excess of originating outside the United States and distributing here. We are talking about originating in almost any foreign currency and being able to distribute those products in almost any financial market in the world."

Foreign nationals who manage Merrill Lynch's branches are being brought to the firm's Princeton, New Jersey, training center to learn its way of doing business. Says Komansky, "Visit our offices, whether it be Thailand, Malaysia, South Africa, or Germany, and you will see the same plaques on the wall with those same Merrill principles in the local language." Sample Merrill homily: "Integrity: No one's personal bottom line is more important than the reputation of our firm."

It is an article of faith at Merrill Lynch that what works for the American middle and upper classes will work abroad, too. "After you get past

superficial differences, people are basically the same in their needs, wants, and desires," says Komansky.

Since the days of Charles Merrill, who put the company together through scores of mergers in the 1920s, the company has built management systems that provide checks and balances on the power of any one person. This system doesn't depend on getting and holding a handful of brilliant individualists. Any intelligent, motivated person from anywhere in the world can absorb the firm's culture and become a Merrill Lynch person.

This type of organization is inherently easier to expand than one that depends on a constellation of stars. Merrill Lynch has a long tradition of cloning its organization and training young people—Americans and foreigners alike—in the "Merrill way."[27]

* * *

To learn more about Merrill Lynch, visit the company's home page at

www.ml.com

The upgraded technology will further enhance the ability of employees to communicate with each other and the firm's customers, almost on a real-time basis throughout the world.

6. Foreign managers need to be promoted into senior ranks at corporate headquarters.[28]

POLITICAL-LEGAL FORCES

4

EXPLAIN THE IMPACT OF POLITICAL-LEGAL FORCES IN INTERNATIONAL BUSINESS

Organizations that engage in international business must cope with a web of political and legal forces. Therefore management must diagnose these forces accurately in order to understand the risks and uncertainties involved in international business. Recall from Chapter 3 that managers may use one or more of five political strategies—negotiation, lobbying, alliance, representation, and socialization—to reduce political risk.

Political risk is the probability that political decisions or events in a country will negatively affect the long-term profitability of an investment. Of concern to all international and multinational corporations is the political risk associated with resource commitments in foreign countries.

Domestic Instability	Low				High
Foreign Conflict	Low				High
Political Climate	Stable				Unstable
Economic Climate	Stable				Unstable

ASSESSING POLITICAL RISK

Political risk factors may be grouped into four principal categories: domestic instability, foreign conflict, political climate, and economic climate. As Figure 4.5 shows, managers may estimate the seriousness of the political risk associated with conducting business in a country by assessing various factors in each category.

DOMESTIC INSTABILITY

The amount of subversion, revolution, assassinations, guerrilla warfare, and government crisis in a country.

FOREIGN CONFLICT

The degree of hostility one nation shows toward others.

POLITICAL CLIMATE

The likelihood that a government will swing to the far left or far right politically.

ECONOMIC CLIMATE

The extent of government control of markets and financial investments, as well as government support services and capabilities.

Domestic instability is the amount of subversion, revolution, assassinations, guerrilla warfare, and government crisis in a country. Haiti's long history of domestic instability has generally discouraged foreign investment.

Foreign conflict is the degree of hostility that one nation expresses to others. Such hostility can range from the expulsion of diplomats to outright war. The invasion of Kuwait by Iraq is one of the more dramatic recent examples. In August 1990, then President George Bush determined that the actions of the government of Iraq were an unusual and extraordinary threat to the national security and foreign policy of the United States. Under authority granted by the U.S. Export Administration Act of 1979, the government imposed a ban on trade with Iraq, which directly affected many firms. This ban and the tensions with Iraq continue. In one composite rating of political risk for 1997, Iraq's risk rating was very high.[29]

Political climate is the likelihood that a government will swing to the far left or far right politically. Managers may evaluate variables such as the number and size of political parties, number of factions in the legislature, role of the military in the political process, amount of corruption in government, effectiveness of political leadership, influence of organized religion in politics, extent of racial and nationality tensions, and quality of the governmental bureaucracy. Currently, Russia is considered to have a risky political climate because of the instability of the government, opposing political forces, and widespread corruption.

The *economic climate* reflects the extent of government control of markets and financial investments, as well as government support services and capabilities. Such include government regulatory and economic control policies (wages, prices, imports, and exports); government ability to manage its own economic affairs (inflation budget surpluses or deficits, and amount of debt); government provision of support services and facilities (roads, airports, electricity, water, and refuse and sewage disposal), often referred to as *infrastructure;* and government capabilities in general.

The U.S. government has had a greater tendency than most other governments to impose export controls unilaterally as a way to advance its foreign policy. Opponents claim that unilateral U.S. export controls cost U.S. businesses billions of dollars per year in sales. One executive asserts, "The theory is everybody else in the world will follow our lead. They have not, and they continue to export a lot of things."[30] Pressure groups continually lobby the U.S. government to impose sanctions on various countries, which generally means limiting the ability of U.S. headquartered companies to do business with or in those countries. For example, some unions want trade sanctions against countries that don't follow U.S. labor standards. Environmental groups want sanctions applied to countries that violate environmental standards. Human rights groups want sanctions imposed to combat political oppression. Many of these groups aren't content for the sanctions to restrict the activities of U.S. companies only. They also want to target every company in every foreign country that trades with the nation whose actions offend their sensibilities. For example, consider some of the political quagmires that oil companies face.

- An international consortium led by British Petroleum and Amoco hopes to tap Azerbaijan's huge Caspian Sea oil reserves but must use pipeline routes through war-torn Chechnya and unstable Georgia.

- Royal Dutch/Shell Group operates in Nigeria for nearly sixty years and then finds itself in an international firestorm over human rights issues in the oil-rich country.

- Mobil and a group of other oil companies pay the U.S. government $296 million for the right to drill for oil off the North Carolina coast and then are delayed for fifteen years and counting—without reimbursement.

In Algeria, where foreigners—and journalists—are favorite assassination targets, expatriate workers sign on for a soldier's life. Bechtel employees, working on a major international pipeline project, lived in compounds protected by trenches, barbed wire fences, and guard towers. No women, children, or visits to neighboring towns were allowed.

Shell, the largest foreign operator in Nigeria, came under fire from human rights groups that called—in vain—for the giant oil company to withdraw from the country. If Shell had agreed, withdrawal would have been very difficult. It has been working in Nigeria, Africa's most populous nation, for sixty years. Shell and its partners employ 5,000 workers and produce half the oil in this country, which is a member of the Organization of Petroleum Exporting Countries (OPEC).

The federal Overseas Private Investment Corporation (OPIC) sells risk insurance and lends money to U.S. companies venturing into politically risky countries. According to Ruth Harkin, president of OPIC, since 1992, the agency has sold $1.6 billion worth of political-risk insurance for forty different overseas oil and gas projects. "We will go up to $200 million per project," Harkin said. "And we'll charge you plenty for it too, but nonetheless, it's worth it. I can assure you."[31]

POLITICAL MECHANISMS

Governments and businesses utilize a variety of political strategies, as we discussed in Chapter 3, to cope with political and legal forces. In this section, we go beyond those strategies to explain two significant types of international political mechanisms: (1) protectionism and (2) bribery and extortion. In doing so, we want you to be aware of actual practices that you are bound to encounter someday in international business.

Protectionism. *Protectionism* covers the many mechanisms designed to help a home-based industry or firms avoid (or reduce) potential (or actual) competitive or political threats from abroad. Tariffs, quotas, subsidies, and cartels are among the most widely used political mechanisms.

PROTECTIONISM
The mechanisms designed and used to help a home-based industry or firms avoid (or reduce) potential (or actual) competitive or political threats from abroad.

A **tariff** is a government tax on goods or services entering the country. Its primary purpose is to raise the price of imported goods or services. As a result, domestic goods and services gain a relative price advantage.

Consider just this one example. Until 1997, Korea's domestic automobile market was protected by a financial and regulatory wall. Tariff and import taxes added 118 percent to the price of an imported car (e.g., the Ford Taurus). Foreigners were prohibited from owning auto retail financing operations. Prime-time TV advertising was forbidden. Autos entering the country had to meet complex standards and certification processes. The government ran a fierce anti-import campaign in the press. It even threatened—at one point—to audit tax returns of consumers who bought foreign cars. A trade agreement signed in late 1996 initially lowered tariffs by 15 percent and significantly erased or eased most of the other restrictions. The government has pledged not to audit foreign-car buyers and to refrain from anti-foreign-auto rhetoric. Even so, tariffs remain high.[32]

A **quota** is a restriction on the quantity of a country's imports (or sometimes, on its exports). Import quotas generally are intended to guarantee home-country manufacturers access to a certain percentage of the domestic market. Most experts agree that, if protectionism is politically unavoidable, tariffs are preferable to quotas. The reason is that quotas fix the levels of imports entering a country and thus freeze markets. Domestic producers then are under less pressure to become more productive and efficient. Quotas are a hidden tax on consumers, whereas tariffs are a more obvious tax.

U.S. sugar import quotas have existed for more than fifty years. The intent is to preserve about half the domestic market for U.S. sugar producers. Domestic sugar cane and sugar beet growers are guaranteed 22.5 cents a pound, or about twice the world market price for sugar. Hence U.S. consumers pay an estimated $3 billion per year in extra food costs because of sugar quotas. However, these quotas do preserve some U.S. jobs that would probably be lost with no quotas. In addition, Archer Daniels Midland and others in the corn sweetener business can readily sell their products at an inflated price to manufacturers looking for a cheaper commodity to satisfy America's sweet tooth.[33]

A **subsidy** is a direct or indirect payment by a government to its country's firms to make selling or investing abroad cheaper for them—and thus more profitable. Indirect payments are illustrated by some of OPIC's activities. This self-sustaining U.S. government agency helps qualified U.S. investors establish commercial projects in developing countries by offering reinvestment assistance and financing. Its political-risk insurance program provides coverage for eligible projects against losses from government seizure of assets; nonconvertibility of local currency into U.S. dollars; and damage caused by war, revolution, insurrection, or strife.[34]

Many countries provide subsidies to farmers whose products are then able to compete on price in global markets. Consider the worldwide average subsidies given to farmers for six products: wheat, 48 percent; rice, 86 percent; sugar (refined white), 48 percent; beef, 35 percent; and pork, 22 percent.[35]

A **cartel** is an alliance of producers engaged in the same type of business, which is formed to limit or eliminate competition and control production and prices. Governments impose tariffs and quotas and grant subsidies. In contrast, cartels operate under agreements negotiated between firms or governments, as in the case of OPEC. A primary goal of any cartel is to protect its members' revenues and profits by controlling output and therefore prices. International cartels currently exist in oil, copper, aluminum, natural rubber, and other raw materials. The best-known cartel is OPEC, which was formed in 1960. The recent history of the oil industry and OPEC clearly demonstrates that cartels often face uncertainty and have to cope with rebellion among their members. In recent years, OPEC hasn't been very effective in controlling oil production by member countries. Members often can't agree on prices or quantities to be produced, especially Nigeria and Venezuela. For example, Venezuela produced about 3.4 million barrels a month in 1997, but had an OPEC quota of about 2.7 million barrels. Venezuela has passed Saudi Arabia as the largest exporter of oil to the United States.[36] By law, U.S. firms are forbidden to form or participate directly in cartels because their purpose is at odds with preserving competitive markets and individual rights based on private property.

Protectionism has both strong advocates and opponents. Generally, it works against consumers' interests by raising prices. Advocates claim that it protects home-country industries and jobs against unfair competition from countries with subsistence wages and special subsidies. Therefore whether companies, business associations, and employee groups favor or oppose a particular protectionist measure depends on how it may affect their interests.

BRIBE

An improper payment made to induce the recipient to do something for the payer.

EXTORTION

A payment made to ensure that the recipient doesn't harm the payer in some way.

Bribery and Extortion. A *bribe* is an improper payment made to induce the recipient to do something for the payer. Bribes are illegal in Canada and the United States but not in some countries. By offering a bribe, the payer hopes to obtain a special favor in exchange for something of value (e.g., money, a trip, or a car). In recent years, the growing moral revulsion against bribery and other forms of corruption has swept politicians from office in Brazil, Italy, and Japan. In Italy, state prosecutors exposed an elaborate web of relationships among the Mafia, politicians, and business executives. Bids for highways, sewers, and other public projects now come in as much as 40 percent below past bids for comparable projects. However, this example is not to suggest that Italy—or any country for that matter—is free from political and business corruption.[37]

Extortion is a payment made to ensure that the recipient doesn't harm the payer in some way. The purpose of extortion is to obtain something of value by threatening harm to the payer. When Coca-Cola entered the Russian market, it refused to respond to extortion efforts by the Russian Mafia. In retaliation, the Russian Mafia launched a bazooka attack on the bottling plant that Coca-Cola was building in Moscow. In addition, the Mafia attempted to intimidate many of the company's Russian distributors.[38]

Bribery and extortion are practiced throughout the world. They occur most frequently in Nigeria, Pakistan, Kenya, Bangladesh, China, Venezuela, Russia, India, Indonesia, and several other countries. In fact, some countries culturally define certain forms of bribery and extortion as an acceptable, appropriate, and an expected form of gift giving. Belgium, France, Sweden, Greece, and Germany allow or tolerate the tax deductibility of foreign bribes. The United Nations and the World Bank are attempting to get members to criminalize bribery and extortion—as has the U.S. government.[39]

The U.S. Foreign Corrupt Practices Act of 1977 makes it a crime for U.S. corporations or individuals to offer or make payments to officials of foreign governments or companies for the purpose of obtaining or retaining business. The act established specific record-keeping requirements for publicly held corporations, making difficult the concealment of political payments prohibited by the act. Violators—both corporations and individuals—face stiff penalties. A company may be fined as much as $1 million, and a manager who directly participates in or has knowledge of any violations of the act faces up to five years in prison and/or $100,000 in fines. Furthermore, the act prohibits corporations from paying any fines imposed on their directors, managers, employees, or agents.[40]

The act doesn't prohibit grease payments to employees of foreign governments whose duties are primarily procedural or clerical. ***Grease payments*** are small payments—almost gratuities—used to get lower level government employees to speed up required paperwork. Such payments may be required to persuade employees to perform their normal duties. Prohibiting grease payments would put U.S. firms at an extreme competitive disadvantage when conducting business abroad. Such a prohibition also would be very difficult to enforce. For example, Paul Gimona of Rome, Italy, is a manufacturer's representative and sole distributor of a high-tech Swedish oil flow detector. His territory includes the United Arab Emirates, Egypt, and other Mideast oil-producing countries. To get his company's device installed in pipelines as they are built, he must pay an unofficial fee to local officials who then approve the projects.[41]

COMPETITIVE FORCES

5

DISCUSS HOW THREE MAJOR TRADE AGREEMENTS AFFECT COMPETITIVE FORCES

We discussed five competitive forces in Chapter 3: competitors, new entrants, substitute goods and services, customers, and suppliers. These forces apply whether a firm competes locally (say, in the Seattle, Washington, area), nationally (say, in Canada), regionally (say, in Asia), or worldwide. In this section we briefly review three significant agreements that directly affect one or more of the five competitive forces. These agreements heighten the market-based competitive pressures on firms.

GENERAL AGREEMENT ON TARIFFS AND TRADE

The General Agreement on Tariffs and Trade (GATT) represents a series of negotiated understandings regarding trade and related issues among the participating countries. Twenty-three countries signed the first GATT in 1947, and seven rounds of negotiations have followed. The most recent round, called the *Uruguay Round,* began in 1986 and continued through the end of 1993. By 2000, world trade in merchandise and commercial services is forecasted to exceed $8 trillion (1 trillion is 1,000 billion), or $2 trillion more than in 1995.

GATT proposed to cut tariffs and other barriers to trade on 8,000 categories of manufactured goods. It also attempted to strengthen intellectual property right (copyright, trademark, and patent) protections and extend world trade rules to services. It set up the World Trade Organization (WTO), which replaced GATT. Under GATT, the United States and other nations had been able to block adverse rulings by arbitration panels, but cannot do so under WTO. By 2000, WTO is expected to have at least 130 member countries, which account for about 95 percent of world trade. A key WTO goal is to progressively reduce the remaining trade barriers. Making trade freer will increase competitive forces throughout the world.[42]

Three principles were fundamental to the various rounds of GATT negotiations. The most *favored nation principle* means that when country A grants a tariff concession to country B, the same concession automatically applies to all other countries that are members of GATT. The *reciprocity principle* means that each member country will not be forced to reduce tariffs unilaterally. A tariff concession is made only in return for comparable concessions from the other countries. The *transparency principle* means that tariffs are to be readily visible to all countries. Presumably, tariffs are the only permitted form of restriction. Thus GATT doesn't allow internal taxes and regulations to be applied to imported goods if they aren't equally applied to domestic goods. However, GATT provides for exceptions to these principles. For example, the *escape clause* provides that, if a product is being imported into a country in such increased quantities that it causes or threatens to cause serious injury to domestic producers of that product, the importing country may temporarily increase the tariff on that product.

Under GATT, trade negotiations also may take place directly between two or more countries.[43] One significant trade dispute between the United States and China relates to the lack of enforcement of intellectual property rights. Global losses caused by software piracy (mostly through direct copying of software products) were estimated at $13 billion in 1995. In China, Russia, the Philippines, and nineteen other countries, 90 percent of the software sold in 1995 was illegally produced (pirated).

After intense negotiations that were filled with threats, China signed an accord in late 1995 to police and enforce U.S. intellectual property rights. As part of the agreement, China agreed to establish at least twenty-two task forces to oversee an antipiracy campaign, and agreed to consult with the U.S. regularly over a three- to five-year period. China agreed to

- launch raids against retail outlets and inspect factories alleged to be engaging in piracy;

- strengthen penalties against enterprises found to be producing pirated products and increase the power of enforcers to crack down on violators;

- end quotas and licensing requirements on audiovisual and software imports; and

- allow audiovisual and computer software companies to form joint ventures in China.

Although some progress has been made, critics claim that China hasn't vigorously enforced the provisions of the agreement. Trade controversies continue unabated with China.[44]

NORTH AMERICAN FREE TRADE AGREEMENT[45]

The North American Free Trade Agreement (NAFTA) went into effect in 1994 to increase free trade among the United States, Canada, and Mexico. It created a trade zone of 8.2 million square miles, 380 million consumers, and billions of dollars worth of economic activity. NAFTA represents an extension of the Canada–United States Free Trade Agreement, which went into effect in 1989.

Over a fifteen-year period, NAFTA is to reduce and eliminate numerous tariffs and most nontariff barriers among the three countries. Although full elimination of certain tariffs will take fifteen years, over 70 percent of the goods imported from Mexico may now enter the United States without tariffs. At the same time, over 50 percent of U.S. exports to Mexico are now tariff-free. The agreement also realizes long-held goals of liberalizing trade in services and foreign investment rules abroad. NAFTA tightens the protection of intellectual property (copyrights, trademarks, and patents, in particular).

Although NAFTA further opens Canadian and U.S. markets, the most significant liberalization applies to Mexico. NAFTA expands Canadian and U.S. companies' ability to establish or purchase businesses in Mexico and increases their ability to sell if they want to leave. NAFTA loosens previous restrictions on expanding operations in Mexico and removes restrictions on transferring profits to other countries.

Despite much liberalization, NAFTA retains protectionist provisions, some of which may persist with no time limit. NAFTA temporarily protects sensitive industries (e.g., agriculture, minerals, banking, textiles, and apparel) by stretching out the phase-in time. NAFTA also contains other types of protection that are permanent and appear to raise trade barriers above pre-NAFTA levels. In some industries—notably automobiles, textiles, and apparel—NAFTA imposes higher North American content rules. Under the previous Canada–United States Free Trade Agreement, for example, automobiles could be imported duty-free if they contained at least 50 percent Canadian and U.S. inputs. For auto imports to receive NAFTA benefits, the North American rule is now 62.5 percent. For textiles or apparel to qualify for "free" trade under NAFTA, all components—beginning with the yarn or fiber—must be produced in North America.

The service industries that received the most attention during NAFTA negotiations were finance, insurance, transportation, and telecommunications. NAFTA doesn't change requirements for foreign banks' entry into the United States and Canada. But the opening of the Mexican financial system is among the agreement's most significant achievements. Requirements for entry into brokerage, bonding, insurance, leasing, and warehousing were liberalized even more than they were for banking.

NAFTA and GATT certainly don't eliminate all trade problems among the member countries. But they do provide frameworks through which such problems can be resolved. By increasing the competitive forces that act on firms, the ultimate intent of GATT and NAFTA is to achieve greater efficiency and consumer satisfaction. However, as legal documents that were politically negotiated, they contain provisions, loopholes, and exceptions that will be tested over the decades to come. The provisions of these agreements no doubt will be welcomed or resisted, depending on their effect on a particular country, industry, or firm.

The following Global Awareness Competency account describes how Alvin Segal, CEO, and his top management team at Peerless Clothing stay informed of political, social, and economic trends and events around the world, and recognize the impact of global events on their organization.

EUROPEAN UNION

The European Union (EU), called the European Community (EC) until 1994, has fifteen members: Austria, Belgium, Denmark, Finland, France, Germany, Greece, Ireland, Italy, Luxemburg, the Netherlands, Portugal, Spain, Sweden, and the United Kingdom. These countries contain some 400 million consumers.[46] Additional countries that may join the EU are Hungary, Iceland, Poland, and the Czech Republic. The potential membership of other countries (Turkey, Slovakia, Estonia, Latvia, Lithuania, and other newly independent countries from the former Soviet Union) remains to be determined.

The goals of the European Union include creating a single market among member countries through the removal of trade barriers (such as tariffs) and establishing the free movement of goods, people, services, and investment capital. The implementation of these and other goals officially began at the end of 1992. In addition, the changes go beyond economic interests to include social changes as well. Educational degrees have already been affected. The EU Council of Ministers issued a directive that recognizes diplomas of higher education across national boundaries. This action makes it easier for professionals to work in different countries. Most member countries have developed master's degree programs in business administration that are compatible with the others' and those in the United States.

The EU clearly is more than an economic union: It is a state of mind and a political force. Eventually, it should lead to less government interference in economic activities. Meeting uniform quality standards through ISO and worker safety and environmental controls will be expected of all companies who trade in the EU.

An essential stage of the EU program is to complete formation of the common internal market. That involves eliminating

Peerless Clothing of Montreal, Quebec, seized an opportunity created by NAFTA. Peerless imports wool cloth and then fashions it into low- and medium-priced suits, which are sold

by various retailers under their own private labels.

Wages in the apparel industry are typically lower in the United States than in Canada. The United States maintains a high duty on wool textiles, but Canada doesn't. As a result, Canadian suit makers such as Peerless enjoy a tremendous cost advantage. "If the Americans lowered their duty on raw materials, I'd have to move to the States instantly, maybe sooner," said Peerless Chief Executive Alvin Segal.

Anticipating such a problem for domestic apparel makers, U.S. negotiators during the free-trade talks insisted on placing a quota on the number of suits that could be exported from Canada to the United States. Peerless, the largest suit maker in Canada, controls a large share of the quota. Before NAFTA

went into effect, Peerless sold few suits in the U.S. market. Today, U.S. buyers account for 98 percent of Peerless's export sales.

But in the United States, Peerless faces strong opposition from the Union of Needle Trades, Industrial and Textile Employees. "The unions are against NAFTA and free trade, and they're using me as a guinea pig," Segal said. Officials with the union, which is trying to organize at Peerless's Montreal plant, say they aren't protesting free trade, merely decrying working conditions at Peerless's operation. Segal debates this view.[47]

* * *

To learn more about the North American Free Trade Agreement, visit the following home page:

www.wiretap.spies.com/11/Gov/ NAFTA

1. **physical barriers** at each country's borders, which prevent the free flow of goods and people;

2. **technical barriers,** which prevent goods and services produced or traded in one member nation from being sold in others;

3. **fiscal barriers,** such as red tape and the different national tax systems, which hinder cross-border trade; and

4. **financial barriers,** which prevent the free movement of investment capital.

The EU also intends to introduce a common currency. Owing to nationalistic and other economic factors, conflicts among nations are intense over the formation of the Economic Monetary Union (EMU). The central feature of EMU is a single currency, to be called the *euro,* supervised by an independent central bank in Frankfurt, Germany. If all goes as planned, the euro will be implemented in 2002.

The European Commission is the EU's executive body and sole initiator of legislation. The commission claims that 95 percent of the legislative measures set out in the 1992 program have been adopted. However, the toughest issues weren't addressed in the 1992 program, including agreement on a common immigration policy. Some member nations are concerned that they'll be flooded with immigrants as the result of an open door policy. As unemployment has risen, the external frontiers of the union have been tightened. It is now virtually impossible to legally enter the member nations as an economic migrant. An applicant rejected by one member can no longer apply to others.

The EU has already increased market opportunities, fostered competition, and encouraged competition from the outside. The removal of transnational trade restrictions and the relaxation of border controls based on economic restraints have had a considerable impact on U.S. and Canadian companies. For example, NBC, with no previous global experience, acquired controlling interest in Europe's Super Channel. It is now beaming its programs to about 60 million homes and hotels across Europe.

Many non-Europeans continue to be concerned that the supposedly free market of Europe will be anything but free to outsiders. The EU Commission has pressured U.S. and Japanese firms to conduct more R&D and production in Europe or face the risk of increased tariffs and other barriers. Restrictions still apply to non-EU banks and security firms unless foreign countries (e.g., the United States, Canada, and Japan) grant reciprocal rights. These restrictions range from limiting the right to acquire banks in EU countries to special taxes on foreign banks operating there.

Various alternative strategies are available to U.S. and Canadian enterprises. One is to export goods and services to the EU. In general, though, North American firms have had only limited success in doing so. The most successful strategy has been to set up subsidiaries or branches in one or more of the EU countries. The advantages of subsidiaries have been demonstrated by well-established companies such as Opel (a subsidiary of GM in Germany), Ford, and IBM. Some companies have consolidated their previous positions in Europe. For example, United Parcel Service (UPS) purchased eleven companies in EU nations to strengthen its market position.

CULTURAL FORCES

6

DESCRIBE HOW CULTURAL FORCES AFFECT INTERNATIONAL MANAGEMENT

The cultural forces that we discussed in Chapter 3 underlie the day-to-day competitive and political forces operating within and among nations. Four aspects of a culture that have direct implications for international management are views of social change, time orientation, language, and value systems.[48]

VIEWS OF SOCIAL CHANGE

Different views of the need for social change and its pace can have a significant impact on an organization's plans for international operations. The people of many non-Western cultures, such as those of India, Saudi Arabia, and China, view change as a slow and natural progression. For them change is part of the evolution of human beings and the universe, guided by a Supreme Being, and the attitude toward it tends to be passive (or even reactive). In contrast, the people of Western cultures tend to view change differently. For them change can be shaped and controlled to achieve their own goals and aspirations, and the attitude tends to be active. Therefore Western managers assigned to non-Western countries often run into difficulty when trying to introduce innovations too rapidly. In cultures that hold a passive/reactive view of change, new ways of doing things often must go hand in hand with a painstaking concern for their effect on interpersonal relationships. Moreover, people in nations such as India, Italy, and Turkey that are characterized by high uncertainty avoidance also are likely to resist or react cautiously to social change. Managers plunged into these cultures have to recognize this viewpoint, plan for it, and manage change accordingly.

TIME ORIENTATION

Many people in the United States and Canada think of time as an extremely scarce commodity. They often say that "time is money," or that "there is too little time." Several popular books on time management show an almost frenetic concern with how managers should plan their days. The need to set and stick to tight deadlines for accomplishing tasks is a basic tenet of this style of management.

In some cultures, however, time is viewed more as an unlimited and unending resource. For example, Hindus believe that time does not begin at birth or end at death. The Hindu belief in reincarnation gives life a nontemporal, everlasting dimension. Because of such attitudes, employees, customers, and suppliers in some cultures are quite casual about keeping appointments and meeting deadlines—an indifference that can be highly frustrating to Canadian and U.S. managers who have to deal with them.

Traditionally, the Mexican attitude toward time can best be summed up in the word *mañana,* meaning "not today"—but not necessarily tomorrow either! A manager in Mexico might say: Yes, your shipment will be ready on Tuesday. You arrive on Tuesday to pick it up but find that it isn't ready. No one is upset or embarrassed; they say politely that the paperwork hasn't been processed yet or offer some other explanation. Time commitments are considered desirable but not binding promises. This attitude toward time is changing among Mexican businesspeople and professionals. As life-styles become more complex and pressures for greater productivity increase, many more people in Mexico are paying attention to punctuality and meeting time commitments.

LANGUAGE

Language serves to bind as well as to separate cultures. Fluency in another language can give an international manager a competitive edge in understanding and gaining the acceptance of people from the host culture. However, the ability to speak a language correctly isn't enough: A manager must also be able to recognize and interpret the nuances of phrases, sayings, and nonverbal gestures.

The story is told of several U.S. executives who were trying to negotiate with their Japanese counterparts. The American head negotiator made a proposal. The Japanese head negotiator was silent. His silence meant that he was considering the offer. The American, however, took his silence to mean that the offer wasn't good enough. So the American raised the offer! Again the Japanese considered in silence, and again the silence prompted the American to raise the offer. Finally, the American reached his limit, and an agreement was struck. The Japanese head negotiator had obtained several concessions simply because the American negotiator had misread his silence. The following Teamwork Competency feature provides additional perspective on the need to be sensitive to unique patterns of language and communication with those from other cultures. As you will see, Mike Burgess needed to act more as a coach, counselor, and facilitator than as a boss.

VALUE SYSTEMS

In Chapter 3, we discussed the importance of value systems and described five value dimensions: power distance, uncertainty avoidance, individualism (versus collectivism), masculinity (versus femininity), and Confucian dynamics. Obviously, differences in cultural values affect how managers and professionals function in international business.

Because of continuing interest in the competitive challenge of Japanese firms, let's look at some of the differences in Japanese and U.S. values and a few of the management implications of these differences. Although the Japanese economy has been in a recession and the halo of the superiority of Japanese management is badly tarnished, one expert warns: "Average American middle managers think we've beaten the Japanese. They think we've won. They think we're smarter. But they don't understand the nature of the competition. The Japanese have a proven ability to cope with crisis."[49]

Mike Burgess, a U.S.-born program manager, came to Indonesia to manage a multicultural venture. When Burgess arranged his first Friday meeting with team members of various nationalities, he expected everyone to appear at 9 A.M. But three of the six Indonesian members didn't arrive until 9:20 A.M. Worse, the three Indonesians brought along three uninvited members from their own staffs. Meanwhile, the four Japanese members of the team had rearranged their seats so that they could sit together.

When the meeting finally got underway at 9:45 A.M., Burgess moved from discussing the agenda and goals to inviting his guests to pose questions. No one volunteered a question—until Burgess remembered that, as the senior Indonesian, Mr. Budi had to be invited to present his comments before anyone else could pose a question.

During the discussion that followed, Burgess became annoyed by the tendency of Indonesian members to get sidetracked from discussions of results and goals. Then, Burgess and

Robert Griffin, the American technical director, became engaged in a heated, open disagreement that surprised both the Indonesian and Japanese teams. During the break that followed, the Indonesians were offended that Burgess had ordered coffee—but no snacks. When the meeting reconvened, Burgess tried to call the participants to a vote on a key decision. Mr. Yamaguchi, the Japanese group leader, asked for a delay of a week. He wanted to consult with his headquarters in Tokyo. Burgess openly expressed his frustration at this further delay. Yamaguchi seized the opportunity to state an annoying workplace habit: Why, Yamaguchi asked, did Burgess send so many e-mail messages to him, even though he worked only twenty-five feet away?

At the core of all these tensions are the widely diverse cultural values and habits of the U.S., Japanese, and Indonesian members—so ingrained in the various individuals that they rarely recognize them without professional guidance.[50]

* * *

To learn more about conducting business abroad, visit the following home page:

www.getcustoms.com

which is the Web site for the authors of *Dun & Bradstreet's Guide to Doing Business Around the World*. Englewood Cliffs, N.J.: Prentice-Hall, 1997.

U.S. and Japanese Societies. Collectivism means that people identify strongly with the groups to which they belong—from the family unit to the society as a whole. It emphasizes group goals and interdependence with others. Groups aren't thought of as collections of individuals. Rather, groups exist first and absorb individuals into them. Consequently, the individual is governed by the norms (rules) of each group. The Japanese form of collectivism leads to greater group cohesion than is usually found in the United States. The short-term sacrifice of the individual's wants for the benefit of the group is commonly accepted. As a result, Japanese achievements tend to be group-oriented. Furthermore, because the Japanese value system is less diverse than that in the United States, severe conflicts caused by underlying differences in values occur less frequently.

In contrast, much (but not all) of the population in the United States—as well as countries such as Canada, Australia, and Great Britain—is relatively individualistic. Many years ago, James Hodgson, former U.S. ambassador to Japan, explained one fundamental difference between U.S. and Japanese societies. His observation continues to be relevant today.

American society is first and foremost underpinned by that venerable Judeo-Christian objective of individual justice. The Japanese, however, spurn individual justice as a priority goal. Instead, they seek something in many ways the opposite; they seek group harmony. We American justice-seekers speak proudly of our rights. The harmony-minded Japanese stress not rights but relations. They reject our emphasis on individual rights as being divisive and disruptive.[51]

U.S. and Japanese Organizations. The fundamental societal differences that we've been discussing are reflected in some very basic differences between U.S. and Japanese organizations. Do these differences mean that U.S. or Japanese managers can't transfer to their organization *any* of the ideas that have worked so well in each other's countries? Not at all. For example, several Japanese management practices—such as the widespread use of team management—have been successfully adapted to U.S. operations. Over the years, U.S. organizations have created their versions of team management that reflect the need for timely decision making. Some Japanese organizations are now adopting some of these modifications. Consider, for example, Nippondenso's alternator and starter factory in Anjo, Japan. Each morning, the plant manager and a small team of employees meet. In an exercise known as a *scramble*, the group discusses a production problem—say, a drill bit on the starter assembly line that breaks too often—and approves a solution. A scramble compresses into thirty to sixty minutes an authorization process that used to take several months as it meandered from department to department. In the case of the drill bit, the group approved a worker's proposal to coat the bit with titanium, a step that increased the tool's longevity tenfold and saved the company $12,500. Says Tsutomu Maekawa, a departmental general manager, "There is one problem, one meeting, and one solution."[52]

In identifying differences between the two nations' organizations and management practices, we are painting with a broad brush. Table 4.1 broadly characterizes and compares U.S. and Japanese organizations based on six dimensions that are strongly influenced by the contrasting values of the two nations. The themes of individualism in the United States and collectivism in Japan are readily apparent.

Changing Landscape. As suggested, exceptions to the traditional patterns in Japanese organizations are becoming more numerous. Highly capable and assertive individuals do leave their organizations and start businesses of their own or join smaller organizations. In the past, firms started by such individualistic entrepreneurs included Honda, Sony, and Matsushita. Small Japanese enterprises (300 or fewer employees) can't afford to offer extensive fringe benefits as do the giant corporations. Small firms also are able to offer less job security because they are less secure in their markets. Owing to the recent recession in Japan, even large corporations, such as Toyota, have had to create a new category of temporary (contract) professional workers. Also, even large Japanese organizations have had to (painfully) lay off regular employees.

Some young Japanese workers aren't as devoted as the preceding generation is to long hours of hard work. Many young Japanese realize that some aspects of Western life-styles are preferable to their own. Some accept the concept of *flexible individualism*—not the rugged U.S. variety but a simple desire for self-expression in their work, life-styles, and possessions.

Child rearing and other household duties, once relegated completely to women, are now sometimes shared by husband and wife. Materialism is leading some families to have two wage earners. These trends in Japan appear to be a result of its increasingly global economic participation, which is modifying its once homogeneous culture.

Throughout this book, we discuss the important and unique role of value systems to management in many parts of the world.

Dimensions	Many (Not All) Major U.S. Organizations	Many (Not All) Major Japanese Organizations
Employment	Short term on average, but varies widely; unstable and insecure	Long term for males (recent decline in lifetime employment), moderately secure and stable
Salary and promotion	Merit pay based on individual contribution; rapid promotion in career	Seniority-based early in career; more merit pay later
Attitude toward work	Individual responsibilities	Collective responsibilities; group loyalty, duty-oriented
Decision making	Individual-oriented; relative top-down emphasis	Consultation oriented; bottom-up emphasis
Relationship with employees	Depersonalized; emphasis on formal contacts	Personalized; employee treated more as family member; paternalism
Competition	Relatively free and open among individuals	Low among individuals within groups; high among groups

CHAPTER SUMMARY

In this chapter, we focused on various global considerations for those engaging in international business. Organizations and individuals—both as employees and consumers—are increasingly touched by global forces and issues.

1. STATE SEVERAL CHARACTERISTICS OF THE GLOBAL ECONOMY.

Over one-fourth of world output is now traded, and middle-class consumers are emerging throughout the world. Organizations are locating operations in many countries to serve growing consumer demand. New technologies are helping create the *global village*. Quality expectations increasingly cut across national boundaries, as illustrated by the ISO 9000 quality standards.

2. DESCRIBE FIVE WAYS OF ORGANIZING TO ENGAGE INTERNATIONAL BUSINESS.

Organizational approaches to international business continue to evolve. *Involvement* in international business often begins with a commission agent and may culminate in a multinational corporation, which views issues and opportunities from a global perspective. Between the two ends of the continuum are the export manager, export department, and international corporation approaches. These organizational approaches increase in relative complexity and in the relative resource commitments required.

3. EXPLAIN SIX STRATEGIES USED IN INTERNATIONAL BUSINESS.

Such strategies include exporting, licensing, franchising, alliances, multidomestic, and global. They also vary in both relative complexity and in the relative resource commitments required.

4. EXPLAIN THE IMPACT OF POLITICAL-LEGAL FORCES IN INTERNATIONAL BUSINESS.

International business operations create new complexities, risks, and uncertainties. Broad categories of political-legal issues include domestic instability, foreign conflict, political climate, and economic climate. Political mechanisms utilized in international business include tariffs, quotas, subsidies, cartels, bribes, and extortion.

5. DISCUSS HOW THREE MAJOR TRADE AGREEMENTS AFFECT COMPETITIVE FORCES.

The General Agreement on Tariffs and Trade (GATT) helps open markets and reduce barriers (such as tariffs) among its 123 member nations. The North American Free Trade Agreement (NAFTA) further reduces barriers, encourages investment, and stimulates trade among Canada, Mexico, and the United States. The European Union (EU) is an organization of fifteen member countries. Its primary goals are to create a single market and allow the free movement of goods, services, people, and capital among its member countries. The ultimate goal is to improve the standard of living and quality of life for the citizens of the member countries.

6. DESCRIBE HOW CULTURAL FORCES AFFECT INTERNATIONAL MANAGEMENT.

The primary cultural factors that can influence how an organization is managed include views of social change (passive or active), time (scarce or unlimited), language (verbal and nonverbal differences), and value systems (individualism versus collectivism). Special attention was given to understanding how cultural issues have led to differences in the management system in Japan and the United States.

QUESTIONS FOR DISCUSSION

1. How important is it to speak the native language of a country to which you have been assigned? How would you prepare yourself for the assignment?

2. Should business school students have more formal education in international business? Why or why not?

3. What approach might a company such as Peerless Clothing use to begin doing business in India? in Russia? in Mexico?

4. Is Russia likely to be permitted to join the European Union in the foreseeable future? Why or why not?

5. Suppose that Kodak wanted to open four new plants overseas. Name four countries that might represent a high degree of risk for such operations. Would Kodak be better off exporting to those countries? Explain.

6. Which portions of the Japanese management system might be applied successfully to a U.S. car manufacturer? Could the Japanese system be applied successfully to Roadway Trucking Company? Explain.

EXERCISES TO DEVELOP YOUR MANAGERIAL COMPETENCIES

1. **Global Awareness Competency.** In response to an increasingly global economy and to capitalize on foreign markets, many U.S. firms have established international operations. This push toward globalization often results in a high demand for business professionals with international backgrounds. One way that you can take advantage of this demand is to gain some international experience of your own.

   Through its International Traineeship Exchange Program, one international student organization, the Association Internationale des Etudiants en Sciences Economiques et Commerciales (AIESEC), helps its members prepare for futures in international business. AIESEC is the largest student-run organization in the world, with 50,000 members from eighty-seven countries. It promotes internship exchanges for its members, and among its international corporate supporters are Price Waterhouse and Lufthansa.

   Find out whether your university is one of the 730 global university affiliates. Then visit the AIESEC home page at

   www.aiesec.org

   What does membership in the organization entail? What are some of the member countries? How does AIESEC strive to create cultural understanding and produce internationally marketable students? How might the organization benefit you?

2. **Communication Competency.** Imagine that you have just become an export manager of a firm and are on an overseas business trip. Your primary goal is to finalize the trade agreement that your company has been working on for the past six months. Negotiations begin as scheduled

and run fairly smoothly until you reach the final point of your presentation. Then, your bilingual foreign counterparts begin an animated discussion among themselves in their native language. The proceedings take a turn for the worse, and they state that they can't agree to your terms. What went wrong?

The most obvious way to avoid the frustration of this situation is to have a translator present. Another way is to learn the language of the host country before entering an international assignment. First, consider several countries that an employer might want you to do business in. Then, examine the foreign language (preferably conversational rather than formal) courses available at your college or university. What is offered? In addition, for a wider selection, investigate such organizations as the Boston Language Institute. The Institute offers many programs of various lengths in more than 140 languages. Decide how you can become fluent in the foreign languages that you identified as potentially relevant to an employer. You can visit the Boston Language Institute's home page at

www.boslang.com

3 **Strategic Action Competency.** With its green store interiors and fragrant aromas, The Body Shop is instantly recognizable in shopping centers around the world. Founded by Anita Roddick in 1976 and headquartered in Littlehampton, England, it has grown into a multinational corporation with 1,436 retail outlets in some forty-six countries. The Body Shop markets soaps, lotions, and cosmetics created from natural ingredients that are not tested on animals. Roddick researches formulas in diverse areas, such as the Masai in Africa. With a company culture built around environmental and human rights activism, The Body Shop actively supports international causes such as Greenpeace, Amnesty International, and rain-forest activist Survival International. Each franchise around the world is expected to uphold these fundamental values, carry the same product lines, and provide the same container-recycling program in every country. The Body Shop is rapidly expanding into new markets, with a recent entry into Singapore.

What type of international strategy is The Body Shop pursuing? Explain your conclusion. To learn more about The Body Shop, visit the company's home page at

www.the-body-shop.com

4. **Self-Management Competency.** More and more firms in many countries are conducting business overseas in an ever-expanding global marketplace. As a result, an increasing number of large organizations throughout the world are placing a premium on employees with a sense of self-awareness and a willingness to accept responsibility for continuous self-development and learning. Overseas business etiquette and cross-cultural awareness can make or break an international alliance, as rules for conducting business among countries in various regions of the world differ considerably. Take the greeting for instance. Although a simple handshake would suffice in most of the world, a bow is traditional in Asia. The term *business lunch* is interpreted much differently in the United States than in Mexico. U.S. executives tend to rush through a meal in order to talk business. Mexican executives view lunch as a time to relax and enjoy getting to know their colleagues. In Mexico, a business lunch may take as long as two- to-three hours.

Overseas business etiquette encompasses everything from wearing the correct attire to knowing what topics to avoid in conversation with international hosts. As a manager engaged in international business, you must understand the cross-cultural nuances and customs of the countries in which you do business. Select a foreign country and conduct a brief cultural audit detailing four business practices that differ from those in your country. Then find answers to the questions: Is it permissible to ask your host about his or her family? How important is punctuality? Do generally accepted nonverbal gestures in your country have different meanings elsewhere? For answers to such questions and more, consult *Trade and Culture* magazine; *Do's and Taboos Around the World*. Roger E. Axtell (ed.). New York: John Wiley & Sons, 3d ed., 1993: and Terri Morrison, Wayne A. Conway, and George A. Borden. *Kiss, Bow, or Shake Hands: How to Do Business in Sixty Countries*. Holbrook, Mass.: Adams, 1994.

5. **Teamwork Competency.** To create a "cultural dialogue," conduct a round-table or panel discussion with students from at least two (preferably more) different cultures to focus on the use of teams in organizations. Propose this activity at your next student business association meeting and have it select the countries of greatest interest. What other steps should you take to plan such an event? Based on the dimensions of the teamwork competency presented in Chapter 1, develop four culture-related topics or issues that you would like to have discussed by this round-table or panel discussion.

REAL-TIME CASE ANALYSIS

ESTEÉ LAUDER

The Esteé Lauder Companies, Inc., is one of the world's leading manufacturers and marketers of prestige skin care, makeup, and fragrance products. Sold in more than 100 countries, Esteé Lauder markets popular brands such as Clinique, Aramis, Origins, Prescriptives, Bobbi Brown essentials, and Tommy Hilfiger fragrance.

The company has long maintained a strong international cosmetics presence in Western Europe. It still achieves double-digit sales growth in the United Kingdom, Spain, Germany, and France. With this successful international experience under its belt, Esteé Lauder is rapidly moving into emerging markets. Its recent expansion into Russia, Eastern Europe, China, and Japan has broken new ground in these previously closed markets, as consumers are eagerly snapping up U.S. goods.

Russia has proven to be an extremely lucrative market for Western cosmetics companies. An estimated 81 percent of its population of 63 million women use cosmetics products regularly. Esteé Lauder has made dramatic moves to strengthen its foothold in this market by opening two shops in Moscow's prestigious GUM department store, the first Clinique boutique in St. Petersburg, and counters in Siberia and Kiev. Even though the Clinique brand was new to the Russian market, Esteé Lauder more than doubled its initial projections for its first year. Competition is fierce, however, as Christian Dior, L'Oreal, and Revlon are all rushing to sow the previously barren beauty products landscape. Each cosmetics company is attempting to adapt its colors to the tastes of the Russian market while delivering the high-quality products and services long available to other parts of the world.

Eastern Europe is at the top of Esteé Lauder's priority list. Since being introduced in Romania in May 1997, the company's Clinique line has dominated the market, selling an average of two items per transaction. Romania is a country of 23 million with a per capita income of only $100 a month. Robert Eickmeyer, senior vice-president for store design of Clinique International notes that this market is an incredible opportunity for prestige cosmetics, stating that there is "no such thing as service" in Romania and that the "whole upper end is wide open." The major draw in most of Esteé Lauder's foreign markets is the $40 gift-with-purchase. Jeanette Wagner, president of

Esteé Lauder International, recalls that a long line had formed by 8 A.M. when Clinique offered a gift-with-purchase promotion at its Prague, Czech Republic, boutique. Esteé Lauder is also examining expansion opportunities in Sofia, Bulgaria, and Belgrade, Serbia.

China is experiencing an explosion in consumerism. More than thirty stores that each contain more than 50,000 square feet serve the Shanghai metropolitan area alone. On average, Shanghai residents spend generously on cosmetics, clothing, and entertainment. To cater to this market, Esteé Lauder has installed large shops within a shop in nine Chinese department stores. Hermia Pavanetto, managing director of Esteé Lauder Hong Kong Ltd., says that these shops generate a lot of interest and traffic. However, she adds that her patrons "still do not see the difference in a $1 lipstick and a $10 lipstick."

In Japan, Esteé Lauder is taking a completely different tack. It is currently testing the open-sell concept in Tokyo's upscale Odakyu department store. Here, its cosmetics, fragrances, and accessories are available to consumers who don't have time to talk to sales personnel. This self-service concept allows customers to purchase products at their leisure, with salespeople present only as support to answer questions and perform makeovers. Within the first five days of operation, some 30,000 people visited the Esteé Lauder shop. If the open-sell concept is successful in Tokyo, the company will introduce it in other key markets worldwide.

Esteé Lauder continues to broaden the scope of its markets by expanding its product offerings and adding services such as in-store spas. Rochelle Bloom, senior vice-president and general manager of Esteé Lauder observes that success in foreign markets hinges on employee training and customer service. Because the population may be unfamiliar with the product and its attributes, she concludes, "You need to spend more time educating the consumer."[53]

QUESTIONS

1. Is Esteé Lauder an international corporation or a multinational corporation? Explain.

2. What international strategy (or strategies) is (are) being used by Esteé Lauder? Explain.

3. What political-legal forces might impact Esteé Lauder's international growth? Explain.

VIDEO CASE

DOING BUSINESS IN CHINA: GETTING PAST GREAT WALLS

A vast and tantalizing market, China is nonetheless a forbidding business challenge. A U.S. business that is considering the Chinese market faces numerous obstacles, from language to correctly appreciating consumers' interests to repatriating profit.

In 1997, Prodigy won a bid to provide Internet services throughout China. However, the contract requires that Prodigy enable the Chinese government to monitor and censor content flowing over the network. And the government recently enacted new rules against "defaming government agencies," spreading pornography and violence, and revealing state secrets, apparently out of concern for the ease by which that could occur over the Internet. The laws apply both to Internet users and providers.

Prodigy might face a clash between nations' laws and business practices similar to that between CompuServe and Germany. CompuServe was charged under German law with enabling hate crimes for allowing users to access Web sites denying the existence of the Holocaust. In the United States, even Holocaust denial is free speech protected by the First Amendment.

However, the *lack* of some legal and regulatory structures may be an impediment. In the United States, telecommunications policy has a long history under legislation and regulations administered by the National Telecommunications and Information Administration and the FCC. A rich set of services has been created in the spectrum bands allocated by the regulatory agencies. They include pagers, cell phones, commercial and citizen band radio, and the like. In many countries, China included, the spectrum is much less formally managed, and fear, uncertainty, and doubt have hindered market entrants, who fear that an early investment might be lost in the chaos of later change.

In thinking about international trade, don't assume that countries are monolithic or that a business environment will be uniform across a vast, continent-sized country with a fifth of the world's population. (Imagine trying to explain to a foreign visitor why so many U.S. corporations are chartered in tiny Delaware.) In China, the southern coastal areas present dramatically different business environments than that of Beijing or the sparsely settled, mountainous northwest region.

In 1997, China also reabsorbed the former British colony of Hong Kong, which is to be administered as a special economic zone. The fact that the handover occurred fairly uneventfully is likely a testament to the importance of economic priorities: China realizes that Hong Kong is a powerful economic engine and that any abrupt changes could trigger a market collapse or an exodus of foreign firms and investors. Similarly, the U.S. government has continually awarded China "most favored nation" (MFN) status, even while complaining about its human rights policies. "Communist China" is a multibillion-dollar market for U.S. imports and exports, whereas less economically significant "Communist Cuba" remains under a decades-long U.S. embargo.

China is steadily driving toward a market-based economy. Ironically, one of the largest business entities in the country is the People's Liberation Army, which a 1997 ABC News analysis described as owning more than 15,000 business enterprises and 50,000 factories. Recognizing that customs, attitudes, and even basic business rules may differ fundamentally is the challenge to the international business manager.

ON THE WEB

Amnesty International (***www.amnesty.org***) addresses human rights issues and documents human rights abuses around the world (including the United States, where it opposes the imposition of the death penalty in criminal cases). In 1996, one of its campaigns was aimed at China, under the slogan "No One Is Safe."

Prodigy China (***www.prodigychina.com***) is Prodigy's joint venture with Sino Telecomm. The U.S. China Business Council (***www.uschina.org***) is an association of American companies looking to do business in China. The Council, headquartered in Washington, D.C., also has offices in Beijing, Hong Kong, and Shanghai. Its work includes attempting to influence U.S. legislation relating to China and helping its members break into Chinese markets.

QUESTIONS

1. How can a U.S. company find qualified individuals to serve as its representatives abroad?

2. When China's MFN status again comes up for review, what sorts of stakeholders would have an interest in the decision?

3. Which of the managerial competencies would be important for the manager sent to establish a company's first Chinese office?

Case contributed by Ross Stapleton-Gray, President, TeleDiplomacy, Inc., a technology and policy consultancy, and Adjunct Professor in Georgetown University's Communication, Culture, and Technology program.

Chapter

5

Entrepreneurs and Small-Business Owners

LEARNING OBJECTIVES

AFTER STUDYING THIS CHAPTER, YOU SHOULD BE ABLE TO:

1. DESCRIBE HOW THE BUSINESS ENVIRONMENT SHAPES ENTREPRENEURIAL ACTIVITY.

2. EXPLAIN WHO ENTREPRENEURS ARE.

3. EXPLAIN HOW ENTREPRENEURS DEVELOP AND RECOGNIZE HOW MANAGERIAL COMPETENCIES CONTRIBUTE TO THEIR SUCCESS.

4. DESCRIBE THE PLANNING ISSUES ASSOCIATED WITH BECOMING AN ENTREPRENEUR.

5. RECOGNIZE THE ORGANIZATIONAL CHARACTERISTICS THAT ENCOURAGE INTRAPRENEURSHIP.

Outline

Opportunity in Outsourcing

Corporate Express is the world's largest direct-to-business office supply company. CEO Jirka Rysavy built this company from a money-losing stationery store, which he bought by paying $100 and agreeing to assume the store's $15,000 in debts. In the course of a year, he closed down the stationery storefront, dropped the company's small accounts, and focused on corporate clients. Sales grew by 800 percent that year. Rysavy's vision of becoming "the IBM of office supply companies" was beginning to seem feasible.

Corporate Express wasn't Rysavy's first start-up attempt. By the time he bought the Boulder stationery store, he already had opened another company to distribute environmental products and was a founding partner of Traders of the Lost Arts shop that sold Third World crafts. His success with these other small businesses may have helped him convince First Inter-state Bank to finance a $7.8 million purchase of the poorly performing stationery division of Denver's NBI. Through this and similar acquisitions, Corporate Express grew from 11 employees to 23,000 employees, and from $2 million in annual revenues to $3.2 billion. Now, companies such as Hewlett-Packard, Sun Microsystems, and Exxon save millions of dollars annually by outsourcing their stockrooms to Corporate Express.

How did this Czechoslovakian émigré who was flat broke in 1984 make his assets grow to nearly $50 million by 1997? His ability to stay focused is surely part of the story. Despite his wealth, he chooses to live alone in a small mountain cabin with no TV or running water. Being comfortable with risk also helps. Even when Corporate Express's stock price fell by 41 percent in one day, he just went home at the end of the day and followed his usual routine—a vegetarian dinner, a few hours of meditation, and a good night's sleep. "To panic in a crisis is the worst thing you can do," he explains. Instead of panicking, Rysavy has his mind on expansion and growth. With Corporate Express's operations now in the capable hands of a boyhood pal, the next frontier for this mountain-man entrepreneur is to lead the company's diversification into software distribution services and overseas growth.[1]

* * *

For additional information about Corporate Express, visit the company's home page at

www.corporate-express.com

THE RISE OF ENTREPRENEURSHIP

1

DESCRIBE HOW THE BUSI-
NESS ENVIRONMENT
SHAPES ENTREPRENEUR-
IAL ACTIVITY

ENTREPRENEUR
Someone who creates a new business activity in the economy.

One of every six business students say that owning their own company is one of their goals, and forecasters predict a large number of organizational births well into the future. In particular, an explosion in venture creation by women, immigrants, and members of minority groups is anticipated. The proportion of new business start-ups involving female entrepreneurs rose from 24 percent in 1975 to 32 percent in 1997.[2] **Entrepreneur** is the label usually given to someone who creates new business activity in the economy. During the past ten years, entrepreneurs have created several million new businesses throughout the world. Entrepreneurs are particularly active in Asia, eastern and western Europe, and increasingly so within Russia and the republics that formerly comprised the Soviet Union. In 1984, Holland registered 15,000 start-ups. In 1994, it registered 39,600, which accounted for 60 percent of the county's 100,000 newly created jobs. Gijs Donders, a 29-year-old Dutch entrepreneur who started his own mop factory says, "It's like the American dream. There is something happening here you didn't see a few years ago. Now it's cool to have your own business."[3]

Does this explosion reflect a boom in "born entrepreneurs" a generation ago? No. Rates of entrepreneurship ebb and flow with environmental conditions, and rapid technological change tends to stimulate entrepreneurship. In the United States, entrepreneurship rates rose dramatically during the 1920s and then declined during the 1930s. They rose again after World War II, but then declined during the 1950s until the 1980s. The past decade has been another period of rising entrepreneurship, initiated by innovations in microelectronics, computers, telecommunications, and information technologies. Low interest rates and higher levels of immigration also seem to contribute to higher rates of entrepreneurial activity. As more and more people become successful entrepreneurs a more favorable social climate is created that spurs others to take the entrepreneurial plunge.[4] According to some futurists, entrepreneurial Generation Xers are likely to fuel entrepreneurship in the coming decade as they seek to make the business world more responsive to social and environmental concerns.[5] Jirka Rysavy is an example of this type of entrepreneur. Money doesn't drive him. His aim is to "contribute to society [and] contribute to consciousness" and through these contributions produce a return to shareholders.

Local conditions can also stimulate entrepreneurship. Economists often argue that costs (i.e., tax rates) are an important factor, but CEOs suggest that other factors are more important. For some industries, such as entertainment, easy networking is crucial. Easy networking is what makes Culver City, California, such an attractive location for Nick Rothenberg. Positioned between Hollywood and the video production centers of Venice and Santa Monica, this Web entrepreneur says that Culver City is the kind of place where he can say to another CEO or potential client, "Let's meet at the coffee shop down the street." North Carolina's Research Triangle, near Raleigh, Durham, and Chapel Hill, has a different type of special appeal. It attracts engineers and software people and has become a mecca for science-based start-ups, taking advantage of its close proximity to the three major universities in those cities (North Carolina State, Duke, and University of North Carolina).[6] This region also is home to many new-venture incubators.

INCUBATOR ORGANIZATION

An organization that supports entrepreneurs.

The term **_incubator organization_** applies to organizations that support entrepreneurs. They rent space to new businesses or to people wanting to start businesses. They often are located in recycled buildings, such as warehouses or schools. In addition to making space available, they serve fledging businesses by offering administrative services and providing management advice. An incubator tenant can be fully operational the day after moving in, without having to buy phones, rent a copier, or hire office employees. Studies show that people tend to start businesses in the same general geographic area as their incubator organizations and to use the skills and knowledge they gained from those organizations.

SMALL-BUSINESS OWNER

Someone who owns a major equity stake in a company with fewer than 500 employees.

Even if you don't start your own company, you might work for a small, growing company someday, and that's a good reason for you to learn about management in the context of entrepreneurial firms. The U.S. government defines a small business as a company employing fewer than 500 people. So, a **_small-business owner_** is simply anyone who owns a major equity stake in a company with fewer than 500 employees. An example of one such company is Second-Chance Body Armor, which manufactures bulletproof vests and other body armor used by police officers and the military. Although it was established in 1973, this company still employs only about seventy people. The Small Business Administration (SBA) is the agency of the federal government responsible for supporting the development of small-business activity, and it offers many useful resources to help people establish and effectively manage such businesses. According to SBA statistics, in 1997 there were 22.56 million small businesses in the United States, and 1.3 million of them were started during the previous year alone. About 47 percent of all U.S. employees work in organizations having fewer than 100 employees. At a time when larger companies were laying people off, small businesses were growing in both number and size.[7] So understanding this type of company and the type of people who might run them can be useful.

THE DIFFERENCE BETWEEN ENTREPRENEURS AND SMALL-BUSINESS OWNERS

This chapter is about entrepreneurs *and* small-business owners, but keep in mind that they aren't the same. Often entrepreneurs create new business activity by starting new companies. But entrepreneurs can also create new business activity by introducing a new product or creating a new market. Thus managers in large corporations engage in entrepreneurial activity when they develop new product lines or establish new divisions to enter markets they hadn't penetrated before. In the broadest sense, then, entrepreneurs manage resources in order to create something new—a new business, a new product or service, or even a new market. Within this broad category, highly successful entrepreneurs often are differentiated from less successful entrepreneurs by how quickly they increase their new business activities. The most successful entrepreneurs are generally considered to be those whose business activities grow most rapidly.

Often people use the term *entrepreneur* incorrectly to mean *small-business owner*. Many entrepreneurs are small-business owners for a while, but not all small-business owners become entrepreneurs. That is, not all small-business owners introduce new business activity. People can become owners of small businesses by purchasing companies, inheriting them, buying franchises, and other means. Furthermore, many such owners are content to keep their businesses small. They don't expand their businesses like successful entrepreneurs do.

Another type of business that people often think of as being a small business is the family business. But actually, a family business may be large or small. And it may be growing fast or slow. There are no government definitions of ***family business,*** but usually the term is used to describe a business owned and managed mostly by people who are related by blood and/or marriage. Often these businesses are passed down from one generation to the next. As described in the Global Awareness Competency piece, in Asia the meaning of *family business* is quite different from that in North America.

FAMILY BUSINESS
A business owned and managed mostly by people who are related by blood or marriage.

WHO BECOMES AN ENTREPRENEUR?

Each year, *Inc.* magazine identifies the 500 most rapidly growing private companies in the United States. To qualify for this list, a company must be at least five years old. About 80 percent are between five and ten years old. In 1997, the average size of these 500 privately owned, rapidly growing firms was sixty-two employees, they generated $9.5 million in annual revenues, and the CEO held 56 percent of the equity.

Who are these CEOs? Most are between the ages of thirty and fifty. Only 3 percent are younger than thirty. These highly successful entrepreneurs are well educated, with 80 percent having a college degree and one-third having some type of graduate degree. Only 16 percent held an MBA, however. On average they say they sleep six hours per night and take two weeks vacation per year. Most (90 percent) didn't set out to expand their companies fast enough to qualify for the *Inc. 500* list. Instead, when they first started, they hoped to merely survive (22 percent) or grow slowly (45 percent). Finally, although most *Inc. 500* entrepreneurs are men, 10 percent were women in 1997.[8] Thus the number of women in the *Inc. 500* list is ten times greater than the number of women CEOs on the Fortune 500 list. Martha Diaz Askenazy, a thirty-eight-year-old Latina, is an example of a successful female entrepreneur. In 1993, she founded Pueblo Contracting Services in Los Angeles, employed four people, and generated $250,000 in revenue. By its fifth year, the company employed twenty-five people and generated $14 million in revenue annually. "I'm part of a growing group—I don't feel I'm alone," she says.[9]

The Chinese Family Enterprise

In Southeast Asia, family business is big business, and it means entrepreneurship. The family enterprise is the basic unit of economic activity, and 90 percent of the billionaires in Southeast Asia are ethnic Chinese. For example, Liem Sioe Liong, as founder of the Salim Group, controls Indonesia's largest ethnic Chinese enterprise. It accounts for 5 percent of Indonesia's gross domestic product, and its $3 billion in assets span seventy-five companies in twenty-four countries.

The rapid growth of Chinese family businesses reflects their entrepreneurial approach. Unlike the traditional large U.S. business, a Chinese family enterprise often consists of a vast network of businesses. Despite their size, however, these businesses bear little similarity to a complex corporation. They are managed more like a small business, held together by strong personal ties instead of formal structures, policies, and procedures. Close relatives fill most top management positions and other strategic posts. These managers accept the authority of the family head, deferring to his decisions. Professional managers (outsiders) are almost never entrusted with the business. Financial arrangements and connections among these companies are kept secret, and strategic planning activities take the form of family discussions, with the head of the family making the key decisions. Even when one of these enterprises decides to sell stock on a major stock exchange, the owners release as little information as necessary. The constant, circuitous flow of assets makes these enterprises difficult for western financial analysts to understand.

Although highly successful, this form of organizing does have its downside. For one thing, effectiveness may be needlessly limited when incompetent and untrained relatives are given jobs that require professional expertise. Even if nonfamily members are eventually hired, they may not be very productive. They have little real authority, even over those who report to them. So it isn't surprising that they generally are unsatisfied and spend their energy thinking about leaving to start their own companies. Increasingly, however, professional managers may be found within the family, as Chinese sons and daughters take their western business-school training back home. Their challenge will be to find ways to blend professional management techniques with the highly successful family approach that has worked so well for hundreds of years of Chinese enterprise.[10]

*   *   *

To learn more about business opportunities throughout Asia, visit the home page of the World Business Network at

www.wbn.org/asiaopportunities.htm

If so few highly successful entrepreneurs started out with the goal of heading a rapidly growing company, how did they get started? When today's most successful entrepreneurs were asked to explain why they started their own companies, only 16 percent said that making money was the reason. The most frequent reason given was to work for themselves and control their lives (41 percent). Other reasons included creating something new (12 percent), proving that they could do it (9 percent), not feeling rewarded in their old jobs (8 percent), being laid off (5 percent), and a variety of miscellaneous reasons (11 percent). The desire to be their own bosses often becomes strong when people discover that they can't accomplish their career goals in a large organization. For example, when Ron Canion's employer, Texas Instruments, nixed a design idea, he and a group of TI employees quit and formed Compaq Computer Company. Canion's entrepreneurial talents ensured success for almost a decade, but then the competition caught up with Compaq and the board felt that it had to replace the entrepreneurial founder.

HOW DO EMPLOYEES FEEL ABOUT WORKING IN A SMALL BUSINESS?

It's easy to imagine that working for yourself might be better than working for someone else. But even if you aren't the business owner, working in a small company is different from working for a large company. Satisfaction is one big difference. According to a Gallup poll, companies with fewer than fifty employees have the most satisfied workforces. The breakdown of "extremely satisfied" employees was as follows.

- In companies with fewer than 50 employees, 44 percent were extremely satisfied.

- In companies with 50–999 employees, 31 percent were extremely satisfied.

- In companies with 1,000+ employees, 28 percent were extremely satisfied.[11]

Table 5.1 helps explain why employees enjoy working in small companies. Obviously, small companies have some drawbacks—such as fewer benefits. But for most people, the drawbacks are offset by a more favorable work climate.

WHAT DO SUCCESSFUL AND UNSUCCESSFUL ENTREPRENEURS DO?

Successful entrepreneurs find market opportunities that others may have overlooked and form a vision of how to exploit these opportunities. Entrepreneurs position themselves well in markets that are shifting or are untapped. In this sense, they are innovative and creative. They accurately predict the direction markets are moving and then prepare to serve those markets before others are ready to do so.

People often think that entrepreneurs succeed primarily because they invent new products, but that isn't the case according to a recent study. They are more likely to succeed by offering a higher quality product or service, rather than by introducing something completely new.[12] Offering exceptional quality led to success for Ben Cohen and Jerry Greenfield. They started Ben & Jerry's Ice Cream in 1978 after enrolling in a $5 correspondence course on ice cream making from Penn State. They started making superpremium ice cream with chunks of fruit, which appealed to customers who didn't like regular ice cream. At that time, the big ice cream manufacturers (e.g., Kraft, Pillsbury, Sealtest, and Borden's) weren't in the superpremium market.[13]

Although more than two-thirds of new businesses survive at least ten years, not all new ventures are successful. Each year, thousands of owners decide to close their small businesses, and about 18 percent are forced to close because of financial difficulties.[14] According to Dun & Bradstreet and other credit-reporting agencies, the majority of failures can be traced to poor management. Also, many of those who fail don't have the stomach for hard work. In a firm just starting up, there's no substitute for hard work, which must often include sixty-plus-hour weeks. One investor remodeled a vacant service station, filled it with cases of beer, hired a few part-time college students at minimum wage to collect the customers' money, and sat back to wait for the profits to roll in. They never did. The owner's absence and failure to exert leadership led to low sales, theft, and general physical deterioration of the business.

Big Companies	Small Companies
Higher guaranteed pay	Lower guaranteed pay
Little opportunity to become very rich, for most employees	More opportunity to become very rich, e.g., through stock options
Better medical and insurance benefits	Fewer medical and insurance benefits
Expected to develop and use deep expertise in one area	Expected to use many skills and wear many hats
Little fluctuation in income	Large fluctuation in income possible when based on company performance
Feel like a cog in a machine	Feel job is important to the company and its mission
Feel insecure because of frequent organizational restructuring	Feel more secure on the job
Can gain some prestige by being associated with a well-known company	Possible difficulty in moving to a big company after working only in small companies
Less autonomy for employees to do things their own way because of hierarchy and administrative oversight	More autonomy to get the job done with less emphasis on how it gets done
Bosses' evaluation of performance and chances for advancement often unclear	Standing with boss seldom a problem

Sources: J. A. Tannenbaum. Worker satisfaction found to be higher at small companies. *Wall Street Journal,* May 5, 1997, p. B2; S. N. Mehta. It's easier for MBAs to find jobs at small firms. *Wall Street Journal,* July 8, 1997, p. B2; J. P. Kotter. *The New Rules: How to Succeed in Today's Post-corporate World.* New York: Free Press, 1995; D. Whitford. Is Fidelity losing it? *Fortune,* January 13, 1997; L. A. Winokur. Big doubts: Small business isn't necessarily a steppingstone to a corporate career. *Wall Street Journal,* May 22, 1997, p. R24; E. Felsenthal. High court makes it easier for workers to sue small firms because of job bias. *Wall Street Journal,* January 15, 1997, p. B2; J. A. Tannenbaum. The pocketbook issue: Striking it rich. *Wall Street Journal,* May 22, 1997, p. R4; and S. N. Mehta. Top down: Two entrepreneurs talk about how they try—sometimes with limited success—to provide workers with the benefits many of them seek. *Wall Street Journal,* May 22, 1997, p. R25.

However, hard work alone isn't enough, either. The entrepreneur must "work smart" and use time effectively. Some of the owner–managers who put in the most hours lose their businesses because their efforts are misdirected. They also aren't able to put the right management team together. A typical example is the inventor who spent all his time trying to sell a new product rather than hiring someone with marketing expertise to stimulate sales. Doing so would have freed the inventor to spend time in the workshop doing what he did best.

Unsuccessful entrepreneurs also fail to plan and don't prepare for expansion.[15] They don't recognize that their role must change as their organization changes. As a company grows from a one-person enterprise to a team effort to an organization requiring more than one level of management, the entrepreneur must be flexible enough to change managerial styles. The owner starts out as a creator, becomes an operator and manager, and gradually evolves into a leader. Each role draws on different competencies.

Poor money management can cripple an organization from the start. Too much capital may have been put into fixed assets (e.g., land, buildings, or equipment). Record keeping may be sloppy and haphazard. The owner may be taking too much money out of the company in salary, perks, and expenses. Cash flow problems may be caused by poor credit-granting practices or by faulty inventory management. All these factors may spell doom for a business just as it is on the verge of success.[16]

ENTREPRENEURIAL CHARACTERISTICS

3

EXPLAIN HOW ENTREPRE-
NEURS DEVELOP AND
RECOGNIZE HOW MANAGE-
RIAL COMPETENCIES
CONTRIBUTE TO THEIR
SUCCESS

The many studies of entrepreneurs that have been conducted over the years indicate that those who succeed have several characteristics in common. These characteristics include personal attributes, good technical skills, and strong managerial competencies. As shown in Figure 5.1, the combination of all of these characteristics increases the probability of entrepreneurial success.

KEY PERSONAL ATTRIBUTES

Because entrepreneurial activity is so important to economic growth, researchers have sought to understand what contributes to successful entrepreneurship. Obviously, business conditions are one important factor. But even in the best of business conditions, not everyone becomes an entrepreneur nor do all entrepreneurs become successful. A study of inventors who worked for three of the country's largest national research laboratories documented this point. The researchers were interested in explaining the differences between inventors who eventually left the labs to start their own companies, and those who didn't. This question is important because the mission of these particular labs is to improve U.S. competitiveness internationally through the transfer of technology to the prospective users of that technology. Was it something about the environment within a lab that caused some inventors to leave and become entrepreneurs? Or was it the personal attributes of the inventors? The study showed that both were important but that differences in personal attributes were more important than differences among the labs.[17]

Entrepreneurs: Made, Not Born. Entrepreneurs are different from the rest of the population, but they probably weren't born that way. Although they develop personal attributes over many years, entrepreneurs develop many of their key attributes early in life, with the family environment playing an important role. For example, women who were born first into a family tend to be more entrepreneurial than women born later into a family, perhaps because the first child receives special attention and thereby develops more self-confidence. Entrepreneurs also

Figure 5.1 **Characteristics of Entrepreneurs**

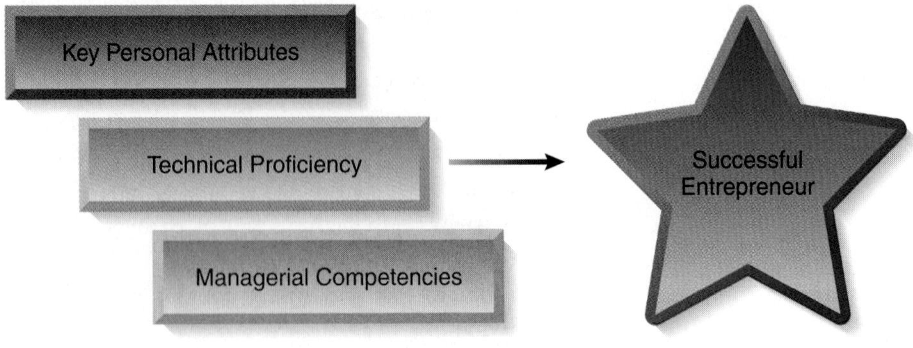

tend to have had self-employed parents. The independent nature and flexibility shown by the self-employed mother or father is learned at an early age. Such parents are supportive and encourage independence, achievement, and responsibility.[18]

Although changing personal attributes isn't easy, especially by the time people reach adulthood, developing some of these attributes may well be worth the effort. The best way is to engage in entrepreneurial behavior. Successful experiences with entrepreneurship may itself lead to the development of beneficial ways of thinking and motivation. This belief is the founding principle for organizations such as The Entrepreneurial Development Institute (TEDI), a nonprofit organization that seeks to teach entrepreneurship to at-risk youth. It was founded by twenty-three-year-old Melissa Bradley, who started a consulting company that earned $1 million her first year out of college. "I envisioned starting TEDI as a for-pay service," she admits, "but the kids I wanted to help couldn't afford it."[19] Details about the developmental experiences offered through the Institute are available on the Internet.

Entrepreneurial Careers.

The idea that entrepreneurial success breeds more entrepreneurial activity may explain why many entrepreneurs start multiple companies over the course of their lifetimes. When the successful founder of the retail catalog Gardeners Eden sold her business to Williams-Sonoma, she didn't stop being an entrepreneur. She launched another new business—the mail-order flower company, Calyx & Corolla. For some people entrepreneurship itself becomes a career. Rather than managing a business solely for income or growth, these individuals use their companies as springboards to start or acquire other ventures and then repeat the process, which is known as the **corridor principle**.[20] That is, opening a business is analogous to entering a passageway. As these individuals walk along it, they notice new corridors to explore. Had they not entered the first one, they would never have learned of the others. Once they're hooked on exploring the corridors, they become serial entrepreneurs. As the phrase suggests, a **serial entrepreneur** is a person who founds and operates multiple companies during the course of a career. Steward Edwards is one. He's founded or cofounded seven startups in five years. "I can't stop starting companies," he says. "I enjoy managing a company up to a point; then I want to go do another one." An inventor who likes bringing new products to market, he says he isn't in it for the money: "What I like to do is create," he insists.[21]

Need for Achievement.

Heading the list of key personal attributes is the need for achievement—a person's desire either for excellence or to succeed in competitive situations. High achievers take responsibility for attaining their goals, set moderately difficult goals, and want immediate feedback on how well they have performed.

David McClelland and others have conducted extensive research into the human needs for power, affiliation, and achievement. Their findings indicate that perhaps only 5 percent of the U.S. population is characterized by a predominant need to achieve.[22] Yet this need is consistently strong in successful entrepreneurs.

Entrepreneurs strive to achieve goals and measure success in terms of what those efforts have accomplished. Entrepreneurs learn to set challenging but achievable goals for themselves and for their businesses and, when they achieve them, to set new goals. Texas entrepreneur and self-made millionaire Sam Wyly recalls, "In high school, my goal was to make the football team. Having made the team, my goal was to beat Tallulah. Having beat Tallulah, my goal was for us to win the state championship. At age seventeen, I decided my new goal was to be governor of Louisiana."[23]

Olga Ramashko also liked to work toward goals. For years she toiled in Moscow as a biophysics researcher. But with the fall of communist rule, she and many other

CORRIDOR PRINCIPLE
Using one business to start or acquire others and then repeating the process.

SERIAL ENTREPRENEUR
A person who founds and operates multiple companies during the course of a career.

Russian women chose to try the entrepreneurial route. Ramashko was tired of watching her male colleagues, who she says, "were sitting there drinking tea all day, waiting to get five more, ten more, twenty more rubles. I said, 'What for? You don't deserve it. You don't do anything.'" Now she runs a skin-care products company with sales of $20,000 per month. She used her profits to build a three-story house, and began urging her daughter to start her own construction company. "Everything we earn we earn from zero," she says. "But I also like that. I like tough conditions, where you set your goals and overcome obstacles."[24]

Desire for Independence. Entrepreneurs often seek independence from others. As a result, they generally aren't motivated to perform well in large, bureaucratic organizations. They have internal drive, are confident of their own abilities, and possess a great deal of self-respect.

Many of these feelings were familiar to Joseph Khoshabe when he started United Financial Mortgage, which grew to have sales of $7 million in its tenth year. He had worked for food giant Bordens, Inc., for twenty years and was superintendent of national distribution for its Cracker Jack division. When Bordens decided to close that division, Khoshabe was prepared. He had anticipated this action and had started a mortgage brokering business on the side. He had also taken out a large mortgage to buy a 100-unit apartment complex. Unfortunately, the lender didn't like Khoshabe's choice of business partners, and on the same day he lost his Cracker Jack job, the lenders started foreclosure proceedings on the apartment building. Thinking through what he wanted to do next, Khoshabe decided he wanted to work for himself, be his own boss, gain control over his life, and prove that he could bounce back. He recalled, "If I was going to succeed or fail, it was going to be on my own." He succeeded and now looks forward to passing the company he built on to his son.[25]

Self-Confidence. A successful track record does much to improve an entrepreneur's self-confidence and self-esteem. It enables that person to be optimistic in representing the firm to employees and customers alike. Expecting, obtaining, and rewarding high performance from employees is personally reinforcing, and it also provides a role model for others. Most people want an optimistic and enthusiastic leader—someone they can look up to. Because of the risks involved in running an entrepreneurial organization, having an "upbeat" attitude is essential.

Self-Sacrifice. Finally, successful entrepreneurs have to be self-sacrificing. They recognize that nothing worth having is free. That means giving up the every Saturday golf game or the occasional trip to the mountains. Success has a high price, and they are willing to pay it. Such sacrifice can be a tough reality for entrepreneurs like Kathy Dawson, who started her own business partly because she wanted to spend more time with her family. After one particularly stressful day of juggling her work and family commitments, Dawson decided to leave the corporate scene to start her own personnel consulting firm. Three years later, her $100,000 annual income is only about half what it was when she was a corporate executive. Her husband gave up his country club membership and plays at a public course instead. She misses the perks of working for a big company—such as using the company charge card without thinking about the cost of a meal or airline ticket. Now, to keep costs down, she arranges business trips on weekends, and once again finds that being successful in her work means sacrificing time with her family.[26]

TECHNICAL PROFICIENCY

Entrepreneurs often demonstrate strong technical skills, typically bringing some related experience to their business ventures. For example, successful automobile dealers usually have acquired a fair amount of technical knowledge about selling and servicing automobiles before opening their dealerships.

Technical skills are especially important in the computer industry, which is home to about 30 percent of the fastest growing firms. Both David Filo and Jerry Yang were Ph.D. candidates in electrical engineering at Stanford University when they first began developing the software and databases that eventually became Yahoo!. As students, Filo and Yang systematically started to keep track of all the Web sites they found useful or interesting. As their list of sites grew longer and longer, they needed a way to locate and edit efficiently the material they found. They developed a search engine to locate material and the software that allowed them to classify and organize all the material. Like many entrepreneurs, Filo and Yang used their technical skills to create something they found useful. In this case, their own needs coincided with those of thousands of other Internet users, so their service was an instant success when it became available to the public in March 1995.[27]

MANAGERIAL COMPETENCIES

Managing a rapidly growing entrepreneurial company can be immensely challenging. To succeed, however, requires developing and drawing on various competencies.

Strategic Action Competency. Entrepreneurial success is often attributed to opportunistic behavior and being in the right place at the right time. Opportunity and luck may play some role in success, but sound strategic decisions also are important. A study of 906 CEOs who were winners of awards in the Ernst & Young LLP Entrepreneur of the Year Program revealed several leading strategic practices they had used to sustain rapid growth for their companies. Some of the most common strategic practices identified were

- delivering products and services that were perceived as the highest quality to expanding market segments;

- cultivating pace-setting new products and services that are first to market;

- delivering products and services that demand average or higher pricing;

- using new products and services to expand revenue by about 20 percent annually;

- generating new customers that expand revenue by about 30 percent annually;

- focusing marketing expenditures on a high-quality sales force that can rapidly expand the company's geographic presence;

- maintaining financial control of the firm; and

- linking the entrepreneur's long-term objectives to a defined exit strategy.

Although the study identified these common strategic practices, the entrepreneurs hadn't necessarily formulated them as goals early in the lives of their firms. For many, these practices emerged through their daily actions. As described in the following Strategic Action Competency feature, making decisions that support growth is an ongoing activity that occurs day in and day out. Thus a good approach is to treat a new venture like an experiment. It should be guided by a clear strategic plan focused on satisfying customers, but decisions about how to achieve the goals should be based on trying various approaches and learning by observing what happens.[28]

Margot Fraser discovered Birkenstock sandals while visiting Germany more than thirty years ago. She bought a pair, and they felt so comfortable that she arranged a meeting with the president of the company, Karl Birkenstock. He had taken over his family's 192-year-old business and was making orthopedically correct sandals for his friends and customers.

Birkenstock agreed to let Fraser have exclusive rights to distribute his sandals in the United States. She and a friend started selling the sandals in health-food and hole-in-the wall stores, offering 5 percent discounts to

retailers who paid their bills within ten days. Soon after several women's magazines featured them, the leather-strapped, molded cork–base shoes became the casual shoe of choice. Companies such as The Gap and Timberland distributed the shoe, and annual sales climbed from $9 million to $50 million. By 1989, Fraser's company had grown to almost 100 employees, and she was buying large quantities of the footwear produced by Birkenstock's German factory.

When the Berlin Wall fell in 1989, the German government offered financial incentives for companies to move into what was once East Germany. Birkenstock moved, but he encountered unexpected production problems. Former garment workers had to be trained to read leather hides for imperfections, and Birkenstock had to wait weeks or even months to get machine parts. While Birkenstock was patching up inconsistent supply lines, knockoff companies were able to copy the sandal and offer them to customers at a quarter of the price. More than 10,000 pairs of shoes at a time were showing up at European flea markets and in U.S. discount chains. At the same time, other manufacturers started producing sandals that were similar in price and style.

To counter such attacks, Fraser

pledged extraordinary service, which included shipping single pairs to retailers overnight to satisfy them. Providing the highest level of service to retailers has always been a priority at Birkenstock and catalogs and marketing material have traditionally focused more on education than selling. Fraser also ran ads in local newspapers and dropped in store names and addresses for a small fee. More recently, like many retailers, she has exploited the Internet to create an additional method of communication with both consumers and retailers. The Birkenstock home page for North America makes it easy for customers to determine their correct size, locate a store nearby, and contact shoe repair services that specialize in rejuvenating worn out, well-loved sandals.[29]

* * *

For additional information about Birkenstock, you can visit the company's German-language home page at

www.gehen.com

or you can visit the home page of the U.S. distributor of Birkenstock footwear at

www.birkenstock.com

Planning and Administration Competency. As the experiences of Fraser and Birkenstock illustrate, unexpected events often disrupt well-laid plans. Though plans may have to change, planning is nevertheless important for entrepreneurial companies, and nearly 80 percent of successful entrepreneurs put their plans in writing. As you might expect, the planning horizon is relatively short. Half the time it covers less than three years. Written monthly plans that cover periods of twelve to twenty-four months are common. As the time frame grows longer, the plans tend to become more general. For example, some may state only annual goals.

Administering the plan is important, too. Here staffing activities can be key.[30] In the start-up phase, when funds are scarce and the company has no track record, attracting top-notch employees is difficult. The founders often do most of the crucial work themselves. But to grow, they soon must hire new talent. Once the talent is on board, successful entrepreneurs tie management compensation to performance against the plan, on a monthly or quarterly basis. They also use the plan to work with employees to set job performance standards jointly.[31]

Yahoo!'s founders acknowledge that their company's rapid growth is "as much a function of serendipity as it is planning,"[32] but they wouldn't have progressed from a company with $1.4 million in annual revenue in 1995 to a company with more than $20 million in annual revenue in 1998 without using their combined planning and administration competency. In the first year, they used this competency to put in place the company's infrastructure—its technological, capital, and human resources. In the second year, they began to execute an advertising strategy. By the third year, their planning activities focused on increasing revenue to fund expanding sales and marketing activities. Planning at this stage was difficult, however, owing to the company's limited operating history and the unpredictable nature of its newly created market. For example, based on observations of other industries, they could expect seasonal fluctuations in advertising costs, but couldn't predict the pattern with any confidence. Cancellation or deferral of a few major advertising contracts could have severe consequences, yet they couldn't let this risk deter them from investing heavily to pursue new opportunities.[33] Thus, compared to more established companies, Yahoo! and other start-ups must base plans and make administrative decisions on very little hard data. Founders can't avoid uncertainty, but they can't allow it to paralyze them.

Teamwork Competency. Successful entrepreneurs are extremely hard working and task oriented, but they aren't lone wolves—one person can do only so much alone. Unless they can build an effective team, their organizations' growth will eventually reach a limit. Successful entrepreneurs are self-starters who usually support subordinates and their programs enthusiastically.[34] Entrepreneurs also maintain good relationships with their venture partners.[35] The study of 906 entrepreneurs previously described found that the majority of successful companies had a particularly effective top management team. Only 3 percent of these CEOs acted alone in their top management role. Such teams tended to be small, with 67 percent ranging in size from three to six managers, and diverse in terms of functional background. These teams were balanced by including people who had previously worked together and people who hadn't worked closely together before. These management teams used a collaborative decision-making style.

Many day-to-day problems that entrepreneurs encounter require the application of teamwork competency for effective resolution—both by top management and by lower levels of management. For instance, the owner of a small-parts manufacturing firm had to deal with a constantly recurring scheduling problem involving the production control manager and the manufacturing superintendent. Several meetings and procedural changes later, the "problem" still existed. Only in-depth interviews with the two men conducted by an outside consultant exposed the real, human problem: The older superintendent resented the younger production control manager telling him what to manufacture and when. Neither the entrepreneur nor his employees had the teamwork competency needed, so the problem persisted until the entrepreneur called in an expert with the needed competency to resolve it. In the meantime, relationships within the company and with external customers were strained.

As described in the following Teamwork Competency account, some successful entrepreneurs also use their teamwork competencies to reach beyond their own firm.

A Helping Hand

Successful entrepreneurs often enjoy extending a helping hand to someone else and watching the business grow. Michael Fields is one such entrepreneur. Fields left his position as president of U.S. operations at Oracle, a computer company, when he and CEO Larry Ellison disagreed over sales strategy. Drawing on his years of experience in the computer industry, he founded Open Vision Technologies, which specialized in storage backup and security systems. In four years, he and his management team developed the company into a $40 million enterprise that went public in 1996 and later merged with another software firm. Now he spends much of his time teaching younger entrepreneurs what he's learned, acting as coach and mentor. "Those of us who are African American in this field and have achieved certain levels of success bear a responsibility to reach back and encourage the success of others," he believes. Those whom he mentors appreciate the introductions he gives them to sources of potential capital, as well as the inspiration he offers. As one of them recalls his feelings before he met Fields, "Operating a small company, I didn't have any black mentors and I desperately needed that. I desperately needed that."[36]

* * *

To learn more about executives who are eager to extend a helping hand to new business owners, visit the home page of Service Corp of Retired Executives (SCORE) at

www.score.org

Communication Competency. For a budding entrepreneur with an idea and ambition, but little else to work with, being able to communicate effectively is essential to gaining the cooperation and support needed to turn a vision into reality.[37] Konosuke Matsushita, who built Panasonic from a start-up company to a $42 billion empire, understood the importance of communication. His competency in this area is legendary and is described in the Communication Competency account.

Much of the communication that occurs in larger companies takes the form of speeches, written reports, formal proposals, and scheduled reviews. In small companies, most communication is direct and less formal. When Paul Ralston moved from his marketing job at Body Shop International PLC to Autumn Harp, where he later became president, he noticed the difference immediately. Communications often got bogged down at Body Shop in a proliferation of memos and e-mail. According to Ralston, "You would get a lot of stuff to read, and you didn't know where it fit in." At Autumn Harp, communication was mostly face to face. "If you needed to talk to someone, you put your head around a wall," Ralston explains.[38]

For global entrepreneurial firms, communicating effectively can be more challenging. A maker of premium pet foods, IAMS, meets this challenge by sending its handful of expatriate employees home-country magazines and newsletters and keeping in touch through frequent phone calls. Director of employment, Anita Wray, realizes that this approach won't continue to work with further growth, however: "As we move forward and more people are on [overseas] assignment, we're going to have to formalize this a little more. We're going to have to assure we keep communications open. It's key," she says.[39]

The Matsushita Mindset

Konosuke Matsushita created an organization whose revenue growth was greater than that of Henry Ford, Ray Kroc, or Sam Walton, yet his name is largely unknown outside his native Japan. In 1917, Matsushita used his savings of ¥100 to start his business, with the help of his wife and four assistants. He quit his former job at Osaka Light, an electric utility, after his boss rejected his idea for a new kind of light socket. He decided to take a risk and try to make the new product himself, although neither he nor his partners knew much about how to manufacture light sockets. With considerable persistence and the help of a former Osaka Light colleague, the small team eventually found a way to produce the new socket. But because they were strapped for cash, one day they agreed to set aside their work on the socket in order to produce a large order of insulator plates needed by a distributor, who approached Matsushita about filling an order for Kawakita Electric. The Matsushitas worked eighteen hours a day, seven days a week to produce 1000 plates. The customer was so satisfied that he ordered 2000 more.

In the years that followed, Matsushita's business grew steadily as he introduced new products to meet his customers' needs. All along,

even during the trying times of the Great Depression, his actions communicated loudly the value that he placed on his employees. In 1929, there was no tradition in Japan of avoiding layoffs by shifting manufacturing employees to sales. But that's what Matsushita did when it became clear that his company needed to cut back on production and reduce rising inventories. After a visit to a religious temple, Matsushita developed the idea of increasing productivity by somehow making work as meaningful to employees as religion. He used communication to begin creating this mindset in the company. At a meeting of office workers and executives, he pointed to their collective achievement and encouraged them to think of their work as fulfilling a larger vision. "The mission of a manufacturer should be to overcome poverty, to relieve society as a whole from misery, and to bring it wealth," he said. Using tap water to illustrate his point, he continued, "This is what the entrepreneur and the manufacturer should aim at: To make all products as cheap as tap water. When this is realized, poverty will vanish from the earth." He later asked that this and his other business principles be spoken aloud each morning. He inspired his employees and succeeded in aligning them with his

vision. Many felt that they were associated with a noble and just cause, and their commitment to the company became a source of significant competitive advantage. Today, Matsushita Electric is a premier electronics company. In the United States, this company and its products are known as the Panasonic brand.[40]

* * *

To learn more about Matsushita Electric, visit the company's home page at

www.mei.co.jp

ASSESSING YOUR ENTREPRENEURIAL POTENTIAL

By now, you may be wondering whether you have what it takes to be a successful entrepreneur. Although no one can predict your success, the characteristics that many entrepreneurs have in common—including family background, motivation, and personality traits—can give you a rough idea of your potential. To learn more, take the quiz presented in the following Self-Management Competency account. Northwestern Mutual Life Insurance Company in Milwaukee prepared this quiz to help you and others like you to get an idea of whether you might have a head start or a handicap if you go into business for yourself.

SELF-MANAGEMENT COMPETENCY
Do You Have the Right Stuff?

Begin with the score of zero. Add or subtract from your score as you respond to each item.

1. Significantly high numbers of entrepreneurs are children of first-generation U.S. citizens. If your parents were immigrants, score plus 1. If not, score minus 1. _____

2. Successful entrepreneurs were not, as a rule, top achievers in school. If you were a top student, subtract 4. If not, add 4. _____

3. Entrepreneurs were not especially enthusiastic about participating in group activities in school. If you enjoyed group activities—clubs, team sports, and so on—subtract 1. If not, add 1. _____

4. Studies of entrepreneurs show that, as youngsters, they often preferred to be alone. Did you prefer to be alone as a youngster? If yes, add 1. If no, subtract 1. _____

5. Those who started an enterprise during childhood—lemonade stands, family newspapers, greeting card sales—or ran for elected office at school can add 2 because enterprise usually appeared at an early age. Those who didn't initiate enterprises, subtract 2. _____

6. Stubbornness as a child seems to translate into determination to do things one's own way—certainly a hallmark of proven entrepreneurs. So, if you were a stubborn child, add 1. If not, subtract 1. _____

7. Caution may involve an unwillingness to take risks, a handicap for those embarking on previously uncharted territory. Were you cautious as a youngster? If yes, subtract 4. If no, add 4. _____

8. If you were daring, add 4. _____

9. Entrepreneurs often speak of pursuing different paths—despite the opinions of others. If the opinions of others matter to you, then subtract 1. If not, add 1. _____

10. Being bored with a daily routine is often a precipitating factor in an entrepreneur's decision to start an enterprise. If an important motivation for starting your own enterprise would be changing your daily routine, add 2. If not, subtract 2. _____

11. If you really enjoy work, are you willing to work long nights? If yes, add 2. If no, subtract 6. _____

12. If you would be willing to work "as long as it takes" with little or no sleep to finish a job, add 4. _____

13. Entrepreneurs generally enjoy their activity so much they move from one project to another—non-stop. When you complete a project successfully, do you immediately start another? If yes, add 2. If no, subtract 2. _____

14. Successful entrepreneurs are willing to use their savings to start a project. If you would be willing to spend your savings to start a business, add 2. If not, subtract 2. _____

15. If you would be willing to borrow from others, too, add 2. If not, subtract 2. _____

16. If your business failed, would you immediately work to start another? If yes, add 4. If no, subtract 4. _____

17. If you would immediately start looking for a good paying job, subtract 1. _____

18. Do you believe entrepreneurship is "risky"? If yes, subtract 2. If no, add 2. _____

19. Many entrepreneurs put long-term and short-term goals in writing. If you do, add 1. If you don't, subtract 1. _____

20. Handling cash flow can be critical to entrepreneurial success. If you believe you have more knowledge and experience with cash flow than most people, then add 2. If not, subtract 2. _____

21. Entrepreneurial personalities seem to be easily bored. If you are easily bored, add 2. If not, subtract 2. _____

22. Optimism can fuel the drive to press for success. If you're an optimist, add 2. Pessimists subtract 2. _____

Your Entrepreneurial Quotient

A score of 35 or more: You have everything going for you. If you decide to become an entrepreneur, you ought to achieve spectacular success (barring acts of God or other variables beyond your control).

A score of 15 to 34: Your background, skills, and talents give you excellent chances for success in starting your own business. You should go far.

A score of 0 to 14: You have a head start on the ability and/or experience in running a business and ought to be successful in opening an enterprise of your own if you apply yourself and develop the necessary competencies to make it happen.

A score of minus 15 to minus 1: You might be able to make a go of it if you ventured on your own, but you would have to work extra hard to compensate for a lack of advantages that give others a "leg up" in beginning their own businesses.

A score of minus 43 to minus 16: Your talents probably lie elsewhere. You ought to consider whether building your own business is what you really want to do because you may find yourself swimming against the tide if you make the attempt. Another work arrangement—such as working for someone else or developing a career in a profession or an area of technical expertise—may be far more congenial to you and, therefore, allow you to enjoy a lifestyle appropriate to your abilities and interests.[41]

BECOMING AN ENTREPRENEUR

4

DESCRIBE THE PLANNING ISSUES ASSOCIATED WITH BECOMING AN ENTREPRENEUR

BUSINESS PLAN
A step-by-step outline of how an entrepreneur or the owner of an enterprise expects to turn ideas into reality.

Research has shown that, before going into business, entrepreneurs who are successful typically plan more carefully than those who fail.[42] One tool that helps them do so is the business plan.[43] A ***business plan*** is a step-by-step outline of how an entrepreneur or business owner expects to turn ideas into reality. A business plan also provides prospective investors with information about the new or expanding business. Table 5.2 shows the major components of a business plan.

Fledgling entrepreneurs must answer the following types of questions in their business plans.

1. What are my motivations for owning a business?

2. Should I start or buy a business?

3. What and where is the market for my product or service?

4. How much will it cost to own the business, and where will I get the money?

5. Should my company be a domestic or global company?

6. How will growth be managed?

7. What is involved in running a successful family business?

MOTIVATIONS FOR OWNING A BUSINESS

People become business owners for various reasons. Some want to make a hobby or craft pay off. Others enter businesses owned by family members. Still others choose an industry on the basis of their assessments of the growth and profit potential in that industry. One way to think about business opportunities is to classify them as lifestyle ventures, smaller profitable ventures, and high-growth ventures.

You've already read about several high-growth ventures in this chapter. These organizations have created substantial wealth for their founders, as well as others who hold a financial stake in them. By comparison, smaller profitable ventures may grow slowly over time, but the owners are content not to push constantly for growth. Family businesses and franchise operations often fall within this category.

Business concept

Describe the product

Identify the market and target customers; provide descriptive and economic data regarding demand

Define competition and present completed market analysis

Clearly articulate marketing strategy

Include location information on business, facilities, outlets, and service

Describe proposed management, leading entrepreneur profile, and key employees

Financial support

State financial needs and planned sources of capital, debt, and personal equity positions

Provide supporting documentation of financial plans:

- Projected income statement (profit-and-loss operating statement)
- Projected cash flow statement
- Projected balance sheet
- Break-even analysis of sales quantity

Incidental information

Include customer surveys, market information, and forecasts of demand and sales

Provide personal data sheets on owners, lead entrepreneurs, and key skilled managers

Give supporting information on materials purchasing, vendors, quotes, and prices

Insert facility plans, layouts, manufacturing requirements, and equipment needs

Supply credit reports, bids, contracts, and other appendices helpful to investors

Source: Adapted from J. G. Longenecker, C. W. Moore, and J. W. Petty. *Small Business Management: An Entrepreneurial Emphasis.* Cincinnati: South-Western, 1997.

LIFESTYLE VENTURE
Often a small company designed to meet the founder's desire for independence, autonomy, and control.

A **lifestyle venture** is designed to meet the founder's desire for independence, autonomy, and control. Such ventures often remain small and may even be limited to a sole proprietor. Michael Bryant's business fits this description. Bryant is CEO and sole employee of Career Transition, located in Baltimore on the second floor of his home. A consultant, Bryant helps people decide what to do with their lives. Many of his clients are sent by organizations that hope he will be able to help the employees they are laying off find new jobs, but some come to him on their own. Bryant also helps downsizing organizations with their strategic planning and offers seminars on time management and communication. He has few expenses, works a four-day week and brings in about $100,000 in a good year.

He describes himself as being as happy as "a pig in slop!" His satisfaction comes from practicing his craft, running his own business, and enjoying a lifestyle that permits him to be around when his kids come home from school and when the sun sets on his property. As a child, Bryant moved frequently—whenever his father's employer transferred him to a new location. Bryant wanted something different for his own family, so when he and his wife Nancy got married, they chose to live in a place where they were willing to set down roots.

Bryant believes that his small business is nearly ideal. "My meetings are great," he says. They are held where he wants them, with only the people he wants to attend, and they end when he says. "My personnel problems are under control. . . . There are no disturbances. And the employees are really mature about what the boss needs to get done." His administrative system is simple—and tailored to his personal needs. And he distributes all his profits to himself.

To keep his motivation high and make things fun, Bryant started playing games and using his business results to keep score. When he meets his monthly revenue goals, he rewards himself with prizes, such as a new camera or CD-ROM player for the kids or a freezer for the kitchen. He explains, "This is how I get pleasure. When I look at these numbers and say, 'I need to do something to move these numbers' and then I do something and they move, I feel terrific."[44]

Bryant clearly is satisfied with his small business operation, and in this regard he isn't unique. In general, research suggests that entrepreneurs who emphasize noneconomic goals, such as "to do the kind of work I want to do," are more satisfied than those whose motivation is primarily economic gain.[45] Of the millions of small-business owners like Bryant in the United States, many find that staying in touch with other CEOs who run similar businesses is useful and rewarding. Networking among these small-business owners is facilitated by the Small Business Advancement National Center and several affiliated regional Small Business Development Centers, which enable owners to learn about resources available locally. Local Chambers of Commerce also facilitate networking. Besides holding meetings at which local business owners can get to know each other personally, the local Chambers of Commerce often support other activities that help small businesses get good public exposure. For example, the Michigan Chamber of Commerce sponsors the ATHENA Award, which recognizes companies that make significant contributions to the professional advancement of women. Second Chance Body Armor has won this award. You might not expect a manufacturer of bulletproof vests to employ a lot of women, but Second Chance Body Armor does. About 75 percent of its workforce are women. More unusual, however, is the fact that 50 percent of the board of directors are women.

DECIDING WHETHER TO START OR BUY A BUSINESS

Prospective entrepreneurs who have the option to "start or buy" begin by weighing the advantages and disadvantages of each strategy. Sometimes, of course, the decision to start a business is made for them because they don't have the financial resources necessary to purchase an existing company.

FRANCHISE

A business run by an individual (the franchisee) to whom a franchiser grants the right to market a certain good or service.

A middle ground between starting a business and buying an existing business is to run a franchise. A *franchise* is a business operated by someone (the franchisee) to whom a franchiser grants the right to market a good or service. The franchisee pays a franchise fee and a percentage of the sales.[46] The franchisee often receives financial help, training, guaranteed supplies, a protected market, and technical assistance in site selection, accounting, and operations management. McDonald's, Domino's Pizza, Jiffy Lube, AAMCO Transmissions, and Jenny Craig Diet Centers, to name but a few, all use franchises to market their products. Whoever enters a franchise agreement obtains a brand name that enjoys recognition among potential customers. However, franchisees are their own bosses only to a degree. They can't run their businesses exactly as they please. They usually have to conform to standards set by the franchiser, and sometimes they must buy the franchiser's goods and services. But many people want to operate a franchise in the first place for these very reasons.

Buying an existing firm is more complex and may involve more risk. The seller may not reveal some hidden problems—and may not even be aware of others.

Also, many a new owner has thought that he or she was buying goodwill, only to have the previous owner open a competing firm and lure away the established clientele. The prospective buyer is wise to specify, in the purchase agreement, restrictions limiting the previous owner's ability or right to compete with the new owner. Such restrictions may limit the types of businesses that the previous owner can operate in a certain area and/or for a stipulated period of time.

As we have noted, new ventures frequently spring from an incubator organization, where entrepreneurs may develop the skills and knowledge needed for starting their own businesses. When deciding what type of business to own, people should begin by examining the abilities, interests, and contacts they can bring to their future company. Prospective entrepreneurs should examine various alternatives carefully in terms of expected revenue, the initial investment required, and the intensity of competition. This analysis often turns up existing businesses that may be purchased. In addition to exploring the Internet, business magazines, such as *Inc., Entrepreneur,* and *Venturing,* can be good sources of ideas for new ventures.

Learning about businesses available for purchase and negotiating the purchase agreement often require the assistance of experts. Bankers, accountants, attorneys, and other professionals may be aware of an opportunity to buy a business before it is publicly announced. A business broker may help the prospective owner find a firm and act as intermediary for the sale. Usually, an attorney prepares or reviews the sale documents.

In deciding whether to start a business, the prospective owner should consider the following questions, among others.

- Is there a way that I can begin the enterprise in stages or with a limited investment?

- Can I run the company at first as a home-based business?

- Can I continue working for someone else and put in time on my own business after hours?

- To what extent can I draw on relatives to help me, perhaps simply by answering the phone while I work at my regular job?

THE MARKET

The forecasting techniques described in Chapter 9 often are overlooked in planning for business ownership. Entrepreneurs frequently are so excited about their business ideas that they assume others will feel the same way. Their market research may consist of asking the opinion of a few friends or relatives about the salability of a product. Such discussions convinced CEO Nancy Deyo, founder of Purple Moon, that money was to be made by selling entertainment software for girls. Moreover, a formal market analysis supported the idea. The emerging market for software entertainment for girls aged seven to twelve was estimated to be worth $4 billion to $6 billion in 1997—a year in which CD-ROMs and online products for girls increased tenfold over the previous year.[47]

Help in targeting and analyzing markets is available to the prospective entrepreneur from numerous sources. The federal government compiles an enormous amount of data on products, industries, consumers, and other market-related categories. Public opinion and market polls also provide information. For example, a recent Harris poll commissioned by *Business Week* revealed that 21 percent of adults were using the Internet and/or the World Wide Web. In just two years, the population of users had shifted from being mostly men to almost equally split between men and women. And the age of users had shifted to include a much greater proportion of middle-aged and older users. With some 2 percent of users older than 65 making purchases over the Internet, the evidence suggests new electronic marketing channels are worthy of consideration for many entrepreneurs.[48]

How should a business plan identify the target market? Typical questions derived from a business plan (see Table 5.2) are listed in Table 5.3. These questions focus on the attractiveness of the market and on the firm's ability to capture a share of that market.

John Doerr, one of the most successful venture capitalists of all time, says that the best business plans are short. He likes to learn the details by talking with the people who will implement the plan. When he meets people to talk about their business plans, he asks himself, "Are these the people I want to be in trouble with for the next five, ten, fifteen years of my life?" Knowing that any start-up will experience unforeseeable problems, he says that for him the investment decision comes down to the management team. "I always turn to the biographies of the team first. For me, it's team, team, team." Doerr and his partners read about 2,500 plans a year, meet with about 100 teams, and invest in about 25. Among those he backed are the likes of Sun Microsystems, Compaq, Lotus, Intuit, Genentech, Netscape, and Amazon.com. Apparently, he is an excellent judge of whether a start-up team has what it will need to be a success.[49]

SOURCES AND USES OF FUNDS

Entrepreneurs are likely to overestimate their income and tend to underestimate their costs. The new-venture plan should identify anticipated costs of opening the business (e.g., deposits, fixtures, and incorporation fees). It should also include a month by month projection of the cost of goods or services sold and the firm's operating expenses for the first one to three years.

The entrepreneur must plan for obtaining funds to handle expenses, such as those associated with the start-up phase, that revenues can't initially cover. Getting

T a b l e 5 . 3	*Market Issues Facing the Entrepreneur*

- Who exactly constitutes your market? Describe the characteristics (age, gender, profession, income, and so on) of various market segments.

- What is the present size of the market?

- What strategy will you use to attract, expand, and keep this market?

- How are you going to price your products or services to make a fair profit and, at the same time, be competitive? Will you have different pricing for different market segments?

- What percentage of your annual revenue will you try to generate from *new* products and services?

- What percentage of annual revenue will you invest in developing new products and services?

- How will you market your products and services?

Source: Adapted from D. L. Sexton and F. I. Seale. *Leading Practices of Fast Growth Entrepreneurs: Pathways for High Performance.* Kansas City, Mo.: National Center for Entrepreneurship Research, 1996.

financial support is one of the most important activities that differentiates people who just think about having their own business from those who actually start one.[50] Furthermore, the larger the amount of resources obtained, the better the odds are of being able to continue in business for the long term.[51]

Common sources of funds include the entrepreneur and other members of the venture team, family and friends, financial institutions such as banks and venture capital firms, and angels. An **angel** is a private individual who invests directly in firms and receives an equity stake in return. Often such a person also acts as a business advisor to the founder. Angels seem to have some altruistic motives and often make less stringent demands than do venture capitalists. Like serial entrepreneurs, angels truly enjoy seeing a business grow and watching a start-up venture mature into a viable business. Angel Norm Brodsky has had this experience many times as an entrepreneur himself and now enjoys supporting others. "Yes, making money is important," he says. "I wouldn't go into deals unless I thought I could get my capital back and make a good return. But I really don't do this type of investing for the money anymore. I'm more interested in helping people get started in business."[52]

In the United States, venture capitalists are investing more heavily in start-ups than they did in the past, although start-ups represent only a small portion of their total business. According to a survey by Price Waterhouse, venture capitalists invested $9.5 billion in some 2,000 companies in 1996, or more than 25 percent over the preceding year.[53] To get information about venture capitalists, entrepreneurs can contact investment research firms, venture capital clubs, or the Entrepreneurial Development Institute. Sources of funds are regularly identified on the Web and in various business publications.

A sound business plan is essential to demonstrate to potential lenders and investors the viability of the proposed enterprise. Once funding is obtained, entrepreneurs should provide their financial backers with timely information and establish a trust relationship with them. This approach tends to reduce the extent to which investors feel the need to intrude into the business, and it enhances the likelihood of their reinvesting in the future.[54]

GLOBAL START-UPS

Most new ventures begin with a domestic focus, but increasingly entrepreneurs found their firms as global enterprises. Logitech—which many people know as the firm that manufactures a widely used computer mouse—is a well-known global start-up. Founded in 1982 by a Swiss and two Italians, this firm was headquartered in California and Switzerland and then spread to Ireland and Taiwan. Within seven years, it had captured 30 percent of the computer mouse market.

Global start-ups pose some special challenges to management, so the decision to found a global firm should be made only after careful analysis. A recent study of twelve global start-ups suggests some of the considerations involved in choosing between domestic and global structures. Figure 5.2 depicts the key factors affecting the decision about whether to found a domestic or global start-up. Specific considerations include the following.[55]

1. Are the best human resources dispersed among various countries? If yes, it may be easier to operate as an international company than to convince potential employees to move to your hometown.

2. Would foreign financing be easier or more suitable? If yes, consider whether the advantages of foreign financing are sufficient to offset the advantages of relying on domestic sources to meet other resources needs.

ANGEL

An individual who invests directly in firms, receiving an equity stake, and often acts as a business advisor to the founder.

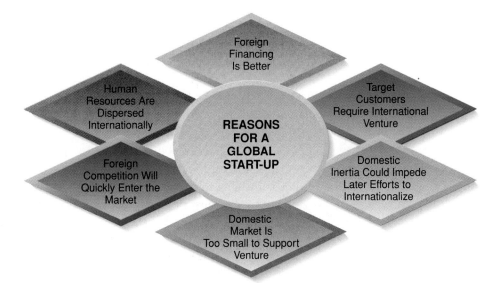

3. Do target customers require a venture to be international? If yes, a global approach may be necessary to acquire a reasonable share of the market.

4. Will worldwide communication lead to quick responses from competitors in other countries? If yes, the best domestic defense may be an international offense.

5. Will worldwide sales be required to support the venture? If initial expenses, such as R&D, will be high, worldwide sales may be necessary to generate sufficient revenue to support the venture.

6. Will domestic inertia be crippling if internationalization is postponed? Changing the ethnocentric policies, procedures, product designs, and advertising strategies of your established domestic company may be more difficult than building a globally effective firm from the beginning.

Even entrepreneurs who decide not to start with a global enterprise may quickly find that they are contemplating a change. Wendy Wigtil is president of Barnyard Babies, which produces cloth designs for children to color and is headquartered in Annapolis, Maryland. She was forced to begin marketing her toys overseas because of the declining demand in the United States for her goods and greater domestic competition, which occurred at the same time. She has positioned her company to be a successful exporter by (1) establishing a small, but financially viable market in the United States, (2) adapting her product and offering it at competitive prices in various countries, (3) realizing that success wouldn't come instantly and setting up a financial plan to help the firm, and (4) committing her firm to quality. Her plan called for the use of foreign distributors to find lucrative markets for Barnyard Babies' products instead of doing her own market research. Having distributors allows her to concentrate on designing new toys instead of flying all over the world trying to sell her toys to individual stores.[56]

GROWTH PRESSURES ON ENTREPRENEURS

Entrepreneurs often find that, as their businesses grow, they feel more and more pressure to use formal methods to lead their organizations. Entrepreneurial and formal organizations differ in terms of six business dimensions: strategic orientation, commitment to opportunity, commitment to resources, control of resources, management structure, and compensation policy.[57] These differences are compared in Table 5.4

To illustrate these differences, let's consider the experience of Gail Ray, founder of Personal Computer Rentals. It's hard to imagine a more entrepreneurial endeavor than Personal Computer Rentals (PCR) when Gail Ray founded it in 1983. She was the stereotypic "one-woman band." She met with customers; negotiated with suppliers; picked up, delivered, and installed equipment; answered the phone; and handled correspondence. She did anything and everything to get her company off the ground. Her PC rental business was an immediate success because it satisfied a significant customer need. In emergency situations, people were willing to pay almost anything to regain access to a PC, yet companies such as IBM chose not to get into the business of leasing personal computers. Ray was swamped with orders as she tried to run her business from the file room of her accountant's office.

Ray's initial backer, Edward Miranda, a stockbroker, encouraged her to expand through franchising. But before it could become a national company, PCR had to get its own house in order. Gail hired Bruce Minker to manage rentals in 1984. He found what he later described as a "scat-of-the-pants operation." Everything from equipment purchases to marketing to collections was handled on an ad hoc basis. Minker and Ray overcame the disorganization by putting in long hours and scrutinizing every detail. PCR sold its first franchise in 1985.

Immediately obvious was the fact that growth required more financing. Banks weren't interested in making loans to unproven ventures in industries that have high failure rates. With Miranda's help, Ray was able to get more equity investors. In 1987, she sold the company to a group of venture capitalists who made PCR their only investment, renaming the company PCR International. These investors wanted PCR International to become the Hertz of the computer rental market. They intended to achieve this goal by aggressively franchising Ray's concept. It worked! One of its most successful franchisees soon had more than seventy offices nationwide.[58]

Looking at the dimensions listed in Table 5.4 reveals how well a venture such as PCR in its early stages fits the pattern of an entrepreneurial organization. Gail

Table 5.4	Business Dimensions of Entrepreneurial and Formal Organizations	
Business Dimension	**Entrepreneurial Organization**	**Formal Organization**
Strategic orientation	Seeks opportunity	Controls resources
Commitment to opportunity	Revolutionary and of short duration	Evolutionary and of long duration
Commitment to resources— capital, people, and equipment	Lack of stable resource needs and bases	Systematic planning systems
Control of resources	Lack of commitment to permanent ventures	Power, status, and financial rewards for maintaining the status quo
Management structure	Flat, with many informal networks	Clearly defined authority and responsibility
Compensation policy	Unlimited; based on team's accomplishments	Short-term driven; limited by investors

Sources: Adapted from H. H. Stevenson, M. J. Roberts, and H. I. Grousbeck. *New Business Ventures and the Entrepreneur,* 3d ed. Boston: Irwin, 1994; and H. H. Stevenson and J. C. Jarillo. A paradigm of entrepreneurship: Entrepreneurial management. *Strategic Management Journal,* 11 (Summer Special Issue), 1990, pp. 27–17.

Ray sought an opportunity that larger corporations ignored or weren't in a position to seize. Actually, her first idea was to start a chain of personal computer service centers. She abandoned that plan when she learned that Xerox intended to do the same thing. She expected competition in the rental business from computer retail chains. Her timing turned out to be an advantage, though, because the retail market hit a saturation point in the early 1980s; the big retailers had to concern themselves with controlling their existing resources and couldn't expand into rentals. That gave her an opportunity to launch her firm.

Ray's management of PCR focused on market potential, refusing to be restricted by limited resources. She was even willing to sacrifice ownership of the company to obtain the resources necessary to finance its growth. Ray recognized that she was giving up the security offered by IBM for the risks associated with business ownership. She also recognized that the rewards could be virtually limitless. She and her investors foresee a time when they will sell off the enterprise for an enormous return.

For a growing number of entrepreneurs operating successful domestic companies, continued expansion eventually requires going global.[59] Wally Tsuha, CEO of auto parts supplier Saturn Electronics and Engineering, faced this fork in the road several years ago. During his tenth year of business, he realized that the auto industry was undergoing a dramatic shift—from domestic to global. To compete in this environment, he decided to acquire an ailing manufacturing company to gain access to its Mexican plant and workforce. Three years later, he expanded into China through a joint venture with Beinei Group, China's largest engine manufacturer.

Although Wally Tsuha's global expansion is still in its early stages, future growth clearly can't be assured through globalization alone. Already, another change is underway in the auto industry. Whereas carmakers once were interested in buying parts like those that Saturn Electronics and Engineering produced, they now demand systems. Large manufacturers who have bought up several parts producers and restructured them into more vertically integrated organizations are meeting many of those demands. These new organizations produce larger modules or systems, which require less assembly by the auto companies. To grow in this new competitive landscape, Tsuha began merging with other producers of electromagnetic parts in order to offer a complete electrical subsystem. His keen strategic insight and effective implementation have put Saturn Electronics and Engineering on the *Inc. 500* list for the past half dozen years. Only three other companies can match that record. Soon, however, Tsuha may have to give up some control and take this rapidly growing private company public in order to raise more funds for acquisitions.[60] According to one study of recent initial public offerings (IPOs), the fact that Tsuha's company is already operating internationally will contribute positively to earnings of the publicly traded company.[61]

MANAGING A FAMILY BUSINESS

Family-owned businesses are an integral part of the U.S. economy, responsible for nearly half the nation's gross domestic product (GDP).[62] Of CEOs on the *Inc. 500* list, 12 percent describe their companies as family businesses, and 49 percent employ family members.[63] When families enter a business, friends and others often say, Isn't it great that you all can work together? Unfortunately, however, a family business often begets a family feud, which can destroy both the family and the business. For the employees of such a firm, getting caught in the cross fire is an occupational hazard, which no one really knows how to prevent. Family feuding often leaves employees wondering whether to look for new employment. Karen Langley (not her real name) explains why she eventually left the small family-owned apparel company that she once worked for. The father, his sons, and their cousins fought constantly over the business, engaging in behavior that could best be described as back-stabbing. "It was very uncomfortable," she says. Distrust within the family was high, and it eventually spread beyond the family. One family member began accusing employees of stealing and began lurking around trying to watch everyone. "It really became impossible for me to stay there," she explained.[64]

To increase their probability of success, families should take actions to ensure that the conditions shown in Figure 5.3 are in place. The following are some specific steps to take.

1. Decide who is responsible for what. Jobs in companies just starting up shouldn't be too narrowly defined. Families should recognize each other's areas of expertise to determine who is best able to make each decision.

2. Draw up a legal agreement specifying how to dispose of, or reallocate, the equity in the business when the current head of the business steps down or dies. This task may include developing a specific plan for deciding succession issues. Investors and other outsiders have an interest in family member accord on how to handle management transitions.

3. Agree on how a decision will be made about whether and when to sell the business.

4. If the business will employ other family members, agree on the hiring criteria to be used before considering any particular family member.

5. Settle fights as they come up. If a family member does something on the job that makes another angry, correcting the problem requires that it be brought into the open.

6. Establish a board of advisers. Sometimes outsiders are needed to mediate a conflict or at least to provide a fresh perspective.[65]

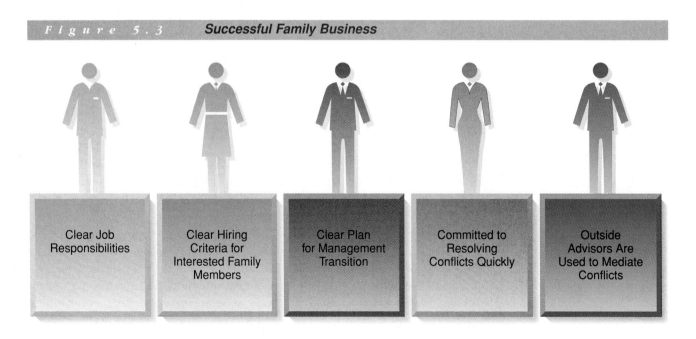

Figure 5.3   *Successful Family Business*

| Clear Job Responsibilities | Clear Hiring Criteria for Interested Family Members | Clear Plan for Management Transition | Committed to Resolving Conflicts Quickly | Outside Advisors Are Used to Mediate Conflicts |

Similar to other types of businesses, family businesses have to address issues of survival and operational issues. Survival issues may arise only once in the lifetime of the owners and the enterprise, but the way they are resolved may determine whether the firm will continue to exist. More than two-thirds of family-business owners want family ownership to continue into the next generation, but few have tackled the issues that need to be addressed to make that happen, which include

1. ensuring equitable estate treatment,

2. preparing for ownership transfer,

3. minimizing estate taxes,

4. ensuring the financial security of the senior generation, and

5. selecting and developing a successor.

Operational issues arise almost daily. Left unattended, they may become survival issues. Many operational issues that cause problems in family businesses are similar to those that might cause conflict in other types of businesses. However, because family members often are affected, emotional reactions can be more unpredictable. Particularly problematic is how to balance the need to make decisions that acknowledge both economic and "rational" criteria and personal relationship and family obligation criteria. Various family members may feel differently about the importance of these two sets of criteria, making disagreements difficult to resolve through consensus. In addition, whereas severing a relationship completely is a reasonable path to take when normal business relationships become frayed, severing relationships is an extreme and sometimes devastating way to react to frayed relationships in a family business.

If they aren't resolved, the family itself may not survive. The experiences of Mary and Phil Baechler, unfortunately, aren't uncommon. Six months after Mary and Phil had their first child, Travis, Phil invented a jogger's stroller. When Phil and Mary took turns jogging, with Travis in the stroller, people would ask where they could purchase one. Mary's father finally convinced them to start a business. So with $8,000, they founded Racing Strollers in 1984.

Mary was talked into running the office from the couple's kitchen table. Phil and Jim, a close friend of the family, rented a small garage and built strollers every weekend. They often worked until the wee hours of the morning trying to fill orders.

After the Baechlers placed a small ad in Runner's World, customers started calling at all times of the day and night, assuming that operators were standing by to take orders. Mary couldn't stand putting a customer on the answering machine and spent countless hours taking orders. Phil just let customers put their orders on the answering machine. Mary had the ambition to make it big, always going that extra mile for a customer. Phil wasn't as driven and didn't go that extra mile. He enjoyed being an artist and designer, wanting only a sense of fulfillment and reasonable financial security. Mary wanted Phil to become a manager and take as much interest in their employees and customers as she did. She viewed the business as a religion and got hooked on making money. Phil wanted a life away from work once they got home. He didn't want to hear about problems at Racing Strollers. He'd been there all day and was bored with the employees' and customers' problems. Mary took all the problems home and wanted to discuss them.

After several years of nearly going broke, the business became profitable in 1988. In 1994, the ten-year-old company had sales in excess of $5 million. The Baechlers' family income rose, enabling them to move into a larger house. Both were working long, hard hours and joked that they each needed a spouse. While the business was doubling at least once a year, the marriage paid the price. When the strain, urgency to move the business forward, and neglect of the family clearly put too much strain on their marriage, the Baechlers had to make a choice. Mary finally chose business over marriage, and the couple started divorce proceedings. The company now operates under the new name, The Baby Jogger Company, with Mary as the CEO. The new company continues to sell the original stroller invented by her husband, as well as several other models developed since then.[66]

Anyone employed in a family firm—whether a family member or an outsider—is affected by how the family gets along. Their relationships and interactions influence the company's competitive position and survival prospects, career advancement opportunities, employee motivation and morale, and employee quality of life at work as well as at home.

CORPORATE INTRAPRENEURSHIP

5

RECOGNIZE THE ORGANI-
ZATIONAL CHARACTERIS-
TICS THAT ENCOURAGE
INTRAPRENEURSHIP

CEOs of large organizations recognize that entrepreneurial behavior within their companies can produce growth and profits. In fact, such behavior may be necessary for long-term survival.[67] Thus corporate entrepreneurship, once considered a contradiction in terms, is becoming more and more widespread.

Consider for a moment why an organization exists. It has some mission—some goals to be accomplished—that requires the efforts of more than one person. At the very least, a business has the goal of satisfying customers so that it can be profitable over the long run.

Fundamental to organizing is dividing up the work. Managers may think that they have organized successfully when they have brought different interests together, minimized conflict, increased stability, and reduced uncertainty. But they often overlook the effects of those organizing efforts on entrepreneurial tendencies. Is the new climate conducive to change? Will disruption be tolerated? Is redirection possible?

Large organizations usually are formally structured, for efficiency. Their managers run operations in such a way that the same activities will continue indefinitely into the future. Obviously, this approach often is at odds with innovation and change. Employees come to take the working environment for granted, and individual efforts to foster change may be met with resistance. What then can be done to encourage entrepreneurship when a company needs to be revitalized? The answer lies in changing—perhaps even inciting a revolution in—an organization's practices. One way to do so is for the company to support intrapreneurs.

INTRAPRENEUR

Someone in an existing organization who turns new ideas into profitable realities.

Gifford Pinchot III coined the term *intrapreneur* to describe someone in an organization who turns ideas into profitable realities.[68] Jacques Robinson and Howard R. Stevenson, Jr., who teamed up to rejuvenate General Electric's video products division, are intrapreneurs. Robinson provided the risk-taking environment in which Stevenson was able to design circuitry that brought the quality of standard television sets up to the level of computer monitors. This advance made using ordinary sets with home computers, video games, and video cameras more practical than it had been.

The introduction of the IBM personal computer represents another intrapreneurial activity. The company assigned development of the PC to Philip Estridge. He and his group proceeded to violate many time-honored IBM traditions. They used outside suppliers to speed up development and hold down costs, rather than depending solely on other IBM divisions. And they marketed PCs directly through retailers, rather than relying on IBM's sales organization. Estridge was able to accomplish his vision because initially he had the support of top management. Owing to differences that eventually arose between Estridge and corporate management, however, he later left IBM.

COMPETENCIES OF INTRAPRENEURS

Not every employee can become a successful intrapreneur. It requires unusually well-developed strategic action, teamwork, and communication competencies. The person who is going to establish a new intrapreneurial venture must have a dream. Yet this dream, almost of necessity, is going to be at odds with what the rest of the organization is doing. So, to establish the new venture, the individual will have to sell that dream to others while simultaneously challenging the organization's beliefs and assumptions. Having successfully communicated a dream that others buy into, developing the venture requires that the intrapreneur build a team to work on the venture, crossing departmental lines, structures, and reporting systems. Intrapreneurial activities can cause some disruption, particularly in large organizations where each manager's "turf" has been staked out carefully over the years, so being diplomatic and avoiding win–lose conflicts is essential. Even diplomats aren't immune to the frustrations that occur throughout the establishment of any new intrapreneurial venture, so a strong support team is needed to carry the intrapreneur through endless trials and tribulations.

FOSTERING INTRAPRENEURIAL ACTIVITY

Top management can foster an intrapreneurial culture by eliminating obstacles and providing incentives for intrapreneurship.[69] Organizations that redirect themselves through innovation have the following characteristics.

- **Commitment from senior management.** Such commitment must include a willingness to tolerate failure. Top managers must regularly communicate their commitment to intrapreneurial activities—and back their words with actions.

- **Flexible organization design.** Intrapreneurial organizations are designed for fast action. Management gives information—and the authority to make decisions—to those best positioned to react to changing market conditions. These people often are first-line managers.

- **Autonomy of the venture team.** Closely aligned with flexibility is maintaining a hands-off policy in day-to-day management of the team charged with implementing an innovation. Successful intrapreneurs usually are allowed considerable leeway in their actions.

- **Competent and talented people who exhibit entrepreneurial behaviors and attitudes.** A willingness to volunteer isn't sufficient reason to assign someone to a venture team—that person also must be competent in that or a related area. Competent volunteers usually have experience in, or have received training for, new-venture creation. Some companies conduct formal training programs; others establish mentor or coaching relationships. Even so, most intrapreneurs have experienced at least one failure before achieving successes that more than offset early losses.

- **Incentives and rewards for risk taking.** Intrapreneurs may not be willing to risk their careers and undergo the frustration of forcing change only for the satisfaction of giving life to their ventures. The developers of successful ventures should be generously compensated. Intrapreneurship should not be a dead-end activity; rather, it should be linked to an identifiable career path of advancement.

This recognition is especially important because it helps ensure that the intrapreneur's next new venture won't become a spin-off from the company!

- **An appropriately designed control system.** Nothing is more stifling to an intrapreneurial activity than bureaucratic controls. Nevertheless, despite the potential contradiction between strong controls and the intrapreneurial spirit, senior management can't give up its accountability for new-venture projects. Controlling internal innovations means collecting and analyzing data that enable management to predict, to a reasonable degree, where the new-venture team is headed. It also involves ensuring that the team understands the difference between intrapreneurial behavior and irresponsible risk taking. Obstacles that inhibit intrapreneurial management generally are structural and deeply ingrained within the firm. Unfortunately, those obstacles are considered to be appropriate practice under some styles of management.

INTEGRATING INTRAPRENEURSHIP INTO AN ORGANIZATION

SKUNKWORKS
Islands of intrapreneurial activity within an organization.

Top management must allow intrapreneurial activities to flourish as a part of the organization's normal day-to-day operations if it wants to reap long-term rewards. These islands of intrapreneurial activity have been called *skunkworks.* The subculture within skunkworks is similar to those in many incubator organizations. Formal rules and procedures are ignored in favor of experimentation and innovation. Violations of reporting policies and review procedures are tolerated by top management, however, as long as the team stays focused on helping the company bring new products and services to market ahead of competitors.[70] As is true for standalone new ventures, tying performance to rewards can keep the skunkworks team focused on its goal. Incentives should reward its cooperation with other parts of the organization and those units that cooperate with and support the intrapreneurial project. Finally, in order for intrapreneurial activities to occur, top management must provide appropriate leadership. People generally are recruited to intrapreneurial activities by charismatic leaders, who support norms and values that foster innovative activity.

Of course, a large organization isn't likely to support a particular skunkworks operation forever. If the effort succeeds, operations will be formalized, and the team might become the nucleus around which a new department is formed. If the effort fails to meet expectations, it might be closed down. A third possibility is to spin off the skunkworks and allow it to operate as a separate division or subsidiary. This approach allows the parent organization to obtain a return on its investment while keeping the entrepreneurial spirit alive.

Thermo Electron's CEO George Hatsopoulos has used this spin-off strategy for the past decade with great success. Founded in 1956, Hatsopoulos's idea was to create a company that would develop and bring to market technologies to address society's needs. Currently, the company is a leading manufacturer of environmental monitoring and analysis instruments and a major producer of paper-recycling equipment. It also is involved in various other businesses related to environmental quality, health, and safety. More important to the CEO than these particular current products is that Thermo Electron continue to create new businesses that serve society's emerging needs. As a result of the spin-off strategy, Thermo Electron's structure is much like that of a network organization. It included eight spin-offs in 1995 and nineteen by 1997. By 1997, Thermo Electron's family of companies operated in twenty-two countries with 20,000 employees and generated nearly $3 billion in annual sales.

If the managers at Thermo Electron could have their way, they would spin off all the company's divisions. They would prefer to run their own businesses because they're very much aware of the rewards of doing so. But Hatsopoulos has strict criteria for deciding what to spin off. These criteria generally are the same as those any investor might use when evaluating the likelihood of a new venture's success: a solid business plan for growth, a solid top management team that he can trust, and a receptive market.[71]

CHAPTER SUMMARY

In this chapter we showed how the business environment can encourage small-business and entrepreneurial activity. People choose to work in small businesses and entrepreneurial organizations for many reasons, but a common thread is the desire of individuals to be their own boss and feel in control of their work life.

1. DESCRIBE HOW THE BUSINESS ENVIRONMENT SHAPES ENTREPRENEURIAL ACTIVITY.

Entrepreneurial activity fluctuates over time, but currently is on the rise in the United States and around the world. Rapid technological change, low interest rates, and high immigration rates all stimulate entrepreneurial activity. Local conditions that meet the needs of entrepreneurs—such as a good labor force and easy networking—also can stimulate entrepreneurial activity.

2. EXPLAIN WHO ENTREPRENEURS ARE.

Entrepreneurs are people who create new business activity in the economy. If they do so by starting a new company, entrepreneurs are also small-business owners. Other entrepreneurs create new business activity within large organizations. Often the reasons that entrepreneurs give for starting their own companies are to be their own bosses and have more control over their lives. When they start their companies, the goal of many entrepreneurs is to grow slowly. When their companies grow rapidly for a sustained period of time, however, they are considered to be more successful. Offering a high-quality product or service is the most common strategy used by successful entrepreneurs. The reality is that many new businesses fail. Poor management, not putting in enough effort, ineffective top management, and failing to plan for expansion are some of the reasons that new businesses fail.

3. EXPLAIN HOW ENTREPRENEURS DEVELOP AND RECOGNIZE HOW MANAGERIAL COMPETENCIES CONTRIBUTE TO THEIR SUCCESS.

Personal attributes that characterize entrepreneurs include the need for achievement, desire for independence, self-confidence, and willingness to make personal sacrifices. These attributes often are developed early in life and seem to be shaped greatly by the family environment. Having a parent who was an entrepreneur and being involved in entrepreneurial activities increase the likelihood that a child will become an entrepreneur. Among the attributes that characterize successful entrepreneurs are need for achievement, a desire for independence, self-confidence, and a capacity for self-sacrifice. Entrepreneurs usually are technically proficient in areas related to their businesses. Managerial competencies are as important for entrepreneurs as they are for other managers. Strategic action, planning and administration, teamwork, and communication competencies seem to be especially important for entrepreneurs.

4. DESCRIBE THE PLANNING ISSUES ASSOCIATED WITH BECOMING AN ENTREPRENEUR.

Entrepreneurs can improve their chances for success by creating a business plan and following it. A prospective entrepreneur must consider questions such as: (1) What are my motivations for owning a business? (2) Should I start a business or buy one? (3) Is there an adequate market for my product or service? (4) How much will it cost, and where will I obtain the start-up funds? (5) Should I start a domestic or global organization? (6) How will I manage growth? (7) What is involved in running a successful family business? Operating a family business leads to some unique opportunities and some special problems. Failure to manage them can spell doom for the company as well as the family.

5. **RECOGNIZE THE ORGANIZATIONAL CHARACTERISTICS THAT ENCOURAGE INTRAPRENEURSHIP.**

Intrapreneurship involves turning ideas into marketable products and services. Fostering intrapreneurship and successfully marketing new ventures require a commitment by management, flexible organizational structures, competent and talented intrapreneurs, incentives and rewards for risk taking, and appropriate control systems. To encourage innovation and prevent formal rules and procedures from interfering with the development of new ideas, large organizations often set up skunkworks teams. Their activities are less formalized, and they usually have unique subcultures.

QUESTIONS FOR DISCUSSION

1. What does it take to start an entrepreneurial business? Why do so many entrepreneurs fail?

2. What are the advantages and disadvantages of working for a small company?

3. A study of the practices of successful entrepreneurial firms found that offering high-quality products and services is the most common strategy of fast-growing companies. Why is this strategy so effective, compared to, for example, a strategy of offering a lower cost product or service or introducing a completely new product or service without regard to quality?

4. Why would an entrepreneur prefer to launch an entirely new venture rather than buy an existing firm?

5. What special challenges do global start-ups pose for their founders? What are some ways to address these special challenges?

6. Increasing numbers of women are choosing to start their own businesses. Why are they doing so? What are the social implications of large numbers of women becoming successful entrepreneurs?

EXERCISES TO DEVELOP YOUR MANAGERIAL COMPETENCIES

1. **Strategic Action Competency.** Imagine that you're thinking about starting a new business. Your idea is to use home-based sales representatives to sell educational toys directly to parents of young children. However, you aren't sure whether the market for toys is likely to grow or shrink during the next decade. Gather some data to help you predict the market for children's toys. Begin by studying data provided by the Bureau of the Census at

   www.census.gov

2. **Global Awareness Competency.** Regardless of the size of the domestic market for toys, you know that the world population is increasing rapidly, so you need to consider the possibility of a global start-up. Your idea is to use recent immigrants to the United States as sources of sales to people in other countries. Use data available from the U.S. Bureau of the Census to choose a country in which you might be able to use this strategy. Describe the advantages and disadvantages that you would likely face if you were attempting to sell toys in the country you chose. General information about issues related to direct selling and network marketing is available from the Direct Selling Association at

   www.dsa.org.uk

3. **Planning and Administration Competency.** Obtaining funding for a new venture is one of the key first steps toward success. Investigate what you should do to increase your chances of developing a business plan that would appeal to venture capitalists and angels and identify some specific possible sources of funds. Begin your research by visiting sources such as the National Association of Young Venture Capitalists at

   www.capitalventure.com

4. **Self-Management Competency.** Imagine that you're interested in starting your own company

someday but that you're not ready to do so just yet. Instead, you want to get a job in a large company known for being highly innovative and supportive of intrapreneurship. As you learned in this chapter, Thermo Electron (**www.thermo.com**) is one such company. Others known for their intrapreneurial cultures include 3M (**www.mmm.com**) and Xerox (**www.xerox.com**). Using the Internet or other means, visit these or other intrapreneurial companies to identify the types of jobs available and the qualifications needed by those hired. Develop a list of things you could do during the next year to increase your chances of being able to land a job that interests you.

5. **Teamwork Competency and Communication Competency.** Working with a small group of other students, develop a mission statement for a new business venture. Then prepare a ten-minute oral presentation that you could give to a potential angel, explaining why you think your business could succeed and the reasons why the angel might be particularly interested in working with your management team. To develop more insight into what angels might be looking for, visit the two Web sites

www.venturesite.co.uk

and

www.nebib.nl

REAL-TIME CASE ANALYSIS

HARVEY'S PRO HARDWARE

Bigger is better, and biggest is best. That seems to sum up the changes in retailing during the decade of the 1990s. With mega-competitors like Home Depot and Wal-Mart, is there any way that a small family hardware store can survive, let alone thrive? Brothers Gary and Jeff Katz think that there is. Selling hardware is in their blood, it seems. Back in 1923, their great-grandfather opened a hardware store in Revere, Massachusetts. Eventually that store was passed down to their grandfather. When their father returned home from service in the Korean conflict, he worked for a while in the family store, too. But before history could repeat itself again, Harvey Katz decided to strike out on his own. If he would assume the $5,000 debt being carried by the owner of a paint-and-wallpaper store, the store was his. He took the risk and made the move twenty miles down the road to Needham. After a year of spending his days helping customers pick the perfect pastel paint to match their flowery wallpaper borders, Harvey decided that he was in the wrong business. Hardware was more his style, he thought, and he soon converted his store.

Harvey Katz has since retired. He still hangs around his old store, but now his oldest son is the primary owner. Together, the two sons run the place. And, as any local will tell you, it's quite a place. Every nook and cranny is stuffed with stuff. The value of its inventory, measured in dollars per square foot, is three times the industry average for similar stores. And sales per square foot is quadruple the industry average. The variety of merchandise is tremendous, and that's one reason customers keep coming to Harvey's. In a region where people live in homes built before the Revolutionary War, demand for the old and the odd is high. Nevertheless, if customers left the store having bought only what they came in for, Harvey's probably couldn't survive. Thanks to Harvey's expert sales staff, many customers find more than they were looking for when they came in. That's how the store generates annual sales of $228,000 per employee and $2.5 million net. Both figures are about twice the industry average.

With thousands of items in stock, the sales staff is a key asset. Salespeople lead customers through the steel jungle to find desired items. Along the way, chances are they'll discover a few additional items. If it isn't actually in the store, the staff probably can find it in one of the business's nearby warehouses. In addition to its unsurpassed inventory, Harvey's offers unsurpassed service. The staff is knowledgeable and eager to educate customers. Extending their service strategy, the owners recently added a service center to the store. Appliance repairs, minor home repairs, warranty work, and locksmithing—all are now available. Today, Harvey's is thriving. Will the same continue to be true when Gary and Jeff Katz retire?[72]

QUESTIONS

1. Is Harvey's Hardware a dinosaur on the brink of extinction? Or is it the ideal antidote to the frustration that many consumers experience when shopping at suburban supercenters? Use the Internet to learn more about the competitive

forces shaping the selling of hardware. If Gary and Jeff Katz asked for your advice about tactics and strategies to use in going forward, what would you tell them? Should this fourth generation of managers continue to rely on the tried and true strategy that has worked for fifty years, or should they develop new ideas to carry them into the years ahead? To answer this question, study the information about the industry provided by the National Retail Hardware Association at

www.NRHA.org

2. Compare the successful managerial competencies Harvey Katz used to those his sons are likely to need in the years ahead. Do the Katz brothers need the same competencies as the owner of a Home Depot store? Explain. For more information about Harvey's Pro Hardware, visit the company's home page at

www.barveysprohardware.com

For more information about Home Depot, visit the company's home page at

www.HomeDepot.com

3. As their inventories continue to grow, Gary and Jeff Katz might wonder whether they could increase the family's fortunes if they opened another store in the same general region. What issues would this idea raise for the family? How should the family decide whether doing so is a good idea and, if so, who would run the new store? Use the Internet to develop some suggestions for the family to consider. A good way to begin your exploration is by visiting the Net Marquee Family Business Net Center at

www.nmq.com

VIDEO CASE

SECOND CHANCE BODY ARMOR: TRUSTING YOUR GUT

Second Chance Body Armor's story is a classic "bullet-proof rags-to-riches" tale of American entrepreneurship. Entrepreneurs may launch a new venture for any number of reasons. Some entrepreneurs are former salaried workers who might have left a job in order to gain more creative control over their ideas. Some are seemingly addicted to the creation of new companies and will launch, develop, and exit many new businesses in the course of their careers. In Richard Davis's case, Second Chance grew out of a dramatic personal experience: a shoot out with robbers attempting to hold up his previous small business.

The U.S. economy is extremely friendly to the entrepreneur, with minimal impediments to start-ups. Second Chance began as a "doing business as" venture; that is, an unincorporated business. Other structures, such as Subchapter S corporations, have been created to make formation of new, small businesses possible.

Davis launched his business on a shoestring: Second Chance's assets were little more than a roll of ballistic nylon and $70 in cash. However, many entrepreneurs also secure more substantial start-up capital through loans, venture investors, friends, and family. In addition to being a source of funding, an entrepreneur's family can be an important source of critical moral support.

The entrepreneur can find him- or herself spread across the spectrum of corporate roles. While most may sport "president" or "CEO" on their business cards, they may also be wearing a half-dozen other hats. Like Davis, the entrepreneur will often serve as marketing impresario, though most stop short of shooting themselves in the stomach as Davis has done more than a hundred times!

Second Chance's use of actual customers in the company's advertising (as is shown on the corporate Web site, where products are modeled by "Save No. 450," etc.) conveys a powerful message: "These people do what you do and this product could save your life, too." And Second Chance's rationale for lighter, flexible products—that many of those killed in shootings may have had body armor but chose not to wear it because of its weight or bulk—distinguishes it from its competition. Even as an established industry leader, the company still has the feel of an entrepreneurial start-up: lean and mean and highly attuned to its customers' needs.

Entrepreneurs can rapidly dive into a perceived new business niche, but they may need to react just as quickly to a negative development. In 1997, a bill was introduced in California to ban mail-order sales of body armor in an attempt to keep it out of the hands of felons. If such a law were enacted, Second Chance's current marketing and sales practices might be jeopardized. It might have to quickly restructure itself for retail store sales in California or shift its efforts to other jurisdictions. Larger companies might resort to lobbying to head off such legislation; smaller companies like Second Chance might do so as members of a coalition of similarly affected companies.

ON THE WEB

Second Chance has a simple Web site which conveys the company's philosophy and product and contact information. The Michigan Chamber of Commerce at ***www.voyager.net/mcofc/*** honored Second Chance with its ATHENA award, given for "significant contributions to the professional advancement of women in the workplace."

The Web provides a wealth of information for the new entrepreneur and is an ideal medium for entrepreneurs to gauge the markets and niches they may seek to enter. The Internet is also an efficient and effective means for small businesses to seek out the service providers—for tax preparation, training, or other contact help—they may need to round out a new start-up venture. The Morino Foundation, a non-profit organization, established the "Netpreneur" program at ***www.netpreneur.org*** to promote new information technology ventures in the Washington, D.C., region and has developed resources and forums to serve the needs of entrepreneurs.

Many venture capital firms, particularly those seeking to fund Internet and new-media-oriented start-ups, are also on the Web. At the higher end of the entrepreneurial scale, several companies have even used the Internet to promote direct public offerings—sale of the company's stock without resorting to the resources of an underwriter.

QUESTIONS

1. How does Second Chance market its product?

2. How might a new entrant into Second Chance's market compete?

3. What problems might have threatened Second Chance as an infant company?

To help you answer these questions and learn more about Second Chance Body Armor, visit the company's home page at

www.secondchance.com

Case contributed by Ross Stapleton-Gray, President, TeleDiplomacy, Inc., a technology and policy consultancy, and Adjunct Professor in Georgetown University's Communication, Culture, and Technology program.

Chapter

6

Ethics and Corporate Social Responsibility

AFTER STUDYING THIS CHAPTER, YOU SHOULD BE ABLE TO:

1. STATE THE IMPORTANCE OF ETHICS FOR ORGANIZATIONS AND THEIR EMPLOYEES.

2. DESCRIBE HOW THE SOCIETAL, LEGAL, ORGANIZATIONAL, AND INDIVIDUAL PERSPECTIVES FOR ASSESSING ETHICAL CONDUCT INFLUENCE DECISIONS AND BEHAVIOR.

3. DISCUSS THE STANDARDS AND PRINCIPLES OF UTILITARIAN, MORAL RIGHTS, AND JUSTICE MODELS OF ETHICS.

4. EXPLAIN HOW THE STAKEHOLDER APPROACH CAN BE USED TO GUIDE ETHICAL DECISION MAKING AND ACTION.

5. RECOGNIZE WHEN WHISTLE-BLOWING MAY BE AN EFFECTIVE WAY TO STOP WRONGDOING AND BE ABLE TO MAKE A WELL-REASONED DECISION ABOUT WHETHER YOU SHOULD BLOW THE WHISTLE.

Outline

Can Patagonia Change the World?

A recent visit to Patagonia's home page revealed that the company wanted to fill two positions: Director of Supply Chain Integration and Internet Program Manager. Hundreds of possible job applicants could have the technical skills and managerial competencies needed for these jobs, but how many would fit this description: "Demonstrated environmental activism is a requirement"? At Patagonia, a company that designs and manufactures specialty sportswear, social responsibility and activism seem to be more important than financial success. And as long as founder and entrepreneur Yvon Chouinard is still around, that's not likely to change at this privately held company. Chouinard spends most of his time far away from the company, leaving day-to-day management tasks to professional managers. But even those managers who are directly responsible for watching the company's financial health have been carefully screened to ensure that their values are in line with those of the activist founder. A CFO who thinks the bottom line is all she needs to worry about might find it difficult to adjust to working in a company that is used as a tool for social change. In the past, Chouinard openly expressed his disrespect for traditional business values—he referred to most businesspeople as "greaseballs." Nevertheless, a company the size of Patagonia, which faces strong competition from companies such as L. L. Bean, REI, and Lands' End, can't thrive if it ignores the advice of its accountants and financial experts. But can CFOs who care as much about the environment as they do about the bottom line really be counted on to keep the company financially sound?

For years, Patagonia did extremely well, growing steadily to reach $24 million in annual sales by the mid-1980s. Then it quickly tripled in size. Chouinard had set a goal of $250 million in annual sales because he wanted more funds in order to pursue his social causes. To encourage growth, he seemed to hire everyone he met whose values fit the company's goal, despite warnings from his professional management team. Eventually, the financial problems mounted to a point where they could no longer be ignored. In 1991, Patagonia was forced to lay off 20 percent of its workforce and Chouinard was forced to rethink his approach to business. Can a company that wants to make the best quality outdoor clothing in the world become the size of Nike? Was the idea of improving the environment incompatible with manufacturing clothing—when the process of producing such goods is itself a process that pollutes the environment? Which is the more socially responsible course of action: trying to use a business to lead the process of change or getting out of business altogether?

Back in 1991, Chouinard spent several months thinking long and hard about questions such as these. In the end, he decided to stay in business and continue to use Patagonia as a tool for creating change. He also committed his company to a course of action that was intended to ensure the company's survival for another 100 years. It dropped 30 percent of its clothing lines, reduced its advertising, and began making major changes in its manufacturing processes, based on the results of its environmental audit results. Because Chouinard owns Patagonia, he can run the company in a way that is consistent with his values and passion for the environment, even if doing so means being somewhat inefficient. Nevertheless, some people wonder whether Patagonia can continue to stay in business as a clothes manufacturer and, at the same time, have a net positive impact on the environment.[1]

* * *

To learn more about Patagonia, visit the company's home page at

www.patagonia.com

IMPORTANCE OF ETHICS

1

STATE THE IMPORTANCE OF ETHICS FOR ORGANIZATIONS AND THEIR EMPLOYEES

Patagonia's approach to ethics and corporate social responsibility represents a proactive strategy designed to go beyond the minimum standards of integrity imposed by laws and government regulations. The program is based on the assumption that managers and employees are guided by more than economic interests; that personal and societal values should also guide a company's actions. The day-to-day decisions and actions of people at various levels of an organization can make real a stated mission of to "do no harm."

The ethical issues facing managers and employees have grown in significance in recent years. By some estimates, fraudulent activities cause 30 percent of U.S.

business failures.[2] No industry seems to be immune. In recent years, business scams have brought down financial institutions such as Kidder Peabody, discount retailers such as Phar-Mor, and even businesses based on religion, such as Jim Bakker's PTL ministry. These and numerous other high-profile scandals have drawn stakeholders' attention to the effects of unethical business practices and fueled demands for reform.[3]

In a world of increasing local and global competition for both employees and customers, being in step with society's expectations can be beneficial to everyone over the long run. In a survey of MBA students at fifty schools, half the respondents said that they would accept lower pay to work for a company they believed was "very socially responsible." Forty-three percent said that they wouldn't take a job at a company that wasn't socially responsible.[4] Patagonia's commitment to ethical practices makes it highly attractive to many students seeking employment. Customers, too, appreciate companies that don't take economic advantage of them. In the aftermath of Hurricane Andrew, Home Depot's nineteen Southeast Florida stores sold storm-related building materials, such as plywood and roofing shingles, at cost plus freight. Home Depot's policy contrasted strikingly to the widespread price gouging that occurred in the area at the time. By forsaking short-term profits derived from the tragedy of the storm, Home Depot strengthened its long-term bond with customers. As one Home Depot customer said to the *New York Times:* "If they had spent $50 million on advertising, they couldn't have bought the goodwill they got by doing this."[5]

In this chapter we focus on the complex ethical and social responsibilities facing organizations, managers, and employees alike. We begin by outlining four perspectives—societal, legal, organizational, and individual—that both influence and define ethical and unethical decisions and behavior. The potential conflicts inherent in organizational ethics become even more evident when we review the utilitarian, moral rights, and justice ethical models. We then describe the stakeholder approach to considering issues of ethics. An analysis of stakeholders' interests can help decision makers recognize the unavoidable conflicts among them and aid in the search for solutions that balance and respect those interests. Finally, we discuss the issue of how you should behave if you witness unethical or illegal business practices.

ETHICS
A set of rules and values that define right and wrong conduct.

PERSPECTIVES FOR ASSESSING ETHICAL CONDUCT

2

DESCRIBE HOW THE SOCIETAL, LEGAL, ORGANIZATIONAL, AND INDIVIDUAL PERSPECTIVES FOR ASSESSING ETHICAL CONDUCT INFLUENCE DECISIONS AND BEHAVIOR

MORAL PRINCIPLES
General rules of acceptable behavior that are intended to be impartial.

In the most elementary sense, *ethics* is a set of values and rules that define right and wrong conduct. They indicate when behavior is acceptable and when it is unacceptable. In a broader sense, ethics includes (1) distinguishing between fact and belief, (2) defining issues in moral terms, and (3) applying moral principles to a situation.

Moral principles prescribe general rules of acceptable behavior that are intended to be impartial. They are of great importance to a society and can't be established or changed by the decisions of powerful individuals alone; nor are they established as "true" solely by appeals to consensus or tradition.[6] Moral principles and the values they represent are fundamental to ethics. As you will learn in this chapter, some moral principles concerning managerial and employee behavior are widely shared, but others are not.[7]

What is considered ethical may depend on the perspective from which ethical issues are considered. Figure 6.1 identifies the four basic perspectives from which ethical values and decisions can be evaluated. Rarely can the ethical implications

Figure 6.1   *Ethical Perspectives for Evaluating Behavior*

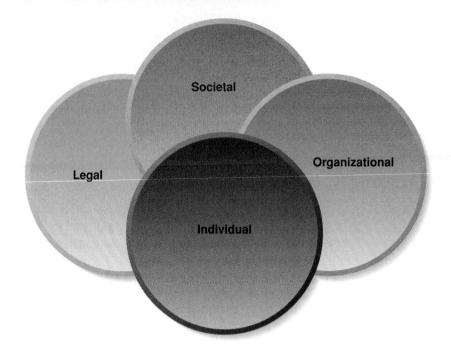

of decisions or behaviors be understood by considering only one of these perspectives. In other words, ethical decisions and behavior need to be evaluated from a systems viewpoint. In this section we explore the perspectives shown in Figure 6.1 and describe their interplay in terms of ethical decisions and behavior.

SOCIETAL PERSPECTIVE

A large part of any view of what is ethical comes from the society in which the behavior occurs. In the United States, the results of various public opinion surveys suggest growing disenchantment with the lack of ethical behavior in general and with managerial ethics in particular. Do you agree or disagree with the following statements?

1. The ethical standard of business managers and executives is only fair or poor.

2. White-collar crime is common or somewhat common.

3. The lack of ethics in businesspeople is contributing to crumbling moral standards.

4. People are less honest today than they were ten years ago.

5. Businesspeople harm the environment to maintain profits.

6. Executives and managers put workers' health and safety at risk to maintain profits.

These statements were presented to adults in several surveys. The following percentages of those surveyed *agreed* with the statements: item 1, 58 percent; item 2, 90 percent; item 3, 76 percent; item 4, 54 percent; item 5, 47 percent; and item 6, 42 percent.[8]

In contrast to these relatively negative survey results, a comprehensive survey of managers revealed that 80 percent thought their organizations were "guided by highly ethical standards."[9] However, the lower level managers responding to the survey were more likely than top managers to say that their organizations were not guided by highly ethical standards. These survey results suggest that the general public perceives serious ethical problems in the way that business is conducted generally, whereas managers tend to see serious ethical problems in business as exceptions that grab headlines.

Managers and employees work in more of a fishbowl than ever before. The media expose and report on decisions and behavior, which then are judged publicly by many different pundits and interest groups. In 1966, public interest groups through the U.S. Surgeon General forced tobacco companies to put warning labels on cigarette packaging. In 1971, pressure from these same groups forced tobacco companies to agree to ban tobacco ads on TV and radio. More recently, continued pressure from groups working on behalf of the public interest has resulted in even more severe restrictions on this industry. Dozens of studies have shown that smoking and chewing tobacco have negative health consequences, including an estimated 400,000 deaths annually in the United States alone. Tobacco-related health problems, in turn, generate huge medical costs, which ultimately are paid for by taxpayers and anyone who pays for private health insurance.

When the Attorneys General of forty states decided that the tobacco companies should be held legally liable for such costs, the potential financial implications were so great that the tobacco companies agreed to a settlement, which Congress and the president have to approve. Initial estimates put the costs to the industry at $368.5 billion. The tobacco companies are to get immunity from class-action lawsuits and a limit on damage claims. In exchange, the tobacco companies agreed not to oppose a new tax on cigarettes, to take actions to attempt to reduce teen smoking, to withdraw advertising believed to be especially appealing to youth, and to set aside funds to settle future lawsuits.[10] No one expects the restrictions placed on tobacco companies to affect their activities in foreign markets. In fact, the American public has paid little attention to what U.S. tobacco companies do abroad. The same isn't true in other industries, however.

Public interest groups concerned about human rights have protested conditions in offshore apparel manufacturing, affecting a wide range of companies. Conditions in a shoe manufacturing plant in Donguann, China, illustrate the problem. Some 50,000 employees, many of them younger than the Chinese minimum age of sixteen for working in factories, make products for Nike, Adidas, Reebok, LA Gear, Puma, and New Balance. Many aren't even paid the Chinese minimum wage of $1.90 per day, with no benefits. They work under conditions that are typical in the region but are harsh by global standards. Mandatory overtime hours typically amount to eighty hours per month, or double the amount allowed by Chinese law. Meal breaks last only ten to fifteen minutes. At other factories in the area, conditions are even worse. Some of those employers attempt to reduce employee turnover by requiring employees to pay a "deposit" equivalent to two weeks pay. Employees forfeit the deposit if they leave before their contracts expire. Other employers confiscate migrant workers' identification papers so that they can't job hop or even remain in the city.[11]

If a company operates in many different countries, local standards for ethical conduct may differ greatly from one location to the next. Hence developing ethical guidelines that make sense in various settings can be a complex task.[12] Some companies apply U.S. standards for ethical conduct universally in the belief that this approach won't violate ethical principles elsewhere. Other companies adapt to local practices, arguing that ethical standards make sense only when considered within a particular societal context.

Even in the same society the view of what is ethical and legal changes over time. Changing societal views of ethical behavior eventually result in new legal requirements. However, before laws and government regulations are changed, managers and their organizations may take voluntary actions that reflect their personal and corporate values and beliefs and their assessments of the public's changing ethical stance. Consider, for example, alcoholic beverages. During prohibition (1919–1932), buying and drinking alcohol was illegal throughout the United States. Now, buying and drinking alcohol are illegal for people of particular ages and for people living in some "dry" localities. Although such actions aren't uniformly banned by federal law and regulations, society's concerns about the consequences of alcohol use are still felt.

As is true for tobacco, federal laws regulate corporate advertising of alcoholic beverages. Organizational decision makers in companies that produce and distribute alcohol, in turn, must decide how to navigate society's shifting ethical and legal currents. One approach is to be as aggressive as possible, while staying within the letter of the law. Another approach is to carve out an advertising strategy that is sensitive to society's opposition to using advertisements to encourage the nation's youth to engage in behaviors that are potentially dangerous. Both approaches can satisfy legal codes of conduct, but either approach might be viewed as unethical, depending on an individual's values and perspective.

LEGAL PERSPECTIVE

LAWS

Society's values and standards that are enforceable in the courts.

What a society interprets as ethical or unethical frequently ends up being expressed in laws, government regulations, and court decisions. ***Laws*** are simply society's values and standards that are enforceable in the courts. The legality of actions and decisions doesn't necessarily make them ethical, however. At one time, for example, U.S. organizations could legally discriminate against women and minorities in hiring and promotions. As a consensus developed that such discriminatory practices were unethical, laws such as the Civil Rights Act of 1964 were passed to stop the practices and ensure equal employment opportunities for all citizens. In addition, the federal government issued regulations requiring government agencies and federal contractors to work at correcting the effects of past discrimination. Affirmative action programs were one outcome of such regulations. During the 1970s and 1980s, large corporations invested millions of dollars designing, implementing, and evaluating affirmative action programs intended to reverse the effects of decades of employment discrimination against women and minorities.

However, in recent years, the equity and effectiveness of affirmative action have been called into question. Although the principle of equal employment opportunity is still widely accepted, people disagree about how best to apply it. Opponents of affirmative action argue that such programs also are discriminatory (causing reverse discrimination) and should be discontinued. California voters outlawed state-sponsored affirmative action programs by passing Proposition 209. That action doesn't affect businesses directly, but, because California is known as a bellwether state on social issues, it can't be ignored. It is forcing business leaders to take a stand on the issue of affirmative action.

Another recent California initiative that affects businesses more directly is the City of San Francisco's requirement that companies that do business with the city must offer benefits to domestic partners of employees. Cities such as San Francisco argue that imposing such restrictions on business is their prerogative. If companies want to take advantage of such benefits as the tax incentives that cities often offer to businesses, they may have to be responsive to local social issues that are important to city residents and that influence their local regulations.[13]

EMPLOYMENT-AT-WILL

A traditional common-law concept holding that employers are free to discharge employees for any reason at any time and that employees are free to quit their jobs for any reason at any time.

The legal concept of employment-at-will provides another example of the interplay between changing societal views and changes in the law. ***Employment-at-will*** is a traditional common-law concept holding that employers are free to discharge employees for any reason at any time and that employees are free to quit their jobs for any reason at any time. Historically, employers often dismissed employees, especially those in managerial positions, without explanation (at will). During the past twenty-five years, though, courts have modified the freewheeling notion that employees can be fired for any reason. Besides prohibiting discriminatory firings, employers have been held liable for firing employees for reasons that violate an important public policy.[14] For example, employers cannot legally fire people for refusing to lie in a legislative hearing, for blowing the whistle about illegal conduct by their employers, or for filing workers' compensation claims.

With respect to dealing with customers, the classic legal concept of *caveat emptor*—"let the buyer beware"—used to be the defense for a variety of shady business practices. During the 1950s and 1960s, an increasingly aware public began to challenge the ethics of such a position. Shifting societal attitudes and values concerning *appropriate* behavior by businesses led to a flood of U.S. consumer legislation during the late 1960s and early 1970s, which substantially diminished the concept of *caveat emptor*. In the 1990s, quality improvement practices and customer-oriented practices make such an approach to customer relations almost inconceivable.

On some issues, both societal opinions and legal precedents clearly define whether a behavior is ethical. When behavior is clearly unethical and illegal, taking a stand that satisfies both the courts and the public is relatively easy for companies. In that case individual employees also have clear knowledge of what's right and what's wrong. In such situations, societal values and standards of behavior are clearly understood and are reinforced by the law. But in many areas of business practices, judgments about right and wrong fall within a gray area of ambiguity. How should employees behave when the laws are unclear or conflicting, or when societal opinions have shifted and old laws are being questioned as unethical? Under these circumstances, employees must look to their personal values and beliefs and the standards, policies, and practices of their organization.

ORGANIZATIONAL PERSPECTIVE

To provide guidance for employees, an organization can define ethical and unethical behaviors.[15] Organizations can also guide employee actions both formally and informally. The most fundamental informal source of guidance is top management's behavior, which demonstrates the ethical principles that are important to the organization. Even within the same company, however, different departments may have different ethical subcultures.[16] In other words, the behaviors of middle and lower level managers can also send signals about what is considered ethical conduct. More formal sources of guidance include policy statements, codes of ethics, speeches, publications, the content of training programs, and disciplinary actions taken against employees who act unethically. The nature of an organization's culture, leadership, reward systems, and practices can work for or against ethical conduct.[17] An organization isn't likely to design reward systems intentionally that will encourage unethical behavior, but often that's just what happens. Consider what happened at Columbia Hospital Corporation of America. Managers at headquarters set quotas for doctors. The quotas were reasonable and most doctors achieved their goals. Management then decided to set more difficult "stretch" goals. These goals were challenging, and most doctors worked hard enough to achieve them. Managers set the next round of goals even higher. Some doctors fell short of the goals, and began to fear the consequences. Out of fear, they figured out ways to "game" the system and appeared to be meeting their goals. Managers again increased quotas so that even the most hard-working doctors couldn't reach them. They, too, began to game the system. The process continued until eventually no one could achieve the goals honestly. By then, almost all the employees had learned how to play the "game," and everyone felt entitled to cheat to protect their jobs.

Situations like the one just described are common. One survey of more than 4,000 employees found that 29 percent felt pressure to engage in conduct that violates their companies' business standards in order to meet business objectives. About 25 percent reported that their managers looked the other way and ignored unethical conduct in order to achieve their business objectives.[18]

Whereas some managers are willing to look the other way, other managers believe that business organizations can be a powerful force for positive change. Members of the Caux Round Table agree with this perspective, as explained in the Global Awareness Competency feature.

INDIVIDUAL PERSPECTIVE

Despite prevalent societal, legal, and organizational interpretations of what is ethical, individuals have their own values and a sense of what is right or wrong. Lawrence Kohlberg (1927–1987) probably is the best-known scholar in the field of the psychology of ethical decision making and behavior. Kohlberg's model of moral development is useful for exploring questions about how members of an organization regard ethical dilemmas, including how they determine what is right or wrong in a particular situation.[19] Kohlberg held that people develop morally, much as they do physically, from early childhood to adulthood. As they develop, their ethical criteria and patterns of moral reasoning go through *stages of moral development.* Figure 6.2 shows these stages of moral development, ranging from the lowest (obedience and punishment orientation) to the highest (universal ethical principles). Kohlberg didn't assume that everyone progresses through all the stages. For example, an adult criminal could be stuck in the first stage.

A person at the *obedience and punishment stage* does the right thing mainly to avoid punishment or to obtain approval.[20] In other words, only the immediate consequences of an action determine whether it's good or bad. An employee stuck at this stage might think that the only reason not to steal money from an employer is the certainty of getting caught and then fired or even arrested. Most organizations

STAGES OF MORAL DEVELOPMENT

According to Kohlberg, people develop morally by going through six stages of moral development: obedience and punishment, instrumental, interpersonal, law and order, social contract, and universal principles.

Figure 6.2 **Kohlberg's Stages of Moral Development**

Universal Principles

Social Contract

Law & Order

Interpersonal

Instrumental

Obedience & Punishment

Childhood ⟶ Through ⟶ Adulthood

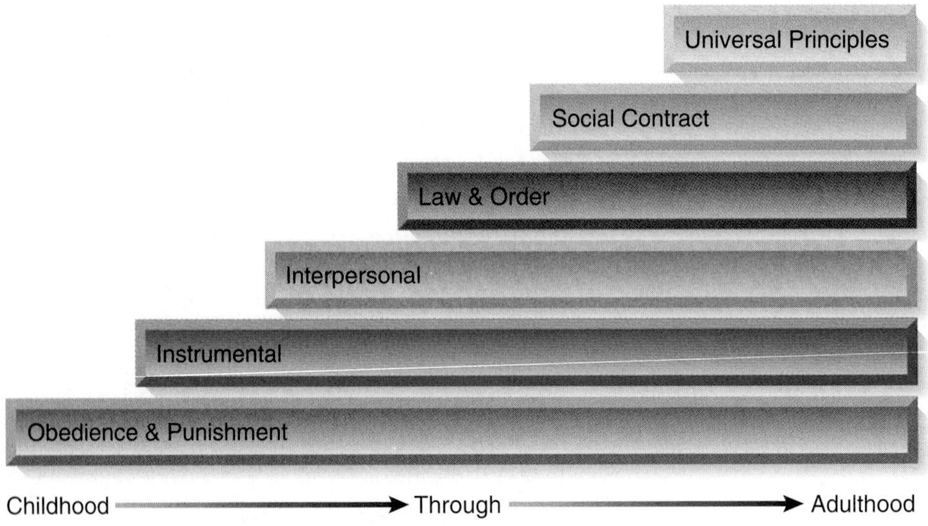

Principles of the Caux Round Table

The Caux Round Table refers to an international group of executives who collaborated to develop general principles for businesses to follow in their activities around the world and now promote their adoption. The framers of these principles sought to establish a set of standards against which socially responsible organizational performance can be evaluated.

The principles are rooted in the Japanese concept of *kyosei,* or the idea of "living and working together for the common good." The Caux Round Table General Principles are summarized as follows.

- **Responsibilities of Businesses:** Beyond Shareholders toward Stakeholders: Businesses are viewed as having value to the extent they create employment and marketable products and services. The role of business includes sharing the wealth it generates to improve the lives of customers, employees, and shareholders.

- **Economic and Social Impact of Businesses:** Beyond Shareholders toward Justice and World Community: Businesses established in foreign countries should contribute to the social advancement of those countries.

- **Business Behavior:** Beyond the Letter of Law toward a Spirit of Trust: Sincerity, candor, and truthfulness contribute to the efficiency of business transactions, especially at the international level.

- **Respect for Rules:** Businesses should respect international and domestic rules and recognize that some behaviors that are legal may, nevertheless, have adverse consequences.

- **Support for Multilateral Trade:** Business should support multilateral trade systems, such as GATT/World Trade Organization, and cooperate in efforts to promote global commerce.

- **Respect for the Environment:** Businesses should protect and improve the environment, promote sustainable development, and prevent wasteful use of natural resources.

- **Avoidance of Illicit Operations:** Businesses should avoid participat-ing in corrupt practices such as bribery, money laundering, drug trafficking, and trading arms used for terrorist activities and should seek to eliminate them.[21]

* * *

The Caux Round Table is an initiative supported by the Minnesota Center for Corporate Responsibility (MCCR), an affiliate of St. Thomas University. For additional information, visit the MCCR home page at

www.stthomas.edu

don't want employees who use such simple reasoning to guide their behavior when faced with ethical dilemmas.

A person at the *instrumental stage* becomes aware that others also have needs and begins to defer to them to get what the individual wants. Proper behavior is what satisfies the person's self-interest. At times, self-interest can by satisfied by making deals or exchanges with other people. An employee at this stage might be willing to defer to the needs of the employer to reduce absenteeism, but only if the employer gives something in return.

A person at the *interpersonal stage* considers appropriate behavior as what pleases, helps, or is approved by friends or family. Proper behavior exhibits conformity to conventional expectations, often of the majority. At this stage, being seen as a "good person" with basically good motives is important. An employee at this stage might focus on the importance of being a loyal employee and colleague who is always friendly and who avoids or smoothes conflict. If absence creates conflicts or work overload for other employees, some people at this stage might be willing to reduce their absences even if that meant not using all of their allotted sick days.

A person at the *law and order stage* recognizes that ethical behavior is not determined only by reference to friends, family, co-workers, or others whose opinions the individual might value. Proper behavior consists of doing a person's duty, showing respect for authority, and maintaining the social order for its own sake. Loyalty to the nation and its laws are paramount. The person sees other people as individuals and also as parts of the larger social system that gives them their roles and obligations. An employee at this stage may rigidly adhere to organizational rules and regulations and legitimate orders from superiors. The employee is likely to resist or criticize the efforts of co-workers or superiors to bend or break the rules. For example, in some organizations employees commonly take paid sick days even when they aren't sick. Employees may even encourage each other to take all their sick days. They view these leave days as something the company owes them. However, the company policy or union contract may state that sick days are allowed only for legitimate illnesses. In this situation, employees at the law and order stage might resist peer pressure to take a day off if they aren't ill. They would view company rules or the union contract as overriding the somewhat selfish interests of their peers. At this stage of moral reasoning, rules are considered to be necessary for the effective functioning of the entire organization, and they should be followed even when it requires some self-sacrifices or resisting pressures from peers.

A person at the *social contract stage* is aware that people hold a variety of conflicting personal views that go beyond the letter of the law. A person at this stage understands that, although rules and laws may be agreed upon and for the most part must be impersonally followed, they can be changed if necessary. Some absolute values, such as life and liberty, are held regardless of different individuals' values or even majority opinion. "The greatest good for the greatest number" is the characteristic ethical norm at this stage.[22] People at this stage would recognize that employees of organizations are expected to follow the rules but would also accept the notion of breaking the rules when those rules conflict with accepted social values. They might accept the notion of a company permitting employees to be absent for only a specified number of days. But if they believe that the absentee rules unduly restrict employees' freedoms, they might also feel justified in breaking the rule or might actively work to modify the rule to make it less restrictive. For example, they might encourage their employer to specify an allowable number of days off per year and allow employees to take these days for whatever reasons they choose.

Finally, someone at the *universal principles stage* views appropriate conduct as determined by a person's conscience, based on universal ethical principles. Kohlberg felt that universal principles are founded in justice, the public welfare, the equality of human rights, and respect for the dignity of individual human beings. In his model, people at the most advanced stage of ethical reasoning recognize these universal principles and act in accordance with them rather than rules or laws.

ETHICAL MODELS

3

DISCUSS THE STANDARDS AND PRINCIPLES OF UTILITARIAN, MORAL RIGHTS, AND JUSTICE MODELS OF ETHICS

Kohlberg's stages of ethical development describe how people develop an approach to determining what is right and wrong. His model doesn't directly address the question of what behaviors are ethical in organizations. Other scholars who address this question have identified three models for describing the ethical frameworks used in organizations: the utilitarian, moral rights, and justice models.[23] Like Kohlberg's stages, these models describe different approaches to thinking about ethics. But unlike Kohlberg's, the assumption here is that anyone can adopt these different models to guide his or her behavior. In other words, which model people use when making judgments of right and wrong is unrelated to their level of development or maturity. Moreover, these models can be applied to issues that involve ethical questions and used to describe ethical decision making and behavior from the perspective of individuals, organizations, and society. Thus each model provides a different but somewhat related set of principles or standards for judging the right or wrong of managerial and employee decisions and behavior.

The three models can, at times, reinforce and support particular decisions and behavior. At other times, certain decisions and behavior may be ethical from the perspective of only one model. In general, a proposed course of action that is supported by all three models is probably the ideal solution. However, in complex decision-making situations with conflicting individual and group interests, the ability to find such an ideal solution may be more the exception than the rule.

Before continuing to study this chapter, please take a moment to fill out the questionnaire in the Self-Management Competency feature on pages 190–191. Then calculate your score.

UTILITARIAN MODEL

The *utilitarian model* focuses on actions (behaviors), not on the motives for such actions.[24] It is most consistent with Kohlberg's social contract stage. A manager or employee guided by this model considers the potential effects of alternative actions from the perspective of the accepted social contract. The alternative chosen is supposed to benefit the greatest number of people, although such benefit may come at the expense of the few or those with little power. In other words, this alternative may help some individuals but harm others. As long as potentially positive results outweigh potentially negative ones, the decision maker considers the decision to be both good and ethical.

In the U.S. economic system, the principles of capitalism have defined the social contract that governs business decisions. Under capitalism, the primary managerial obligation is to maximize shareholders' profits and their long-term interests. Nobel Prize–winning economist Milton Friedman is probably the best-known advocate of this approach.[25] Friedman argues that using resources in ways that do not clearly maximize shareholder interests amounts to spending the owners' money without their consent—and is equivalent to stealing. According to Friedman, a manager can judge whether a decision is right or wrong by considering it's consequences for the company's economic needs and financial well-being. If it improves the financial bottom line it's right, but if it detracts from the financial bottom line, it's wrong. The utilitarian model drives companies to assess constantly how activities—even so-called "charitable" contributions—are related to business performance. A recent survey of contributions managers found that two-thirds were struggling to show how the company's donations and community service programs contribute to corporate goals.[26]

According to the utilitarian model, all employees should strive to use the company's resources to increase its profits and engage in activities designed to do so, while staying "within the rules of the game. These rules include open and free competition without deception or fraud."[27] The utilitarian model prescribes ethical standards for managers and employees in the areas of organizational goals, efficiency, and conflicts of interest.[28]

Organizational Goals. Providing the greatest good for the greatest number in a competitive market system means focusing on maximizing profits. Achieving high

SELF-MANAGEMENT COMPETENCY
Managerial Values Profile

The Managerial Values Profile is designed to help managers identify the value premises that guide their managerial actions. The results can be useful for people who wish to better understand the determinants of their own actions, as well as those who want to broaden their perspectives on managerial ethics.

Instructions

Twelve pairs of statements or phrases follow. Read each pair and check the one that you most agree with. For example, do you agree with 1 or 2? 3 or 4? 5 or 6? You may, of course, agree with neither statement; in that case, you should check off the statement that you least disagree with, the "lesser of the two evils."

It is essential that you select one and only one statement or phrase in each pair; your Managerial Values Profile cannot be scored unless you do so.

_____ 1. The greatest good for the greatest number	or	_____ 2. The individual's right to private property	
_____ 3. Adhering to rules designed to maximize benefits to all	or	_____ 4. Individuals' rights to complete liberty in action, as long as others' rights are similarly respected	
_____ 5. The right of an individual to speak freely without fear of being fired	or	_____ 6. Engaging in technically illegal behavior in order to attain substantial benefits for all	
_____ 7. Individuals' rights to personal privacy	or	_____ 8. The obligation to gather personal information to insure that individuals are treated equitably	
_____ 9. Helping those in danger when doing so would not unduly endanger oneself	or	_____ 10. The right of employees to know about any danger in the job setting	
_____ 11. Minimizing inequities among employees in the job setting	or	_____ 12. Maintaining significant inequities among employees when the ultimate result is to benefit all	
_____ 13. Organizations must not require employees to take actions that would restrict the freedom of others or cause others harm	or	_____ 14. Organizations must tell employees the full truth about work hazards	
_____ 15. What is good is what helps the company attain ends that benefit everyone	or	_____ 16. What is good is equitable treatment for all employees of the company	

(Continued)

profits is thought to result in the highest quality products and the lowest prices for consumers. Profits are seen as the reward for satisfying consumers. If profits get too high, new competitors will enter the market, thereby increasing the supply of high-quality goods and pushing prices down. According to Friedman, no firm *unilaterally* should go beyond what the law requires—for the sake of helping preserve the environment, for example. Doing so would only reduce that firm's profits and would do nothing to eliminate the pollution caused by its competitors. They would obtain a greater share of the market and profits because of lower costs and thus lower prices. Friedman contends that the government is responsible for protecting the environment and should pass environmental laws and regulations that apply to *all* companies.

Efficiency. Managers and employees alike should try to attain organizational goals as efficiently as possible. Efficiency is achieved by both minimizing inputs (e.g., labor, land, and capital) and maximizing productive outputs. For example, if technologies are available that allow a firm to produce goods or deliver services at

	17.	Organizations must stay out of employees' private lives	or		18.	Employees should act to achieve organizational goals that result in benefits to all
	19.	Questionable means are acceptable if they achieve good ends	or		20.	Individuals must follow their own consciences, even if it hurts the organization
	21.	Safety of individual employees above all else	or		22.	Obligation to aid those in great need
	23.	Employees should follow rules that preserve individuals' freedom of action while reducing inequities	or		24.	Employees must do their best to follow rules designed to enhance organizational goal attainment

Scoring Your Managerial Values Profile

Below, circle the numbers of the statements or phrases that you checked off. When you have circled the numbers of all of your choices, add up the *number of circled items* in each column. Put this number in the row marked "Total." The total for any column can range from zero to eight. The higher your score, the more these values are important to you.

Utilitarian	Moral Rights	Justice
1	2	4
3	5	8
6	7	9
12	10	11
15	14	13
18	17	16
19	20	22
24	21	23
Total: _____	_____	_____

Source: Copyright © 1997, Marshall Sashkin. No further reproduction without written permission.

a lower cost, it should use them. It should do so regardless of the consequences in terms of layoffs, retraining costs, or moving production overseas to obtain lower wages and be subject to fewer restrictive regulations.

Conflicts of Interest. Managers and employees alike should not have personal interests that conflict with the organization's achievement of its goals. A purchasing agent having a significant financial interest in one of the firm's major suppliers faces a potential conflict of interest. Again, the reason for this proscription relates to profitability. In this case, the purchasing agent might be motivated to purchase from that supplier, even when the price or quality isn't the best available.

In the wake of a 50 percent plunge in the price of Boston Chicken shares, apparent conflicts of interest resulted in bad press for many stock analysts and their firms. In 1993, the initial public offering (IPO) of Boston Chicken shares made headlines. Shares that sold for $10 at the beginning of the day sold for almost $25 by the end of the day. During the years that followed, the stock continued to do well, thanks in part to "buy" recommendations issued by analysts who happened to work for the brokerages that had backed the Boston Chicken IPO and underwrote subsequent stock offerings. As the stock began to fall in 1997, these analysts continued to endorse it. As one investor put it, the analysts "were in bed with the investment bankers and the company management on this one." "I feel ripped off," said another major investor. "People have a right to be upset. Some of these problems had to be going on for months. I can't believe the analysts didn't see it."[29]

Conflicts of interest can sometimes be difficult to judge. Analysts involved in the Boston Chicken debacle felt that they were able to exercise their professional judgments about the financial health of that company, regardless of the fact that their employers had other reasons for wanting to see the stock do well. Similarly, when J.P. Morgan & Company was accused of letting a conflict of interest hamper the city of San Diego's financial decisions, its managers felt badly misunderstood. They defended their actions by pointing out that there was no conflict of interest under California law. Independent experts tended to agree with that conclusion, but some also acknowledged that there was an "appearance of impropriety."[30]

Identifying conflicts of interest can be even trickier when cultural differences are added to the mix, as one American discovered when on assignment in Russia. The American was working with a senior Russian partner, who also happened to own some other businesses. When the Russian began to "borrow" company materials and equipment, the American viewed his behavior as unethical. The Russian saw no conflict of interest; using the equipment in two companies in which he was an owner seemed both reasonable and efficient.[31]

The utilitarian model is consistent with strong values of individualism, acceptance of uncertainty, and masculinity, as defined in Chapter 3. These values support profit maximization, self-interest, rewards based on abilities and achievements, sacrifice and hard work, and competition.[32] Many economists espouse the utilitarian model, but it receives less support from the general public. During the past twenty-five years, utilitarian ethics have been increasingly challenged and tempered by the moral rights and justice models.

MORAL RIGHTS MODEL

MORAL RIGHTS MODEL
Judging decisions and behavior by their consistency with fundamental personal and group liberties and privileges.

The *moral rights model* holds that decisions should be consistent with fundamental rights and privileges (e.g., life, freedom, health, privacy, and property), as set forth in documents such as the first ten amendments to the U.S. Constitution (the Bill of Rights) and the United Nations' Declaration of Human Rights.[33] Several U.S. laws enacted during the past twenty-five years require managers and other employees to consider these rights as guides for their decision making and behavior. The moral rights model is consistent with Kohlberg's universal principles stage of moral development. That is, respect for certain moral rights is equivalent to defining these moral rights as universal principles that should guide ethical decisions and behavior.[34]

Life and Safety. Employees, customers, and the general public have the right not to have their lives and safety unknowingly and unnecessarily endangered. In the United States, many laws require businesses to comply with society's view of appropriate standards for quality of life and safety. For example, this moral right in large part justifies the U.S. Occupational Safety and Health Act (OSHA) of 1970, which contains many requirements designed to increase the safety and healthfulness of work environments. Among other things, OSHA and its implementing regulations restrict the use of asbestos, lead-based paint, and various toxic chemicals in the workplace. Businesses operating in other countries often find that laws are less restrictive there, so they must choose whether to meet only the standards of the host country or exceed those legal requirements. General Motors chose to use a higher standard than required for its operations in Mexico. Although it wasn't legally required to do so, the company spent more than $10 million to install small stand-alone sewage treatment systems in towns throughout the country. According to Lee Crawford, a managing director working there, "It was just something we felt was the right thing to do. . . . Water is one of the biggest single problems in Mexico." As an indication of how important these projects were to Mexico, the Mexican government honored General Motors with its Aguila Azteca award for humanitarian service.[35]

Truthfulness. Employees, customers, and the general public have the right not to be intentionally deceived on matters about which they should be informed. For example, in 1994, critics claimed that code sharing on computer screens by airlines was highly deceptive. Code arrangements between two airlines occurred when one of the carriers involved operated the flight, but both sold tickets on it. Often, passengers booked flights that involved transferring from, for example, American Airlines to either a small regional airline or a non-U.S. airline, such as Qantas or Air Canada. An asterisk next to the item indicated that it was a code-sharing flight, but the asterisk was so subtle that travel experts said that it was easily missed. And, even then, busy agents had to take extra time to look up which airline actually was flying the route. Thus passengers often found themselves unexpectedly having to switch airlines.[36] In late 1994, as a result of government and public pressure, when code sharing occurred, it was made obvious to agents and customers.

Privacy. Citizens have the right to control access to personal information about themselves and its use by government agencies, employers, and others. This moral right was the basis for the U.S. Privacy Act of 1974. The act restricts the use of certain types of information by the federal government and limits those to whom this information can be released. The 1988 Video Privacy Protection Act is an example of a more specific law designed to ensure that privacy rights are respected. This act forbids retailers from disclosing video rental records without the customer's consent or a court order. For example, a customer who rents exercise videos need not worry about getting on mailing lists for exercise equipment catalogues, fitness magazines, and the like.

With the availability of an array of new information technologies (especially computers and videos), enormous concern has been expressed about invasions of privacy at the societal, legal, organizational, and individual levels.[37] A few of these privacy issues include drug testing, honesty testing, confidentiality of medical and psychological counseling records, managerial monitoring of e-mail and work performed on computers, and access to credit records. The prevalence of several forms of monitoring and surveillance are shown in Table 6.1.

T a b l e 6 . 1	*Prevalence of Electronic Monitoring and Surveillance*

	Percent of Companies
Voice mail taped and reviewed	5
Telephone conversations taped and reviewed	10
Computer files stored and reviewed	14
Electronic mail messages stored and reviewed	15
Employee performance videotaped	16
Work areas videotaped to counter theft	34

Source: Bureau of National Affairs. *Bulletin to Management: Electronic Monitoring.* June 19, 1997, p. 197.

Video monitoring is an example of the use of one technology that has become widespread, despite the negative reaction many people have to the idea of having everything they do recorded on tape. For example, at hundreds of Dunkin' Donuts shops, the walls have ears that can hear conversations between customers as they wait in line to be served, as well as monitor conversations among employees. Franchise owners believe that this form of intrusion is necessary to increase security and keep employees on their toes. But some employees and customers have expressed concerns. Thalia Hondrogen, a customer, said, "It's like spying. . . . It's not American. Many times you say things to close friends you don't want overheard."[38] People react in a similar way when they hear about software programs designed to keep track of people's Internet travels.[39]

Freedom of Conscience. Individuals have the right to refrain from carrying out orders that violate their moral or religious beliefs. An Oregon court ruled in favor of a woman who had been fired because she insisted on serving as a juror. Her boss had ordered her not to serve, knowing that she could get out of jury duty because of her young children.[40]

Free Speech. Employees have the right to criticize the ethics or legality of their employers' actions. This right holds only if the criticisms are conscientious and truthful and do not violate the rights of others within or outside the organization. Virtually all U.S. federal legislation passed concerning occupational safety, pollution, and health has contained provisions designed to protect employees who report violations of laws by their employers.[41]

The principle of free speech has been at the center of controversies associated with new media, such as the Internet. Should executives at Yahoo! and Lycos accept advertisements from companies engaged in pornographic activity? Advertisements for pornographic products and services have long been banished from broadcasts of the major television networks. Consistent with this ban, Lycos declined to accept such advertisements for more than a year. But the culture of the Internet has supported a more aggressive adherence to principles of free speech, and Lycos eventually changed its policy. Management's explanation for allowing advertising for pornographic material was: "There are only about 20 or 30 keywords that would lead to that ad, and they're pretty raunchy—nothing you could print in a newspaper." Yahoo! gives a similar rationale. Referring to his company's advertisements on prominent Web sites, the president of one producer of X-rated material says that such advertising has been great for business, yielding 25,000 new memberships in just three months.

Permitting such advertising may be consistent with the principle of free speech, but parents whose children are exposed to pornography on the Web often express other concerns. Major corporations advertising on these sites may also eventually express concerns. If a blue-chip firm knows that its logo might appear next to a pornography ad, it might think twice about whether to advertise on that Internet site.[42]

Private Property. The legal and value systems of the United States, Canada, the United Kingdom, Germany, Japan, and many other societies recognize the individual's right to private property. This right allows people to acquire, use, and dispose of shelter and have life's basic necessities. British philosopher John Locke (1632–1704) believed that human beings by nature have rights to life, political equality, and property. The extension of that belief is that the state should not interfere with these rights and that it should protect those rights.[43]

As a guide to ethical decision making in organizations, the moral rights model serves as an effective counterweight that protects the nonbusiness sectors of society from enthusiastic capitalists following the utilitarian model. However, as a guide to ethical behavior in organizations, the moral rights model says more about what organizations should *avoid* doing—that is, violating the moral rights of employees, customers, and members of society—than it does about what *to* do. The justice model provides more guidance in this regard.

JUSTICE MODEL

JUSTICE MODEL

Judging decisions and behavior by their consistency with an equitable, fair, and impartial distribution of benefits (rewards) and costs among individuals and groups.

The *justice model* evaluates decisions and behavior with regard to how equitably they distribute benefits and costs among individuals and groups.[44] It is consistent with Kohlberg's universal principles stage. To ensure just decisions and behavior, the proponents of this model argue that three principles should be followed when designing management systems and making organizational decisions: the distributive justice principle, the fairness principle, and the natural duty principle.

DISTRIBUTIVE JUSTICE PRINCIPLE

A moral requirement that individuals not be treated differently because of arbitrarily defined characteristics.

Distributive Justice Principle. The *distributive justice principle* morally requires that individuals not be treated differently on the basis of arbitrarily defined characteristics. This principle holds that (1) individuals who are similar in relevant respects should be treated similarly, and (2) individuals who differ in relevant respects should be treated differently in proportion to the differences between them. As already mentioned, the U.S. Civil Rights Act of 1964 forbids employers from considering personal characteristics such as race, gender, religion, or national origin in decisions to recruit, hire, promote, or fire employees. Another legal regulation that supports the distributive justice principle is the U.S. Equal Pay Act of 1963. It made illegal the payment of different wages to women and men when their jobs require equal skill, effort, and responsibility and are performed under similar working conditions. Prior to the passage of this act, it was common for women to be paid at two-thirds the rate of men doing the same work. The practice of unequal pay for men and women doing equal work was a holdover from practices adopted during World War II, when many women entered the workforce to replace men who left the factories to go into the armed services.[45]

Perceptions about what constitutes distributive justice also were behind recent concerns over the growing disparity between the compensation packages that CEOs receive and the pay levels of everyone else. When wage gains are compared to gains in corporate profits, the problem is even more obvious. During the first half of the 1990s, average corporate profits rose 75 percent, CEO pay rose 92 percent, and factory pay rose 39 percent.[46] In recent years, CEO pay at large companies has increased by about 10 percent annually while total wages and benefits have increased by less than 5 percent annually, on average.[47]

FAIRNESS PRINCIPLE

A moral requirement that employees support the rules of the organization when certain conditions are met.

Fairness Principle. The *fairness principle* morally requires employees to support the rules of the organization when two conditions are met: (1) the organization is just (or fair); and (2) employees have voluntarily accepted benefits provided by the organization or have taken advantage of opportunities offered in order to further their own interests.[48] Employees are then expected to follow the organization's rules, even though those rules might restrict their individual choices. For example, if a job applicant was informed that accepting a job offer would later involve being subjected to random drug testing and continuous video monitoring, the organization could expect the employee to accept these conditions of employment. Under the fairness principle, both the organization and its employees have obligations and both should accept their responsibilities. Their mutual obligations can be considered fair if they satisfy the following criteria.

- **They result from voluntary acts.** Employees cannot be forced to work for a particular organization, and employers cannot arbitrarily be forced to hire a particular person.

- **They are spelled out in clearly stated rules.** These rules should specify what both the employee and the organization are required to do.

- **They are owed between individuals who are cooperating for mutual benefit.** The employees and managers share a common interest in the survival of the organization.[49]

Perceptions of fairness often reflect people's reactions to the procedures used to resolve problems. Acceptable processes lead to perceived *procedural justice*. For example, a company's management practices are more likely to be perceived as fair when a formal process is in place for investigating employees' grievances and taking remedial actions, when needed.[50] Similarly, top managers working in foreign subsidiaries are sensitive to issues of procedural justice. Believing that their multinational employers use fair procedures in making resource allocations inspires them to go beyond the call of duty in their work and leads to more cooperative and creative behavior.[51]

NATURAL DUTY PRINCIPLE

A moral requirement that decisions and behaviors be based on a variety of universal obligations.

Natural Duty Principle. The ***natural duty principle*** morally requires that decisions and behavior be based on universal principles associated with being a responsible member of society: (1) to help others who are in need or in jeopardy, provided that the help can be given without excessive personal risk or loss; (2) not to harm or injure another; (3) not to cause unnecessary suffering; and (4) to support and comply with just institutions. One way to think of a natural duty is as a responsibility that is accepted in exchange for certain rights. For example, if you have a right to safety, as suggested by the moral rights model, this right can best be assured if members of society also agree that they have a duty not to harm others. Thus the natural duty principle complements the moral rights model.

ASSESSMENT OF ETHICAL MODELS

Each of the three ethical models—utilitarian, moral rights, and justice—has strengths and weaknesses. Utilitarian views are most compatible with the goals of efficiency, productivity, and profit maximization—all strong managerial values in the United States. Managers in many U.S. organizations overwhelmingly value this ethical model. In contrast, the moral rights and justice models emphasize individual rights and obligations and the need to distribute benefits and burdens fairly among individuals. These models give greater weight to long-term employee welfare than to short-term organizational efficiency. Employment conditions in many European countries reflect policies developed in cultures whose values are relatively more consistent with the moral rights and justice models. For example, in Spain employers aren't able to fire their employees "at-will" if they have been on the job several months. This policy (which has come under attack from employers who argue that it is too constraining) reflects cultural values that are more consistent with the moral rights and justice models than with the utilitarian model.

Those who attempt to reach the *ideal* in making ethical decisions face many difficulties.[52] Using these three models in combination increases the probability that decisions and behavior will be judged as ethical by others. Many changes in organizational practices reflect solutions that were developed by managers who accepted the utilitarian model but also believed that doing what was right was one way for the company to do well. Managers who take this approach often find themselves collaborating with other individuals and groups who are willing to help managers find cost effective ways of doing good. The adoption of pollution prevention technologies that exceed government requirements illustrates this approach. To achieve the goals of being both a clean manufacturer and remaining profitable, many U.S. and Japanese-affiliated transplants have used employee involvement in continuous improvement activities. For example, Quad/Graphics used employee teams to find low-cost ways to reduce hazardous waste. Safety-Kleen used teams of engineers and production workers to redesign their equipment to reduce pollution.[53]

CORPORATE SOCIAL RESPONSIBILITY

4

EXPLAIN HOW THE STAKE-
HOLDER APPROACH CAN
BE USED TO GUIDE ETHI-
CAL DECISION MAKING
AND ACTION

STAKEHOLDERS
Individuals or groups that have interests, rights, or ownership in an organization or its activities.

Managers have many responsibilities, which engage them in a wide range of activities. One way to organize these activities is according to the groups of people who are affected by the decisions made by managers and the actions they take. That is, a manager's job can be thought of as a series of attempts to address the concerns of multiple stakeholders.[54]

STAKEHOLDERS

Stakeholders are individuals or groups that have interests, rights, or ownership in an organization and its activities. Stakeholders who have similar interests and rights are said to belong to the same stakeholder group. Customers, suppliers, employees, and strategic partners are examples of stakeholder groups. Each has an interest in how organizations perform and is interdependent with them. These stakeholder groups can benefit from a company's successes and can be harmed by its failures and mistakes. Similarly, the organization has an interest in maintaining the general well-being and effectiveness of these stakeholder groups. If one or more of the stakeholder groups were to break off their relationships with the organization, the organization would suffer.

For any particular organization, some stakeholder groups may be relatively more important than others. The most important groups—the primary stakeholders—are those whose concerns the organization must address in order to ensure its own survival. Secondary stakeholders are also important because they can take actions that can damage—but not destroy—the organization. Public opinion leaders, political action groups, and the media are secondary stakeholders for many organizations.[55]

Figure 6.3 identifies the many stakeholders that may have an interest in a particular corporation. Note that no distinction is made between primary and secondary stakeholders. The reason is that the importance of each stakeholder group varies from one firm to the next. In general, employees, shareholders, customers, government regulators, and society or the local community are primary stakeholders for most U.S. companies.

STAKEHOLDER CONCERNS

Each group of stakeholders has somewhat different concerns. That is, each cares more about some aspects of an organization's activities and less about others.

Customers. Many organizations say that they put the concerns of their customers or clients first. For U.S. companies, that often means improving the quality of products and services while keeping costs in check. Managers have introduced TQM for both external customers who purchase the product or service and internal customers in other departments. These programs extend to the entire company and frequently involve both suppliers and customers. As the following Teamwork Competency account illustrates, using teams to improve quality is one approach that organizations can use to address the concerns of customers.

At Motorola Teams Defeat Defects

Christopher Galvin, now CEO of Motorola, is a firm believer in teamwork. As the company's third-generation leader, he has been reshaping a corporate culture long based on internal competition. His predecessors were so confident that competitive behavior was needed for success that they urged units to try to steal business away from each other. From a company where employees felt that the different business units were best described as "a loose confederation of warring camps," Galvin wanted to build a global giant with a cohesive strategy and corporate culture to match. Galvin has succeeded in instilling a culture based on teamwork. As general manager of paging during the 1980s, he used teamwork and quality improvement techniques

to reduce from twenty-eight to two days the time required to manufacture pagers. In the mid-1980s Galvin coined the phrase "an answering machine in your pocket" and used it as the vision statement for his group's goal. Since then, pagers and paging devices have become an integral part of the 1990s telecommunications revolution. No longer limited to medical doctors and emergency personnel, these small devices are used by dual-career families who need to maintain contact with each other and their children, salespeople who must be on call to their customers, and millions of others in all walks of life.

At Motorola's plant in Boynton Beach, Florida, all pagers are custom built in unique job lots for the purchaser. They are built by robots and teams of workers. The robots tune the crystals inside the pagers to the proper frequencies and inspect the finished products. The workers monitor the robots. Several minifactories exist within the larger "plant." Each factory produces a specialized type of pager. One group, for example, builds a wristwatch pager that has little attraction for the Western consumer but that is extremely popular with the Japanese.

This plant didn't always function as well as it does now. In 1987, the Paging Division was producing large numbers of defective products. The company decided to use its Boynton Beach plant as an experiment. To be fair to those who were going to

become part of the experiment, all employees were permitted to stay on the payroll as long as they met the basic human resources requirement of third-grade reading and writing skills. Rather than fire those who didn't have the skills needed to work with the high-tech robots, the company trained workers in how to monitor robots and take full responsibility for the product as it was assembled. Their quality target was to lower the defect level to *six sigma* (about 1 defect in 14 million pagers).

With a clear goal and the assurance that taking risks would not cost them their jobs, self-managed work teams experimented with workflow and product assembly procedures. As the number of defects fell toward targeted levels, management expanded the project to include interdepartmental teams that volunteered to solve problems involving nonproduction issues.

Now Galvin is pushing the rest of Motorola to work together as a team. His brother Michael observes, "Chris is very, very committed to the team process. He's always saying that the essence of successful partnerships in life, whether it's marriage, business, or sports, is trust."[56]

* * *

To learn more about Motorola, visit the company's home page at

www.motorola.com

Although most companies want to please their customers, pressures to improve profits and be responsive to shareholders may mean that customers' concerns are temporarily forgotten. Sears discovered just how powerful its customers were when the company set up an incentive system for its automotive repair and service business that had severe unintended consequences. In 1992, consumers filed hundreds of complaints against Sears, accusing the company of selling unnecessary parts and

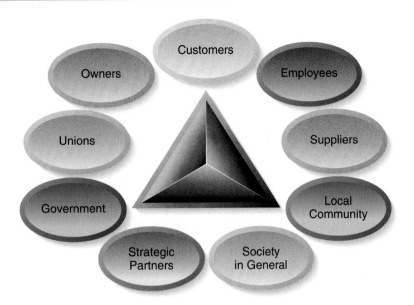

services in more than forty states. Sears's management didn't set out to deliberately defraud customers—so what went wrong?

Faced with declining revenues and reduced market share, management adopted new incentive goals and performance programs to improve profitability. Service representatives received higher sales quotas and mechanics received higher minimum work quotas. Goals called for larger numbers of parts and services such as springs, shocks, alignments, and brake jobs—to be sold each shift. Pressures from top management on service managers and mechanics left some of them few legitimate options for meeting their goals. Under these pressures, some employees resorted to unethical behaviors and careless repairs to meet their goals.

Customer complaints alerted Sears to the problem. Management discontinued the sales commissions and quotas for selling specific parts and services. The company took out full-page ads in newspapers across the country apologizing for its mistake, hoping to win customers back. In addition, Sears agreed to repay customers who had had unneeded work done and to pay all related court costs.[57]

Understandably, consumers in general expect companies to maintain high standards of conduct. Consumers may punish companies that fail to do so by boycotting them. Cheating and not satisfying customers obviously tarnished Sears's reputation. Solving those problems was costly, time-consuming, and embarrassing to the company and its employees.

Some consumers make a special point of purchasing products and services only from companies that have outstanding reputations for ethics issues and social responsibility. Many consumers of Ben & Jerry's ice cream feel better knowing that the company is a supporter of Vermont's dairy farmers and an advocate of environmental causes. If Ben & Jerry's ever acts contrary to its socially responsible approach to business, the company might lose many of its socially aware customers.

Employees. Many of the concerns that employees have today reflect changes in the structure of organizations and the fact that work is a major activity in their lives.

How a company should treat employees during times of change is a key issue raised by this group of stakeholders. When IBM restructured its organization in the early 1990s, it terminated more than 100,000 employees, many at the middle management level. The company had long been known for its policy of job security, so employees were shocked when IBM replaced some of its managers with temporary people hired to finish ongoing projects.[58] Just as the economy was absorbing the shock of layoffs at IBM, AT&T announced that it expected to lay off 40,000 employees. Like IBM, AT&T had been known for job security. Employees felt betrayed, and the media vilified AT&T's former CEO Bob Allen. In the end there were fewer layoffs than he had originally announced. Many people believe that Allen decided against laying off so many people because of the public's adverse reaction. It sent a clear message that laying off so many people was ethically untenable.

Pay is another area of concern to employees. The desire to receive equal pay for equal work is among the most important of workplace issues, according to a national survey of 40,000 women. As already noted, the Equal Pay Act of 1963 makes it illegal to pay men and women differently for doing equivalent work. Nevertheless, many women feel that their employers don't live up to the principle on which this law is based. Of nearly equal importance were a desire for secure and affordable health insurance, paid sick leave, and assured pension and retirement benefits. Some people were surprised that child-care issues were considerably less important than these other concerns for the majority of women surveyed.[59] However they go about it, progressive companies understand that meeting such concerns is a responsibility they should take seriously.

Society and the Environment. Conducting business in a way that protects the natural environment while making economic progress is referred to as *sustainable development.*[60] In addition to local laws and regulations that govern business actions related to pollution and the use of natural resources, international standards for environmental management have been developed. The European Union's Eco-Management and Audit Scheme (EMAS) and the International Organization for Standardization's ISO 14000 standards are examples of environmental policy statements designed to provide guidance to multinational businesses. By meeting the ISO 14000 standards, companies can certify that they have developed responsible environmental policies. Such certification may, in turn, be used by local community decision makers when deciding whether to permit a business to operate in the area.[61]

Recently, industry analysts and the media have put more pressure on companies to be responsive to community and environmental concerns. When *Fortune* magazine publishes its annual list of "Most Admired Companies," it spotlights companies having the best records in those areas (e.g., Coca-Cola, Herman Miller, and Dupont) and points a finger at the worst (e.g., Flagstar, Columbia/HCA Healthcare, and Great Western Financial).[62]

For many industries, being profitable while addressing society's need for a healthy environment has been a difficult challenge. For those that depend on the environment to sustain their businesses, meeting this challenge is a strategic imperative. One approach to meeting this challenge is described in the following Strategic Action Competency selection describing an environmental initiative in the forest products industry.

Increasingly, environmental issues affect managerial decisions and behavior. Companies such as 3M, McDonald's, Kodak, Volvo, and many of the leading chemical companies now include principles of industrial ecology in their strategic plans. For example, 3M's strategic policy formalizes the company's commitment to

SUSTAINABLE DEVELOPMENT

To conduct business in a way that protects the natural environment while making economic progress.

Creative solutions for responsible management of the environment are necessary in the forest products industry, where trees are an essential resource. The American Forest and Paper Association's Sustainable Forestry Initiative is one example of how concern about the environment is being translated into good business practices. Companies who produce forest products understand that the public has an interest in maintaining the quality of forests, which also are used for recreation purposes. If the industry isn't responsive to these concerns, it knows that government will eventually enact and enforce stricter laws and regulations to control its activities. Serving 200 corporate members, the Association's goal is to convince the public that loggers can clean up their act without government intervention. How? By requiring its members to practice and promote responsible forestry, protect wildlife habitat, and produce reports that document these efforts.

Middle managers such as A. Bradford Wyman are the key to the Initiative's success. A wood operations manager at Crown paper mills, Wyman manages the wood cut from that company's 85,000 acres of land (15 percent of the total) and the wood delivered by independent loggers (85 percent of the total). He believes that the greatest threat to his industry is the public's negative attitude toward cutting down trees. By cooperating with environmental groups, he expects to develop timber-management techniques that such groups will accept. In addition to changing the way his own company manages its timberlands, he plans to enforce his standards by purchasing wood only from independent loggers who have completed programs in environmental safety and protection.[63]

* * *

For additional information about the American Forest and Paper Association efforts to promote sustainable forestry practices, visit its home page at

www.afandpa.org

1. solve its own pollution and conservation problems beyond compliance requirements;

2. prevent pollution at the source, whenever possible;

3. conserve natural resources through waste reclamation and other methods;

4. assist regulatory and government agencies concerned with environmental activities; and

5. develop products that have a minimal negative effect on the environment.[64]

The environment is only one of several issues that concern communities. Many also expect businesses to contribute to a community's quality of life in other ways. Charitable contributions are one way that corporations can respond to this concern. Being able to give back to the community is one of the few reasons to bother making a profit, according to cofounder Ben Cohen's "values-led" view of capitalism. Each year, 7.5 percent of Ben & Jerry's pretax profits go to social causes.[65]

Ben & Jerry's approach to doing business is unusual in the United States, but in other countries showing concern about society's well-being isn't as rare for a company. In Italy, for example, charitable foundations own many banks. Without shareholders constantly pressing for increased profitability, Italy's banks have been considered successful as long as they were able to make charitable donations and still have some money left to reinvest. This tradition will likely change with progress toward European monetary union and privatization of the banking industry. Forced to compete with more profitable banks in Germany and France, Italian bankers will soon face increased shareholder pressures.[66]

Owners and Shareholders. For many organizations, such as public schools, nonprofit foundations, and government agencies, the concerns of owners—that is, taxpayers and contributors—often are essentially those of society at large. But for privately owned companies and those whose shares are publicly traded, the concerns of owners—that is, shareholders—may be quite different from those of society in general.

Most shareholders invest their money in companies for financial reasons. At a minimum, they want to preserve their capital for later use. During the past decade, the majority of publicly traded shares have moved from the hands of individual investors to institutional investors, who trade on behalf of individuals.[67] Because the job of institutional investors is to make money by choosing which companies to investment in, their perspective on corporate issues is to make profit generation the firm's top priority. As professional investors, these shareholders have considerable power to influence management's decisions.

CONFLICT AND CONSENSUS AMONG STAKEHOLDERS

Clearly, the primary concerns of the stakeholder groups differ somewhat. So do their views about the appropriate role of business in society. Some managers would agree with Chrysler Chairman Robert Eaton, who says, "The idea of corporations taking on social responsibility is ridiculous. You'll simply burden industry to a point where it is no longer competitive." Other managers would agree with the view of the average American, who rejects the idea that making money is the only role of business. In fact, socially responsible corporations are the more attractive alternative for prospective employees.[68] Such differences in perspectives make managing effectively a challenge.

Solutions to the management issues that arise day in and day out are seldom simple. Wal-Mart Stores, Inc., the Canadian subsidiary of the well-known U.S. company, discovered this truth the hard way when it decided to pull Cuban-made pajamas from shelves in 136 stores. The company did so because of concern that selling the pajamas might violate U.S. laws, which prohibit trading with Cuba by U.S. companies and their subsidiaries. Although U.S. trade officials endorsed the decision, Canadian customers protested the move, saying that it violated NAFTA. Caught between the conflicting interests of these important stakeholder groups, Wal-Mart is now trying to find an acceptable solution.[69]

Conflict among stakeholders is common, but so are shared interests. Effective managers use their communication competency to determine the interests of key stakeholders and work with them to find a solution that addresses each set of concerns. The next Communication Competency article illustrates this point.

The successes of other customer-driven companies support this view. Michael Treacy and Fred Wiersema studied the performance of thirteen well-known customer-oriented firms, and compared their performance to others in the same industries. Over a period of five years, the revenues of these thirteen companies grew 3.2 times faster than their competitors'. Profitability was 2.1 times as great as their competitors'.[70]

Paying attention to the concerns of employees is good for business too. When Aaron Feuerstein, owner, president, and CEO of Malden Mills, spent $15 million to pay wages and benefits to 1,000 employees who weren't even working, some

Townspeople Turned Investors

For Robert "Joe" Murphy, president of Community Grocers, Inc., in Mount Ayr, Iowa, satisfying customers goes hand-in-hand with satisfying shareholders and being a socially responsible business. When Murphy decided to open his supermarket, he was responding to the townspeople, who had expressed concern when one in-town supermarket closed. Then, when the only surviving grocery store moved to the outskirts of town, their concerns deepened. Murphy was listening; convinced that the town needed a local grocery store, he sought financing from members of the community. In a town of only 1,700 men, women, and children, Murphy persuaded 322 to invest in his grocery venture. Through these contributions, he raised more than $640,000. One person observed that "it got to the point where if you were at a ball game or a restaurant or on a golf course, if you weren't an investor, you were in the minority." Now the townspeople-turned-investors are also Murphy's customers. They want great service, fresh produce, and of course, healthy returns. So far, Murphy has found that he can satisfy these multiple stakeholders successfully. "Keeping a shareholder happy is no more than keeping the general public happy," he observed.[71]

observers thought he was acting more like a saint than an intelligent businessman. Malden Mills, located in Lawrence, Massachusetts, suffered a catastrophic fire, forcing the plant to close for several months. Rather than close the old plant permanently, or take the opportunity to move it to a lower cost site, the seventy-year-old Feuerstein chose to rebuild the plant and keep his employees on the payroll while the plant was being rebuilt. "Why would I go to Thailand to bring the cost lower when I might run the risk of losing the advantage I've got, which is superior quality?" he asked. Corporate customers—including Lands' End, L.L. Bean, Patagonia, and North Face—rely on Malden Mills to manufacture and supply high-tech fabrics created in its R&D labs. This CEO believes that the financial success of his company depends on consistently producing high-quality products, which in turn requires employing superior technology and employees.[72]

When making decisions and implementing organizational changes to improve sales or profits, managers must take into account the effects of the changes on employees, customers, community, shareholders, and other relevant stakeholders. Paying attention exclusively to profitability is a mistake that only the inexperienced are likely to make. When researchers at Cornell University surveyed 250 executives of large companies and 250 business school students about what made a great leader, the executives clearly appreciated the need to address the concerns of employees and society at large. Great leaders, they believed, were those capable of managing issues such as diversity, the environment, and balancing work and family. In contrast, students admired "results-oriented" leaders, including so-called slash-and-burn downsizers. The unidentified reporter who wrote up these results for a major news publication added this editorial comment: "Yikes!"[73]

Shareholder and employee interests often seem to conflict, especially over restructuring and downsizing. Decisions to reduce layers of management or sell off a poorly performing division usually are made to improve efficiency and profitability in order to satisfy shareholders. The employees who lose their jobs in the process are victims of the conflict between their needs for employment and shareholders' desire for financial gain. However, when employees are owners themselves, management may put more effort into finding a solution that minimizes disruption for employees while also meeting the organization's financial goals. Employees, in turn, may recognize the importance of improving productivity in order to maintain their employment. As in the example of Crown paper mills, employees often recognize that their own long-term employment depends on the ability of their company—and even an entire industry—to satisfy the concerns of the communities affected by their business.

Would you be surprised to learn that investors want to know that a company treats its employees well? A study of 275 portfolio investors, conducted by Ernst & Young's Center for Business Innovation, found that "ability to attract and retain" talented employees ranked as the fifth of thirty-nine most important factors for deciding where to invest. The California Public Employees Retirement System (CALPERS) is one investor that has begun to base stock purchase decisions on how companies treat their employees. Perhaps these investors know that having satisfied employees goes along with having satisfied customers, especially in the services sector. Managers and employees who hate their jobs can't give the best possible service to customers. Conversely, when customers are happy, employees feel a sense of pride and satisfaction at being part of the company.[74]

Employee-friendly companies also have a competitive advantage in attracting the highly skilled workers they need. After being on the job for a while, employees who are more satisfied with how they are treated are more willing to do a little extra for the organization. Managing employees well can also benefit shareholders in other ways. For example, companies that have good records of equal employment opportunity and nondiscrimination perform better in the stock market and have higher annualized returns than those with poor records. Other research suggests that good economic performance goes hand-in-hand with being environmentally responsible. Studies such as these support the idea that economic concerns need not be divorced from ethical concerns. Behaving ethically can be profitable.[75]

EVALUATING CORPORATE SOCIAL PERFORMANCE

With heightened public interest in corporate social responsibility, many companies are discovering that they can't avoid having people evaluate how well they perform in this respect. As we have noted already, business publications such as *Fortune* magazine rank various aspects of organizational performance annually. The federal government also recognizes corporate social performance. In 1997, it established the **Ron Brown Award for Corporate Leadership,** which rewards leadership in employee and community relations. Named after the late Secretary of Commerce, who died in an airplane accident while on government business in Bosnia, the Ron Brown Award complements the Malcolm Baldrige National Quality Award. The Ron Brown Award defines excellence in terms of three basic principles.

1. Top management must demonstrate commitment to corporate citizenship.

2. Corporate citizenship must be a shared value of the company that is visible at all levels.

3. Corporate citizenship must be integrated into a successful business strategy.

When evaluating companies, a select committee of judges looks for employee and community centered programs that meet five criteria.

- The programs are distinctive, innovative, and effective. They represent "best practices" when compared to competitors.

RON BROWN AWARD FOR CORPORATE LEADERSHIP
A federal government award that recognizes demonstrated corporate leadership in employee and community relations.

- They have had a significant, measurable impact on the people they were designed to serve.

- The programs offer broad potential for social and economic benefits for U.S. society.

- They are sustainable and feasible within a business environment and mission.

- They can be adapted to other businesses and communities.

Affirmative Social Responsibility. The Ron Brown Award encourages business leaders to move away from the traditional, utilitarian model of business and take a more proactive stance with respect to contributing to society. Rather than deny their social responsibility, or resist it by doing the least possible amount, many companies are choosing to do everything that is required and to look for areas in which they can do even more for the mutual benefit of all stakeholders.

A proactive, or affirmative, approach to social responsibility is the most difficult, complex, and expensive concept for organizations to implement. It involves accepting five categories of obligations.[76]

- **Broad Performance Criteria.** Managers and employees must consider and accept broader criteria for measuring the organization's performance and social role than those required by law and the marketplace.

- **Ethical Norms.** Managers and employees must take definite stands on issues of public concern. They must advocate ethical norms for the organization, the industry, and business in general. These ethical norms are to be advocated even when they seem detrimental to the immediate profits of the organization or are contrary to prevailing industry practices.

- **Operating Strategy.** Managers and employees should maintain or improve the current standards of the physical and social environment. Organizations must compensate victims of pollution and other hazards created, even in the absence of clearly established legal grounds. Managers and employees need to evaluate possible negative effects of the organization's plans on other stakeholders and then attempt to eliminate or substantially reduce such negative effects before implementing the plans.

- **Response to Social Pressures.** Managers and employees should accept responsibility for solving current problems. They need to be willing to discuss activities with outside groups and make information freely available to them. They also need to be receptive to formal and informal inputs from outside stakeholders in decision making.

- **Legislative and Political Activities.** Managers must show a willingness to work with outside stakeholders for enactment, for example, of environmental protection laws. They must promote honesty and openness in government and in their own organization's lobbying activities.

SOCIAL AUDIT

An attempt to identify, measure, evaluate, report on, and monitor the effects that an organization is having on its stakeholders and society.

Social Audit. Managers concerned about their company's social performance may undertake a social audit. A ***social audit*** is an attempt to identify, measure, evaluate, report on, and monitor the effects that the organization is having on its stakeholders and society as a whole—information not covered in traditional financial reports.[77] In contrast to a financial audit, a social audit focuses on social actions rather than fiscal accountability and measures achievement under the affirmative social responsibility concept. Table 6.2 shows some of the areas that Levi Strauss & Company considers in its audit. Other firms that undertake social audits include

Stakeholder Group	Examples of Concerns
Owners and investors	Financial soundness
	Consistency in meeting shareholder expectations
	Sustained profitability
	Average return on assets over five-year period
	Timely and accurate disclosure of financial information
Customers	Product/service quality, innovativeness, and availability
	Responsible management of defective or harmful products/services
	Safety records for products/services
	Pricing policies and practices
	Honest, accurate, and responsible advertising
Employees	Nondiscriminatory, merit-based hiring and promotion
	Diversity of the workforce
	Wage and salary levels and equitable distribution
	Availability of training and development
	Workplace safety and privacy
Community	Environmental issues
	Environmental sensitivity in packaging and product design
	Recycling efforts and use of recycled materials
	Pollution prevention
	Global application of environmental standards
	Community involvement
	Percentage of profits designated for charitable contributions
	Innovation and creativity in philanthropic efforts
	Product donations
	Availability of facilities and other assets for community use
	Support for employee volunteer efforts

AT&T, The Body Shop, McDonald's, and Johnson & Johnson. As Table 6.2 illustrates, the concerns of important stakeholder groups can provide a framework for developing a social audit.[78] Such audits are necessary because even the most conscientious companies can have some employees who fail to meet ethical standards of conduct. At Levi Strauss, for example, a small group of employees in El Paso, Texas, accused company managers of harassing them after they filed for workers' compensation benefits. These employees had suffered work-related injuries. They claimed that they were being pressured into returning to work before they were ready and that the company discouraged injured workers from taking the time necessary to fully recuperate.

BLOWING THE WHISTLE ON UNETHICAL BEHAVIOR

5

RECOGNIZE WHEN
WHISTLE-BLOWING MAY
BE AN EFFECTIVE WAY TO
STOP WRONGDOING AND
BE ABLE TO MAKE A WELL-
REASONED DECISION
ABOUT WHETHER YOU
SHOULD BLOW THE
WHISTLE

WHISTLE-BLOWERS
Employees who report unethical or illegal actions of their
employers to management,
external stakeholders, or the
public.

Even in the best-run organizations, ethical lapses may occur. Employees who hold a traditional utilitarian perspective may be particularly likely to engage in behaviors that benefit the firm but impinge on the concerns of other stakeholders. These employees aren't necessarily less ethical than everyone else in their personal lives.[79] But their view of business decisions, based solely on economics, may lead them to discount negative, noneconomic outcomes associated with economic gains. Thus many employees find themselves in a position of knowing that unethical behavior is going on and having to decide what to do about it.

Employees who report unethical or illegal actions of their employers to other people or organizations that are capable of taking corrective action are referred to as **whistle-blowers.** If you knew that a co-worker was behaving illegally or unethically, would you report it to someone? If yes, who would you tell—someone inside the company or someone on the outside?

Researchers Janet Near and Marcia Miceli have been studying whistle-blowing for several years. Based on their studies and research by others, they are convinced that whistle-blowers aren't very different from other employees. They don't seem to be at a higher stage of moral development, nor are they either more or less loyal to the company than their peers. Instead, they tend to be people who happen to know about the wrongdoing and believe that by acting they can do something to stop it.[80] That is, they believe that they can be effective whistle-blowers.

Encouraging people to blow the whistle doesn't always make sense. When you see wrongdoing occur, your goal should be to find a way to stop it. Simply confronting the person involved may be all that you need to do. Whistle-blowing is a step that you should take only after making other less drastic efforts to change the situation. That is, blow the whistle only as a last resort and when you're likely to achieve a useful outcome—and in full recognition of the possible consequences to yourself. Table 6.3 lists some of the questions to ask yourself if you're considering blowing the whistle.

If your answers to these questions indicate that your whistle-blowing isn't likely to stop the wrongdoing, you should consider other courses of action. For example, you might try to persuade other employees to act with you; ignoring or firing a group of employees who report wrongdoing is more difficult than taking action against one person. Another alternative is to consider leaving the company. This action may not stop the wrongdoing, but at least it will ensure that you don't get caught up in the situation and possibly end up being drawn into the wrongdoing yourself.

In addition to considering whether they will be effective whistle-blowers, employees often consider whether they are likely to experience retaliation for blowing the whistle.[81] In many states, whistle-blowers are legally protected from retaliation by their employers. Some states protect only those whistle-blowers who go outside the company (e.g., telling a newspaper reporter) to report wrongdoing. Other states protect only whistle-blowers who report wrongdoing to someone inside the company (e.g., writing a letter to the CEO). Regardless of such laws, fear of retaliation is a reasonable concern. In particular, retaliation against whistle-blowers is likely to occur under the following circumstances.

- The allegation of wrongdoing has little merit. Accusations of wrongdoing can be very harmful to both the individuals who are accused and the company. People who make accusations without much convincing evidence may be destructive instead of helpful.

Do the characteristics at the right describe you, the whistle-blower?	Do you have credibility with middle and upper managers in the organization?
	Do you have power in the organization (professional status, long tenure, or control over resources)?
	Are you willing to identify yourself?
	Are you prepared to leave the organization if that becomes necessary?
Do the characteristics at the right describe the person to whom you plan to report the wrongdoing?	Does the person have credibility?
	Is the person powerful?
	Is the person supportive of you?
Do the characteristics at the right describe the person being accused of wrongdoing?	Is the person's credibility questionable?
	Does the person have relatively low power and status?
Do the characteristics at the right describe the wrongdoing you intend to report?	Does the organization depend on the wrongdoing to achieve its goals? (If yes, then you will be more effective if you report the wrongdoing to an external source instead of an internal source.)
Do the characteristics at the right describe the evidence you have?	Do you have written documents?
	Does your evidence come from more than one source?
	Is the evidence unambiguous?
	Do you have evidence of illegal behavior?
Do the characteristics at the right describe the organizational context?	Is reporting the wrongdoing related to doing a normal part of your job?
	Does the organization have a strong ethical culture and clear rules for how wrongdoing will be treated?
	Do you feel you can trust your superiors to not retaliate against you?

Adapted from: J. P. Near and M. P. Miceli. Whistle-blowing: Myth and reality. *Journal of Management,* 22, 1996, pp. 507–526; J. P. Near and M. P. Miceli. Effective whistle-blowing. *Academy of Management Review,* 20, 1995, pp. 679–708; and M. P. Miceli and J. P. Near. *Blowing the Whistle: The Organizational and Legal Implications for Companies and Their Employees.* New York: Lexington Books, 1992.

*The more times your answer is "Yes," the more likely your whistle-blowing efforts will be effective.

- The accusations are made to someone outside the company. If the whistle-blower doesn't make accusations to someone within the company before making those accusations public, the company has no opportunity to address the problem before it becomes the object of public scrutiny.

- The whistle-blower has little support from top management or middle management. Having the support of someone in management often means that the whistle-blower has a powerful ally who can help protect him or her from retaliation—for example, by offering advice about how to go about disclosing the wrongdoing in a responsible way.

Giving whistle-blowers legal protection isn't enough to encourage whistle-blowing, however.[82] The corporate culture must also encourage whistle-blowing. As shown in Table 6.4, putting policies and practices in place that protect whistle-blowers is just one of many things an organization can do to minimize wrongdoing and support ethical behavior. Arthur Martinez, the CEO of Sears, for one, learned that creating such a culture can be difficult. Martinez took his job shortly after the company learned that its auto service centers had treated customers unethically. Then another scandal hit the news. In its efforts to collect delinquent accounts, Sears had been overly aggressive and threatening toward customers who owed the company money and had also filed for bankruptcy. Some of the collection techniques were clearly illegal.[83] Did the company's corporate culture and reward systems seduce loyal, well-intentioned employees into using illegal collection tactics for the benefit of the firm? If so, how many people were involved? Who knew about the ethical misconduct, and why didn't they do something to stop it? Martinez had worked hard to change the Sears culture to avoid such problems. Despite his efforts, some people in the company continued to behave unethically and illegally. Perhaps no company's ethical culture is strong enough to guarantee that employees will always behave appropriately. Nevertheless, the practices listed in Table 6.4 are among the many things that a company can do to minimize ethical misconduct. If you aspire to work for an organization with a strong ethical culture, you can use that list to evaluate how serious an organization is about preventing ethical lapses.

Table 6.4   *Organizational Practices for Minimizing Wrongdoing*

- Signal the importance of ethical conduct through the organization's vision and values statements.

- Document the organization's ethical rules through a written Code of Ethics.

- Have someone designated as the Ethics Officer, who is responsible for monitoring the organization's adherence to its stated standards.

- Appoint an ethics committee to oversee the organization's ethics initiatives and supervise the ethics officer.

- Use integrity tests when screening job applicants.

- Emphasize the importance of ethical conduct in training and development programs to ensure that employees understand what behaviors are considered unethical by the organization.

- Evaluate employees' adherence to ethical guidelines and use these evaluations when making decisions about pay and promotions.

- Provide ways for employees to report the questionable actions of peers and superiors, such as by providing an ethics hot line.

- Conduct ethical audits and take visible steps to address concerns that such audits might uncover.

- Develop enforcement procedures that contain stiff disciplinary and dismissal procedures and follow through by using these procedures when appropriate.

- Constantly communicate the organization's ethical standards and principles, using all channels of communication possible. Recognize that the actions of top managers are especially important in communicating ethical standards.

- Treat allegations of wrongdoing seriously, while at the same time ensuring that both the whistle-blower and the person accused of wrongdoing are treated fairly.

CHAPTER SUMMARY

In this chapter we examined the importance of ethical and socially responsible business decisions. What is viewed as ethical is likely to vary among an organization's many stakeholders, as well as among different cultures. These differences mean that, ultimately, individuals must accept responsibility for their own conduct.

1. STATE THE IMPORTANCE OF ETHICS FOR ORGANIZATIONS AND THEIR EMPLOYEES.

An explicit concern with ethical issues and guidelines represents a positive strategy to minimize ethical problems and to react quickly and effectively when they do occur. Stakeholders, such as customers, are increasingly holding organizations responsible for ethical decision making and conduct. However, there are differing perspectives on what being *ethical* and *socially responsible* means in various situations.

2. DESCRIBE HOW THE SOCIETAL, LEGAL, ORGANIZATIONAL, AND INDIVIDUAL PERSPECTIVES FOR ASSESSING ETHICAL CONDUCT INFLUENCE DECISIONS AND BEHAVIOR.

The ethics of any decision or behavior can rarely be understood by considering a single ethical perspective. All four perspectives must be considered. The societal perspective includes shared values and how they affect individual and group standards for acceptable behavior. The legal perspective includes the enactment of new laws and regulations and the interpretation of current laws and regulations that define ethical behavior. The organizational perspective includes decisions and actions that go beyond those mandated by law and demonstrate an organization's ethical standards. The individual perspective includes values and behavior that reflect a person's stage of moral development.

3. DISCUSS THE STANDARDS AND PRINCIPLES OF UTILITARIAN, MORAL RIGHTS, AND JUSTICE MODELS OF ETHICS.

Managers and employees commonly rely on one or some combination of three ethical models to guide decision making and behavior. The utilitarian model focuses on decisions or behavior that are likely to affect an organization's profitability. For businesses, the bottom line includes indicators of financial and economic performance. The moral rights model upholds a member of society's fundamental rights to life and safety, truthfulness, privacy, freedom of conscience, free speech, and private property. The justice model advocates impartial, equitable distribution of benefits and costs among individuals and groups, according to three principles: distributive justice, fairness, and natural duty.

4. EXPLAIN HOW THE STAKEHOLDER APPROACH CAN BE USED TO GUIDE ETHICAL DECISION MAKING AND ACTION.

The diverse values and ethical approaches prevalent in advanced economies introduce a great deal of complexity for organizations that attempt to act in a socially responsible way. One approach that an organization can use to ensure socially responsible actions is to consider how its actions affect primary and secondary stakeholders. Each group of stakeholders has different concerns. Sometimes these concerns conflict; at other times they mesh. Thus finding solutions that address the concerns of multiple stakeholders becomes an important strategic task. Effective managers use their communication and strategic action competencies to ensure the well-being of their organizations in terms of both economics and ethics.

5. RECOGNIZE WHEN WHISTLE-BLOWING MAY BE AN EFFECTIVE WAY TO STOP WRONGDOING AND BE ABLE TO MAKE A WELL-REASONED DECISION ABOUT WHETHER YOU SHOULD BLOW THE WHISTLE.

The objective of whistle-blowing is to stop illegal or unethical wrongdoing. A whistle-blower is more likely to be effective when he or she has credibility, power, and support within the organization; when written evidence of the wrongdoing is available; when the business doesn't depend on the wrongdoing to achieve its objectives; and when the person being accused of wrongdoing has relatively low credibility and power. Organizations that seek to minimize wrongdoing should have procedures in place to encourage whistle-blowers to take action and assure them that such action won't result in retaliation against them.

QUESTIONS FOR DISCUSSION

1. Each year in the United States, college students engage in excessive drinking on campus. Besides the many negative behaviors associated with the misuse of alcohol, sometimes drinking too much results in death from alcohol poisoning. In the interests of their students and in response to parental concerns, some colleges have rules that prohibit the sale and consumption of alcohol on campus, in sports facilities, and in college-affiliated sororities and fraternities. What are the pros and cons of such college policies? How do the policies of colleges affect the types of ethical decisions that their students are likely to face? If members of a sorority or fraternity disagree with each other about whether to allow alcohol at their parties, how should they resolve this ethical dilemma?

2. Do you prefer the utilitarian model or the moral rights model as a guide for decisions and behavior? Explain. What personal decisions and actions within the past three months can you point to that illustrate your personal preference?

3. What is the difference between judging a decision from an individual perspective and a legal perspective? Is one perspective better than the other? Explain your logic.

4. Can the ethical culture of an organization be improved? If so, how? If you don't think it can be improved, why not?

5. Recruiters who search for job candidates on campus have been reporting a new trend. In the past, students usually didn't make a decision to accept a job offer until they had completed all the interviews they had scheduled. Now, it seems, students may actually accept several job offers, knowing that at some point they will have to decide which job to show up for. As one student put it: "My only responsibility is to myself. If I get a better offer, I'm going to take it. Do you think the company wouldn't rescind its offer if it found someone better who would work for the same amount? Please!" Analyze the decision to accept multiple job offers and later renege on all but one of those agreements. Do you consider this behavior unethical? Explain your reasoning.

6. Are people with particular types of jobs more or less likely to break the law or behave unethically? If yes, explain why.

7. What can you do to avoid being pressured into acting in ways that go against your own ethical principles?

EXERCISES TO DEVELOP YOUR MANAGERIAL COMPETENCIES

1. **Strategic Action Competency.** As the general public puts more pressure on businesses to behave in socially responsible ways, new business opportunities are created. For example, numerous consulting firms now offer assistance to organizations that are interested in developing and implementing ethics policies. Investigate the types of consulting services being offered. Can an organization significantly change its culture by utilizing this type of consulting service? For an example of what one consulting firm, KPMG, offers, visit its home page at

   www.usserve.us.kpmg.com/ethics

2. **Self-Management Competency.** Students for Responsible Business is an organization that was created for business students and alumni who believe that people in business should be at the

   forefront of changing the role of business in society. This organization is involved in numerous activities, ranging from providing information to sponsoring conferences and internships. Is this organization one that you should join? Why or why not? To learn more about the organization, visit its home page at

   www.srb.org

3. **Planning and Administration Competency.** One way that organizations can contribute to the community is by encouraging employees to participate in community activities. Genentech, a biotech company that uses human genetic information to develop and manufacture pharmaceuticals, is an example of a company that takes this approach. Investigate the specific types of community activities that Genentech supports. Does

this company's approach to corporate responsibility represent a sincere concern about its role in society, or are the motives behind the company's activities primarily commercial? To learn about Genentech's involvement in community activities, visit its home page at

www.gene.com

4. **Communication Competency.** Organizations communicate their ethical principles in a variety of ways: through the behavior of leaders, in writing, by offering training programs, through performance assessment methods, and so on. Using your college or university as an example, describe the ethical principles that it communicates to its members. If your school has a Web site, be sure to visit it to determine whether ethical concerns are represented there.

5. **Global Awareness Competency.** Many U.S. companies have located some or all of their manufacturing facilities in other countries. As described in this chapter, employment conditions at those facilities may not meet the standards we have come to expect in the United States. Nike, the athletic apparel manufacturer, is an example of a company that has received a great deal of criticism for the actions of its foreign suppliers. How has Nike responded to this criticism? Compared to some of its competitors, does Nike seem to be more or less concerned about its global social responsibilities? Compare Nike at

www.nike.com

to Reebok at

www.reebok.com

and New Balance at

www.newbalance.com

REAL-TIME CASE ANALYSIS

ETHICAL ASPIRATIONS AT LEVI STRAUSS & COMPANY

In 1872, Levi Strauss received a letter from Jacob Davis. A Nevada tailor, who had been buying bolts of fabric from Strauss's dry goods company, Davis wrote to explain how he used metal rivets to strengthen the construction of the overalls he made. Because Davis couldn't afford to file for a patent, he invited Strauss to become a partner. Strauss knew a good idea when he saw it and the two were granted the patent in 1873. Today, Levi Strauss & Company is still privately owned, and the company's approach to ethical management is as familiar to business leaders as their jeans are to teenagers. Its mission statement begins, "The mission of Levi Strauss & Co. is to sustain responsible commercial success as a global marketing company of branded apparel." Its Aspiration Statement goes on to say, "We all want a company people can be proud of, . . ." which includes "leadership that epitomizes the stated standards of ethical behavior." At Levi Strauss, ethical leadership extends well beyond company walls, to its dealings with some 500 cutting, sewing, and finishing contractors in more than 50 countries. Despite cultural differences in what is viewed as ethical or as common business practices, the company seeks business partners "who aspire as individuals and in the conduct of all their businesses" to ethical standards compatible with those of Levi

Strauss. In addition to legal compliance, the company will do business only with partners who share a commitment to the environment and conduct their business consistent with its own Environmental Philosophy and Guiding Principles. In the area of employment, partners must pay prevailing wage rates, require less than a sixty-hour week, not use workers under age fourteen and not younger than the compulsory age to be in school, not use prison labor, and not use corporal punishment or other forms of coercion. Levi Strauss regularly conducts contractor evaluations to ensure compliance. It helps companies develop ethical solutions when noncompliance is discovered.

Closer to home, Levi Strauss actively promotes ethical business practices through activities such as membership in Business for Social Responsibility—an alliance of companies that share their successful strategies and practices through educational programs and materials. The company's domestic employment policies also are known for being ahead of the times. For example, it was among the first companies to offer insurance benefits to its employees' unmarried domestic partners. Through this and other policies, the company has taken a strong stance in favor of the diversity that employees bring to the workplace.[84]

QUESTIONS

1. Based on what you know about Levi Strauss & Company's approach to ethics, what model of ethics does the company seem to endorse? Explain.

2. Suppose that Levi Strauss were a public company. Knowing that its managers are willing to trade some economic efficiencies in order to operate according to their collective view of what is "ethical," would you buy shares of stock in this company? Why or why not?

3. Managers at Levi Strauss believe that they run an ethical company, but some critics view their liberal employment and benefits policies as immoral. These critics object to the policies because they are inconsistent with the critics' religious views. Analyze the pros and cons of adopting socially liberal employment policies that are viewed by some members of society (including potential employees and potential customers) as immoral.

To learn more about managing ethically at Levi Strauss & Company, visit the company's home page at

www.levi.com

VIDEO CASE

THE BODY SHOP: LATHER, RINSE, REPATRIATE?

The Body Shop has made a reputation on its corporate ethical conduct, pursuing a policy of "trade not aid," that is, establishing relationships with its suppliers that stress mutual respect and that don't merely distribute benefits without a valued *quid pro quo.*

Collaboration goes beyond the simple exchange of money for products made by peasant workers: The Body Shop is also interested in new-product proposals, and it has invested heavily in education. In addition to trade, the company inspires a partner's belief in the right to expect this form of exchange, not a simple dictation of economic dependence. The Body Shop expects its ideals to extend beyond immediate relationships, both to future partners and in the work of its current partners after they may have moved on.

The Body Shop faces unusual challenges in its work, requiring innovative application of managerial competencies. The effective use of communication competency is essential in all organizations, but for The Body Shop it necessarily extends to a facility with foreign languages. Planning and teamwork are conducted with foreign partners for whom The Body Shop's knowledge of traditional business practices may indeed be foreign. Thus, reconciling both operations and perceptions requires the skillful listening and insight of global awareness competency. The Body Shop also initiates strategic actions, from its perspective as the international partner in its many relationships with local suppliers.

The Body Shop not only attempts to establish a fair price for the products it buys (e.g., from Mexican farmers), but it also takes steps to ensure that the money paid will actually reach the workers. It does so by setting up a banking mechanism that prevents profit skimming by corrupt government officials. The Body Shop's strategy might be contrasted with other international businesses, which shop the global market to find governmental policies (e.g., with respect to labor or pollution laws) most favorable to their immediate, corporate needs. Many companies in the apparel industry have shifted production offshore to low-labor-cost countries, such as Vietnam and Malaysia. Although this utilitarian approach may have an effect in raising some of the "lowest boats"—even the cheapest labor will become more expensive as these companies compete for it—enormous income disparities remain. Such behavior also draws fire for the often wholesale loss of jobs in the country or state from which production has been shifted.

Many international and multinational companies, along with noncommercial, nongovernmental organizations, are taking an increased role in what was formerly more the province of governments: instituting international development programs, either for social equity or to promote sustainable (ecologically stable) economic development.

"Doing well by doing good" may have its limits, however. The Body Shop has had a significant—and positive—impact on the Mexican village that manufactures cactus-fiber scrubs. But what should The Body Shop do if consumer demand for cactus-fiber scrubs unexpectedly drops? Should The Body Shop "take a bath" (so to speak!) on an unsuccessful product or terminate its relationship with the supplier, for whom this may be the difference between subsistence and disaster?

ON THE WEB

The Body Shop's Web site (***www.the-body-shop. com***) provides all the information that you might expect of an online retailer, including a catalog of its products and information to inspire and promote political activism. The Body Shop also uses its Web site to promote nonproduct materials. These materials, such as its *Full Voice* campaign magazine, further underscore its reputation for going against the traditional utilitarian views of industry generally, to comment on the cosmetics industry itself and how it "promotes insecurity and peddles false hopes."

In recent years, Mexico has experienced considerable strife that is related to economic inequities, particularly among native populations such as those in the state of Chiapas. Proponents of NAFTA anticipated that it would dramatically change U.S.–Mexican economic relations; critics of NAFTA expected it to cause a more rapid migration of jobs to Mexico, where protections for workers are less, benefits are virtually nonexistent, and wages are extremely low.

The Institute for Global Communications (***www.igc.org***) is a progressive political organization that uses information technology to promote its causes; it hosts several online communities organized around issue themes. Its EcoNet and ConflictNet networks provide coverage of political and economic development in the areas where The Body Shop finds its suppliers.

QUESTIONS

1. When it needs to end a relationship with a supplier, what options might The Body Shop have?

2. What benefits does The Body Shop accrue from its "trade not aid" policy?

3. What negative consequences might arise from The Body Shop's close association with its sources?

To help you answer these questions and learn more about The Body Shop, visit the company's home page at

www.the-body-shop.com

Case contributed by Ross Stapleton-Gray, President, TeleDiplomacy, Inc., a technology and policy consultancy, and Adjunct Professor in Georgetown University's Communication, Culture, and Technology program.

PART 3

Strategic Decision Making

Chapter

7

Planning and Strategy Formulation

LEARNING OBJECTIVES

AFTER STUDYING THIS CHAPTER, YOU SHOULD BE ABLE TO:

1. STATE THE FEATURES OF EFFECTIVE PLANNING.
2. DIFFERENTIATE THE CHARACTERISTICS OF STRATEGIC AND TACTICAL PLANNING.
3. IDENTIFY AND EXPLAIN THE BASIC LEVELS OF PLANNING AND STRATEGY FORMULATION.
4. EXPLAIN THE EIGHT TASKS OF THE STRATEGIC PLANNING PROCESS.
5. APPLY TWO MODELS OF BUSINESS-LEVEL STRATEGY TO HELP DEVELOP COMPETITIVE STRATEGIES.

Outline

Dick Clark Productions

Dick Clark Productions, Inc., is a profitable and diverse entertainment enterprise with 1998 revenue estimated at $90 million. The company operates in three core business segments.

- **Television productions.** This business division produces TV programming for broadcast networks, cable networks, syndicators, and advertisers. Programming includes awards shows, entertainment specials and series, comedy specials and series, talk and game show series, and made-for-television movies.
- **Corporate productions.** This business division specializes in marketing, event, and business communications services. Through this unit, the firm provides services for sales and recognition meetings, new product introductions, special events and event marketing, trade shows and exhibits, and film and video production to many Fortune 500 companies.
- **Theme restaurants.** Dick Clark's

American Bandstand Grill is an entertainment-themed restaurant group featuring The Great American Food Experience served in a contemporary setting. These entertainment-themed casual dining restaurants are based on the "American Bandstand" concept with classic to contemporary rock 'n' roll music playing in an environment decorated with memorabilia covering the early years of rock 'n' roll to the present. As of early 1998, the firm had ten such theme restaurants in ten cities, including Kansas City, Indianapolis, St. Louis, Dallas, and Philadelphia.

The Rock and Roll Hall of Fame and Museum recognizes Dick Clark, founder and CEO of Dick Clark Productions, Inc., as a major force in transforming the record business into a global industry. The Hall of Fame tribute to him states, in part:

> Though his demeanor was low-key and agreeable, Clark did not shrink

when it came time to defend rock and roll. He stood up for the music when it was under attack from censorious voices who branded it immoral. By playing rhythm and blues records by the original artists on his show, Clark helped stop the long-standing practice whereby records by black artists were "covered" in lame, sanitized versions by white artists, thereby robbing the former of income and recognition. Such figures as *Buddy Holly* and *James Brown* made their national debut on American Bandstand.[1]

To learn more about Dick Clark Productions, Inc., visit the company's home page at

www.dickclark.com

Dick Clark Productions has developed new strategies and lines of business—such as corporate productions and theme restaurants—since its formation in 1977. Because of its effective planning and strategies formulation process, the company has become highly successful. In this chapter, we describe how it and other organizations use their planning processes to formulate and implement their strategies.

EFFECTIVE PLANNING

1

STATE THE FEATURES OF EFFECTIVE PLANNING

Planning is the most basic managerial function. When done properly, it sets the direction for the organizing, leading, and controlling functions. In Chapter 1, we stated that planning involves defining organizational goals and proposing ways to reach them. Now we present a more comprehensive definition. **Planning** is the formal process of (1) choosing the organization's vision, missions, and overall goals for both the short run and long run; (2) devising divisional, departmental, and even individual goals based on organizational goals; (3) choosing strategies and tactics to achieve those goals; and (4) allocating resources (people, money, equipment, and facilities) to achieve the various goals, strategies, and tactics.[2]

Dick Clark Productions has been successful, in part, because Dick Clark and other key managers developed well thought out strategic and tactical plans. In tele-

PLANNING

PLANNING

The formal process of choosing an organizational mission and overall goals for both the short run and long run; devising divisional, departmental, and even individual goals based on the organizational goals; formulating strategies and tactics to achieve those goals; and allocating resources (people, money, equipment, and facilities) to achieve the various goals, strategies, and tactics.

vision production, the firm's strategic plan calls for a diversified programming mix that includes awards specials; event and entertainment specials and series; music, talk, and game show series; and made-for-television movies. This set of related products, together with the company's reputation for developing quality shows within budget, differentiates the firm from many television producers. In fact, bringing in a show within budget is a competitive advantage with the growing demand for cost-efficient, original programming from new cable networks, advertisers, and syndicators.

If undertaken properly, planning should assist in (1) identifying future opportunities, (2) anticipating and avoiding future problems, (3) developing courses of action (strategies and tactics), and (4) understanding the risks and uncertainties associated with various options.[3] Thus the organization will have a better chance of achieving its general goals. These goals include adapting and innovating in order to create desirable change, improving productivity, and maintaining organizational stability. Achieving these goals should enable the organization to achieve long-term growth, profitability, and survival.[4] In sum, planning creates a process for organizationwide learning, including the discovery of key issues and options for their resolution. A key theme of this chapter is to help you develop the competencies that you need to plan effectively.

TYPES OF PLANNING

2

DIFFERENTIATE THE CHARACTERISTICS OF STRATEGIC AND TACTICAL PLANNING

Planning is concerned with developing courses of action, improving effectiveness and productivity, and ensuring profits. There are many types of planning, but for now we concentrate on two of the basic types: strategic planning and tactical planning.

STRATEGIC PLANNING

STRATEGIC PLANNING

The process of analyzing the organization's external and internal environments; developing the appropriate mission, vision, and overall goals; identifying the general strategies to be pursued; and allocating resources.

Strategic planning is the process of (1) analyzing the organization's external and internal environments, (2) developing a mission and a vision, (3) formulating overall goals, (4) identifying general strategies to be pursued, and (5) allocating resources to achieve the organization's goals. In developing strategic plans, managers take an organization or divisionwide approach. The overall purpose of strategic planning is to deal effectively with environmental opportunities and threats as they relate to the organization's strengths and weaknesses.[5]

CONTINGENCY PLANNING

Preparation for unexpected and rapid changes (positive or negative) in the environment that will have a significant impact on the organization and that will require a quick response.

In some organizations, such as Royal Dutch Shell,[6] the strategic planning process includes *contingency planning,* or preparation for unexpected and rapid changes (positive or negative) in the environment that will have a large impact on the organization and require a quick response. This process begins with managers developing scenarios of major environmental events that could occur. A contingency plan for a negative dramatic event could be developed for responding to a disaster (e.g., an earthquake, flood, or fire destroying a company's largest refinery) or for managing a crisis (e.g., the strike at UPS parcel service in 1997). Similarly, a contingency plan for a positive dramatic event could be developed for responding to customer demand for products (goods and/or services) that overwhelms the firm's current capacity (e.g., the surge in demand for FedEx's services as a result of the UPS strike). Generally, no more than five potentially critical events should be considered because too many events can make the planning process unmanageable. Contingency planning forces managers to be aware of possibilities and outline strategies to respond to them. It supports orderly and speedy adaptation, in contrast to panic-like reactions, to external events beyond the organization's direct control.[7]

Recall that we discussed at length in Chapter 3 the scanning and analysis of the external environment, over which managers have little control. Let's now consider briefly the four main aspects of strategic planning that managers can directly influence: mission and vision, goals, strategies, and resource allocation.

MISSION
An organization's current purpose or reason for existing.

Mission and Vision. The *mission* is the organization's purpose or reason for existing. A statement of mission may answer basic questions such as (1) What business are we in? (2) Who are we? and (3) What are we about? It may describe the organization in terms of the customer needs it aims to satisfy, the goods or services it supplies, or the markets that it is currently pursuing or intends to pursue in the future. Some mission statements are lengthy, but others are quite brief. The following statements illustrate how five organizations define their missions.

- **Dick Clark Productions:** We are a diverse entertainment enterprise.

- **Sony Music Canada:** Our passion is music. Our commitment is to our artists. Our focus is customer service. Our edge is innovation. Our success is in our attitude.

- **Newport Shipping Company:** We will build great ships. At a profit if we can. At a loss if we must. But we will build great ships!

- **AT&T:** We are dedicated to being the world's best at bringing people together—giving them easy access to each other and to the information and services they want—anytime, anywhere.

- **Walt Disney:** To make people happy.[8]

A mission statement has meaning only if it serves as a unifying and driving force for guiding strategic decisions and achieving the organization's long-term goals. The mission statement should stimulate those in an organization to think and act strategically—not just once a year but every day.

VISION
An organization's fundamental aspirations and purpose that usually appeals to its members' hearts and minds.

Some organizations develop vision statements that are different from their mission statements. A *vision* expresses an organization's fundamental aspirations and purpose, usually by appealing to its members' hearts and minds. A vision statement adds "soul" to a mission statement if it lacks one. Over time, traditional statements of mission (such as stating the business the organization is in) may change, but the organization's vision may endure for generations. The following statements represent the visions of five organizations.

- **3M:** To solve unsolved problems innovatively.

- **Hewlett-Packard:** To make technical contributions for the advancement and welfare of humanity.

- **Mary Kay Cosmetics:** To give unlimited opportunity to women.

- **Merck:** To preserve and improve human life.

- **Wal-Mart:** To give ordinary folk the chance to buy the same things as rich people.[9]

GOALS
What an organization is committed to achieving.

Goals. An organization's *goals* are what it is committed to achieving. Goals may be expressed both qualitatively and quantitatively (what is to be achieved, how much is to be achieved, and by when it is to be achieved). A qualitative goal at Southwest Airlines is to earn a profit associated with expansion into a new city within six months. Two of its quantitative goals are (1) to turn each plane around within twenty minutes from the time of arrival at an airport gate, and (2) to maintain costs per available seat mile at least $0.01 below the nearest competitor.[10]

STRATEGIES

The major courses of action that an organization takes to achieve its goals.

Strategies. The major courses of action that an organization takes to achieve its goals are called **strategies.** In Chapters 3 and 4, we presented various competitive strategies that organizations use to cope with threats and take advantage of opportunities. They include the alliance strategy, exporting strategy, licensing strategy, multidomestic strategy, and global strategy. Throughout this chapter, we present additional general and firm-specific strategies.

A key challenge is to develop strategies that are at least partially *unique* relative to competitors or to pursue strategies similar to those of competitors but in *different ways*.[11] For example, Wal-Mart and Kmart have some common strategies. However, Wal-Mart is much more efficient in pursuing them through the use of advanced information technologies. Dick Clark's growing chain of restaurants, the American Bandstand Grill, is utilizing various interrelated strategies to make this entertainment-themed restaurant concept somewhat unique relative to other theme restaurants, such as Planet Hollywood and the Hard Rock Café. The Bandstand Grills are located in suburban areas, where many of the restaurants' family patrons live. Steve Pirato, the company's vice-president of operations, stresses the uniqueness of its strategies:

> We have a strong following with families, and Dick's name sends out certain messages in that area. It's all age groups, from young families to grandparents. We draw large parties, too, usually family reunions, class reunions. The music is a big part of that. We fit into what I call 'family-gathering days.' Dick is very much a part of the concept. He preaches to us that he has treated everybody like a star. That's his success. We teach our employees that every guest is a star. Every person who comes in is a special person. We generate a certain entertainment, though it's not interactive entertainment. We're not in downtowns, so we haven't positioned ourselves from a tourist standpoint. We position ourselves in the community itself. Summer is our busiest time of year because that's when families are visiting family. And we're a family attraction. With "American Bandstand" reruns airing on cable television's VH1 channel, a children's market for Bandstand Grills is growing. We keep music in the foreground rather than the background.[12]

RESOURCE ALLOCATION

The earmarking of money, through budgets, for various purposes.

Resource Allocation. When an organization allocates resources, it assigns money, people, facilities and equipment, land, and other resources to various functions and tasks. As part of the strategic planning process, **resource allocation** generally involves the earmarking of money, through budgets, for various purposes.[13]

Careful budgeting and resource allocation decisions are a strategic component in the selection and development of television productions at Dick Clark Productions. In a business noted for extravagance, Clark stopped filming "American Bandstand" in 1989 when the faster paced MTV came into the picture, but reruns are generating pure gold for Dick Clark Productions. The reruns are a daily hit on VH1, Viacom's adult music cable channel. A show-business production can hit it big but still lose money if costs are too high. Clark sticks to ideas that can be executed at low cost. If they fail, the firm doesn't lose much. If they succeed, the firm grows with them. Consistent with spreading risks and keeping budgets for any one show low and controllable, the company's television productions in 1997 included seven awards specials, five entertainment specials, a game show series, a primetime country music variety series, a primetime network dramatic anthology series, a made-for-television movie, three new Bloopers' specials, and a series utilizing vintage "American Bandstand" episodes. The company also began production of a new children's series.[14]

DOWNSIZING STRATEGY

Signals an organization's intent to rely on fewer resources—primarily human—to accomplish its goals.

When an organization announces a **downsizing strategy,** it signals its intent to rely on fewer resources—primarily human—to accomplish its goals. Organizations often implement such a strategy through layoffs, early retirement programs, not filling vacant positions, reassignment of personnel, and the like. For example, to cut the financial resources allocated to personnel, Levi Strauss reduced (downsized) its workforce from about 20,000 in the United States and Canada in 1977 to about 11,000 employees in 1998—a reduction of 45 percent. In addition, the company closed eleven manufacturing plants. The downsizing strategy was necessary, in large part, because of reduced sales as a result of accelerating competition in the jeans market.[15]

TACTICAL PLANNING

Tactical planning is the process of making detailed decisions about what to do, who will do it, and how to do it—with a normal time horizon of one year or less. Middle and first-line managers and teams often are heavily involved in tactical planning. The process generally includes

- choosing specific goals and the means of implementing the organization's strategic plan,

- deciding on courses of action for improving current operations, and

- developing budgets for each department, division, and project.

Departmental managers and employee teams develop tactical plans to anticipate or cope with the actions of competitors, to coordinate with other departments, customers, and suppliers, and to implement strategic plans. As Table 7.1 suggests, tactical planning differs from strategic planning primarily in terms of shorter time frames, size of resource allocations, and level of detail. Despite their differences, they are closely linked in a well-designed planning system.

The following Planning and Administration Competency feature demonstrates the importance of information gathering, analysis, and problem solving in strategic and tactical planning. Information and its use are vital to the identification of symptoms, underlying problems, and alternative solutions. Note, also, how management empowered the team.

T a b l e 7 . 1	*Focus of Strategic and Tactical Planning*	
Dimension	**Strategic Planning**	**Tactical Planning**
Intended purpose	Ensure long-term effectiveness and growth	Means of implementing strategic plans
Nature of issues addressed	How to survive and compete	How to accomplish specific goals
Time horizon	Long term (usually two years or more)	Short term (usually one year or less)
How often done	Every one to three years	Every six months to one year
Condition under which decision making occurs	Uncertainty and risk	Low to moderate risk
Where plans are primarily developed	Middle to top management	Employees, up to middle management
Level of detail	Low to moderate	High

PLANNING AND ADMINISTRATION COMPETENCY
CSX's Asset Utilization Strategy

The CSX Corporation is primarily a railroad company but also conducts ocean shipping, inland barging, and distribution operations. Its rail system is the third largest in the United States, linking twenty states and Ontario, Canada. CSX Transportation, one of the company's strategic business units, is the largest coal hauler in the United States.

CSX's top management wanted to improve the asset utilization of its rail service to its Appalachian coal field customers (mining firms). The initial strategic goal focused exclusively on obtaining a 10 percent return on assets. A team formed to help the company reach this goal found that current practices focused on reducing direct expenses, such as salaries. Coal cars were held at the mine collection point until there were enough cars to form a single train—in many instances, more than 160 cars. Although this practice reduced the total cost of train

crews, coal cars, either full or empty, were idle much of the time.

The team took a radically different approach, focusing on improving coal car utilization. The team actually increased labor costs by running more but shorter trains with as few as seventy-eight cars. However, these trains moved out, reached their destinations, were unloaded more quickly, and thus were returned to the mines sooner than they had been previously. As a result, CSX Transportation was able to eliminate more than 9,000 coal cars, use twenty-five fewer locomotives, and free more than $150 million of capital that had been tied up in equipment—all while hauling nearly the same amount of coal.

These financial benefits were achieved only after top management allowed the team to develop its own strategies and gave the team the freedom to make the changes needed to meet the overall goal. The funds that

became available from the sale of the excess coal cars were used to further improve plant and equipment, helping other parts of the railroad.[16]

* * *

To learn more about the CSX Corporation, visit the company's home page at

www.csx.com

LEVELS OF PLANNING AND STRATEGY

3

IDENTIFY AND EXPLAIN THE BASIC LEVELS OF PLANNING AND STRATEGY FORMULATION

The scope and complexity of strategic planning, strategy formulation, and strategic decisions vary from organization to organization. They depend primarily on the amount of diversification and the levels within the organization at which strategic planning takes place and strategic decisions are made.

EFFECTS OF DIVERSIFICATION

DIVERSIFICATION
The variety of goods and/or services produced and the number of different markets served by the organization.

Diversification refers to the variety of goods and/or services produced by an organization and the number of different markets it serves. Strategic changes in the amount of diversification should be guided by answers to questions that help top managers identify the potential risks—and opportunities—that diversification presents. The following are four such questions.

- **What can we do better than any of our competitors if we enter a new market?** Managers may base diversification on vague definitions of their businesses rather than on a systematic analysis of what sets them apart from their competitors.

- **What strategic assets are needed to succeed in the new market?** Excelling in one market doesn't guarantee success in a new one. The competencies required to be competitive in one type of business often do not transfer to another type of business.

- **Will we simply be a player in the new market or will we emerge a winner?** Diversifying companies may be outmaneuvered by their new competitors. The reason is that managers may have failed to consider whether their organizations' strategic assets can be easily imitated, purchased on the open market, or replaced by other competitors.

- **What can we learn by diversifying, and are we sufficiently organized to learn it?** Astute managers know how to make diversification a learning experience. They anticipate how new businesses can help improve existing ones, act as stepping-stones to markets previously out of reach, or improve organizational efficiency.

An organization may be a single business (even a dominant business) in a market or diversified into related businesses or unrelated businesses. As Figure 7.1 indicates, diversification and the scope of strategic planning are directly related. A firm that produces varied goods or services for unrelated markets often must have a broadly based planning process. A firm involved in a single product line or service needs a less elaborate planning process.

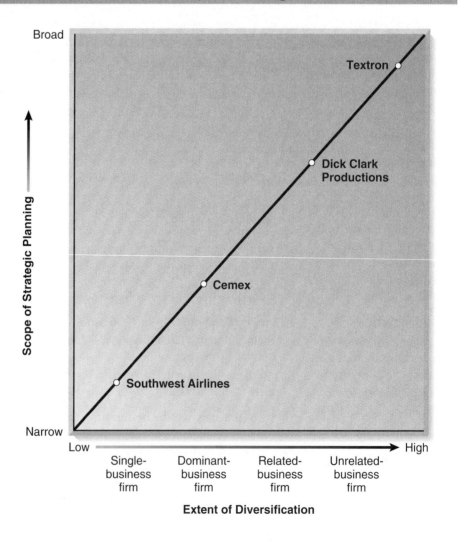

Figure 7.1   **Extent of Diversification and Scope of Planning**

SINGLE-BUSINESS FIRM
Provides a limited number of goods or services to one segment of a particular market.

DOMINANT-BUSINESS FIRM
Serves various segments of a particular market.

RELATED-BUSINESS FIRM
Provides a variety of similar goods and/or services.

UNRELATED-BUSINESS FIRM
Provides diverse products (goods and/or services) to many different markets.

A *single-business firm* provides a limited number of goods or services to one segment of a particular market. Southwest Airlines provides one type of transportation service to travelers seeking high value for a low price.

A *dominant-business firm* serves various segments of a particular market. Reuters, the 148-year-old British news agency, has evolved into a global financial information enterprise. It recently acquired Tibco to extend its competencies in providing such information. The acquired firm provides information management software to distribute and manipulate real-time data for trading rooms.[17] Similarly, Cemex, headquartered in Monterrey, Mexico, has become the third largest cement maker in the world by steadily acquiring plants, distribution terminals, and marine terminals in twenty-two countries throughout the world. Cemex recently followed through on its strategic plan to move into Asia by purchasing a 30 percent share in Rizal, a Philippine cement maker. The company follows a strategy of selectively buying cement companies, then increasing their efficiency through companywide computerization and information system—CemexNet—to share operating data between companies on a real-time basis. Cemex offers a variety of cement products (mixes) to all types of cement users—from builders of skyscrapers to road builders to homeowners putting in new sidewalks.[18]

A *related-business firm* provides a variety of similar goods and/or services. Its divisions generally operate in the same or similar markets, use similar technologies, share common distribution channels, or benefit from common strategic assets. Dick Clark Productions approximates a related-businesses firm. Its three primary business segments are interrelated: television productions, corporate productions, and entertainment-theme restaurants.

An *unrelated-business firm* provides diverse products (goods and/or services) to many different markets. Often referred to as a conglomerate, such a firm usually consists of distinct companies that have no relation to each other. During the past ten years, many North American firms have backed away from such diversification by selling off unrelated businesses. For the most part, the volume and diversity of information needed to manage such firms was overwhelming. As a result, their top managers often reverted to financial data and controls that focused on the past and near-term for making strategic decisions. Many other types of problems also arose, such as too little investment in long-term research and development.

Research shows a strong connection between extensive diversification and a decline in a firm's competitiveness. One of the most dramatic examples of this pattern was the sell off (divestiture) of 250 businesses by ITT since 1977. In 1996, it then split the remaining businesses into four independent enterprises: Rayomier (pulp and paper), ITT Enterprises (automotive components, pumps, and defense), ITT Hartford (insurance), and ITT Corporation (Sheraton hotels, casinos, sports, television, and telephone directories). For each share of stock owned in the old ITT, shareholders received a share of stock in each of the four newly created firms.[19]

Textron, Inc., headquartered in Providence, Rhode Island, is one of the better performing global multi-industry companies. It has about 57,000 employees and $10 billion in annual revenues. Textron has four general business segments.

- **Aircraft:** Commercial and military helicopters, tiltrotor aircraft, business jets, single-engine piston aircraft, and piston engines are provided by three firms (strategic business units) owned by Textron.

- **Automotive:** Instrument panels, interior and exterior plastic components, and functional components and systems are provided by seven firms (strategic business units) owned by Textron.

- **Industrial:** Fastening systems, golf course and turf-care products, industrial components (which includes systems and components businesses), and fluid and power systems are provided by ten firms (strategic business units) owned by Textron.

- **Finance:** Consumer and commercial lending and related insurance are provided by two firms (strategic business units) owned by Textron.[20]

CORPORATE LEVEL

Dominant-business, related-business, and unrelated-business firms normally develop plans and strategies at three levels: corporate, business, and functional. Figure 7.2 shows these levels for Dick Clark Productions, Inc., a related-business firm.

CORPORATE-LEVEL STRATEGY
Guides the overall direction of firms having more than one line of business.

Core Focus. At the top, *corporate-level strategy* guides the overall direction of firms having more than one line of business. The amount of diversification determines the complexity of the planning and strategy formulation required. Corporate-level strategies focus on the types of businesses the firm wants to engage in, ways to acquire or divest businesses, allocation of resources among the businesses, and ways to develop synergy or learning among those businesses. Top corporate managers then determine the role of each separate business within the organization.[21]

Dick Clark Productions' corporate strategy is to utilize the strength of its trademarks, goodwill, and related assets from its television business in order to capitalize on other entertainment-related businesses. These other businesses are intended to complement the core television business, contribute to each other's development, and support the company's growth as a whole.

Figure 7 . 2	**Dick Clark Production, Inc., Strategy Levels**

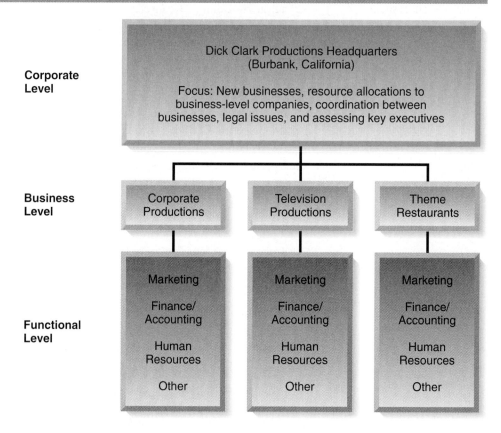

Corporate-level management provides guidance and reviews the performance of strategic business units. A **strategic business unit** (SBU) is a division or subsidiary of a firm that provides a distinct product or service and often has its own mission and goals. An SBU may have a well-defined set of customers and/or cover a specific geographic area. An SBU is usually evaluated on the basis of its own income statement and balance sheet. The top managers of each SBU are responsible for developing plans and strategies for their unit. These proposals normally are submitted to corporate headquarters for review. Top corporate management, as at Textron, is heavily involved in determining which SBUs to start, acquire, or divest. Corporate-level management also decides whether to allocate the same, less, or more capital and human resources to the various SBUs. Figure 7.2 shows three of the primary strategic business units (there are others) at Dick Clark Productions. Television Production, the core SBU, focuses on programming that has the potential both to be profitable in the first year of release and to be renewed year after year. The television SBU is cautious in developing situation comedies and dramatic programs. The reason is that these types of programs require substantial development and production financing and have a greater risk of not being profitable, which would divert resources from other, promising ventures.

Common Growth Strategies. Five common corporate-level growth strategies are forward integration, backward integration, horizontal integration, concentric diversification, and conglomerate diversification. **Forward integration** occurs when a company enters the businesses of its customers, moving it closer to the ultimate consumer. For example, Merck & Company, the world's preeminent pharmaceutical company, acquired Medco Containment Services, a successful mail-order distributor of discount prescription drugs, for more than $6 billion.[22]

Backward integration occurs when a company enters the businesses of its suppliers, usually to control component quality, ensure on-time delivery, or stabilize prices. This strategy is implemented by acquiring suppliers or by creating new businesses that provide the same goods or services as the organization's suppliers.

Amazon.com bills itself as the "Earth's biggest Bookstore" because it offers a selection of 2.5 million books. However, as of 1997, Amazon.com stocked just a few thousand titles in its Seattle, Washington, warehouse. Amazon works with a dozen wholesalers but had been obtaining 60 percent of all the books it sold through the Ingram Book Group, which has seven warehouses strategically located throughout the United States. To lessen its dependence on Ingram, Amazon implemented a plan to obtain more books directly from publishers, rather than through wholesalers. Its Seattle warehouse has been enlarged by 70 percent and a new one has been leased in New Castle, Delaware. The result is a sixfold increase in Amazon's warehouse capacity. This expansion enables the company to stock 200,000 to 300,000 titles and to buy most of its books directly from publishers, rather than through the Ingram Book Group.[23]

Horizontal integration occurs when a company acquires one or more competitors to consolidate and extend its market share. Travis Boats & Motors, Inc., headquartered in Austin, Texas, is growing by purchasing established boat dealers and getting special discounts from boat manufacturers by buying year-round. "We're gonna consolidate this industry," says Travis' chairman, Mark Walton. "We're gonna get better and better." Travis—which now owns seventeen stores in six southern states—is constantly on the lookout for more stores to acquire. Walton targets the best boat dealership in a town and tries to buy it. Some dealers don't want to sell, in which case, according to Walton, "We make it clear, not in a mean way, that we sure like that market and we would like them to join us, but if they elect not to, that we would be friendly competitors, but—nonetheless—competitors."[24]

The *alliance strategy,* as through joint ventures, is an alternative to traditional forms of backward, forward, and horizontal integration. Quincy Jones—the entertainer, arranger, composer, producer, and entrepreneur—has made extensive use of the alliance strategy. He owns five separate enterprises, which generally make use of that strategy. For example, Qwest Records—co-owned with Warner Records—produces jazz, pop, rock, rap, gospel, inspirational, and R&B albums. It's home to artists such as Tevin Campbell, the Winans, and Keith Washington. Also, Quincy Jones–David Salzman Entertainment (QDE)—a joint venture with Time Warner—has produced films and television programs, including the *Fresh Prince of Bel-Air* and the *Jenny Jones Show.* Distribution and access to consumers is imperative in this industry. Quincy Jones comments, "Distribution, that's where the real power is. I partnered with other major media companies to form new entities so that I could have access."[25]

CONCENTRIC DIVERSIFICATION

Occurs when a firm acquires or starts a business related to the organization's existing business in terms of technology, markets, or products.

Concentric diversification, sometimes called *related diversification,* occurs when a firm acquires or starts a business related to the organization's existing business in terms of technology, markets, or products. Generally, a related-business enterprise acquires another company or starts a new venture. Some common thread must link the two firms, such as the same general set of customers, similar technology, overlapping distribution channels, compatible managerial competencies, or similar goods or services. Boeing's recent acquisition of McDonnell Douglas for about $13 billion in Boeing stock is a good example of concentric diversification. The two firms long had been fierce competitors in the aircraft industry. The merger was driven by global competitive forces, consolidation (mergers) by competitors, the changing economics of the defense industry related to aircraft procurement, and the like. Phil Condit, the CEO of Boeing, stated that both firms were faced with a deceptively simple question: "How do you position yourself in a global economy?"[26]

CONGLOMERATE DIVERSIFICATION

Occurs when a firm adds unrelated goods or services to its line of businesses.

Conglomerate diversification occurs when a firm adds unrelated goods or services to its line of businesses. Generally one company acquires another company or starts a venture in a totally new field. Diversified enterprises operating unrelated businesses most often use this strategy. As mentioned previously, this corporate-level strategy is usually viewed with skepticism. United Technologies Corporation, headquartered in Hartford, Connecticut, is one of the few conglomerates still operating in the United States. The primary strategic business units in this conglomerate include Pratt & Whitney Engines, Otis Elevators, Carrier Air Conditioners, Hamilton Standard Aviation Systems, Sikorsky Helicopters, and UT Automotive Systems.[27]

BUSINESS LEVEL

BUSINESS-LEVEL STRATEGY

The interconnected set of key commitments and actions intended to provide value to customers and gain a competitive advantage for an organization by using its core competencies (abilities) in specific markets.

Business-level strategy is the interconnected set of commitments and actions intended to provide value to customers and gain a competitive advantage by using the company's core competencies (abilities) in specific markets.[28] A single-business firm, such as the Kropf Fruit Company or an SBU, provides a particular line of goods or services to a specific industry or market segment. Top managers of an enterprise or SBU are constantly involved with planning and formulating strategies for (1) maintaining or gaining a competitive edge in serving its customers, (2) determining how each functional area (e.g., production, human resources, marketing, and finance) can best contribute to its overall effectiveness, and (3) allocating resources among its functions.

A focus on customers is the foundation of successful business-level plans and strategies. When planning and formulating strategies that focus on customers, management must address three basic questions.

- **Who will be served?** Customer needs and demand may vary according to demographic characteristics (e.g., age, gender, income, occupation, education, race, nationality, and social class); geographic location; life-style choices (e.g., single or married, with or without children); type of customer (e.g., manufacturers, wholesalers, retailers, or end customers); and so on. Callaway Golf primarily serves consumers of golf equipment (golfers).

- **What customer needs will be satisfied?** Callaway Golf serves the needs of average and skilled golfers for high-quality premium clubs.

- **How will customers' needs be satisfied?** Callaway Golf uses its core competencies in product innovation, marketing, and distribution to serve its customers.[29]

The following Strategic Action Competency account provides a vivid example of what happens when a firm loses touch with both its customers and new, more economical technologies that serve its customers' needs better. The strategic action competency requires that managers stay informed of the actions of competitors, analyze general trends in the industry and their implications for the future, recognize when changes in the industry create significant threats and opportunities, understand the strengths and limitations of various business strategies, and recognize the management challenges of alternative strategies and address them systematically. Encyclopaedia Britannica management failed to rethink the strategic fundamentals of its business and paid the price.

Britannica's vulnerability was mainly the result of its continued dependence on the economics of intensive personal selling, which no longer was effective in that particular industry. However, many businesses, including automobile, insurance, real estate, and travel agencies still sell their goods and services that way.[30]

FUNCTIONAL LEVEL

FUNCTIONAL-LEVEL STRATEGY

The set of highly related commitments and actions intended to provide value and help an organization gain a competitive advantage through its operations (manufacturing), marketing, human resources, and finance.

Functional-level strategy is the set of highly related commitments and actions established for operations (manufacturing), marketing, human resources, finance, and the organization's other functional areas. Functional-level plans and strategies should be designed to complement business-level strategies and plans. At the functional level, these tasks often involve a combination of strategic and tactical planning. Table 7.2 provides examples of the issues that management in various types of firms usually address in developing functional-level plans and strategies.

Let's briefly consider one functional area. Operations strategies specify how the firm will utilize its production capabilities to support its business-level strategies. Similarly, marketing strategies address how the firm will sell and distribute its goods and services. Finance strategies identify how best to obtain and allocate the firm's financial resources. As discussed further in Chapter 21, typical operations plans and strategies address the following issues.

- Capacity requirements: amount, timing, and type.

- Facilities: size, location, and specialization.

- Technology: equipment, automation, and linkages.

- Vertical integration: extent of use of outside suppliers.

- Quality: defect prevention, monitoring, and intervention.

- Inventory management and control: amount, storage, and replenishment frequency.

- Environmental standards: noise, pollution levels, and waste.[32]

Encyclopædia Britannica was one of the strongest and best-known brand names in the world. Since 1990, sales of Britannica's printed multivolume sets have fallen by more than 50 percent. Recently, CD-ROMs have devastated the traditional printed encyclopedia business.

The printed *Encyclopædia Britannica* set used to sell for about $1,500 to $2,200. An encyclopedia on CD-ROM, such as the Microsoft Encarta, sells for about $50. Some people get Encarta at no extra cost when they buy personal computers or CD-ROM drives. The production cost for a set of encyclopedias—printing, binding, and physical distribution—is about $200 to $300. The production cost for a CD-ROM is about $1.50. This example illustrates but one way in which new information technologies and competition can disrupt the conventional strategies of an established business.

Britannica's management appeared to view CD-ROMs as noth-

ing more than electronic versions of inferior products. Encarta's content is licensed by Funk & Wagnalls, whose encyclopedia historically had been sold in supermarkets. Microsoft added slightly to that content with simple public-domain illustrations and movie clips. Britannica's editors apparently viewed Encarta as a toy, not an encyclopedia.

Judging from their initial inaction, Britannica's executives failed to understand what their customers were really buying. Parents had been buying the *Encyclopædia Britannica* less for its intellectual content than out of a desire to do the right thing for their children. When parents want to "do the right thing today," they buy their children a computer.

The PC appears to be Britannica's real competitor. With many computers come a dozen or so CD-ROMs, one of which may happen to be—as far as customers are concerned—a reasonable substitute for the printed version of *Encyclopædia Britannica*.

When the threat became overwhelming, Britannica did create a CD-ROM version of its encyclopedia. Initially, to avoid undercutting its sales force, the company included it free with the printed version and charged $1,000 to anyone buying the CD-ROM by itself. The largest part of Britannica's cost structure was not for the content, including editorial work—which constituted only about 5 percent of total costs—but that of the direct sales force. The encyclopedia sets were sold door-to-door by salespeople who were paid a significant commission. Revenues continued to decline, and the best salespeople left. Britannica's owner, a trust controlled by the University of Chicago, finally sold the enterprise. Under new management, the company is rebuilding around the Internet.

In 1996, the new management disbanded the company's North American sales force—140 company employees and 410 independent contractors. The sales force was no longer selling enough encyclopedias to justify the cost. The money saved is going toward further development of its Web-based product, Britannica Online, and its CD-ROM edition. Britannica now markets its products through direct-mail advertising, television commercials, and its Web site. The 1998 CD-ROM version of the entire Britannica was marketed for about $350. It includes, among other features, all the words of the 1998 thirty-two volume printed set (some 44 million words), about 8,000 photographs and illustrations, 15,000 related Internet links, 1.4 million hyperlinks, 1,200 animated maps, and the Merriam-Webster *New Collegiate Dictionary*.[31]

* * *

To learn more about the *Encyclopædia Britannica*, visit the company's home page at

www.ebig.com

Herman Miller, Inc., is an office furniture manufacturer headquartered in Zeeland, Michigan. Over the past decade, the firm has developed many plans and implemented many strategies to improve its operations. More recently, the company has waged a campaign among its 7,000 employees to reduce waste, which the company defines as "materials that enter the manufacturing facility but are not shipped to customers." The company aims to eliminate all waste going to landfills

Sample Functions	Sample Key Issues
Human resources	• What type of reward system is needed?
	• How should the performance of employees be reviewed?
	• What approach should be used to recruit qualified personnel?
	• How is affirmative and fair treatment ensured for women, minorities, and the disabled?
Finance	• What is the desired mixture of borrowed funds and equity funds?
	• What portion of profits should be reinvested and what portion paid out as dividends?
	• What criteria should be used in allocating financial and human resources to projects?
	• What should be the criteria for issuing credit to customers?
Marketing	• What goods or services should be emphasized?
	• How should products be distributed (e.g., direct selling, wholesalers, retailers, etc.)?
	• Should competition be primarily on price or on other factors?
	• What corporate image and product features should be emphasized to customers?
Operations (manufacturing)	• What should be the level of commitment to total quality?
	• How should suppliers be selected?
	• Should the focus be on production runs for inventory or producing primarily in response to customer orders?
	• What production operations should be changed (e.g., automated or laid out differently) to improve productivity?

by the end of 1998 and substantially reducing materials going into incinerators, composting, recycling or any form of disposal—all the while continuing to grow. Herman Miller has dramatically reduced emissions of pollutants from its adhesives, coatings, and solvents. It has worked with customers and suppliers to halve the amount of packaging without sacrificing product protection. Its facilities use the latest energy- and cost-saving technologies, including passive solar techniques. Nonrecyclable materials are burned to heat and cool its Zeeland headquarters and to produce some of the electricity used there. Its Ethospace line of office systems is largely made of recycled steel and is designed for easy repair to avoid premature disposal.[33]

STRATEGIC PLANNING PROCESS

4

EXPLAIN THE EIGHT TASKS OF THE STRATEGIC PLANNING PROCESS

We have presented various concepts and issues involved in planning and strategy formulation. In this section, we expand on some of those concepts and issues and present them as a process of strategic planning. The focus is on business-level planning, with some consideration of functional-level planning.

Considerably more attention is given to functional-level issues and planning in Chapters 9, 10, 12, and 21.

The process of strategic planning is presented for single-business firms (or SBUs) as a sequence of eight core tasks, which are summarized in Figure 7.3. In practice, managers and teams, such as at the Kropf Fruit Company, involved in business-level strategic planning often jump back and forth between tasks, or even skip tasks, as they develop strategic plans. Also, a proposed strategy may be abandoned if it can't be implemented for some reason that wasn't apparent initially.

TASK 1: DEVELOP MISSION AND GOALS

As indicated previously, organizational mission and goals are developed by answering questions such as: What business are we in? What are we committed to? and What results do we want to achieve? General goals provide broad direction for decision making and may not change from year to year. The mission and goals are not developed in isolation, as indicated by the two-way arrows in Figure 7.3. They are influenced by diagnosis of environmental threats and opportunities (task 2) and diagnosis of the organization's strengths and weaknesses (task 3).

The Meredith Corporation, headquartered in Des Moines, Iowa, has a clear sense of its mission and general goals. The firm defines itself as America's leading home and family media company. "We're an old company, but we're not old-fashioned," says Chairman Jack Rehm. He sums up in a short sentence the company's mission: "Provide information on the home and family to the people in this country who want it." The great issues of the day are not its focus. Meredith offers instead a continuous stream of tips on how families can lead more desirable lives. The heart of the firm is *Better Homes and Gardens*. It and Meredith's other big seller, *Ladies' Home Journal,* belong to the highly competitive group of women's service magazines. Meredith's 63-million-name database provides a competitive advantage when it launches new magazines, sixteen in the last ten years. Those names are people that it knows a lot about: what they've subscribed to, what they've purchased, whether they've ordered a certain type of product, and the like.[34]

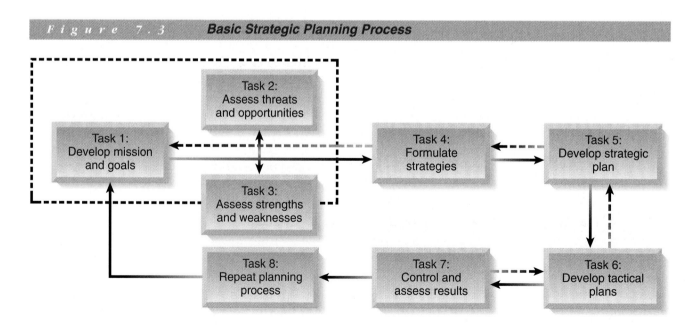

| Figure 7.3 | **Basic Strategic Planning Process** |

TASK 2: ASSESS THREATS AND OPPORTUNITIES

In Chapters 3 and 4, we discussed environmental forces—internal and external, domestic and global—that can affect an organization. These forces represent significant threats or opportunities for an organization. Strategic planning helps managers identify these threats and opportunities and to take them into account in developing the organization's mission, goals, plans, and strategies. Political forces and stakeholders within and outside the organization play a key role in determining the organization's mission and goals, as well as exerting pressures for changing them. Top managers negotiate with powerful stakeholders (boards of directors, banks, governments, major customers, and suppliers) in an attempt to influence those forces.

The task environment exerts the most direct influence on an organization's strategic planning process. In Chapter 3, we reviewed the framework suggested by Michael Porter for diagnosing the competitive forces that a firm faces at any particular time.[35] Recall that this framework (see Figure 3.4 and related discussion) includes five competitive forces: threat of new competitors, customer bargaining power, supplier bargaining power, threat of substitute products, and rivalry among existing firms in the industry. The combined strength of these forces affects the long-run profit potential in an industry. That, in turn, affects each individual firm's (or SBU's) overall profit potential, growth prospects, and even likelihood of survival. To be effective, strategic planning must include a careful diagnosis of these forces. Several specific variables affect the strength of each force, but a review of all the variables is beyond the scope of this book. Here, we simply review each force and highlight its potential impact on a firm's strategic planning.

Threat of New Competitors. The entry of new competitors often is a response to high profits earned by established firms and/or rapid growth in an industry. The difficulties that new competitors face depend mainly on the barriers to entry and the reactions of established competitors. Barriers to entry are factors that make entering an industry relatively easy or relatively difficult. Two important barriers are economies of scale (lower costs of volumes increase) and capital requirements.

Nortel, formally known as Northern Telecom, and headquartered in Brampton, Ontario, Canada, designs, builds, and integrates wireless enterprise, public carrier, and broadband networks for information, education, entertainment, and commerce. "A World of Networks" is the company's vision for creating digital networks for a wide range of public and private sector customers worldwide.

The telecommunications industry and Nortel, as one of its largest businesses, have gone through a revolution since the mid-1980s. Nortel's management recognizes that absolute or even clear distinctions no longer exist in the markets or among the customers of telecom-service providers, cable operators, computer companies, software developers, and some entertainment conglomerates. The convergence of information-related industries is evident in the global trend of cross-investments, mergers, and alliances that include

- phone companies owning cable systems abroad and at home and cable companies offering telephone service;

- satellite TV and data networks being launched by a defense contractor, a computer manufacturer, and a media company;

- consumer electronics manufacturers buying movie and music producers;

- software companies acquiring the rights to images, data, and entertainment content; and

- marketing companies, Web page designers, and entrepreneurs creating new frontiers for electronic commerce, with virtual transactions across global online networks.[36]

The technological drivers for these changes are the computer revolution and *digital convergence*—the coming together of previously distinct products that use digital technologies. For example, the telephone and the computer both utilize digital technologies. However, they historically served completely different markets with entirely different functions. The process of digital convergence means that a computer begins to incorporate the functionality of a communicating device and that the telephone takes on the functionality of a computer.[37] The dramatic declines in the cost of computer power and digital convergence have greatly helped to reduce economies of scale and capital requirements as barriers to new competitors in providing the increasing array of telecommunications services.

Customer Bargaining Power. The bargaining power of customers depends on their relative ability to play one firm off against another in order to force down prices, obtain higher quality, or buy more goods or services for the same price. As a result of deregulation, new computer-based technologies, digital convergence, and new competitors, the power of customers in purchasing telecommunications services has increased substantially over the past dozen years.

The bargaining power of customers is likely to be great in the following situations.

- A small number of customers purchase relatively large volumes from the seller. Major automobile firms buy original equipment tires from a few makers.

- Customers purchase standard and undifferentiated goods or services. Customers perceive little difference between many telecommunications services, such as long distance service.

- Customers can easily switch from one seller to another. Long distance telephone service providers, such as MCI and AT&T, make switching easy.

Supplier Bargaining Power. The bargaining power of suppliers increases when they can increase or protect market share, raise prices, or eliminate certain features of their goods or services with little fear of losing customers. The situations that tend to make suppliers more powerful are similar to those that make customers more powerful. The bargaining power of suppliers is likely to be great in the following situations.

- A small number of suppliers sell to a large number of customers in an industry. Boeing and Airbus are the primary suppliers of airplanes to commercial airlines worldwide.

- Suppliers don't have to worry about substitute goods or services that their customers can readily buy. Airlines can't substitute another product for a jet liner.

- Suppliers' goods or services are differentiated. A Boeing 767 is substantially different from an Airbus A300 in terms of the number of passengers it can carry and its range.

Headquartered in Santa Clara, California, and a giant manufacturer of microprocessors (computer chips), Intel is generally viewed as having substantial supplier power. Intel's power extends in two directions. Horizontally its reach extends to an 88 percent market share in PC microprocessor chips. The firm's reach is expanding vertically, too. Electronic functions once left to ancillary chips made by other chip companies are now being absorbed into Intel's core processor chips. Because those surrounding chips mainly perform multimedia and communications functions, Intel calls its vertical integration policy MMX (for "multimedia extensions"). Customers seem to feel that this policy best serves their interests. The reason is that the more functions that are combined on a microprocessor, the faster the computer runs, the cheaper it is to make, and the more reliable it is.[38]

Threat of Substitute Goods or Services. The seriousness of the threat of substitute goods or services depends on the ability and willingness of customers to change their buying habits. Substitutes limit the price that firms in a particular industry can charge for their products without risking a loss in sales. Cable television operators are being challenged by providers of digital satellite television transmission. Brinks and other armored car and guard operators are being increasingly threatened by the increase in the number of electronic surveillance firms.

Rivalry among Existing Firms. The rivalry among existing firms in an industry varies with top management's view of threats or opportunities, the strategies a firm pursues, and competitors' reactions to those strategies. These reactions and strategies include price increases or decreases, advertising campaigns, introduction of improved or new goods, changes in customer service, and so on. Three of the variables affecting the strength of rivalry among firms within an industry are the number of firms, the rate of industry growth, and level of fixed costs.

The many manufacturers (mostly assemblers) of personal computers, high rate of growth in demand for PCs, and ever improving computer-based capabilities have combined—along with other factors—to create intense rivalry among firms in the industry. Through endless combinations of price cuts, improved features, and service enhancements, global and local suppliers of PCs attempt to gain a competitive edge over their competitors. Global PC firms include—among others—AST, Compaq, Dell, Gateway, Hewlett-Packard, IBM, Micron, NEC, Packard Bell, Sony, and Toshiba. By 1998, manufacturers were aggressively marketing models costing less than $1,000 to the millions of consumers who did not yet own personal computers.[39]

TASK 3: ASSESS STRENGTHS AND WEAKNESSES

The assessment of internal strengths and weaknesses enables managers to identify an organization's core competencies and to determine which need to be improved. This assessment covers factors such as the organization's relative competitive position, ability to adapt and innovate, human resource skills, technological capabilities, financial resources, managerial depth, and the values and background of its key employees.

CORE COMPETENCIES
The strengths that make an organization distinctive and more competitive by providing goods or services that have unique value to its customers.

Core competencies are the strengths that make an organization distinctive and more competitive by providing goods or services that have unique value to its customers. Let's consider just three of the ways that core competencies may strengthen the competitiveness of an enterprise.[40] First, core competencies may provide access to more markets. Toyota has implemented a Toyota Production System (TPS) in all of its auto plants. The system produces high-quality autos at competitive prices for each of its market segments throughout the world. The TPS applies not just to manufacturing but to almost everything that Toyota does, from product development to supplier relations and distribution. Michael Cusumano, a professor at MIT's Sloan School and an expert on the auto industry comments: "I don't know of a [car] company that better combines superior skills in all the critical areas: manufacturing, engineering, and perhaps marketing."[41] Second, core competencies may make a major contribution to customers' perceived benefits from the good or service. Model for model in the auto market segments in which Toyota competes (e.g., economy—Toyota Corolla; family—Toyota Camry; luxury family sports sedan—

Lexus GS300; and luxury—Lexus GS400), customers believe that its autos possess an array of high-quality features and dependability.[42]

Third, a firm's core competencies may make simple imitation difficult if that firm is highly successful. Nobody has been able to match the TPS. GM, Ford, and Chrysler have all borrowed bits and pieces of it, and Honda's system comes the closest, resembling Toyota's in many respects. "Even though TPS has been studied to death, it is not properly understood," says John Shook, an American who went to work for Toyota in Japan back in 1983 and now directs the Japan Technology Management Program at the University of Michigan. "Remember how Vince Lombardi always said he would share his playbook with anyone, but nobody could execute like the old Green Bay Packers? It is the same thing with Toyota. Everybody has techniques and practices, but nobody has a system like Toyota's."[43] We discuss the main features of the TPS in Chapter 21.

Core organizational competencies represent strengths, as do the individual's managerial competencies. Most individuals find that assessing their strengths is easier than assessing their weaknesses. The same is true of organizations when assessing their strengths and weaknesses. Weaknesses often are blamed on specific managers and employees. As a result, statements of organizational weaknesses may be perceived as personal threats to their positions, influence, and self-esteem. But weaknesses are not self-correcting and are likely to become worse if not openly dealt with in the strategic planning process. Recall from Chapter 1 that *outsourcing* means letting other organizations perform a needed service and/or manufacture needed parts or products. An increasing number of firms are outsourcing activities that are not a core competency and/or represent a current or potential weakness. For example, Nova Gas Transmission, Ltd.—headquartered in Calgary, Alberta, Canada—signed outsourcing contracts in 1997 worth $550 million with IBM and the DMR Consulting Group, Inc. Nova is one of the largest carriers of natural gas in North America. This new strategy will let Nova trim a little off the $100 million it spends on information technology operations annually. But the main drivers of the outsourcing strategy were quick access to advanced computer-based expertise, specialized application development expertise, and additional personnel to help with an overhaul of Nova's information technology applications. Bruce McNaught, vice president of internal resources at Nova, comments: "We are moving Nova into new technologies and application development processes. Rather than reinvent the wheel, we decided we could use these two organizations to help put these things together. Playing into that decision was the difficulty in attracting, training and retaining skilled personnel."[44]

Table 7.3 shows a basic framework for assessing some business-level and functional-level strengths and weaknesses. This framework is best suited to a single-business firm or an SBU. In some companies, top, middle, and first-level managers are required to develop statements of opportunities, threats, strengths, and weaknesses for their areas of responsibility. The specific issues identified by mid-level plant managers may be different from those raised by top managers. Plant managers may focus on manufacturing opportunities, threats, strengths, and weaknesses, whereas top managers are more likely to focus on current and potential competitors, legislation and government regulations, societal trends, and the like. Ideally, the key issues raised, regardless of their source, are addressed in the organization's strategic plan.

TASK 4: FORMULATE STRATEGIES

The assessment process and development of organizational goals are closely linked to formulating organizational strategies. Potential strategies, in turn, must be evalu-

Instructions: Evaluate each issue on the basis of the following scale.

A = Superior to most competitors (top 10%)

B = Better than average. Good performance. No immediate problems.

C = Average. Equal to most competitors.

D = Problems here. Not as good as it should be. Deteriorating. Must be improved.

F = Major cause for concern. Crisis. Take immediate action to improve.

		Scale				
Category	**Issue**	**A**	**B**	**C**	**D**	**F**
Information Technologies	Networking capabilities	—	—	—	—	—
	Speed of introduction	—	—	—	—	—
	Enhance service to customers	—	—	—	—	—
	Enhance product features	—	—	—	—	—
Human resources	Employee competencies	—	—	—	—	—
	Reward systems	—	—	—	—	—
	Commitment to learning	—	—	—	—	—
	Team orientation	—	—	—	—	—
	Other	—	—	—	—	—
Marketing	Share of market	—	—	—	—	—
	Channels of distribution	—	—	—	—	—
	Advertising effectiveness	—	—	—	—	—
	Customer satisfaction	—	—	—	—	—
	Other	—	—	—	—	—
Finance	Ability to obtain loans	—	—	—	—	—
	Debt-equity relationship	—	—	—	—	—
	Inventory turnover	—	—	—	—	—
	Usefulness of financial reports	—	—	—	—	—
	Other	—	—	—	—	—
Manufacturing	Per unit cost	—	—	—	—	—
	Inventory Control	—	—	—	—	—
	Flexibility	—	—	—	—	—
	Quality process	—	—	—	—	—
	Other	—	—	—	—	—

ated in terms of (1) environmental forces, (2) the organization's strengths and weaknesses, and (3) the likelihood that the strategies will help the organization achieve its mission and goals.

As noted previously, firms such as Textron and United Technologies have many strategic business units. Thus the task of creating and evaluating alternative strategies for such organizations is very complex. Therefore, to simplify the discussion, we consider the task of formulating and evaluating alternative strategies only for a single-business firm or an SBU.

Three basic growth strategies are common to business-level planning and strategy. A ***market penetration strategy*** involves seeking growth in current markets with current products. A firm might increase market share by increasing the use of the product (e.g., getting current AT&T customers to use its long distance service more often), attracting competitors' customers (e.g., getting Kmart customers to

MARKET PENETRATION STRATEGY

Seeking growth in current markets with current products.

shop at Wal-Mart), or buying a competitor (e.g., Boeing buying McDonnell Douglas). Market penetration also may be achieved by increasing the total size of the market by converting nonusers into current users (e.g., Compaq's introduction of an under $1,000 PC made to attract new PC customers).

A *market development strategy* involves seeking new markets for current products. Three of the principal ways to do so include entering new geographic markets (e.g., Nortel's expansion from North American operations to global manufacturing and sales), target markets (e.g., Meredith Corporation's introduction of an online magazine—*Successful Farming*—for farmers because half of them have PCs connected to an Internet service), and uses for current products and facilities (e.g., AT&T's use of its regular phone lines to carry new multimedia products and services, such as videoconferencing).

A *product development strategy* involves developing new or improved goods or services for current markets. Approaches that can be used to develop enhanced products include improving features (e.g., the reduction of noise in the interior of the 1998 Toyota Camry); improving quality in terms of reliability, speed, efficiency, or durability (e.g., Dell Computer's steady introduction of new lines of PCs); enhancing aesthetic appeal (e.g., introduction by several manufacturers of flat-panel CD monitors for PCs, which require one-tenth the depth of regular monitors); or introducing new models (e.g., Kodak's introduction of panoramic film and digital cameras).

TASK 5: DEVELOP A STRATEGIC PLAN

After formulating alternative strategies and selecting among them, management is ready to develop a strategic plan. The plan should contain (1) a statement of organizational mission and goals; (2) strategies for obtaining and utilizing the necessary technological, marketing, financial, and human resources to achieve those goals; (3) strategies for manufacturing processes and conducting R&D; and (4) strategies for developing and utilizing organizational and employee competencies. The strategic plan may also include a summary of the diagnosis of external opportunities and threats and internal strengths and weaknesses.

The following Global Awareness Competency feature provides insights into the environmental assessment, mission and goals, strategies, strengths, and core competencies that are elements of Citicorp's plans and strategies. Citicorp's managers and key employees are expected to (1) stay informed of political, social, and economic trends and events around the world; (2) recognize the impact of global events on the organization; and (3) understand the nature of national, ethnic, and cultural differences and be open to examining and accepting these differences.

TASK 6: DEVELOP TACTICAL PLANS

The purpose of tactical plans is to help implement strategic plans. As indicated in Figure 7.3, middle and first-line managers and employee teams normally base tactical plans on the organization's strategic plan. Also, you might want to refer back to Table 7.1 for a summary of the features of tactical planning.

Graphic Solutions is a small custom printer in Burr Ridge, Illinois (near Chicago), with about seventy employees. In anticipation of its growth and to capture the knowledge of its employees, owners Suzanne Zaccone and her brother, Bob, developed a tactical plan to maintain strong communication between employees and managers. Their primary mechanism for doing so was to create a team environment. Their actions focused on (1) creating an environment characterized by empowerment, in which effective teamwork is expected, recognized, praised, and rewarded and (2) bringing issues and dissent into the open and using it to

New York–based Citicorp, with its affiliates and subsidiaries (such as Citibank), is a global financial services organization having assets of more than $300 billion. Its staff of 85,000 serves individuals, businesses, governments, and financial institutions in more than 3,400 locations in ninety-eight countries and territories throughout the world.

Dennis Martin, executive vice-president of Citicorp/Citibank, notes that its mission is mainly to be a local bank with a global reach. Other large banks focus more on the global aspects of banking and finance. The difference is that the great majority of Citibank's revenue and sales comes from local indigenous companies. The bank's strategy is to serve more and more local customers, as well as its global customers.

Multinational customers want Citicorp to deliver as many products as possible in as many markets as feasible. Citicorp is dedicated not only to commercial banking products, but also to investment banking products. It is making an effort to extend the power of global investors to local customers. Citicorp also has developed ways to transfer successfully what works in one country to another country. This strategy also has a conceptual framework that suggests—stage by stage—the products to be offered in various countries. The ability to find and assign people who are familiar with those products and local customs is important to the firm's success.

Key employees come from various backgrounds and countries. Dennis Martin is an Argentinean who had studied in Argentina and had never worked or studied in the United States before being promoted. Today, Martin deals with some ninety-five ethnic groups in seventy-five countries. In Citibank's culture, regardless of color of eyes, skin, or religion, employees speak the same language in serving the bank's customers. Martin indicates that Citicorp looks for leaders because leaders bring foresight and change.

One of Martin's cardinal rules is that he is a private businessman, and as such he conducts business in emerging markets under the terms and regulations set by governments. Thus Citibank may not be able to enter some markets, such as Vietnam, where Martin feels the bank has good opportunities to invest, as soon as it would like.

Katuri Rangan, a marketing professor at the Harvard Business School, made the following observations about Citibank's (Citicorp's) consumer strategies in the diverse Asian market.

Citibank identified a global consumer who behaves quite similarly wherever he is. They dine out, go to concerts and movies, take vacations and buy consumer durables and clothing. Even though they may not all be Westernized, they all have Western spending habits. In Asia, getting a Citibank card is like gaining admission to a club.[45]

To learn more about Citicorp/Citibank, visit the company's home page at

www.citibank.com

enhance the quality of decisions, while at the same time facilitating cooperative behavior and keeping the group moving toward its goals. The following Teamwork Competency account describes these activities and also indicates a high level of communication competency.

TASK 7: CONTROL AND ASSESS RESULTS

Strategic and tactical planning must be accompanied by controls to ensure implementation of the plans and evaluation of their results. If the plans haven't produced the desired results, managers and teams may need to change the controls, mission, goals, or strategies, or the plans themselves. The lack of planning can lead to extinction by instinct, and poor, drawn-out planning can lead to paralysis by analysis. A thorough assessment of the results of planning should reveal whether either of these conditions exists. In Chapter 19 we discuss controlling in organizations.

Employees at Graphic Solutions meet regularly with their managers. Each month several workers from each department are chosen by lottery to meet with Suzanne and Bob Zaccone, president and vice president, respectively. Workers' questions and comments at the meetings touch on everything from daily workplace issues to the company's overall agenda.

The Zaccones also let employees know when the company's budget is being developed so that workers can make recommendations on equipment purchases and other expenditures. For the first time in 1996, the Zaccones asked employees to evaluate the company, express their views on company policies, and make suggestions for improving productivity and quality—a program that they plan to continue.

They also are asked for comments—whether positive or negative—about the performance of managers and the Zaccones themselves. To protect anonymity and thus encourage candor, survey forms are mailed to employees' homes and are returned by mail—typed and unsigned, if employees prefer. "It's like a corporate report card for us," says Suzanne Zaccone. "Sometimes it really opens our eyes."

Suzanne Zaccone also urges employees to communicate with her by electronic mail when she's on the road.[46]

* * *

To learn more about Graphic Solutions, visit the company's home page at

www.graphicsolutions.com

TASK 8: REPEAT THE PLANNING PROCESS

The forces that affect organizations are constantly changing. Sometimes these changes are gradual and foreseeable. At other times they are abrupt and unpredictable, as financial firms discovered in late 1997 and 1998. Many Asian economies, including those of Japan, Korea, and Indonesia, experienced an economic crisis and had to be rescued by the International Monetary Fund. Whatever the nature of change, managers and other employees need to be ready to adapt or innovate by repeating the planning process. Hence planning is an ongoing process—it is always a *means*, never an *end* in itself.

MODELS OF BUSINESS-LEVEL STRATEGY

1

APPLY TWO MODELS OF BUSINESS-LEVEL STRATEGY TO HELP DEVELOP COMPETITIVE STRATEGIES

In this section, we present two models of business-level strategy: the product life cycle model and the generic strategies model. Each provides a different way to generate and evaluate alternative strategies (task 4 in Figure 7.3). In combination, these models can be powerful aids in the business-level planning, strategy formulation, and management process.

PRODUCT LIFE CYCLE MODEL

PRODUCT LIFE CYCLE MODEL
Identifies the market phases that products usually go through during their lifetimes.

Basic Model. The *product life cycle model* identifies the market phases that products may go through during their lifetimes. Figure 7.4 shows one version of the basic product life cycle that has five phases: introduction, growth, maturity, decline, and termination. The vertical axis shows whether market demand (sales volume) for the product is increasing, stable, or decreasing. The horizontal axis shows time. For fad products, the time span for four of the five phases often is three years or

Figure 7.4 **Basic Product Cycle Model**

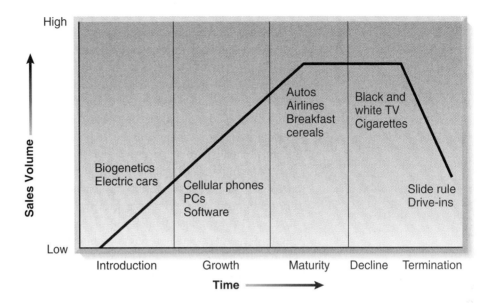

less. A fad product, as in the case of cabbage patch dolls, doesn't necessarily totally disappear (termination phase). Some current products that appear to qualify as fads include hemp clothing, clear products (e.g., clear dish soap and hair products), and carbohydrate diets—one of many fad diets that come and go. In contrast, automobiles have been marketed for more than eighty years. Within North America, the auto industry now appears to be in the maturity phase, which usually means that the total number of units sold is constant or is increasing by no more than 3 percent per year. However, automakers are beginning to experience a new stage of growth as a result of increasing income levels in many countries (e.g., Brazil, China, Mexico, and Poland).

Strategic planning for each category of goods or services is influenced by its life cycle and the phase of that cycle the product is in. The basic product life cycle isn't intended to apply to a specific brand (e.g., a particular PC model and make), but rather to a product class (e.g., PCs, sports passenger cars, bicycles, and cigarettes). According to the basic model, the emphasis on strategies and functional areas (e.g., marketing, production, R&D, and finance) needs to change for different phases of the product life cycle.[47]

During the introduction phase, the dominant strategic concerns are with product development (R&D), finding customers (marketing), and paying for start-up, expansion, and marketing programs (finance). Few versions of the good or service exist as competitors struggle to build volume to a break-even level. Marketing often is aimed at educating potential customers about the product rather than pointing out product differences or building identity for the firm's product. Risk and the possibility of failure are great in this initial phase for a single-business firm or SBU.

In the growth phase, new distribution channels are sought (e.g., getting Wal-Mart to carry the product) and marketing activity tends to remain at a high level. However, the nature of marketing changes from educating consumers to an emphasis on product differences and brand identity (e.g., the strategies being used by Compaq Computer). One competitor's sales growth doesn't have to come at the expense of other and new competitors. However, as a business's sales increase, the market share of any one competitor is likely to decline. In the later growth phase, some firms may seek a competitive advantage by lowering prices (as PC manufacturers have done). Significant price cuts may further stimulate product demand, as with PCs.

During the maturity stage of a good or service, a major strategic issue is the need to reduce per unit costs. Cost cutting may involve closing plants or eliminating the provision of services at unprofitable locations, laying off employees, reducing levels of management, and automating. Automakers and telecommunications (especially phone companies) are among the industries that have used such measures extensively to cut per unit costs. Another strategy is to maintain, or even try to increase, market share at the expense of competitors. Phone companies and automakers also are among those who have used this strategy successfully. Further cost reductions may be made by reducing the number of product lines to achieve efficiency. Sears cut the variety of goods that it provides—including termination of the Sears catalog—to create greater focus and efficiency as part of its turnaround strategy.[48] Pricing also is likely to be more competitive. The horizontal integration strategy (mergers between direct competitors) becomes a more common method of eliminating direct price competition, achieving greater efficiency in marketing and management, and protecting market share. The 1996 purchase of West Publishing (of Egan, Minnesota) by International Thomson Corporation (the Canadian publishing and information services firm) is a notable example. Distribution to a large number and a wide range of customers may be crucial during the maturity stage, particularly if a competitive advantage is difficult to achieve through either lower per unit costs or product differentiation.

During the decline phase of a product's life cycle, the strategic emphasis on efficiency (reduced costs per unit) continues to be strong. This effort may be associated with reducing capital investment, rather than holding it steady (or increasing it to achieve substantial improvements in efficiency), as in the maturity phase. Product options and variations often are standardized and their number reduced. Efforts are also made to improve marketing efficiency. Mergers or acquisitions and many failures among competing firms occur because of overcapacity. For example, over the past ten years, many firms providing services related to oil and gas drilling have either failed or merged. Cutthroat price competition may occur as firms try to increase their capacity utilization and drive competitors from the industry.

In the termination phase, product availability is reduced sharply, and the product may even be eliminated altogether. Drive-in theaters throughout North America closed during the past two decades, as the popularity of television, VCRs, and other home electronics products exploded.

Modified Model. The modified product life cycle model, as shown in Figure 7.5, suggests that product, service, or marketing modifications by firms may change the pattern of the life cycle. In the modified model, the vertical axis shows new strategic initiatives being introduced rather than a range of sales volumes. The horizontal axis shows trigger points rather than uniform increments in time.[49]

For simplicity, Figure 7.5 shows two versions of the product—A and B, although in reality, there may be numerous versions over time. They may be based on product redesigns with new features, additional customer services that come with the product (e.g., many restaurants have added take-out and home delivery services, or new marketing initiatives). They may also involve providing a product that is in the mature stage in one part of the world to customers in other parts of the world who can afford to buy it as a result of rising incomes. The wave effect results from varying strategic initiatives that have positive impacts on sales volume over time.

The modified model is based on the fundamental assumption that the management of one or more firms can intervene in the life cycle of products through new

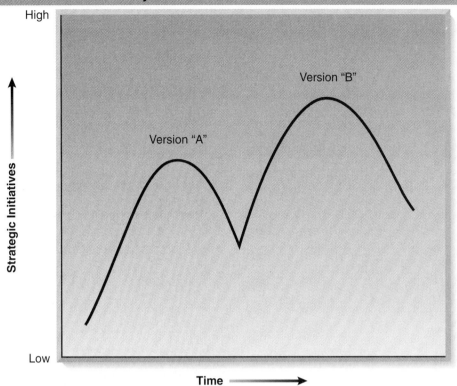

strategic initiatives. Such initiatives can shift a mature or declining good or service into a new growth stage. For example, some years ago Japanese manufacturers, unlike U.S. manufacturers who thought that motorcycles and radios were entering the decline stage, developed new markets (reentered a growth stage) for motor scooters, all-terrain vehicles (ATVs), and Walkman radios.

GENERIC STRATEGIES MODEL

GENERIC STRATEGIES MODEL

A framework of three basic business-level strategies that can be applied to a variety of organizations in diverse industries.

The *generic strategies model* comprises a framework of three basic business-level strategies that can be applied to a variety of organizations in diverse industries.[50] This model is called *generic* because all types of organizations can use it, whether they are involved in manufacturing, distribution, or services. Figure 7.6 shows the basic parts of this model. The strategic target dimension (vertical axis) indicates how widely the good or service is intended to compete—throughout the industry or within a particular segment of the industry. The source of advantage dimension (horizontal axis) indicates the basis on which the good or service is intended to compete: uniqueness as perceived by the customer or low cost (price) to the customer. The various combinations of these two variables—strategic target and source of advantage—suggest three different generic strategies: differentiation strategy, cost leadership strategy, and focus strategy.

DIFFERENTIATION STRATEGY

Competing with all other firms in the industry by offering a product that customers perceive to be unique.

Differentiation Strategy. The *differentiation strategy* emphasizes competing with all other firms in the industry by offering a product that customers perceive to be unique. This strategy is dominant in the auto industry. Most automakers attempt to create unique value (benefits) by influencing customer perceptions and/or providing real differences. Various approaches are associated with the differentiation strategy. They may include, among others, innovative product design (BMW), high quality (Toyota), unique brand image (Mercedes-Benz), technological leadership (Honda's four-wheel steering), customer service leadership (Lexus), an extensive dealer network (Ford and GM), and product warranty (Mazda's introduction

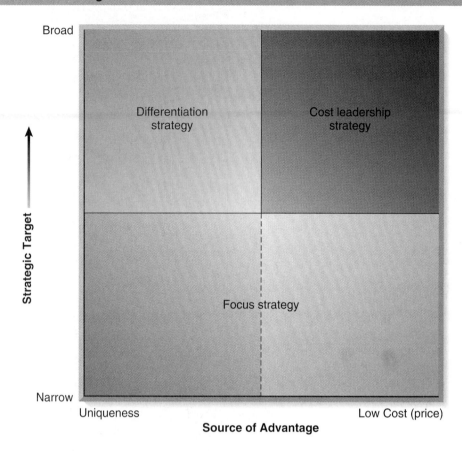

Source of Advantage

of the bumper-to-bumper warranty concept). The long-term effectiveness of the differentiation strategy depends on how easily competitors can imitate the unique benefits provided by the firm. As soon as most or all competitors imitate the offering (such as a bumper-to-bumper car warranty), it no longer is an effective means of differentiation.

COST LEADERSHIP STRATEGY

Competing in the industry by providing a product at a price as low as or lower than competitors.

Cost Leadership Strategy. The **cost leadership strategy** emphasizes competing in the industry by providing a product at a price as low as or lower than competitors. This strategy requires a constant concern with efficiency (reduction in per unit costs). Several essential actions are associated with a cost leadership strategy: (1) utilizing facilities or equipment that yield high economies of scale; (2) constantly striving to reduce per unit overhead, manufacturing, marketing, and follow-up service costs; (3) minimizing labor-intensive personal services and sales forces; and (4) avoiding customers whose demands would result in high personal selling or service costs. High volume and/or rapid growth often are needed for profitability with the cost leadership strategy.

In the retail banking industry, the Wells Fargo Bank has recently adopted the cost leadership strategy. It believes that it can attract money and customers by offering the lowest cost, most automated consumer banking operations. While competitors have been increasing their payrolls and number of branches, Wells Fargo has closed branches and slashed some 13,000 jobs since acquiring First Interstate Bank in 1996. Joseph Stiglich, the Wells Fargo executive vice president who oversees retail branch banking, says that when customers think "service," they think about which bank offers the easiest, quickest, least expensive access to money.

They don't think about some nice, well-dressed person explaining why the loan officer needs five days to approve a loan application. At Wells Fargo, a small business anywhere in the country can apply for a loan of up to $100,000 by faxing in a simple, two-page application form; approval can take as little as a few hours.

Wells Fargo had more than 600 low-cost minibranches in California supermarkets in January 1998, most of them not much more than a bank of ATMs and two to four employees. The number of traditional branches had declined from 600 to only 450 by the end of 1996.[51]

FOCUS STRATEGY

Competing in a specific industry niche to serve the unique needs of certain customers or a narrowly defined geographic market.

Focus Strategy. The *focus strategy* emphasizes competing in a specific industry niche by serving the unique needs of certain customers or a specific geographic market.[52] A niche is a specialized group of customers (e.g., teenagers, physicians, or retirees) or a narrowly defined market segment that competitors may overlook, ignore, or have difficulty serving (e.g., a specific geographic area). Organizations attempt to create a unique image for their products by catering to the specific demands of the selected niche, ignoring other potential customers. Strategic actions associated with the focus strategy are adaptations of those associated with differentiation and cost leadership strategies but are applied to a specific market niche.

Table 7.4 summarizes the key features of the generic strategies model and gives further examples of organizations that have used them successfully.

Small firms that assemble PCs and provide excellent personal services base their focus strategies on a narrowly defined geographic market and low cost. For example, after Jennifer Zihlman observed a flicker on the monitor of her new personal computer, she didn't have to explain the problem to a salesperson or wait forever on a toll-free line. Instead, she got in her car and returned the computer to its manufacturer, Dallas-based Adam Computers, Inc. She watched a technician substitute some circuit cards on the PC. In twenty minutes, Zihlman was returning to her small embroidery business, her problem solved at no expense. For eight years, such

Table 7.4	Applications of the Generic Strategies Model	
Business-Level Strategy	**Feature**	**Company Examples**
Differentiation	Premium quality	Lexus—autos
	Brand image	Compaq—PCs
	Technological leadership	Gillette—razors
	Customer service	Maytag—appliances
		Nike—sports shoes
Cost leadership	Tight cost controls	Discount Tires—tire replacement
	Efficient scale of facilities	Motel 6—travel accommodations
	Efficient service, sales force, and advertising	Wal-Mart—retailing
	Competitive pricing	UPS—package delivery
Focus	Careful identification of target market (niche)	Nieman Marcus—elite retailing
	Cost leadership emphasis or differentiation emphasis	Dick Clark Productions
	Constant review of customer demand in niche	Polo—clothing
		Rolex—watches

service has kept Zihlman coming back to Adam Computers, a sixteen-employee company located in a strip shopping center.

The small companies "don't have all the quality checks, but they can manage smaller gross margins, can be fast and cheap, and they're all over the place," says Ted Waitt, CEO of Gateway 2000, Inc., the seventh-largest PC maker. Interestingly, Gateway grew to its present size from just Waitt and a friend assembling machines on a cattle farm near Sioux City, Iowa, starting in 1986. The twenty largest PC makers have about 75 percent of the market share. The remaining market is served by thousands of niche providers such as Adam Computers, which produces about 7,000 PCs a year.[53]

CHAPTER SUMMARY

In this chapter, we presented an overview of how firms may develop plans and formulate strategies. Strategic planning may be characterized as a complex decision-making process with two major branches: corporate-level planning and business-level planning. Strategic plans are further refined by tactical planning and implemented through action plans.

1. STATE THE FEATURES OF EFFECTIVE PLANNING.

Planning is the most fundamental managerial function. Effective planning can help an organization adapt to change by (1) identifying future opportunities, (2) anticipating future problems, and (3) developing appropriate strategies and tactics. Effective planning also facilitates entrepreneurship and helps employees deal with risk and uncertainty.

2. DIFFERENTIATE THE CHARACTERISTICS OF STRATEGIC AND TACTICAL PLANNING.

Strategic planning focuses on the development of an organization's mission and vision, goals, general strategies, and major resource allocations. Tactical planning is concerned with shorter term detailed decisions regarding what to do, who will do it, and how to do it. Tactical planning provides the specific ideas for implementing strategic plans.

3. IDENTIFY AND EXPLAIN THE BASIC LEVELS OF PLANNING AND STRATEGY FORMULATION.

The four primary types of diversification are (1) single-business firm, (2) dominant-business firm, (3) related-business firm, and (4) unrelated-business firm. As organizations diversify, their range of goods, services, and markets increases which, in turn, increases the scope and complexity of their

strategic planning. Corporate-level strategy guides the activities of various businesses (or product lines) within a parent organization. Corporate-level growth strategies include forward integration, backward integration, horizontal integration, concentric diversification, and conglomerate diversification. Business-level strategy directs the operations and performance of a single-business firm or strategic business unit (SBU). It addresses issues such as, How do we compete? Functional-level strategy establishes guidelines and tactics for managing each functional area and specifies how each will contribute to the organization's business-level strategies and goals.

4. EXPLAIN THE EIGHT TASKS OF THE STRATEGIC PLANNING PROCESS.

The strategic planning process comprises eight interrelated core tasks: (1) develop the organization's mission and goals, (2) assess threats and opportunities, (3) assess strengths and weaknesses, (4) formulate strategies (e.g., market penetration, market development, or product development), (5) develop a strategic plan, (6) develop tactical plans, (7) control and assess the results of both strategic and tactical plans, and (8) repeat the planning process as necessary.

5. APPLY TWO MODELS OF BUSINESS-LEVEL STRATEGY TO DEVELOP COMPETITIVE STRATEGIES.

The product life cycle model emphasizes planning and strategies according to the life cycle that many products go through—introduction, growth, maturity, decline, and termination. The generic strategies model provides a framework of three basic business-level strategies (differentiation, cost leadership, and focus) that are applicable to a variety of organizations in diverse industries.

QUESTIONS FOR DISCUSSION

1. What are the key differences between strategic planning and tactical planning for an organization such as Dick Clark Productions?

2. Review the mission statement for Newport Shipping Company. What are three strategic implications that follow from this mission statement?

3. What is the amount of diversification at the college or university that you attend? Explain the basis for your conclusion.

4. Identify three differences in the key management issues associated with managing a single-business firm versus managing an unrelated-business firm.

5. Review the discussion of the Adam Computers Corporation in the section on focus strategy. To what extent is this enterprise diversified? Where do this firm's services seem to fall in the product life cycle model? What are the primary implications of your answers for the firm?

6. If a quick copy firm in your area wanted to engage in backward integration, what are three possible strategic actions that it might consider?

7. What are the main differences between corporate-level, business-level, and functional-level strategies? Give an example of each for companies that you know about.

8. What are the primary forces driving industry and market competition for companies in the telecommunications industry?

9. Review the discussion of the Meredith Corporation in the section on the strategic planning process. What are three possible threats that this firm should consider in its strategic planning process?

EXERCISES TO DEVELOP YOUR MANAGERIAL COMPETENCIES

1. **Planning and Administration Competency.** To some, the term *corporate vision* is just another buzzword. In fact, many companies craft a statement of corporate vision, describing where the company wants to be in the future, but that's where the matter ends. Albert R. Gamper, Jr., president and CEO of the CIT Group, Inc., holds a different view. When he first came to CIT, a New Jersey-based financial services company, the firm's vision was defined in terms of return on equity, return on assets, and net income. Gamper felt that it wasn't an adequate vision statement. He broadened the firm's vision to include company culture and management style. In other words, What type of corporate culture should the company have? What kind of working environment should the company foster? How should management motivate employees? He likens corporate vision to asking a person, What do you want to be when you grow up?

   Gamper has trouble with the notion that the company's vision is to come directly from the CEO. That view implies that the CEO has some kind of magical power and insight. He comments that he is "not sure that is the case—that the CEO can see so much farther than anyone else, that he or she has such a dynamic grasp of the future." Instead, he believes that the success of a long-term corporate vision depends on teamwork. He also believes that the CEO should jointly develop with others basic operations strategies, determining which businesses to be involved in, and deciding how to position the company.[54] Do you agree? Explain. To learn more about the CIT Group, Inc., visit the company's home page at

   www.citigroup.com/index

   Pick a company and review its Web site (and other sources, if necessary). Does the company present a vision statement? If so, is it based primarily on financial standing? Does it address culture and management style? Does it provide direction for the organization? How does it seem to compare with the views of Albert Gamper, Jr.?

2. **Global Awareness Competency.** As domestic markets mature, many companies look overseas for expansion. The latest catch-phrase in retailing is *globalization*. Retailers are frantically learning the major differences and subtleties involved in conducting business in new international markets. In the case of U.S. retailers, the fact that 95 percent of the world's population lives elsewhere serves as a strong incentive for international trade.

   Several strategic decisions must be made in the transition of the home country retailer into international markets. One strategic decision revolves around timing. It may help to be ahead of competitors in entering new markets. Toys "Я" Us captured the lead with its early entry into Europe and Japan. A second strategic decision involves market selection. Retailers must carefully evaluate the economic and market climates of the target countries and balance their risks accordingly. For example, Wal-Mart's operations in Canada and the United States (stable environments) will offset the effects of a major currency devaluation experienced in their Mexican operations (an unstable environment). A third strategic decision involves assessing the overall retailing concept of the firm in relation to the characteristics of the particular market. Retailers must evaluate and match their concepts to each international market. In developed retail markets, where consumers are more conscious of fashion and quality, specialty stores are enjoying considerable success. The Gap caught on immediately in France and Pier 1 Imports has performed well in Japan. However, in less developed markets such as Brazil, discount stores, including Carrefour of France, have been successful. Most consumers in countries such as Brazil, China, and Mexico are more concerned with price, value, and convenience than fashion.[55]

Select one major retailer—such as Carrefour, Pier 1, Sears, Wal-Mart—and investigate its home page (and other sources, if necessary). What in-store concepts and practices have been transferred intact and what, if any, have been modified—either globally or in a particular country? Have any changes in the size of its stores been necessary? If yes, why? Are there any differences in the level of services provided in its international markets?

3. **Communication Competency.** Even though business protocol in Russia differs from that of the United States, many managers have trouble recognizing the differences and adjusting. Traces of its nineteenth century aristocracy remain in Russian society, despite more than seventy years of communism. Russians place a high value on courtesy and formality when building a business relationship.

To initiate business proceedings, Russians will expect a formal invitation. A foreign manager can expect two types of meetings when in Russia: the brief, one-on-one negotiation (which may last an hour) and the more intense official visit (which may consist of a formal meal, conference, and factory visit). It is not appropriate to just drop in for fifteen minutes to chat or schedule meetings on a tight timetable. It is a good idea to have an upper level manager meet with a Russian official

of the same rank. A project manager meeting with the director of research would be viewed as a breach of protocol.

Traditional Russian culture is more formal than U.S. or European culture. It is an insult to address a Russian by his or her first name unless invited to do so. U.S. managers often like to "get down to business," and feel comfortable with a direct approach. Russians will often want to make an initial presentation to place the meeting in context, taking their time to "get to the point." During this portion of the meeting, the visiting manager is advised to listen attentively and refrain from interrupting.

Hospitality is another core element of Russian tradition. To Russians, meals are a vital part of building a strong relationship. Many times, Russians will be relatively silent during the formal dinner meeting, only to make concessions later over dessert. To conclude business proceedings, a toast and gifts are in order. The toast is an important part of the Russian business ceremony. Guests are expected to offer a sincere and brief toast in response. As a gift, the visiting managers might present pens bearing the company logo to their Russian hosts.[56]

Identify four additional communication tips for participating in Russian business meetings. What personal communication skills do you need to focus on or develop to be effective in Russian business meetings?

To learn more about the communication and related cultural aspects of Russian business meetings, investigate issues of BISNIS Bulletin, under *Russian business meetings,* BISNIS Online at

www.itaiep.doc.gov/bisnis/bisnis

This Web site is the U.S. Department of Commerce's Business Information Service for the Newly Independent States (BISNIS). The online series on Russian business meetings in the BISNIS Bulletin by Richard Steffens, a staff professional with the Commercial Service at the U.S. Embassy in Moscow, is particularly helpful.

4. **Teamwork Competency.** An emerging trend in strategic management today is the virtual team. Members of a virtual team may live continents apart and may not engage in teamwork in the traditional sense, but they serve strategic needs in today's work environment. For example, one team member in Japan may communicate the diagnosis of an important problem via video and then e-mail another member with a proposed solution. Corporate downsizing has left companies with less expertise to cover their global operations, while mergers have created skill imbalances

within the resulting consolidated organizations. Virtual teams are often cross-functional and allow global companies to assemble specialists quickly to tackle key international projects and transfer technology between their various locations.

The merger of Martin Marietta, Lockheed, and General Electric Aerospace Division created Lockheed Martin Corporation, a Bethesda, Maryland, strategic business unit. The result was an SBU with a variety of competencies and problems that rarely matched geographically. "Having the wrong skills in the wrong place most of the time was what drove us to think about virtual teams," recalls Joe Cleveland, president of Lockheed Martin Enterprise Information Systems. At Lockheed, virtual teams are composed of members from the client services, applications, and infrastructure divisions of MIS. For example, a client in Orlando may want a team to build a company World Wide Web site. "If you tried to do it with the dedicated expertise in Orlando, you may not have the best experts," explains Cleveland. A virtual team would combine the experience of the most suitable consultants Lockheed could offer, regardless of what part of the world they live in.[57]

What do you see as the personal advantages and disadvantages of working in a virtual team versus working in a traditional team? What difficulties are there in forming cross-cultural virtual teams? What are the likely challenges of a virtual team that addresses strategic issues and doesn't regularly meet face to face? For more information on multicultural strategic virtual teams, see the paper by Geert Hofstede and associates at their home page at

www.info.ware.nl/people/Geert_Jan_Hofstede/wired

The paper (1997) is entitled: "Wired International Teams: Experiments in Strategic Decision Making by Multi-Cultural Virtual Teams."

On the frontier of this new way of thinking is W. J. Hagerty and Sons, Ltd., a 101-year-old international manufacturer and distributor of jewelry-care products based in South Bend, Indiana. Once run by the head of the family, the company now operates under the management of twenty-three members of the fourth generation of Hagertys. "We have a common interest," says Shelley Hagerty Meszaros, president of W. J. Hagerty, USA, when describing the key to the company's continued success. "We love this business, we're here to work, and we're here to sell."[58] To learn more about W. J. Hagerty & Sons, visit the firm's home page at

www.hagerty-polish.com/History/index

Imagine running a business with your parents, siblings, and cousins. What actions would you take to ensure a positive and effective relationship? How would you organize the strategic leadership of your family business? What do you think you need to develop about yourself in order to participate effectively in the strategic decision making of this family business?

5. **Strategic Action Competency.** Consumer products giant Procter & Gamble has an array of established brands that people use to perform mostly basic tasks. Tide laundry detergent has been "new and improved" more than sixty times over the years, Pampers is now thirty-six years old, Jif peanut butter was introduced in 1956, and Ivory soap has been around since before the turn of the century. In the United States, demand for such basic products grows at only about 2 percent per year.

The company is setting its sights elsewhere for growth—to fresh products, more countries, and new businesses. Procter & Gamble is striving to be more innovative, more outward looking. Since about 1990, China has developed into a mass market, and P&G is winning the race to be a major player in it. In the process, the company also found a way to rejuvenate mature brands and products. The detergent Tide has a new lease on life and Pantene shampoo sales account for a significant share of P&G's sales. Also, P&G now has the largest daily-use consumer products company in China, domestic or foreign.

Part of P&G's success in China stems from management's accurate reading of the market and modifying products to satisfy consumer demand. For example, Pantene (the world's best-selling hair-care product) is formulated especially for straight Asian hair. Chief Executive Officer John Pepper estimates that, if the average Chinese consumer doubles spending on laundry detergent by the year 2000, as P&G predicts, the company's sales will rise to $500 million in that category alone within China. Of course, P&G sells in virtually all regions of the world.[59]

Assume that you were a member of P&G's top management team. What strategic factors and issues would you want to consider in deciding how to market and operate in various countries? Based on Chapter 4 and this chapter, identify four specific strategies that P&G likely would find useful. Explain your selection of those strategies. For more information on Procter & Gamble, visit the firm's home page at

www.pg.com

REAL-TIME CASE ANALYSIS

CHARGEURS' CORPORATE AND SBU STRATEGIES

Chargeurs is a French textile corporation with four major strategic business lines (units).

- **Wool:** produces and markets wool tops through its industrial activities; scouring, carding, and combing raw sheep's wool direct from the fleece.

- **Fabric:** produces innovative wool-based garment fabrics and focuses primarily on stretch, wool, and lycra-mix fabrics.

- **Interlining:** designs and manufactures interlining for the apparel industry. These highly technical products play a key role in the shape and suppleness of garments.

- **Protective Films:** develops and produces adhesive films designed as temporary protection for surfaces during manufacturing, handling, and storage.

This firm is headquartered in Paris. Eighty-four percent of Chargeurs' sales are generated outside France. Its worldwide operations comprise 110 companies in five continents. The corporation has an international management team, and its 7,000 employees represent forty-five nationalities. Top management at the corporate and SBU levels operates on the principles of decentralization and accountability throughout the network of companies. Accelerating international development is one of Chargeurs' major priorities and is a cornerstone of its growth strategy.

Let's review some background information on one of its SBUs—Chargeurs Wool. Wool processing involves purifying the wool of grease and then combing it into fine strands of yarn. The wool yarn is then sold to many of the 1000 weaving, spinning, or knitting companies worldwide. Chargeurs broke into this market by acquiring the leading French wool processor, Prouvost, in 1988. Subsequent acquisitions of competitors in Argentina and Uruguay strengthened the SBU's position. Chargeurs Wool is the only firm that competes in all the top wool producing regions (South Africa, South America, Australia, and New Zealand) *and* all the top wool consuming regions (North America, Europe, and the Far East). This competitive advantage helps Chargeurs maintain its number one ranking in this global industry.

Owing to its global presence, Chargeurs Wool is in a position to offer its customers more than seventy different varieties of wool, mixed from the raw wool

of its producing regions. To accommodate its customers' unique and stringent quality and product requirements, Chargeurs Wool operates processing plants in all major markets. Units in the Southern Hemisphere cater to primarily local demand, whereas those in Europe and the United States produce for the global market. As with all of Chargeurs' SBUs, Chargeurs Wool management is decentralized, with each regional subsidiary manager responsible for the local market. Each geographic subsidiary is further partitioned into two semi-independent units: trade (buying and selling raw wool) and processing (manufacturing the finished product).

The wool industry is extremely competitive. Chargeurs Wool utilizes its extensive international network of trade and processing units to keep a close watch on market trends and competitors' activities. The SBU's ease of access to all international buying channels in all the wool producing countries and its high quality of finished wool differentiate it from the competition. Top SBU management has encouraged greater international coordination of its processing operations by allowing different subsidiaries to specialize in different products. However, Chargeurs Wool manufactures its main products close to its primary customers. To strengthen its international strategy, management at the corporate and SBU levels are working toward establishing a global brand for all the corporation's products.

Chargeurs Wool's primary strategic goals are a direct result of the corporate-level acquisition strategy that boosted this SBU to its current leadership position. To maintain its top ranking, the SBU has attempted to create a unified organization involving three former competitors. A main goal of Chargeurs Wool management is to standardize internal processes around the world so that all its geographic subsidiaries will generate the same quality products and services.

The corporate-level acquisition strategy is designed to exploit further a major competitive advantage: the corporation's global presence. Chargeurs Wool relies on the economies of scale of its trade organization and the synergies gained by pooling the processing technology of all its international combing mills. Utilizing its combined assets, all of Chargeurs' SBUs are able to respond flexibly to changes in the market environment and customer demand.

At the corporate level, Chargeurs maintains a "lean headquarters," depending largely on the input of the SBUs' top-level managers for strategic direction. To develop corporate strategies, top corporate management meets with all the SBU top-level managers twice a year for a week. The first meeting involves discussion of specific issues and goals, leading to overall strategy formulation for Chargeurs' corporate level future focus. Based on these strategic issues and goals, budget formulation is the focus of the second weeklong meeting. At that time the fairly autonomous SBUs are expected to challenge each other's budgets. Financial transactions between SBUs are exchanged at the going market rate for the same goods and services. This approach limits intraorganizational conflicts and interdependencies among the SBUs.[60]

To learn more about Chargeurs, visit the firm's home page at

www.chargeurs.fr

QUESTIONS FOR DISCUSSION

1. What corporate-level competitive advantage does Chargeurs possess?

2. What are the characteristics of Chargeurs' global wool strategy?

3. How does Chargeurs plan to promote its corporate identity while retaining its regional focus?

VIDEO CASE

KROPF FRUIT COMPANY: HOW DO YOU LIKE THEM APPLES?

Kropf Fruit Company's management knows that the company needs to modify its way of doing business in light of changed circumstances. Kropf is planning changes and weighing the options and consequences—looking hard before leaping.

Kropf's challenge arises from customer bargaining power. Its customers are less interested in establishing a particular price than a mode of operations: They will purchase only in large lots to simplify their own operations. Kropf might be able to deliver a better, cheaper product, but, factoring in the cost of doing business with many small producers, the big buyers have elected not to shop there. (Kropf is facing a form of oligopsony, in which a relatively small group of buyers control the market for a product.)

For a company in need of strategic redirection, Kropf is in an enviable position. It both recognizes its dilemma (perhaps half the battle!) and has already established a degree of backward integration. It helps growers by using its economy of scale to purchase fertilizers for them. It also encourages growers to anticipate its needs, in both quantity and type of produce. Because of the long production cycle (apple trees take years to grow from seedlings to mature, productive trees), long-term planning is important.

Kropf could consider horizontal integration as one element of its plan to grow large enough to attract customers: The easiest way do so might be to merge with or acquire a rival of comparable size. Because of the bind that Kropf finds itself in— healthy, but not quite large enough to command attention from a consolidating customer market—it may find that other businesses in its region share a similar concern.

An increase in size through consolidation may not ultimately please customers, especially if it results in produce of lower quality that is more suited to mass-production methods. Tomatoes bred to be handled more easily by machine and to have longer shelf lives, for example, have been criticized as bland and tasteless. Kropf might consider the alternative of staying small and adopting a strategy of differentiation: a higher priced, but tastier and more attractive, apple. Although this strategy apparently has worked for some organic farms, catching a wave of consumer interest in healthier foods, the market trends that Kropf's management has observed apply here too. Whole Foods Market has emerged as a dominant organic food retailer, consolidating smaller firms and chains and threatening the survival of "mom and pop" organic stores and small co-ops.

Kropf's management will need to apply its planning and administration competencies in the course of improving the company's position. Expanding by

50 percent or more will stretch the company's existing structure, requiring that it be duplicated or redesigned. Establishing a new management tier may even be necessary to preserve a workable span of control.

Kropf might also consider changing its marketing channels. Tradition may have bound it to buyers in its region, but the World Wide Web has opened world markets to smaller producers. Kropf might carve out a niche, in partnership with an international shipping services provider, by selling more exotic and high-quality fruits in specialized markets.

Kropf's management also needs to be attuned to global developments that might affect its markets, so as not to be blind-sided by, say, the next kiwi fruit. Kiwis, though not a staple in the United States, have become a popular import. Only a few years ago, before a savvy importer renamed them (from "Chinese gooseberry"), they were all but nonexistent in supermarkets and grocery stores. Similarly, Canadian rape seed oil took off only when it was renamed "canola" oil.

Although Kropf aggregates apples from numerous growers and in turn delivers them to mass buyers, certain commodities are often marketed by the industry (e.g., as pork is marketed by the Pork Producers Council and dairy products are marketed by the California Milk Processor Board). Commodity producers can gain by their inclusion under industry-level umbrellas, although entire industries can suffer, as apple growers did during the scare over the chemical Alar.

ON THE WEB

Kropf Fruit Company is on the Web (*www.kropf-inc.com*). The Michigan Apple Committee (*www.michiganapples.com*) represents companies like Kropf, and the Apple Hill Growers Association (*www.applehill.com*) is a comparable community of growers in California.

A recent Supreme Court case, *Glickman v. Wileman,* provides an interesting look at industry-level marketing. In that case the Court ruled that compelling producers (California peach growers) to pay a share of marketing products as an industry under a U.S. Department of Agriculture (USDA) program didn't violate the First Amendment. You can find information on that case by using a Web search engine such as HotBot (*www.hotbot.com*) or AltaVista (*www.altavista.digital.com*).

QUESTIONS

1. In what industries might producers face a similar challenge of matching the needs of large consumers?

2. Kropf directly owns only a small percentage of the orchards producing for it. Why might this be?

To help you answer these questions and learn more about Kropf Fruit Company, visit the company's home page at

www.krpf-inc.com

Case contributed by Ross Stapleton-Gray, President, TeleDiplomacy, Inc., a technology and policy consultancy, and Adjunct Professor in Georgetown University's Communication, Culture, and Technology program.

Chapter

8

Fundamentals of Decision Making

LEARNING OBJECTIVES

AFTER STUDYING THIS CHAPTER, YOU SHOULD BE ABLE TO:

1. DEFINE DECISION MAKING.

2. EXPLAIN THE CONDITIONS OF CERTAINTY, RISK, AND
    UNCERTAINTY UNDER WHICH DECISIONS ARE MADE.

3. DESCRIBE A FRAMEWORK FOR UNDERSTANDING ROUTINE,
    ADAPTIVE, AND INNOVATIVE DECISIONS.

4. EXPLAIN HOW GOALS AFFECT DECISION MAKING.

5. DESCRIBE THE RATIONAL, BOUNDED RATIONALITY, AND POLITICAL
    MODELS OF DECISION MAKING.

Outline

Tandy's Incredible Flop

Admitting that its ambitious fleet of Incredible Universe stores has turned into an incredible failure, Tandy Corporation pulled the plug on the seventeen-store chain in 1997. In 1992, with the strong approval of CEO John Roach, Tandy touted it as the largest electronics store in the world. Incredible Universe stores sold televisions, VCRs, computers, video games, refrigerators, washers, dryers, microwave ovens, bread makers, vacuum cleaners, and exercise equipment—and many even had their own McDonald's restaurant inside. With such an assortment of goods, stores had to rack up annual sales of some $65 million dollars just to break even.

To make shopping a memorable experience, Tandy followed the Disney World model. Incredible Universe employees were called "cast members." Managers were called "producers," and "directors." As customers roamed the aisles, employees would say to customers, "Welcome to Incredible Universe. We hope you enjoy the show." The average store contained 184,000 square feet. Because each store and its parking lot were so huge, Tandy needed to draw customers from major metropolitan areas, such as Houston, Dallas, San Diego, and Phoenix, to shop seven days a week. Often more than 50,000 people showed up for the grand opening of a store. What went wrong?

First, many customers had to drive past competitors, such as Circuit City or Best Buy, to reach an Incredible Universe store. Many felt that the extra drive wasn't worth the advantages offered. Second, electronic sales were soft and competition was brutal. Customers could call Gateway, Dell, and other manufacturers to get prices and delivery of computers that Incredible Universe couldn't match. Overambitious expansion prevented it from operating stores efficiently. Training of new cast members and producers couldn't keep up with demand to open stores and provide customers with quality service. As a result, since 1995, Incredible Universe had lost more than $287 million. Third, many stores frequently ran short on stocks of new equipment and products for computers. Although the company tried to improve product supply, started a low-price guarantee, and launched a new marketing campaign with the slogan, "It's worth the drive," none of these initiatives stopped the financial losses. Fourth, McDuff, Circuit City, and other stores in the Tandy chain were losing money. Therefore Roach made the decision to return Tandy to profitability by focusing on its original business—Radio Shack.[1]

*   *   *

To learn more about Tandy's decision, visit the company's home page at

www.tandy.com

WHAT IS DECISION MAKING?

Under less dramatic conditions, managers and employees make decisions every day, as John Roach did, using a process that contains the same basic elements. They define the problem (e.g., highly competitive industry and falling demand for electronic devices), gather information (e.g., getting financial reports on store losses), identify and assess alternatives (e.g., improve inventory control and start a new marketing campaign), and then decide what to do. Roach's decision was to close all the Incredible Universe stores, try to find jobs for all their employees in Radio Shack stores, and give severance packages to managers who couldn't find jobs within the Tandy organization. He had to act because he was under heavy pressure from shareholders and creditors alike to strengthen Tandy's financial position. Fortunately, when most managers make decisions, relatively few face such dire prospects. All, however, encounter a wide range of decision-making situations.

In this chapter, we present the fundamentals of ***decision making,*** which include defining problems, gathering information, generating alternatives, and choosing a course of action. We demonstrate how managers and employees can systematically base various types of decisions on the nature of the problem to be solved, the possible solutions available, and the degree of risk involved. In Chapter 9, we present

DECISION MAKING
The process of defining problems, gathering information, generating alternatives, and choosing a course of action.

various decision-making tools that managers can use to guide them in their decision-making processes.

An effective manager relies on all six managerial competencies to make a decision. Conversely, decision-making processes are basic to all managerial competencies. In 1992, Roach's decision to create Incredible Universe demonstrated his strategic action competency. He had a vision that Incredible Universe would provide a unique service to customers by giving them something like a Consumers Electronics Show. In 1997, he relied on his planning and administration competency to close all those stores and provide for the people affected. His managers didn't have the competencies—planning and administrative, self-management, and teamwork—to overcome customer complaints and a soft electronics market.

CONDITIONS UNDER WHICH DECISIONS ARE MADE

2

EXPLAIN THE CONDITIONS OF CERTAINTY, RISK, AND UNCERTAINTY UNDER WHICH DECISIONS ARE MADE

The conditions under which individuals in an organization make decisions reflect the environmental forces (developments and events) that individuals can't control but that may in the future influence the outcomes of their decisions.[2] In the discussions of general and global environmental forces in Chapters 3 and 4, we introduced many of the forces that managers and employees often confront. In Chapter 6, we described how various stakeholders affect decisions involving ethical and social responsibility issues. Thus decisions are affected by forces that can range from new technologies or the entrance of new competitors into a market to new laws or political turmoil. Besides attempting to identify and measure the magnitude of these forces, managers must estimate their potential impact. For example, managers at Johnson & Johnson's ad agency had to motivate eyeglass and hard contact wearers to go soft with Acuvue. The choice of ads for television was critical.

The impact of such events always is felt in the future, either sooner or later. Managers and others involved in forecasting and planning may be hard-pressed to identify those events and their impacts, especially when they may not occur until years later. More often than not, people have to base their decisions on limited available information. Hence the amount and accuracy of information and the depth of individuals' managerial competencies (see Chapter 1) are crucial to sound decision making.

We can broadly classify the conditions under which decisions are made as certainty, risk, and uncertainty.[3] Figure 8.1 shows these conditions as a continuum. When individuals can identify developments and events and their potential impact with great confidence, they make decisions under the condition of certainty. As information dwindles and becomes ambiguous, the condition of risk enters into decision making. Individuals begin to base their decisions on either objective (clear) or subjective (intuition and judgment) probabilities. The condition of uncertainty occurs when individuals have little or no information about developments and events on which to base a decision. Because of that uncertainty, the decision makers may be able to make only a reasonable guess rather than an informed decision.

CERTAINTY

CERTAINTY

The condition under which individuals are fully informed about a problem, alternative solutions are obvious, and the possible results of each solution are clear.

Certainty is the condition under which individuals are fully informed about a problem, alternative solutions are obvious, and the likely results of each solution are clear. The condition of certainty at least allows anticipation (if not control) of events

and their outcomes. This condition means that both the problem and alternative solutions are known and well defined. Once an individual identifies alternative solutions and their expected results, making the decision is relatively easy. The decision maker simply chooses the solution with the best potential outcome. For example, purchasing agents at the State Farm Insurance Company are expected to order standard-grade paper from the supplier who offers the lowest price and the best service. Of course, the decision-making process usually isn't that simple. A problem may have many possible solutions, and calculating the expected outcomes for all of them might be extremely time-consuming and expensive.

Decision making under the condition of certainty is the exception for most middle and top managers and various professionals. However, first-line managers make most day-to-day decisions under conditions of certainty or near certainty. For example, a tight production schedule may cause a first-line manager at Exxon's Baytown, Texas, plant to ask ten employees to work four hours of overtime. The manager can determine the cost of the overtime with certainty. The manager also can anticipate with near certainty the number of additional barrels of refined crude oil that will be produced. Thus the labor costs for the extra units can be figured with near certainty before the overtime is scheduled.

RISK

RISK

The condition under which individuals can define a problem, specify the probability of certain events, identify alternative solutions, and state the probability of each solution leading to the desired results.

Risk is the condition under which individuals can define a problem, specify the probability of certain events, identify alternative solutions, and state the probability of each solution leading to the desired result.[4] Risk generally means that the problem and alternative solutions fall somewhere between the extremes of being relatively common and well defined and being unusual and ambiguous.

PROBABILITY

The percentage of times that a specific outcome would occur if an individual were to make a particular decision a large number of times.

Probability is the percentage of times that a specific outcome would occur if an individual were to make a particular decision a large number of times. The most commonly used example of probability is that of tossing a coin: With enough tosses of the coin, heads will show up 50 percent of the time and tails the other 50 percent.

The amount and quality of information available to an individual about the relevant decision-making condition can vary widely—as can the individual's estimates of risk. The type, amount, and reliability of information influence the level of risk and whether the decision maker can use objective or subjective probability in estimating the outcome (see Figure 8.1).

OBJECTIVE PROBABILITY

The likelihood that a specific outcome will occur, based on hard facts and numbers.

Objective Probability. The likelihood that a specific outcome will occur, based on hard facts and numbers, is known as *objective probability.* Sometimes an individual can determine the likely outcome of a decision by examining past records. For example, although Northwestern Mutual Life, Allstate, Farmer's, and other life insurance companies can't determine the year in which each policyholder will die, they can calculate objective probabilities that specific numbers of policyholders, in various age categories, will die in a particular year. These objective probabilities are based on the expectation that past death rates will be repeated in the future.

SUBJECTIVE PROBABILITY
The likelihood that a specific outcome will occur, based on personal judgment and beliefs.

Subjective Probability. The likelihood that a specific outcome will occur, based on personal judgment and beliefs, is known as ***subjective probability.*** Such judgments vary among individuals, depending on their intuition, previous experience with similar situations, expertise, and personality traits (e.g., preference for risk taking or risk avoidance). John Klipfell, president of American Greeting Cards, thought that by giving people a chance to make their own personalized greeting cards sales would increase. Through its marketing research department, American found that women forty years old and older tend to buy cards off the rack, whereas young adults, who are more at ease with computers, are more likely to create their own cards. American Greeting Cards purchased computerized card-making kiosks and placed them in locations where young adults spend time and money—shopping malls and mass market retailers. Using cartoon graphics from Warner Brothers, American Greeting Card has found that CreataCard hasn't been the big success it hoped for. It installed 10,000 CreataCard machines in 1995 and expected to install about 7,500 in 1997. Follow-up surveys showed that consumers generally were disenchanted with the amount of time required to make a card (about eight to ten minutes from start to finish) and the card's cost (about $2.95 per card) and that older consumers in particular wouldn't use a computer. A poor implementation process, along with an overoptimistic belief that shoppers would use the technology, can be blamed for the poor results.[5]

A change in the conditions under which decisions are made can alter expectations and practices. Such a change may shift the basis for judging the likelihood of an outcome from objective probability to subjective probability or even to uncertainty. Consider how the decisions of some motorists have changed as a result of objective and perceived changes in highway driving conditions. Sandy Stubbs, a Delta flight attendant, runs red lights driving home from the airport late at night. Patti Cantwell, a doctor, didn't stop recently when her Jeep was bumped by a truck early in the morning. Both drivers broke the law, according to the Florida Driver's Handbook. But following the well-publicized murders of several tourists on the state's highways, some drivers say they'd rather break the law than risk their lives. In this climate of fear, driving rules are being ignored. Obeying the old rules—stop for red lights, stop for accidents, or pull over and nap if you get sleepy driving at night—can now be very risky or even deadly at certain times and in certain locations. Thus the conditions under which drivers make such decisions, especially at night, has changed. "Years ago they'd tell you to pull over and take forty winks if you were tired," Judge Harvey Baxter said. "I won't do that any more."[6]

UNCERTAINTY

UNCERTAINTY
The condition under which an individual does not have the necessary information to assign probabilities to the outcome of alternative solutions.

Uncertainty is the condition under which an individual doesn't have the necessary information to assign probabilities to the outcomes of alternative solutions. In fact, the individual may not even be able to define the problem, much less identify alternative solutions and possible outcomes. Uncertainty often suggests that the problem and the alternative solutions are both ambiguous and highly unusual.[7]

Dealing with uncertainty is an important facet of the jobs of many managers and various professionals, such as research and development engineers, market researchers, and strategic planners.[8] In 1992, John Roach of Tandy faced uncertainty when he announced that Tandy Corporation would open Incredible Universe stores. By 1997, that decision had proved to be very costly because of the soft market for electronic goods and Tandy's inability to operate the new stores efficiently. Frito-Lay and other food processing organizations faced uncertainty when they launched their new chips with Procter and Gamble's olestra, a fat-free ingredient. Would consumers buy these chips? The jury is still out. Uncertainty is present even when organizations do considerable research and planning before committing resources to projects. As the philosopher K. E. Boulding put it, "The impossibility of total prediction is clearly illustrated by the principle that if we had tomorrow's newspaper today, a good deal of [the events reported] would not happen."[9] Yet individuals often must make decisions under the condition of uncertainty. They may base these decisions on a combination of research, experience, and hunches that they hope will lead to desirable results.

Whirlpool's management experienced many uncertainties as it wrestled with whether to become a global corporation. Long a North American company, Whirlpool today has manufacturing operations in eleven countries, with facilities in the United States, Europe, and Latin America. Whirlpool markets products in more than 120 locations as diverse as Thailand, Hungary, and Argentina. The following Global Awareness Competency account presents a snapshot of the analysis that Whirlpool's management undertook in confronting the uncertainties and that led to its eventual decision to go global.

FRAMEWORK FOR DECISION MAKING

3

DESCRIBE A FRAMEWORK FOR UNDERSTANDING ROUTINE, ADAPTIVE, AND INNOVATIVE DECISIONS

Managers and employees must make decisions in a variety of situations, and no single decision-making method will cover all of them. In general, though, the decision maker should begin by defining accurately the problem at hand, move on to evaluating alternative solutions, and finally make a decision.

The conditions under which decisions are made—certainty, risk, and uncertainty—provide a foundation for a comprehensive framework for decision making. Decisions may be classified as routine, adaptive, or innovative. These categories reflect the types of problems encountered and the types of solutions considered. Figure 8.2 illustrates the different combinations of problem types (vertical axis) and solution types (horizontal axis) that result in the three decision-making categories. In addition, the conditions of certainty, risk, and uncertainty appear along the diagonal line from lower left to upper right.

TYPES OF PROBLEMS

The *types of problems* that managers and other employees deal with range from the relatively common and well defined to the unusual and ambiguous. The bank teller with an out-of-balance cash drawer at the end of the day faces a common and well-defined problem. In contrast, the problem of women and minorities not moving faster into management positions is ambiguous: Some people maintain that it is caused by both overt and hidden forms of discrimination. Others believe that women and minorities just need more time in the management pipeline and that gender and/or racial discrimination no longer has anything to do with the problem.[10]

TYPES OF SOLUTIONS

The *types of solutions* available also range from the known and well defined to the untried and ambiguous. The bank teller with an out-of-balance cash drawer follows a specific, well-defined procedure—check all deposit slips against deposit receipts and cash tickets and recount all the cash. In contrast, Weyerhaeuser Company recently decided to experiment with the then-untested concept of "high-yield forestry" on some of its land in the Pacific Northwest and South. The idea was not to leave forests to nature and chance, but to manage trees like an agricultural crop. If successful, Weyerhaeuser would be able to grow a lot of high-quality timber.

GLOBAL AWARENESS COMPETENCY
Whirlpool Goes Global

Whirlpool's senior management started with the knowledge that, if the company continued down the path it was on, the future would be neither pleasant nor profitable. Even though Whirlpool had dramatically lowered costs and improved product quality, profit margins in North America had been declining because everyone in the industry was pursuing the same course and the domestic market was mature. The four main players—Whirlpool, General Electric, Maytag, and White Consolidated, which had been acquired by Electrolux—were beating one another up every day on price and service warranties.

Whirlpool's senior management explored several strategies. One was to restructure the company financially and pay large dividends to the shareholders. Another was to diversify into other businesses. If the appliance industry didn't offer growth, were there other durable goods industries that did? Among the alternatives considered were horizontal expansion (buy-

ing other appliance makers) and vertical expansion (buying suppliers). In the process of examining alternatives, it became clear to management that the basics of managing the business were the same in Europe, North America, Asia, and Latin America. Whirlpool was already very good at what it did. Thus what it needed to do was to enter appliance markets in other parts of the world and learn how to satisfy different kinds of customers.

Previously, Whirlpool's management hadn't identified the potential power of its existing capabilities in global marketing. Whirlpool had been limiting its definition of the appliance market to the United States and Canada. The company's eight months of analysis turned up a great deal of evidence that, over time, the industry would become global, whether or not Whirlpool chose to become global. Thus Whirlpool faced three choices. It could ignore the inevitable—a decision that would have condemned Whirlpool to a slow death. It could

wait for globalization to begin and then try to react, which would have forced Whirlpool to play catch up, technologically and organizationally. Or Whirlpool could control its own destiny and try to shape the very nature of globalization in the industry. Whirlpool chose the latter.[11]

* * *

To learn more about Whirlpool, visit the company's home page at

www.whirlpool.com

However, growing cycles of trees are thirty years—a long time horizon for spending resources on caring for trees before they begin to earn a return. Even so, Weyerhaeuser's managers decided that the experiment would pay off and began to replant its timberlands, using this new method of growing trees. William Corbin, Weyerhaeuser's executive vice president for timberlands, says that, by 2020, high-yield forestry will mean a 70 percent increase in yields per acre. High-yield forestry could also permit Weyerhaeuser to grow appearance-grade lumber—knot-free wood used in window trim, doors, moldings, and furniture. He also forecasts that, by 2020, more appearance-grade wood will be imported from Brazil, Chile, and New Zealand. Thus imported wood could have an impact on Weyerhaeuser's production schedule and the prices it charges customers.[12]

ROUTINE DECISIONS

Standardized choice made in response to relatively well-defined and common problems and alternative solutions.

ROUTINE DECISIONS

Routine decisions are standard choices made in response to relatively well-defined and common problems and alternative solutions. Often a solution is available in established rules or standard operating procedures (discussed in more depth in Chapter 9) or, increasingly, in computer software, such as computerized airline reservation systems. Cleaning buildings, processing payroll vouchers, packing and

Figure 8.2 **Framework for Decision Making**

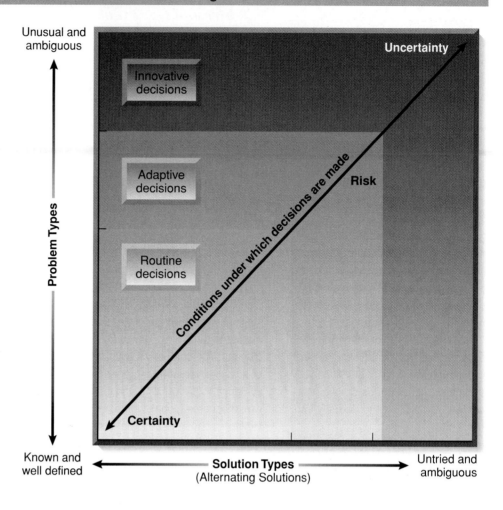

shipping customers' orders, and making travel arrangements are but a few examples of tasks requiring routine decisions.

Employees need to guard against the tendency to make routine decisions when a problem actually calls for an adaptive or innovative decision.[13] Eckard Pfeiffer, founder and former CEO of Compaq Computers, believed that he dramatically increased Compaq's profitability by advertising and strategically positioning it as the company that provided networking equipment for systems, not just individual pieces of hardware. But this form of routine thinking was based on faulty logic. In fact, sales at Compaq rose because its customers spent a record 42 percent of their capital equipment budgets on new computers and state-of-the-art software. The organizations that are the primary buyers of Compaq's computers wanted systems that could help them invent totally new ways of delivering products. Thus the proposal for increasing advertising requires firmer proof of effectiveness, and the causes of lagging sales require deeper analysis. At a minimum, the need for adaptive decision making exists.

ADAPTIVE DECISIONS

Adaptive decisions are choices made in response to a combination of moderately unusual and only fairly uncommon problems and alternative solutions. Adaptive

ADAPTIVE DECISIONS
Choices made in response to a combination of moderately unusual and only partially known problems and alternative solutions.

CONTINUOUS IMPROVEMENT

Streams of adaptive decisions made over time in an organization that result in a large number of small, incremental improvements year after year.

INNOVATIVE DECISIONS

Choices based on the discovery, identification, and diagnosis of unusual and ambiguous problems and the development of unique or creative alternative solutions.

decisions often involve modifying and improving upon past routine decisions and practices. In fact, the concept of continuous improvement is a key to total quality management.

Continuous improvement involves streams of adaptive organizational decisions made over time that result in a large number of small, incremental improvements year after year. Continuous improvement requires a commitment to constant diagnosis of technical, organizational, and managerial processes in search of improvements.[14] In part the process resembles the wheel in a hamster cage—a ladder wrapped onto a cylinder, with no beginning and no end. Each "turn of the wheel" improves an existing product and/or its production methods. Year after year the organization's products keep getting better, more reliable, and less expensive.

Continuous improvement is driven by the goals of providing better quality, improving efficiency, and being responsive to customers. Accordingly, improvements typically

1. enhance value to the customer through improved and new products and services;

2. reduce errors, defects, and waste;

3. increase responsiveness to customer changes and expectations; and

4. elevate productivity and effectiveness in the use of all resources.[15]

Continuous improvement is a cornerstone of Rubbermaid's approach to planning and administration. The company's managers have continuously developed goals and plans for new products and taken calculated risks to improve Rubbermaid's products. Rubbermaid is consistently viewed as one of the most admired, adaptive, and innovative corporations in the Corporate Reputations Survey conducted each year by *Fortune* magazine.[16] The following Planning and Administration Competency feature provides some examples of how Rubbermaid's managers achieve the organization's continuous improvement goals.

INNOVATIVE DECISIONS

Innovative decisions are choices based on the discovery, identification, and diagnosis of unusual and ambiguous problems and/or the development of unique or creative alternative solutions. The solutions frequently involve a series of small, interrelated decisions made over a period of months or even years. In particular, leading-edge innovations may take years to develop and involve numerous professional specialists and teams. Because innovative decisions normally represent a sharp break with the past, they normally don't happen in a logical, orderly sequence. They often are based on incomplete and rapidly changing information and, in fact, may be made before problems are fully defined and understood. To be effective, decision makers therefore must be especially careful to define the right problem and recognize that earlier actions can significantly affect later decisions.

Recall the 1992 Gulf War when the Hummer was launched with great fanfare and Arnold Schwarzeneger's and General Norman Schwartzkopf's enthusiastic endorsements. Its advertisements said that people who drive hummers like to boast that nothing can stop them—that these tanklike vehicles climb over fallen trees, drive through water 2½ feet deep, and plow through bogs with ease. But the Hummer's maker, AM General, has found the terrain tough going in the marketplace. The following Strategic Action Competency piece highlights some of the strategic blunders the company made.

Rubbermaid's success depends on making small improvements to some 5,000 unspectacular products: mailboxes, window boxes, storage boxes, toys, mops, dust mitts, spatulas, snap-together furniture, desk organizers, step stools, wall coverings, playhouses, drink coasters, lint brushes, ice cube trays, stadium seats, garbage pails, bath mats, sporting goods, dinnerware, playground equipment, laundry hampers, dish drainers,

and more. For example, the company took a mop bucket, added an *antimicrobial* agent to its plastic, and it became the only antimicrobial mop bucket on the market at the time.

Rubbermaid profits by taking seriously the basic products that others dismiss as trivial. For example, a team at Rubbermaid focused on ways to improve the common mailbox. The team developed a new model with a double-wide floor that lets magazines lie flat and a little flag that pops up, automatically, to show homeowners that their mail has arrived. Another "household" product Rubbermaid improved is the lunch box. To ensure that the lunch box (known as Sidekick) keeps food well insulated, Rubbermaid engineers adapted the design from its existing line of plastic coolers, which feature high-density polyethylene liners.

In product development, Rubbermaid makes extensive use of focus groups (small groups of customers that meet face-to-face with company

personnel to discuss products). No customer gripe is too small to consider. When focus group participants complained of puddles in their dish drainers, Rubbermaid responded with a drain tray made a bit higher in back to help water flow into the sink.

However, most ideas for improved and new products flow from the company's own teams. Twenty 5–7 person teams (one person each from marketing, manufacturing, R&D, finance, and other departments) focus on specific product lines, such as bathroom accessories. A highly innovative company, Rubbermaid introduces about 350 new products each year. It typically spends 14 percent of profits on research and development. A competitor in the cookware industry states: "They're in a class by themselves."[17]

* * *

To learn more about Rubbermaid, visit the company's home page at

www.rubbermaid.com

GOALS AND DECISION MAKING

4

EXPLAIN HOW GOALS AFFECT DECISION MAKING

Decision making in organizations under the conditions of risk and uncertainty are coupled directly with goals in one of two ways: (1) the decision-making process is triggered by a search for better ways to achieve established goals; or (2) the decision-making process is triggered by an effort to discover new goals, revise current goals, or drop outdated goals. Let's return to Whirlpool. David Whitwam stated that the Whirlpool's overall goal now is to achieve "world-class performance in terms of delivering shareholder value, which we define as being in the top 25 percent of publicly held companies in total returns through a given economic cycle."[18]

Goals are crucial in giving employees, managers, and organizations a sense of order, direction, and meaning. In fact, the six managerial competencies would be relatively ineffective if they weren't directed at achieving goals. Setting goals is especially important in adaptive and innovative decision making. As suggested in Chapter 7, the planning process is vitally concerned with identifying possible new goals, revising goals, and finding better ways to accomplish existing goals.

No one at AM General expected to sell the 7-foot wide, 6,840-pound Hummer in large numbers. These machines were targeted at niched markets. Last year, it sold 1,400 vehicles and lost nearly $20 million dollars on sales of $462 million. Industry analysts claim that AM General needs to sell between 2,500 and 3,000 Hummers a year to make a profit. Why aren't the vehicles selling better?

In addition to being huge and exotic looking, they're expensive, ranging in price from $52,000 for a pickup truck to about $90,000 for a fully loaded wagon. Buyers tend to be baby-boomers eager for a new toy or companies, such as Quaker Oats, that use the vehicles to advertise their products, such as Gatorade and Pizza A Go Go, a restaurant that delivers pizzas in Palo Alto, California. Analysts argue that AM General erred by trying to build a commercial business on a rarefied market segment and should have emphasized fleet sales to potential buyers such as Barrick Gold

and other mining companies, rural fire departments, and British Petroleum, Exxon, Shell, and other oil exploration firms. To sell in the fleet market, the company must convince buyers that the Hummer is worth a 28 percent premium price over, for example, a four-wheel drive Ford F-10 pickup.

The commercial failure of the Hummer is only one of AM General's strategic problems. The company's military sales have been off because many nations are cutting their defense budgets. AM General managers believed that its commercial enterprise would shore up revenues as military orders diminished. Unfortunately, turning the spartan Hummer into a civilian vehicle proved costly—adding many features, such as air conditioning and door locks, drove the price up by 70 percent.

One way for AM General to survive is to change its strategy. To succeed in the civilian marketplace, the Hummer needs to be smaller, more practical, and more affordable. But the

company doesn't have the capital for such a strategic change, and top management worries that introducing a smaller truck would undercut the Hummer's tough image. But unless AM General makes an innovative decision, the Hummer might be an oversized, out-of-production curiosity much like Ford's infamous Edsel.[19]

* * *

To learn more about the Hummer, visit AM General's home page at

www. hummer.com

THE NATURE OF GOALS

GOALS
Results to be attained.

Goals are results to be attained, and thus indicate the direction in which decisions and actions should be aimed. Clear goals specify the quality or quantity of the desired results. Recall from the Preview account that John Roach's goal for Tandy's Incredible Universe stores was to create a consumer electronic show for shoppers by using a Disney theme. Unfortunately, consumers didn't embrace this concept. Many goals guide people's behavior without their giving the goals much thought. For example, most drivers automatically go through the motions of driving—observing the speed limit, looking out for other cars and pedestrians, using seat belts, and so on—when pursuing the goal of getting to and from work or school safely. When individuals deliberately choose to modify or change goals, they often engage in a conscious, full-blown decision-making process.

Goals also are called objectives, ends, purposes, standards, deadlines, targets, and quotas. Whatever they're called, goals specify results and outcomes that someone believes to be desirable and worth achieving. Ralph Strayer, CEO of Johnsonville Foods, wanted to create an organization that resembled a flock of geese flying in a unified V with a common goal. Each individual should pull his or her own weight and take turns leading. He learned that the employees weren't committed to this goal and disliked working weekends and that many didn't want to lead. He also discovered that machine downtime of between 30 and 40 percent was a major cause of weekend work. To rectify that situation, he and the employees jointly set a goal of reducing machine downtime to 10 percent. When this goal was reached, no weekend work was needed. Strayer also found that about 5 percent of the time air leaked into vacuum-packed plastic packages of sausages. This leakage shortened the shelf life of the product. The employees took a leadership role and set a goal of reducing leakage by half. Within a few weeks, the employees achieved this goal and set another goal of 0.5 percent. Strayer concluded from these incidents that nothing matters more than a shared goal.[20]

Goals can cover the long run (years) or the short run (minutes, hours, days, or months). Long-range, or general, organizational goals such as survival, growth, and profitability often remain stable. However, the development of specific, short-range goals for departments and projects requires constant managerial and employee attention. Specific production, human resource, marketing, and financing goals usually change from year to year or even quarter to quarter.

WHY PEOPLE SET GOALS

Setting goals can yield several benefits, which are the same whether the goals apply to an entire organization, a specific department or division, a team, or an individual employee. First, goals serve to focus individual and organizational decisions and efforts. Ken Thuerbach, the successful founder and CEO of Alpine Log Homes, Inc., of Victor, Montana, states: "Every successful person is an obsessive goal setter. Once you have goals, you have a pattern of opportunity. You can't hit a target that you can't see. You must have focus."[21] In terms of the organization, goals provide a set of stated expectations that everyone can understand and work to achieve. Second, goals aid the planning process, as discussed in Chapter 7. After diagnosing problems and the competition, managers usually establish goals as a part of their planning efforts. Third, goals motivate people and stimulate better performance. Clear and specific goals often raise productivity and improve the quality of work.[22] Fourth, goals assist in performance evaluation and control. To modify an old saying, "If you don't know where you're going, you'll never know when you get there."

Managers and employees in organizations aren't the only ones who can benefit from setting goals, evaluating progress toward achieving them, and taking corrective action as needed. For example, let's say that your goal is to get a B in this course but that you get a D on the first exam. This feedback should serve as a powerful incentive to assess your efforts so far and determine how to avoid the same result on the next exam. This type of assessment, and acting on it, is a self-controlling way of working toward your goal.

GENERAL AND OPERATIONAL GOALS

GENERAL GOALS
Broad direction for decision making in qualitative terms.

OPERATIONAL GOALS
What is to be achieved in quantitative terms, for whom, and within what time period.

General goals provide broad direction for decision making in qualitative terms. For example, one of the general goals of the Smithsonian Library in Washington, D.C., is to serve as an educational resource for the people of the United States and the rest of the world. *Operational goals* state what is to be achieved in quantitative terms, for whom, and within what time period. An operational goal for someone enrolled at Jenny Craig or some other diet center might be: to reduce my weight by ten pounds within three months. It specifies what in quantitative terms (lose ten pounds), for whom (me), and a measurable time period (three months).

The following Self-Management Competency article highlights how Michael Dell used his personal drive, resilience, and self-awareness skills to lead Dell Computer. As many shareholders know, owning stock in Dell Computer has been like holding a winning lottery ticket. Someone who purchased $10,000 worth of stock in

Dell Sells

Michael Dell started Dell Computer in his University of Texas dorm room in Austin in 1983. He was enrolled as a premed student but was really interested only in tinkering with computers. He spent his first two semesters buying outmoded IBM PCs from local retailers, then upgrading them in his dorm room and selling them—not just on campus, but literally hawking them door to door to local law firms and small businesses. His growing inventory caused his roommate to move. He told his parents that he wanted to drop out after his freshman year, and they were furious. He agreed to go back to school if summer sales were less than $50,000. He sold more than $180,000 worth of PCs the first month and never returned for his sophomore year.

He quickly realized that instead of upgrading older machines, he could buy components and assemble a whole PC more cheaply. Then he could sell the machine with his name on it directly to customers at a 15 percent discount to established brands. The reason that Dell has become such a profitable company has nothing to do with exotic software or cutting-edge chip technology. Instead, it's a matter of execution. Selling computers directly to customers is hardly an earth-shattering concept. But Dell's goal was to ship newly ordered PCs to customers within eight hours of receiving their orders. His goal for

1998 is to bring that figure down to seven hours.

Although the company's computers have had some of the highest quality ratings in the PC industry, Dell became obsessed with finding a way to reduce the failure rate even further. Design flaws emerged in Dell's notebook computer that cost the company $36 million. The key, he believed, was to reduce the number of times that each hard drive was being handled during assembly. He set a goal that dramatically reduced the number of "touches" from thirty to fifteen and revamped production lines to achieve this goal. Soon thereafter, the rate of rejected hard drives fell by 40 percent, and the overall failure rate for the company PCs dropped by 20 percent.

His deliberate goal-setting approach and mastery of details allows him to focus on little things that keep Dell moving forward. It was his idea to try to sell PCs on the Web when others on his staff were skeptical that a market would materialize. When orders are downloaded from the Web, they are instantly relayed to one of Dell's three plants. There is no parts inventory; suppliers know that all components must be delivered within an hour. There is no finished goods inventory; trucks back into one of the thirty-five bays at the Austin plant to load PCs for delivery to customers immediately after the units have been assembled.

Dell Computer ships about four million PCs, notebooks, servers, and workstations a year. Most are sold to businesses, not individual consumers. Buyers call Dell's 800 number or log onto the company's Web site, where they can configure their own model and then watch as their customized PCs are priced by feature on the screen. Enter a credit card number, hit Return, and you're done. Big customers such as Boeing—which buys an average of 160 PCs a day—e-mail Dell sales reps working inside their companies to place orders.[23]

* * *

To learn more about Dell, visit the company's home page at

www.dell.com

1989 now has stock worth more than $1 million, a gain of more than 20,000 percent. The company's annual sales exceed $7.8 billion dollars, and it employs more than 10,350 people around the world.

ROLE OF STAKEHOLDERS

Goals aren't set in a vacuum. As mentioned in earlier chapters, various stakeholders (e.g., customers, shareholders, suppliers, and government agencies) have an impact on an organization and its employees. This impact is felt in the goal-setting and revision process. As suggested in Figure 8.3, stakeholders play a crucial role in

Figure 8.3   **Stakeholders, Alternatives, and Goals**

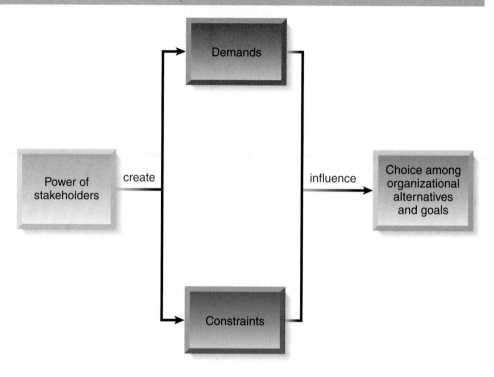

shaping the demands, constraints, and choices of alternatives that managers and employees face when setting goals.[24]

Demands are the desires expressed by powerful stakeholders that an organization make certain decisions and achieve particular goals.[25] Even stakeholders within an organization don't always agree with the goals of their departments, divisions, or organization as a whole—or the means for achieving them. When Ed Brennen was the CEO of Sears, some board members disagreed with him over the goals he set for Sears' financial brokerage arm, Dean Witter, and real estate brokerage arm, Caldwell Banker, and the high-priority given to the corporate resources devoted to achieving those goals.[26] When profits declined, the board, with the support of the shareholders, encouraged Brennen to retire. The board quickly appointed Arthur Martinez CEO, and he immediately downsized Sears by selling both companies.

Constraints limit the types of goals set, the decisions made, and the actions taken. Two important constraints are laws and ethics. A salesperson facing declining sales can't legally obtain a government contract by giving the contracting officer a kickback. Likewise, for a salesperson to promise customers a product that can't be delivered at the quoted price is unethical.

Choices are goals and alternatives that organizations and individuals are free to select, but don't have to. Michael Dell chose not to produce state-of-the-art computer chips and software. Instead, his company relies on Intel, Microsoft, Motorola, and other suppliers to furnish PC components. Dell chooses to focus on ways of reducing the cost of distributing technology. In doing so, the company draws closer to customers and suppliers alike. It helped Motorola, for example, set up a manufacturing plant in Penang, Malaysia, because Dell already had an assembly plant there.

The relative range of choices that organizations have in setting goals varies greatly, depending on the magnitude of stakeholder power. Organizations can have many choices in setting goals when external stakeholder power is relatively low, as, for example, at Rubbermaid and Dell Computer. They are leading competitors in their markets and have sufficient human, technological, and financial resources to shape *and* satisfy stakeholders. Conversely, some organizations face powerful external stakeholder demands and constraints and have few choices in setting goals. Brooklyn Union, a utility company that uses natural gas to generate electricity, seems to be in this category. Government bodies and environmental pressure groups have made strong demands and placed strict constraints (governmental regulations) on where the utility can build power plants, how these power plants are to be constructed, how they are to be operated, how wastes are to be disposed of, and so on.

DECISION-MAKING MODELS

4

DESCRIBE THE RATIONAL, BOUNDED RATIONALITY, AND POLITICAL MODELS OF DECISION MAKING

Our discussion of the circumstances surrounding most decision making has set the stage for examining three decision-making models: rational, bounded rationality, and political. Management theorists developed these models to describe various decision-making processes. Goal setting and achievement are important in all three models.

RATIONAL MODEL

RATIONAL MODEL

A series of steps that individuals or teams should follow to increase the likelihood that their decisions will be logical and well founded.

The ***rational model*** prescribes a series of steps that individuals or teams should follow to increase the likelihood that their decisions will be logical and sound. A rational decision permits the maximum achievement of goals within the limitations of the situation. This definition addresses means (how to best achieve goals), not ends (the goals themselves). Consider the situation of Neutrogena Corporation, a soap manufacturer. Neutrogena makes a residue-free soap formulated for pH balance. It had a large sales force that called on dermatologists and attended medical conventions, it advertised in medical journals and sent direct mail to doctors, and it performed basic research at its own Skincare Institute. The company originally sold its soap only through drugstores and avoided price promotions. In choosing this position, Neutrogena didn't add the deodorants and skin softeners that many customers desire in their soap. It passed up the large volume potential of selling through supermarkets, Wal-Mart, Target, Kmart, and other mass merchandisers. It made these rational decisions for three reasons. First, such tactics would be inconsistent with the company's "medical" image. Second, Neutrogena had gained efficiency by focusing on a single product; producing different soaps would require different equipment, employee behaviors, and distribution systems. Third, it makes organizational priorities clear; by choosing not to offer a wide variety of soap products, it avoided the confusion that would come from trying to be all things to all people.

Unfortunately, Neutrogena's shareholders were concerned about the company's slow growth and the profitability of its product. They pressured top management into broadening the company's product line and including mass merchandisers in its distribution strategy. Under the Neutrogena name, the company began producing a variety of products—eye-makeup remover and shampoo, for example—for which it had no unique competency and which diluted its image. Neutrogena has since engaged in price promotions and watched its profitability fall.[27]

Figure 8.4 shows the rational decision-making model as a seven-step process. It begins with defining and diagnosing the problem and moves through successive

Figure 8.4 **Rational Decision-Making Model**

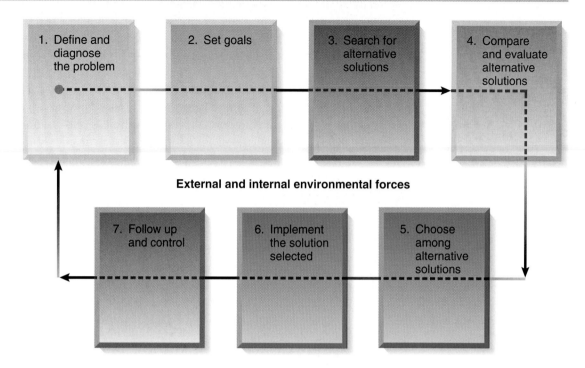

steps to following up and controlling. When making routine decisions, individuals can follow these steps easily. In addition, people are more likely to utilize this process in situations involving conditions of near certainty or low risk, that is, when they can assign objective probabilities to outcomes. Routine decisions under conditions that approximate certainty obviously don't require using all the steps in the model. For example, if a particular problem tends to recur, decisions (solutions) may be written as standard operating procedures or rules. Moreover, individuals or teams rarely follow these seven steps sequentially when making adaptive or innovative decisions.[28]

Step 1: Define and Diagnose the Problem. If managers, teams, or individual employees are unaware of the true problems and their possible causes, no effective decision making can occur. Problem definition and diagnosis involves three skills that are part of a manager's planning and administration competency: noticing, interpreting, and incorporating. *Noticing* involves identifying and monitoring numerous external and internal environmental forces and deciding which ones are contributing to the problem(s). *Interpreting* involves assessing the forces noticed and determining which are causes, not merely symptoms, of the real problem(s). Finally, *incorporating* involves relating those interpretations to the current or desired goals (step 2) of the department or organization. If noticing, interpreting, and incorporating are done haphazardly or incorrectly, the individual or team eventually is likely to choose a poor solution.

Let's consider two examples of the need for sound problem definition and diagnosis. Taking aspirin for headaches may do the trick in the short run, but headaches usually are a symptom, not the problem. The problem underlying the symptom could be physiological (e.g., eyestrain) or psychological (e.g., stress). Also, problems are sometimes incorrectly defined in terms of proposed solutions. For example, the members of a marketing department at Apple Computer believed that slow sales were the result of understaffing. Acting on this definition of the problem, department members focused on the obvious goal of obtaining funds for new positions. However, the basic problem was that Dell's, Gateway's, and Compaq's superior products and customer services had rendered Apple's product and marketing strategies ineffective.

Fundamental to problem definition and diagnosis is asking numerous probing questions. Let's pause for a moment and consider the definition of the word *question*. Our use of the word goes beyond the dictionary definition: an act or instance of asking. We like the following multiple meanings expressed by two creativity experts.

- A question is an invitation to creativity.

- A question is an unsettled and unsettling issue.

- A question is a beginning of adventure.

- A question is a disguised answer.

- A question pokes and prods that which has not yet been poked and prodded.

- A question is a point of departure.

- A question has no end and no beginning.[29]

By asking a variety of *who, when, where, how,* and *why* questions, individuals and teams will improve the odds of effective problem definition and diagnosis.

Step 2: Set Goals. After individuals or teams have defined a problem, they can set specific goals for eliminating it. For example, let's say that top management has defined excessive manufacturing costs as a problem but that it actually is merely a symptom of the real problem. The real problem could be defective materials (inputs) getting into the production process, production workers' inadequate quality control (inspection) skills, or any of numerous other possibilities. Management could set a hierarchy of goals for the various levels in the organization, from the division manager to the lathe operator, to solve the *seeming* problem. Or management could identify the *real* problem and then set a hierarchy of goals to correct it. In both cases, the goals would spell out the desired results: what is to be achieved and by what date (see Figure 8.3)—but only in the latter case would they be worth pursuing and devoting significant resources to.

Under the condition of uncertainty, setting precise goals can be extremely difficult. Individuals or teams may have to identify alternative goals, compare and evaluate them, and choose among them as best they can. For example, a business career might be your overall goal, but you could be uncertain about which specific path to follow. Should you become an accountant or a sales representative or choose one of many other occupations that can lead to a satisfying career in business? To arrive at an answer, you'll have to consider the alternative paths for achieving your general goal, often without all the information you might want for making a decision.

Step 3: Search for Alternative Solutions. Individuals or teams must look for alternative ways to achieve a goal. This step might involve seeking additional information, thinking creatively, consulting experts, undertaking research, and similar actions. However, when there seems to be no feasible solution for reaching a goal, there may be a need to modify the goal. For example, some people set impossible goals for themselves and then try harder and harder to achieve them, often without success. The solution selected might be to work longer and longer hours, literally seven days a week. The ultimate result could be high levels of stress and dissatisfaction that eventually force these individuals to reexamine their goals and decide which ones are really important.

Step 4: Compare and Evaluate Alternative Solutions. After individuals or teams have identified alternative solutions, they must compare and evaluate these alternatives. This step emphasizes expected results and determining the relative cost of each alternative. In the Neutrogena Soap example, pressure from shareholders led management to compromise its original goals and target market. The result was to undermine the organization's focus and profitability. In Chapter 9, we present several aids for rationally comparing and evaluating alternative solutions.

Step 5: Choose Among Alternative Solutions. Decision making is commonly associated with having made a final choice. Choosing a solution, however, is only one step in the rational decision-making process. Many managers complain that when recent college graduates receive a project assignment, they tend to present and discuss only one solution. Instead of being able to compare and evaluate several alternatives, a manager can only accept or reject the choice being presented. Although choosing among alternative solutions might appear to be straightforward, it may prove to be difficult when the problem is complex and ambiguous and involves high degrees of risk or uncertainty.

Step 6: Implement the Solution Selected. A well-chosen solution isn't always successful. A technically correct decision has to be accepted and supported by those responsible for implementing it if the decision is to be acted on effectively. If the selected solution can't be implemented for some reason, another one should be considered. We explore the importance of participation in making a decision by those charged with implementing it in Chapters 15 and 16.

Step 7: Follow-Up and Control. Implementing the preferred solution won't automatically achieve the desired goal. Individuals or teams must control implementation activities and follow up by evaluating results. If implementation isn't producing satisfactory results, corrective action will be needed. Because environmental forces affecting decisions change continually, follow-up and control may indicate a need to redefine the problem or review the original goal. Feedback from this step could even suggest the need to start over and repeat the entire decision-making process.

The following Teamwork Competency account illustrates how Sony Electronics designed teams that were able to formulate clear objectives and systems to monitor their performance. To develop teamwork competency among its employees, Sony relied on many of the steps of the rational model.

You might think of the rational model as an ideal, nudging individuals or teams closer to rationality in making decisions. At best, though, human decision making only approximates this ideal. When dealing with some types of problems, people don't even attempt to follow the rational model's seven steps.[30] Instead, they may apply the bounded rationality or political models. Observations of actual decision-making processes in organizations suggest that individuals modify or even ignore the rational model, especially when faced with making certain types of adaptive and innovative decisions.

BOUNDED RATIONALITY MODEL

The **bounded rationality model** refers to an individual's tendencies (1) to select less than the best goal or alternative solution (i.e., to *satisfice*), (2) to engage in a limited search for alternative solutions, and (3) to have inadequate information and

BOUNDED RATIONALITY MODEL

An individual's tendency (1) to select less than the best goal or alternative solution (i.e., to satisfice), (2) to engage in a limited search for alternative solutions, and (3) to have inadequate information and control over external and internal environmental forces influencing the outcomes of decisions.

New System Solves Problems at Sony

In 1989, Sony's San Diego trinitron picture-tube and color assembly plant was regarded as the worst in Sony's system. Symptoms were low morale, including lack of employee concern for results, poor communication from management, low productivity, high costs, and lagging quality. Absenteeism was almost 7 percent, personnel turnover was 6 percent a month, and the plant was losing money.

Sony's top management recognized that significant change was required and decided to introduce a "high-performance work system" in the plant. To learn how teams at other organizations operated under this system, San Diego managers benchmarked the best managerial practices at Clark Equipment, Sherwin Williams, TRW, and the San Diego Zoo. There, managers had realized that a top-down management approach to problem solving wasn't effective. Participation and teamwork had become basic practices in all of these organizations. Returning to their plant, Sony's top managers asked employees to help make radical changes at the plant.

Several employee groups volunteered for the change. Consultants then trained managers and employees in teamwork skills, such as conflict resolution, negotiation, coaching, and ways to achieve cooperative behavior. Individual process-design teams, consisting of technicians, operators, and maintenance employees were created. These teams were responsible for all day-to-day operations, including setting work schedules, scheduling maintenance, ordering equipment, and suggesting promotions. The success of these initial efforts sparked expansion of the concept throughout the San Diego plant.

Within three years, the "high-performance work system" produced results. In addition to building morale and trust among employees, the new system improved the company's profitability. Two redesign teams implemented shift-synchronization schedules that increased profitability by $5 million annually. The mixing team, after solving its employee turnover problems, solved its chemical waste problem, developed a new purchasing strategy, and reduced the amount of city water used. These practices saved Sony more than $869,000 a year. Employees producing CRT tubes increased their production by 50 percent. Comprehensive managerial competency building efforts throughout the plant virtually eliminated turnover and resulted in higher productivity and greater safety.[31]

* * *

To learn more about Sony, visit the company's home page at

www.sony.com

control over external and internal environmental forces influencing the outcomes of decisions.[32] Herbert Simon, a management scholar, introduced this model in the mid-1950s. It contributed significantly to the Swedish Academy of Sciences' decision to award him the 1978 Nobel Prize in economics for his "pioneering research into the decision making process within economic organizations." The bounded rationality model is particularly useful because it emphasizes the limitations of rationality and thus provides a better picture of the day-to-day decision-making processes used by most people. This model partially explains why different individuals make different decisions when they have exactly the same information.

Satisficing. The practice of selecting an *acceptable* goal or alternative solution is called ***satisficing.*** An acceptable goal might be easier to identify and achieve, less controversial, or otherwise safer than the best available goal. The factors that result in a satisficing decision often are limited search, inadequate information, and information processing bias, as shown in Figure 8.5. However, the achievement of quality improvement goals often is a result of a series of satisficing decisions. Recall from Chapter 2 that W. Edwards Deming taught management that the greatest cause

SATISFICING

The practice of selecting an acceptable goal or alternative solution.

Figure 8.5 **Factors Influencing a Satisficing Decision**

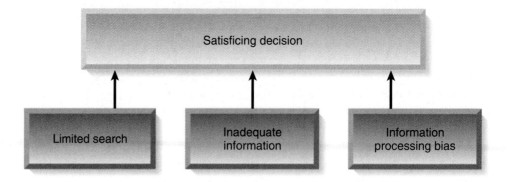

of defective products was poorly designed processes. Many successful organizations map, measure, and continuously improve their processes incrementally to reach a high level of quality. Introducing statistical quality controls in a series of satisficing steps, for example, enabled Exxon's Baytown plant to reduce chemical air emissions by 50 percent. This plant is now in compliance with "Clean Texas 2000," a statewide air pollution program to decrease the amount of emissions in the air by 2000. Exxon's employees receive twenty days of training per year, which Exxon officials believe is acceptable to meet its continuous-improvement goals.[33]

In an interview almost thirty-five years after introducing the bounded rationality model, Herbert Simon described satisficing for a management audience:

> *Satisficing is intended to be used in contrast to the classical economist's idea that in making decisions in business or anywhere in real life, you somehow pick, or somebody gives you, a set of alternatives from which you select the best one—maximize. The satisficing idea is that first of all, you don't have the alternatives, you've got to go out and scratch for them—and that you have mighty shaky ways of evaluating them when you do find them. So you look for alternatives until you get one from which, in terms of your experience and in terms of what you have reason to expect, you will get a reasonable result.*
>
> *But satisficing doesn't necessarily mean that managers have to be satisfied with what alternative pops up first in their minds or in their computers and let it go at that. The level of satisficing can be raised—by personal determination, setting higher individual or organizational standards [goals], and by use of an increasing range of sophisticated management science and computer-based decision-making and problem-solving techniques. As time goes on, you obtain more information about what's feasible and what you can aim at. Not only do you get more information, but in many, if not most, companies there are procedures for setting targets, including procedures for trying to raise individuals' aspiration levels [goals]. This is a major responsibility of top management.[34]*

Limited Search. Individuals usually make only a limited search for possible goals or alternative solutions to a problem, considering options until they find one that seems adequate. For example, when trying to choose the "best" job, college seniors can't evaluate every available job in their fields and probably would reach retirement age before obtaining all the information available. In the bounded rationality model, individuals stop searching for alternatives as soon as they hit on an acceptable one. Even the rational decision-making model recognizes that identifying and assessing alternative solutions costs time, energy, and money.

Inadequate or Misinterpreted Information. Bounded rationality also recognizes that individuals frequently have inadequate information about problems and that events that they can't control will influence the results of their decisions. Faced with increasing customer resistance to high automobile prices, management at Honda and Toyota believed that the only way to produce a less-expensive car was to skimp on features. In the United States, Honda replaced the rear disk brakes on the Civic with lower cost drum brakes and used cheaper fabric for the back seat, hoping that customers wouldn't notice. Toyota tried to sell a version of its best-selling Corolla in Japan with unpainted bumpers and cheaper seats. Management at both Honda and Toyota made these decisions without adequate information, and, as soon as customers rebelled, quickly reversed their decisions.

Information Processing Biases. Consistent with the bounded rationality model, individuals often fall prey to information processing biases when they engage in bounded rationality decision making. The following are five of these biases.[35]

1. The ***availability bias*** means that people who easily recall specific instances of an event may overestimate how frequently the event occurs. People who have been in serious automobile accidents often overestimate the frequency of such accidents.

2. The ***selective perception bias*** means that what people expect to see often is what they *do* see. People seek information consistent with their own views and downplay conflicting information. Some people eagerly leap from a tower 100 feet above the ground with only a bungee cord between them and certain death. Yet these same people may not be willing to live near a closed plant that has been declared a superfund cleanup site.

3. The ***concrete information bias*** means that vivid, direct experience usually prevails over abstract information. A single personal experience can outweigh statistical evidence. An initial bad experience on the job may lead a worker to conclude that most managers can't be trusted and are simply out to exploit their subordinates.

4. The ***law of small numbers bias*** means that people may view a few incidents or cases as representative of a larger population (i.e., a few cases "prove the rule") even when they aren't. A number of Arab-Americans experienced hostility from some non-Arabs after the invasion of Kuwait by Iraqi forces. Apparently the non-Arabs incorrectly attributed the unsavory characteristics of Saddam Hussein (sample of 1) to Arab-Americans in general.

5. The ***gambler's fallacy bias*** means that seeing an unexpected number of similar events can lead people to the conviction that an event not seen will occur. For example, after observing nine successive reds turn up on a roulette wheel, a player might incorrectly believe that chances for a black on the next spin are greater than 50/50. They aren't!

POLITICAL MODEL

The ***political model*** describes the decision-making process in terms of the particular interests and goals of powerful external and internal stakeholders. Before considering this model, however, we need to define power. ***Power*** is the ability to influence or control individual, departmental, team, or organizational decisions and goals.[36] To have power is to be able to influence or control (1) the definition of the problem, (2) the choice of the goal, (3) the consideration of alternative solutions, (4) the selection of the alternative to be implemented, and ultimately (5) the actions and success of the organization. Political processes are most likely to occur when

AVAILABILITY BIAS
Recall of specific instances of an event, which may overestimate how frequently the event occurs.

SELECTIVE PERCEPTION BIAS
Seeing what a person expects to see.

CONCRETE INFORMATION BIAS
Vivid, direct experience dominating abstract information.

LAW OF SMALL NUMBERS BIAS
Viewing a few incidents or cases as representative of a larger population (a few cases "prove the rule") even when they aren't.

GAMBLER'S FALLACY BIAS
Believing that an unexpected number of similar chance events can lead to an event not seen.

POLITICAL MODEL
A description of the decision-making process in terms of the particular interests and goals of powerful external and internal stakeholders.

POWER
The ability to influence or control individual, departmental, team, or organizational decisions and goals.

decisions involve powerful stakeholders, disagreement over choice of goals, and people not searching for alternative solutions. These factors are highly interrelated, as shown in Figure 8.6.

Problem Definition. In the political model, external and internal stakeholders try to define problems for their own advantage. As external stakeholders, the Teamsters tried to block the passage of the Motor Carriers Act of 1980 that began deregulation of the trucking industry. The U.S. government's study found that rates were 75 percent higher in countries with regulated trucking rates, such as the United States and Germany, than in unregulated countries, such as Great Britian, Belgium, and the Netherlands. Regulation supported higher wages for U.S. drivers because it strictly limited the entry of new firms and prohibited price competition between particular locations. The Teamsters Union made major contributions to various congressional campaigns in an attempt to block passage of this legislation. However, the act did pass, thousands of new nonunion trucking fims have entered this industry, and the percentage of Teamster drivers has dropped from 60 to 28 percent. As a result, trucking rates have dropped by an average 25 percent. Service to small communities has improved, and service complaints have decline.[37]

When things go wrong within politically based or oriented organizations, one or more individuals may be singled out as the cause of the problem. This finger pointing is called ***scapegoating,*** which refers to the process of casting blame for problems or shortcomings on an innocent or only partially responsible individual, team, or department. Individuals or units may use scapegoating to preserve a position of power or maintain a positive image. Flour Corporation used this tactic, scapegoating one of its engineers, when it was convicted of financial fraud during cleanup work at a closed nuclear-weapons fuel factory near Cincinnati. The General Accounting Office (GAO)—the investigative arm of Congress—cited Flour for cost overruns, missing inspection records, leaking containers of hazardous waste, and substance abuse problems. Flour originally denied the allegations, noting that they were overstated and highly prejudicial. It also alleged that the U.S. Department of Energy impeded the company's own internal investigation. It finally settled the lawsuit brought by the U.S. Justice Department to preserve the continuity of its operations.[38]

SCAPEGOATING

The process of casting blame for problems or shortcomings on an innocent or only partially responsible individual, team, or department.

Figure 8.6   *Factors Affecting Political Decision-Making Processes*

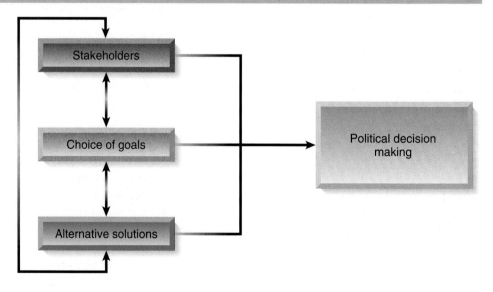

Choice of Goals. The political model recognizes the likelihood of conflicting goals among stakeholders and that the choice of goals will be influenced strongly by the relative power of stakeholders. Often no clear "winner" will emerge, but if power is concentrated in one stakeholder, the organization's primary goals will likely reflect that stakeholder's goals. The goals of Dell Computer reflect those of Michael Dell. Similarly, the goals of The Body Shop have been shaped by its founder Anita Roddick.

In contrast a balance of power among several stakeholders may lead to negotiation and compromise in the decision-making process. It's then characterized by the push and pull of the stakeholders who have both power and conflicting goals. Although a balance of power may lead to compromise, as in most union–management negotiations, it also may lead to stalemate. In the UPS strike in the summer of 1997, both union and management had to compromise their original positions to break the stalemate and settle the strike. Recall that a common political strategy is to form a coalition (alliance) when no one person, group, or organization has sufficient power to select or implement its preferred goal. Many health-related organizations and associations—such as the American Cancer Society, American Heart Association, and American Medical Association—have formed an informal coalition with Congress to fight smoking and tobacco interests.

Search for Alternative Solutions. Some goals or the means used to achieve them may be perceived as a win–lose situation; that is, my gain is your loss, and your gain is my loss. In such a situation, stakeholders often distort and selectively withhold information to further their own interests, as both management and union officials did in the Teamsters strike against UPS. Such actions can severely limit the ability to make adaptive and innovative decisions, which, by definition, require utilizing all relevant information, as well as exploring a full range of alternative solutions.[39]

Stakeholders within the organization often view information as a major source of power and use it accordingly. The rational decision-making model calls for all employees to present all relevant information openly. However, employees operating under the political model would view free disclosure as naive, making achievement of their personal, team, or departmental goals more difficult. To complicate the picture, information often is (1) piecemeal and based on informal communication (Did you know that . . . ?); (2) subjective rather than based on hard facts (Those computer printouts don't really matter around here.); and (3) defined by what powerful stakeholders consider to be important (What does the boss think? or How will the board respond?).

One of the common political strategies used by stakeholders to achieve their goals is co-optation. **Co-optation** involves bringing new stakeholder representatives into the strategic decision-making process as a way to avert threats to an organization's stability or existence.[40] An example is placing a banker on a firm's board of directors when the firm needs to borrow money. Also, some organizations have created *junior* executive committees as a way to involve middle managers in selected strategic issues and gain their support in implementing a chosen course of action.

The political model of decision making sometimes reflects the pursuit of short-term and narrowly defined self-interests. In this situation, an individual or organization is prone to behave in ethically questionable ways. Table 8.1 provides a short checklist of questions that you can use to help you decide whether personal use of your organization's supplies and equipment is ethical. What decision-making rule(s) did you follow? Would you be proud to have others see your choices?

CO-OPTATION

Bringing new stakeholder representatives into the strategic decision-making process as a means of averting threats to an organization's stability or existence.

How do you rate the ethics of a decision to make personal use of each of the following organizational resources. Assume that the organization has no formal policy on personal use of any of these resources. Place an X in the appropriate blank.

	Highly Ethical	Ethical	Gray Area	Unethical	Highly Unethical
Taking a box of paper clips home	___	___	___	___	___
Using a copy machine for personal use	___	___	___	___	___
Using e-mail for personal messages	___	___	___	___	___
Using a fax machine for personal use	___	___	___	___	___
Playing games on the computer during business hours	___	___	___	___	___
Creating and maintaining a local club newsletter on company time	___	___	___	___	___
Buying a competitor's software product, taking it apart, and redesigning your software to become more competitive	___	___	___	___	___
Having an assistant edit your term paper	___	___	___	___	___

Source: Adapted from A. A. Conger, K. D. Koch, and B. L. Helft. Ethical attitudes toward IT: A factor analysis of computer use attitudes. *Information Systems Journal,* 5, 1995, pp. 161–184.

CHAPTER SUMMARY

The purpose of this chapter was to introduce you to the fundamentals of decision making and to help you develop your planning and administration, strategic action, global awareness, self-management, and teamwork competencies. We presented and discussed various decision-making models that managers often use. In Chapter 9, we present various planning and decision aids that managers can use to help them make good decisions.

1. **DEFINE DECISION MAKING.**

Decision making involves identifying problems, gathering information, considering alternatives, and choosing a course of action from the alternatives generated.

2. **EXPLAIN THE CONDITIONS OF CERTAINTY, RISK, AND UNCERTAINTY UNDER WHICH DECISIONS ARE MADE.**

Decisions are made under conditions that reflect the likelihood that developments and events will occur over which the decision maker has no control but which may influence the outcomes of decisions. These conditions may be characterized as a continuum from certainty to risk to uncertainty. The greater the risk and uncertainty of future events, the more difficult and challenging is decision making.

3. DESCRIBE A FRAMEWORK FOR UNDERSTANDING ROUTINE, ADAPTIVE, AND INNOVATIVE DECISIONS.

Routine decisions involve relatively well-defined and common problems and solutions. Adaptive decisions involve somewhat unusual problems and/or solutions of low to moderate risk. Innovative decisions involve very unusual and ambiguous problems and/or solutions of high risk or uncertainty.

4. EXPLAIN HOW GOALS AFFECT DECISION MAKING.

Goals indicate the direction that decisions and actions should take and the quality or quantity of the results desired. Four benefits derived from setting goals are (1) focusing decisions and efforts, (2) aiding the planning process, (3) motivating people and stimulating performance, and (4) assisting performance evaluation and control. Stakeholders are crucial in selecting or changing organizational goals.

5. DESCRIBE THE RATIONAL, BOUNDED RATIONALITY, AND POLITICAL MODELS OF DECISION MAKING.

The rational model is a sequence of seven steps for making decisions: (1) define and diagnose the problem, (2) set goals, (3) seek alternative solutions, (4) compare and evaluate alternative solutions, (5 choose among alternative solutions, (6) implement the solution selected, and (7) follow up and control the results. The three constraints of the bounded rationality model are (1) satisficing, (2) limited search, and (3) inadequate or misinterpreted information. This model recognizes the practical limitations on individuals' decision making. The political model emphasizes the role of powerful stakeholders in decision making. In particular, political clout tends to influence decision making in terms of identifying problems, setting goals, generating alternative solutions, and even choosing which solution to implement.

QUESTIONS FOR DISCUSSION

1. What were some of the conditions that led John Roach to pull the plug on Tandy's Incredible Universe operations? Do these conditions exist in other industries? Explain.

2. Did your decision to enroll in this course involve certainty, risk, or uncertainty? Explain your answer.

3. Identify five routine decisions that you made before attending this class today. Under which of the three conditions did you make them?

4. Why can individuals, whose rationality is limited according to the bounded rationality model, be expected to make reasonably rational decisions at times?

5. What did you learn about general and operational goals from reading the account of Dell Computer?

6. Choose an organization that is facing pressure from external stakeholders, such as any of the U.S. tobacco companies, to change the way it conducts its business. What tactics have they used to manage these stakeholders? Were they successful? Explain.

EXERCISES TO DEVELOP YOUR MANAGERIAL COMPETENCIES

1. **Global Awareness Competency.** Terry Prindiville, a JCPenney executive, believes that Penney's future growth will be in foreign countries. The company is negotiating with potential licensees in Greece and Portugal and is considering anchoring a new regional mall in Taiwan. It

offers catalogs in Iceland and Brazil and is translating a trimmed-down catalog into Spanish to tap the Latin American market. However, it hasn't been smooth sailing for Penney. In Belgium, its plan to build giant stores were stopped by local zoning boards—stacked with competing merchants. The boards' zoning decisions left Penney with small, outdated spaces in congested downtown areas while competitors built spacious suburban stores. Penney also tried to buy a retail chain in Belgium and assumed that it could turn the chain around by slashing bloated payrolls and raising productivity. The labor laws in Belgium made layoffs prohibitively expensive and time-consuming. Under what conditions is Penney's top management making these decisions? Using the framework for decision making, what type(s) of decisions is Penney's top management making? To learn more about JCPenney's global expansion, visit the company's home page at

www.jcpenney.com

2. **Planning and Administration Competency.** McDonald's is facing tough U.S. competition from Wendy's and Burger King. McDonald's has been trying to reduce costs, but can't raise prices because many of its customers will shift to its competitors. Over the next two years, it plans to save $750 million by revamping the routes of its trucks that deliver French fries. Visit the company's home page at

www.mcdonald's.com

and list the general and operational goals it has set for company-owned restaurants.

3. **Strategic Action Competency.** Far into the decision-making process, Robert Lutz, president of Chrysler, decided to scrap the company's new luxury car. The LX would have been a rear-wheel drive luxury car, would have featured a new 32-value, V-8 300 horsepower engine, and would have been priced in the high $30,000s to low $40,000s, against the Cadillac Seville STS. Part of the rationale for killing the design was cost, but another part reflected Chrysler's strategy. What did Chrysler want to be known for in the market? If many other carmakers produce luxury cars, did Chrysler need one too? Do you agree with Chrysler's decision? What framework did you choose in making your decision? To learn more about Chrysler's decision, visit the company's home page at

www.chrysler.com

4. **Self-Management Competency.** After selling Blockbuster to Viacom for $8.4 billion in 1994, Wayne Huizenga began thinking about what to do. Running a small company wouldn't do; he wanted to take on an industry. The $310 billion-a-year new-car business sounded intriguing until he learned of the control that manufacturers exercise over franchisees and their ban against publicly owned dealers. He and a friend hit on the idea of a used-car superstore. He visualized setting up a chain of used-car operations that could utilize the talents of his Blockbuster team in scouting real estate and building outlets. He wanted the highest quality used cars and realized that they would come from new-car dealers who had leased cars to individuals or as fleets to organizations. He also discovered that 30 percent of the 40 million people who brought used cars last year did so through classified ads. Armed with these data, he founded AutoNation. What self-management competency skills and knowledge did he draw on to make the decision to found AutoNation? What are his goals? What did he learn from his experiences at Blockbuster? To learn more about Huizenga's self-management competency and his decisions to found AutoNation, read *Business Week*, January 27, 1997, pp. 34–35, and *Fortune,* June 9, 1997, pp. 93–96.

5. **Teamwork Competency.** Texas Instrument's (TI's) former CEO, Jerry Junkins, said, "Teams are the wave of the future." What makes teams work at TI is their ability to draw people from different functional areas, such as marketing, engineering, finance, and human resources, and to learn from each other. Management is responsible for clarifying the performance challenges for the team, but management must also be flexible enough to allow the team to develop a commitment to its goals and its approaches to solving problems. The best teams at TI translate their purposes into specific performance goals. If a team fails to establish specific performance goals or these goals don't relate directly to the organization's goals, team member and overall team performance suffers. What type of goals do teams establish at TI? What decision-making models do teams use? To answer these questions, visit Texas Instrument's home page at

www.ti.com

REAL-TIME CASE ANALYSIS

CADILLAC CATERA

In 1994, General Motors' executive board made several decisions to reverse GM's downward sales. It hired Ronald Zarrella, formerly president of Bausch & Lomb, as head of marketing. Zarrella set out to dispel the long-held assumption at GM that the product was everything. Instead, he advocated a strategy emphasizing brand identity. He pointed out that Saturn, which has won praise for its straightforward selling practices and unconventional ads for its sedans and coupes, used a strategy that built brand identity.

As a part of this strategy of brand name positioning, GM adopted a concept known as "needs-based marketing." It required surveying car buyers about their preferences in order to give customers what they say they need and want rather than what engineers think they should have. Customers were asked about features, styling, advertising, dealer service, and their buying experiences. According to Zarrella, decisions should be made on facts and data instead of emotions and history.

GM targeted Cadillac to implement its brand name positioning strategy. Why Cadillac? Cadillac had sold 351,000 cars in 1978 but sold only 201,275 in 1997. Cadillac's share of the 1.2-million-unit luxury-car market had slipped from 24 percent in 1989 to 15 percent in 1997. The average Fleetwood owner is sixty-two, and the average Seville owner is fifty-two. The solution to this problem was to attract the segment of the luxury market—aged about forty-four—that currently buys Lexus, BMW, and Infiniti. Last year, this market of forty- to fifty-year-old baby-boomers accounted for more than one-third of all the luxury cars sold; by 2000, GM estimates that it will be 40 percent. The targeted market is younger, somewhat wealthier than present Cadillac buyers, and more likely to be college educated and female. In addition, the target market has very definite "psychographic" characteristics. That is, the average baby-boomer was raised on imports and retains a youthful and active lifestyle in middle age. Baby-boomers are confident in their ability to negotiate deals and have little brand loyalty. They expect high quality and reliability from their cars, and tend to avoid what they consider common.

GM's answer to its sliding sales was to introduce a new car, the Catera, in the fall of 1996. The Catera is an Americanized version of the Opel Omega MV6, which is built at the Adam Opel AG plant in Rus-

selsheim, Germany. Under the direction of GM's brand management team, GM is targeting international market segments and giving them a product that best meets customers' needs, regardless of where parts are made and assembled. The brand management team virtually had to reengineer the Opel to meet American safety standards and tastes. However, the Catera contains more than 150 parts from the Omega. Parts are being obtained from GM's plants in France, Germany, Great Britain, and the United States. Each part must meet world-class standards of excellence. The instrument panel is put together and tested separately by workers and then installed by a robot on the main assembly line. This arrangement reduces the chance of loose parts and squeaks and rattles showing up later. Each of the 170 Cateras built each day gets a special inspection before being trucked to Antwerp, Belgium, and shipped to Savannah, Georgia.

GM also launched a $40 million dollar marketing campaign. The TV advertisement features the theme: the "Caddy that Zigs" and a cute cartoon character, the Catera Duck. Since GM forecast that many Catera buyers would be women, ads feature things that women want, including antilock brakes, remote keyless entry, airbags, and heating, air-conditioning, and radio dials that are more fingernail friendly. To avoid the need for owners to bring their cars into dealerships for servicing, the Catera has long intervals between routine maintenance, including 100,000-mile durability and a "limp home" feature that allows it to be driven 50 miles without engine coolant.

How well has the Catera sold? Although Cadillac said that it expected to sell about 30,000 Cateras the first year, it actually sold only 23,201, compared to first-year sales of 39,367 for the Lexus ES 300 and 23,793 for the Mercedes C Class. GM also forecast the target age for the Catera to be 35–50, whereas actual buyer age was 58. The problem for Cadillac is that older buyers have fewer cars left to buy, whereas younger buyers can support sales for many years. Based on these results, what did Cadillac do? First, it decided to shoot the Catera Duck. Many dealers felt that the duck didn't accurately portray Cadillac quality. Many GM managers believed that the duck did a good job of spreading the Catera name but conceded that the duck didn't do as well in bringing in new buyers or publicizing the merits of the Catera. Second, GM intends to show customers taking their

Cateras to golf and tennis tournaments, which affluent young adults attend in large numbers.[41]

QUESTIONS

1. List all the decisions described in this real-time case. Under what conditions were these decisions made?

2. What general and operational goals did GM set for the Catera? Are they realistic? Explain.

3. Illustrate examples of GM managers' use of bounded rationality.

4. Karen Sehee-Licari, assistant product brand manager of Catera, said: "Men fall in love with cars, and women want to depend on their cars. Women have a relationship with their cars; men have a romance with their autos." What decisions did GM make to support her statement?

To learn more about Catera, visit GM's home page at

www.gm.com

VIDEO CASE

BEHIND THE SCENES: JOHNSON & JOHNSON'S ACUVUE

Johnson & Johnson, the developers of the Acuvue disposable contact lens, are gambling on the introduction of a new product. Technically, it is a fairly modest gamble because much of Acuvue's existing technology and expertise is applicable to the new product. However, the company is committing substantial sums, exposing its corporate image to potential damage (Ford will be forever tagged as the manufacturer of the Edsel), and relying on its customers to extend their trust to the new product. To be reasonably sure that its message is clear, Acuvue created a television commercial and used focus groups to get a sense of how the market might receive that message.

But decisions made in crafting a marketing campaign are only the tip of the iceberg. The decision to develop, manufacture, and introduce such a product would have been made months or years earlier and would have been backed by extensive research. Contributing to the decision would have been researchers, engineers, production supervisors, financial analysts, and marketing analysts. The company's engineers would have been given the task of developing cost and performance estimates. For any new mass consumer product, especially one associated with health, both medical and legal experts would have been consulted. (In the pharmaceutical industry, a diligent investigation of medical risks and possible liability could consume years and millions of dollars.)

Numerous decisions will be made during the product development stage. They will range from the superficial (e.g., the focus group hated avocado but thought that sea green was charming) to the substantive (e.g., a decision to abandon a product, even after millions of dollars had been invested).

Effective use of all the managerial competencies may be necessary to ensure sound decisions and success of the venture. Strategic action competency certainly is involved, as is global awareness competency for an international firm. Communication competency—envision a senior executive, backed by a stack of research, demonstrating at the right moment to a group of stakeholders the advantages of disposable (imagine!) contact lenses with the help of a multimedia presentation—is essential. Many other activities will also demand attention. For example, generating a feeling of corporate teamwork may be challenging when some managers and teams will benefit more from the new product than others. In fact, some might face the scrapping of their own projects because of the new offering.

The stakeholders and the nature and consequences of decisions will change as the product progresses from concept to a commitment to develop and market it to the final shaping of the product to its introduction and promotion. Stakeholders' interests in decisions can be great, and differences among individuals or groups might even be irreconcilable. Sometimes when a product is being abandoned, executives responsible for it may even leave the company and attempt to take the product to market by forming a new start-up company. Many entrepreneurs have gotten their inspiration within large firms and then left them because of disagreements over how product decisions should have been made.

In the final analysis, the magnitude of many variables will likely be unknown. For example, Acuvue might exhaustively test its product and commercial message with focus groups, only to see a successful Hollywood movie spark a resurgence in glasses or a famous person set a style (as did the hatless John F. Kennedy in the late 1950s and early 1960s).

ON THE WEB

As an inexpensive publishing medium, the Web gives organizations and individuals the opportunity to collect and disseminate information on any topic they choose. Johnson & Johnson presents information about Acuvue contact lenses on its Web site (*www.jnj.com*). Some Web sites have been created for ideas before their time and for products that later "flopped." You can use a search engine such as Hot-Bot (*www.hotbot.com*) to find them. Simply pair the keyword "failure" with products such as the Edsel, Ford's disaster; the Apple Lisa, the commercially failed predecessor to the spectacularly successful Macintosh; or Snapple, which Quaker Oats bought and then sold at a $1.4 billion loss.

Yahoo! (featured in Chapter 13's video case) provides an easy means of examining stock histories, which can be a gauge of the decision-making skills of corporate executives. These histories also graphically demonstrate another sort of decision—by shareholders. Fundamentally, a share price reflects shareholders' assessments of a company's prospects, based on what they know of its products, strategies, and markets. You can use the Yahoo! stock quote page (*quote.yahoo.com*) to investigate companies that have had significant recent changes in share values, such as Sunbeam (SOC) or Apple (AAPL).

QUESTIONS

1. What does the phrase "to shoot the messenger" mean in the context of decision making?

2. How can companies encourage active participation by all employees in decision making?

To help you answer these questions and learn more about Johnson & Johnson's Acuvue, visit the company's home page at

www.jnj.com

Case contributed by Ross Stapleton-Gray, President, TeleDiplomacy, Inc., a technology and policy consultancy, and Adjunct Professor in Georgetown University's Communication, Culture, and Technology program.

Chapter

9

Planning and Decision Aids

LEARNING OBJECTIVES

AFTER STUDYING THIS CHAPTER, YOU SHOULD BE ABLE TO:

1. EXPLAIN THE ESSENTIALS OF THE SCENARIO, DELPHI TECHNIQUE, AND SIMULATION FORECASTING AIDS.

2. APPLY TWO AIDS FOR FOSTERING CREATIVITY—OSBORN'S CREATIVITY MODEL AND THE CAUSE AND EFFECT DIAGRAM.

3. DESCRIBE THREE AIDS FOR HELPING TO ACHIEVE TOTAL QUALITY MANAGEMENT—BENCHMARKING, DEMING CYCLE, AND PARETO ANALYSIS.

4. EXPLAIN ONE PROJECT MANAGEMENT AID—THE PROGRAM EVALUATION AND REVIEW TECHNIQUE.

Outline

Electronic Commerce

After a long day of telecommuting (working at home on her networked PC), Susan James mouse-clicks her TV from computer to television mode. It is the year 2010 and, outside, satellites drift across the sky. She settles into her self-molding couch to watch "Omaha Beach 68102," and a jacket on one of the characters catches her eye. She clicks on the jacket with a remote. Sizes, colors, and prices appear in the lower right corner of the screen. She clicks on the corner, and an image of herself—already scanned into the TV—wearing the jacket fills the screen.

James likes what she sees. With a click she orders the jacket custom-tailored instead of off the rack. Her name, address, order, measurements, and credit information—stored in her computer—speed to the retailer with the best price, who ships the jacket to her for next-day delivery.

Predictions on the future of the electronic marketplace vary wildly. Though an extreme shift is unlikely, some forecasters believe that by 2010 shopping malls will be in the decline stage and that 55 percent of shopping will occur through nonretail channels—the Internet, CD-ROM catalogs, and interactive television. Bill Gates, CEO of Microsoft, forecasted recently that one-third of all food sales will be conducted electronically by 2005.

Forrester Research has made a more conservative forecast: Internet shopping will rise from about $520 million in 1997 to more than $7 billion by 2001. Although this amount of growth is impressive, the $7 billion is not an immediate threat to retail stores that sell $300 billion in apparel alone. It does, however, threaten the $60 billion plus nonstore retail industry, which Arthur Andersen's *Analysis of Retailing in North America* calls one of the retail industry's fastest-growing segments.[1]

* * *

To learn more about Forrester Research, visit the company's home page at

www.forrester.com

In this scenario, Susan James didn't have to drive, park, wait, enter a store, and shove through crowds. Shopping was bundled with entertainment. Online retailers offered a variety of product and delivery options, including a customized product. James shopped from home, but could have shopped from any online computer at any hour of the day—including an electronic kiosk in a mall, on a street corner, or in a store. Within minutes, she received product consultation and found the lowest price in the country.

Two things are clear about such scenarios. One, interactive retailing is a long-term real threat to traditional retailers and a real opportunity, both now and in the future, for progressive ones. Two, interactive retailing will change the very nature of shopping for many consumers. Interactive retailing is part of a broader development and trend known as electronic commerce. ***Electronic commerce*** encompasses all types of commercial transactions via computer-based networks that involve the processing and transmission of data—including text, sound, and visual images. Such transactions take place between retailers and end-users (e.g., Amazom.com, the book retailer, and its customers), business to business (e.g., between manufacturers, wholesalers, and retailers), and business to government (e.g., regarding purchasing, taxes, and meeting regulatory requirements).[2]

Scenarios such as the one just described are but only one type of the many planning aids and techniques available and being used. One study identified forty-nine specific types of planning aids and techniques.[3] In addition, literally hundreds of decision-making aids are commonly used to resolve specific issues, solve problems, and improve the operations of functional areas. Throughout this book we discuss various planning and decision aids that apply to specific situations. However, we do not discuss general planning and decision aids (e.g., break-even analysis and payoff matrix) in this book. They are commonly presented and discussed in depth

ELECTRONIC COMMERCE
All types of commercial transactions via computer-based networks that involve the processing and transmission of data—including text, sound, and visual images.

in other business courses (e.g., accounting, finance, and marketing). In this chapter, we review a sample of planning and decision aids that can be used (1) at various organizational levels, (2) in virtually all functional areas (e.g., marketing, finance, human resources, and auditing), and (3) for aiding in the analysis essential to planning and decision making associated with many types of organizational issues and problems.

We begin by discussing the basics and limitations of forecasting and the essentials of three commonly used forecasting techniques: scenarios, the Delphi technique, and simulation. Then, we address the need for creativity in many situations through the review of two—among dozens of aids—used to foster creativity, namely, Osborn's creativity model and the cause and effect diagram. Next, we present three aids that are designed to improve quality. These aids include benchmarking, the Deming cycle, and Pareto analysis. We conclude the chapter with discussion of a technique useful in project planning and implementation.

FORECASTING AIDS

1

EXPLAIN THE ESSENTIALS
OF THE SCENARIO, DELPHI
TECHNIQUE, AND SIMULA-
TION FORECASTING AIDS

FORECASTING
Predicting, projecting, or estimating future events or conditions in an organization's environment.

EXTRAPOLATION
The projection of some tendency from the past or present into the future.

Forecasting involves predicting, projecting, or estimating future events or conditions in an organization's environment. Forecasting is concerned primarily with external events or conditions beyond the organization's control that are important to its survival and growth. As noted in the Preview feature, forecasts related to electronic commerce will soon become fundamental to planning and decision making by traditional retailers. Forecasts suggest that electronic commerce and related information technologies will create both threats and opportunities for traditional retailers in the future.

Most forecasting is based on extrapolation. **Extrapolation** is the projection of some tendency from the past or present into the future. The simplest, and at times most misleading, form of extrapolation is a linear, or straight-line, projection of a past trend into the future.[4] The Preview feature scenario related to one prediction of the electronic marketplace—the description of how Susan James and perhaps many thousands if not millions of others are likely to shop in 2010—portrays an extreme shift in shopping patterns that could threaten the survival of some shopping malls.

Cheryl Russell is former editor of *American Demographics* magazine and current editor in chief of New Strategists Publications, an Ithaca, New York–based publisher of demographic reference books for businesses. She warns of four forecasting pitfalls.

- **Listening to the media.** If you track trends through the headlines, you're in trouble. The media often distort trends, blow fads up into trends, or completely miss trends.

- **Assuming things are going to return to the way they used to be.** There's this concept that trends are like a swinging pendulum—that we go one way, then the other. That's a nice concept, but it really doesn't work that way.

- **Hearsay.** It's the mentality that the neighbors are doing it, or everyone says they know someone doing this, so therefore a trend must exist.

- **Tunnel vision.** You need to read materials in areas you wouldn't typically think of. If all you read is the business press, you need to expand your [scope].[5]

Even though forecasting is uncertain, it's still necessary. Managers and teams at all levels have to use whatever is available to them in anticipating future events and conditions. Three forecasting aids—scenarios, the Delphi technique, and simulation—are often used in planning and decision-making situations. Because all of them focus on understanding possible futures, they aren't mutually exclusive.

SCENARIOS

SCENARIO

A written description of a possible future.

MULTIPLE SCENARIOS

Written descriptions of several possible futures.

A **scenario** is a written description of a possible future. **Multiple scenarios** are simply written descriptions of several possible futures. Planners at JCPenney, Wal-Mart, and other retailing firms might use scenarios to address questions such as: What future opportunities might exist for electronic commerce? How could developments in electronic commerce dramatically change traditional retailing? and, What types of strategies might be useful in preventing, diverting, encouraging, or dealing with the possible future for electronic commerce? Thus scenarios are intended to

- provide a wide range of possibilities against which to evaluate strategies,

- provide a broad vision of possible events,

- assist in the identification of events that warrant the development of contingency plans, and

- help managers and others identify patterns, generalizations, and interrelationships.[6]

Scenarios are quite useful in forcing those involved in planning to evaluate preliminary plans against future possibilities. As reported in the following Global Awareness Competency account, Royal Dutch/Shell management uses scenarios to stimulate and guide its long-range thinking about possible worldwide developments and the strategic implications of those developments. Thus Royal Dutch/Shell's managers and professionals attempt to (1) stay informed of political, social, and economic trends and events around the world; (2) recognize the impact of global events on the organization; and (3) understand the nature of national, ethnic, and cultural differences, be open to examining these differences honestly and objectively, and respect those differences in their dealings with others.

Scenarios are usually developed for possible futures five to twenty years ahead. To keep the process manageable, three scenarios are usually sufficient: the most probable scenario, a pessimistic scenario, and an optimistic scenario.

DELPHI TECHNIQUE

DELPHI TECHNIQUE

A forecasting aid based on a consensus of a panel of experts.

Named after an ancient Greek oracle, the **Delphi technique** is a forecasting aid based on a consensus of a panel of experts. The experts refine their opinions, step by step, until they reach a consensus. Because the technique relies on opinions, it obviously isn't foolproof. But the consensus arrived at tends to be much more accurate than a single expert's opinion. The Delphi process replaces face-to-face communication and debate with a carefully planned, orderly program of sequential discussions. The first decision that has to be made involves the selection of a group of experts.

The method was developed by the Rand Corporation in the early 1950s to obtain expert judgments on how many Soviet atomic bombs would be required to do a specific amount of damage to the United States.[7] The Delphi technique is now recognized as an important aid to strategic planning.

Basic Steps. The Delphi technique involves three basic steps.

1. **A questionnaire is sent to a group of experts.** These experts remain unknown to one another. The questionnaire requests numerical estimates of

Royal Dutch/Shell's Scenario Planning

Scenario planning began at Royal Dutch/Shell in 1968. An ad-hoc study group within Shell undertook a study on *The Year 2000*. The impetus was the question: How soon would the world run out of oil? And, if those resources were depleted, would that condemn oil companies to an unexciting, low-growth future? As Shell people put it, "Is there life [for our company] after oil?"

Scenarios at Royal/Dutch Shell are used as tools for foresight—discussions and documents whose purpose isn't to produce a prediction or a plan, but a change in the mindset of the people who use them. The telling of stories about the future in the context of their own perceptions of the present opened the eyes of managers and professionals to developments that otherwise might be unthinkable.

The scenario planners at Royal/Dutch Shell try to grasp the meaning of changes in social values, technology, consumption patterns, political thinking, and international finance in various parts of the world. There is little duplication with the planning still done by Shell's supply or finance people, who look only at oil-related developments. The scenario planners don't ignore oil and energy concerns, but they are looking for "driving forces," that might come from anywhere and ultimately affect the world of energy and oil. They analyze these forces to determine whether, and how, the resulting changes might affect Shell. In short, scenarios provide tools by which unfashionable and weak signals may be picked up and considered, without overwhelming the managers who use them.

Once written, scenarios are tested and quantified with the help of simulation models and the company's energy and economics data banks. The quantification helps focus the scenarios and demonstrate whether they are internally consistent. The end result is a small set of consistent plausible futures for the organization.

Shell's scenario planners recognized the future ahead of its time. They foresaw: the energy crises of 1973 and 1979; the growth of energy conservation and the reduction of demand for oil; the evolution of the global environmental movement; and even the breakup of the Soviet Union.

Thus Shell's management became aware of the possibility of such changes in the world early enough to make crucial decisions to help the company adapt to them when they actually occurred. Many people believe that this type of planning gives Royal Dutch/Shell an important competitive advantage.[8]

* * *

To learn more about Royal Dutch/Shell, visit the company's home page at

www.shell.com/Home.html

specific technological or market possibilities. It asks for expected dates (years) and an assignment of probabilities to each of these possibilities. Respondents are asked to provide reasons for their expressed opinions. This process may be conducted through e-mail and other electronic means.

2. **A summary of the first round is prepared.** This report may show the average, medium, and quartile ranges of responses. The report, along with a revised questionnaire, is sent to those who completed the first questionnaire. They are asked to revise their earlier estimates, if appropriate, or to justify their original opinions. The reasons for the possibilities presented in the first round by the experts are subjected to a critique by fellow respondents in writing. The technique emphasizes informed judgment. It attempts to improve the panel or committee approach by subjecting the views of individual experts to others' reactions in ways that avoid face to face confrontation and provide anonymity of opinion and of arguments advanced in defense of those opinions.

3. **A summary of the second round is prepared.** This report often shows that a consensus is developing. The experts are then asked in a third questionnaire to indicate whether they support this emerging consensus and the explanations that accompany it. To avoid blind agreement, they are encouraged to find reasons for *not* joining the consensus.[9]

Three rounds generally are recommended. Although more rounds could be used, the experts often begin dropping out after the third round because of other time commitments. The number of participating experts may range from only a few to more than 100, depending on the scope of the study. A range of fifteen to twenty is recommended for a very focused issue. As the sample size (number of experts) increases, the amount of coordination required also increases, as do costs.

Delphi Questionnaires. The heart of the Delphi technique is the series of questionnaires. The first questionnaire may include broadly worded questions. In later rounds, the questions become more specific because they are built on responses to the preceding questionnaires.

Table 9.1 shows a Delphi technique questionnaire developed for student and classroom use. It is concerned with possible developments in electronic commerce during the next twenty years as applied to automobile dealerships. You might want to take a few minutes now to answer the questions in Table 9.1.

Table 9.1 **Delphi Questionnaire: Implications of Electronic Commerce for Automobile Dealers**

Introduction: The seven questions here are concerned with future possible developments for automobile dealerships as a result of electronic commerce (EC) over the next twenty years or so. In addition to giving your answer to each question, you are asked to rank the questions from 1 to 7. The ranking 1 means you think that you have the best chance of making an accurate projection for this question relative to the others. The ranking 7 means you regard your answer as least probable relative to other years identified. Please rank all questions, using every number from 1 to 7 only once. "Never" is also an acceptable answer.

Rank (1–7)		Questions	Year
_____	1.	By what year will 40 percent of new automobile sales take place through EC?	_____
_____	2.	By what year will 35 percent of used car sales take place through EC?	_____
_____	3.	By what year will 30 percent or more of automobile loans be obtained through EC?	_____
_____	4.	By what year will the number of new car dealerships be reduced by one-third as compared to 1999?	_____
_____	5.	By what year will 50 percent or more of appointments for new car warranty work be scheduled through EC?	_____
_____	6.	By what year will 40 percent or more of new car sales occur directly between the manufacturer and consumer through EC?	_____
_____	7.	By what year will 35 percent or more of new car sales be custom ordered for manufacture through EC rather than purchased from inventory (e.g., a dealer's lot)?	_____

The Australian Science, Technology and Engineering Council (ATEC) recently applied the Delphi process in a novel way to conduct a technological foresight exercise of the needs of Australian maritime industries to 2010. The Shipping Partnership Study involved participants from groups comprising industry, government, research, and academic and professional societies in Australia. The study group comprised the 135 who responded to a survey of 550 individuals originally selected. Possible developments were identified in seventy-six *topic statements* that were divided into nine *subtopics* for investigation. These subtopics were ship design, ship manufacture, ship ownership and operation, research and development, transport, warship design and production, industry suppliers, the exclusive zone (EEZ), and cargo handling.

The Shipping Partnership Study focused on *determining priorities, consensus generation,* and *communication and education.* Through analysis of the Delphi survey results, combined with strategic thinking by the partners, the Partnership eventually identified thirty-six issues having first claim for consideration. Consensus generation was promoted by the Delphi procedures and encouraged in Partnership discussions. Communication and education, a key part of the process fostered by the Delphi survey, was underway in early 1998.[10]

SIMULATION

SIMULATION
A representation of a real system.

A *simulation* is a representation of a real system. A simulation model usually describes the behavior of the real system (or some aspect of it) in quantitative and/or qualitative terms. For example, a simulation at Ford Motor Company may show how changes in external variables (e.g., inflation rate, competitors' price changes, and unemployment rate) may affect Ford's sales, profits, and employment levels. Computers often are used in simulation. In contrast to scenarios, simulations are based on specific cause and effect relationships between factors or variables.[11]

Advanced business simulations are relatively expensive, complex, custom-designed, and often require the use computers to perform hundreds of thousands of calculations. Taking their cue from the military, the developers and users of these simulations refer to them as business war games. For example, Advanced Competitive Strategies (ASC), a consulting firm headquartered in Portland, Oregon, developed computer simulation software called *Value War.* ASC gathers data about a company and its market and then divides a company's staff into opposing *armies* to fight out a particular strategy. In one case, Shell Oil used this simulation to figure out whether building unstaffed service stations would increase market share (the simulation determined that it wouldn't). The cost of advanced war game simulations typically starts at about $80,000. Mark Frost, a senior associate at Booz, Allen & Hamilton (a strategy consulting firm), comments, "Simulations provide a real chance for senior decision makers to take a walk into the future, to see where the company may succeed and where it may fail."[12]

Simulation often is used to forecast the effects of environmental changes and internal management decisions on an organization, department, or SBU. The goal of simulation is to reproduce or test reality without actually experiencing it. Most simulations are intended to let management ask numerous "what if" questions. For example, What profits can we anticipate next year if inflation is 8 percent and we continue current pricing policies? or, What profits can we expect next year if inflation is 2 percent and we open two new plants? To answer such questions, analysts often develop complex equations and use computers to perform many of the step-by-step computations required. Such models can be used to simulate virtually any issue of interest (e.g., profits, sales, and earnings per share) for which a forecast is needed.

Typical Questions and Variables. A simulation can help planners deal with three common strategic questions.

1. What general effect will certain changes in the economy (e.g., an increase in interest rates from 6 to 10 percent) have on the organization if its primary strategies remain unchanged?

2. What will be the specific effects on the organization if a particular strategy (e.g., low cost, focus, or differentiation) is selected in anticipation of those changes in the economy?

3. Are there any particular combinations of strategies that will enable the organization to gain a competitive advantage?

Types of environmental variables used in a simulation might include inflation rate, short-term interest rate, tax rate, and unemployment level. Strategies used in a simulation could affect price, sales, dividends, cash flow, depreciation, or production capacity. The performance measure used to present the outcome of a simulation model might be an income statement, a financial ratio (e.g., debt-to-equity ratio, return on equity, or earnings per share), or a balance sheet (assets and liabilities).

Manufacturing processes have been studied with computer simulation. In the past, simulations of manufacturing systems were performed mainly by mathematical experts who believed in the results. However, managers often didn't believe in them because the results were presented in the form of hard-to-interpret computer printouts. Simulation of manufacturing systems now utilizes a new technology—computer graphics—that is much clearer and easier to understand. With the help of graphic displays, the simulation evolves step by step on the screen for the user and others to see. As a result, many managers are gaining confidence in simulation results.[13]

VIRTUAL REALITY

A surrogate environment created by communications and computer systems.

Virtual Reality. A new technology, *virtual reality*, is a surrogate environment created by communications and computer systems.[14] The term denotes a simulated environment into which a user "enters," moves around, and interacts with objects. Virtual reality fulfills the sensory requirements of human beings for sight, sound, and movement. One of the earliest practical uses of virtual reality was the training of pilots in flight simulators. Entertainment manufacturers are increasingly using it in their video games. Some dentists are even using it to relax their patients while performing oral surgery.

The advantage of virtual reality as a planning aid is the freedom it allows for experimentation. The pace of action may be slowed down or speeded up. Processes that occur rapidly can be slowed down for more careful study. Processes that extend over long periods of time can be speeded up to reveal more clearly the consequences of particular actions. Actions that can't be replayed in the real world can be redone countless times. Complexity can be simplified by uncoupling variables that are interlocked in reality.

Virtual reality can be as simple as a computer-based representation of an architect's sketchpad. The architect can draw and talk through moves in a spatial-action language, leaving traces that represent the forms of buildings on a site. Because the drawing reveals qualities and relations unimagined beforehand, moves can function as experiments—for example, discovering that certain building shapes don't fit the slope of the land or that classrooms are too small.

Greg Bookout, whose small firm *Digital Visions* is headquartered in Mt. Shasta, California, sells real-time 3D simulation and virtual reality environments to developers, academicians, and governments around the world. Corporate customers include GM, Hughes Training, and Lockheed Martin. For example, he developed a simulated ship engine room that enables Lockheed engineers and maintenance technicians wearing virtual reality goggles to conduct walk-through training in ship's engine rooms. Constructing its accurate simulations from Lockheed's photos and drawings took Bookout one month. In another project, he developed a virtual drive down streets in Melbourne for an Australian insurance company to simulate ways to improve traffic safety. It replicates lifelike city streets, with moving vehicles, pedestrians, and working traffic lights.[15]

The following Planning and Administration Competency feature summarizes how IBM PC Company's management used simulation to help identify, analyze, and recommend the most cost-effective changes for IBM Europe's PC manufacturing and distribution operations. As part of this project, an IBM team developed a supply-chain simulation model designed to quantitatively assess the impact of various operational strategies on cost and customer service levels. This simulation helped management identify symptoms, underlying problems, and alternative solutions; make timely decisions; take calculated risks and anticipate the consequences; and develop plans and schedules to achieve specific goals efficiently

CREATIVITY AIDS

2

APPLY TWO AIDS FOR FOSTERING CREATIVITY— OSBORN'S CREATIVITY MODEL AND THE CAUSE AND EFFECT DIAGRAM

CREATIVITY
The ability to visualize, foresee, generate, and implement new ideas.

All forecasting aids need to be supported by a healthy dose of creativity. *Creativity* is the ability to visualize, foresee, generate, and implement new ideas. Creative thinking increases the quality of solutions to many types of problems, helps stimulate innovation, revitalizes motivation and commitment by challenging individual competencies, and serves as a catalyst for effective team performance. For organizations creativity is no longer optional—it is imperative. In particular, for total quality management initiatives to succeed, managers and employees alike need creative thinking skills.[16] The creative process comprises five interconnected stages: preparation, concentration, incubation, illumination, and verification.

Preparation involves a thorough investigation to ensure that all parts of an issue or problem are identified or understood. This stage involves searching for and collecting facts and ideas.

Concentration occurs when energies and resources are focused on identifying and solving an issue or problem. A commitment must be made in this stage to implementing a solution.

Incubation involves an internal and unconscious ordering of gathered information. This stage may involve an unconscious personal conflict between what is currently accepted as reality and what may be possible. Relaxing, sometimes distancing yourself from the issue, and allowing the unconscious to search for possible issues or problems and solutions is important. A successful incubation stage yields fresh ideas and new ways of thinking about the nature of an issue or a problem and alternative solutions.

Science fiction writer Ray Bradbury once said that he often had flashes about good material during the half-awake state before real sleep. Often he forced himself completely awake to make notes of these ideas. In fact, you can coach yourself to receive dream images by telling your unconscious, Give me a dream about [the issue or problem you are working on]. Wake me as soon as the dream is over. (With practice, you will be able to dream and awaken yourself in this way.) As soon as you're awake, *do not* open your eyes but *do* review your dream. Then open your eyes and, using the pad and pencil you have left by your bedside, quickly write down the main elements of the dream.[17]

This project was prompted by management's concerns about the distribution process for the European division of the IBM PC Company. First, service levels—measured as the fraction of on-time order shipments—were low. Distribution centers often didn't have the right finished goods on hand to fill customer orders and thus had to wait for shipments. Shipment delays, especially at trans-shipment points, weren't uncommon. Second, the costs of the distribution network were high. Freight rates that were negotiated

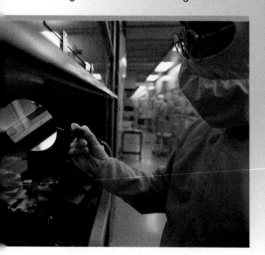

weren't necessarily the best. The operational costs of the transshipment points and country distribution centers were high. Significant inventory was being held by the distribution centers. Third, IBM managers thought that increasing competition would require meeting service expectations that couldn't be satisfied at a reasonable cost through the existing distribution process.

A team was formed to attack these problems. It first had to gain a detailed understanding of all in-place manufacturing and distribution processes in the European division before it could develop a model. These included planning processes, manufacturing processes, and finished goods distribution processes.

Next, the team developed a detailed supply-chain simulation model of the relevant processes so that it would have a foundation for evaluating proposed changes and directly assessing their effect on costs and service levels. The team first validated the simulation model against the existing business processes and then

explored alternative processes. It viewed the simulation model as a vehicle for convincing team members and others that proposed changes in operational processes were appropriate.

With this model, the team was able to compare different manufacturing strategies, examine the effect of different planning and forecasting methods, and identify lower cost distribution processes. Ultimately, the analysis led to significant changes in both manufacturing and distribution. These changes included adoption of a build-to-order (BTO) manufacturing strategy, implementation of a direct-ship distribution process that bypassed costly country distribution centers, and rejection of a cost-inefficient idea that had been gaining currency among IBM executives—the introduction of a new "customization" assembly plant in Europe.[18]

* * *

To learn more about the IBM PC Company, visit its home page at

www.pc.ibm.com

The *illumination stage* is the moment of discovery, the instant of recognition, as when a light seems to be turned on mentally. The mind instantly connects an issue or a problem to a solution through a remembered observation or occurrence. Ray Jones, the research lab director for a chemical firm, describes the illumination stage in this way:

> *Somebody came to me recently with the problem of making silicon nitride powders. We can make silicon nitride fibers, but could we make very fine powders? We came up with some solutions that we thought could do it, but neither of us was satisfied with them. About a month later an idea popped into my head which I think solves the entire thing.*[19]

Verification is the testing of the created solution or idea. At this stage, confirmation and acceptance of the new approach is sought.

These five interconnected stages apply to various types of creativity.[20] One type is *novelty,* or an original approach to a problem. Novelty involves seeing a possibility before anyone else does. Arthur Fry, a researcher at 3M, was the first to use Post-it Notes to mark pages in his church hymnal. He then recognized the tremendous potential for Post-it Notes applications. A second type of creativity is *synthesis,* or the combining of existing ideas from various sources into a new whole. Some organizations have expanded their markets by synthesizing new services or products to complement existing lines. When Walter Young, Jr., became CEO of Champion Enterprises in 1990, the company was going broke selling inexpensive, factory-built houses. "People thought we were in the trailer park business," says Young. "It was a real perception problem, and it was all of our own making.[21] Young's new viewpoint: Mobile homes might be downscale, but *manufactured housing* can be anything you want. The company began building bigger houses in its factories, betting that millions of families who couldn't afford a house built by a developer on-site, would be thrilled to have a factory-built full-sized home trucked to their lots. This synthesis of traditional manufactured mobile home housing with larger houses on owners' lots has been a major success for Champion. A third type of creativity is *extension,* which involves extending an idea to another application. Microsoft has consistently modified its software products to extend their applications to solve new problems and meet new users' needs—and to capitalize on planned obsolescence.

The self-management competency exercise at the end of this chapter provides a way for you to assess your own barriers to creative thought and innovative action. For now, we present A. F. Osborn's creativity model and the cause and effect diagram as aids for fostering creative planning and decision making in organizations.

OSBORN'S CREATIVITY MODEL

Osborn's creativity model is a three-phase decision-making process that involves fact finding, idea finding, and solution finding. It is designed to help overcome blockages to creativity and innovation, which may occur for a variety of reasons. It is intended to stimulate cooperation and freewheeling thinking that lead to innovative decisions.[22] It can be used with all types of groups (e.g., a manager and subordinates or a team of employees). Sufficient time and freedom must be allowed for the model to work well, and some degree of external pressure and self-generated tension are helpful. However, too much pressure or too many threats from the wrong sources (e.g., an order from top management to determine within ten days why quality has deteriorated) can easily undermine the process. Osborn's creativity model stimulates novel ideas and curiosity. It is one of several aids for finding new ways of identifying and considering problems and generating solutions.

Fact-Finding Phase. Fact finding involves defining the issue or problem and gathering and analyzing important data. Although the Osborn creativity model provides some fact-finding procedures, they aren't nearly as well developed as the idea-finding procedures.[23] One way to improve fact finding is to begin with a broad view of the issue or problem and then proceed to define subissues or subproblems. This phase requires making a distinction between a symptom of an issue or a problem and an actual issue or problem. For example, a manager might claim that negative employee attitudes constitute a problem. A deeper investigation might reveal that negative employee attitudes are only symptoms of a festering issue. The issue may be a lack of feedback on how well employees are performing their jobs.

Idea-Finding Phase. Idea finding starts by generating tentative ideas and possible leads. Then, the most likely of these ideas are modified, combined, and added to, if necessary. Osborn maintained that individuals can generate more good ideas by following two principles. First, defer judgment: Individuals can think up almost twice as many good ideas in the same length of time if they defer judgment on any idea until after creating a list of possible leads to a solution. Second, quantity breeds quality: The more ideas individuals think up, the more likely they are to arrive at the potentially best leads to a solution.

To encourage uninhibited thinking and generate lots of ideas, Osborn developed seventy-five general questions to use when brainstorming a problem. **Brainstorming** is an unrestrained flow of ideas in a group with all critical judgments suspended. The group leader must decide which of the seventy-five questions are most appropriate to the issue or problem being addressed. Moreover, the group leader isn't expected to use all of the questions in a single session. Examples of questions that could be used in a brainstorming session are:

- How can this issue, idea, or thing be put to other uses?

- How can it be modified?

- How can it be substituted for something else, or can something else be substituted for part of it?

- How could it be reversed?

- How could it be combined with other things?[24]

A brainstorming session should follow four basic rules.

1. **Criticism is ruled out.** Participants must withhold critical judgment of ideas until later.

2. **Freewheeling is welcomed.** The wilder the idea, the better; taming down an idea is easier than thinking up new ones.

3. **Quantity is wanted.** The greater the number of ideas, the greater is the likelihood that some will be useful.

4. **Combination and improvement are sought.** In addition to contributing ideas of their own, participants should suggest how ideas of others can be turned into better ideas, or how two or more ideas can be merged into still another idea.[25]

These rules are intended to separate creative imagination from judgment. The two are incompatible and relate to different aspects of the decision-making process. The leader of one brainstorming group put it this way: "If you try to get hot or cold water out of the same faucet at the same time, you will get only lukewarm water. And if you try to criticize and create at the same time, you will not do either very well. So let us stick solely to *ideas*—let us cut out *all* criticism during this session."[26]

A brainstorming session should have from five to twelve or so participants in order to generate diverse ideas. This size range permits each member to maintain a sense of identification and involvement with the group. A session should normally run not less than twenty minutes nor more than an hour. However, brainstorming could consist of several idea-generating sessions. For example, follow-up sessions could address individually each of the ideas previously generated. Table 9.2 presents the guidelines for leading a brainstorming session.

Solution-Finding Phase. Solution finding involves generating and evaluating possible courses of action and deciding how to implement the chosen course of action. This phase relies on judgment, analysis, and criticism. A variety of planning and decision-making aids—such as those presented in this chapter—can be used. To initiate the solution-finding phase, the leader could ask the group to identify from one to five of the most important ideas generated. The participants might be asked to jot down these ideas individually on a piece of paper and evaluate them on a five-

Basic leadership role	• Make a brief statement of the four basic rules.
	• State the time limit for the session.
	• Read the problem and/or related question to be discussed and ask, "What are your ideas?"
	• When an idea is given, summarize it by using the speaker's words insofar as possible. Have the idea recorded by a participant or on an audiotape machine. Follow your summary with the single word "Next."
	• Say little else. Whenever the leader participates as a brainstormer, group productivity usually falls.
Handling problems	When someone talks too long, wait until he or she takes a breath (everyone must stop to inhale sometime), break into the monologue, summarize what was said for the recorder, point to another participant, and say "Next."
	• When someone becomes judgmental or starts to argue, stop him or her. Say, for example, "That will cost you one coffee or soda for each member of the group."
	• When the discussion stops, relax and let the silence continue. Say nothing. The pause should be broken by the group and *not* the leader. This period of silence is called the *mental pause* because it is a change in thinking. All the obvious ideas are exhausted; the participants are now forced to rely on their creativity to produce new ideas.
	• When someone states a problem rather than idea, repeat the problem, raise your hand with five fingers extended, and say, "Let's have five ideas on this problem." You may get only one or you may get ten, but you're back in the business of creative thinking.

Source: Adapted from A. F. Osborn. *Applied Imagination,* 3d rev. ed. New York: Charles Scribner's Sons, 1963, pp. 166–196.

point scale. A very important idea might get five points; a moderately important idea could get three points; and an unimportant idea could be assigned one point. The highest combined scores may indicate the actions or ideas to be investigated further.

Osborn's creativity model has been modified often and applied in a variety of ways. The following Teamwork Competency piece highlights how IDEO Product Development, headquartered in Palo Alto, California, uses brainstorming. IDEO is a professional services firm that helps clients design and develop new products and, in the process, become more innovative. The creative process at IDEO is fostered through the extensive use of empowered design teams. Teams are staffed to take advantage of diverse perspectives, technical and creative skills, and achieving goals jointly. Diverse views are encouraged and used to enhance the quality and creativity of decisions. At the same time, cooperation is fostered, and the teams are kept moving toward their goals.

IDEO projects last from a few weeks to several years, with the average being ten to twelve months. Depending on the client's needs, results can range from sketches of products to crude working models to complete new products. Clients vary from venture-funded start-ups to multinational corporations in North America, Europe, and Japan. IDEO developed part or all of more than 3,000 products in dozens of industries, including Apple's first computer mouse, AT&T's new consumer telephones, Oral B's "Squish Grip" toothbrushes for children, and Nike's latest sports sunglasses.

IDEO is unique in encouraging clients to participate in brainstorming sessions conducted within design teams. By going to a "brainstormer," clients gain insight and learn because they join IDEO designers in the creative process. Brainstorming sessions usually are initiated by a design team.

The team members then invite other IDEO designers to help generate ideas for the project. These sessions are held in rooms with five brainstorming rules written on the walls: defer judgment, build on the ideas of others, one conversation at a time, stay focused on the topic, and encourage wild ideas.

Designers who are also skilled facilitators lead the brainstorming sessions; they enforce the rules, write suggestions on the board, and encourage creativity and fun. Nearly all the designers are experienced at brainstorming. Typically, project members (or clients) introduce the project and describe the design issue or problem they face (e.g., How do you make fishing more fun and easy for neophytes?). Participants then generate ideas (e.g., Use the "slingshot" method to launch lures.), often sketching them on paper or whiteboards. Many new projects start with a flurry of brainstorming sessions. Clients often attend them to describe their existing products and the new products that they want designed. Clients may also give detailed demonstrations before a brainstormer to explain the product or service, such as clients from a chain of hair salons who did haircuts at the Palo Alto office to demonstrate their work process. Twenty or so IDEO employees may be invited to brainstorming sessions in the early weeks of a project.

Clients are usually invited to brainstorming sessions or to live at IDEO because their knowledge is needed to complete a project. As generalists rather than specialists, IDEO designers often design and develop products that they knew little or nothing about before the project began. This ignorance may have short-term costs while IDEO designers learn about the product and industry at the outset of a project. But it also benefits clients because designers have fewer preconceived assumptions about what can and can't be done with a specific product or in a particular industry.

Brainstorming sessions elicit cooperation between clients and IDEO designers and thus can be useful in breaking down stereotypes. One designer, for example, grumbled before a brainstorming session for a personal services firm: "This is boring, I want to do something fun, I want to meet some smart people, I want to learn something." After the session, the same designer talked about what an interesting industry it was, how smart the client was, how much fun he had, and how many interesting designs could be done for the client. Ninety minutes of interaction and collaborative learning dissolved this cynical designer's negative view of the client and the industry.[27]

* * *

To learn more about IDEO Product Development, visit the company's home page at

www.ideo.com

Assessment. The Osborn creativity model is based on the assumption that most people have the potential for greater creativity and innovation in decision making than they use. Some research suggests that the same number of individuals working alone may generate more ideas and more creative ideas than do groups.[28] However, most of this research was conducted with students rather than employees and employee teams on the job. Unlike employees who have diverse knowledge and skills and who are brought together to brainstorm problems that have serious long-term consequences (as at IDEO), student groups are relatively homogeneous. Most students have a limited range of knowledge of the problems given to them and limited skills to apply to their solution. Because students don't have to be concerned with real-world consequences, they may be less than fully committed to the process. Thus whether group brainstorming in a work setting is more or less effective than individuals working alone to generate ideas remains an open question.

A growing amount of evidence suggests that in some work settings electronic brainstorming may be a better way to generate ideas than traditional face-to-face brainstorming.[29] **Electronic brainstorming** makes use of technology to input and automatically disseminate ideas in real time over a computer network to all team members, each of whom may be stimulated to generate additional ideas. For example, individuals may input their ideas on the keyboard as they think of them. Every time an idea is entered, the team's ideas appear in random order on each person's screen. An individual can continue to see new sets of ideas in random order by pressing the appropriate key.[30] The random order format prevents the system's users from identifying who generates each idea.

CAUSE AND EFFECT DIAGRAM

The **cause and effect diagram** helps team members display, categorize, and evaluate all the possible causes of an effect, which is generally expressed as a problem.[31] Kaoru Ishikawa proposed this type of analysis. Hence the cause and effect diagram is called an *Ishikawa diagram*. It also is called a *fishbone diagram* because of its appearance. Figure 9.1 shows the general framework of a cause and effect diagram, the construction of which usually involves four steps.

- **Step 1:** The team needs to agree on the "effect," which should be stated in terms of the problem (e.g., files out of place, late delivery of merchandise to a customer, or job cost exceeding estimate). Brainstorming or other techniques may be needed if the team isn't able to begin with a clear, common view of the nature of the problem. The problem, or effect, is then shown on the right side of the diagram, as in Figure 9.1.

Figure 9.1   *General Framework of Cause and Effect Diagram*

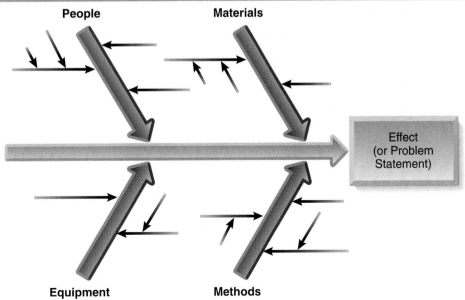

- **Step 2:** The team identifies all the general factors of categories that contribute to the problem, which will help the team organize the specific causes. Figure 9.1 shows the four commonly used categories: people, equipment, methods, and materials. These categories are only suggestions, and the team may use any categories that aid creative thinking. The assumption is that for every effect there are likely to be several major categories of causes. These are the main "bones of the fish." Sometimes this step isn't taken until all the possible causes have been brainstormed. At that time, they are placed in major categories.

- **Step 3:** The team may also use brainstorming or other techniques to generate all the possible causes that contribute to the problem (or effect) in that category. The session leader or members repeatedly ask, What causes this cause? In theory, the team will ask this question five times as it moves from *surface* causes to *root* causes.

- **Step 4:** This step involves reaching agreement on the top three to five root (critical) causes in each major category. These are written on the diagram and connected to the appropriate main category with arrows.

Using this diagram, the team can then focus on collecting additional data to determine whether the relationships between the assumed causes and the effect are valid. Team members' hunches and perceptions about what causes the problem will be either supported or refuted by the data. Solutions can then be developed to address and eliminate genuine causes.

Figure 9.2 shows a cause and effect diagram developed by a team at the Rush–Presbyterian–St. Luke's Medical Center (in Chicago) that was considering the possible causes of patients having to wait for beds after arriving at the hospital. The vision of this medical center is to be recognized as Chicago's premier health ser-

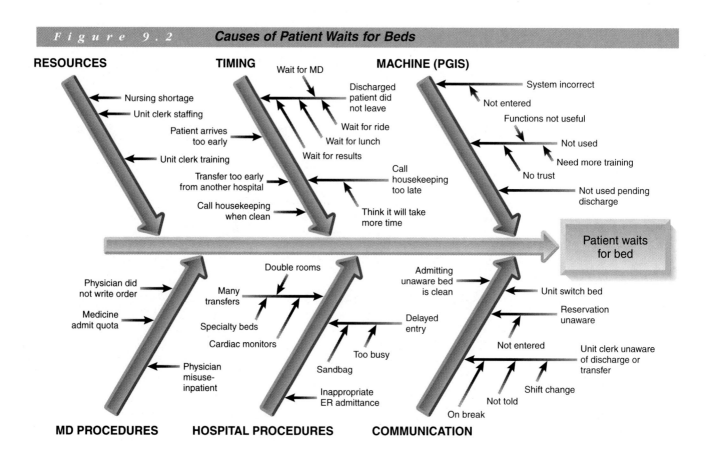

Figure 9.2   *Causes of Patient Waits for Beds*

vices organization based on the superiority of its clinical programs, its application of the latest medical technologies, the excellence of its education and research, and its emphasis on health promotion and patient education, disease prevention, and cost-effective outcomes.[32]

Note in Figure 9.2 that the major categories of causes related to resources, timing, machines, MD (doctor) procedures, hospital procedures, and communication. Based on this analysis, the hospital took a whole series of actions to reduce the frequency of patients having to wait for beds.

Assessment. The cause and effect diagram, Osborn model, or any other aid intended to stimulate creativity in planning and decision making can't guarantee innovative outcomes. However, the proper use of such aids in supportive organizations, such as IDEO, usually increases the likelihood of more innovative plans and decisions. Use of the cause and effect diagram encourages individuals and teams to spend more time searching for root causes. This effort reduces people's tendency to identify symptoms as causes. If the process is successful, resources won't be spent exploring or trying to correct the wrong things (e.g., symptoms or superficial causes).

TOTAL QUALITY AIDS

Planning and decision making starts with the recognition that there is no single indicator of quality. **Quality** may be defined as value (linking different grades of products and price), conformance to specifications or standards, excellence (providing the best), and meeting or exceeding customers' expectations. The most common definition of *quality* is the extent to which a good or service meets and/or exceeds customers' expectations.[33] Consumers often apply the value definition of quality when making purchasing decisions. *Consumer Reports* ranks products and services on both quality and price to arrive at recommendations of "best-buys." Thus alternative perspectives of quality are appropriate in different circumstances. Three planning and decision aids focus specifically on enhancing total quality: benchmarking, the Deming cycle, and Pareto analysis.

BENCHMARKING

Benchmarking is the continuous process of comparing an organization's strategies, products, or processes with those of *best-in-class* organizations. It helps employees learn how such organizations achieved excellence and then set out to match or exceed them.[34] Benchmarking has been used to assess most aspects of organizations' operations. It identifies the "best" that is occurring elsewhere and helps organizations determine how to develop their own strategic or tactical plans and processes to reach that level.

QUALITY
Value, conformance to specifications or standards, excellence, and meeting or exceeding customers' expectations.

BENCHMARKING
The continuous process of comparing an organization's strategies, products, or processes with those of *best-in-class* organizations.

Basic Steps. As noted in Figure 9.3, benchmarking includes seven basic steps.[35] Step 1 involves *defining the domain* to be benchmarked. This step includes a careful study of the organization's own products and processes that are to be compared to benchmark products and processes. In the advertising for the 1998 Dodge Ram pickup (a new model), the company claimed that about 100 different aspects of the pickup were improved upon to meet or exceed current benchmarks in pickup design. Improvements included the new four-door option called the "quad cab" design.

Functions such as manufacturing, finance, marketing, inventory management, transportation, accounting, legal services, human resources, and marketing may be benchmarked. Also, various functional processes may be benchmarked. Each function

Figure 9.3   **The Benchmarking Process**

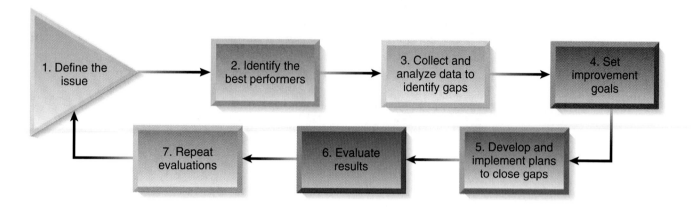

or process may be broken into more specific categories or processes for that purpose. For example, benchmarking in human resources may include the processes of recruiting, diversity enhancement, training, compensation, performance appraisal, recognition programs, and job design.

Benchmarking can be expensive and time-consuming. Thus some people recommend that benchmarking be directed at the specific issues and processes that are likely to yield the greatest competitive advantage (e.g., core strategic competencies, managerial competencies, and the like).[36] Others suggest that benchmarking be applied to all functions and processes to instill total quality throughout the organization.

Step 2 involves *identifying the best performers,* or best-in-class, for each function, process, and product to be benchmarked. They may include organizations in the firm's own industry or in other industries. For example, Xerox compared its warehousing and distribution process with that of L. L. Bean, the catalog sales company, because of its excellent reputation in this area.

Step 3 involves *collecting and analyzing data to identify gaps,* if any, between the function, product, or process being evaluated and that of the best-in-class organizations. The data collected need to focus on specific methods utilized, not simply on the results obtained. It is one thing to know that Wal-Mart has a superb warehouse distribution system. It is another thing to learn how Wal-Mart has achieved this level of excellence. There are many sources of information for learning about best-in-class organizations. They include customers, suppliers, distributors, trade journals, company publications, newspapers, books on total quality, consultants, presentations at professional meetings, and even on-site interviews with people at the best-in-class organizations. This last source usually is easier to tap if the organizations aren't direct competitors.

The remaining steps are consistent with the typical planning phases: Step 4 involves *setting improvement goals;* step 5, *developing and implementing plans to close gaps;* step 6, *evaluating results;* and step 7, *repeating the evaluations as necessary.* Step 7 suggests that benchmarking needs to be an ongoing process. Over time, the things benchmarked may remain the same or need to be revised. Revisions may include dropping and/or adding functions, products, or processes as issues, conditions, technology, and markets change.

Rank-Xerox provides an interesting example of internal benchmarking among its operating divisions in Europe, the Middle East, and Africa. It is 80 percent owned by Xerox and sells several lines of copiers, document processors, and services. A team of some two-dozen people from the sales, service, and administrative staffs was formed. The team set up a simple internal benchmarking program, gathering various types of sales data and making country-by-country comparisons. In only two weeks the team found eight instances in which the division serving one country dramatically outperformed the divisions serving others. In France five times more color copiers were sold than in any other country. In Switzerland sales of Xerox's top-of-the-line DocuPrint machines—digital copiers that can receive documents electronically and store them so copies can be made at any time—were ten times greater than those in any other country. The Dubai division, on the Persian Gulf, was the only one making telephone sales. In one country, when service contracts came up for renewal, the customer attrition rate was 15 percent, but in Austria it was only 4 percent.

Next, team members visited each benchmarked division. Their instructions: Simply find out how it was done; don't try to figure out why it worked. The team then put together a book for each division's sales and service managers, showing each benchmark, how their territory compared with it, and how the top performer's system worked. In most cases, division managers visited the benchmarked division and copied and installed its method in a matter of weeks.

The results were breathtaking. For example, by copying the French division's practices in selling color copiers—chiefly by improving sales training and making sure that color copiers were pushed through dealer channels as well as direct sales—the Swiss division increased its unit sales by 328 percent, the Dutch division by 300 percent, and the Norwegian division by 152 percent. The Rank-Xerox team developed a 200-page handbook of best practices, showing how to improve market databases and how to mix personal selling with direct mail and telemarketing to use sales time better.[37]

Limitation. Benchmarking should be linked to other sources of information, such as changing customer expectations and preferences. Benchmarking always looks at the present in terms of how some process (logistics) or quality dimension is being performed by others. This approach may not be adequate for determining what should be done in the future or whether an organization should retain a function or process or contract it out. For example, an organization could contract out its computer operations to Electronic Data Systems (EDS) or some other firm. When used simply to copy the best-in-class competitors, benchmarking may lead only to short-term competitive advantage. Finally, benchmarking needs to be used to complement and aid, not to substitute for, the creative and innovative efforts of the organization's own employees.[38]

DEMING CYCLE

In Chapter 2, we provided some information on W. Edwards Deming, considered by some to be the "godfather" of the quality movement. One of the aids he advocated for improving quality is commonly known as the Deming cycle. Originally developed by Walter Shewhart, some call it the Shewhart cycle. Others refer to it as the PDCA cycle because it involves the four stages of plan (P), do (D), check (C), and act (A). As Figure 9.4 suggests, these stages unfold in sequence and continuously. Thus the **Deming cycle** comprises four stages—plan, do, check, and act—that should be repeated over time to ensure continuous improvements in a function, product, or process.

Three questions need to be answered during the *plan* stage of the Deming cycle: (1) What are we trying to accomplish? (2) What changes can we make that will result in improvement? and (3) How will we know that a change is an improvement?

DEMING CYCLE

The four stages of improving quality; planning, doing, checking, and acting.

Figure 9.4　**The Deming Cycle**

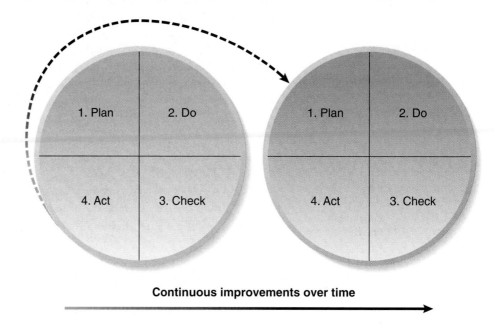

Continuous improvements over time

The plan stage involves analyzing the current situation, gathering data, and developing ways to make improvements. The *do* stage involves testing alternatives experimentally in a laboratory, establishing a pilot production process, or trying it out with a small number of customers. The *check* stage requires determining whether the trial or process is working as intended, any revisions are needed, or it should be scrapped. The *act* stage focuses on implementing the process within the organization or with its customers and suppliers.[39] Benchmarking may be one of the aids used in the plan stage. Other tools that may be used to support the Deming cycle include the program evaluation and review technique presented in the last section of this chapter.

The following Communication Competency account shows how the owner of the Deluxe Diner applied the Deming cycle to solve the problem of customers having to wait too long to be seated. It demonstrates the crucial role of communication in the Deming cycle. Owner Billie Boyd promoted two-way communication by soliciting feedback; listening; seeking out contrary opinions; creating give-and-take conversations; informing employees of relevant data and activities and keeping them up to date; and appearing to be persuasive and comfortable in her managerial role.

PARETO ANALYSIS

Pareto analysis focuses on the sources and relative priorities of the causes of problems. It is frequently used to assess the causes of a quality problem or TQM programs. The **Pareto principle** states that a small number of causes (usually 20 percent of the total) accounts for most of the impacts of the problems (usually 80 percent of the total) in any situation. It is based on research done by a nineteenth century Italian economist, Vilfredo Pareto, and often is referred to as the "80/20 rule." Pareto analysis separates the "vital few" from the "trivial many." Thus it improves the analyst's chances of getting the greatest results for the least amount of time and effort.[40]

Pareto Diagram. One of the tools of Pareto analysis is the **Pareto diagram,** which is a chart used to determine the relative priorities of issues, defects, or prob-

PARETO PRINCIPLE

States that a small number of causes (usually 20 percent of the total) account for most of the problems (usually 80 percent of the total) in any situation.

PARETO DIAGRAM

A chart used to determine the relative priorities of issues, defects, or problems.

Deming Cycle at Deluxe Diner

The owner of Deluxe Diner, Billie Boyd, decided to do something about the long lines at lunchtime that occurred every day. One process in the plan stage involved several team meetings with her employees. They identified four main aspects of this problem: (1) customers were waiting in line for as long as fifteen minutes; (2) usually, tables were available; (3) many of the customers were regulars; and (4) people taking orders and preparing food were getting in each others' way.

The employees offered various ideas. Boyd developed a plan that involved the following changes: (1) allow customers to fax their orders in ahead of time (rent a fax machine for one month); (2) install a preparation table for fax orders in the kitchen, where there was ample room; and (3) devote one of the two cash regis-

ters to handling fax orders. To assess whether these changes improved the situation, Boyd collected data on the number of customers in line, the number of empty tables, and the delay before customers were served. The length of the line and the number of empty tables were measured every fifteen minutes during the lunch hour. When the fifteen-minute line check was done, she noted the last person in line and the time until that person was seated.

Next, the results of the these measurements were observed for three weeks. Three improvements were detected during the check stage. Time in line dropped from fifteen minutes to five minutes, on average. The line length was cut to a peak average of twelve people, and the number of empty tables declined slightly. Boyd held another team meeting with her

employees to discuss the results. They decided to purchase the fax machine, fill the fax orders, and use both cash registers to handle walk-up and fax orders. Boyd thought that the Deming cycle was very helpful in resolving the problem and intends to use it again.[41]

lems. They are arranged in descending order of magnitude of importance, indicating which problems to address first. Pareto diagrams also can be used to highlight the before and after results of projects by comparing multiple diagrams. Let's consider the steps involved in constructing a Pareto diagram related to defects.

1. Count the number of occurrences for each defect observed.

2. Display your results in a defect table. Be sure to place the defects in descending order according to the number of occurrences. Also, calculate the percentage of all defects that are accounted for by each individual defect.

3. Construct a bar chart displaying each defect and its relative frequency. Be sure to place the defect that occurs most to the left and all others in descending order toward the right.

4. The defect that occurs most should be investigated first. After correcting the causes of that defect, if the system is still producing an unacceptable number of defects, perform another Pareto analysis by gathering new data and repeating the steps.

Consider this example. A company produced 325,000 parts during a five-month period. The plant runs two eight-hour shifts, five days a week. During the five months, 78 rejects were detected. This reject rate exceeded the company's threshold for investigation. The quality assurance engineer gathered data on the rejected parts, categorized the data by defect, and plotted a Pareto diagram, as shown in Figure 9.5. The diagram showed six types of defects, including rough finish, undersize, oversize, and out of round.

The engineer was disappointed in the results, because solving the "rough-finish" defect would only cure about a fourth of the problems. She then concluded that, in this case, the defect symptom might not be directly related to the problem's root cause. After some thought, she categorized the data by the shift during which the defective parts were produced, came up with a time distribution, and plotted the Pareto diagram shown in Figure 9.6.

The engineer quickly saw that the problem was related to the first shift, 8 A.M. to 4 P.M., on Mondays, with 45 percent of the defects occurring during 10 percent of the work time of that shift. She then drew another Pareto diagram, as shown in Figure 9.7, based on 35 defective parts that were generated during the first shift on Mondays. This diagram showed that size variations were the main problem, with almost 90 percent, in 40 percent of the categories, concentrated during the targeted period of time.

The analysis showed that the defective parts were being made during start-up on Monday mornings, after the machines had been idle for two days. The engineer talked to the production department, which did some quick testing the following Monday. The test confirmed that the excessive size variation was caused by insufficient machine warm-up. Production easily changed its procedures and eliminated the problem, returning the defect rate to an acceptable level.[42]

Assessment. The preceding example shows that the 80/20 rule doesn't always hold absolutely in practice. For it to do so, exactly 80 percent of the defects would need to be reflected in exactly 20 percent of the categories. Thus analysts must be insightful and creative and exercise good judgment when interpreting a Pareto diagram. For example, in the previous example, the engineer looked more deeply into the situation when the initial Pareto diagram (Figure 9.5) analysis revealed the prob-

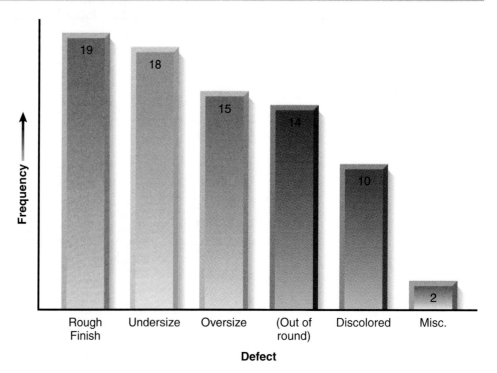

Figure 9.5   **Pareto Diagram: Data Categorized by Defect**

Frequency

19   18   15   14   10   2

Rough Finish   Undersize   Oversize   (Out of round)   Discolored   Misc.

Defect

Figure 9.6 **Pareto Diagram: Data Categorized by Shift**

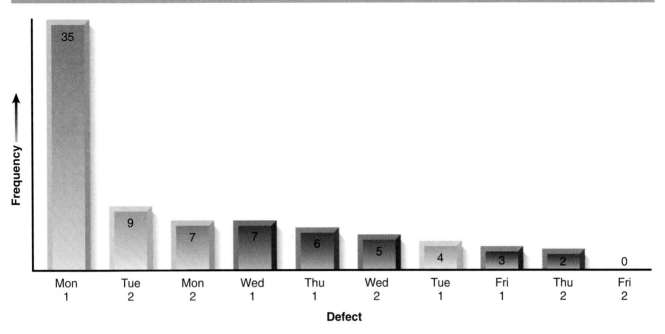

lem's root cause. The initial broad categories of identified problems often need to be analyzed further to verify that specific categories of problems, not just symptoms, are being considered. Generally, two or three Pareto analyses must be developed before the process of identifying alternative solutions can begin, as demonstrated in the example.

Figure 9.7 **Pareto Diagram: Data Categorized by Size-variation Problem for Second Monday Shift**

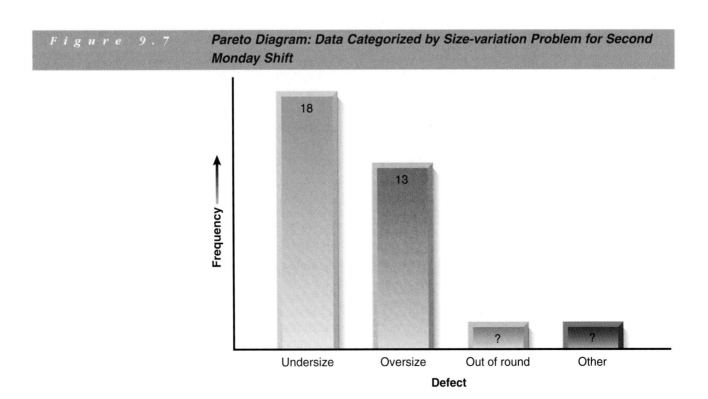

5

EXPLAIN ONE PROJECT
MANAGEMENT AID—THE
PROGRAM EVALUATION
AND REVIEW TECHNIQUE

PROJECT
A one-time activity with a well-defined set of desired results.

PROJECT MANAGEMENT
The principles, methods, and techniques used to establish and implement a project and achieve its goals.

PROGRAM EVALUATION AND REVIEW TECHNIQUE (PERT)
A method of scheduling the sequence of activities and events required to complete a project, estimating their costs, and controlling their progress.

A *project* is a one-time activity with a well-defined set of desired results. Other characteristics of a project include a definite start and finish, a time frame for completion, uniqueness, involvement of people on a temporary basis, a limited set of resources (people, money, and time), and a sequence of activities and phases. *Project management* consists of the principles, methods, and techniques used to establish and implement a project and achieve its goals. The essentials of project management can be applied to projects as simple as developing a thirty-page business plan in an entrepreneurship course or as complex as constructing a sixty-story office tower.[43] The following Self-Management Competency feature suggests the types of professional ethics that are expected by the Project Management Institute of those who work in project management. It spells out the importance of personal integrity, ethical conduct, and applying state-of-the art tools and techniques.

PROGRAM EVALUATION AND REVIEW TECHNIQUE

The *program evaluation and review technique (PERT)* is a method of scheduling the sequence of activities and events required to complete a project, estimating their costs, and controlling their progress. It is one of the most useful aids in project management. In its first major application in 1958, PERT was used in the U.S. Navy's ballistic missile program, more popularly known as the Polaris missile program. The Navy's prime contractor cited PERT as a major reason for completing the program two years ahead of the original schedule. Several government agencies now require companies with which they have contracts to use PERT.

The technique normally is used for one-of-a-kind projects (such as the construction of a theme area at Disney World), projects that involve a new production process (such as a robotic automobile plant), or projects that require interlocking building processes (such as an apartment complex). Project managers use PERT to analyze and specify in detail what is to be done, when it is to be done, and the likelihood of achieving the goal on time. As commonly used in practice, PERT consists of four major elements: (1) a network, (2) a critical path, (3) resource allocations, and (4) cost and time estimates.[44]

PERT NETWORK
A diagram showing the sequence and relationship of the activities and events needed to complete a project.

Network. A *PERT network* is a diagram showing the sequence and relationships of the activities and events needed to complete a project. As shown in Figure 9.8, events (the boxes) are points where decisions are made or activities are completed. Activities (the arrows) are the physical or mental tasks performed in order to move from one event to another.

The network is the basis of the PERT approach. To build one, the project team must identify key project activities, determine their sequence, decide who will be responsible for each activity, and calculate the amount of time needed to accomplish each activity. The network diagram identifies the relationship among the sequence of events and the activities. For example, the arrows in Figure 9.8 show that event 3 can't occur until activities A, B, and C have been accomplished. A PERT network clearly shows how the different managers and teams responsible for the various activities must coordinate their work.

CRITICAL PATH
The path with the longest elapsed time, which determines the length of the project.

Critical Path. Every project follows paths, or sequences of events and activities. The *critical path* is the path with the longest elapsed time, which determines the length of the project. To shorten the time for project completion, the project team must give the most attention to activities along the critical path. A delay in any other path that would lengthen the time for the critical path would delay the completion

SELF-MANAGEMENT COMPETENCY
Professional Ethics in Project Management

Like many other professional areas, project management is concerned with ethical behaviors and decisions. Much of this attention has been directed through the Project Management Institute, a nonprofit professional organization dedicated to advancing the art of project management. It publishes *Project Management Journal, PM Network,* and provides other professional resources.

The association champions a code of ethics for the project management profession. The following is an excerpt from the code. According to this code of ethics, project management professionals shall

- accept responsibility for their actions;
- provide the necessary project leadership to promote maximum productivity while striving to minimize costs;
- apply state-of-the-art project management tools and techniques to ensure that quality,

costs, and time objectives, as set forth in the project plan, are met;
- treat fairly all project team members, colleagues, and co-workers, regardless of race, religion, sex, age, or national origin;
- protect project team members from physical and mental harm;
- seek, accept, and offer honest criticism of work and properly credit the contribution of others; and
- assist project team members, colleagues, and co-workers in their professional development.

These ethical standards, for the most part, apply to team leaders of any type of project, including student group projects.[45]

* * *

To learn more about the Project Management Institute, visit its home page at

www.pmi.org

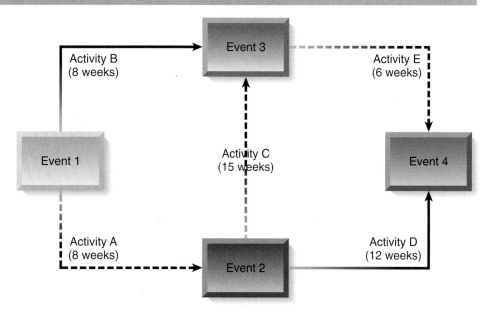

Figure 9.8   **A Basic PERT Network**

Event 1

Activity B
(8 weeks)

Event 3

Activity E
(6 weeks)

Activity C
(15 weeks)

Event 4

Activity A
(8 weeks)

Event 2

Activity D
(12 weeks)

date. A complex project such as construction of a theme park at Disney World or the new Hong Kong International Airport consists of thousands of activities and hundreds of paths. Work goes on concurrently along each separate path. In the case of such huge projects, a master PERT network and individual PERT networks for each path are common.

The wide-band arrows in Figure 9.8 identify the critical path, which requires a total elapsed time of twenty-nine weeks. It equals the sum of the times required to complete the activities between events 1 and 2, events 2 and 3, and events 3 and 4. Any delay in activity completion along the critical path will delay project completion.

Resource Allocation. Project teams require a variety of resources to undertake their assigned activities. Resource availability greatly influences the length of time between events and the costs associated with each activity. Project leaders must estimate types and amounts of required materials, equipment, facilities, and human resources. For example, the first major activity in constructing a house without a basement is excavating and pouring footings. A contractor may estimate that this activity will require one backhoe, one backhoe operator, and three laborers for four days, as well as specific amounts of sand for fill, wood for concrete forms, steel reinforcing rods, and concrete.

Cost and Time Estimates. PERT's ability to help reduce project costs and time is of particular value. The project team prepares cost estimates for each activity (task), such as excavating and pouring footings for a house. Similarly, the team estimates the amount of time needed for each activity. For example, Figure 9.8 shows that activity A *should* take eight weeks.

Four time estimates often are made for each activity. The *most likely time* is the estimated time required to complete an activity, taking into consideration normal problems and interruptions. The *optimistic time* is the estimated time required to complete an activity if everything goes right. The *pessimistic time* is the estimated time required to complete an activity if unusual problems and interruptions occur. Based on Murphy's law, the assumption is that serious problems may arise, although even the pessimistic estimate normally doesn't take into account rare, catastrophic events, such as fires, tornadoes, floods, and war. The *expected time* represents a weighted average of the most likely, optimistic, and pessimistic time estimates. By developing alternative time estimates, the project team can anticipate and react quickly to problems or opportunities. If an activity is running behind schedule, having people work overtime or hiring additional people might be advantageous. If an activity is ahead of schedule, the project manager might speed up deliveries of supplies that are needed for later activities. Without a PERT network, project managers may not perceive that further action is required.

PERT becomes a control mechanism after a project is underway. Using PERT's reporting procedures, a project team can monitor differences between actual and planned times and costs for each activity.

ASSESSMENT OF PERT

PERT is most useful when projects are complex and require tight coordination. This project management aid helps reduce project time and costs under the following conditions.

- The project consists of a well-defined collection of job or team activities.

- The job or team activities may be started and stopped independently of one another. Continuous-flow processes—such as oil refining, where jobs or operations follow each other in a strict time sequence day after day—do not lend themselves to the use of PERT.

- The job or team activities are ordered; that is, they must be performed in a particular sequence or often in multiple simultaneous sequences that create complex networks. For instance, the foundation of a house must be laid before the walls are erected.[46]

Several PC and mainframe software systems are available for PERT and other project management aids. For example, Open Plan, provided by Welcom Software Technology, enables the user to handle projects with as many as 100,000 activities. Open Plan creates easy-to-read graphics and can provide as many as 256 calendar schedules per project. Open Plan and similar project management software systems also offer many other features, such as cost scheduling and control aids.

CHAPTER SUMMARY

In this chapter, we focused on forecasting, creativity, quality, and project management aids that may be used to support planning, decision making, and implementation activities in organizations. Of the hundreds of planning and decision-making aids, we focused on a small group of aids that are useful in most organizations and functional areas.

1. EXPLAIN THE ESSENTIALS OF THE SCENARIO, DELPHI TECHNIQUE, AND SIMULATION FORECASTING AIDS.

Forecasting is the process of estimating future events and conditions in an organization's environment. Scenarios are written descriptions of possible futures. The Delphi technique is a process of consensus building among experts to arrive at estimates of future events and conditions. Simulation involves the use of models of real systems that permit the testing of alternatives, often on a computer.

2. APPLY TWO AIDS FOR FOSTERING CREATIVITY—OSBORN'S CREATIVITY MODEL AND THE CAUSE AND EFFECT DIAGRAM.

Osborn's creativity model and the cause and effect diagram help decision makers solve unstructured and ambiguous problems, which often call for unique and innovative decisions. The creative process as a whole includes five interconnected elements: preparation, concentration, incubation, illumination, and verification. Osborn's creativity model is designed to stimulate and reduce blocks to creativity and innovation. The cause and effect diagram provides a process for getting at the root causes of a problem (an effect).

3. DESCRIBE THREE AIDS FOR HELPING TO ACHIEVE TOTAL QUALITY—BENCHMARKING, DEMING CYCLE, AND PARETO ANALYSIS.

Benchmarking is the process of comparing an organization's functions, products, or processes with those of *best-in-class* organizations. The process includes a sequence of seven steps, as shown in Figure 9.3. The Deming cycle includes four stages—plan, do, check, and act—that should be repeated over time to ensure continuous improvement in functions, products, and processes. Pareto analysis is based on the 80/20 rule, such as 80 percent of the personnel problems in an organization may be caused by 20 percent of the employees. The Pareto diagram is a graph that helps individuals and teams determine which problems should be solved and in what order. The Pareto diagram is frequently used in total management quality programs to establish priorities for quality-related problems.

4. DISCUSS ONE PROJECT MANAGEMENT AID—THE PROGRAM EVALUATION AND REVIEW TECHNIQUE.

Project management refers to the principles, methods, and techniques used to establish and implement a project. PERT has four main elements: (1) network, (2) critical path, (3) resource allocation, and (4) cost and time estimates. It is a valuable tool for planning and decision making in implementing one-of-a-kind and large or complex projects.

QUESTIONS FOR DISCUSSION

1. It is January 2020, and the Dinkels have settled down for an evening of television. Mary Dinkel aims her remote control at a 3-by-5-foot screen across the room and taps in a four-digit code to call up the fifth rerun of her all-time favorite flick, Titanic. The family doesn't drive to Blockbuster for a movie anymore, and the number of such outlets continues to shrink. Network TV is free, but nothing much there interests the Dinkels tonight. It is time for a rerun of Titanic. Or almost anything else on film that the Dinkels can think of. The shows are all there—thousands of them—ready to be punched up by computer. Do you agree with this scenario? Why or why not? What are three implications of your assessment for firms in the entertainment industry?

2. Are there any potential ethical concerns with the increasing use and applications of virtual reality (one form of simulation)? Explain.

3. Describe a personal situation that occurred within the past six months for which Osborn's creativity model would have been useful. Why would it have been?

4. How does Osborn's creativity model differ from the cause and effect diagram?

5. Develop a cause and effect diagram related to one problem that you have experienced at your college or university. You may also undertake this assignment with four to six other students in this class.

6. Develop a cause and effect diagram for one career problem, such as selecting a major or getting the type of job you desire.

7. Describe how benchmarking could be used to help plan improvements in one service or process (such as registration, advising, or financial aid) at your college or university. Who might you benchmark? Explain why.

8. You should do this activity in a discussion group with four to six other students. Each person should take five minutes and write down the five things that irritated them most while eating at local restaurants during the past three months. From this information, the group should develop a Pareto diagram. Does it offer any clues for needed changes to restaurant operators in the area? What are the limitations of your findings?

9. Use the program evaluation and review technique (PERT) to develop an action plan for successful completion of your next academic year.

EXERCISES TO DEVELOP YOUR MANAGERIAL COMPETENCIES

1. **Self-Management Competency.** This exercise provides you the opportunity to assess, reflect on, and reduce possible personal barriers to creativity. For each of the statements in the questionnaire, use the following scale to express which number best corresponds to your agreement or disagreement with the statement.[47] Write that number in the blank to the left of each statement. Please do not skip any statements.

Strongly Agree	Agree Somewhat	Agree	Disagree	Strongly Disagree
1	2	3	4	5

_____ 1. I evaluate criticism to determine how it can be useful to me.

_____ 2. When solving problems, I attempt to apply new concepts or methods.

_____ 3. I can shift gears or change emphasis in what I am doing.

_____ 4. I get enthusiastic about problems outside of my specialized area of concentration.

_____ 5. I always give a problem my best effort, even if it seems trivial or fails to arouse enthusiasm.

_____ 6. I set aside periods of time without interruptions.

_____ 7. It is not difficult for me to have my ideas criticized.

_____ 8. In the past, I have taken calculated risks and I would do so again.

_____ 9. I dream, daydream, and fantasize easily.

_____ 10. I know how to simplify and organize my observations.

_____ 11. Occasionally, I try a so-called unworkable answer in hopes that it will prove to be workable.

_____ 12. I can and do consistently guard my personal periods of privacy.

_____ 13. I feel at ease with peers even when my ideas or plans meet with public criticisms or rejection.

_____ 14. I frequently read opinions contrary to my own to learn what the opposition is thinking.

_____ 15. I translate symbols into concrete ideas or action steps.

_____ 16. I seek many ideas because I enjoy having alternative possibilities.

_____ 17. In the idea-formulation stage of a project, I withhold critical judgment.

_____ 18. I determine whether an imposed limitation is reasonable or unreasonable.

_____ 19. I would modify an idea, plan, or design, even if doing so would meet with opposition.

_____ 20. I feel comfortable in expressing my ideas even if they are in the minority.

_____ 21. I enjoy participating in nonverbal, symbolic, or visual activities.

_____ 22. I feel the excitement and challenge of finding solutions to problems.

_____ 23. I keep a file of discarded ideas.

_____ 24. I make reasonable demands for good physical facilities and surroundings.

_____ 25. I would feel no serious loss of status or prestige if management publicly rejected my plan.

_____ 26. I frequently question the policies, goals, values, or ideas of an organization.

_____ 27. I deliberately exercise my visual and symbolic skills in order to strengthen them.

_____ 28. I can accept my thinking when it seems illogical.

_____ 29. I seldom reject ambiguous ideas that are not directly related to the problem.

_____ 30. I distinguish between trivial and important physical distractions.

_____ 31. I feel uncomfortable making waves for a worthwhile idea even if it threatens team harmony.

_____ 32. I am willing to present a truly original approach even if there is a chance it could fail.

_____ 33. I can recognize the times when symbolism or visualization would work best for me.

_____ 34. I try to make an uninteresting problem stimulating.

_____ 35. I consciously attempt to use new approaches toward routine tasks.

_____ 36. In the past, I have determined when to leave an undesirable environment and when to stay and change the environment (including self-growth).

Transfer your responses to the statements above and record them in the blanks provided below. Then add the numbers in each column, and record the column totals.

	A		B		C		D		E		F
1. ___		2. ___		3. ___		4. ___		5. ___		6. ___	
7. ___		8. ___		9. ___		10. ___		11. ___		12. ___	
13. ___		14. ___		15. ___		16. ___		17. ___		18. ___	
19. ___		20. ___		21. ___		22. ___		23. ___		24. ___	
25. ___		26. ___		27. ___		28. ___		29. ___		30. ___	
31. ___		32. ___		33. ___		34. ___		35. ___		36. ___	

Totals: ___   ___   ___   ___   ___   ___

Take your scores from the scoring sheet and mark them with a dot in the score categories (cells) on the following graph. The vertical axis, which represents the possible column totals, ranges from 6 to 36. The horizontal axis represents the columns on your scoring sheet and ranges from A to F. The *Key to Barriers* at the end of this exercise identifies the category of barriers in each column. Connect the dots you have marked with a line. The high points represent your possible personal barriers to creativity as you see them. The higher the number in each column, the greater the barrier that factor represents in realizing your creative potential.

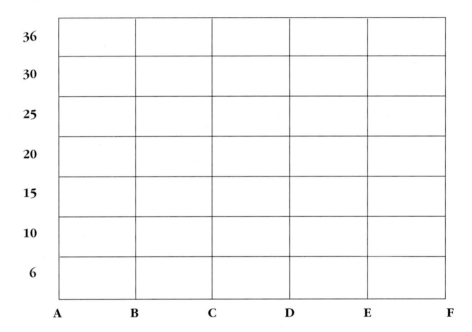

KEY TO BARRIERS

A = Barriers related to self-confidence and risk taking

B = Barriers related to need for conformity

C = Barriers related to use of the abstract

D = Barriers related to use of systematic analysis

E = Barriers related to task achievement

F = Barriers related to physical environment

Based on these results, are there any actions that you can and want to take to improve your creativity?

2. **Teamwork Competency.** You are part of a management team for the PBJ Corporation, which produces peanut butter and jelly sandwiches.

One of PBJ's largest customers is MegaSnack, a company that supplies hundreds of vending machines across the city.[48]

A number of businesses that rent MegaSnack's machines have reported that customers are dissatisfied with "too little peanut butter" on the sandwiches. Consequently, MegaSnack is unhappy with PBJ's current performance and has announced that it will look for another supplier if PBJ can't rectify the situation. Assume that you and your fellow team members in management class have been given the task of determining possible reasons for *why so many sandwiches have less peanut butter than MegaSnack has specified they should*. Later a team will investigate these possible reasons and recommend actions to solve the problem.

The following are the specifications that MegaSnack has given PBJ to use for each sandwich.

- White bread, two 1.0-ounce slices per sandwich

- Grape jelly, 1.0 ounce per sandwich

- Smooth peanut butter, 1.0 ounce per sandwich

- Total sandwich weight 4.0 ounces, ±0.25-ounce variance

The white bread is purchased from a vendor that slices to exact weight specifications of 1.0 ounce per slice. The weight of the bread is checked randomly at delivery; so far weight variance has been extremely rare and virtually insignificant. The bread is set up on the assembly line so that sandwiches can be made. A tube dispenser system applies jelly in a 1.0-ounce amount to every other slice of bread on the assembly line (one slice has jelly, the next one does not, and so on). Each application is weighed electronically by computer and automatically ejected. The dispenser system is checked for calibration hourly and tuned daily.

After the application of jelly, the bread continues down the assembly line. Numerous on-site checks

have shown that each sandwich meets MegaSnack's weight specifications up to the point at which peanut butter is added. Peanut butter in the amount of 1.0 ounce is applied and spread manually to each slice of bread that has not had jelly added. (A number of automatic machine tubes have been tried for dispensing and spreading the peanut butter, but all have had a tendency to clog and have been abandoned.) After the peanut butter has been spread, the slices of bread with jelly and the slices with peanut butter are put together manually to form sandwiches. Then each completed sandwich is weighed. MegaSnack has allowed for a total sandwich weight variance of 0.25 ounce, but PBJ's sandwiches are frequently 0.20 ounce underweight, with all of the variance attributable to peanut butter.

You and your team members are to come up with four lists of ideas, each list covering one of the major factors affecting this process problem: *methods, personnel, materials,* and *machinery.* If you think that other factors might be affecting the process, create lists for them as well. To create your lists for the factors, use the brainstorming process described in this chapter. You must follow the rules of brainstorming. After the final brainstorming session, discuss the following questions

- What were your reactions to the brainstorming process?

- What were the advantages and disadvantages of brainstorming?

- How would the task have been different if you had not been given the four categories of methods, personnel, materials, and machinery? What can you learn from that?

- What have you learned about brainstorming as an aid to planning and decision making?

3. **Strategic Action Competency.** A necessary first step in learning about and implementing total quality management (TQM) is to assess the emphasis that an organization places on the eight basic criteria presented in the following questionnaire. The Total Quality Management (TQM) Inventory is designed for use as a diagnostic tool rather than as a rigorous data-gathering instrument.[49] Please read carefully the six statements listed under each criterion. Select the statement that best describes how that criterion applies to an organization for which you now work or have previously worked. Write the letter of that statement in the blank to the left of each criterion. Another approach is to interview experienced individuals in that organization by asking them to respond to the instrument. The choices given range from exceptionally strong commitment to the absence of performance for each criterion.

QUESTIONNAIRE

———— 1. *Top-Management Leadership and Support Criterion*
   A.   Top managers are directly and actively involved in activities that foster quality.
   B.   Top managers participate in activities that foster quality.

C. Most top managers support activities that foster quality.

D. Some top managers are supportive of and interested in quality improvement.

E. A few top managers are tentatively beginning to support activities that foster quality.

F. No top management support exists for activities involving quality.

_____ 2. *Strategic Planning Criterion*

A. Long-term goals for quality improvements have been established across the organization as part of the overall strategic planning process.

B. Long-term goals for quality improvement have been established across most of the organization.

C. Long-term goals for quality improvement have been established in key parts of the organization.

D. Short-term goals for quality improvement have been established in parts of the organization.

E. The general goals of the organization contain elements of quality improvement.

F. No quality improvement goals have been established anywhere in the organization.

_____ 3. *Focus on the Customer Criterion*

A. A variety of effective and innovative methods are used to obtain customer feedback on all organizational functions.

B. Effective systems are used to obtain feedback from all customers of major functions.

C. Systems are in place to solicit customer feedback on a regular basis.

D. Customer needs are determined through random processes rather than by using systematic methods.

E. Complaints are the primary methods used to obtain customer feedback.

F. No customer focus is evident.

_____ 4. *Employee Training and Recognition Criterion*

A. The organization is implementing a systematic employee training and recognition plan that is fully integrated into the overall strategic quality planning process.

B. The organization is assessing what employee training and recognition is needed, and the results of that assessment are being evaluated periodically.

C. An employee training and recognition plan is beginning to be implemented.

D. An employee training and recognition plan is under active development.

E. The organization has plans to increase employee training and recognition.

F. There is no employee training and there are no systems for recognizing employees.

_____ 5. *Employee Empowerment and Teamwork Criterion*

A. Innovative, effective employee empowerment and teamwork approaches are used.

B. Many natural work groups are empowered to constitute quality improvement teams.

C. A majority of managers support employee empowerment and teamwork.

D. Many managers support employee empowerment and teamwork.

E. Some managers support employee empowerment and teamwork.

F. There is no support for employee empowerment and teamwork.

_____ 6. *Quality Measurement and Analysis Criterion*

A. Information about quality and timelines of all products and services is collected from internal and external customers and from suppliers.

B. Information about quality and timelines is collected from most internal and external customers and from most suppliers.

C. Information about quality and timelines is collected from major internal and external customers and from major suppliers.

D. Information about quality and timelines is collected from some internal and external customers.

E. Information about quality and timelines is collected from one or two external customers.

F. There is no system for measuring and analyzing quality.

_____ 7. *Quality Assurance Criterion*

    A.   All goods, services, and processes are designed, reviewed, verified, and controlled to meet the needs and expectations of internal and external customers.

    B.   A majority of goods, services, and processes are designed, reviewed, verified, and controlled to meet the needs and expectations of internal and external customers.

    C.   Key products, services, and processes are designed, reviewed, verified, and controlled to meet the needs and expectations of internal and external customers.

    D.   A few goods and services are designed, reviewed, and controlled to meet the needs of internal and external customers.

    E.   Goods and services are controlled to meet internally developed specifications that may or may not include customer input.

    F.   There is no quality assurance in this organization.

_____ 8. *Quality and Productivity Improvement Criterion*

    A.   Most significant performance indicators demonstrate exceptional improvements in quality and productivity over the past five years.

    B.   Most significant performance indicators demonstrate excellent improvement in quality and productivity over the past five years.

    C.   Most significant performance indicators demonstrate good improvement in quality and productivity.

    D.   Most significant performance indicators demonstrate improving quality and productivity in several areas.

    E.   There is evidence of some quality and productivity improvement in one or more areas.

    F.   There is no evidence of quality and productivity improvements in any areas.

To determine your scores on the inventory, complete the following three steps.

1.   For each of the *Total Quality Management Criteria* listed in the left column, find the letter under the heading labeled *Response Categories/Points* that corresponds to the one you chose on the questionnaire.

2.   Then circle the one- or two-digit *point* number that corresponds to the letter you chose.

3.   Finally add the points circled for all eight criteria to determine your *overall score.*

    The numbers that you are about to circle correspond to the relative weights attached to individual Quality/Productivity Criteria in the U.S. President's Award for Quality and Productivity Improvement Guidelines. Therefore, in addition to helping to score your responses, the points also identify the categories that are more significant than others. For example, scores on Criterion 8 (Quality and Productivity Improvement Results) are better indicators of an organization's orientation toward quality and productivity than are its scores on Criterion 4 (Employee Training and Recognition).

	Response Categories/Points					
Total Quality Management Criteria	**A**	**B**	**C**	**D**	**E**	**F**
1. Top-Management Leadership and Support	20	16	12	8	4	0
2. Strategic Planning	15	12	9	6	3	0
3. Focus on the Customer	40	32	24	16	8	0
4. Employee Training and Recognition	15	12	9	6	3	0
5. Employee Empowerment and Teamwork	15	12	9	6	3	0
6. Quality Measurement and Analysis	15	12	9	6	3	0
7. Quality Assurance	30	24	18	12	6	0
8. Quality- and Productivity-Improvement Results	50	40	30	20	10	0
Scores for Choice Categories	—	—	—	—	—	—
Overall Score:	—	(range: 0–200)				

INTERPRETATION OF SCORES

160–200 points: A score in this range may indicate a "world-class" organization with a deep, long-term, and active commitment to improving quality and productivity.

120–159 points: A score in this range may indicate that an organization with a sound, well-organized philosophy of quality and productivity improvement is beginning to emerge.

80–119 points: A score in this range may indicate an organization that is starting to learn about and plan quality and productivity improvements.

40–79 points: A score in this range may indicate an organization that is vaguely aware of quality and productivity improvement but has no plans to learn about or implement such activity. Scores at this level approach the danger level.

0–39 points: A score in this range may indicate an organization that currently has neither an awareness of nor an involvement with quality and productivity improvement programs. Unless an organization has an absolute, invulnerable monopoly on extremely valuable goods or services, this level represents a de facto decision to go out of business.

REAL-TIME CASE ANALYSIS

CALIBER LEARNING NETWORK—AN OUTSOURCER OUTSOURCES

Sylvan Learning Systems and MCI Communications joined forces in late 1996. Sylvan launched an international network dedicated to adult professional education—the Caliber Learning Network (or simply Caliber). This enterprise focuses on academic and corporate education services through a network of professional education centers in all major U.S. cities. As of 1998, Caliber had forty-six centers and a goal of an additional fifty partner extension sites (such as the on-site capability at Johns Hopkins University) by 1999, including some abroad. Caliber changes the traditional classroom experience by the unique integration of three communication technologies: satellite broadcast, audio and video conferencing, and PC networking. Caliber's mission is to facilitate the delivery of expert content to a global audience within a dynamic, interactive learning environment.

Caliber is an example of how focusing on core organizational competencies can result in a new model of business—being both an outsourcer and a provider of services that takes advantage of strategic outsourcing. As an affiliate of Sylvan Learning Systems, Inc., Caliber is focused on creating a distance learning network for adult professional education and training services. As both an outsourcer and a provider of its core business—state-of-the-art distance learning classrooms and services—Caliber serves institutions such as the Wharton School of Business and Teachers College at Columbia University

When considering outsourcing the networking services crucial to delivering its core business, Caliber had to ensure that all the services would function reliably. The firm turned to MCI Systemhouse to provide the full range of networking services necessary to provide seamless education courses via satellite, video conferencing, PC networking, and the Internet.

All the way up and down the line, the company is outsourcing services that are not part of its core competencies, says Chris Nguyen, Caliber's chief operating officer. Although Caliber's core business serves thousands of professionals, the company knows which areas of business are better left to other specialists, such as MCI Systemhouse.

Nguyen states, "My job is to deliver high-quality education services on a global basis. I can't afford to have an executive of a major corporation walk into one of our centers and have the system crash. In my business, network reliability is a critical factor that depends on the hardware, network, and computing infrastructure."

Caliber has partnered with MCI Systemhouse for single-source networking and help-desk management and support through its network/MCI Enterprise Management (nEM) services. Under nEM, MCI Systemhouse assesses and makes recommendations about Caliber's information technology. For example, MCI installs reliable, industry-standard equipment and software, upgrades office suite software, and ensures interoperability throughout Caliber's system.

A deciding factor in Caliber's choice of MCI Systemhouse was the global information technology company's reputation in its core market. "When we tell our educational partners that we have outsourced the design, development, maintenance, and support of the hardware and data communications layer to MCI Systemhouse, they respond "great,'" says Nguyen. His associates believe that the technical reliability of Caliber's business is strengthened by outsourcing to MCI Systemhouse. The decision to outsource first-line support for procedural, knowledge-based, and software/hardware help-desk functions is also a relief to Nguyen, especially in terms of mind-share, which, he says, "is as good as money."

Caliber is developing a sales operation, marketing, and finance—and every area is new and untested. "That I don't have to deal with the networking infrastructure is a huge blessing," Nguyen says. "Plus MCI Systemhouse fits into our price constraints and service requirements."

Nguyen helped build Sylvan Learning Systems' worldwide computer-based testing network, with 1,800 computerized testing centers, and networking needs similar to Caliber's. But that business didn't outsource the networking and infrastructure services. "I know what happens when you undertake a large-scale deployment that extends your organization beyond its core competencies," Nguyen says. "If we had outsourced infrastructure, hardware, and support from the beginning, we may have gotten off to an even stronger start."[50]

To learn more about the Caliber Learning Network, visit the company's home page at

www.caliberlearning.com/welcome

QUESTIONS

1. Develop two scenarios: (1) a scenario that would focus on the possible environmental (competitive, political, cultural, etc.) forces that would help to make the Caliber Learning Network highly successful; and (2) a scenario that would focus on the key environmental forces that would make it difficult for Caliber to grow and earn a profit. Use the time horizon of 2010.

2. Assume that you are a member of Chris Nguyen's management team and have been asked to join multiple brainstorming sessions to identify the issues, potential opportunities and advantages, and potential problems and disadvantages associated with the possibility of outsourcing the networking services, as Caliber eventually did. For example, separate brainstorming sessions might be held on "issues to consider," "potential opportunities and advantages," and "potential problems and disadvantages."

3. Construct a cause and effect diagram that could have helped Caliber management assess the problem of providing reliable networking services.

4. Develop a benchmarking process that would enable Caliber to assess the outsources services that it is receiving from MCI Systemhouse.

5. Develop the basics (outline) of a PERT diagram for bringing MCI Systemhouse on board as the provider of Caliber's networking services.

VIDEO CASE

UNITED PARCEL SERVICE: DELIVERY ACCORDING TO PLAN

United Parcel Service (UPS) is a shipping empire. With 300,000 employees, its workforce could populate a small country, and it constitutes the tenth largest airline in the world, even without passengers. In managing empires, information is crucial. For an extremely time- and schedule-sensitive organization such as UPS (where shipments might be freshly cut flowers from Mexico headed to markets in New York City or a Gateway 2000 monitor being flown in for just-in-time integration with the rest of a PC order), planning and decision aids are vital.

UPS rival FedEx was a market innovator when it established its original hub in Memphis, Tennessee. FedEx's strategy was based on analysis of the nature of its business at the time and a realization that, by forcing all its traffic through an optimized central facility, it could guarantee overnight delivery even while shipping packages hundreds of extra miles. Such a decision might not have required complex analysis—prior to FedEx's innovation, shipping was much less organized. FedEx's simple slice through the Gordian knot of routing probably erased a lot of hidden inefficiencies. However, the efficiencies gained by single-hub routing end at some point, and a company might decide to create more hubs or pursue several different strategies at the same time. In calculating how best to do so, managers are increasingly using decision aids, such as simulation and other tools.

Another major freight shipper, Union Pacific Railroad, found itself in crisis owing to insufficient planning that all but paralyzed its operations in October 1997. The railroad had recently acquired a large regional rival, Southern Pacific Railway, and for that and various other reasons found itself 40,000 rail cars over its traffic capacity. The resulting backup of freight in the system meant that ships were unable to unload at ports in California. The traffic jam was so bad that the Federal Surface Transportation Board declared a formal "traffic emergency" (i.e., a state of crisis significant enough to be of national concern). UPS experienced a somewhat similar situation during its 1997 workers' strike. Because of UPS's size and enormous share of all package shipping, there was some speculation that the federal government might need to intervene.

Decision aids (e.g., scenario exercises or simulations) might have helped Union Pacific's executives forecast how the acquisition of Southern Pacific would affect the company's ability to deliver freight. UPS certainly made use of planning and decision tools in responding to the strike. They ranged from financial planning (to determine how long the company could afford to shut down) to how certain high-priority contracts could still be executed with its remaining staff.

The RAND Corporation, a federally funded R&D center and "think tank," conducts a scenario exercise called "The Day After," wherein participants are asked to play various roles. The RAND staff pushes them through a series of possible events in a simulated crisis. Most recently, it has conducted scenario exercises concerning "critical national infrastructure." These scenarios dealt with how critical national systems such as telecommunications or transportation may be at risk in the future from criminals, terrorists, foreign nations, or simply from natural disasters and systemic failures (such as occurred with Union Pacific)—and how to counteract such situations.

Planning and decision aids are becoming ever more useful as information systems are integrated, with the Internet as the "glue" that links countless organizations and their data. Increased data availability and information technologies have taken a great deal of uncertainty out of certain types of operations. For example, UPS customers can now determine the location and status of their packages within the UPS system from their own computers with tracking software. Knowing that an overnight package (guaranteed for delivery by 10:30 the next morning) had left a loading dock in Des Moines that morning at 6:50 would let a manager in Waterloo use actual values in a PERT chart for a project. Without such sophisticated tracking systems, the manager could only make a less certain estimate based on knowing that the package had been shipped and how long it usually took a package to arrive.

Shipping is still a largely inexact science. Start-up information services provider RouteLink, which uses the World Wide Web to let companies broker opportunities for freight shipping, estimates that commercial trucks travel empty on the order of 30 *billion* miles each year.

ON THE WEB

United Parcel Service is on the Web (***www.ups.com***). RAND, with offices in California and Washington, D.C., also is on the Web (***www.rand.org***). The President's Commission on Critical Infrastructure Protection (***www.pccip.gov***) has made use of RAND's scenario services in examining transportation as one of eight critical national infrastructures. Transportation—especially air transportation—is of primary concern, owing to the risk of terrorism, aging air traffic systems, and plans to remove restrictions on the airlines that have kept them flying in narrow flight corridors, now that computers and radar provide more current information. RouteLink is on the Web (***www.routelink.com***).

QUESTIONS

1. The Internet will certainly challenge UPS, as more and more information is shipped electronically instead of on paper in packages. What techniques might UPS utilize to forecast its future in light of the Internet?

2. How might UPS management use the PERT technique in planning for creation of a new shipping hub in its system?

3. How might UPS utilize "virtual reality" in its operations?

To help you answer these questions and learn more about UPS, visit the company's home page at

www.ups.com

Case contributed by Ross Stapleton-Gray, President, TeleDiplomacy, Inc., a technology and policy consultancy, and Adjunct Professor in Georgetown University's Communication, Culture, and Technology program.

PART 4

Organizing

Chapter

10

Fundamentals of Organization Design

LEARNING OBJECTIVES

AFTER STUDYING THIS CHAPTER, YOU SHOULD BE ABLE TO:

1. DESCRIBE THE MAIN ELEMENTS OF ORGANIZATIONAL STRUCTURE AND HOW THEY'RE SHOWN ON AN ORGANIZATION CHART.
2. DISCUSS THE MOST COMMON TYPES OF DEPARTMENTALIZATION.
3. STATE THE BASIC PRINCIPLES OF COORDINATION.
4. DESCRIBE THE AUTHORITY STRUCTURE OF AN ORGANIZATION.
5. EXPLAIN THE FACTORS THAT AFFECT THE CENTRALIZATION OR DECENTRALIZATION OF DECISION MAKING.
6. STATE THE DIFFERENCES BETWEEN LINE AND STAFF AUTHORITY.

Outline

PepsiCo Spins Off Restaurants

On October 7, 1997, PepsiCo completed its independence day for the world's largest collection of restaurants. Tricon Global Restaurants now owns more than 30,000 Pizza Hut, KFC, and Taco Bell outlets, with annual sales exceeding $4 billion and is almost 70 percent the size of McDonald's. Why did PepsiCo sell its restaurants?

According to PepsiCo Chairman Roger Enrico, PepsiCo is getting out of the restaurant business so that it can dramatically sharpen its focus on soft drinks and snack foods. Although its Pepsi-Cola brand runs a distant second to Coca-Cola, Frito-Lay is the nation's dominant maker of salty snacks. The spin-off also gets PepsiCo away from the ups and downs of sales in the restaurant business, which hasn't been especially profitable. Enrico also found little synergy between PepsiCo's soft drink and snack operations, which heavily rely

on marketing, and its restaurants, for which customer service is the key to success. Although many of the Tricon restaurants can serve other soft drinks, they plan to stick with Pepsi.

For Tricon, turning around lagging sales for Pizza Hut is a big challenge. In some places, it's a full-service, dine-in restaurant. In others, it offers delivery only. Adding to consumer confusion is a menu that in some locations includes sandwiches and even Buffalo wings. Today, 75 percent of the chain's business is carryout and delivery. Another challenge for Tricon's managers is cobranding, the increasingly popular practices of having two or more restaurants share the same location. Although customers find the concept exciting, employees find that taking directions from two different managers is confusing.

Overseas, Tricon plans to concentrate on major Asian markets. Both KFC and Pizza Hut are strong in

Japan, Hong Kong, and Singapore. Moving into Australia and China will require Tricon to capitalize on its economies of scale for purchasing ingredients and training managers. Some 44 percent of these restaurants are operated by franchisees who have the right to purchase ingredients from local vendors. Tricon wants to reduce that number by half to save an estimated $1.5 billion in five years by purchasing food for all its restaurants in certain countries. [1]

* * *

To learn more about PepsiCo, visit the company's home page at

www.pepsico.com

ORGANIZATIONAL STRUCTURE

1

DESCRIBE THE MAIN ELEMENTS OF ORGANIZATIONAL STRUCTURE AND HOW THEY'RE SHOWN ON AN ORGANIZATION CHART

All too often managers are too far removed from day-to-day operations to apply their competencies effectively and structure their organizations for greater productivity. Only a dramatic turn of events, such as plunging sales and/or profits, may motivate managers to identify and deal with problems of organizational structure. When PepsiCo's management recognized that declining sales in its three restaurant chains were a cause of declining profits, it changed the organization's structure by spinning off its restaurants to make the company more flexible for today and into the future. In this chapter we focus on organizational structure, or the formal system that enables managers to allocate work, coordinate tasks, and delegate authority and responsibility in order to achieve organizational goals efficiently. First, we examine elements of an organization's structure and various types of departmentalization that allow managers to determine who should perform which activities. Then, after discussing how managers or teams allocate work and coordinate tasks, we look at lines of authority that affect the flow of organizational decisions and their implementation. In doing so we consider the need to relate responsibility, authority, and accountability. We then explore delegation and questions of centralized versus decentralized authority. Finally, we examine the roles of line and staff authority. Many aspects of this chapter revisit concepts based on the traditional views of management introduced in Chapter 2.

Organizational structure is a formal system of working relationships that both separates and integrates tasks. Separation of tasks makes clear who should do what, and integration of tasks indicates how efforts should be meshed. Organizational structure helps employees work together effectively by

1. assigning human and other resources to tasks;

2. clarifying employees' responsibilities and how their efforts should mesh through job descriptions, organization charts, and lines of authority;

3. letting employees know what is expected of them through rules, operating procedures, and performance standards; and

4. establishing procedures for collecting and evaluating information to help managers make decisions and solve problems.

ELEMENTS OF ORGANIZATIONAL STRUCTURE

For our purposes, organizational structure includes four basic elements: specialization, standardization, coordination, and authority.[2]

Specialization is the process of identifying particular tasks and assigning them to individuals or teams who have been trained to do them. At Frito-Lay, for example, middle managers are responsible for directing the work of teams in production, quality control, and management information systems. Functional managers usually supervise a particular department, such as marketing, accounting, or human resources. First-line managers usually are in charge of a specific area of work, such as printing, medical records, or data processing. Thus one person can specialize in any of a number of different management jobs. Later in this chapter we describe how the principle of specialization is applied in terms of different forms of departmentalization.

Standardization refers to the uniform and consistent procedures that employees are to follow in doing their jobs. Written procedures, job descriptions, instructions, rules, and regulations are used to standardize the routine aspects of jobs. Standards permit managers to measure an employee's performance against established criteria. Job descriptions and application forms standardize the selection of employees. On-the-job training programs develop standardized skills and reinforce values important to the organization's success. This approach may seem mechanical, but if jobs weren't standardized, many organizations couldn't achieve their goals. Just walk into any McDonald's, Wendy's, or Burger King, where every person has a job with well-defined standards: from how long a customer may be kept waiting for service to the length of time food stays on the warming trays to the amount of French fries that go into an order of "regular fries."

Coordination comprises the formal and informal procedures that integrate the activities separate individuals, teams, and departments in an organization. In bureaucratic organizations, such as United Parcel Service (UPS), written rules are enough to link such activities. In less structured organizations, such as the San Diego Zoo, 3M, and Jian (a software development and marketing company), coordination requires managerial sensitivity to companywide problems, willingness to share responsibility, and effective interpersonal communication. Later in this chapter we examine some specific principles of coordination.

ORGANIZATIONAL STRUCTURE

A formal system of working relationships that both separates and integrates tasks (clarifies who should do what and how efforts should be meshed).

SPECIALIZATION

The process of identifying particular tasks and assigning them to individuals or teams who have been trained to do them.

STANDARDIZATION

The uniform and consistent procedures that employees are to follow in doing their jobs.

COORDINATION

The formal and informal procedures that integrate the activities of separate individuals, teams, and departments in an organization.

AUTHORITY
The right to decide and act.

Authority is basically the right to decide and act. Various organizations distribute authority differently. In a centralized organization, such as Pier 1, top managers make decisions about what merchandise to buy and where to locate a new store—and communicate these decisions to lower level managers. In a decentralized organization, such as Jian, decision-making authority is given to lower level managers and employees working in teams. Firms often combine the two approaches by centralizing certain functions (e.g., accounting and purchasing) and decentralizing others (e.g., marketing and human resources). We also discuss authority in more detail later in this chapter.

THE ORGANIZATION CHART

ORGANIZATION CHART
A diagram showing the reporting relationships of functions, departments, and individual positions within an organization.

One way to visualize the interrelationships of these four basic elements of organizational structure is to create an ***organization chart.*** It is a diagram showing the reporting relationships of functions, departments, and individual positions within an organization. Figure 10.1 is the organization chart for FedEx, a market leader in the small-package delivery service industry. The chart could be expanded to show even greater detail by including the titles of departmental managers and identifying work teams within the departments according to the specific tasks they perform. For example, the managers of various departments, such as express products, retail marketing, cooperative marketing, and customer service, report to the senior vice-president of marketing and customer service.

In general, an organization chart provides four important pieces of information about an organization's structure.

1. **Tasks.** The chart shows the range of different tasks within the organization. For instance, tasks at FedEx range from personnel to properties and logistics to satellite systems to line haul operations.

Figure 10.1 ***Organizational Structure of FedEx***

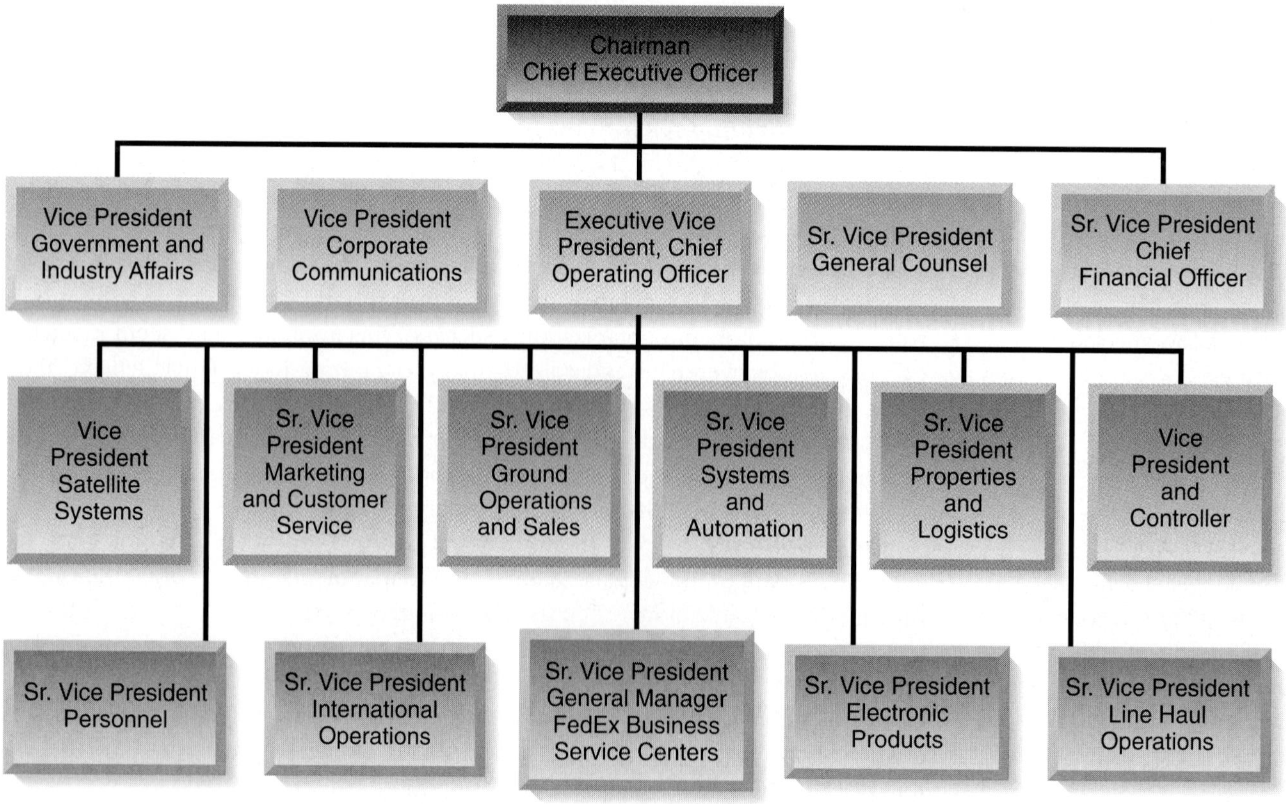

2. **Subdivisions.** Each box represents a subdivision of the organization that is responsible for certain tasks. For example, the senior vice-president for line haul operations at FedEx is responsible for maintenance services, quality programs, flight operations and support, and aircraft acquisition and sales.

3. **Levels of management.** The chart shows the management hierarchy from the chairman of the board to the various divisional managers. All those directly subordinate to the same individual usually appear at the same management level and report to that individual.

4. **Lines of authority.** Vertical lines connecting the boxes on the chart show which positions have authority over others. At FedEx, the executive vice-president reports to the president. The senior vice-presidents of marketing and customer service, ground operations and sales, properties and logistics, and international operations, among others, report to the executive vice-president.

The advantages and disadvantages of organization charts have been debated for years.[3] One advantage is that such a chart shows employees how the pieces of the entire organization fit together. That is, it indicates how their own specialized tasks relate to the whole. Thus everyone knows who reports to whom and where to go with a particular problem. The chart also may help management detect gaps in authority or duplication of tasks.

A major disadvantage of the organization chart is that it's just a piece of paper—sometimes without much validity. It simply can't show everything about an organization's structure nor much about the way things often really get done. For example, it can't show who has the most political influence or where the vital informal channels of communication operate. In addition, employees may incorrectly read status and power into their jobs, based on the proximity of their boxes to that of the CEO. These disadvantages can be overcome if the chart is used for its intended purpose—to *illustrate* the basic, formal structure of the entire organization.

DEPARTMENTALIZATION

2

DISCUSS THE MOST COM-
MON TYPES OF DEPART-
MENTALIZATION

DEPARTMENTALIZATION
Subdividing work into tasks and assigning them to specialized groups within an organization.

Departmentalization addresses two of the four basic elements of organizational structure: *specialization* and *standardization*. **Departmentalization** involves subdividing work into tasks and assigning them to specialized groups within an organization. It also includes devising standards for the performance of tasks.

Management can use any of four basic types of departmentalization: by function, by place (location), by product (goods and/or services), and by customer. Division of work is the first step in departmentalization, but *how* people are grouped depends on the goals of the organization. At Taco Bell, employees now work in self-directed teams. Many of the daily tasks they previously performed, such as dicing or otherwise preparing ingredients, are now performed by outside suppliers, who prepare these items to Taco Bell's standards.

The key to effective departmentalization lies in organizing people and activities in such a way that decisions easily flow throughout the organization. Large, complex organizations, such as Johnson & Johnson, Chevron, and Levi Strauss, actually use different forms of departmentalization at various organizational levels to facilitate this flow. Levi Strauss, for instance, has eight product divisions, including Jeanswear, Womenswear, and Menswear, that reflect a product structure. Each division is then broken into functional departments (e.g., accounting, production, and marketing) that support the division's products.

FUNCTIONAL DEPARTMENTALIZATION

Recall that functions are the groups, or sets, of tasks that an organization performs, such as production, marketing, and finance. ***Functional departmentalization*** groups employees according to their areas of expertise and the resources they draw on to perform a common set of tasks. Functional grouping is the most widely used and accepted form of departmentalization.[4]

Functions vary widely, depending on the nature of the organization. For example, hospitals don't have product development departments, but they do have admitting, emergency room, and nursing departments. Churches don't have production departments, but they do have youth, education, and choir departments. Delta Airlines has operations, traffic, and finance departments. Toys "R" Us and other large retail chains have general merchandising, physical distribution, and support services departments (e.g., legal, human resources, and accounting).

Marshall Space Flight Center is one of NASA's largest facilities in the United States. Located in Huntsville, Alabama, its employees are responsible for the propulsion systems used in manned space flights. It employs more than 3,000 people, including space exploration and payload specialists and certified flight operators, who perform a variety of functions. The following Planning and Administration Competency feature highlights how the human resources and administrative support division is organized at Marshall to achieve its mission.

Grouping tasks and employees by function can be both efficient and economical. It is particularly efficient for small organizations making a single product because it creates a clear hierarchy of authority and decision making. Large firms organized by function often assign responsibility and authority for several departments to one senior manager. PetsMart is a leading provider of products and services for pet owners, with 345 superstores in thirty-five states. The company is organized by function—real estate, finance, general merchandise, and store operations—and key decisions are made by the chairman of the board and the president.

Functional departmentalization has both advantages and disadvantages. Table 10.1 shows several of each.

T a b l e 1 0 . 1	*Advantages and Disadvantages of Functional Departmentalization*

Advantages

- Promotes skill specialization.

- Reduces duplication of resources and increases coordination within the functional area.

- Enhances career development and training within the department.

- Allows superiors and subordinates to share common expertise.

- Promotes high-quality technical problem solving.

- Centralizes decision making.

Disadvantages

- Emphasizes routine tasks.

- Reduces communication between departments.

- May create conflict over product priorities.

- May make interdepartmental scheduling difficult.

- Focuses on departmental rather than organizational issues and goals.

- Develops managers who are experts in narrow fields.

The organization chart for the human resources and administrative support division is shown in Figure 10.2. Each department has its own specialized area of expertise. The training and development department selects specific employees to attend executive development programs to develop the managerial competencies required for their next assignments. It also identifies and organizes the necessary resources for these managers and keeps an accurate record on each person's development. The personnel management department focuses on recruiting college graduates, the movement of employees throughout the organization (promotions, demo-

tions, and retirements), and implementation of NASA's diversity program. The security department creates security guidelines for all employees and works within the guidelines established by Congress for all federal employees. The property management department is concerned with the physical plant—buildings, grounds, airstrips, and space museum—located at Huntsville. This functional design enables the director of the Huntsville Center to make timely financial and personnel decisions, monitor changes in the federal budget that could affect the Center's operations, and delegate responsibility to various departments for task completion.[5]

* * *

To learn more about NASA, visit this organization's home page at

www.nasa.gov

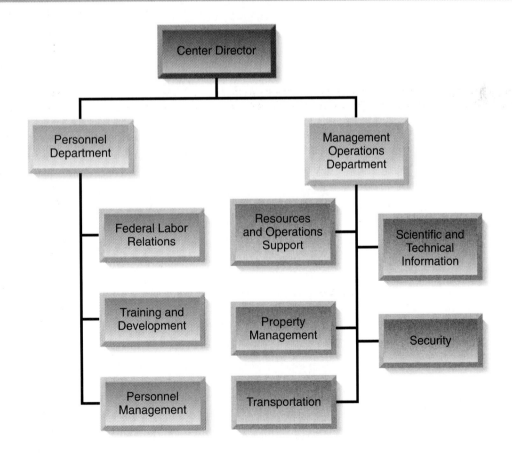

Figure 10.2   **Marshall Space Center's Functional Departmentalization**

Advantages of Functional Departmentalization. Departmentalization by function is economical because it results in a simple structure. It is often the best form for organizations that sell a narrow range of goods and/or services mainly in one market (product and geographic). Management creates one department for each primary task to be performed (e.g., engineering, sales, and R&D). This structure keeps administrative expenses low because everyone in a department shares training, experience, and resources. Job satisfaction may increase if employees can improve their specialized skills by working with others in the same functional area. Employees can see clearly defined career paths within their own departments. As a result, the organization can more easily hire and promote personnel who have or develop good problem-solving skills in each area of specialization.

Disadvantages of Functional Departmentalization. The disadvantages of functional departmentalization become obvious when an organization has diversified products or markets. For instance, General Electric offers a variety products, ranging from light bulbs to refrigerators. Making decisions quickly becomes difficult when employees have to work their way through layers of structure for approvals. For example, a sales representative may lose a good account because she has to wait for the sales manager to get the production manager to make a scheduling decision. In addition, when there's friction between departments, managers have to spend time resolving the issues involved. Pinpointing the accountability and performance levels of employees who are performing separate functions may also be difficult. In other words, a top manager may not be able to determine easily which department—production, sales, or credit—is responsible for declining profits.

Another disadvantage is that top management may have a hard time coordinating the activities of employees in different departments. Functional departmentalization tends to de-emphasize the goals of the entire organization. Employees may focus on departmental goals, such as meeting their own budgets and schedules, and lose sight of the big picture. Moreover, when functional employees begin to worry about their own areas of expertise, they may have trouble seeing others' points of view. Employees develop a loyalty to their own departments, which in turn may erect barriers instead of encouraging identification and coordination with their counterparts in other departments.

PLACE DEPARTMENTALIZATION

PLACE DEPARTMENTALIZATION
The grouping of all functions for a geographic area at one location under one manager.

Place departmentalization groups all functions for a geographic area at one location under one manager, rather than dividing functions among different managers or grouping all tasks in one central office. It is commonly used by organizations with operations in many different locations. Many large companies, including Procter & Gamble, Arthur Andersen, and Metropolitan Life Insurance, have set up regional and district offices. Similarly, federal agencies such as the IRS, the Federal Reserve Board, and the U.S. Postal Service use place departmentalization to provide nationwide services. Multinational firms often use this form of departmentalization to address cultural and legal differences in various countries, as well as the lack of uniformity among geographic markets.[6]

Starbucks CEO Howard Schultz crafted a business strategy that enabled the company to become the largest specialty coffee retailer and roaster in the world. He stays abreast of the actions of competitors and has formed strategic partnerships with other firms. For example, Starbucks coffee is now served on all United Airline flights, and ITT Sheraton Hotels has its own catalogue of Starbucks products, offering shoppers espresso and cappuccino makers, cups, and the like. Starbucks' strategy is implemented for its retail stores through a combination of functional (e.g., human resources, real estate, coffee) and place departmentalization. The following Strategic Action Competency piece focuses on Starbucks' organizational structure and retail operations.

Short Decaf Mocha Latté, Please

Starbucks is a billion-dollar organization that has more than 1,400 stores in the continental United States and elsewhere around the world, including ten in Tokyo, four in Hawaii, and three in Singapore, that serve more than 3 million people each week. Each store sells coffee beans, beverages, coffee-making equipment, pastries, and accessories. Management likes to position the stores in high-traffic locations. Starbucks is vertically integrated and controls its coffee sources, roasting, and retail sales to ensure adherence to its strict principles.

Figure 10.3 shows the company's basic organization chart. At its headquarters in Seattle, vice-presidents of the various functions report to the CEO. To ensure consistent customer service in all locations, seven district managers report to the vice-president of retail operations. The district managers receive operating guidelines, ranging from roasting practices to sales training, but are accountable for the specific operations and profitability of the stores in their areas. The district managers are responsible for store locations, staffing and compensation, sales, store operations, and all other functions related to a store's profitability. They also are responsible for seeing that each new employee receives at least twenty-five hours of formal training. This training covers customer service, cash register operations, coffee brewing methods, and how to scoop coffee beans correctly.[7]

* * *

To learn more about Starbucks, visit the company's home page at

www.starbucks.com

Starbucks' Organization Structure

Starbucks CEO

- Vice President Retail Operations
  - Southwest
  - Northwest
  - South Central
  - Midwest
  - Northeast
  - Canada
  - East Coast
- Vice President Human Resources
- Vice President Marketing
  - Vice President Real Estate
- Vice President Management Information Systems
  - Vice President New Business Development
- Vice President Coffee
  - Vice President Finance

Advantages of Place Departmentalization. Table 10.2 summarizes the advantages of place departmentalization, which are primarily those of efficiency. If each unit is relatively small and in direct contact with its customers, it can adapt more readily to market demands. For production, place departmentalization might mean locating plants near raw materials or suppliers. In addition, because their attention is more focused, managers are likely to use their planning and administration competency to organize subordinates' efforts to meet customer demands.

Disadvantages of Place Departmentalization. Table 10.2 also shows some disadvantages of place departmentalization. Organizing by location clearly increases problems of control and coordination for top management, which often is far away. To ensure uniformity and coordination, organizations that use place departmentalization, such as Blockbuster Video, Southland (7-Eleven stores), and Hilton Hotels, make extensive use of rules that apply to all locations. One reason for doing so is to guarantee a standard level of quality regardless of location, which would be difficult if units in various locations went their own separate ways. Also, employees may emphasize their own units' goals or focus only on problems that occur within their own geographic areas without some direction from headquarters. Because most of an organization's functional departments must be duplicated at each location, costs are higher than for an organization that adopts a functional form of departmentalization.

PRODUCT DEPARTMENTALIZATION

As an organization grows, the weaknesses of functional and place departmentalization begin to overshadow their strengths. These weaknesses become apparent when an organization expands its product lines and attracts diverse customers. In response, top management often turns to product departmentalization. **Product departmentalization** divides the organization into self-contained units, each capable of designing, producing, and marketing its own goods and/or services.

Organizations that have worldwide operations often use this form of departmentalization. Large multiproduct companies such as Procter & Gamble, Novartis, and Samsung also use this approach. Each of these companies started with a combination of functional and place departmentalization, but growth and an increasing inability to serve the needs of particular customers made those structures unworkable or uneconomical.

PRODUCT DEPARTMENTALIZATION
The division of an organization into self-contained units, each capable of designing, producing, and marketing its own goods and/or services.

Table 10.2	*Advantages and Disadvantages of Place Departmentalization*

Advantages

- Equipment used for products is all in one place, saving time and costs.
- Managers develop expertise in solving problems unique to one location.
- Managers know customers' problems.
- Method is suited to multinational organizations.

Disadvantages

- All functions—accounting, purchasing, manufacturing, customer service—are duplicated at each location.
- May cause conflicts between each location's goals and corporate goals.
- May require extensive rules and regulations to coordinate and ensure uniformity of quality among locations.

Harrisons & Crosfield operates manufacturing facilities around the world. To implement its global strategy successfully, its managers must develop global awareness competency. They have to be able to communicate fluently in two languages (one of which has to be English). They must also recognize and understand great variations in cultures and be able to adapt their behavior to the cultural conditions of host countries. For example, in Singapore, new plants should be opened only on "lucky" days; in Japan, no business is conducted during "Golden Week." Harrisons & Crosfield has chosen a combined product and place form of departmentalization, as highlighted in the following Global Awareness Competency account.

Table 10.3 shows the advantages and disadvantages of product departmentalization.

Advantages of Product Departmentalization. Increased specialization allows managers and employees to concentrate on a particular product line. Management also can pinpoint costs, profits, problems, and successes more accurately for each product line. Moreover, management can develop a distinctive competence, or strategic advantage, for each product line (see Chapter 7). Other potential gains include lower costs for materials, freight rates, and labor. For marketing, locating near customers can mean better service for them. Salespeople can spend more time selling and less time traveling. Being closer to customers also can help sales managers identify the marketing tactics most likely to succeed in a particular region.

Disadvantages of Product Departmentalization. Because functions are duplicated for each product line (i.e., each business), resource utilization is relatively inefficient. In addition, products with seasonal highs and lows in sales volumes may result in high personnel costs. For example, Jostens has high demand for high school yearbooks in the spring but low demand the rest of the year, so fewer workers are needed much of the year. Hence the company faces the choice of transferring employees to other product lines or laying them off. Either solution means higher personnel costs than if product demand were less seasonal.

Coordination across product lines usually is difficult. Employees tend to focus on the goals for their particular product, rather than on broader company goals. This situation often creates unhealthy competition within an organization for scarce

Table 10.3	Advantages and Disadvantages of Product Departmentalization

Advantages

- Suited to fast changes in a product.

- Allows greater product visibility.

- Fosters a concern for customer demand.

- Clearly defines responsibilities.

- Develops managers who can think across functional lines.

Disadvantages

- May not use skills and resources effectively.

- Doesn't foster coordination of activities across product lines.

- Fosters politics in resource allocation.

- Restricts problem solving to a single product.

- Limits career mobility for personnel outside their product line.

Harrisons & Crosfield

Based in London, Harrisons & Crosfield has divisions in many parts of the world. Figure 10.4 illustrates how it uses place and product departmentalization to achieve its success. It owns rubber, cocoa, coffee, and tea plantations in Indonesia and Papua-New Guinea. The commodities produced on those plantations are marketed through division headquarters in Singapore. Weather, stability of the nations' economic systems, and labor unrest are the primary problems that this division faces.

The chemicals and industrials division manufactures chrome chemicals, zinc products, and numerous organic chemicals. It has manufacturing plants and offices in Europe, the United Kingdom, and the United States. Waste, pollution, energy use, and accident frequency are the main problems that this division faces.

The foods and agriculture division produces animal feed, pet foods, malt, flour, and other consumer foods for people living in the United Kingdom. Stiff competition from other global companies who sell consumer products there is the toughest problem that this division faces.[8]

resources. For example, at Harrisons & Crosfield, discussions might range from the acquisition of a new sugar cane plantation in Indonesia to building a new malt plant in the United Kingdom. The debate over which project should be undertaken may revolve around what each division manager believes would be best for that product line, not what might be best for the company as a whole.

Career mobility is restricted when employees develop skills that are relevant only to a particular product line. Specialization doesn't allow people to develop the skills needed to move up in the organization's hierarchy or into its other businesses.

Top management may set common profit standards for *all* product lines, which may not be realistic for the industries in which some of them have to compete. PepsiCo's managers had put tremendous pressures on its restaurant divisions—Pizza Hut, KFC, and Taco Bell—to generate profits comparable to those earned by its soft drink and snack divisions. When the restaurant divisions were unable to generate such profits, PepsiCo decided to sell its restaurants to Tricon and focus on its soft drink and snack food businesses.

Figure 10.4   **Harrisons & Crosfield's Place and Product Departmentalization**

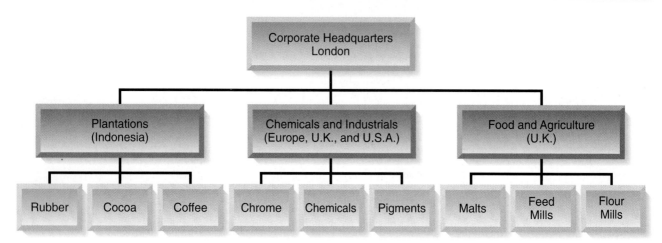

CUSTOMER DEPARTMENTALIZATION

Organizing around the type of customer served.

Customer departmentalization involves organizing around the type of customer served. It is used when management wants to ensure a focus on the customer's needs rather than on the organization's skills (functional) or the brands it produces and sells (product). In the increasingly service-oriented U.S. economy, the customer form of departmentalization is becoming more and more common.[9] Customer departmentalization is generally used to differentiate products and offer different terms to different customers (production of different models and volume discounts to large customers and not-for-profit customers, etc.). This form of departmentalization indicates that management is sensitive to the needs of each customer segment and that it has identified segments that have substantial sales potential.

Fluor Corporation, a global engineering, construction, and maintenance organization with 20,000 employees, uses customer departmentalization to organize its operations. Fluor offers its customers a full range of technical services that allows it to respond to customer needs anywhere in the world. Fluor has developed a global communications network that identifies customer needs by market area. With this system, Fluor can allocate human and financial resources to customer opportunities that have the greatest potential. The decision to use customer departmentalization began with top management's belief that Fluor has the skilled people required to solve customers' many and varied technical problems. Because each customer has specific needs, Fluor's management organized the company to listen to the customer, analyze the customer's needs, and deliver cost-effective services. Fluor identified five types of customers—hydrocarbon, industrial, government, process, and power—as shown in Figure 10.5. In the industrial area, Fluor made the site selection studies for the new Mercedes-Benz plant in Tuscaloosa, Alabama. It also designed a new plant at the Pernis Refinery in the Netherlands for Shell. In the power area, it operates A. T. Massey, a coal company that produces high-quality, low-sulfur coal for the electric generating and steel industries.[10]

Advantages and Disadvantages of Customer Departmentalization.
Table 10.4 shows the advantages and disadvantages of customer departmentalization. The primary advantage of this form is that the organization can focus on

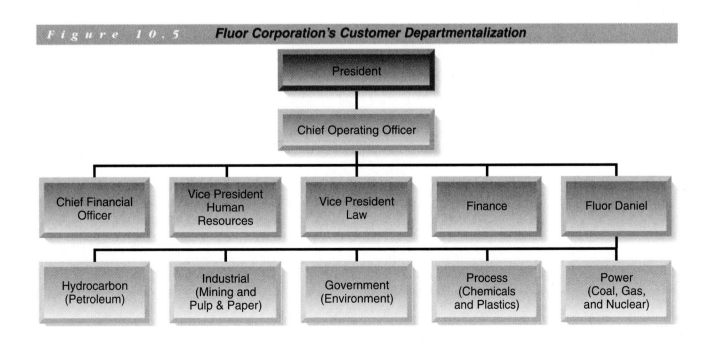

Figure 10.5 **Fluor Corporation's Customer Departmentalization**

Advantages

- Allows greater customer focus.
- Clearly identifies key customers.
- Suited to understanding customer needs.
- Develops managers who become customer advocates.

Disadvantages

- Doesn't foster coordination between customers.
- Fosters politics in resource allocation.
- Employees feel pressure from customers to give them privileges.
- Restricts problem solving to a single type of customer.

customers' needs. Various customers have specialized needs, and this form of departmentalization helps the organization cater to those needs.

However, customer departmentalization can lead to pressure on the organization to meet too many specialized customer demands. Attempting to do so can overly complicate production scheduling and result in short, expensive production runs.

SELECTING AN ORGANIZATIONAL STRUCTURE

No particular type of departmentalization—functional, place, product, or customer—is best in all circumstances. Managers must select the organizational structure that matches the firm's specific needs.[11] Table 10.5 lists characteristics that can help managers decide which structure is best for their particular situations.

Alphagraphics, Sir Speedy, other quick-printing firms, and many other types of small organizations that have standard products and diverse customers, probably would find functional departmentalization the best. Procter & Gamble, Johnson & Johnson, and other organizations with large and diverse product lines probably

Organizational Characteristic	Type of Departmentalization Favored
Small size	Functional
Global or national scope	Place
Depends on customer needs	Customer
Essential to use scarce resources appropriately	Customer
Customer base is	
Diverse	Product
Stable	Functional or customer
Makes use of specialized equipment	Product
Requires skill specialization	Functional
High transportation costs for raw materials	Place or customer

would find product departmentalization most useful. Merck and other organizations in the pharmaceutical industry that utilize numerous complex technologies probably would find product and customer departmentalization most appropriate. Disney, Exxon, and other organizations that operate internationally in numerous regions probably would benefit from place departmentalization.

Clearly, the choice depends on the situation.[12] Some organizations even use all four types of departmentalization. For example, Novartis is a $24.3 billion global biological and chemical company headquartered in Basel, Switzerland, with operations in more than seventy countries. Because of cultural and product line differences, it is organized by country (France, United States, Canada, and Australia), product line (health-care, agriculture, and chemicals), function (R&D, marketing, and finance), and customer (hospitals and other institutions).[13]

COORDINATION

3

STATE THE BASIC PRINCIPLES OF COORDINATION

Departmentalization divides the organization's work and allows for specialization and standardization of activities. However, to achieve organizational goals, people, projects, and tasks have to be coordinated. Without it, people's efforts are likely to result in delay, frustration, and waste. For precisely that reason, coordination is one of the basic elements of organization design.

Many managers believe that good people can make any organization design work. Although such managers may be overstating the case, people who work well together are an extremely valuable asset. A good analogy is football, where teamwork is essential. During practice sessions, coaches try to transform the individual players into one smoothly functioning team. Players learn their functions as part of a cooperative effort, see how each task relates to every other task, and relate these tasks to the whole. Coordination is required as the players execute their functions, particularly when they are called on to innovate or adjust to the unexpected in a game situation. Similarly, managers have to encourage employees to subordinate their individual interests to the organization's broader goals and yet be able to innovate when the situation demands.

In this section we present three basic principles of coordination: the unity of command principle, the scalar principle, and the span of control principle. These principles are directly related to planning and administration competency.

UNITY OF COMMAND PRINCIPLE

UNITY OF COMMAND PRINCIPLE

The principle that states that an employee should have only one boss.

The **unity of command principle** states that an employee should have only one boss. Every employee is supposed to know who is giving direction and to whom he or she reports. According to this precept, managers must minimize any confusion over who makes decisions and who implements them because uncertainty in this area can lead to serious productivity and morale problems.

SCALAR PRINCIPLE

SCALAR PRINCIPLE

The principle that states that a clear and unbroken chain of command should link every person in the organization with someone at a level higher, all the way to the top of the organization.

The **scalar principle** states that a clear and unbroken chain of command should link every person in the organization with someone at a level higher, all the way to the top of the organization. Tasks should be delegated clearly, with no overlapping or splitting of assignments. We illustrate this principle in Figure 10.6, which shows part of Comair Holdings, Inc.'s, organization chart. Headquartered in Cincinnati, Comair has six product divisions. Its Comair, Inc., division offers 600 weekly flights to seventy-eight cities in twenty-seven states and three countries. Within that division are various functional vice presidents. Reporting to the vice president for

Figure 10.6 **Comair Holdings, Inc., Organization Chart**

Figure 10.6 Comair Holdings, Inc., Organization Chart

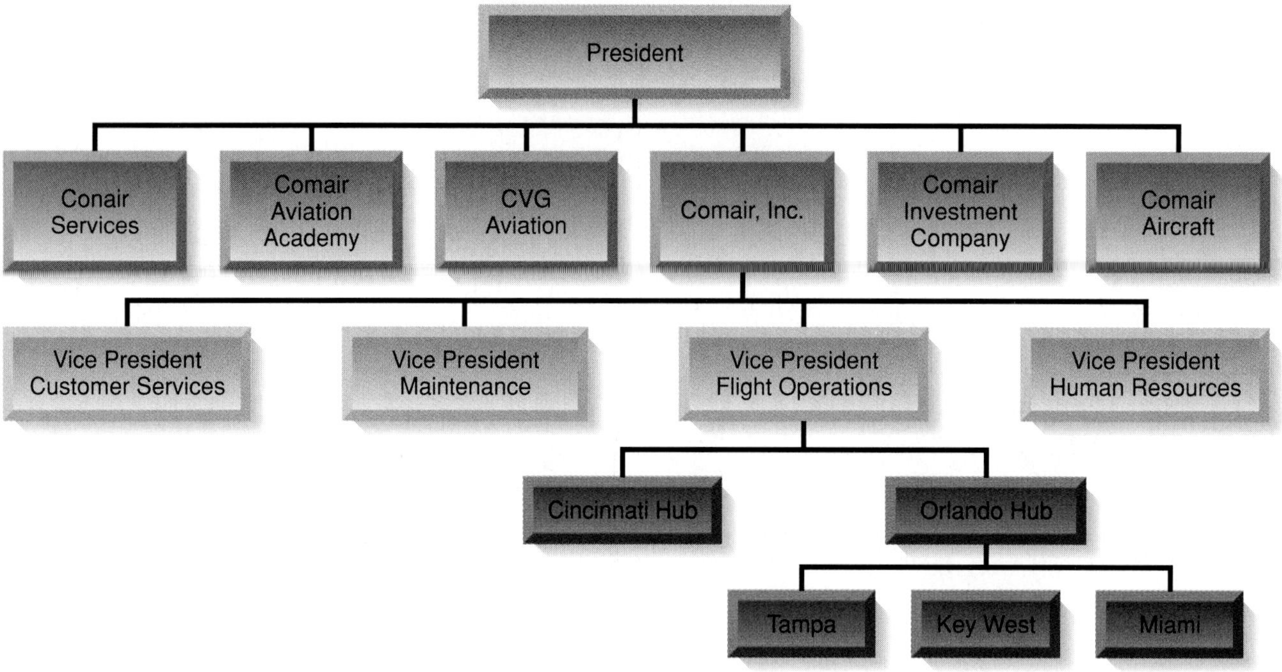

flight operations are employees who work at two major hubs (cities) served by Comair. Application of the scalar principle means that managers at the Orlando hub are responsible for the company's employees in Key West, Tampa, Miami, and other cities served from that hub.[14]

If followed rigidly, the scalar principle would require that all job-related communications between employees in different product departments at the same level (e.g., the aviation academy division and the services division at Comair Holdings) be approved by their respective superiors. Obviously, strict adherence to this principle would waste time and money—and be extremely frustrating. In practice, informal relationships across departmental lines spring up to facilitate problem solving and communication within the organization.

SPAN OF CONTROL PRINCIPLE

SPAN OF CONTROL PRINCIPLE

The principle that states that the number of people reporting directly to any one manager must be limited.

The **span of control principle** states that the number of people reporting directly to any one manager must be limited because one manager can't effectively supervise a large number of subordinates. Span of control is a concept as old as organizations. In fact, it began with Roman military commanders' belief that narrow spans of control were effective in combat. The traditional viewpoint of management (Chapter 2) holds that the ideal number of subordinates reporting to any one manager should be no fewer than four and no more than twelve.

For the most part, successful organizations in the future will have flat structures, that is, few levels of management. Many companies (Lucent Technologies, Boeing, and Xerox, among others) already have flattened their structures by reducing the number of management layers between the CEO and first-line managers. This approach broadens the span of control, with a much larger number of people reporting to each manager. For example, when Lee Byung-Chull founded Samsung in 1938, it had a total of 40 employees. Its business was to produce fertilizer for farmers in South Korea. He personally knew each employee and customer. Today,

Samsung is led by Lee Kun Hee who oversees Samsung's more than 160,000 employees who are employed in one of Samsung's twenty-eight different companies, ranging from memory chips to autos. Hee has delegated decision-making authority to the president of each company. The company presidents have clear goals and assignments that can be divided into manageable parts.[15]

There is no "correct" number of subordinates that a manager can supervise effectively.[16] However, four key factors determine the best span of management for any situation.

1. **The competence of both the manager and the employees.** If a manager and/or employees are new to a task, they obviously require more supervision than knowledgeable veteran managers and employees do. The less experienced the manager and/or employees, the narrower the span of control should be.

2. **The similarity or dissimilarity of tasks being supervised.** A process focus means widely varying products and tasks, whereas a product focus means more standardization. For example, at Starbucks, the span of control in the retail store area is broad because all managers can focus on one product: coffee and its accessories. The more numerous and dissimilar the products, the narrower the span of control should be.

3. **The incidence of new problems in the manager's department.** A manager should know enough about the operations of the department to understand precisely the problems that subordinates are likely to face. The more the manager knows about these factors, the broader the span of control can be.

4. **The extent of clear operating standards and rules.** Clear rules and standard operating procedures (SOPs) leave little to chance and lessen the need for adaptive decisions. For example, at Jiffy Lube, extensive rules govern the tasks and behaviors of employees. The greater the reliance on rules and SOPs, the broader the span of control may be because the rules do much of the controlling.[17]

COORDINATION VERSUS DEPARTMENTALIZATION

In any organization tension exists between coordination and departmentalization. When forces for coordination are stronger than those for departmentalization, functional departmentalization works best. Pep Boys, the self-service automotive repair chain, has kept pace with the changing needs of car owners by stocking a large assortment of automotive tires, parts, and accessories for domestic and imported cars and trucks. It provides speedy, efficient service to customers by smooth coordination of departmental activities. In general, when a problem arises, top managers must be able to coordinate the actions of various functional departments (e.g., merchandising, marketing, and distribution) quickly to find a solution. Under such conditions, functional departmentalization helps ensure the necessary degree of coordination.

When forces for coordination and departmentalization are equal, a customer form of departmentalization works best. The customer structure addresses the conflict between, say, the product manager's need to satisfy a customer and the functional department's need to provide technical help. Employees move from customer to customer, depending on the customer's needs. At Fluor Corporation, engineers could work on a power plant for Enron in the Philippines and an oil refinery in Thailand for Rayong Refinery Company. Additionally, some of these same employees may be assigned to work on building a 250-mile trans-Andean crude oil pipeline from Argentina to Chile.

When forces for departmentalization are stronger than those for coordination, place or product departmentalization is best. Managers decide what is appropriate for only their market area or product, without having to consider the impact of their decisions on other areas or product lines. At Novartis, each division faces its own unique problems. Because each market is unique, programming activities between divisions isn't needed. However, some coordination is necessary in the use of the same or similar methods for financial, accounting, or environmental reporting so that the corporate level receives comparable data from all three divisions.

For multinational companies (e.g., Texas Instruments, Kraft Foods, and Royal Dutch Shell), the use of several types of departmentalization and methods of coordination is common. In such organizations there is no single best way to balance the tension between coordination and departmentalization. Recall that Comair Holdings is organized into six product groups, or divisions. Comair, Inc., is further departmentalized by function and then by place. The methods of coordination vary for each division, depending on its circumstances. In some of the functional departments, the scalar principle and narrow spans of control are effective. In departments that reflect place departmentalization, violation of the scalar principle is common, and wide spans of control are effective.

AUTHORITY

4

DESCRIBE THE AUTHORITY STRUCTURE OF AN ORGANIZATION

As discussed earlier, *authority,* the fourth element of organizational structure, is the right to make a decision and act. Authority is exercised, for instance, when a board of directors authorizes a bond issue to raise capital, when an executive approves a new advertising campaign, when a sales manager signs a contract with a client, when a production manager promotes a worker to first-line manager, and when a supervisor fires someone. In short, authority is the glue of organizational structure.

As we pointed out in Chapter 2, Chester Barnard, president of New Jersey Bell Telephone Company from 1927 to 1948, held a somewhat different view of authority.[18] He maintained that authority flows from the bottom up, rather than from the top down. This view is known as the *acceptance theory of authority.* Barnard didn't think that an employee should analyze and judge every decision made by an immediate superior before either accepting or rejecting it. Rather, he thought that most decisions or orders fall within the subordinate's **zone of indifference,** which means that the subordinate will accept or obey them without serious question. If a decision or directive falls outside that zone, however, the subordinate will question whether to accept or reject it. For example, a manager's request that a secretary type a report probably falls within the secretary's zone of indifference—it's part of the job description. But the manager's request that the secretary work on Sunday probably falls outside that zone, and the secretary may refuse.

Authority implies both responsibility and accountability. That is, by exercising authority, managers accept the responsibility for acting and are willing to be held accountable for success or failure. Furthermore, when delegating tasks to others, managers should take care to match the responsibility they confer with authority and then insist on accountability for results.

ZONE OF INDIFFERENCE
The decisions or orders that a subordinate will accept without question.

RESPONSIBILITY

RESPONSIBILITY
An employee's obligation to perform assigned tasks.

Responsibility is an employee's obligation to perform assigned tasks. The employee acquires this obligation upon accepting a job or a specific assignment. A manager is responsible not only for carrying out certain tasks but also for the actions of subordinates. Sherry Detwiler, vice-president, human resources, at Ace Cash Express, is responsible for developing policies relating to diversity issues for the company. She felt that Ace Cash Express should develop programs to enable it to attract and retain employees in the face of increasing diversity with respect to values, expectations, lifestyles, and family responsibilities. She now is responsible for programs involving

1. child-care subsidies that provide partial reimbursement to employees for the cost of child care;

2. improved part-time benefits, including medical and dental coverage, group life insurance, and short- and long-term disability insurance; and

3. flexible work arrangements that let people share jobs, work compressed work weeks (ten hours a day for four days), and gradually return to work after an illness.[19]

The seventeen local personnel managers are allowed flexibility in phasing in these programs, but Detwiler is responsible to Jay Shipowitz, chief operating officer (COO) for overall implementation of these programs. She also is held accountable for program results.

ACCOUNTABILITY

Accountability is the expectation that employees will accept credit or blame for the results of their work. Employees are expected to report those results, and this feedback enables management to determine whether effective decisions are being made and tasks are being done properly. No supervisor can check everything an employee does. Therefore management establishes guidelines within which responsibilities are to be carried out. Employees are accountable for performance within these limits. Thus, unlike authority, accountability *always* flows from the bottom up. The news assistant of a newspaper is accountable to the senior reporter, the senior reporter is accountable to the editor, the editor is accountable to the publisher.

Accountability is the point at which authority and responsibility meet and is essential for effective performance. For example, the state grants you the authority to drive an automobile and assigns you the responsibility for obeying traffic laws. You are then held accountable for your behavior while driving a car. If you drive without mishap, your license is renewed and your insurance coverage is extended; if you continually disobey traffic laws and are caught or cause accidents, your license and insurance may be revoked. When either authority or responsibility are lacking, managers cannot judge a subordinate's accomplishments fairly. And when managers are reluctant to hold subordinates accountable for their tasks, subordinates can easily pass the buck for nonperformance.

DELEGATION OF AUTHORITY

Delegation of authority is the process by which managers assign to subordinates the right to make decisions and act in certain situations. Thus, in addition to assigning a task to a subordinate, the manager also gives the subordinate adequate decision-making power to carry out the task effectively. Delegation starts when the structure of the organization is being established and tasks are divided. It continues as new tasks are added during day-to-day operations.

Delegation of authority occurs in conjunction with the assignment of responsibilities, as when a company president assigns to an executive assistant the task of preparing a formal statement for presentation to a congressional committee, or when the head of a computer department instructs a programmer to debug a new management reporting system. In each case a manager gives decision-making power to a subordinate. The basic components of the delegation process are determining expected results, assigning tasks and the authority needed to accomplish them, and holding those to whom the tasks were assigned accountable for results achieved. These components shouldn't be separated.

Improving Delegation. The following six principles are useful for improving delegation of authority.

1. **Establish goals and standards.** Subordinates should participate in developing the goals that they will be expected to meet. They should also agree to the standards that will be used to measure their performance.

2. **Define authority and responsibility.** Subordinates should clearly understand the work delegated to them, recognize the scope of their authority, and accept their accountability for results.

3. **Involve subordinates.** The challenge of the work itself won't always encourage subordinates to accept and perform delegated tasks well. Managers can motivate subordinates by involving them in decision making, by keeping them informed, and by helping them improve their skills and abilities.

4. **Require completed work.** Subordinates should be required to carry a task through to completion. The manager's job is to provide guidance, help, and information—not to finish the job.

5. **Provide training.** Delegation can be only as effective as the ability of people to perform the work and make the necessary decisions. Managers should continually appraise delegated responsibilities and provide training aimed at building on strengths and overcoming deficiencies.

6. **Establish adequate controls.** Timely, accurate feedback should be provided to subordinates so that they may compare their performance to agreed-upon standards and correct their deficiencies.[20]

Organizations in which decisions are effectively delegated have managers whose communication competencies build strong interpersonal relationships across departmental or product lines. At Jian, CEO Burke Franklin relies on other organizations to produce and distribute Jian's disks and operate its human resources department. He has found that, to delegate decision making effectively, Jian must create avenues for communication to flow freely between organizations. In seeking out controversial ideas and approaching situations from varying positions, managers need to be skilled at influencing their superiors, as well as suppliers and customers. The following Communication Competency account indicates how ARAMARK, a $6-billion organization in the food service, uniform rentals, and health-care industry, uses its Executive Leadership Institute to develop its managers' communication competencies.

Barriers to Delegation. Delegation can only be as effective as the ability of people to delegate.[21] Table 10.6 lists excuses that managers make for not delegating. The greatest psychological barrier to delegation is fear. A manager may be afraid that if subordinates don't do the job properly, the manager's own reputation will suffer. Such a manager may rationalize: I can do it better myself. or My subordinates aren't capable enough. or It takes too much time to explain what I want done. In addition, some managers also may be reluctant to delegate because they fear that subordinates will do the work their own way, do it too well, and outshine the boss!

Failing to delegate can be justified only if subordinates are untrained or poorly motivated. However, it is the manager's responsibility to overcome such deficien-

ARAMARK Execs Lead with Open Communication

ARAMARK's Executive Leadership Institute is a nine-month leadership development experience. Participants from various divisions are given the opportunity to share best practices across divisions and learn the latest management concepts from consultants and academics. Participants are formed into teams that tackle issues and problems that cross divisional boundaries. A division that wants a team to investigate an issue is asked to provide the team with a history of the issue, courses of action taken in the past and their outcomes, information regarding marketplace trends, relevant financial information, and any other relevant material.

Two examples of proposed interdivisional cooperation illustrate the usefulness of this approach. A major division of ARAMARK, campus dining, provided an opportunity for undertak-ing initiatives with the Children's World Learning Center. ARAMARK would not only provide food service to a campus, but also would operate a day-care center on that campus. Similarly, the corrections division operates prisons for local and state governments and the Crest Uniform division provides professional uniforms. Together, the two divisions could operate the institution and provide uniforms.

To improve the flow of communication across divisions, participants can't work on issues or problems affecting their own divisions. This restriction helps bring new perspectives to problem solving and also challenges the participants to create informal networks with others to gather and analyze information. At the conclusion of project development, each team makes a presentation to senior managers. If they believe that the project is worthy of implementation, members of the appropriate division are delegated authority and responsibility to carry it out.[22]

*   *   *

To learn more about ARAMARK, visit the company's home page at

www.aramark.com

cies. Gabrielle Bush, owner of a small computer software company, had to delegate responsibility and authority to others when she realized that she couldn't directly manage all thirty-two employees in three functional departments. She had to overcome her fear of delegating if her organization was to grow and prosper.

Among the organizational barriers that may block delegation is a failure to define authority and responsibility clearly. If managers themselves don't know what is expected or what to do, they can't properly delegate authority to others. The

T a b l e 1 0 . 6	*Excuses Managers Make for Not Delegating*

- Employees lack experience.

- It takes more time to explain than to do the job myself.

- A mistake by an employee could be costly.

- Employees are already too busy.

- Delegating is terrifying to me.

Source: Adapted from R. B. Nelson. *Empowering Employees Through Delegation.* Burr Ridge, Ill.: Irwin, 1994, 20-26.

financial scandal that rocked Columbia-HCA Healthcare Corporation centered on top management's failure to delegate responsibility and authority for developing and implementing effective decision-making procedures that would prevent unethical and illegal billing practices. The federal government claimed that Columbia defrauded the federal government for years by inflating the cost of treating Medicare patients by *upcoding* the severity of medical procedures billed to Medicare. Upcoding is the practice of indicating that the patient's case is more complicated than it actually is, requiring excessive numbers of tests and more intensive or longer treatment than needed. This practice increased patients' bills and Columbia's reimbursement from Medicare. Furthermore, the government claimed that Columbia allowed physicians to perform unneeded surgical procedures in order to obtain annual bonuses that could add as much as 35 percent to their salaries. The government claimed that physicians might have sacrificed patient care for profits in some instances.[23]

Overcoming Barriers to Delegation. Table 10.7 lists five factors that can help managers become better delegators. Effective delegation requires that employees be given some freedom to accomplish assigned tasks. Managers must accept that there are several ways to deal with problems and that their own ways of solving them aren't necessarily those their subordinates will choose. Subordinates will make mistakes, but, whenever possible, they should be allowed to develop their own solutions to problems and learn from their mistakes. This approach is very difficult for many managers, but unless they use it, they won't be able to delegate effectively. They'll be so busy with minor tasks or with checking on subordinates that they'll fail to complete their own important assignments. Thus managers must always keep in mind that the advantages of delegation justify giving subordinates freedom of action, even at the risk of letting mistakes occur.

Improved communication between managers and subordinates also can overcome barriers to delegation. Managers who make it a point to learn the strengths, weaknesses, and preferences of their subordinates can more effectively decide which tasks can be delegated to whom. Such knowledge will give them greater confidence in their delegation decisions. In addition, subordinates who are encouraged to use their abilities and who feel that their managers will back them are likely to accept responsibility eagerly.

T a b l e 1 0 . 7	*The Art of Delegation*

- Delegate strategically by measuring employees' successes against jointly set goals.

- Treat delegation as a career-building tool that provides employees with the needed experiences to prepare them for greater responsibility.

- Find the right person for the task.

- Let employees establish their own plan(s) of action.

- Make sure that you stay on top of things and hold employees accountable.

Source: R. Ayres-Williams. Mastering the fine art of delegation. *Black Enterprise*, April 1992, 91–93.

CENTRALIZATION AND DECENTRALIZATION OF AUTHORITY

**CENTRALIZATION OF
AUTHORITY**
The concentration of decision
making at the top of an organization or department.

**DECENTRALIZATION OF
AUTHORITY**
A high degree of delegated
decision making through-
out an organization or
department.

Centralization and decentralization of authority are basic, overall management philosophies of delegation, that is, of where decisions are to be made.[24] **Centralization of authority** is the concentration of decision making at the top of an organization or department. **Decentralization of authority** is a high degree of delegated decision making throughout an organization or department. Decentralization is an approach that requires managers to decide what and when to delegate, to select and train personnel carefully, and to formulate adequate controls.

ADVANTAGES OF DECENTRALIZATION

Decentralization has several potential advantages.

1. It frees top managers to develop organizational plans and strategies. Lower level managers and employees handle routine, day-to-day decisions.

2. It develops lower level managers' self-management competencies. According to Jack Welch, president of GE, decentralization prepares managers for positions requiring greater judgment and increased responsibility.[25]

3. Because subordinates often are closer to the action than higher level managers, they may have a better grasp of all the facts. This knowledge may enable them to make sound decisions quickly. Valuable time can be lost when a subordinate must check everything with the boss.

4. Decentralization fosters a healthy, achievement-oriented atmosphere among employees.

Neither centralization nor decentralization is absolute in an organization. No one manager makes all the decisions, even in a highly centralized setting. Total delegation would end the need for middle and first-line managers. Thus there are only degrees of centralization and decentralization. In most organizations some tasks are relatively centralized (e.g., payroll systems, purchasing, and human resources policies), and others are relatively decentralized (e.g., marketing and production).

Under Norman Brinker's leadership, Chili's operates four different restaurant chains—Chili's, Bennigan's, Macaroni Grill and Cozymel's—in the casual dining segment of the restaurant industry. Each restaurant chain has its own president who has the authority to delegate marketing, location, personnel, and other functional decisions to lower level managers. However, Chili's centralizes purchasing and advertising decisions, enabling the company to use its vast buying power to get the best prices from suppliers and generate the most customers for the advertising dollars spent.[26]

FACTORS AFFECTING CENTRALIZATION AND DECENTRALIZATION

Several factors can affect management's decision to centralize or decentralize decision-making responsibilities. Let's briefly consider six of these factors.

Costliness of Decisions. Cost is perhaps the most important factor in determining the extent of centralization. As a general rule, the more costly it is to the organization, the more likely top management will make the decision. For instance, the PepsiCo decision to sell its restaurants to Tricon was made by CEO Roger Enrico and his staff. Costs may be measured in dollars or in intangibles, such as the company's reputation in the community, social responsibility, or employee morale.

Uniformity of Policy. Managers who value consistency favor centralization of authority. These managers may want to assure customers that everyone is treated equally in terms of quality, price, credit, delivery, and service. At Home Depot, a nationwide home improvement sales promotion on paint requires that all stores charge the same price.

Uniform policies have definite advantages for cost accounting, production, and financial departments. They also enable managers to compare the relative efficiencies of various departments. In organizations with unions, such as General Motors and American Airlines, uniform policies also aid in the administration of labor agreements regarding wages, promotions, fringe benefits, and other personnel matters.

Organization Culture. A firm's culture will play a large part in determining whether authority will be centralized or decentralized. ***Organization culture*** comprises the norms, values, and practices that characterize a particular organization.[27] Caring about its employees and serving its customers are the dominant values in JCPenney's corporate culture. Management actions have reinforced these values ever since founder James Cash Penney laid down the seven guiding principles, called the "Penney Idea." For instance, one store manager was criticized by a top manager for making too much profit—it was unfair to customers. Customers can return merchandise with no questions asked. Everyone within the company is treated as an individual. Employees are encouraged to participate in decisions that will affect them, and layoffs are avoided at all costs. Long-term employee loyalty is especially valued. Decision making at Penney is decentralized in merchandising but centralized in finance.

PepsiCo has a very different corporate culture, reflecting its desire to overtake Coca-Cola's share of the soft drink market. Managers compete fiercely against one another to gain market share, to squeeze more profit from a product line, and to work harder. Employees who don't succeed are fired. Even the company picnic is characterized by intensely competitive games, which teams strive to win at all costs. Everyone knows the organization culture and either thrives on the creative tension it creates or leaves. At PepsiCo each brand manager is responsible for his or her decisions. Decentralizing decision making to those closest to the customer clearly establishes accountability in the company.[28]

Availability of Managers. Many organizations work hard to ensure an adequate supply of competent managers and employees—an absolute necessity for decentralization. Such organizations believe that practical experience is the best training for developing managerial potential. They are willing to permit employees to make mistakes involving small costs.

Control Mechanisms. Even the most avid proponents of decentralization, such as DuPont, GE, and Marriott, insist on controls and procedures to determine whether actual events are meeting expectations. Each hotel in the Marriott chain collects certain key data, including number of beds occupied, employee turnover, number of meals served, and the average amount that guests spend on food and beverages. Analysis of the data helps each manager control important aspects of the hotel's operation and compare it against the performance of others in the chain. If a hotel's operations don't fall within certain guidelines, top management may step in to diagnose the situation.[29]

Environmental Influences. External factors (e.g., unions, federal and state regulatory agencies, and tax policies) affect the degree of centralization in an organization. Laws and government regulations regarding hours, wages, and the employment of minorities make decentralizing hiring authority difficult for an orga-

---

ORGANIZATION CULTURE
Shared assumptions, values, and norms that characterize a particular organization.

---

nization. Unions with long-term contracts also exert a centralizing influence on many organizations. When unions bargain on behalf of the employees of an entire organization, such as UPS or Delta Airlines, top management can't risk decentralizing labor negotiations. But when small local or regional unions represent employees in various departments, top management may delegate the authority to negotiate the terms of labor contracts to departmental managers.

LINE AND STAFF AUTHORITY

LINE AUTHORITY
The right to direct and control the activities of subordinates who perform tasks essential to achieving organizational objectives.

Line authority belongs to managers who have the right to direct and control the activities of subordinates who perform tasks essential to achieving organizational goals. Line authority thus flows down the organization through the primary chain of command, according to the scalar principle. In contrast, **staff authority** belongs to those who support line functions through advice, recommendations, research, technical expertise, and specialized services.

Line functions are closely tied to organizational goals and processes. These functions differ from one type of organization to another. For example, Figure 10.7 shows an abridged version of the Toys "Я" Us organization chart. In this case, line departments perform tasks such as marketing, store merchandising, and physical distribution. Staff departments provide specialized information and services to the line departments, including finance and administration, real estate, and management information systems. The line departments follow the line of authority from

Figure 10.7 **Line and Staff Structure at Toy's "Я" Us**

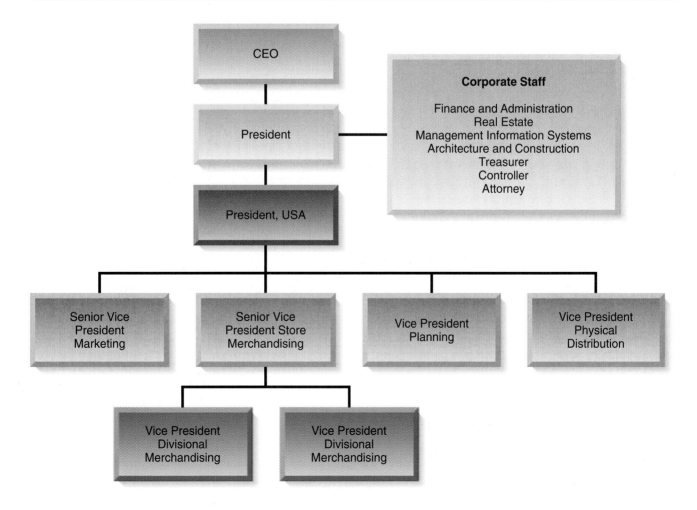

STAFF AUTHORITY
The right to direct and control subordinates who support line activities through advice, recommendations, research, technical expertise, and specialized services.

the office of CEO to the vice-presidents for divisional merchandising, and so on. All staff departments at Toys "Я" Us exist at the corporate level and support the line managers in the performance of their tasks.

LOCATION OF STAFF DEPARTMENTS

Usually, the location of staff departments within an organization is determined by the differences between generalized and specialized functions.[30] If staff services are used extensively throughout an organization, staff departments may need to be located relatively high up in the hierarchy. In fact, most large organizations centralize general staff functions at the top. At Toys "Я" Us, for instance, corporate staff handles finance and administration, real estate, management information systems, treasury functions, and corporate legal functions. The vice presidents who manage these staff functions usually are in corporate policy-making positions. For example, the vice president for real estate at Toys "Я" Us is responsible for developing store locations companywide.

If a staff department provides necessary services to a specific line function, it should be located near that function both physically and in terms of managerial authority. A staff specialist who performs some support functions that a line manager would otherwise have to perform usually reports directly to that line manager.

CHAPTER SUMMARY

In this chapter we highlighted the traditional ways of structuring organizations. As organizations get more involved in global activities, incorporate new information technology, compete for customers, and respond to new employee expectations, the need will be great to rethink fundamental organizational structures.

1. DESCRIBE THE MAIN ELEMENTS OF ORGANIZATIONAL STRUCTURE AND HOW THEY'RE SHOWN ON AN ORGANIZATION CHART.

The four basic elements of organizational structure are specialization, or the process of identifying tasks and assigning them to individuals or teams trained specifically to perform them; standardization, or the process of developing the procedures by which the organization promotes uniform and consistent performance; coordination, or the formal and informal procedures that integrate tasks performed by separate groups; and authority, or the right to make decisions and take action. An organization chart shows the interrelationships among these four elements.

2. DISCUSS THE MOST COMMON TYPES OF DEPARTMENTALIZATION.

The four primary types of departmentalization are functional departmentalization, which groups employ-

ees according to common tasks to be performed; place departmentalization, which groups functions and employees by geographic location; product or service departmentalization, which groups employees in self-contained units, each responsible for its own product or service; and customer departmentalization, which groups employees to focus on specific customer needs.

3. STATE THE BASIC PRINCIPLES OF COORDINATION.

Three principles can be used in coordinating employee activities: the unity of command principle, which states that each employee should report to only one boss; the scalar principle, which states that a clear, unbroken chain of command should link every person in the organization with his or her superior; and the span of management principle, which states that the number of subordinates who report directly to a particular manager should be limited.

4. DESCRIBE THE AUTHORITY STRUCTURE OF AN ORGANIZATION.

Three factors comprise the authority structure of an organization: authority, or the right to make decisions and take action; responsibility, or the obligation to perform assigned tasks; and accountability, or the expectation that each employee will accept credit or blame for the results of his or her performance. Delegation is the assignment of authority to employees.

5. **EXPLAIN THE FACTORS THAT AFFECT THE CENTRALIZATION OR DECENTRALIZATION OF DECISION MAKING.**

Six factors affect managers' decisions to centralize or decentralize authority: costliness of decisions, uniformity of policy, corporate culture, availability of tal-

ented employees and managers, control mechanisms, and environmental influences.

6. **STATE THE DIFFERENCES BETWEEN LINE AND STAFF AUTHORITY.**

Line authority flows down through the primary chain of command, according to the scalar principle, and is held by managers whose activities are essential to achieving organizational goals. Staff authority is held by managers whose offices support line activities by providing specialized information and services.

QUESTIONS FOR DISCUSSION

1. What are the major differences between the four types of departmentalization?

2. What other factors did PepsiCo likely consider when it spun off its restaurants?

3. Under what conditions would a product structure be most suitable?

4. What are the advantages and disadvantages of delegating decision making?

5. What factors influence the extent to which an organization is decentralized?

6. Will the trend likely be toward centralization or decentralization in organizations over the next few years? Why?

7. What other form of departmentalization might Starbucks choose to continue its growth?

8. What are the advantages of NASA's form of departmentalization?

9. What is the difference between line and staff positions? Are the differences always clear in organizations? Explain.

EXERCISES TO DEVELOP YOUR MANAGERIAL COMPETENCIES

1. **Global Awareness Competency.** Kimberly-Clark is a global organization that manufactures and markets products for personal, business, and industrial use. It has annual sales of more than $12 billion and more than 42,000 employees. Headquartered in Dallas, Texas, it operates more than thirty-three plants in the United States and more than thirty-six plants in seventeen foreign countries.

Kimberly-Clark is organized around two product lines. The first includes tissue paper products for households, commercial, institutional, and industrial uses; infant- and child-care products and adult-incontinence products; and health-care products. This line faces fierce competition from Johnson & Johnson and Procter &

Gamble. The costs of doing business overseas, coupled with poor economic conditions in Europe, are major challenges. The second product line includes newsprint, printing papers, premium business and correspondence paper, and tobacco industry papers. The U.S. market's demand for these products has been weak. Offsetting it, however, has been an increased demand for newsprint and technical paper in foreign countries. With NAFTA, Kimberly-Clark also expects improvements in the Mexican market. To meet growing Mexican demands for printing, school notebook, and tobacco industry papers, it opened a plant in Ramos-Arizpe, near Monterrey. To satisfy Mexico's growing demand for medical products, it recently acquired Tecnol, a Fort

Worth, Texas, medical supply firm. What are some challenges facing Kimberly-Clark's management because of its form of departmentalization? In terms of global awareness competency, is the product form of departmentalization the best structure for the company's continued growth? To learn more about Kimberly-Clark, visit the company's home page at

www.kimberly-clark.com

2. **Strategic Action Competency.** Carmike Cinemas own more than 2,700 movie theatres in cities of less than 200,000 population. It serves its customers through standardized low-cost theatre complexes requiring few screens and unsophisticated projection technology. A single manager can run an entire theatre. Operating in small cities and towns allows Carmike to use a highly personal form of marketing through personal contacts, such as sponsoring Little League teams. Based on its strategy, what form of departmentalization is most likely to lead to high profitability? To learn more about Carmike Cinemas, visit the company's home page at

www.carmike.com

3. **Planning and Administration Competency.** 3M is a $12-billion global organization with more than 85,000 employees. It is known as an organization that encourages employees to work around and even defy their superiors to satisfy customer needs and develop innovative products. According to William L. McKnight, 3M's founder, "Top management believes that if they delegate authority and responsibility to employees, they will develop good ideas. People are going to have ideas of their own and want to do their jobs in their own way. Mistakes will be made, but these will probably not be so serious in the long run as the mistakes management makes if it is dictatorial." As a result, 3M doesn't have a well-developed strategy that integrates its departments. For example, the production of tape for disposable diapers

and the production of reflective materials for traffic signs were located in the same department. Some managers believed that these responsibilities were given to the same department so that employees in the diaper products area could help employees in the traffic products area invent adhesives that could be used on road signs. What principles of coordination are violated with this structure? How is 3M departmentalized? To learn more about 3M, visit the company's home page at

www.mmm.com

4. **Communication Competency.** "Historically, we have worked pretty much in a vacuum," says Jeryl Schornhorst, director of washer engineering at Whirlpool Corporation. His department worked on new designs without much input from manufacturing engineering. "We would design the parts and send prints out to manufacturing," he explains. "Whatever it took to make things, that was their business." Today, product planners first develop a concept, but as soon as they have done so, manufacturing and other functions (e.g., quality control, home economics, and logistics) become involved. The design itself faces a committee comprising people selected from various departments that have a stake in the concept. Once it clears them, a manufacturing team starts working on the production process for it. And to further integrate departments, a multifunctional review committee is established to go over the final plans. Despite some early mistakes, communication barriers between departments has been broken down. How are decisions made at Whirlpool? Who has the final authority and responsibility to make them? What departmental differences did Whirlpool's management have to overcome to make this new system work? To learn more about Whirlpool, visit the company's home page at

www.whirlpool.com

REAL-TIME CASE ANALYSIS

R. R. DONNELLEY & SONS

R. R. Donnelley and Sons was founded in 1864 outside of Chicago. It has become the world's largest commercial printer, with more than 41,000 employees in twenty-two countries and annual sales exceeding $6 billion. Donnelley prints telephone directories, magazines (e.g., *Reader's Digest, Farm Journal,* and

TV Guide), books, and direct-mail advertisements. The company is organized into thirty-eight divisions; the divisions, in turn, are organized into eight product groups, which are part of three sectors. Historically, division managers were highly autonomous and could choose the printing jobs they wanted to run and the equipment they wanted to buy. Donnelley's competitive advantage come from its ability to use its large presses, often costing million of dollars, efficiently. These presses were purchased by plant managers, whose decisions weren't subject to review by the company's top management. As a result, plant managers sought the most profitable jobs they could attract because they were held accountable for operating profits. They screened projects carefully to ensure that they would earn a profit for their own plants and often didn't share "best practices" with other plant managers for fear that their own profitability might suffer. Because most of the sales force was assigned to product groups, expenses involved in each sale were applied to the work at the plants in each group. Division managers' incentives were tied to their particular divisions' profits. Donnelley's 500 salespeople worked solely on commission and were paid for what they sold, regardless of the plant to which the work went.

In 1995, there were about 55,000 printing companies in the United States. Most had fewer than twenty-five employees. Donnelley's management was aware that smaller companies entering the printing market were using new digital technologies. Building partnerships among themselves and utilizing software packages capable of making four-color pages, these companies were providing stiff competition for Donnelley. Its management believed that by 2000, publishers would send files of their manuscripts to a printer where they would be retained in a database. When Barnes and Noble and other bookstores needed copies of a particular book, they would contract with the printer and the books would be printed, bound, and shipped. The printer would simultaneously send a check to the publisher to cover the necessary royalties.

This vision was radically different from what Donnelley had done for the past 136 years. To make it a reality, Donnelley would need to develop and manage four basic systems: a sales organization for capturing sales and managing the purchasing process; a system for royalty accounting and payment; an object-oriented database for managing the intellectual property; and a manufacturing database for directing the digital presses. Once the digitized document was in the database, virtually no time or setup costs would be required to convert it to a final product in nearly any quantity. Cost per copy would drop because of savings in customers' warehousing, transportation, obsolescence, and throwaways. The total cycle time would be reduced from 20 days to, if necessary, a single day.[31]

QUESTIONS

1. What philosophy of delegation is practiced at Donnelley? Why had it been effective for 136 years?

2. What type of departmentalization has Donnelley used historically?

3. If Donnelley's management wants to pursue the new digital technology, what obstacles might it need to overcome? What type of departmentalization would you recommend?

To learn more about R. R. Donnelley & Sons, visit the company's home page at

www.rrdonnelley.com

VIDEO CASE

JIAN: PLAYING WELL WITH OTHERS

Jian is a software company whose products support business processes and is itself a model of the versatile, flexible business of the future. Jian's organizational design relies on outsourcing several key functions to strategic partners.

In his farewell address, President George Washington warned his countrymen to avoid "entangling alliances," recalling the strategic military and political webs that had doomed Europe to endless wars and intrigues. But business alliances, in the form of strategic partnerships, are an increasingly important tool for information age ventures. Jian has two primary partnerships: Bindco (discussed in detail in Chapter 11's video case) functions as Jian's production arm, and Execustaff acts as its human resources department.

The two outsourcing partners mesh with Jian in different ways. The relationship between Bindco and Jian is clearly defined, and the two companies have designated key individuals as single points of contact to ensure effective communication and coordination in passing Jian's content into Bindco's production processes.

But people are a bit more complicated than computer software, and Execustaff's interactions with Bindco are necessarily more complex. The more of a management role that Execustaff assumes in developing Jian's human capital, the knottier the interactions may become.

Jian's reliance on its outsource partners gives it great flexibility and the ability to shift directions aggressively as strategic developments might dictate. On the one hand, Jian CEO Burke Franklin can devote more effort to developing and refining his strategic vision. But, on the other hand, he has to maintain the stability of the outsource relationships.

Ultimately, neither Bindco nor Execustaff owe their first allegiance to Jian; each must be primarily concerned with its own investors, employees, and profitability. The companies are, in fact, three separate companies, and circumstances might eventually dictate that the strategic partnerships be terminated.

Serious financial difficulties for one of the partners might dictate severing ties. Or one of the partners' business interests may diverge (e.g., if Bindco chose to shift from hardcopy publishing to an entirely softcopy service). Or another company might acquire one of the partners; if the acquirer were a competitor of a remaining partner or had different strategic interests (e.g., in serving only larger, or smaller, customers) the original partnership might unravel.

Again, the clear-cut Jian/Bindco relationship might make for an easy separation. Another company with comparable printing and distribution skills might easily be substituted or even taken on in parallel for a transitional period. Jian might also resume performing certain of the functions now outsourced (e.g., shifting package design or media duplication in-house).

When working in an outsourced environment, managers must use communication and teamwork competencies both with their own employees and with employees of the outsource partners. Formal lines of authority may be traditional, but one company's manager may be the most important managerial presence for an employee of another (e.g., in the day-to-day activities of the liaisons between Jian and Bindco).

ON THE WEB

Both Jian (*www.jianusa.com*) and Bindco (*www.bindco.com*) are on the Web. Jian's Web site contains a list of professional advisors who are familiar with its products and who may be able to assist customers. These advisors aren't an integral part of Jian's operations or outsource arrangements and pay Jian a fee for the exposure. Jian doesn't vouch for their expertise (although it does suggest a list of interview questions that a customer might use to verify that an advisor is appropriate). The World Wide Web is, by its nature, a tool for strategic networking (e.g., building a network of service suppliers for mutual promotion) and creating a linked community of interest based on a company's customers.

QUESTIONS

1. Jian's strategic partners will experience their own business cycles. How should Jian respond to a partner's financial troubles?

2. What concerns might a manager need to address if a strategic partnership is to be ended?

3. What conditions would make outsourcing a more or less desirable strategy for a company?

To help you answer these questions and learn more about Jian, visit the company's home page at

www.Jianusa.com

Case contributed by Ross Stapleton-Gray, President, TeleDiplomacy, Inc., a technology and policy consultancy, and Adjunct Professor in Georgetown University's Communication, Culture, and Technology program.

Chapter

11

Contemporary Organization Designs

LEARNING OBJECTIVES

AFTER STUDYING THIS CHAPTER, YOU SHOULD BE ABLE TO:

1. STATE WHY AN ORGANIZATION'S DESIGN IS IMPORTANT.

2. EXPLAIN HOW DIFFERENT ENVIRONMENTS INFLUENCE ORGANIZATION DESIGN.

3. DESCRIBE THE DIFFERENCES BETWEEN MECHANISTIC AND ORGANIC ORGANIZATION DESIGNS.

4. DISCUSS THE EFFECTS OF TECHNOLOGY ON THE DESIGN OF MANUFACTURING AND SERVICE ORGANIZATIONS.

5. EXPLAIN HOW ENVIRONMENT AND TECHNOLOGY COMBINE TO DETERMINE THE AMOUNT OF INFORMATION THAT AN ORGANIZATION MUST PROCESS.

6. INTEGRATE THE KEY FACTORS THAT AFFECT AN ORGANIZATION'S DESIGN.

Outline

GE Appliances

Many organizations pursue a one-size-fits-all approach to its organization design. GE, however, believes that it can adequately design each manufacturing plant, including its organizational structure, only after carefully studying the culture of the country in which each is to be located, along with the marketing and retail methods used there. GE measures the quality and strength of local competitors, the market's growth potential, and the availability of skilled labor. Its goal is to obtain the best possible plant with the smallest financial investment.

GE's approach to organization design in its appliance division grew out of a failure. In the early 1990s, GE believed that it could build one factory to serve all of Asia. It would then extend its geographic departmentalization from country to country as its competitors—Whirlpool, Maytag, and Electrolux—were doing. GE quickly discovered the fallacy of this approach when it tried to develop joint ventures in China. These efforts failed because

of manufacturers' overcapacity, numerous local brands, outdated technology, and horrific distribution problems (China has notoriously bad roads and primitive transportation systems). To overcome these problems, GE formed a joint-venture with an old-line distributor called Shanghai Communication & Electrical Appliances Commercial Group. Because the Shanghai Group understood China, it took on the task of identifying factories scattered throughout China that were capable of producing GE products. To ensure that GE standards are met at each factory, the company flies teams of experts in quality, technology, service, manufacturing, billing, collecting, and other skills to a plant. Each team spends as long as needed—a week to six weeks—to bring the suppliers into compliance with GE's standards. In addition to helping local plants reach GE's world-class manufacturing standards, the teams help them cut costs. A refrigerator that used to cost $10,000 now costs less than $4,000 to produce.

GE adopted a different organization design in India and the Philippines. In each of these countries, GE was able to form a joint venture with a single partner that was strong enough to supply GE appliances to the entire nation. Bombay-based Godrei, the top Indian makers of refrigerators and laundry products, and Philacor of Manila, which is number two in Philippine appliance sales, met and surpassed GE's criteria for costs and quality. By designing each organization to satisfy the requirements of its region, the GE appliance division has been profitable in Asia since its first weeks of operations there in 1994.[1]

* * *

To learn more about GE's appliance division, visit the company's home page at

www.ge.com

WHAT IS ORGANIZATION DESIGN?

1

STATE WHY AN ORGANIZATION'S DESIGN IS IMPORTANT

ORGANIZATION DESIGN
Determining the structure and authority relationships for an entire organization.

Organization design involves determining the structure and authority relationships for an entire organization in order to implement the strategies and plans embodied in the organization's goals (see Chapter 7). For example, Carlton Cards has redesigned the way it makes greeting cards. It did away with functional departments and created teams for particular holidays, such as Valentine's Day. A team of artists, writers, lithographers, operations personnel, merchandisers, and accountants are assigned to each holiday. Team members work together at Carlton's Cleveland, Ohio, plant until the card or group of cards has been produced.

The practice of matching organization design to a firm's strategy isn't new. In his landmark study of seventy large organizations, Alfred Chandler found that organization design follows strategy.[2] The choice of organization design makes a difference because not all forms support a particular strategy equally well. This structure-follows-strategy theory is based on the idea that, like a plan, an organization's design should be a means to an end, not an end in itself. Thus there are few hard and fast rules for designing or redesigning an organization. Every firm's organization design is the result of many decisions and historical circumstances.

To some extent managers and other employees make design decisions all the time—not just during major upheavals, such as expansions, reorganizations, or downsizing. In any organization, every time a new department is formed, new methods of coordination are tried, or a task is assigned to a different department, the organization design is being tested or tinkered with. This type of change isn't necessarily bad. In fact, you might think of design features as tools with which managers work, just as sailors use the sails, rigging, and rudder as tools to steer their boats. Sailors frequently *fine-tune* their boats, even when sailing a relatively steady course. The effective manager also constantly fine-tunes the organization's design in light of changes in the environment and technology.

In one sense organization design is the sum of managerial decisions for implementing a strategy and, ultimately, achieving the organization's goals. Hence the design of an organization acts both as a "harness," helping people pull together in performing their diverse tasks, and as a way to coordinate efforts. When we talk about organization design, then, we are referring to managers' decisions concerning the organization's very nature.[3]

Figure 11.1 shows the key factors that affect organization design. We discuss the environment, technology, and information processing in depth in this chapter. We discussed strategy in Chapters 3, 4, and 7, and refer to topics in those chapters as appropriate.

ENVIRONMENT AND ORGANIZATION DESIGN

2

EXPLAIN HOW DIFFERENT ENVIRONMENTS INFLU-ENCE ORGANIZATION DESIGN

In a sense, everything outside the organization comprises its external environment, as illustrated in Figure 11.2. Recall our discussion in Chapters 3, 4, and 7 of forces that shape the environment within which an organization operates. In this section we concentrate on how environmental stability or change influences an organization's design—that is, shapes its departmental, information processing, and control systems.

An organization that provides goods and/or services in an environment with slow technological innovation and relatively few competitors has problems that are

Figure 11.1   **Overall Factors Affecting Organization Design**

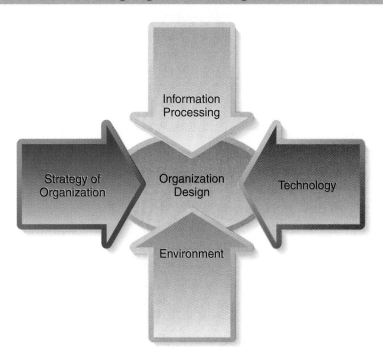

Figure 11.2   **Forces That Affect an Organization's Design**

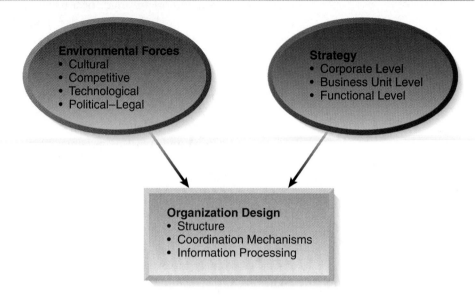

different from those of an organization in a growing, changing, and highly competitive market. The first environment is stable; the second, changing and uncertain. Recall that the relative stability of an organization's environment has major implications for its strategy and structure. The competitive forces—customers, competitors, suppliers, new entrants, and substitute goods and services—dictate the type and amount of information that managers need in order to make decisions. Most firms, however, operate in both stable and changing environments. As a result, some functions may undergo little structural change, whereas others may change considerably.

STABLE ENVIRONMENT

STABLE ENVIRONMENT
A setting characterized by few changes in products, technology, competitive forces, markets, and political forces.

A ***stable environment*** is characterized by few changes, and the changes that do occur have minimal impact on the organization's internal operations. No environment is perfectly stable, and all undergo some change. With good environmental scanning techniques (see Chapters 8 and 9), managers should be able to anticipate many such changes and help their operations and employees adjust to them without major structural changes. A stable environment is reflected in

- products that haven't changed much in recent years,

- little technological innovation,

- a fixed set of competitors, customers, and other stakeholders, and

- consistent government policies.[4]

In a stable environment, top management can easily keep track of what's going on. For example, companies in the brewing, ice cream, fast-food, glass container, and farm equipment industries operate in relatively stable technological environments. Although companies in these industries may make slight changes in their products, the changes can be incorporated easily into their existing manufacturing processes. Changes in the quantity of goods and services produced and sold, rather than product quality, are likely to occur in a stable environment and usually have little impact on the organization's design. Because the product itself doesn't change significantly from year to year, production managers don't have to alter entire manufacturing processes. Firms in highly stable environments are likely to develop extensive distribution systems and invest heavily in capital equipment. They adapt to fluctuations in demand by changing the size of their workforces, not by introducing a new product line or changing production methods.

The pizza industry has experienced a stable annual growth rate of 5.7 percent throughout the 1990s, with current annual sales of more than $23.2 billion. The industry is segmented by method of preparation: ready-to-eat, frozen, refrigerated, and shelf-stable. The ready-to-eat segment accounts for 90 percent of sales, frozen pizza accounts for 8.5 percent, refrigerated pizza holds close to a 1 percent share, and shelf-stable (pizza shells, dry mixes/flours) accounts for 0.5 percent. Sales in the ready-to-eat segment have grown by 6 percent annually, frozen by 3.5 percent, refrigerated by 7 percent, and shelf-pizza by 5.8 percent.

The major pizza providers include Pizza Hut, Little Caesars, Domino's, and Papa John's. These four organizations account for more than 25 percent of all the ready-to-eat pizza sold in the United States. There are roughly 60,000 ready-to-eat pizza outlets in the United States, with more than 25,000 owned by families or friends. Annual revenues per store for the majors range from $417,900 for Domino's to $528,700 for Papa John's. The reason for the steady rise in U.S. pizza consumption can be linked to workplace and life-style changes. Both spouses in most families and most single heads of households now work. They have been increasingly attracted to pizza because of its ease of preparation, whether having it delivered to the home or buying it at the store and heating it up when they get home. Baby boomers are the first generation of Americans raised on pizza, and in turn, they are passing their liking for it on to their children. In fact, pizza has replaced hot dogs as the most popular kids' choice for meals.[5]

What happens when an organization misreads trends in its market place? Although few companies can boast of the global consumer clout of Kellogg, sales of twelve of its top fifteen cereal brands have plummeted around the world. Since 1988, when Kellogg had a 40.5 percent share of the U.S. ready-to-eat cereal market, its market share has slipped to 33.2 percent. One reason for this downturn is that Kellogg didn't align its strategy with its consumer base. The following Strategic Action Competency feature highlights some of the market trends that CEO Arnold Langbo and his top management team failed to recognize.

CHANGING ENVIRONMENT

CHANGING ENVIRONMENT
A setting that is unpredictable because of frequent shifts in products, technology, competitive forces, markets, or political forces.

A **changing environment** is unpredictable because of frequent shifts in products, technology, competitors, markets, and/or political forces. This type of environment is reflected in

- products that are continuously changing or evolving,

- significant technological innovations that make production processes or equipment obsolete,

- sets and/or actions of competitors, customers, or other stakeholders that change continually, and

- government actions that reflect the current level of political clout wielded by various interest groups for consumer protection, product safety, pollution control, and civil rights.[6]

As the GE Preview feature showed, firms operating in a changing environment usually experience *constant* pressure to adapt their products to meet new customer

Kellogg's Strategic Blunders

The $8 billion U.S. cereal market is barely growing. Busy Americans are substituting bagels, muffins, pastries, and other on-the-go breakfast foods for a bowl of cereal. Big-brand competitors, including General Mills (Wheaties and Cheerios), Philip Morris (Post Grape-Nut and Shredded Wheat) and Quaker Oats, are struggling not only because of the stability of the total market, but also because lower priced store brands have increased their market share by 10 percent. Today's consumers are tired of the hassle of clipping coupons and are demanding everyday low prices.

What happened? Most analysts believe that Kellogg needs to shift away from an emphasis on market share to profitability. The cost to Kellogg of distributing coupons, reimbursing clearinghouses and retailers, and subsidizing executives' time comprise 20 percent of its sales costs. That's more than Kellogg spends on advertising. Kellogg must also reduce the confusing proliferation of cereal line extensions. Small changes in flavors as "new products" should be stopped in favor of tangible improvements, such as healthier and better tasting products. Perhaps cereal should be offered as a healthy snack or late dinner for exhausted couples. What Kellogg also lacks is a clear strategic focus. Langbo and his top management team, who live in Battle Creek, Michigan, seem insulated from changes in the industry's structure and consumer tastes. In an effort to gain more profitability, they closed plants and laid off more than 1,000 employees instead of examining Kellogg's strategy and realigning its design to fit that strategy.[7]

* * *

To learn more about Kellogg, visit the company's home page at

www.kelloggs.com

preferences and demands—and they often do so. Organizations in the telecommunications, computer hardware and software, electronics, and fashion industries operate in rapidly changing environments. The GE appliance division faced a changing environment as it expanded internationally. Initially, management thought it could build one factory to serve all of Asia. It soon discovered that it needed different organization designs to fit the unique and changing requirements in various countries.

When a technology is changing, organizations that depend on it must be able to respond quickly, generating new ideas that can affect either the product itself or the way it is manufactured and marketed. In the electronics industry, breakthroughs in integrated circuits and miniaturization significantly transformed the computer, telecommunications, and transportation industries.

Computer communications used to be simple. A company simply leased a few phone lines from AT&T and bought some modems from a supply house. It then began sending data between its home office and its branches. If service failed, the company called the modem supplier or AT&T. Today data communications are a whole new world. Service and equipment providers have proliferated, including local phone companies, satellite suppliers, microwave vendors, and local-area network companies—and the Internet has exploded onto the scene. As a result, corporate and institutional computer networks are far more complex, often containing analog and digital links of all types, as well as intermixed voice, data, and video traffic.

In changing environments, managers should constantly seek to satisfy the needs of customers whose demands and needs are changing. Success depends on the

In Athens, Greece, a VeriFone employee had a competitor raise doubts about whether VeriFone could deliver a new payment-service technology on time to a new customer. The employee located the nearest phone at 4:40 P.M. and hooked his laptop to it. He e-mailed an SOS to all VeriFone employees, which created a virtual team to gather customers' testimonials and other data while he slept.

In San Francisco, the e-mail arrived at 6:30 A.M. An employee organized a conference call with marketing employees, one in Atlanta where it was 9:30 A.M. and one in Hong Kong, where it was 10:30 P.M. Together they decided how to handle data coming in from customers. A few hours later, these employees had drafted a sales presentation. Before the person in San Francisco left for the day, he passed the presentation on to the Hong Kong team so that it could add Asian data. When the Greek sales rep awakened a few hours later, he retrieved the presenta-tion from the network and showed the customer the data on his laptop. Impressed by the speedy reply, the customer placed an order with VeriFone.

Pape designed VeriFone's global organization specifically to use virtual teams. They can be short-lived, as in the preceding example, or permanent. Any employee at VeriFone may orga-nize a virtual team according to the following guidelines. First, a team must have a purpose. The purpose will largely determine who should be on the team, what information needs to be collected, what the team will and will not try to accomplish, and what defines success. Second, virtual teams should have only three to five members because more members make effective communication diffi-cult. Members should also be selected from different time zones so that the team can be productive throughout much, if not all, of the day. Third, the duration of the team must be stated. Finally, knowing how to use various communications tools (espe-cially electronic tools) effectively is essential. Team members have to remember that some tools are great for communicating, such as e-mail, but not very effective for arguing points and arriving at a consensus.[8]

* * *

To learn more about VeriFone, visit the company's home page at

www.verifone.com

VIRTUAL TEAM

Any task-focused group that meets without all members necessarily being in the same room or even working at the same time.

organization's ability to anticipate market trends and respond to them quickly. To do so may mean partial or complete redesign of the organization.

One organization that has adapted its information gathering and analysis proce-dures in a changing environment is VeriFone. William Pape, VeriFone's cofounder, has built the company into one of the largest payment-service organizations in the world by creating virtual teams. A ***virtual team*** is any task-focused group that meets without all its members necessarily being in the same room or even working at the same time. These teams may meet through e-mail, conference calls, videoconfer-ences, or the use of other communications tools. In the above Planning and Admin-istrative Competency account, note in particular how Pape designed VeriFone's vir-tual teams to handle customers' challenges. These teams delegate tasks to the employees who can best handle the customer and solve the problem.

MATCHING DESIGN AND ENVIRONMENT

3

DESCRIBE THE DIFFER-ENCES BETWEEN MECHA-NISTIC AND ORGANIC ORGANIZATION DESIGNS

Organizations operating effectively in stable environments tend to choose organization designs that differ from those chosen by firms operating in changing environments. Researchers Tom Burns and Gene Stalker labeled these contrasting designs *mechanistic* and *organic,* respectively. Table 11.1 highlights the differences between the two.

Table 11.1 — Differences Between Mechanistic and Organic Structures

Mechanistic	Organic
• Tasks are highly specialized.	• Tasks tend to be interdependent.
• Tasks tend to remain rigidly defined unless changed by top management.	• Tasks are continually adjusted and redefined through interaction.
• Specific roles (rights, obligations, and technical methods) are prescribed for each employee.	• Generalized roles (responsibility for task accomplishment beyond specific role definition) are accepted.
• Structure of control, authority, and communication is hierarchical.	• Structure of control, authority, and communication is a network.
• Communication is primarily vertical, between superior and subordinate.	• Communication is both vertical and horizontal, depending on where needed information resides.
• Communication primarily takes the form of instructions and decisions issued by superiors and of information and requests for decisions supplied by subordinates.	• Communication primarily takes the form of information and advice among all levels.

Source: Adapted from T. Burns and G. M. Stalker. *The Management of Innovation.* London: Tavistock, 1961, 119–122.

MECHANISTIC ORGANIZATION

An organization design in which activities are broken into specialized tasks and decision making is centralized at the top.

A **mechanistic organization** is one in which management breaks activities into separate, specialized tasks.[9] Tasks, authority, responsibility, and accountability for both managers and subordinates are defined by level in the organization. Firms using this design resemble bureaucratic organizations, and decision making is centralized at the top. Top management decides what is important and how to share this information with everyone else in the organization. The objective of this type of organization design is to train employees to work efficiently. When one employee leaves, another can slip into the empty spot—like interchangeable machine parts. Thus the mechanistic organization seems best suited to firms operating in stable environments, such as McDonald's and reservation system offices at large hotels and credit card companies. In such environments, where employees tend to perform the same tasks over and over, job specialization and standardization are particularly appropriate to drive the costs of training and operations down. In Figure 11.3, block A shows the match between an organization's stable environment and mechanistic design.

ORGANIC ORGANIZATION

An organization design that stresses teamwork, open communication, and decentralized decision making.

An **organic organization** places less emphasis on giving and taking orders and more on encouraging managers and subordinates to work together in teams and to communicate openly with each other. In fact, employees are encouraged to communicate with anyone who might help them solve a problem. Decision making is decentralized, with authority, responsibility, and accountability flowing to employees having the expertise required to solve problems as they arise. An organic organization is well suited to a changing environment. In Figure 11.3, block D shows this relationship. Phil Knight, Nike's CEO, has structured the company along product lines: athletic apparel and footwear. Using an organic management approach, he encourages people to take risks, delegates to employees the authority to make decisions, holds them accountable for results, and has few levels of management.

In changing environments, the organization needs to respond quickly to changing markets and/or create new markets for its products. Thus Nike promoted Michael Jordan as "Air Jordan" and Tiger Woods as "Tiger" and quickly developed

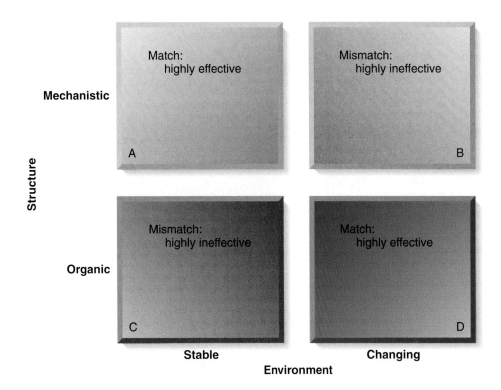

a line of shoes and athletic apparel to capture a large share of the markets generated by these superstars. Moreover, because employees need to respond quickly to environmental changes, job descriptions are broad rather than narrow, and teams (not managers) make decisions.

Differentiation and Integration. Burns and Stalker's findings were supported and extended by Paul Lawrence and Jay Lorsch, who examined the organization designs of three departments—production, research and development (R&D), and marketing—in ten different companies.[10] They found that departments in companies operating in stable environments, such as can manufacturers, were designed differently than the same departments in companies operating in unstable environments, such as plastics manufacturers. They also found that all three departments in the same company wouldn't be affected to the same extent by the firm's environment. That is, employees in R&D departments in the can companies viewed their environments as more unstable than employees in the production departments of the same companies did.

The researchers found that the key to organization design for a manager was to structure the department to match the challenges posed by its external environment. Production departments in both stable and unstable environments were structured more mechanistically than R&D departments were. Departments designed to fit their environments were more effective than those that hadn't been so designed. To describe the character of design differences between departments, Lawrence and Lorsch used the terms *differentiation* and *integration*.

Differentiation is the measure of the differences among various departments with respect to structure, tasks, and goals. If departments have different structures, tasks, and goals, an organization can be classified as highly differentiated or specialized by function. For example, Michelle Pagnotto, a production team leader at WearGuard, a division of ARAMARK, is concerned about reducing costs, meeting daily production quotas, and following rules that ensure efficient delivery of direct mail uniforms to customers. In contrast, George MacNaughton, WearGuard's president, and his management team are concerned about maintaining customer relationships, forming strategic alliances with other uniform companies, introducing innovative products, and choosing the appropriate business strategy to foster WearGuard's growth.

Liz Claiborne, a manufacturer of men's and women's clothing, is a highly differentiated organization operating in a changing environment. Marketing department employees try to stay abreast of the latest fashion trends. They attend trade shows and ask customers for their design preferences. Their goal is to be in the forefront with the latest styles. However, once a decision is made to produce a certain item, it is communicated to the production department. Employees in that department are concerned with meeting the production quotas required to supply the more than 3,500 Liz Claiborne clothing outlets around the world. Changes in style at the production level are expensive and must be avoided if at all possible.

Integration is the measure of coordination among departments with respect to structure, tasks, and goals. If departments have similar goals, are organized similarly, and work together as a team to accomplish organizational goals, an organization is highly integrated or coordinated. The three important principles of integration—unity of command, scalar principle, and span of control—apply especially in integrated organizations. In contrast, organizations that are highly differentiated require the use of more integrating devices and tactics to achieve a coordinated effort because, internally, their goals and structures vary.

Lawrence and Lorsch found that the production department of a plastics firm operating in a *changing environment* retained long-standing production processes and was organized along formal, mechanistic lines because production needed to be stable to be efficient. However, the R&D department in the same firm faced constant demand for *new ways to make* and use plastics and, as a result, was organized more organically.

Research thus supports the importance of designing an organization's structure to fit its environment. It also emphasizes the importance of integration. Depending on the situation, successful firms use a variety of integrative tools. In stable environments, following the chain of command is most effective. In unstable environments, the use of task forces greatly improves coordination among departments. Moreover, the presence of a mechanistic structure in certain departments and an organic structure in others doesn't necessarily reduce the firm's overall effectiveness. In fact, when the environment includes both stable and unstable elements, organizations need to utilize practices that both integrate and differentiate its design.

The following Global Awareness Competency piece explores how Black & Decker redesigned itself to become a global organization in a changing environment by using various types of differentiation and integration to achieve its goals. Recall that a *global corporation* looks at the entire world as its market. It manufactures, conducts research, raises capital, and buys supplies wherever it can achieve the best results. It stays closely in touch with technology and market trends around the world. National boundaries and differences tend to be irrelevant, and corporate headquarters might be located anywhere.

Black & Decker (B&D), maker of power tools for home and professional users, had manufacturing plants in ten countries and sold its products in more than ninety in the 1990s. Design centers, manufacturing plants, and marketing programs focused on making and selling products worldwide. But it wasn't always that way.

In 1981, earnings had begun to slip, and a worldwide recession caused a significant downturn in the power tools segment of B&D's business, its bread and butter. However, B&D's problems were partly a result of its own strategy. By 1982, B&D operated twenty-five manufacturing plants in thirteen countries on six continents. It had three operating groups and a headquarters group in Maryland. Each group had its own staff, which led to duplication and overstaffing. In addition, individual B&D companies, such as B&D of West Germany, operated autonomously in each of the more than fifty countries where B&D sold its products. The company's philosophy had been to let each country company adapt products and product lines to fit the unique characteristics of each market. The Italian firm produced power tools for Italians, the U.K. subsidiary made power tools for Britons, and so on.

As a result, these companies didn't communicate well with each other. Successful products in one country often took years to introduce in others. For example, the highly successful Dustbuster, introduced in the United States in the late 1970s, wasn't introduced in Australia until 1983. When efforts were made to introduce B&D home products into European markets, the European managers refused to comply. They felt that home appliances and products were uniquely American and wouldn't do well outside the United States.

Because of the tailor-made specifications for different markets, design centers weren't being used efficiently. At one point, eight design centers around the world were producing 260 different motors, even though market research had revealed that the firm needed fewer than 10 different models. Plant utilization was quite low, employment levels were high, and output per employee was unacceptably low.

As B&D moved into the mid-1980s, management realized that something had to be done. One area in which the Japanese hadn't made significant inroads was in housewares and small appliances. So B&D acquired the small-appliances division of General Electric in 1984 to give itself more shelf space in housewares and also a large enough line of products to provide economies of scale in manufacturing.

To gain some efficiencies from being a global corporation, starting in 1987, B&D tried to match staffing requirements with sales and limited the number of motors that it was going to market. Standardizing motors allowed B&D to develop a global product strategy: to change certain features for local market demand but retain a product's essential design. B&D is organized along product lines (e.g., vacuum cleaners), which have common distribution channels, technologies, customers, competitors, or geographic markets. Product-line managers are responsible for all functions, including manufacturing, advertising, and sales, for their product lines. In 1998, because of a slump in kitchen products, it hopes to sell that division.[11]

* * *

To learn more about Black and Decker, visit the company's home page at

www.blackanddecker.com

TECHNOLOGY

4

DISCUSS THE EFFECTS OF TECHNOLOGY ON THE DESIGN OF MANUFACTURING AND SERVICE ORGANIZATIONS

In Chapter 2 we noted that technology is an important contingency variable that affects the design of an organization. Recall that, in general, technology is the process that transforms information and raw materials into finished products. Most people associate it only with the machinery used in manufacturing plants, but technology greatly influences all types of organizations and their products. Schools, banks, hospitals, governments, and retail stores all now rely heavily on technology.

Therefore we can analyze its impact on organization design in a variety of settings. Its importance cannot be overstated.

TECHNOLOGICAL INTERDEPENDENCE

A firm's technology has a significant impact on its organization design because different types of technologies generate various types of internal interdependence. ***Technological interdependence*** is the degree of coordination required between individuals and departments to transform information and raw materials into finished products.[12] There are three types of technological interdependence: pooled, sequential, and reciprocal. Figure 11.4 shows how they operate to coordinate the efforts of employees in order to achieve desired results.

Pooled interdependence, illustrated in Figure 11.4(a), involves little sharing of information or resources among individuals within a department or among departments. Although the various departments contribute to overall organizational efforts, they work on their own specialized tasks. At NationsBank, for example, the savings, loan, and real estate departments work independently of one another. NationsBank achieves coordination by requiring each department to meet certain standards and follow certain rules. These rules are consistent for all its banks in various states and apply to all routine transactions, such as check cashing and receiving deposits, with few exceptions.

Sequential interdependence, illustrated in Figure 11.4(b), serializes the flow of information and resources between individuals within the same department or between departments. That is, the output from department A becomes the input for department B, the output from department B becomes the input for department C, and so on. Mercedes-Benz uses standard methods and procedures at its Vance, Alabama, plant to manufacture its sports-utility vehicle. These methods and procedures spell out the single exact and proper way to do every task. They were drawn up by engineers and posted at workstations for easy reference. Everything is spelled out, down to the proper way to tighten a lug nut. When an employee is finished with a hammer, guides, like chalk body outlines, indicate exactly where it is to be laid. To ensure coordination of its departments (or workstations), managers must carefully schedule when parts arrive and leave each department (workstation).[13]

Reciprocal interdependence, illustrated in Figure 11.4(c), encourages every individual and department to work with every other individual and department;

Figure 11.4   *Three Types of Technological Interdependence*

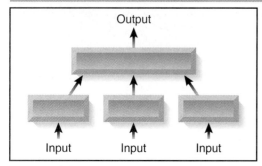

(a) Pooled interdependence

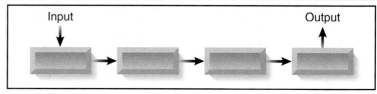

(b) Sequential interdependence

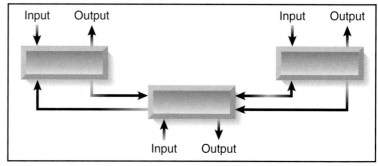

(c) Reciprocal interdependence

information and resources flow back and forth freely until the task is completed. For example, hospitals use resources from several departments (e.g., x-ray, nursing, surgery, and physical therapy) to restore a patient's health. Each specialist and department supplies some of the resources needed to help the patient. Doctors and professionals from each specialized area meet to discuss the patient's recovery. The method of coordination is mutual adjustment, achieved through group meetings.

Designing an organization to handle reciprocal interdependence and then managing it is very challenging. The structure of the organization must allow for frequent communication among departments, and planning is essential. Because management can't easily anticipate all customer demands or solve all the problems that arise, managers must continually communicate face to face to be sure that they understand the nature and scope of issues and problems—and to devise solutions.

SERVICE TECHNOLOGIES

The use of technology is fairly obvious in a manufacturing assembly line. Technology's role in the design of service organizations often is less obvious. The service sector of the U.S. economy now employs far more people than manufacturing. In fact, services now account for 74 percent of the nation's total employment and over 71 percent of its gross domestic product. Service organizations have grown so rapidly in number and size that they account for nearly 90 percent of all new, nonfarm jobs created in the United States since 1953. Some are quite large: American Express has more than 73,000 employees, Citicorp has 89,400 employees, and Kroger has more than 160,000 employees.[14]

Two characteristics distinguish service organizations from manufacturing organizations:[15]

- **Intangibility.** The output of a service firm is intangible and thus cannot be stored. The output must be used immediately or lost forever. Holding seats in inventory on a plane or train is impossible. If these seats aren't sold prior to departure, the revenue is lost forever. Manufactured goods such as cars, TVs, and computers can be stored and sold later.

- **Closeness of the customer.** The customer and client are involved simultaneously in the coproduction of services. Clients are consuming and evaluating services as they are being produced. In a very real sense, the employees of a travel agency are simultaneously producing and selling a service to their customers. Service employees deal directly with customers, but production employees in manufacturing are separated from their firms' customers.[16]

These two features have an important implication for managers: The simultaneous production and consumption of services means that quality control cannot be achieved by the inspect-and-reject method traditionally used in manufacturing plants. Instead, quality control must occur at the point of service delivery. The service provider is responsible for ensuring quality of service during each interaction with the client.

ROUTINE SERVICE TECHNOLOGIES
Methods used by organizations operating in relatively stable environments and serving customers who are relatively sure of their needs.

Types of Service Technologies. There are two basic types of service technologies: routine and nonroutine. Organizations operating in relatively stable environments and serving customers who are relatively sure of their needs use *routine service technologies.* Such organizations include retail stores, fast-food restaurants, banks, travel agencies, gas stations, and bookstores. They aren't so much involved with producing the service as with dispensing it. The information being exchanged is simple, and the tasks are standardized. The demand on the service provider is fairly precise, and thus employees interact with customers for only short periods of time. For example, the interaction between a bank teller at BankAmerica and a customer who wants to make a deposit has all these characteristics.

Organizations operating in complex and changing environments and serving customers or clients who are unsure of their needs or imprecise about their problems use ***nonroutine service technologies.*** Customers or clients usually don't know how to solve their problems even when they can identify them. In this context, service providers—usually professionals—continually encounter new problems and variety is the norm, not the exception. Thus creativity and novelty are essential as the service provider develops techniques to fit the situation at hand. The types of service providers using nonroutine technologies include legal, accounting, brokerage, marketing and advertising, medical, and architectural firms. The focus is on meetings between the service provider and the client and the tasks and skills needed to serve the client's needs. Each meeting between the client and the provider lasts a relatively long time. A successful outcome depends on the client's willingness to give the service provider the information needed to find a satisfactory solution and to participate in its development.

Organization Design and Service Technology. Selected organization design features discussed in Chapter 10 (specialization, standardization, coordination, and authority) and their relationships with the two types of service technologies are shown in Table 11.2. Firms using nonroutine service technologies tend to be organic. They are organized informally, and decision making is decentralized. Because problems facing such a firm are unique, reciprocal interdependence among employees is common. However, firms utilizing routine service technologies can be designed along more mechanistic lines. Specialization is low and standards are common because customers' needs are known. Decision making is centralized in top management. Pooled technological interdependence, which stresses routine tasks and standardization, ensures efficiency.

NONROUTINE SERVICE TECHNOLOGY

Methods used by organizations operating in a complex and changing environment and serving customers or clients who are unaware of their needs or imprecise about their problems.

Table 11.2	Matching Design Features and Service Technologies		
		Service Technology	
Design Feature		**Routine**	**Nonroutine**
Needs of client		Known	Unknown
Structural characteristics			
Specialization		Low	High
Standardization of activities		High	Low
Span of management		Wide	Moderate
Authority		Centralized	Decentralized
Organizational structure		Mechanistic	Organic
Environment		Stable	Changing
Technological interdependence		Pooled and/or sequential	Reciprocal
Examples		Banks, retail stores, fast-food chains, and hotels and motels	Law firms, brokerage houses, marketing and advertising firms, and accounting firms

We can further examine not only the way in which a service technology affects the design of an organization, but also the role of the customer in the service production process. Figure 11.5 illustrates the amount of customer participation in the process and the degree to which the organization tries to customize its offerings to satisfy unique customer needs.[17] Each combination presents the organization with different choices of technology. Let's explore the organization design implications for several different types of service.

In quadrant A, customers simply need to tell the organization's employees what they want. The employees can routinely adjust their methods and behavior to satisfy customers' needs. Organizations that provide services for a variety of customers who desire to have a home cleaned, lawn mowed, or car repaired would be examples. Customers are price sensitive, and in many instances they could provide the service for themselves. They usually don't observe the actual performance of the work. Rather, they inspect the final product for quality. Sequential task interdependence permits standardization of tasks, and extensive rules and regulations govern employee behavior. The customer initially calls on the organization for service and then turns the process over to it.

If customers have complex and unique problems, they are typically less price sensitive and able to provide the service themselves; they will want the organization to provide customized solutions to their problems. Quadrant B of Figure 11.5 indicates that the client's problems require an organization's complex services, as in the provision of legal advice or medical treatment. The client (or patient) must actively participate by providing sensitive information before alternatives can be discussed. As the service provider learns more and more about the client's problem, various alternatives may become obvious, including the need for behavioral changes. As the client's behavior changes or other changes occur, the client communicates the effect of these changes back to the provider. This type of exchange leads to reciprocal interdependence between client and service provider. In such cases, the provider should have multiple skills for helping the client deal with the problem. Through conversations with the client, the service provider gains immediate feedback, which can help avoid costly and embarrassing misunderstandings.

Figure 11.5   *Service Technology*

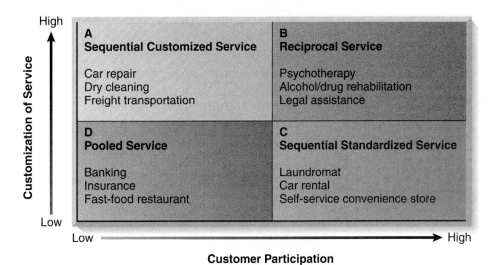

Source: Adapted from Larsson, R., and Bowen, D. E. Organization and customer: Managing design and coordination of services. *Academy of Management Review,* 1989, 14, 213–233.

Many services are purchased for mere convenience and are delivered with the use of sequential standardized service technology. Quadrant C in Figure 11.5 represents situations in which an employee greets the customer to find out what the customer wants. The employee notes the customer's desires on a document (e.g., a work order) and then passes it on to other employees to handle. Pizza Hut, Domino's, and Papa John's pizza parlors are examples of firms that use sequential standardized service technology to satisfy customer demand. The customer evaluates the organization's quality against known standards, such as time, cost, store hours, availability, and accessibility.

Banks, insurance companies, and movie theaters represent organizations in quadrant D of Figure 11.5. The interdependence between customer and organization is pooled. Customers don't participate in the process after their initial request for service. The organization uses standard procedures to achieve low-cost mass production. An example of an organization design that matches a low customization of services and requires little customer participation is PETsMART, a retailer of pet products. The company estimates that U.S. households spend more than $15.3 billion annually on pet food and related pet items. More than 54 million households have at least one pet, with 40 percent having more than one type of pet. PETsMART targets middle- to upper-income households with children aged five to nineteen. The primary shoppers are women. To capture a share of this market, PETsMART currently operates 410 superstores around the world. Its goal is to offer pet owners a complete assortment of pet products, at prices that are typically 10 to 20 percent below those offered by supermarkets and traditional pet food and pet supply stores.

PETsMART has standardized many key aspects of its operations, such as accounting, store layouts, merchandise displays, purchasing, advertising, and pricing. Doing so ensures that all stores look similar and that all operations are consistent throughout the chain. Each store manager is responsible for all store operations, including hiring, work scheduling, and maintenance activities. The company prefers to hire individuals who have proven experience in high-volume retail stores such as Sam's or Home Depot. Once hired, employees are put through an extensive training program, which gives them the knowledge they need to answer customers' questions fully. The company views the quality of its customer service as essential to its success.

PETsMART has recently suffered financial losses because it tried to use its low customer participation and low customization of service technology in its Discovery Center stores. These stores have interactive kiosks for children's education. Customers (children) and employees must jointly participate in activities for the children's learning to occur. The service technology appropriate for these stores was high customer participation and low customization of service (quadrant C in Figure 11.5).[18] PETsMART needed to change its design to match its strategy. In Chapter 13, we discuss how such changes can be made.

INFORMATION PROCESSING STRATEGIES

5

EXPLAIN HOW ENVIRON-
MENT AND TECHNOLOGY
COMBINE TO DETERMINE
THE AMOUNT OF INFOR-
MATION AN ORGANIZATION
MUST PROCESS

Part of technology's impact is that it determines an organization's information needs and, conversely, helps meet those needs. Information is important because nearly every activity in an organization involves information processing. Managers spend nearly 80 percent of their time actively exchanging information as they attend meetings, talk on the telephone, dictate letters and memos, receive and send e-mail, receive reports, read computer printouts, and so on. Information is the glue that holds the organization together.

The design of an information processing system is *contingent* on the stability of an organization's environment and its technology.[19] The basic effect of rapid change (or instability) in an organization's environment and technology is to create uncertainty. With respect to organization design, *uncertainty* refers to the gap between the amount of information needed to perform a task and the amount of information available.

Uncertainty limits managers' ability to plan for the effects of change. Three factors contribute to uncertainty: (1) the diversity of the organization's outputs, (2) the number of different technical specialists on a project, and (3) the level of difficulty involved in achieving objectives. The greater the diversity of high-quality products and the number of different technical specialists utilized, the greater the number of factors a manager must assess prior to making a decision.

Although organization design should ensure the provision of the information needed for decision making, sometimes it fails to do so. To solve this problem, managers can turn to one of two general approaches: (1) increase the organization's ability to process information, or (2) reduce the need to process information. These two general approaches and specific ways to implement them are shown in Table 11.3.

INCREASING THE ABILITY TO PROCESS INFORMATION

Managers can increase an organization's ability to process information by creating vertical information systems or lateral relations.[20] These strategies are especially useful when the people or departments involved are either sequentially or reciprocally interdependent.

VERTICAL INFORMATION SYSTEM

An information processing strategy that managers can use to send information efficiently up the organization.

Vertical Information Systems. A *vertical information system* is an information processing strategy that managers can use to send information efficiently up the organization. Rapidly changing information can be constantly updated, giving managers the right information at the right time for planning and coordinating. By bringing information up to top management, vertical information systems support centralized decision making.

Types of organizations that have effectively used vertical information systems include Ticketmaster outlets, airline reservation departments, off-track betting parlors, and supermarkets. Most of these information systems are computerized. For example, Kroger, Safeway, and other supermarkets now use optical scanners at their checkout counters. As purchases pass over the eye of the scanner, the cost, item type, and related data are read directly from the Universal Product Code (UPC) into a computer. When the store manager wants to know how a special coupon affected a product's sales volume, the computer readily provides the information.

Table 11.3	*Information Processing Strategies*	
General Approach	**Strategy**	
Increase the organization's ability to process information	1. Create vertical information systems 2. Create lateral relations	
Reduce the organization's need to process information	1. Create slack resources 2. Create self-contained tasks or departments	

Source: Adapted from J. R. Galbraith. *Designing Complex Organizations.* Reading, Mass.: Addison-Wesley, 1973, p. 15. Reprinted with permission.

The manager also can determine the percentage of sales from each department (e.g., produce, meat, and dairy). Finally, these systems process the prices of items much faster than manual keying and virtually eliminate checkout errors.

One of the largest and most successful vertical information systems in use today is that of Harrah's Entertainment, Inc. Through the use of Winners Information Network (WINet), Phil Satre, Harrah's CEO, formally communicates with customers to entice them to increase their loyalty to Harrah's. WINet keeps track of a customer's gaming activity, show and restaurant patronage, and room occupancy, among other things. In addition to supporting Harrah's target marketing efforts, this information is utilized with its point and reward program, which works in much the same way that airline mileage incentive programs work. The following Communication Competency feature illustrates how Harrah's uses its vertical information system to track customer activities and influence their choices of gaming experiences. To protect its strategic investment in the innovative nature of the WINet system architecture and its core processes, Harrah's has applied for a patent.

LATERAL RELATIONS

An information processing strategy by which decision making is placed in the hands of those who have access to the information needed to make the decision.

Lateral Relations. Another information processing strategy, *lateral relations,* cuts through the chain of command by placing decision making in the hands of those who have access to the information needed to make the decision. In contrast to vertical information systems, which centralize decisions by bringing information up to top managers, lateral relations tend to decentralize decision making. The two methods of implementing this strategy are to (1) establish direct contact between employees or departments, or (2) create a new position to integrate information.

The simplest form of lateral relations is to allow direct contact between employees or departments that need to solve a common problem, in order to facilitate joint decision making. Figure 11.6 illustrates lateral relations. If department A is falling behind in its production of parts needed by department D, A's manager would contact D's manager directly, instead of referring the problem up through E and G's managers and back down to D's manager through F's manager. If A and D's managers can agree on a solution, the number of communications flowing through the hierarchy regarding problems can be reduced significantly. This process also frees top managers to devote more of their attention to problems that lower level managers can't solve, such as dealing with environmental change.

Figure 11.6 **Lateral Relations in Organizations**

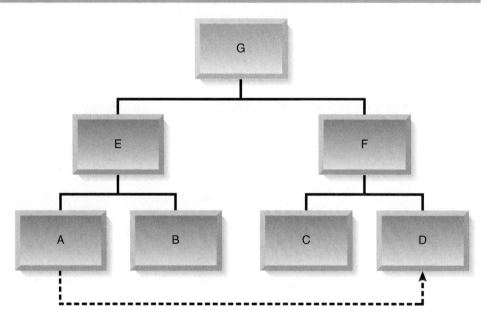

Harrah's WINet Database

If you're one of the 6 million people already in its database, Harrah's is likely to know about the type and preference of hotel room you last stayed in, the time and place of a casino show you last attended, and how much you can be expected to game during your next visit. This information is in the WINet, a sophisticated customer database developed and maintained by Harrah's. The information in WINet is shared by all of the company's sixteen casinos.

Harrah's devised the WINet system to master the arts of the "soft

sell" and customer relationship management. Prior to WINet, information about Harrah's customers was not shared among its locations. Each casino used its own independent system, sales force, and marketing team to track customer activity and develop individual promotions. As a result, Harrah's didn't have a complete picture of customer activities at all its locations. With WINet, customer information is consolidated and summarized nightly from all sixteen of Harrah's locations. The corporate marketing department in Memphis, Tennessee, uses this information to develop brandwide promotions, leaving the individual casinos to develop specific, local promotions. An example of a brandwide promotion that might be available at all Harrah's locations would be a Harrah's Super Bowl party with a free hotel night.

Each customer is given a gaming worth score based on the customer's level of gaming activity and the cost of attracting the customer to a casino. That cost may include a free room, shows, a limousine, and other complimentary services that the customer has qualified for. Customers also accumulate points based on their gaming activity. These points can be redeemed for various complimentary services at any Harrah's location.

Customer preferences, such as type of room, line of credit, and type of gaming are also captured in WINet. In addition, convention and group junket activity is stored to track the profitability of various groups of customers.

To inform employees of customer habits, appropriate personnel (casino, hotel, restaurant, and show personnel) have access to the customer's gaming worth score, points, preferences, bank and credit information, and qualification for complimentary services by means of computer terminals located throughout the casino. Also, marketing personnel can determine the effectiveness of their promotion programs through WINet, as all promotion redemptions are recorded in the system. This information, coupled with that on customer activities, determines the profitability of the promotion. All in all, Harrah's employees have the information they need to recognize and serve their customers well. As a result of the WINet system, Harrah's personal communications with customers have improved greatly, as has customer satisfaction.[21]

* * *

To learn more about Harrah's, visit the company's home page at

www.harrahs.com

MATRIX ORGANIZATION
A design that combines the advantages of the functional and product structures to increase the ability of managers and other employees to process information.

Matrix Organization. Yet another alternative is to create a matrix organization. A *matrix organization* combines the advantages of functional and product organization design to increase the ability of managers and employees to process information. In a matrix organization, functional managers (e.g., engineering, manufacturing, and sales) and product managers (individual product lines) report to a matrix manager. The matrix manager's job is to coordinate the activities of the functional and product managers. Instead of reporting to separate higher level managers, they report to one general matrix manager who consolidates and integrates their activities.

A matrix design integrates activities and holds down costs by eliminating duplication of key functional activities for each product line. The functional manager's responsibility is to identify the resources needed to perform a job, and the product manager's responsibility is to identify products that the organization can make to satisfy customers' needs. The matrix manager's job is to achieve an overall balance by coordinating the organization's functional and product activities to ensure delivery of the product on time and within budget. Figure 11.7 illustrates this balance. The functional and product managers need to work closely with each other (reciprocal interdependence) to make a matrix design work well.[22]

Matrix organizations require managers to demonstrate high levels of communication, teamwork, and self-management competencies. Often, human resources managers work with managers and employees to help them learn how to make decisions *organically* rather than *mechanistically*. That is, they need to base decisions on expertise and persuasion rather than on rules, SOPs, formal roles, and hierarchical position. Disagreements must be dealt with through confrontation and problem solving rather than getting passed "upstairs." Coordination is achieved through extensive formal and informal meetings or in one-to-one conversations. Teams consisting of both product and functional managers and employees decide who will do what and when.

Advantages of a Matrix Design. The advantages of a matrix design are highlighted in Table 11.4.[23] Basically, a matrix design permits the flexible sharing of employees across product lines. The job of the matrix manager is to assess new products, obtain resources for the entire division, and integrate the efforts of product and functional personnel.

Disadvantages of a Matrix Design. The disadvantages associated with the matrix design include the reality that the maintenance of two management hierarchies (functional and product) is expensive. Further, the employees involved typically have two bosses: a functional boss and product boss. Trying to decide who to listen to often creates confusion and ambiguity for the employee. When the

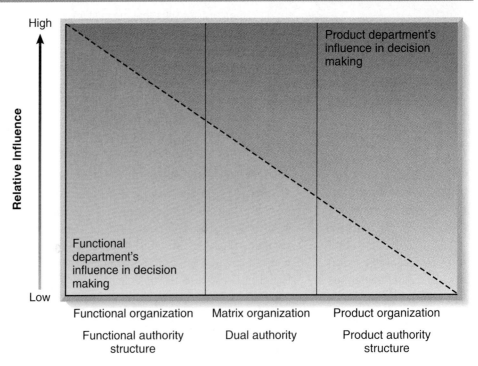

Figure 11.7   **Matrix Organization Design**

Advantages

- Achieves coordination to meet dual demands of efficiency and changing customer preferences

- Encourages flexible sharing of human resources across product lines

- Allows employees to learn new skills in different areas

- Works best in organizations with limited resources and multiple products

Disadvantages

- Requires people to work for two bosses—functional and product—which can be frustrating and confusing

- Requires people to develop good interpersonal skills

- Requires managers and other employees to understand and accept organic rather than mechanistic management

- Requires a skilled matrix manager who can maintain a balance between functional and product interests

product is delivered and there are no new products to work on, layoffs usually follow. Therefore employees sometimes tend to prolong their tasks so that they can keep their jobs. The expense of training employees to behave as coaches and facilitators and not bosses can be high. And many employees and managers simply can't give up assumptions about clear lines of authority and accountability and thus are unable to function effectively in a matrix design.

REDUCING THE NEED TO PROCESS INFORMATION

Managers can reduce the need to process information by either reducing the number of exceptions (problems) that occur or reducing the number of factors to be considered when exceptions do occur. Two strategies used to implement this approach are slack resources and self-containment.

SLACK RESOURCES

Extra resources—materials, funds, and time—that an organization stockpiles in order to be able to respond to environmental changes.

Slack Resources. *Slack resources* are extra resources—materials, funds, and time—that organizations stockpile in order to be prepared to respond to environmental changes. Slack resources can reduce the need to process information by minimizing the problems that are likely to arise. One form of slack resources is an organization's ability to lengthen production and delivery schedules or increase lead times. When an organization overestimates the length of time needed to complete a project, it creates slack—extra time—in the schedule that can be used for dealing with unexpected difficulties. The student who writes a term paper well in advance of the due date builds slack into his or her schedule—extra time that can be used for editing and typing or for something else entirely.

One effect of slack resources is to reduce departmental interdependence. For example, Eljer Industries, manufacturers of plumbing, heating, and ventilation products, maintains extra inventory of plumbing and ventilation products to meet unexpected demand. Less communication is needed among the purchasing, production, and sales departments because of this extra inventory. However, if only a minimal amount of finished goods inventory is kept on hand (no slack), the three departments must coordinate activities closely to avoid creating an unmanageable backorder situation. If backorders pile up, customer satisfaction drops because customers must wait longer than they anticipated for what they ordered.

Creating slack resources also has negative cost and customer relations implications.[24] Increasing manufacturing lead time generates inventories that are expensive to store. At Eljer Industries, this extra cost is reflected in warehousing expenses, such as building construction or leasing costs and employee and energy costs to maintain the buildings. The money thus tied up isn't available for other purposes. Extending planning, budgeting, and scheduling time horizons may lower performance expectations. Moreover, some customers may not be able to live with extended schedules because of their own plans, commitments, or cost considerations.

Self-Contained Tasks or Departments. The second strategy for reducing the need to process information is to assign *all* activities concerning a specific product, project, or geographic region to one group. This approach effectively reduces the number of factors to be dealt with when exceptions, or problems, arise. The self-contained strategy involves choosing product or place rather than functional departmentalization. Recall that some organizations choose a product form of departmentalization because they are having problems with their functional organization. In a firm organized around products (e.g., Procter & Gamble, General Foods, and PepsiCo) each product group has its own resources for the functional areas of accounting, marketing, manufacturing, personnel, and finance. That is, each product line contains all the resources needed to satisfy its customers' needs.

Organization by product lines enables a company to achieve flexibility and adaptability. It also reduces the amount of information a manager needs to process, in two ways. First, product departmentalization limits the number of products and consumer demands that each group must deal with. Within the organization, managers have little need to share information concerning manufacturing costs, delivery schedules, distribution channels, and the like with managers in other groups. One manager's concerns aren't relevant to another's. Second, specialization across product lines is reduced. In functional departmentalization, an accountant must know something about all the organization's products; in product departmentalization, an accountant needs to know something about only one product line. Thus uncertainty is reduced because all necessary information will pertain only to a limited set of product problems.

NETWORK ORGANIZATIONS

Another form of organization design, the network organization, permits the effective and efficient processing of information. The ***network organization*** subcontracts some or all of its operating functions to other firms and coordinates their activities through managers and other personnel at its headquarters.[25] The traditional functions of sales, accounting, and manufacturing are no longer under one roof but are provided by separate organizations connected by computer to the firm's headquarters. Contacts and working relationships in the network are maintained by electronic means, not personal meetings. Use of the Internet permits managers to locate suppliers, designers, manufacturers, and others quickly through online clearinghouses.

Network organizations can't operate effectively unless they can communicate quickly, accurately, and over great distances. When this capability exists, managers of network organizations can

- search globally for opportunities and resources;

- maximize the use of resources, whether owned by the organization or not;

- have the organization perform only those functions for which it has or can develop expertise; and

NETWORK ORGANIZATION

An organization that contracts some or all of its operating functions to other organizations and coordinates their activities through managers and other employees at its headquarters.

- outsource those activities that can be performed better and at less cost by others.

This design means that contractors are added or dropped as they are needed. Organizations in the fashion, toy, publishing, motion picture, and software industries have used this design effectively. Virtually all large retailers outsource the manufacturing function and many outsource the distribution function. At Kmart, Wal-Mart, JCPenney, and other large retailers, corporate headquarters aggregates sales each night, as reported by each store over the electronic cash register point-of-sale information system. The system breaks product-line sales into item, cut, size, material, color, style, and number sold. Those data are then transmitted from corporate headquarters to contractors around the world. Within a few days, replacement merchandise is on the shelves.

An example of a network organization is Nike. With annual sales of more than $8 billion and an 18 percent market share in the global footwear industry and a 41 percent market share in the athletic apparel industry, Nike employs few people at its Beaverton, Oregon, headquarters. The company's success lies in its ability to design technologically advanced athletic shoes and get them to the market quickly. Designers and market researchers at headquarters introduce new models. A small plant at headquarters makes prototype shoes, which employees and athletes wear and test. Once the design has been finalized, it is faxed to suppliers in the Pan-Pacific region for mass production. Nike then distributes them to retailers throughout the world from its huge distribution warehouse in Memphis, Tennessee, home of FedEx.[26]

Implications for Global Organizations. The evolution of global organizations has been characterized by a growing need to balance several conflicting goals: meeting requirements for economic survival, adjusting to demands from host countries, and integrating operations throughout the world.[27] Galoob Toys is one global organization that uses a network design, as shown in Figure 11.8. Only

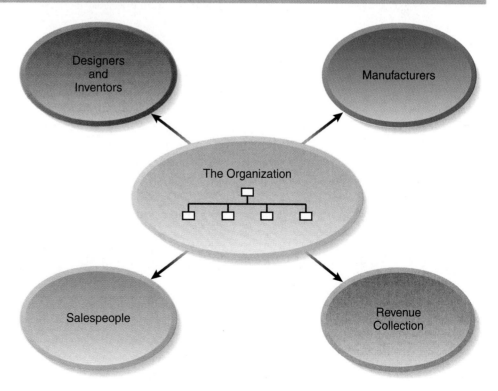

Figure 11.8   Galoob Toys' Network Design

100 employees in California run the entire business, relying on contractors and subcontractors to perform all its operations. Independent inventors and entertainment companies conceive most of Galoob's toys, and outside specialists do most of the design and engineering work. Galoob contracts manufacturing and packaging to firms in Hong Kong, who in turn subcontract most of the labor-intensive work to factories in China. When the toys arrive in the United States, Galoob distributes them through commissioned sales representatives. Galoob doesn't even collect its own money. Commercial Credit Corporation collects from the sales representatives, subtracts its handling fee, and remits the rest to Galoob. In short, Galoob is simply a broker for all these contractors and subcontractors.[28]

Advantages of a Network Design. A network design has several advantages. First, the structure is unbelievably lean. There are very few employees on the payroll because most production and services are contracted for and coordinated by means of vertical information processing systems. Moreover, workforce flexibility and challenge are high because employees are contractors who respond to changing tasks and new demands. In addition, some network organizations preserve highly specialized teams and always use them. For example, Bindco is a leading manufacturer and distributor of computer software. It developed **turnkey manufacturing,** a process of designing, manufacturing, assembling, warehousing, and filling orders for another organization. Jian, the software development company discussed in Chapter 10, uses Bindco's systems to handle all customer contacts, including receiving deposits and invoicing. Thus Jian is free to focus exclusively on software development.

Disadvantages of a Network Design. This unusual organization design also has some disadvantages.[29] For one thing, there is little hands-on control. Operations aren't under one roof, and managers must adjust to relying on independent contractors and subcontractors to do the work.

Second, the network organization runs the risk that a contractor will drop the ball and not report it. For example, when Intel worried about not being able to make the necessary financial commitment to introduce a new line of computer chips, it enlisted two contractors to manufacture its flash chips. NMB Semiconductors had trouble getting its manufacturing process up and running just as the demand for the chips was exploding. As a result, Intel couldn't get nearly enough chips and lost market share to competitors who didn't outsource their manufacturing.

Third, defining the organization is difficult because it changes rapidly. As contractors change, new relationships need to be formed and these take time to develop. Finally, commitment to the organization is low because employees tend to be committed to the contractor that employs them, not to the brokering firm. They realize that they may be dismissed at any time if the brokering firm decides to use a different contractor.

TURNKEY MANUFACTURING

A process of designing, manufacturing, assembling, warehousing, and fulfilling customer orders for another organization.

FITTING AN ORGANIZATION WITH A DESIGN

6

INTEGRATE THE KEY FACTORS THAT AFFECT AN ORGANIZATION'S DESIGN

To conclude our discussion, let's look at how the key design factors we've presented in this chapter affect the design of some of the organizations highlighted so far in this book. We've said that an organization's design should reflect the organization's environment, strategy, technology, and information processing needs and that no single design is going to be appropriate for an organization all the time.[30] Rather, managers should choose a design that fits the organization's needs at a particular time, and as these needs change, so must the design. An organization design is a blueprint to help an organization achieve its goals; it's not an end in itself.

In any organization, some activities and skills are always more crucial to success than others. For instance, L.L. Bean provides its customers with a high-quality product in a very competitive, but somewhat stable, market. Its business strategy is to differentiate itself from other catalogue retailers, such as Eddie Bauer and JCPenney, by providing customers with extraordinary service and a wide variety of name brand products. Bean's managers have chosen a routine service technology and a vertical information system to implement this strategy. This choice of design enables employees to monitor the sales of each item, the number of times a customer has called, type of payment, and other relevant information.

For McDonald's, Burger King, and Hardee's, the environment is stable, and competitors are well known and established. These firms have chosen a low-cost business strategy to attract and maintain customers. Customers can shop around to find the best price and quality. These organizations also have fit their design to a routine service technology. This service technology is appropriate because many of the jobs performed by employees, such as processing customers' orders, are routine. A mechanistic structure fits the needs of their technology and the conditions of their environments.

GROUPING AND COORDINATING ACTIVITIES

We've indicated that managers can put in place one of four types of departmentalization, or a mix of them, to achieve their organization's goals. A functional form of departmentalization is appropriate when the organization is small. Information can be processed easily within each function. Top managers coordinate the various decisions made by the functional managers. Pooled interdependence supports functional departmentalization.

The place departmentalization utilized by Harrisons & Crosfield is appropriate when the organization is large, mature, and operates in various locations around the world. To coordinate its various divisions, Harrisons & Crosfield uses pooled interdependence. It allows each division to focus on the customers buying a particular product, minimizing the communication required between product lines. Key activities can be grouped by product line, each being self-contained, with its own engineers, accountants, manufacturing processes, marketing campaigns, and other functions. Top managers rely on rules, regulations, and standards to coordinate activities among divisions.

If the organization operates in several geographic areas, each with its own special needs, place departmentalization also is appropriate. American Airlines is organized geographically, but it uses vertical information systems extensively to transmit information simultaneously to everyone concerned with changes in flight schedules, weather, and other conditions. The company has chosen a routine service technology to deliver products to its customers. This type of service technology relies extensively on rules and standard procedures that dictate the ways in which employees are to perform their tasks.

Organizations may implement a matrix design to gain the benefits of both functional employees' expertise and the need to change its products constantly to appeal to its customers. Reciprocal interdependence serves a matrix organization best because it promotes the integration of both functional and product managers' activities. The stage of the project becomes the basis for the type of interdependence and the assignment of employees. In the engineering design stage, GE uses reciprocal interdependence. Employees from engineering, marketing, and manufacturing are brought together to discuss the financial implications of a new product. After the product has been designed and approved for production, employees in the manufacturing department actually produce it. Mass production relies on sequential technological interdependence to coordinate employees' efforts. Finally, employees and their managers in the sales department jointly set sales goals. If all the salespeople achieve their goals, GE will achieve its goals.

The network form of design allows an organization to use contractors and subcontractors to perform many of its functions, including design, manufacturing, sales, and finance. The advantage is that the organization itself doesn't have to perform all these functions and can select contractors who have the expertise needed to solve specific types of problems. An extensive vertical information processing system links various subcontractors to the firm.

DETERMINING THE AUTHORITY STRUCTURE

Determining how much authority and freedom employees should have to make decisions is an integral part of choosing an organization design. In the case of small entrepreneurial firms, the owner usually makes the decisions. In larger firms that are organized by function, such as Toys "Я" Us, a vertical information system efficiently transmits information up the chain of command. A mechanistic structure supports the centralization of decision making.

Place departmentalization divides the organization by location. Often this decision is a function of the product marketed and the difficulty of transporting it over large distances, as in construction and meat packing. Global organizations also recognize the trade-offs between centralized control and the complexity of operating in different environments. Authority to commit the organization's resources resides with employees within each geographic region. Local management is closer to the customers and can satisfy their specialized needs better than can some manager far away.

The product form of structure places the authority to make decisions with those individuals in charge of a "business." At Harrisons & Crosfield, divisional managers are totally responsible for their own businesses, including finding raw materials, financing new plants, manufacturing, distribution, marketing, and sales. They have the authority to organize their divisions in the most appropriate manner for the environments they operate in.

Departmentalization by customer is used when managers want to focus on customers' needs rather than on producing a product (functional form) or products (product form) to sell. Managers have the authority to make decisions regarding their customers. Pillowtex, a manufacturer of pillows and other bedding products, quotes different prices for the same goods to different types of customers. For example, it differentiates pricing for discount stores, small retailers, and large customers, including large-volume discounts. This practice signals that management is sensitive to the needs of its customer segments and can make decisions to satisfy their varying needs.

In a matrix structure, decisions are delegated to the managers closest to the action. The crucial administrative skill is selecting managers to head each project and delegating enough authority to enable them to carry out their tasks. At GE, decision making is delegated to each matrix manager in the appliance division. An organic, as opposed to a mechanistic, structure supports the project manager's role in GE's matrix. To increase the manager's ability to process information, matrix structures rely on lateral relations, which allow product and functional managers to coordinate their tasks. Reciprocal interdependence characterizes the relationships among managers.

Authority is centralized in the network form of design. The organization's use of contractors dictates that most major decisions be made at headquarters. Contractors and subcontractors simply implement these decisions within the guidelines established by the organization.

CHAPTER SUMMARY

In this chapter, along with Chapter 10, we focused on alternative ways that managers can design an organization's structure in order to achieve the organization's goals. The external environment greatly affects organization design because of the pressures for change that it exerts. These pressures also require managers to process large amounts of information when making decisions about goals, strategy, and structure. Matching organization design and strategy is affected by managers' choices of (1) technology and (2) information processing methods. Both organization design and strategy directly affect the ways in which managers structure and coordinate various organizational activities.

1. DEFINE ORGANIZATION DESIGN.

Organization design is the process of determining the structure and authority relationships for an entire organization. It is undertaken only after a firm's strategy and goals have been established.

2. EXPLAIN HOW DIFFERENT ENVIRONMENTS INFLUENCE AN ORGANIZATION'S DESIGN.

Organizations operate in relatively stable or changing environments. A stable environment is characterized by few product changes, little technological innovation, a fixed set of competitors and customers, and consistent government policies. A changing environment is characterized by continuous product changes, major technological innovation, an ever-changing set of competitors and customers, unpredictable government policies, and rapid changes in individual values and expectations.

3. DESCRIBE THE DIFFERENCES BETWEEN MECHANISTIC AND ORGANIC ORGANIZATIONS.

Firms operating in stable and changing environments tend to choose mechanistic and organic organizational designs, respectively. In a mechanistic organization, management concentrates on specialization, standardization, and centralized authority. The organization tends to be highly differentiated. In an organic organization, management concentrates on teamwork, communication, constant job redefinition, and decentralized authority. The organization tends to be well integrated.

4. DISCUSS THE EFFECTS OF TECHNOLOGY ON THE DESIGN OF MANUFACTURING AND SERVICE ORGANIZATIONS.

Three types of technological interdependence affect organizational structure: pooled, sequential, and reciprocal. Pooled interdependence requires little sharing of information and other resources by departments. Individuals work on specialized tasks. Sequential interdependence serializes the flow of information and other resources between individuals and departments to accomplish tasks. Reciprocal interdependence encourages the flow of information and other resources back and forth between individuals and departments to accomplish tasks.

5. EXPLAIN HOW ENVIRONMENT AND TECHNOLOGY COMBINE TO DETERMINE THE AMOUNT OF INFORMATION AN ORGANIZATION MUST PROCESS.

In a stable environment, technological interdependence is likely to be pooled or sequential. There is relatively little need to share information internally or to process greatly varying amounts of externally generated information. In a changing environment, technological interdependence more often is reciprocal, with great need for sharing information internally and also for processing large amounts of externally generated information. To deal with uncertainty, firms can either increase their ability to process information by creating vertical information systems or lateral relations, or reduce their need to process information by utilizing slack resources or forming self-contained tasks or departments. To be effective, matrix and network designs require vertical information systems.

6. DESCRIBE THE FACTORS THAT AFFECT THE DESIGN OF AN ORGANIZATION.

Designing an organization is a complex task. The manager must consider environmental forces and the organization's goals and strategies before choosing a design. Choosing a design requires selecting a type of departmentalization and technology. Different combinations of these two design features affect the amount of information that an organization can process.

QUESTIONS FOR DISCUSSION

1. What are the organization design implications for a manager whose organization is operating in a stable environment? a changing environment?

2. How does the environment affect the way in which large airlines (e.g., Delta, American, United, and USAirways) are designed?

3. How does the environment influence a manager's organization design choice?

4. What types of problems do managers of virtual teams face?

5. How do environmental and technological factors influence the selection of the most effective information processing strategy?

6. What competencies are needed to manage employees effectively in a matrix structure?

7. What are the advantages and disadvantages for your management career if you work in an organization using a network design?

EXERCISES TO DEVELOP YOUR MANAGERIAL COMPETENCIES

1. **Communication Competency.** Anthony Rucci, chief administrative officer at Sears, defines his job as helping its employees understand the business and its customers. After visiting forty stores, he quickly realized that Sears employees had lost sight of the importance of serving their customers and therefore the company's profitability. He believed that unless it had a trained, literate, motivated, competent workforce, and empowered employees to make decisions, Sears wouldn't be able to satisfy its customers. He also knew that employees at every level would need to have their pay linked to customer satisfaction. In March 1997, cash registers began randomly printing out a special coupon along with a customer's receipt asking the customer to call an 800 number. Because each call was linked to a salesperson and a transaction, meaningful data on the salesperson's performance was collected. Customers who called were rewarded with a $5 rebate for their next purchase. How did Anthony Rucci use his communication competency to accomplish this task? You might want to read "Bringing Sears into the New World," *Fortune,* October 13, 1997, pp. 183-184, and visit the company's home page (www.sears.com) before answering that question.

2. **Self-Management Competency.** The millions of workers who are now telecommuting need to develop skills and attitudes that other workers don't need. According to some experts, the "ideal" telecommuter is moderately sociable, moderately neat, can set his or her own schedule, and has the fortitude to draw the line when a manager oversteps the boundary between home and work. To learn whether you have what it takes to be a telecommuter, complete Gil Gordon's questionnaire in Delta Airlines' in-flight magazine, *Sky,* October 1997, p. 41, or consult his home page at

   www.gilgordon.com

3. **Planning and Administration Competency.** In the world of new-product development, organizations have formed consumer groups to help them solve problems that arise with product use and to suggest new products that the organization should offer. Hitachi Data Systems, a $2 billion mainframe, storage devices, and service company, organized an advisory panel from its most important customers. During three-day meetings, the customers talk about their plans and the products and services that they will require. Hitachi is looking for its customers to give it clear signals on what state-of-the-art service means to them. Customers have helped Hitachi design various delivery systems and training programs. Customers also share best practices and identify improvements that they have made in their own operations. In addition, customers have benefited from communicating with each other. How did Hitachi's managers use their planning and administration competencies to make its customer advisory panel? To learn more about Hitachi, visit the company's home page at

   www.hitachi.co.jp/

4. **Global Awareness Competency.** British Airlines carries more international passengers than any other airline. But if it is to improve on this performance, it must find new ways to please international travelers. Even with its arrival lounges complete with showers and valets, its first-class seats with inflatable lumbar support mechanisms, and seats that can recline into a fully horizontal bed, it hasn't been able to form effective strategic alliances with other carriers, such as American, Lufthansa, and United. For British Airlines to become a truly global airline, it needs route structures that span the world and to overcome government regulations that preclude joint ventures in some countries. What are some of the organization design issues facing British Airlines as it attempts to become a global airline? How can its management use its global awareness competency to solve the problems the airline faces? To learn more about British Airlines, visit the company's home page at

www.british-airways.com

5. **Strategic Action Competency.** How is PepsiCo designed to implement its strategy? Does its organization design match its environment? What strategic action competencies must its managers utilize to increase the company's effectiveness? Before visiting PepsiCo's home page (www.pepsico.com) you might want to refer to our discussion of PepsiCo in Chapter 10.

REAL-TIME CASE ANALYSIS

FEUDING PARTNERS AT ARTHUR ANDERSEN

Imagine a company that a few years ago didn't even exist and that now employs 50,000, operates on six continents, competes against IBM and AT&T but is neither a computer maker nor a telecommunications organization, leads its industry with annual revenues of more than $6 billion, and is growing more than 25 percent annually. What's more, it isn't listed on any stock exchange. The organization is Andersen Consulting, which specializes in management strategy and information technology. Andersen Consulting emerged in 1989 from Arthur Andersen, the accounting firm. The two parts of the organization have been feuding over the partnership's strategic direction. The accounting business has more partners, but the consulting business generates the most revenue. The debate focuses on who is best positioned to lead the partnership in the years ahead.

The situation is complicated by the fact that people on the two sides don't trust each other or even seem to like each other. It's the kind of conflict that can destroy an organization, with one part that's aging and operating in an entrenched and stable environment and another part that's young and growing in a changing environment. Money is also an issue. Each partner on the accounting side brings in or manages $3 million worth of business, whereas each partner on the consulting side brings in or manages $6 million worth of business annually. The young Turks on the consulting side are offended by a portion of their profits being diverted to older, less productive partners on the accounting side. Many consultants view auditing and tax accounting as a commodity and, although the business isn't going to go away, it isn't growing much.

The conflict has grown since the appointment of George Shaheen as leader of Andersen Consulting. He and the other consulting partners see themselves as agents of change. Andersen Consulting's headquarters is in Palo Alto, California, far from the accounting headquarters in Chicago. The location is no accident. From the beginning, Andersen Consulting viewed its competitors as IBM, EDS, Bain, and McKinsey, not other large accounting firms, such as Ernst & Young, Coopers and Lybrand, and Price Waterhouse. Andersen Consulting's clients were Fortune 500 companies whose global operations and complex technology requirements demanded expert advice on the best computer system to do the job. Shaheen envisions retooling clients' management systems, reorganizing business processes, restructuring workforces, and leveraging knowledge that can transform entire industries. The consultants run their division as if the accountants didn't exist.

The strategic direction of the firm is still in debate. However, at a worldwide meeting of all 2,700 partners in Paris, the partners elected Jim Wadia, an accounting partner based in London, as managing partner of the entire organization.[31]

QUESTIONS:

1. How have the different environments of Arthur Andersen's accounting and consulting operations contributed to the feud?

2. If you were Jim Wadia, what organization design alternatives would you consider? Which one would you choose to resolve the feud? Explain your choice.

To learn more about Arthur Andersen, visit its home page at

www.arthurandersen.com

VIDEO CASE

BINDCO: MIND YOUR OWN BUSINESS

Bindco, a printing and packaging company, was an early arrival in the recent wave of outsourcing of services. It uses economies of scale and its own managerial and core competencies to let other companies efficiently and effectively focus on why they were founded—to mind their own businesses, so to speak.

Bindco's expertise cuts broadly across a content provider's needs. Whether it's a PC software package, human resources training program, or one of many other types of media presentations, the nature of the content is immaterial; the ability to format artfully, package, label, and ship is all. (Bindco's outsource relationship with software developer Jian is discussed in Chapter 10's video case.)

Bindco can address its customers' concerns regarding scale. For example, during its growth from a garage-based start-up, to a going concern, and eventually, perhaps, to a publicly traded company, a software developer might have radically different production and distribution needs. By pooling production work for various customers, Bindco can realize economies of scale and return substantial savings to them, even as it smoothly increases the level of effort required for any one customer. Knowing that even a dramatic fluctuation in demand for its products is buffered by its gross capacity and its ability to reschedule quickly its many tasks, Bindco can devote a great deal of attention to its own unique core competencies.

If Bindco's customers can benefit from its scale, for its part Bindco can develop a mix of customers that best allows it to minimize risk (e.g., by ensuring that its customers' production cycles guarantee a steady level of aggregate work). Unlike, say, a seasonal labor supplier or tax preparer, which may have to all but shut down after the harvest season or once the IRS has been dealt with, Bindco can maintain a level of work that fosters workforce stability and continual full production. Bindco management also is alert to strategic opportunities to diversify further its customer base to meet the needs of prospective clients with services that Bindco can best provide.

Although Bindco's corporate culture may be quite distinct from that of any of its customers, the resulting union of capabilities can function effectively as a whole. Bindco's mechanistic, task-oriented structure might seem extremely rigid to a small software shop. That would be especially true if the shop were loosely structured on the "egoless programming team" model that's possible when programmers can easily embrace an entire project, communicate easily, and work closely in a collegial setting. (Larger organizations, where moderating bureaucracy is necessary to complete larger, more complex projects, might more resemble Bindco.)

A strategically savvy outsource services provider anticipates its customers' needs and interests, as industry requirements change. For example, in the publishing industry, companies that have traditionally taken publishers' content from digital bits to printed materials are considering new approaches. Services now include producing multimedia offerings with text, graphics, and sound for use on the World Wide Web. Printing had been a relatively stable industry for decades; the Web, expanding spectacularly and doubling in scope every few months, is creating a vast new electronic market.

Outsourcing isn't without its dangers. For example, many of the larger companies in the petroleum industry, frustrated by the difficulties of managing personal computers and networks, have turned that work over to outsourcers. In some cases, that even involved turning over all the company's existing computer assets to the service provider. In turn, the service provider would maintain them in place and replace and upgrade them as necessary, using its economies of scale (by providing similar services to many companies) to achieve savings and efficiencies.

The outsourcer often bought the existing computers from a company and then leased them back, resulting in a temporary profit for the company and letting the operations headaches become someone else's. Although this scheme seemed attractive in the short term, some companies found that they were captive to the outsourcer for years and that getting out of an unsatisfactory arrangement often was costly and time-consuming.

ON THE WEB

Bindco is on the Web (*www.bindco.com*). Its Web site is intended to give prospective customers (primarily corporate decision makers responsible for services planning) a sense of its capabilities. As Bindco is a business–business service provider, with no services of its own to market directly to a mass consumer market, the company's site receives only modest traffic.

According to its Web site, many of Bindco's customers are providers of information technology goods and services, concentrated in California where Bindco is headquartered. However, Bindco also maintains offices in Boston and San Diego and targets international markets as well.

QUESTIONS

1. What do companies who employ an outsourcer such as Bindco give up?

2. How might Bindco's market change in light of Internet advances and the exploding use of the vast amount of information the Internet makes available?

3. What concerns might arise if Bindco took on two clients that were competitors?

To help you answer these questions and learn more about Bindco, visit the company's home page at

www.bindco.com

Case contributed by Ross Stapleton-Gray, President, TeleDiplomacy, Inc., a technology and policy consultancy, and Adjunct Professor in Georgetown University's Communication, Culture, and Technology program.

Chapter

12

Human Resources Management

LEARNING OBJECTIVES

AFTER STUDYING THIS CHAPTER, YOU SHOULD BE ABLE TO:

1. DEFINE HUMAN RESOURCES MANAGEMENT AND DESCRIBE ITS ROLE IN AN ORGANIZATION'S STRATEGY.

2. DESCRIBE SEVERAL IMPORTANT LAWS AND GOVERNMENT REGULATIONS THAT AFFECT HOW ORGANIZATIONS MANAGE THEIR HUMAN RESOURCES.

3. DESCRIBE THE PHASES OF THE STAFFING PROCESS AND THE STAFFING TOOLS AND TECHNIQUES USED BY ORGANIZATIONS.

4. EXPLAIN HOW TRAINING AND DEVELOPMENT PROGRAMS CAN IMPROVE EMPLOYEE PERFORMANCE.

5. DISCUSS SEVERAL USES AND METHODS OF APPRAISING PERFORMANCE.

6. EXPLAIN THE COMPONENTS OF A TOTAL COMPENSATION PACKAGE.

Outline

Managing the Clowns at Cirque du Soleil

Do you remember the last time you sat under the big top, watching clowns entertain children and acrobats tumbling across the floor? Perhaps you have even seen a performance of Cirque du Soleil—one of the most unique circus acts in the world. With corporate headquarters in Montreal and offices in Las Vegas and Amsterdam, Cirque du Soleil is an international entertainment company that employs more than 1,200 people representing seventeen nationalities and speaking at least thirteen different languages. Its major "products" include a permanent show that runs in Las Vegas and three touring shows—an American tour, an Asian tour, and a European tour. Growth plans include adding permanent shows at Disney World and in Berlin. These shows highlight the talents of Cirque's 230 full-time artists. But these artists could not have delighted more than 10 million spectators worldwide without the efforts of the company's other 1,000 employees.

In a business where people are clearly its most important asset, managing human resources effectively is essential. Success is possible only with careful planning, recruitment, and selection. For its tours, Cirque relies heavily on temporary staff (temps). In each city where it performs, Cirque hires 125 to 150 people to work as ushers, ticket sellers and takers, and security personnel. For a year of tours, that adds up to some 1,800 temps. Although Cirque employs them for only a few days, good temps are essential to the company's reputation because they have the most direct personal contact with customers. To be hired, applicants must conduct themselves well during an interview designed to assess attitude, experience, and skills.

For positions in the touring groups, the selection process is more intensive. "When a person applies for a touring position, it's not just a job, but a way of life," explains one of Cirque's managers. These positions involve traveling 50 percent of the time and working with performers from many different cultures. Each day, the company receives unsolicited résumés from 30 to 50 people eager to run off and join this circus. After screening applicants for experience and skills, interviews are used to assess per-sonal characteristics. Is this a person who will thrive in the turbulent environment of entertainment? How well is this person likely to get along with people from other cultures? To find out, Cirque's selection process involves multiple stages of interviews—some that are one-on-one and others with a whole group of Cirque employees posing "what if" and "how would you handle this" questions. Once accepted, the fun begins for new employees. For those who thrive in this environment, there will be many opportunities to gain experience and move into other jobs. In fact, 90 percent of all job openings at Cirque du Soleil are filled by current employees with demonstrated track records and an interest in advancing their careers or simply trying something different.[1]

* * *

To learn more, visit the company's home page at

www.cirquedusoleil.com

WHAT IS HUMAN RESOURCES MANAGEMENT?

1

DEFINE HUMAN RESOURCES MANAGEMENT AND DESCRIBE ITS ROLE IN AN ORGANIZATION'S STRATEGY

HUMAN RESOURCES MANAGEMENT
The philosophies, policies, and practices that affect the people who work for an organization.

Human resources management (HRM) is a system of philosophies, policies, and practices that affect the people who work for an organization. It includes activities related to staffing, training and development, performance review and evaluation, and compensation. Effective human resources management satisfies the concerns of multiple stakeholders. For shareholders, an effective human resources management system is essential for an organization to achieve its strategic goals.[2] The reason is that numerous studies have found that effective HRM translates directly into bottom line results.[3] Figure 12.1 shows the results of one of these studies. Firms that have only average HRM systems (those in the middle quintile) aren't as highly valued by the market as those that have truly effective HRM systems (those in the top quintile).

The firms with truly effective HRM systems, such as Southwest Airlines and General Electric, have developed their own unique approaches to managing people. Their HRM systems fit their strategies and respond to a broad range of external environmental influences. Human resources management systems evolve over long periods of time, and people outside the organization often have difficulty fully

Source: Adapted from M. A. Huselid and B. E. Becker. The impact of human resource management practice on turnover, productivity, and corporate financial performance. *Academy of Management Journal,* 38, 1995, pp. 635–672.

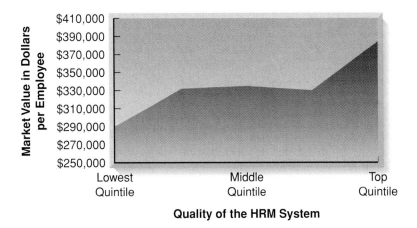

Quality of the HRM System

understanding them. Thus competitors can't easily copy others' approaches, which gives the truly effective firms a competitive advantage. In this chapter we can't discuss all the factors that affect various HRM systems. Nevertheless, as you study this chapter, keep in mind that no two organizations are identical in their approaches to human resources management.[4]

As described in Chapter 6, employees want to be treated fairly, they need to be able to balance the demands of work with other demands in their lives, and they want to feel confident about their long-term employability. Effective HRM systems address these concerns, helping an organization attract and retain employees with the skills and motivation needed for high-level performance.

Although specific HRM philosophies, policies, and practices vary greatly, every organization faces a few common challenges. In particular, organizations must operate within the constraints of the law, recruit and hire people to staff the organization, be sure that employees are trained to do the work they were hired to do, assess employee performance, and compensate employees fairly for the work they do. We describe the activities involved in addressing these challenges in detail in this chapter. As you will learn, many of these activities revolve around an organization's need for a workforce that has the competencies needed to create, produce, and deliver products and services. Just as we have identified managerial competencies needed in most managerial jobs, many companies have identified other sets of competencies needed by their employees. Once the needed competencies have been identified, other human resources management activities can be designed to ensure that these competencies are in place. Table 12.1 lists some of the objectives that companies say they can achieve by using a competency-based approach. Note that the numbers to the right indicate the percentage of companies that use a competency-based approach to achieve each objective.

THE LEGAL AND REGULATORY ENVIRONMENT

2

DESCRIBE SEVERAL IMPORTANT LAWS AND GOVERNMENT REGULATIONS THAT AFFECT HOW ORGANIZATIONS MANAGE THEIR HUMAN RESOURCES

In the United States, Canada, and some other countries, governments have determined that equal opportunity in all aspects of employment is a worthy goal. As a result, executive orders, laws, and court rulings specify acceptable and unacceptable human resources actions. These legal requirements affect not only recruitment, selection, and placement, but also pay plans, benefits, penalties, and terminations. For an international company such as Cirque du Soleil, compliance with the laws and regulations of every country it visits is essential. International differences in

Objective	Percentage of companies that say it is an important reason for using a competency-based approach
Communicating valued behaviors	48%
Raise the level of competency of all employees	45
Emphasize people (versus job) capabilities to gain competitive advantage	42
Reinforce new company values	27
Close skill gaps	26
Focus people on total quality/customer-centered behaviors	22

Source: Adapted from M. A. Bennett. Competencies under the microscope: New research examines how and why organizations are using them to shape HR. *ACA News,* June 1996, pp. 7–10. Additional discussion of these results can be found in: The state of competencies: ACA's research one year later. *ACA Journal,* Autumn, 1997, pp. 54–61.

employment regulations are too complex to summarize here, so instead we'll focus on the primary regulatory influences shown in Figure 12.2 for the United States.[5]

EQUAL EMPLOYMENT OPPORTUNITY

Collectively, the laws regulating ***equal employment opportunity (EEO) laws*** are intended to eliminate discrimination in employment. The basic principle is to ensure that job applicants and employees are judged solely on characteristics that

F i g u r e   1 2 . 2   **Significant Legal and Regulatory Influences on Human Resource Management in the United States**

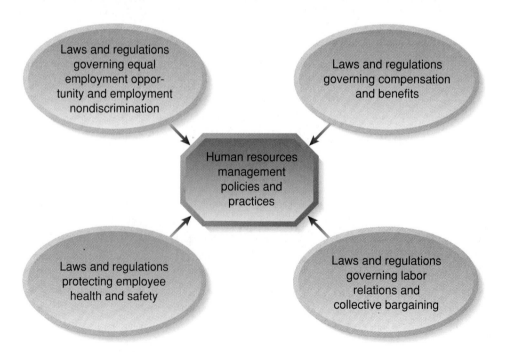

EQUAL EMPLOYMENT OPPORTUNITY LAWS
Laws intended to eliminate discrimination in employment. The basic principle is to ensure that job applicants and employees are judged solely on characteristics that are related to the work that they are being hired to do and on their job performance after being hired.

are related to the work that they are being hired to do and on their job performance after being hired.

The most important legislation pertaining to equal employment opportunity and employment discrimination is Title VII of the Civil Rights Act of 1964, and its subsequent amendments. The original act prohibits discrimination in all phases of employment on the basis of race, color, religion, sex, or national origin. That is, generally employers can't use information about these personal characteristics when making employment decisions such as whether to hire, fire, promote, train, or give a raise to someone. However, there are some exceptions to this general rule. For example, if any of these factors is a valid occupational qualification, it can be used in making employment decisions. Religious discrimination is permitted in filling certain key administrative positions in religiously affiliated colleges and universities. Similarly, a theatre production company can specify that actors hired for a role be the same sex as the fictitious character. Compliance with Title VII is monitored by the Equal Employment Opportunity Commission (EEOC) and enforced by the Justice Department.

Additional legislation modified and extended Title VII. The Equal Employment Opportunity Act of 1972 gave the EEOC the power to sue employers in federal court on behalf of an aggrieved individual or class of people. The Pregnancy Discrimination Act of 1978 requires employers to treat pregnant women as they would any other employee. Employers cannot use pregnancy, childbirth, or related medical conditions to justify differential treatment if the employee can otherwise perform the job. Finally, a main feature of the Civil Rights Act of 1991 permits the awarding of both compensatory damages (for the loss of income and/or emotional pain and suffering) and punitive damages (to penalize the employer financially for illegal acts) to aggrieved employees. Prior to passage of this act, only compensatory damages were allowed.

Other important employment discrimination laws cover age and disabilities. The Age Discrimination in Employment Act of 1967, as amended, protects people aged forty or over against discrimination because of age. These workers are protected with regard to recruiting, hiring, promotion, termination, and most other terms and conditions of employment. The Americans with Disabilities Act of 1990 prohibits employers with more than fifteen employees from discriminating against disabled individuals.

The principle of basing employment decisions on job-relevant competencies rather than irrelevant factors, such as a person's race or sex, is easy to grasp. More difficult is assessing whether illegal discrimination actually affected a particular employment decision, unless the action was extreme and the evidence is clear. That was the situation with regard to the history of hiring practices of symphony orchestras. In 1970, some 95 percent of the musicians in the best U.S. symphony orchestras were men. Then orchestras began to change their auditioning procedures. In an effort to base hiring decisions only on the quality of music a person produced, the orchestras eventually decided to use a "blind" procedure for auditions. Today, job applicants are heard but not seen—they play from behind a screen so that the evaluating committee can't be biased by whom they see playing the music. As a result, women now have a significant presence in the best orchestras, comprising about 25 percent of their members.[6]

Although the United States has numerous laws and regulations designed to prevent discrimination based on personal attributes, many other countries don't. Moreover, in some countries the culture treats members of different groups (e.g., men and women, or members of particular ethnic groups) quite differently—sometimes in ways that U.S. employers and employees would consider discriminatory. So, a question that often arises is whether doing business in another culture ever justifies using information about a person's sex, religion, ethnicity, and other personal characteristics when making employment decisions. A typical situation is described in the following Global Awareness Competency feature.

Suppose that you are a senior partner in Midland Ashby, a consulting firm. You are writing a proposal for an assignment halfway around the world, and as part of the proposal you need to describe the members of the team that would work with your client. The client is located in a country with very "traditional" views about men and women. The person with the most expertise on the client's problem is a woman, so you list her as one of the team members. Your potential client comments on this aspect of the proposal, stating that a woman team member is unacceptable. What should you do? Should you remove the woman from consideration and give her another assignment, or should you refuse to play by the client's rules?

When a panel of managers was asked this question, here's how they responded.

1. Business is business. Leave her on the team, where you need her. It would be ridiculous to assume that she could not be on the team even in a culture with very different attitudes about women.

2. Two other managers chose to begin by trying to persuade the client to accept the woman. But if the client would not accept her, they would take her off the team in order to respect the culture of the client.

3. Acknowledging that this is one of the toughest business decisions, another manager said that the consulting company's principles against discrimination should not be compromised. He would leave her on the team and let her make presentations to the client to prove her expertise. He thought that this would probably result in loss of the contract, but that was better than discriminating against his employee.

4. Two managers thought that the woman's suggestions and input should be sought before she was written into the proposal. If she was interested in the assignment knowing the extra challenges she would face, these managers would keep her on the team. They would handle the client by stressing the importance of making a sound business decision—in this case, that means making use of the expert on the topic.

5. One manager agreed that the consultant should be responsive to the cultural norms of clients. But she noted that the consultant might want to reconsider where and with whom they were willing to do business.

6. One manager proposed handling the situation by explaining the situation to the woman and asking her to serve as a ghost member of the team. Her input would be sought and used by the team, but the client would never see her.

7. One manager stated that legally, the consultant had no option but to use the best qualified person. Under Title VII, denying her the assignment because she was a woman would be illegal.[7]

What's your opinion?

* * *

To learn more about issues in international human resources management, visit the home pages of the International Association for Human Resource Information Management at

www.ihrim.org

and the International Personnel Management Association at

www.ipma-hr.org

COMPENSATION AND BENEFITS

Of the several laws that influence compensation and benefits practices, the primary one is the Fair Labor Standards Act (FLSA) of 1938. The FLSA is a federal law that specifies a national minimum wage rate ($5.15 per hour in 1998) and requires payment for overtime work by covered employees. Individual states can, and often do, set higher standards than those set at the federal level.

Not all employees are covered by the FLSA. The act distinguishes between ***nonexempt employees***—those covered by the act—and ***exempt employees***—those not covered by the act. Exempt employees include, among others, outside salespeople, and executive, administrative, and professional personnel. Such employees usually are paid an annual salary or work on commission and tend to earn much more than the minimum wage. They understand that they may need to work more than forty hours a week in order to meet their responsibilities and that they don't get paid overtime for such work.

Another important regulation affecting compensation practices is the Equal Pay Act of 1963. This act requires men and women to be paid equally when they are doing equal work (in terms of skill, effort, responsibility, and working conditions) in the same organization. Suppose for example, that a software company had mostly men programmers designing computer games and mostly women programmers designing Web sites for those games. If the levels of skill, effort, and responsibility were similar in these two jobs, the men and women programmers should be paid equally—despite the fact that they weren't doing identical work.

Some legislation mandates that employers provide employees with certain benefits. For example, the Federal Insurance Contribution Act (FICA) of 1935 and later amendments require most employers to make Social Security contributions on behalf of their employees. The act also requires employers to participate in an unemployment compensation system. The Workers' Compensation Act requires employers to pay into a fund to be used to compensate people for work-related injuries or diseases. Retirement plans, a benefit provided voluntarily by employers, are regulated by the Employee Retirement Income Security Act (ERISA) of 1974. Under ERISA, employees who are twenty-one years of age and have completed one year of service must be allowed to participate in a company's retirement plan if it has one.

EMPLOYEE HEALTH AND SAFETY

The Occupational Safety and Health Act (OSHA) of 1970 requires employers to provide a safe and healthful workplace with adequate protection against hazards that are likely to cause serious physical impairment or death. These hazards could be dangerous equipment, unsafe production processes, exposure to noxious chemicals, and the like.

For jobs that are inherently dangerous (e.g., construction, foundry work, metal stamping, and coal mining) OSHA calls for the use of all appropriate safety precautions. In metal stamping, for instance, safety devices must be used so that the operator's limbs are in a safe zone before the machine can be operated. Spray painters commonly wear respirators to protect themselves from paint fumes. No matter how risky the job, the intent of OSHA is to ensure that employers do not expose employees to unsafe practices, thereby endangering their physical well-being.

LABOR RELATIONS AND COLLECTIVE BARGAINING

The right to unionize and bargain collectively is an important part of the regulatory aspect of human resources management. Different laws govern labor relations for public sector (federal, state, and local government) and private sector employees. Of these, the most significant laws are the Wagner Act of 1935 and the Taft-Hartley Act of 1947. The Wagner Act (also known as the National Labor Relations Act) gives employees the right to form or join labor unions, to bargain collectively, and to strike in order to secure better economic and/or working conditions. For example, in 1997, United Parcel Service (UPS) truck drivers went on strike to pressure management to reduce the use of lower paid part-time jobs. The NLRA also prohibits employers from engaging in unfair labor practices such as

- interfering with or threatening employees who exercise their rights as guaranteed by labor law;

- discriminating against employees because of their union activities;

- refusing to bargain in good faith with union representatives concerning employees' wages, hours, and terms and conditions of employment; and

- attempting to control or interfere with union affairs.

The NLRA did not prohibit unfair labor practices by unions. However, the Taft-Hartley Act, which amended the NLRA, was enacted to counteract union abuses. Under Taft-Hartley, unions can't

- refuse to bargain in good faith,

- threaten or restrain employees in exercising their rights to join or not join a union,

- charge discriminatory dues or entrance fees, and

- force employers to discriminate against employees who are not union members.

Currently, about 15 percent of employees belong to unions. The percentage varies greatly from state to state and across occupational groups. For example, in South Carolina only about 3 percent of employees belong to unions whereas in New York nearly 30 percent do.[8]

Occupationally, most union members work in manufacturing and government jobs. But this pattern may change in the future. In 1996, the first national union for doctors was formed by a podiatrist who believed that a union would give doctors more power to negotiate employment conditions with managed care organizations. The new union, called the First National Guild for Health Care Providers of the Lower Extremities, is affiliated with the AFL-CIO.[9]

Traditionally in the United States, relations between unions and management have been contentious and adversarial. However, this condition is gradually changing. Many union leaders now recognize that, in order for them to achieve their goal of protecting jobs, union–management cooperation and problem solving are necessary. Similarly, many managers realize that union members can help a company find ways to work more effectively and enlarge their common "pie" of resources.[10]

INDEPENDENT CONTRACTORS

Since the mid-1980s, organizational restructuring and downsizing have created new challenges in human resources management. One such challenge is simply determining whether someone who works for an organization should be considered to be an employee. Most of the laws that we've described specifically protect the employees of an organization—they weren't written to protect independent contractors that an organization might employ on a project basis. As more and more jobs are outsourced to independent contractors, such as consultants, the federal government has developed guidelines for companies to use to determine whether a person is an employee.

Why should the government care whether an employer considers someone to be an employee or an independent contractor? Taxes are one big reason. For example, if a person is an employee, the employer is responsible for withholding (i.e., collecting and paying) federal income taxes and FICA contributions on behalf of the government and for paying workers' compensation insurance. But employers don't have to withhold taxes or pay worker's compensation insurance for independent contractors. Independent contractors are responsible for making quarterly income tax and FICA payments, but employers are responsible for reporting the amounts that they paid during the calendar year to such contractors. Compared to employees, people who work as independent contractors have fewer legal rights and protections. For example, a painting contractor who worked a fifty-five-hour week to finish a job wouldn't be entitled to overtime pay.

The administrative and cost implications, as well as other responsibilities associated with employees, give employers an incentive to call the people who work for them independent contractors instead of employees. The Internal Revenue Service (IRS) in particular wants to be sure companies don't evade their responsibilities by disclaiming people who should be considered employees. The IRS regulations use several factors to define *employee,* as shown in Table 12.2

T a b l e 1 2 . 2	**Factors to Be Used in Determining Whether a Person Is an Employee or an Independent Contractor**
Employees are more likely to	**Independent contractors are more likely to**
Follow instructions about when, where, and how to do the work	Be responsible only for delivering the end result, using whatever means they want in order to get the work done
Do work that is highly integrated into the main business	Do work that isn't central to the main business
Receive significant training	Be responsible for their own training
Render the service personally	Be permitted to subcontract the work out to someone else
Be required to devote full time to one employer	Devote less than full time to one employer, and work for multiple employers
Use the employer's space, equipment, and tools to do the work	Do the work off the premises using their own equipment and tools
Submit regular reports	Submit just one report at the end of the project
Be paid at regular intervals	Be paid when the project is completed
Be subject to discharge at any time and be free to terminate their employment at any time	Be subject to discharge only for failing to fulfill their contracts and be free to terminate the relationship only upon completion of the contract or breach of the contract by the other party

Source: Adapted from: When is an independent contractor actually an employee? *Workforce* (Supplement to the September issue), 1997, pp. 6-7; and G. Flynn. Independent contractor vs. employee: Get it right. *Workforce,* September 1997, pp. 125–130.

THE STAFFING PROCESS

STAFFING
The process by which organizations meet their human resources needs, including forecasting future needs, recruiting and selecting candidates, and orienting new employees.

Staffing is the process by which organizations ensure that they have the number and type of people needed—at the times and places they're needed—to create, produce, and deliver the organization's products and services. Figure 12.3 illustrates the basic components of the staffing process, which include the following activities.

- **Planning.** Before hiring anyone, an organization should forecast its human resources requirements. By doing so, it can determine the number of employees to hire and the types of competencies they will need. Moreover, management will be able to determine when it will need these employees.

- **Recruitment.** The organization next develops a pool of job candidates from which to select qualified employees. Candidates are recruited, for example, by running ads, contacting employment agencies, and visiting college campuses.

- **Selection and hiring.** After recruiting candidates for available positions, the organization selects and hires those who are most likely to perform well on the job.

- **Orientation.** After employees have been hired, they must be oriented to their jobs and to the organization in general. Effective orientation programs familiarize new employees with company policies, safety rules, and work expectations. They also include explanations of compensation and employee benefits.

- **Movement.** After completing the orientation process, employees continue to participate in the staffing process. Promotions, demotions, and transfers are all part of the process that spans employees' careers.

- **Separation.** The final stage is separation of employees from the organization. Separation can occur as a result of employees finding new jobs, retiring, becoming disabled, or being fired or laid off.

As vacancies occur, the process is repeated.

Those in an organization who have primary responsibility for staffing varies. In some organizations, staffing activities are centralized in the human resources

---

Figure 12.3   **The Staffing Process**

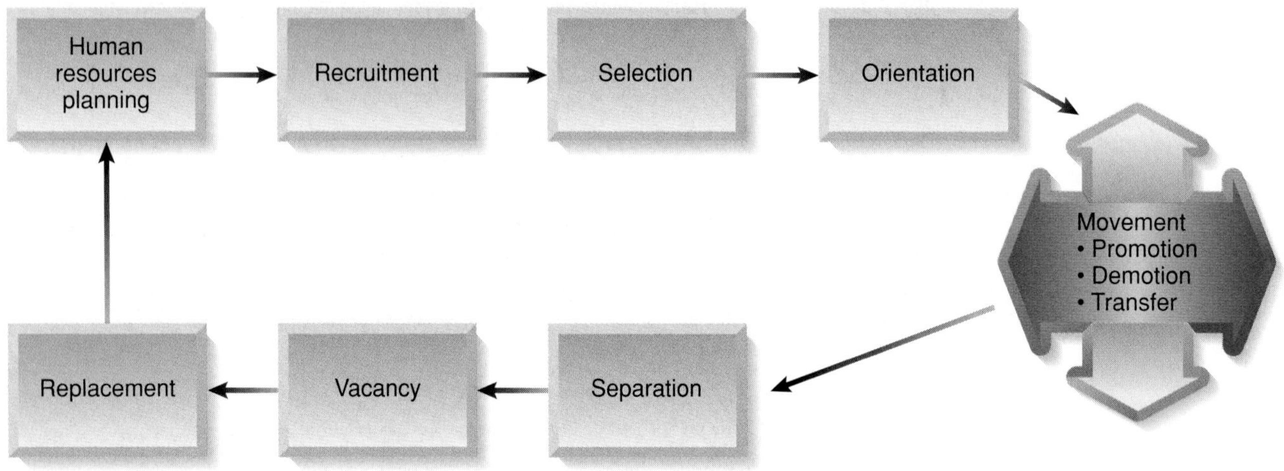

department, and professional HR staff members do the recruiting and hiring. In less centralized organizations, however, line managers often have some responsibility for staffing activities. In decentralized organizations, work teams may have even more responsibility for staffing activities. For example, at IBAX, a health-care information systems software vendor, self-managed work teams carry out many of the staffing activities described in this section, including assessing their own staffing needs and making hiring decisions.

HUMAN RESOURCES PLANNING

The first stage of the staffing process, **human resources planning,** involves forecasting the organization's human resources needs and developing the steps to be taken to meet them. It consists of setting and implementing goals and actions needed to ensure that the right number and type of individuals are available at the appropriate time and place to fulfill organizational needs. As described in the Preview feature, Cirque du Soleil needs to do two types of human resources planning: for temporary and permanent staff. The circus must continually plan for its staffing needs in the cities it tours. What are the days and hours during which temps will be needed? How many ticket sellers and takers, ushers, and security personnel will be needed? In addition, because the circus is growing rapidly, it must make plans to add permanent staff for both its traveling and permanent shows.

Human resources planning is tied directly to strategic planning (see Chapter 7). Typically, business goals are established first, followed by goals for managing human resources that will be consistent with the broader goals. Table 12.3 illustrates how several specific business goals might be translated into goals for managing an organization's human resources.

Determining an organization's human resources needs is the foundation of human resources planning. Let's consider some of the tools and techniques used for planning and forecasting these needs: competency inventories, job analyses, replacement charts, and expert forecasts.

Competency Inventory. A **competency inventory** is a detailed file maintained for each employee that lists level of education, training, experience, length of service, current job title and salary, and performance history. Also included are assessments of the employee's competency levels in terms of the factors included

Table 12.3	Examples of Business Goals and Associated Human Resources Goals

Business Goal	Human Resources Goal
Increase market share	Attract new applicants
Improve efficiencies	Reduce staffing levels
Improve customer service	Push decision making down to lower level employees
Grow through acquisitions and alliances	Provide continuous employment for all employees and rewards for success in line with their achievements
Reduce costs as percentage of revenues	Encourage employees to take on increasing job responsibilities

Source: Adapted from R. S. Schuler. *Managing Human Resources.* Cincinnati: South-Western, 1998.

in the competency model used throughout this book.[11] Our competency model is only one of many that could be used. In fact, a recent survey of 217 companies revealed a total of 148 different competency models in use. However, the purpose of all these competency models is the same: to keep track of the talent in the organization so that it can be nurtured and used effectively.

Many organizations use computerized human resources information systems for storage and easy retrieval of such vital job-related information. For example, Texas Instruments (TI) maintains such files on its thousands of employees. These files help the firm's top managers spot human resources gaps. They also help TI demonstrate that it followed legal requirements when filling a job or taking some other type of personnel action.

Job Analysis. A *job analysis* is a breakdown of the tasks for a specific job and the personal characteristics necessary for their successful performance. A thorough job analysis has two parts: a description and a specification. A *job description* is an outline of a position's essential tasks and responsibilities. Job descriptions are used most often to develop sound and fair compensation and performance appraisal systems. Job descriptions also allow recruiters to give potential candidates realistic descriptions of vacant positions. A *job specification* is a list of the personal characteristics, competencies, and experience a worker needs to carry out a job's tasks and assume its responsibilities. It helps human resources professionals and department managers identify the right person for the job.

Replacement Chart. A *replacement chart* is a diagram showing each management position in the organization, along with the name of the person occupying each position and the names of candidates eligible to replace that person. These charts, which are usually confidential, provide a simple means of forecasting management needs and identifying internal availability of candidates.

Sometimes, holders of lower level positions may not be considered suitable replacements for higher level jobs. In that event, gaps in a firm's replacement chart—positions for which there are no suitable replacements—point to the need for better management development programs or, perhaps, outside recruiting. Jack Welch, CEO of General Electric, says that one of his assessment practices is to have each vice president name a potential replacement. He believes that a vice president who can't name a successor hasn't spent enough time grooming subordinates for advancement.

Expert Forecasts. A variety of expert forecasting methods—some simple, some complex—can be used to determine an organization's demand for human resources. The forecasting method to be used depends on the time horizon, the type, size, and strategy of the organization, and the accuracy of the information available. More than 60 percent of all large firms utilize some type of expert forecasting to project HR needs. Such forecasts may not be very accurate, however. For example, in 1980, IBM forecasted rapid growth in its business and began hiring thousands of new employees. When the forecasts proved to be wrong, IBM kept the new employees anyway, consistent with its policy of no layoffs. Employing people who really weren't needed cost the company a lot of money and may have prevented IBM from making needed strategic corrections sooner. Eventually, the company had to take corrective action because of changes in the industry. Doing so meant that it had to break its commitment of job security to thousands of employees, an action that badly tarnished the corporation's employee-friendly reputation.[12]

Experiences such as IBM's make many companies skittish about hiring too many people. To avoid having to disappoint employees who thought that they had

JOB ANALYSIS
A breakdown of the tasks and responsibilities for a specific job and the personal characteristics, skills, and experience necessary for their successful performance.

JOB DESCRIPTION
An outline of a position's essential tasks and responsibilities.

JOB SPECIFICATION
A list of the personal characteristics, skills, and experience a worker needs to carry out a job's tasks and assume its responsibilities.

REPLACEMENT CHART
A diagram showing each position in the organization, along with the name of the person occupying the position and the names of candidates eligible to replace that person.

a permanent job, companies are now much more likely to hire temporary workers or independent contractors. For example, a recent survey showed that 70 percent of high-tech firms and financial institutions and 50 percent of insurance companies employed temporary accountants.[13] Many companies that reduced their workforce by laying off employees later found that, to achieve their goals, they needed to rehire these same people. According to one large study, approximately 25 percent of the companies that had trimmed their workforces were rehiring people the next year—either for their former jobs or for new permanent jobs.[14] These companies are now learning the true costs associated with forecast errors. For example, to rehire a laid-off staff person, a company may have to offer higher pay. But though they may be paid better, such employees now feel less loyalty to the firm. So, if a better opportunity comes along, they may be more willing to change jobs than to stay put in anticipation of a promotion or pay raise.

RECRUITMENT

RECRUITMENT

The process of searching, both inside and outside the organization, for people to fill vacant positions.

When there aren't enough potential candidates among current employees to meet the demand that human resources planning predicts, the organization must recruit people to fill those jobs. **Recruitment** is the process of searching, both inside and outside the organization, for people to fill vacant positions. Recruitment also should be concerned with identifying potential employees' needs. In this way recruitment not only attracts individuals to the organization, but also increases the chances of retaining them once they're hired. For companies facing labor shortages of key talent, effective recruitment is essential to survival, making it a central strategic issue. As the Planning and Administration Competency account demonstrates, at Cisco Systems maintaining a competitive advantage requires beating other companies in the race for technical employees.

HOW THE ENVIRONMENT AFFECTS RECRUITING

The external environment is particularly important for managers to consider when developing a recruiting program. Three aspects of the external environment that affect recruiting are laws and government regulations, labor unions, and the labor market.

AFFIRMATIVE ACTION PROGRAMS

Efforts intended to ensure that a firm's hiring practices and procedures guarantee equal employment opportunity, as specified by law.

RELEVANT LABOR MARKET

The geographic and skill areas in which an employer usually recruits to fill its positions.

Government Regulations. An organization's recruiting policies and practices are influenced heavily by laws and government regulations. The EEOC requires employers to maintain records on the number of openings in various job groups and the number of applicants for them, broken down by race, ethnicity, sex, and other characteristics. An affirmative action program may require an organization's workforce to reflect the composition of the relevant labor market. **Affirmative action programs** are efforts intended to ensure that a firm's hiring practices and procedures guarantee equal employment opportunity, as specified by law. An employer's **relevant labor market** is the geographic and skill areas in which an employer usually recruits to fill its positions. Thus, if the racial composition of the relevant labor market is 60 percent white, 30 percent black, and 10 percent other, an organization's workforce should approximate the percentages for minority workers. When, in the EEOC's opinion, a company underemploys members of a designated minority, the agency may require the company to engage in special recruiting efforts. However, affirmative action programs, set-asides, and similar types of programs increasingly are coming under attack as reverse discrimination. For example, California voters passed Proposition 209, which outlaws state-sponsored affirmative action programs. In 1997, the U.S. Supreme Court chose not to consider a lawsuit charging that Proposition 209 was unconstitutional. Laws such as Proposi-

Reeling in the Best of the Best at Cisco Systems

Silicon Valley needs two things to keep it going: bright ideas and bright people. Bright ideas are needed for continuous innovation and new products, and bright people are needed to fuel the growth of the booming high-tech industry. These days, finding enough talented people seems to be more of a problem than coming up with new ideas, especially for a company trying to grow. Cisco Systems is one of those companies. During one growth spurt, it was taking on about

1,000 new hires each quarter, which amounted to nearly 10 percent of total job growth in Silicon Valley. CEO John Chambers is clear on this point: "Cisco has the overall goal of getting the top 10 percent to 15 percent of people in our industry. Our philosophy is very simple—if you have the best people in the industry to fit into your culture and you motivate them properly, then you're going to be an industry leader."

Usually, the best people already have good jobs, and often they're happy with their employers. Rather than rely on the pool of applicants that actively are looking for work, Cisco focuses on enticing passive job seekers. To figure out how to locate good potential employees, Cisco first needed to learn how they spend their time. The company did so by holding focus group discussions with some of its current employees—the kind of people Cisco wanted more of. These folks don't spend their time looking through job ads. They're more likely to

be surfing the Internet or attending art festivals and local home and garden fairs. At such events, Cisco recruiters work the crowds, collect business cards and talk up the company. When an interested prospect is identified, Cisco pairs that person with a current employee who has similar interests and skills—a "friend." Friends serve both as screeners to help filter out unsuitable applicants and as advocates to convince the best candidates to accept job offers from Cisco. A thousand Cisco employees have volunteered to be part of the friends program. Do they do this to combat their own loneliness? Probably not. More likely, they're attracted to the generous referral fee and the free-trip lottery ticket that they receive if someone they've befriended is eventually hired.[15]

* * *

To learn more, about Cisco Systems, visit the company's home page at **www.cisco.com**

---

tion 209 remind employers who seek to increase the representation of underrepresented groups (e.g., women and minorities) that their employment practices must not use irrelevant personal attributes as a basis for their decisions. This requirement holds even when the employer's intent is to prevent discrimination against members of protected groups.

UNION SHOP

An organization whose agreement with a union stipulates that, as a condition of continued employment, all employees covered by the contract must already be or must become union members within a specified period of time.

Labor Unions. About three-fifths of the states permit a ***union shop*** provision in management-labor contracts. A union shop is an organization whose agreement with a union stipulates that, as a condition of continued employment, all employees covered by the contract must already be or must become union members within a specified period of time—usually 60 or 90 days.[16] (In states with right-to-work laws, however, employees can't be forced to join a union.)

Labor Market. The labor market itself greatly influences recruiting efforts. If the local supply of qualified employees in a job category exceeds local demand, recruitment will be relatively easy. But when the local supply of qualified employees is limited, recruiting efforts intensify. In recent years, U.S. unemployment has been low by historical standards, hovering near 5 percent. Most employers face a shortage of skilled workers and managers. Some forecasters expect this condition to continue into the foreseeable future.[17] A tight labor supply can make recruiting more difficult for employers, but it generally benefits employees. Employers offer more training to upgrade their employees' skills, and they may have to raise compensation levels and improve working conditions.

Failure to find effective ways to cope with a tight labor supply can doom an organization, which haunts many U.S. corporations. Qualified executives seem particularly scarce. Yet acquiring the best top executives is essential for strategic success. The talent shortage is described in the Strategic Action Competency article.

SOURCES OF RECRUITMENT

Faced with the cost of recruiting, organizations try to identify and attract qualified employees who will stay with them as long as the organization wants them to. Typically, a department manager submits a personnel requisition to the organization's human resources department. The requisition identifies the department in which the opening exists, job title, job specification, salary range, and similar information. Using such requisitions, a recruiter searches for candidates, either inside or outside the organization. Table 12.4 lists several of the more common recruitment sources. Some, such as unsolicited applications, are relatively inexpensive. In contrast, executive search firms typically charge 35 percent of a person's first year's salary as their fee. Which source a recruiter turns to is usually determined by the type of job to be filled. For example, a position at Arthur Andersen specifying an undergraduate accounting degree will be more readily filled through on-campus recruiting efforts or ads in professional journals than through classified ads in Sunday newspapers. To recruit software programmers and multimedia engineers, Internet ads and electronic job fairs are better bets these days.

Although recruitment activities can often seem bureaucratic, informal social processes also play a part. Many people find their jobs through friends who inform them of job openings they know about. In China, this custom is well established. There, people routinely use their personal networks of relationships to influence the hiring process.[18]

Some U.S. companies actively encourage employees to recruit their friends, knowing that friendships can serve as a good information conduit. Silicon Valley firms take the idea of reaching out to friends one step further. In the Valley, engineers are in very short supply, and competition for Stanford University graduates is fierce. To recruit them, some firms stake out particular classes and pursue an elaborate recruiting strategy. One such class is a computer science course that teaches people how to teach others to use computers. Students who complete this class then go on to work as teaching assistants in another computer course. If a company can hire one of these teaching assistants—or better yet, one of the two students who coordinate the work of the teaching assistants—it wins in two ways. First, it gains an employee who has excellent technical skills. Even better, it gets someone who has a direct connection to the students in the introductory class, who will be graduating in the next two years.[19]

SELECTION AND HIRING

The next step in the staffing process is filling the vacant position. Jack Welch, CEO of General Electric, appreciates how important this activity is: "All we can do is bet on the people whom we pick," he says. "So my job is picking the right people."[20] Table 12.5 lists seven information sources available to managers making selection decisions. Many organizations use a combination of information sources.

Résumés. A well-written résumé is clear, concise, and easy to read and understand. It gives (1) personal data (name, address, and telephone number); (2) career

Executive Poaching Pays Off

When Charles Thomas, CEO of Pittsburgh-based Solid State Measurements, Inc., considered what it would take to achieve his objective of significant growth, he realized that he had a problem. "We had very good talent for running a $3 to $5 million company," he observed, "but we didn't have the talent for taking it to $25 million to $50 million in annual sales." At the time, Thomas was doing much of the top-level managerial work related to both day-to-day operations and marketing. To free up time for other things, he needed someone to help him create a top management team to

take on some of this work. But even with the help of a search firm, it took nine months to find someone with the right strategic action competency. What Thomas needed was a manager with the experience required to manage a company that generated 65 percent of its sales overseas and the drive that would guide the company through a period of major growth.

Thomas was surprised by how small the executive talent pool was, and he isn't alone. Despite all the talk of downsizing and layoffs, executives say that the market for top talent is the tightest it's been in twenty-five years. The number of searches being done by executive search firms is up by about 25 percent over past years, and finding the right candidate often takes twice as long as it did just a few years ago. One explanation for the current problem is that downsizing has had an unexpected negative effect on the development of top-level managers. Downsizing usually involves reducing the ranks of middle managers, as well as the number of rungs on the career ladder. As a result, people now have fewer oppor-

tunities to gain the middle management experience they need in order to take on top-level jobs. According to one vice president of an executive search firm, "Forty-five-year-olds are basically doing the same thing they did when they were thirty." Other changes also contribute to the problem. Owing to heightened levels of competition, CEOs and boards don't want to risk hiring someone who merely has high *potential*—they want proven leaders. At the same time, they are quick to dump an executive who doesn't work out and often look outside the company when making top-level hiring decisions. Consequently, talented managers within the company are now less likely to hang around patiently, hoping for a promotion. If a competitor dangles an offer in front of them, chances are they'll take it unless they have strong incentives to stay where they are. Poaching talent from other companies may not be polite, but it's definitely popular.[21]

* * *

To learn more about recruiting, visit the Recruiters Online Network at

www.ipa.com

objectives; (3) education (including grade point average, degree, and major and minor fields of study); (4) work experience, highlighting special skills and responsibilities; (5) descriptions of relevant competencies, activities, and personal information; and (6) the names, addresses, and telephone numbers of references. Keep in mind that many companies now accept electronic résumés, submitted over the Internet. These companies may specify a format for your résumé, or even provide an electronic form for you to complete. In such cases, complying with all the requirements for submitting your résumé is especially important because some of the companies also use software programs designed to scan for information and route your résumé to the appropriate person.

Reference Checks. Because résumés can be falsified easily, managers should request references and conduct reference checks. Many human resources professionals routinely check educational qualifications, including schools attended, study major or majors, degrees awarded, and dates. An applicant's work experience is more difficult to check because employers often are reluctant to provide evalua-

Table 12.4 **Usual Sources for Recruitment of Job Candidates**

Source	Comment
Advertisements	Newspapers carry many help-wanted ads, particularly in their Sunday editions. Available professional positions that require specialized backgrounds are advertised in many professional journals.
Educational institutions	High schools can be an excellent source of office, clerical, and secretarial employees. Trade and vocational schools and community colleges provide many machinists, mechanics, and paraprofessionals. Colleges and universities provide most management trainees and professionals.
Electronic recruitment sites	Many company home pages include information about job openings, as well as a system for electronic submission of résumés.
Employee referrals	One of the best and most consistently used sources of new employees is referral of candidates by current employees. However, reliance on employee referrals may perpetuate past discrimination, if the workforce is homogeneous. A predominantly white male workforce may refer mostly white males, thereby inviting an EEOC investigation.
Job fairs	Job fairs usually involve a large number of companies, all of whom are seeking job applicants with similar sets of skills. For example, one job fair might target computer programmers while another targets people with backgrounds in accounting and financial analysis.
Unsolicited applications	Many jobs are filled by walk-in or write-in candidates. Walk-ins tend to seek lower level jobs, but many professionals submit unsolicited résumés.
Private employment services	These services differ according to who pays for them. Search consultants, or "headhunters," are paid by the organization and tend to focus on upper level professionals and managers. In contrast, employment agencies collect their fees from job seekers.
Public employment services	Many states and the federal government provide employment services at no charge. Such services list primarily the unemployed and to a lesser extent those seeking job changes. The military also provides some placement assistance for veterans.

tions of former employees. Their concern stems from cases in which former employers who have given references have been successfully sued by those who were given bad references. In fact, by law, organizations are required to provide only the job title and dates of employment of a former employee.

Job Applications. Most organizations require candidates to fill out a job application. Increasingly, this step too can be taken over the Internet. Regardless of whether you apply in person, through regular mail, or electronically, the job application is used to gather information about job-related experiences and accomplish-

- **Résumés**
- **Reference checks**
- **Job applications**
- **Realistic job previews**
- **Interviews**
- **Tests**
- **Assessment centers**

ments. In many cases this application serves the same purpose as a résumé. In addition, employers also can use it to gather information for EEOC reports.

Realistic Job Previews. A screening technique gaining in popularity is the *realistic job preview,* which clearly shows candidates a job's tasks or requirements, thus pointing out its good and bad aspects. American Airlines has one of its industry's best realistic job previews. Potential flight attendants are shown a variety of tasks that they would be required to learn and perform, such as safety procedures and serving techniques. In a full-sized cabin mockup at the Dallas-Fort Worth Learning Center, they get a realistic look at the job.

REALISTIC JOB PREVIEW
A screening technique that clearly shows candidates a job's tasks or requirements.

Especially when labor is in short supply, the temptation is to give an optimistic preview to job applicants, instead of a realistic one. This happened to Andrew Lazear, who was lured away from his job on Long Island by the offer of a job in Los Angeles. Recruiters for Rykoff-Sexton, Inc., a specialty food manufacturer, offered Lazear a raise and the promise of both rapid future pay raises and promotions. After six months of being wooed, Lazear took the job and moved his family. He met his goals and performed well for two years, but then Rykoff-Sexton had financial difficulties and needed to reorganize. Lazear was fired, and decided to sue. The California Supreme Court ruled that he had a right to do so because he gave up a job based on false promises. In this case, the unrealistic job preview gave the employee a basis for holding the employer accountable, despite the fact that Lazear had no written employment guarantee.[22]

Interviews. In making a final selection, most human resources professionals rely on a combination of interviews and tests. Although commonly used, interviews vary in their ability to predict on-the-job performance accurately. In general, situational interviews that probe what the applicant would do in different situations are better predictors of performance than interviews that focus on past work.[23] Nevertheless, an interview can be misleading. Most people can remain alert and pleasant for a thirty-minute interview, but that doesn't mean that they can perform well eight hours a day, day in and day out.

CONTRAST ERROR
Basing a candidate's rating on a comparison with the preceding interviewee.

SIMILARITY ERROR
A bias in favor of candidates that look or act like the interviewer.

HALO ERROR
Judging a candidate's overall potential on the basis of a single characteristic, allowing it to overshadow other characteristics.

Research indicates that interviewers tend to decide about a person early in the interview and then spend the rest of the time seeking information to support that decision. Furthermore, early impressions often are erroneous. Three types of judgment errors are especially common in interviews: A ***contrast error*** occurs when an interviewer bases the rating of a particular candidate on a comparison with the preceding interviewee. A ***similarity error*** occurs when an interviewer forms a bias in favor of a candidate who looks or acts like the interviewer. A ***halo error*** occurs when an interviewer judges the candidate's overall potential on the basis of a single characteristic (e.g., how well the candidate dresses or talks or where she or he attended college), allowing it to overshadow the candidate's other characteristics.

Despite its potential drawbacks, an interview does serve some useful purposes. It allows the interviewer and applicant to learn what each has to offer the other. Although it may not determine whether someone will perform well, an interview may indicate how well an applicant will fit in with other members of a work group. Finally, human nature is such that most people simply won't hire someone they haven't met.[24]

When you first enter the world of work, you probably will be interviewed many times before you're in a position to conduct interviews yourself. You can learn a lot about how to conduct a successful interview by carefully observing and analyzing how interviewers interact with you. Typically, someone about to graduate from college goes through three types of employment interviews: on-campus, plant or office, and final selection. Candidates should be aware that the interviewer's approach can affect how they conduct themselves during the interview.[25] An aloof approach may stifle responses, but a gregarious interviewer might get the interviewee to open up and be more expressive.

COGNITIVE ABILITY TEST
A written test that measures general intelligence, verbal ability, numerical ability, reasoning ability, and so on.

PERFORMANCE TEST
A test that requires job candidates to perform simulated job tasks.

Tests. Many organizations use tests in addition to interviews to screen and select candidates. Tests may be oral, written, or performance based. A common type of written test, the **cognitive ability test,** measures general intelligence; verbal, numerical, and reasoning ability; and the like. Such tests have proved to be relatively successful in predicting which applicants are qualified for certain jobs. Another type of test commonly used is the performance test. A **performance test** requires a candidate to perform simulations of actual job tasks. One example is a code-writing test for computer programmers. Another example is an in-basket exercise. In this case, job candidates receive a stack of letters, notes, memos, telephone messages, faxes, and other items and are told to imagine that they have been promoted to a new position. They are given a specific amount of time to deal appropriately with these items. In most cases they will have the opportunity to explain or discuss their decisions in a follow-up interview.[26]

A performance test is an excellent selection method, but giving one can be difficult to do for some jobs. Nucor, a steel manufacturer, found a creative way to use performance testing when hiring new steelworkers. When Nucor has construction work done in its own plants, Nucor managers watch the construction workers at the job sites. They look for plumbers, carpenters, electricians, and other skilled workers who demonstrate good work habits and then attempt to hire these people to take jobs as steelworkers.[27]

Having good work habits means that workers do more than just complete assigned tasks well. Having good work habits also means assisting others and generally contributing to the success of the entire team or organization. Although Nucor has to train the skilled craftspeople that it hires in how to work with steel, it does so knowing that the training investment is likely to pay off in terms of gaining an employee who will fit well into Nucor's demanding organizational culture.

When a manager can't actually watch potential employees doing a job, watching them perform a simulation may be the next best thing. At the BMW auto plant in South Carolina, job candidates work for 90 minutes on a simulated assembly line. To be hired, they must show more than their technical skills. They also must show the mental and physical stamina required to perform well in BMW's "aerobic workplace."[28]

Unlike cognitive ability and performance tests, personality tests have no right or wrong answers. Recall that personality refers to the unique blend of characteristics that define an individual. In jobs that involve a great deal of contact with other people, such as sales agents and many types of service jobs, a personality characteristic referred to as *extraversion* is a good predictor of future job performance. Extraverts tend to be talkative, good-natured, and gregarious—characteristics that facilitate smooth interactions with customers and clients. Another personality characteristic of interest to many employers is conscientiousness. Conscientious people seem to have a strong sense of purpose, obligation, and persistence—all of which lead to high performance in almost any type of work situation.[29]

Many organizations now routinely test for drugs. Testing positive for drugs usually keeps an applicant from being hired. Penalties for existing employees who test positive depend on the organization's policies and procedures. Some organizations fire employees with positive test results. Other organizations provide counseling and treatment programs for employees who test positive. Once a hotly contested issue, particularly the random testing of existing employees, drug testing by organizations is now more widely accepted. It's often accepted because of the benefits of a drug-free workplace, including reduced insurance premiums, lower turnover, and fewer workers' compensation claims. Additionally, substance abuse can lower workplace productivity. Although the full extent of the impact is uncertain, workplace substance abuse is estimated to cost American businesses about $120 billion annually.[30]

As part of the selection process, honesty tests are becoming more common because employee theft costs U.S. businesses an estimated $40 billion annually.[31] An honesty test is a specialized paper-and pencil measure of a person's tendency to behave dishonestly. Some honesty tests also attempt to predict the likelihood that people will break rules, abuse sick leave privileges, or use drugs at work.[32]

ORIENTATION

Upon completion of the selection and hiring process, the employee enters orientation. *Orientation* either formally or informally introduces new employees to their job responsibilities, their co-workers, and the organization's policies. When orientation programs are effective, both the newly hired employees and the organization benefit in several ways. An effective orientation program can accomplish the following goals.

- **Promote realistic job expectations.** Even experienced employees must gain a fundamental understanding of their new organization and "how things really work" because every organization has unique norms, networks of co-workers, and ways of getting things done.

- **Promote functional work behavior.** Properly oriented employees can become effective quickly because they know which behaviors are valued and which aren't.

- **Reduce employee turnover.** Properly oriented new employees are eased into their jobs and therefore, feeling reassured, are more apt to stay than employees thrust hurriedly into their new jobs with little orientation.

PUTTING IT ALL TOGETHER

Having the right employees in the right jobs at the right time and place requires a fully integrated staffing process. All the activities that we've described must be coordinated and used intelligently to meet the organization's human resources needs. To see the whole picture, consider how Marriott Hotels handle the staffing process.

Quality of service in the hotel industry depends on the quality and competencies of the organization's employees. Recognizing this fact, Marriott Hotels staffing process designed to provide the organization with the best qualified, cated, and enthusiastic workforce it can find. What is its staffing process like? Let's consider a typical hotel in the Marriott chain.

The process begins when applicants respond to a self-administered test on a personal computer. The computer program asks questions such as: Why did you leave your last job? How well do you get along with co-workers? How well do you get along with superiors? How frequently do you get frustrated at work? How would you rate your organizational skills? Do other people think that you're adaptable? The computer program is designed to analyze the applicant's responses and prepare a list of questions to be used by a manager in conducting a later interview. The computer analysis also reports the questions on which the applicant paused longer than normal—viewed as a potential red flag that the applicant may not be telling the complete truth. The test responses and the interview are used to select employees who fit Marriott's needs and who are likely to remain with the company for a reasonable period of time. This selection process has contributed to a steady decline in Marriott's turnover rate.

Marriott also emphasizes orientation. It begins with a formal eight-hour training program. During the next ninety days each new employee is assigned to a mentor for guidance. Each new employee attends refresher training sessions at the end of the first and second months. When each class of new employees completes the ninety-day orientation period, the hotel treats them to a banquet.[33]

TRAINING AND DEVELOPMENT

4

EXPLAIN HOW TRAINING AND DEVELOPMENT PROGRAMS CAN IMPROVE EMPLOYEE PERFORMANCE

TRAINING AND DEVELOPMENT
Activities aimed at helping employees overcome the limitations, current or anticipated, that are causing them to perform at less than the desired level.

In addition to their orientation programs, many organizations offer employees more extensive training and development experiences. The main purpose of ***training and development*** is to overcome the limitations, current or anticipated, that are causing an employee to perform at less than the desired level. An organization may save money by recruiting trained individuals, but many organizations have found that training and development programs are preferable to hiring experienced employees. For example, EDS found that hiring "green" recruits is better than hiring experienced workers from other organizations because it doesn't have to *retrain* the new employees to do things its way.

When organizations undergo major changes, training and development activities often are necessary to help employees make the transition to a new way of doing things. Redesigning work around teams is one type of change that creates high demand for training and development. IBAX discovered the importance of training and development when it went through a restructuring from a traditional hierarchy to six autonomous product-based units. The restructuring included a shift to self-managed teams that were accountable for their own business performance. In many cases jobs were also redesigned, giving employees additional tasks and responsibilities. Training often was needed before employees were capable of taking on these new tasks.

In addition to changing the specific technical tasks of employees, team-based designs require employees to make the shift from working more or less independently to collaborating and working closely with others. The following Teamwork Competency piece describing British Petroleum's experience with self-managed teams illustrates the role of training in this type of situation.

When the Norwegian arm of British Petroleum (BP Norge) decided that it needed to dismantle its hierarchy and move toward becoming a network of collaborators, it decided to restructure the organization around self-managing teams. If employees were willing to assume leadership and work across functions, the company believed that it could speed up decision making, reduce costs and cycle times, and increase innovation. Despite the strong business argument supporting a change to teamwork, the

organization found that pushing the change was difficult.

Nine months of frustration led management to conclude that a systematic training initiative was needed to educate the organization and support the development of new teamwork competencies. The first phase of training focused on changing old thought patterns and helping people understand the link between BP Norge's business strategy and need for self-managed teams. Because employees had been through many change efforts in the past, they had become skeptical and resistant. To convince them that more change was needed, a team of American and Norwegian facilitators conducted two-day workshops, which were attended by a mix of people from all levels and functional specialties. Oil rig workers and senior managers sat side-by-side, as did Norwegians and Americans—even if they couldn't speak each other's language. Prior to the workshop, everyone completed a prework assignment.

First, they watched a video that explained self-managed teams and showed how other organizations had used them successfully. They also interviewed a few colleagues to find out what they thought about self-managed teams. At the workshop, discussion focused on understanding the process through which teamwork develops. Participants were taught that denial about the need for change and resistance to it are natural reactions, but they were also encouraged to share their concerns with each other and seek answers to their questions. Throughout the two-day workshops, participants also began practicing the behaviors that they would need in their new team environment. These behaviors included taking risks, communicating about their feelings, and teaching others as well as learning from others.[34]

* * *

To learn more about BP Norge, visit the company's home page at

www.bp.com

TRAINING FOR THE JOB

Training refers to improving an employee's skills to the point where he or she can do the current job more effectively. Training methods often used by organizations are listed in Table 12.6, along with their primary advantages and disadvantages.

For employees who are unable to read, write, do arithmetic, or solve problems well enough to perform even simple tasks, basic skills training will be needed. Such employees can't write letters to customers, read warning labels on chemical containers, or understand machine operating symbols. Organizations spend large sums of money on remedial training for employees because they believe that, if employees can master certain basic skills, they can perform a variety of jobs and be able to deal with some of the new technologies.[35]

DEVELOPMENT PROGRAMS

The intent of development programs is to improve an employee's competencies in preparation for future jobs. Before sending an employee to a development program, a needs analysis is made to identify that person's particular strengths and developmental needs. For supervisors and managers, developmental needs often include inability to set goals with others, negotiate interpersonal conflicts, and conduct performance appraisal reviews.[36]

Method	Advantage	Disadvantage
Job rotation	Provides exposure to many jobs; real learning experience can help develop many competencies at once.	Doesn't convey full sense of responsibility; time on each job is too short.
Programmed instruction	Provides individualized learning and feedback.	Time-consuming to develop; cost effective only for large groups.
Videos	Conveys consistent information to all employees.	Doesn't allow for individualized pacing and feedback.
Simulation	Creates lifelike situations to teach team-work and communication competencies.	Can't always duplicate real situations; costly to design and run.
Role-playing	Gives insights into others' jobs; often focuses on communication and global awareness competencies.	Can't fully create real situations.
Interactive media	Allows self-paced learning; is involving and can include individualized feedback.	Costly to develop; requires sophisticated technology and equipment to deliver the training.

Some development programs are tailored to fit specific individual and organizational needs. For example, Hoechst requires its managers to attend at least forty hours of management development programs each year at one of its development centers. Such programs often help the managers gain insight into how the organization operates, thereby improving their planning and administration competency. They may also teach teamwork competency, especially the components needed for managers to work in a TQM environment. Many large companies, such as GE, McDonald's, and Motorola, provide so many hours of development activities to so many employees that they have built company "universities," complete with classrooms, "dorm" rooms, and other amenities of a typical college campus.

Development programs sometimes are intended to help employees gain a broader perspective than that needed in the current or next job. Organizations may encourage employees to attend these more general development programs as part of a long-term strategy for developing a cadre of high-potential employees and lower level managers who, several years in the future, may eventually become upper level managers. For example, many organizations send selected managers to university-sponsored management development programs. The organization wants to broaden these managers' perspectives and prepare them for general (as opposed to functional) management positions. Because employees from various organizations are involved in such programs, participants learn not only from the instructor but also from their peers. Training in these programs often is designed to help participants develop strategic action competency.

TRAINING AND DEVELOPMENT FOR GLOBAL ASSIGNMENTS

One of the increasingly important challenges for organizations is preparing people to be expatriate employees working in a nation other than their home country. Without this preparation, such employees may not be able to take on and successfully complete an overseas assignment. Table 12.7 identifies some of the issues that organizations must address in preparing their employees for a foreign assignment. Particularly important is cross-cultural training, including cultural awareness, lan-

Table 12.7 **Typical Issues Facing Expatriate Employees**

- What is the host country's business culture like? What is its management style? Do I have the skills I'll need to handle relationships with my employees?

- Will this assignment be good for my long-term career prospects? Can I expect to be promoted when I return? How will I be treated if I don't perform well in my new overseas job?

- What is the country like? What are its customs? Will I be able to adjust to the culture?

- Will my family be able to adjust to the new situation? Will my spouse be able to find suitable employment? Will my children be able to adjust to going to school in another country? How good is the educational system there?

- How will we learn enough of the new language to communicate effectively?

- Where will we live? How will the new housing arrangements compare to our current home? What will happen to our current home when we leave for the new assignment?

- What are the tax and other financial issues I will have to address as an expatriate? Who will be available to advise me on these topics? Will the company pay me in a way that protects my income from high foreign tax rates?

- How will our medical needs be taken care of? If someone in my family becomes seriously ill, will we be able to come back and receive treatment from our family physician?

Source: Adapted from S. Taylor and N. Napier. Working in Japan: Lessons from women expatriates. *Sloan Management Review,* Spring 1996, pp. 76–84; C. Gould. What's the latest in global compensation? *Global Workforce,* July 1997, pp. 17–20; Executives overseas. *HR Focus,* March 1997, pp. 6–7; and L. Grant. That overseas job could derail your career. *Fortune,* April 14, 1997, p. 166.

guage instruction, and practical assistance with matters of daily living.[37] Such training improves employees' global awareness competency by creating sensitivity to the host country's culture and appreciation for it. Language training improves an expatriate employee's communication competency. Practical assistance with matters of daily living helps employees and their families adjust to life in the new environment, thereby enhancing their self-management competency.

Colgate-Palmolive is one organization that effectively prepares employees throughout the world for job assignments in other countries. The New York-based Colgate-Palmolive Company operates in more than 170 countries and derives over 70 percent of its $7 billion of annual revenue from overseas markets. Colgate-Palmolive's success is due in part to its global human resources strategy of selecting and preparing people for job assignments around the world. And not just its U.S. workers are being prepared for overseas assignments—people from many countries are being prepared for assignments somewhere other than their homelands. About 60 percent of Colgate's expatriate employees are from countries other than the United States.

In preparing its employees for global assignments, Colgate-Palmolive considers both the needs of the company and the needs of its employees. HRM professionals help determine the competencies that employees will need to meet Colgate's business goals. They also help identify and develop employees who have what the company calls *global talent.* These are people who are interested in the global environment, want the challenge of a global assignment, and are motivated to work toward the company's global business goals. They also are people who would contribute to the country in which they live and would be likely to experience personal growth from the assignment.[38]

5

DISCUSS SEVERAL USES AND METHODS OF APPRAISING PERFORMANCE

PERFORMANCE APPRAISAL

The process of systematically evaluating each employee's job-related strengths, developmental needs, and progress toward meeting goals and determining ways to improve the employee's job performance.

360-DEGREE APPRAISAL SYSTEM

A performance review system that gathers feedback from an employee's colleagues inside the organization and from people outside the organization with whom the employee does business.

One of the primary responsibilities of managers is to assess their employees' performance. Their evaluations influence who is promoted, demoted, transferred, and dismissed, and the size of raises that employees receive. Managers usually have to explain ratings to their subordinates, who may—in fact, probably will—disagree with them in at least some respects.[39]

Performance appraisal is the process of systematically evaluating each employee's job-related strengths, developmental needs, and progress toward achieving goals, and then determining ways to improve the employee's job performance. This function is essential if the organization is to reward fairly the efforts of good performers, redirect the efforts of struggling performers, and know when to dismiss inadequate performers.

An important part of performance appraisal involves an assessment of each employee's progress toward achieving his or her goals. To be effective, those goals must be clear and specific so that an employee knows what is to be achieved—and they should be challenging. However, goals alone aren't sufficient. For goals to lead to improved performance, employees also need feedback about how well they are doing, and suggestions for how they can improve. Regular assessment of progress toward attaining goals helps employees remain motivated and solve problems as they arise. Regular feedback also encourages periodic reexamination of goals to determine whether they should be adjusted.

One popular way to provide employees with feedback is the ***360-degree appraisal system.*** The organization gathers assessments of the employee from a variety of sources—supervisors, subordinates, colleagues inside the company, people outside the organization with whom the employee does business, and even a self-appraisal by the employee. Usually, several people in each of these roles provide assessments. The identities of specific individual assessors aren't disclosed to the employee. The assessments might focus on specific areas of job performance, or they might be judgments about the person's competencies. Feedback to the employee involves explaining how other people view the employee, comparing these perceptions to the employee's self-assessments, and developing action plans for how to improve in the future. Thus, in this instance, the performance appraisal process is closely aligned with training and development activities.

USING PERFORMANCE APPRAISALS

Performance appraisals can be invaluable aids for making many types of human resources management decisions. As we have just indicated, decisions about the types of training and development experiences that an employee needs can be influenced by the results of performance appraisal. Pay decisions are another use of performance appraisal information. Many organizations try to motivate employees by basing pay, bonuses, and other financial rewards on performance. To do so, organizations must have a method for accurately measuring employee performance. Performance appraisal information also helps guide decisions about personnel movement. Who should receive a promotion? Who should be transferred, demoted, or terminated? All such personnel movements should be based on performance-related factors, not gender, race, age, or other factors unrelated to the job.

Most people who have given or received performance appraisals would agree that a serious problem with them is their subjective nature. Let's briefly examine four errors commonly made when giving performance appraisals: rater characteristics, leniency, halo effect, and central tendency.

RATER CHARACTERISTICS
The personal attributes that a performance appraiser brings to the task, which often exert a subtle and indirect influence on performance appraisals.

LENIENCY
A rating error that occurs when an individual rates all employees in a group higher than they deserve.

HALO EFFECT
A rating error that occurs when knowledge of performance on one dimension colors the ratings on all others.

CENTRAL TENDENCY
A rating error that occurs when all employees are given an average rating, even when their performances varies.

RANKING METHOD
A type of performance appraisal that compares employees doing the same or similar work.

GRAPHIC RATING METHOD
A type of performance appraisal that evaluates employees on a series of performance dimensions, usually along a 5- or 7-point scale.

BEHAVIORALLY ANCHORED RATING SCALE
A type of performance appraisal that describes specific job behaviors along a continuum of intensity.

Each person engaged in rating the performance of others brings his or her own characteristics to the task. Thus **rater characteristics** often exert a subtle and indirect influence on performance appraisals. Younger and less experienced managers, who may have received low evaluations themselves, tend to rate others more strictly than do older, more experienced managers. Managers who have high self-esteem, low anxiety, good social skills, and emotional stability give more accurate performance appraisals than managers with the opposite personality traits.[40]

Leniency occurs when an individual rates all employees in a group higher than they deserve. Leniency is particularly likely to occur when there are no organizational norms against high ratings and when rewards aren't tied to performance appraisals. Tying rewards to appraisals places a natural limit on the number of high ratings that a manager can give and the organization can afford.

The **halo effect** occurs when the rater's knowledge of an employee's performance on one dimension colors the rating on all others. In some cases an equal rating on all dimensions doesn't reflect an error in judgment—an employee may actually perform all tasks equally well or equally poorly. However, most people do some tasks better than other tasks, so their ratings should vary from one performance dimension to another.

Central tendency is a rating error that occurs when a manager rates all employees "average," even when their performances vary. Managers with broad spans of control and little opportunity to observe behavior are likely to play it safe by rating most of their subordinates in the middle of the scale rather than high or low.

METHODS OF PERFORMANCE APPRAISAL

The problems that we've discussed highlight the difficulties encountered in assessing employee performance objectively. Most attempts to solve these problems have focused on devising new methods of appraising performance. As a result, many different types of rating formats and evaluation techniques are used. Here we focus on three general types: the ranking, graphic rating, and behavioral rating methods.

Ranking. The **ranking method** is used to appraise performance by comparing employees doing the same or similar work. In simple ranking, the rater lists employees from best to worst and thus is easy to use. It also reduces the effects of leniency because the rater can't give everyone a high evaluation. Rankings are especially useful for making defensible promotion decisions or reducing the size of the workforce. The manager can simply select names from the top down on the list until all promotion vacancies are filled—or from the bottom up until all necessary workforce reductions are made. Because rankings tend to be based on overall performance, however, they aren't very useful in providing specific feedback. Knowing that she is ranked fourth out of ten people, for example, doesn't tell an employee what she needs to do to become the top-ranked employee, or even number two.

Graphic Rating. The **graphic rating method** of performance appraisal evaluates employees on a series of performance dimensions, usually along a 5- or 7-point scale. Such scales are the most widely used form of performance evaluation. A typical rating scale may be from 1 to 5, with 1 representing poor performance and 5 representing outstanding performance.

Behavioral Rating. A **behaviorally anchored rating scale** (BARS) describes specific job behaviors along a continuum of intensity. It is similar to the graphic rating method in that a numerical scale typically is used to measure a range of performance. However, BARS differs from graphic rating in terms of the level of descriptive detail for each point on the scale. An example of a behaviorally anchored rating scale that can be used to assess student oral presentations is shown in Figure 12.4.

The specificity of BARS is both an advantage and a disadvantage. The advantage is that performance-related behaviors are described carefully and in detail. Therefore it is useful in providing specific performance feedback to the person being evaluated. The disadvantage is that developing a behavioral scale can be time-consuming and costly because of the precise observable descriptions of behaviors that are required.

PERFORMANCE APPRAISAL INTERVIEWS

After evaluating an employee, a manager must communicate his or her performance appraisal judgments to the employee. The manager usually does so in a performance appraisal interview.

During the interview, the manager and the employee should exchange information about the employee's strengths and developmental needs. The focus should be on job-related performance, not on personality, habits, or mannerisms that don't affect job performance. Managers often keep a diary to record actual events that illustrate effective and ineffective behaviors of the employee. Allowing the employee to respond to these observations makes the session meaningful to both the manager and employee. Finally, the manager and employee should mutually agree on goals for improvement.

Figure 12.4 **Sample of a Behaviorally Anchored Rating Scale (BARS)**

Behavioral Focus: Oral Presentation Style

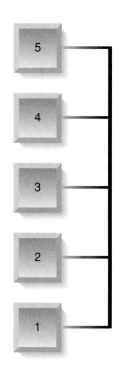

Speaks with clarity; tone and pitch of voice conveys interest and excitement; knows material so well that notes aren't needed; maintains good eye contact with many people in audience — 5

Pleasant and entertaining speaking voice; speaks largely without notes; good eye contact with audience but concentrates on certain people — 4

Occasional lapses into monotone voice; varies between reading from written speech and speaking without written materials; when not relying on written materials, stares at selected people in the audience or stares over the heads of entire audience — 3

Nervous edge in voice, particularly when not reading from prepared script; some use of distracting speech patterns and mannerisms; relies heavily on reading from prepared materials; occasional glances at audience — 2

Speaks in monotone voice; uses distracting speech patterns and mannerisms; reads prepared speech; virtually no eye contact with members of audience — 1

CHOOSING THE RIGHT APPROACH TO PERFORMANCE APPRAISAL

Like all the other human resources management activities, the review of employee performance should be consistent with and support the organization's strategic goals, culture, and operating systems and procedures. For example, in organizations having a low-cost strategy, such as Wal-Mart, ways to increase employee efficiency should be stressed. In organizations pursuing a differentiated strategy based on outstanding customer service, such as Nordstrom or BMW, employees must be able to work in teams, solve customer problems collaboratively, and work without direct supervision.

Some advocates of total quality management (TQM) suggest that traditional performance appraisals are incompatible with TQM. They argue that traditional performance appraisal focuses on individual goals and performance standards and so may undermine teamwork. In contrast, TQM focuses on the process and the system, emphasizing team, departmental, and organizational performance. Also, traditional performance appraisal places responsibility for failure on the individual. Many TQM experts attribute up to 90 percent of all performance problems to management practices, including poor selection and inadequate training. Finally, traditional performance appraisal may encourage some people to manipulate or avoid the system for personal gain. TQM focuses on improving the system for collective gain.[41]

Do these differing viewpoints mean that companies adopting a TQM approach should no longer assess individual performance? Not at all. Ensoniq Corporation, a maker of electronic keyboards for musicians, adopted a TQM approach in order to compete effectively in the global market. In doing so, Ensoniq followed W. Edwards Deming's philosophy that *traditional* performance appraisal can hurt motivation, morale, and performance by pitting employees against each other in a competitive battle for approval. Competition arises because individual-focused performance appraisal usually means that the performance of about half the employees will be rated below average and about half above average. So Ensoniq doesn't use traditional performance appraisals.

At Ensoniq the purpose of the performance review is to encourage dialogue between employee and manager regarding ways to enhance performance. Reviews occur every four months. Focussing on an employee's total effectiveness in terms of communication, leadership, adaptability, and initiative, the reviews are qualitative rather than quantitative. That is, no numbers are assigned to the supervisor's evaluations. This approach helps the employee focus on how to improve and avoids the distraction of wondering about how he or she stacks up against other employees. Quantitative measures of individual-level performance aren't needed in Ensoniq's review system because the company's TQM system provides immediate and direct quantitative feedback to employees. Thus, although Ensoniq doesn't use a traditional performance appraisal system, it still assesses individual performance and uses these assessments to promote behaviors that contribute to TQM's effectiveness.[42]

As the Ensoniq example illustrates, the performance appraisal system should foster the behaviors that an organization needs in order to remain competitive. Different strategies may call for different types of behaviors and different approaches to performance appraisal. Nevertheless, almost all organizations use some form of performance measurement that involves subjective evaluation of employee performance.

The purpose of any compensation system is to reward employees equitably, to provide the means to attract potential new employees, and to motivate and retain good employees. A total compensation system has two major components: direct compensation and indirect compensation. **Direct compensation** is a person's base wage or salary and any incentive pay received. **Indirect compensation** refers to benefits required by law (e.g., Social Security contributions and unemployment compensation) and those provided voluntarily by the employer (e.g., medical insurance, retirement plans, and life insurance).

BASE WAGE OR SALARY

The two main approaches to establishing the base wage or salary for employees are job-based pay and competency-based pay. With **job-based pay,** compensation is linked to the specific tasks that a person performs. To establish the pay level, a job evaluation is done to determine the job's comparative monetary worth. Job-based pay has been widely used in the past, but it presents some serious problems for organizations. In particular, job-based pay

- reinforces an organizational culture that emphasizes hierarchy and centralized decision making and control, and limits employee participation;

- creates status differentials that can foster competition rather than cooperation among employees; and

- may fail to reward the work behavior that is necessary for organizations to adapt and survive in a rapidly changing environment.[43]

Competency-based pay links compensation to people's competencies—that is, their job-relevant skills, knowledge, and experience. Employees with higher competency levels receive higher pay than those with lower competency levels. Thus competency-based pay encourages employees to develop their competencies, thereby becoming more valuable to the organization. As a result, the organization can be more flexible and adaptable to changing demands. With a more flexible workforce, the organization may need fewer employees and thus reduce human resources costs. Also, flexibility can enhance productivity and product or service quality.

Whether an organization uses job-based pay or competency-based pay for establishing the base wage or salary, it should strive for equity in its compensation system. Equity, which concerns fairness, can dramatically affect employee motivation and performance. (We discuss the motivational basis of equity in Chapter 14.) When employees perceive the compensation system to be equitable, they are more likely to do their jobs well and be committed to the organization than when they perceive the compensation system to be inequitable. In fact, inequitable pay can result in a variety of counterproductive employee behaviors.[44]

Sometimes a company will establish a reward system with the best of intentions only to discover that it creates perceptions of inequity—and thus is ineffective. Modern of Marshfield is a furniture manufacturer with 100 employees in Marshfield, Wisconsin. The company tried two different reward systems to motivate employees to submit cost-saving suggestions. Initially, Bill Mork, Modern's CEO, implemented a reward system that was run by management and relied on recognition. After reviewing all employee suggestions that had been implemented during the month,

DIRECT COMPENSATION
An employee's base wage or salary and any incentive pay received.

INDIRECT COMPENSATION
Benefits that are required by law and those that are provided voluntarily by the employer.

JOB-BASED PAY
Compensation that is linked to the specific tasks a person performs.

COMPETENCY-BASED PAY
Compensation that is linked to people's competencies.

the company's managers selected a "colleague of the month." This person didn't receive any cash but was honored with a special parking place and a handshake in front of the assembled employees. The results of the reward program were disappointing—few suggestions were offered, and winners were called "brown-nosers" by their co-workers.

Mork decided to change the reward system so that an employee would get a cash award plus 10 percent of the estimated savings whenever the company implemented that employee's suggestion. An additional 10 percent of the estimated savings went into a fund, the proceeds of which were distributed annually to all employees who made useful suggestions. Employees who had their suggestions implemented participated in monthly drawings for prizes ranging from T-shirts to TV sets. A colleague of the month was still selected, but a panel of the six previous winners made the selection. The employee selected as colleague of the year won an expenses-paid trip for two to an exotic location. Employee suggestions increased to 1,200 per year—approximately one per employee per month. Employee attitudes changed when they saw people getting checks. The winners weren't perceived as brown-nosers any longer. As Mork says, "Suddenly, the winner became someone who could buy a round of beer."[45]

The employees of Modern of Marshfield probably were unmotivated by the first reward system because they perceived it to be inequitable. Employees whose suggestions were implemented didn't perceive the reward to be large enough to be meaningful and worth the scorn of their fellow workers. This situation of perceived inequity changed with the second reward system. Employees then perceived that they were being rewarded fairly for their suggestions.

INCENTIVE PAY

Incentive pay is intended to link at least a portion of pay to job performance to encourage superior performance. To be effective, incentives must be aligned with the behaviors that help achieve the organization's goals. In addition to increasing employee motivation to perform well, incentive pay can reduce turnover among good performers. High performers are more motivated to stay with an organization when they are rewarded more generously than poor performers. In addition, incentive pay can be cost effective. Savings result from productivity improvements and from the organization's ability to match compensation costs and performance levels better.[46]

Although incentive pay is an attractive compensation option for organizations, it isn't problem free. It works best, for example, when employees trust the system to work properly. The organization must have an effective performance appraisal system, and employees must trust management to use the system equitably. Also, administering a pay-for-performance system is more time-consuming than using a base wage or salary system with periodic across-the-board increases. Finally, unions tend to oppose pay-for-performance systems based on individual performance or demand strict rules to guide their use. Unions are more receptive to systems that are based on team, plant, or companywide performance.[47]

Individual-Based Incentive Pay. Individual-based incentive pay includes piece-rate incentives, commissions, bonuses, and merit pay. Piece-rate incentives involve the adjustment of a fixed amount of money paid for each unit of output produced when the number of units produced exceeds a standard output rate.[48] Piece rate incentives tend to focus employees on those aspects of the job that increase their output. Thus other useful activities such as machine maintenance or the training of new employees may be neglected.

Typically used with salespeople, commissions are compensation based on a percentage of total sales. Some salespeople work on a base salary plus commission. Others work on a straight commission basis, with all their direct compensation being incentive pay. Unfortunately, this creates a temptation for some individuals to use high-pressure sales tactics or to behave unethically in order to generate income.

BONUSES
Lump-sum payments given for achieving a particular performance goal.

Bonuses are lump-sum payments given for achieving a particular performance goal. Bonuses may be one-time payments linked to nonrepetitive goals. For instance, the Lawrence, Kansas, plant of Quaker Oats bases part of its annual lump sum payouts on the achievement of goals, such as completing plant training on schedule, maintaining employee participation levels, and developing departmental mission statements.[49] Bonuses also may be linked to the annual achievement of continuing performance goals. At Duke Power Company, cash awards to employees in thirty different business units are based on the company's achieving its targeted return on equity and the business unit's realizing its specific goals.[50]

MERIT PAY
A permanent increase in base pay linked to an individual's performance during the preceding year.

Merit pay is a permanent increase in base pay linked to an individual's performance during the preceding year. Often merit increases are based on subjective measures of performance, such as supervisory ratings. Although employees generally prefer permanent pay raises, such raises can be costly for employers. In recent years, many companies have reduced their reliance on merit pay in favor of incentives and bonuses because they believe that such pay systems are more effective methods for managing performance.

Team- or Organizationally Linked Incentive Pay. Three types of team- or organizationally linked incentive pay are gainsharing, profit sharing, and stock ownership. In a gainsharing reward system, teams of employees share in the gains (or cost savings) realized by measurable improvements in productivity. Typically, the amount of the reward varies from team to team because of differing amounts of improvement. In one hospital, for instance, departments (e.g., cardiac care, intensive care, and medical management) that substantially exceeded their productivity improvement targets received a larger share of the gain than departments (e.g., dietary, rehabilitation, and home health care) that just met their goals. Departments that didn't meet their productivity improvement goals didn't receive a reward under the gainsharing system.[51]

Unlike gainsharing, profit sharing isn't linked to measurable productivity improvements that teams of employees can control. Rather, profit sharing is based on the actual profits that a business earns and rewards employees with a share of those profits. The link between individual performance and an organization's profits may be relatively weak; thus profit sharing may not affect individual performance as much as a gainsharing system. Profit sharing may be restricted to managers and/or key executives, or it may involve all employees.

STOCK OPTIONS
The right given to an employee to buy the company's stock at a specified price.

EMPLOYEE STOCK OWNERSHIP PLANS
Incentive plans whereby the company funds the purchase of its stock to be held in individual employee investment accounts.

Like profit sharing, stock ownership may be restricted to certain levels in an organization or made available to all employees. Stock ownership may take the form of stock options or an employee stock ownership plan. ***Stock options*** give employees the right to buy the company's stock at a specified price. Traditionally, stock options have been limited to key managers, but companies now are making stock options available to most, if not all, of their employees. Companies such as Rockwell International, Kroger food stores, and AT&T use ***employee stock ownership plans*** (ESOPs) to provide employees throughout the organization with shares of their stock. A company with an ESOP either contributes shares of its stock or cash to purchase shares on the open market. The shares owned by the ESOP are then allocated among individual employee accounts. Employees become shareholders just like anyone else who invests in the company. Stock ownership may increase motivation and commitment but not unless employees perceive a clear linkage between individual and organizational performance.[52]

For those taking a job for the first time, the type and amount of pay they receive is determined largely by labor market conditions and company policy. But for more experienced workers, pay becomes an issue to be negotiated. Like any type of negotiation, pay negotiations require excellent communication. For Gordon Gould, a good pay package meant owning a piece of the company. His approach to negotiating this pay arrangement is described in the Communication Competency account.

BENEFITS REQUIRED BY LAW

Employers are obligated by law to provide certain benefits for their employees. These legally mandated benefits include Social Security, unemployment compensation, workers' compensation, and family and medical leave.

Social Security. Under the Federal Insurance Contribution Act (FICA) of 1935 (commonly called the Social Security Act) and subsequent amendments, most employers are required to contribute financially to the social security of their employees. The Social Security system provides retirement income, disability income, survivors' benefits, and Medicare coverage to employees and their dependents—if they meet certain eligibility criteria.

Unemployment Compensation. As a benefit for employees, unemployment compensation is intended to offset lost income during involuntary unemployment and to help unemployed workers secure new jobs. Employers must pay into this program, though the contribution rate varies from state to state. Additionally, companies with a history of periodically laying off large percentages of their workforces pay more unemployment tax than organizations with histories of fewer layoffs.

Workers' Compensation. As specified by the Workers' Compensation Act, this benefit is designed to compensate people for work-related injuries or diseases. The benefits that employees could receive include disability income, medical care, rehabilitative services, and death benefits for their families. Like unemployment compensation, the cost of workers' compensation for an employer varies by state and the organization's record.

Family and Medical Leave. The Family and Medical Leave Act of 1993 requires employers with fifty or more employees to grant up to twelve weeks unpaid leave annually for the birth or adoption of a child, to care for a spouse or an immediate member of the family with a serious health condition, or when the employee is unable to work because of a serious health condition. Employers are required to maintain preexisting health coverage during the leave period and, once the leave is concluded, to reinstate the employee to the same or an equivalent job. To be eligible, employees must have worked for the organization for at least one year.

BENEFITS NOT REQUIRED BY LAW

A variety of benefits are provided voluntarily by employers or as a result of union negotiations. Health insurance is probably the type of insurance most often included in a benefits package. Coverage of major medical costs and hospitalization is the most common component of health insurance. In addition, many employers' insurance plans provide dental, vision, and/or psychiatric coverage.[53] In addition to the retirement benefits provided by Social Security, many companies sponsor retirement plans for their employees. Most employers also offer pay for

In California, the hub of the high-tech industry is called Silicon Valley. In New York City, the hub of the new-media industry is called Silicon Alley. That's where people like Gordon Gould, a twenty-something "information architect," toil in a cavernous loft space called "the Pit." Along with other programmers, engineers, and marketing specialists, he works for a start-up company called Thinking Pictures. In order to take this job, he had to give up a comfortable job at Sony. So what could entice him to leave a large, successful company for the risky world of a start-up new-media company? Put simply, equity. Says Gould, "I'm young, but I'm not dumb. I know I'm a prime producer and I want my compensation to reflect that. If I'm going to spend sixteen hours a day in an office, I want to be rewarded for the upside value my work generates. I want to feel that the company is partly my baby." Gould set his negotiating target at 5 percent equity in Thinking Pictures, and negotiated from there. He ended up with a 3.5 percent stake—enough to make him rich at a young age if the company does well.

Leigh Steinberg also knows a thing or two about negotiating pay packages. He's a superagent who negotiates deals for top players in the National Football League. Here are his seven tips for how to negotiate a great deal.

1. **Know what you want before you ask.** Short-term economic gain? Long-term economic security? To work for a top-quality company? Autonomy? Before you begin to negotiate, make a list of what matters to you.

2. **If you think you're an MVP (most valuable player) act like one.** In other words, *show* that you are essential to the company's success, don't just claim to be.

3. **Become a free agent.** This involves two things. Getting multiple offers and being willing to move.

4. **Don't be dishonest.** Never misrepresent yourself or pump up the size of competing offers. A relationship that starts with lying will not last.

5. **Know who's across the table.** Knowing their background and current situation will give you more power during negotiations.

6. **Control yourself, don't fumble.** The challenge here is to walk a fine line between not being too modest and becoming angry if the other person doesn't seem to appreciate your skills.

7. **Live to fight another day.** One thing that's certain is that another negotiation will follow this one. So keep your emotions at a distance and try to operate under a paradigm of cooperation.[54]

To learn more about Thinking Pictures, visit the company's home page at

www.thinkpix.com

some amount of time when the employee is not actually working. Paid coffee breaks, lunch breaks, and vacation time all are examples.

In the United States, employees receive relatively little paid vacation compared to those in other countries. In most U.S. organizations, someone with one year on the job would be eligible for one to two weeks of paid vacation. After five years, most U.S. employers offer two to three weeks of paid vacation. After fifteen years, most U.S. employers offer three full weeks of paid vacation. In most other industrialized countries, vacation time is mandated by law, and employees with one year on the job generally get much more vacation than U.S. employees do. Figure 12.5 illustrates how vacations for U.S. workers compare to those in several other countries.

In addition to these typical benefits, employers may offer many other benefits to make their organizations more appealing to employees. For example, providing tuition reimbursement may attract people who want to continue their education

Figure 12.5 **Average Number of Vacation Days in Several Countries**

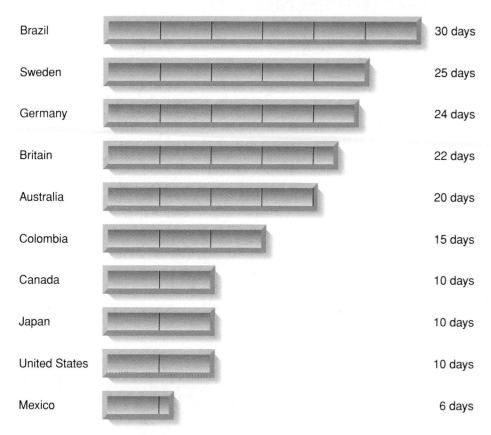

Brazil	30 days
Sweden	25 days
Germany	24 days
Britain	22 days
Australia	20 days
Colombia	15 days
Canada	10 days
Japan	10 days
United States	10 days
Mexico	6 days

Source: Based on a study of 1005 large companies, conducted by Hewitt Associates, as reported in L. B. Ward. Working harder to earn the same old vacation. *New York Times,* May 11, 1997, p. 12.

part-time while working full-time. Extra benefits provided for managers and executives (often referred to as "perks") may include company cars, country club memberships, professional or trade association memberships, financial planning advice, and expense accounts.

CHAPTER SUMMARY

An effective human resources management (HRM) system satisfies the needs of multiple stakeholders, including those of shareholders and employees. Its main components include staffing, training and development, performance appraisal, and compensation—all of which must be conducted in accordance with myriad legal regulations intended to protect the rights of employees. Managers are directly involved in most of these HRM activities, so the effectiveness of the HRM system depends ultimately on them. In global organizations, such as Cirque du Soleil, both the HRM system and individual managers must be responsive to cultural differences in how employees relate to

their work environments and to differences in the legal protections granted by different societies.

1. **DEFINE HUMAN RESOURCES MANAGEMENT AND DESCRIBE ITS ROLE IN AN ORGANIZATION'S STRATEGY.**

Human resources management (HRM) is concerned with the philosophies, policies, programs, practices, and decisions that affect the people who work for an organization. The various HRM functions should help the organization achieve its strategic goals. Effective HRM has a positive impact on an organization's financial bottom line.

2. **DESCRIBE SEVERAL IMPORTANT LAWS AND GOVERNMENT REGULATIONS THAT AFFECT HOW ORGANIZATIONS MANAGE THEIR HUMAN RESOURCES.**

The regulatory aspect of human resources management encompasses equal employment opportunity and employment discrimination, compensation and benefits, employee safety and health, and labor relations. Although their most pervasive impact is on the staffing and compensation functions, government regulations also influence performance appraisals and training and development activities.

3. **DESCRIBE THE PHASES OF THE STAFFING PROCESS AND THE STAFFING TOOLS AND TECHNIQUES USED BY ORGANIZATIONS.**

The staffing process normally includes six phases: (1) planning and forecasting human resources needs, (2) recruitment, (3) selection, (4) orientation, (5) movement, and (6) separation. The primary tools and techniques used to plan and forecast human resources needs are the competency inventory, job analysis, replacement charts, and expert forecasts.

4. **EXPLAIN HOW TRAINING AND DEVELOPMENT PROGRAMS CAN IMPROVE EMPLOYEE PERFORMANCE.**

The purpose of training programs is to maintain and improve current job performance. The intent of development programs is to teach competencies that employees will need in the future. Both training and development can be conducted on or off the job. Two of the greatest challenges facing organizations are remedial skills training and grooming people for global job assignments.

5. **DISCUSS SEVERAL USES AND METHODS OF APPRAISING PERFORMANCE.**

Four important uses of performance appraisals are (1) to make reward decisions (raises, bonuses, and other rewards), (2) to make personnel movement decisions (promotions, demotions, transfers, and lay-offs), (3) to give subordinates constructive feedback on their performance over a specified period of time, and (4) to identify training and development needs. The performance appraisal methods most commonly used are ranking, graphic rating, and behavioral rating.

6. **EXPLAIN THE COMPONENTS OF A TOTAL COMPENSATION PACKAGE.**

The compensation package is used to attract, motivate, and retain qualified employees. Total compensation includes both direct compensation and indirect compensation. Direct compensation consists of the base wage or salary and incentive pay. Job-based pay and competency-based pay are two methods of determining the base wage. Incentive pay is designed to link at least part of employee pay to job performance. Incentive pay can be linked to individual, team, department, or organizationwide performance. Indirect compensation includes benefits that are mandated by law and those that employers provide voluntarily or as a result of contract negotiations with unions. Social Security, unemployment compensation, and workers' compensation are benefits that employers must provide. Insurance, retirement, vacation pay, and a variety of other benefits are not required by law, although some legislation does regulate how these benefits are managed if they are provided.

QUESTIONS FOR DISCUSSION

1. How does the international nature of Cirque du Soleil affect its human resources practices?

2. How does effective human resources management address shareholders' concerns?

3. What are the primary legal and regulatory influences on human resources management?

4. Which recruitment sources are likely to be most effective for filling (a) jobs in the fast-food industry, (b) positions in Silicon Valley and Silicon Alley, and (c) professional jobs that require advanced educational degrees (e.g., physicians, lawyers, and professors)?

5. What are the advantages of on-the-job training and development programs? Do such programs eliminate the need for off-the-job training? Why or why not?

6. A manager once said: "Let's just say that there are a lot of factors that tug at you and play on your mind that cause you to soften the ratings you give. It may not have a great impact all the time, but when you know a 5 will create problems and a 6 will not, many managers give a 6." Why do managers inflate performance appraisals? What problems does this cause for employees and employers?

7. Describe the options that an organization has in designing its total compensation system. What advantages and disadvantages do they have for employers? For employees? What types of compensation would you like to receive? Why?

EXERCISES TO DEVELOP YOUR MANAGERIAL COMPETENCIES

1. **Self-Management Competency.** The following ten questions might be asked during an employment interview. Some of them are illegal and should never be asked. Employers who ask illegal questions may be subject to legal prosecution for employment discrimination. Place a check mark in the appropriate column to indicate whether the question is legal or illegal. Before taking this quiz, visit the home page of the Equal Employment Opportunity Commission (EEOC) at

www.eeoc.gov

	Legal	Illegal
1. How old are you?	_____	_____
2. Have you ever been arrested?	_____	_____
3. Do any of your relatives work for this organization?	_____	_____
4. Do you have children, and if you do, what kind of child-care arrangements do you have?	_____	_____
5. Do you have any handicaps?	_____	_____
6. Are you married?	_____	_____
7. Where were you born?	_____	_____
8. What organizations do you belong to?	_____	_____
9. Do you get along well with other men [or women]?	_____	_____
10. What languages can you speak and/or write fluently?	_____	_____

ANSWERS

The following evaluations provide clarification rather than strict legal interpretation because employment laws and regulations are constantly changing.

1. How old are you?
   This question is legal but inadvisable. An applicant's date of birth or age can be asked, but telling the applicant that federal and state laws prohibit age discrimination is essential. Avoid focusing on age, unless an occupation requires extraordinary physical ability or training and a valid age-related rule is in effect.

2. Have you ever been arrested?
   This question is illegal unless an inquiry about arrests is justified by the specific nature of the organization—for instance, law enforcement or handling controlled substances. Questions about arrests generally are con-

sidered to be suspect because they may tend to disqualify some groups. Convictions should be the basis for rejection of an applicant only if their number, nature, or recent occurrence renders the applicant unsuitable. In that case the question(s) should be specific. For example: Have you ever been convicted for theft? Have you been convicted within the past year on drug-related charges?

3. Do any of your relatives work for this organization?
   This question is legal if the intent is to discover nepotism.

4. Do you have children, and if you do, what kind of child-care arrangements do you have?
   Both parts of this question are currently illegal; they should not be asked in any form because the answers would not be job-related. In addition, they might imply gender discrimination.

5. Do you have any handicaps?
   This question is illegal as phrased here. An applicant doesn't have to divulge handicaps or health conditions that don't relate reasonably to fitness to perform the job.

6. Are you married?
   This question is legal, but may be discriminatory. Marriage has nothing directly to do with job performance.

7. Where were you born?
   This question is legal, but it might indicate discrimination on the basis of national origin.

8. What organizations do you belong to?
   As stated, this question is legal; it is permissible to ask about organizational membership in a general sense. It is illegal to ask about membership in a specific organization when the name of that organization would indicate the race, color, creed, gender, marital status, religion, or national origin or ancestry of its members.

9. Do you get along well with other men [or women]?
   This question is illegal; it seems to perpetuate sexism.

10. What languages can you speak and/or write fluently?
    Although this question is legal, it might be perceived as a roundabout way of determining an individual's national origin. Asking how a particular language was learned isn't permissible.

2. **Planning and Administration Competency.** The Family and Medical Leave Act of 1993 requires some employers to grant up to twelve weeks of unpaid leave for various family-related situations (e.g., the birth or adoption of a child). The law states only the minimum leave that employers must allow. Some employers have more generous policies. Visit the home pages of three companies that interest you. Based on the information provided, what is each company's philosophy concerning the relationship between work demands and family needs. How important is it to you to work for a company that has a progressive approach to managing work-family issues? To see the full text of the Family and Medical Leave Act, visit

   www.dol.gov/dol/esa/fmla

3. **Global Awareness Competency.** Going overseas to work as an expatriate can be an exciting experience, but it can also be stressful. Employers can reduce the stress associated with expatriate experiences by providing a wide range of services to address the needs of someone who is relocating to another country. Because the inter-

national environment is so complex, many employers rely on consulting companies to provide expatriation and repatriation services. After visiting the following Web sites, describe the various human resources management services available to firms sending employees overseas. Under what conditions should a company outsource these services to a consulting firm?

   Hewitt Associates:
   www.hewittassoc.com/resc
   Windham World: www.windham.com/expat
   Arthur Andersen:
   www.arthurandersen.com/bus-info/services/IES

4. **Teamwork Competency.** Measuring the performance and productivity of teams is a challenge that many organizations face. Measuring individual performance is difficult enough, let alone measuring group performance. How can team performance be assessed? An approach called PROMes is one solution. After visiting the following Web site, describe the PROMes approach to measuring team performance.

   acs.tamu.edu/~promes

5. **Strategic Action Competency.** For IBM, the past decade has been a time of significant change. After downsizing during the early part of the decade, the company rebounded by 1996, with much of its new growth coming from acquisitions. Read the chairman's letter to shareholders in IBM's most recent annual report. Identify one or two current strategic issues facing IBM and explain how these issues are likely to affect human resources practices at the company (e.g., HR planning, recruitment, training, and compensation). You can view an online version of IBM's annual report at

www.ibm.com/AnnualReport

REAL-TIME CASE ANALYSIS

THE MAGIC OF DISNEY BEGINS WITH HRM

The theme parks of the Walt Disney Company bring smiles to millions of customers from around the world. The company's sophisticated technical and creative staff makes experiences like Sleeping Beauty's Castle possible, but for most customers these employees are out of sight and out of mind. Visitors are more immediately impressed by the costumed hosts and hostesses who take their tickets and help them on and off rides. Most of these hourly employees are high school and college students. But they aren't just your typical students. They are an elite cadre who have been carefully selected, trained, and rewarded to deliver "Disney Courtesy."

Because most potential employees already know about the clean-cut and conservative image portrayed by Disneyland or Disney World employees, the company finds that most job applicants who wouldn't fit the image have already self-selected themselves from consideration. To be sure that everyone knows what to expect, however, one of the first steps in the hiring process involves showing applicants a video that details dress codes and rules of grooming and discipline. Next come forty-five-minute interviews. Interviewers ask standard questions and watch how well applicants listen, smile, and respond. From the interviews, they judge how well applicants are likely to handle "guests" and how well they are likely to get along with other employees. Disney screens for communication and teamwork competencies, not technical skills.

Once hired, "cast-members" attend an eight-hour orientation program where they learn the company's history, philosophy, and standards for customer service. Here they also are introduced to their role in creating happiness—the most important, but least tangible aspect of a successful Disney experience. The message is delivered by trainers who exude the Disney spirit. You won't find corporate types in these classrooms. Instructors are more likely to be some of the best veteran cast members, dressed in full costume and showing through example what a job at Disney involves. Following orientation, new cast members receive sixteen to forty-eight hours of "paired-training." This aspect of the training is essentially one-on-one coaching by respected members of the troupe. Successful completion of this training is required before new cast members are allowed to interact with customers on their own.

When a role is learned, it's performed repeatedly day after day. Supervisors and managers work hard to keep cast members fresh and focused on creating a feeling of magic. For example, one day a contest may be held to find the guest who has traveled the farthest, with a token prize for the winner. Disney also works hard to find ways to tell workers how much they are valued. For example, they offer service recognition awards, attendance awards, and banquets to mark the anniversaries of long-time employees. And one night a year the park is open only to employees and their families. Managers say thanks by dressing in costume and operating the park themselves.[55]

QUESTIONS

1. Why does Disney think that selecting people with communication and teamwork competencies is essential? Why don't they assess technical skills for their cast members?

2. Many of the jobs at Disney's amusement parks are routine and could easily lead to boredom. If you were a manager at Disney, how could you use performance appraisal and feedback to help keep cast members from letting the routine of their jobs interfere with the magical feeling that they're expected to create?

3. The Disney approach to managing human resources seems to give employees little freedom to be creative or develop new ways of doing things. Strict rules guide all aspects of behavior. Is this tight rein really necessary for the Disney

parks to succeed? Why or why not? What problems might this approach to human resources management create for the company as it expands into other countries and cultures?

To learn more about the Disney Company, visit its home page at

www.disney.com

VIDEO CASE

IBAX HEALTH: IS THERE A DOCTOR IN THE HOUSE?

IBAX was formed as a joint venture of two larger companies, computer systems titan IBM and health-care provider Baxter. Its first organizational structure reflected the mushing, not meshing, of cultures. Only by restructuring the company to reflect the new joint venture's "personality" as a provider of a set of products and services has IBAX been made to click. The effort included both refocusing existing staff and bringing some executives in to fill gaps that had existed.

Prior to its restructuring, IBAX was missing several key senior managers, probably a consequence of its birth as a joint venture. Those positions weren't at the top of IBAX's organizational pyramid so much as somewhere lower in IBM and Baxter's hierarchies. Executives in both companies, perhaps, felt little urgency about filling them, leading to external politics that delayed decision making. IBAX was drifting, rudderless, and probably demanding a great deal of its lower level managers, as they struggled intuitively to operate without the direction that would normally have come from above.

IBAX and its parent companies recruited Jeff Goodman as CEO to turn the joint venture around. Upon arriving at IBAX, Goodman faced challenges that were almost all human resources–related. Filling the vacant senior positions was a top priority. As challenging would be the twin tasks of unifying the disparate pieces brought to the joint venture into a single, unified culture and preparing for painful, but necessary, staff cuts.

In establishing IBAX's identity, Goodman would hardly be able to work from a clean slate: Employees brought to the venture from either parent would have their own perceptions and world views, and those hired by IBAX after its creation would have still other perceptions. Goodman realigned the company in several significant ways (e.g., along product lines and through reassigning support staff to the line departments).

IBAX itself was subsequently acquired by HBOC, another provider of patient care, clinical, financial and strategic management software, and other health-care–related services. Initially capitalized by its parents at $80 million, HBOC acquired IBAX for less than $50 million, suggesting that as valiant as the effort to turn the company around had been, its losses had been significant. But according to health industry technology coverage of the sale, CEO Jeff Goodman's efforts had paid off—HBOC wouldn't even have considered buying the company prior to its restructuring.

ON THE WEB

Baxter Healthcare is on the Web (***www.baxter.com***), as is (no surprise!) IBM (***www.ibm.com***). IBAX itself is difficult to find on the Internet: As a subsidiary joint venture, it was better known through its parents, and it was being absorbed into HBOC even as the Web was arriving. HBOC is on the Web (***www.hboc.com***).

QUESTIONS

1. Which aspects of human resources management do you think would be most difficult to address when merging two companies: Legal issues? Staffing? Training and development? Performance appraisals or compensation? Why?

2. How might the human resources practices at an entrepreneurial start-up (such as Second Chance Body Armor, discussed in Chapter 5) differ from that of IBAX?

3. If you were Jeff Goodman, how much time would you allocate in your new-employee orientation program for a discussion of IBM and Baxter? Explain.

Case contributed by Ross Stapleton-Gray, President, TeleDiplomacy, Inc., a technology and policy consultancy, and Adjunct Professor in Georgetown University's Communication, Culture, and Technology program.

Chapter

13

Organizational Innovation and Change

LEARNING OBJECTIVES

AFTER STUDYING THIS CHAPTER, YOU SHOULD BE ABLE TO:

1. EXPLAIN THE RELATIONSHIP BETWEEN INNOVATION AND ORGANIZATIONAL CHANGE.

2. DESCRIBE THE FEATURES OF LEARNING ORGANIZATIONS THAT ENABLE THEM TO ANTICIPATE AND EFFECTIVELY DEAL WITH CHANGE.

3. ASSESS YOUR OWN REACTIONS TO INNOVATION AND CHANGE.

4. EXPLAIN THE PROCESS OF PLANNED ORGANIZATIONAL CHANGE.

5. DESCRIBE FOUR APPROACHES TO ORGANIZATIONAL CHANGE.

Outline

After 40 Years, XBS Is Still Learning

In 1996, Xerox gave its prestigious President's Award to Chris Turner, XBS's Learning Person. In 1997, President Clinton awarded Xerox the 1997 Malcolm Baldrige National Quality Award. Winning the Baldrige award wouldn't have been possible without the years of effort devoted to changing the 40-year-old XBS organization. XBS is Xerox Business Services, the fast growing part of the Xerox company. Unlike other Xerox employees, 80 percent of the 15,000 employed by XBS go to work at the sites of the customers' businesses. Their jobs involve operating on-site document processing centers for companies that outsource this function to XBS. It already has 40 percent of the market share for document outsourcing, and its customers give XBS a 95 percent satisfaction rating. But its employees want more, and they view learning as their key to greater success.

To get where it is today, XBS had to change. And for XBS to change, its employees had to change. Turner describes the XBS change strategy as "creating a community of inquirers and learners." This community is global, working in 4,000 companies in 36 countries. Turner helped these employees become customer-focused business partners capable of continuously changing what they do—creating and applying cutting edge document services—and how they do it. What does the XBS learning organization look like? Turner describes it as an organization built on trust: "To me, trust is one of the essentials of learning." People at XBS consider the consequences of their decisions in terms of whether they are likely to build or diminish trust levels in the company. This approach frees people to ask questions and share solutions. Camp Lur'nin—an annual event that employees created and participate in—is one forum for information exchange. Learning also occurs through intentional experimentation. When XBS managers realized that better computer equipment was needed to improve customer satisfaction, they handed the problem to three sites (dubbed "learning laboratories"), gave each site $1,000, and asked them to experiment. Their solution? Keep the $1,000 and have customers buy the computers! This revolutionary idea is just the kind of solution that Turner expects from XBS employees.[1]

* * *

To learn more about XBS, visit its home page at

www.xerox.com/XBS

THE NATURE OF INNOVATION AND CHANGE

1

EXPLAIN THE RELATIONSHIP BETWEEN INNOVATION AND ORGANIZATION CHANGE

INNOVATION
The process of creating and implementing a new idea.

At XBS and other fast-moving organizations, innovation and change go hand-in-hand. **Innovation** is the process of creating and implementing a new idea. Because new ideas can take many forms, many types of innovation are possible. The creation of new products and services is one major type of innovation and is often referred to as *technical innovation*. Even in the absence of a new product or service, innovation can still occur. *Process innovation* involves creating a new means of producing, selling, and/or distributing an existing product or service. *Administrative innovation* occurs when creation of a new organization design better supports the creation, production, and delivery of products and services. Examples of administrative innovation include virtual teams and other information management systems, which we discussed in Chapter 11. These types of innovation focus on the organization as the target for change. Although they're beyond the scope of this chapter, more extensive forms of innovation also are possible. For example, the innovations of some organizations are aimed at fundamentally reshaping the industry in which they compete.[2]

In Chapter 5, we described the important role of entrepreneurs and intrapreneurs as sources of innovation. XBS's Chris Turner is an intrapreneur, working to help her company change through administrative and process innovations. Entrepreneurs often start new businesses to bring technical innovations to the marketplace. Significant technical innovations are the ones that often make headlines and sound bytes, but process and administrative innovations are the more common types of innovation in typical organizations.

Innovation of any type is likely to require organizational change. **Organizational change** refers to any transformation in the design or functioning of an organization. Thus, if an organization creates or adopts a substantially new method of production, implementing the innovation is likely to require major organizational change. For example, when employees told Nucor Steel's CEO Ken Iverson about a new low-cost technology for making steel, they stimulated a massive organizational change. After studying the idea carefully, Nucor built a $270 million plant for a thin-slab minimill. The decision to build the new plant represented a key strategic decision, which has had consequences for almost every aspect of steel making. Jobs of production workers and managers alike have changed significantly, as have the competencies needed to perform those jobs. Nucor now makes a ton of sheet steel in forty-five minutes, versus three hours for other big steelmakers.[3]

Sometimes organizational change involves smaller adjustments. When Frito-Lay created a new low-fat chip, only minor modifications in production and sales activities were required. Though small in magnitude, those changes were essential to customer acceptance of the new product. Successful companies are equally adept at making both minor and major changes. Furthermore, successful companies understand that change may be needed even in the absence of significant innovation.

Unsatisfactory performance is another common reason for change.[4] When Custom Foot first started up, it set out to provide customers with moderately priced, custom-fit shoes. Flexible manufacturing—also used by Levi Strauss to make custom-fit jeans—makes this new approach to selling shoes possible. A customer creates his or her own unique product by choosing among several basic features, such as color, type of leather, and type of heel. A high-tech scanner takes foot measurements and determines the customer's correct shoe size. The order is then transmitted electronically to one of several factories that have contracted with Custom Foot to do a few production runs each week. Custom Foot guarantees delivery to the customer within three weeks.

Custom Foot carried no inventory when it first opened. With the high-tech scanner to determine correct shoe sizes, customers weren't supposed to need to try on shoes. But Custom Foot had some learning to do. When customers complained that their custom shoes didn't fit well, Custom Foot learned that the customer, not a machine, determines the "correct" shoe size. Some people like a tighter fitting shoe, but others like a looser fit. Now stores carry enough inventory to enable customers to try on shoes before placing their orders. Custom Foot also had to learn how to make accurate forecasts about the leather needed to produce the shoes people ordered. If the necessary type of leather wasn't available when the factory received an order, it wouldn't be able to produce the shoe in time to meet the three-week delivery promise. In the first year, inaccurate forecasts about the types of leather that people would choose caused many missed delivery dates. To solve that problem, the company designed new databases to provide an instant tally and analysis of customer preferences.[5] For Custom Foot, many of the needed changes were small. They weren't made in response to an innovation—they were simply part of an ongoing process of improving customer service and satisfaction.

As the examples of XBS and Custom Foot illustrate, innovation and change often occur in response to the concerns of external stakeholders. A shortage of qualified employees may lead an organization to change its human resources management system in order to attract more job applicants. Pressure from environmentalists may lead to a change in materials acquisition processes or even to the

ORGANIZATIONAL CHANGE

Any transformation in the design or functioning of an organization.

creation of an innovative waste management system. More and more organizations are using the Internet to reach customers pressed for time with new marketing and sales approaches.

As we suggested in Chapter 11, changing an organization's design is one way for the organization to adjust to a changing environment. Merging with another firm, spinning off a business unit, and flattening the hierarchical structure all involve transforming the organization's basic design.[6] A dynamic, changing environment makes innovation and change as important—if not more important—for established organizations as they are for new organizations. Even the most successful organizations can't rest on prior successes. If they become complacent, competitors are sure to woo customers away. Now that Custom Foot has entered the shoe market, more established shoe companies face increased pressure to provide customized fits. Decline and even extinction result when organizations fail to adapt. Handy Dan Home Improvement Center, Pan Am, Herman's Sporting Goods, and many savings and loan associations have failed. Other companies are going through wrenching downsizing now because they were slow to adapt. When a large employer in a community is forced to downsize because of declining sales and profits, the organizational change can affect the entire community. Eastman Kodak, headquartered in Rochester, New York, was the biggest employer in the region and the country's best known name in photography. But when its main competitor, Tokyo-based Fuji, reduced the price of its color film by as much as 30 percent, Kodak's profits plummeted. To cut costs, Kodak announced that it would reduce its workforce by more than 10,000 people worldwide. Worried about job security, some of the 34,000 local employees cut back on their lunches at local restaurants, and when they did go to lunch they brought fewer smiles with them. CEO George Fisher, who had been praised for his pro-growth strategy just a few years earlier, acknowledged the pain: "The anxiety that we create when we do things like we're doing is immense, and you can't help but generate some degree of ill will."[7]

Most people—whether students, employees, managers, or consultants—are involved with organizations that need to change. To be effective, organizations and their managers, employees, and contractors must learn how to deal creatively with day-to-day conditions that require adaptation. The primary purpose of this chapter is to help you understand how organizations can use innovation and change to survive—and even to thrive—in a changing world.

LEARNING ORGANIZATIONS

2

DESCRIBE THE FEATURES
OF LEARNING ORGANIZA-
TIONS THAT ENABLE THEM
TO ANTICIPATE AND
EFFECTIVELY DEAL WITH
CHANGE

Successful innovation and change aren't events with clear-cut beginnings and endings. Rather, they are never-ending processes. In some of the best organizations, these processes are becoming part of the daily routine. Innovation and change are not infrequent and special—they are built into the organizations' ways of doing things. In recent years, such organizations have been referred to as learning organizations.

A *learning organization* has both the drive and the capabilities to improve its performance continuously, based on experience.[8] Learning organizations add value for customers by identifying new needs—in some instances, even before customers have done so—and then developing ways to satisfy those needs. Sometimes the process seems chaotic. When the environment is complex and dynamic, learning may require a lot of exploration and experimentation. Failures are frequent, but so are unexpected achievements. When the environment is more stable, learning is more likely to occur through a systematic process of testing alternative approaches.[9] Regardless of whether the process is chaotic or systematic, through

LEARNING ORGANIZATION
Involvement of all employees in identifying and solving problems, thus enabling the organization continuously to experiment, improve, and increase its capacity to deliver new and improved goods or services to customers.

continuous innovation and change a learning organization creates sustainable competitive advantage in its industry.

Figure 13.1 presents the five interrelated building blocks of a learning organization:

- shared leadership,

- culture,

- strategy,

- organization design, and

- use of information.

SHARED LEADERSHIP

In bureaucratic organizations, top-level managers take responsibility for making decisions, directing operations, and achieving organizational goals. Employees are treated as simply another factor in production, along with capital and equipment. Often they perform routine tasks that give them little opportunity to share in decision making and leadership.

In learning organizations, all employees share at least some leadership responsibilities. Everyone is encouraged to find ways to improve products and services and to experiment with new methods to serve the organization. At Yahoo!, a provider of Internet search engines and other services, all employees experiment constantly to satisfy customer demand. Yahoo! receives thousands of suggestions and comments from users who are eager for sites that suit their particular needs. Employees who read these submissions are fully empowered to make changes as they see fit. The sharing of decision making and leadership creates a culture that fully supports the goals and efforts of a learning organization.

CULTURE

In bureaucratic organizations, workers often are assigned to routine tasks that allow little experimentation. In learning organizations, empowered employees are encouraged to identify and experiment with new methods and approaches.

Figure 13.1 **Characteristics of a Learning Organization**

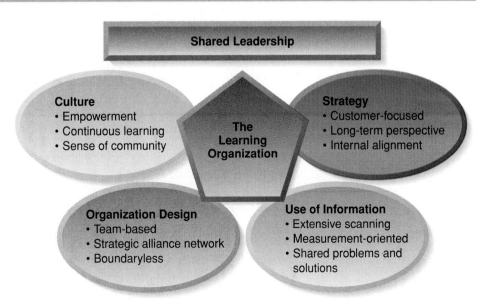

Empowerment provides a way to integrate tasks and allow employees to buy into the organization's goals. Max DePree, CEO of the Herman Miller Company, believes that leaders in learning organizations should liberate employees. Leaders can do so by removing roadblocks that keep them from doing their jobs to the best of their abilities and supporting employees who experiment with new approaches to satisfy customers. Herb Kelleher, CEO of Southwest Airlines, shares this view. At Southwest, empowered employees are always looking for better ways to meet customers' needs for low-cost, reliable air travel. When clerks suggested doing away with tickets, Kelleher encouraged them to experiment with the innovative idea on selected routes. Now, a customer calling for a reservation receives a PIN number. When the passenger arrives at the gate, an attendant asks for that PIN number and issues a plastic, reusable boarding pass, color coded for seat selection (first come, first served). Passengers who need a receipt get one promptly through the mail.[10]

Community. Learning organizations develop a sense of community and trust. Everyone needs to work together, respecting each other and being able to communicate openly and honestly. Problems can't be avoided or handled by just passing them along to another department or up the hierarchy. Conflict and debate are accepted as responsible forms of communication. A sense of community also gives employees the feeling that they are important and are being treated fairly. Employees cooperate because they want to, not because they have to.[11]

When people feel that they are part of a community, they are more willing to make the extra effort needed to find and fix problems. They are also less likely to leave the organization or to break up an alliance, taking their accumulated knowledge with them. Short-term learning is of little use if it is followed by long-term memory loss. Organizational memory loss is a problem facing many learning organizations, as described in the Planning and Administration Competency feature.

Continuous Learning. Obviously, a learning organization can't succeed without employees who are willing to learn and change. Hence learning organizations encourage individual learning in numerous ways. The culture of empowerment places responsibility on employees for problem finding and problem solving.[12] Empowerment requires more involvement and learning than does simply having someone else make all the decisions. The flat, team-based structure found in learning organizations facilitates learning because employees are involved in a broad range of activities and work with others from whom they can learn. Formal training is another way to ensure continuous learning. For managers in particular, continuous learning is essential to develop the competencies needed by generalists who are knowledgeable in several areas, as opposed to specialists who understand only finance, production, marketing, or some other function.

STRATEGY

Several strategies are available to learning organizations. Regardless of which strategies are used, however, they need to address three key issues: customer focus, long-term perspective, and internal alignment.

Customer Focus. Whether a learning organization's primary goal is satisfying current customers or gaining new customers, customer-focused strategies reflect a clear understanding of how important customers are to success. With more than two dozen newspapers under its umbrella, Knight-Ridder, Inc., is one of the largest newspaper chains in the United States. Like many other newspaper companies, it grew concerned as readership levels declined throughout the 1980s. To rebuild its

After a decade of downsizing by U.S. organizations, many employees have come to accept the idea that they will be moving from one organization to another several times during their careers. Professionals who enter the job market today can expect to change jobs about every five years, working for as many as ten different employers during their careers. In each job, the professional learns a great deal. Some of the learning is of a technical nature, which will probably be useful regardless of where the next job happens to be. But much of the professional's learning will be specific to the organization left behind: What are the rules of behavior that characterize the organization culture? How are decisions made in the organization? What was the real reason that the last client wasn't completely satisfied? Where are the inefficiencies in the system that should be eliminated? Unless this knowledge has somehow been captured by the employer and passed on to others, it walks out the door when the professional leaves. Soon, the organization finds itself left with mainly new employees, all of whom are struggling to learn their jobs and, at the same time, how the organization really operates. Few people—including managers at the top of the organization—personally remember what happened at the organization more than five years ago. When decisions have to be made, they are likely to rely on their experiences with previous employers. Often the result is poor decision making. When McKinsey & Co., a consult-ing firm, studied this problem at an automotive company, it discovered that 30 percent of the time spent solving problems was wasted. The problems had been solved before. The real problem, it seemed, was that no one was around who remembered!

Organizational memory loss is particularly severe when turnover is high. However, reducing turnover isn't the only way to preserve what employees learn. Many organizations try to retain what employees have learned by capturing that knowledge before they leave. One approach is to use intensive exit interviews. A skilled interviewer can probe and record an employee's knowledge and recollections. N. M. Rothschild PLC, a London-based firm, used this approach when its director of corporate affairs left before a successor had been found. The interview was recorded, edited for clarity, and then made widely available in the company.

Learning audits are another technique used to capture organizational memories. Kraft General Foods has used this technique for years, accumulating huge archives of information in the process. Learning audits typically center on a project. Throughout the project, key people periodically record what they are doing and thinking. The records capture their reasoning and can be studied by others in the company, enabling them to draw important lessons and inferences about the project.

A government-owned research center in New Mexico didn't conduct learning audits during the many years it carried out nuclear weapons testing, but now it wishes that it had. Weapons testing has stopped, and management is concerned that the knowledge and skills of weapons specialists eventually will be lost. To avoid that possibility, in case testing is ever resumed, management at the facility decided to interview its retired engineers and technicians. The director of nuclear weapons technology explained, "We don't want to press the erase button on our memory and go back to where we were fifty years ago."[13]

*   *   *

To learn more about Kraft General Foods, visit the company's home page at

www.kraftfoods.com

readership, it launched a project called 25/43—so named because the goal was to increase readership among people between the ages of 25 and 43. Based on extensive input from readers, this project revolutionized the way the company produces newspapers. Articles became shorter, topics were selected in part because of their potential interest to readers, and page layouts were redesigned. Equally significant was the change from a culture that gave priority to the preferences of editors and journalists to one that recognized that success required responding to the preferences of readers.[14]

Long-Term Perspective. At a time when many organizations and shareholders look no farther than the next quarterly report, acceptance of the need for a long-term perspective is crucial for a learning organization. The processes of learning and change simply take time. At Knight-Ridder, for example, declining newspaper circulation was anticipated long before it became a reality. As early as the 1970s, the company began experimenting with other forms of news delivery, including TV broadcasts, but eventually abandoned them as failures. During the 1980s, the company experimented with online business services and again had little success at first. Eventually, the learning paid off. With several years of experience behind it, the company bought Dialog Information Services, the world's largest online full-text information service. Used by many technicians and scientists, as well as students and professors, Dialog gives users the ability to search and access more than 10,000 publications and data sources. With this acquisition, Knight-Ridder was transformed from a traditional newspaper company to a leader in the provision of online business information.[15]

Internal Alignment. For learning organizations, the business strategy drives the design of all systems within the organization—human resources management, communications, and logistics. When that is done, the learning that occurs is far more likely to translate into success. At Xerox, the human resources management system is closely aligned with the company's goals and is called "Managing for Results." Each manager, supervisor, and front-line associate has goals, action plans, and performance measures that flow directly from the company's strategic goals. Monthly customer reviews help the company assess employees. Xerox's family-friendly policies—which include child-care subsidies, leaves of absence, and flexible work arrangements, among other things—are an essential part of its concern for its employees. These policies incorporated what the company had learned from its research on the causes of inefficiency and nonproductive work practices. By adopting the new policies that addressed work-family conflicts, Xerox reaped the benefits of reduced absenteeism and increased customer satisfaction. Every year, when *Working Mother* magazine publishes a list of the best companies for working mothers, Xerox is on the list.[16]

ORGANIZATION DESIGN

The design of learning organizations often reflects their emphasis on organic rather than mechanistic systems. In particular, they emphasize the use of teams, strategic alliances, and boundaryless networks.

Teams. In learning organizations, "bosses" are practically eliminated as team members take responsibility for training, safety, scheduling vacations, and purchases. In its Bayamon, Puerto Rico, plant, GE employs 172 hourly workers and just 15 salaried "advisors," in addition to its plant manager. Advisors have technical knowledge that may be helpful to employees when they are trying to solve specific problems. Team members come from all the plant's departments. Every six months workers rotate through the plant's four main operations. To support this team-based design, GE found that it needed to change its reward system to support the individual learning that was needed. Upon beginning a new job, the employee gets a $0.25 per hour raise. Upon learning the job of, say, statistical quality control, and declaring themselves "masters," they get a $0.50 per hour raise. Promotions, demotions, and firings are based on competence, not on seniority.[17]

Strategic Alliances. In addition to experimenting on their own, many learning organizations use strategic alliances with suppliers, customers, and even competitors as a method of learning. In Japan, Amgen, a biotech company, has joined in an alliance with Kirin Brewery. From Kirin, Amgen learns about fermentation processes, which are crucial for producing synthetic blood clotting protein. From Amgen, Kirin learns about amino-acid/protein combinations that can act as catalysts to speed up the brewing process.[18]

Boundaryless Networks. An extreme design option for learning organizations is to become a network of cooperating units connected by complex interdependencies and separated by few boundaries. Network structures, which we described in Chapter 11, maximize the linkages between organizations. Such linkages, in turn, provide learning opportunities and generate innovation in products and services.[19] Network structures seem to work in part because they create a sense of community among a larger pool of people who share their diverse knowledge and expertise, using it to find creative solutions to difficult problems.[20]

USE OF INFORMATION

Information is the lifeblood of learning organizations. To be effective they must undertake extensive scanning, be measurement oriented, and foster shared problems and solutions.

Extensive Scanning. Staying attuned to relevant changes is a passion for learning organizations. To ensure that they don't miss an important new trend or change, learning organizations aggressively scan both the external and internal environments for information. As a result, large amounts of information are obtained from the external environment on how customers are reacting to current products and services, how customers compare them to those of competitors, and whether new competitors may be on the horizon. Such information is essential to judgments concerning the need to create new products or services to meet customer demand. Information obtained from the internal environment indicates how employees feel about the organization, whether their attention is focused on customers, whether they feel energized to solve difficult problems, and the likelihood that key employees will defect to competitors. These are just a few of the concerns that learning organizations address by scanning their environments and evaluating the information received from the scanning process.

Measurement Oriented. Organizations learn in order to improve performance. To judge improvement, an organization needs to know where it was before and where it is now. Performance measurements make assessing improvement possible. In learning organizations, employees have access to data about customer satisfaction, profits and losses, market share, employee commitment, and competitors' strategies, among other things. Data are gathered, monitored, disseminated, and used throughout the organization. Employees believe that too much information is better than too little so that they can pick and choose what they need to perform their tasks. At Springfield Remanufacturing, managers make available all production and financial figures, and employees are encouraged to ask tough questions about them. Employees also have access to daily printouts that provide detailed cost information on all products. The days of managers hoarding information are long gone in learning organizations.[21]

Shared Problems and Solutions. Numerical data (measurements) aren't the only type of information considered important in learning organizations. "Soft" information is valued too. Says XBS's Chris Turner, "I'm more interested in anecdotal evidence than hard data. If you get 1,000 anecdotes and they all begin to fit together, then you've got a pattern that makes sense."

Whereas measurements help an organization judge how much progress has been made, soft information is the stuff that learning is made of. By sharing information about the problems they face and the solutions they discover, employees minimize the number of times they reinvent the wheel and speed up the process of organizational learning. Coopers & Lybrand (which has since merged with Price Waterhouse) identified a way to increase the amount and effectiveness of soft information sharing as one of its key strategic challenges. Its clients were scattered around the world, and they all demanded service that reflected cutting-edge practice. In this environment, Coopers & Lybrand knew that its success depended on finding ways to transfer quickly the learning that occurs. With each consulting engagement, employees gain new insights and experiment with new solutions. The learning that occurs is useful for that specific engagement, and it may also be useful to another team sometime in the future. But transferring the lessons learned by one team to other teams working elsewhere around the world isn't easy. These lessons can't be taught with numbers alone—detailed narrative explanations are also needed.

The challenge is to find effective ways to record and transmit narrative explanations of what has been learned. Several organizations now use computer-aided systems for managing narrative information. Companies such as Tandem Computer and Office Equipment used computer-aided systems for best-practice sharing. Like e-mail, these systems allow for rapid and wide distribution of information. In addition, they enable the organization to store shared solutions in an electronic library. Later, users can access the library, using index catalogs in which problems and solutions are grouped in meaningful categories. Although this technology is in its infancy, it promises to enhance organizational learning even when knowledge is widely dispersed in both space and time.[22]

DO YOU ENJOY INNOVATION AND CHANGE?

3

ASSESS YOUR OWN REACTIONS TO INNOVATION AND CHANGE

In the next section, we describe further the process of change. Before continuing, however, take a moment now to answer the questions posed in the following Self-Management Competency account. These questions are designed to provide insight into how you respond to innovation and change. If you're uncomfortable with innovation and change, working in a learning organization may be quite difficult for you. But, if you enjoy innovation and change, you might discover that you would enjoy working in a learning organization. In fact, you might become bored and restless in a traditional organization.

A PROCESS OF PLANNED CHANGE

4

EXPLAIN THE PROCESS OF PLANNED CHANGE

As we've already noted, innovation and change can be somewhat chaotic or planned and relatively smooth. By its very nature, chaotic change is difficult to describe. Nevertheless, large-scale organizational changes seldom occur without a bit of chaos. Organizations usually strive to minimize it by imposing some order on the change process. Change is most likely to be orderly when it has been planned. The process of planned organizational change comprises the nine steps shown in Figure 13.2. Although planned changes don't always proceed exactly as shown, these steps constitute the basic components of a change process, regardless of the sequence followed.[23]

SELF-MANAGEMENT COMPETENCY
How Innovative Are You?

Instructions

To find out how innovative you are, use the following scale in responding to the eighteen statements. In each case, there is no right or wrong answer. Rather, the intent is to help you explore your attitudes.

SA = Strongly Agree

A = Agree

? = Undecided

D = Disagree

SD = Strongly Disagree

Statement	Response				
1. I try new ideas and new approaches to problems.	SA	A	?	D	SD
2. I take things or situations apart to find out how they work.	SA	A	?	D	SD
3. I can be counted on by my friends to find a new use for existing methods or existing equipment.	SA	A	?	D	SD
4. Among my friends, I'm usually the first person to try out a new idea or method.	SA	A	?	D	SD
5. I demonstrate originality.	SA	A	?	D	SD
6. I like to work on a problem that has caused others great difficulty.	SA	A	?	D	SD
7. I plan on developing contacts with experts in my field located in different companies or departments.	SA	A	?	D	SD
8. I plan on budgeting time and money for the pursuit of novel ideas.	SA	A	?	D	SD
9. I make comments at meetings on new ways of doing things.	SA	A	?	D	SD
10. If my friends were asked, they would say I'm a wit.	SA	A	?	D	SD
11. I seldom stick to the rules or follow protocol.	SA	A	?	D	SD
12. I discourage formal meetings to discuss ideas.	SA	A	?	D	SD
13. I usually support a friend's suggestion on new ways to do things.	SA	A	?	D	SD
14. I probably will not turn down ambiguous job assignments.	SA	A	?	D	SD
15. People who depart from the accepted organizational routine should not be punished.	SA	A	?	D	SD
16. I hope to be known for the quantity of my work rather than the quality of my work when starting a new project.	SA	A	?	D	SD
17. I must be able to find enough variety of experience on my job or I will leave it.	SA	A	?	D	SD
18. I am going to leave a job that doesn't challenge me.	SA	A	?	D	SD

Scoring

Give yourself the following points for each circled response.

SA = 5 points

A = 4 points

? = 3 points

D = 2 points

SD = 1 point

Interpretation

Total your scores for all responses. The higher the score, the more willing you are to be innovative and welcome change. A score of 72 or greater is high; a score of 45 or less is low. People who aren't innovators have a tendency to maintain the status quo. Innovative people like to create changes in their organizations to increase performance.[24]

Figure 13.2   **The Process of Organizational Change**

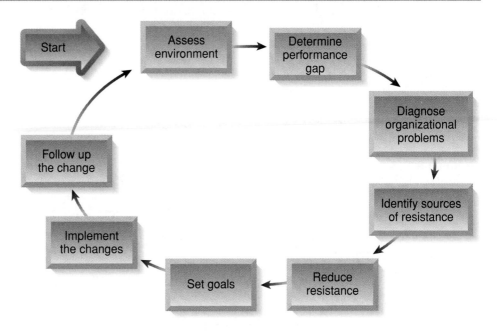

ASSESS THE ENVIRONMENT

Learning organizations are keenly aware of the need to scan the environment for information that may signal the need for change. As we described in Chapter 3, both the degree and rate of change in the environment have implications for organizations. The four environmental factors most responsible for stimulating organizational change are customers, technology, competitors, and the workforce. Other factors that may pressure organizations to change include globalization and the actions of important stakeholders, such as shareholders, government regulators, unions, and political action groups.[25]

Organizational change often is a response to the external environment, but not always. Sometimes the internal environment creates a need for change, as was true at Manugistics. When it was founded in 1969, Manugistics sold computer time on a mainframe to companies that didn't have computers of their own. Since then, it has gone public, was bought by a Fortune 500 company, merged with GTE, and eventually was bought back by its own managers. Operating now as a software company in Maryland, it has been on a growth binge for the past decade. Much of its growth has been achieved through acquisitions, including companies in Germany, France, Japan, Australia, and the United Kingdom. With each purchase comes the challenge of assimilating the newly acquired employees into the Manugistics culture. Later in this chapter, we show how Manugistics responds to this internally driven need for change.

DETERMINE THE PERFORMANCE GAP

PERFORMANCE GAP

The difference between what the organization wants to do and what it actually does.

With information about the environment in hand, the next step in the change process is to determine the performance gap. A ***performance gap*** is the difference between what the organization wants to do and what it actually does. When Fidelity Institutional Retirement Services Company (FIRSCo) reorganized and automated virtually all its systems and procedures, it quickly realized savings in costs. However, a performance gap in the area of customer satisfaction continued to be troublesome, indicating that still more changes were needed. To address this performance gap, FIRSCo needed to learn more about the reasons for customer dissatisfaction.[26]

DIAGNOSE ORGANIZATIONAL PROBLEMS

The aim of diagnosis is to identify the nature and extent of problems before taking action. The idea that diagnosis should precede action may seem obvious, but its importance is often underestimated.[27] All too often results-oriented managers begin the change process prematurely and impatiently push for solutions before the nature of the problem itself is clear.

FIRSCo's philosophy was that loyal, satisfied employees create loyal, satisfied customers. So when customer satisfaction was low, management turned its attention to employee performance. Management discovered that the reorganization had caused many employees to lose direct contact with their customers. As they became more removed from customers, they also lost a sense of being able to affect customer satisfaction directly. In addition, many employees now were working in new jobs and were being managed by people who had recently been promoted.[28] Taken together, these conditions worked against the employees being able to satisfy customers.

Most organizational problems have multiple causes; seldom is there a simple and obvious cause, and seldom does only one perspective need to be considered. Using a variety of information gathering techniques is the best approach. Attitude surveys, conferences, informal interviews, and team meetings all can be used to gain insights from people with varying perspectives.

Organizations often hire outside consultants to assist with problem diagnosis. For example, interpersonal problems often require gathering sensitive information from employees. Outside consultants may be better able to conduct interviews and interpret data in an unbiased manner. In addition, consultants often have the expertise that the organization lacks to conduct and analyze attitude surveys properly.

IDENTIFY SOURCES OF RESISTANCE

Few planned organizational change efforts go as smoothly as managers would like. Most run into some amount of resistance. Experienced managers are all too aware of the various forms that resistance can take: immediate criticism, malicious compliance, sabotage, insincere agreement, silence, deflection, and in-your-face defiance are just a few examples.[29] Some managers don't even initiate needed changes because they feel incapable of overcoming expected resistance. Successful managers understand why people resist change and what can be done to overcome such resistance.

In general, people—and sometimes even entire organizations—tend to resist change for five reasons: fear, vested interests, misunderstandings, different assessments of the situation, and interorganizational agreements.[30]

Fear. Some people resist change because they fear that they'll be unable to develop the competencies required to be effective in the new situation. A common obstacle to organizational change is the reluctance of managers and nonmanagers alike to change their attitudes and learn the new behaviors that their organizations require. Even when employees understand and accept that they need to change, doing so often is difficult because they fear the consequences. When Mercedes-Benz Credit Corporation set out to restructure its operations in the United States, employees seemed to have good reason to be fearful of the future. Restructuring usually involves layoffs. The company's president, Georg Bauer, knew that fear could be a problem and would make getting needed help from employees difficult.

"It was absolutely essential to establish a no-fear element in this whole change process," he said. Rather than resist change, he wanted employees to help create a new, more efficient organization by expressing their ideas about where to cut and how to do work differently. Besides empowering employees to make decisions about how to change their work, he offered an incentive to convince employees that even cutting their own jobs wouldn't harm them financially. The incentive was to offer the security of a new—and probably better—job to anyone bold enough to eliminate his or her current position. The approach worked. Four entire layers of management vanished at the suggestion of the employees themselves.[31]

Vested Interests. Fear often goes hand-in-hand with vested interests. People who have a vested interest in maintaining things as they are often resist change.[32] Downsizing, cost cutting, and restructuring begun by many organizations in the 1980s to improve performance has continued throughout the 1990s. At times, downsizing has hurt product quality, alienated customers, and actually cut productivity. Georg Bauer understood that successful change requires getting people to let go of vested interests and consider how a different future might actually be a better future.

Misunderstandings. People resist change when they don't understand its implications. Unless quickly addressed, misunderstandings and lack of trust build resistance. Top managers must be visible during the change process to spell out clearly the new direction for the organization and what it will mean for everyone involved. Getting employees to discuss their problems openly is crucial to overcoming resistance to change. As the Communication Competency piece suggests, organizational changes that involve bringing rivals together must be especially sensitive to the possibility of misunderstandings. In this situation, effective informal communication is essential.

Assessments. Employees also may resist change if they assess the situation differently than do their managers or team members. Some people initiate change believing that anyone with the same information would make the same decision. This assumption isn't always correct. Often top-level managers see change as a way to strengthen the organization. They may also believe that change will offer them new opportunities to develop their own competencies as they tackle new challenges. In contrast, employees may view proposed changes as upsetting the implicit and explicit compacts between themselves and their employer. In particular, they may expect increased workloads and longer hours to be the only rewards for staying around to help implement a major organizational change.[33]

Employees and managers may also have different assessments because of different experiences with change. In some organizations, initiating change efforts is seen simply as something that new managers do to make their mark. Over time, employees see change efforts come and go much like the seasons of the year, as managers implement one fad after the other. Eventually, cynicism sets in and employees refuse to support yet another change "program." Without employee support the change efforts fail, which further contributes to cynicism.[34]

Interorganizational Agreements. Labor contracts are the most common examples of interorganizational agreements that create resistance and limit options for change. Actions once considered major rights of management (e.g., to hire and fire, assign personnel to jobs, and promote) have become subjects of negotiation. Advocates of change also may find their plans delayed because of agreements with competitors, suppliers, public officials, or contractors. Although agreements sometimes are ignored or violated, the legal costs of settlement can be expensive.

In the engine-building business, many joint ventures have been attempted, and almost as many have failed. On paper, joint ventures between companies with different strengths promise big rewards. But, in reality, establishing cooperative relationships between former rivals often proves difficult. Despite its history of modest success with joint ventures, GE decided to enter into a new joint venture with United Technologies' Pratt & Whitney unit. Whether this venture succeeds will depend in part on whether employees can overcome their distrust of each other. Each company suspects the other of spreading information about defects in its rival's engines. The suspicions may be valid. According to one newspaper account, a GE executive once showed a reporter a video of a Pratt engine backfiring and belching flames. Ironically, the same competitive forces that kept these two companies apart in the past are now responsible for them getting together.

Boeing, a potential buyer of large quantities of the engines these companies make, had announced that it would require new engines to meet a stricter standard. Operating costs for new 747s would have to be reduced by 10 percent. While at an air show in Singapore, employees of the two companies were complaining about this new standard. But being engineers, their conversation eventually moved toward speculation about how a new type of engine might be what was needed. Someone apparently said, "let's do it together," and soon officials from the two companies were exploring the possibilities. The venture's president is a thirty-four-year veteran of GE. The top team is filled out with two co-general managers—one from each company. The co-general managers each have extensive experience with alliances and should be capable of setting the tone for cooperation. Time will tell whether managers farther down in the hierarchy can set aside the past and begin to trust each other enough to share information and work together effectively. According to research by the Conference Board, when companies merge top-level managers, they usually are careful to explain their actions to customers and shareholders. Employees, however, often are left feeling uninformed as the change process unfolds.[35]

* * *

To learn more about these two companies, visit their home pages at

www.ge.com

and

www.pratt-whitney.com

When Sir Colin Marshall, CEO of British Airways (BA), declared that the company would become the "world's favourite airline," many employees saw little reason to change. They felt secure in their jobs at this government-subsidized airline. Before its turnaround in the late 1980s, the airline had been dubbed by customers as BA for "Bloody Awful." Sir Colin needed to convince BA's employees that their jobs would be secure only when their customers were satisfied. Being best in customers' eyes meant everything from making sure that the concourse lights were always on to making sure that meals on short flights were easy to deliver and unwrap. It also meant that employees had to change their attitudes toward customers from that of moving "packages" to a concern for passengers as human beings.

To make the changes needed, customer service training was provided to all employees. Flight crews attended language training classes to help them become proficient in French, Italian, German, or Spanish. The trainers themselves were crew members who flew half the year and taught the other half. Thus they knew and understood customer service problems, the questions most likely to be asked, and the vocabulary most often used. This program helped British Airways attain its goal of being one of the best airlines in the world.[36]

REDUCE RESISTANCE

Resistance to change will never disappear completely, but managers can learn to overcome its negative consequences. In fact, some resistance to change may actually be useful. The first lesson in reducing resistance is not to be afraid of it. Employees can operate as a check-and-balance mechanism to ensure that management properly plans and implements change. Justifiable resistance that causes management to think through its proposed changes more carefully may result in better decisions. Four commonly used methods for managing resistance are education, participation, negotiation, and cooptation.

Education. One method for overcoming resistance to change is through education and communication. This method is ideal when resistance is based on inadequate or inaccurate information and analysis and the resisters are the ones who must carry out the change. British Airways and FIRSCo used this method to help implement change.

Participation. Organizations often meet with less resistance to change when they allow participation and involvement. Resistance is lower when employees are involved in identifying where change is needed and implementing proposed changes. Participation in the change process usually requires teamwork.

At IBM, which has undergone a major transformation during the past few years under CEO Lou Gerstner, full employee participation is credited with the company's revival. People like John Patrick, a thirty-year IBMer who also knew a lot about teamwork, were the unlikely leaders of this change. John Patrick's use of participation and teamwork are described in the Teamwork Competency feature.

Research shows that participation usually leads to commitment, especially when it is voluntary.[37] Nevertheless, participation can have its drawbacks. If participation isn't carefully managed, it can lead to poor solutions and waste a lot of time and money.

Negotiation. Another way to deal with resistance to change is to negotiate and offer incentives or rewards to potential or active resisters. This method of dealing with resistance is especially appropriate when someone clearly is going to lose as a result of the change. For example, at Oryx, an oil and gas producer, the company eliminated rules, procedures, reviews, and reports that had little to do with exploration for hydrocarbons. As the price of oil continued to drop, the company had to cut 1,500 managerial jobs. The company also negotiated wage and benefits concessions with those who remained. They were committed to the changes and began to look for ways to further increase Oryx's efficiency.[38]

Cooptation. In some situations, management attempts to manipulate others to reduce their resistance to change. Cooptation is a political maneuver that brings people into the decision-making process to obtain their endorsement of change or, at least, get them not to resist it. Coopting a group involves giving one of its leaders a role in the change process. This method isn't a form of participation because those who are proposing the change don't really want advice from those coopted.

Cooptation can be a dangerous response to resistance, however. People who feel that they have been tricked, are not being treated fairly, or are being lied to are likely to respond negatively to a change.[39] Many managers have found that, by manipulating subordinates, they have ultimately created more resistance to the change than they would have had they chosen another tactic.

Selecting a Method. There is no sure-fire approach to reducing resistance. Each approach has some potential strengths and weaknesses, as summarized in Table 13.1 Therefore five issues need to be considered in the selection of a method to overcome resistance to change.

The development of personal computers has permanently changed the world of computing. But IBM, once the dominant force in the industry, failed to realize the significance of the changing environment until it was too late. When he took over as CEO in 1993, everyone in the organization knew that Gerstner's job was to save a company that seemed to be on the brink of destruction. In only five years-a short amount of time for transforming a behemoth like IBM—Gerstner had returned IBM to a respected competitor.

Gerstner was helped by managers such as John Patrick, who rallied people throughout the company around a common vision for the future. Patrick had already put in thirty years at IBM. While others around him argued about who was to blame for IBM's fall, Patrick was experimenting with Gopher, one of the early software programs used on the Internet. As he played with Gopher, he realized that the Internet would change completely the future of computing. He shared this insight and a six-point plan for what IBM needed to do in a manifesto titled "Get Connected." His message generated immediate enthusiasm, and before long a virtual community of excited employees had formed.

Although it had no budget and no formal authority, within six months the Get Connected team had created one of the first significant corporate Web sites. That month Patrick attended an industry event called Internet World, then in its infancy. He signed up IBM as a major participant for the next meeting. He had no authority to do so, but he was counting on the Get Connected team to design and staff the show. Although the activity never appeared on anyone's budget, seven months later fifty-four people from twelve IBM units presented their accomplishments at the next Internet World gathering. In another few months, IBM would create an Internet division and make John Patrick vice president and chief technology officer. Patrick has learned a great deal about change through his experiences. He uses four principles to summarize his learning.

- The less you ask for the more you get: If you have a budget, someone else may be able to question your activities. Naysayers can't kill projects they don't fund.
- Just enough is good enough: Don't wait until your project is perfect. Get it out so people can react.
- Nowhere beats somewhere. Patrick never puts a business unit name on his card. He prefers to operate with the motto, "If IBM wins, everyone wins."
- Lose a teammate, gain a division. Teams involved in change efforts often worry when their best members are "hired away" by other parts of the company. Patrick loves to see this happen because he knows that he'll have an ally wherever that person ends up. "I refer to it as colonization," Patrick says.[40]

* * *

To see what IBM's corporate Web site looks like today, visit the company's home page at

www.ibm.com

- **Amount and types of resistance anticipated.** All other things being equal, the greater the anticipated resistance, the more difficult that overcoming it will be. Education and participation probably are the most appropriate methods of combating strong resistance.

- **Power of resisters.** The greater the power of the resisters, the more the proponents of change must involve the resisters. Conversely, the stronger the proponent's position, the greater is the opportunity for negotiation.

- **Location of needed information and commitment.** The greater the need for information and commitment from others to help design and implement change, the more the advocates of change should use education and participation. Gaining vital information and commitment from others requires time and their involvement.

Table 13.1   Methods of Overcoming Resistance to Change

Method	Situations	Advantages	Drawbacks
Education	When there is a lack of information or inaccurate information and analysis.	Once persuaded, people will often help with the implementation of the change.	Can be very time-consuming if many people are involved.
Participation	When the initiators do not have all the information they need to design and others have considerable power to resist.	People who participate will be committed to implementing change, and any relevant information they have will be integrated into the change plan.	Can be very time-consuming if participants design an inappropriate change.
Negotiation	When someone or some group will clearly lose out in a change and that person or group has considerable power to resist.	Sometimes it is a relatively easy way to avoid resistance.	Can be expensive in many cases if it alerts others to negotiate before complying.
Cooptation	When other tactics will not work or are too expensive.	It can be a relatively quick and inexpensive solution to resistance problems.	Can lead to future problems if people feel manipulated.

Source: Adapted from J. P. Kotter and L. A. Schlesinger. Choosing strategies for change. *Harvard Business Review,* March-April, 1979, p. 111.

- **Stakes involved.** The greater the short-run potential for damage to the organization's performance and survival if the situation isn't changed, the greater is the need for managers to negotiate and/or use cooptation to overcome resistance.

- **Short-term and long-term effects.** Accurate assessment of the first four factors still leaves the manager with the choice between short-term and long-term effects. Forcing change on people can have many negative effects, both in the short term and the long term. Education and negotiation often can overcome initial resistance and can lead to long-term benefits. Participation can lessen both short-term and long-term resistance. Cooptation may be quickest in the short run but can lead to long-term resistance.[41]

SET GOALS

For change to be effective, goals should be set before the change effort is started. If possible, the goals should be (1) based on realistic objectives, (2) stated in clear and measurable terms, (3) consistent with the organization's overall goals and policies, and (4) attainable. For example, when a take-out pizza business in Virginia decided that it needed to improve driver safety, it began by collecting systematic information about behaviors, such as the extent to which drivers came to complete stops at intersections. Management shared the information with employees and gave them the task of setting specific goals for improvement. During the months that followed, driving behavior was monitored and charts were used to inform employees of their progress toward those goals. Employees participating in goal setting showed improvement in several areas of behavior, including some for which they hadn't even set specific goals.[42]

Continental Airlines also stressed the importance of setting goals. These goals are presented in the company's Go Forward plan, which is described in the following Strategic Action Competency account.

You know times are bad when even the vice president of corporate communications admits things like, "This airline was probably, candidly, one of the least-respected airlines in corporate America. It could *not* get any worse than Continental in 1994." Then some mechanics ripped the company logo off their uniforms so that they could run errands after work without being identified as Continental employees. Two years later, Continental was celebrating its highest pretax profits ever. How did the company do it? With the leadership of a new CEO whose battle cry was "From worst to first." The Go Forward plan set out the following strategic goals.

1. **Fly to win.** The goal was to achieve top-quartile industry margins.

2. **Fund the future.** To do so required reducing interest expense by owning more hub real estate.

3. **Make reliability a reality.** Specific goals included ranking among the top airlines on the four measurements used by the U.S. Department of Transportation (DOT).

4. **Working together.** Have a company where employees enjoy working and are valued for their contributions.

When Bethune took over, he let nearly every vice president go. (That's one way to reduce resistance!) Eventually, some 7,000 of the 40,000 employees were cut, leaving the others a bit concerned. To signal that a new future lay ahead, the 800-page corporate policy manual was hauled out to a parking lot and set aflame with a torch as employees, managers, and executives watched. Burning a policy manual is a good way to embark on a change process, but it's just a beginning. Specific goals, linked to specific rewards, were what made the strategy meaningful.

In 1995, one goal was to be ranked in the top five of the DOT on-time performance ratings. For each month the goal was reached, employees would earn an extra $65. Two months later, Continental was in first place. The next year the goal and the reward were changed. Now employees could earn $100 for each month the company ranked first and $65 for each month it ranked second or third. These goals and rewards were still in place as of 1998. Executives have goals and associated rewards, too. Employees regularly rate their managers on an employee survey. How well does the manager communicate the plan to employees? Does the manager treat employees with respect and dignity? An outside consulting group analyzes the results and executives' bonuses reflect their performance.

Performance measured against these goals isn't the only type of information given to employees. In a complete shift from the past, the company now disseminates data about baggage handling performance, on-time performance, complaints, and stock performance daily. The data are faxed to 350 locations, e-mailed to 2,000 locations, and available through voice mail from any location an employee happens to be. Though not yet perfect, Continental is proud of the fact that its customer satisfaction was high enough in 1997 to earn it the number one spot among major airlines for flights of 500 or more miles and the "Airline of the Year" title from a leading industry magazine.[43]

* * *

To learn more about Continental Airlines, visit the company's home page at

www.flycontinental.com

IMPLEMENT THE CHANGE

The next step in planned organizational change is to select and implement a practical approach to achieve it. Later in this chapter we describe four interrelated approaches to change: technology, design, task, and people. Regardless of which approach is used, the ability to sustain change depends primarily on how well the organization reinforces newly learned behaviors during and after the change effort. A combination of money, pats on the back, and new job opportunities help create a climate that reinforces new behaviors.[44] If employees view the rewards as fair, they are likely to improve their competencies and maintain their new behaviors.

For Continental Airlines to maintain and build on the results of its change efforts, executives must be sensitive to employees' sense of fairness and be careful not to raise performance goals without increasing the rewards for achieving them.

At Manugistics change is constant because of its growth through acquisition strategy. The software that Manugistics sells is used to integrate planning activities for product demand, distribution, manufacturing, and transportation throughout the supply chain. It integrates operations both within a firm and among separate entities. For Manugistics, implementing change supports and maintains a corporate culture that thrives on continual change. Guiding Manugistics through all the changes that have accompanied its growth are three core values, referred to as its Elements of Excellence.

- We treat others as we would like to be treated.

- Partnership with our clients results in superior products.

- Team success is more important than personal glory.

Today, the company focuses on instilling these values in the companies it acquires. Doing so usually means changing the culture of the acquired company. "It's critical that whatever company we're involving ourselves with internationally is going to embrace, can embrace, and must embrace our Elements of Excellence, our values," explains a manager. "Being the same in terms of processes and procedures isn't so important."

When Manugistics makes an acquisition, it does so because it values the employees and wants them to stay. Free-flowing communication helps instill the company culture that includes empowerment and continuous learning. "Empowerment is an important concept here because it's absolutely mandatory that we rely on these good people that we've hired to make decisions that move us forward," explained one manager. Learning also is important for these employees, who often are selling software plus service packages that cost clients $1 million to $2 million. Before making such significant purchases, clients want to be convinced that Manugistics' employees have the latest knowledge and the capabilities needed to meet the clients' needs. To keep current, employees are required to take courses at Manugistics University and encouraged to use a generous tuition reimbursement program to take advantage of other learning opportunities. By offering public training, Manugistics also helps customers learn.[45]

FOLLOW UP THE CHANGE

During follow-up, managers need to monitor results to ensure that the change process has been successful. This determination may be based on measures of customer and employee satisfaction, productivity, new-product development, market share, or other results that the change process was intended to achieve. The speed, degree, and duration of improvement should also be monitored.

The results of a change process should be monitored continuously. However, because that usually is too costly and time-consuming, assessments typically are made at predetermined intervals. One assessment should be made immediately after a change is implemented.[46] To avoid jumping to premature conclusions, another assessment should be made later. Sometimes the second assessment reveals that the positive effects of change have worn off. Alternatively, a second assessment could reveal delayed positive effects. Misjudging the amount of time needed to see the positive results of a change process is perhaps the most common mistake that managers make.

As this description of the change process reveals, organizational change is a complex undertaking. For the process to lead to desired outcomes, each step must be completed satisfactorily, even if the order of the steps is different from that shown in Figure 13.2. Once a decision to undertake change has been made, the change process can be started more easily if the organization has been prepared for it in advance. Effective leaders ensure that an organization is ready for change even before substantial changes are considered. Table 13.2 describes several actions that managers should take in order to create an organization that is in a continual state of readiness for change.

APPROACHES TO CHANGE

5

DESCRIBE FOUR APPROACHES TO PLANNED ORGANIZATIONAL CHANGE

We next discuss the four major approaches to change depicted in Figure 13.3. Although we describe each separately, some combination of these approaches is involved in most large organizational change efforts. Seldom can significant change be based on one of these approaches alone.[47]

T a b l e 1 3 . 2	*Preparing for Organizational Change: Guidelines for Managers*

Managers can prepare their organizations for successful organizational change by following these guidelines prior to initiating a change effort. Several of these guidelines presume that managers will engage in preparing for change well in advance of the decision that a particular change is needed. The objective for managers should be to ensure that their organization maintains a state of readiness for change so that it can move quickly and effectively when major changes are needed.

Develop a Prolearning Orientation Among Employees

- Provide frequent opportunities for employees to take responsibility for problem identification and problem solving.

- Develop open communication channels and ensure that they are used frequently to inform employees of organizational successes and failures.

- Do everything possible to keep employees informed of customers' preferences and the evaluations of the services and products offered by the organization.

- Encourage small-scale experimentation to produce solutions to emerging problems before large-scale solutions are needed.

Develop a Resilient Workforce

- Use resilience-to-change as a basis for hiring and promotion decisions.

- Educate the workforce about the fundamentals of organizational change processes.

- Train employees to understand the symptoms and causes of resistance and cynicism, and train managers in effective means for reducing resistance and cynicism.

- Celebrate successful change efforts—large and small—to build confidence in the organization's capacity for change.

Build the Architecture to Support Change Initiatives

- Develop a means for recording lessons learned from change efforts and ensuring these lessons are used to guide future change efforts.

- Train managers in structured approaches to change rather than allowing them to rely on their intuition and instincts.

- Create opportunities for employees to work in cross-functional teams as a means of developing the teamwork and communication competencies often needed for large-scale change efforts.

- Identify key measures that can be used to regularly assess organizational performance. Regularly assess the organization against these measures to establish a baseline against which future change can be assessed.

Sources: J. L. McCarthy. *A Blueprint for Change: A Conference Report.* (No. 1149-96-CH). New York: Conference Board, 1996; T. J. Galpin. *The Human Side of Change.* San Francisco: Jossey-Bass, 1996; Price Waterhouse. *Better Change: Best Practices for Transforming Your Organization.* Burr Ridge, Ill.: Irwin, 1995; and B. Schneider, A. P. Brief, and R. A. Guzzo. Creating a climate and culture for sustainable organizational change. *Organizational Dynamics,* 24 (4), 1996, pp. 6–19.

Figure 13.3 **Approaches to Organizational Change**

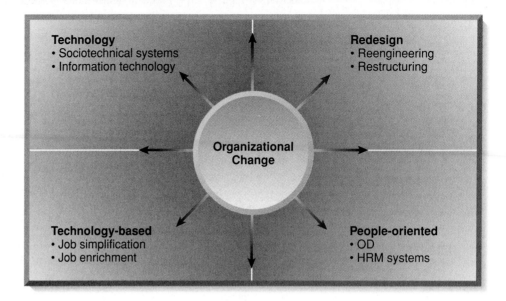

The technology-based approach focuses on change in workflows, production methods, materials, and information systems. The redesign approach emphasizes internal structural changes: realigning departments, changing who makes decisions, and merging or reorganizing departments that sell the company's products. The task-based approach concentrates on changing specific employee job responsibilities and tasks. The people-oriented approach includes a wide range of activities intended to improve individual competencies and performance levels. The people-oriented approach often has implications for all components of the human resources management system.

TECHNOLOGY-BASED APPROACH

At the turn of the century, Frederick Taylor changed the workplace with his ideas of scientific management. Recall that his basic aim was to increase organizational efficiency by the application of scientific principles. In 1908, Henry Ford launched the mass production of cars. In an age of mass consumption, assembly lines were ideal for making identical goods in volume. No longer were skilled craftsmen needed to piece together one-of-a-kind vehicles from nonstandard parts. Employees became replaceable parts.

In many of today's markets, customers and competition are pushing companies to add niche items and shorten production schedules.[48] Hence many organizations—forced to turn out goods in smaller lots and change lines quickly—can't mass produce the quantities needed to make traditional assembly lines profitable. If traditional mass-production assembly lines are posing problems for organizations, what's a better approach? Sony, USAA, and Stanley Works are among those that have dismantled their assembly lines and replaced them with sociotechnical systems.

SOCIOTECHNICAL SYSTEMS

Consideration of the needs of both employee and organization in devising ways to satisfy customer demand.

Sociotechnical Systems. *Sociotechnical systems* involve consideration of the needs of both employee and organization in devising ways to satisfy customer demand. That is, employees must be able to satisfy their needs at the same time that the organization must be able to produce the goods or services desired by its customers. An essential aspect of the sociotechnical approach to change is to give teams of employees the responsibility for a product or service and allow them to make decisions about task assignments and work methods.[49] Team members are expected to learn all the jobs within their team's area of responsibility. Frequently, they are paid on the basis of their competencies, rather than on seniority. We have referred to the growing use of teams repeatedly in the preceding chapters and describe it in more detail in Chapter 17.

INFORMATION TECHNOLOGY

Complex networks of computers, telecommunications systems, and remote-controlled devices.

Information Technology. Coping with competition often requires information flexibility. *Information technology* (IT) comprises complex networks of computers, telecommunications systems, and remote-controlled devices. An organization now can have electronic links to its suppliers and customers. It can link its manufacturing and inventory functions so that, as soon as the supply of a part runs low, a central computer automatically executes an electronic purchase order signaling the supplier to ship a new quantity of the part. Such technologies enable learning organizations to diffuse their best practices instantly throughout a country or around the world. For organizations with Web sites, it provides an efficient method for communicating with customers. In addition to providing comments and feedback to the company, Web sites can be used to educate customers about changes in the organization's products and services. At the Yahoo! site, employees and customers hold a continuing electronic conversation about both the changes that customers request and the actions that Yahoo! takes in response.

Computer-integrated manufacturing (CIM) is another type of technology that can facilitate organization change. CIM links sales, production, and shipping functions. This technology breaks down barriers between departments, improves quality control, and reduces inventory costs by creating just-in-time manufacturing processes. The employees involved can use their computers to "talk" to each other and monitor the manufacturing process as the product moves through the system.[50]

Harley Davidson Motorcycle Company used this approach to attack its quality problems, which had resulted in drastic declines in market share. Managers and employees designed a just-in-time (JIT) inventory system and statistical process control techniques. The JIT system scheduled raw materials to arrive only as needed, which produced huge inventory savings. Harley gradually invested money in other new technologies, such as robots and computer-aided manufacturing (CAM) techniques, to help employees improve quality. Statistical process controls enabled employees to monitor quality and make corrections immediately rather than waiting for them to show up in a dealer's showroom. Dealer satisfaction improved dramatically as customer complaints about quality dropped. Dealers were able to stock fewer parts because of higher quality, and, when needed, parts were shipped immediately. These improvements allowed Harley to slash production and service costs while greatly improving the quality of its bikes.[51] We describe other uses of information technology further in Chapter 21.

REDESIGN APPROACH

We discussed the fundamentals of organization design and described contemporary design practices in Chapters 10 and 11. As we pointed out, in the 1990s, many organizations have experimented with changing their organization designs. Sometimes the need for redesign follows directly from implementing new technologies. As Mellon Bank's customers became more comfortable using Automatic Teller Machines (ATMs), the bank found that it needed 30 percent fewer branches. The remaining branches were redesigned to focus more on selling new products and offering new services than on cashing checks.[52]

Managers are bombarded by ideas on how to redesign their organizations to improve customer satisfaction. These ideas include delayering, downsizing, reengineering, restructuring, and becoming networked. Regardless of the redesign chosen, the intent usually is to clarify what gives the organization its leadership position with its customers. In other words, design changes should capitalize on the capabilities that distinguish the organization from its competitors. Businesses, products, or services that don't contribute to this goal are candidates for elimination or sale.

REENGINEERING
Creating new ways to get work done, often involving redesigning the processes related to logistics, distribution, and manufacturing.

Reengineering. *Reengineering* focuses on creating new ways to get work done. It often involves the redesign of processes related to logistics, manufacturing, and distribution. The goal is to design the most effective process for delivering a service or product.[53] Effective processes are those that cost the least while at the same time producing goods and providing services of excellent quality rapidly. Thus the starting point is to assess current processes from the customer's point of view.

Successful reengineering requires managers and employees to examine the breadth of activities to be redesigned and the depth of the changes needed. In terms of *breadth,* although reengineering a single activity or function may be important to an organization, including more activities is likely to extend its benefits throughout the organization.[54] Often, reengineering a process is interrelated with other key activities. Recall that many organizations are structured by function and that employees' ideas about change typically are based on its effect on their departments. However, reengineering requires employees to think across functions. Reengineering can reduce the amount of "hand-offs" between departments by increasing the amount of resources that are brought together simultaneously to meet customers' needs. Benefits may include faster delivery time, more accurate billing, and fewer defective products that must be returned.

The *depth* of a reengineering effort is measured by the number of roles, responsibilities, rewards, incentives, and information technologies to be changed. Successful reengineering requires in-depth changes. If reengineering efforts are sufficiently deep, the old support systems (e.g., accounting, performance measurement, training, and compensation) will become obsolete. Starting from scratch, in effect, the organization can redesign itself and new support systems will emerge. In the short run, the change process may create excess capacity and financial stress. Unless the organization is growing, such pressures can lead to layoffs.[55]

Firms capable of growth can undergo changes to improve efficiency without having to suffer this short-term side effect. With 85 percent of Banca di America's (BAI) revenues coming from retail banking, its managers chose reengineering as the way to improve customer satisfaction. Two teams of BAI employees diagnosed customer transactions and categorized them as payments, deposits, withdrawals, money orders, and the like. By carefully documenting the processes for each transaction (e.g., depositing a check drawn on another bank in a customer's account), they discovered that a simple deposit transaction required sixty-four activities and nine forms. After reengineering this process, the same transaction required only twenty-five activities and two forms. The average number of employees per branch has dropped from nine to three or four. These savings allowed BAI to open fifty new branches and increase revenues by 24 percent without adding personnel.[56]

RESTRUCTURING
Reconfiguring the levels of authority, responsibility, and control in an organization.

Restructuring. *Restructuring* typically means reconfiguring the distribution of authority, responsibility, and control in the organization.[57] Entire businesses or divisions might be combined or spun off. When Sears, Roebuck & Company recently restructured, it sold off interests in insurance (Allstate Insurance Company), real estate (Coldwell Banker), and finance (Dean Witter Reynolds). The objective was to refocus on merchandising. In addition, Sears took drastic measures to reduce overhead and improve productivity.

Managers often assess what needs to be restructured through the computation of ratios. Such ratios include total employees to sales, corporate staff to operating employees, and managerial span of control. An organization typically benchmarks competitors to determine how their ratios compare.

Restructuring isn't guaranteed to work. Several studies indicate that restructured firms end up in worse financial shape after the restructuring than they were before. Obviously, no one knows whether the firms would have even survived without the radical changes undertaken. Regardless of how effective it may be in the long run, when restructuring involves layoffs, it is a painful experience for both those who were let go and those who survive the cuts. The survivors often feel guilty because, somehow, they have been spared, but they also are anxious because they might be next. Survivors often have trouble maintaining a commitment to an organization when they might be "doing time" until the next round of layoffs is announced.[58]

TASK-BASED APPROACH

Whenever a job is changed—whether because of new technology or a redesign effort—tasks also change. Two dramatically different ways of changing a task are job simplification and job enrichment.

Job Simplification. The oldest task approach to change is job simplification. *Job simplification* involves the scientific analysis of tasks performed by employees in order to discover procedures that produce the maximum output for the minimum input. The job specification states the tasks to be performed, the work methods to be used, and the work flow to be obtained. Recall that the scientific management techniques developed by Frederick Taylor defined jobs and designed tasks on the basis of time-and-motion studies (see Chapter 2). Like process reengineering, job simplification is founded on engineering concepts. But there is a big difference between these two approaches to change. Reengineering focuses on an entire process, which may involve many employees working in many parts of the organization. For example, at BAI, the deposit transaction that was reengineered involved tellers in the front office and data processors in the back room. In contrast, the focus of job simplification is the work done by employees in a particular job.

Many fast-food restaurants, such as McDonald's, Burger King, and Hardee's, use job simplification because (1) employees can learn tasks rapidly, (2) short work cycles allow task performance with little or no mental effort, and (3) low-skilled and low-paid employees can be hired and trained easily. The downside of job simplification is that it leads to low employee commitment and high turnover. Most current competitive challenges require a committed and involved workforce that is able to make decisions and experiment with new ways to do things. Many people seek jobs that allow greater discretion and offer more of a challenge. Designing jobs with employee needs in mind requires a different approach.

Job Enrichment. Changing job specifications to broaden and add challenge to the tasks required in order to increase productivity is called *job enrichment.* Job enrichment has four unique aspects. First, it changes the basic relationships between employees and their work. Job enrichment is based on the assumption that interesting and challenging work can be a source of employee satisfaction and involvement. We describe the motivational benefits of job enrichment in more detail in Chapter 14.

Second, job enrichment directly changes employee behaviors in ways that gradually lead to more positive attitudes about the organization and a better self-image. Because enriched jobs usually increase feelings of autonomy and personal freedom, employees are likely to develop attitudes that support the new job-related behaviors.

Third, job enrichment offers numerous opportunities for initiating other types of organizational change. Technical problems are likely to develop when jobs are

JOB SIMPLIFICATION
Scientific analysis of tasks performed in order to develop ways to produce the maximum output for the minimum input.

JOB ENRICHMENT
Changing job specifications to broaden and add challenge to the tasks required in order to increase productivity.

changed, which offers management an opportunity to refine the technology used. Interpersonal problems almost inevitably arise between managers and subordinates and sometimes among co-workers who have to relate to one another in different ways. These situations offer opportunities for developing teamwork and communication competencies.

Finally, job enrichment can humanize an organization. Individuals can experience the psychological lift that comes from developing new competencies and doing a job well. Individuals are encouraged to grow and push themselves.

PEOPLE-ORIENTED APPROACH

On the one hand, technology, design, and task approaches try to improve organizational performance by changing the way work is done. The assumption is that employees will change as required by the changes made in their work settings.[59] People-oriented approaches, on the other hand, attempt to create organizational change by focusing on changing employee perceptions, attitudes, competencies, and expectations. As these factors change, employees may then seek changes in the organization's technology, design, or tasks. According to this view, employees are the captains of change, not just the vessels for carrying it out.

People-oriented change can involve individuals, groups, or the entire organization. Many people-oriented approaches are commonly grouped under a broad label—organization development. ***Organization development (OD)*** is a planned, long-range behavioral science strategy for understanding, changing, and developing an organization's workforce in order to improve its effectiveness.[60] Although OD methods frequently include design, technological, and task changes, their primary focus is on changing people. Three core sets of values define the OD approach to organizational change and are consistent with learning organizations.

- **People values.** People have a natural desire to grow and develop. Organization development aims to overcome obstacles to individual growth and enable employees to give more to the organization. It stresses treating people with dignity and respect, behaving genuinely rather than playing games, and communicating openly.

- **Group values.** Acceptance, collaboration, and involvement in a group lead to expressions of feelings and perceptions. Hiding feelings or not being accepted by the group diminishes the individual's willingness to work constructively toward solutions to problems. Openness can be risky, but it can usually help people effectively plan solutions to problems and carry them out.

- **Organization values.** The way groups are linked strongly influences their effectiveness. Organization development recognizes the importance of starting the change process at the top and gradually introducing it throughout the rest of the organization. Top-level managers shouldn't attempt to introduce change at lower levels of the organization until they have begun to change themselves.

Of the many OD methods available, one of the most commonly used is survey feedback. ***Survey feedback*** allows managers and employees to provide feedback about the organization and receive feedback about their own behaviors.[61] Such information becomes the basis for group discussion and the stimulus for change. Accurate feedback from others about behaviors and job performance is one of the primary characteristics and values on which OD is based.

Feedback is obtained by means of a questionnaire, which is developed and distributed to all employees, who complete it and turn it in anonymously. The con-

ORGANIZATION DEVELOPMENT

A planned long-range behavioral science strategy for understanding, changing, and developing an organization's workforce in order to improve its effectiveness.

SURVEY FEEDBACK

An OD method that allows managers and employees to provide feedback about the organization and receive feedback about their own behaviors.

tent of the questionnaire depends on the areas of most concern to the organization. Typically, however, employee surveys tap into employees' feelings of commitment and satisfaction, their assessments of the climate for innovation, the degree to which employees feel that the organization is customer-oriented, and attitudes toward supervision and management practices.

Surveys used for obtaining feedback may be custom-designed for the organization. Alternatively, standardized questionnaires can be used. The advantage of custom-designed questionnaires is that they focus specifically on the topics of interest to the organization. A disadvantage is that they can be difficult to interpret unless the same questions have been asked over a period of a few years. When information is available for a period of several years, a custom-designed questionnaire can be used to assess whether the organization is or isn't generally improving.

An alternative to a custom-designed questionnaire is a standardized questionnaire. A standardized questionnaire is one that has been developed for use in a wide range of organizations. Often a standardized questionnaire has been developed according to scientific principles, so users of the questionnaire can be confident that the assessments it yields are valid reflections of the organization. Because standardized questionnaires often have been used by several organizations in the past, they allow an organization to compare its employees' responses to those of employees in other organizations. Benchmarking permits management to assess the degree to which employee attitudes match or diverge from the attitudes of employees in other organizations. Table 13.3 describes a standardized questionnaire developed to assess employee perceptions of their organization's climate for creativity.

| *T a b l e   1 3 . 3* | *Survey Feedback Using KEYS: A Survey for Assessing an Organization's Climate for Creativity* |

KEYS is a newly developed survey that organizations can use to assess the extent to which employees perceive their workplace to be supportive of creativity and innovation. Based on the diagnosis that KEYS provides, organizations can determine whether changes are needed to improve the existing climate. If improvements are needed, the results of the survey also provide information about which specific aspects of an organization's culture require change in order to be more supportive of creativity and innovation.

KEYS includes seventy-eight statements designed to assess perceptions of encouragement for creativity, autonomy and freedom, available resources, pressures, and impediments to creativity. Employees use a four-point scale to indicate the extent to which they agree with statements. Sample questions are shown below.

Examples of statements included in KEYS:

People are encouraged to solve problems creatively in this organization.

My supervisor serves as a good work model.

There is free and open communication within my work group.

Generally I can get the resources I need for my work.

I have too much work to do in too little time.

There are many political problems in the organization.

During the past ten years, more than 15,000 employees from dozens of organizations have completed the KEYS survey. Research of employees who work on creative projects has shown that scores on the KEYS questionnaire are higher in work units that produce creative results and lower in work units that produce less creative results.

Source: Adapted from T. M. Amabile, R. Conti, H. Coon, J. Lazenby, and M. Herron. Assessing the work environment for creativity. *Academy of Management Journal, 39,* 1996, pp. 1154–1184; and T. M. Amabile. *KEYS: Assessing the Climate for Creativity.* Greensboro, N.C.: Center for Creative Leadership, 1995.

Survey feedback works best as a bridge between the diagnosis of organizational problems and the implementation of other people-oriented approaches to change. There is little evidence to suggest that survey feedback alone will result in changes in individual behavior or organizational effectiveness. However, it does enable managers to collect information from a large number of employees and feed that information back to them for purposes of solving organizational problems.

There are too many people-oriented approaches to change to list them all here. In general, however, people-oriented approaches usually involve changing the organization's human resources management practices (see Chapter 12). When large-scale organizational change is the objective, changes in many aspects of the human resources management system might be considered. For example, if an organization seeks to improve customer satisfaction, it should consider using selection and training techniques that increase the levels of customer-oriented competencies among new recruits, as well as redesigning compensation and reward systems. If an organization changes the technologies, design, and tasks of employees to increase the quality of products and services, it should also offer appropriate training and make changes to both the performance measurement and compensation components of the human resources management system.

CHAPTER SUMMARY

Whether they are newly established or mature, organizations of all types maintain their vitality by innovating, changing, and learning from their experiences. As the external environment becomes increasingly competitive and turbulent, the most effective organizations will be those that build innovation, change, and learning into their normal operations.

1. EXPLAIN THE RELATIONSHIP BETWEEN INNOVATION AND ORGANIZATIONAL CHANGE.

Innovation is the process of creating and implementing a new idea. Three basic types of innovation are technical, process, and administrative. Organizational change refers to any transformation in the design or functioning of an organization. Generally, innovations require organizational change. Innovation and change are important to both new and established organizations, owing to the dynamic nature of the external environments of most organizations.

2. DESCRIBE THE FEATURES OF LEARNING ORGANIZATIONS THAT ENABLE THEM TO ANTICIPATE AND EFFECTIVELY DEAL WITH CHANGE.

Organizations are redesigning themselves to become learning organizations capable of quickly adapting their practices to satisfy the needs of their customers. The basic features of such organizations are culture,

leadership, strategy, organization design, and information sharing.

3. ASSESS YOUR OWN REACTIONS TO INNOVATION AND CHANGE.

Learning organizations require employees who are comfortable with innovation and change. Your score on the survey quiz titled "How Innovative Are You?" indicates whether you tend to enjoy innovation and change or prefer stability and routine.

4. EXPLAIN THE PROCESS OF PLANNED ORGANIZATIONAL CHANGE.

Planned organizational change consists of (1) assessing changes in the environment; (2) determining whether a performance gap exists and, if so, its nature and magnitude; (3) diagnosing organizational problems; (4) identifying sources of resistance to change; (5) selecting methods for reducing resistance; (6) setting clear, realistic, and attainable goals for change; (7) implementing a change strategy that will accomplish the stated goals; and (8) following up to determine whether the change has been successful.

5. DESCRIBE FOUR APPROACHES TO ORGANIZATIONAL CHANGE.

Technology-based change includes sociotechnical systems and information technology. The sociotechnical system balances the needs of employees with those of the organization. The redesign approach involves reengineering, which is concerned with changing the way work is carried out, and restructuring, which involves changing levels of authority, control, and responsibility. Redesign changes normally affect large portions of an organization. Task-based approaches include job simplification, which uses scientific management principles to redesign tasks, and job enrichment, which permits employees to satisfy their needs by doing work that involves various tasks. People-oriented approaches can be used to change employee attitudes and behaviors. Survey feedback permits managers and employees to provide information about a range of topics, including job satisfaction, organizational commitment, and perceptions of supervisory and managerial behaviors. Major organizational change often involves using all four approaches.

QUESTIONS FOR DISCUSSION

1. What approaches to change did management at Xerox Business Services use to sustain its growth?

2. How are the basic features of a learning organization different from those of a bureaucratic organization?

3. Evaluate the following statement: "We trained hard, but it seemed that every time we were beginning to form into teams, we would be reorganized. We tend to meet any new situation by reorganizing, and what a wonderful method it can be for creating the illusion of progress while producing confusion, inefficiency, and demoralization." (Petronius, 210 B.C.)

4. What are the main differences among the four approaches to achieving change? How are these approaches similar?

5. Is the way you react to innovation and change a fixed aspect of your personality? Do you think you can develop the competencies needed to be effective in organizations experiencing change? Explain.

6. Describe a situation in which you resisted change. Why did you do so? What were the consequences of your resistance?

EXERCISES TO DEVELOP YOUR MANAGERIAL COMPETENCIES

1. **Planning and Administration Competency.** Imagine that your school has decided to make a rather drastic change in how courses are structured. Under the new system, courses can be of varying lengths (from a one-day course to a course that spans two years) and offered on any days of the year. Working with a partner, develop twenty questions that should be included in a survey feedback instrument to be used by your school. Keeping in mind that the school has already made the decision to implement the change, indicate who you would ask to complete the survey and explain why. Before you begin, explore your school's Web site. Learn as much as you can about how the organization is currently structured and what types of course schedules currently exist. (If your school doesn't yet have a Web site, obtain the information in other ways.)

2. **Strategic Action Competency.** *FastCompany* is a business magazine that describes itself as the "Handbook of the Business Revolution." This company was based on two ideas: A global revolution is underway that is changing the world of business, and business is changing the world. The company's founders believed that the current revolution will be as far-reaching as the industrial revolution. Besides having fun, *FastCompany's* founders set out to chronicle this revolution and stimulate conversations about it. Through their magazine, they hoped to disseminate innovative best practices and leading ideas, identify the values of the revolution, debunk old myths, and discover new legends. What are the newest ideas being discussed in this handbook? To find out, visit the electronic version of *FastCompany* at

www.fastcompany.com

3. **Communication Competency.** The process of organizational change requires extensive communication among all parts of an organization. For global organizations, communications can be particularly challenging. First, explain why communication is important to change efforts and describe how differences in cultures, locations, and time zones can interfere with effective communication during the process of a planned organizational change. Second, describe how information technology can be used to address these issues. To learn about the current capabilities of communication technology, visit the home page of Computer Mediated Communications Magazine at

www.december.com/cmc/mag

4. **Self-Management Competency.** When Xerox (and the XBS division in particular) hires new employees, it wants to be sure that it selects people who will fit into a learning organization. Investigate the current job openings at Xerox. What characteristics and competencies seem to be valued for job applicants? What could you do to develop the competencies that Xerox values? Does Xerox seem to discourage applicants who might not be effective in this learning organization? Explain. You can find lists of job openings by visiting the home pages of Xerox at

www.com.xerox/employment

and XBS at

www.xerox.com/XBS

For a more general listing of job openings, visit the home page maintained by the National Association of Colleges and Employers at

www.jobweb.org

5. **Global Awareness Competency.** Grace Cocoa was created by merging six leading manufacturers of cocoa and chocolate brands that were spread throughout some sixteen countries. In the early 1990s, the organization operated as six nearly autonomous companies with almost no collaboration. However, to be most effective, the managers in these firms needed to work together as parts of one smoothly running company. Then top management announced an organizational redesign. At the time, the lower level managers expressed little interest in changing. After investigating the problem further, the company began an intensive managerial learning and development process designed to integrate the units. The process was designed to address issues that had been identified in a survey of key managers. By 1997, Grace Cocoa had made the transition to a new design—one that it believed was appropriate for an organization that needed to operate as a global entity. The new design is based on functional groupings. Thus, regardless of where they are located around the world, everyone within the same functional area reports to the same executive.[62] Why were managers initially reluctant to make changes in the way they operated? Is the new functional structure likely to facilitate organizational learning across cultures and countries? Explain.

REAL-TIME CASE ANALYSIS

KINKO'S GOES CORPORATE

Ever wonder where the name Kinko's came from? The nickname was given to Paul Orfalea, inspired by his red hair. In 1970, Orfalea founded Kinko's, the copy shop company, by setting up one copier in a converted taco stand. Until 1996, Kinko's culture was as casual as its name suggests. Decisions were made by consensus, which took a lot of time but also seemed to build a committed community of partners. But much has changed during the past couple of years. To celebrate Kinko's twenty-sixth birthday, CEO Orfalea decided to sell a 30 percent stake of the privately held company to Clayton, Dublier & Rice (CDR), a New York investment firm. Before CDR came on the scene, Kinko's was owned by 128 partners, who operated a total of 851 stores. Now those partners own an estimated 35 percent of the company, with Orfalea holding the remaining 35 percent of shares. Orfalea compared that day to his wedding day: "It's scary and happy at the same time," he said.

Kinko's was phenomenally successful under Orfalea's leadership. A champion of innovation, he gave annual awards (e.g., all-expense-paid vacations to Disneyland) to the employees of the copy shop that came up with the most innovative idea during the year. While the employees enjoyed their reward, Orfalea and his board would stay behind to attend to customers. Among the new services developed was digitized document services, allowing customers to send electronic text and image documents over the Internet for instant printing anywhere in the world. Charlotte McManus and C. Rollin Buchanan, owners of a Kinko's store in Irvine, California, started and developed this service, which has grown to become a division of Kinko's. In Atlanta, Kinko's stores operate a center for learning and training, which can be accessed via the Internet. However, as some stores grew rapidly as a result of the innovations they made, others lagged behind. In 1996, nearly a third of the stores were unprofitable.

Now that Orfalea is no longer in charge, the culture of the firm is changing. To cut costs, CDR consolidated partners' debts, centralized purchasing, and is financing overseas expansion. Daily management of the firm is in the hands of professional outside managers, leaving Orfalea with more time to think up new ideas. Kinko's partners know that the change from entrepreneurial autonomy to corporate oversight won't always be easy. "There will be turmoil in the transition," observed Orfalea's cousin, who also was one of the first Kinko's partners. "Once in a while you have a twinge, but the other side is we can gain a lot."[63]

QUESTIONS

1. Was the old Kinko's a learning organization? Is it important for the new Kinko's to be a learning organization? Why or why not?

2. Of the four approaches to learning described in this chapter, which ones is Kinko's most likely to use to make the change from a decentralized, entrepreneurial firm to a more centralized, professionally managed corporation?

3. How much and what type of resistance to change would you expect from the 128 Kinko's partners? Why? What should CDR do to reduce resistance to change?

4. Orfalea says his goal for the new Kinko's is to have 2,000 stores by 2000. Is that an achievable goal? What factors might determine whether the company succeeds in achieving this goal or fails to do so?

5. Review Chapter 5. Based on what you know about entrepreneurs, what is Paul Orfalea likely to do next: Sell his stake in Kinko's? Start a new business? Attempt to retake control of the firm? Simply retire? Become an "angel"? Explain your choice.

To learn more about Kinko's, visit its corporate home page at

www.kinkos.com

its Atlanta learning center home page at

www.tlckinkos.com

and its document solution division home page at

www.edp.com

VIDEO CASE

YAHOO!: LEARNING OUT LOUD

Yahoo! is the model learning organization. From an idea dreamed up by two Stanford graduate students to one of the first ventures to derive revenues from Web-based advertising to a spectacular public offering and rapid growth through alliances and acquisitions, Yahoo!'s managers and employees have steadily absorbed and applied lessons from an industry involved in explosive growth.

Yahoo!'s industry—services based on the Internet and its World Wide Web—requires that the company be continually innovative and meet demanding schedules. (In the industry's jargon, a "Web year" occurs every three months.) Its innovativeness and success have attracted people who are both willing to work with change and throw themselves unstintingly into their work. In fact, many of the people attracted

to the information technology industry are extremely self-motivated—self-management is already an integral part of their basic philosophy and competency.

Although Yahoo! can maintain a crazy corporate culture—with employees camped out for the night in their cubicles—it also has to deal with other companies with more traditional cultures. Some Internet start-ups have had to hire older, experienced employees just to give the impression of "adult supervision" and to appear less weird to strategic partners. Many acquire more traditional executives as they seek to attract investment partners, especially if they attempt to go public with an initial stock offering. Senior managers in Internet start-ups need to understand how their organizations can best function internally while, at the same time, meshing with other organizations in necessary outside alliances and vendor relationships.

A company that encourages its employees to learn, yet fails to provide an environment in which those employees can see their ideas become reality, may risk losing those employees to other companies or to forming their own ventures. Apple Computer, which might have served as an inspiration to Yahoo!'s entrepreneurs—Apple's cofounders had similarly started their future billion-dollar company in a garage two decades earlier—has lost large numbers of highly skilled employees and has cut projects and innovation efforts as it's fallen on hard times.

Yahoo!'s services have expanded from its core Web catalog service into a number of other areas, including

- city-localized and country-specific Web cataloging,

- co-branding with other major information services,

- customer-capturing services such as free e-mail, and

- traditional print publishing.

Almost certainly some of these new ventures won't succeed or will require modification to succeed. In localized services, Yahoo! is competing head to head with Microsoft's Sidewalk services, as well as with established "traditional" media organizations (newspapers, magazines, radio, and television) that are expanding to the Web. That Yahoo! management needs to exercise a broad vision and execute strategic decisions goes without saying. As Yahoo! blazes trails in cyberspace, the rapidity of development and economies of the Web mean that competition will come drafting in its wake.

As an information age company—nearly every employee uses a computer every day in his or her work—Yahoo! is well situated to be a learning organization: Employees can rapidly interact via e-mail or reach out and touch colleagues through the Internet. Even better, Yahoo! is in the business of receiving, maintaining, and serving others' content and in so doing can absorb and understand trends and innovations in its industry.

According to cofounder Jerry Yang, the company seeks out generalists with the capacity to comprehend multiple disciplines and to be "confident, but not arrogant." Individuals at Yahoo! can take actions affecting the lives of millions of users. A manager, surrounded by enthusiastic, self-motivated, "renaissance" individuals, faces a unique challenge, requiring, in particular, excellent communication and teamwork competencies.

Yahoo!'s cofounders, Yang and Filo, have already used the fruits of their learning to prime the pump for future learning, having endowed Stanford University—from which they had dropped out to launch their business—with a $2 million "Yahoo! Founders" chair.

ON THE WEB

As one of the World Wide Web's primary features, the Yahoo! site (*www.yahoo.com*) is the obvious place for a Web surfer to start. The site itself is parent to a host of related subsites (e.g., Yahoo! Washington D.C. and Yahooligans!, a "Web guide for kids").

Yahoo! is allied in partnerships with other Web ventures that complement its services and make its site more complete and compelling. For example, Yahoo! provides Web search services through a partnership with Digital Equipment Corporation"s "Alta-Vista" subsidiary and stock market quotes and news from Reuters.

Yahoo!'s competitors on the Web include Microsoft Sidewalk (*www.sidewalk.com*), which is looking to strip away Yahoo!'s city-specific, local audience; and other search engines such as Excite (*www.excite.com*) and Lycos (*0*).

QUESTIONS

1. How might universities serve as incubators for learning organizations?

2. What constraints or concerns might an organization encounter in learning from its customers?

3. How much emphasis should a learning organization's management place on employee retention?

To help you answer these questions and learn more about Yahoo!, visit the company's home page at

www.yahoo.com

Case contributed by Ross Stapleton-Gray, President, TeleDiplomacy, Inc., a technology and policy consultancy, and Adjunct Professor in Georgetown University's Communication, Culture, and Technology program.

PART 5

Leading

Chapter

14

Motivating for Performance

Outline

What Motivates Steve Dorner?

Steve Dorner isn't a household name, but Eudora, the e-mail software he invented, is. In fact, more than 18 million people use Eudora, a product owned by Qualcomm, Dorner's employer. A telecommunications company based in San Diego, Qualcomm purchased licensing and development rights, and eventually the Eudora trademark, from the University of Illinois at Champaign–Urbana. The university was Dorner's employer when he invented Eudora and it held all rights to his invention. When the university sold those rights for less than $1 million, he received no royalties. Today, his invention is the world's leading Internet e-mail package, providing complete connectivity among virtually all types of personal computers. Contrast Dorner's situation with that of Mark Andreesen, who was an undergraduate student at Illinois. While Dorner was working on Eudora, Andreesen was working on a software program called Mosaic. Mosaic eventually became Netscape Navigator. As founder and CEO of Netscape, Andreesen was a millionaire by age twenty-four.

After Eudora became a Qualcomm product, Dorner gave up his position at the university to go to work for Qualcomm so that he could continue working on Eudora. His wife didn't want to move to San Diego, however, so he arranged to be a telecommuter. Giving employees wide latitude and respect is central to Qualcomm's culture. For his first two years as a Qualcomm employee, Dorner chose to work out of a small windowless room that had been built as a bomb shelter under his house and was entered through a trap door. Then he moved into the family's woodworking shop, which has windows and heat, but still affords the isolation needed for him to stay focused on his work. These conditions suit Dorner fine. "After working four years at home," he said, "I never want to move back to an office."

Software programming is highly skilled work. According to one expert, "It's a young person's skill. It requires intense concentration. To do a good job, you have to have your mind wrapped around the whole program.

. . . You have to be constantly focussed on the goal." Dorner enjoys the creative aspects of the task, which he says include "figuring out the real problem people are trying to solve and the best way to solve the problem." Dorner also enjoys the contact he has with Eudora users, who send about 100 e-mail messages a day. "It's very gratifying," he says, "but it can also make me feel a little hunted sometimes. I'm the one who has to, in the final analysis, deal with every single problem."[1]

* * *

To learn more about Qualcomm, visit the company's home page at

www.qualcomm.com

To learn more about Eudora, visit its home page at

www.eudora.com

OVERVIEW OF WORK MOTIVATION THEORIES

1

COMPARE AND CONTRAST FOUR APPROACHES TO UNDERSTANDING WORK MOTIVATION

MOTIVATION
Any influence that brings out, directs, or maintains goal-directed behavior.

Motivation is any influence that triggers, directs, or maintains goal-directed behavior. This chapter is about motivated performance, like that of Steve Dorner. As a manager, you'll be responsible for helping employees perform effectively at work. But you can't fulfill this responsibility until you understand what motivates both you and them. In this chapter, we introduce you to various factors that generate the employee behaviors needed for effective performance.

The question of what motivates people at work is a fundamental one that has long been of interest to managers and researchers alike. Interest in the topic has led to the development of many different theories about work motivation. Each theory offers some insight into this complex topic. However, no single theory adequately addresses all aspects of motivation. The theories described in this chapter fall into four general categories.

1. Theories about individual differences in motivation address questions such as: Are the things that motivate Steve Dorner different from those that motivate Mark Andreesen?

2. Theories about how the job and organization contexts affect motivation address questions such as: Do people who work at Qualcomm find their work more

satisfying than the people who work at Netscape? and Are software programming jobs more motivating than jobs on a chip assembly line?

3. Theories about how managerial behavior affects motivation address questions such as: How can Steve Dorner's boss use goals and rewards to improve Dorner's productivity?

4. Theories that consider the entire motivation process address all of these questions and can be used to design effective motivation systems.

Figure 14.1 lists the theories in each of the four categories. Insights from all of them help in understanding how employees feel about their work and how effective performance management systems can be developed.[2]

As you read about these theories, keep in mind that they were developed and tested primarily in the United States and Canada. Only recently have researchers begun to consider whether these theories also can be used to explain motivation in other cultures. Moreover, management researchers in other countries have just begun to develop theories of motivation that reflect their unique cultures. A discussion of cultural differences in work motivation is beyond the scope of this chapter. Nevertheless, keep in mind that other theories may be needed to explain work motivation elsewhere in the world.[3]

The theories discussed in this chapter focus on the motivation of individuals. U.S. and Canadian theories of motivation reflect the individualism characteristic of this region's culture, as well as the nature of the jobs that employees in these two countries have held during most of this century. Although jobs are now becoming increasingly team oriented, theories of team motivation are not yet as well developed as theories of individual motivation. We address team motivation in Chapter 17.

Figure 14.1 **Approaches to Understanding Motivation**

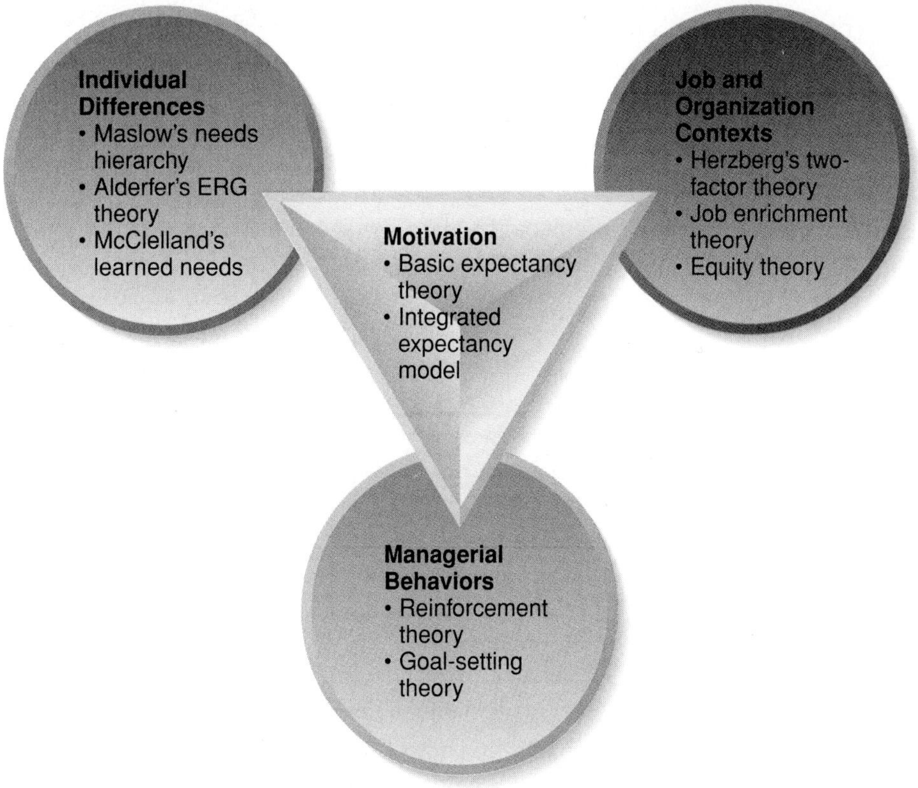

Individual Differences
- Maslow's needs hierarchy
- Alderfer's ERG theory
- McClelland's learned needs

Job and Organization Contexts
- Herzberg's two-factor theory
- Job enrichment theory
- Equity theory

Motivation
- Basic expectancy theory
- Integrated expectancy model

Managerial Behaviors
- Reinforcement theory
- Goal-setting theory

INDIVIDUAL DIFFERENCES

Individual differences are the needs, values, competencies, and other personal characteristics that people bring to their jobs. These characteristics vary from person to person. Each person is different in terms of the needs that are most salient, the values that are most important, the competencies that are most developed, and so on. The specific content of individual differences is what makes each person unique.

The common thread is that these individual differences are important determinants of how people think, feel, and behave. One person may be motivated by an opportunity to earn more money and prefer a job that offers such an opportunity. Another may be motivated by security, preferring a job that involves less risk of unemployment.[4] Yet another may thrive on challenges and seek a position that stretches her competencies to the limit and helps her develop new ones. Effective managers understand the individual differences that shape each employee's unique view of work and use this understanding to maximize each employee's effectiveness.

THE JOB AND ORGANIZATION CONTEXTS

Job characteristics determine the extent to which employees experience work to be meaningful, the level of personal responsibility that employees feel, and the knowledge that employees gain about how well they are performing. As we described in Chapter 13, job enrichment is one method of improving performance. In this chapter, we look more closely at how job design affects employee motivation.

The way jobs are designed determines the immediate context of work, but the job itself isn't the only such determinant of motivation. The organizational context—in particular, the organization's human resources management policies and managerial practices—also affects employee motivation. The appropriate benefits (e.g., paid vacations, sick leave, insurance, and child or elder care), reward structure (e.g., bonuses or commissions), and development opportunities (e.g., training, education, and mentoring) may attract new employees to the organization. Whether such policies serve to motivate and retain existing employees depends on whether employees perceive them as fair and equitable.

MANAGERS' BEHAVIORS

In many organizations, only top-level managers have responsibility for making decisions about how to design jobs and which policies to adopt. Middle and first-line managers then work within the framework created by those decisions. Nevertheless, middle and first-line managers can directly motivate employees through more personal, one-on-one communication. For example, they can work with employees to set realistic goals, and they can use both monetary and nonmonetary means to reward employees for achieving those goals or punish employees for failing to do so. James Taylor, a food-service manager for ARAMARK Corporation, and his employees jointly set goals for serving food to college students. These goals include maintaining food portion sizes, ensuring dining room cleanliness, improving cashiers' speed, preventing theft, and reducing absenteeism. When employees reach their goals, they receive rewards such as tickets to sporting events, golf balls, free dinners at local restaurants, and athletic jackets. When employees don't achieve their goals, Taylor discusses with the employees how they can improve their performance.

AN INTEGRATIVE APPROACH TO MOTIVATION

Many theories of motivation address how one factor (e.g., an individual's needs or the design of a job) affects motivation at any particular time. Few, however, consider the ways in which many factors combine to affect the ebb and flow of a person's motivation over time. Expectancy theory is one that does so. It accounts for individual differences in employee needs, the way work is designed, human resources management policies, and managerial behaviors. Because this theory incorporates ideas from several simpler theories, we describe it near the end of the chapter.

THEORIES ABOUT INDIVIDUAL DIFFERENCES

2

DESCRIBE HOW INDIVIDU-ALS' NEEDS AFFECT MOTIVATION AND PERFORMANCE

NEED

A strong feeling of deficiency that creates an uncomfortable tension. That tension causes a person to take actions to satisfy the need. Satisfying the need reduces the intensity of the motivating force.

mployees differ from each other in many ways. They have different abilities, personalities, values, and needs. During the past century, psychologists have conducted thousands of studies about such differences. Based on those studies, they have created numerous theories to describe the nature of differences among people, the development of individual differences, and the consequences of such differences both on and off the job.

Here, we describe three theories of individual differences that attempt to explain how individual differences affect employee motivation in the workplace. Furthermore, all three of these theories consider individual differences in terms of *needs* as particularly important for explaining what motivates people. The three theories are Maslow's hierarchy of needs, Alderfer's ERG theory, and McClelland's theory of learned needs.

MASLOW'S HIERARCHY OF NEEDS

A *need* is a strong feeling of deficiency in some aspect of a person's life that creates an uncomfortable tension. That tension becomes a motivating force, causing a person to take actions to satisfy the need, reduce the tension, and diminish the intensity of the motivating force.

Figure 14.2   **Maslow's Hierarchy of Needs**

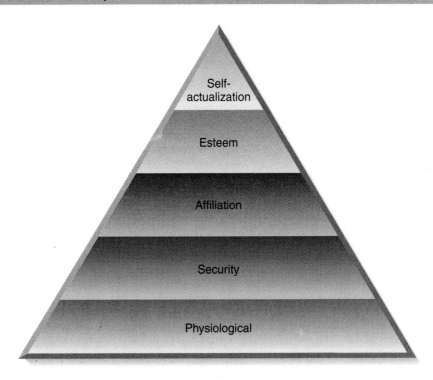

PHYSIOLOGICAL NEEDS
The most basic human desires for food, clothing, and shelter.

SECURITY NEEDS
The desires for safety and stability and the absence of pain, threat, and illness.

AFFILIATION NEEDS
The desires for friendship, love, and belonging.

ESTEEM NEEDS
The desires for self-respect, a sense of personal achievement, and recognition from others.

SELF-ACTUALIZATION NEEDS
The desires for personal growth, self-fulfillment, and the realization of the individual's full potential.

Psychologist Abraham Maslow believed that people have five types of needs, which he arranged in a **hierarchy of needs,** as shown in Figure 14.2: physiological (at the base), security, affiliation, esteem, and self-actualization (at the top). He suggested that, as a person satisfies each level of needs, motivation shifts to satisfying the next higher level of needs.[5]

Physiological needs are those for food, clothing, and shelter. As the most basic human needs, they occupy the first level in Maslow's hierarchy. People try to satisfy physiological needs before all others. For example, the primary motivation of a hungry person is to obtain food rather than, say, gain recognition for achievements. Thus people work for wages that will allow them to meet these needs first.

Security needs include the desire for safety and stability, and the absence of pain, threat, and illness. People deprived of the means to satisfy security needs become preoccupied with obtaining them. Many workers express their security needs as a desire for a stable job with adequate medical, unemployment, and retirement benefits. Organizations that provide stability and such benefits are likely to have relatively low turnover and little dissatisfaction among employees who are striving to meet these needs.

Affiliation needs are the desire for friendship, love, and belonging. This level in Maslow's hierarchy represents a clear step up from the truly basic physiological and security needs. Employees with high affiliation needs enjoy working closely with others. Employees with low affiliation needs may be content to work on tasks by themselves. Steve Dorner seems to fit this description. When an organization doesn't meet affiliation needs, an employee's dissatisfaction may be expressed in terms of frequent absenteeism, low productivity, stress-related behaviors, and even emotional breakdown. A manager who recognizes that a subordinate is striving to satisfy affiliation needs should act supportively. The manager might encourage others to work more closely with the employee and suggest that the employee participate in the organization's social activities.

Esteem needs are the desire for self-respect, a sense of personal achievement, and recognition from others. To satisfy these needs, people seek opportunities for achievement, promotion, prestige, and status—all of which symbolize their competence and worth. Managers who perceive that employees are motivated by esteem needs should emphasize the hard work and finely honed skills that are required for success. They may publicly reward achievement with published achievement lists, bonuses, praise, lapel pins, and articles in the organization's paper. These and other forms of recognition help build employee pride. When the need for esteem is dominant, managers can promote job satisfaction and high-quality performance by providing opportunities for exciting, challenging work and recognition for accomplishments.

Self-actualization needs are the desire for personal growth, self-fulfillment, and the realization of the individual's full potential. Traits commonly exhibited include initiative, spontaneity, and problem-solving ability. Managers who recognize this motivation in employees can help them discover the growth opportunities available in their jobs, or they can create special growth opportunities. For example, at Merck, scientists can attend law school and become patent attorneys; at Hewlett-Packard, a parallel technical ladder was established so that scientists can earn higher salaries without taking on management tasks. At both companies, managers also can offer employees special assignments, such as working on a task force that reports to top management. Such assignments often represent growth opportunities through which employees can develop their managerial competencies while continuing to utilize to the fullest their technical knowledge and skills.[6]

WHICH NEEDS MOTIVATE YOU?

SATISFACTION–PROGRES-SION HYPOTHESIS

The idea that a lower level need must be reasonably satisfied before the next higher level need emerges as a motivator of behavior.

Maslow's theory predicts the needs that will drive a person's behavior, based on consideration of which needs have been satisfied and which remain to be satisfied. A key hypothesis of the theory is the ***satisfaction–progression hypothesis,*** which proposes that a satisfied need is no longer a motivator and that, once a need has been satisfied, another emerges to take its place. In general, lower level needs must be satisfied before higher needs become strong enough to motivate behavior. Thus people are always striving to satisfy some higher need.

Research supports Maslow's view that, until their *basic* needs are satisfied, people won't be concerned with higher level needs.[7] However, little evidence supports the view that people meet their needs precisely as suggested by Maslow's hierarchy (see Figure 14.2). For example, not everyone satisfies social needs (aspects of Maslow's affiliation and esteem needs) before moving on to satisfy self-actualization needs. Some people pay little attention to social needs as long as they are free to do what they do best (e.g., play chess, participate in sports, do handicrafts, or solve computer programming problems).

Do you know which needs are most influential in motivating you at this point in your life? To identify their relative importance to you, complete the questionnaire presented in the Self-Management Competency feature. After you have completed the questionnaire, refer to Tables 1.2 through 1.7 in Chapter 1. What are the implications of your scores for the competencies that you need to develop? For example, strengthening your teamwork competency may enable you to satisfy strong affiliation needs. Developing the drive and persistence component of your self-management competency may improve your chances of satisfying a strong need for self-actualization.

ALDERFER'S ERG THEORY

ERG THEORY

Alderfer's approach to motivation, which specifies a hierarchy of three needs categories: existence, relatedness, and growth.

Like Maslow, Clay Alderfer looked at motivation from a needs perspective. Instead of five categories of needs, however, his ***ERG theory*** specifies three needs categories: existence, relatedness, and growth.[8]

EXISTENCE NEEDS

The desires for material and physical well-being.

Existence needs are the desires for material and physical well-being that are satisfied through food, water, air, shelter, working conditions, pay, fringe benefits, and the like. They are similar to Maslow's physiological and security needs, combined. ***Relatedness needs*** are the desires to establish and maintain interpersonal relationships with other people, including family, friends, supervisors, subordinates, and co-workers. Relatedness is similar to Maslow's affiliation needs. ***Growth needs*** are the desires to be creative, to make useful and productive contributions, and to have opportunities for personal development. They are similar to Maslow's esteem and self-actualization needs.

RELATEDNESS NEEDS

The desires to establish and maintain interpersonal relationships with other people.

GROWTH NEEDS

The desires to be creative, make useful and productive contributions, and have opportunities for personal development.

The ERG model recognizes Maslow's satisfaction–progression hypothesis, but it also contains a frustration–regression hypothesis. The ***frustration–regression hypothesis*** holds that, when individuals are frustrated in meeting higher level needs, the next lower level needs reemerge and again direct behavior. For example, a finish carpenter who does highly creative trim work in houses may work for a contractor who builds from a limited number of floor plans with few trim work options. Because the job doesn't provide a creative outlet, the frustrated carpenter may stop pursuing satisfaction of growth needs at work and instead regress to pursuing activities that satisfy his relatedness needs. An example would be socializing with other construction workers..

FRUSTRATION–REGRES-SION HYPOTHESIS

The idea that frustration in fulfilling a higher level need will result in the reemergence of the next lower level need as a motivator of behavior.

Figure 14.3 illustrates the satisfaction–progression and frustration–regression components of the ERG model. On the right is the satisfaction–progression hypothesis,

SELF-MANAGEMENT COMPETENCY
Work Motivation Questionnaire[9]

This questionnaire is designed to assess the needs that are important to you. There are no right or wrong answers. The best response to any item is simply the one that best reflects your feelings—either as you have experienced them or as you anticipate that you would experience them—in a work situation. Respond to the twenty statements by indicating the degree to which each is true for you. Use the following key and circle the number that best indicates how true and accurate the statement is.

> 1 = Not true and accurate.
>
> 2 = Slightly true and accurate.
>
> 3 = Partly true and accurate.
>
> 4 = Mostly true and accurate.
>
> 5 = Completely true.

1. I believe that the real rewards for working are good pay, working conditions, and the like. 1 2 3 4 5

2. The most important thing to me in evaluating a job is whether it gives me job security and employee benefits. 1 2 3 4 5

3. I would not want a job in which I had no co-workers to talk to and share work stories with. 1 2 3 4 5

4. I want a job that allows rapid advancement based on my own achievements. 1 2 3 4 5

5. Searching for what will make me happy is most important in my life. 1 2 3 4 5

6. Working conditions (office space, equipment, and basic physical necessities) are important to me. 1 2 3 4 5

7. I would not want a job if the equipment was poor or I was without adequate protection against layoffs. 1 2 3 4 5

8. Whether the people I was going to work with were compatible would affect my decision about whether or not to take a promotion. 1 2 3 4 5

9. A job should offer tangible rewards and recognition for a person's performance. 1 2 3 4 5

10. I want a job that is challenging and stimulating and has meaningful activities. 1 2 3 4 5

11. If I took a job in which there were strong pressures to rush and little time for lunch, coffee breaks, and the like, my motivation would suffer. 1 2 3 4 5

12. My motivation would suffer if my fellow employees were cold or held grudges toward me. 1 2 3 4 5

13. Being a valued member of the team and enjoying the social aspects of work are important to me. 1 2 3 4 5

14. I'm likely to work hardest in a situation that offers tangible rewards and recognition for performance. 1 2 3 4 5

15. Going as far as I can, using my skills and capabilities, and exploring new ideas are what really drive me. 1 2 3 4 5

16. An important factor for me is that my job pays well enough to satisfy the needs of my family and me. 1 2 3 4 5

17. Fringe benefits, such as hospitalization insurance, retirement plans, and dental programs, are important to me. 1 2 3 4 5

18. I would likely work hardest in a job where a group of employees discuss and plan their work as a team. 1 2 3 4 5

19. My accomplishments give me an important sense of self-respect. 1 2 3 4 5

20. I would work the hardest in a job where I could see the returns of my work from the standpoint of personal interest and growth. 1 2 3 4 5

Scoring Directions

In the following table, insert the number you circled for each of the twenty statements. Then add each column to get your summary scores.

1. _____	2. _____	3. _____	4. _____	5. _____
6. _____	7. _____	8. _____	9. _____	10. _____
11. _____	12. _____	13. _____	14. _____	15. _____
16. _____	17. _____	18. _____	19. _____	20. _____
Totals: _____	_____	_____	_____	_____
Motives Basic Creature Comfort	Safety and Security	Social or Affiliation	Self-esteem	Self-actualization

Interpretation

For each of the five motives, there is a minimum of 4 and a maximum of 20 points. Scores of 18 or more are quite high and suggest that the motives measured by that scale are very important to you. Scores from 13 to 17 suggest that the motives measured are moderately important to you. Scores from 9 to 12 suggest that the motives are not especially important to you. Scores below 9 are quite low and suggest that the motives measured are not at all important to you.

and on the left is the frustration–regression hypothesis. Even though an individual has regressed to seeking satisfaction of a lower level need, the higher level need may reemerge as an important motivator of behavior. When that happens, the person will progress to the next higher level need, seeking again to satisfy that need, though perhaps in a different way.

Several studies support the three categories of needs identified by Alderfer, and some research indicates that individuals move among the three needs levels as

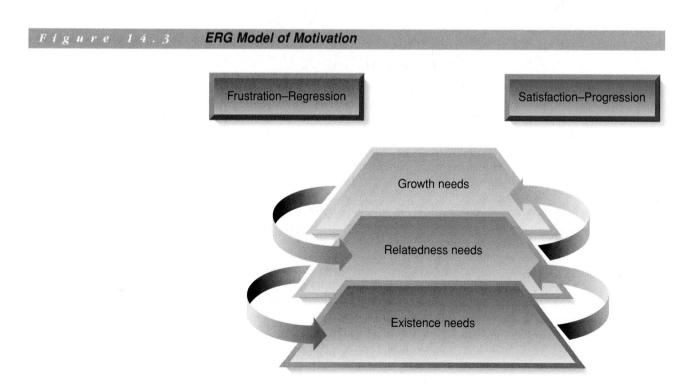

Figure 14.3 ERG Model of Motivation

Alderfer proposed. Also, research suggests that engaging in activities related to psychological growth actually increases the importance of growth needs. That is, growth needs are somewhat unique in that engaging in relevant activities can actually stimulate rather than satisfy these needs.[10]

Perhaps the most important contribution of the ERG model is the frustration–regression hypothesis, which indicates how managers can approach employee motivation. When employees are frustrated in fulfilling their needs, managers should try to determine the cause of the frustration and, if possible, work to remove blockages to needs satisfaction. If blockages can't be removed, managers should try to redirect the employees' behavior toward satisfying a lower level need. For example, a company's production technology may limit the growth opportunities for people in their jobs. If employees are frustrated because they can't be creative or develop new skills, they could be encouraged to focus on relating to their co-workers.

McClelland's Learned Needs

David McClelland's **learned needs theory** specifies that people acquire needs through interaction with the surrounding environment. In other words, the social contexts in which people live and work influence the learning of motivating needs and their strength. In contrast to the theories of Maslow and Alderfer, McClelland didn't view needs as a hierarchy through which people move.

When a need is acting as a determinant of a person's behavior, it is referred to as a *motive*. McClelland believed that three key motives were particularly useful for understanding the differences among individuals: achievement, affiliation, and power.[11]

Achievement. The *achievement motive* is the desire to succeed relative to some standard of excellence or in competitive situations. People with a high need for achievement often like to assume personal responsibility for setting their goals, prefer to pursue moderately difficult goals, and desire immediate and concrete feedback. Being achievement oriented may be necessary in order to succeed at work in an increasingly competitive business world. If employees aren't achievement oriented, they may well be let go when their organizations eliminate positions, departments, and/or layers of management.

Affiliation. The *affiliation motive* is a person's desire to develop and maintain close, mutually satisfying interpersonal relationships with others. Individuals with a strong affiliation motive tend to seek approval and reassurance from others and conform to group norms. Increasingly, organizations are using teams of managers and other employees to solve problems and meet goals. The affiliation motive affects people's willingness to work together in teams. People who dislike interacting with others won't be able to function effectively as a team member.

Power. The *power motive* is an individual's desire to influence and control others and the social environment. The power motive is expressed in two ways: as *personal power* and as *socialized power*.[12] With personal power, people try to influence and control others merely to assert their dominance. With socialized power, individuals use their power to solve organizational problems and help the organization reach its goals. The power motive also may affect how employees react to team operations, particularly with regard to self-managed work teams. Self-managed work teams comprise groups of employees who must work together daily to produce a product (or major component) and who perform various managerial tasks (e.g., setting team goals, scheduling work assignments, ordering materials,

---

LEARNED NEEDS THEORY
McClelland's approach to motivation, which specifies that people acquire three needs or motives—achievement, affiliation, and power—through interaction with their social environments.

ACHIEVEMENT MOTIVE
The desire to succeed relative to some standard of excellence or in competitive situations.

AFFILIATION MOTIVE
A person's desire to develop and maintain close, mutually satisfying interpersonal relationships with others.

POWER MOTIVE
An individual's desire to influence and control others and the social environment.

JOB AND ORGANIZATION CONTEXTS AS MOTIVATORS

3

EXPLAIN HOW THE JOB AND ORGANIZATION CONTEXTS AFFECT MOTIVATION AND PERFORMANCE

The needs theories of Maslow, Alderfer, and McClelland emphasize individual differences as explanations for motivation. They are based on the assumption that the situation is less important than individual differences as a determinant of behavior. In contrast to this approach are theories that emphasize the importance of the environment and play down differences in how individuals respond to the same situation. Three theories that view the job and organization contexts as important determinants of behavior are Hertzberg's two-factor theory, Hackman and Oldham's job enrichment theory, and equity theory.

HERZBERG'S TWO-FACTOR THEORY

TWO-FACTOR THEORY
Herzberg's approach to motivation, which states that distinct types of experiences produce job satisfaction (motivator factors) and job dissatisfaction (hygiene factors).

Herzberg's **two-factor theory** identifies aspects of the job and organizational contexts that contribute to satisfaction and motivation.[13] Herzberg initially examined the relationship between job satisfaction and productivity for 200 accountants and engineers. In carrying out their research, Herzberg and his associates asked participants to describe job experiences that produced good and bad feelings about their jobs. The researchers discovered that the presence of a particular job characteristic, such as responsibility, might increase job satisfaction. However, the lack of that same characteristic didn't necessarily produce dissatisfaction. Conversely, if lack of a characteristic, such as job security, produced dissatisfaction, high job security didn't necessarily lead to satisfaction.

The study's results led Herzberg to conclude that two separate and distinct aspects of the environment were responsible for creating feelings of job satisfaction and job dissatisfaction. He used the terms *motivator factors* and *hygiene factors* to refer to these two aspects of the environment, giving the theory its name: the two-factor theory.

MOTIVATOR FACTORS
Job characteristics that, when present, should create high levels of motivation.

Motivator Factors. *Motivator factors* are aspects of the job and organizational contexts that create positive feelings among employees. Motivator factors are job characteristics (challenge of the work itself, responsibility, recognition, achievement, advancement, and growth) that, when present, should create high levels of motivation. These factors determine whether a job is exciting and rewarding. However, their presence alone doesn't guarantee that employees will be productive. Motivators lead to superior performance *only* if no dissatisfiers are present.

HYGIENE FACTORS
Characteristics of the work environment outside the job that, when positive, maintain a reasonable level of job motivation but don't necessarily increase it.

Hygiene Factors. *Hygiene factors* are the nontask characteristics of the work environment that create dissatisfaction. They include aspects of the environment that are closely associated with the job (e.g., compensation and level of responsibility) and certain aspects of the broader organization (working conditions, company policies, supervision, co-workers, salary, formal status, and job security). They need to be present, at least to some extent, to avoid dissatisfaction. Lack of dissatisfaction is essential for motivator factors to be effective. However, lack of dissatisfaction alone will not motivate employees. The Associates, a company in Irving, Texas, provides free parking, excellent health and life insurance, a retirement plan, and time off for child or elder care. Will its employees be more highly motivated to perform than if those benefits weren't provided? Herzberg's theory suggests that, although these positive environmental factors will prevent feelings of dissatisfaction, they won't generate feelings of excitement about the job and organization. Motivator factors must also be present.

Figure 14.4 illustrates these basic components of Herzberg's two-factor theory. Note that hygiene factors tend to be aspects of the work environment that would satisfy the lower level needs identified by Maslow and Alderfer. Motivator factors tend to be conditions that would satisfy higher level needs. Despite this parallel, however, Herzberg's view of motivation was quite different from the view of the needs theorists. He believed that the factors he identified were universally applicable. In his view, individual differences among employees weren't very important. That is, most employees would be dissatisfied in jobs lacking in hygiene factors and, if hygiene factors were addressed, most employees would be satisfied and productive if motivator factors were present.[14] Therefore, in Herzberg's view, managers should be able to motivate all employees in the same way—by ensuring the presence of both hygiene and motivator factors.

JOB ENRICHMENT

In Chapter 13 we discussed how redesigning work to create more enriched jobs is one type of organizational change that many U.S. organizations are making. The most popular and extensively tested job-enrichment model was developed by J. Richard Hackman and Greg Oldham.[15] Figure 14.5 illustrates the components of this theory. Numerous studies have shown that the theory provides a good explanation for both understanding how employees feel about their work (satisfaction) and how well they do their work (performance).[16]

Critical Psychological States. The Hackman–Oldham theory states that three *critical psychological states* are needed to create high levels of motivation in the workplace. *Experienced meaningfulness* refers to whether employees perceive their work as valuable and worthwhile. *Experienced responsibility* refers to whether employees feel personally responsible for the quantity and quality of their work. *Knowledge of results* refers to the extent to which employees receive feedback about how well they are doing. Feedback can come from the task

---

CRITICAL PSYCHOLOGICAL STATES
In the Hackman–Oldham theory the identification of experienced meaningfulness, experienced responsibility, and knowledge of results as the psychological states needed to create high levels of motivation in the work-place.

EXPERIENCED MEANINGFULNESS
The extent to which employees perceive their work to be valuable and worthwhile.

EXPERIENCED RESPONSIBILITY
The extent to which employees feel personally responsible for the quantity and quality of their work.

KNOWLEDGE OF RESULTS
The extent to which employees receive feedback about how well they are doing.

Figure 14.4 **Herzberg's Two-Factor Theory**

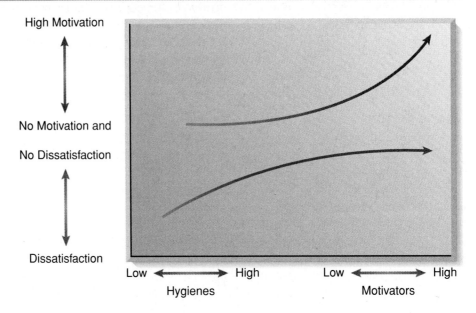

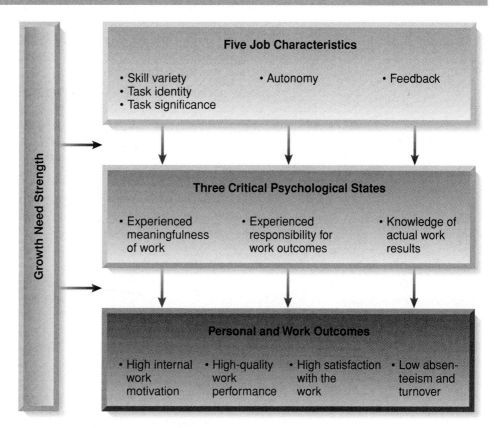

Source: J. R. Hackman and G. R. Oldham. *Work Redesign,* Reading, Mass.: Addison-Wesley, 1980, p. 83. Reprinted with permission.

itself or from other sources, such as supervisors and customers. When all three of these psychological states are experienced, employee motivation is high.[17]

KEY JOB CHARACTERISTICS

Hackman and Oldham's view that the three critical psychological states are affected by five key job characteristics: skill variety, task identity, task significance, autonomy, and feedback.

SKILL VARIETY

The degree to which the job involves many different work activities or requires several skills and talents.

TASK IDENTITY

The extent to which a job involves completing an identifiable piece of work, that is, doing a job with a visible beginning and outcome.

We can illustrate the concepts represented by these psychological states with an analogy to the game of golf. Players hit the ball and follow its flight. They receive immediate feedback in the form of their scores on each hole, which tells the golfers how well they are playing against a standard (par). Personal responsibility for performance is high even though golfers may make excuses for poor performance. Experienced meaningfulness also may be high when golfers see their efforts translated at once into scores that can be compared to par and to the scores of their playing partners. Because all three psychological states usually are high among regular players, motivation usually is high. In fact, some golfers exhibit motivated behavior rarely seen at work: getting up before dawn, playing in rain and snow, feeling despair or joy (depending on how the round went), and even aggression (throwing a club after a muffed shot). How can these same feelings be created at work?

Key Job Characteristics. Hackman and Oldham argued that the three critical psychological states are affected by five key job characteristics. ***Key job characteristics*** are objective aspects of the job design that can be changed to improve the critical psychological states. ***Skill variety*** is the degree to which the job involves many different work activities or requires several skills and talents. ***Task identity*** is present when a job involves completing an identifiable piece of work, that is, doing a job with a visible beginning and outcome. ***Task significanc***e is

Chapter 14 *Motivating for Performance* | **473**

TASK SIGNIFICANCE
The extent to which a job has a substantial impact on the goals or work of others in the company.

AUTONOMY
The extent to which the job provides substantial freedom, independence, and discretion to the individual in scheduling work and determining the procedures to be used in carrying out tasks.

FEEDBACK
When employees receive direct and clear information about their work performance from the task itself or from others.

GROWTH NEED STRENGTH
A desire for personal challenges, a sense of accomplishment, and learning.

present when a job has a substantial impact on the goals or work of others in the company. ***Autonomy*** is present when the job provides substantial freedom, independence, and discretion to the individual in scheduling work and determining the procedures to be used in carrying out tasks. Finally, ***feedback*** is present when work results give the employee direct and clear information about his or her performance.[18]

Hackman and Oldham argued that employees are motivated to the extent that their jobs have all five of these key job characteristics. When all are present at a significant level, employees feel involved in their work, and involved employees exert more effort.[19] In this regard, the Hackman–Oldham theory is similar to Herzberg's—that is, both theories recognize the importance of the job context in motivation. Like the needs theorists, however, Hackman and Oldham also believed that individual differences played a role. In particular, they identified the strength of an employee's growth needs as an individual difference that would influence how people reacted to enriched jobs.

Growth Need Strength. Figure 14.5 indicates that the strength of an employee's growth need influences the relationships among job characteristics, critical psychological states, and work motivation. ***Growth need strength*** refers to a desire for personal challenges, a sense of accomplishment, and learning. Employees with a strong growth need are likely to respond positively to enriched jobs. However, employees with a weak growth need may experience enriched jobs as frustrating and dissatisfying. This point is illustrated by a study in which autoworkers from Detroit worked in Sweden as engine assemblers in a SAAB plant. These jobs allowed them a great deal of freedom and responsibility in performing their jobs. After a month, however, 75 percent of the U.S. workers reported that they preferred their traditional assembly-line jobs. As one worker said, "If I've got to bust my a__ to have a meaningful job, forget it; I'd rather be monotonous [sic]."[20]

Clearly, enriched jobs aren't for everyone. However, as Laura and Pete Wakeman have found, many people thrive in an environment characterized by jobs designed to give workers a sense of responsibility and meaningfulness. The Wakemans' approach to operating their chain of bread stores reflects many principles of job enrichment, as described in the following Strategic Action Competency piece. When deciding how to operate their franchise businesses, the Wakemans faced a key strategic decision: how much control to exercise over franchisees. Reasoning that giving franchisees a great deal of autonomy would make them more committed and creative in the long run, the Wakemans devised an unusual franchise contract.

The objective of job enrichment is to create jobs that employees will enjoy doing. People who enjoy the tasks they perform may not need the extra motivation of high pay and impressive job titles. Nevertheless, if such rewards aren't distributed equitably, dissatisfaction may result.

EQUITY THEORY

EQUITY THEORY
An approach to motivation that is concerned with individuals' beliefs about how fairly they're treated compared with their peers, based on their relative levels of inputs and outcomes.

Equity theory relates to how employees make judgments about whether the organization is treating them fairly. The primary research on equity theory was done by J. S. Adams.[21] He stated that individuals mentally form ratios to compare their inputs and outcomes with those of others doing similar work to determine whether they are being treated fairly. Inputs are what an employee gives to the job (e.g., time, effort, education, and commitment to the organization) to obtain desired outcomes. Outcomes from work include the feelings of meaningfulness and responsibility associated with enriched jobs as well as rewards (e.g., such as recognition, promotions, and increased pay).

Usually, the idea behind a franchise is to have consistency and similarity among the stores within the franchise family. Giving franchise operators autonomy to do their own thing is seldom high on the franchise owner's list of key objectives. Twenty years ago, when Laura and Pete Wakeman decided to open franchise stores for their Great Harvest Bread Company, they chose to be different. Printed in big bold letters in every franchise contract is this message:

ANYTHING
*not expressly prohibited by
the language of this agreement*
IS ALLOWED

Why? Because the Wakemans believe that freedom and autonomy inspire creativity, and ultimately, better ways of doing business. "Innovation happens overnight in our company," says Laura.

What links the 151 Great Harvest Bread stores is little more than the fact that each one bakes the company's signature honey-wheat bread on the premises, using whole wheat flour ground on site. Compared to

bakeries that make bread by simply adding water to a prepackaged mix, task identity is high for employees who bake Great Harvest Bread. Anything else that a franchisee wants to try is up to the individual. For example, a store in Wayne, Pennsylvania, added cookies, invented new breads, and started a coloring contest for kids, which draws 5,000 entries per month. A Detroit franchisee came up with a new way to package products in gift boxes. Other franchisees have developed everything from new signs to new approaches to child care.

The Wakemans encourage people to innovate, but they also want franchisees to share their innovations with each other. They support sharing of ideas and information about how well those ideas have worked when tried in various locations. E-mail and telephone are the most common means of information sharing and feedback. But the Wakemans also pay 50 percent of the travel costs when any franchisee or employee visits another store in the system.

Great Harvest Bread Company store operators give this approach to

running a franchise high marks. Explains one, "Yeah, we're part of a franchise, but we're also growing a business on our own." The feeling of responsibility among franchisees for succeeding with their stores and the sense of accomplishment that comes with doing well have proved to be a winning recipe for motivation.[22]

* * *

To learn more about Great Harvest Bread Company, visit its home page at

www.greatharvest.com

An example of the equity comparison process is presented in Table 14.1. It's a simple dollars per hour example to illustrate how the ratios work. In reality the ratios can be quite complex, involving factors that are quite difficult to quantify and compare. As a result of such a comparison, an employee or even a team will feel equitably rewarded, underrewarded, or overrewarded. Feelings of being overrewarded are probably rare, but when they occur they have beneficial consequences for employers. Overrewarded employees tend to perform better in their jobs and are better citizens of the organization than employees who haven't been so well rewarded.[23]

More typical are situations that result in employees feeling underrewarded. When employees remark that their employer treats them unfairly, that's usually what they mean! Many Japanese workers have begun to feel unfairly treated. They consider their inputs to be the long hours they spend commuting on crowded trains, the seemingly endless hours they spend at the office and in afterwork socializing, and the years of loyalty they show their employers. Until recently, they could count on receiving in exchange the valuable outcomes of employment security and large year-end bonuses. During the past few years, however, some Japanese

	Ratio Comparison	Perception
Equity	$\dfrac{\$50}{5 \text{ hrs. work}} = \dfrac{\$100}{10 \text{ hrs. work}} = \$10/\text{hr.}$ $\dfrac{\text{Outcomes (self)}}{\text{Inputs (self)}} = \dfrac{\text{Outcomes (other)}}{\text{Inputs (other)}}$	"I'm being treated equally."
Inequity	$\left[\dfrac{\$50}{5 \text{ hrs. work}} = \$10/\text{hr.}\right] < \left[\dfrac{\$100}{4 \text{ hrs. work}} = \$20/\text{hr.}\right]$ $\dfrac{\text{Outcomes (self)}}{\text{Inputs (self)}} < \dfrac{\text{Outcomes (other)}}{\text{Inputs (other)}}$	"I'm getting less than I deserve for my efforts."
Inequity	$\left[\dfrac{\$50}{5 \text{ hrs. work}} = \$10/\text{hr.}\right] > \left[\dfrac{\$25}{4 \text{ hrs. work}} = \$5/\text{hr.}\right]$ $\dfrac{\text{Outcomes (self)}}{\text{Inputs (self)}} > \dfrac{\text{Outcomes (other)}}{\text{Inputs (other)}}$	"I'm getting more than I deserve."

employers have shown a willingness to lay off workers in response to competitive pressures. Thus employees can no longer count on the job security that they enjoyed in the past. In response, many Japanese employees have begun to question whether the exchange is fair. According to a recent poll of Japanese employees, only one-third now feel that they are equitably paid.[24]

When people perceive that they are being treated unfairly, they are likely to look for justifications for the treatment. Failing to find any, they may behave in ways that harm the organization. For example, when high performers leave the organization, the company loses their productive talents.[25] If dissatisfied employees stay, they may react by withholding effort in order to restrict output or lower quality.[26] Being hostile toward customers is another way that employees deal with unfair treatment. Sometimes employees resort to more drastic, and even illegal, ways of dealing with the perceived inequity. Deliberate sabotage of equipment and even killing former colleagues and managers are examples of drastic employee reactions.[27]

Generally, six alternatives are available to employees who want to reduce their feelings of inequity:

- increase their inputs to justify higher rewards when they feel that they are over-rewarded in comparison with others;

- decrease their inputs to compensate for lower rewards when they feel under-rewarded;

- change the compensation they receive through legal or other actions, such as leaving work early, forming a union, and so on;

- modify their comparisons by choosing another person to compare themselves against;

- distort reality by rationalizing that the inequities are justified; or

- leave the situation (quit the job) if the inequities can't be resolved.

Perceived inequities can arise in many ways. In U.S. companies, they often occur with respect to promotions, pay raises, perquisites (perks), and other human resources management practices in organizations. For example, merit pay systems may cause feelings of inequity. Although it is supposed to be based on performance, merit pay can be a source of bitter disputes among employees. Many companies put aside a set amount for merit increases or allocate only a certain number of merit increases to be given companywide. Thus, if an organization has many deserving employees, but its funds are limited, some employees may feel that their performance (input) has gone unrecognized.[28]

Issues of pay equity often arise in organizations that compete in the international labor market. Nortel's solution to international equity issues is described in the Global Awareness Competency account. Nortel's managers stayed informed of the economic conditions that affected employees on both sides of the U.S.–Canadian border. As a result, they developed a compensation policy that enabled them to retain employees who are in high demand and relatively short supply around the world.

To be effective in their roles, managers must strive to treat all organization members fairly. Doing so can pay huge dividends. People who are paid and treated fairly are more likely to believe in and be committed to what they do. In turn, they will become more trusting, honorable, and loyal employees and will work harder to exceed the expectations that managers have of them.[29]

HOW MANAGERS' BEHAVIORS AFFECT MOTIVATION

4

EXPLAIN HOW MANAGERS CAN USE REWARDS AND GOALS TO MOTIVATE EMPLOYEES

Decisions about how jobs are designed and policies about how people are to be paid have important consequences for employee motivation. In large organizations, managers at fairly high levels often make these decisions. Regardless of whether decisions made by high-level managers are good or bad for employee motivation, they place constraints on how much middle and first-line managers can change the type of work that people are asked to do or the general level of pay that they will receive. Even when managers aren't able to redesign jobs or create new pay structures, they can affect employee motivation through their use of reinforcers and goals.

REINFORCEMENT THEORY

REINFORCEMENT THEORY
An approach to motivation that suggests that behavior is a function of its consequences (rewards or punishments).

Reinforcement theory states that behavior is a function of its consequences (rewards or punishments). This approach to understanding what motivates behavior was developed most extensively by noted psychologist B. F. Skinner,[30] who gained much public attention when he revealed that he raised his children strictly by reinforcement theory principles. These principles hold that behavior followed by pleasant consequences is more likely to be repeated and that behavior followed by unpleasant consequences is less likely to be repeated. If you receive a reward (e.g., a bonus, a compliment, or a promotion) for superior performance, you are likely to continue performing well in anticipation of future rewards. However, if the consequences of a particular behavior are unpleasant (e.g., management's disapproval or a demotion), you will tend to modify that behavior.

Figure 14.6 shows the process by which rewards and punishments influence behavior. A person's response (behavior) to a stimulus (situation) results in specific consequences (rewards and punishments), which in turn shape future behavior. For instance, suppose that you work for a high-tech firm. You come to a monthly staff

Borderline Pay at Nortel

Northern Telecom, Ltd. (Nortel) is Canada's leading telecommunications company. It's 63,000 employees are spread around the world, so dealing with pay differences between countries is nothing new for Nortel. Ironically, however, the company found that some of its most difficult motivation and reward problems arise from pay differences between Canada and its nearest neighbor, the United States. Like other Canadian companies, Nortel faces a significant challenge in deciding what is equitable pay for managers and professionals.

Demand for managers and professionals is strong in the United States, so many Canadians consider the option of moving across the border. Typically, Canadian professionals and managers earn one-third less than their U.S. counterparts, as shown in the table below. In contrast, employees who hold jobs at lower pay levels are paid more in Canada than in the United States.

A Canadian manager comparing inputs and outcomes to those of a similar executive in the United States may conclude that she is underpaid and seek employment across the bor-

der. As more Canadian professionals and managers seek employment in the United States, companies such as Nortel face the possibility of a "brain drain."

In order to attract new talent and avoid losing its best employees, Nortel has adopted a new approach to setting salaries. Because Nortel employees use their U.S. counterparts when assessing whether they are paid fairly, Nortel now utilizes a formula that blends the pay levels in the United States and Canada to set salaries for higher level jobs, giving more weight to U.S. salary levels. An example of the formula used to determine the salary of a top information systems executive, who the company believes is vulnerable to offers from the United States, is as follows.

Weighted blending. A weight of 0.2 is given to pay rates in Canada, and a weight of 0.8 is given to pay rates in the United States. The exchange rate used to convert U.S. to Canadian dollars is 1.37. Thus

$$(0.2 \times \$98,000) + (0.8 \times \$110,000 \times 1.37) = \$140,160 \text{ Canadian}$$

Using this formula, Nortel hopes to prevent the perception of two types of inequity. First, the new formula takes into account the manager's natural tendency to compare his or her inputs and outputs to those of similar U.S. managers. Second, the Canadian manager who has subordinates in the United States knows that they are paid at U.S. rates. Using the blended approach to setting the manager's pay helps reduce any perceived inequity that might arise from a manager's comparing inputs and outputs and knowing that subordinates are being paid as much as or more than the manager.[31]

* * *

To learn more about Northern Telecom, visit the company's home page at

www.nortel.com

To learn more about issues of international compensation, visit the home page of the American Compensation Association at

www.acaonline.org

Examples of Pay Differences in Canada and the United States

Job	Canada	United States	Canadian Pay as a Percentage of U.S. Pay
CFO of $300-million packaging company	$161,000	$247,500	65%
Information system executive	$ 98,000	$150,300	65%
Treasurer	$109,100	$153,200	71%
Machine operator	$ 27,000	$ 19,900	136%
Salesclerk	$ 24,500	$ 16,800	146%

Note: Amounts are in Canadian dollars.

meeting with a proposed style sheet for diagrams that are to be inserted in user manuals, much like the existing style sheets for text. If your manager praises your initiative and creativity, your behavior is rewarded. You probably will be motivated to come up with other innovations. However, if your manager gives you a disapproving look and says that the firm is perfectly happy with existing methods, you probably would feel put down or embarrassed in front of your colleagues. In effect, your behavior has been punished. You probably will conclude that new ideas lead to unpleasant consequences and that the best way to earn a reward is just to follow orders.

According to reinforcement theory, a manager who wants to change an employee's behavior must also change the specific consequences of that behavior. Behaviors that managers can most easily change by using reinforcement principles are those that can be easily measured.[32] Measurable behavior is action that can be observed and counted. Examples include smiling when a customer approaches, using a seat belt when driving a delivery truck, and wiping up spills when they occur on the shop floor. For 7-Eleven store operators, the measurable behaviors of interest to the company's management include how often the stores' computers are used to determine which products are moving and which are simply sitting on the shelf. Management wants store operators to adopt this behavior because it will result in better inventory control and decisions about ordering products from suppliers. Therefore the company's managers closely monitor store managers' use of the computer. If a store manager isn't using the computer often enough, managers at headquarters express their disapproval.[33]

Whether a consequence is pleasant or unpleasant is determined by two factors: the action that follows the behavior and the nature of the outcome. These two factors combine to modify behavior through positive reinforcement, negative reinforcement, punishment, and extinction. Positive reinforcement and negative reinforcement are consequences that strengthen or maintain behaviors. Punishment and extinction are consequences that reduce or stop behaviors.

Positive Reinforcement. *Positive reinforcement* creates a pleasant consequence by the use of rewards to increase the likelihood that a behavior will be

POSITIVE REINFORCEMENT

A pleasant consequence in the form of a reward to increase the likelihood that a behavior will be repeated. Any rewarding outcome that encourages an individual to repeat a behavior can be classified as a positive reinforcer.

Figure 14.6 **Reinforcement Process**

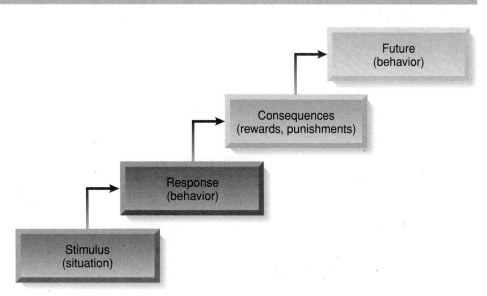

repeated. Any reward that encourages an individual to repeat a behavior can be classified as a positive reinforcer. Some common positive reinforcers used by organizations are praise, recognition of accomplishment, promotion, and salary increases. Many people regard these reinforcers as desirable.

Steve Kerr, chief learning officer at GE, points out that positive reinforcers can be extremely effective when they are made public. "Start spreading the news," he says. "When you give a deserving worker a reward, broadcast it! If you hand out a $1,000 spot bonus, but no one knows it except you and the recipient, the total number of people you've motivated is somewhere between zero and one." But if co-workers see good performance being reinforced, they may become motivated by the reinforcement, too. Through a program called Quick Thanks!, GE Medical Systems encourages employees to reward their peers on the spot. They can nominate any colleague to receive a $25 gift certificate in appreciation for exemplary work, and often they deliver the reward themselves. In one year, GE gives as many as 10,000 such awards.[34]

Punishment. *Punishment* is an attempt to discourage a behavior by the application of negative outcomes whenever it does occur. The purpose of punishment is to reduce the likelihood that an individual will repeat the target behavior. For example, disciplinary actions may be taken against an employee who comes to work late, neglects to clean up the work area, or turns out too many defective parts. The disciplinary action might take the form of a verbal reprimand, a monetary fine, a demotion, or, if the employee persists, a suspension—all with the intention of discouraging the behavior. Whatever form it takes, punishment should match the nature of the infraction and should be consistent with what other employees have received.[35]

The concepts of reinforcement and punishment are easy for most people to understand because most individuals can readily recall examples of their behaviors being reinforced or punished. The concepts of negative reinforcement and extinction are sometimes more difficult to grasp, however. The reason is that both refer to the *absence* of behavioral consequences.

Negative Reinforcement. When people engage in behavior to avoid unpleasant consequences, they experience *negative reinforcement.* Some students may come to class on time to avoid a reprimand from the instructor. Similarly, most employees follow coffee break and lunch hour guidelines to avoid the disapproval of managers or co-workers. In both cases, these individuals are acting to avoid unpleasant results; when they are successful they are negatively reinforced. Note that, whereas punishment causes a behavior to occur less frequently, negative reinforcement causes the behavior to be repeated.

Extinction. *Extinction* is the absence of any reinforcement, either positive or negative, following the occurrence of a behavior. Usually, extinction occurs when the positive reinforcement that once normally resulted from the behavior is removed. Because the behavior no longer produces reinforcement, the employee stops engaging in it.

Extinction is a common problem for managers, who often become victims to their own successful attempts be more systematic in delivering rewards and punishments. A manager who seeks to reduce tardiness may put in place a plan to reward employees for coming to work and not taking days off. The manager begins to offer a small monetary bonus for a perfect attendance record. Eventually, when experiencing more pressure to reduce costs, the manager decides to eliminate the bonus program. Soon absenteeism is higher than ever. Even employees who had low absentee rates prior to the bonus program may now be absent more often.

What happened? Unfortunately, the manager has trained everyone to overcome any barriers they encounter in order to get to work on time and receive their bonuses. Removing the opportunity to earn a bonus caused extinction of the behavior.

Guidelines for Managers. Positive reinforcement is the preferred approach for influencing work behavior. However, an effectively designed and administered disciplinary system usually is necessary in organizations. Managers can use positive reinforcement or punishment to improve efficiency, cut costs, increase attendance, and raise productivity by following the guidelines shown in Table 14. 2.

Dan Caulfield is founder and CEO of Hire Quality, a Chicago-based job-placement firm. He's spent hundreds of thousands of dollars and countless hours trying to move his workforce of about fifty people from print to electronic communication. Unfortunately, in his attempts to change behaviors, he relied almost exclusively on punishment. In a business that screens some 35,000 candidates per month, operating without paper is both a major challenge and a way to cut costs and speed up processing. Caulfield's investments in computer systems that could do much of the processing electronically were a good first step toward becoming paperless, but no matter how much he pleaded with employees, they still relied on paper for many of their daily activities. When Caulfield was confident that his employees had all the electronic tools they needed to work without paper, he tried using punishment. He walked through offices removing yellow paper stickers from computer monitors, crumpled up papers that he found on people's desks, and scrounged through desk drawers looking for whatever paper he could find. He threw it all into a

Table 14.2	**Five Guidelines for Using Reinforcement Theory**
Guideline	**Comment**
Don't reward all individuals equally.	To be effective, reinforcers should be based on performance. Rewarding everyone equally in effect reinforces poor or average performance and ignores high performance.
Failure to respond can also modify behavior.	Managers influence their subordinates by what they do not do as well as by what they do. For example, failing to praise deserving subordinates may cause them to perform poorly the next time.
Tell individuals what they can do to receive reinforcement.	Setting performance standards lets individuals know what they should do to be rewarded; they can then adjust their work habits to get these rewards.
Tell individuals what they are doing wrong.	If managers withhold rewards from subordinates without indicating why they're not being rewarded, the subordinates may be confused about what behaviors the manager finds undesirable. The subordinates may also feel that they're being manipulated.
Don't punish in front of others.	Reprimanding subordinates might sometimes be a useful way of eliminating an undesirable behavior. Public reprimand, however, humiliates subordinates and may cause all the members of the work group to resent the manager.

barrel, dragged the barrel to the fire escape and set it ablaze as employees watched. He explained, "I had to do something dramatic or people would have gone on using paper forever." Fines were introduced as a further deterrent: $1.00 per line for using the fax machine and 25 cents per page for printing a résumé. But as Caulfield eventually learned, this approach caused resentment among employees.[36] With a better understanding of reinforcement theory, Caulfield would have known that offering rewards to the employees who used the least paper or found new ways to reduce the use of paper could have yielded the results he wanted.

Although the reinforcement model has many positive features, it also has some drawbacks.[37] First, the model may oversimplify behavior by not recognizing individual characteristics, such as needs and values.[38] Second, it may unduly emphasize manipulating and controlling subordinates. Third, with its heavy emphasis on external rewards, the model tends to ignore the fact that an increasing number of employees are motivated by the job itself. Like each of the other theories described, this one also presents only a partial explanation for behavior. Nevertheless, the basic principles identified in Table 14.2 provide useful aids for managers.

GOAL SETTING

Goal-setting theory was introduced by Edwin A. Locke in the 1960s and further developed during three decades of research as a reaction to the reinforcement theory.[39] Whereas reinforcement theory focuses attention on the consequences of behavior, Locke's goal-setting theory focuses attention on the aspirations that people have. *Goal-setting theory* states that managers can direct the performance of their employees by assigning specific, difficult goals that employees accept and are willing to commit to. Providing feedback to employees about their progress toward achieving those goals also is important if the goals are to be an effective motivator. According to this theory, managers can improve performance without directly controlling all the consequences of employee behaviors.

Goal-setting theory views employees as rational beings who control their own behaviors, which they choose in order to achieve their goals. Goals affect motivation in two ways: by increasing the amount of effort people choose to exert and by directing or channeling that effort. When employees accept a goal as something to strive for and commit to achieving the goal, they essentially agree to exert the amount of effort required to do so. If goals are too easy or so difficult that employees reject them as impossible, the goals will have no motivational effects.

Specific goals are more effective motivators than are vague, ambiguous goals. Specific goals help focus attention on a well-defined task so that any effort expended by employees is more likely to translate into goal achievement. Specific goals also make it easier for employees to gauge how well they're doing. If a goal is specific, employees can quickly judge whether their efforts are paying off in terms of performance. Employees can then use this feedback to decide whether to continue using the same methods or try new approaches.

Numerous studies have documented that performance is improved when employees are guided by specific and difficult goals. These studies have investigated the effects of goals on employees in a wide range of jobs, including roofers and pizza deliverers.[40] In one study, goals were used to improve the efficiency of truck drivers hauling logs to lumber mills. Before goals were introduced, loggers were carrying loads that were well below their trucks' legal weight capacities. Goals were introduced to encourage the loggers to transport fuller loads. At first, drivers were given a vague, easy goal that was stated as "do your best." This goal had almost no effect on the size of the loads the drivers hauled. Three months later, drivers were given the goal of carrying loads that were 94 percent of their trucks' capaci-

GOAL-SETTING THEORY
An approach to motivation that states that managers can direct the performance of their employees by assigning specific, difficult goals and providing feedback to employees about their progress in achieving those goals.

ties. Within a month, the average load had increased from less than 60 percent to more than 80 percent of capacity. Six months later, truckers were carrying loads that averaged over 90 percent of capacity. This improvement in efficiency was achieved without changing the compensation system or introducing organizational rewards for goal achievement. The goals themselves—and the competition they created among the logging crews—provided the motivation needed to improve performance.[41]

Done correctly, goal setting can be an effective motivational tool. In the original statement of goal-setting theory, assigned goals were considered to be just as effective in motivating employees as goals that are jointly set by a manager and subordinate. However, many managers believe that goals work best when employees participate in the goal setting. Participation increases the employees' willingness to accept goals, which is essential in order for the goals to be motivating. In addition, goal setting can be effective only if employees have the competencies needed to achieve the goal, receive feedback about how they are doing, and receive rewards for achieving the goal. These basic principles are the foundation for management by objectives (MBO).

Management by objectives is a management technique used in many types of organizations in the United States. Generally, the MBO process begins with a conversation between manager and employee. During this conversation, past performance is reviewed and objectives (goals) for the future are identified. The manager and employee agree to a set of goals that both parties accept as appropriate, with the understanding that future performance evaluations and rewards will reflect the employee's progress toward the agreed-upon goals. As described in the Planning and Administration Competency article, this approach to management can yield big improvements. The Etec approach shows how the use of goal-setting principles encourages managers to gather and analyze information systematically, make timely decisions, and plan and organize projects effectively.

MANAGEMENT BY OBJECTIVES

A management technique whereby a manager and employee set objectives (goals) for the future. Both parties accept the objectives as appropriate, with the understanding that future performance evaluations and rewards will reflect the employee's progress in meeting the agreed-upon goals.

MOTIVATION: AN INTEGRATED VIEW

5

DISCUSS WAYS IN WHICH THE COMBINATION OF INDIVIDUAL DIFFERENCES, THE JOB AND ORGANIZATION CONTEXTS, AND MANAGERIAL BEHAVIORS AFFECT MOTIVATION

Each of the motivation theories described so far offers useful insights into motivation. Effective managers can use all of these theories and insights to motivate employees. To take maximum advantage of the theories, however, managers must be able to integrate them. In this section we describe an integrated view of motivation that incorporates many of the specific principles discussed so far in this chapter. But, before we do so, we need to present yet another theory of motivation—basic expectancy theory. This simple theory is the basis for the integrated view of motivation.

BASIC EXPECTANCY THEORY

BASIC EXPECTANCY THEORY

The view that people tend to choose behaviors that they believe will help them achieve desired outcomes (e.g., a promotion or job security) and avoid behaviors that they believe will lead to undesirable outcomes (e.g., a demotion or criticism).

One of the most widely accepted models for explaining how people make decisions about how to behave is Victor Vroom's basic expectancy theory. It suggests that people choose among alternative behaviors by considering which behavior will lead to the more desired outcomes (e.g., recognition or new challenges).[42] Thus it combines ideas from both reinforcement theory and goal-setting theory. More specifically, *basic expectancy theory* states that people tend to choose behaviors that they believe will help them achieve their goals (e.g., a promotion or job security) and avoid behaviors that they believe will lead to undesirable consequences (e.g., a demotion or criticism).

The theory is formulated as a general theory that can explain a wide range of behavioral choices, but here we focus on behaviors related to work performance.

Stephen Cooper, CEO and Chairman of Etec Systems, a high-tech manufacturer of expensive electronic equipment, used a combination of goal setting and MBO to turn around that company. In 1993, when Cooper took over, the company was losing $1 million a month. Believing in the power of goals both to motivate employees and to direct their attention, he set the goal of generating annual revenues of $500 million by 2000. To get there, he made sure that 800 employees had written personal plans to guide their daily work. These one-page plans included five to seven goals, to which employees assigned priority rankings.

For each goal, the employee had to state how progress would be measured. Cooper views this system as essential to the company's success. He explains, "We operate on the leading edge of technology with very demanding customers. If you're going to be a technology leader, you have to execute on schedule."

For Phil Arnold, a precision optics manager, executing on schedule means achieving goals such as increasing production volume by 30 percent and reducing cycle times by 10 percent. The six junior managers who report to him, in turn, each have goals that they must achieve. And the people supervised by the junior managers all have daily checklists that reflect the junior managers' goals. Every Monday, the junior managers give a four-minute status report to Arnold. Problems are identified and solutions for dealing with them are developed immediately.

Arnold learned the hard way to monitor progress and identify problems before they turn into crises. Before he began holding his Monday meetings, Arnold didn't find out about a problem with a vendor until it was far too late to take corrective actions. He then had to spend months dealing with the damage caused by the vendor. With the current system, every week everyone knows what they should be doing, how much weight to give each assignment, and how their goals relate to the goals of other people in the company. The company operates efficiently, yet can respond quickly to changes in the environment.

Cooper says that the key to Etec's success is doing the little things right: "You do the big things by doing the little things right. If you execute, you can do anything. When a company has a clear mission, and people know how their individual mission fits into the big picture, everyone paddles in the same direction." In this case, Cooper and everyone else at Etec Systems paddled themselves out of their decline and have returned to their former status as a fast growing, highly profitable company.[43]

* * *

To learn more about Etec Systems, visit the company's home page at

www.etec.com

Examples of behavioral choices that are related to work performance include whether to go to work or call in sick, whether to leave work at the official quitting time or stay late, and whether to exert a great deal of effort or to work at a more relaxed pace. When making behavioral choices such as these, employees normally consider three questions, perhaps unconsciously at times.

1. **The expectancy question:** If I make an effort, will I be able to perform the intended behavior?

2. **The instrumentality question:** If I perform the intended behavior, what will be the outcomes?

3. **The valence question:** How much do I value the outcomes associated with the intended behavior?

EXPECTANCY
The belief that a given level of effort will lead to improved performance.

Expectancy. Before acting, an employee must assess whether expending the required effort will result in improved performance. *Expectancy* is the belief that a certain level of effort will lead to improved performance. We use the term *performance* broadly here, as the level of the individual's work-related achievements. It could involve making more sales, creating a satisfied customer, and/or helping another salesperson do his or her job more effectively. At Granite Rock, a stone supply company in Watsonville, California, performance refers to what the employee has learned.[44] As described in Chapter 13, this definition of performance is typical in learning organizations. *Effort* is the amount of physical and/or mental energy exerted to perform a task or to learn something new. In other words, how hard is the employee trying? At Nordstrom department stores, a salesperson's attempts to find a medium-sized blue-striped shirt is an example of effort. Effort refers solely to the energy expended—not to how successful it is. However, employees who believe that exerting more effort results in better performance generally show higher levels of performance than employees who don't believe that their efforts will pay off.[45]

INSTRUMENTALITY
The perceived usefulness of performance as a means for obtaining desired outcomes (or avoiding undesired outcomes).

Instrumentality. *Instrumentality* is the perceived usefulness of performance as a means for obtaining desired outcomes (or avoiding undesired outcomes). To be willing to expend the effort needed to achieve the desired performance, employees must believe that the performance is instrumental to them. If you make more sales, will your pay be greater? If you develop an innovative product design, will you receive public recognition for this accomplishment? If you arrive to work on time, rather than being a few minutes late, will anyone else really care? If your performance rating says that your work is outstanding, will you get paid more?

Finding ways to ensure that employees believe that better performance will result in greater rewards is a source of continual challenges for employers. Increasingly, employers are experimenting with pay plans that tie pay increases for all workers to the company's financial performance. For example, at Dial, employees are eligible for an annual cash bonus that is based on net revenue growth, operating margin, and asset turnover. Employees who in previous years could expect a pay raise of approximately 5 percent can now look forward to a bonus as large as 11 percent of salary if the company performs well. The pay system promises greater rewards for success, but it also means that bonuses might be very small if the company does poorly for any reason.[46]

Pay systems such as the one at Dial are intended to create perceptions of high instrumentality, but they don't always succeed. For employees at lower levels in the organization, the link between their individual job performance and the company's overall financial performance may be tenuous. Unexpected changes in market conditions or a bad management decision can have devastating consequences for the company, despite excellent performance by the typical employee. The result is that employees may experience feelings of low instrumentality. Nevertheless, pay systems designed around the principles of expectancy can be quite effective. The key is to design a system that is sensitive to perceptions of both expectancy and instrumentality.

The performance appraisal and reward system used at Lincoln Electric, a Cleveland-based manufacturer of electric motors, is effective in creating feelings of high expectancy and instrumentality. This company is well-known for its highly motivated and productive employees. Supervisors rate employees on four performance dimensions: quality, dependability, ideas and cooperation, and output. The appraisal system is designed to force managers to identify the best employees, average employees, and below average employees. Managers keep records regarding behaviors such as tardiness (which affects the dependability score) and the number of motor defects that can be directly traced to the employee's work (which affects the quality score). Consequently, employees expect that, if they put in the effort to arrive on time and avoid making errors as they assemble motors, they'll be rated as superior performers. In addition, they know that their supervisors' ratings will be used to calculate their annual bonuses, which represent a large portion of their annual pay. In fact, they even know the formula that will be used to calculate their bonuses. Lincoln Electric has performed extremely well in most years, so bonuses are usually sizable. Compared to the industry average, Lincoln Electric's workforce is about twice as productive as those of other companies.[47]

VALENCE

The weight that a particular employee attaches to outcomes.

Valence. The *valence* of an outcome associated with performance is the weight that a particular employee attaches to the outcome. Valences are subjective; the same outcome may have a high valence for one person and a low valence for another. For example, a promotion from museum curator to the higher paying position of museum director would appeal more to an individual who values (places a high valence on) financial gain and increased responsibility than to an individual who values creativity and independence.[48]

Like goal-setting theory, expectancy theory gives great weight to how people think about the future. The assumption is that people base rational choices about how to behave on the information available to them. One implication of this view is that employers who offer incentives for performance must do more than simply design a good incentive plan. They must also communicate it effectively. Allstate Insurance Company's approach to communicating a new executive compensation package is described in the Communication Competency feature. Many Allstate executives didn't fully understand how their pay was determined and weren't motivated by the way their pay was structured. So, when the board decided to restructure executive pay packages, they paid a great deal of attention to explaining the bases for the new packages. Allstate management worked with communication experts to design and use a formal communication plan that would be informative, persuasive, and clear.

THE INTEGRATED EXPECTANCY MODEL

Lyman Porter and Edward Lawler realized that basic expectancy theory could serve as a good foundation for a more fully developed model of motivation. Figure 14.7 shows the Porter–Lawler integrated expectancy model. It recognizes that employee satisfaction and performance are two different, but related, phenomena. Note that, in this model, satisfaction isn't viewed as a cause of high performance. Instead, the model suggests that employees who perform well will feel more satisfied, assuming that their performance is rewarded appropriately.[49]

Figure 1 4 . 7 **The Integrative Expectancy Model**

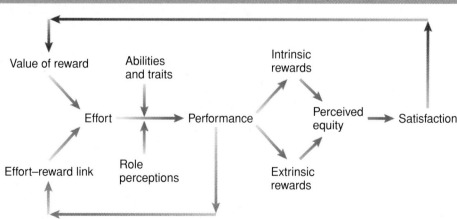

Source: From L.W. Porter and E. E. Lawler III. *Managerial Attitudes and Performance.* Homewood, Ill.: Irwin, 1968, p. 165. Used with permission.

Explaining Allstate's New Pay Plan

In 1931, Sears, Roebuck and Company established the Allstate Insurance Company. But like many other companies, in the 1990s Sears pursued a more focused strategy and spun off Allstate. Although sixty years old, Allstate came face-to-face with the demands of Wall Street for the first time. When Allstate went public, an outside board of directors was established. Evaluating executive pay packages was among its first tasks. The board commissioned a study of key executives to learn how they perceived their pay and their views about how pay should be determined. A team of Allstate managers and external compensation consultants went to work. Their study revealed a weak link in the system. Because the pay of Allstate executives was tied to the stock movement of Sears, they felt that they had little control over it. "In many cases, our executives were not really motivated by Sears' executive pay," concluded the assistant vice president of compensation.

Allstate needed a new, simpler plan that linked pay directly to Allstate's business results. Equally important, the plan needed to be communicated clearly. Allstate's board knew that executives wouldn't be appropriately motivated by the plan if they didn't understand it. When the new pay plan was ready, experts were brought in to develop a communication strategy. They collaborated with a team of Allstate managers who hadn't been involved in developing the pay plan and who represented a variety of specialty areas. The communication strategy developed by this team focused on conveying to executives how great the future could be for them individually and collectively if adequate results were achieved.

Before devising its formal communication strategy, team members began by making sure they understood the new pay plan themselves. "We ripped (the plan) apart, we took the staples out if it—we literally ripped it apart, not figuratively—and stuck the pages up on the walls. . . . We tried to understand the plan and draw it on the board," explained one of the communication experts.

Once the team members were sure that they understood the new pay plan, the principle that proved most important as they developed the formal communication strategy was "Keep it Simple." Rather than overwhelm people with all the details, the communicators emphasized the link between achieving business objectives and the pay that the executives would receive. To ensure that the executives could see "the big picture," the written material included a foldout page showing how all the pieces of the package fit together. To give personal meaning to the package, each executive received an individualized statement that showed the maximum amounts that he or she could earn if individual and group targets were achieved.

A second survey conducted after the new package was explained revealed that 85 percent of the executives felt that they now had a better understanding than before of their annual incentive pay, their stock options, and the total pay package.[50]

* * *

To learn more about Allstate, visit the company's home page at

www.allstate.com

ABILITY

A person's mastery of competencies required to do a job.

TRAITS

Individual personality characteristics (e.g., the strength of various needs) that can affect a person's job performance.

Briefly, this model begins with the idea that employees will exert effort when they believe that increased effort will lead to a reward and that the reward is something they value. If increased effort is needed to perform at a level that will allow you to keep your job, then keeping your job is the reward, and the value of this reward is the importance you attach to friendships with your co-workers, your pay, or your feelings of accomplishment. Some workers might prize the friendship of co-workers; others might value money more highly.

Of course, employee effort isn't the only variable that affects performance; abilities, traits, and role perceptions also influence performance. **Ability** refers to the individual's mastery of competencies required to do a job. **Traits** are individual personality characteristics (e.g., the strengths of various needs) that can affect a person's job performance. Thus abilities and traits are relatively independent of the work situation. Although employees can learn new skills on the job, they generally acquire basic abilities and traits before beginning work.

The Ritz–Carlton Hotel chain, a winner of the Malcolm Baldrige National Quality Award, is noted for providing exceptional service to its customers. Hotel management influences the abilities and traits that employees bring to the workplace through a careful hiring process. The selection process also helps communicate and clarify role perceptions. Following it is a rigorous orientation program and extensive training. Continual on-the-job training includes a daily lineup in every department of the hotel. In the lineup, which lasts ten to fifteen minutes, employees stand at attention and receive communications and training from the department head. The result is exceptional performance, which results in outstanding ratings from the hotel chain's customers.

ROLE PERCEPTIONS

Beliefs about what is required to do the job successfully, including both the specific tasks that an employee believes are part of the job and the attitudes and behaviors that an employee thinks are appropriate in terms of the organization's culture.

Role perceptions are the employee's beliefs about what is required to do the job successfully. Role perceptions include both the specific tasks that an employee believes are part of the job and the attitudes and behaviors that an employee thinks are appropriate in terms of organizational culture. Role perceptions are formed by many types of employee experiences, including interactions with customers, co-workers, and supervisors. As the Etec Systems example illustrates, managers can help clarify role perceptions by ensuring that employees have specific goals to strive for and by ensuring that an employee's various goals don't conflict.

EXTRINSIC REWARDS

Outcomes supplied by the organization, such as a good salary, status, job security, and fringe benefits.

Performance can be rewarded in two ways. **Extrinsic rewards** are outcomes supplied by the organization, such as a good salary, status, job security, and fringe benefits. These rewards arc similar to the job context items that Herzberg called hygiene factors. **Intrinsic rewards** are personally satisfying outcomes, such as feelings of achievement and personal growth. These rewards are similar to Herzberg's motivator factors. In the Porter–Lawler model, both intrinsic and extrinsic rewards are desirable. Employees' perceptions of whether their rewards are equitable include their evaluations of both extrinsic and intrinsic rewards.

INTRINSIC REWARDS

Personally satisfying outcomes, such as feelings of achievement and personal growth.

Finally, satisfaction is an employee's attitude about the work situation. Porter and Lawler believed that this attitude was determined by the difference between the rewards employees receive and the rewards they believe that they *should have* received; the smaller the difference, the greater is the employee's satisfaction. People often compare the rewards they receive to the rewards that others receive. If an employee believes that the comparison shows unfair treatment, dissatisfaction results.

Satisfaction is important to organizations because it's related to absenteeism, tardiness, turnover, and commitment. The more satisfied that employees are, the less likely they are to be absent or late or to leave the company. Satisfied employees focus on the positive aspects of their work, not the negative. They are therefore more likely to make a commitment to the organization than are dissatisfied employees. This commitment, in turn, translates into continued effort, better performance, and increasing rewards. Conversely, dissatisfied employees exert less effort, which results in declining performance and a general downward spiraling to ineffectiveness.[51]

GUIDELINES FOR PERFORMANCE MANAGEMENT

5

DESCRIBE THE DESIGN AND IMPLEMENTATION OF AN EFFECTIVE PERFORMANCE MANAGEMENT SYSTEM

When researchers develop theories such as those described in this chapter, their intent usually is to propose explanations for why people behave as they do. They focus on developing accurate descriptions of human behavior. Managers can use the descriptions to design performance management systems that enhance employee motivation. They can also use the theories that we have described to help diagnose causes of performance problems.

Companies use performance management systems to focus on, reward, and provide feedback about employee job performance. A recent study of more than 400 companies that had adopted performance management systems revealed them to be quite beneficial. This study compared changes in performance for companies that had adopted performance management systems to those that hadn't. For companies with performance management programs, improvements in financial performance indicators (e.g., stock price, book value, and return on investment) were substantially greater than those of companies without such systems.[52]

ENHANCING EMPLOYEE MOTIVATION

Recruiting and retaining employees who are highly motivated is an important first step in maximizing employee performance. Maximizing employee performance through motivation requires several actions.

Design Jobs with High Motivating Potential. Fully enriched jobs may not be appropriate in all situations, but the evidence indicates that enriched jobs tend to be more satisfying than unenriched jobs. Jobs that may be candidates for enrichment are those characterized by repetitive tasks requiring few skills, narrow in scope, and restrictive in terms of the amount of freedom they give employees as they carry out their tasks. To determine whether jobs need to be redesigned, managers should assess the degree to which employees experience their work as meaningful, feel personally responsible for their work outcomes, and receive adequate feedback.

Clearly Identify the Behaviors and Performance Achievements That Will Be Rewarded. For employees to be energized by their work, they must have a clear understanding of what performing well requires. Too often, managers assume that employees understand how best to direct their efforts. More likely, employees feel uncertain about what is most important. By working with employees to set specific and measurable goals, managers can clarify their expectations for employees. These goals may include job-specific performance goals as well as behaviors that extend beyond job tasks but are necessary for the organization to function effectively.[53] At manufacturing companies such as Pratt & Whitney, goals related to learning new skills are just as important as getting the job done. To make sure that employees understand the importance of developing their skills, Pratt & Whitney began to peg pay increases to the amount of training that employees undergo.[54]

When setting goals, managers should be careful not to fall into the trap of focusing only on goals that are easily quantified.[55] Rose Arnone, a Merck employee, described a boss she once had as confusing productivity goals with "face time" goals. Rose's work involved 30 percent travel time, which meant she put in long hours away from the office, including some weekends. Nevertheless, her boss expected her to be at her desk at 8 A.M. sharp Monday morning. Rose kept working but her motivation plummeted. She felt, Okay, I'll do the best I can, but you're not getting any more from me. That boss has since left the company, and her new boss has a better approach. She sets clear goals for getting the job done and doesn't try to dictate the methods that Rose is to follow nor the amount of time that she must put in to get the job done.[56]

Align Rewards with What Employees Value. To be motivators, rewards must be aligned with the things that employees value. The rewards that employees want can be determined simply by asking them. Some employees value monetary rewards above everything else, whereas others value scheduling flexibility, the opportunity to work on special projects, training and development opportunities, and so on. Whenever possible, effective managers find ways to use various rewards to motivate a variety of employees.

Provide Plenty of Feedback. Feedback is essential to motivation, regardless of whether employees are performing well or poorly. When employees are performing well, feedback telling them so spurs them on. When employees are performing poorly, feedback to that effect suggests that they consider a different approach to the task or intensify their efforts. Giving appropriate feedback can be difficult, however, and inappropriate feedback may actually decrease motivation. How does a manager know what type of feedback to give? One general rule is to focus on task performance and avoid criticizing personal characteristics that are difficult for employees to change.[57]

Provide Equitable Rewards. Employees' perceptions of whether rewards are equitable are affected by many factors, and managers must be aware of all of them. Employees make two types of comparisons when evaluating whether they have been rewarded fairly. One type of comparison involves employees assessing their own accomplishments in terms of the rewards they receive. Insufficient rewards may demotivate employees, causing them to do little more than go through the motions. Conversely, major rewards can motivate superior performance.

A second type of comparison involves assessing their own accomplishments and rewards in terms of those of other employees. Effective managers recognize that employees' assessments of equity and fairness are basically subjective perceptions. Perceptions may partially reflect objective facts, but inaccurate assumptions and beliefs often play a role, too. Effective communication about rewards is essential. A well-designed reward system will have little motivational value if employees misunderstand the system and rely on inferences and rumor when assessing whether the system is fair.

DIAGNOSING PERFORMANCE DEFICIENCIES

By clarifying performance expectations, linking performance to rewards that employees value, and paying attention to employee perceptions of equity, managers can increase employee motivation levels. Even when employees are highly motivated, however, other barriers to effective performance may exist. To remove these barriers, managers must first identify them. The theories described in this chapter suggest that barriers to performance may be caused by underdeveloped competencies, inappropriate performance goals, or lack of feedback about performance.

Assess Whether Employees Have the Necessary Competencies. To perform well, people must know more than simply what is expected of them. They must know how to do their assigned tasks. That is, they must have the competencies required to translate their efforts into achievements. Motivated employees who lack the required competencies perform just as poorly as competent employees who are unmotivated. Organizations that take a systematic approach to recruitment, selection, and placement usually are less likely to put employees in jobs for which they aren't qualified. But because jobs can change over time, managers must also consider whether additional training is needed in order for employees to remain competent in the context of their changing jobs.

Verify That Employees Perceive Their Goals as Feasible Yet Challenging. Managers who set specific goals (with or without employee participation) help employees focus on the most important aspects of their jobs. However, specific goals can sometimes backfire and become barriers to performance, especially if the goals are either too easy or too difficult. In general, difficult goals are more motivating than easy goals. But, if the goals are too difficult, employees will feel that they have no chance of achieving them and exert little or no effort trying. Specific goals that conflict with each other also create barriers to performance. Like goals that are too difficult, conflicting goals cause employees to feel that the goals are impossible to achieve.

Verify That Employees Believe That the Performance Desired by Managers Is What Will Be Rewarded. To maintain or increase motivation, the link between rewards and performance must be clear. On the one hand, managers seldom believe that they fail to reward good performance. On the other hand, employees frequently report that good performance isn't what counts in their organization. Putting in time at the office, socializing with the boss, being agreeable, and not making waves are just a few of the behaviors that employees list when asked about who gets rewarded. When such perceptions are discovered, managers must do more than simply assert that employees are wrong if they believe that performance isn't being rewarded. A manager's responsibility includes uncovering the roots of such perceptions and working to change them.

CHAPTER SUMMARY

Ensuring that employees are motivated to work productively is a primary managerial responsibility. Managers who are able to do so will be rewarded for their efforts with a workforce that expresses little dissatisfaction and exerts high levels of effort. To be effective, managers must understand the many factors that, in combination, can enhance or squelch motivation. The four approaches to motivation described in this chapter provide useful insights about how to enhance the motivation and productivity of an organization's workforce.

1. DESCRIBE FOUR APPROACHES TO UNDERSTANDING WORK MOTIVATION.

Four approaches to understanding work motivation are (1) understanding individual differences in employees' needs, (2) understanding how the job and organization contexts affect motivation, (3) understanding how managers' behaviors affect employee motivation, and (4) understanding how the separate approaches can be integrated into a single, comprehensive approach.

2. DESCRIBE HOW INDIVIDUALS' NEEDS AFFECT MOTIVATION AND PERFORMANCE.

Maslow's hierarchy of needs identifies five categories of individual needs: physiological, security, affiliation, esteem, and self-actualization. This theory holds that people are motivated to satisfy these needs according to their importance at specific times in their lives. Its framework includes the satisfaction–progression phenomenon. Alderfer's ERG model identifies three, rather than five, categories of needs: existence, relatedness, and growth. ERG theory includes a description of the frustration–regression phenomenon. McClelland's learned needs model suggests that people acquire three motives—achievement, affiliation, and power—by interacting with their social environment. These motives have implications for what people want from their work experiences and how they interact with others, but they are not arranged in a hierarchy.

3. EXPLAIN HOW THE JOB AND ORGANIZATION CONTEXTS AFFECT MOTIVATION AND PERFORMANCE.

Herzberg's two-factor model states that factors in the work situation strongly influence satisfaction and performance. Motivator factors—including the challenge of the work itself, responsibility, recognition, achievement, and advancement and growth—reflect the nature of the job and can create high levels of motivation and satisfaction. Hygiene factors—such as reasonable working conditions, company policies, and benefits—involve the context in which the job occurs and relate to feelings of dissatisfaction. Hygiene factors can hurt employee performance if not present but don't necessarily increase performance when present.

The job-enrichment model states that three critical psychological states—experienced meaningfulness, experienced responsibility, and knowledge of results—lead to high motivation and job satisfaction. In turn, five job characteristics—skill variety, task identity, task significance, autonomy, and feedback—influence critical psychological states. Individuals with strong growth needs and the necessary knowledge and skills to perform the job are more likely to respond positively to job-enrichment programs than individuals who do not have these characteristics.

Equity theory is based on the assumption that people want to be treated fairly. A fair or equitable situation is one in which people with similar inputs experience similar outcomes. When inequities exist, people aren't satisfied, performance drops, and they then choose one of several actions to reduce their inequity: modify their inputs, modify their outcomes, rationalize the inequities, or leave the situation.

4. **EXPLAIN HOW MANAGERS CAN USE REWARDS AND GOALS TO MOTIVATE EMPLOYEES.**

Reinforcement theory states that behavior is a function of its consequences. There are four types of consequences: positive reinforcement, negative reinforcement, punishment, and extinction. Positive reinforcement provides rewards to increase the probability of a behavior occurring. Negative reinforcement occurs when an employee engages in a behavior to avoid or escape from unpleasant outcomes. Punishment applies negative outcomes to discourage repetition of a behavior. Extinction withdraws the reinforcement that previously had been applied to a behavior. Positive and negative reinforcement should be used to encourage desired work behaviors, whereas punishment and extinction should be applied to discourage undesired work behaviors.

Goal-setting theory states that managers can direct the performance of their employees by assigning specific, difficult goals that employees accept and are willing to commit to. Goals affect motivation in two ways: by increasing the amount of effort that people choose to exert and by directing or channeling that effort. Specific goals are more effective than vague, ambiguous goals. Providing feedback to employees about their progress toward those goals also is important to their effectiveness. Management by objectives is a goal-setting technique used by managers who set goals jointly with employees.

5. **DISCUSS WAYS IN WHICH THE COMBINATION OF INDIVIDUAL DIFFERENCES, THE JOB AND WORK CONTEXTS, AND MANAGERIAL BEHAVIORS AFFECT MOTIVATION.**

The Porter–Lawler expectancy model of motivation suggests that people make conscious decisions about their own behavior and select a course of action because they expect a certain behavior to lead to a desired outcome. The model explains motivation in terms of value of reward, perceived effort–reward probability, effort, abilities and traits, role perceptions, performance, rewards, perceived equitable rewards, and satisfaction.

6. **DESCRIBE THE DESIGN AND IMPLEMENTATION OF AN EFFECTIVE PERFORMANCE MANAGEMENT SYSTEM.**

Effective performance management systems reflect the key principles of several theories of motivation. These principles include designing enriched jobs, clarifying performance expectations, providing rewards that employees value, giving feedback, and ensuring equitable treatment. In addition, managers must be able to diagnose the causes of poor performance. In doing so, managers need to consider whether employees have the competencies required to do the job, whether goals are viewed as challenging and feasible, and whether employees and managers alike have the same view of what is rewarded.

QUESTIONS FOR DISCUSSION

1. Using Maslow's needs hierarchy and McClelland's learned needs model, explain what motivates Steve Dorner (see the Preview feature). What needs seem to be most important to him? How do his job and organization meet these needs?

2. Explain how you can use the equity model to determine your level of satisfaction with your grade in this course.

3. Choose a behavior of yours that you would like to change. What does the reinforcement model suggest about how you could do so? Can you change the behavior on your own, or would you need someone else to help you? Explain.

4. Suppose that you were the mayor of a city. You target garbage removal and disposal as an area for improvement. Explain how you could use goal-setting theory to improve the performance of your city's sanitation department. Be specific.

5. Think about a specific job that you've had. Use the integrative model of expectancy theory to explain your motivation and performance. What aspects of the situation were motivating for you? What aspects of the situation interfered with your performance? How could a manager have used expectancy theory to improve your motivation and/or your performance?

EXERCISES TO DEVELOP YOUR MANAGERIAL COMPETENCIES

1. **Global Awareness Competency.** Visit the home page of Northern Telecom (Nortel) at

   www.nortel.com

   and explore the career opportunities offered around the world. Select two jobs in two different countries. Use Alderfer's ERG theory to analyze the motivational aspects of the two jobs from your perspective.

2. **Planning and Administration Competency.** Visit the Hire Quality home page at

   www.hire-quality.com

   to learn about how this employment firm helps match job candidates and employers. Click on the box addressed to employers seeking qualified candidates and read the description of how Hire Quality identifies suitable candidates. Describe the basic steps in the company's unique approach. If you were an employer looking for highly motivated employees, would you use Hire Quality to find them? Why or why not?

3. **Self-Awareness Competency.** Sunrise Consulting is a firm that designs "customized programs to motivate and reward employees." Visit the company's home page at

   www.ro.com

   and read the descriptions of its numerous program offerings. Choose three programs that you would like your current or future employer to adopt. For each program that you select, explain how it relates to your scores on the Work Motivation Questionnaire on page 468.

4. **Strategic Action Competency.** As we noted in Chapter 12, hiring qualified employees is a key strategic action for high-tech firms, which depend on highly talented employees to create new products and services. Unless these firms can attract the very best talent, they won't be able to compete successfully. Visit the home pages of several high-tech companies. Evaluate how effective these companies are likely to be in getting people to apply for jobs with them and eventually accepting job offers from them. Select one company and offer three suggestions for how they could improve their electronic job posting and recruiting efforts. The home pages of three companies that you might visit are those of Etec Systems at

   www.etec.com

   IBM at

   www.ibm.com

   and Microsoft at

   www.microsoft.com

5. **Teamwork Competency.** Working with two members of your class, use Hackman and Oldham's job enrichment theory to analyze the motivational aspects of this course. To what extent does the design of the course enhance your feelings of meaningfulness, responsibility, and knowledge of results. Explain how various elements of the course design affect these three psychological states.

REAL-TIME CASE ANALYSIS

EDDIE BAUER SATISFIES

To most people, the Eddie Bauer company brings to mind images of outdoor clothing and casual business wear. Located in Redmond, Washington, Eddie Bauer is a rapidly growing catalog and retail company. The past five years have seen double-digit revenue growth for the catalog division, which brings in about 30 percent of the company's $1.5 billion in annual sales. Retail stores selling clothing and furniture make up the rest of the business. Throughout this growing company, employee satisfaction is given high priority, earning it a spot among *Business Week*'s top 10 places to work as well as inclusion in *Working Mother* magazine's list of Top 100 Employers.

Among the many Eddie Bauer strategies for attracting new employees (called associates) and keeping the current workforce satisfied is the firm's family-friendly approach. Dealing with family issues is a part of the company's strategic business plan. Its success in this regard is part of what led *Business Week* to conclude that it's such a good place to work. "The pay isn't great," the magazine acknowledged, "but employees like the hours and say management demonstrates impressive family support." Company spokeswoman Liz Gorman elaborates: "Balance is at the core of what Eddie Bauer is all about. We believe there really is a need to have a balance in work and life."

How does the company help associates achieve work and life balance for 12,000 people working in more than 450 locations throughout the United States, Canada, Japan, and Germany? The benefits it offers include

- flexible work day that allows workers at the corporate headquarters to choose an 8-to-5 workday or a 6:30 A.M.-to-3:30 P.M. workday;

- a cafeteria that will prepare takeout food for associates who work into the evening;

- special summer hours that allow associates to work a four-day week, so they can have long weekends;

- one "Balance Day" per year, in addition to normal vacations and holidays, intended to encourage employees to schedule "call in well" absences;

- a casual dress code, which has been in place for more than a decade;

- job sharing and telecommuting arrangements;

- a 40 percent subsidy of transportation costs for associates who use a vanpool;

- emergency child-care services;

- child- and elder-care consulting and referral services;

- dry cleaning services that pick up and deliver at the associate's place of work;

- special in-home heath services for new parents;

- an Outdoor Experience Allowance, which provides 50 percent subsidies for a variety of activities, ranging from golf lessons to horseback riding; and

- a Group Mortgage HOME program that assists employees with financial transactions associated with selling or purchasing a home.

These are just a few of the many benefits developed by Eddie Bauer in response to its associates' preferences. Five years ago, when the company decided to aim for being an employer of choice, management held focus group sessions with associates to get their input. What became clear was that juggling work and nonwork activities was a struggle for a large portion of the workforce.

President Rick Fersch responded to employees' concerns by giving his full support to creating change quickly and with as little red tape as possible. Management believes that these benefits pay for themselves because many of them result in lower health-care costs. In addition, the programs enable associates to be more focused and productive at work because they know that they will have the resources they need to manage their personal needs.[58]

QUESTIONS

1. Which needs are addressed by each of the benefits listed? To what extent do these benefits address hygiene factors and motivator factors?

2. Imagine that you are an Eddie Bauer associate. Would the benefits offered by Eddie Bauer motivate you to work harder in order to keep your job? Explain.

3. Companies that offer extensive family benefits sometimes experience unexpected backlash from employees who live alone or have no children to support. Use equity theory to explain the source of such backlash reactions and the possible consequences of such backlash. What can companies such as Eddie Bauer do to avoid such backlash?

4. As more and more companies adopt family-friendly policies in response to pressure from workers, Eddie Bauer may lose the competitive advantage that it currently enjoys as an employer of choice. What other cutting-edge approaches to keeping employees satisfied and motivated should the company consider? Relate your recommendations to one or more of the motivational theories described in this chapter.

To learn more about Eddie Bauer, visit the company's home page at

www.eddiebauer.com

VIDEO CASE

LANIER OFFICE PRODUCTS: CUSTOMER VISION IS 20/20

The most visible expressions of Lanier's purpose are its mission statement and quality vision. Various methods could be used to motivate employees individually to meet the company's goals and advance its corporate image. Because of the nature of Lanier's business—generating small profit margins on the sale of other manufacturers' equipment—it's likely not to produce any entrepreneurs. But modest monetary rewards could still be powerful motivators. Management could establish various forms of financial incentive (e.g., corporate profit sharing, and sales bonuses). In some retail firms, commissions make up the largest part of sales staff's compensation.

Many companies now rely on employee stock ownership to motivate performance, in some cases, even when a company *isn't* publicly traded. Science Applications International Corporation (SAIC), an employee-owned defense contractor, has established an "internal stock market" to express the company's valuation and reward employees by awarding stock options. The stock's price is reset four times a year; in fiscal year 1997, internal stock trading amounted to 1.8 million shares worth $41 million. Employees' profits from their shares of SAIC represent extrinsic rewards, but the company's internal stock market might also aid in generating intrinsic rewards, as employees more closely associate themselves with their corporate family and its collective fortunes.

Managers need to be attuned to problems that might arise from "perks" that benefit employees disproportionately, however. Workers without children may not begrudge on-site daycare, but such a service shouldn't appear to be an opulent windfall. A sensible approach to awarding perks is to offer a menu of benefits, some of which could be of interest and use to any of the employees, and allow them to choose from among them up to a maximum amount of "benefits capital." This method could also allow the employee with less of an interest in community benefits, or a more pressing need for income, to opt for a (perhaps discounted) cash equivalent.

The Lanier Team Management Process embodies Lanier's corporate vision for quality. Translating abstract concepts into tangible, teachable tasks can transform them from vague feel-good statements into concrete charters. Many companies' mission statements amount to little more than window dressing (e.g., nice sounding words strung together, often under the tutelage of a hired consultant). The Lanier executive who can rattle off the company's vision, point by point, and discuss what each point means in concrete terms suggests a firm commitment to that vision. The company's workforce is likely to be motivated to participate in achieving such clearly visible goals.

Lanier's corporate vision for quality, which is an important element in its approach to prospective customers (and well outlined on the company's Web site), is also likely to be a powerful motivator within the company. Like that of Wainwright Industries (see Chapter 2), a strategy of companywide attention to quality at Lanier is mandatory in customer service; the company rewards individual achievement in delivering quality service through special recognition.

ON THE WEB

Lanier Office Products' parent company, Harris Corporation, is on the Web (**sol.corp.harris.com**). Lanier's own Web site (**www.lanier.com**) document's employment opportunities and outlines the motivational methods it uses (e.g., commissions for sales positions). SAIC also is on the Web (**www.saic.com**);

its Web site gives details on employee stock owner-ship options and the company's internal stock market.

QUESTIONS

1. Lanier management decides to offer an incentive bonus to increase sales—a week's paid vacation for the top salesperson each quarter. How might this incentive motivate different employees differently?

2. How might the absence of key managers (e.g., as occurred with IBAX; see Chapter 12) lead to motivational problems?

3. An employee working on a key part of a company's new service is performing poorly and is seemingly disinterested in meeting a looming deadline. Give examples of both positive and negative reinforcements that the employee's manager might apply.

To help you answer these questions and learn more about Lanier's Customer Service, visit the company's home page at

www.lanier.com

Case contributed by Ross Stapleton-Gray, President, TeleDiplomacy, Inc., a technology and policy consultancy, and Adjunct Professor in Georgetown University's Communication, Culture, and Technology program.

Chapter

15

The Dynamics of Leadership

LEARNING OBJECTIVES

AFTER STUDYING THIS CHAPTER, YOU SHOULD BE ABLE TO:

1. DESCRIBE THE BASICS OF LEADERSHIP.

2. STATE THE CONTRIBUTIONS OF THE TRAITS MODELS OF LEADERSHIP.

3. DESCRIBE THE PRIMARY BEHAVIORAL MODELS OF LEADERSHIP.

4. EXPLAIN THE PRINCIPAL CONTINGENCY MODELS OF LEADERSHIP AND THE SITUATIONAL FACTORS THAT DETERMINE A LEADER'S EFFECTIVENESS.

5. STATE THE UNIQUE BEHAVIORS OF TRANSFORMATIONAL LEADERS AND THEIR IMPACT ON FOLLOWERS.

6. DESCRIBE HOW ORGANIZATIONS DEVELOP EFFECTIVE LEADERS.

Outline

K a t h e r i n e   H u d s o n ' s   V i e w   o f   L e a d e r s h i p

By the time Katherine Hudson took over as CEO of W. H. Brady, she had already proven herself to be an outstanding general manager. Earnings of the business units that she had headed at Kodak, her former employer, more than tripled under her direction. As Hudson transforms W. H. Brady into a more global company, similar results can be expected. Headquartered in Milwaukee, Wisconsin, W. H. Brady manufactures audio, visual, and data storage tapes, as well as a variety of coated and adhesive specialty tapes and materials. The old Brady's culture was conservative and risk-averse—characteristics that Hudson thought detrimental for a company competing in a global market with innovative giants like 3M. Hudson created a looser culture that thrives on participation rather than a controlling management style. To make the point that no one is better than anyone else in the company, at her first major staff meeting she had all fifty executives wear Groucho Marx glasses with big noses and mustaches. She's the idea generator, but she lets her management team decide which ideas to use and which to toss aside. "The most important thing in trying to have change occur is generating the feeling that we're all in this together," she explains. "Maybe in the past you could have the all-knowing CEO who actually made decisions and affected what was going on in dramatic detail, but the world is too complex right now. The best thing I can do is set a direction and a tone for what they're trying to accomplish. If they feel that I'm not with them, or that they can't approach me and actually make a comment—even a negative one—then I don't think we'll have the degree of team spirit and energy needed to go forward."

What is the direction being set? Her strategy has four key components: geographic expansion, increased market penetration, joint ventures and acquisitions, and new products and new markets. To ensure that employees understand their roles in carrying out the strategy, Hudson tries to keep her explanations simple: "We tell our employees that business is not that complicated, that it's not this big intellectual exercise for which you have to bring in heavy duty consultants and have them show you what to do. All you have to do is three things: grow the top line, control your costs, and use your assets wisely." She and her management team have worked hard consistently to communicate this simple message. Do all 2,500 Brady employees have the message? Hudson says not yet. "But we are making a big dent and consistency is the key. It has to be simple enough so that you can tick it off with no notes. And it has to be consistent across the management team and over time."

So far, the members of her board of directors seem pleased. "We are extremely happy with her accomplishments," says one board member. "She uses unconventional approaches to problem solving and has brought to the company a lively style and participative management approach that encourages thinking 'outside the box.' She surrounds herself with the best and the brightest, and then gives them the latitude to do their jobs."[1]

* * *

To learn more about W. H. Brady, visit the company's home page at

www.whbrady.com

BASICS OF LEADERSHIP

1

DESCRIBE THE BASICS OF LEADERSHIP

LEADERSHIP

Influencing others to act toward the attainment of a goal.

*L*eadership involves influencing others to act toward the attainment of a goal. As Katherine Hudson knows, over the long run a leader can't simply threaten or coerce people into complying. Leadership is based on interpersonal relationships, not administrative activities and directives. Leadership can be exercised by people throughout an organization, and the best organizations have effective leaders at all levels. W. H. Brady would not succeed if CEO Hudson were its *only* leader; middle managers and even machine operators also must lead effectively.

Much can be learned about the conditions for successful leadership from the experiences of Katherine Hudson. First, trust must be established. Giving employees more freedom to act autonomously and make decisions is a necessary first step. Second, leaders must clarify the direction in which people should be headed. Clear, consistent communication helps people feel confident that they can make the right decisions. Third, effective leaders encourage others to take risks. A project's failure shouldn't derail a person's career. By celebrating failures, Hudson encourages her employees to accept occasional failure as a normal, and potentially valuable aspect of risk taking. Finally, leaders must have a source of power.[2]

TYPES OF POWER

POWER

The ability to influence the behavior of others.

Power is the ability to influence the behavior of others. Leaders exercise power, and effective leaders know how to use it wisely. The types of power used by a leader reveal a great deal about why others follow that individual. One of the most useful frameworks for understanding the power of leaders was developed by John French and Bertram Raven.[3] They identified five types of power: legitimate, reward, coercive, referent, and expert. Effective leaders may find it necessary to use all five types of power at different times.

LEGITIMATE POWER

Influence based on the leader's formal position in the organization's hierarchy.

Legitimate Power. Influence based on the leader's formal position in the organization's hierarchy is *legitimate power.* Access to resources, information, and key decision makers gives some leaders legitimate power in influencing events and passing on information and rewards to subordinates. Such leaders are often said to have clout or political influence within an organization. Legitimate power can

- get a good job for a talented employee,

- obtain approval for expenditures beyond the budget,

- provide easy access to top people in the company, and

- ensure knowing early about important decisions and policy shifts.

REWARD POWER

Influence stemming from a leader's ability to reward followers.

Reward Power. The influence stemming from a leader's ability to satisfy followers' needs is *reward power.* In other words, employees act on a supervisor's requests in the belief that their behaviors will be rewarded. The supervisor may be able to reward them with favorable job assignments, preferred vacation schedules, promotions, and/or raises.

COERCIVE POWER

The ability of a leader to obtain compliance through fear of punishment.

Coercive Power. The ability of a leader to obtain compliance through fear or punishment is *coercive power.* Punishment may take the form of official reprimands, less desirable work assignments, pay cuts, demotions, suspensions, or even termination.[4] This approach is familiar to Dale Davis, a facilities manager at Rodel, Inc., a manufacturing company in Delaware. Before managers at Rodel received intensive leadership training, he described the place as "a real meat grinder—an environment of intense emotion. If you could dominate a situation or grab the most resources, you were the winner. My own style—and I wasn't alone—was to yell and scream and beat people into submission."[5] Coercive power usually is less effective than, say, reward power for the same reasons that punishment has a limited effect as a motivator (see Chapter 14). Some employees respond to coercion by falsifying performance reports, stealing company property, and exhibiting similar negative behavior, rather than improving their performance.

REFERENT POWER

Influence based on followers' personal identification with the leader.

Referent Power. Influence based on followers' personal identification with the leader is *referent power.* The followers are apt to like, admire, and want to emulate the leader. Referent power usually is possessed by leaders who have admirable personal characteristics, charisma, and/or excellent reputations.

EXPERT POWER

Influence based on a leader's specialized knowledge.

Expert Power. A leader's specialized knowledge grants that person *expert power.* It is a key source of power for managers at the present time and will continue to be so in the future. Subordinates act on the leader's recommendations because of the leader's knowledge. Andy Grove, chairman and cofounder of Intel, was able to lead his company in part because he knows so much about microchip processors. After earning his Ph.D. at the University of California, Berkeley, Grove worked with a team of engineers who discovered how to use silicone as a medium for long-term information storage. This discovery was fundamental to the success of the industry and earned awards for the team. Named "Time's Man of the Year" in 1997, Grove is still recognized as a visionary thinker.[6]

USING POWER EFFECTIVELY

The leader's use of different types of power, or clout, can lead to one of three types of behavior in followers: commitment, compliance, or resistance. *Committed* subordinates are enthusiastic about meeting their leader's expectations and strive to do so. Subordinates who merely *comply* with their leader's requests will do only what has to be done—usually without much enthusiasm. In most cases, *resistance* by subordinates will be expressed as appearing to respond to their leader's requests while not actually doing so or even intentionally delaying or sabotaging plans.[7]

As Figure 15.1 shows, expert and referent power tend to result in subordinate commitment, legitimate and reward power tend to result in compliance, and coercive power tends to result in resistance. Referent power usually leads to high levels of performance. Hence effective leaders are likely to rely on expert, referent, and reward power, using legitimate and coercive power only minimally. Legitimate power is effective when a manager simply requires an employee to perform a task that is within the employee's capabilities and job description. In some situations coercive power may be effective in getting subordinates to comply with rules. In general, however, when leaders threaten or punish, the response is anger.

In organizations that rely on teamwork, some of these forms of power are more useful than others. Consider the situation at Mary Kay Cosmetics. In this company the consultants, as the sales force is called, work for themselves and are fully empowered. Nevertheless, teamwork is essential to the company's success. Local and national sales directors provide coaching and mentoring, creating a supportive environment. From the CEO down, the company's leaders realize that their role is to give recognition and praise to keep the entire team motivated to achieve personal and overall economic goals. The way in which leaders at Mary Kay Cosmetics use the five types of power in this team-oriented organization is described in the following Teamwork Competency feature.

| *Figure 15.1* | **Consequences of Using Five Types of Power** |

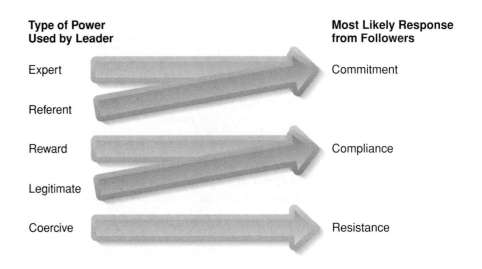

The book, *Forbes Greatest Business Stories of All Time,* profiles twenty business leaders. Mary Kay Ash is the only woman in the book. Now chairman emeritus of Mary Kay Cosmetics, Ash founded her company in 1963, a month after she retired from a successful twenty-five-year sales career. Her goal? It's to provide women with an unlimited opportunity for personal and financial success. Technically, Mary Kay Beauty consultants don't work for the company that Ash founded. Each is an entrepreneur who owns and controls her own business. Mary Kay sells its products directly to the sales force, who then sell the products to customers. The most successful consultants (about 9,000 people in 1998) advance to become sales directors for a group of consultants, and eventually national sales directors.

In a company where everyone's her own boss, how do Mary Kay and the sales directors influence and motivate the others to work together as a team? What types of power do they wield? One thing is certain: No one uses coercive power. That would never be accepted in a company that uses the Golden Rule—Do unto others as you would have them do unto you—as its guiding philosophy. With everyone being her own boss, legitimate power, also, is basically irrelevant. However, reward power plays a big role. Annual sales meetings, well-known for their extravagance and party-like atmosphere, are held in each country where the organization does business to recognize outstanding achievements. Typical awards are cars, trips, office equipment, and cash. Pink cars are considered the signature award—a pink Cadillac in the United States, a pink Mercedes-Benz in Germany, a pink Toyota in Taiwan, and a pink Ford in Argentina.

Expert power is particularly important to leadership within the organization. Ash understood the importance of training as a way to improve sales figures. Providing such training is one of the key roles of the sales directors, who hold weekly meetings with the consultants. These sales experts are entrusted with passing along proven selling techniques. But the success of Mary Kay Cosmetics is due to more than good sales techniques. Motivation plays a huge role in the company's success.

The nearly half million Mary Kay Beauty consultants around the world admire the company's founder and are eager to use her as their role model (and for this reason, it's easy to spot a Mary Kay sales meeting when it's in town!). Lisa Madson expressed the inspiration Mary Kay gave her: "I was a secretary. I was not voted most likely to succeed in high school. But she reaches so many people by talking about the living potential that everyone has inside. And she's the living example." Janice Bird, who works at headquarters, elaborated: "People understand that for Mary Kay, it was bigger than just her. They've increased their own self-esteem by being around her, and they want to pass that on to others in the same way she did." Mary Kay Ash retired a millionaire many times over, and many of her followers also have succeeded beyond their wildest dreams. For ten consecutive years they have set new sales records, selling more than $2 billion worth of products in 1997 alone. Mary Kay Beauty consultants continue to show a strong commitment to their retired leader and her original goals.[8]

*   *   *

To learn more about Mary Kay Cosmetics, visit the company's home page at

www.marykay.com

Several different models describe how effective leaders influence others. There is no single or simple answer to which style of leadership works best, although research has been extensive and numerous articles and books have been written on the subject. We have grouped the results of this research into four categories of models: traits, behavioral, contingency, and transformational. Fifty years ago, traits models of leadership were the most popular. Gradually, as evidence accumulated, traits models were replaced—first by behavioral models and then by contingency models. Currently, the transformational model has many supporters, reflecting efforts of many leaders to transform outdated forms of organizations into more competitive ones.

TRAITS MODELS

2

**STATE THE CONTRIBU-
TIONS OF THE TRAITS
MODELS OF LEADERSHIP**

TRAITS MODELS
Leadership models based on
the assumption that certain
physical, social, and personal
characteristics are inherent in
leaders.

Many early studies of leadership were directed at identifying the personal traits of leaders. **Traits models** are based on the assumption that certain physical, social, and personal characteristics are inherent in leaders.[9] According to this view, the presence or absence of these characteristics distinguishes leaders from nonleaders. Some of the key traits are

- **physical:** young to middle-aged, energetic, striking appearance, tall, slender;

- **social background:** educated at the "right" schools, socially prominent, or upwardly mobile; and

- **personality:** adaptable, aggressive, emotionally stable, dominant, self-confident, and sociable.

There is some common-sense support for the notion that effective leaders have certain traits. However, research hasn't proved that traits consistently separate potential leaders from nonleaders.[10] For example, physical characteristics don't correlate with successful leadership; they relate only to *perceived* leadership ability. Physical characteristics still may be helpful in the performance of some manual-labor jobs, but effective leadership rarely depends on a person's height, strength, or weight.

Personality traits found to relate to a sales manager's effectiveness include gregariousness, risk taking, impulsiveness, exhibitionism, and egocentrism. Anthony Bartarse, owner of an auto dealership in Oakland, California, is a good example. Named the 1997 National Hispanic Business Entrepreneur of the Year, Bartarse describes himself as a very sociable guy. "I love the different types of people, from the very nice to the very obnoxious. I enjoy myself with all kinds. I act. I play low key, and that makes friends," he says.[11] However, these same traits aren't common to successful coaches of sports teams. Their personality traits usually include self-assertion, self-assurance, a strong need for power, and a low need for security. Besides, many successful sales managers and coaches have personality profiles completely different from those mentioned. This lack of proof doesn't mean that certain traits have nothing to do with effective leadership.[12] It simply means that traits must be evaluated in relation to other factors, such as the situation and followers' needs.

BEHAVIORAL MODELS

3

**DESCRIBE THE BEHAV-
IORAL MODELS OF
LEADERSHIP**

BEHAVIORAL MODELS
Leadership models that focus
on differences in the actions
of effective and ineffective
leaders.

After discovering that leaders don't have a uniform set of personal traits, researchers turned their attention to isolating *behaviors* that are characteristic of effective leaders. **Behavioral models** of leadership focus on differences in the actions of effective and ineffective leaders. In other words, they are based on what effective and ineffective leaders actually do: how they delegate tasks to subordinates, where and when they communicate to others, how they perform their roles, and so on. Unlike traits, behaviors can be observed and learned. Because leadership behaviors can be learned, individuals can be trained to lead more effectively.

THEORY X AND THEORY Y

Assumptions and beliefs about individuals and how to motivate them often influence a leader's behavior. Figure 15.2 lists two contrasting sets of assumptions that

- The typical employee dislikes work and will avoid it if possible
- Employees want direction whenever possible
- Managers must coerce employees to get them to work

- People like to work
- Employees who are committed to the company's objectives will exercise self-direction and self-control
- Employees learn to accept and even seek responsibility at work

THEORY X

A leadership style whereby leaders tell subordinates what's expected of them, instruct them in how to perform their jobs, insist that they meet certain standards, and make sure that everyone knows who's boss.

THEORY Y

A leadership style whereby leaders consult with their subordinates, seek their opinions, and encourage them to take part in planning and decision making.

leaders hold about their subordinates. These sets of assumptions are called Theory X and Theory Y.

Managers who believe that people are motivated mainly by money, are lazy and uncooperative, and have poor work habits will treat them accordingly. Such managers tend to use a directive leadership style: They tell people what to do. They lead by telling their subordinates what's expected of them, instructing them in how to perform their jobs, insisting that they meet certain standards, and being sure that everyone knows who's boss. Douglas McGregor, author of *The Human Side of the Enterprise,* labeled this leadership style ***Theory X.***[13]

In contrast, leaders who believe that their people work hard, cooperate, and have positive attitudes will treat them accordingly. Such leaders use a participative leadership style: They act by consulting their subordinates, seeking their opinions, and encouraging them to take part in planning and decision making. According to McGregor, these leaders practice ***Theory Y.*** By and large, employees clearly prefer Theory Y behaviors because of the opportunities afforded them for getting involved in the decision-making process. When Mort Meyerson was CEO of EDS, he used the Theory X approach. But now, when he reflects on those days, he realizes that his boot camp mentality made a lot of people unhappy. Although the company was a financial success, the culture was destructive, and sometimes it led people to act against the long-term interests of the company and its customers.

Katherine Hudson is an example of a Theory Y leader. All of her staff is salaried (no clock punching) and many telecommute. When asked about whether placing this much trust in employees has a downside, she replied, "The question here is: What are the assumptions under which you operate with other human beings? I may be naïve, but my main belief is that 99 percent of people want to take pride in their work, make a contribution, and look back at the end of the day and say, 'I did something to contribute to the success of this enterprise.' If you believe that and trust that people really want to make a contribution, then the paradigm by which you manage changes dramatically."[14]

OHIO STATE UNIVERSITY AND UNIVERSITY OF MICHIGAN MODELS

Researchers at Ohio State University took another approach to studying leadership styles. They asked employees to describe the behaviors of their supervisors. Based on the responses, the researchers identified two leadership styles: considerate and initiating-structure.[15]

CONSIDERATE LEADERSHIP STYLE
Exhibiting concern for employees' well-being, status, and comfort.

A *considerate leadership style* is characterized by concern for employees' well-being, status, and comfort. Typical behaviors of a considerate leader include

- expressing appreciation when employees do a good job,

- not demanding more than employees can achieve,

- helping employees with their personal problems,

- being friendly and accessible, and

- rewarding employees for jobs well done.

A considerate leader seeks to create a friendly and pleasant working climate. Such a leader assumes that subordinates want to do their best and that the leader's job is to make it easier for them to do theirs. A considerate leader seeks acceptance by treating subordinates with respect and dignity and tends to downplay the use of both legitimate and coercive power. Bruce Moravec leads a team of 300 people, building a Boeing jet aircraft. Moravec has little formal power, so he relies heavily on consideration. "Ninety-five percent of my people get their paychecks from other departments," he explains. "All I can do is influence them." How? "I work with them on an informal basis, walk around, ask how it's going. Most people want to do a good job. You have to let them know that you're there to help, not just to give them orders."[16]

Not surprisingly, the considerate leadership style usually is readily accepted by subordinates. Advocates contend that this style of leadership generates goodwill and leads to job satisfaction for subordinates. Other positive outcomes include closer cooperation between leader and subordinates, increased motivation of subordinates, more productive work groups, and low turnover and grievance rates.

INITIATING-STRUCTURE LEADERSHIP STYLE
Actively planning, organizing, controlling, and coordinating subordinates' activities.

The *initiating-structure leadership style* is characterized by active planning, organizing, controlling, and coordinating subordinates' activities. Typical behaviors of an initiating-structure leader include

- assigning employees to particular tasks,

- establishing standards of job performance,

- informing employees of job requirements,

- scheduling work to be done by employees, and

- encouraging the use of uniform procedures.

PRODUCTION-CENTERED LEADERSHIP STYLE
Setting standards, organizing and paying close attention to employees' work, keeping production schedules, and stressing results.

Used as the only approach, a forceful initiating-structure leadership style can lead to employee grievances, turnover, and lower employee satisfaction. However, research suggests that effective leaders may exhibit both considerate and initiating-structure behaviors.[17] Employees' reactions to initiating-structure leaders tend to depend on whether they also believe that their leaders are considerate. If so, they view their leader's behavior as effective. However, if employees believe a leader to be inconsiderate, they tend to view the leader's behavior as "watching over employees' shoulders" or *micromanaging*.

EMPLOYEE-CENTERED LEADERSHIP STYLE
Encouraging employees to participate in making decisions and making sure that they are satisfied with their work.

Researchers at the University of Michigan undertook similar studies of leadership behaviors. They classified leaders' behaviors as either production-centered or employee-centered. Leaders who utilize a *production-centered leadership style* set standards, organize and pay close attention to employees' work, keep production schedules, and stress results. Those who have an *employee-centered leadership style* encourage employees to participate in making decisions and make sure that they're satisfied with their work. This type of leader's primary concern is with employees' welfare. The researchers found that employee-centered leaders were more likely to be in charge of high-performance teams than were production-centered managers. More effective leaders were those who had supportive relationships with their team members and encouraged them to set and achieve their own goals.[18]

Many people seem to think that men are more likely to use a production-centered style and that women are more likely to use an employee-centered style. The results of dozens of research studies into whether men and women use different leadership behaviors do suggest that some gender differences exist. Men tend to act and be perceived as being slightly more production-centered (task oriented), whereas women tend to act and be perceived as slightly more employee-centered. In most organizations, such differences are quite small, but some situations magnify them. In particular, women are likely to emerge as effective leaders in groups that are working on long-term, socially complex tasks.[19]

MANAGERIAL GRID MODEL

MANAGERIAL GRID MODEL

A model that identifies five leadership styles, each combining different proportions of concern for production and concern for people.

Developed by Robert Blake and Jane Mouton, the ***managerial grid model*** identifies five leadership styles that combine different proportions of concern for production (similar to the initiating-structure and production-centered styles) and concern for people (similar to the consideration and employee-centered styles).[20] These styles are plotted on a grid in Figure 15.3.

At the lower left-hand corner of the grid, point (1, 1) is the *impoverished style*, characterized by low concern for both people and production. The primary objective

| *Figure 15.3* | **The Managerial Grid Model** |

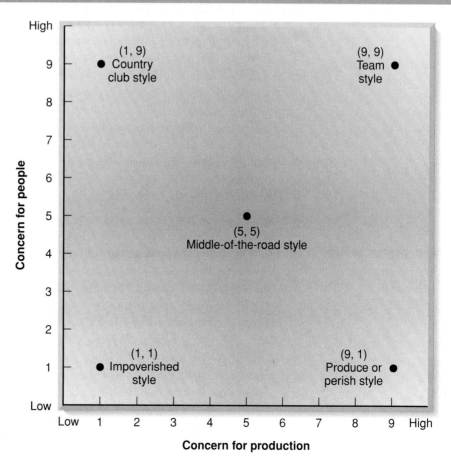

Source: R. R. Blake, J. S. Mouton, and L. E. Greiner, Breakthrough in organization development. *Harvard Business Review*. November– December 1964.

of managers who use this style is to stay out of trouble. They pass orders along to employees, go with the flow, and make sure that they can't be held accountable for mistakes. They exert the minimum effort required to get the work done and avoid being fired or demoted.

At the upper left-hand corner, point (1, 9) is the *country club style*, identified as a high concern for people and a low concern for production. Managers who use this style try to create a secure and comfortable atmosphere and trust that their subordinates will respond positively. Attention to the need for satisfying relationships leads to a friendly, if not necessarily productive, atmosphere and work tempo.

A high concern for production and a low concern for people are reflected at point (9, 1), in the lower right-hand corner. This style is the *produce or perish style*. Leaders who use this style don't consider employees' personal needs to be relevant to achieving the organization's objectives. They use their legitimate and coercive powers to pressure subordinates to meet production quotas. They believe that operational efficiency results from arranging the work so that employees merely have to follow orders. When a company's profitability is falling, showing more concern for production may seem like the best thing a leader can do to turn the company around. Effective leaders realize that this approach is only a short-term solution, however.

In the middle of the grid, point (5, 5) indicates the *middle-of-the-road style*. Leaders who use this style seek a balance between workers' needs and the organization's productivity goals. Adequate performance is obtained by maintaining employee morale at a level sufficient to get the work done.

The upper right-hand corner, point (9, 9), represents the *team style*, which shows high levels of concern for both people and production. Leaders who use this style attempt to establish cohesion and foster feelings of commitment among workers. By introducing a "common stake" in the organization's purposes, the leader builds relationships of trust and respect.

Honda employees have been exposed to different leadership styles during the company's fifty-year life. During the first forty years, employees grew accustomed to founder Soichiro Honda's people-centered leadership. When he retired and Nobuhiko Kawamoto took over, the employees had to adjust to a new style. After analyzing industry trends, Kawamoto decided to change the company's strategy. Then, using a more production-centered style, he changed the organization's design, shook up its culture, and improved its profitability. Kawamoto's bold leadership approach is described in the following Strategic Action Competency account.

EMPOWERMENT MODEL

EMPOWERMENT MODEL
Sharing influence and control with followers.

The behavioral models described so far were developed prior to the 1990s. More recently, a new behavioral model has appeared on the scene: the empowerment model. The **empowerment model** reflects a leader's sharing of influence and control with followers. In doing so, the leader involves employees (individually or in teams) in deciding how to achieve the organization's goals, thus giving them a sense of meaning, competence, self-determination, and impact. A sense of meaning results when employees' hearts are in their work and when their values don't conflict with their work activities. A sense of competence means that employees believe that they have what it takes to do their jobs. A sense of self-determination means that employees feel that they control their own actions and aren't being coerced into doing things. Finally, a sense of impact is experienced when employees can see the results of their efforts. Empowerment helps satisfy the basic human needs for achievement, a sense of belonging, and self-esteem. Empowered workers feel more satisfied with their work and less stressed.[21]

Honda's founder, Soichiro Honda, was known as a brilliant engineer. From the company's start in 1948 until its founder's death in 1991, the company's culture put engineers on a pedestal, indulging their originality and creative tinkerings and letting profits take care of themselves. The approach worked for many years, as the company's engineers designed cars that consumers liked. But competition from more efficient companies, such as Toyota, began eroding Honda's sales. By the early 1990s, Honda's profits were only one sixth of what they had been ten years earlier. Kawamoto, himself a brilliant engineer, was promoted to CEO with a mandate to turn the company around.

Before Soichiro Honda's death, Kawamoto visited him several times. On one visit he said to the founder, "You left behind lots of good things but also things that are not right for the present," to which the old man replied, "Times change. You should do the things you want to." Kawamoto took this to mean that he was free to ignore the existing consensus-style management approach and make whatever changes he felt were needed. "I told people that we have to think about efficiency and speed and effectiveness, and for this it's okay to throw away our old identity." He was

aggressive, even confrontational, in making his point. "In emergencies, you can't wait around saying 'what does everyone think we should do?'" he says by way of explanation.

Car dealers were told to stop their incessant complaining, "You're the ones who have made the company go bad, aren't you? You're not trying hard enough." A new performance appraisal system was put in place to measure individual performance throughout the company. Communication and measurement processes were standardized as the company installed a total quality management (TQM) approach to manufacturing. Production lines were reconfigured to speed the process and allow greater flexibility. Engineers were expected to create designs that could be manufactured more efficiently. Kawamoto admits that these changes weren't easy, saying that "R&D, which stressed creativity and originality, naturally put up great resistance." Factory workers had to change too. "Kawamoto sets high targets and puts an emphasis on speed in reaction time," noted one factory manager. To avoid missing hot trends, like the boom in demand for sport utility vehicles that Honda had missed out on, power in the company was shifted from R&D to marketing.

Honda's new strategy, which Kawamoto describes as customer focused, has increased sales and improved profits. But in his mind, the race has just begun: "The world condition is very difficult. I have to look for weak points that might cause fatal defects. The real competition to survive in the world is starting now. Now that we've turned the corner, we have to accelerate."[22]

* * *

To learn more about Honda, visit the company's home page for its Japanese operations, Honda Motor Company, Ltd., at

www.honda.co.jp

and the company's home page for its North American operations, Honda Motor Company, at

www.honda.com

In a study of one Fortune 50 company, followers reported feeling more empowered when their leaders were clear about their expectations, when their leaders gave them plenty of information about what was happening in the organization, and when they involved the followers in making *important* decisions.[23] Really important decisions include defining jobs (see Chapter 14), determining tasks for which employees will be held accountable, and even deciding who will be hired to work with present employees and how they will be paid.

Empowered employees are essentially self-managing and self-leading. W. L. Gore, the company that makes Gore-Tex fabrics, has empowered employees. One employee recalled her first day at work: "My supervisor said, 'Well, here's your office'—it's a wonderful office—'and here's your desk' and walked away. And I thought now what do I do, you know? I was waiting for a memo or something, or a job description. Finally, after another month I went to my supervisor and said, 'What the heck do you want from me? I need something from you,' and he said, 'If you don't know what you're supposed to do, examine your commitments and opportunities.'" Although this employee was frustrated at first, most of Gore's 6,500 employees love being empowered—so much so that *Fortune* ranked it number seven in its 1998 list of "Best Companies to Work For."[24]

A company with completely empowered employees may seem like it has no leaders, but that isn't so. What it has are leaders who recognize that their job isn't to create followers who are dependent on them. Instead, their job is to help people learn to lead themselves. Self-leaders—that is, self-managed employees—have been taught by their supervisors to use many of the techniques described in Chapter 13 to manage their *own* behaviors. They set goals for themselves, they monitor and evaluate their own performance, and they reward themselves for a job well done.[25]

Sunshine Cleaning Systems is another company with leaders who believe in empowerment. This Florida company provides janitorial and cleaning services to organizations such as the Smithsonian Institution, the Florida Turnpike, various sports centers, restaurants and banks. CEO Larry Calufetti is a former baseball player and coach who believes that people perform best when they feel a sense of personal responsibility for their work. Like a coach, he sees his role as helping his people perform to their full potential, but he realizes that empowering employees doesn't relieve him of responsibility. Rather, he and the other company managers must be sure that employees have been trained in the skills they need on the job and that they have the tools and equipment needed to get the work done effectively and efficiently.

LEADER–MEMBER EXCHANGE MODEL

The behavioral models described so far are based on the assumption that a leader behaves the same way toward all the followers in a group. However, researcher George Graen has theorized that leaders use different styles with different followers. When the theory was first introduced, it was called the vertical-dyad linkage model.[26] It is now called the leader–member exchange (LMX) model. The **leader–member exchange model** states that a leader forms with each follower a somewhat unique one-on-one relationship.[27] In organizations, the leader and follower are usually a supervisor and subordinate. Their relationship centers on how they will perform their respective work roles.

The quality of a relationship between a leader and follower can vary from low (an ineffective relationship) to high (an effective relationship). In a low-quality relationship, the basis for exchanges between supervisor and subordinate is their economic contract. Subordinates in low-quality relationships tend to give to the organization only what is specified in their formal or implied employment contracts. The supervisor in a low-quality relationship gives the subordinate little latitude and avoids delegating to the subordinate.

In high-quality relationships, the supervisor and subordinate develop a more positive relationship, in which each trusts the other. Subordinates in high-quality relationships express greater loyalty and commitment. Supervisors in high-quality relationships give the subordinate better assignments and greater latitude. In effect, subordinates in high-quality LMX relationships are more empowered than those in low-quality LMX relationships. Subordinates in high-quality relationships perform better on required job tasks, have better attendance records, and in general are viewed as good organizational citizens who are willing to exceed the minimum required of them.[28]

If the followers' performance is better when leaders and followers develop more positive relationships, why would a leader develop positive relationships with some followers but not others? To answer this question, researchers have followed recent college graduates as they took their first job after graduation. Based on research of more than 100 graduates and their supervisors, more leaders and followers apparently develop high-quality relationships when they have similar personalities. Early in the relationship, such similarities may cause the leader initially to evaluate the subordinate favorably and trust the subordinate's ability to perform well. Trusting the subordinate, the supervisor freely delegates to the subordinate and gives the subordinate considerable latitude. This freedom gives the subordinate an early opportunity to demonstrate his or her competencies. Achievements by the subordinate strengthen the relationship. In other words, personality similarity may help the leader–follower relationship get off to a good start. Then, if both leader and follower behaviors build trust, a high-quality relationship will develop. Low-quality relationships are more likely to occur when the leader and follower have different personalities or when initial performance is unsatisfactory.[29]

SUMMARY

Behavioral models have added greatly to the understanding of leadership. The focus has shifted from who leaders *are* (traits) toward what leaders *do* (behaviors). However, leadership behaviors that are appropriate in one situation aren't necessarily appropriate in another. Because the behavioral models failed to uncover leadership styles that were consistently appropriate to all situations, other models of leadership were devised. The next step in the evolution of knowledge about leadership was the creation of contingency, or situational, models.

CONTINGENCY MODELS

4

EXPLAIN THE PRINCIPAL CONTINGENCY MODELS OF LEADERSHIP AND THE SITUATIONAL FACTORS THAT DETERMINE A LEADER'S EFFECTIVENESS

CONTINGENCY MODELS
Leadership models based on the idea that the situation determines the best style to use.

FIEDLER'S CONTINGENCY MODEL
A model that suggests that successful leadership depends on matching a leader's style to a situation's demands.

LEAST PREFERRED CO-WORKER
The employee with whom the manager can work least well.

According to **contingency models** of leadership, the situation determines the best style to use.[30] The situational factors contained in these models are shown in Figure 15.4. However, no single contingency model encompasses all these factors. The four most influential contingency models of leadership are Fiedler's contingency model, Hersey and Blanchard's situational model, House's path–goal model, and the leader–participation model.

FIEDLER'S CONTINGENCY MODEL

The first contingency model was developed by Fred Fiedler and his associates.[31] **Fiedler's contingency model** suggests that successful leadership depends on matching a leader's style to a situation's demands. In other words, each leadership style is most effective when it is used in the right situation. According to this model, the manager has to understand his or her own leadership style, diagnose the particular situation, and then match style and situation. That may mean either changing the situation to match the manager's style or giving the leadership role to someone whose style does match the situation.

Leadership Styles. Fiedler viewed leadership style as a trait that is difficult to change. Leadership style is determined by asking the manager to describe his or her **least preferred co-worker** (LPC), that is, the employee with whom the manager can work least well. By seeing how a leader describes this least preferred co-worker, the leader's style can be determined.

A leader who recognizes the importance of developing strong and positive emotional ties with followers is called a **relationship-oriented leader.** This type of

Figure 15.4 **Situational Factors Influencing a Leader's Effectiveness**

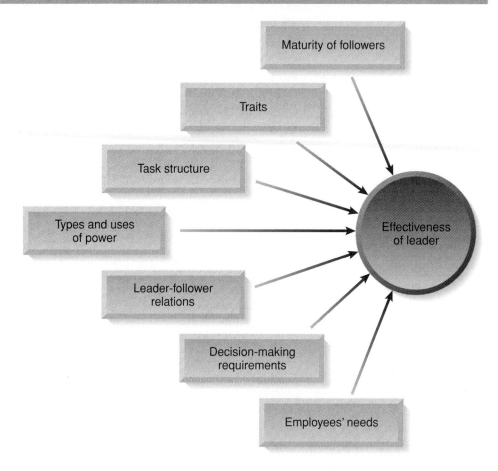

RELATIONSHIP-ORIENTED LEADER
A person who recognizes the importance of developing strong and positive emotional ties with followers.

TASK-ORIENTED LEADER
A person who structures the job for employees and closely watches their behavior.

LEADER–MEMBER RELATIONS
The extent to which followers accept the leader.

TASK STRUCTURE
The degree to which a job is routine.

LEADER POSITION POWER
The extent to which a leader has legitimate, coercive, and reward power.

leader would always use a considerate or an employee-centered style. A leader who doesn't value relationships and instead focuses only on the task is called a *task-oriented leader.* This type of person structures the job for employees and closely watches their behavior. Such a leader simply wants to get the job done.

Situational Variables. Fiedler identified three variables in the work situation that help determine which leadership style will be effective: leader–member relations, task structure, and the leader's position power. Each can be described as either favorable or unfavorable for the leader.

Leader–member relations is the extent to which followers accept the leader. A leader who gets along well with employees and whose expertise is respected is in a favorable situation. A leader who is disliked and isn't trusted is in an unfavorable situation.

Task structure is the degree to which a job is routine. When giving directions, the leader can refer to standard operating procedures. Fiedler considered this situation to be favorable for a leader. In contrast, for a complex and nonroutine job, the leader has no clear guidelines or procedures to point to. In this case the leader has to guide and direct employees. This situation is considered to be unfavorable for a leader.

Leader position power is the extent to which a leader has legitimate, coercive, and reward power. Having strong position power is favorable for a leader because it simplifies the leader's ability to influence subordinates. Low position power makes the leader's task difficult because the leader has to rely on personal sources of influence.

Figure 15.5 illustrates Fiedler's contingency model of leadership. The basic situational variables are shown on the far left. The numbered columns represent possible combinations of the three variables and are arranged from the most favorable situation (1) to the least favorable situation (8) for the leader. The leadership style, task-oriented or relationship-oriented, best suited to each combination of variables is indicated by T or R in the bottom row.

A leader will have the most control and influence in situations represented by column 1. A leader will have progressively less control and influence in situations represented by columns 2–7. A leader's control and influence are quite limited in situations represented by column 8.

Effective Leadership Styles. As suggested in Figure 15.5, task-oriented leaders perform most effectively in the most favorable situations (columns 1, 2, and 3) and in the least favorable situation (column 8). In the most favorable situations the leader is well respected, has freedom to reward and punish subordinates, and subordinates' activities are clear and specific (e.g., payroll, data entry, and maintenance). In the least favorable situation (column 8), tasks are unstructured, group support is lacking, and the leader's position power is low. The unpopular president of a school PTA or a manager who has to downsize the public relations department are examples. In such cases, the only hope for achieving *any* results appears to be task-oriented leadership.

Relationship-oriented leaders generally are most effective in moderately favorable situations. In such cases, tasks are structured, but the leader is disliked or vice versa. Regardless of the situation, the leader must depend on employees' willingness and creativity to accomplish the required tasks.

Limitations. Fiedler's model, like any other, has its limitations.[32] First, the situational variables are complex and difficult to assess. Second, the model pays little attention to the characteristics of subordinates. Whether they are highly skilled professionals or unskilled laborers could make a big difference in determining an appropriate leadership style. Finally, Fiedler asserts that a leader can't easily change his or her leadership style to fit a situation. When a leader's style and the situation

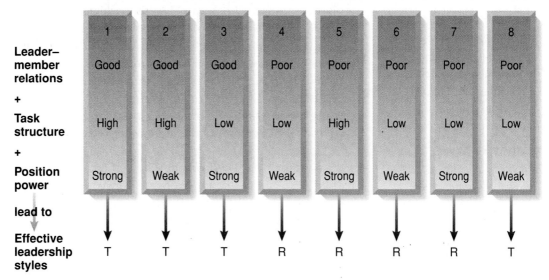

Figure 15.5 **Fiedler's Contingency Model**

	1	2	3	4	5	6	7	8
Leader–member relations	Good	Good	Good	Poor	Poor	Poor	Poor	Poor
+								
Task structure	High	High	Low	Low	High	Low	Low	Low
+								
Position power	Strong	Weak	Strong	Weak	Strong	Weak	Strong	Weak
lead to								
Effective leadership styles	T	T	T	R	R	R	R	T

T = task-oriented style   R = relationship-oriented style don't match, he argues, the situation, *not* the leader, should be changed to fit the leader's style. However, this approach often isn't practical.

Organizational Implications. Even though it remains controversial, Fiedler's contingency model is an interesting approach to understanding leadership and one that many managers find appealing. Its greatest contribution may be its redirection of research in the field, rather than provision of any concrete answers. It has caused researchers to examine a situation more closely before attempting to find the leadership style most appropriate to the situation. Fiedler pointed out that a leader can't be labeled good or poor. Rather, the leader may perform well in one situation but not in others. Hence organizations can gain better leadership by making the situation more favorable or shifting the leader to a situation that better matches the individual's style.[33]

HERSEY AND BLANCHARD'S SITUATIONAL LEADERSHIP MODEL

Hersey and Blanchard's situational leadership model suggests that the levels of directive (similar to initiating-structure and production-centered) and supportive (similar to considerate and employee-centered) leader behaviors be based on the level of readiness of the followers.[34] In contrast to Fiedler, who believes that a leader's style is relatively rigid, Hersey and Blanchard emphasize a leader's flexibility to adapt to changing situations.

Directive behavior occurs when a leader relies on one-way communication, spelling out duties and telling followers what to do and where, when, and how to do it. Directive leaders structure, control, and supervise subordinates.

Supportive behavior occurs when a leader relies on two-way communication, listening, encouraging, and involving followers in decision making. Being supportive doesn't mean just being nice. Raymond Gilmartin, Merck's CEO, is sometimes called Mr. Nice Guy because of his supportive style. It makes Gilmartin bristle. "Nice guy sort of implies that you want to get along, have camaraderie, make everybody happy. That's not the way I operate. The way I operate is to be receptive to other people's ideas and to basically respect what they do," he explains. "It's very important for people to be able to challenge, to be very open."[35]

Readiness is a subordinate's ability to set high but attainable task-related goals and a willingness to accept responsibility for reaching them. Readiness is related to the task and not to the person's age. People have varying degrees of readiness, depending on their backgrounds and the specific task they are trying to accomplish.

This model prescribes different combinations of directive and supportive leader behaviors for different levels of subordinates' readiness. Figure 15.6 portrays the relationship between Hersey and Blanchard's leadership styles and levels of follower readiness. The curve running through the four leadership quadrants (S4–S1) indicates the level of directive and/or supportive behavior that characterizes each style. The readiness level of the individual or team ranges from low to high.

A leader with a *directive style* (lower right-hand quadrant) provides clear instructions and specific direction. When an employee first enters an organization, directive leadership is most appropriate. Newcomers usually are committed, enthusiastic, and energetic. They are anxious to get started and learn. Because commitment is high, a lot of support from the leader isn't needed *or* appropriate.

As employees learn their jobs, a directive style is still important because the employees aren't yet ready to assume total responsibility for doing the job. At this point, however, a leader needs to begin using supportive behavior, or the coaching style, in order to build employees' confidence and maintain their enthusiasm.

HERSEY AND BLANCHARD'S SITUATIONAL LEADERSHIP MODEL
A model that suggests that the levels of directive and supportive leader behaviors should be based on the readiness level of followers.

DIRECTIVE BEHAVIOR
Reliance on one-way communication, spelling out duties, and telling followers what to do and when and how to do it.

SUPPORTIVE BEHAVIOR
Reliance on two-way communication, listening, encouraging, and involving followers in decision making.

READINESS
A subordinate's ability to set high but attainable goals and a willingness to accept responsibility for reaching them.

DIRECTIVE STYLE
Providing clear instructions and specific directions to others.

Figure 15.6 **Hersey and Blanchard's Situational Leadership Model**

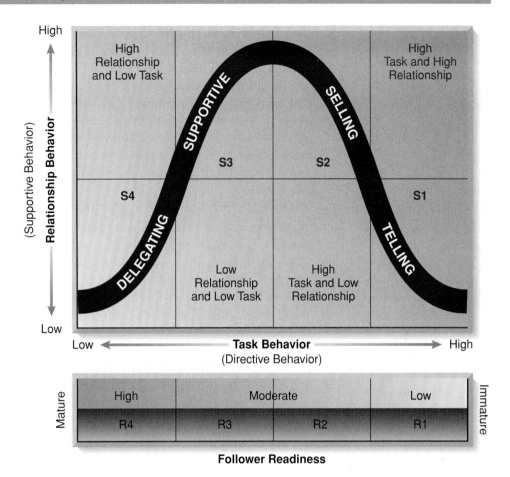

Source: P. Hersey and K. H. Blanchard. *Management of Organizational Behavior: Utilizing Human Resources,* 6th ed. Englewood Cliffs, N.J.: Prentice-Hall, 1993. Used by permission from Ronald Campbell, President, Leadership Studies, Escondido, California, 1995.

COACHING STYLE
Building confidence and motivation through supportive behavior.

SUPPORTING STYLE
Sharing decision making when directive behavior no longer is required.

DELEGATING STYLE
Recognition that others are ready to accomplish a particular task and are both competent and motivated to take full responsibility for it.

The **coaching style** encourages two-way communication and helps build confidence and motivation on the part of the employee, although the leader still has responsibility for and controls decision making. When followers feel confident performing their tasks, the leader no longer needs to be directive. However, the leader does need to maintain open communication by actively listening and supporting subordinates' efforts to use what they have learned. In the **supporting style,** the leader and followers share decision making.

The **delegating style** is appropriate for a leader whose followers are ready to accomplish a particular task and are both competent and motivated to take full responsibility for it. Even though the leader may still identify problems, the responsibility for carrying out plans is given to experienced followers. They are permitted to manage projects and decide how, when, and where tasks are to be done.

Limitations. Hersey and Blanchard's model also has some limitations. First, can leaders actually choose a leadership style when faced with a new situation? The answer to this question has important implications for management selection, placement, and promotion. Some people can read situations better and adapt their leadership style more effectively than others. For those who can't, what are the costs of training them to be able to do so? Do these costs exceed the potential benefits? Second, in the same group, different employees are likely to be at different levels of readiness. Under this condition, what is the best style? Finally, the model doesn't distinguish among the reasons for low readiness. Does lack of readiness reflect a lack of motivation, a lack of competencies, or some combination of both?[36] Additional research is needed to begin to answer these questions.

Organizational Implications. Hersey and Blanchard's situational leadership model has generated a lot of interest.[37] The idea that leaders should be flexible with respect to the leadership style they use is appealing. However, the leader must constantly monitor the maturity level of followers in order to determine the combination of directive and supportive behaviors that is most appropriate. An inexperienced employee may perform as well as an experienced employee if properly directed and closely supervised. If the leader's style is appropriate, it should also help followers gain more experience and become more competent. Thus as a leader helps followers evolve, his or her leadership style also needs to evolve.

HOUSE'S PATH–GOAL MODEL

HOUSE'S PATH–GOAL MODEL
A model that indicates that effective leaders specify the task and clear roadblocks to task achievement, thereby increasing subordinates' satisfaction and job performance.

Another contingency model was developed by Robert House. ***House's path–goal model*** indicates that effective leaders clearly specify the task, reduce roadblocks to task achievement, and increase opportunities for task-related satisfaction, thereby clarifying the paths, or means, by which employees can attain job satisfaction and improve performance. The leader's function is to motivate subordinates and help them reach their highly valued, job-related objectives. The specific style of leader behavior exhibited should be determined by two contingency variables: employee characteristics and task characteristics. A version of the path–goal model is shown in Figure 15.7.

Like the other two contingency models, the path–goal model doesn't provide a formula for the best way to lead. Instead it stresses that, to be effective, a leader should select the style most appropriate to a particular situation and the followers' needs. The model identifies four styles of leadership.

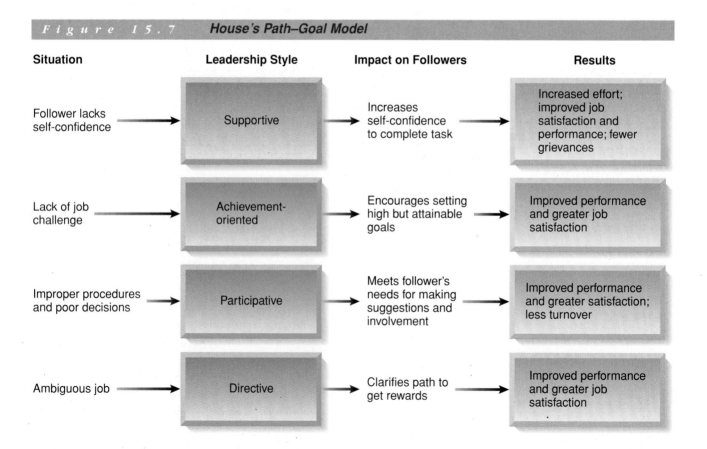

Figure 15.7   House's Path–Goal Model

Situation	Leadership Style	Impact on Followers	Results
Follower lacks self-confidence	Supportive	Increases self-confidence to complete task	Increased effort; improved job satisfaction and performance; fewer grievances
Lack of job challenge	Achievement-oriented	Encourages setting high but attainable goals	Improved performance and greater job satisfaction
Improper procedures and poor decisions	Participative	Meets follower's needs for making suggestions and involvement	Improved performance and greater satisfaction; less turnover
Ambiguous job	Directive	Clarifies path to get rewards	Improved performance and greater job satisfaction

Figure 15.8 **Vroom-Jago Decision Tree**

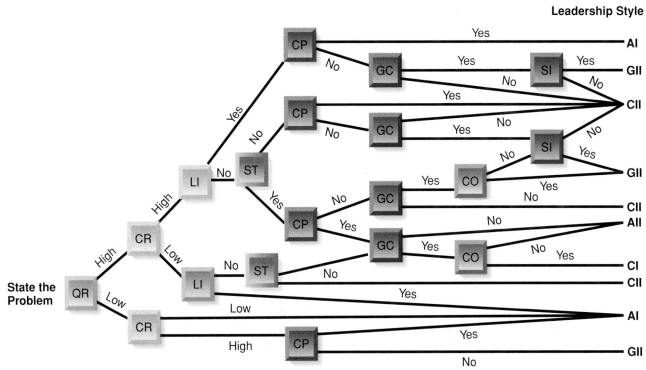

Leadership Style

Problem Attributes

QR	Quality requirement:	How important is the technical quality of this decision?
CR	Commitment requirement:	How important is subordinate commitment to the decision?
LI	Leader's information:	Do you have sufficient information to make a high-quality decision?
ST	Problem structure:	Is the problem well structured?
CP	Commitment probability:	If you were to make the decision by yourself, is it reasonably certain that your subordinate(s) would be committed to the decision?
GC	Goal congruence:	Do subordinates share the organizational goals to be attained in solving this problem?
CO	Subordinate conflict:	Is conflict among subordinates over preferred solutions likely?
SI	Subordinate information:	Do subordinates have sufficient information to make a high-quality decision?

Source: Reprinted from Victor H. Vroom and Arthur G. Jago. *The New Leadership: Managing Participation in Organizations.* Englewood Cliffs, N.J.: Prentice-Hall, 1988. Used with permission of the authors.

leader goes to the next question, and so on until the eighth question is asked and answered and an appropriate leadership style is determined. The leadership style should then lead to a high-quality decision that will be accepted by subordinates.

Organizational Implications. The leader–participation model provides an excellent guide for determining the type and degree of subordinate participation in decision making. It confirms the findings of other research. Leaders use participation when the quality of the decision is important, when subordinates should accept the decision and they're unlikely to do so unless they're allowed to have some say in it, and when subordinates can be trusted to strive for organizational rather than individual goals.[41]

This model also stresses that the situation—not the leader—should receive attention. Along with Hersey and Blanchard's and House's models, the leader–participation model states that a leader can adopt different styles of leadership to meet the demands of different situations. But, before choosing a leadership style, the leader must assess the situation. However, not all leaders can do what's suggested by the model. Although they may know how they *should* behave, they may lack the ability to tailor their behavior to meet the specific situation. Research suggests, for example, that women may be more comfortable and better able to use higher levels of participation, whereas men are more comfortable and better able to use more autocratic methods for making decisions.[42]

COMPARING CONTINGENCY MODELS

To recap, leaders need to be able to direct and motivate others to achieve both high productivity and greater job satisfaction. The four contingency models just discussed offer somewhat different advice about choosing an effective leadership style. Table 15.2 compares the elements of these models.

Table 15.2 **A Comparison of Four Contingency Models**

	Fiedler's Contingency Model	Hersey and Blanchard's Situational Model	House's Path-Goal Model	Leader–Participation Model
Key situational variables	Task structure Leader–member relations Leader position power	Level of followers' maturity	Task characteristics Employee characteristics	Eight diagnostic questions concerning time, quality, and acceptance
Leadership styles	Task-oriented Relationship-oriented	Telling Selling Participating Delegating	Achievement Directive Participative Supportive	Autocratic I and II Consultative I and II Group II
Implications	Leader's style is matched to situation or situation is changed to fit leader's style. High or low control situations favor task-oriented leader. Moderate control situations favor relationship-oriented leader.	Effective leaders choose a style to match the maturity level of their followers.	If tasks are routine and simple, supportive or participative leadership is best for team members who want to satisfy their social needs. If tasks are nonroutine and complex, directive or achievement-oriented leadership is best for team members who want to self-actualize on the job.	Effective leaders analyze the situation by answering the eight contingency questions and then choosing among the five styles, depending on their answers.

The contingency models demonstrate the importance to a leader of situational factors and follower characteristics. Successful leaders are adept at recognizing the requirements of the situation and the needs of their followers and then adjusting their own leadership style (or the situation) accordingly. Contingency models imply that leaders should be able to adapt their behavior to the different conditions they may face. Can leaders realistically be expected to be so flexible? One study of more than 500 managers in a public utility indicates that managers can and do use different leadership styles in different situations. Managers who displayed a broad range of leadership behaviors were more effective in their jobs.[43]

TRANSFORMATIONAL AND CHARISMATIC LEADERSHIP

5

STATE THE UNIQUE BEHAVIORS OF TRANSFORMATIONAL LEADERS AND THEIR IMPACT ON FOLLOWERS

TRANSFORMATIONAL LEADERSHIP
Leading by motivating. Key behaviors are vision, framing, and impression management.

Clearly, the leadership models presented so far don't agree on ways in which leaders can best influence followers. Early models focused on personality traits, and most of the later ones look at leader behaviors as determined by contingency, or situational, factors. In the past few years, many top managers around the world have realized that they'll have to make significant changes in the way things are done if their organizations are to survive. Many now believe that the type of leadership needed by top managers for tomorrow's organizations is what has been labeled *transformational*.[44]

Quite simply, **transformational leadership** is leading by motivating. Transformational leaders provide extraordinary motivation by appealing to followers' ideals and moral values and inspiring them to think about problems in new ways.[45] Joan of Arc, Abraham Lincoln, Franklin D. Roosevelt, John F. Kennedy, and Martin Luther King, among others, have transformed entire societies through their words and by their actions. Followers of these leaders felt trust, admiration, loyalty, and respect for them and were motivated to do more than they thought they could, or *would,* do. A leader can motivate followers by making them more aware of the importance and value of their tasks and the need to place them ahead of their own self-interests. Transformational leaders' influence rests on their ability to inspire others through their words, visions, and actions. In essence, transformational leaders make tomorrow's dreams a reality for their followers.

What methods do transformational leaders use to affect their followers profoundly and generate this type of response? Transformational leaders exhibit three behaviors: vision, framing, and impression management.[46] Figure 15.9 shows these behaviors and followers' reactions to them.

VISION

Perhaps the most important characteristic that transformational leaders possess is their ability to create a *vision* that binds people to each other. Dr. Martin Luther King's famous "I Have A Dream" speech galvanized a generation to support the civil rights movement in the United States. But transformational leaders must have more than just a vision: They also have to have a road map for attaining it. What is important is that followers "buy into" that vision and that the leader has a plan to energize them to reach it.[47]

CHARISMATIC LEADERS
Individuals that have an unshakable belief in their mission, are supremely confident that they and their followers can succeed, and have the ability to convey these certainties to their followers.

Leaders who are totally committed to their vision and course of action often are called charismatic. **Charismatic leaders** have an unshakable belief in their mission, are supremely confident that they and their followers can succeed, and have the ability to convey these certainties to their followers. Followers of charismatic leaders demonstrate unquestioning loyalty and obedience.[48]

Figure 15.9 **Transformational Leadership Model**

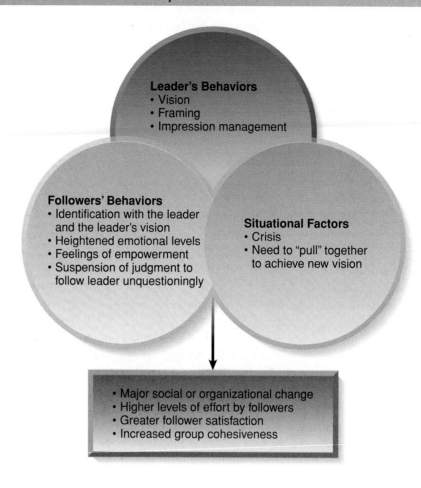

* Major social or organizational change
* Higher levels of effort by followers
* Greater follower satisfaction
* Increased group cohesiveness

FRAMING

When changes in the environment occur slowly, many top managers fail to recognize them as threats to their organizations. To make members of an organization aware of environmental changes, transformational leaders often *frame* their vision by giving employees a new purpose for working. **Framing** is a process whereby leaders define the group's purpose in highly meaningful terms. In organizations, framing often involves identifying the core values and purpose that should guide employees. At Mary Kay Cosmetics, the core purpose is "to give unlimited opportunity to women." At Walt Disney, the core purpose is simply "to make people happy." At Medtronic, a company that specializes in medical equipment, it is "restoring patients to full life."[49]

IMPRESSION MANAGEMENT

Impression management involves an attempt to control the impressions that others form about the leader through behaviors that make the leader more attractive and appealing to others. Impression management sounds manipulative and calculating—and sometimes it is. But, more often, impression management is a natural and sincere expression that reveals to followers an alignment between the vision and the person. When observers of effective leaders refer to the importance of integrity, that often is what they mean—revealing to followers how the message they are hearing relates to the personal experiences of the messenger. Telling sto-

FRAMING

A process whereby leaders define the purpose of their movement in highly meaningful terms for their followers.

IMPRESSION MANAGEMENT

A leader's attempt to control the impressions that others form about the leader through practicing behaviors that make the leader more attractive and appealing to others.

ries and anecdotes is a particularly effective way to manage impressions, and according to some it is the essence of charisma.[50]

Strong communication competency enables leaders to engage in effective storytelling and impression management in general. Anthony Mark Hankins is an especially good communicator, who many expect to be recognized soon as one of the next leaders in the fashion industry. In informal settings, he loves to tell stories. When the situation calls for something more formal, he's great at that too, as described in the Communication Competency piece.

SIGNIFICANCE FOR PRACTICE

Transformational leaders are most effective when an organization is new or when its survival is threatened. The poorly structured problems that these organizations face call for leaders with vision, confidence, and determination.[51] Such leaders must influence others to assert themselves, to join enthusiastically in team efforts, and arouse their feelings about what they are attempting to do.

However, transformational and charismatic leadership have several drawbacks. First, overzealous followers can become blind to conditions surrounding the leader and the movement—a bit like the children who followed the Pied Piper of Hamelin. Such leaders emotionally manipulate followers and so can create visions for their own self-aggrandizement. Sometimes these visions can wreak havoc with the rest of the world (e.g., Attila the Hun, Adolph Hitler, or Joseph Stalin). Second, because followers and movements become dependent on the transformational or charismatic leaders, the danger is that such leaders will surround themselves with "yes people" and fail to receive information that challenges the decisions that they make to achieve their visions. Finally, many charismatic leaders are known for their autocratic styles of leadership.[52]

LEADERSHIP DEVELOPMENT

6

DESCRIBE HOW ORGANIZATIONS DEVELOP EFFECTIVE LEADERS

A 1998 study conducted by the Conference Board asked executives to rate the leadership capacity of their organizations. The results were disturbing, showing that less than 10 percent rated their companies as excellent and half rated their companies as fair or poor. This pessimism, combined with recognition of the importance of effective leadership, seems to explain why organizations invest millions of dollars and untold hours on efforts to improve leadership effectiveness.[53] These investments fall into three general categories: assigning people to positions to promote learning on the job, offering assistance through coaching and mentoring, and sending employees to formal leadership assessment and training programs.

LEARNING ON THE JOB

As we noted in Chapter 1, on-the-job learning is important for all aspects of managerial work. To develop leadership on the job requires that employees take jobs or project assignments that include leadership responsibilities. Early in a person's career, working as an individual contributor on team projects provides many opportunities for learning effective leadership. Being a formal leader of a project allows an employee to use different types of power and observe how people react to the employee's attempts to influence them. Team leaders also can ask team members for candid feedback and suggestions for improvement. Team members who aren't designated as the formal leader also can learn, by observing the relationship between the leader and team and by practicing the use of referent and expert power.

Anthony Mark Hankins Gets Rich on Cheap Chic

Anthony Mark Hankins's energy is the first thing that people notice when they meet him. As one person put it, "Watching him is like channel surfing." But watch long enough and you realize he's all business underneath. He decided in kindergarten that he wanted to be a fashion designer and began experimenting soon after. Cheap chic is his fashion niche. Inspired by his mother, he designs clothes for a market that has traditionally been underserved—Hispanic and African-American women. Drawing on his training at Yves Saint Laurent's couture house in Paris, he uses vivacious colors and prints to design fashions that look good on the average woman and that sell at prices that the typical hard-working woman can afford.

At age 28, and only four years after leaving his job as JCPenney's first in-house designer to start his own business, Hankins is making his dreams come true. To hear his story, those dreams began when he was a child spending summers on his grandmother's farm. She would take him to the local textile mill and buy damaged sheets, from which he created his first designs. Today, more than 1,200 stores—including military PXs around the world—carry his designs, racking up annual sales exceeding $40 million.

For many organizational leaders, employees are the most important target of their communication. Not so for Hankins. To be a leader in the fashion business, he needs to convince retailers to promote his line. He uses his show on the Home Shopping Network to convince potential customers that his fashions should be in their closets. Customers and business partners alike seem mesmerized by his style. According to the firm's vice president of merchandizing, every time Hankins is on Home Shopping Network, sales are double the amount the network had estimated. His enthusiasm and storytelling seem to be what attract people the most. "He's just a terrific talent, with this unbelievable personality that makes everyone just love him," exuded one executive. He also knows how to negotiate. The deals that he's closed so far include retailing giants Nordstrom, Sears, Marshall Field, and Target. "He's a very good business partner," said a Sears vice president who praised him for showing "so much passion for the business."[54]

When jobs with supervisory responsibilities become available, opportunities for learning on the job expand considerably. Supervisory jobs almost always involve leadership—that is, they involve influencing others to make progress toward a goal. Although the goal may be set by someone else, supervisors are charged with inspiring others to become committed to the goal and to strive to achieve it.

FORMAL ASSESSMENT AND TRAINING

Learning on the job is an excellent method for developing leadership capacity, but most large organizations don't rely solely on this approach to leadership development. In addition, they ensure that their most talented employees receive formal leadership assessments and attend leadership training programs. Formal assessment and training may be conducted at the organization's own educational facilities, at a college or university, or by organizations such as the Center for Creative Leadership—a nonprofit organization dedicated to leadership research and education. Regardless of location, formal assessment and training programs generally include evaluating the individual's current approach to leadership and providing educational experiences designed to improve the individual's effectiveness as a leader.

AT&T's Leadership Development Program is typical of formal training approaches. High-potential employees at mid-level or above attend a two-week program, which focuses on promoting a collaborative approach to leadership and developing leaders who are both empowered and empowering. AT&T leaders receive plenty of feedback from the people who know their leadership styles best, using 360-degree assessment and feedback techniques. As described in Chapter 12, 360-degree feedback involves asking an employee's peers, supervisors, and subordinates to provide evaluations and then using these assessments to provide feedback to employees about how others perceive them. For employees in roles that involve leadership, providing such feedback is a popular approach to improving leadership effectiveness. Not surprisingly, most leaders see themselves in a more positive light than their followers do. The best leaders have a realistic view of themselves and use feedback about their behavior constructively to make improvements.[55]

At FedEx, selecting and developing a person to enter a leadership role takes fourteen months. Each year, some 3,000 FedEx employees interested in leadership positions enter the company's Leadership Evaluation and Awareness Process (LEAP). Only 20 percent make it to the final stage. Why? According to a senior official at the company, three reasons account for people dropping out. First is realizing that leaders put in very long hours. Second is realizing that leadership carries an unrelenting sense of obligation—they are always representatives of FedEx, even when they aren't at work. And third is realizing that leadership involves intensive interactions with people. The self-evaluation included in LEAP opens the eyes of many potential leaders. According to the managing director of the FedEx Leadership Institute, "Too many people get into leadership for all the wrong reasons. They want power. They think it's the only way to advance. LEAP is a gate that everyone has to pass through. And those who pass through it are attuned to what it means to lead and to work effectively with other people."[56]

COACHING AND MENTORING

Whether held on a college campus or a corporate campus, most formal leadership development programs take place in traditional classroom settings. Leaders who prefer a more personal approach can hire a personal leadership coach or work with a mentor. When Debi Coleman left her position as CFO of Apple Computers to take a job as CEO of an Oregon-based start-up company named Merix, she knew that she had several weaknesses as a leader. So intent was she on improving that she even made up flash cards to remind herself about how to behave in situations that caused her the most problems. To assist her, she hired Kay Stepp of Executive Solutions to coach her. As her coach, Stepp helps Coleman become aware of areas that need improvement. "She is very good at bringing you to the point of asking yourself questions that you should probably have been asking yourself before," explains Coleman. Stepp even attends meetings of Coleman's executive team, to give her real-time feedback: "Kay will give me a look that says, 'Debi, you're cutting off conversation.'"[57]

Personal coaches can provide an intensive leadership development experience, but they can be quite expensive. Few people can afford this method of leadership development. For many managers, having a mentor is more feasible. Mentors are most often supervisors or senior colleagues in the organization who provide advice and guidance about a variety of career-related concerns. For managers, talking with mentors about how to develop into a more effective leader is important to career advancement. In particular, mentors can help the manager understand how others respond to his or her behaviors and point out weaknesses or blind spots. Mentors

SELF-MANAGEMENT COMPETENCY
Your Leadership Style Preference[58]

This questionnaire measures your preferences for certain styles of leadership behavior. It is intended to help you better understand, and perhaps control, your leadership actions. To be useful, you must answer the questions honestly. There are no "right" or "wrong" answers. Trying to figure out the best answer only makes the results useless for improving your self-awareness and understanding. These questions may ask you to make difficult choices. Please make the choices based only on your personal preferences.

The questions ask you to describe how you treat employees. If you have never supervised other employees, try to imagine what you probably would do if you were supervising someone. For example, think of a work situation that you have experienced and imagine that you are the supervisor. Pick the statement that best describes how you think you would behave.

Instructions

Read each pair of statements. For each pair, pick the statement that best describes your own management behaviors and preferences. In some cases you will probably feel that both statements describe you pretty well, but you still must pick only the one that describes you best. In other cases you might feel that neither statement describes you at all. Even so, you must pick one—the one that is the least inaccurate. You will not be able to score this questionnaire when you finish unless you have picked only one statement from each pair.

Place an X in the space to indicate which statement describes you best.

1. a. ———— I take the time to explain to employees exactly what I expect of them.
   b. ———— Employees should be responsible for determining what is expected of them on the job.

2. c. ———— I am pleasant toward employees but I avoid getting too friendly.
   d. ———— I respond to employees in a warm and friendly manner.

3. e. ———— I help employees set specific high goals for themselves.
   f. ———— I allow employees to find their own ways to do their jobs better.

4. g. ———— I try to get employees to work together as a team.
   h. ———— I try to keep a proper distance from individual employees.

5. a. ———— I make clear to employees exactly how I want the job done.
   b. ———— As long as the job gets done I don't care how employees go about doing it.

(Continued)

also serve as role models that a manager can emulate and provide valuable advice concerning the styles of leadership favored in the organization. Finally, mentors often assist a manager in developing leadership capabilities by helping the manager find assignments that will foster on-the-job learning.[59]

By now, perhaps you're eager to begin developing your own leadership effectiveness and wondering what you can do immediately. Reflecting on your own strengths and weaknesses and accepting responsibility for making improvements are two actions that you can take to promote your own leadership development. To begin that process, respond to the questions in the Self-Management Competency feature on pages 526–529.

6. c. _____ Employees know when they have done a good job and don't need me to tell them.

    d. _____ I tell employees how much I appreciate their efforts.

7. e. _____ I provide employees with the information needed to plan the work effectively.

    f. _____ I take employees' limits into account and don't expect too much of them.

8. g. _____ I provide opportunities for employees to get together to share ideas and information.

    h. _____ I make productive use of the time when others are speaking, to prepare my own arguments.

9. a. _____ I encourage employees to try out new work-related ideas.

    b. _____ I expect employees to adhere to and maintain standard work procedures.

10. c. _____ I respect effective employees but I don't pretend to be at their level.

    d. _____ I treat employees with respect and as equals.

11. e. _____ I make sure that employees have the resources they need to do a good job.

    f. _____ I expect employees to solve their own work problems.

12. g. _____ I am understanding when employees come to me with their problems.

    h. _____ I emphasize to employees their own responsibility for their work.

13. a. _____ I express clearly to employees my views about the ways things should be done.

    b. _____ I expect employees to figure out for themselves how things should be done.

14. c. _____ There's little point in encouraging employees' ideas since almost all that they come up with were tried out long ago.

    d. _____ I ask employees for their ideas and let them know that their suggestions are desired and appreciated.

15. e. _____ I expect a great deal from employees in terms of performance.

    f. _____ I avoid giving employees specific numerical goals or targets.

16. g. _____ I show employees that I am personally concerned about them.

    h. _____ I prefer to deal with employees privately and one-to-one rather than involving a group.

17. a. _____ If employees want to know how to do a specific task or activity, they know there are established procedures they can follow.

    b. _____ I decide myself what will be done as well as how to do it.

18. c. _____ With so much always changing, there's no point in worrying employees with the details too far in advance.

    d. _____ I let employees know of changes well in advance so that they can prepare.

19. e. _____ I help employees get the training they need to perform the job effectively.

    f. _____ I let employees know that I expect them to do their best.

20. g. _____ I show employees that I really listen to them.

    h. _____ I rarely spend time in group meetings with employees.

21. a. _____ I make clear assignments of particular employees to specific tasks.

    b. _____ I find it best to let employees sort out informally who is best for which task assignment.

(Continued)

22. c. _____ I screen out all the unimportant interactions with employees and attend only to those that are really important, to minimize disruptions to my own work.

    d. _____ I make sure that employees find me accessible to them and interested in their concerns.

23. e. _____ I make sure that employees clearly understand my role and responsibilities.

    f. _____ When employees know and carry out their job responsibilities, there is little need for me to get involved.

24. g. _____ I show a great deal of concern for employees' personal welfare.

    h. _____ I respect employees' privacy and right to have personal concerns left alone.

25. a. _____ I prepare specific work schedules for employees to help define responsibilities and to coordinate work activities.

    b. _____ As long as the work gets done employees can keep to their own schedules.

26. c. _____ I permit employees to try out new ideas that seem unlikely to have an adverse effect on productivity.

    d. _____ I listen to employees' ideas for doing things better and make changes based on their suggestions.

27. e. _____ I make sure that all employees understand the specific standards of performance that apply to their work.

    f. _____ I ask employees to do their best without setting overly specific standards.

28. g. _____ I make sure that when I take actions or make decisions affecting them, employees understand the reasons.

    h. _____ Employees accept the fact that I'm the boss, so there is no need for constant explanations of my actions.

29. a. _____ I let employees know just what are the standards and regulations I expect them to follow.

    b. _____ Employees can develop their own informal standards and work rules, as long as the job gets done.

30. c. _____ I try to get all of the relevant information before making an important decision.

    d. _____ I consult with employees before making important decisions about the work.

Directions for Scoring

1. Count the number of times you picked "a." Put the number here: _____

2. Count the number of times you picked "e." Put the number here: _____

3. To get your Task Behavior Score, add the two numbers above and put the total here: _____

Task Behavior Score

4. Count the number of times you picked "d." Put the number here: _____

5. Count the number of times you picked "g." Put the number here: _____

6. To get your Relationship Behavior Score, add the two numbers above and put the total here: _____

Relationship Behavior Score

7. Plot your scores on the chart on page 529. Find your Task Behavior Score on the vertical axis first, and draw a horizontal line across the chart at this level. Then find your Relationship Behavior Score on the horizontal axis and from this point draw a vertical line up the chart.

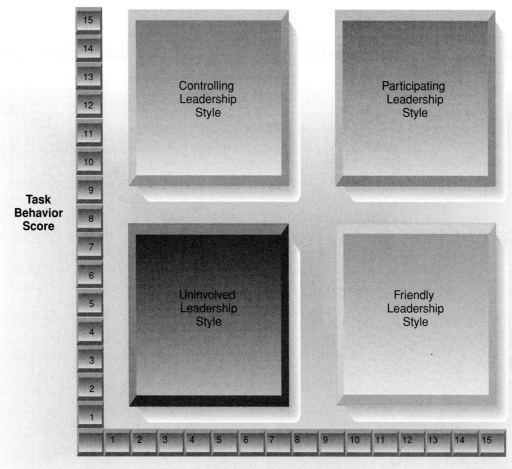

Task Behavior Score (vertical axis, 1–15)

Controlling Leadership Style

Participating Leadership Style

Uninvolved Leadership Style

Friendly Leadership Style

Relationship Behavior Score (horizontal axis, 1–15)

Interpreting Your Score

Most research on leadership suggests that the best style of leadership depends a lot on the situation. The scores on this questionnaire cannot tell you how well you are able to adapt your leadership style to different situations. What it can tell you is something about the leadership style that is most natural to you. By plotting your scores on the chart, you can see clearly just what your overall tendency is.

Uninvolved: Low on both Task and Relationship Behaviors
Participating: High on both Task and Relationship Behaviors
Friendly: Low on Task and High on Relationship Behaviors
Controlling: High on Task and Low on Relationship Behaviors

By understanding your own typical pattern of behavior, you will probably find it easier to learn how to improve on it or change it to meet varying situations.

DEVELOPING LEADERS FOR GLOBAL ORGANIZATIONS

Increasingly, managers at all levels and in many types of organizations have jobs that involve exercising leadership in various cultures. At American Express, Ken Chenault is responsible for global advertising and brand management. Anointed as the most likely successor to CEO Harvey Golub, Chenault's leadership skills have been praised as outstanding. They need to be, because nearly all the heads of the company's business units report directly to him. At PRT Group, a custom software engineering company, project leaders work with programmers from countries as diverse as Malaysia, Canada, Germany, and India. An American, Doug Mellinger, founded the company and chose Barbados for his headquarters location, in part because he wanted to be in a location that would let him attract the best programming talent from all over the world.[60]

In global companies such as American Express and PRT, what type of leadership is effective? Do people from different countries prefer different types of leadership? Do leaders need to behave differently with each employee, depending on the employee's cultural background? Historically, for example, Japanese leaders have been portrayed by others as using a more participative style than managers in Western countries. Is this stereotype about differences accurate, or are changes occurring throughout the world that are creating convergence in leaders' styles?[61]

Research addressing these questions is still scarce, but answers are beginning to emerge. To the surprise of many people, the nature of leadership appears to be similar around the world.[62] As General Norman Schwartzkoff observed, anytime a group of people come together, a leader emerges. Furthermore, in work organizations, a hierarchy almost always exists—flat or vertical—with a single leader at the top. And within organizations, the functions that leaders perform (planning, organizing, leading, and controlling) seem to be similar for managers around the world.[63]

The transformational and charismatic leadership models have been studied the most in different cultures. Based on studies of managers and military leaders in the United States, Africa, the Netherlands, India, Spain, Singapore, China, and Austria, among others, people worldwide apparently have images of leaders that match the transformational approach to leadership. And around the world, transformational leadership seems to be effective in creating satisfaction and inspiring effort.[64]

The most comprehensive worldwide study of leadership is the Global Leadership and Organizational Behavior Effectiveness Research Program, which is referred to as the GLOBE project. The brainchild of Robert House, this massive study is a collaborative effort involving 170 social scientists and management scholars who have been collecting data on leadership around the world. Results from this project are just beginning to be made public. Some of the earliest conclusions from this project are described in the following Global Awareness Competency account.

The volume of data generated by the GLOBE project is enormous. Several years will be required to analyze and interpret all the data. Nevertheless, preliminary results from the project suggest that managers who develop a few essential behavioral styles—charismatic/value based, team-oriented, and humane—can be reasonably effective in many different countries and cultures.

Nevertheless, many culturally specific behaviors also must be learned by leaders working in various cultures. Can a manager give performance-related feedback the same way in every country? Probably not. In the United States, supervisors usually provide negative feedback directly in a face-to-face conversation. But in Japan, supervisors usually channel negative feedback through a peer of the subordinate's. Although effective leaders in many different countries seem to portray similar images to their followers, they create these images while adhering to the cultural norms of a specific region.

Some Leadership Styles Are Universal[65]

The GLOBE project seeks to address several interesting questions about the nature of leadership in organizations around the world. One key question under investigation is whether some leader behaviors are considered effective by managers worldwide. To answer this question, the project collected data from approximately 16,000 middle managers working in more than 800 organizations in sixty-four countries. They were asked to describe behaviors that facilitated or impeded effective leadership. Leadership behaviors were grouped into six general patterns. Specific behaviors and attributes associated with each category also were identified. Middle managers' responses were analyzed to determine which leadership behavior patterns were universally considered positive or universally considered negative. The table below shows the results of the study.

General Leadership Behavior Patterns	Specific Leader Behaviors and Attributes	Universally Positive or Negative?
Charismatic/value-based	Visionary Inspirational Self-sacrificing Shows integrity Decisive Performance-oriented	Positive
Team-oriented	Collaborative team orientation Team integrator Diplomatic Not malevolent Administratively competent	Positive
Humane	Modest Generous Compassionate	Positive in most countries
Participative	Not dictatorial Not bossy Not elitist	Mixed; somewhat positive in some countries and somewhatnegative in other countries
Autonomous	Individualistic Independent Unique	Mixed; somewhat positive in some countries and somewhat negative in other countries
Narcissistic	Self-centered Status conscious Conflict inducer Face saver Procedural	Negative

CHAPTER SUMMARY

Leadership is an integral component of organizations. People at all levels of an organization can exercise leadership, which can take many forms. Because it is so important, researchers have conducted numerous studies in attempts to understand the secrets of effective leadership. Based on their studies, they have developed various theoretical models. Each of these models explains some—but not all—aspects of leader effectiveness. Organizations interested in developing effective leaders often use these models as the basis for their leadership development activities.

1. **DESCRIBE THE BASICS OF LEADERSHIP.**
Leadership involves influencing others to act toward the attainment of a goal. Leaders rely on five types of power to exert influence: legitimate, reward, coercive, referent, and expert. The most effective use of power results in followers who are committed to the leader's goals. The improper use of power can also result in mere compliance and even resistance.

2. **STATE THE CONTRIBUTIONS OF THE TRAITS MODELS OF LEADERSHIP.**
Traits models of leadership were early attempts to identify the personal characteristics that make a leader successful. The characteristics studied included physical, social background, and personality. Research has failed to show that traits consistently separate potential leaders from nonleaders. Thus other models of leadership have replaced the traits models.

3. **DESCRIBE THE PRIMARY BEHAVIORAL MODELS OF LEADERSHIP.**
Behavioral models of leadership provide a way of identifying effective leaders by their actions. There are five primary behavioral models. The Theory X and Theory Y model states that leaders' behaviors reflect their basic assumptions about people. Theory X and Theory Y represent two quite different ways that leaders view their subordinates and thus manage them. The Ohio State University and University of Michigan models also identify two leadership behavior styles. These styles were called considerate and initiating structure by the Ohio State researchers and production-centered and employee-centered by the Michigan researchers. The managerial grid model identifies various combinations of concern for people and production. The empowerment model states that leaders share influence and control with followers and thereby satisfy basic human needs for achievement, belonging, and self-esteem. Finally, the leader–member exchange model states that leaders form unique relationships with each follower.

4. **EXPLAIN THE PRINCIPAL CONTINGENCY MODELS OF LEADERSHIP AND THE SITUATIONAL FACTORS THAT DETERMINE A LEADER'S EFFECTIVENESS.**
There are four principal contingency leadership models. Fiedler's contingency model suggests that successful leadership depends on matching the demands of the situation to leadership style. Hersey and Blanchard's situational leadership model indicates that leaders must adapt their leadership style to the readiness level of their followers. House's path–goal model holds that effective leaders clarify the paths, or means, by which subordinates can attain job satisfaction and perform well. The leader–participation model suggests that leaders can choose one of five leadership-decision styles, depending on the situation.

5. **STATE THE UNIQUE BEHAVIORS OF TRANSFORMATIONAL LEADERSHIP AND THEIR IMPACT ON FOLLOWERS.**
Transformational leadership involves inspiring, and thereby motivating, individuals to reach the leader's highest goals. Leaders influence others by creating a vision that appeals to subordinates' emotions, framing the problem in ways that others can easily understand, and using impression management tactics to increase their attractiveness to followers. These behaviors create feelings of identification with the leader, heightened emotions, empowerment, and willingness to follow the leader unquestioningly.

6. **DESCRIBE HOW ORGANIZATIONS DEVELOP EFFECTIVE LEADERS.**
Organizations use three approaches to develop effective leaders: placing employees in positions that promote learning on the job, providing employees with formal leadership assessments and training, and offering mentoring and coaching. In global organizations, these activities must take into account the leadership behaviors and attributes that are viewed positively throughout the world. They also must recognize that some behaviors may be desirable in one region of the world but ineffective in others. In addition to

what organizations do to develop leaders, individuals can develop their own leadership capabilities by assessing their current approaches to leadership, developing action plans for improvement, and carrying out those plans.

QUESTIONS FOR DISCUSSION

1. How do the different types of power a leader can exercise influence followers' behaviors?

2. Would you prefer to work with a Theory X or Theory Y leader? Explain why.

3. Describe the basic elements in the Ohio State University and University of Michigan leadership models. How can these concepts help you become a more effective leader?

4. Describe Fiedler's three situational variables and his contingency approach to leadership.

5. Explain how Hersey and Blanchard's situational leadership model relates to the readiness of followers.

6. What behaviors would you look for in a transformational leader? How would you know whether a transformational leader is present in your class? What behaviors and skills might such a person show to others?

7. If you were considering taking a job in an organization based in Italy, what questions might you ask to determine whether the organization was likely to help you develop into a more effective leader?

8. What can you do to learn how to be a more effective leader?

EXERCISES TO DEVELOP YOUR MANAGERIAL COMPETENCIES

1. **Self-Management Competency.** Leadership development is a growing field, and programs are offered by numerous organizations. Investigate several leadership training programs being offered. For each one that you investigate, state whether the program utilizes a leadership model based on traits, behaviors, contingencies, transformation, or a combination of them. To begin, visit the Education, Training and Development Resource Center for Business and Industry's home page at

   www.tasl.com

   the Center for Creative Leadership's home page at

   www.ccl.org

   and the American Society for Training and Development's home page at

   www.astd.org.

2. **Global Awareness Competency.** When entrepreneur Doug Mellinger had difficulty finding computer programmers to work for his company, he solved the problem by moving to a location to which people from all over the world might be willing to move—Barbados. His plan worked. He has been able to hire programmers from Germany, India, Ireland, China, and many other countries. Now his company is thriving. What type of leadership approach is appropriate for a company with a workforce that is so culturally diverse? To learn about how Doug Mellinger approaches his leadership responsibilities, visit the company's home page at

   www.prt.com

   You can also read about Mellinger by obtaining the January 1998 issue of *Inc.* magazine; see the article by Michael Hopkins, "The antihero's guide to the new economy."

3. **Teamwork Competency.** As organizations reorganize work around teams, more and more companies are looking for employees with demonstrated leadership capabilities. Choose an industry of interest to you and explore the job announcements. Are companies looking for employees who can demonstrate their effectiveness as leaders? Does leadership seem to be more important for some companies than others? Several Web sites provide extensive listings of job openings,

including job listings from classified newspaper ads, which can be found at

www.careerpath.com

jobs posted by more than 600 companies at

www.jobfind.com

and the job seekers Web site of the National Association of Colleges and Employers at

www.jobweb.org

4. **Planning and Administration Competency.** Although the workforce of many companies includes a diverse mix of people, this diversity is not yet well represented in high-level leadership positions of Fortune 500 companies. To assist companies interested in developing a pool of demographically diverse leaders, the U.S. government's Glass Ceiling Commission developed twelve recommendations for business and government organizations. What are its twelve recommendations? What are the implications of these recommendations for the design of a company's leadership development and mentoring programs? The Commission's recommendations are described at

www.ilr.cornell.edu/library/e_archive/Glass Ceiling

and at

www.dol.gov/dol/_sec/public/media/reports/ceiling.htm

5. **Communication Competency.** Effective leaders make sure that their formal communications project an inspiring vision and instill confidence about the organization's ability to achieve that vision. Many corporate annual reports include a vision or mission statement. Look at the annual reports of three companies referred to in this chapter. Based on the vision statement and any other information contained in the annual report, what type of leadership style does the CEO of the company seem to have? To start your investigation, visit American Express's home page at

www.americanexpress.com

and W. H. Brady's home page at

www.whbrady.com

and Gore Fabric's home page at

www.gorefabrics.com

REAL-TIME CASE ANALYSIS

HERB KELLEHER FLIES SOUTHWEST AIRLINES

Southwest Airlines is flying high: *Fortune* ranks it the number 1 best company to work for in America. Customers rank it number 1 in customer service and appreciate the airline's low, low prices. The Federal Aviation Administration ranks it number 1 in on-time arrivals and safety. And many leadership experts rank CEO Herb Kelleher the number 1 business leader. What type of leadership style does Kelleher use? You be the judge after reading some examples of how Kelleher runs his company.

- Kelleher insists that employees have fun at work. He sets the example, and then makes sure everyone else has fun too. How? Kelleher says that hiring decisions are key: "We are looking for attitudes that are positive and for people who can lend themselves to causes. We are looking for people who have a good sense of humor and people who are interested in performing as a team and take joy in team results instead of individual accomplishments." In her job interview, Mary Ann Adams, a finance executive, had to recount a practical joke. She passed this interview test by telling how she

created a screen-saver for her computer, using an unflattering picture of her old boss.

- A promotional video for the company, which refers to itself as the "LUV (love) airline," is a nonstop musical production that features a zany Kelleher doing the boogie and employees from each department of the company singing jingles that explain their responsibilities and how they serve the customers.

- Kelleher cultivates the impression he makes on employees. He says, "It is important to spend a lot of time with your people and communicate with them in a variety of ways. And a large part of it is demeanor. Sometimes we tend to lose sight of the fact that demeanor—the way you appear and the way you act—is a form of communication." Kelleher makes sure that he radiates a demeanor that says he is proud of his employees.

- Kelleher always seems to be crusading, as if he were the underdog fighting off an enemy. In the company's early days, he had to battle major airlines and politicians for the right to take off and land his fleet of three aircraft. "I was a crusader freeing Jerusalem from Saracens," he recalls. He thinks that this spirit is central to the company's culture. "The people who work here don't think of Southwest as a business. They think of it as a crusade."

- He's been quoted as saying, "Fun is a stimulant to people. They enjoy their work and work more productively. You don't have to surrender your individuality to work for Southwest Airlines." He admits that he finds it more fun to chat with his mechanics than do the things CEOs are expected to do, like sit on government panels.

- At 3 A.M. one Sunday, Kelleher brought donuts to the cleaning crew and put on overalls to help it clean a plane.

- One pilot pointed out that "It's not a Mary-Kay type atmosphere where we're all starry eyed. It's mutual respect." Unlike Robert Crandall, former CEO of American Airlines, Kelleher would never belittle his pilots to the press or treat them like "units of expense."

- When a gate supervisor was asked what makes Southwest different from other airlines she said, "We're empowered to make on-the-spot decisions. For example, if a customer misses a flight, it's no sweat. We have the latitude to take care of the problem. There's no need for approvals."

- When asked about the company's profit sharing, Kelleher explained that his employees are very aware of the company's stock performance. He recounts an incident in Los Angeles where an agent from another airline asked to borrow a stapler. The Southwest agent went over with the stapler, waited for it to be used, and brought it back. The other agent asked, "Do you always follow staplers around?" The Southwest agent replied, "I

want to make sure we get it back. It affects our profit sharing." The airline has been consistently more profitable than other airlines.

- Kelleher insists on *not* setting departmental goals or numerical targets. Goals and targets always are set for the performance of the company as a whole. "At Southwest, we all work toward the same goal, and setting up different goals for different areas is likely to create a schism within the company," he asserts. Employee productivity at the company is about twice the industry average, measured in terms of the ratio of number of employees per number of passengers served.[66]

Questions

1. Where would you put Herb Kelleher in the managerial grid? Explain your answer.

2. Historically, employee turnover at Southwest Airlines has been only 50 percent as high as the airline industry average. Is Kelleher's approach to leadership part of the reason? Explain.

3. According to contingency models of leadership, Kelleher should be using a leadership style that matches the specific situation in his company. Use Fiedler's contingency model to analyze the situation at Southwest Airlines. According to the model, is Kelleher's leadership approach appropriate for the situation?

4. Does Kelleher believe in Theory X or Theory Y? Justify your opinion.

5. Does Kelleher exhibit the three behaviors of transformational leadership? Explain.

To learn more about Herb Kelleher, visit Southwest Airlines' home page at

www.iflyswa.com

VIDEO CASE

SUNSHINE CLEANING SYSTEMS: THE TEAM WHERE EVERYONE BATS CLEANUP

Sunshine Cleaning Systems, with an enthusiastic, involved CEO, shares some of the "family" feel of Southwest Airlines. The sense of family that CEO Larry Calufetti engenders likely accounts for the company's low turnover rate in an industry where high turnover is the rule.

Employees at Sunshine Cleaning are encouraged both to excel in their work—exercising their abilities to innovate—and to pull together as a team. Management believes that no one will know the job better

than the employees who do it day in and day out, and presumably if there's a better way, those same employees will be likely to find it. Sunshine is clearly in the Theory Y camp, as shown in the company's attitude toward employee discretion. The "codes" use a considerate leadership style, giving the "what," and not the "how."

Encouraging personal initiative is important at Sunshine. Although management can't be sure that it won't have a staffing glitch (e.g., an employee calling in sick at the last minute), it *can* be sure that the task (e.g., prepping a stadium for the next day's event) won't disappear. As with a baseball team whose members can be shifted to cover weaknesses, Sunshine's ideal for its employees is that they should all be able to pick up someone else's chores if the need arises. However, Sunshine's management also knows that its team members are individuals, that some roles will be difficult to fill, and that other roles come naturally.

Sunshine offers only modest monetary bonuses for outstanding behavior, but with the award comes public recognition as "Employee of the Month." Non-monetary reward is likely to have a stronger motivating effect at Sunshine, where employee relations are close and earning praise from the "coach" commands respect. Line managers at Sunshine likely have strong communication and teamwork competencies; all employees at Sunshine are encouraged to develop planning and administration competencies, as they collectively apportion, undertake, and complete tasks.

Employees should also be inspired by the support they get in doing their jobs. Some organizations lay out requirements for what employees must do. In contrast, Sunshine's managers clearly focus on what employees must be given: the support, training and tools necessary to complete their tasks, the responsibility and leeway to innovate to do what they think is necessary and right, and the opportunity for development and promotion. Completion of large, important tasks is an integral part of Sunshine's work, but its managers seem more inclined toward a relationship-oriented rather than a task-oriented style, pushing responsibility and autonomy down in the workforce and reaping the reward of aggressive and productive team players.

The use of the sports team metaphor fits Sunshine well: Employees wear uniforms, and all pitch in until the task at hand is finished. Management's interpretation of how "coach" differs from "manager" gives a hint as to why Sunshine's team shows a relatively low attrition rate for its industry: A coach needs to work with *all* the players, whereas a manager can selectively choose only certain people to do certain tasks. Emphasizing the team also allows Sunshine's "coaches" to ask for extra effort from individuals, with a high likelihood of receiving it on behalf of the team.

ON THE WEB

As a privately held company focused on contracts with municipal and corporate customers, Sunshine Cleaning hasn't yet created a Web site for itself. The International Window Cleaning Association is on the Web (***www.iwca.org***). Sunshine Cleaning Systems President Larry Calufetti is past president of the Association.

QUESTIONS

1. As a Sunshine manager, you've been assigned a work team and the company's newest contract, servicing the city's convention center. How would you address the job in a participative leadership style?

2. Is Sunshine likely to be a good company for on-the-job leadership training? Why or why not?

3. The night before a John Tesh concert at Miami's municipal arena, one member of Sunshine's service team fails to show—the team leader. How might the team react?

Case contributed by Ross Stapleton-Gray, President, TeleDiplomacy, Inc., a technology and policy consultancy, and Adjunct Professor in Georgetown University's Communication, Culture, and Technology program.

Chapter

16

Organizational Communication

Outline

Martinez Communicates Sears' Turnaround Strategy

The 1980s were a decade of declining sales at Sears, but the 1990s seemed to be a much better time for the company. Old rules had been stripped away, and employees had been both empowered and intensively trained. Stock prices rose steadily for three years running, following the appointment of CEO Arthur C. Martinez in 1992. Then, suddenly, Sears' stock prices took a plunge, tumbling almost 10 percent. Sluggish sales, flattening customer service ratings, complaints from overworked store managers, and a weak profit picture all led investors to wonder whether the company had lost its focus again. In an interview about how he planned to respond to recent events, Martinez shared his plan. "I want to revisit and intensify the theme of our customer being the center of our universe," he explained. "There will be no new initiatives, no new big ideas." He just wanted to send a clear, simple message.

In recent years, Martinez had learned how difficult it was to communicate even a very simple message. Misunderstandings were common in the company. Random surveys of employees revealed that many thought their main function was to protect the assets of the company, not to be obsessive about customer service. These surveys also revealed how little employees knew about the company's performance. When Sears was earning only two cents on the dollar, many employees thought it was earning fifty or sixty cents on the dollar.

With these facts in hand, Martinez shifted into overdrive in an effort to achieve a key strategic objective: "develop a winning culture." Employees were soon being bombarded with information from headquarters. Training programs intended to teach employees about the company's products and goals mushroomed. The company completely revamped its approach to communicating with employees. Store managers began receiving e-mail messages about everything that was going on in the company, even if it had little relevance to them. Morale improved at first, energizing managers to intensify their customer service efforts. But soon everyone was frustrated by information overload. To make the point that too much information was as bad as too little, one executive went to a meeting pushing a wheelbarrow filled with memos, surveys, videos, and various other communiqués received during the past month.

The point was made. With so many messages flooding the workplace, focusing on the customer had become difficult. According to Anthony Rucci, executive vice-president of administration, headquarters promptly responded to the feedback. More than 100 planned initiatives were removed from the 1997 fourth-quarter agenda and e-mail was shut down entirely during the busy holiday season. Consistent with putting customers first, future holiday seasons will be free from surveys, product training sessions, and benefits requiring managers' attendance. Store managers also have been assured that they can respond to mundane messages from headquarters as their time permits.[1]

* * *

To learn more about Sears, Roebuck & Company, visit the company's home page at

www.sears.com

THE COMMUNICATION PROCESS

Whether in a retail store, school district, bank, transportation system, or manufacturing plant, effective communication is essential. Communication is to an organization as the bloodstream is to a person. Just as a person can develop hardening of the arteries, which impairs physical efficiency, an organization can develop blockages of communication channels, which impair its effectiveness. Just as heart bypass surgery may be necessary to save a person's life, an organization may have to revamp its communication system to survive. And, just as heart patients can do more harm than good if they overreact to their health problems by exercising too strenuously, an organization such as Sears may go overboard trying to repair a history of poor communication with employees.

Without *effective* communication, managers can accomplish little, which is why we included communication as one of the six key managerial competencies. Recall that communication can be formal or informal, verbal or nonverbal, and may take many forms, including face-to-face interactions, phone calls, faxes, e-mail, notes posted on bulletin boards, letters, memos, reports, videos, and oral presentations. In this chapter, we examine how communication takes place, identify some barriers to communication, and explore ways of improving communication in organizations.

Communication is the transfer and exchange of information and understanding from one person to another through meaningful symbols. It is a way of exchanging and sharing ideas, attitudes, values, opinions, and facts. Communication is a process that requires both a sender, who begins the process, and a receiver, who completes the communication link. When the receiver understands the communication, the cycle is complete.

In organizations, managers use the communication process to carry out their four functions (planning, organizing, leading, and controlling). Because they must have access to relevant information in order to make sound decisions, effective managers build networks of contacts who facilitate information gathering, interpretation, and dissemination. These contacts help managers become the nerve centers of their organizations. Much like radar screens, managers scan the environment for changes that could affect the organization and share this information with others. Once made, decisions are quickly disseminated to those who will help carry them out.

In contrast, ineffective managers often leave employees in the dark about what is happening. Poor communication seems to be a particular problem during downsizing, when managers' and employees' stress levels soar. Poor communication allows rumors to replace facts, fosters animosities between departments and work teams, and impedes successful organizational change. Under such circumstances, poor communication seems to be the single most important reason for poor strategy implementation.

However, effective communication also is necessary during times of expansion and growth. At AMC Entertainment, the movie theatre chain that created the multiplex and megaplex establishments, as many as fifteen theatre managers report directly to a general manager. A primary responsibility of the general managers is to learn what makes going to the movies enjoyable for customers and then deliver that service. When AMC did an assessment to find out why some general managers were more effective than others in terms of customer service, they learned that listening skills were the most important characteristic of the best managers.[2]

Most managers spend a large part of their working day communicating with superiors, peers, customers, and others; writing memos, letters, and reports; and talking to others on the phone. In doing so, they are engaged in the communication process, which involves six basic elements: sender (encoder), receiver (decoder), message, channels, feedback, and perception.

Figure 16.1 shows how these elements interact during the communication process.[3] Managers and employees who are concerned with improving their communication competency need to be aware of these elements and how they contribute to successful communication. We discuss the roles of the sender and the receiver first because they are the actors in the process.

SENDER (ENCODER)

The ***sender*** is the source of information and the initiator of the communication process. The sender tries to choose the type of message and the channel that will be most effective. The sender then encodes the message.

Encoding translates thoughts or feelings into a medium—written, visual, or spoken—that conveys the meaning intended. Imagine that you are planning to apply for a summer job. You will get the best response by first learning about the channels of communication used by the organization. Many employers now prefer to accept applications via the Internet, so you should begin by visiting the organization's Web

COMMUNICATION
The transfer of information and understanding from one person to another through meaningful symbols.

SENDER
The source of information and initiator of the communication process.

ENCODING
Translating thoughts or feelings into a medium—written, visual, or spoken—that conveys the meaning intended.

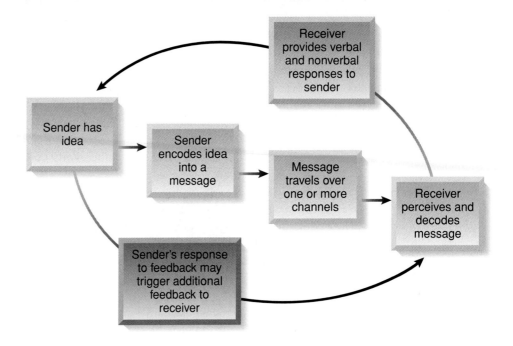

site. From there, you often can determine which job openings exist and the procedures that the company uses to process applications for employment. If the organization accepts electronic applications, you're likely to get a faster response from your inquiry by using this method.[4] If the organization has no Web site, you can begin the process by calling to find out whether an opening exists, then writing a letter, and then phoning again to confirm that your letter was received.

Regardless of whether you apply electronically or use a traditional letter, your application should convey certain ideas and impressions. For example, you should explain why you're interested in that particular company. You also need to provide background information about your qualifications for the job and explain how you believe the job will further your career. When you transfer these ideas to an electronic memo or to paper, you are encoding your message. To increase encoding accuracy, follow those parts of the five communication principles that apply to the form of communication you're using:

1. **Relevancy.** Make the message meaningful and significant, carefully selecting the words, symbols, or gestures to be used.

2. **Simplicity.** Put the message in the simplest possible terms, reducing the number of words, symbols, or gestures used to communicate your intended thoughts and feelings.

3. **Organization.** Arrange the message as a series of points to facilitate understanding. Complete each point in a message before proceeding to the next.

4. **Repetition.** Restate key points of the message at least twice. Repetition is particularly important in spoken communication because words may not be clearly heard or fully understood the first time.

5. **Focus.** Focus on the essential aspects, or key points, of the message. Make the message clear and avoid unnecessary detail. In spoken communication, empha-

size significant points by changing your tone of voice, pausing, gesturing, or using appropriate facial expressions. In written communication, underline or italicize key sentences, phrases, or words.

RECEIVER (DECODER)

RECEIVER
The person who receives and decodes (or interprets) the sender's message.

The **receiver** is the person who receives and decodes (or interprets) the sender's message. **Decoding** translates messages into a form that has meaning to the receiver. The person who receives your electronic application or letter about a summer job reacts to it first on the basis of whether there are any openings. If there aren't, the receiver probably won't pay much attention to your inquiry. If there are openings, the receiver probably will compare what you wrote about yourself to the type of person the organization wants to hire. Jack Green is one of Hewlett-Packard's corporate recruiters. Responsible for recruiting at more than sixty colleges and universities around the country, he's learned to decode messages efficiently. He takes no more than twelve seconds to judge a résumé. He prefers a standard résumé—if he receives one printed on pink paper with a color photo he'll "try to look beyond it." He searches for key information, including job experience, campus leadership, grades, and hometown. Why hometown? He says that it helps him judge the likelihood of a student's accepting a job in one of thirty cities where Hewlett-Packard has facilities.[5]

DECODING
Translating encoded messages into a form that has meaning to the receiver.

LISTENING
Paying attention to a message, not merely hearing it.

One of the main requirements of the receiver is the ability to listen. **Listening** involves *paying attention to* the message, not merely hearing it. Of the 75 percent or more of their time that managers spend in communicating, about half is spent listening to others. Becoming a better listener is an important way for people to improve their communication skills. Studies have shown that most people can recall immediately only about 50 percent of what someone tells them. Two months later, they can recall only about 25 percent. That's why effective communication often involves the use of several media, such as newsletters, e-mail, and the telephone.

Ten guidelines for effective listening are presented in Table 16.1. Try using them the next time that you're trying to communicate with someone else. You'll be surprised at how much effective listening improves the communication process.

Table 16.1	*Guidelines for Effective Listening*

1. Remember that listening is not just about receiving information—how you listen also sends a message back to the message sender.

2. Stop talking! You can't listen if you're talking.

3. Show a talker that you want to listen. Paraphrase what's been said to show that you understand.

4. Remove distractions.

5. Avoid pre-judging what the person thinks or feels. Listen first, then make judgments later.

6. Try to see the other person's point of view.

7. Listen for total meaning. This includes both the content of the words and the feeling or attitude underlying the words.

8. Attend to both verbal and nonverbal cues.

9. Go easy on argument and criticism, which put people on the defensive and may make them "clam up" or become angry.

10. Before each person leaves, confirm what has been said.

MESSAGE

MESSAGE

The verbal (spoken and written) symbols and nonverbal cues that represent the information that the sender wants to convey to the receiver.

The **message** contains the verbal (spoken and written) symbols and nonverbal cues representing the information that the sender wants to convey to the receiver. Like a coin, a message has two sides, and the message sent and the message received aren't necessarily the same. Why? First, encoding and decoding of the message may vary because of differences between the sender's and the receiver's backgrounds and viewpoints. Second, the sender may be sending more than one message.

Recruiters such as Jack Green, as well as managers and employees generally, use three types of messages: nonverbal, verbal, and written. The use of nonverbal messages is extremely important, although many individuals don't recognize this fact. Accordingly, we discuss nonverbal messages at greater length than the other two types.

NONVERBAL MESSAGES

The use of facial expressions, movements, body position, and physical contact (often called *body language*) to convey meaning.

Nonverbal Messages. All messages not spoken or written constitute nonverbal messages. **Nonverbal messages** involve the use of facial expressions, body movement, gestures, and physical contact (often called *body language*) to convey meaning. When people communicate in person, as much as 60 percent of the content of the message is transmitted through facial expressions and body movement.

Recruiter Jack Green sees each student for only thirty minutes, so every bit of information he can get is important. A strong handshake creates the first impression. Green admits that first impressions based on nonverbal cues can be misleading but that they are hard to ignore. He recalls one hiring recommendation that he made in 1983 based on the "strong presence" of the candidate. He later came to regret his recommendation. "If you sat in the room with him, like I did, you would see that he was this all-American college boy—handsome, polite, friendly. His GPA was 3.8. I can still remember it," he says. Why the regret? Six months after he was hired he was a prime suspect for the murder of his ex-girlfriend. It took four more years and another attempted murder before the police could make their case. The man was a Hewlett-Packard employee the entire time. Green acknowledges now that he should have paid more attention to the fact that the student's grades had slipped during his last semester in school. "So you can be wrong. A mistake like that puts you on your guard. It makes you realize that you are not as good as you think you are."

In the incident recalled by Jack Green, nonverbal messages had a very powerful effect on the receiver, with unfortunate circumstances. Nevertheless, the incident provides a vivid example of how important such messages can be. Let's look at three of the many kinds of nonverbal messages that you should be aware of: use of space, personal appearance, and body language.

PROXEMICS

The study of ways that people use physical space to convey a message about themselves.

With regard to *space,* how close you are to another person, where you sit or stand, and how you arrange your office can have a real impact on communication. The term **proxemics** refers to the study of ways people use physical space to convey messages. Think of how you would feel if you walked into class midway through the term and someone was sitting in "your" seat. You'd probably feel angry because your space, or territory, had been invaded. Space and the use of space have communicative importance. To test how important your territory is to you, complete the questionnaire shown in Figure 16.2.

In Japan, strict rules of etiquette guide seating behavior. If businesspeople are traveling together on a train, the most senior executive sits next to the window, facing the direction in which the train is moving. In a taxi, the "top" seat is behind the driver and the most junior seat is next to the driver. In elevators, the senior person stands in the rear in the center facing the door and the most junior person stands near the buttons.[6]

Instructions: Circle one number to answer each question as follows:

1   Strongly agree
2   Agree
3   Not sure
4   Disagree
5   Strongly disagree

	1	2	3	4	5
1. If I arrive at my apartment (room) and find my roommate sitting in my chair, I am annoyed if he/she doesn't at least offer to get up immediately.	1	2	3	4	5
2. I do not like anyone to remove anything from my desk without first asking me.	1	2	3	4	5
3. If a stranger puts a hand on my shoulder when talking to me I feel uncomfortable.	1	2	3	4	5
4. If my suit jacket is lying on the back of a chair and another student comes in and chooses to sit in the chair, I feel that he or she should ask me to move my jacket or choose another seat.	1	2	3	4	5
5. If I enter a classroom and "reserve" a chair with a notebook, I am annoyed and offended upon my return to find my book moved and someone sitting in "my" seat.	1	2	3	4	5
6. If a person who is not a close friend of mine gets within a foot from my face to talk to me, I will either back off or uncomfortably hold my ground.	1	2	3	4	5
7. I do not like strangers walking into my room (apartment).	1	2	3	4	5
8. If I lived in an apartment, I would not want the landlord to enter for any reason without my permission.	1	2	3	4	5
9. I do not like my friends or family borrowing my clothes without asking me first.	1	2	3	4	5
10. If I notice someone staring at me in a restaurant, I become annoyed and uncomfortable.	1	2	3	4	5

To score and interpret your responses, add the numbers you circled for all 10 statements. Then compare your total with the following definitions:

10–25 points: *Highly territorial.* Your instincts for staking out and protecting what you consider yours are high. You strongly believe in your territorial rights.

26–39 points: *Ambiguous but territorial.* You may act territorial in some circumstances but not in others. You feel differently about different types of space.

40–50: *Not territorial.* You disagree with the entire concept of territoriality. You dislike possessiveness, protectiveness, and jealousy. The concept of private ownership is not central to your philosophy of life.

Spatial arrangements in corporate offices in North America can send many signals to members of the organization. In some organizations, such as Royal Dutch Shell and NationsBank, top managers have larger offices, windows with better views, plusher carpets, and higher quality furnishings than middle managers. Meriting a personal secretary, a head of the table seat at meetings, a chauffeured limousine, use of a private dining room, and the ability to summon employees for discussion—all send messages via the use of space. Organizations that seek to have a more egalitarian culture, such as Lucent Technologies and JCPenney, intentionally avoid these status symbols. Not all managers have opportunities to plan and design the building in which people will work, but many managers have opportunities to plan the arrangements of elements within a building, such as the tables and chairs used to furnish meeting rooms.

As the following Planning and Administration Competency feature illustrates, making decisions about the environment in which people work can be an important administrative responsibility. The shape of tables and seating arrangements can affect more than just the flow of conversation; they also send messages that reinforce (or contradict) the desired corporate culture.

Table arrangements are important outside the boardroom, too. At the Bank of Alma, a small community institution in Michigan, many of the managers have small round tables in their offices, in addition to their desks. When they want to make customers feel at ease and establish good rapport, the managers avoid talking across their desks and instead hold the conversation at the round table.

In terms of *personal appearance,* you've undoubtedly heard the expression, "Clothes make the person." Style consultants for major corporations believe that the way a person dresses definitely communicates something to others. You should ask yourself: Is the way I'm dressed going to hurt or help my business relationships? Like it or not, people still judge you partly on the basis of how you look. If you're dressed appropriately, customers and others may see you as a more competent person than someone who dresses inappropriately. Of course, what is *appropriate* depends on the organization. A conservative suit fits in well on Wall Street but looks out of place in Silicon Valley.

A study of female administrative employees at the University of Michigan revealed that deciding how to dress can be complex. On days of important meetings or when executive education classes are being held, business school staff "dress up," more than on other days. Staff who spend much of their time with students "dress down." As one receptionist in the admissions office explained, "I don't want to dress too nice because students will come in wearing their slacks and jeans and I don't ever want to give them the impression that I'm superior over them. I want to look like I am kind of at their level, so they aren't intimidated and so they will use our office as a resource."[7]

With regard to *body language,* the body and its movement—particularly movements of the face and eyes, which are very expressive—tell other people a lot about you. As much as 50 percent of the content of a message may be communicated by facial expression and body posture; another 30 percent by inflection and the tone of the speech. The words themselves may account for only 20 percent of the content of the message.[8]

The ability to interpret facial expressions is an important part of communication. Eye contact is a direct and powerful way of communicating nonverbally. In the United States, social rules suggest that in most situations, brief eye contact is appropriate. However, if eye contact is too brief, people may interpret you as being aloof or untrustworthy. Conversely, people often interpret prolonged eye contact as either a threat or a sign of romantic interest, depending on the context. A good poker player watches the eyes of the other players as new cards are dealt. Pupil dilation often betrays whether the card(s) just dealt improved the player's hand.

Posture also communicates meaning by signaling a person's degree of self-confidence or interest in what is being discussed. The more interested you are, the more likely you are to lean toward the person who is talking. Conversely, leaning

Squaring Off in Corporate Boardrooms

To illustrate how space is used in organizations, a Dutch artist named Jacquiline Hassink spent six years photographing tables—dining tables, courtroom tables, and boardroom tables were all part of the project. "Tables are objects that organize people," she says. "You study the table and then you know something about the structure of the people who gather around it."

After photographing the boardroom tables of thirty multinational companies, she concluded that the shape of the table often reflected the corporate culture. McDonald's boardroom, called the Mac room, felt very egalitarian to Hassink. The boardroom itself is round (like a hamburger?). The table is designed much like that of the United Nations, with two rings of seats. The inner ring is formed of brown seats and the outer ring is formed of green seats. There are no assigned seats for the directors, who sit wherever they please. The glass walls allow employees to watch what's going on and to see whether the CEO looks happy or angry. "It was one of the most democratic tables I've seen," observed Hassink.

Levi Strauss also uses round tables in its boardroom. Unlike most companies, however, it has four tables instead of one. This arrangement promotes interaction and discussion among board members, who often break into discussion teams during board meetings. CEO Robert Haas usually sits at the front table near the door.

General Motors and Procter & Gamble have more traditional rectangular boardroom tables, with the CEO positioned at the head. The exotic green table at General Motors is protected by a leather cover between meetings. The hall leading into the Procter & Gamble boardroom is lined with paintings of previous CEOs.

According to Hassink, the rectangular tables are clear signs of corporate autocracy, and the paintings reflect a respect for past history and tradition.[9]

The home page of Work Space Resources, a business that specializes in office design, is recommended as a source of additional information at

www.workspace-resources.com

away may communicate a lack of interest. Similarly, tension and anxiety typically show in a person's legs and feet. People often are able to hide tension from the waist up but may give themselves away by crossing their legs tightly and tapping their feet.

Verbal Messages. Employees communicate verbally (speaking and writing) more often than in any other way. Spoken communication takes place face-to-face and over the telephone. Most people prefer face-to-face communication because nonverbal messages are an important part of it. But some people prefer written communications because it allows them to choose and weigh their words more carefully before sending the message. When emotions run high, or you are writing in a second language, weighing your words carefully can be advantageous.

Effective verbal communication requires the sender to (1) encode the message in words (and nonverbal cues) that will convey it accurately to the receiver, (2) convey the message in a well-organized manner, and (3) try to eliminate distractions. At the Bank of Alma, loan officers must be especially good at sending verbal messages. Many customer transactions involve the use of long written documents, filled with legal and financial jargon. The loan officers assume that most customers won't read these documents, even though they are required to sign them. Therefore, the loan officers take responsibility for conveying verbally the messages contained in the written documents. They translate the jargon into everyday language and then summarize what the documents say for the customer, checking to make sure that the customer understands the key points.

In daily interactions, nonverbal and verbal messages are sent and received simultaneously. Effective communication requires attending to both types of messages when encoding and decoding information. Sarah McGinty is a professor at Harvard University's school of education who also consults with clients about developing effective communication styles. As the Communication Competency account explains, McGinty believes that body language is an important aspect of both formal and informal communication. Appropriate body language makes public presentations more persuasive. She also stresses that good linguistic habits facilitate both formal and informal communication but that poor linguistic habits may put an individual at a disadvantage when negotiating.

You should always consider general principles such as those offered by Sarah McGinty to be guidelines, not rules. These guidelines may serve you well in U.S. business settings, but they could get negative reactions in other settings and other cultures.

Hisako Nagashima uses many of the forthright communication methods suggested by McGinty, but her style isn't appreciated by everyone. Nagashima's superb strategic action competency is credited with having built the overseas businesses of Japan's number one cosmetics company, Shiseido. She also improved the working conditions for women salespeople of the company, by confronting management and demanding that women be paid the same as their male counterparts. Eventually her message got through, and two years later the company dropped it's practice of paying women one-tenth the amount of severance pay that men received. Many older, traditional Japanese men found her style abrasive, however. "Some of her former bosses and colleagues hate her guts," observed a Shiseido manager. Even the senior vice-president that she reports to admits that he isn't always comfortable with her style. "There are times when I think she is a bit too mouthy," he acknowledged. But she get things done. Her current responsibilities include making Shiseido more relevant to American consumers and increasing overseas sales to 25 percent of revenues by the year 2000.[10]

Written Messages. Although spoken communication is quicker than written communication and allows the sender and receiver to interact, organizations use many forms of written messages (e.g., reports, memoranda, letters, e-mail, and newsletters). Such messages are most appropriate when information has to be collected from or distributed to many people at scattered locations and when keeping a record of what was sent is necessary. The following are some guidelines for preparing effective written messages.

1. The message should be drafted with the receiver clearly in mind.

2. The contents of the message should be well thought out ahead of time.

3. The message should be as brief as possible, without extraneous words and ideas. Important messages should be prepared in draft form first and then polished. If the message has to be long, include a brief summary on the first page. This summary should clarify the main points and contain page references to details on each item.

4. The message should be carefully organized. State the most important point first, then the next most important point, and so on. This way, even if the receiver reads only the first few points, the essentials of the message will get across. Make the subject clear by giving the message a title. Make the message more readable by using simple words and short, clear sentences.

McGinty Speaks on the Power of Speech

For better or worse, how we speak affects how we are perceived. Listeners feel more confident when they hear proposals offered by a person who shows self-confidence. In meetings, confident people tend to speak more, fend off interruptions, make jokes, argue, and laugh. Less confident people tend to ask more questions during meetings, defer when someone tries to interrupt, leave their sentences unfinished, and encourage others to speak. They may be appreciated for offering empathy, but they are not perceived as people with solutions.

Speech patterns can be affected by many factors, including gender, age, and even corporate culture. To learn which communication styles are effective in a specific organization, Professor Sarah McGinty suggests that you try acting like a researcher. If you can sit in on a meeting, watch who talks, who changes the course of

a discussion, and who gets noticed and why. How do people express their disagreements with each other? Does politeness always rule the day, or do people seem to enjoy and expect energetic debate?

Can you determine which style of communication you use? McGinty says that doing so can be difficult, but insights can be gained by making tapes of yourself speaking and then listening carefully to them. Telephone conversations and meetings are easy to record. Communication workshops also are a good way to learn more about your style and practice improving it.

To begin improving immediately, McGinty suggests avoiding some common bad habits. One habit she considers ineffective is always seeking consensus by saying things such as "As Sheila said" and "I pretty much agree with Shabir." Also avoid under-

mining your own ideas with phrases such as "I may be way off base with this, but. . . ." In general, she suggests that people strive to be bolder in their speech and worry less about offending someone. But be careful. Saying "You're completely wrong" is less effective than saying "I have a plan that I think will solve this problem."[11]

CHANNELS

CHANNEL

The path that a message follows from sender to receiver.

INFORMATION RICHNESS

The information carrying capacity of a channel of communication.

The **channel** is the path a message follows from the sender to the receiver. **Information richness** is the information carrying capacity of the channel. Not all channels can carry the same richness of information. Written communications are low in richness. Customer and employee surveys are a form of written communication that many organizations rely on heavily despite their lack of information richness. Surveys usually ask people to express their opinions about various topics by choosing among a fixed set of opinions. Customers might be asked to indicate whether they were "delighted," "just satisfied," or "disappointed" with the customer service they received. Employees might be asked to indicate whether they "strongly agree," "agree," "disagree," or "strongly disagree" with a statement such as "My supervisor treats me with respect." This form of communication facilitates quantitative analyses, but it limits the type and amount of information received from customers and employees. Only the information written down is received. Channels low in richness are considered to be *lean* because they are effective mainly for sending specific data and facts.

As Figure 16.3 indicates, face-to-face interaction is the richest communication channel. It conveys several cues simultaneously, including spoken and nonverbal information. Face-to-face interaction also provides immediate feedback so that comprehension can be checked and misinterpretations corrected. Managers can gather additional information about how customers and employees feel about the organization and its products by speaking with them personally. Focus groups are a structured form of face-to-face communication that often are used to gauge customers' reactions to products. The telephone is somewhat less rich than face-to-face communication, but not as lean as written surveys. The First National Bank of Chicago changed its approach to customer satisfaction surveys in order to obtain richer information. The bank discontinued its mail survey and began to conduct telephone surveys. Managers were trained to interview customers and were responsible for acting on their responses. Directly hearing the voices of customers added richness and perspective to the information provided.[12]

In addition to selecting a level of information richness, individuals must choose among several types of channels for communicating with others. They include downward, upward, and horizontal formal channels and informal channels, such as the grapevine and networking or caucus groups.

DOWNWARD CHANNELS
Communication paths that managers use to send messages to employees or customers.

Downward Channels. Managers use ***downward channels*** to send messages to employees. For instance, the L.L. Bean mail-order headquarters in Freeport, Maine, receives more than 165,000 phone calls a day during the holiday season for 16,000 outdoor items ranging from socks to flannel shirts to hunting bows to tents.[13] To communicate effectively with L.L. Bean's 3,000 employees, its managers use downward channels to convey

- how to handle special promotional items;

- job descriptions, detailing duties and responsibilities;

- policies and procedures, explaining what is expected of employees and the organization's rules and employee benefits;

- feedback about an individual's job performance; and

- news of activities and events that management believes employees should participate in (charitable organizations, blood drives, and the like).

Managers frequently use downward communication effectively as a channel, but it may be the most misused channel because it provides little opportunity for employees to respond. In fact, the fundamental problem with downward communication is that it is too often one-way: It's a lean channel that doesn't encourage feedback from those on the receiving end. To correct this problem, managers should urge employees to use upward channels.

| Figure 16.3 | **Information Richness of Channels** |

Source: Adapted from R. L. Daft and R. H. Lengel. Information richness: A new approach to managerial behavior and organization design. In. B. M. Staw and L. L. Cummings (eds.), *Research in Organizational Behavior,* vol. 6. Greenwich, Conn.: JAI Press, 1984, pp. 191–233.

Information Channel	Information Richness
Face-to-face discussion	Highest
Telephone conversations	High
Written letters/memos (individually addressed)	Moderate
Formal written documents (unaddressed bulletins or reports)	Low
Formal numeric documents (printouts, budget reports)	Lowest

UPWARD CHANNELS
Communication paths that
subordinates use to send
information to superiors.

Upward Channels. Some managers don't see the value of encouraging employees to participate in setting goals, planning, and formulating policies. The result is a failure to provide upward channels of communication. Subordinates use ***upward channels*** to send messages to superiors. Such channels may be the only formal means that employees have for communicating with higher level managers in the organization. Upward communication provides feedback on how well employees understand the messages they have received. Moreover, it enables employees to voice their opinions and ideas. If effective, upward communication can provide an emotional release and, at the same time, give employees a chance to participate, the feeling they are being listened to, and a sense of personal worth. Most important, employees often have excellent suggestions for improving efficiency and effectiveness.

At Cirque du Soleil, upward communication is as strong as downward communication. Specific methods for communicating upward include direct personal contacts as well as three publications circulated regularly within the company. One publication is *The Ball,* which features a column called BYOB—Be Your Own Bitch. Employees use it to complain, gripe, and rib without censorship. "This is part of the way we do things," explained Marc Gagnon, vice-president of human resources. One message indicated that the writer felt that the Dutch employees were being treated better than the Canadians. This information was quite useful because it allowed the company to head off certain issues before they could blow up. *The Ball* also informs employees of events and activities taking place at company locations around the world.

Besides its three publications, Cirque du Soleil uses employee focus groups to help design new initiatives and develop new policies. "We look for three things," explained Gagnon. "Make sure the policy is clear and they understand it; see if they agree with it, or if they disagree with it and why; and see if we have any chance to get people to use it. People are allowed to say 'no' to a policy."[14]

Upward communication has many benefits, but managers need to be aware of the problems that can plague upward communication. First, few employees want their superiors to learn anything negative about them, so they may screen out bad news. Most employees try to impress their superiors by emphasizing their contributions to the company. Some may even try to make themselves look better by putting others down. Second, an employee's personal anxieties, aspirations, and attitudes almost always color what is communicated. How many of you would tell a potential employer of the bad things you have heard about the organization? If you really wanted the job, you probably wouldn't be so bold. Finally, the employee may be competing for the manager's job and thus be willing to remain silent and let the manager stumble.

Realizing that employees aren't always comfortable giving direct upward feedback has led many companies to provide another alternative—anonymously contacting a third party. At Pillsbury, employees can call a recording machine and sound off. Verbatim transcripts are prepared of each call and forwarded to the CEO and other top-level managers, with no identification about the gender or any other detectable caller characteristics. The objective was for the company's senior managers to hear the views of employees, without causing employees to be fearful of what might happen to them for voicing their concerns and criticisms. Employees began using the service to share all sorts of information. They noted that a clock in one bakery always ran five minutes fast, identified locations that didn't carry particular products on the shelves, suggested new pizza toppings, and complained so much about slow expense reimbursements that the company overhauled some of its accounting procedures. By calling to express their appreciation, employees also made a hero of a manager who closed down operations during a snowstorm.[15] Other companies that actively encourage upward communication include Rite Aid, Eastman Kodak, and Brown-Ferris Industries. In each case, the CEO encourages open griping and pays particular attention when the same comment is made repeatedly.[16]

Horizontal Channels. Managers and other employees use *horizontal channels* when communicating across departmental lines, with suppliers, or with customers. This type of channel is especially important in network organizations (see Chapter 11). Essential to the success of a network organization is maintaining effective communication among customers, suppliers, and employees in various divisions or functional areas. For example, as Nike continues to outsource the manufacturing of its athletic shoes and apparel to manufacturers throughout the world, it needs an effective horizontal communication channel to link suppliers with information about market demand in order to schedule production and shipping efficiently.

Horizontal channels are formal if they follow prescribed organizational paths.[17] Messages communicated horizontally usually are related to coordinating activities, sharing information, and solving problems. Horizontal channels are extremely important in today's team-based organizations, where employees must often communicate among themselves to solve their clients' production or process problems.

Informal Channels. So far we have concentrated on formal channels of communication. However, never underestimate the importance of informal channels of communication. The *grapevine* is an organization's informal communication system, along which information can travel in any direction. The term comes from a Civil War practice of hanging telegraph lines loosely from tree to tree, like a grapevine. In organizations, the path that messages follow along the grapevine is based on social interaction, not organization charts.

At Xerox's Palo Alto Research Center (PARC), informal communications are essential to productivity. The company learned just how important informal communications were when it began looking for ways to boost productivity. Management hired a social anthropologist to observe closely the behavior of technicians that repaired copiers (tech reps) in an effort to improve efficiency. The consult saw that tech reps often made a point of spending time with each other but not with customers. They would hang around the parts warehouse or the coffee pot and swap stories from the field. The consultant recognized the importance of these informal conversations to tech rep performance. Through their stories, the reps shared knowledge and generated new insights about how to repair machines better. Xerox concluded that tech rep performance could be improved by increasing this type of communication, so the company issued two-way radio headsets to the reps.[18]

Informal channels of communication have been recognized by many organizations as so important that they encourage and support employees' efforts to strengthen them. *Employee network groups* are informal groups who organize regularly scheduled social activities that promote informal communication among employees who share a common interest or concern. In many organizations, network groups—also called caucus groups—form to bring together minority employees. For example, at Xerox and many other large organizations, numerous caucus groups exist for members of particular ethnic groups. Caucus groups for women also are quite common. According to a survey of Fortune 500 companies, such groups have grown rapidly during the past decade. Participants benefit from the business information shared during meetings, as well as from the friendships they form and contacts they make. As one black manager explained, a network group provided him with a "non-threatening atmosphere for expressing what you're experiencing."[19]

Networking Outside the Organization. Managers and employees also spend considerable time meeting with peers and others outside the organization. They attend meetings of professional associations, trade shows, and other gatherings. As a result, they may develop various close, informal relationships with talented and interesting people outside the organization. People use these networks to help each other, trading favors and calling on each other's resources for career advancement or other types of information and support.

Mervyn Morgan, founder of a mortgage finance company, recognized how important networking is to growing businesses but felt that he had too few networking opportunities. So he organized The Bronx Business Breakfast Club, which meets once a month to network and discuss business issues. The Club's activities are supported by organizations such as *Black Enterprise* magazine, American Express, and Chase and draw some seventy attendees per meeting. "The goal is to provide the means and resources for local businesses to come together," explained Pamela Goodman, the Club's executive director. "We are helping them create business opportunities amongst themselves." Morgan's initiative has already paid off. He networked with people in Atlanta, where his company was considering opening a branch. Through those contacts, he met others in Atlanta, including a black architectural firm. Said Morgan, "I am looking to build long-term relationships with all of them."[20]

FEEDBACK

FEEDBACK

The receiver's response to the sender's message.

Feedback is the receiver's response to the sender's message. It's the best way to show that a message has been received and to indicate whether it has been understood. You shouldn't assume that everything you say or write will be understood exactly as you intend it to be. If you don't encourage feedback, you're likely to misjudge how much others understand you. Thus you'll be less effective than those who encourage feedback.

Whenever a message is sent, the actions of the sender affect the reactions of the receiver. The reactions of the receiver, in turn, affect the later actions of the sender. If the sender receives no response, the message was never received or the receiver chose not to respond. In either case, the sender is alerted to the need to find out why the receiver didn't respond. Upon receiving rewarding feedback, the sender continues to produce the same kind of message. When feedback is not rewarding, the sender eventually changes the type of message.

Receiver reactions also tell the sender how well goals are being achieved or tasks are being accomplished. However, in this case the receiver exerts control over the sender by the type of feedback provided. The sender must rely on the receiver for an indication of whether the message was received and understood. Such feedback assures the sender that things are going as planned or brings to light problems that have to be solved. Procter & Gamble, 3M, IBM, and other companies have guidelines for providing effective feedback. According to these guidelines, feedback should have the following characteristics.

1. **It should be helpful.** If the receiver of the message provides feedback that adds to the sender's information, the feedback is likely to be helpful.

2. **It should be descriptive rather than evaluative.** If the receiver responds to the message in a descriptive manner, the feedback is likely to be effective. If the receiver is evaluative (or judgmental), the feedback is likely to be ineffective or even cause a breakdown in communication.

3. **It should be specific rather than general.** The receiver should respond specifically to points raised and questions asked in the message. If the receiver

responds in generalities, the feedback may indicate evasion or lack of understanding.

4. **It should be well timed.** The reception—and thus the effectiveness—of feedback is affected by the context in which it occurs. Giving performance feedback to a person during halftime of a football game or at a luncheon is different from giving the same person feedback in the office. Informal settings usually are reserved for social as opposed to performance-based feedback.

5. **It should not overwhelm.** Spoken communication depends heavily on memory. Accordingly, when large amounts of information are involved, spoken feedback is less effective than written feedback. People tend to "tune in and out" of conversations. They may fail to grasp what the speaker is saying if the message is too long and complex.[21]

PERCEPTION

PERCEPTION
The meaning ascribed to a message by a sender or receiver.

Perception is the meaning ascribed to a message by either sender or receiver. Perceptions are influenced by what people see, by the ways they organize these elements in memory, and by the meanings they attach to them. The ability to perceive varies from person to person. Some people having entered a room only once can later describe it in detail, whereas others can barely remember anything about it. Thus the mental ability to notice and remember differences is important. How people interpret what they perceive is affected by their past. A clenched fist raised in the air by an employee on strike and walking the picket line could be interpreted as either an angry threat to the organization *or* an expression of union solidarity and accomplishment. The attitudes that people bring to a situation color their perceptions of it. By following the communication tips offered by Sarah McGinty, a speaker can gain more control over the perceptions of an audience.

Some problems in communication can be traced to two problems of perception: selective perception and stereotyping. *Selective perception* is the process of screening out information that a person wants or needs to avoid. Many people "tune out" TV commercials. Most everyone has been accused at one time or another of listening only to what they want to hear. Both are examples of selective perception. In organizations, employees sometimes do the same thing. Manufacturing employees pay close attention to manufacturing problems, and accounting employees pay close attention to debits and credits. Such employees tend to filter out information about other areas of the organization and focus on information that is directly related to their own jobs.[22]

SELECTIVE PERCEPTION
The process of screening out information that a person wants or needs to avoid.

STEREOTYPING
Making assumptions about individuals solely on the basis of their belonging to a particular gender, race, age, or other group.

Stereotyping is the process of making assumptions about individuals solely on the basis of their belonging to a certain gender, race, age, or other group. Stereotyping distorts reality by suggesting that all people in a category have similar characteristics, which simply isn't true.

Elgin Clemons described an incident he experienced while working as an attorney at the prestigious law firm of Shearman & Sterling. A graduate of Princeton University and New York University Law School, Clemons worked as an associate for the law firm for two years. One day he decided not to call for a messenger and instead personally delivered to the firm's mail room a stack of work to be sent to a client. A mail clerk told him he would have to get an attorney's signature. "What makes you think I'm not an attorney?" Clemons, who is black, asked. He knew that the mail clerk was reacting to his race. The stereotyping was even more painful because the mail clerk also was black.

A mail clerk's stereotyping habits may have little consequence for an attorney, but when the firm's partners engage in stereotyping, the consequences are significant. At Shearman & Sterling, the partners, all of whom were white, acknowledged that they assume that blacks as a group have more problems with legal writing than whites. Melida Hodgson, another black associate at the firm, illustrated how such stereotyping can create behaviors that are self-reinforcing. Hodgson learned through a secretary that a litigation memo she had written received some criticism from a partner. When she queried the higher ranking associate and partner on the case, she was told not to worry and was given no feedback about the problem. But then when she was speaking to the senior partner who doled out assignments, he told her that there had been some problems with her work and that he was having difficulty getting partners to give her assignments. Clemons saw this type of stereotyping and lack of communication as a real problem. In his view, if a black associate wrote one bad memo, the associate was confirming the stereotype and immediately was put into a category of people that partners didn't want to work with. In contrast, if a white associate made the same mistake, it would be interpreted as an exception, and the associate would be given another chance.[23]

During the 1990s, organizations have become increasingly sensitive to the potential negative consequences of stereotyping based on a person's gender, race, ethnicity, age, or sexual orientation. As they have sought to manage workforce diversity more effectively, many organizations—including Shearman & Sterling—have developed training programs and other initiatives designed to reduce the negative personal and organizational consequences of stereotyping. We discuss workforce diversity further in Chapter 18.

In summary, then, the message sent, the channel of communication used, and the ability to respond all depend on a person's perceptions. Encoding and decoding skills are based on a person's ability to perceive a message and situation accurately. Developing the ability to send and receive messages accurately is central to being an effective manager.

IMPACT OF INFORMATION TECHNOLOGY

2

DESCRIBE THE IMPORTANCE OF INFORMATION TECHNOLOGY IN THE COMMUNICATION PROCESS

New information technologies are rapidly changing the methods of communication available to managers and employees alike—and thus the channels of communication they use. These technologies are changing the manner in which employees communicate with each other and make decisions. Telephone answering machines (voice mail), fax machines, teleconferencing, closed-circuit television systems, computerized report preparation, videotaping, and computer to computer transmission are examples of communication methods developed during the past twenty-five years. Here, we review three of these technologies: electronic mail (e-mail), the Internet, and teleconferencing.

ELECTRONIC MAIL

ELECTRONIC MAIL
Use of computer text composition and editing to send and receive written information.

Electronic mail (e-mail) uses computer text composition and editing to send and receive written information quickly, inexpensively, and efficiently. In seconds, messages are transmitted from the sender's computer to the receiver's. They are read at the receiver's convenience. Senders and receivers usually process their own e-mail. They don't have to give messages to, or receive messages from, secretaries or telephone operators. Messages appear on (and disappear from) video screens with no hard copies produced, unless one is specifically desired.

Electronic mail has become popular with managers for several reasons. First, a manager doesn't have to wait long for a response because information usually can be sent, returned, and recalled in moments. Second, e-mail is relatively inexpensive because it can "piggyback" on computer, telephone, and other equipment that companies already have in place. Third, it increases productivity by eliminating the need for the paper-handling steps required in traditional interoffice or intercompany communication systems. One significant disadvantage has been observed in companies that use e-mail extensively: Employees who might never confront co-workers face to face are less hesitant to explode at others via e-mail, a phenomenon called *flaming*.

Intel Corporation began using e-mail more than a decade ago. Today thousands of PCs connect Intel's more than 29,500 employees at locations throughout the world, along with its more than 2,000 customers. The system covers the United States and plants in more than twelve foreign countries. If Intel's chairman Andrew Grove needs to send a message to a manager in Tsukuba, Japan, he can call Tsukuba. However, 5:00 P.M. in California is equivalent to 4:00 A.M. in Tsukuba, so timing (as well as cost) make the telephone a less than optimal method. E-mail enables Grove to send a message before leaving work in the evening and to have an answer waiting on his computer when he arrives for work the next morning. In terms of cost, e-mail is 90 percent less expensive than overseas calls and letters and 75 percent less costly than telex. Grove believes that e-mail and other automated office techniques have had positive effects on research and development at Intel. Producing state-of-the-art products and services at affordable prices requires that everyone in the organization have access to global information that could improve their performance.[24]

E-mail has dramatically changed the way people can work. No longer is it necessary for a person to live within commutable distance of an organization to be employed by it. Telecommuting allows organizations to recruit and hire people who may never come to the office and can live anywhere in the world. Allowing employees to telecommute expands the pool from which an employer can select new hires and can also help in promoting existing employees who prefer not to relocate. When Northern Telecom wanted to hire William Holtz as vice president of global operations, he expressed an interest but was unwilling to move from Philadelphia to Nashville. So he became a "distant staffer." Working from home, he manages approximately 2,000 people, including several other telecommuters.[25]

THE INTERNET

INTERNET
A loosely configured, rapidly growing web of 25,000 corporate, educational, and research computer networks around the world.

The ***Internet*** is a loosely configured, rapidly growing web of thousands of corporate, educational, and research computer networks around the world. The U.S. Department of Defense created it in 1969, and it was designed to survive a nuclear war. Rather than route messages through central computers, the Internet makes use of thousands of computers linked by thousands of different paths. Anyone with a computer and modem can get on the Internet. Each message sent bears an address code that speeds it toward its destination. Messages usually arrive in seconds; only on rare occasions do they vanish into cyberspace. The Internet is like any other communications device in that a user can get a busy signal. With thousands of Internet groups and e-mail lists, sometimes the traffic is heavy and a user might have to wait a short time to connect to the system.

There is little privacy of information sent over the Internet, although finding methods to make information secure is a high priority of researchers and users. But because information on the Internet is potentially available to almost anyone in the world, it offers many communication opportunities. If you have been completing the Exercises to Develop Your Managerial Competencies at the end of each chapter in this textbook, you are already quite familiar with the Internet.

TELECONFERENCING

Communicating via e-mail offers many conveniences, but a major drawback is that the information sent is primarily in written form. The Internet is more information rich, easily transmitting video pictures and, increasingly, sound. New technological developments are quickly transforming the Internet into a high-fidelity, communications tool. Teleconferencing technology, which combines television and telephone technologies, is another high-fidelity communications tool that organizations use to facilitate discussions among people dispersed around the world. Unlike traditional conference calls over the telephone, teleconferencing allows participants to see each other's body language and to jointly view materials such as blueprints, charts, graphs, or even product prototypes. Also, it can be used in combination with other information technology, such as *group ware,* which is an aid to group problem solving and decision making.

THE DOWNSIDE OF INFORMATION TECHNOLOGY

Information technologies can expand the communication capabilities of individuals and organizations exponentially. In recent years, organizations have spent billions of dollars on these technologies in the hope of improving communication among employees and among employees and external stakeholders, such as suppliers and customers. Decisions regarding the acquisition and use of information technology usually are made by an organization's middle- and upper-level managers. Such decisions take into account the organization's overall strategy and the role that information technology should play in meeting its goals. As revealed in the Strategic Action Competency piece, organizations that have invested heavily in information technology are sometimes surprised to learn that it isn't a cure-all for improving communication.

BARRIERS TO EFFECTIVE COMMUNICATION

3

DEFINE BARRIERS TO COMMUNICATION AND DESCRIBE WAYS TO OVERCOME THEM

One of the first steps in communicating more effectively is to identify barriers to the process. These barriers hinder the sending and receiving of messages by distorting, or sometimes even completely blocking, intended meanings. We divided these impediments into organizational and individual barriers—although there is obviously some overlapping—and listed them in Table 16.2.

ORGANIZATIONAL BARRIERS

Channels of communication, both formal and informal, are largely determined by organization design. Hierarchical organizations have more levels of authority and

Table 16.2	*Barriers to Communication*
Organizational	
Authority and status levels	
Specialization of task functions by members	
Different goals	
Status relationships among members	
Individual	
Conflicting assumptions	
Semantics	
Emotions	

Devoting resources to acquiring information technology (IT) and training people to use it represent important strategic actions. Because information technology makes many types of communication easier, managers often assume that it will result in improved communication. The motto of many managers in recent years has been "the more the better." Do

investments in information technology actually improve the quality of communication? Is more better?

To learn their views, the Academy of Management polled 350 executives in a wide variety of organizations. The percentages of executives who were using each of several types of technology are shown in Exhibit A.

Although they were experienced users of information technologies, many of these executives expressed frustration and skepticism about their overall effectiveness. Exhibit B shows the percentage of executives who indicated each type of concern listed.

Combined with other studies showing no relationship between the amount spent on information technology and business success, these findings need to be considered carefully before a manager decides to invest heavily in information technology. Nevertheless, many companies have suc-

cessfully used new information technologies to improve their performance. Debbie Fields, CEO and president of Mrs. Fields cookies, is an example. She uses information technology to coach her managers on how to make and sell cookies. The technology helps her convey both business information and her charismatic leadership style, making her presence felt throughout the organization.

The key to using information technology successfully may be to use it to supplement more personal forms of communication. According to Patricia Brudick, coauthor of *Megatrends 2000,* "The more technology you have in your office and at home, the more you need to balance that with the high touch of a personal meeting." Debbie Fields's understanding of this need is reflected in her frequent store visits, for which she is well-known.[26]

Exhibit A

Type of Information Technology (IT)	Percentage Using It
E-mail	90%
Voice mail	88%
Fax	82%
Internet	53%
Cellular phone	46%

Exhibit B

Type of Concern	Percentage Who Expressed the Concern
IT has made our lives busier, but not better	58%
ITs ability to add value is vastly overrated	55%
IT produces more misunderstandings than real-time human conversation	54%
IT has caused relationships to deteriorate	51%
IT means serious information overload and redundancy for me	50%
IT has caused the work environment to become too cold and impersonal	44%

greater differences in status among their members. Flat organizations have relatively few authority levels and tend to be more egalitarian in terms of status. The degree of specialization present in the organization also may affect clear communication, as can the presence of conflicting goals.

Authority and Status Levels. When one person holds a higher formal position than another, that person has a higher level of authority. When one person is held in higher esteem than another, regardless of their positions in the organizations, that person has a higher status level. Authority level and status often go hand-in-hand, but not always. *Status* is a person's social rank in a group, which often is determined by a person's characteristics, in addition to the person's formal position. When status and authority levels differ, communication problems are likely to occur.

The more levels in the organization—and the farther the receiver is from the sender—the more difficult effective communication becomes. Figure 16.4 illustrates the loss of understanding as messages are sent downward through a formal communication channel. To help reduce this problem, top managers increasingly are using live video presentations or videotapes to deliver the same message to employees at all the organization's locations. In doing so, these managers use both verbal and nonverbal messages and cut out intervening receivers and senders to increase the probability that the original messages will be received intact. Many organizations use videotapes when trying to move managers to new locations. The presentations can reinforce the reason(s) for the relocation and the need for employee cooperation during the changeover.

Even when communicating with others at the same level of authority, status can interfere with the process. In group discussions, members having higher status speak more and have more influence than members having lower status. This phenomenon is difficult to overcome, and it has been observed in both computer-mediated and face-to-face discussion groups. When computer-mediated group discussion techniques were first introduced, many people expected them to mute the effects of status on communication. Instead, information technologies often reinforce existing status relationships and magnify their effects on communication.[27]

STATUS

A person's social rank in a group.

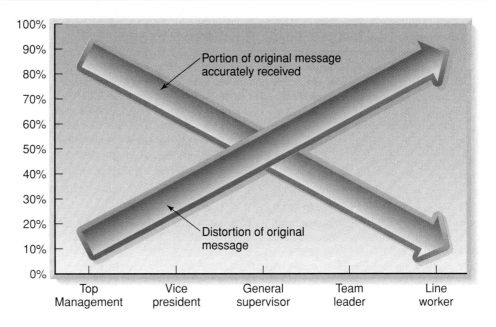

Figure 16.4 **Levels of Understanding for a Message from the CEO**

Portion of original message accurately received

Distortion of original message

Top Management — Vice president — General supervisor — Team leader — Line worker

In flat, egalitarian organizations, authority levels may not interfere with communication, but status is likely to come into play. Temporary employees, for example, often report feeling as if they are being treated as second-class citizens. Often they are excluded from meetings, not invited to social functions, and denied team-based reward systems. In other words, they seldom hear news as it travels through the grapevine and miss the many advantages of informal communication networks. Not surprisingly, then, nearly one of four managers report that frictions between permanent and temporary workers is a significant disadvantage of relying on temporary employees to create flexible staffing levels.[28]

Specialization. As knowledge becomes more specialized, professionals in many fields develop their own jargon, or shorthand, to simplify communication among themselves. That often makes communication with people outside a particular field difficult. For example, a tax accountant and a marketing research manager might have trouble communicating successfully. Moreover, in an attempt to make themselves indispensable, some people intentionally use the language of specialization to obscure what is going on. Employees often use specialized language when trying to "snow" others. When a plumber wrote to the U.S. Department of Housing and Urban Development (HUD) to find out whether using hydrochloric acid to unclog drains was safe, a HUD bureaucrat wrote back: "The efficacy of hydrochloric acid is indisputable, but corrosive acid is incompatible with metallic permanence." The plumber wrote back saying he agreed and was using it. A fax message from the bureaucrat arrived immediately at the plumber's shop. It read: "Don't use hydrochloric acid. It eats the hell out of pipes." Then the plumber understood.

Different Goals. Recall from Chapter 15 Herb Kelleher's view of how differing goals can interfere with organization performance. Kelleher doesn't set departmental goals because he believes that they would create conflicts between departments. Such conflicts can be direct consequences of competing interests, or may simply arise from misunderstandings created by the different perspectives of the parties involved. Open communication between people with differing goals speeds problem solving and improves the quality of solutions. A study of fifty-two self-employed dentists illustrates this point. The research assessed the relationships between dentists and other people who comprised a network of professionals important to their businesses, such as bankers, other members of the dental profession, and suppliers. The study showed that dentists who viewed their goals as differing from the other network members discussed issues with them less openly and constructively. Lack of open discussion, in turn, interfered with the development of strong relationships within the network.[29]

INDIVIDUAL BARRIERS

The Center for Creative Leadership at Greensboro, North Carolina, estimates that half of all managers and 30 percent of top managers have some difficulty in communicating with others. Through an intense training session at the center, managers can learn how to improve their communication competency. The center's staff works with participants who believe that their messages are clear and effective when, in fact, they aren't. Their words, phrases, and references may be clear to some individuals, puzzling to others, and obscure to still others. These problems can be caused by semantics and emotions.

Semantics. The study of the way words are used and the meanings they convey is called **semantics.** Misinterpretation of word meanings can play a large role in communication failure. When two people attribute different meanings to the

SEMANTICS
The study of the way words are used and the meanings they convey.

same words but don't realize it, a barrier exists. Consider what happened when a sales representative phoned in a special order to the company's shipping department. He asked that it be shipped "as soon as possible," expecting these words to ensure that the order was given top priority. Five days later, the sales rep got a call from the irate customer wanting to know when the order would be delivered. Upon checking with the shipping department, the sales rep found that the order was being shipped that day. After some shouting, the sales rep realized that in the shipping department, "as soon as possible" meant that the request did *not* need to be given top priority.

Problems caused by semantics are compounded when people who speak different languages attempt to communicate. As described in the Global Awareness Competency feature, imprecise translations cause many blunders in international business dealings.

To avoid such blunders, companies should routinely have messages translated back to the original language to ensure the accuracy of the original translation—a process called *backtranslation*. If the original message and the backtranslated version agree, the translated version probably will not have unexpected meanings. Even backtranslation is not foolproof, however, because the meanings of words often depend on the context in which they are used—especially in high-context cultures (e.g., Arabic, Japanese, and Chinese). In high-context cultures, communication involves sending and receiving many subtle cues. Nonverbal cues, intonation subtleties, and inferences are all essential aspects of communication. The Japanese often talk around a point without ever stating it directly. From their perspective, it is the responsibility of the listener to discern the message from the context. German, Scandinavian, and Anglo cultures are low-context cultures that place more emphasis on the precise meanings of words and terms.

EMOTION

A subjective reaction or feeling.

Emotions. An *emotion* is a subjective reaction or feeling. Remembering experiences, an individual recalls not only events but also the feelings that accompanied them. Thus when people communicate, they convey emotions as well as facts and opinions. The sender's feelings influence encoding of the message and may or may not be apparent to the receiver. The receiver's feelings affect decoding of the message and the nature of the response.

Misunderstandings owing to differences in what arouses people's emotions often accompany cross-cultural communications. In Japan, for example, feelings of embarrassment and shame are more easily aroused during social interactions than they are in Western cultures. Furthermore, these emotions aren't easily detected by people not socialized in the Japanese culture. Consequently, Westerners are likely to create situations that cause their Japanese counterparts to feel embarrassment and shame without realizing it, and thus seem insensitive.

Although there are many other cultural differences in how people experience and express emotions, there are also many similarities. Rather than being barriers to communication, these similarities aid communication. In particular, the antecedents of some emotions—anger, happiness, disgust, fear, sadness, and surprise—seem to be similar in most cultures, as are the facial expressions that accompany the emotions.[30] These similarities mean that nonverbal cues are less likely to be misinterpreted when emotions are involved.

Gender-based differences in emotions and the misunderstandings that result may explain much of the confusion that employees experience with respect to the issue of sexual harassment. As described in the Self-Management Competency account, organizations can ensure that employees understand what constitutes harassment and help prevent it through training and development programs. But ultimately, employees themselves must take responsibility for ensuring the integrity of their communication.

Lost in the Translation

The largest number of blunders in advertising promotions in foreign countries are caused by faulty translation. Slang terms, idioms, and local dialects have all contributed to the many marketing mishaps that have occurred as organizations expanded into global markets. Here are some examples that illustrate how small language differences create big advertising blunders.

- Exxon's original Japanese brand was Esso, which means stalled car when pronounced phonetically in Japanese. Discovering this problem, Exxon chose Enco as a replacement, not realizing that it referred to a sewage disposal truck.

- When Budweiser tried to translate it's slogan, King of Beer, into Spanish it discovered that beer (cerveza) is a noun of the feminine gender, leaving them with Queen of Beer as a slogan.
- In France, Colgate-Palmolive introduced a toothpaste called Cue, not realizing this is a pornographic word in French.
- Also in France, a mistranslation of the U.S. film *City Slicker* resulted in a French title that meant Life, Love, and Cows.
- When the Japanese introduced a coffee creamer called Creap, they were disappointed by slow sales.[31]

OVERCOMING BARRIERS

People *can* overcome barriers to effective communication. They must first be aware that barriers exist and can cause serious organizational problems. Then they must be willing to invest the effort and time necessary to overcome the barriers. Several ways of overcoming barriers to communication are presented in Table 16.3.[32]

Regulate the Flow of Information. If you receive too much information you will suffer from information overload. How much information is too much varies from one person to the next, and may even be different for today's X-generation and baby-boomers. The X-generation has grown up in an environment dominated by the media. Homework was often completed sitting in front of a television and/or while listening to music on a Walkman. MTV and video games that may constitute information overload by members of previous generations are normal for the current generation. Some observers believe that these differences in experiences have significantly changed the speed with which people can process information and the amount of information that they can process simultaneously.[33]

Table 16.3	*Overcoming Barriers to Communication*

- Regulate the flow of information.
- Encourage feedback.
- Simplify the language used in the message.
- Listen actively.
- Restrain negative emotions.
- Use nonverbal cues.
- Use the grapevine and informal networks.

SELF-MANAGEMENT COMPETENCY
A Harassment-Free Workplace

Many organizations didn't begin to consider sexual harassment to be a significant problem until Anita Hill testified against Supreme Court Justice Clarence Thomas during his Senate confirmation hearings. But by then, Delaware-based E.I. du Pont de Nemours (Du Pont) had already been battling sexual harassment for several years as part of its efforts to improve the company. It didn't set out to be on the cutting edge of this issue; it was just trying to do what was right for Du Pont. Nevertheless, its program won the 1997 *Workforce* magazine Optimas Award for *Vision.* Called "A Matter of Respect," the program's centerpiece is its sexual harassment workshops. Gender-balanced groups of twenty to twenty-five employees view and discuss a variety of workplace incidents that involve communications with various possible interpretations. The workshops are given in Japan, China, Mexico, Puerto Rico, and throughout Europe and the United States, with each country adapting the specific material to fit the local cultural context. More than 65 percent of Du Pont's workforce have attended the workshops.

The following vignettes are taken from videos that employees watch and

discuss. Key questions for them to consider are whether the vignette represents sexual harassment and how they would have handled the situation.

- A Du Pont employee is dining with a customer. He proposes signing the final contract in his hotel room.
- A female employee is waiting for her male counterpart to give her instructions on a lab procedure. Instead, he comments on how good she smells and comments that his wife wouldn't want the two of them to go together on a business trip. When she tries to change the subject, he tells her how smart and pretty she is.
- A female employee appears to proposition a male employee.
- While considering whether to give a woman a particular assignment, two male managers discuss her looks and her divorce.

Janet Staats, who serves as one of the discussion facilitators, says that employees struggle to draw conclusions, going back and forth in their opinions. For one employee, the situation may definitely be viewed as harassment, but for another it isn't. By exposing employees to people's differing perspectives, the company seeks to make everyone more sensitive to

some of the emotional consequences that their actions can have on other people.

The workshops sometimes stimulate memories of previous incidents of harassment, and for a few participants they confirm that uncomfortable experiences they are having currently need not be tolerated. Such employees often need someone to talk to. With that in mind, DuPont has trained more than 100 facilitators in how to listen, how to talk to worried employees, how to guide employees toward professional help, and how to conduct the early stages of the investigative process that is followed when a formal complaint is made.[34]

Regardless of how much information is needed to create feelings of overload in individuals, every organization is capable of producing that volume of information and more. Therefore you should set up a system that identifies priority messages for immediate attention. One way of doing so is to ask others to bring you information only when significant deviations from goals and plans occur (known as *exception reporting*). When everything is going as planned, you don't need a report. And if you want to empower your subordinates, let them know that they don't need to send you a copy of all those e-mail messages.

Encourage Feedback. You should follow up to determine whether important messages have been understood. Feedback lets you know whether the other person understands the message accurately. Feedback doesn't have to be verbal; in fact, actions often speak louder than words. The sales manager who describes desired changes in the monthly sales planning report receives feedback from the report itself when it is turned in. If it contains the proper changes, the manager knows that the message was received and understood. Similarly, when you talk to a group of people, look for nonverbal feedback that will tell you whether you are getting through to them.

Simplify the Language of the Message. Because language can be a barrier, you should choose words that others will understand. Your sentences should be concise, and you should avoid jargon that others won't understand or that may be misleading. In general, understanding is improved by simplifying the language used—consistent, of course, with the nature of your intended audience.

Listen Actively. You need to become a good listener as well as a good message sender. Recently, several organizations have developed training programs to improve employee listening. Such programs often emphasize that listening is an active process in which listeners and speakers share equal responsibility for successful communication. The following are some characteristics of active listeners.[35]

- **Appeciative:** listens in a relaxed manner, seeking enjoyment or inspiration.

- **Empathic:** listens without judging, is supportive of speaker, and learns from the experiences of others.

- **Comprehensive:** listens to organize and make sense of information by understanding relationships among ideas.

- **Discerning:** listens to get complete information, understand main message, and determine important details.

- **Evaluative:** listens in order to make a decision based on the information provided.

Restrain Negative Emotions. Like everyone else, you convey emotions when communicating, but negative emotions can distort the content of the message. When emotionally upset, you are more likely than at other times to phrase the message poorly. When emotionally upset, both manager and subordinate are likely to misinterpret a message. The simplest answer in such a situation is to call a halt until the people involved can restrain their emotions.

Use Nonverbal Cues. You should use nonverbal cues to emphasize points and express feelings. Recall the methods of nonverbal communication that we've presented. You need to be sure that your actions reinforce your words so that they don't send mixed messages.

Use the Grapevine. As a manager, you couldn't get rid of the grapevine in an organization even if you tried, so you should use it to send information rapidly, test reactions before announcing a final decision, and obtain valuable feedback. Also, the grapevine frequently carries destructive rumors, reducing employee morale and organizational effectiveness. By being "plugged into" the grapevine, you can partially counteract this negative effect by being sure that relevant, accurate, meaningful, and timely information gets to others.

GUIDELINES FOR EFFECTIVE COMMUNICATION

4

STATE THE GUIDELINES FOR EFFECTIVE COMMUNICATION

To be an effective communicator, you must understand not only the process of communication depicted earlier in Figure 16.1, but also the guidelines for effective communication. These guidelines, presented throughout the chapter, are summarized in the following list. We have expressed them in terms of the American Management Association's eight guidelines that you can use to improve your communication skills.[36]

- **Clarify your ideas before communicating.** Analyze the topic or problem to clarify it in your mind before sending a message. Communication often is ineffective because the message is inadequately planned. Part of good message planning is considering the goals and attitudes of those who will receive the message.

- **Examine the true purpose of the communication.** Before you send a message, ask yourself what you really want to accomplish with it. Decide whether you want to obtain information, convey a decision, or persuade someone to take action.

- **Consider the setting in which the communication will take place.** You convey meanings and intent by more than words alone. Trying to communicate with a person in another location is more difficult than doing so face-to-face.

- **Consult with others, when appropriate, in planning communications.** Encourage the participation of those who will be affected by the message. They can often provide a viewpoint that you might not have considered.

- **Be mindful of the nonverbal messages you send.** Tone of voice, facial expression, eye contact, personal appearance, and physical surroundings all influence the communication process. The receiver considers both the words and the nonverbal cues that make up your message.

- **Take the opportunity to convey something helpful to the receiver.** Considering the other person's interests and needs often presents opportunities to the sender. You can make your message clearer by imagining yourself in the other's position. Effective communicators really try to understand the message from the listener's point of view.

- **Follow up the communication.** Your best efforts at communication can be wasted unless you succeed in getting your message across. You should follow up and ask for feedback to find out whether you succeeded. You can't assume that the receiver understands; feedback in some form is necessary.

- **Be sure that your actions support your communication.** The most effective communication is not in what you say but in what you do. Actions do speak louder than words.

CHAPTER SUMMARY

Effective communication is essential to many aspects of human endeavor, including life in organizations. For managers, communication competency is the foundation upon which managerial effectiveness is built. Through communication, managers gather and interpret information that they then use to set a strategic direction. Strategic decisions, in turn, must be communicated throughout the organization, where they are used to guide planning and teamwork activities. In cross-cultural situations, the global awareness competency supports effective communication.

1. DEFINE THE MAIN ELEMENTS OF THE COMMUNICATION PROCESS.

The communication process comprises six elements: the sender (encoder), the receiver (decoder), the message, channels, feedback, and perception. Of the many possible forms of nonverbal communication, managers should be particularly aware of—and able to use effectively—space, physical appearance, and body language. Channels of communication are both formal and informal. Formal channels are downward, upward, and horizontal. Managers most frequently use downward channels to send messages to the various levels of the organization. Upward channels allow employee participation in decision making and provide feedback to management. Horizontal channels are used among peers in different departments and are especially important in network organizations. Informal channels—the grapevine and network groups—often are as important as formal channels of communication. Managers can never eliminate the grapevine and thus should learn to use it to send messages and receive feedback.

2. **DESCRIBE THE IMPORTANCE OF INFORMATION TECHNOLOGY IN THE COMMUNICATION PROCESS.**

Information technology increases the speed and convenience of communication and information transfer. E-mail, the Internet, and teleconferencing are three types of information technology that affect the communication process in organizations. Although information technology often makes communication eas-

ier, it can lead to information overload, lower quality communication, and deteriorating social relationships.

3. **DEFINE BARRIERS TO COMMUNICATION AND DESCRIBE WAYS TO OVERCOME THEM.**

Barriers to communication hinder the sending and receiving of messages by distorting or even blocking intended meanings. Barriers can be either organizational or individual. Organizational barriers may result from the design of the organization itself, from differences in social status, from the jargon that often grows up around highly specialized tasks, and from differing goals. Individual barriers may result from conflicting assumptions on the part of the sender and receiver, from misinterpretation of meaning, and from misunderstanding of emotional reactions.

4. **STATE THE GUIDELINES FOR EFFECTIVE COMMUNICATION.**

Guidelines for effective communication include clarifying your ideas, examining your purpose in communicating, considering the setting, consulting with others, being mindful of nonverbal messages, taking the opportunity to convey something helpful to the receiver, following up, and being sure that your actions support your communication.

QUESTIONS FOR DISCUSSION

1. What are the three most commonly used information channels in organizations? When is each channel most effective?

2. What are some of the communication problems that arise in doing business in a foreign country?

3. What are the primary barriers to communication and how can individuals . . . overcome them?

4. Why do communication difficulties arise in organizations?

5. The world is a busy and confusing place, and people are constantly bombarded by multiple messages. How do people simplify these messages in order to handle the confusion?

6. Many organizational change efforts involve redesigning jobs to include more teamwork. How does a change from individual jobs to team-based jobs affect communication in an organization?

7. Open office designs are becoming increasingly popular in organizations. Describe the pros and cons of open office designs for communication processes.

8. Besides taking language lessons, what other activities could you participate in to improve the cross-cultural aspects of your communication competency? What benefits would be associated with improving this competency?

EXERCISES TO DEVELOP YOUR MANAGERIAL COMPETENCIES

1. **Global Awareness Competency.** International business communications often are conducted in English. When executives of U.S. international companies write to their counterparts in other countries, they write in English 97 percent of the time. When they receive correspondence from other countries, it is in English 60 percent of the time. Although English is used regularly in international business, that doesn't relieve English-speaking managers of the need to word their international messages carefully. Communication experts Mary Ellen Guffey and Sondra Ostheimer offer the following tips for international correspondence.

   - Avoid all metaphors, cliches, jargon, idioms, and slang.

   - Be direct and straightforward in low-context cultures such as the United States, Scandinavia, Switzerland and Germany, but be less direct in high-context cultures such as Japan, Arabia, and Latin America.

   - Don't refer to seasons because they vary around the world. Instead state the month.

   - Avoid references to the weekend, dinner, and lunch time, as these terms can mean very different times in other countries.

   These writing tips and a wealth of other useful information can be found at

   www.westwords.com/guffey/students.html

   As assistant to Shiseido's Hisako Nagashima, you have been asked to prepare a memo that will be sent to several executives around the world who work in key jobs at major luxury department stores and women's magazines. The purpose of the memo is to invite these executives to attend an exclusive event at Shiseido's Les Salons du Palais Royal Shiseido, the company's world-class perfumery in Paris. Dress for the event is formal evening wear. The major activity will be to introduce the company's newest fragrances. You don't know whether the executives you are contacting will be able to attend this event, which is scheduled to coincide with a major fashion show. Ms. Nagashima wants only very high-level executives to attend the event. She isn't interested in having these executives send representatives from lower levels in their organizations. Prepare one version of a memo that would be suitable for sending to executives in Germany and a second version that would be suitable for sending to executives in Brazil. To learn more about Shiseido's products and their perfumery, visit the company's home page at

   www.shiseido.com

2. **Communication Competency.** Public speaking is a type of formal communication that many people find intimidating. Yet many organizations expect employees to be able to make formal presentations as part of their normal jobs. One good way to develop your formal speaking competency is to take a course. Another way is to join an organization such as Toastmasters International. This global organization includes 8,000 local clubs in more than fifty countries. How could joining this organization help you improve the formal aspect of your communication competency? Describe other benefits of participating in Toastmasters International. Begin your investigation by visiting the organization's home page at

   www.toastmasters.org

3. **Planning and Administration Competency.** Shearman & Sterling is an international law firm headquartered in New York City, with offices in Abu Dhabi, Beijing, Dusseldorf, Tokyo, Paris, and elsewhere. Like other law firms, much of the work that must be done is carried out by entry-level professionals, including student interns and associates who have just completed law school. The firm is dependent on these sources of labor and is eager to attract the best and the brightest. Visit the Web site for Shearman & Sterling to investigate the professional opportunities described (e.g., summer programs, continuing education, and career development). Analyze the firm's formal communication, using the five principles of encoding: relevancy, simplicity, organization, repetition, and focus. What nonverbal messages are conveyed through the Web site? Describe the specific cues that you react to as part of the nonverbal message. Prepare a one-page memo to Shearman & Sterling describing the strengths and weaknesses of its approach to communicating via the World Wide Web. How could improving its Web site contribute to its human resource planning and staffing activities? The home page for Shearman & Sterling is at

   www.shearman.com/opportunities/opportunities

4. **Communication Competency.** Use the following questionnaire to assess your communication habits in informal communication settings. What are the implications of your scores? If you think that you may need to improve your communication competency, use the Internet to investigate the types of communication training services available in your locality.

ASSESSING INFORMAL COMMUNICATION COMPETENCY

Informal communication is especially important to working in teams. Think back to a specific work team that you belonged to, either in school or at a job. Respond to each statement by circling the response that best fits your skills, attitudes, and behaviors.

5 Strongly Agree

4 Slightly Agree

3 Not Sure

2 Slightly Disagree

1 Strongly Disagree

Statement	Rating				
1. I prefer to avoid conflicts by not discussing my opinions with people who have a different point of view.	1	2	3	4	5
2. I tend to talk more than others do.	1	2	3	4	5
3. If the other person seems not to understand me, I try to speak more slowly and more distinctly.	1	2	3	4	5
4. I tend to forget that some words have many meanings.	1	2	3	4	5
5. When I give feedback, I respond to the facts and keep the feelings out of it.	1	2	3	4	5
6. I am not embarrassed by periods of silence when I'm talking to someone.	1	2	3	4	5
7. I concentrate hard to avoid distracting nonverbal cues.	1	2	3	4	5
8. Listening and hearing are the same things.	1	2	3	4	5
9. I make sure that the person wants feedback before I give it.	1	2	3	4	5
10. I avoid saying "Good," "Go on," etc., while the other person is speaking.	1	2	3	4	5
11. I try to delay giving feedback so that I can have more time to think it through.	1	2	3	4	5
12. I enjoy using slang and quaint local expressions.	1	2	3	4	5
13. My feedback focuses on how the other person can use my ideas.	1	2	3	4	5
14. Body language is important for speakers, not listeners.	1	2	3	4	5
15. I use technical jargon only when talking to experts.	1	2	3	4	5
16. When someone is wrong, I make sure that she or he knows it.	1	2	3	4	5
17. I try to express my ideas in general, overall terms.	1	2	3	4	5
18. When I'm listening, I try not to be evaluative.	1	2	3	4	5

SCORING YOUR SURVEY

Transfer your numeric responses from the survey onto this scoring sheet, add the categories, and obtain the total. For instance, your Feedback score is the sum of your responses to statements 1, 4, 7, 10, 13, and 16.

	Feedback		**Listening**		**Flexibility**
1. _____		2. _____		3. _____
4. _____		5. _____		6. _____
7. _____		8. _____		9. _____
10. _____		11. _____		12. _____
13. _____		14. _____		15. _____
16. _____		17. _____		18. _____
Subotals _____		_____		_____
Total _____				

Place an X on each of the three category continuums to mark your subtotals.

Feedback   (High) _____ (Low)

Listening   (High) _____ (Low)

Flexibility   (High) _____ (Low)

                 30   25   20   15   10   5   0

Place an X on the overall continuum to mark your total score.

(High) _____ (Low)

   90   80   70   60   50   40   30   20   10   0

Develop an action plan that will help you improve in each area. Then describe this action plan to a friend and explain how you can use it to improve your communication competency. During your discussion, practice the guidelines for effective communication presented in the chapter.

REAL-TIME CASE ANALYSIS

SIEMENS BUSINESS COMMUNICATIONS SYSTEMS[37]

Siemens AG is one of the world's largest technology companies. Founded in Germany in 1847, it now has operations in 170 countries. Since its founding, Siemens has helped people around the world communicate with each other. Siemens installed the transatlantic cable between the United States and Europe in 1874. And Siemens provided the first commercial telegraph system, which included a 7,000-mile telegraph link between London and Calcutta. The company also introduced the world's first ISDN PBX into the European market, thereby greatly expanding the capacity for Internet communication worldwide.

Located in Santa Clara, California, is one of this firm's many business units—Siemens Business Communications. This business unit provides telecommunications systems to meet a variety of business goals. Its customers include organizations that want to improve their internal communications systems, increase customer satisfaction, or improve profitability. Siemens recognizes that communications systems are most effective when they meet an organization's specific needs.

To help customers judge the fit between their business needs and the products that Siemens sells, the company built an executive briefing center. The center was designed to promote effective communication between Siemens's representatives and customers. It features comfortable seating, an open layout, and all the communication technologies the company has to offer. According to President and CEO Karl Geng, "We have designed the Executive Briefing Center with the customer in mind. To maintain our reputation for excellence, we provide an avenue to jointly explore solutions that will drive a company's bottom line. Our company listens very carefully to its customers. As a result, we tailor each visit to the Executive Briefing Center to ensure that customers' business concerns are met and addressed."

One of the new communications products being demonstrated is a multimedia kiosk that can be used in retail establishments. It can process a credit card, access the company's database about the customer's buying preferences, issue discount coupons to the shopper, and handle a video call from the shopper to the retailer's centralized call center. Siemens believes that single purpose/single channel kiosks are a thing of the past. So does Brian Woolf, president of the Retail Strategy Center, who says: "It all boils down to one thing: Behavior follows rewards. The more rewards you put in kiosks, the more behavior occurs."

A new service offered allows a company to route the telephone calls that come into its centralized calling stations (e.g., the 800 numbers you call when you want to order something from a catalog or inquire about the status of your credit account). According to President Geng, the system compares caller criteria with the agent database and establishes a *virtual group* for every call. This virtual group is made up of the agents who are best suited to take specific types of calls. Calls are queued to the first and best agent of the virtual group. This system could, for example, automatically determine that a caller needs a French-speaking agent and then create a virtual group of agents who can speak French.

The executive briefing center is more than a facility for displaying the company's state-of-the-art products. It also facilitates the company's information gathering efforts. As products are demonstrated, Siemens's staff members pay careful attention to how customers respond and the concerns they express. This approach is central to the company's vision, which is "Complete Customer Satisfaction." Once you have purchased a product and have become a customer, you are invited to join a club of other users of Siemens Business Communications. The club, called NRUG, has evolved into an active group of customers that has its own president and executive board. Members of the NRUG executive board meet regularly with the Siemens Business Communications board to express their concerns and offer their opinions.

To learn more about Siemens Business Communication Systems, visit the company's home page at

www.siemensrolm.com

To learn more about Siemens AG, visit the company's home page at

www.siemens.com

To learn more about NRUG, visit the organization's home page at

www.nrug.org

QUESTIONS

1. Siemens Business Communications conducts recruiting interviews on many college and university campuses. You can check the schedule by visiting the company's Web site. The company also posts job openings on its Web site and accepts electronic résumés via the Internet. Explore the job openings listed currently. Choose four jobs and read about their requirements and duties. How important is communication competency for the four jobs?

2. Suppose that you were invited to interview for a job at this communications company. What would you do to prepare for the interview to ensure that you were perceived as an excellent communicator?

3. You were a hit! You got the job at Siemens Business Communications. Your first assignment is at the Executive Briefing Center, where you will meet customers from around the world in many different lines of businesses and interested in a broad range of products. Communicating with customers is what you will be doing 90 percent of the time. Make a list of communication "rules of thumb" that you can refer to as you begin this new job. The rules of thumb should include all aspects of communication.

4. Many of the products being developed by this company are intended to be used by businesses to "get closer to" their customers. New technologies allow retailers, for example, to build databases with detailed information about each customer (e.g., Does the customer speak French? Does the customer often call with some highly technical question? Is the customer a big spender?). Suppose that you call and that these databases are now being accessed by the customer service rep who handles your call. What are the advantages and disadvantages of the growing use of customer databases? Is it likely to improve or detract from the quality of communication that occurs between businesses and their customers? Consider this question from the perspective of both the customer and the business.

VIDEO CASE

BANK OF ALMA: IF MONEY TALKS, LISTENING PAYS

The Bank of Alma is a friendly neighbor in its community, listening to the interests and concerns of its customers. Its CEO and president, John McCormack, is aware that the bank is unable to change many of the factors affecting its operations (e.g., documents dictated by banking regulations). He also is aware that how the bank interacts with its customers is its greatest selling point. As a result, he encourages the bank's employees to make human interaction a cornerstone of its operations.

Many companies have headed *away* from the "high-touch" interaction with customers favored by the Bank of Alma. The banking industry, in fact, has led the adoption of automated customer service (e.g., in the use of automatic teller machines—ATMs). On the one hand, ATMs are a bargain: An ATM, at some $50,000 or so, is available twenty-four hours per day, never calls in sick, doesn't receive benefits, and gets depreciated on the books rather than drawing a pension. On the other hand, banks lose interaction with customers that could point them toward offering new services or providing feedback on customer satisfaction.

However, some banks are "listening" (e.g., sifting through mountains of demographic and other types of data) to identify prime customers and distinguish them from other customers. Credit card issuers have begun to drop customers who always pay the balance due on their bills on time because they can make a great deal more money by charging extremely high interest rates to those who carry balances forward. In some cases, banks have been accused of "red lining" (i.e., using demographic mapping) to discriminate systematically against groups that the law obligates them to serve.

Some companies have experimented with strategic partnerships to maintain close customer contact (e.g., moving their services to places their customers already frequent) and cut costs at the same time. Some police forces, for example, have instituted community policing efforts by placing beat officers in fast-food restaurants, where they can do their paperwork, be seen in the community, and become well known to citizens where they meet, eat, and socialize. Pacific Bell announced plans to close *all* its current customer service offices and move various functions, such as billing dispute resolution, into convenience stores.

The interface between customers and service providers is changing in many ways and blurring (as if spotting your phone service representative behind the deli counter isn't confusing enough!). In U.S. business today, there's a steady retreat from the previous generations' suit-and-tie uniform toward "casual days" or uniformly "business casual" working attire. However, moving to less formal attire may make for less comfortable interactions (in some businesses, employee disagreements over what constitutes "casual" have led to reimposition of a more severe dress code), and may be confusing to customers. Some customers will always expect their banker to look like a banker.

Ultimately, the Bank of Alma's strategy may be a good one. The homeowner who has a pleasant experience in securing a construction loan might consider the bank first when other needs arise (e.g., a home equity loan to pay for a child's college education or to launch a new business). Referrals to friends and neighbors—and to children—can maintain the bank as a partner in the community.

Bank of Alma's management, however, is likely to have to increasingly utilize its strategic action competency and rely on information technology to position the bank for continued success in the information age. Microsoft's Bill Gates has set his sights on banking and the transformation of traditional practices with PC-based resources and the Internet. Another industry titan, IBM, is promoting the Integrion Financial Network, a service network for the banking industry, as a counter to Microsoft's efforts.

ON THE WEB

The Bank of Alma isn't yet on the Web. Such banks will face increasing competitive pressures from banks and other financial institutions that are making use of the Internet. Home Financial Network (***www.homeatm.com/home***) is attempting to deliver a familiar, ATM-like interface through individual banks to Internet users. Customers who have become accustomed to the convenience of ATMs and are shopping more for price than the human touch may be lured to banks offering services in the comfort of the home.

The Integrion Financial Network is on the Web (***www.integrion.com***). This service eventually will include "traditional banking functions through remote channels plus new capabilities uniquely defined to accommodate electronic commerce transactions."

QUESTIONS

1. How might the Bank of Alma use information technology to advance its strategy of making interactions with customers friendly and personal?

2. How might a bank use the World Wide Web to "listen" to customers?

3. Why might a bank make cross-cultural awareness training a priority in employee development?

Case contributed by Ross Stapleton-Gray, President, TeleDiplomacy, Inc., a technology and policy consultancy, and Adjunct Professor in Georgetown University's Communication, Culture, and Technology program.

Chapter

17

Groups and Teams
in Organizations

LEARNING OBJECTIVES

AFTER STUDYING THIS CHAPTER, YOU SHOULD BE ABLE TO:

1. EXPLAIN THE IMPORTANCE OF GROUPS AND TEAMS.

2. DESCRIBE THE BASIC TYPES OF GROUPS AND WORK TEAMS FOUND IN ORGANIZATIONS.

3. DISCUSS THE MAJOR COMPONENTS OF A MODEL OF WORK TEAM FUNCTIONING.

4. DESCRIBE THE ROLE OF A WORK TEAM LEADER.

5. EXPLAIN HOW TWO KEY ASPECTS OF HUMAN RESOURCES MANAGEMENT SYSTEMS—TRAINING AND REWARDS—CAN SUPPORT WORK TEAM EFFECTIVENESS.

Outline

Jostens manufactures a variety of products, the most well-known being quality class rings. In 1990, Jostens' employees were producing sixteen rings per employee per day. After the entire facility switched to self-managing teams, the employees produced twenty-five rings per person per day. The entire process—from order receipt to shipping—was shortened from thirty calendar days to just ten calendar days from receipt of a work order to shipping of the finished product.

Like many other companies, reducing costs and responding more quickly to customers were key reasons for Jostens' organizing around teams. Jostens quickly recognized the power of teams. The company also

realized that, if teams could help it be more effective, teams could help customers be more effective too. Besides class rings, Jostens produces class yearbooks. Typically, a team of students and faculty volunteers develop the content and layout of a yearbook. Effective teams create attractive and interesting yearbooks, and they finish their tasks on time. High-quality, exciting yearbooks sell well and reflect well on Jostens. Unattractive, sloppy, or late yearbooks cut into Jostens' profits. By helping yearbook teams be more effective, Jostens improves its own image and profitability.

To help yearbook teams be more effective, Jostens provides extensive guidance to faculty advisors. Through its *Advisor & Staff* magazine and Web

site, Jostens shares what it knows about effective teamwork with its customers. Recent features have addressed topics such as how to staff a team, how to motivate and reward volunteer team members, how to run a brainstorming session, and how to keep the team on schedule. Jostens understands that providing such guidance is just as useful to yearbook teams as advice on cropping photos, laying out headlines, and selecting a cover.[1]

IMPORTANCE OF GROUPS AND TEAMS

1

EXPLAIN THE IMPORTANCE OF GROUPS AND TEAMS

Groups and teams are fundamental to human existence. Without at least one other person to support it, an infant could not survive. Without friendship groups, young children could not develop into emotionally healthy adults. Without help from others, a firefighter could never put out a raging forest fire and a surgeon could never successfully implant an artificial heart. Jostens is only one of many organizations that has switched to teams as a way to improve productivity. In a recent study of U.S. and Canadian companies, half the managers responding believed that improving teamwork processes to focus on customers was the strategic initiative with the greatest potential for ensuring their organizations' success.[2]

Automakers estimate that developing a new model requires as many as 7 million engineering hours. Even at companies known for their product development skills, such as Toyota and Honda, developing a new car requires as many as 1,000 engineers working in teams for three to five years. At Microsoft, creating a new version of Windows requires writing more than 10 million lines of code. Producing that amount of code takes 400–500 people working together for approximately three years.

Figuring out how to divide up the mountains of work involved in such complex projects is the first challenge that management must meet. The second challenge is to integrate the efforts of the individuals working on the projects. At Microsoft, management meets these challenges by organizing employees into numerous work teams and then carefully synchronizing their activities. Each team has a clear and limited product vision and time limit for completing its work. Teams working on

Table 17.1 *Why Organizations Use Work Teams*

The Most Common Reasons for Having Employees Work in Teams

- Improve on-time delivery of results
- Improve customer relations
- Facilitate innovation in products and services
- Essential for management and employee development and career growth
- Reinforce or expand informal networks in the organization
- Improve employees' understanding of the business
- Reduce costs and improve efficiency
- Quality improvement
- Increase employee ownership, commitment, and motivation

the same project are in constant communication with each other. Almost all major development efforts take place at Microsoft headquarters, which makes face-to-face communication and problem solving easy.[3] At Microsoft, teams are essential to innovation and product development. At Jostens, manufacturing teams reduce production costs and ensure on-time delivery of products.

According to a survey conducted by the Conference Board, innovation and on-time delivery were the two most common reasons for the increasing use of work teams. Table 17.1 lists several of the other reasons for organizing employees into work teams instead of having them work on small tasks that they can complete alone.[4]

The importance of teams is reflected in the amount of time that managers and others spend in team meetings. Many top managers report spending 50 percent or more of their time in team meetings; first-line managers and professionals may spend between 20 and 50 percent of their time in such meetings.[5] The good news about team meetings is how varied they are in purpose, style, length, format, and even technology. They range from quick huddles in someone's office to voice-mail exchanges to multiday planning retreats.

Signicast Corporation is an example of a company that adopted a team-based organizational design as a strategic move. The company was poised for continued growth, except that it needed more space in order to do so. When management decided to build new facilities, it also rethought the firm's strategy and the logic of its operations. As described in the following Strategic Action Competency feature, the design of the new facilities was based on utilization of work teams and reflected many of the principles of a learning organization.

The increasing popularity of team-based organizational structures (described in Chapter 11) reflects the belief that teamwork can achieve outcomes that could not be achieved by the same number of individuals working in isolation. But as many organizations are discovering, the payoff from teams isn't automatic. Although teams offer great potential for increased innovation, quality, and speed, that potential isn't always realized. Even when teams do fulfill their potential in these areas, team members and their organizations may experience unanticipated negative side effects, such as lingering unproductive conflicts and turnover.[6]

Signicast Creates a Team-Based Learning Organization

Headquartered in Milwaukee, Signicast Corporation is a manufacturer of castings. Using the blueprints supplied by customers such as Harley Davidson and John Deere, it manufactures precision metal parts. In 1992, top management decided to build a new facility, which would allow the company to grow. These executives decided not just to replicate the existing plant. Instead, they wanted to design the best facility in the world. To guide their decisions, they first investigated their customers' concerns arising from Signicast's history of long lead times, high costs, and unreliable delivery dates. To respond to these concerns, top management adopted speed, low cost, and flexibility as its strategic goals. Achieving these goals would require that production be switched from the batch process design of the old plant to an automated, continuous-flow process.

To take advantage of the employees' expertise, Signicast's executives involved them in designing the new facilities. A team of five executives would develop an idea and then ask employees to evaluate it and suggest revisions. The employees were volunteers from each department in the Milwaukee facility, and when asked for suggestions they had plenty to say. "Sometimes those meetings would go on for hours," recalled Robert Schuemann, a member of the executive team. "Sometimes there were even multiple meetings to discuss one item. Employees would come up with suggestions; we'd implement them, and bring them back [to employees] for confirmation." This approach was new to the company, so some learning was expected.

Rather than build one huge facility that could handle all the processes and products involved, the company decided to build small modules that could operate independently. The first module has been operating since 1993, and in 1998 the second module was under construction. In the first module, one supervisor oversees the entire plant, which is organized into two day teams and two night teams. Many of the plant's policies and procedures were adopted only after the teams had an opportunity to vote on them. Supporting the new team design are a new pay system that rewards employees for developing a variety of skills, extensive cross-training for technical skills, and a ten-week team-building course that is mandatory for team leaders and open to everyone else.[7]

TYPES OF GROUPS AND WORK TEAMS

2

DESCRIBE THE BASIC TYPES OF GROUPS AND WORK TEAMS FOUND IN ORGANIZATIONS

GROUP

Two or more individuals who come into personal and meaningful contact on a continuing basis.

INFORMAL GROUP

A small number of people who frequently participate in activities and share feelings for the purpose of meeting their mutual needs.

In everyday conversation, the terms *group* and *team* often are used interchangeably, but in this chapter we distinguish between the two. Here, *group* is the more general term, and *team* is a special type of group.

A **group** is two or more individuals who come into personal and meaningful contact on a continuing basis.[8] Five strangers who happen to be waiting on the street corner for a bus are not a group. Five employees who by chance happen to sit at the same lunch table in their company's cafeteria are not a group either. Although these two sets of people may have personal contact, the contact isn't likely to be highly meaningful and most likely is just a one-time event. Suppose, however, that the five strangers always meet at the same bus stop and ride to work together regularly. As their interactions become more meaningful and they develop expectations for each others' behavior, the five strangers are transformed into a group. Similarly, if the five employees begin to seek each other out and regularly eat together, they would become a group.

INFORMAL GROUPS

There are two types of groups within organizations: informal groups and work teams. An **informal group** consists of a small number of individuals—usually three to twelve—who frequently participate together in activities and share feelings for the purpose of meeting their mutual needs. They may support, oppose, or have no interest in organizational goals, rules, or higher authority. A social group is one of the most common types of informal groups, within or outside organizations. An organization's design often influences the development of informal groups. It does so by the physical layout of work space, departmental structure, and type of technology used. In many automobile plants, the use of rigid assembly-line technology along with autocratic managers often has resulted in employee dissatisfaction and the formation of hostile informal groups. These groups may attempt to slow production by agreeing to work at a reduced pace and taking time to socialize.[9] Alternatively, an organization may encourage development of more positive informal groups, such as those based on shared hobbies or other interests. The friendships formed in such informal groups are greatly valued by many employees and may result in their feeling a greater sense of loyalty toward their employer.

A **work team** consists of a small number of identifiable, interdependent employees who are held accountable for performing tasks that contribute to achieving an organization's goals.[10] Members of a work team have a shared goal, and they must interact with each other to achieve it. At Amerade Hess, for example, the goal of exploration and prospect teams is to locate oil reservoirs and evaluate their size and accessibility. The requirement that team members interact with each other differentiates work teams from organizations (see Chapter 1). Members of an organization share a goal but not all of them need to interact with each other in order to achieve that goal.

Generally, work teams range in size from two to about twenty members. Work teams have an identity, both to their members and to others in the organization. A very small organization could function as a work team, but most organizations have several work teams. Among the types of work teams found in organizations are functional, problem-solving, self-managing, and multidisciplinary teams.[11]

Work teams differ in many respects. Three key differences are the nature of their goals, their duration, and their membership. The differing *goals* of work teams may focus on product development, quality assurance, or problem solving. The *duration* of work teams may vary from short term (e.g., a four-month project team) to permanent (e.g., a staff planning team). Some teams, such as NASA's mission control, exist over an extended period of time. Other teams, such as one comprising lawyers, investment bankers, and other specialists to help a company go public, have relatively short lives. The *membership* of work teams may be functional (employees in the same department), multidisciplinary (employees from various functions), or even cross-organizational (employees working with suppliers and customers). To illustrate these differences, let's consider four of the most common types of work teams: functional, problem-solving, multidisciplinary, and self-managing.

FUNCTIONAL WORK TEAMS

A *functional work team* includes members from a single department who jointly consider issues and solve problems common to their area of responsibility and expertise. For example, at ConAgra, a diversified international food company, a functional team could be the purchasing manager and the purchasing agents in the department. Their goals might include minimizing costs and ensuring that beef supplies are available to stores when needed. To achieve their goals, these work team members need to coordinate their activities constantly, sharing information on price changes and new products. At Next Door Food Stores, the audit department formed functional teams in order to improve their relationships with the customer—in this

---

WORK TEAM

A small number of identifiable, interdependent employees who are held accountable for performing tasks that contribute to the achievement of organizational goals.

FUNCTIONAL WORK TEAM

Members from a single department or unit who jointly consider issues and solve problems common to their area of responsibility and expertise.

case, the customers are store managers. Functional work teams formed for the purpose of completing their daily work, such as those at Jostens and Next Door Food Store, are quite stable, enduring for as long as the organization maintains its same basic structure. A functional work team brought together as a *task force* to look at a specific issue or problem would disband as soon as it had completed its specific assignment.

PROBLEM-SOLVING WORK TEAMS

PROBLEM-SOLVING WORK TEAM
Five to twenty employees from different areas of a department who consider how something can be done better.

A ***problem-solving work team*** usually consists of five to twenty employees from different areas of a department who consider how something can be done better. Such a team may meet one or two hours a week on a continuing basis to discuss ways to improve quality, safety, productivity, or morale. Or it might meet intensively during the course of a few weeks and then disband.

Sears CEO Arthur Martinez used temporary problem-solving teams to implement his turnaround strategy for the ailing retailer. As the company celebrated the 100th anniversary of its most famous product—the Sears catalog—it was struggling to stay alive. In 1995, the job of rescuing Sears was handed to a new CEO, Arthur Martinez. Within a year, Sears was making money again. But for Sears to continue to succeed, every employee needed to focus on continued innovation, shareholder return, and customer satisfaction. Martinez wanted the firm to meet world-class standards in these aspects of performance. To determine the levels of performance that Sears would have to achieve to qualify as world-class, Martinez organized several task forces, staffing them with senior executives, to find the answer. He explained his long-term vision for the company and assigned them the task of figuring out how it could be achieved. One task force built a model to explain shareholder return over a twenty-year period and determined what Sears needed to do to be in the top quartile of *Fortune 500* companies. Another task force studied several years of customer service surveys and formed eighty customer focus groups around the country to find out how customers viewed Sears and what they thought needed to be improved. A third task force, charged with addressing innovation, conducted research on the nature of organizational change and came up with a plan to generate a million suggestions from employees.[12]

Task forces such as those used by Sears' CEO are perhaps the most common type of problem-solving work team. Task forces often are used by organizations to help accomplish strategic reorientation, to help gather data about the external environment, and to help design approaches for implementing a new strategy.

QUALITY CIRCLE
A group of employees from the same work area, or who perform similar tasks, who voluntarily meet regularly to identify, analyze, and propose solutions to problems in the workplace.

Quality circles are another form of problem-solving work team. A ***quality circle*** (also called a TQM team) is a group of employees who meet regularly to identify, analyze, and propose solutions to various types of workplace problems. Meetings usually lasting an hour or so are held once every week or two during or after regular working hours. Unlike task forces, quality circles do not address just one problem and then disband. They are expected to look for and propose solutions to quality-related problems *continually*. Members often are given overtime pay if a quality circle meets after work. They normally receive eight or more hours of formal training in decision-making and team processes, which they apply in their meetings. Quality circles normally don't have the authority to implement their proposed solutions, which are presented to management for further consideration and action.[13]

Western Contract Furnishers provides furnishings and interior design services to both corporations and private individuals. At one of its annual retreats, management decided to reorganize according to the principles of TQM. Membership in the first TQM teams was drawn from specific functional areas, with no cross-representation.

The teams considered how to improve the compensation system, warehouse operations, the computer system, sales administration, and product installation. The success of these work teams eventually led the company to create multidisciplinary work teams to address companywide concerns.[14]

MULTIDISCIPLINARY WORK TEAMS

A ***multidisciplinary work team*** may consist of five to thirty employees from various functional areas and sometimes several organizational levels who collectively have specific goal-oriented tasks. These tasks may include designing and introducing process reforms and new technology, meeting with customers and suppliers to improve quality, developing new products, linking separate functions (marketing, finance, manufacturing, and human resources) to increase rate and amount of product innovation, and/or improving links among strategic and tactical decisions and plans. The use of such teams is spreading rapidly and crosses all types of organizational boundaries.[15]

A multidisciplinary work team may be permanent or temporary, depending on its goals and tasks. Some TQM teams have members from interrelated functions who meet regularly to improve continuously the product or process for which it is responsible. After Western Contract Furnishers completed its reorganization, it began relying on multidisciplinary TQM teams. When a team is needed, volunteers are solicited from each department. Once formed, the team sets a timeline, chooses a facilitator, researches the issue, and recommends a course of action to management. Almost everyone in the company has served on one or more of these teams in recent years.

Product development teams are another common type of multidisciplinary work team. A *product development team* exists for the period of time required to bring a product to market, which could vary from a couple of months to several years. As already noted, Microsoft is one of many companies using product development teams extensively. In the telecommunications and electronics industries, multidisciplinary R&D teams bring together experts with a variety of knowledge and backgrounds to generate ideas for new products and services. To ensure that the products appeal to customers, the work teams may include representatives from marketing and the eventual end-users.[16] Multidisciplinary work teams provide several important competitive advantages if they are properly formed and managed. Let's consider two of these potential advantages in more depth: speed and creativity.[17]

Speed is vital in product development and customer service at AT&T, GTE, MCI, and other telecommunication companies. In product development, multidisciplinary work teams reduce time by replacing serial development with parallel development. In the past, the development process involved completion by one function (e.g., basic research) of its task and then forwarding the item to the next function (e.g., prototyping), and so on until all the functions had completed their tasks in sequence. With parallel development, many tasks are done at the same time and are closely coordinated among the functions. This method cuts the amount of time spent in the development cycle, or what is often called *time to market*. When the European unit of Digital Equipment Company (DEC) of Maynard, Massachusetts, decided to guarantee delivery of its new P/VAX systems, it needed to design a completely new process for obtaining the necessary components from its plants in various countries, assembling these components, and delivering a product that met customers' specifications. To design and implement that new process, DEC created a multidisciplinary, multinational management work team that met regularly in different countries. Members were all from the same level in the organization. They worked as equals throughout the process, and no one in the team had formal authority to direct or discipline the others.[18]

In service-based organizations also, multidisciplinary customer service teams speed response time. When Trade Insurance Services reorganized into teams, it played up its expectations for speedier services, calling the new initiative *FAST*—for flexible account services teams. These work teams include policy underwriters, salespeople, and claims specialists who work together to serve each customer.[19]

Creativity is increased by bringing together people having a variety of experiences and expertise to address a common problem or task. Boeing decided to use a hierarchy of work teams in the design and development of its new 777 jet liner. This project involved 10,000 employees and 500 suppliers working in more than 200 multidisciplinary work teams. Each team was made up of people from engineering, manufacturing, finance, and other departments, depending on its task. At the top of the hierarchy was a management team of the five or six top managers from each discipline. It has the overall responsibility for the plane being built correctly and on time. Reporting to this management team is a large group of the fifty or so team leaders—half each from engineering and operations. They are set up in 25 to 30 two-person work teams and oversee the more than 200 operational multidisciplinary work teams that have responsibility for producing specific parts of the plane. These work teams typically include five to fifteen workers and include a wing team, a flap team, a tail team, and so on.[20]

SELF-MANAGING WORK TEAMS

A ***self-managing*** (or self-directed) ***work team*** normally consists of five to fifteen employees who work together daily to make an entire product or deliver an entire service. The members all may be from a single functional area, as at Next Door Food Store, but more often self-managing work teams are multidisciplinary, as illustrated in Figure 17.1. These teams often perform various managerial tasks, including scheduling their members' work and vacations, rotating job tasks and assignments among members, ordering materials, deciding on team leadership (which may rotate among members), and setting production goals. In other words, to a large extent, they decide both what they need to do and how to do it.[21]

In the United States, manufacturers have been rapidly adopting self-managing work teams during the past two decades. The DEC team described earlier is but one of many self-managing work teams in that company, with most of the others working on the shop floor. During the 1990s, self-managing work teams spread into the service sector. For example, Allstate, Metlife, and many other insurance companies have reorganized their employees into self-managing customer service teams that can handle all aspects of a customer's dealings with the company.[22]

Frequently, each member of a self-managing work team learns the multiple skills required by all the tasks performed by the team. The use of these teams fundamentally changes how work is organized, and the impact can be enormous. Self-managing work teams have raised productivity in some cases by 30 percent or more and have increased quality substantially. Typically, one or more managerial levels are eliminated with the introduction of such work teams, thereby creating a flatter organization. The result has been downsizing at many organizations, including the elimination of many middle management positions.[23]

Self-managing work teams composed of highly skilled members who are fully empowered to accomplish major tasks are sometimes called *high-performance teams*. The Tokyo String Quartet, the U.S. Navy Seals, and the Emergency Trauma team at Massachusetts General Hospital are examples of high-performance work teams.[24] Central to the effectiveness of high-performance work teams are members who submerge their individual egos and become totally committed to the team and its objectives.

SELF-MANAGING WORK TEAM

Five to fifteen employees who work together daily to make an entire product or deliver an entire service.

Figure 1 7 . 1 **Members of a Self-Managing Work Team**

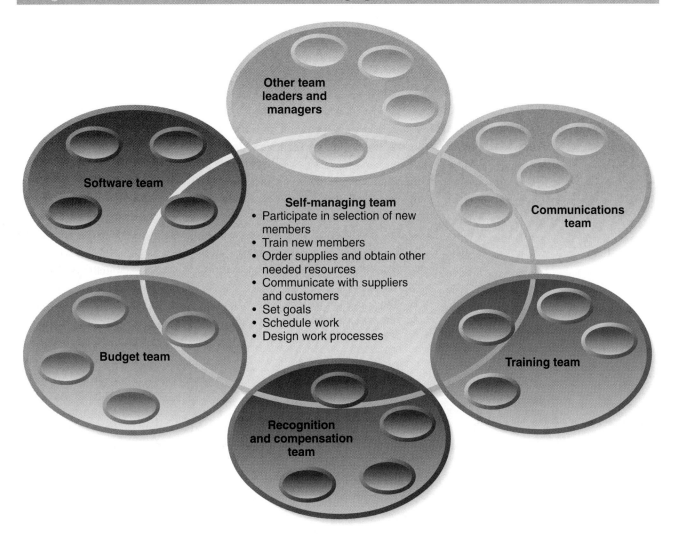

Other team leaders and managers

Software team

Self-managing team
- Participate in selection of new members
- Train new members
- Order supplies and obtain other needed resources
- Communicate with suppliers and customers
- Set goals
- Schedule work
- Design work processes

Communications team

Budget team

Training team

Recognition and compensation team

The U.S. Navy Seals are a highly trained underwater unit that often is called on to carry out top secret and highly dangerous military assignments. They have long been considered to be among the finest soldiers in military history. To weed out people who won't make a total commitment to the team, the Seals put potential team members through Hell Week, during which they swim endless miles in the cold Pacific waters, paddle rubber boats for hours in life-threatening conditions, perform grueling calisthenics, and get so little sleep that hallucinations are common after the first couple of days. This process weeds out about 30 percent of the trainees. As Rear Admiral Raymond Smith explains, "We are talking here about a seminal event, something that is the core of our vetting process." Hell Week starts after four weeks of basic training, and is followed by another nine weeks of weapons and explosives training and a three-week parachuting course. The rigorous training isn't intended primarily to identify the best athletes or musclemen. In fact, the fastest and strongest often quit first because they can't adapt to working in a setting that values the team's accomplishments more than an individual's outstanding abilities.[25]

SELECTING THE BEST TYPE OF WORK TEAM FOR THE JOB

Different types of work teams suit different purposes, so there is no one-best way to organize a work team.[26] Instead, an organization is likely to tailor different types of work teams to various needs and goals at various times. Texas Instruments Malaysia (TIM) produces about three million high-volume integrated circuits per day, many of which are shipped to companies in Japan. This operation employs 2,600 people, almost all Malaysian nationals. At TIM, the use of quality improvement teams started in the management and engineering offices. The first ones were multidisciplinary, consisting of managers and professionals from different departments. Following early successes of these work teams at the management and professional support levels, quality circles were created among lower-level employees. At TIM, quality is achieved through the combined efforts of a multidisciplinary quality steering team of high-level managers, a process management support team of middle managers and engineers who provide guidance and expertise, and self-managing work teams of employees who manufacture the circuits. Mohd Azmi says, "All quality activities here are aimed at trying to satisfy customers. Customers look at quality, cost, service, and so forth. But at TIM, people development shares equal priority with customer satisfaction. Why? If our people are not developed and trained to deliver, you cannot have customer satisfaction. Personnel development is the cause and customer satisfaction is the effect or result."[27]

A MODEL OF WORK TEAM FUNCTIONING

3

DISCUSS THE MAJOR COMPONENTS OF A MODEL OF WORK TEAM FUNCTIONING

Figure 17.2 illustrates our general model of work team functioning. The four key components are the external support system, team design, internal team processes, and criteria for assessing the team's effectiveness. These four components are highly interrelated and, considered together, they provide a full understanding of how well a particular work team functions. The model provides a way to diagnose work team problems, identifies key contingency factors that are likely to affect the work team's functioning, and provides guidance for managers interested in assessing whether a work team is achieving all of the various outcomes that are possible.[28]

Figure 17.2   A Model of Work Team Functioning

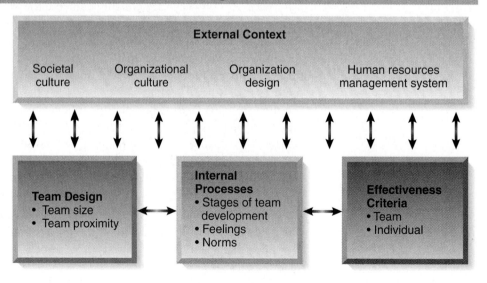

EXTERNAL SYSTEM

Organizational conditions and influences outside the team that exist before and after the team is formed, including societal and organizational culture, organization design, and the human resource management system.

The *external system* comprises outside organizational conditions and influences that exist before and after the work team is formed. These influences may include societal and organizational culture, organization design, and the human resources management system. The conditions encountered in the external system usually continue even after the work team ceases to function.

Culture. The societal culture in which the work team operates is one major aspect of the external system. For example, in collectivistic cultures, such as Korea, people are very comfortable working in teams. In contrast, forming effective work teams in individualistic cultures such as the United States is more of a challenge. Nevertheless, even in individualistic societies, work teams can function well if they are supported by the organizational culture. When individualistic employees are empowered through self-managing work teams, they gain more control and influence over their work. This result is consistent with their valuing of individualism—and thus may increase their satisfaction.[29] Organizational values that support participation by lower-level employees increases the likelihood that work team members will embrace organizational goals and authority relations, rather than attempt to undermine them.[30]

Organization Design. Organization design also directly influences the formation and functioning of work teams. As we described in Chapters 10 and 11, traditional organizations rely heavily on stable, functional work teams with a designated leader. In organizations striving to be more adaptive, temporary multidisciplinary work teams greatly increase the organizations' flexibility. A team may choose its own leader, or the leadership role may be shared among several members. In traditional organizations, employees seldom are members of more than one work team at a time. In innovative organizations, working on several different teams simultaneously or in rapid succession is typical.

Redesign efforts may impose the conditions of the work team's survival. For instance, a workforce reduction could create havoc for work teams and informal groups by removing many of their members. When employees believe that procedures for implementing a reduction in force or other change are unfair, informal groups may form to resist further attempts at organizational change. Alternatively, effective redesign efforts create feelings of trust and openness and the desire to create a more positive future (see Chapter 12).

Human Resources Management System. As we described in Chapter 13, organizations use a variety of HRM practices to foster employee performance, including long-term planning, recruitment and selection of employees, performance assessment, training and development, and reward systems. Until recently, these practices focused almost exclusively on managing the performance of individual employees, with little consideration of how they work when employees are organized into teams. However, organizations have quickly learned that practices designed to enhance individual performance can be detrimental to teamwork and recognized that new performance management systems were needed. For example, the characteristics needed in an employee who works in relative isolation are different from those needed in an employee who must work in a team environment. More technical skills—or at least a willingness to learn new skills—often are needed in self-managed work teams that share all aspects of performing a task. Nevertheless, the *importance* of technical abilities in making hiring decisions often is actually less in team-based organizations. The reason is that getting people to develop their technical skills is relatively easy. Much more difficult is changing people's basic personality traits or the levels of their managerial competencies, which develop slowly over time.[31] When Mercedes opened its new plant in Alabama, its recruiting ads attracted 45,000 applications for 1,500 jobs. Charlene Paige remembers feeling intimidated by the technical skills of some applicants. "A couple of guys were doing the [tire changing] test real fast," she recalled. "They were trying to be very impressive, taking shortcuts. I barely knew how to operate a hammer." Yet Charlene got the job, and the two guys were passed over because Mercedes was looking for people who listen when they are given instructions, follow instructions, and get along well with others.

Of the six managerial competencies, communication and teamwork will become even more important in organizations where employees work in teams rather than alone. For Boeing's self-managed work teams, however, planning and administration competency also is essential for scheduling and performance monitoring tasks. When teams are used to coordinate the activities of work units spread throughout the world, global awareness is increasingly important.[32] In addition to changing the criteria used to select new employees, team-based organizations may also change the basic procedures used to assign people to jobs. Some self-managed work teams have the authority to make their own hiring and firing decisions. In such cases, employees must be trained in how to make valid human resources decisions and adhere to legal constraints. Without an effective external support system to ensure that they are capable of making appropriate hiring decisions, self-managed work teams may be doomed from the start.

Two other key HRM practices that can support or hinder effective teamwork are the training given to teams and the organization's reward system. Training should develop behaviors that build an effective internal team process. Rewards should be linked to the assessment of the work team's accomplishments. We return to these two aspects of the external system after looking more closely at the other components in our model of effective work team functioning.

TEAM DESIGN

The design choices involved in creating a work team are numerous. We have already discussed the importance of choices concerning team duration, team goals, and team membership. Here we focus on two additional design choices: team size and team location.

Team Size. As the number of team members increases, changes occur in the team's internal decision-making processes. The optimal team size seems to be from five to twelve members, depending on the team's tasks. A good rule of thumb to remember is that understaffed teams tend to outperform overstaffed teams.[33] Members of larger teams generally have difficulty communicating directly with each other. Increasing team size also causes the following effects.

- Demands on leader time and attention are greater. The leader becomes more psychologically distant from the other team members. This problem is most serious in self-managing work teams, where more than one person can take on leader roles.

- The team's tolerance of direction from the leader is greater, and the team's decision making becomes more centralized.

- The team atmosphere is less friendly, the actions are less personal, more cliques form within the team, and, in general, team members are less satisfied.

- The team's rules and procedures become more formalized.[34]

For innovative decision making, the ideal work team size is probably between five and nine members.[35] If a work team has more than nine members, cliques might form. If larger teams are required for some reason, the use of subteams may be a solution to the problem of size. The purpose of subteams is to encourage all team members to share ideas when analyzing task-related problems, information, and alternative solutions. The full team can then meet to discuss subteam assessments and recommendations. In some instances, different subteams work on the same set of problems and then share and discuss their conclusions with the entire team. The leader of a large work team needs to be aware of the possibility that subteams, or cliques, may form on their own, each with its own leader and agenda. Although more resources are available to large teams, these resources can create a backlash that hurts overall team effectiveness if each unofficial subteam or clique lobbies strongly for its own position.

Team Proximity. *Team proximity* refers to the location of a team's members. Two aspects of proximity are relevant when designing a work team: proximity to other work teams and members of the organization, and team members' proximity to each other. When many teams are working together on a single project, as they do at Microsoft, teams benefit from being near others in the organization. Members from different teams can meet at the snack shop or water cooler to fill each other in on developments within their respective teams. Problem solving readily occurs as the need arises. For some work teams, however, performance is improved when the team is removed from the daily activities of the organization. Recall the discussion of corporate intrapreneurship in Chapter 5. Innovation and creativity are essential to successful intrapreneurship, but these attributes can be stifled by the bureaucracy and political intrigue often found in large corporations. Consequently, intrapreneurial teams at 3M and Black & Decker frequently set up skunk works operations in a remote location—such as an old warehouse or someone's garage. Isolated from outside distractions, the intrapreneurs are able to focus on the future without having to battle the status quo of the present.

Virtual Work Teams. Most people have a mental image of a team. Some envision a group of people sitting around a table discussing ideas. Others think of people engaged in demanding, yet exhilarating physical activities. Still others imagine a team of factory workers putting together a major component of an engine or a dance troupe performing. All of these images have one thing in common: The team members are in close proximity to each other. When asked to think of a team, few people imagine individuals working in offices that are scattered across the country or even around the world. However, as virtual work teams become more common, images of teams may begin to change.

A *virtual work team* is simply a work team that meets and does its tasks without everyone being physically present in the same place or even at the same time. Virtual work teams can be functional, problem-solving, multidisciplinary, or self-managing. In Chapter 16, we described how new communications technologies are being used by virtual work teams to extend the reach of organizations far beyond their traditional physical and cultural boundaries. In Chapter 11, we highlighted how VeriFone, a worldwide supplier of Transaction Automation software and communications systems, depends on virtual work teams for many types of work. The company has sixty quality improvement teams that address problems identified by employees who then agreed to lead virtual work teams to solve the problems.

Many of the principles of effective teamwork that apply to face-to-face team activities also apply to virtual work teams. However, other principles for designing and managing virtual work teams address the special nature of such teams.[36] As organizations expand into global consumer and labor markets, managing virtual work teams will be an increasingly important managerial responsibility. It is an aspect of global awareness competency that managers can develop by staying informed of developments in communications technology and in practices being adopted by the companies with the most experience in this aspect of organization design. Some of the current best practices for managing virtual work teams are described in the Global Awareness Competency feature.

INTERNAL PROCESSES

INTERNAL PROCESSES
The activities that enable a team to coordinate and integrate the efforts of team members, including the development of the team over time, personal feelings, and behavioral norms.

Work teams are effective only when their activities are coordinated and integrated.[37] Simply putting people together and assigning them a task doesn't ensure coordination and integration. *Internal processes* include the development of work team norms over time, personal feelings, and behaviors. These components are interrelated: A change in one may result in changes in others.

Observations of newly formed work teams reveal that coordination and integration tend to develop over a period of time. People with little experience working in teams often expect a team to be fully functioning immediately. Those who understand the stages of team development realize that team members usually need to spend some time together before the team can jell and begin to function most effectively—knowing this fact of team life reduces needless frustration. The establishment of clear norms and positive feelings precede effective task completion. Paying attention to norms and feelings is as important as understanding the task. Effective work team leaders help shape the development of effective internal processes.

Stages of Work Team Development. Social scientists have developed many different models to explain how teams develop.[38] Because many of these models overlap, we present only one of them, as outlined in Figure 17.3. The vertical axis indicates that work teams develop on a *continuum of maturity,* which ranges from low, or immature (e.g., inefficient and ineffective) to high, or mature (e.g., efficient and effective). The horizontal axis represents a *continuum of time together,* which ranges from start (e.g., the first team encounter) to end (e.g., the point at which the team adjourns).

No particular period of time is needed for a team to progress from one stage to the next. For example, a team whose members have effective interpersonal skills and high initial commitment to the team's goals could move rapidly to the performing stage. In contrast, an informal group may never make much progress and quickly disband voluntarily if its members aren't satisfied with it. A work team may be discontinued in a variety of ways. It may simply stop meeting and continue to exist only on paper. It may meet rarely and only engage in routine tasks. Its membership may change (e.g., adding, losing, or changing members), weakening its purpose or commitment. It may be terminated officially by the authority that created it. In general, however, the speed of team development seems to reflect the team's deadlines. Work teams develop slowly at first. As deadlines approach, team members feel more pressure to perform and often respond by resolving or setting aside personal differences in order to complete the task.

Figure 17.3 also shows the possibility of a team ending at each stage or recycling to a previous stage. For example, a mature work team could lose the majority of its members in a short period of time to promotions, retirements, and/or rotation of membership. With so many new members, the team may recycle to an earlier stage of development. The stages identified represent general tendencies, and teams may develop by going through repeated cycles rather than linearly, as

Companies such as VeriFone, Price Waterhouse, and Whirlpool are among a growing number of organizations that face challenges that can best be met by drawing on the ideas and knowledge of people who happen to live all over the world. In the past, face-to-face meetings were the only feasible way to bring such talent to bear on a project or problem. But today, people who are geographically dispersed can be readily formed into a team that will work together for as long as needed. Such teams are more likely to function effectively if they follow some simple guidelines:[39]

- *The following guidelines apply to all virtual work teams, regardless of whether they will work together for a short or long period of time.*

  1. Whenever possible, use a variety of communication technologies. Software designed especially for electronic meetings can be a good way to supplement video or telephone conference calls. Software that facilitates language translations can make written communication easier for team members.

  2. Pay attention to the quality of the communication transmissions. Low-quality speaker phones are frustrating and demotivating for team members, especially when they are listening to someone speaking with a strong accent. Video images should be clear and large enough to reveal subtle expressions and body language. If poor-quality equipment makes interaction unpleasant, the team's final product will suffer.

  3. Keep the team as small as possible—preferably no more than seven or eight people. To the extent possible, take similarities and differences in time zones into account when assembling the team.

  4. Encourage the team members to discuss cultural differences. These differences usually become apparent quickly when people meet face to face. Cultural differences may be less salient during electronic meetings, but they are no less important.

  5. Be sure that someone is responsible for facilitating the communication process. A good facilitator doesn't allow participants to lapse into becoming passive observers. A facilitator also may occasionally contact participants individually to learn how they are reacting to the experience of working as part of a virtual team and to be sure they feel that their opinions are being heard.

  6. Encourage team members to interact one on one, without feeling obligated to copy every e-mail message to the entire team. This approach can help prevent misunderstandings from needlessly escalating into crises.

  7. Train team members to match their choice of technology to the task. Fax, e-mail, and a company's intranet work well for disseminating information. Conference calls and video conferencing are more appropriate for holding important discussions and making major decisions.

- *For virtual teams that will be working together for several months or years, a few additional principles should be followed, within time and budget constraints.*

  1. Hold an initial face-to-face meeting to discuss the team's purpose and clarify the roles and responsibilities of each team member. Doing so will help the team members develop trust and social bonds more quickly.

  2. Whenever possible, individual team members should visit others, even if the entire team can't be assembled.

  3. Schedule periodic face-to-face meetings to refresh connections and minimize "out-of-site, out-of-mind" attitudes.

Figure 17.3   **The Development of Work Teams**

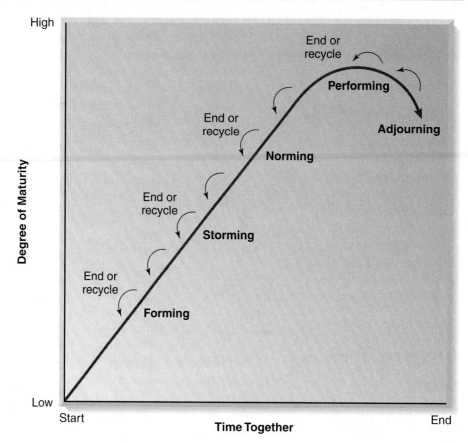

Source: Adapted and modified from B. W. Tuckman and M. A. C. Jensen. Stages of small-group development revisited. *Group and Organization Studies,* 2, 1977, pp. 419–442; and B. W. Tuckman. Developmental sequence in small groups. *Psychological Bulletin,* 63, 1965, pp. 384–389.

shown. Also, each stage simply reveals the *primary* issues facing team members. Behaviors from other stages may occur at times within each stage.[40] Let's now examine each stage of work team development.

During the *forming stage,* a work team focuses on orientation to its goals and procedures. The amount of information available and the manner in which it is presented are crucial to work team development. Most members may be anxious about what the team and they, as individual members, are supposed to do. In the audit department at Next Door Food Store, team members initially were concerned that some members might dominate team discussions and that others would feel intimidated and not participate. In newly formed teams, task relationships often are guarded, cautious, and noncommittal. Understanding leadership roles and getting acquainted with other team members facilitate development.[41] At Next Door Food Store, training and team building experiences helped the audit team move to the next stage of development.

The *storming stage* begins when competitive or strained behaviors emerge. Initially, the storming process may involve resistance and impatience with the lack of progress. A few dominant members may begin to force an agenda without regard for the needs of other team members. Team members may challenge the leader, or they may isolate themselves from team discussion. If conflict spreads, frustration, anger, and defensive behavior (especially the self-serving "look out for yourself"

FORMING STAGE

The earliest stage of team development, at which the work team focuses on orientation to its goals and procedures.

STORMING STAGE

The stage of team development that begins when competitive or strained behaviors emerge and may involve resistance and impatience with the lack of progress.

kind) may appear. Team members might think: Our problem is that we don't want to resolve our conflicts. We thrive on them. It may be counterproductive, but conflict seems to be a way of life for now.

If conflict is suppressed and not permitted to occur, resentment and bitterness may result, which in turn can lead to apathy or abandonment. Although conflict resolution often is the goal of work teams during the storming stage, conflict management generally is what is achieved. In fact, conflict management is a more appropriate goal because maintaining conflict at a manageable level is a desirable way to encourage a work team's growth and development.

In the **norming stage,** team members become increasingly positive about the team as a whole, the other members as individuals, and what the team is doing. At the beginning of the norming stage, the dominant view might be: We are in this together, like it or not. Let's make the most of it. Thus the team members may begin to develop a sense of belonging and commitment. Task-related and role behaviors of members increasingly are resolved through cooperation, open communication, and the acceptance of mutual influence. The rules of behavior that are widely shared and enforced by the members of the work team develop. If the work team gets to the end of this stage, most members may like their involvement a great deal.

Sometimes, however, the work team focuses too much on "we-ness," harmony, and conformity. When that happens, team members may avoid task-related conflicts that need to be resolved to achieve optimal performance. That in turn may cause the quality and/or quantity of performance to slip.

Some work teams never reach their full potential, regardless of how long they exist. Nevertheless, by the **performing stage,** members usually have come to trust and accept each other. To accomplish tasks, diversity of viewpoints (rather than we-ness) is supported and encouraged. Members are willing to risk presenting "wild" ideas without fear of being put down by the team. Careful listening and giving accurate feedback to others focus team members on the team's tasks and reinforce a sense of clear and shared goals. Leadership within the team is flexible and may shift among members in terms of who is most capable of solving a particular problem. In terms of relationship behaviors, the team accepts the reality of differences and disagreements and works on them cooperatively and enthusiastically. The team tries to reach consensus on important issues and to avoid internal politics. The following characteristics lead to high levels of team performance.

- Members direct their energies toward the twin goals of getting things done (task behaviors) and building constructive interpersonal ties and processes (relationship behaviors).

- Members have adopted procedures for making decisions, including how to share leadership.

- Members have achieved trust and openness among themselves.

- Members have learned to receive help from and give help to one another.

- Members experience a sense of freedom to be themselves while feeling a sense of belonging with others.

- Members have learned to accept and deal with conflicts.

- Members know how to diagnose and improve their own functioning.[42]

The degree to which one or more of these characteristics is absent determines the extent to which teams are likely to be ineffective.

NORMING STAGE

The stage of team development at which team members become increasingly positive about the team as a whole, the other members as individuals, and what the team is doing. The rules of behavior that are widely shared and enforced by the members of the work team develop.

PERFORMING STAGE

The stage of team development by which members usually have come to trust and accept each other, members are willing to risk presenting "wild" ideas without fear of being put down, and giving accurate feedback to each other helps focus the team on its tasks and goals.

ADJOURNING STAGE
The stage of team development that involves terminating task behaviors and disengaging from relationships.

The ***adjourning stage*** involves terminating task behaviors and disengaging from relationships. This stage isn't always planned and may be rather abrupt. However, a planned team conclusion often involves recognition for participation and achievement and an opportunity for members to say personal good-byes. Adjournment of a work team charged with a particular task should be set for a specific time and have a recognizable ending point. However, many work teams (e.g., the executive committee of an organization's board of directors) are ongoing. As members turn over, some recycling through earlier stages rather than adjournment may occur. Staggered terms of appointment can minimize the amount of recycling required.

Throughout the stages of a work team's development, team members experience a variety of feelings. Next, we discuss these feelings in more detail.

FEELINGS
The emotions that reflect how team members feel about each other, including anger, happiness, trust, and distrust.

Feelings. *Feelings* reflect the emotional climate of a group. The four feelings most likely to influence work team effectiveness and productivity are the feelings of trust, openness, freedom, and interdependence. The more these feelings are present, the more likely the work team will be effective and the members will experience satisfaction.[43] These feelings probably are present in a formal or informal group to which you belong if you *agree* with the following statements.

- **Trust:** Members have confidence in each other.

- **Openness:** Members are really interested in what others have to say.

- **Freedom:** Members do what they do out of a sense of responsibility to the group, not because of a lot of pressure from others.

- **Interdependence:** Members coordinate and work together to achieve common goals.

COHESIVENESS
The strength of members' desires to remain in the group or team and their commitment to it.

The greater the degree to which the four feelings are present, the higher is the level of group cohesiveness. ***Cohesiveness*** is the strength of members' desires to remain in the group and their commitment to it. Cohesiveness can't be dictated by managers or other work team members. It is a reflection of the members' feelings toward one another and the team as a whole. A cohesive team can work effectively for or against organizational goals.[44] For example, a cohesive team with negative feelings toward the organization may promote performance standards that limit productivity and pressure individual members to conform to them. In contrast, a cohesive team with positive feelings toward the organization may support and reinforce high quality and productivity.

How people feel is one important aspect of working in a team but how people actually behave may be even more important. Let's now turn to a discussion of behavior patterns within work teams.

BEHAVIORAL NORMS
The informal rules of behavior that are widely shared and enforced by the members of a group.

Behavioral Norms. ***Behavioral norms*** are the informal rules of behavior that are widely shared and enforced by members of a work team. They set standards for members' behaviors under specific circumstances. Their main function is to regulate and standardize the behaviors viewed as important by team members.[45] Norms may specify how much members should do, how customers should be treated, the importance that should be assigned to quality, what members should wear, what kinds of jokes are acceptable, how members should feel about the organization, how they should deal with their managers, and so on.

A work team norm exists when three criteria have been met.[46] First, there is a standard of appropriate behavior for team members. For example, there may be a standard for the lower and upper limits of production for the team as a whole and for individual members. Second, members must generally agree on the standard.

That doesn't mean that all team members need to agree. But, if most members have widely varying opinions about how much work is enough, for example, the team doesn't have a productivity norm. Third, the members must be aware that the team supports the particular standard through a system of rewards and punishments—rewards for compliance and punishments for violations. For example, a member who produces more integrated circuit boards per day than the work team norm may get the silent treatment until he or she complies with that norm. Of course, someone who doesn't care about the work team and its sanctions may continue to violate the productivity norm.[47] In contrast, a team member could engage in *free riding* by not contributing fully to team performance but still sharing in team rewards despite making less effort than the others.[48] An example of free riding is the individual on a six-person team in class who contributes much less than the others in producing a term paper or case analysis, yet receives the same high grade as the others.

Most norms develop as the result of one or more of four factors.[49] Superiors or co-workers may make an *explicit statement* with respect to the rules of behavior to enable the work team to meet its goals. For example, management at Mobil Oil bans smoking (except in designated areas) at its refineries for safety reasons. If team leaders and members accept and help enforce this prohibition, it becomes a team norm as well as a formal rule of the organization. *Critical events* in a group's history may lead to the development of norms. Group members may view a whistle-blower with scorn, thus establishing a norm for what may and may not be communicated to higher levels of management and outsiders. The *first behaviors* in new work teams may emerge as norms, setting future expectations and standards. For example, the seating arrangement at a team's first meeting may lead to norms dictating where each team member is to sit. Even if the initial seating arrangements are changed, norms that developed early in the life of the team will continue to influence who talks to whom, how often, and who starts the conversation.

The carryover of norms from *past experiences* also influences the formation of norms in a new situation. Students and professors do not have to create new norms about acceptable classroom behavior as they go from class to class; they simply carry them over. Similarly, as explained later in this chapter, some organizations use formal training to develop organizationwide norms about how team members should behave. This training establishes companywide norms, which employees carry into each new work team they enter.

Norms govern both task-oriented behaviors and relationship behaviors.[50] Jostens now has dozens of self-managing work teams. Their interactions are likely to focus on task-oriented behaviors. For the work teams to be effective, however, important relationship behaviors also must be present: warmth, praise, and acceptance of others; encouragement of participation by all members; and resolution of team conflict and tension.[51] The student teams that develop the content for the yearbooks produced by Jostens also develop norms about both task-oriented and relationship behaviors. However, the volunteer student teams are likely to be affected more by relationship norms than task-oriented norms. Hence one objective of Jostens is to provide advice to faculty about how to help these teams develop appropriate task-oriented norms, which support task completion. By assigning tasks and setting goals, faculty advisors can partially influence the interactions that develop within the yearbook team.

Norms concerning how to handle conflicts within the team are especially important for teams that engage in a lot of problem solving and decision making. In some cultures, such as China, Malaysia, and Thailand, societal values support avoiding open conflict and instead striving for harmony and cohesiveness. In the more individualis-

FREE RIDING
Not contributing fully to group performance because the team member can share in group rewards despite making less effort than the others.

tic culture of the United States, people feel more comfortable when they are able to express their opinions and have their views taken seriously by other team members. At the same time, however, U.S. culture values friendly relationships among co-workers, so too much conflict feels uncomfortable.

A study revealed that, even among executive teams, norms concerning conflict differed greatly from one team to the next. About half the teams studied reported that they argued most of the time. In these teams, everyone felt free to voice opinions and share ideas. One executive described his team's pattern for handling conflict this way: "We scream a lot, then laugh, and then resolve the issues." In several other teams, however, there was little open conflict—in fact, some teams actually had too little conflict.[52] Social pressures to maintain friendships and avoid disagreements can lead to work team members agreeing to a decision based more on personal feelings than on facts and analysis.

When decision-making work teams are so cohesive that conflict is stifled, groupthink can develop. *Groupthink* is an agreement-at-any-cost mentality that results in ineffective work team decision making and may lead to poor solutions. The fundamental problem underlying groupthink is pressure on members to concede and accept what other members think. The likelihood of groupthink increases when

GROUPTHINK

An agreement-at-any-cost mentality that results in an ineffective team decision-making process and may lead to poor solutions.

- peer pressure to conform is great,

- a highly directive leader presses for a particular interpretation of the problem and course of action,

- the need to process a complex and unstructured issue under crisis conditions exists, and

- the group is isolated.[53]

Falling between the extremes of all-out warfare and groupthink are teams with norms that support productive controversy. *Productive controversy* occurs when team members value different points of view and seek to draw them out to facilitate creative problem solving. To ensure constructive controversy, work team members must establish ground rules to keep them focused on issues rather than people and defer decisions until various issues and ideas are explored. By framing decisions as collaborations aimed at achieving the best possible results and following procedures that equalize sharing of power and responsibility, team members can focus on their common goal and avoid becoming embroiled in battles of egos.[54]

PRODUCTIVE CONTROVERSY

Valuing different points of view and seeking to draw them out to facilitate creative problem solving.

When a team leader and individual team members learn how to manage the work team's internal processes, they improve the likelihood of the team being effective. A tool for assessing a work team's internal processes is presented in the following Teamwork Competency account. A team leader can use the Team Assessment Survey to pinpoint problems that the team needs to address. With a better understanding of specific problem areas, teams members can then be encouraged to develop their own approaches to addressing those problems.

EFFECTIVENESS CRITERIA

Some people believe that work teams are a waste of time and should be used only when the politics of the situation demand it. Such people probably have been members of work teams that scored low on most of the questions in the Team Assessment Survey. Others view work teams as superior to individual efforts and believe they should be used whenever possible. Perhaps they have been members of work teams that scored high on most of the questions in the Team Assessment Survey. The reality about work teams lies somewhere between these two extremes.

SELF-MANAGEMENT COMPETENCY
Team Assessment Survey

Instructions

This survey should be completed individually by each member of a team. Each person should indicate the extent to which he or she thinks the team exhibits the following characteristics and behaviors.

Questions	To a Very Small Extent		To Some Extent		To a Very Large Extent
1. Team members understand the range of backgrounds, skills, preferences, and perspectives in the team.	1	2	3	4	5
2. Team member differences and similarities have been effectively harnessed toward achieving team goals.	1	2	3	4	5
3. The team cannot integrate diverse viewpoints.	5	4	3	2	1
4. Members view themselves as a team, not as a collection of individuals with their own particular jobs to do (e.g., they work interdependently, have joint accountability, and are committed to joint goals).	1	2	3	4	5
5. Team members have articulated a clear set of goals.	1	2	3	4	5
6. The team's goals are not motivating to members.	5	4	3	2	1
7. Team members agree on what goals and objectives are important.	1	2	3	4	5
8. The team has an effective work structure. It understands what work needs to be done, when work needs to be completed, and who is responsible for what.	1	2	3	4	5
9. It is not clear what each person in the team is supposed to do.	5	4	3	2	1
10. Team members have devised effective timetables and deadlines.	1	2	3	4	5
11. Team members have a clear set of norms that cover most aspects of how to function.	1	2	3	4	5
12. Team members take arguments personally and get angry easily.	5	4	3	2	1
13. Every team member does his or her fair share of the work.	1	2	3	4	5
14. A few members do most of the work.	5	4	3	2	1
15. A few people shirk responsibility or hold the team back.	5	4	3	2	1
16. Team members are imaginative in thinking about new or better ways to perform team tasks.	1	2	3	4	5
17. All team members participate in decision making.	1	2	3	4	5
18. Team members have the resources, information, and support they need from people outside team boundaries.	1	2	3	4	5
19. Team meetings are well organized.	1	2	3	4	5
20. Team meetings are not productive.	5	4	3	2	1
21. Coordination among members is a problem. People seem not to know what to do and when to do it for smooth team functioning.	5	4	3	2	1
22. Team members express their feelings freely in the team.	1	2	3	4	5
23. Team members support each other.	1	2	3	4	5
24. Team members are not effective at decision making.	5	4	3	2	1

Scoring and Interpretation

After everyone in the team has completed the survey, the team leader should compute the team's average score for each question. For example, suppose that a team had four members and that they gave these responses to question 1: The first person circled 3, the second person circled 4, the third person circled 5, and the fourth person circled 4. Then the team's average for question 1 is: $(3 + 4 + 5 + 4)/4 = 4$.

After computing the average score for each question, the team leader should be sure to provide feedback to the team. Effective feedback involves acknowledging the things the team seems to be doing well (e.g., questions with an average of 4 or higher), and identifying the things that need to be improved immediately (e.g., questions with an average of 2 or lower). Questions with an average of between 2 and 4 represent areas that should become targets for eventual improvement, but these issues can be addressed after the more immediately pressing issues have been resolved.

After setting priorities for which areas need improvement, together the team leader and team members should agree on a schedule for making those improvements. At the end of that time, the leader should again ask team members to respond to the Team Assessment Survey. When results for the reassessment have been calculated, team members should assess whether they have made satisfactory progress in addressing the issues previously identified. If they find that they haven't, they should continue to make adjustments and reassessments, as needed.

EFFECTIVENESS CRITERIA
Measurements of the outcomes achieved by individual members and the team as a whole.

Figure 17.4 shows several effectiveness criteria for evaluating work teams. *Effectiveness criteria* measure the outcomes achieved by individual members and the team as a whole. A particular work team may be effective in some respects and ineffective in other respects. For example, a team may take longer than expected to make a decision. Thus, on speed and cost criteria, the team may seem ineffective. But the team's decision may be highly creative and make the team's primary customer feel very satisfied with the output. Thus, on creativity and customer satisfaction, the team would be viewed as effective. Similarly, individual members of the team may feel that their own work is slowed by having to get agreement from other team members before they proceed. But through such discussions, the individual develops a better understanding of other perspectives and gains new technical knowledge and skills. Whether the work team is viewed as effective overall depends on the relative importance of the various effectiveness criteria shown in Figure 17.4.[55]

WORK TEAM LEADERSHIP

4

DESCRIBE THE ROLE OF A WORK TEAM LEADER

Informal social groups tend to be leaderless, but work teams almost always have a designated leader. Sometimes the leader comes from a higher level in the organizational hierarchy than the other work team members; at other times the leader is simply designated from among a team of peers. In some work teams, one person remains the leader throughout the life of the team, whereas in others the leadership role is rotated among team members.

In Chapter 15, we discussed issues of leadership in depth. The theories and principles of leadership described there generally apply to leadership of work teams. Here we discuss three leadership roles that new work team leaders sometimes find particularly difficult: empowerment, managing the external boundary of the team, and disbanding an ineffective work team.

EMPOWERMENT

Perhaps the most difficult aspect of being a work team leader is empowerment of team members. Work teams may be more successful in achieving organizational goals if their members are empowered (given authority and responsibility) to do

Figure 17.4   **Effectiveness Criteria for Work Teams**

Team Effectiveness		
Task completion	**Team development**	**Stakeholder satisfaction**
Accuracy	Team cohesiveness	Customer satisfaction with team's procedures and outputs
Speed	Team flexibility	Team satisfaction with team's procedures and outputs
Creativity	Team preparedness for new tasks	Satisfaction of other teams with the team's procedures and outputs
Cost		

Individual Effectiveness		
Task performance	**Relationships with others**	**Personal development**
Speed	Increased understanding of other perspectives	Develop competencies (teamwork, communication, strategic action, global awareness, planning and administration, and self-awareness)
Accuracy	Build others' trust in you	Develop network of colleagues within and outside the organization
Creativity	New friendships	Gain technical knowledge and skills
Efficiency		

their jobs. Conversely, if their authority and responsibility are restricted, team members may well reduce their levels of commitment. They might continue to perform satisfactorily but with little enthusiasm for improving quality and productivity.

For some leaders, accepting the idea of empowerment is difficult. Ford Motor Company's Alex Trotman is an example. When Ford was developing its Taurus model, the company had already adopted empowerment as a cornerstone of its corporate culture, but many long-time executives were uncomfortable with giving so much autonomy to work teams. Trotman, for example, was concerned about cost-cutting. Rather than convince the Taurus design team of the importance of keeping costs low, and then empowering the team to make design decisions that reflected this objective, Trotman used his veto power to achieve his objectives. He overrode the design team, demanding that it reconfigure the back end of the original Taurus wagon design and move the side-view mirrors.[56] David Nadler, chairman of Delta Consulting Group, would have expected Trotman to have difficulty adjusting to an empowerment philosophy. "Even the most capable managers have trouble making the transition because all the command-and-control-type things they were encouraged to do before are no longer appropriate. There's no reason to expect them to have any skill or sense of this. But they can learn it," he says. At Ford, for example, the old culture reflected the military training that shaped many of its executives' view of how to lead. For these managers, learning how to empower team members meant learning how to hand control over to employees.

J. D. Bryant, a thirty-three-year-old manager at a Texas Instruments plant, found the idea of empowerment difficult to grasp at first, too. He had been told to hand over more responsibility to the operators who assembled circuit boards. His response was to discontinue his practice of calling up his staff's e-mail messages and let them do it themselves. "I never let the operators do any scheduling or any ordering of parts because that was mine. I figured as long as I had that I had a job," he admits. Frustrated by this experience, Bryant eventually transferred to another plant where the role of leader was rotated within the team. At this plant, he was able to observe other effective leaders and learn about planning, setting milestones, and transferring responsibility among team members. Eventually Bryant became an enthusiastic team leader whose teamwork competency was so admired that he became a roving troubleshooter. If other teams are having problems, they call him in for help. After talking with team members and sitting in on a few of their meetings, he offers his advice.[57]

For some managers, learning how to empower team members means realizing that empowerment of self-managed work teams doesn't imply adopting a strictly hands-off style. Especially for a newly empowered work team, a leader needs to take responsibility for ensuring that the team has clear goals. Some planning and monitoring of the team's work also is necessary. Leaders of newly created self-managing work teams should take responsibility for explaining the organization's business plan and then help the team define the results to be achieved. Initially, the work team leader may also need to handle the budget, monitor team results, provide feedback to team members, and provide coaching as needed.[58]

As work team members become more experienced, the leader's role changes. A mature self-managed work team will take over responsibility for establishing team performance goals, assigning responsibilities to individual team members, monitoring the performance of the team and its members, and addressing many of the performance problems that arise.[59] But even when a self-managed work team is fully mature, the leader normally retains a few administrative responsibilities, or at least shares them with team members. These duties include preparing and managing the team's budget, conducting formal performance appraisals and providing feedback, handling persistent individual performance problems, and making compensation decisions.[60]

MANAGING THE EXTERNAL BOUNDARY

Many team activities involve the interface between the work team and the external system within which the team operates. Work team members and leaders alike naturally focus much of their attention on the team's internal processes: Is the work moving along? Are team members getting along? Experienced work team leaders realize that they also must be concerned with matters outside the team's purview. Even the most mature work teams may continue to look to the leader for information about business plans and other external conditions. In particular, work team leaders often serve as liaisons with top management, other teams within the organization, key clients and suppliers, and even competitors. Some of these constituencies (e.g., suppliers, top management, and other teams within the organization) are important because they control valuable resources that the team may need to complete its work. Some may be important because their evaluations of the team indicate the team's effectiveness. And some may be important because they can actively oppose the team's actions and prevent it from achieving its goals.

Effective leaders actively manage relationships with all of these important external groups. To start the process, a leader should lead a team discussion to generate a list of the important external groups and their concerns of interest to the team.

The leader should also encourage team members to identify the information they need about these groups and the types of relationships the team should establish with them. Such relationships can be formal or informal, and contact may be frequent or occasional. The purpose of maintaining external relationships with other groups—such as obtaining and/or providing information, attempting to influence them, coordinating activities with them, involving them in decisions, and/or obtaining their permission to implement decisions made by the team—should be determined.

After identifying key external groups and clarifying why each is important to the work team, the leader should develop strategies for maintaining such relationships. For example, to verify that the team has a clear and accurate understanding of what management expects it to accomplish, and when, the team may decide to invite a key top-level manager to one of its early meetings. The team might also agree to prepare a progress report and have a follow-up meeting with that person at agreed upon intervals. To stay in touch with other work teams, specific team members could be designated to establish informal relationships with members of those teams and/or propose a more formal mechanism for maintaining a relationship.

The work team leader may be deeply involved in establishing and maintaining these various external relations, or team members themselves may take much of that responsibility. Regardless of how the work team decides to manage external relationships, the team leader should be sure that the team is attuned to the external context of its responsibilities and is being responsive to appropriate external groups.

DISBANDING AN INEFFECTIVE WORK TEAM

Finally, work team leaders must learn to recognize when a poorly functioning work team has reached the point of no return. Occasionally, despite all efforts to build an effective team, conflicts between team members escalate beyond repair. Reed Breland experienced such conflicts when he became a team facilitator at Hewlett-Packard's financial services center in Colorado Springs. According to Breland, "It was a classic case of personality conflict. They just didn't like each other." The conflict between two people affected not only themselves but also the other six team members. Breland let the team try to work it out at first. And he made sure that the team understood they were responsible for getting the work done, no matter what. But after nine months of continued squabbling, Breland concluded that the work team simply wasn't effective. Rather than making judgments about who was to blame for the problems, he dissolved the team and had its members placed elsewhere. "If the chemistry isn't right, it doesn't matter how good or bad the players are," says Breland. "It's not going to work. As a team leader, you have to know when it's reached that point." Breland's decision seems to have been a good one, as team members all are doing fine in their new assignments.[61]

ADMINISTRATIVE SUPPORT FOR WORK TEAMS

5

EXPLAIN HOW TWO KEY
ASPECTS OF HUMAN RE-
SOURCES MANAGEMENT
SYSTEMS—TRAINING AND
REWARDS—CAN SUPPORT
WORK TEAM EFFECTIVENESS

Work teams of all types are being empowered to perform tasks that previously weren't employees' responsibility. Figure 17.5 shows a wide range of tasks that could be assigned to teams in a manufacturing plant. The vertical axis indicates the degree of empowerment (i.e., authority, responsibility, and general decision-making discretion) for tasks. The horizontal axis indicates the amount and range of competencies required of team members for handling an increasing number and complexity of tasks.

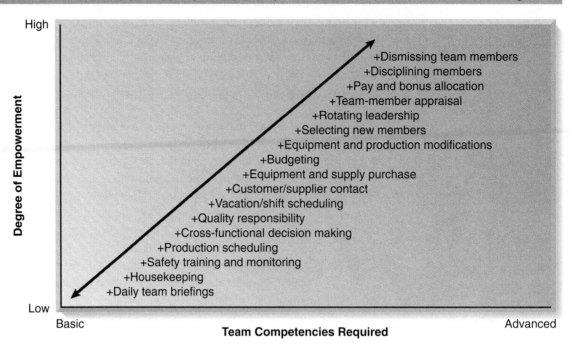

Source: Adapted from L. Holpp. Applied empowerment. *Training,* February 1994, 39–44; and D. M. Bakersfield. Why business loves work teams. *Black Enterprise,* April 1993, 85–90.

As organizations move toward more highly empowered work teams, the organization's success becomes more tightly linked to work team effectiveness. Organizations that invest resources to train teams can increase both team and organizational effectiveness. Even the best trained work team can misdirect its energy, so organizations must also be sure that expectations and rewards align with the work team's responsibilities and results. Often work team leaders are held accountable for ensuring that team members have the training they need. Team leaders also may be expected to make decisions about the pay of team members and distribute other rewards among them. How well team leaders fulfill these responsibilities depends in part on their own individual competencies and in part on the administrative support available. Team leaders can more easily address issues of training and rewards when their organizations' human resources management systems include formal team training and appropriately designed compensation plans.

TEAM TRAINING

Management often rushes to form work teams without considering how the behaviors needed for effective teamwork differ from those needed for effective individual contributions. Team members may receive little or no training to ensure that they can perform the required tasks and achieve the goals set.[62] As Displaymasters discovered, this approach to work teams often leads to failure. Displaymasters is a small Minneapolis-based company that manufactures displays. When managers put workers into teams for the first time, they did so without explaining their expectations or defining the team members' new roles. They provided no training in how to be an effective work team member and paid no attention to employees' feelings. The result was chaos. Employees became skeptical of teamwork and frustrated with the managers. Displaymasters has since regrouped and offered team training. Although the company is organized into cross-functional work teams, no one dares to call them that because of their initial failure. Instead, they are called departments to avoid any negative associations with the chaos that "teams" caused in the past.[63]

Team training can take many forms. Three main goals of team training programs are to develop team cohesiveness, effective teamwork procedures, and work team leaders. Although some training efforts address all three of these objectives simultaneously, here we discuss them in sequence for clarity.

Training to Develop Team Cohesiveness. Perhaps more than any other organization, NASA understands that training comes before effective teamwork. Before astronauts are sent into space to live in a community that relies heavily on teamwork for survival, NASA has them working together every day for one to two years to become a team. They share office space, spend countless hours together in flight simulators, and rehearse everything from stowing their flight suits to troubleshooting malfunctions. Formal training in procedures is part of the experience, but it isn't everything. NASA realizes that teamwork training also involves helping teammates get to know each other and developing confidence in each other.

Most organizations can't afford to give work team members a year or two of training before the teams begin working on their tasks. They look for quicker ways to achieve the same objectives that NASA has for its training program. To develop team cohesiveness, many organizations use experientially based, adventure training. Evart Glass Plant, a division of Chrysler Corporation, involved its entire 250-person staff in such training as a way to prepare them for working in self-managed work teams. Some of the planning and administration competencies that Chrysler needed to develop (problem-solving, organizing projects, and time management) are described in the Planning and Administration Competency piece.

Was the training effective? Surveys and personal interviews were conducted to assess employees' reactions, and the results were positive. Employees commented that people now were going out of their way to help others and felt that people were doing a better job of seeking out opinions from employees at all levels. Employees also got to know each other. Explained one engineer, "Personally, I hadn't been on third shift very long and found there were three people on that shift that I had the wrong opinion of. I saw they were real go-getters and they stayed positive throughout the experience; I was surprised." Other employees expressed similar feelings. Overall, the training helped break down personal walls that people had built around themselves and helped them see the benefits of being a contributing member of a team.[64]

Training in Team Procedures. Experiential training is an effective way to develop cohesiveness, but used alone it isn't likely to result in optimal work team effectiveness. Work teams can also benefit from more formal training. For example, team members who are taught about the stages of team development are less likely to become easily frustrated during the early forming and storming stages of team development. They will also realize the importance of norms to their performance and therefore strive to develop norms that aid rather than hinder it.

In addition to explaining the evolution of team development, formal training programs often cover how to

- use a variety of techniques for generating creative ideas (e.g., brainstorming),

- identify and discuss problems and their possible causes (e.g., using fishbone diagrams and other decision-making aids described in Chapter 9),

- choose one solution from among the many available (e.g., when to resort to voting and compromise), and

- ensure that solutions are implemented according to an agreed upon schedule.

PLANNING AND ADMINISTRATION COMPETENCY
Teams that Play Together Stay Together at Chrysler

Like many manufacturing facilities, Chrysler's Evart Glass Plant division began restructuring around teams during the mid 1990s. "Team effort is what counts," according to plant manager Bert Burtolozzi. "As a society, we have focused on the individual, but in the workplace no one individual can do it—we must focus on our greatest asset: our teams."

Many companies put their top executives through programs such as Outward Bound, but Evart had the entire workforce participate. Union members and managers were trained side by side. They spent the day at a nearby camp learning a variety of teamwork lessons. The training took place during employees' normal work hours, which in this case meant that training took place across three 8-hour shifts. Everyone received normal pay for the time spent in training. The training teams were cross-functional.

For example, a hi-lo driver (similar to a forklift operator), a maintenance person, a shift supervisor, and a receptionist found themselves working together as a team throughout their training. After each activity, trainers led a discussion about the experience to identify the lesson to be learned from it. Below are a few of the activities and associated lessons from the specially designed one-day program.

The Challenging Activity	The Teamwork Lesson
Juggle several objects simultaneously (e.g., tennis balls, hackey sacs, and koosh balls) as a team.	Although everyone has a different role, each person touches and affects the outcome.
Find the path hidden in a carpet maze and move each member through it in a limited amount of time.	Teams must find and use each individual's hidden strengths (e.g., a good memory and the ability to move quickly). Doing so allows the team as a whole to succeed.
Balance fourteen nails on the head of a nail that has been pounded into a supporting block of wood, creating a free-standing structure without supports.	Things that may seem impossible can be achieved when people work together.
Draw a vehicle that represents the training teams and signify which part of the vehicle each member represents.	To validate the different strengths of each member and recognize that bringing these strengths together leads to success on the task.

For self-managing work teams, formal training may also include company-specific procedures for obtaining resources, cost accounting, progress reports, and team evaluations. When Western Contract Furniture created TQM teams, it hired a consultant to train its managers and associates. The training covered basic teamwork principles and included discussions about the importance of modifying the company's culture to support the new TQM teams. The objective of the training was to prepare managers and employees to work on autonomous ad hoc task forces. The task forces were formed from volunteers interested in addressing an issue needing attention, as identified by the company's quality council. Employees were trained in how to choose a facilitator, research an issue, and develop recommendations. Following this training, almost everyone in the company has served on a TQM team.

Training to Develop Work Team Leaders. We have already described leadership development in some detail in Chapter 15. Most of that prior discussion applies to team leadership. Nevertheless, a few points about training team leaders are worth noting.

New team leaders often misunderstand their role. Good team leaders are receptive to member contributions and don't reject or promote ideas because of their own personal views. Good team leaders summarize information, stimulate discussion, create awareness of problems, and detect when the team is ready to resolve differences and agree to a unified solution. Training in how to support disagreement and manage meetings are especially useful for new work team leaders.

- **Supporting disagreement.** A skillful work team leader can create an atmosphere for disagreement that stimulates innovative solutions while minimizing the risk of bad feelings. Disagreement can be managed if the leader is receptive to differences within the team, delays the making of decisions, and separates idea generation from idea evaluation. This last technique reduces the likelihood that an alternative solution will be identified with one individual rather than the team. The absence of disagreement on a work team may be as destructive to its proper functioning as too much disagreement. The use of decision-making aids, such as brainstorming, the nominal group technique, devil's advocacy, and dialectical inquiry, creates productive controversy and can result in better quality decisions that are fully accepted by members of the team. Training team leaders to use these simple techniques is a good first step toward stimulating constructive controversy within teams.[65]

- **Managing meetings.** People who resist teamwork often point to time wasted in meetings as a big source of dissatisfaction. True, teams do need to meet, one way or another, but team meetings should never be a waste of time. Training team leaders in the tactics of running meetings can make meetings more efficient. In addition, training can help team leaders learn how to strike a proper balance between permissiveness and control. Rushing through a team session can prevent full discussion of the problem, lead to negative feelings, and result in poor solutions. However, unless the leader keeps the discussion moving, members will become bored and inattentive. Unfortunately, some leaders feel that pushing for an early solution is necessary because of time constraints. Such a move ends discussion before the team has had a chance to work through a problem effectively.

TEAM REWARDS

As we described in Chapters 12 and 14, reward systems inform employees about how to direct their energies and reinforce them for making valuable contributions to the organization. In the United States, the formal compensation systems in most organizations have been designed to reward individual and/or business unit performance. Systems designed to specifically reward team efforts are relatively new. According to a recent survey by William M. Mercer, a consulting company that helps companies design compensation systems, only about one-fourth of companies currently offer "small group incentives," and another fourth of them are considering their use.

In part because they are so new, there is little agreement concerning how best to design these systems. The basic principles that apply to creating any reward system also apply to systems for teams. Both monetary and nonmonetary rewards should be used, taking into account differences in what individuals value most. However rewards are distributed, employees should understand the system, feel that it is fair and equitable, and understand the link between their performance and their rewards.

When employees work in a single team most of the time and this teamwork is essentially the employee's entire job, establishing team performance measures and using them to determine rates of pay is relatively easy. At most companies, however, people aren't assigned full time to a single work team. Their primary responsibilities may derive from a job that they perform essentially as an individual, with work team activities tacked onto their regular duties. Or, most of a person's regular duties may require working in teams, but over the course of a year the person may serve on five or six different work teams. Most experts agree that different team structures call for different reward systems. Thus, rather than prescribe a specific approach to rewarding work teams, it is more useful to understand the basic choices involved in tailoring a reward system to an organization's situation.[66]

Table 17.2 lists several questions that managers should consider when designing work team rewards. With so many choices, perhaps the best way to develop an appropriate reward system is to assign the task to an empowered, multidisciplinary, well-trained work team.

T a b l e 1 7 . 2	*Choices for Rewarding Work Teams*

- How can nonmonetary rewards be used to recognized excellent team performance?

- Should *any* monetary rewards be linked to team performance? If yes, what portion of a person's total monetary rewards should be linked to performance of the team (versus the performance of the individual or the business unit)?

- Should rewards for teamwork be linked to results that aren't under the complete control of the team or to behaviors that team members can more directly control?

- If rewards are to be linked to results, which effectiveness criteria should be used to evaluate team results?

- Should all members of the team receive equal rewards? If not, on what basis should people receive differential rewards (e.g., use a formula and conduct 360-degree appraisals)?

- Who should be responsible for the allocation of rewards among team members: team members, a team leader, someone outside the team?

- For global teams, how should cultural differences among members of the team and the pay systems used in different countries be addressed?

For examples of how some companies have answered these questions, see P. Pascarella. Compensating teams. *Across the Board,* February 1997, pp. 16–22.

CHAPTER SUMMARY

Contemporary organization designs differ from traditional organizations in many ways. One of the most striking differences is the increasing reliance on work teams. This trend is the reason that teamwork competency is one of the six key managerial competencies that are the focus of this book. Understanding the model of work team functioning presented in this chapter is one way to begin improving your teamwork competency.

1. ### EXPLAIN THE IMPORTANCE OF GROUPS AND TEAMS.

Teams may serve many important purposes. One of the most important reasons for using teamwork is to achieve greater customer focus. Teams are proving to be especially effective as a way for organizations to satisfy customers' demands for innovation and faster response times. The popularity of team-based organizational structures reflects the belief that teamwork offers the potential to achieve outcomes that couldn't be achieved by individuals working in isolation.

2. DESCRIBE THE BASIC TYPES OF GROUPS AND WORK TEAMS FOUND IN ORGANIZATIONS.

A group is two or more individuals who come into personal and meaningful contact on a continuing basis. There are two basic types of groups in organizations: informal groups and formal work teams. An informal group consists of a small number of individuals who frequently participate in activities together and share feelings for the purpose of meeting their mutual needs. A work team consists of a small number of identifiable, interdependent employees who are held accountable for performing tasks that contribute to achieving an organization's goals. Members of a work team have a shared goal and must interact with each other to achieve it. The four most common types of work teams are functional, problem-solving, multidisciplinary, and self-managing teams. Three key differences among work teams are the nature of their goals, their duration, and their membership. Different types of work teams suit different purposes. There is no one-best way to organize a work team.

3. DISCUSS THE MAJOR COMPONENTS OF A MODEL OF WORK TEAM FUNCTIONING.

The primary components of a model of work team functioning are the external system, team design, internal team processes, and criteria for assessing the team's effectiveness. These four components are highly interrelated and must be considered together in order to understand fully how a particular team functions.

The external system comprises outside conditions and influences that exist before and after the team is formed. These external influences may include societal and organizational culture, organization design, and the human resources management system.

The team design choices involved in creating a team are numerous. In addition to choices concerning team duration, goals, and membership are choices concerning size and location. Virtual work teams are an increasingly common choice in global and hi-tech organizations.

Internal processes include the development of the work team over time, personal feelings, and behavioral norms. Through these processes, the members of a work team develop and integrate their behaviors. Coordination and integration tend to emerge over time and in several stages. Feelings reflect the emotional climate of a group. The four feelings most likely to influence work team effectiveness and productivity are trust, openness, freedom, and interdependence. Behavioral norms are the informal rules of behavior that are widely shared and enforced by the members of a group. They set standards for members' behaviors under specific circumstances.

Effectiveness criteria measure the outcomes achieved by individual members and the work team as a whole. A particular work team may be effective in some respects and not in others.

4. DESCRIBE THE ROLE OF A WORK TEAM LEADER.

The theories and principles of leadership described in Chapter 15 generally apply to leadership in work teams. Three leadership functions that new work team leaders sometimes find particularly difficult to carry out are empowerment, managing the external boundary of the team, and disbanding an ineffective work team.

5. EXPLAIN HOW TWO KEY ASPECTS OF HUMAN RESOURCES MANAGEMENT SYSTEMS— TRAINING AND REWARDS—CAN SUPPORT WORK TEAM EFFECTIVENESS.

Addressing issues of training and rewards is easier for team leaders when their organizations' human resources management systems include formal team training and sound compensation plans. Team training can take many forms. Three predominant goals of team training programs are to develop team cohesiveness, effective teamwork procedures, and team leaders. Formal compensation systems in most organizations reward individual and/or business unit performance. Systems designed to specifically reward team efforts are relatively new and involve making several choices. The choices made should reflect the specific organizational context of the work teams.

QUESTIONS FOR DISCUSSION

1. What are some of the advantages and disadvantages of organizing employees into work teams?

2. Describe the stages of group development. Which stage is most crucial?

3. Raj Kashish described his workplace as ". . . friendly, just great. All the people get along together, and we bowl and play softball after work." Quality records show that Kashish's team produces high-quality results but that its costs are high and its output of work is low. Is this an effective work team? Explain why or why not.

4. What are the primary differences between functional work teams and multidisciplinary work teams?

5. What are the main differences between problem-solving work teams and self-managing work teams?

6. You have an opportunity to take a new job as work team leader in an organization. Before you accept the offer, you want to assess whether the organization is likely to provide a supportive environment for the team. What questions would you ask about the organization to determine whether the environment is supportive?

7. Roberta Mack has been asked to head a task force. The assignment is to evaluate the company's practices in terms of whether they support or interfere with employees' desires for a high-quality life, at work as well as away from work. List eight important guidelines that Mack should follow in her role as leader of this task force.

EXERCISES TO DEVELOP YOUR MANAGERIAL COMPETENCIES

1. **Planning and Administration Competency.** Many organizations require their employees to work in teams but offer them no specific training in-house. Such organizations often encourage managers to send employees to training programs offered at universities or by consultants. Investigate three training programs designed to develop teamwork competencies. List the strengths and weaknesses of each. Then rank order the three programs, assigning 1 to the program that you think is most comprehensive and 3 to the program that you think is least comprehensive. To get started, visit the home pages of the International Institute for Learning at

    www.iil.com

    Team Leadership Resources at

    www.team-leadership.com

    American Association for Training and Development at

    www.astd.org

    and Outward Bound at

    www.outwardbound.org

2. **Strategic Action Competency.** When weather, fire, or other forms of disaster strike, businesses can find themselves closed down for weeks at a time. Each day of lost business cuts into profits and may threaten employees' jobs. High-speed disaster recovery teams address the need to rebuild businesses following major disasters. Imagine that your business has just been struck by a disaster and that you're investigating disaster recovery contractors. To begin, list the effectiveness criteria that you would want a disaster recovery team to satisfy. Use the Internet to investigate the services available. Many communities offer the services of a community emergency recovery team (CERT). Is one available in your community? How important does teamwork seem to be in the disaster recovery business? How do disaster recovery organizations describe their services? To begin, explore the home pages of the Evans Team at

    www.evans-team.com

    Life Safety Associates at

    www.lifesafety.com

Disaster Recovery Journal at

www.drj.com

and Associated Lane Emergency Response Teams at

www.alertweb.org

3. **Self-Management Competency.** Jobweb is one of many electronic services that provide information about job openings for recent college graduates. This particular Web site often also lists the results of recent surveys concerning the competencies and experiences that employers are looking for. Visit Jobweb and similar Web sites to learn more about how your teamwork competency is likely to affect employers' evaluations of you as a job candidate. Compared to other competencies, how important is the teamwork competency? What types of experience should you try to get now in order to convince potential employers that you have developed your teamwork competency? The Jobweb home page is at

www.jobweb.org

4. **Global Awareness Competency.** The Project Management Forum is a nonprofit professional organization dedicated to advancing the quality of project management. Among its services is an electronic journal that includes case studies describing successful project management practices. Its Web site also contains links to many other resources for project managers around the world. Using this Web site as a starting point, explore the resources available to project managers. If you were to become a professional project manager, how could you use the resources available to improve your ability to manage a global, virtual project management team? List five steps that you could take to prepare for serving as the leader of a global, virtual project. The Project Management Forum's home page is at

www.pmforum.org

5. **Communication Competency**. For this exercise, you'll need to select a team of which you are a member and ask the other team members to participate with you. Everyone in the team should answer the following questions and then spend some time sharing the responses. The answers to these questions indicate the perceptions that members have about the team and how it is developing. The answers also may reveal some difficulties that are blocking its progress.

INSTRUCTIONS

Circle the number below each question that you believe to be most descriptive of your team.

1. How clear are the goals?

2	4	6	8	10
No apparent goals	Goal confusion, uncertainty, or conflict	Average goal clarity	Goals mostly clear	Goals very clear

2. How much trust and openness are present in the team?

2	4	6	8	10
Distrust, a closed team	Little trust, some defensiveness	Average trust and openness	Considerable trust and openness	Remarkable trust and openness

3. How sensitive and perceptive are team members?

2	4	6	8	10
No awareness or listening in the team	Most members self-absorbed	Average sensitivity and listening	Better than usual listening	Outstanding sensitivity to others

4. How much attention is paid to process (the way the team is working)?

2	4	6	8	10
No attention to process	Little attention to process	Some concern with team process	A fair balance between content and process	Very concerned with process

5. How are team leadership needs met?

2	4	6	8	10
Not met, drifting	Leadership concentrated in one person	Some leadership sharing	Leadership functions distributed	Leadership needs met creatively and flexibly

6. How are team decisions made?

2	4	6	8	10
No decisions could be reached	Made by a few	Majority vote	Attempts at integrating minority vote	Full participation and mostly by consensus

7. How well are team resources used?

2	4	6	8	10
One or two contributed, but most silent	Several tried to contribute, but were discouarged	Average use of team resources	Team resources well used and encouraged	Team resources fully and effectively used

8. How much loyalty and sense of belonging to the team exist?

2	4	6	8	10
Members have no team loyalty or sense of belonging	Members not close, some friendly relations	About average sense of belonging	Some warm sense of belonging	Strong sense of belonging among members

9. How much discretion (empowerment) is provided to the team for determining the methods, procedures, and schedules used to accomplish its goals?

2	4	6	8	10
No discretion	Some discretion	Balance between team and higher management	Substantial discretion	Total discretion

10. How important is the work performed by the team in terms of serving *customers'* needs, either internal (other units) or external to the organization?

2	4	6	8	10
No importance	Some importance	Average importance	Significant importance	Great importance

INTERPRETATION

Add the points for all ten questions to arrive at a team development score. Scores of 20 to 60 or so suggest that your team is ineffective to marginally effective. Scores of 70 to 80 suggest an average to good team, but one that falls short of reaching its full potential. Scores of 90 to 100 suggest that this team is remarkable and that you are enthusiastic about its effectiveness. Compare team members' total scores and the responses to each item. Where differences in perceptions exist, discuss the possible reasons for these differences. Rather than arguing about whose views are right or wrong, focus on trying to understand each person's perspective.

REAL-TIME CASE ANALYSIS

AES POWERS UP WITH TEAMS

AES Corporation supplies electricity to public utilities and steam to industrial companies. Headquartered in Virginia, it was owner or part owner of thirty-five power plants worldwide as of 1998, with continued rapid growth expected in the years ahead. Plant locations as of 1998 are as follows.

Location	Number of Plants
United States	7
China	9
Argentina	5
Britain	4
Brazil	4
Hungary	3
Pakistan	2
Kazakhstan	1

To create a work environment that is both fun and supportive of its strategy of operational excellence, AES adopted a decentralized structure. Every employee is encouraged to participate in strategic planning and new plant design. To minimize layers of management, the company chose to organize around multiskilled teams and to have no functionally organized corporate staff. Scott Gardner graduated from Dartmouth and joined an AES plant that was developing a $200 million cogeneration plant in San Francisco. "It involved a lot of work and few people to do it," he recalled. Among the tasks he took on were negotiating with the community over the plant's water system and buying and selling pollution credits. Most of the company's plants operate without shift supervisors. Cofounder and Chairman Roger Sant explains the logic: "If Dennis [his partner and CEO] and I had to lead everything, we couldn't have grown as much as we have. People would bring deals for us to approve, and we would have a huge bottleneck." As a result, in five years the company grew from 600 to 6,000 employees. These employees have enriched jobs and plenty of authority to make decisions. At AES, managers and their teams make the decisions. The team leader is expected to seek the advice of whoever they think is appropriate and then take responsibility for the decisions that are made. AES believes that its team-based structure fits with the company's four basic values:

- *Integrity and wholeness.* The goal is that the things AES people say and do in all parts of the company should fit together with truth and consistency.

- *Fairness.* AES wants to treat its people, customers, suppliers, shareholders, governments, and communities fairly. This value requires that employees routinely question the relative fairness of alternative courses of action.

- *Fun.* AES wants employees to flourish in the use of their gifts and skills and thereby enjoy the time they spend at AES.

- *Social responsibility.* The company believes that it should be involved in projects that provide social benefits, such as lower costs to customers, safety, reliability, and environmental cleanliness.

AES's approach has worked well in the United States, but it doesn't always transfer well to other cultures. This issue is a challenge for the company because over two-thirds of its operations are now overseas. When AES joined with a Belgian company and purchased a plant in Ireland, the Irish managers found that relinquishing their authority was difficult. A U.S. employee had to go to Ireland to instill the company's values at the new location. Slowly, some managers began to see that their employees could make good decisions, but CEO Bakke says the changes have taken too long. "The managers just didn't trust the employees to turn over power," he observed.

In many countries, the biggest problem that AES faces is the overstaffing of existing facilities. When AES buys these facilities or enters into a joint venture relating to them, AES must cut staff. Central to the AES philosophy is the idea of giving people big jobs with big responsibilities and getting rid of as many bosses as possible. According to employee Michael Cranna, "There are two reasons why teams are successful at AES: the type of people we have here and the environment in which they work. People tend to be independent and thrive in a loose environment where roles and responsibilities are not always clearly defined. The environment at AES is one where responsibility is pushed down to the lowest level possible, encouraging everyone to take ownership for not only their piece of the project, but for the project in its entirety." To succeed employees must be willing to accept these responsibilities and then draw on a team of people who can help them make the right decisions.

In 1998, AES began to initiate changes in its pay systems to support its team environment. Bakke is critical of U.S. laws that require nonmanagement employees to be paid strictly on an hourly basis. He believes that such laws are a major hindrance to creating a fun, meaningful, and empowered workplace. Although he can't do much to change those laws, in other countries AES has begun to introduce changes.

Plants in Argentina, Pakistan, England, and South America are moving to an all-salaried format. Oscar Prieto described his experience with changing the pay system in Argentina: "We broke all the rules. No bosses. No time records. No shift schedule. No assigned responsibilities. No administration. And guess what? It worked!" His next challenge was to do the same thing in Brazil.

QUESTIONS FOR DISCUSSION

1. What work team effectiveness criteria seem to be most important to AES cofounders Dennis Bakke and Roger Sant?

2. Suppose that you were in charge of campus recruiting for AES. What qualities would you look for in job candidates and how would you determine whether a candidate possessed these qualities?

3. In which countries or cultures is AES likely to have the most difficulty applying its management principles? In which countries is it likely to have the least difficulty? Explain why.

4. Do you agree with Dennis Bakke's opinion concerning the negative consequences of paying people on an hourly basis? Is an all-salaried system more appropriate for a team-based organization? Why or why not?

5. Besides pay, what other aspects of the external system at AES are likely to be important to the success of its work teams.

To learn more about AES, visit the company's home page at

www.aes.com

VIDEO CASE

NEXT DOOR FOOD STORES: TEAM SPIRIT

Next Door Food Stores' DGIT team has been a successful experiment in creating a self-directed team, uniting the resources and skills of auditors who had previously worked separately. Upon completion of its task, the team was dissolved. However, the company is better for having undertaken the experiment and, presumably, is inclined to spawn new, self-directed teams.

Author and journalist Tracy Kidder described the history of a similar team at Data General, a midsized computer manufacturer, in the late 1970s in his book, *The Soul of a New Machine*. The multidisciplinary and self-directing team was created as internal competition in the development of a new computer model at a time when Data General's competitor, DEC, was dominating the market with its VAX "superminicomputer." Data General already had its own model in development, but the independent team's computer ultimately became Data General's first choice. The team went through peaks and valleys, created subteams (for hardware and software), and, like the DGIT team, had a natural end point. Both teams disbanded after delivering the product, but the Data General team seemed almost to fall apart once its load—the stress and excitement of the task—had been removed. The DGIT team's members are making a smooth transition along a course that they themselves plotted.

As DGIT team members are reassigned to a closer relationship with individual stores, they probably will carry with them the lessons learned as team members and leaders for use in forming new store-level teams. Their experience from working as part of a team effort—planning and communicating team goals, taking turns at leadership, and developing their teamwork competencies—should increase the likelihood that similar teams will succeed in the future.

Working in teams, employees can gain a better appreciation of the company's goals and processes—each member brings different life and work experiences and perspectives to the team—and, collectively, they have a better chance of instituting significant change than if they were working individually. A team approach to organizational improvement might be contrasted with (but it can complement as well) the approach taken at Wainwright Industries in continuous improvement through individual employee suggestions (Chapter 2).

Even after teams disband, an organization can continue to benefit from the experience of team members through their actions as a group. The Central Intelligence Agency's "Career Trainee" program assigns future executive-track officers (usually new hires, but some more seasoned veterans as well) into classes. At various points throughout the yearlong program, the trainees are organized into teams, for example, to simulate a task force responding to a foreign affairs crisis or to undergo military familiarization training. At the end of the training, they are all released back to their original offices or sent (in the case of new hires) to their first formal assignment. All are better prepared to both serve in and create teams; each has also been educated on the roles and functions of others throughout the organization. The returnees, like the alumni of a college or university, form a virtual network of contacts that might be tapped, and former career trainees often serve a liaison function in future teams, based on their broad knowledge of other organizational components.

Next Door Food Stores might take advantage of information technologies to preserve the DGIT team as a team, even after dispersal of its members in the field. Using e-mail, telephone conference calls, and other information technologies, the DGIT team veterans could be reconvened as a task force to solve corporate-level problems, such as brainstorming about the possible impact that the Year 2000 problem might have on store financial reporting. (The Year 2000 problem, which arises because computers programmed for two-digit dates will fail to recognize the difference between the years 1900 and 2000, is described in Chapter 20. Problems with two-digit dates began to crop up several years ago when customers presenting credit cards with expiration dates in 2001 or 2002 had them rejected at gas pumps or cash registers.)

ON THE WEB

As a regional convenience food store chain, Next Door Food Stores is on the Web as much to attract potential employees as to promote its services to its far-flung customers. Information about job opportunities and benefits and a "mini" job application form are site mainstays. The CIA is on the Web (**www.odci. gov/cia/**); its employment listings include a fascinating range of occupations, from military analysts and computer engineers, to "Leather and Fabric Craft Specialists."

QUESTIONS

1. As a manager at a troubled firm, you've been tapped to head a task force to come up with a strategy to turn the company around. Representatives of each of the company's divisions comprise the task force. What do you do first? Explain why you chose that action.

2. How do municipal services utilize team structures?

3. What other types of teams might Next Door Food Stores consider creating? Why?

To help you answer these questions and learn more about Next Door Food Stores, visit its home page at

www.nextdoor1.com

Case contributed by Ross Stapleton-Gray, President, TeleDiplomacy, Inc., a technology and policy consultancy, and Adjunct Professor in Georgetown University's Communication, Culture, and Technology program.

Chapter

18

Organizational Cultures and Workforce Diversity

LEARNING OBJECTIVES

AFTER STUDYING THIS CHAPTER, YOU SHOULD BE ABLE TO:

1. DESCRIBE THE CORE ELEMENTS OF CULTURE.

2. IDENTIFY THE LEVELS OF CULTURE AND SUBCULTURE THAT ARE IMPORTANT TO MANAGING ORGANIZATIONS.

3. DISCUSS SEVERAL GENERAL TYPES OF ORGANIZATIONAL CULTURES.

4. EXPLAIN THE MEANING AND IMPORTANCE OF WORKFORCE DIVERSITY.

5. DESCRIBE SEVERAL ACTIVITIES REQUIRED TO MANAGE WORKFORCE DIVERSITY SUCCESSFULLY.

Outline

Counter Culture at Amy's Ice Creams

Scooping ice cream for a job may not be glamorous, but it can be fun. In fact, if you want a job at Amy's Ice Creams, you'll need to prove that you can *make* it fun. Having fun is key to Amy's strategy. Back in 1984, when Amy's first opened, superpremium ice cream shops were hard to find, but today they're everywhere. To survive, owner Amy Miller needed to differentiate her shop from all the others. How? Miller's strategy is to give customers a memorable "experience" with every scoop of ice cream. Examples of some of the experiences customers look forward to are Sleep-Over night (when employees dress in pajamas), Disco night (with strobe lights going), and Romance night (when the store is lit with candles). The strategy may sound crazy, but it's working. Annual sales for her seven-store chain have topped $2 million and continue to grow at about 20 percent per year.

Miller's strategy requires a special organizational culture. It's just as important for employees of Amy's Ice

Creams to buy into making their work fun as it is for customers to buy into the idea of having fun. To make her strategy work, Miller keeps close tabs on her company's culture. Job interviews are a powerful tool. When hiring, she looks for people who will support the culture. She wants creative types, so she tests for creativity by giving job applicants a white paper bag and telling them do something interesting with it. They have a week to work on their creations. Winning creations have included board games, works of art, and a pop-up jack-in-the-box. If job applicants can't be creative with the bag, she figures they won't be entertaining on a hot night with a long line of customers waiting for service.

For those who are eventually hired, the interview clearly signals the high value that Miller places on fun. And every day on the job, she makes sure that her message is remembered. To remind current employees of how many creative people are looking for jobs, Miller occasionally passes

around some of the applicants' best creations. Such reminders seem to stimulate employees to come up with new entertainment ideas on their own. If the line is long, time seems to go by more quickly when customers are doing their best imitations of barnyard animals in order to win free ice cream. When they have to wait while an empty ice cream tub is replaced with a refill, customers seem to mind less when they're trying to think of the answer to a pop trivia quiz, or watching someone break-dance on a freezer top. Of course, fun isn't the only reason that people come to Amy's Ice Creams. They also know that the fun doesn't cost them more or interfere with the speed or quality of customer service.[1]

THE ELEMENTS OF CULTURE

1

DESCRIBE THE CORE ELE-
MENTS OF CULTURE

CULTURE

A unique pattern of shared assumptions, values, and norms that shape the socialization activities, language, symbols, rites, and ceremonies of a group of people.

A *culture* is the unique pattern of shared assumptions, values, and norms that shape the socialization activities, language, symbols, rites, and ceremonies of a group of people.[2] Cultures develop in both large and small groups of people. In this chapter, we focus on one specific type of culture—organizational—but in doing so we recognize that organizational cultures are influenced by larger societal and industry cultures and smaller employee group subcultures. At Amy's Ice Creams, an element of the organizational culture is a shared assumption that customers enjoy being entertained—that everyone values fun and creativity. One of the company's strongest norms is that employees are expected to shed the ordinary habits of interaction and become performers who sometimes do outrageous things, such as wearing pajamas to work. Amy Miller's job interview process and the paper bag task are socialization activities that support this culture.

One way to think about culture is to compare it to personality. Like personality, culture affects in predictable ways how people behave when no one is telling them what to do. At Amy's Ice Creams, customers can expect the employees to be having fun with each other and with the customers even when no supervisor is there to tell them to perform. Shared assumptions, values, socialization experiences, symbols, language, narratives, and practices are the cultural elements that unite members of the culture and maintain a distinction between members and nonmembers.

When people belong to the same culture, there still can be great variation among its members. A society can have its own unique culture while at the same time subcultures can exist in it. In many countries, for example, distinct tribal, ethnic, and regional subcultures have developed over time. Similarly, an organization may have its own unique culture while also having distinctive subcultures in some departments or among members of some professions. In most large organizations, multiple cultures exist side by side. Accountants and designers may work together on a multidisciplinary work team. Customers and employees from multiple societal cultures and subcultures may interact daily. People from different corporate and industry cultures may be brought together through mergers, acquisitions, joint ventures, and other forms of strategic alliances. As a relatively small organization, Amy's Ice Creams doesn't have subcultures nor does it have operations in widely scattered locations. All its shops are located in or close to Austin, Texas. Nevertheless, even at Amy's Ice Creams, people from many cultures interact. Like most cities in the United States, the population of Austin comprises a variety of racial, ethnic, religious, and national backgrounds.

Managing cultural diversity effectively has emerged as a key business issue during the past decade. The effective management of cultural diversity begins with an understanding of the elements of culture.

SHARED ASSUMPTIONS

SHARED ASSUMPTIONS
Underlying thoughts and feelings that members of a culture take for granted and believe to be true.

Shared assumptions are the underlying thoughts and feelings that members of a culture take for granted and believe to be true. Societies differ in their assumptions about time, for example. In India, Hindus believe that time is everlasting and frequently arrive late to meetings, to the frustration of U.S. managers. Industries differ in their assumptions about customers. At Lucent Technologies, Lockheed Martin, and other high-tech companies in their industry, a common assumption is that engineers, not customers, are the best source of new product ideas. In contrast, consumer products firms such as Colgate and Procter & Gamble give relatively more weight to the input they receive from consumers. Organizations also may differ in their assumptions about what the notion of effectiveness means, and so on.

SHARED VALUES

VALUE
A basic belief about a condition that has considerable importance and meaning to individuals and is stable over time.

A *value* is a basic belief about a condition that has considerable importance and meaning to individuals and is stable over time. A value system comprises multiple beliefs that are compatible and support one another. For example, the societal values of private enterprise and individual rights are mutually supportive. In organizations with cultures that support TQM, employees value continuous improvement and information sharing.[3] As we described in Chapter 6, many contemporary organizations are striving to ensure that all employees value ethical and socially responsible conduct.

The shared values in an organization may be described in various ways. The organization culture profile (OCP) provides one way.[4] The OCP contains fifty-four statements that express a value, with each statement printed on a card. Several of the values measured by the OCP are shown in Table 18.1. To determine which values describe the organization, employees sort the statements into categories ranging from most characteristic to least characteristic of the organization. The results can then be analyzed to determine which values are shared most strongly throughout the organization. The unique combination of values found in an organization contribute to its identity and also reflect the values of the larger society.[5]

Table 18.1   *Sample of Organizational Culture Value Statements*

- Flexibility
- Informality
- Stability
- Being easygoing
- Predictability
- Being supportive
- Being innovative
- Being aggressive
- Risk taking
- Taking initiative
- Being careful
- Being reflective
- Autonomy
- Being demanding
- Being rule-oriented
- Taking individual responsibility
- Being analytical
- Security of employment
- Paying attention to detail
- Low level of conflict
- Being team-oriented
- Confronting conflict directly
- Sharing information freely
- Enthusiasm for the job
- Emphasizing a *single* organizational culture
- Working long hours
- An emphasis on quality
- Being people-oriented
- Being socially responsible
- Respect for the individual's rights
- Being results-oriented
- Being highly organized
- Tolerance

Source: Adapted from C. A. O'Reilly III, J. A. Chatman, and D. F. Caldwell. People and organizational culture: A profile of comparison approach to assessing the person–organization fit. *Academy of Management Journal,* 34, 1991, p. 516.

SHARED SOCIALIZATION

SOCIALIZATION
The systematic process by which new members are brought into a culture.

Socialization is a systematic process by which new members are brought into a culture.[6] Individuals learn the ropes and are introduced to the culture's behavioral norms. The most powerful way to socialize people into a culture is through consistent role modeling, teaching, coaching, and enforcement by others in the culture. At the societal level, socialization takes place within the family, in schools and religious organizations, and through the media. At the industry level, socialization often occurs through organized activities conducted by industry associations. The Printing Industry Association is more than 100 years old. Like many industry associations, it socializes members through regularly scheduled meetings, courses and workshops, social events, and awards ceremonies.

SHARED SYMBOLS

SYMBOL
Anything visible that can be used to represent an abstract shared value or something having special meaning.

A *symbol* is anything visible that can be used to represent an abstract shared value or something having special meaning. Symbols are the simplest and most basic observable form of cultural expression. Prudential Life Insurance uses the Rock of Gibraltar to represent continuity and dependability, which have great meaning to both its employees and policyholders. Symbols may be expressed through logos, architecture, parking priorities (e.g., assigned versus unassigned spaces, in or out of the garage, and close versus far from building), uniforms, office (e.g., spaciousness, location, furniture, and carpeting), open versus closed door norms, common cafeteria or separate dining facility for higher management, plaques, lapel pins, type of art on walls, and types of awards (e.g., emphasizing quality and customer service achievements).

SHARED LANGUAGE

LANGUAGE
A shared system of vocal sounds, written signs, and/or gestures used to convey special meanings among members.

From a cultural perspective, *language* is a shared system of vocal sounds, written signs, and/or gestures used to convey special meanings among members.[7] The elements of this system include shared jargon, slang, gestures, signals, signs, songs, humor, jokes, gossip, rumors, proverbs, metaphors, and slogans. In general, the greater the number and use of such language elements, the deeper is the culture.[8] Herb Kelleher, CEO of Southwest Airlines, believes that his company's culture is the key to its success. Once, when asked whether the real secret to his success wasn't simply keeping costs low, Kelleher slammed his fist on the table and shouted back that culture has *everything* to do with Southwest's success because competitors can't copy its culture.[9] Kelleher is a master at using language to maintain and differentiate his company's culture. Consider these cultural statements: "Work should be fun . . . it can be play . . . enjoy it." "Work is important . . . don't spoil it with seriousness." "We give more for less, not less for less." "Fly the luv airline." "We dignify the CUSTOMER." The word *customer* is always capitalized. Letters of commendation and appreciation to employees are known as "Love Reports." "We are family" is a metaphor used to refer to all employees.

SHARED NARRATIVES

NARRATIVES
The unique stories, sagas, legends, and myths in a culture.

Narratives are the unique stories, sagas, legends, and myths in a culture. Narratives often describe the unique accomplishments and beliefs of leaders over time, usually in heroic and romantic terms.[10] The basic story may be based on historical fact, but as the story gets told and retold, the facts may be embellished with fictional details. One well-known saga, which now appears on the company's Web site, is the one about how Mary Kay Ash founded a successful company while struggling to support herself and her children as a single parent.

SHARED PRACTICES

The most complex but observable cultural form is shared practices. These practices include taboos or rites and ceremonies. **Taboos** are behaviors that are forbidden in the culture. A taboo at Merck is to put profits ahead of ethical responsibilities to doctors, nurses, and patients. **Rites and ceremonies** are elaborate and formal activities designed to generate strong feelings. Usually they are carried out as special events.[11] In most societies, important rites and ceremonies celebrate the birth, marriage, and death of the society's members. In the entertainment industries, at the annual ceremonies that bestow the Oscar, Grammy, and Emmy awards, the recipients always thank many other people who made their success possible. This rite is a way of recognizing many people in the industry who aren't called to the stage for formal recognition.

LEVELS OF CULTURE

2

IDENTIFY THE LEVELS OF CULTURE AND SUBCULTURE THAT ARE IMPORTANT TO MANAGING ORGANIZATIONS

Culture is a fuzzy concept. It isn't something that you can put in a box and weigh. And you cannot round up all the members of a particular culture in order to count them. The boundaries that separate cultures often are blurred. So too are the boundaries that separate one level of culture from another. Because of its fuzzy nature, the best way to think of culture is in relative terms. Rather than try to describe a culture directly, often the best way to understand a culture is to compare and contrast it with other cultures. With this approach in mind, three levels of culture can be identified as most important to managing organizations: societal culture, industry culture, and organizational culture.

Societal cultures usually encompass the most people—that is, they represent the most general level of aggregation. Industry cultures represent groups of organizations that share common assumptions, values, and so on. Of the three types, organizational cultures usually encompass the fewest people. As we discuss organizational cultures, keep in mind that, to some extent at least, they are shaped by the broader cultural influences of the societies and industries of which the organizations are a part.

The interplay of societal and organizational cultures is illustrated in the Global Awareness Competency feature, which describes the experiences of managers at Pharmacia & Upjohn, Inc. This company was created through a merger of U.S. and Swedish pharmaceutical firms. Because they were in the same industry, the two firms shared some common assumptions and values, but these commonalities seemed small in light of other cultural differences.

To many outsiders, societal-level cultural differences created the conflicts within Pharmacia & Upjohn. But some of the firm's managers argue that differing management philosophies and organizational cultures caused the problems. Most likely, both types of differences contributed to the problems. Thus, for the new company to function effectively, managers and employees alike in both of the original companies have to begin adapting to their differences. Ultimately, Pharmacia & Upjohn will develop its own unique corporate culture—one that blends elements of the U.S. and Swedish approaches to doing business. The sooner that happens, the easier it will be for everyone in this company to work together productively.[12]

SOCIETAL CULTURES AND SUBCULTURES

Recall from Chapter 3 that we broadly categorized societies and individuals in terms of values such as individualism versus collectivism and low versus high uncertainty avoidance. For example, the Canadian and U.S. societies rank relatively high on individualism and low on uncertainty avoidance. In contrast, Japan and Taiwan

Culture Clash at Pharmacia & Upjohn

The headquarters of Pharmacia & Upjohn are just a stone's throw from England's Windsor Castle. It seems to be an odd choice for the headquarters of a company created by merging firms whose individual headquarters were in Kalamazoo, Michigan, and Stockholm, Sweden. The decision about where to locate the new headquarters and its 100-person staff is just one example of what happens when two sides distrust each other. For the managers who have to travel from Stockholm, Kalamazoo, and Milan—the locations of the company's main operations and 30,000 employees—the headquarters decision was just one of many sources of stress. Among the others were the following.

- The hard-driving, mission-oriented U.S. approach of the Upjohn managers clashed with the consensus-oriented Swedish approach of the Pharmacia managers. While the Upjohn managers focused on ambitious cost-cutting goals and numerical accountability, the Pharmacia managers kept their employees informed and sought feedback about how to carry out changes.
- The Upjohn managers scheduled meetings throughout the summer and couldn't comprehend that Pharmacia managers would spend the entire month of August on vacation.
- The internationally experienced Pharmacia managers were surprised by the lack of international savvy and parochial attitudes of the Upjohn managers. Managers

in many European companies are accustomed to working across borders and tend to be more flexible and adaptable than U.S. managers. Upjohn's strict policies subject all workers to drug and alcohol testing and ban smoking. At Pharmacia's Milan location, wine is poured freely in the company dining room and the boardroom in Stockholm is well-stocked with humidors.

- The Upjohn-based CEO put managers on a tight leash, requiring frequent reports, budgets, and staffing updates. The Swedes viewed these tasks as a waste of time and eventually stopped taking them seriously. The Italians felt that the Americans were acting like imperialists and trying to take over.

These conflicts were reflected in the company's bottom line. Everyone had hailed the merger as a wise strategic decision to expand the scale and scope of both firms. The new firm had greater international presence and more products than either firm had alone. But melding the cultures proved more difficult than anticipated, and earnings in the first two years were below expectations, resulting in the resignation of the firm's CEO.

One approach that is helping to bridge the cultures among members of the research units is moving the U.S. and European managers back and forth across the Atlantic. According to Research Executive Vice President Goran Ando, doing so helps speed cultural learning and development of mutual respect. But the basic styles of

the managers are slow to change. "I am a Swede who has lived in both Britain and the United States for a number of years," explained Andro. "I see in Americans a more can-do approach to things. They try to overcome problems as they arise. A Swede may be slower on the start up. He sits down and thinks over all the problems, and once he is reasonably convinced he can tackle them, only then will he start running." Guy Grindborg, a technical trainer for the Swedish firm Ericsson, Inc., has observed similar differences, causing him to adjust the way he conducts training sessions when he's in the United States. "The Swedish approach is more the engineering approach: 'Tell my why and how this thing works.' The American approach is much more direct. Their attitude is: 'Don't teach me to be an expert, just tell me what I need to know to do my job.' "[13]

* * *

To learn more about Pharmacia & Upjohn, visit the company's home page at

www.pharmacia.se

rank lower on individualism and higher on uncertainty avoidance. However, all four countries are somewhat low in terms of power distance.

Societal values have many far-reaching consequences for managing organizations. They shape the preferences and behaviors of customers, employees, and all other members of the communities in which an organization operates. For example, in individualistic cultures, people are more comfortable being given straight-forward feedback about their individual strengths and weaknesses; in collectivistic cultures feedback is given in more subtle and indirect ways and focuses less directly on the individual. At Microsoft, differences such as these mean that the company's U.S. managers must understand a variety of societal cultures and be able work with the local managers who run sales offices in some sixty countries.[14] Expatriates who lack cultural sensitivity and global awareness experience problems in communication and feelings of isolation. Managers working in a culture that they don't understand are likely to make poor decisions about how to staff their organizations and motivate employees.[15]

Experienced travelers know that societal cultures don't necessarily change suddenly when they cross the border between countries. However, experienced managers realize that cultures often change dramatically from one side of a mountain range to the other, from north to south, and from the seashore to the landlocked interior within countries. In China, the United States, and many other countries, distinct regional subcultures are present, and thinking that all members of a society share the same attitudes, values, and norms is a mistake.

For example, China's billion plus people comprise many distinct ethnic groups who speak many dialects and follow myriad local customs. A study of more than 700 managers in large cities in each of the country's six major regions suggests that there are at least three distinct subcultures in China: one in the southeast, another in the northeast, and a third covering much of the central and western parts of the country. The subculture of the southeast region is the most individualistic, whereas the subculture of the central and western areas is the most collectivistic. The culture of the northeast region falls between these two extremes. Bridging this and other differences among the regions, however, is a shared commitment to traditional Confucian values of societal, interpersonal, and personal harmony.[16]

INDUSTRY CULTURES AND SUBCULTURES

Identifying the boundaries between industry cultures can be as difficult as locating the boundaries between regional subcultures. Nevertheless, when employees move between industries they usually can sense, if not identify explicitly, the cultural differences. Researcher Margaret Phillips has studied two industries and documented some of the differences between them. Her research compared the cultures of the art museum industry and the wine-making industry. Through in-depth interviews of employees of six organizations in each industry, she identified several assumptions that distinguished these industries from each other. Among the differences she found are those shown in Table 18.2.[17]

Mergers and acquisitions often reveal differences in industry cultures. Ciba-Geigy, a Swiss pharmaceutical company now known as Novartis, didn't realize that the pharmaceutical and consumer products industries had different cultures until they acquired AirWick, which makes room deodorizers. The chemical basis and production processes for pharmaceuticals and room deodorizers are similar enough, but the two industries operate under very different assumptions and have very different missions. Consumer products are manufactured and sold to make money, whereas pharmaceutical products are created and distributed to save lives. Scientists at Ciba-Geigy were accustomed to thinking of their work in humanitarian terms and found it demeaning to work on developing room deodorizers. The two industry cultures were never successfully brought together, and the AirWick business was eventually sold off.[18]

Dutch researcher Geert Hofstede, who is most well known for improving our understanding of societal cultures (see Chapter 3), has also studied industry cul-

Assumptions in the Art Museum Industry	Assumptions in the Wine Industry
Identification with the industry is grounded in a person's degree of allegiance to the organization's educational mission.	Identification with the industry is grounded in a person's firm and geographic location.
Important constraints on a person's actions and organizational success include time and financial resources.	Important constraints on a person's actions and organizational success include the grape supply, regulators, and the physical environment.
Organizations within the industry enjoy a relationship of friendly interdependence. Similarly, the museum industry is viewed as interdependent with other cultural industries.	Organizations within the industry compete directly with each other, but together they are competing against the beer and distilled spirits industries.
Managers believe that expertise in judging "good" art is best gained through formal education in aesthetic standards.	Managers believe expertise in judging "good" wines is best gained through practical experience, that is, by tasting many different wines.

tures. His research indicates that industry cultures can be compared by using the dimensions shown in Figure 18.1.[19]

When companies from different industries or different segments of the same industry merge, form joint ventures, or enter into any other type of strategic alliance, cultural clashes often flare up unexpectedly. This culture clash seems to

Figure 18.1   *Dimensions for Describing Industry Cultures*

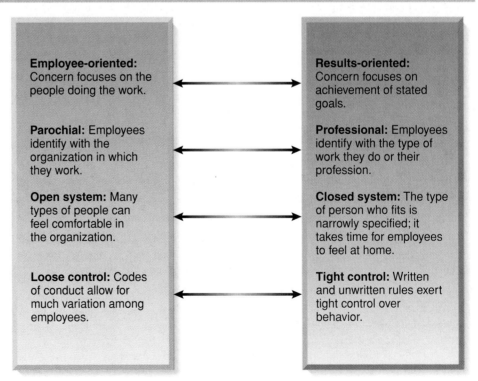

Employee-oriented: Concern focuses on the people doing the work. ⟷ **Results-oriented:** Concern focuses on achievement of stated goals.

Parochial: Employees identify with the organization in which they work. ⟷ **Professional:** Employees identify with the type of work they do or their profession.

Open system: Many types of people can feel comfortable in the organization. ⟷ **Closed system:** The type of person who fits is narrowly specified; it takes time for employees to feel at home.

Loose control: Codes of conduct allow for much variation among employees. ⟷ **Tight control:** Written and unwritten rules exert tight control over behavior.

be one of the primary reasons that so many mergers fail to meet expectations. The financial services industry has undergone restructuring through mergers and acquisitions during the past several years. In general, the trend has been toward consolidation, with the eventual goal being to provide customers with one-stop financial shopping. In the process, financial institutions learned that there are major subcultures within the financial services industry. When American Express, the credit card company, bought Shearson, a brokerage firm, its management didn't anticipate how difficult blending these two cultures would be. Ultimately, Shearson was sold off. More recently, when the brokerage firm of Morgan Stanley bought the brokerage firm of Dean Witter, it ended up with Dean Witter's Discover credit card business. Because of past failures, such as the one at American Express, experts wondered whether Morgan Stanley could make the new merger work. "I've always thought the credit card business didn't mix with the brokerage business," observed analyst Michael Flanagan. "The challenge is to dispel that notion." Analyst Raphael Soifer agreed, "I'm not convinced that Morgan Stanley will be able to sell brokerage services to Discover card [customers]. I think there's perhaps a long-term case to be made for selling the Discover card."[20]

As GE Capital has learned, careful planning about how to deal with cultural differences can increase the success of companies involved in strategic alliances.[21] GE Capital's approach to ensuring the successful integration of cultures is described in the Planning and Administration Competency account. Its Pathfinder model begins with preacquisition information gathering and analysis. If a decision is made to go ahead with an acquisition, a standard procedure for problem solving is then followed and the results are carefully monitored.

ORGANIZATIONAL CULTURES AND SUBCULTURES

Figure 18.2 provides a general framework for examining organizational cultures. It shows that an organization's culture is shaped by the higher level, *macro* cultures of societies and industries. For our purposes, the **macroculture** includes a combination of the assumptions and values of both the society and industry in which the organization (or one of its business units) operates.

The boundaries that separate one organizational culture from another are usually more clear-cut than those that separate societal or industry cultures. For many organizations, membership is *not* ambiguous: Either you belong to the organization, or you don't. In some organizations, however, the boundaries are getting fuzzy

MACROCULTURE

A combination of the assumptions and values of both the society and industry in which the organization (or one of its business units) operates.

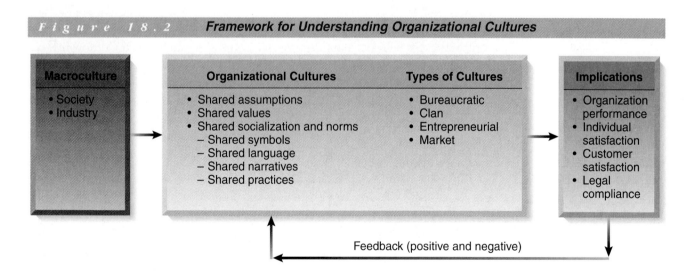

Figure 18.2 **Framework for Understanding Organizational Cultures**

Macroculture	Organizational Cultures	Types of Cultures	Implications

• Society
• Industry
	• Shared assumptions
	• Shared values
	• Shared socialization and norms
	  – Shared symbols
	  – Shared language
	  – Shared narratives
	  – Shared practices
		• Bureaucratic
		• Clan
		• Entrepreneurial
		• Market
			• Organization performance
			• Individual satisfaction
			• Customer satisfaction
			• Legal compliance

Feedback (positive and negative)

GE Capital's Pathfinder Model for Cultural Integration

GE Capital Services has made the successful management of acquisitions a cornerstone of its strategy for growth. Every business group has a business development officer whose job is to find potential acquisition targets. The company has made more than 100 acquisitions during the past five years, growing by 30 percent in the process. GE Capital's experience has shown that acquisitions are much more likely to be successful if the employees who end up working together share the same values and mindsets. Therefore conducting a cultural audit and identifying cultural barriers are tasks that GE Capital's managers complete before an acquisition decision is finalized.

Its cultural audits identify cultural

differences at all levels—societal, industry, and organizational. Regarding industry-level similarities and differences, the companies are compared in terms of costs, brands, technologies, and customers. If the differences seem so great that they could cause the acquisition to fail, GE drops the planned acquisition. If the differences seem manageable and an acquisition deal is finalized, a systematic process for integrating the cultures then begins. One of the first steps is to appoint an integration manager, who is responsible for integrating the cultures and the business and operational systems. As soon as the deal is finalized, key people from the two businesses are brought together to socialize, exchange information, and share their feelings about the new situation. Managers of the acquired company are quickly informed of GE Capital's twenty-five central policies and practices. Integration goals are developed, a 100-day deadline is set, and managers from the two companies meet for a three-day session devoted to exploring the cultural differences. Managers tell each other about their companies' his-

tories, folklore, and heroes. Topics include approaches to market penetration, the amount of focus on cost, and reliance on authority versus shared decision making. These discussions culminate in a written plan for the next six months or more. Such plans generally include short-term projects that require people from the two companies to work together to achieve some quick results, such as reducing costs. The plans, as well as other information related to the integration process, are posted on the company's intranet, whereby managers throughout the company can study them and learn from each new acquisition experience.[22]

* * *

To learn more about GE Capital Services, visit the company's home page at

www.ge.com/gecc18.html

Information about GE Capital Services can also be accessed from the home page of General Electric at

www.ge.com

because of increased reliance on temporary employees, contract workers, and strategic alliances. GE's Jack Welch has even gone so far as to suggest that his ideal organization would be "boundaryless." GE Capital's Pathfinder model for integrating acquisitions is a step in that direction. Despite GE's efforts to minimize its internal and external boundaries, GE retains a strong and distinctive organizational culture. In each of its businesses, everyone understands that the goal is to be number 1 or number 2 in the industry. Numerous specific practices within the company focus attention on this goal and create predictable patterns of managerial and employee behaviors regarding

- how to solve problems, meet goals, and deal with important customers, suppliers, and other stakeholders;

- how employees relate to one another;

- how employees are to perceive, think, and feel about the solutions that have been used in the past for dealing with various problems;

- how results are to be measured; and

- how rewards and punishments are to be determined.[23]

The more predictable that behavior patterns are, the stronger is the organization's culture. A strong organizational culture doesn't just happen, however. It's cultivated by management, learned and reinforced by employees, and passed on to new employees. Over time, it can change, though not easily. This uniformity doesn't mean that a culture simply can be written into a new-employees' handbook and learned by reading it, or even that employees can fully explain the culture. The underlying shared assumptions and values may be unstated and organizational members may have trouble consciously verbalizing some of them.[24]

As is true of societal culture, many organizations have several distinct subcultures. If the members of different subcultures don't trust and cooperate with one another, power struggles and gamesmanship may result. Sometimes organizational subcultures coexist peacefully within the overall organizational culture; at other times subcultures are a major source of continuing conflict.[25] When that happens, teamwork within the organization suffers. As described in the Teamwork Competency piece, conflicting subcultures have made teamwork virtually impossible at Andersen Worldwide. A firm that once was held together by a single strong culture, Andersen is now at war with itself.

Subcultures within organizations often reflect business or functional specialties (e.g., manufacturing, research and development, accounting, engineering, marketing, and human resources). One of the goals of TQM and reengineering efforts is to integrate subcultures that divide functional specialties and thereby reduce the conflicts that so often go hand-in-hand with them. Fragmented subcultures can also be stitched together by changing the physical layout, rotating employees among departments, and linking monetary rewards to the achievement of goals that require collaborative effort.[26]

TYPES OF ORGANIZATIONAL CULTURES

3

DISCUSS SEVERAL
GENERAL TYPES OF
ORGANIZATIONAL
CULTURES

Cultural elements and their relationships create a pattern that is distinct to an organization, just as a personality is unique to an individual. As with a classification of individuals that share some common characteristics, several general types of organizational cultures can be described. Of the many frameworks that have been proposed, one useful one is presented in Figure 18.3. The vertical axis reflects the relative formal control orientation, ranging from stable to flexible. The horizontal axis reflects the relative focus of attention, ranging from internal functioning to external functioning. The extreme corners of the four quadrants represent four pure types of organizational culture: bureaucratic, clan, entrepreneurial, and market.[27] In a culturally homogeneous organization, one of these basic types of culture will be predominant. In a culturally fragmented organization, multiple cultures are likely not only to exist but also to compete for superiority.

As is true of organization designs, different organizational cultures may be appropriate under different conditions, with no one type of culture being ideal for every situation. However, some employees may prefer one culture over another. As you read about each type of culture, consider which best fits your preferences. Employees who work in organizations with cultures that fit their view of an ideal culture tend to be committed to the organization and optimistic about its future.[28]

BUREAUCRATIC CULTURE

BUREAUCRATIC CULTURE
An organization in which employees value formalization, rules, standard operating procedures, and hierarchical coordination.

An organization that values formalization, rules, standard operating procedures, and hierarchical coordination has a **bureaucratic culture.** Recall that the long-term

TEAMWORK COMPETENCY
Andersen Worldwide Has Lost It

Andersen Worldwide has experienced debilitating internal conflicts between its accounting and consulting units. Since its founding in 1913, the accounting firm of Arthur Andersen had built a reputation for being so internally cohesive that employees were sometimes referred to as "Androids." Its consulting activities, which focus on information technology, didn't begin until 1954. During the first years of its existence, the mature accounting business helped smooth out the ups and downs of the entrepreneurial consulting business. For years, people who specialized in accounting and consulting coexisted in relative peace, relying on give and take to resolve conflicts. New recruits were hired straight out of college and socialized through rigorous training and mentorship programs. They were taught to believe that the firm as a whole was greater than the sum of its parts. Consultants, who didn't need in-depth knowledge of accounting, were expected to pass the CPA exam nevertheless. Most of the people who became partners had been with the firm their entire careers.

By the 1980s, the culture had become fragmented. Some partners came to the firm later in their careers and weren't CPAs. The consultants began to question the assumption that the two businesses were better off combined than they would be as separate firms. According to a former board member, "They began to think, 'well, we'd rather not be in one pot.'" In 1989, after several key partners from the consulting business left, the remaining partners negotiated a compromise that established Andersen Consulting as a separate business unit.

Since then, the two business units have continued to grow apart, each with its own culture and vision of the future. News stories have chronicled the in-fighting in detail, and some competitors have tried to use the feud to their own advantage. Deloitte & Touche Consulting Group, for example, ran full-page advertisements that read, "Andersen Consulting: Distracted by infighting. Deloitte Consulting: Focused on our clients. When you hire a consulting firm, you can't afford for them to be more concerned with their own problems than they are with

your well-being . . . since we're not wasting time fighting with each other, we give every client our undivided attention."[29]

* * *

To learn more about Andersen Worldwide, visit the home pages of its two units, Arthur Andersen at

www.arthurandersen.com

and Andersen Consulting at

www.ac.com

You may also find it useful to reread the description of the debate concerning the firm's strategic direction in the Real-Time Case Analysis at the end of Chapter 11.

concerns of a bureaucracy are predictability, efficiency, and stability. Its members highly value standardized goods and customer service. Behavioral norms support formality over informality.[30] Managers view their roles as being good coordinators, organizers, and enforcers of written rules and standards. Tasks, responsibilities, and authority for all employees are clearly defined. The many rules and processes are spelled out in thick manuals, and employees believe that their duty is to "go by the book" and follow legalistic procedures.

Most local, state, and federal governments have bureaucratic cultures, which can impede their effectiveness. The federal personnel manual, which spells out the rules for hiring and firing, runs to thousands of pages. Hundreds of pages are needed just to explain how to fill out some of the forms. The approval process for ordering a computer can take more than a year, during which time the equipment ordered can become technologically obsolete.[31]

Figure 18.3 **Framework of Types of Cultures**

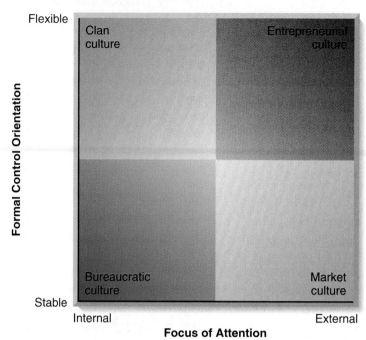

Focus of Attention

Sources: Adapted from R. Hooijberg and F. Petrock. On cultural change: Using the competing values framework to help leaders execute a transformational strategy. *Human Resource Management,* 32, 1993, pp. 29–50; and R. E. Quinn. *Beyond Rational Management: Mastering the Paradoxes and Competing Demands of High Performance.* San Francisco: Jossey-Bass, 1988.

CLAN CULTURE

CLAN CULTURE

The attributes of tradition, loyalty, personal commitment, extensive socialization, teamwork, self-management, and social influence.

Tradition, loyalty, personal commitment, extensive socialization, teamwork, self-management, and social influence are attributes of a ***clan culture.*** Its members recognize an obligation beyond the simple exchange of labor for a salary. They understand that contributions to the organization (e.g., hours worked per week) may exceed any contractual agreements. The individual's long-term commitment to the organization (loyalty) is exchanged for the organization's long-term commitment to the individual (security).

The clan culture achieves unity with a long and thorough socialization process. Long-time clan members serve as mentors and role models for newer members. These relationships perpetuate the organization's values and norms over successive generations of employees. The clan is aware of its unique history and often documents its origins and celebrates its traditions in various rites. Members have a shared image of the organization's style and manner of conduct. Public statements reinforce its values.

In a clan culture, members share feelings of pride in membership. They have a strong sense of identification and recognize their interdependence. The up-through-the-ranks career pattern results in an extensive network of colleagues whose paths have crossed and who have shared similar experiences. Shared goals, perceptions, and behavioral tendencies foster communication, coordination, and integration. A clan culture generates feelings of personal ownership of a business, product, or ideas. In addition, peer pressure to adhere to important norms is strong. The richness of the culture creates an environment in which few areas are left totally free from normative pressures. Depending on the types of its norms, the culture may or may not generate risk-taking behavior or innovation. Success is assumed to depend substantially on sensitivity to customers and concern for people. Teamwork, participation, and consensus decision making are believed to lead to this success. Arthur Andersen originally had a clan culture, as do many traditional Japanese organizations.

Fel-Pro, an auto-parts maker in Skokie, Illinois, had a clan culture. Maintaining that culture was made a condition of selling the company to Federal-Mogul. The Fel-Pro culture valued having a family atmosphere. It operated a summer camp for children of its employees, always sent parents a Treasury Bond upon the arrival of a new child, and funded scholarships for employees and their children. Teamwork among employees was promoted, and turnover was unusually low. The family programs cost the company 57 cents per worker hour, and company data indicated that employees who took advantage of the programs were more likely to participate in team problem solving and offer suggestions for operational improvements. When Chairman Richard Snell of Federal-Mogul approached Fel-Pro about buying the company, he was told that a deal could be worked out only if Fel-Pro's culture was protected. Although he worried about how Federal-Mogul's employees might react, Snell agreed to continue operating Fel-Pro's summer camp for at least two years and to continue the scholarship fund for at least five years.[32]

ENTREPRENEURIAL CULTURE

ENTREPRENEURIAL CULTURE

Exhibits high levels of risk taking, dynamism, and creativity.

High levels of risk taking, dynamism, and creativity characterize an ***entrepreneurial culture.*** There is a commitment to experimentation, innovation, and being on the leading edge. This culture doesn't just quickly react to changes in the environment, it creates change. Effectiveness means providing new and unique products and rapid growth. Individual initiative, flexibility, and freedom foster growth and are encouraged and well rewarded.

Entrepreneurial cultures usually are associated with small to middle-sized companies that are still run by a founder, such as Microsoft, Intel, and Nordstrom. Nordstrom, one of the West Coast's premier department store chains, is an example of a large company that has kept its entrepreneurial culture. Sales personnel are expected to do whatever it takes to please the customer. Writing thank you notes to customers and reminding them of special occasions that may require gift purchases are tasks often done during a salesperson's days off. Stories of heroic deeds are part of the company's culture, too. Examples include changing a customer's flat tire in the parking lot, driving for three hours to deliver a holiday gift, and buying a shirt that met the customer's style preference from a competitor in order to give the customer what he wanted. These heroic deeds are considered part of doing the job, which is meeting customers' needs so that they'll return to buy more. Incentive pay plans motivate everyone at Nordstrom to approach their jobs as opportunities for entrepreneurial risk taking and rewards.[33]

MARKET CULTURE

MARKET CULTURE

Values achievement of measurable and demanding goals, especially those that are financial and market-based.

The achievement of measurable and demanding goals, especially those that are financial and market-based (e.g., sales growth, profitability, and market share) characterize a ***market culture.*** Hard-driving competitiveness and a profits orientation prevail throughout the organization. Pepsico, Aramark, Gulf & Western, among others, are organizations that have created market cultures.

In a market culture, the relationship between individual and organization is contractual. That is, the obligations of each party are agreed on in advance. In this sense, the formal control orientation is quite stable. The individual is responsible for some level of performance, and the organization promises a specified level of rewards in return. Increased levels of performance are exchanged for increased rewards, as outlined in an agreed schedule. Neither party recognizes the right of the other to demand more than was originally specified. The organization doesn't promise (or imply) security; the individual doesn't promise (or imply) loyalty. The contract, renewed annually if each party adequately performs its obligations, is utilitarian because each party uses the other to further its own goals. Rather than promoting a feeling of membership in a social system, the market culture values independence and individuality and encourages members to pursue their own financial goals and, by so doing, to help each other. For example, the salesperson who increases sales will make more money, and the firm will earn more profits through the salesperson's greater sales volume.

The market culture doesn't exert much informal, social pressure on an organization's members. They don't share a common set of expectations regarding management style or philosophy. Superiors' interactions with subordinates largely consist of negotiating performance–reward agreements and/or evaluating requests for resource allocations. Superiors aren't formally judged on their effectiveness as role models or mentors. The absence of a long-term commitment by both parties results in a weak socialization process. Social relations among co-workers aren't officially emphasized, and few economic incentives are tied directly to cooperating with peers. Managers are expected to cooperate with managers in other departments only to the extent necessary to achieve their performance goals. As a result, they may not develop an extensive network of colleagues within the organization. The market culture often is tied to monthly, quarterly, and annual performance goals based on profits.

Colgate-Palmolive has adopted a market culture in order to survive in the highly competitive consumer products business. Lois Juliber is one manager who thrives in that culture. As head of North American operations, she sharply reduced costs and reorganized business processes. The time needed to deliver orders was cut by 25 percent. Before that, as the company's chief technology officer, she had pushed through the FDA the massive documentation required for the new Total toothpaste. The new brand cut deeply into Procter & Gamble's Crest sales and gave Colgate a lead in market share for the first time in thirty-five years. In an earlier assignment as head of Asia operations, Juliber had doubled sales and tripled profits in just three years.[34] With these successes behind her, Juliber was recently given an even tougher assignment—to develop a globally integrated system of manufacturing and operations procedures.

ORGANIZATIONAL IMPLICATIONS

Organizational culture has the potential to enhance organizational performance, individual satisfaction, the sense of certainty about how problems are to be handled, and so on. However, if the organizational culture gets out of step with the changing expectations of external stakeholders, it can hinder effectiveness.[35]

The need to determine which attributes of an organization's culture should be preserved and which should be modified is constant. In the United States during the 1980s, many companies began changing their cultures to be more responsive to customers' expectations of product quality and service. During the 1990s, many organizations began to reassess how well their organizational cultures fit the expectations of the workforce. Since World War II, the U.S. workforce has changed demographically, becoming more diverse. More and more employees have begun to feel that organizational cultures established decades ago are out of step with contemporary values. We address the challenge of adjusting established organizational cultures to meet the expectations of a demographically diverse workforce in the remainder of this chapter.

MEANING AND IMPORTANCE OF WORKFORCE DIVERSITY

4

EXPLAIN THE MEANING AND IMPORTANCE OF WORKFORCE DIVERSITY

DEMOGRAPHIC DIVERSITY
The degree of mix of demographic characteristics of the people who make up an organization's workforce.

CULTURAL DIVERSITY
The full mix of the cultures and subcultures to which members belong.

As we described in Chapter 1, the composition of the U.S. workforce has changed dramatically since about 1950. Many of the changes are summarized by the term *workforce diversity*. Recall that workforce diversity refers to the mix of people from various backgrounds in the labor force. Two important aspects of workforce diversity are demographic and cultural diversity. In large organizations, different staff may be responsible for initiatives related to managing these two types of diversity. However, most managers don't make a sharp distinction between them.

DEMOGRAPHIC AND CULTURAL DIVERSITY

Characteristics such as age, sex, race, and national origin are typically referred to as *demographics*. **Demographic diversity** reflects the degree of mix of characteristics of the people who make up an organization's workforce. An organization that employs mostly high school students or mostly workers who have returned to work from retirement would have very little age diversity. An organization that employs people of all ages in approximately equal numbers would have a great deal of age diversity. The U.S. Department of Labor regularly issues reports that document the demographic characteristics of the U.S. workforce, and most organizations also keep track of the demographic characteristics of their employees. As we described in Chapter 12, numerous EEO laws and regulations prohibit employers from basing employment decisions on a *person's* demographic characteristics. However, affirmative action efforts may be used to ensure that the demographic characteristics of an *organization's* workforce reflect the demographic characteristics of the available labor force. Because of the legal issues associated with demographic diversity, many organizations now consider compliance with EEO laws and regulations to be distinct from the effective management of cultural diversity.

An organization's **cultural diversity** refers to the full mix of the cultures and subcultures to which members of the workforce belong. Subcultures with which employees may identify include those described earlier in this chapter (e.g., occupational and regional). Also included, however, are subcultures associated with demographic characteristics. For example, employees within each generation (or even each age cohort) tend to share a subculture that is distinct from the subcultures of other generations. In addition, subcultures based in religion, marital and family status, sexual orientation, and other unifying life experiences typically are included in the meaning of cultural diversity.

At Dayton Hudson, a Minneapolis-based retailer, appreciating the cultural diversity of customers is as important as appreciating employee diversity. Consequently, the company thinks of diversity very broadly and in ways linked to buying behaviors. For example, management and buyers recognize that people who are unusually large or small may have different perspectives from those who are of average size when it comes to pricing, merchandise selection, and the physical layout of stores.

MONOLITHIC, PLURALISTIC, AND MULTICULTURAL ORGANIZATIONS

In Chapter 1, we defined a multicultural organization as having a workforce representing the full mix of cultures found in the population at large, along with a commitment to fully utilize these human resources. In multicultural organizations, the organizational culture reflects a blending of many cultures and subcultures, with no one culture dominating the others. As a result, a new type of culture emerges from this combination.

MONOLITHIC ORGANIZATION

Dominated by a single majority culture or subculture, and members of other cultures or subcultures are expected to adopt the norms and values of the majority.

Such an organizational culture is in sharp contrast to monolithic and pluralistic organizations. ***Monolithic organizations*** are dominated by a single majority culture or subculture, and members of other cultures or subcultures are expected to adopt the norms and values of the majority. In many large U.S. organizations, the norms and values of white, American, heterosexual men are dominant. Employees who are different in any respect often feel that, in order to succeed, they must adjust their behavior at work to fit those norms. However, in many medium-sized and small businesses, the norms are those of other cultures. For example, Wall Street Strategies, a business that provides advice on stock selection, is a monolithic organization in which the norms reflect the values of the African-American men who work there.[36]

PLURALISTIC ORGANIZATION

Mixed in their cultural composition, but there is still a dominant culture or subculture that members of the organization are expected to adopt.

Compared to monolithic organizations, ***pluralistic organizations*** are more mixed in their cultural composition. The norms are still those of a dominant culture or subculture, which members of the organization are expected to follow, but members from other cultural backgrounds fill a variety of jobs at all levels in the organization. Cultural differences are accepted as part of the work environment, and each subculture attempts to maintain its own set of norms and values. That is, the subcultures aren't fully blended, as in a multicultural organization. Many pluralistic companies are located in large urban centers, such as New York City, where small and medium-sized high-tech companies hire immigrants to fill approximately one-third of their technical jobs. Muffin Head Productions is typical. Owner Haim Ariav describes his small company as the United Nations of multimedia because five of his sixteen employees are immigrants.[37]

Many U.S. organizations are in the process of transforming themselves from monolithic organizations to pluralistic organizations or from pluralistic organizations to multicultural organizations. Fundamentally, these transformations involve changing the organizational culture. The specific approach that an organization uses to transform its culture depends on the organization's goals.

ORGANIZATIONAL GOALS FOR MANAGING WORKFORCE DIVERSITY

We've noted that legal compliance with nondiscrimination laws is one reason that organizations are concerned about managing workforce diversity. Human resources management systems designed to promote the goal of equal employment communicate an organization's commitment to treating employees fairly and have improved the employment status of protected groups.[38] Although many laws and regulations address demographic diversity, few address cultural diversity. The extent to which organizations attempt to manage workforce diversity to comply with EEO laws and regulations or to meet other goals varies greatly. Increasingly, however, concerns about workforce diversity reflect recognition of the potential benefits of diversity for improved organizational performance.[39]

Legal Compliance. Complying with laws and regulations that prohibit discrimination, such as Title VII of the Civil Rights Act, is a necessary first step for any organization. The basic premise of such laws and regulations is that employment decisions should be based on job-related qualifications, not membership in a demographic group. Affirmative action regulations, which have recently become quite controversial, go a bit further. The basic premise of these regulations is that organizations should actively recruit job applicants to build a workforce that reflects the demographics of the qualified labor force locally. To monitor their progress, employers generally assess various employment numbers and ratios. At organizations such as 3M, Philip Morris, and Baltimore Gas and Electric, these measures include female and minority hiring numbers, offer/acceptance ratios, turnover and retention rates, promotion patterns, downsizing decisions, and compensation levels.[40]

Of course, simply monitoring numbers isn't sufficient to ensure legal compliance. As Texaco learned, a company must take action to change the numbers if they suggest a pattern of discrimination. In 1990, the Department of Labor declared that Texaco was deficient in its minority representation, and in 1995 the EEOC issued a similar finding. Although the company's employment numbers indicated that it had been making some progress in hiring a more diverse workforce, promotion and pay rates lagged behind those of other companies in the industry. The problem was that too many managers within the company ignored the company's nondiscrimination policies. They often allowed their personal prejudices to affect their managerial actions. The seriousness of Texaco's problems became public in 1996, when secretly recorded conversations revealed that certain senior executives used racial epithets and plotted to destroy documents demanded by the courts in a discrimination case. Other evidence presented during the case revealed that supervisors commonly referred to members of racial subgroups in derogatory terms. Many employees did nothing to protest such treatment for fear of losing their jobs, and others quit. Eventually, some took their evidence to court. As part of the settlement, Texaco agreed to pay some $140 million to current and former aggrieved employees—the largest settlement ever for a case of racial discrimination. The company also agreed to begin a massive cultural change effort.[41]

Some organizations that initially monitored their numbers primarily because of concerns about legal compliance discovered that the numbers could also be used to gain insights into other problems. At the accounting firm of Coopers & Lybrand, employment numbers alerted the partners to a disturbing trend. The firm was losing women with strong records of accomplishment between the manager and partner levels. Because balancing work and family is something that many women struggle with at midcareer, the partners wondered whether these successful women were leaving to care for their families. As it turned out, they weren't; they were leaving to take jobs at other companies. Coopers & Lybrand's partners realized that the firm's corporate culture wasn't as positive as it needed to be to retain top talent and took steps to correct the situation.[42]

Positive Organizational Culture. By analyzing various employment statistics, an organization can determine whether people from different backgrounds are being given job opportunities that match their capabilities. Research indicates that, as the number of employees who share a subculture increases, its members experience fewer problems and less negative stereotyping.[43] Nevertheless, managers shouldn't fall into the trap of using records kept to monitor legal compliance as a basis for drawing conclusions about how employees are matched to jobs or feel about their work situations.

A positive organizational culture is one in which everyone feels equally integrated into the larger system. Members of majority and minority subcultures feel respected; everyone has an equal chance to express views and influence decisions; and everyone has similar access to both formal and informal networks within the organization. Sergio Peneda, a product manager in the applications and Internet client group, believes that Microsoft has a positive culture in terms of diversity. He describes it this way: "At Microsoft, you're ultimately judged based on your ability to articulate leadership and do a really great job in what you do. And that's irrespective of whoever you are."[44]

Marriott International has a policy aimed at guaranteeing fair treatment to all employees. It allows workers to appeal grievances all the way to the company chairman. Top management regularly gives poor performers second and third chances. A peer review procedure involves workers in reviewing disciplinary actions. Susan Gonzalez, a manager at the New York Times Square hotel is so concerned about ensuring fairness that she keeps records of holiday requests and assignments going back four years to show that choice days are evenly doled out. The hotel's employees come from seventy countries, speak forty-seven languages, and observe many different religious and ethnic events. Thus making assignments of time off for holidays is a particularly challenging responsibility.[45] At both Dayton Hudson and Marriott, cultural diversity among employees is beneficial for customers. Multilingual employees make it easier for store customers and hotel guests to communicate in a language other than English. At Dayton Hudson, the additional languages that employees speak are printed on their name badges.

The most common methods used to assess organizational culture are employee surveys and focus groups. Questionnaires may be used to ask employees individually or in focus group discussions whether they feel valued and whether they feel that everyone is equally valued; the degree of respect, sensitivity, and fairness managers show toward employees from different subcultures; and how employees feel about their future career opportunities. To assess its culture, GE developed a survey designed specifically to measure how members of various subcultures feel about the organization's culture. Questions addressed career development and mobility, management supportiveness and behavior, mentoring, work life, and general perceptions of the organization's stance on diversity. GE compared the responses of employees in its many different locations and units to determine where organizational culture changes were needed. Companies such as American Express and United Technologies benchmark the results of their culture surveys against the responses given by employees in other companies.

In addition to asking employees directly about the organizational culture, some organizations conduct cultural audits to evaluate the language used in organizational documents and advertising, the visible symbols that decorate public spaces, the types of awards given to employees, the types and quality of food available in the company cafeteria, policies regarding holidays and absences, and the types of social activities sponsored by the organization, among other items. Cultural audits often reveal that the organizational culture reflects the values and preferences of some subcultures while ignoring those of other subcultures. When such discrepancies are found, simple changes often can be made to create a more positive culture.

Using Diversity to Create Economic Value. A third reason that organizations are striving to manage diversity effectively is because they believe that they can use diversity to create greater economic value.[46] With a diverse workforce and positive organizational culture in place, many managers believe their companies will be able to

- develop products and services for new markets,

- attract a broader range of customers,

- improve customer satisfaction and increase business from repeat customers, and

- reduce costs, including those associated with litigation.

Sergio Peneda believes that his Latino heritage brings a valuable perspective to the products he helps create at Microsoft, and he believes the same is true for other minorities: "I think any person of color can have a direct and positive influence on certain products, particularly those for the home. As more and more people get on the Web, they'll want to see a variety of content," he explains. "I think, long term, that presents me with an opportunity to influence and help arrange more Latino-directed content so the world can see that the Internet isn't just targeted to one ethnic group." In the United States, Hispanics are the fastest growing, and will soon be the largest, ethnic group. They currently account for 11 percent of the population. Although two-thirds have roots in Mexico, many have roots in Central and South America, Puerto Rico, and Cuba. According to the Census Bureau, by 2020, one of every six U.S. citizens will have an Hispanic heritage.[47]

Denny's is an organization whose negative corporate culture resulted in blatantly poor customer service for African-American customers and several consecutive years of financial losses. In 1993, on the same day that it settled one federal suit for discriminating against customers in California, six black Secret Service agents waited nearly an hour before being served in a Denny's restaurant in Maryland. This wasn't an isolated incidence. Such poor customer treatment was condoned by Denny's managers all over the country. As one news reporter put it, "Diversity was a concept as foreign to its all-white management team as foie gras was to a Denny's menu."[48] The suit that the six agents filed against Denny's was the third such suit filed that year. Meanwhile, competitors such as McDonald's had established strong links to minority communities and developed many loyal customers. The costs to Denny's of settling these and similar suits were enormous. As part of one settlement, Denny's paid $54 million to 295,000 aggrieved customers.

In Denny's case, there is little doubt that corporate culture contributed to the company's decline during the 1980s and early 1990s. Even before Denny's problems were being reported in the media, a consulting firm hired to help the company improve its financial performance told management that its organizational culture was a problem. "The lack of diversity was the first issue we identified," according to Bill Boggs, a managing partner of the consulting firm. "I told the senior managers that Flagstar [the parent company] was in a strategically dangerous position, since their customers are certainly not all white males." Then-CEO Jerry Richardson replied that he had "just never thought about it." Five years later, Richardson was finally replaced by Ron Petty, the former head of Burger King. Since then, Denny's has effected a major cultural and financial turnaround.[49]

To date, little research is available publicly to document the economic benefits of a diverse workforce and positive organizational culture. However, some companies use proprietary information to establish the economic benefits of diversity. Others simply believe that there is a link and don't require research evidence to support their view. St. Paul Companies describes the link between diversity and economic value this way: "The execution of a global marketing strategy that recognizes customer differences and new emerging markets will give us an important edge and create profitable business . . . it is important that we recognize the relationship of diversity to profitability. Growing our business recognizes the importance of redefining or understanding of our customers. Increasingly, we will need to fully measure the impact of this understanding relative to profitability and growth." Their measures include growth in multicultural markets, customer surveys, and agent focus groups.[50]

MANAGING WORKFORCE DIVERSITY FOR SUCCESS

5

DESCRIBE SEVERAL ACTIV-
ITIES REQUIRED TO MAN-
AGE WORKFORCE DIVER-
SITY SUCCESSFULLY

For organizations with diverse workforces in place, the challenges of creating a positive organizational culture and using diversity to create economic value are substantial. Most people simply are more at ease interacting with people who are similar to themselves in various ways. Communication seems easier and misunderstandings, perceptions of unfair treatment, and conflict seem to occur less often. For employees who live and socialize mostly with people who have similar cultural backgrounds, working in a culturally diverse organization may be uncomfortable—especially if they don't have well-developed communication, teamwork, and self-management competencies. As many employers are learning, however, they *can* manage cultural diversity in ways that all employees will feel comfortable and be able to use their talents to the fullest.

As is true for many other managerial responsibilities, effectively managing cultural diversity is a continuing process, not a one-time program or short-term fad. Organizations that succeed in managing diversity do so because top management is committed to achieving legal compliance, instituting a positive organizational culture, and using diversity to create economic value. Such managers recognize that significant organizational changes may be needed to achieve these goals, and they are willing to commit resources to making such changes. Investments of time, money, and people all are necessary to complete any type of large-scale organizational change. As shown in Figure 18.4, the activities required to change from an organization that values cultural homogeneity to one that values cultural diversity

Figure 18.4   **Phases of Diversity Management Change Efforts**

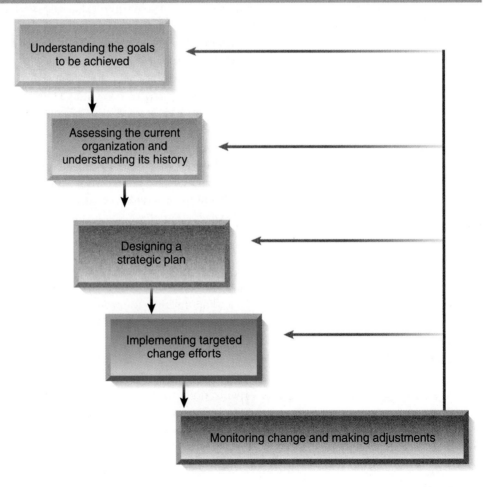

can be undertaken in five phases that involve

- understanding the goals to be achieved,

- assessing the current organization and understanding its history,

- designing a strategic plan for creating change,

- implementing a large number and variety of targeted change efforts, and

- monitoring change efforts against goals, and making adjustments as needed.

UNDERSTANDING THE GOALS TO BE ACHIEVED

When managers set goals related to improving the financial performance of an organization, they generally base them on a reasonably clear understanding of what must be done to meet them. Past experience provides frameworks for thinking about the organization and how changes in one part of it are likely to affect changes in other parts. They know who the key stakeholders are and have a general understanding of the major concerns of those stakeholders. They are working in familiar territory, using familiar language.

When managers set out to change the way an organization manages diversity, the first step often involves identifying new types of goals and methods of achieving them. Diversity consultants often help managers with this phase. Through one- or two-day training sessions, they can help managers think about the types of changes that they can make (e.g., better legal compliance, more positive culture, and greater economic value). The consultants can also help managers develop measures that they can use to assess the effectiveness of the changes made (e.g., employment statistics, cultural audits, and customer satisfaction). For managers such as Denny's former CEO Jerry Richardson, who have never given much thought to the issue of cultural diversity, this early educational phase can also help them identify diversity issues and learn to discuss them. For others, it can help them expand their views of the types of cultural differences that may be important in their organizations. Such fundamental ideas and discussions provide a necessary foundation for beginning to dispel some of the mistaken ideas that managers often have about cultural differences and their importance.

Lucent Technologies understands that managing diversity effectively is essential to the company's success. To work toward this goal, Lucent offers diversity courses, organizes mentoring relationships, and supports a wide array of Employee Partnership Groups, including the Alliance of Black Lucent Employees (ABLE), the Asia/Pacific American Association for Advancement of Lucent (4A-Lucent), and the Hispanic Association of Lucent Employees (HISPA). As described in the Strategic Action Competency feature, Lucent Technologies is now expanding rapidly into global markets. As it does, it confronts new types of diversity.

ASSESSING THE CURRENT ORGANIZATION AND UNDERSTANDING ITS HISTORY

Traditional organizational practices tend to minimize cultural diversity in various ways. Recruiting practices emphasize finding candidates from "reliable" sources. Interviews screen out candidates who "don't fit." Socialization and training practices produce uniform ways of thinking and behaving. Attendance policies and pay practices standardize work schedules. And bureaucratic approaches to management often limit how much discretion managers can exercise in addressing the special needs of employees. Many such practices were adopted by organizations for good reasons. For example, standardization was viewed as a way to increase efficiency

Lucent's Global Diversity Strategy

Lucent Technologies came into being as an autonomous company in 1996 as a result of a major restructuring of AT&T. Headquartered in Murray Hill, New Jersey, Lucent employs over 130,000 people. As a provider of both the hardware and the software that runs the world's communication systems, innovation is at the center of Lucent's business strategy. Today, 20 percent of Lucent employees live outside the United States. Bell Labs, Lucent's R&D unit, is the source of most of the company's breakthrough inventions.

For decades, Bell Labs has enjoyed a reputation as one of the world's most productive research units. To maintain that reputation, Lucent knows it must attract and fully utilize the best scientific talent in the world. Many breakthrough inventions are made by teams of employees who focus their diverse areas of specialized knowledge onto a common problem. One such team invented quantum cascade (QC) lasers that operate at room temperature and are 25 times more powerful than the earlier models, which operated only at -300 degrees Fahrenheit.

Global diversity has long been a part of the culture at Bell Labs, but until recently, the other former-AT&T units that are now part of Lucent focused most of their efforts in the United States. As Lucent seeks to grow by providing its technologies to countries around the world, however, global diversity is beginning to affect everyone. According to Jim Brewington, president of the Micro Electronics group, "It is only through understanding cultural and human differences around the world that we will achieve world-class results. Just as we seek to be best in class in quality, productivity, and innovation, we need to be aggressive in being best in class in fully utilizing the skills and talents of all Lucent people."[51]

* * *

To learn more about Lucent Technologies, visit the company's home page at

www.lucent.com

and fair treatment of employees. As organizations consider how to change their cultures to be more accepting of diversity, practices that create uniformity within the organization often become targets. When the changes are implemented, however, unexpected consequences sometimes follow. Organizations that create multifunctional teams, for example, often are surprised by how much longer these teams can take to reach a decision. If speedy decisions are important to satisfy customers or take advantage of fleeting opportunities, this unexpected consequence may damage the organization's image and even its profitability. Before managers begin designing new approaches to managing diversity, they first need to be sure that they understand how current practices affect the amount and nature of diversity—both in the organization as a whole and within its smaller units. Some types of homogeneity may be appropriate, or even essential to effective operations, and thus should be retained after careful evaluation.

DEVELOPING A PLAN FOR CHANGE

As we described in Chapter 13, managers should begin the process of planned organizational change by assessing the environment and determining performance gaps. This aspect of the planning process calls for setting overall goals for managing cultural diversity, followed by setting more specific goals. Successful plans are guided by a clear vision for the future, involve all relevant stakeholders, and include a clear and realistic timetable.

Vision. Articulating and communicating a clear vision of how the future can be better is essential in developing a plan for change. Until leaders formulate a clear vision and persuade others to join them in being dedicated to that vision, they won't be able to generate the enthusiasm and resources needed for large-scale cultural change.

Involvement. For the plan to be effective, those who are affected must buy into it. The best way to ensure that is through early involvement. It seems obvious that employees should be involved, but often this principle is forgotten, even by experienced managers. Xerox has a long record of enlightened diversity management. One of its earliest successes involved a caucus group for African-American employees. In fact, it was so successful that the company decided to create a caucus group for female employees. However, the first attempt to establish a women's caucus—in the mid 1970s—failed. One explanation for the failure was that the women's caucus was designed to duplicate the existing African-American caucus instead of being designed specifically to address the concerns of female employees. A few years later, female employees at Xerox began to establish caucus groups on their own. Eventually there were a dozen different women's caucuses: Some are national, some are regional, and some are specific to one location; some are for minority women and others aren't; some are for exempt employees and others are for nonexempt employees. At Xerox, at least, women have several caucus groups that meet their needs. Task forces, focus groups, surveys, hot lines, and informal conversations are just a few of the ways managers can involve employees and other stakeholders in planning change efforts.

Timing. Planned organizational change usually follows an evolutionary—not revolutionary—path. Realistic expectations about how quickly change will occur are important to the long-term success of change efforts. Usually, change occurs more slowly than expected. Xerox began changing its culture more than thirty years ago and continues to do so. Digital, another leader in terms of managing diversity, began its change efforts more than twenty years ago. It is doubtful that managers in either of these companies anticipated how long their companies' change efforts would continue to evolve. Although meaningful changes in corporate cultures occur slowly, not all useful initiatives require decades to implement. Furthermore, significant changes in the culture may not be needed to address some diversity issues successfully. Changes designed to help employees balance their work and nonwork commitments might be effective within only a year or two. Sometimes the slowness of change is merely frustrating. At other times unrealistic expectations cause change efforts to be abandoned prematurely. Learning from the experiences of change experts and other organizations may be the best way for a manager to develop a timetable for cultural change.

IMPLEMENTING TARGETED CHANGE EFFORTS

The list of methods that organizations can use to manage cultural diversity is quite long and varied.[52] Thus managers need to target specific efforts and set priorities for implementing them. One targeted change effort that can be used quickly is simply to terminate employees who create a negative climate or otherwise engage in clearly inappropriate behavior. At the brokerage firm of Smith Barney, Nicholas Cuneo was known for his intimidation tactics. One woman recalled being in his office when he casually opened his desk drawer, took out a gun, and laid it on the desk. This and numerous other incidents of intimidation and humiliation eventually resulted in a lawsuit. Cuneo, a twenty-five-year veteran of the company, was immediately given a leave of absence and he later retired.[53]

Assessing compensation levels and making needed adjustments is another type of targeted change effort. Women around the world generally earn less than men in the same types of jobs, according to data collected by the United Nations. Frustrated with this situation, many are leaving the corporate world, often to set up their own businesses.[54] In the United States, numerous studies have shown that women tend be paid less than men even when their education, experience, skills, performance, and job assignments are equivalent. Such pay differentials generally have negative consequences for organizational culture. Female employees often feel unfairly treated and may become resentful. These feelings may result in higher turnover rates for women, which can in turn be demoralizing for other women. By changing their procedures for setting pay rates to reduce the role of subjective judgments, organizations can quickly signal their intention to move from being a monolithic organization toward becoming a pluralistic or multicultural organization.[55]

Perhaps the most common targeted action that organizations take is to send employees to diversity training sessions. Training programs vary greatly, but most attempt to provide basic information about cultural differences and similarities and sensitize participants to the powerful role that culture has on their work behavior. How informed are you about issues of cultural diversity? To get a sense of how well you are able to separate myth from fact, take the Diversity Knowledge quiz presented in the Self-Management Competency feature.

An organization's choice of specific efforts may reflect the nature of diversity that is important for the organization, the goals set, the actions of other organizations in the industry, and so on. At Dayton Hudson much of the focus is on customers, and specific targeted change efforts included providing seating that older customers could use to rest their feet for a few minutes, putting baby-changing stations in the men's lounges, and providing diversity training to demonstrate how mistaken employees can be when they base inferences about customers on appearances alone.

Texaco's comprehensive plan for creating cultural change, agreed to as part of its lawsuit settlement, focuses more on the treatment of employees than the treatment of customers. It includes the activities listed in Table 18.3, many of which are typically found in plans developed by other organizations.

Implementing such changes will take many years, and many challenges will arise along the way. Among the most difficult challenges that Texaco and other companies face as they attempt to implement change are

- managing the reactions of members of the dominant culture, who may feel that they have lost some of the power they had previously held and exercised;

- synthesizing the diversity of opinions from individuals and using them as the basis for reaching meaningful agreement on issues; and

- avoiding real and perceived tokenism and quota systems that can help the organization achieve its quantitative goals but can be destructive to developing a positive culture.[56]

Perhaps the biggest challenge to managers, however, is understanding that cultural diversity can have many organizational consequences. For example, on the one hand diversity can enhance a team's ability to solve problems creatively. On the other hand, the price of such creativity may be heightened conflict within the team. Similarly, changing the mix of men and women in a team or department toward a 50–50 split may improve the attituides of the women involved while irritating the men. Managers shouldn't expect that diversity-related initiatives affect members of the organization in uniformly positive ways. They should be prepared to weigh carefully which costs they are willing to incur in order to achieve other gains.[57]

SELF-MANAGEMENT COMPETENCY
Diversity Knowledge Quiz

Indicate whether each statement is True or False. Correct answers are given later in the chapter.

1.	T	F	Joy and fear are feelings that can be accurately recognized from facial expressions, regardless of which cultures people are from.
2.	T	F	A person who is over age sixty-five and living in one of the world's developing regions is three times more likely to be working than a person of that age living in a developed region.
3.	T	F	Worldwide, about 50 percent of women between the ages of fifteen and sixty-four are in the labor force.
4.	T	F	Most Americans with Japanese heritage come from families who have lived in the United States for at least two or three generations.
5.	T	F	College graduation rates have been declining for men during the past decade and increasing for women.
6.	T	F	Most people could count on their fingers the number of female and minority CEOs who head one of the 500 largest firms in the United States.
7.	T	F	In America's ten largest cities, an average of one of four persons is of Latino origin.
8.	T	F	Compared to other demographic groups, gay men tend to be better educated and hold higher paying jobs.
9.	T	F	Compared to other employees, persons with disabilities have better safety records.
10.	T	F	Mental speed slows down slightly but steadily beginning at about age thirty, but performance of many complex mental tasks continues to improve steadily as people age.
11.	T	F	As recently as 1970, interracial marriages were illegal in some parts of the United States.
12.	T	F	Almost all Fortune 500 firms indicate that they are implementing initiatives to manage diversity.

MONITORING CHANGE AND MAKING ADJUSTMENTS

When an organization offers a new product or service in the marketplace, it almost always uses one or more numerical indicators to measure its success. When the development and sale of a product or service is successful, the people who contributed to that success often are recognized and rewarded. Many organizations apply these same principles to the introduction of diversity-related changes, and doing so seems to pay off. Research shows that the success of diversity training initiatives is greater in organizations that evaluate the effectiveness of the training and in those that offer rewards to managers who make diversity-related improvements in their business units.[58] At Dow Chemical, managers are encouraged to promote women at a rate at least equal to that of men. Hoechst Celanese is more specific. Based on its analysis of graduating college students, management sets numerical targets for its workforce. For example, by 2000, the company wants 34 percent of its managers to be women and minorities. Twenty-five percent of managers' bonuses are tied to their performance on diversity initiatives, which include training programs and mentoring, as well as developing employees for promotion. American Express ties managers' bonuses to their performance as measured by employees' responses to the firm's annual attitude surveys.[59]

Not everyone accepts this approach, however. For example, Colgate-Palmolive doesn't buy the idea of numerical goals. Others worry that attempts to quantify results may backfire because things often get worse before they get better. After

Table 18.3 **Components of Texaco's Cultural Change Initiatives**

Recruitment and Hiring

• Ask search firms to identify wider arrays of candidates

• Enhance the interviewing, selection, and hiring skills of managers

• Expand college recruitment at historically minority colleges

Identifying and Developing Talent

• Form a partnership with INROADS, a nationwide internship program that targets minority students for management careers

• Establish a mentoring process

• Refine the company's global succession planning system to improve identification of talent

• Improve the selection and development of managers and leaders to help ensure that they are capable of maximizing team performance

Ensuring Fair Treatment

• Conduct extensive diversity training

• Implement an alternative dispute resolution process

• Include women and minorities on all human resources committees throughout the company

Holding Managers Accountable

• Link managers' compensation to their success in creating "openness and inclusion in the workplace"

• Implement 360-degree feedback for all managers and supervisors

• Redesign the company's employee attitude survey and begin using it annually to monitor employee attitudes

Improve Relationships with External Stakeholders

• Broaden the company's base of vendors and suppliers to incorporate more minority- and women-owned businesses

• Increase banking, investment, and insurance business with minority- and women-owned firms

• Add more independent, minority retailers and increase the number of minority managers in company-owned gas stations and Xpress Lube outlets

Source: Adapted from V. C. Smith. Texaco outlines comprehensive initiatives. *Human Resource Executive.* February 1997, p. 13; A. Bryant. How much has Texaco changed? A mixed report card on anti-bias efforts. *New York Times,* November 2, 1997, pp. 3–1, 3–16, 3–17; and Texaco's workforce diversity plan, as reprinted in *Workforce,* March 1997 (suppl.).

R. R. Donnelley & Sons started its cultural change efforts, black employment fell from 8 percent to 6 percent. (See Chapter 10 for background information about Donnelley.) The small number of black employees, in turn, led the company to ask those who remained to attend multiple diversity training sessions to ensure that their views were represented. Employees found the training sessions to be stressful, and some resented having to attend multiple sessions, especially in light of the declining minority employment.[60] Some indicators commonly show negative effects, whereas others show the opposite. Managers unfamiliar with such patterns may react to early negative results by withdrawing their support for continued change efforts. Concerns about what the data indicate shouldn't be addressed by halting change efforts. Better ways to avoid such problems include setting realistic timetables and being careful to collect data that are consistent with the goals for change.

Any organizational change effort can run into unanticipated problems, and diversity interventions are no exception. Cultural awareness training programs may backfire if they seem to reinforce stereotypes or highlight cultural differences that employees have tried to obliterate in order to fit into the company's culture. Special skill-building programs offered only to some subgroups also can feed negative stereotyping, or they may be viewed as giving the target group an unfair advantage. Employees assigned to work in markets that match their cultural backgrounds may view that as limiting rather than maximizing the contributions that they can make. Affirmative action programs may create a stigma for all members of groups targeted to benefit. As a result, even the best qualified people are presumed to have acquired their positions because of their demographic attributes rather than on the basis of merit. Networking or caucus groups may lead to increased segregation and fragmentation.[61] Problems such as these seem to arise in organizations when employees become focused on their cultural differences rather than on their common goals. Ultimately, managing diversity successfully involves developing a strong organizational culture that values cultural differences and ensures that the talents of all employees are used to their fullest extent.

Answers for the Diversity Knowledge Quiz
All of the statements are true.

CHAPTER SUMMARY

Effective managers know that the thoughts, feelings, motivations, and behaviors of employees reflect the cultures on which they are based. Societal, industry, occupational, and organizational cultures and subcultures all combine to shape the behavior of individuals and the interactions of individuals and groups within an organization. The greater the number of cultures and subcultures in an organization, the greater is the need to manage cultural diversity effectively.

1. DESCRIBE THE CORE ELEMENTS OF CULTURE.

A culture is the unique pattern of shared assumptions, values, and norms that shape the socialization activities, language, symbols, rites, and ceremonies that unite members of a group and maintain their distinction relative to nonmembers. Assumptions are the underlying thoughts and feelings that are taken for granted and believed to be true. Values are basic beliefs about a condition that has considerable importance and meaning to individuals and is stable over time. Socialization is a systematic process by which new members are brought into a culture and taught the norms for behavior. A symbol is anything visible that can be used to represent an abstract shared value or something having special meaning. Language is a shared system of vocal sounds, written signs, and/or gestures used to convey special meanings among members. Narratives are the unique stories, sagas, legends, and myths in a culture. Shared practices include taboos (forbidden behaviors) and rites and ceremonies (formal activities that generate strong feelings).

2. IDENTIFY THE LEVELS OF CULTURE AND SUBCULTURE THAT ARE IMPORTANT TO MANAGING ORGANIZATIONS.

Cultures can be associated with large or small groups of people. The three primary levels of culture are societal, industry, and organizational. When people belong to the same culture, not everyone shares identical assumptions and values. There can be great variation among members of a culture, and these variations are the basis for subcultures. Just as societies often have geographically defined subcultures, organizations often have subcultures that reflect the levels of people in the organization, their occupations, and/or their business units. However, boundaries between levels and between subcultures may be blurred.

3. **DISCUSS SEVERAL GENERAL TYPES OF ORGANIZATIONAL CULTURES.**

Although all organizational cultures are unique, some general types of cultures can be identified. The four types discussed are bureaucratic, clan, entrepreneurial, and market cultures. They are characterized by differences in the extent of formal control (ranging from stable to flexible) and focus of attention (ranging from internal to external). Thus an organization could represent many blends of these pure cultural types, either as a whole or through its subcultures. Strong cultures may work for or against organizational performance, depending on their fit with the demands of external stakeholders and the competitive environment.

4. **EXPLAIN THE MEANING AND IMPORTANCE OF WORKFORCE DIVERSITY.**

Workforce diversity refers to the mix of people from various backgrounds employed by an organization. Two aspects of workforce diversity are demographic diversity and cultural diversity. The demographic diversity of a workforce refers to the degree of mix of demographic characteristics (e.g., differences in age, gender, and ethnicity) of employees. The cultural diversity of a workforce refers to the full mix of the cultures and subcultures (e.g., based on occupation, organizational level, or locale) to which employees belong. Different subcultures are often associated with different demographic groups. In multicultural

organizations, the organizational culture reflects a blending of all the subcultures found within the organization. Monolithic organizations are dominated by a single majority subculture, and members of other subcultures are expected to follow the norms and accept the values of the majority. Pluralistic organizations are more mixed in their cultural composition. Members of the organization are still expected to adopt the norms of a dominant subculture, but members of other subcultures fill a variety of jobs at all levels in the organization. Cultural differences are accepted as part of the work environment, and each subculture tends to maintain its own set of norms and values.

5. **DESCRIBE SEVERAL ACTIVITIES REQUIRED TO MANAGE WORKFORCE DIVERSITY SUCCESSFULLY.**

Concern about effectively managing workforce diversity reflects three types of organizational goals: complying with EEO laws and regulations, creating a positive organizational culture that makes work enjoyable for employees, and improving organizational performance. Managing cultural diversity in order to achieve these objectives is a long-term process requiring substantial investments of time, money, and people. All are necessary to implement any type of large-scale organizational change. The activities required to change an organization from one that values cultural homogeneity to one that values and leverages cultural diversity include understanding the goals to be achieved, assessing the current organization and understanding its history, designing a strategic plan for creating change, implementing a large number and variety of targeted change efforts, measuring the effects of change efforts, and making adjustments as needed.

QUESTIONS FOR DISCUSSION

1. Should top management explicitly try to shape and change the culture of an organization? Why or why not?

2. Based on the values presented in Table 18.1, identify the seven value statements that are most characteristic of the culture of an organization in which you have been involved. Do these values work for or against achieving the goals of the organization? Explain.

3. Based on the values presented in Table 18.1, identify the seven value statements that you think are most desirable for an ideal organization. Why did you choose them?

4. Would you like to work in an organization that has a strong organizational culture? Why or why not?

5. Which type of organizational culture would you prefer to work in? Why would you choose it?

6. Of three general types of objectives that organizations can have for managing diversity, which do you think is most important? Why?

7. Consider the list of diversity initiatives at Texaco, as shown in Table 18.3. For each item in that list, state which of the three types of organizational diversity goals it addresses. Has Texaco failed to address any such goals? Explain.

EXERCISES TO DEVELOP YOUR MANAGERIAL COMPETENCIES

1. **Self-Management Competency.** Different types of organizational cultures fit different types of environments. Similarly, different types of organizations seem to suit different people. Andersen Worldwide is an organization that has two distinct subcultures: the audit and the consulting units. Visit the Arthur Andersen home page at

   www.arthurandersen.com

   and the Andersen Consulting home page at

   www.ac.com

   to learn more about these two units. How would you categorize these two subcultures—bureaucratic, clan, entrepreneurial, or market? Which type of culture would you prefer to work in? Why?

2. **Strategic Action Competency.** Review Texaco's plan for managing cultural diversity, as described in this chapter. What organizational goals are likely to be achieved, assuming that the plan is fully implemented? Suppose that you've been appointed to a task force to make suggestions for additional diversity initiatives at Texaco. What would you add to its current plan? Be sure to state the goals to be met by the initiatives you recommend adding. You can obtain a description of another comprehensive plan for addressing diversity by visiting the following State of Colorado Web sites, which describe the state's diversity goals and plans, at

   govenor.state.co.us/gov_dir/gss/edo/ diversity/index.html#table

   and

   govenor.state.co.us/gov_dir/gss/edo/ diversity/strastep.html

3. **Planning and Administration Competency.** A person's mobility can be affected by many factors, including age, size, general health, vision, and physical impairments. Select and visit an organization with physical facilities that you can easily access (e.g., a library, museum, restaurant, theater, or store). Evaluate the facility in terms of its ease of access for people with various mobility impairments. Is the facility "friendly" or "unfriendly" to a diverse population of users? How does the mobility–friendliness of the facility affect employees and customers or visitors? Consider the impact of the facility on the organization's image and effectiveness and suggest three changes that could be made to improve the facility. Explain how these changes would contribute to organizational effectiveness. To conduct further research, you may want to visit the home page of the National Organization on Disability at

   www.nod.org

   Links to similar resources on the Internet are available at

   www.pacer.org/natl/yellona.html

   and

   www.disabilityplan.com/ablsempl.html.

4. **Global Awareness Competency.** Choose a country with which you are unfamiliar and learn as much as you can about the core elements (assumptions, values, symbols, and narratives) of the societal culture or one of its regional subcultures. Suppose that your employer were to send you to this culture for two weeks. Your assignment is to evaluate whether a new, high-tech fabric is likely to sell well. How can you use what you learned about the core elements of the culture to help you judge how well the fabric will sell?

5. **Communication Competency.** The Glass Ceiling Commission has issued several reports describing the similarities and differences among a variety of demographically defined groups (e.g., groups defined by ethnicity, age, and gender). These reports can be accessed on the Internet at

   www.dol.gom

and

www.ilr.cornell.edu/lib/bookshelf/e_archive/ GlassCeiling/

Select a report that focuses on a demographic group of which you are *not* a member. Make a list of some of the differences between that target group and other demographic groups. Discuss what you learned from the report with a member of that target group. Ask for the person's opinion about the accuracy and relevance of the general characterization. Then share your own views about similarities between the target group and a demographic group of which you are a member.

REAL-TIME CASE ANALYSIS

DING, DONG. AVON'S CALLING *WHO?*

Avon Products, Inc., employs women from all types of backgrounds. Founded in 1886, the firm's products were familiar to almost everyone in the generations that preceded Generation X. More than 2 million "Avon Ladies" sell its cosmetics door-to-door around the world, and there are more powerful women in executive positions at Avon than at any other Fortune 500 company. Approximately 40 percent of its global managers are women, and more than 20 percent of its professionals and managers are people of color. Those figures indicate what can be achieved after two decades of paying attention to diversity.

In the 1970s and well into the 1980s, Avon's approach to diversity was to strive to "do the right thing." Influenced by the Civil Rights era, the firm has had aggressive affirmative action programs in place for many years. But ironically, managers at the company were slow to realize that the influx of women into corporate America had important consequences for home-based cosmetics sales. Fewer customers were at home to sell to, and fewer women were available to be recruited as Avon representatives. By the mid-1980s, Avon's profitability had slumped.

Financial problems have a way of getting the attention of managers. At Avon, poor financial performance signaled a need to become more responsive to a changing consumer market. Multiculturalism was recognized as an important element in meeting customer demand and gaining competitive advantage. A variety of cultural diversity initiatives were launched. Middle managers were sent to Morehouse College in Atlanta for leadership development training, which included a session on why and how diversity can provide competitive advantage. The entire management team participated in awareness training provided by leading diversity consultants affiliated with the American Institute for Managing Diversity. Management launched a multicultural planning research project to evaluate the company's policies and practices regarding promotion. Its purpose was to identify potential barriers to the advancement of women and minorities. More than 100 people from corporate headquarters and several profit center locations participated in the project, including most of the company's senior managers. Based on findings from the project, management developed a five-year plan with specific goals.

Throughout the 1990s, Avon's approaches to managing cultural diversity were widely reported. Executives' annual hunting trips to the rod and gun club were discontinued. Women got showers and lockers in their bathrooms, just like the men had. The company's season tickets for the Knicks and Yankees were swapped for the New York City Ballet and the New York Philharmonic. The company had earned a reputation for being progressive. Its culture had changed. When other companies sought to benchmark their own diversity efforts, they often compared themselves to Avon. All of these events occurred under the leadership of Chairman and CEO James E. Preston.

In 1997, Preston indicated that he would probably retire within a year. At the same time, he announced several promotions within the company. The promotions put six executives, three of whom were women, in place for possible succession. When speculation arose about whether the next CEO would likely be a woman, Preston said, "I would be very surprised if it wasn't the case. We have more women in senior, middle, and lower-level management than any other company I know of." After that comment, *Fortune* reported that "now the Avon execs who are concerned about whether they will get a fair shot at the top job are *the men.*" *The men* included Avon's president and chief operating officer Ed Robinson. *The men* realized that they had stiff competition. Susan Kropf, president of Avon U.S., had presided over manufacturing and was credited with dominating global markets when she was head of emerging markets. Edwina Woodbury, chief financial and administrative officer, was in the spotlight for her efforts to overhaul Avon's inefficient ways and free cash for growth. Andrea Jung, president of global marketing and new business—and widely considered a hotshot talent—had held previous executive positions at Bloomingdale's, I. Magnin, and Neiman Marcus before Preston lured her to Avon. Christina Gold, a Canadian who had taken over U.S. operations in 1993, was credited with saving the company from a revolt by Avon ladies who were disgruntled with her predecessor's cost-cutting tactics.

On December 12, 1997, the headlines that shocked many observers read: "Avon calls on a man to lead it." The man was Charles Perrin, former CEO of Duracell International, the battery company. Preston explained the decision: "We wanted someone who had been there and done it. We wanted someone who had experience as a chief executive of a global company. A lot has been made of the gender issue. But the first responsibility of the Avon board is to place Avon in the hands of someone who can lead it." And what about the promising men and women with experience inside Avon as well as many executives in the cosmetics and retailing industry? "They are just a few years away," explained Preston.[62]

QUESTIONS FOR DISCUSSION

1. What competencies did Avon's board see in Charles Perrin that set him apart from Avon's female executives who apparently had been in line for promotion?

2. Suppose that Kropf, Woodbury, Jung, or Gold has hopes of succeeding Perrin. What should they do to develop their competencies further so that the Avon board will look at them and conclude that they have "been there, done that"?

3. If you were a top manager at Avon, how would you feel about the appointment of Perrin? What would you do to help him learn about the cosmetics and retailing industries as quickly as possible? What would you try to learn from him?

4. Perrin is 52; the women described vary in age from 39 to 49. Have the women just not been in the pipeline long enough? Or is there a glass ceiling at Avon? To learn more about Avon Products, visit the company's home page at *avon.avon.com*. [Yes, it really is avon.avon.com.]

VIDEO CASE

DAYTON-HUDSON: RESEMBLING AMERICA

Dayton-Hudson is taking steps to ensure that the company resembles America in terms of diversity. In Dayton-Hudson's case, diversity means hiring across the spectrum of races, cultures, and creeds that make up the company's customer base. In addition it means ensuring that any remaining internal obstacles to retention and promotion of women and minorities are dismantled.

The phrase "resembling America" very nearly means "resembling the world" these days. The demographics of the United States have always evolved, as successive waves of immigrants have arrived and as internal migrations have occurred (e.g., movement of African-Americans from the South to the industrializing North during Reconstruction). Within a few years, Anglos are expected to be a minority in the United States; in fact, in parts of the country, they already are. In Detroit, where J. L. Hudson established his first store in 1881, there is even a sizable population of Chaldeans (a Babylonian culture, from the area that is modern Iraq), Hamtramck is heavily Polish,

and many other neighborhoods and communities are enclaves of literally dozens of immigrant groups.

As cultures come together, organizations must learn that stereotypes are likely to cause employees to behave inappropriately toward members of other cultures.

Clothing retailer Eddie Bauer was recently sued by a customer who had been accused of shoplifting and who had been forced to remove his shirt. The customer had actually purchased the shirt on a previous visit to an Eddie Bauer store, but (like virtually anyone else) wasn't carrying the receipt. The customer charged that the store's staff had singled him out for unfair suspicion and treatment because of his race; the jury agreed, and the store found itself directed to pay a $1 million settlement and to issue an apology. "Shrinkage" in retail stores is a very real problem, and stores need to be alert to customer theft, but in this case the courts found evidence that the accusation was made more on the basis of unfounded racial bias than fact.

As Dayton-Hudson's diversity training game shows, you can't always (if ever) "judge a book by its cover." Appropriate workplace diversity training should incline an employee to set aside prejudice and to be open to new experiences. Although it is valuable in most workplaces, diversity training is especially important in services and retail sales, where people skills are at a premium and a salesperson might encounter hundreds of people, of all shapes, sizes, colors, and ethnicity during the day. Cross-cultural awareness can strengthen various of the managerial competencies (e.g., attuning a manager to subtleties in communication or helping to reconcile team members' diverse expectations).

Recruiting a diverse workforce and training it to be aware of the diversity of the company's customers is a first step, but it may be insufficient. Organizations also need to *retain* employees. Stepping up the pace of recruitment among underrepresented minorities could be disastrous if those hired leave just as quickly—and with a negative impression of the experience. Some companies take steps to ensure that newly hired employees are matched with mentors to help them "learn the ropes." A mentor can compensate for the lack of an "old boys' network," explaining corporate policies and culture, providing an ear for venting frustrations, and encouraging personal and professional development.

ON THE WEB

Dayton-Hudson is on the Web (**www.shop-at.com**). The Equal Employment Opportunity Commission (EEOC) is on the Web (**www.eeoc.gov**). According to its Web site, the EEOC's mission is "to promote equal opportunity in employment by enforcing the federal civil rights employment laws through administrative and judicial actions, and education and technical assistance."

QUESTIONS

1. What might a manager look for in selecting a mentor for a new employee?

2. The Walt Disney Company drew protests from religious conservatives when it decided to extend employee benefits to same-sex domestic partners. How else could an organization's decisions to tolerate diversity encounter opposition?

3. How should an organization respond if its policies asserting equality in the workplace are at odds with prevailing community norms?

To help you answer these questions and learn more about Dayton-Hudson Company, visit its home page at

www.shop-at.com

Case contributed by Ross Stapleton-Gray, President, TeleDiplomacy, Inc., a technology and policy consultancy, and Adjunct Professor in Georgetown University's Communication, Culture, and Technology program.

PART 6

Controlling and Evaluating

Chapter

19

Controlling in Organizations

LEARNING OBJECTIVES

AFTER STUDYING THIS CHAPTER, YOU SHOULD BE ABLE TO:

1. EXPLAIN THE FOUNDATIONS OF CONTROL.
2. DISCUSS WAYS THAT ORGANIZATIONS CAN CREATE EFFECTIVE CONTROLS.
3. IDENTIFY THE SIX STEPS OF THE CORRECTIVE CONTROL MODEL.
4. DESCRIBE THE PRIMARY TYPES OF ORGANIZATIONAL CONTROL.
5. DISCUSS ETHICAL CONTROL ISSUES CONFRONTING MANAGERS.

Outline

How FedEx Runs on Time

Annually, U.S. organizations spend more than $67 billion on loading, unloading, sorting, reloading and delivering packages to customers. Frederick Smith, the former Marine who founded and is CEO of FedEx, has been winning the battles against most of his competitors in this intensively competitive industry because of his tight control system. FedEx operates an $11.5 billion delivery system from its Memphis, Indianapolis, and Dallas hubs. It operates more than 590 airplanes and 38,500 other vehicles. When Smith first started FedEx about 20 years ago, he knew that it was in the information business. He stressed that knowledge about the cargo's origin, present whereabouts, destination, estimated time of arrival, price, and shipping cost were as important to customers as safe delivery. Today, FedEx wants to be known as the "Clipper ships of the computer age."

Roger Podwoski handles FedEx's daily operations review. Every weekday at 5:00 A.M., a taped recap of the night's performance is made available by voice mail. His staff checks in before the meeting to review any problems they'll need to discuss and solve. The organization's global operations control and coordination team is composed of fifteen people from key departments—air operations, customer service, computer systems, meteorology—stationed around the globe. Global conference calling allows people to participate in this meeting from around the world. It never runs more than seventy-five minutes. The meeting follows a detailed and formal checklist. Sanders says, "Meteorology," and that representative gives a two-minute report. He then says, "Air Operations," and if it has no issues, its representative will say, "No comment." The meeting follows a disciplined pattern that flows quickly and smoothly. If a problem can't be solved during the meeting, it's listed as an action item for the next meeting. Podwoski makes sure that it is followed up.

The control system that makes FedEx unique is its central sorting facilities in Memphis and Indianapolis. Its newest hub in Dallas mirrors the efficiency of its other hubs. All packages arrive at a hub for sorting by midnight. A DC-10 with more than 50,000 pounds of packages (or some 131,000 packages) is unloaded within thirty minutes. The packages are unloaded directly into a giant warehouse containing an elaborate conveyor belt system; the packages are sorted frantically because all must be loaded onto outgoing planes that take off for their intended destinations by 3:00 A.M. From the time a package is placed on one of the intake ramps, the conveyor system takes six minutes to scan, sort, and redirect the item to a container ready to be loaded onto an outgoing plane. The planes arrive at their local sorting destinations before 6:00 A.M. Ground couriers then transport packages to local offices and on to the receiver. Its barcoding process enables FedEx to monitor a customer's package movement at every step of its journey. FedEx has installed computer terminals in the offices of its largest 100,000 customers, and it has given 650,000 customers its proprietary software so that they can label their own packages. FedEx receives electronic notification from them to pick up and then ships and delivers those packages.

During the day, contact is maintained with ground couriers by means of the digitally assisted dispatch system. This system enables the company to leave messages at the couriers' vans even when they are unoccupied. The use of hand-held transceivers by couriers has enabled FedEx to reduce customer billing errors and maintain constant contact with the courier. FedEx also uses this system to find out how satisfied its 68,000 employees are with its policies.

FedEx realizes that, over the next ten years, the global express-transportation market is likely to grow from more than $12 to $150 billion. Companies are scrambling to establish overseas branches to grab their share of the world's market. Because most manufacturers have shifted to just-in-time inventory, expensive parts must be shipped all over the world constantly. FedEx has therefore established partnerships with global firms. Temic Semiconductor, a division of Mercedes Benz with annual sales of $1 billion, and FedEx formed a partnership that enabled Temic to close eight warehouses and set up one global warehouse in Subic Bay, the Philippines. A customer placing an order with Temic receives confirmation within thirty seconds. Notice is sent electronically to the manufacturing plant, which makes and sends products to Subic Bay where FedEx receives them and ships them to customers. In Asia, orders can be received and shipped within eight hours; it takes forty-eight hours for them to reach their final U.S. and European destinations. This arrangement saves Temic more than $5.5 million annually.[1]

FOUNDATIONS OF CONTROL

CONTROL
Mechanisms used to ensure
that behaviors and performance conform to an organization's rules and proce-
dures.

Control involves the use of mechanisms to ensure that behaviors and perfor-mance conform to an organization's rules and procedures.[2] To most people the word *control* has a negative connotation—of restraining, forcing, delimiting, watching, or manipulating. Many shopping malls employ security guards during the peak season to keep tight surveillance on shoppers' cars and on shoppers themselves when they are returning to their cars with goods. Most convenience stores (e.g., 7-Eleven and self-service gasoline stations, among others) have surveillance cameras that videotape customer movements throughout the store but especially when they approach the cashier. Most employees and many shoppers resent such practices because of their deeply held values of freedom and individualism. For this reason controls often are the focus of controversy and policy struggles within organizations.

However, controls are both useful and necessary. Effective control was one of the keys to FedEx's increased profits over the past decade. An important part of that control system was the ability to track customers' parcels at each stage of collec-tion, shipment, and delivery. We can illustrate the need for controls by describing how control interacts with planning, with specific reference to FedEx's operations.

- Planning is the formal process of developing goals, strategies, tactics, and stan-dards and allocating resources. Controls help ensure that decisions, actions, and results are consistent with those plans. At FedEx, its controls help identify which customers generate the greatest profits and which actually end up cost-ing the company. FedEx closes accounts that aren't profitable to serve, such as those in small, widely scattered locations.

- Planning prescribes desired behaviors and results. Controls help maintain or redirect *actual* behaviors and results. At FedEx, customer service employees are supposed to answer a customer's question within 140 seconds. Managers are evaluated annually by their superiors and workers. If assessments fall below an established level, managers may be replaced.

- Managers and employees can't effectively plan without accurate and timely information. Controls provide much of this essential information. Advances in electronic communications—and particularly the Internet—have enabled firms to attract and hold new customers by providing them with crucial information as needed. By partnering with Temic and other organizations and providing timely information about services and costs, along with parcel tracking, to them and their customers FedEx has been able to expand rapidly its customer base.

Plans indicate the purposes to be served by controls. Controls help ensure that plans are implemented as intended. Thus planning and control complement and support each other.

PREVENTIVE AND CORRECTIVE CONTROLS

There are two general types of organizational controls: preventive and corrective.[3] ***Preventive controls*** are mechanisms intended to reduce errors and thereby min-imize the need for corrective action. For example, convenience store robberies fell by 80 percent in Gainesville, Florida, after the city passed an ordinance to make such stores safer. The ordinance requires two clerks to be on duty from 8:00 P.M. to 4:00 A.M., well-lighted parking lots, a limit of $50 in the cash register, and an unob-structed view into the store. Similarly, air traffic controllers help prevent crashes by ensuring that airline pilots follow well-defined standards, rules, and procedures during takeoffs and landings.

PREVENTIVE CONTROLS
Mechanisms intended to
reduce errors and thereby
minimize the need for corrective action.

Rules and regulations, standards, recruitment and selection procedures, and training and development programs function primarily as preventive controls. They all direct and limit the behaviors of managers and employees alike. The assumption is that, if managers and employees comply with these requirements, the organization is likely to achieve its goals. Thus preventive controls are needed to ensure that rules, regulations, and standards are being followed and are working. FedEx's ability to pick up and deliver more than 3 million packages a day in some 211 countries depends on its employees' ability to conform to FedEx's policies.

Corrective controls are mechanisms intended to reduce or eliminate unwanted behaviors or results and thereby achieve conformity with the organization's regulations and standards. Similarly, an air traffic controller exercises corrective control by instructing a pilot to change altitude and direction to avoid another plane. At FedEx, dipatchers send messages to drivers to change their pick-up routes to satisfy customer needs.

SOURCES OF CONTROL

The four primary sources of control in most organizations are stakeholders, the organization itself, groups, and individuals. These sources are shown in Table 19.1 along with examples of preventive and corrective controls for each.

Stakeholder control is expressed as pressures from outside sources on organizations to change their behaviors. Recall that stakeholders may be unions, government agencies, customers, shareholders, and others who have direct interests in the well-being of an organization. The decisions of global leaders attending the 1997 environmental conference in Kyoto, Japan, called for manufacturers to cut emissions of certain pollutants by as much as 7 percent over the next several years. If these proposals are enacted by their governments, large polluters, such as automobile manufacturers and utilities, in many countries will have to spend billions of dollars on emissions and process controls. In addition, many consumers are demanding that companies provide environmentally safe products and often are willing to pay extra for these "green marketed" products. *Green marketing* is the name for marketing of products and services considered environmentally friendly

CORRECTIVE CONTROLS
Mechanisms intended to reduce or eliminate unwanted behaviors and thereby achieve conformity with the organization's regulations and standards.

STAKEHOLDER CONTROL
Pressures from outside sources on organizations to change their behaviors.

GREEN MARKETING
Sale of products and services considered to be environmentally friendly, which makes the producing organizations environmentally responsible.

T a b l e 1 9 . 1	*Examples of Different Sources and Types of Control*	
	Type of Control	
Source of Control	**Preventive**	**Corrective**
Stakeholders	Maintaining quotas for hiring personnel in protected classes	Changing recruitment policies to attract qualified personnel
Organization	Using budgets to guide expenditures	Disciplining an employee for violating a "No Smoking" safety regulation in a hazardous area
Group	Advising a new employee about the group's norm in relation to expected level of output	Harassing and socially isolating a worker who doesn't conform to group norms
Individual	Deciding to skip lunch in order to complete a project on time	Revising a report you have written because you are dissatisfied with it

that make their organizations "environmentally responsible." Organizations use green marketing not only to increase consumer approval, but also to cut costs. By using recyclable materials for toothpaste cartons, Tom's of Maine reduced its environmental waste by 40 percent. Similarly, by making its drinking straws 20 percent lighter, McDonald's saves one million pounds of waste per year. McDonald's also challenges its suppliers to provide and use recycled products and materials.[4]

Organizational control comprises the formal rules and procedures for preventing or correcting deviations from plans and for achieving desired goals. Examples include rules, standards, budgets, and audits. **Group control** comprises the norms and values that group members share and maintain through rewards and punishments. Examples include acceptance by the group and punishments, such as giving a group member the silent treatment, which we described in Chapters 17 and 18.

Individual self-control comprises the guiding mechanisms that operate consciously and unconsciously within each person. Standards of professionalism are becoming an increasingly important aspect of individual self-control. Becoming a professional involves acquiring detailed knowledge, specialized skills, and specific attitudes and ways of behaving. The entire process may take years of study and socialization. In doing their work, certified public accountants, lawyers, engineers, business school graduates, and physicians, among others, are expected to exercise individual self-control based on the guiding standards of their professions.

PATTERNS OF CONTROL

Stakeholder, organizational, group, and individual controls form patterns that differ widely from one organization to another. As we have pointed out previously, strong organizational cultures usually produce mutually supportive and reinforcing organizational, group, and individual controls. At Southwest Airlines, the culture focuses on treating the customer right. One senior vice president oversees customer contact and personally answers more than 1,000 letters a month—and not with form letters. When five medical students complained that their regularly scheduled flight got them to class fifteen minutes late, Southwest moved the departure time forward by fifteen minutes to enable them to take the most convenient (for them) flight. To maintain such a strong culture, Southwest hires employees who have a good sense of humor, who are broad-minded, and who are tolerant of individual differences. In keeping with its customer orientation, Southwest uses frequent flier customers to help select new flight attendants.[5]

In our discussions of motivation, leadership, and teams, we focused on managerial practices used to achieve employee loyalty, which often is influenced by an organization's control systems. Such controls are executed by means of planning and administrative procedures. Steve Robinson and Truett Cathy, founders of Chick-Fil-A, used their planning and organizing abilities to develop manager loyalty in an industry noted for high manager turnover. Competition for good managers is fierce in the fast-food industry, with annual turnover of store managers running between 30 and 40 percent. The following Planning and Administrative Competency feature highlights the type of control system that Robinson and Cathy installed and the results they achieved.

ORGANIZATIONAL CONTROL
Formal rules and procedures for preventing and correcting deviations from plans and for pursuing goals.

GROUP CONTROL
The norms and values that group members share and maintain through rewards and punishments.

INDIVIDUAL SELF-CONTROL
The guiding mechanisms that operate consciously and unconsciously within each person.

CREATING EFFECTIVE CONTROLS

2

DISCUSS WAYS THAT ORGANIZATIONS CAN CREATE EFFECTIVE CONTROLS

One way to develop and measure the effectiveness of formal organizational controls is to compare their costs and benefits. Such a cost–benefit analysis addresses three basic questions.

1. For what desired behaviors and results should organizational controls be developed?

Chick-Fil-A is a chain of quick-service, shopping-mall restaurants that in a decade has grown from a single diner in Atlanta to more than 600 restaurants and annual sales topping $400 million. This growth is even more stunning because Truett Cathy is a devout Christian who requires all stores to be closed Sundays. Chick-Fil-A managers earn 50 percent more than store operators at other fast-food chains, but the founders' method of

delegating authority and responsibility is the key to operator loyalty.

New operators are required to post $5,000 in earnest money. In return, they are guaranteed a base income of $24,000, and they get 50 percent of store profits after paying 15 percent of revenues for services that the company provides. The reward system at Chick-Fil-A provides the store manager with an incentive that encourages risk taking. Management doesn't have to worry about elaborate bureaucratic controls or managers ignoring relatively small cost savings. To store managers, such savings result in greater profits. Thus Chick-Fil-A aligns its managers' interests with the company's, with both having an incentive for helping each other succeed. Rather than relying on a few creative people at headquarters to come up with marketing ideas, store managers share ideas with each other. Many of these ideas require community involvement and risk taking.

Chick-Fil-A's growth reflects its ability to attract first-rate management candidates. It is very particular about

the people it chooses to run its stores. The company looks for people with character, drive, and a liking for people. Recruiters try to determine whether they would like for their sons or daughters to work for the person being interviewed. The company doesn't even consider people who don't want to continue working for it until they retire. It gives its best operators a chance to manage additional outlets in a local market rather than move them from store to store and then perhaps to headquarters. It also pays them to train new managers for outlets.

The entire corporate field staff consists of only twenty-five people, with little overhead to control. To reduce crew turnover, the company expects store managers to hire and train their employees carefully—to hire crew members who will be proud to work for Chick-Fil-A. Any crew member who stays for at least two years and averages twenty or more hours per week is eligible for a $1,000 scholarship.[6]

2. What are the costs and benefits of the organizational controls required to achieve the desired behaviors and results?

3. What are the costs and benefits of utilizing alternative organizational controls to obtain the desired behaviors and results?

The Prudential Insurance Company used these three questions to decide whether its general fitness program for white-collar workers was a success. The company provided smoke-free offices, an on-site fitness center with an instructor, low-cholesterol food in the cafeteria, and removed all candy and cigarette machines from the premises. A group of employees participated in a study of effects. Doctors measured each participant's level of cardiorespiratory fitness (aerobic capacity) with a treadmill exercise test prior to the experiment. After five years, Prudential reported that employees in the experiment had used 20 percent fewer sick days per year and that medical claims had declined by 46 percent. Annual disability and major medical costs were $120.60 per participant, compared to an average employee cost of $353.88. Prudential concluded that the program improved employees' fitness and saved the company money on medical costs.[7]

COST–BENEFIT MODEL

Figure 19.1 shows a cost–benefit model for gauging the effectiveness of an organization's control system. The horizontal axis indicates the amount of organizational control, ranging from low to high. The vertical axis indicates the relationship between the costs and benefits of control, ranging from zero to high. For simplicity, the cost-of-control curve is shown as a direct function of the amount of organizational control. The two break-even points indicate where the amount of organizational control moves from a net loss to a net benefit and then returns to a net loss. Although the optimal amount of control is difficult to calculate, effective managers probably come closer to achieving it than do ineffective managers.

Managers have to consider trade-offs when choosing the amount of organizational control to use. With too little control, costs exceed benefits and the controls are ineffective. As the amount of control increases, effectiveness also increases—up to a point. Beyond a certain point, effectiveness declines with further increases in the amount of control exercised. For example, an organization might benefit from reducing the average managerial span of control from twenty-one to sixteen employees. However, to reduce it further to eight employees would require doubling the number of managers. The costs of the increased control (managers' salaries) might far outweigh the expected benefits. Such a move might also make workers feel *micromanaged.* That, in turn, could lead to increased dissatisfaction, absenteeism, and turnover.

Eighty-one percent of major U.S. organizations engage in some kind of drug screening of their employees. According to the American Management Association,

---

Figure 19.1   **Cost-Benefit Model of Organizational Control**

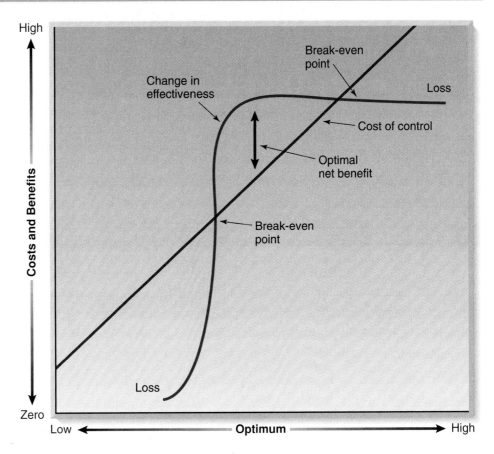

about 2 percent of these organizations use hair analysis. A major selling point is that hair analysis has a so-called wide detection window. Although urine tests generally detect drug use during the previous week, hair tests can reveal any illegal substance use as far back as a month or more. Employees at Bic Corporation, the retail chain Sports Authority, and General Motors have complained that this analysis can expose genetic information contained in DNA, such as hereditary defects or a predisposition to certain diseases. Two employees at Vyvx, an Oklahoma-based fiber-optics firm, lost their jobs because they wouldn't submit to hair testing. Theoretically, insurance companies could use genetic information to deny coverage, or a company could deny a person promotions because he or she is likely to suffer a major illness later in life.[8]

CRITERIA FOR EFFECTIVE CONTROLS

Designing effective organizational controls and control systems isn't simple, because many issues must be considered.[9] However, control systems are more likely to be effective if they are linked to desired goals and are objective, complete, timely, and acceptable. These criteria refine and make more specific the ideas presented in the cost–benefit model.

As suggested by the assessment method shown in Table 19.2, a control may more or less satisfy each of these criteria. The table also implies that a particular control or control system should be designed and evaluated in terms of all five criteria. The total score from such an assessment can range from a low of 5 to a high of 25. The higher the total score, the greater is the likelihood that the control or control system is effective. Organizational controls that fail reasonably to satisfy the five criteria actually may do more harm than good.

Linkage to Desired Goals. Control or control systems should be linked to the desired goals of the organization. These goals often include improving customer service, protecting the organization's assets, and improving the quality of its goods and/or services. FedEx has information systems—including bar codes and hand-held tracking devices—that provide fast and profitable service to its customers. Similarly, Chick-Fil-A treats operators as partners and exercises few controls. It believes that its store operators will manage their stores in ways that will benefit both them and the company.

Objective. An objective control or control system is impartial and can't be manipulated by employees for personal gain. In the United States, the Financial Accounting Standards Board (FASB) and several government agencies devote a great deal

Table 19.2	Method for Assessing the Effectiveness of Organizational Controls				
	Evaluation				
Criteria	Definitely Not	Unlikely	Can't Tell	Probably	Definitely
1. It is linked to desired goals.	1	2	3	4	5
2. It is objective.	1	2	3	4	5
3. It is complete.	1	2	3	4	5
4. It is timely.	1	2	3	4	5
5. It is acceptable.	1	2	3	4	5

of effort to developing and monitoring principles and practices to ensure that financial statements objectively and as accurately as possible reflect reality.

Complete. A complete control or control system encompasses all the desired behaviors and goals. A purchasing manager evaluated solely on the basis of cost per order may allow quality to slip. A computer salesperson evaluated only on the basis of sales volume may ignore after-sales service. Thus balancing quantitative (measurable) and qualitative (subjective) controls is necessary.

Timely. A timely control or control system provides information when it is needed most. Timeliness may be measured in seconds for evaluating the safe movement of trains and planes or in terms of months for evaluating employee performance. Computer-based information systems have played a major role in increasing the timely flow of information. The computerized cash registers at Wal-Mart give store managers daily data on each department's sales, as well as profitability measures for the entire store.

Acceptable. An acceptable control or control system is recognized as necessary and appropriate. If a control system is widely ignored, managers need to find out why. Perhaps the controls should be dropped or modified, should be backed up with rewards for compliance and punishments for noncompliance, or should be linked more closely to desired results.

In 1995, H. Douglas Johns founded Monorail, Inc., a fast-growing start-up company in Marietta, Georgia. He based the company on a daring new competitive strategy. It was to have no warehouses, no credit department, no customer service representatives, and no call center—all to be made possible by focusing on a few core skills—product design, marketing, and logistics—and outsourcing everything else. In just three years Monorail became the fourteenth leading supplier of desktop PCs. Johns believed that most customers would rather buy computers from retailers they know than from catalogs or the Internet. They want to see it, feel it, and touch it. After spending nine years with Compaq, he had a good understanding of the industry and the needs of various stakeholders—and the necessity of maintaining effective controls. The following Strategic Action Competency account demonstrates how Johns created an effective control system at Monorail, Inc.

CORRECTIVE CONTROL MODEL

3

IDENTIFY THE SIX STEPS IN THE CORRECTIVE CONTROL MODEL

CORRECTIVE CONTROL MODEL
A process for detecting and eliminating or reducing deviations from an organization's established standards.

The **corrective control model** is a process for detecting and eliminating or reducing deviations from an organization's established standards.[10] This process relies heavily on information feedback and responses to it. As shown in Figure 19.2, the corrective control model has six interconnected steps: (1) define the subsystem (an individual, a department, or a process), (2) identify the key characteristics to be measured, (3) set standards, (4) collect information, (5) make comparisons, and (6) diagnose problems and make corrections.

DEFINE THE SUBSYSTEM

A formal control subsystem might be created and maintained for an employee, a department, or an entire organization. The control mechanisms could focus on specific inputs, transformation processes, or outputs. Input controls often limit the amount by which raw materials used in the transformation process can vary from the organization's standards. For example, breweries use elaborate controls (including inspections and laboratory testing) to guarantee that the water and grains they

Monorail, Inc.

The typical sale of a PC at Monorail works like this. Retailer CompUSA orders a PC from the company. That order is transmitted electronically through FedEx Logistics Services to

one of Monorail's many contract manufacturers. The manufacturer assembles the PC from an inventory of Monorail parts and ships it directly to the appropriate CompUSA outlet via FedEx. The entire process takes two or three business days.

Meanwhile, FedEx wires an invoice to SunTrust Bank in Atlanta, whose loan department handles Monorail's billing and credit approvals. Monorail quickly receives cash from SunTrust and the bank assumes the risk of collecting the funds from CompUSA customers. Customers who need help call Monorail's 1-800 service center that is staffed and run by Sykes Enterprise, a call-center outsourcing company based in Tampa, Florida. Customers who want

to upgrade their hardware simply call a toll-free number and FedEx picks up the computer the next day, delivers it to an upgrade center, and returns it to a customer—all within four days.

Doug Johns knows that his control system can't operate successfully without two major strategic partners: SunTrust and FedEx. These companies are better at what they do than most others. For example, Monorail's PC can easily fit into a standard FedEx box. Monorail uses FedEx's shipping control system (described in the Preview feature) and SunTrust's financial control system to great advantage. Thus it avoided having to install and maintain its own comparable control systems.[11]

use to make beer meet predetermined standards. Such controls ensure that the correct quantity and quality of inputs enter the production process.

Many formal controls are applied during production (the transformation process). For Coors, Miller, and other brewers, they include timing the cooking of the brew, monitoring temperature in the vats, sampling and laboratory testing of the brew at each stage of the process, and visual inspection of the beer prior to final packing. Finally, output controls are used. For brewers, they range from specifying the levels of distributor inventories to monitoring consumer attitudes toward the beer and related services.

Figure 19.2   *Corrective Control Model*

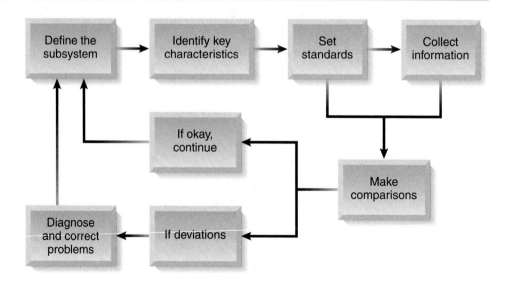

IDENTIFY KEY CHARACTERISTICS

The key types of information to be obtained about a person, team, department, or organization must be identified. Establishing a formal corrective control system requires early determination of the characteristics that can be measured, the costs and benefits of obtaining information about each characteristic, and whether variations in each characteristic are likely to affect performance.

After identifying them, managers must choose the characteristics to be measured. The *principle of selectivity* (also known as Pareto's law) holds that a small number of characteristics always account for a large number of effects. For example, in brewing beer, three characteristics that greatly influence the final product's quality are water quality, temperature, and length of brewing time. The direct control of objectives makes possible the control of the few vital characteristics that can account for major variations in results.

SET STANDARDS

Standards are criteria for evaluating qualitative and quantitative characteristics and should be set for each characteristic measured. One of the most difficult, but important, aspects of doing business in a foreign country is to understand the differences in standards. Owing to the difficulties that they face in setting standards that apply in widely differing cultures and markets, many global organizations have adopted the strategy of *thinking globally, but acting locally.* Cisco, a computer networking organization, discovered that customer standards varied from country to country. In Japan, office buildings often lack the space required for installing the company's complex electrical equipment, so it had to design network routers that would fit under a person's desk. In France, buyers insisted that at least some product components be French made and demanded that Cisco test its products at French-based organizations.[12]

Cultural and cross-cultural differences also are apparent in various human interactions, including language, nonverbal communication, religion, time, space, color, numbers, materialism, customs, status symbols, and food preferences. For example, different time standards are reflected in differing approaches to work. U.S. and Canadian executives expect meetings to begin and end at certain times, but Latins typically arrive later than the stated times and aren't concerned about ending meetings at the specified times. Why? Their standard for time isn't based on deadlines, but rather on a series of events: First, they do a task; when that is finished, they move on to the next task; and so on. Similarly, Indonesians have "rubber time"; to them, time is elastic. If something comes up that is more important than business, such as a wedding, business gets postponed. In Nigeria, a starting time for a meeting is only an approximation, and tardiness is readily accepted. Thus global organizations must observe standards set by cultures, rather than apply standards that the organizations are accustomed to and would prefer to set.

Increasingly, control systems are being based on performance standards (performance goals). Of the many possible types of performance standards, the following are but a few examples from five different functional areas.

- **Inventory:** Monthly finished goods inventory should be maintained at the sales level forecast for the following two-month period.

- **Accounts receivable:** Monthly accounts receivable should be no more than the dollar value of the previous month's sales.

- **Sales productivity:** The dollar value of sales per salesperson should be $1,000 greater than the comparable month for the previous year and $12,000 greater annually.

PRINCIPLE OF SELECTIVITY

A small number of characteristics always account for a large number of effects (also known as Pareto's law).

STANDARDS

Criteria against which qualitative and quantitative characteristics are evaluated.

- **Employee turnover:** The turnover of field sales personnel should be no more than 2 per 100 salespeople per month and no more than 20 per 100 salespeople annually.

- **Production waste:** Waste should amount to no more than $50 per month per full-time production worker, or no more than $600 per year per full-time production worker.

COLLECT INFORMATION

Information on each of the standards can be collected manually or automatically. Examples of the latter are the electronic counting devices used at Disney World to count the number of people who use each ride or the turnstiles at libraries that count the number of people who enter.

If information is collected by the individual or group whose performance is to be controlled, its validity must be checked. Employees and managers have an incentive to distort or conceal information if negative results will be used to criticize or punish them. Moreover, when formal controls emphasize punishment, strong group controls (see Chapter 17 for a list) often emerge to distort the information reported to management. Such reporting often obscures responsibility for failure to achieve goals or meet standards.

Top managers may create special departments or rely on regular departments to collect information by monitoring or auditing certain activities. Mick McGill, senior vice-president of human resources at The Associates, collects data from the U.S. Department of Labor and the company's competitors to determine, for example, whether starting salaries for various jobs are sufficient and affirmative action guidelines are being followed. Similarly, John Stillo, senior vice president in the controller's department of The Associates, collects and analyzes information to verify that income and expenditures are being recorded in accordance with established accounting standards.

MAKE COMPARISONS

Comparisons are needed to determine whether what *is* happening is what *should be* happening. In other words, information about actual results must be compared with performance standards. Such comparisons allow managers and team members to concentrate on deviations or exceptions. At Tom's of Maine, an operator is supposed to package eighty-one tubes of toothpaste a minute. If all operators reach this goal, the production process operates efficiently. If standards are known, overcontrolling becomes less likely and employees can use their time more effectively. If there is no apparent difference between what is and what should be happening, operations normally continue without any change.

DIAGNOSE AND CORRECT PROBLEMS

Diagnosis involves assessing the types, amounts, and causes of deviations from standards. Action can then be taken to eliminate those deviations and correct problems. However, the fact that a characteristic can be controlled doesn't necessarily mean that it should be controlled. At times, the problem may be one of undercontrol because the timeliness of information and the linkage of corrective controls to desired results are inadequate. Computer-based management information systems often help in overcoming inadequacies in corrective controls.

The following Communication Competency piece demonstrates how Ricardo Semler, president of Semco Manufacturing of Brazil, has used many features of the corrective control model. His leadership style has promoted effective two-way com-

Ricardo Semler

When Ricardo Semler took over the family business in 1979, Semco operated like many other Brazilian companies. Managers used fear to motivate and control workers. Armed guards roamed the factory floor, timed workers' trips to the rest rooms, and frisked employees for contraband when they left the building. Employees who broke equipment had their paychecks docked to replace it.

Semler decided to replace fear and management control with an effective communication system. He reduced the organization's hierarchy from eight levels to three and removed barriers, such as reserved parking spaces for managers, that separated workers from managers. The new levels were designed as concentric circles. One circle contained six employees whose task was to develop new business strategies and coordinate the activities of the entire organization. The second circle contained the heads of the various divisions. The third circle contained all other employees.

Employees are called associates. Associates make most of the day-to-day decisions, dress as they want, choose their own superiors, and have no time clocks. Just as Brazilian housewives base their self-esteem on their homemaking abilities and therefore make soup from scratch rather than buying canned soup, Semler realized that he must clearly communicate all financial results rather than reporting accounting summaries. To undertake this task, all associates were required to attend classes to learn how to read and understand financial statements. A union leader teaches the course. Every month, each associate receives a balance sheet, a profit-and-loss analysis, and a cash flow statement. Semler encourages associates to set their own salaries based on their outputs and contributions to the organization. When customers buy products made by Semco, they receive detailed instructions and videos made by the associates on how to use the products.

To foster effective two-way communication, associates evaluate their supervisors. These evaluations are posted for everyone to see. If a manager's evaluation is consistently low, that manager steps down. Semler and his team are evaluated, and these evaluations also are posted.[13]

munication and built strong interpersonal relationships between his top management team and employees. As a result, employees take corrective actions rather than relying on managers to direct them.

PRIMARY TYPES OF CONTROLS

4

DESCRIBE THE PRIMARY TYPES OF ORGANIZATIONAL CONTROL

Throughout this book, we have discussed various aspects of control and have indicated how a firm's strategy helps focus (control) employee behavior.[14] For example, compared to the Ritz Carlton Hotel, Marriott's Hampton Inns provide low-cost accommodations. Therefore Marriott's control systems focus on maintaining a low-cost strategy. In terms of human resources management, performance appraisal systems help managers assess the behaviors of employees and compare them with performance standards. Deviations are noted and corrective controls are used to reduce or eliminate problems.

In this section we explore six primary types of organizational control. Two are basic to the type of organization: bureaucratic and organic controls. One reflects external considerations: market controls. Two are functional: financial and accounting. And one is technological: automation controls. We also provide examples of specific control methods utilized by organizations.

As Figure 19.3 illustrates, all organizations utilize some combination of bureaucratic and organic control methods in conjunction with their market, financial, accounting, and automation-based controls. The methods available have the potential for complementing one another *or* working against one another. Thus management should select and assess control methods in relation to one another.

BUREAUCRATIC VERSUS ORGANIC CONTROLS

Bureaucratic controls involve the extensive use of rules and procedures, top-down authority, tightly written job descriptions, and other formal methods for preventing and correcting deviations from desired behaviors and results. Bureaucratic controls are part of bureaucratic (mechanistic) management (see Chapters 2 and 11). In contrast, ***organic controls*** involve the use of flexible authority, relatively loose job descriptions, individual self-controls, and other informal methods for preventing and correcting deviations from desired behaviors and results. Organic controls reflect organic management (see Chapter 11).

Organic controls are consistent with a clan culture. Recall that a clan is simply a group united by common interests (goals) and characteristics. In clan-type organizational cultures, such as The Associates, Johnson & Johnson, and Home Depot, members share pride in membership and a strong sense of identification with management. In addition, peer pressure to adhere to certain norms is considerable. Teams of self-managed employees control themselves with little direction from a supervisor. These self-managed teams use many organic controls, which create a supportive environment for members to learn new tasks. The following Teamwork Competency article highlights what can happen when management creates systems for team members to monitor their own performance and empowers team members to make decisions,

Table 19.3 contrasts the use of bureaucratic and organic control methods. For example, detailed rules and procedures are used whenever possible as a bureaucratic control method. In contrast, detailed rules and procedures are used only when necessary as an organic control method. However, an organization or its units doesn't have to use totally bureaucratic or totally organic control methods. The la Madeleine French Bakery & Cafe in Dallas has grown to fifty-five restaurants in ten markets since 1991. Bureaucratic methods of control are used to enforce uniform and highly detailed safety rules throughout the organization. In contrast, the manager of each restaurant uses organic controls to build team spirit in day-to-day operations.

BUREAUCRATIC CONTROLS

Extensive rules and procedures, top-down authority, tightly written job descriptions, and other formal methods for preventing and correcting deviations from desired behaviors and results.

ORGANIC CONTROLS

Flexible authority, loose job descriptions, individual self-controls, and other informal methods of preventing and correcting deviations from desired behaviors and results.

Figure 19.3 **Primary Types of Organizational Controls**

TEAMWORK COMPETENCY
A. O. Smith

In the early 1980s, life on the shop floor at A. O. Smith, a Milwaukee automobile parts manufacturer, was dull. Union stewards argued with management over work rules. Workers repeated the same task, either welding or riveting parts to truck frames, every twenty seconds. Absenteeism was running as high as 20 percent on some days. No one paid much attention to quality. Wages were based on piecework pay. Workers were encouraged to get the parts out the door, junk or not. Ford Motor Company was rejecting 20 percent of the door frames produced by Smith because they didn't fit. Something had to happen, or the company would go bankrupt.

Top management decided to involve employees in problem solving and formed several quality teams. The union strongly opposed these teams, but the company pressed ahead. As quality improved, the union's opposition lessened. Clearly, improving quality and cutting costs were the only ways the company was going to survive.

Now there are teams of five to seven workers who rotate from job to job. The members of the team select team leaders who assume managerial duties, such as scheduling production and overtime, ordering maintenance work, and monitoring quality control. All team members are involved in building a quality product. With team members taking over duties and controls from first-line supervisors, the company has been able to reduce their number. In 1980, the ratio of first-line supervisors to workers was 1 to 10; today it is 1 to 34. The company is training the remaining managers to put aside the rest of the bureaucratic methods of control and adopt more organic methods.[15]

Coca-Cola, American Airlines, Gillette, and other large organizations have large numbers of departments, which can differ widely in their emphasis on bureaucratic or organic controls. Mechanistic characteristics in certain departments and organic characteristics in others don't necessarily reduce a firm's overall effectiveness.[16] For example, at Coca-Cola, the syrup production department operates within a relatively stable environment, whereas the bottling department operates within a

Table 19.3	Characteristics of Bureaucratic and Organic Control Methods
Bureaucratic Control Methods	**Organic Control Methods**
Use of detailed rules and procedures whenever possible	Use of detailed rules and procedures only when necessary
Top-down authority, with emphasis on positional power	Flexible authority, with emphasis on expert power and networks of control
Activity-based job descriptions that prescribe day-to-day behaviors	Results-based job descriptions that emphasize goals to be achieved
Emphasis on extrinsic rewards (wages, pensions, status symbols) for controlling performance	Emphasis on both extrinsic and intrinsic rewards (meaningful work) for controlling performance
Distrust of team controls, based on an assumption that team goals conflict with organizational goals	Harnessing of group controls, based on an assumption that group goals and norms assist in achieving organizational goals
Organizational culture not recognized as a source of control	Organizational culture seen as a way of integrating organizational, group, and individual goals for greater overall control

changing environment. Managers of these two departments are likely to choose different ways to divide and manage the work. The syrup production manager probably will choose a mechanistic structure, and the bottling manager probably will choose a more organic system. One consequence of use of the organic system was that bottling managers recognized that consumers in different countries didn't perceive Coca-Cola the same way and had differing product requirements. For example, in Spain, refrigerators are smaller than in other countries. As a result, two-liter bottles didn't fit in the refrigerators, and sales were lost until the bottling department redesigned the bottle.

MARKET CONTROLS

Market controls involve the use of data to monitor sales, prices, costs, and profits, to guide decisions and evaluate results. The idea of market controls emerged from economics, and dollar amounts provide effective standards of comparison. To be effective, market controls generally require that

- the costs of the resources used in producing outputs be measured monetarily,

- the value of the goods and services produced be defined clearly and monetarily priced, and

- the prices of the goods and services produced be set competitively.

Two of the control methods that can satisfy these requirements are profit-sharing plans and customer monitoring.

Profit-Sharing Plans. Recall that profit-sharing plans provide employees with supplemental income based on the profitability of an entire organization or a selected subunit.[17] The subunit may be a strategic business unit, a division, a store in a chain, or other organizational entity. Profit-sharing plans generally have four goals:

- to increase employee identification with the organization's profit goals, allowing greater reliance on individual self-control and group controls;

- to achieve a more flexible wage structure, reflecting the company's actual economic position and controlling labor costs;

- to attract and retain workers more easily, improving control of selection and lowering turnover costs; and

- to establish a more equitable reward system, helping to develop an organizational culture that recognizes achievement and performance.

Many factors influence whether the goals of a profit-sharing plan can be achieved. First, employees must believe that the plan is based on a reasonable, accurate, and equitable formula. The formula, in turn, must be based on valid, consistently and honestly reported financial and operating information. Second, employees must believe that their efforts and achievements contribute to profitability. Third, employees must believe that the size of profit-based incentives will increase proportionally as profitability increases. These factors also are crucial in determining the effectiveness of gain-sharing plans. Recall that gain-sharing plans pass on the benefits of increased productivity, cost reductions, and improved quality through regular cash bonuses to employees.

Customer Monitoring. *Customer monitoring* consists of ongoing efforts to obtain feedback from customers concerning the quality of goods and services. Such monitoring is done to prevent problems or learn of their existence and solve them. Customer monitoring is being used increasingly in corrective control, in an attempt to assess or measure customers' perceptions.[18] Based on such assessments, management may take action to prevent the loss of further business because of customer dissatisfaction.

Customer monitoring often is used by service providers. Staples, the office supply chain founded in 1986, tracks consumer purchases by offering a membership card good for discounts and special promotions. This system allowed Staples to know its customers' purchasing habits well. Because of its cash-register data, which tracks buying preferences, quantities, and frequency, Staples doesn't need to use mass mailings and generic coupons. Instead, it targets specific customer segments for selected coupons, mailings, and promotions. Hotels and restaurants may ask customers to judge the quality of their service by completing a "customer satisfaction card." After purchases of their products, many firms follow up with telephone interviews or mail questionnaires to obtain information from customers. Lexus reimburses dealers for performing 1,000- and 7,500-hundred-mile checkups at no cost to Lexus owners. After the car has been serviced, the customer is asked to fill out a survey regarding the adequacy of the service. An independent marketing research firm enters the data into a computer and then sends it on to Lexus headquarters in California by satellite transmission. As a result, Lexus can track all service work done anywhere in its system and compare the quality of service provided by its dealers.[19]

FINANCIAL CONTROLS

FINANCIAL CONTROLS
A wide range of methods, techniques, and procedures intended to prevent the misallocation of financial resources.

Financial controls include a wide range of methods, techniques, and procedures intended to prevent or correct the misallocation of resources.[20] External auditors, usually certified public accounting firms (e.g., Arthur Andersen, Ernst & Young, and Coopers & Lybrand) and/or internal auditing departments (e.g., accounting, controller, and treasurer) monitor the effectiveness of financial controls. The primary responsibility of external auditors is to the shareholders. The auditors' role is to assure shareholders that the firm's financial statements present its true financial position and are in conformity with generally accepted accounting principles.

Because there are so many financial control methods, techniques, and procedures, we focus on only two of the essential ones: comparative financial analysis and budgeting.

COMPARATIVE FINANCIAL ANALYSIS
The evaluation of a firm's financial condition for two or more time periods.

Comparative Financial Analysis. Evaluation of a firm's financial condition for two or more time periods is called *comparative financial analysis.* When data are available from similar firms, they are used in making comparisons.[21] Industry trade associations often collect information from their members and publish it in summary form. Publicly owned firms publish income statements, balance sheets, and other financial statements. These sources often are used by managers and outsiders to assess changes in the firm's financial indicators and compare its financial health with that of other firms in the same industry. Companies that have multiple production facilities (e.g., GM, Ford, Exxon, and IBM), retail outlets (e.g., Kmart, Wal-Mart, and Sears), restaurants (e.g., McDonald's, Wendy's, and Red Lobster), hotels (e.g., Hilton, Holiday Inn, and Sheraton) compare the financial records of all units for control purposes.

RATIO ANALYSIS
Selecting two significant figures, expressing their relationship as a proportion or fraction, and comparing its value for two periods of time or with the same ratio for similar organizations.

The most common method of comparison is ratio analysis. *Ratio analysis* involves selecting two significant figures, expressing their relationship as a proportion or fraction, and comparing its value for two periods of time or with the same ratio of similar organizations. Of the many types of ratios, those most commonly used by organizations are profitability, liquidity, activity, and leverage. They are summarized in Table 19.4.

Return on investment (ROI) generally is considered to be the most important profitability ratio because it indicates how efficiently the organization is using its resources. A ratio value greater than 1.0 indicates that the organization is using its resources effectively. The *current ratio* indicates an organization's ability to pay bills on time. A current ratio should be well above 1:1 and if a firm has a ratio of 2:1, it should be financially sound. A low current ratio might mean that the organization has unnecessary inventory, a lot of cash sitting idle, or heavy accounts receivable that are difficult to collect. *Inventory turnover* indicates the average number of times that inventory is sold and restocked during the year. A high ratio means efficient operations—a relatively small amount of money is tied up in inventory—enabling the organization to use its resources elsewhere. *Debt ratio* is computed to assess an organization's ability to meet its long-term financial commitments. A value of 0.40 would indicate that the organization has $0.40 in liabilities for every $1.00 of assets. The higher this ratio, the poorer credit risk the organization is perceived to be by financial institutions. Generally, organizations with debt ratios above 1.0 are considered to be relying too much on debt to finance their operations.

Financial ratios have little value unless you know how to interpret them. For example, an ROI of 10 percent doesn't mean much unless you compare it to the ROIs of other organizations in the same industry. A firm with an ROI of 5 percent in an industry where the average ROI is 11 percent might be performing poorly. An inventory turnover rate of 5 at Pep Boys, Chief Auto Parts, and other auto-supply stores might be excellent but would be disastrous for Kroger, Grand Union, Safeway, and other large supermarkets for which an inventory turnover of 15 is common. Organizations can improve their inventory turnover rate by offering "specials" to stimulate customer demand, lowering prices, or not carrying items that move slowly.

Budgeting. The process of categorizing proposed expenditures and linking them to goals is known as **budgeting.** Budgets usually express the dollar costs of various tasks or resources. For example, production budgets may be based on hours of labor per unit produced, machine downtime per thousand hours of running time, wage rates, and similar information. The main budget categories usually include labor, supplies and materials, and facilities (property, buildings, and equipment).[22]

Budgeting has three primary purposes: (1) to help in planning work effectively; (2) to assist in allocating resources; and (3) to assist in controlling and monitoring resource utilization during the budget period. When managers assign dollar costs

BUDGETING

The process of categorizing proposed expenditures and linking them to goals.

Table 19.4	Examples of Financial Ratios		
Type	**Example**	**Calculation**	**Interpretation**
Profitability	Return on investment (ROI)	$\frac{\text{Profit after taxes}}{\text{Total assets}}$	Productivity of assets
Liquidity	Current ratio	$\frac{\text{Current assets}}{\text{Current liabilities}}$	Short-term solvency
Activity	Inventory turnover	$\frac{\text{Sales}}{\text{Inventory}}$	Efficiency of inventory management
Leverage	Debt ratio	$\frac{\text{Total debt}}{\text{Total assets}}$	How a company finances itself

to the resources needed, they sometimes realize that proposed tasks aren't worth the cost; they can then modify or abandon the proposals.

Budgeting for completely new tasks usually requires forecasting conditions and estimating costs. Budgeting for established tasks is easier because historical cost data are available. In either case, those who prepare budgets must exercise judgment. Budgets often are developed for a year and then broken down by month. Managers thus are able to track progress in meeting the budget as the year unfolds—and to take corrective action as necessary.

The control aspect of budgeting may be either corrective or preventive. When budgeting is used as a corrective control, the emphasis is on identifying deviations from the budget. Deviations indicate the need to identify and correct their causes or to change the budget itself.

The power of a budget, especially when used as a preventive control, depends on whether it is viewed as an informal contract that has been agreed to or a club to bludgeon those who don't stay within their budgets. One study asked first-line managers about their companies' budgets. The question was: "Do you feel that budgets or standards are frequently a club held over the head of the manager to force better performance?" Twenty percent of the 204 respondents replied "yes" and 68 percent answered "no." Most employees who must live by budgets accept their use by top management as a control mechanism. However, some employees view budgets with fear and hostility. This reaction usually occurs when an organization enforces budget controls with threats and punishment.[23]

There is no single classification system for budgets. Specific individuals, sections, projects, teams, committees, departments, divisions, or SBUs may be given budgets within which they are expected to operate. The following are the most common types of budgets used in business.

- Sales budget—a forecast of expected revenues, generally stated by product line on a monthly basis and revised at least annually.

- Materials budget—expected purchases, generally stated by specific categories, which may vary from month to month because of seasonal variations and inventory levels.

- Labor budget—expected staffing, generally stated by number of individuals and dollars for each job category.

- Capital budget—targeted spending for major tangible assets (e.g., new or renovated headquarters building, new factory, or major equipment), often requiring a time horizon beyond one year.

- Research and development budget—targeted spending for the development or refinement of products, materials, and processes.

- Cash budget—expected flow of monetary receipts and expenditures (cash flow), generally developed at least once a year for each month of the year.

The types of budgets and budget categories used are strongly influenced by organization design and organizational culture. An organization having a functional structure usually has a budget for each function (e.g., marketing, production, finance, and human resources). However, an organization having a product structure usually has a budget for each product line. For example, American Brands is structured by product—office, tobacco, distilled spirits, hardware and home improvements, specialty, and life insurance—and uses product-line budgeting. Management has found that this type of budgeting enables its control system to measure effectively the contributions of each product line.

Accounting for Quality

Within the past decade, many organizations have needed to change their financial controls to reflect more accurately changes in their products. Coca-Cola, Allied Signal Corporation, Koehler Manufacturing, and others have had to change their accounting systems because of high overhead costs associated with offering customers a diversity of products. These products required numerous variations in production runs and costly setups. Richard Miller, a vice president at Koehler, for example, had no idea that certain administrative costs were being charged to his battery line. Expenses such as dealing with environmental officials, applying for permits, and filing compliance reports were never measured but were equally assigned to all products as overhead expenses. When he found out, he calculated that the product's profitability was nearly 30 percent less than he had thought. He and other managers found that their organizations needed control systems that would enable them to measure accurately the cost of making quality products for the consumer. ***Activity-based costing*** (ABC) is a system that focuses on activities as the fundamental cost centers.[24] Activities become the focal point for the organization. An *activity* is any event that drives costs, including energy consumed, miles driven, computer hours logged, quality inspections made, shipments made, and scrap/rework orders filled.

In contrast to traditional accounting, ABC focuses on the work activities associated with operating a business. The number of these activities usually depends on the complexity of operations. The more complex the organization's operations, the more cost-driving activities it is likely to have. Equally important, managers have discovered that not all products have the same mix of these activities. If a product doesn't require the use of an activity, its cost would be zero for that activity. For example, at Koehler Manufacturing, one low-volume product requires frequent machine setups, has many intricate parts that generate numerous purchase orders, and requires constant inspections to maintain quality. A second, high-volume product requires few machine setups, few purchase orders, and few quality inspections. If Koehler were to ignore the differences in these two products in terms of their cost-driving activities and simply assign a general overhead cost to the products on the basis of volume, the high-volume product would bear most of the overhead cost. This approach would seriously distort actual unit costs for each product. Koehler could make production mistakes and their profitability would hide the impact of these mistakes. It could carry unprofitable products and customers because winners would more than offset losers. The company could survive with misleading cost allocations and without knowing the real costs of its individual business processes—but profits would not be as high as they could be.

Figure 19.4 depicts a model of the flow of information in an activity-based accounting system. The information in this system is viewed from two perspectives: cost and process. The *cost view* reflects the flow of costs from resources to activities and from activities to products and services. At Boeing, one of the activities is materials handling. The resources consumed in moving materials from one location to another at the plant is traced to each product, based on the number of times an item has been moved. This cost view is the key concept underlying activity-based costing: *Resources are consumed by activities, and activities are consumed by products and services.*

The *process view* reflects the lateral flow from costs of input information to activities and from activities to performance evaluation, or the observed transactions associated with an activity. In the case of materials handling at Boeing, information is gathered on the number of times an item is moved to determine the extent of activity during a period. This information provides the activity data needed to com-

ACTIVITY-BASED COSTING
A system that focuses on activities as the fundamental cost centers.

Figure 19.4   **Activity-Based Costing Model**

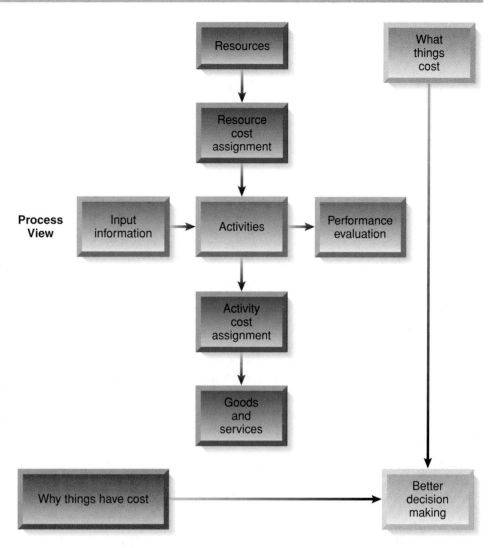

Source: Adapted from C. Cokins. If activity based costing is the answer, what is the question? *IIE Solutions,* 29(8), 1997, p. 41; and S. S. Rao. ABCs of cost control. *Inc. Tech.,* 2, 1997, pp. 79–81.

plete the costing of products. It also provides the data needed for performance evaluation.[25]

Dana Corporation installed an activity-based cost system at its Plymouth, Minnesota, factory to improve the quality of its automobile parts.[26] For six months in all areas of the plant, employees wrote down what they did each day to define their basic activities. For example, in the materials control department, which buys components for products and fills customer orders, a customer representative spends about 30 percent of the time taking orders and 50 percent of the time processing them.

Accountants used these expense data and applied activity-based costing to the department. The differences between the traditional way of accounting for costs and the activity-based cost system are shown in the following table. The data on the left side of the table are the *accounting police,* or command-and-control tools. These data tell managers whether they have overspent their budgets. The right side of the table defines the same costs in *verb-adjective-noun grammar* form. It provides cost information for employees and managers, not for accountants. Employees can relate much better to this language because it is easy to understand and logical.

Traditional		Activity-Based Costing	
Salaries	$371,917	Process sales orders	$144,840
Source parts	118,069	Fringe benefits	136,320
Supplies	76,745	Expedite supplier orders	72,143
Fixed costs	23,614	Expedite internal processing	49,945
Total	$590,345	Resolve supplier quality	47,599
		Reissue purchase orders	45,235
		Expedite customer orders	27,747
		Schedule intracompany sales	17,768
		Request engineering changes	16,710
		Resolve problems	16,648
		Schedule parts	15,390
		Total	$590,345

Dana was able to improve product quality by pinpointing activities that focused on achieving it. By working with suppliers more closely, the company was able to save expediting costs and improve supplier quality. Combined, these activities saved Dana $99,742. As the company develops standards for the cost of each activity, it will be able to determine quickly which activities are driving costs and which are directly related to customer satisfaction. The result will be better products and higher profits.

Benefits. Using an activity-based accounting control system yields at least four benefits.[27] First, costs are pinpointed by activity instead of being charged to overhead. Employees understand that their activities are translated into costs that define the performance level of their units and the organization as a whole. The system also gives them an incentive to think about how to reduce costs. Second, cost allocations are based on the portion of activities that can be directly traced to a product or job itself, as opposed to the volume of production. Third, costs associated with an activity for a particular product can now be traced. This result shows managers that the best way to control costs is to control the activities that generate them in the first place. Managers can see whether they are performing activities that have little impact on profits and are spending a lot of money doing so. Finally, the use of ABC shifts managers' thinking from accounting to managerial decision making. Information technology is essential in gathering ABC information and combining not just cost, but also nonfinancial information and performance measures. As managers and employees become more aware of activity costing and the information available from this accounting system, they will become more proficient in differentiating profitable and unprofitable activities.

Limitations. The benefits of activity-based accounting control systems are offset somewhat by two limitations. First, managers must still make some arbitrary cost allocations based on volume. In many high-volume organizations, such as Intel and Texas Instruments, obtaining accurate product costs is difficult because so many costs relate to buildings, land, and equipment. Second, high measurement costs are associated with multiple activity centers and cost drivers. For example, at a hospital, automatically recording the results each time a nurse takes someone's blood pressure would be unreasonably expensive. Similarly, at NationsBank, BankAmerica, and other banks, recording the length of time that a teller and customer talk would be extremely difficult. Even if it were feasible, it might not be a good idea because most banks don't want tellers rushing customers and minimizing customer contact.

AUTOMATION-BASED CONTROLS

Automation involves the use of devices and processes that are self-regulating and operate independently of people. Automation usually involves linking machines with other machines to perform tasks. **Machine controls** are methods that use instruments or devices to prevent and correct deviations from desired results. The use of machines in business has gone through several significant stages of development. Machines initially increased productivity by giving employees better physical control over certain tasks. Eventually the interaction of employee and machine created a mutual control system. Then, a new threshold was reached with automation.

Machine control of other machines takes over part of the managerial control function. That is, machines can now participate in the control process with managers. For example, computers in oil refineries collect data, monitor, and make automatic adjustments during refining processes. The impact of such automatic machine control on management has been reported in a number of studies. One researcher found that the introduction of an advanced automated system in one large factory reduced the number of middle management jobs by 34 percent.[28]

There has been a steady shift toward machine controls in production operations. It began with machines being given control of some production tasks, as when automatic sensors replaced visual inspection in steel production. With the advent of assembly lines and mass-production technology, machines supplemented rules and regulations as a way of directly controlling production workers. In continuous process or robotic operations, machines actually control other machines.

Advanced machine control is a distinctive feature at Swatch Watch. In 1978 when Ernest Thomke founded the watch company in Bienne, Switzerland, he realized that Swiss manufacturers long ago had lost much of their market share to the Japanese. Although the Swiss still dominated the luxury segment of the market, the Swiss were suffering from the the Far East's onslaught. He decided to revolutionize the industry by making a watch that would sell for no more than $30.00, could be manufactured cheaply, had high quality, required no repair, and would sell 10 million pieces in the first three years. These objectives were so high that to reach them by improving existing technologies was impossible. He designed a manufacturing process that enabled Swatch Watch to use the latest machine controls to reach its goals. The following Global Awareness Competency item highlights how Thomke's recognition of the global forces in the watch industry enabled him to manufacture the Swatch.

AUTOMATION
The use of devices and processes that are self-regulating and operate independently of people.

MACHINE CONTROLS
The use of instruments to prevent and correct deviations from desired results.

COMPUTER MONITORING
The use of special software to collect highly detailed quantitative information on employee performance.

ETHICS AND CONTROL

5

DISCUSS ETHICAL CONTROL ISSUES CONFRONTING MANAGERS

Some methods of control, particularly those aimed directly at the behaviors of individuals, pose potential ethical dilemmas for managers and employees alike. To illustrate this problem, we present three controversial control methods: computer monitoring, drug testing, and undercover security agents.

COMPUTER MONITORING

Computer monitoring is the use of special software to collect highly detailed quantitative information on employee performance. An estimated 12 million U.S.

Ernest Thomke, Swatch Watch

Until Thomke founded Swatch, frequently as many as thirty independent organizations were involved in the production of a single watch. Skilled craftsman made parts of the watch in hundreds of tiny shops, each of them specializing in only a few parts. The parts were then sold to organizations that put entire watches together.

The Swatch differed with regard both to its construction and the

process used to manufacture it. First, the case was not only an outer shell, but also a container to which individual parts could be directly attached. This technology required advanced computer-aided design and computer-aided manufacturing (CAD/CAM) technology and the extensive use of robotics. Second, the number of components was reduced from 91 in a traditional watch to 51. New materials were developed for the case, the glass, and micromotor. Also, a new assembly technology was designed and a pressure diecasting process perfected. Third, parts were no longer attached by screws. Components were riveted and welded together ultrasonically. Because the crystal was also welded to the case, the watch was guaranteed to be water-resistant to a depth of 100 feet. Fourth, the strap was integrated into the case and assembled at the same time the case was made. Finally, the only part with

a limited expectancy of about three years, the battery, was inserted into the bottom of the case and the opening closed with a cover.

The Swatch was officially introduced in Switzerland on March 1, 1983. During the first four months, 25,000 were sold. Sales in the United States of this $30 colorful watch grew from 100,000 pieces in 1983 to more than 4 million pieces by 1998. To further expand sales and utilize its manufacturing process, Swatch recently introduced its Swatch Access, a quartz timepiece with a built-in computer chip and antenna that store and transmit personal account data. For example, skiers can slide the watch in front of a special scanner, the skier's lift fees are electronically deducted from an account, and admission to the lift is granted. If stolen, the watch can easily be deactivated, leaving the thief holding up the lift line with no means of entry.[29]

workers currently are being monitored electronically, often without their knowledge.[30] Employees who work at computer terminals in data processing service bureaus, insurance companies, airlines, telemarketing firms, and telephone companies are those most often monitored in this way. Information collected by computers may include the number of keystrokes, number of customers served, length of time required to serve each customer, minutes away from the computer terminal, number of corrections and changes made, and so on. At FedEx, if employees spend, on average, one second less on each phone call, the organization saves $500,000 a year.

Organizations such as FedEx and GE, among others, that monitor the work of their employees by computer indicate that doing so gives them an objective basis for giving employees precise feedback about their performance and for determining training needs.[31] The conversation between a customer and customer-service representative is that employee's work product. Thus the monitoring of both sides of the conversation may be the most accurate way to measure an employee's performance. However, customers should be asked whether they mind having their conversations monitored. At GE's Answer Center in Louisville, Kentucky, quality is stressed over quantity and counts for 70 percent of an employee's performance evaluations. Handling problems related to warranties over the phone costs GE $4 per call, saving $16 a call by avoiding the need to send out a repair person. Monitoring also makes pinpointing problems easier in call centers, such as directory assistance centers, catalog order centers, and customer service departments of large organizations. These centers often have hundreds of employees who answer thousands of phone calls a day.

Computer monitoring is causing growing concern among unions, civil libertarians, and legislators because it invades employees' privacy to a greater degree than most other control methods used by organizations. Many employees who are monitored by computer complain of depression, anxiety, back pain, shoulder soreness, stiff and sore wrists, and fatigue. Most monitored employees also complain that their managers have little idea about the job pressures because they have never been monitored.[32]

DRUG TESTING

Since passage by Congress of the Drug-Free Workplace Act of 1988, 81 percent of all major U.S. companies test employees for drug use.[33] The act was passed as a reaction to the increased use of illegal drugs in all segments of the society, the reluctance of employers to report known or suspected drug use by former employees for fear of lawsuits, and employer liability for negligent hiring. In addition, the act requires all federal government contractors and fund recipients to certify that they will maintain a drug-testing program. The act doesn't require other organizations to implement drug-testing programs. Instead, the primary focus is on employee awareness and rehabilitation.

Abuse of illegal drugs by employees costs U.S. organizations an estimated $100 billion per year. Drug abuse leads to increased absenteeism, shoddy products, workplace accidents, and skyrocketing insurance claims. Health-care costs and accident rates are more than 10 percent higher for abusers than for nonabusers. According to a recent survey of 1,000 organizations, 48 percent of them test for drugs prior to employment, up from 21 percent just several years ago. This survey revealed that the drug-testing programs of most of the nation's top 1,000 organizations cover both preemployment testing and testing of current employees.[34]

Preemployment Testing. Private sector employers may require any job applicant to submit to a drug-screening test, unless prohibited by state law. Most drug use testing involves the examination of body fluids, although hair analysis, video-based testing of eye–hand coordination, and pupillary reaction tests have been used. Employers can state a preference to hire only qualified candidates. As drug use may negatively affect job performance, organizations can choose to hire only applicants who pass a drug-screening test. FedEx, General Electric, Georgia Power, and others use a plan that involves:

- **Notification.** Applicants are notified of the screening on the physical exam questionnaire to minimize claims of invasion of privacy.

- **No rescheduling of test.** Candidates are not allowed to postpone the test after appearing at the doctor's office and realizing that drug testing is part of the physical exam.

- **Test validity.** In the event of a positive test, the same sample is reanalyzed in order to ensure validity. Records of results usually are kept in the doctor's office for 180 days in case of a lawsuit.

- **Confidentiality.** Confidentiality is maintained by recording positive test results only in the patient's records at the doctor's office. The doctor's office verbally notifies the applicant and a human resource specialist at the firm of the test results. The employing firm doesn't maintain records of test results.

Testing Current Employees. The testing of current employees raises further issues. Employers who test employees usually follow one of three policies.

1. **Random testing.** Employees are tested at random. Those selected at any one time are tested at predetermined dates. Trucking companies report that drugs were found in the systems of nearly a third of all tractor-trailer drivers involved in accidents. Many trucking companies now perform random drug tests on their drivers.

2. **Testing based on probable cause.** Employees are tested only if the manager has reasonable cause to suspect drug abuse. Signs of probable abuse include possession of drug paraphernalia, suspicious behavior, and drastic mood or personality shifts.

3. **Testing after an accident.** Employees involved are tested after any accident or major incident on the job.

Some organizations have established elaborate policies and procedures to control drug and alcohol abuse among their current employees. For instance, Motorola spells out its program in a ten-page document. It requires managers to give employees, in writing, information on employee assistance programs, the effects of alcohol and drug abuse on co-workers and others, and how Motorola will conduct its tests. Capital Cities/ABC, a media conglomerate, also has an extensive program, including educational assistance, employee counseling, the use of various drug tests, drug-sniffing dogs, and undercover operations, if needed.

UNDERCOVER SECURITY AGENTS

Employee theft is the unauthorized taking, control, or transfer of an organization's money and/or property by an employee. It costs employers more than $40 billion annually in the United States alone.[35] An estimated 33 percent of all workers steal from their employers, and approximately 20 percent of business fail (more than 16,000 U.S. firms annually) because of internal theft. A rule of thumb says that any company loses 1 to 2 percent of its sales to employee theft. Employee theft includes pilferage (repeated stealing of small amounts), kickbacks, securities theft and fraud, embezzlement (taking assets entrusted to the employee's care), arson, burglary, vandalism (malicious destruction of assets), shoplifting, insurance fraud, check fraud, and credit card fraud. Although the news media have played up the role of outsiders in computer-related crime, most of it is committed by employees.

The primary reason for the growth of internal security staffs and security firms, such as Pinkerton, Burns, and Guardsmark, is the need to bring the increasing rate of employee theft under control. These security firms provide companies with undercover security agents, often in response to suspicion that theft is taking place. Companies that sell their trash, such as Optigraphics, have used such agents posing as trash collectors because they suspect collusion between employees and trash collectors. Optigraphics manufactures baseball cards and, if a card doesn't meet the firm's standards, it is discarded in the trash. Some retail department stores use undercover agents to verify that salespeople are ringing up sales and not acting in collusion with "customers" in theft. A Pinkerton undercover agent who went to work as a production employee for a manufacturer discovered that continual inventory shrinkage of 1 percent per year was the result of widespread pilfering. Group norms had developed among employees in support of continuous small amounts of stealing at that plant.

Undercover security seems to be tolerated and generally accepted—both legally and socially—as long as there is no hint of entrapment. **Entrapment** involves luring an individual into committing a compromising or illegal act that the person wouldn't otherwise commit.

ENTRAPMENT
Luring an individual into committing a compromising or illegal act that the person otherwise would not commit.

CHAPTER SUMMARY

In this chapter we examined how organizations use various controls to achieve their goals. After considering the basic foundations of control, we highlighted the criteria for effective control systems. Next, we looked at a corrective control model and detailed the steps involved in its use. We then discussed primary types of financial and nonfinancial controls and ended the chapter with a discussion of ethical problems that managers face when using various types of controls.

1. EXPLAIN THE FOUNDATIONS OF CONTROL.

The foundations of organizational control are (1) the type of control, (2) the source of control, (3) the pattern of control, and (4) the purpose of control. Preventive controls, such as rules, standards, and training programs, are designed to reduce the number and severity of deviations that require corrective action. In contrast, corrective controls are designed to bring unwanted behaviors in line with established standards or goals. There are four sources of organizational control: stakeholders, the organization itself, groups, and individuals. Patterns of the different kinds of control vary from mutually reinforcing to independently operating to conflicting.

2. STATE HOW ORGANIZATIONS CAN CREATE EFFECTIVE CONTROLS.

The effectiveness of formal organizational controls is measured in terms of costs and benefits. The cost–benefit model highlights the trade-offs that occur with increases or decreases in control. At some point, increasing controls ceases to be effective. The effectiveness of specific controls is evaluated according to whether they achieve desired results and are objective, complete, timely, and acceptable.

3. IDENTIFY THE SIX STEPS OF THE CORRECTIVE CONTROL MODEL.

The corrective control model comprises six interconnected elements: (1) define the subsystem, (2) identify the characteristics to be measured, (3) set standards, (4) collect information, (5) make comparisons, and (6) diagnose and correct any problems.

4. DESCRIBE THE PRIMARY TYPES OF ORGANIZATIONAL CONTROL.

The primary types of organizational control include (1) bureaucratic, (2) organic, (3) market, (4) financial, (5) accounting for quality, and (6) automation-based. Effective managerial control usually requires using several types and methods of control in combination.

5. DISCUSS ETHICAL CONTROL ISSUES CONFRONTING MANAGERS.

Ethical issues concerning control methods arise from the use of computer monitoring, drug testing, and undercover security agents.

QUESTIONS FOR DISCUSSION

1. How are planning and control linked?

2. What types of control does FedEx use?

3. What are the characteristics of Chick-Fil-A's control systems?

4. What organizational factors create the need for control?

5. Describe the key characteristics of the corrective control model as they apply to a bank.

6. What are the primary types of control? How is each used? Which is most important? Why?

7. What is activity-based costing? Visit a local fast-food restaurant and apply this model of control to that store's operation.

8. Do organizations have the right to monitor their employees by computer without their knowledge? Explain.

9. If you were assigned to look for drug abuse on your campus or in an organization you belong to, what drugs would you look for? Should universities test their students for drug abuse? Why or why not?

10. Recently, China and the United States held talks on intellectual property rights. What controls can a government use to protect such rights?

EXERCISES TO DEVELOP YOUR MANAGEMENT COMPETENCIES

1. **Self-Management Competency.** The following questionnaire lists behaviors that you and others might engage in on the job. For each item, circle the number that best indicates the frequency with which you would engage in that behavior. Then put an X over the number that you think best describes how others you know behave. Finally, put a check mark beside that behavior if you believe that management should design a system to control that behavior.

Behavior	Most of of the time	Often	About half the time	Seldom	Never
1. Blaming an innocent person or a computer for errors	5	4	3	2	1
2. Passing on information that was told in confidence	5	4	3	2	1
3. Falsifying quality reports	5	4	3	2	1
4. Claiming credit for someone else's work	5	4	3	2	1
5. Padding an expense account by more than 5 percent	5	4	3	2	1
6. Using company supplies for personal use	5	4	3	2	1
7. Accepting favors in exchange for preferred treatment	5	4	3	2	1
8. Giving favors in exchange for preferred treatment	5	4	3	2	1
9. Asking a person to violate company rules	5	4	3	2	1
10. Calling in sick to take a day off	5	4	3	2	1
11. Hiding errors	5	4	3	2	1
12. Taking longer than necessary to do the job	5	4	3	2	1
13. Doing personal business on company time	5	4	3	2	1
14. Taking a longer lunch hour without approval	5	4	3	2	1
15. Seeing a violation and not reporting it	5	4	3	2	1
16. Overlooking boss's error to prove loyalty	5	4	3	2	1
17. Asking an aide to lie about one's whereabouts	5	4	3	2	1
18. Telling co-workers that one is going somewhere but actually going somewhere else	5	4	3	2	1

QUESTIONS

1. What are the differences between the most and least frequently occurring behaviors?

2. What are the most important items that should be controlled? Why? What do they reveal about your own preferences for control?

3. How would management go about establishing programs for controlling them?[36]

2. **Strategic Action Competency.** Frito-Lay is a snack food division of PepsiCo, Inc., with annual sales of $10 billion. It uses a computerized executive information system to gather data from two primary sources: scanners at supermarket checkout counters, and 10,000 hand-held computers operated by Frito-Lay's sales representatives. The hand-held computers make daily updates possible. These updates provide real-time trend information for more than 100 product lines in some 450,000 stores. At the end of each day, the hand-held computer is connected to a minicomputer at a Frito-Lay distribution center, and the results are sent to company headquarters in Plano, Texas. The central computer sends back information to the hand-held computers on price changes and promotions for use the next day. This system enables managers to flag problems and opportunities requiring management attention. Frito-Lay's computer system also has enabled it to understand what its competition is doing in the marketplace. After visiting Frito-Lay's Web site at

   www.fritolay.com

   describe its management control system and how it compares itself to the competition.

3. **Global Awareness Competency.** With the Chinese, a contract may not represent finality, but a starting point. The Chinese approach is to negotiate the process to establish an interpersonal relationship, thereby creating a bonding friendship. Consequently, the Chinese negotiate to do business with each other, often leaving specific terms to be determined in the future by the circumstances that occur. A contract is viewed as worthwhile only as long as it is necessary or convenient. When the Chinese suddenly find themselves in a situation where honoring a particular contract will be difficult, they may turn to their partners, expecting not only understanding, but support and help getting them out of their dilemma by changing the terms of the agreement. For example, McDonald's twenty-year contract for a central operation in Beijing didn't keep it from being evicted after two years. What implications does this notion of an agreement have on firms operating in China? To help you answer this question and for illustrations of how two firms changed their management control systems to operate in China, visit McDonald's Web site at

   www.mcdonalds.com

   and KFC's Web site at

   www.kfc.com

4. **Teamwork Competency.** When Skip LeFauve was appointed president of GM's Saturn plant in Spring Hill, Tennessee, he knew that he had to improve quality and enhance worker involvement by placing decision making on the factory floor to make the Saturn venture successful. Through skills training and team-building exercises, work units became self-directed. These units managed most daily activities including production and scheduling, maintenance, inventory control, and record keeping. They also took responsibility for defining and assigning jobs, recruiting and training new hires, and preparing budgets. Saturn's consensus principles required approval by at least 70 percent of the unit's members before a decision could be implemented. These work units also created "decision circles" that were organized around major elements of production, such as the cooling system, and focused on long-term improvement. What kind of control system did LeFauve adopt at Saturn? Why was it successful? To understand Saturn's control system more completely visit its Web site at

   www.saturn.com

REAL-TIME CASE ANALYSIS

IAMS COMPANY

Each year, people spend more than $9.4 billion on pet food. The Iams Company is a premium maker of pet foods, with four plants in Ohio and its headquarters in Dayton. With more than 126 million cats and dogs in the United States, this fifty-five-year-old company caters to pet owners who are serious about good eating habits and nutrition for their pets. Sold only through pet stores and veterinary clinics, Iams promises more calories per bite and higher-quality ingredients based on "pioneering research in animal nutrition" tailored to a pet's "life stage," or age, than do its competitors, such as Hill's and Purina.

Because its products are sold only through pet stores and by vets, Iams underwrites research and studies of animal nutrition, dermatology, geriatrics, kidney disorders, and allergies at various graduate schools of veterinary medicine. It also sends practicing veterinarians to seminars to show them how to gain more sales and offers nutrition certification programs. Iams also donates tons of free food for the pets of cash-poor veterinary students.

What makes Iams different from other organizations is its control system. As a premium cat and dog food manufacturer, its foods must be the same from bag to bag. In contrast, the formulation of standard brands can change, depending on the fluctuation of ingredient prices. The basis of Iams's ability to consistently deliver premium cat and dog food is its control system. Each key function—production, sales, customer service, information technology, finance, and accounting—is measured by a combination of cost, time, volume, and errors. When employees meet or exceed their performance levels, Iams gains a competitive advantage. These measures drive decisions and have become the foundation of the organization's culture.

The heart of Iams's control system is its compensation plan. All employees are covered under its productivity incentive plan (PIP). It is composed of base pay plus incentives for meeting or exceeding sales, profits, and return on investment. Plant performance is measured on various operating factors—machine downtime, absenteeism, and waste—and displayed daily for all employees to see. Employees are assembled to review each quarter's results. The CEO personally discusses these results with the employees.

Production employees rotate from job to job for the purpose of cross-training. When they demonstrate that they have learned new competencies, they are certified to use those competencies. Future merit raises are based in part on certification. An important feature that undoubtedly contributes to its success is that the program is monitored continuously by a team of supervisors and employees.

When the original PIP plan was designed, managers met with every hourly employee to make sure that they understood the plan. Even with this level of personal attention, initially some of the employees were apprehensive about being allowed to make personnel decisions such as hiring, promotions, and transfers. To overcome this apprehension, the human resources staff held counseling sessions with anxious employees and listened to their concerns. They explained the details of the program again and assured employees that the plan could be modified should it be shown to be unfair or unworkable.[37]

QUESTIONS

1. What is the primary type of control system at Iams? Compare it with that used by Chick-Fil-A.

2. How has Iams tried to control major stakeholders that can influence the profitability of the organization? Are these practices ethical? Explain.

3. Apply the corrective control model to Iams. What are the key subsystem elements emphasized in the case?

To learn more about the management control systems at Iams, visit the company's home page at

www.iams.com

VIDEO CASE

TOM'S OF MAINE: BRUSH WITH GREATNESS

Tom's of Maine is a typical small business for which specialized equipment can afford a degree of automation but wherein the employees remain in close contact with the entire production process. At Tom's, measuring employee productivity is fairly straightforward because of the nature of the product and processes—the focus is on discrete batches and a mechanized line. After a shift, total throughput can be calculated, accounting for cases packed and product rejected in quality assurance. In some highly automated service environments, however (e.g., telephone sales or help-desk operations), performance can be measured to the second, or the keystroke.

If Tom's should expand, it might need to change its processes (e.g., to automate its lines more fully to speed throughput). Harvard Business School professor Shoshana Zuboff has explored the introduction of automation into factory processes. She's found that problems arise when employees are displaced from the production process and have to mentally "retool." For example, they may have to learn that a blinking light on a console signals a condition that they used to be able to feel by touching the machinery or sense by listening to the line. The next generation of factory workers may find a panel of blinking lights exactly what they need in order to feel part of a machine.

Computer manufacturer Gateway 2000, which featured its folksy, rural South Dakota roots in much the same manner that Tom's is marketed as a small, Maine business, recently decided to split its operations and move senior managers to San Diego when it grew. Although this split may have been necessary (the claim was that recruiting executive professionals away from urban centers was difficult), such expansion could also be disruptive. It could, in fact, encourage the development of rival, petty fiefdoms away from direct oversight of senior management.

Some of the work at Tom's of Maine is grindingly repetitive. Tube packers get a break every hour, but at 80 tubes per minute streaming from the filler, a team will have processed some 4,800 toothpaste tubes in that hour. Measurement of productivity can be a source for tension between labor and management. Union contracts often contain production quotas, and management attempts to push workers past certain limits (e.g., in upping the speed of a production line) have been the cause of strikes. "Working to rule" is a strategy sometimes used in work slowdown protests, where employees perform the bare minimum of work specified in their contract.

Management may feel that because a factor can be measured, it should be measured. Such an attitude might be counterproductive, especially when employees may resent what they feel to be "workplace surveillance." Exact measurement might aid managers in planning and administration, but they should also utilize communication competency—making clear why and how measurement can assist in making the work more effective and listening to find out when employees' concerns for privacy might indicate practical limits on productivity.

Small businesses such as Tom's of Maine have always enjoyed a certain amount of good will from consumers. There is a presumption that the small business, where production might still reflect hand-

crafting, is something to cherish and a source of high-quality goods. Some large companies have begun to project an image of the small, familylike producer to market certain product lines, as in boutiques. Some of the major breweries, for example, are attempting to capitalize on the microbrewing trend with what seem to be quaint, small-scale companies. Even though Plank Road Brewery sounds like one of the little guys, it is an arm of giant Miller Brewing Company.

ON THE WEB

Tom's of Maine is on the Web (***www.toms-of-maine.com***), as is Gateway 2000 (***www.gateway2000.com***). Gateway's slogan, "You've Got a Friend in the Business," attempts to capture the same, down-home coziness as Tom's of Maine and many other small businesses. However, in 1997, Gateway surpassed Apple Computer in sales to the educational market, and as of early 1998 it was worth in excess of $7 billion.

QUESTIONS

1. Productivity analysis reveals that throughput and quality vary significantly between two teams working the Tom's line. If you were a manager at Tom's, how might you address this difference?

2. In companies with many "knowledge workers," the Internet may be an essential work resource. How might it also pose a management challenge?

3. If computers have made work more measurable, how has the workplace also changed in the last several decades to make it less rigidly structured?

To help you answer these questions and learn more about Tom's of Maine, visit the company's home page at

www.toms-of-maine.com

Case contributed by Ross Stapleton-Gray, President, TeleDiplomacy, Inc., a technology and policy consultancy, and Adjunct Professor in Georgetown University's Communication, Culture, and Technology program.

Chapter

20

Information Management Technology

LEARNING OBJECTIVES

AFTER STUDYING THIS CHAPTER, YOU SHOULD BE ABLE TO:

1. EXPLAIN SEVERAL DRAMATIC IMPACTS OF INFORMATION TECHNOLOGIES ON EMPLOYEES AND ORGANIZATIONS.

2. COMMENT ON THE ROLE OF INFORMATION AS A VALUED RESOURCE.

3. DESCRIBE SIX SELECTED INFORMATION MANAGEMENT TECHNOLOGIES.

4. STATE THE PRIMARY FACTORS INVOLVED IN THE DESIGN OF INFORMATION SYSTEMS.

5. IDENTIFY THE CHARACTERISTICS OF EFFECTIVE INFORMATION SYSTEM IMPLEMENTATION.

6. EXPLAIN SEVERAL ETHICAL ISSUES IN THE APPLICATION OF INFORMATION TECHNOLOGIES.

Outline

United Airlines' Global Information System

One business that doesn't have to go out and collect data is the airline industry. Its data are delivered three times a day. The Airline Tariff Publishing Company (ATPCO) sends data about fare changes to its subscribers, which means that every airline gets a nearly real-time look at what its competitors are doing. This type of data has potential strategic implications. What's less obvious is that the data make it hard to understand what's truly important. That's the reason for data analysis.

Consider United Airlines, headquartered in Elk Grove Village, Illinois, which uses ATPCO's data on competitive airlines to develop responses to their actions. To do that, United must interpret data about those actions with knowledge of special events, such as the air travel implications of the Albuquerque, New Mexico, balloon festival or the High Point, North Carolina, furniture show. Glenn Colville, manager of R&D for the information services division of United, comments, "In our industry, it's easy to get information [data]. The trick is to match up the information [data] with the concepts that drive the business." The goal of the analysis is to determine the best mix of full and discount fares that will maximize revenue from United's 350,000 daily booking alternatives.

United Airlines relies on a two-tiered analysis. The first tier examines competitive data, historical data, cancellations, and bookings as far as 331 days in advance in terms of passenger revenue, aircraft capacity, and current forecasts. This analysis is run on several mainframe computers that process raw transactions data and make complex calculations. Colville comments, "Because we handle more than a million bookings and cancellations each day, even the smallest optimization of the mix of passengers and routes can have a massive impact on revenue."

In United's second tier, the firm's analysts subject the first-tier reports to additional study, based on their own experience and knowledge of local events. To assist them, the analysts have access to printed reports, custom screens, and specialized analysis programs. Colville explains, "Computers keep track of what happened historically, and analysts try to find exceptions that can increase the yield [revenue per passenger mile] and the load factor [percentage of seats filled per plane]. They also look for major competitive changes, such as numerous fare changes that could signal a fare war. Customers and travel agents see the new fares as soon as we do, so we lose business until we react."[1]

* * *

To learn more about United Airlines, visit the company's home page at

www.ual.com

ROLE OF INFORMATION TECHNOLOGIES IN ORGANIZATIONS

1

EXPLAIN SEVERAL DRAMATIC IMPACTS OF INFORMATION TECHNOLOGIES ON EMPLOYEES AND ORGANIZATIONS

In several earlier chapters, we described the impact of computer-based information technologies on various aspects of organizations. Affected are product design and quality, services offered, communications systems used, employee selection, choice of organization designs, and managerial functions (planning, organizing, leading, and controlling), among others. The Preview feature shows both the strategic and operational importance of United Airlines' global information system for achieving its revenue goals and making detailed decisions about its 350,000 daily booking alternatives. It demonstrates how United's analysts utilize computer-generated data and information to assess and make decisions related to the best mix of passengers and routes to optimize revenue. The data gathered about fare changes by the Airline Tariff Publishing Company (ATPCO) are transmitted electronically to most airlines virtually instantaneously. The airline industry is one of many now immersed in the digital world and cyberspace.

DIGITAL WORLD

The linking of people, decisions, tasks, and processes via computers and computers with other computers.

The ***digital world*** is the linking of people, decisions, tasks, and processes via computers and computers with other computers. *Digital* refers to the method of data transmission, through on/off signals. ***Cyberspace*** represents the real-time transmitting and sharing of text, voice, graphics, video, and the like over a variety

CYBERSPACE

Represents the real-time transmitting and sharing of text, voice, graphics, video, and the like over a variety of computer-based networks.

of computer-based networks. Cyberspace is much more than communication connections between points A and B. Its broader capabilities allow (1) people to come together across remote distances to confer in the same three-dimensional virtual electronic space, (2) computers to *talk* to other computers, and (3) individuals to interact with computer-based machines to aid creativity and make decisions.[2] United, American, Continental, and other airlines currently take advantage of many of the capabilities of cyberspace on a daily basis.

PREDICTIONS COME TRUE

In a 1958 issue of the Harvard Business Review, Harold J. Leavitt and Thomas L. Whisler forecast what organizations of the future would look like. Their predictions included the following.

- **The role and scope of middle managers will change.** Many middle-management jobs will become more structured, have less status, and command less compensation. The number of middle managers will decline, creating flatter organizations. The middle-management positions that remain will be more technical and strategic.

- **Top management will focus more on innovating, planning, and creating.** The rate of obsolescence and change will quicken, and top management will continually have to address developments on the horizon.

- **Large organizations will recentralize.** New information technologies will give top managers more information. This advantage will extend top management's strategic control over crucial decisions.[3]

To a substantial degree, these predictions have come true. New and more profound predictions are now being made as a result of the current revolution in information technologies. For example, Frances Cairncross, author of *The Death of Distance,* contends that more businesses will become like Hollywood studios, pulling together individuals and companies for one-time projects. Thus network organizations will become increasingly common. Plummeting communications costs will revolutionize the way business is done, she argues. Lower communications costs lead to lower transactions costs, which in turn reduce the optimal size of firms. Since 1970, the average number of employees in U.S. firms has dropped by a fifth. Competition from the Internet, as well as competition among long-distance providers, will continue to drive down the cost of phone calls, Cairncross predicts. She calls fiberoptic cables the "oil pipelines of the information economy."[4]

IMPACTS TODAY

The information technology revolution is having significant impacts on organizations in various ways. ***Information technologies*** (ITs) are the computer-based electronic systems that help individuals and organizations assemble, store, transmit, process, and retrieve data and information. The new generation of managers and employees are much more knowledgeable than their counterparts of just a decade ago about the uses and benefits of technology. Many organizations are using information technology as a strategic asset to maintain an edge in competitive global markets. Advances in telecommunications and networking allow people to exchange information more freely than ever. Computer-based systems are available that can intelligently link, learn, and make recommendations to decision makers by applications of artificial intelligence, mainly through expert systems.[5]

Leavitt and Whisler's predictions were strongly criticized throughout the 1960s, 1970s, and 1980s as being farfetched. They no longer are so considered because

INFORMATION TECHNOLOGIES (ITs)

The computer-based electronic systems that help individuals and organizations assemble, store, transmit, process, and retrieve data and information.

organizations have indeed undergone radical changes in design and methods of operation, based primarily on new information technologies.[6] One highly significant benefit has been the reduction of the information *float* in organizations. In the past, decision making took a lot of time because information and proposals had to pass through numerous organizational layers before anything could be decided or actually happen. Today's information technologies cut through those layers and across organizational boundaries.

Recall that the streamlining of decision and information flows, especially through the use of horizontal networks, is a key feature of organization redesign. The new information technologies are a vital component of most job and organization redesign initiatives. Managers whose main function was to serve as assemblers and relayers of information are no longer needed. Organizations continue to reduce the number of first-line and middle managers because information technologies streamline many of the communication, coordination, and control functions that such managers traditionally performed. The managers who remain have been freed from many routine tasks and can devote more time and attention to planning and decision making.

The demand for *knowledge workers* is growing rapidly. They are needed to help ensure the successful integration of information systems with other organizational systems. These workers can deliver the appropriate technology and provide instructions for using it efficiently and effectively. The magnitude of the information revolution and the central role of knowledge workers is underscored by output figures. The total tonnage of industrial output in the United States is about the same as it was a century ago, even though real output is some twenty times higher. This difference reflects the increasing knowledge content of goods and services. This "lighter" output, combined with dramatic reductions in transportation costs, suggests that producing close to customers is no longer as important as it was in the past.[7]

Changes in an organization's design, the geographic dispersion of its workforce, and increased reliance on information technologies often lead to decentralization of tactical decisions, but greater centralization of strategic decisions and controls, as predicted by Leavitt and Whisler in 1958. Decentralization results in the empowerment of lower level employees, managers, and teams, allowing them to engage in tactical planning, self- and mutual control, and day-to-day decision making. In some ways, organizations increasingly resemble professional firms (e.g., CPA firms, law firms, and group medical practices). The most successful of such firms attract, motivate, and retain competent employees through a steady stream of challenging projects. In these organizations, few jobs consist solely of overseeing the work of others. Many employees take on managerial roles for short periods of time by serving as team leaders. Employees' jobs change often, depending on the project being worked on.[8]

The current impacts of information technologies aren't all positive, however. Consider the comment made by one manager:

> *Increased use of technology means increased responsibility; e.g., typesetting, electronic files for graphics. Increased responsibility means the high possibility of increased stress. Time saved in one area is lost in another. The new area of responsibility is more demanding because it is dynamic.*[9]

One of the looming negative impacts of computer-based information technology is the Year 2000 computer problem. In brief, many computer systems have been programmed to use two digits to represent a year and will therefore be unable to calculate accurately dates that begin with 2000. A computer that subtracts the year 1999 from the year 2000 will erroneously arrive at a value of minus 99 ("00" − "99") rather than the correct answer of a one-year difference. Such miscalculations could incorrectly determine numerical values (e.g., bank accounts and mortgage payments) of great importance. They could also cause a system to halt or "crash" and thereby interrupt some process (e.g., real-time automatic teller transactions).[10] Table 20.1 presents four of the more common false assumptions made by managers about the Year 2000 problem and the corresponding actual situation. Many large firms, including FedEx and Bank of America, are spending hundreds of millions of dollars to fix their Year 2000 problems.

ROLE OF INFORMATION IN ORGANIZATIONS

2

COMMENT ON THE ROLE OF INFORMATION AS A VALUED RESOURCE

Organizations store and process vast amounts of data, which managers and employees must turn into useful information. This information enables them to make better decisions. The terms *data* and *information* often are used interchangeably but incorrectly.

DATA AND INFORMATION

DATA
Facts and figures.

Data are facts and figures. Every organization, such as United Airlines, processes data about its operations to create current, accurate, and reliable information. Many decisions require data such as market statistics, operating costs, inventory levels, sales figures, and the like. However, raw data are much like raw materials—not very useful until they are processed. Processing data involves comparison, classification,

Table 20.1	False Assumptions and Facts about the Year 2000 Problem
False Assumptions	**Facts**
• Only mainframe and other large systems have the Year 2000 problem.	• Any computer-based system can have the Year 2000 problem, including mainframe-midrange-, and PC-based systems.
• Only older model systems (hardware and software) have Year 2000 problems.	• Systems that are being bought as of 1998 are almost as likely to have the Year 2000 problem as do the older systems that a company already possesses. There is no across-the-board standard for dealing with the Year 2000 problem.
• Organizations have until New Year's Eve of 1999 to find and fix the Year 2000 problem.	• Many systems will encounter the Year 2000 problem long before the end of 1999. If a manufacturing system does two-year forecasts, it might have Year 2000 problems soon or right now, owing to date calculations involving 1999 and the Year 2000.
• Organizations can confine their Year 2000 worries to their own internal systems.	• Organizations must look at outside entities that they depend on or that depend on them. How will the firm be affected if suppliers have Year 2000 problems?

Source: Adapted from L. B. Eliot. Correcting Year 2000 (Y2K) false assumptions. *Decision Line*, December/January 1998, pp. 15–16.

analysis, and summarization to make them usable and valuable. Thus the relationship of data to information is the same as that of raw materials to components of finished goods or aspects of services. Recall the Preview feature. Three times a day United Airlines and most other airlines receive data about fare changes by virtually all airlines from ATPCO. Analysis of this mass of data by United's information services division creates information to help management determine the mix of full and discount fares that is likely to maximize revenue.

INFORMATION

The knowledge derived from data that people have transformed to make them meaningful and useful.

KNOWLEDGE

Concepts, tools, and categories used to create, store, apply, and share information.

Information is the knowledge derived from data that people have transformed to make them meaningful and useful. In effect, data are subjected to a *value-added process* that yields meaningful information for decision making. Individuals use their ***knowledge***—concepts, tools, and categories—to create, store, apply, and share information. Knowledge can be stored in a book, in a person's mind, or in a computer program as a set of instructions that gives meaning to streams of data.[11] In United Airlines' second-tier analysis, analysts base additional study of the first-tier reports on their own experience and knowledge of local events.

VALUE-ADDED RESOURCE

In contrast to that of physical resources, the value of information isn't easily determined. The value added to data, especially through the use of information technologies, is determined by those who use the resulting information to achieve desired goals. Such organizational goals may include (1) maintaining or increasing market share, (2) avoiding catastrophic losses, (3) creating greater flexibility and adaptability, (4) improving the quality of goods and services, (5) maximizing revenue, and (6) minimizing costs.[12] Individuals at different organizational levels and in various units and teams have different information needs. Certain information is essential to the specific types of decisions they must make to serve their customers, whether internal or external to the organization.

Top managers typically are interested in information on overall organizational performance and new product ideas. Detailed information on daily production and quality at each manufacturing site isn't likely to be as useful to them as it is to self-managing teams in the plants. These teams need specific information about the availability of raw materials, changes in productivity, rates of defects, and other operating characteristics. To sales managers, detailed information on various raw materials probably has little value. Sales personnel want to know the amounts and types of goods and services that can be promised for delivery at various times and at what prices.

To be considered a value-added resource, information must possess value over and above that of the raw data.[13] Figure 20.1 shows four common interrelated criteria used to assess the value of information: quality, relevance, quantity, and timeliness.

Quality. The quality of information refers to its accuracy in portraying reality. The more accurate the information, the higher is its quality. The degree of quality required varies according to the needs of those who will use the information. Employees responsible for production inventory control need high-quality (precise) information about the amounts of raw materials available and resupply schedules required to meet customers' delivery expectations. Marketing managers concerned with five-year sales forecasts might be able to use lower quality (less precise) information, such as general market trends and sales projections. Such long-term forecasting can't be developed quickly or easily from detailed daily or weekly sales data.

Relevance. The relevance of information refers to the extent to which it directly assists decision making. Managers and employees often receive information that is

Figure 20.1   **Interrelated Criteria for Valuing Information**

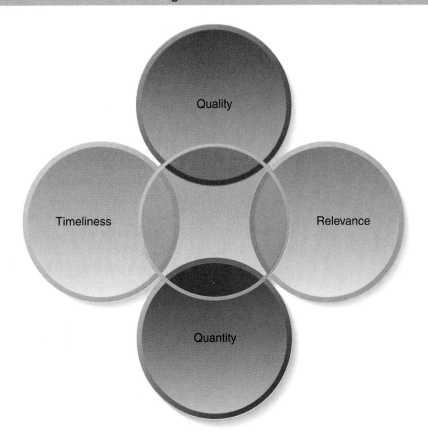

of little use. For example, a self-managing production team needs detailed information about production schedules, inventory levels, and promised delivery dates in order to make good decisions. Such information is relevant to providing quality goods when desired by customers. These team members don't need detailed information about the organization's global strategy. However, the relevance of information can differ for the same person or function at different times. For example, summer sales estimates in January may not be relevant to Mattel managers trying to project next December's demand. But summer sales estimates may be very useful the following October when those same managers are trying to project next summer's demand before setting production goals.

Quantity. Quantity refers to the amount of information available when people need it. More information isn't always better. In fact, too much can lead to information overload, particularly if the extra information isn't relevant to the decisions being made.[14] The provision of information—relevant or not—costs time and money, and information overload can cause stress and reduce effectiveness. For example, Charles Wang, Chairman of Computer Associates International—a software firm that sells e-mail and other software packages—limits his use of e-mail. He also made the decision to shut down the company's e-mail system for five hours a day so that employees wouldn't be distracted by it. He comments, "As a leader in a company, you have to go to an extreme to demonstrate a point. With subordinates copying their bosses on practically every memo they write [using e-mail], it has become a cover-your[self] tool."[15] Headquartered in Islandia, New York, Computer Associates has more than 11,000 employees in 160 offices in 43 countries.

Timeliness. Timeliness means the receipt of needed information before it ceases to be useful for decision-making purposes. Top managers at Corning Glass Works who make strategic plans for new plants and products are interested in quarterly or annual production and sales information. In contrast, production employees and managers at its Bellefonte, Pennsylvania, plant need daily—and sometimes even hourly or minute-by-minute—information concerning operations to ensure that they meet their production schedules. If they received such information only quarterly or even monthly, it wouldn't be timely and could severely harm the quality and amount of outputs and disrupt promised deliveries to customers.

These four criteria—quality, relevance, quantity, and timeliness—are interrelated and are essential to the provision of information that serves as a value-added resource. The following Planning and Administration Competency feature recounts the experience of The Sports Authority, a rapidly growing sporting goods retailer, in applying Lotus Notes, a multifunctional software package. This software improved the quality, relevance, quantity, and timeliness of information flows. Managers and employees improved their abilities to (1) monitor information and use it to identify symptoms, underlying problems, and alternative solutions; (2) make timely strategic and operational decisions; (3) develop schedules to achieve specific goals; and (4) determine the need for resources and organize their acquisition and use.

SELECTED INFORMATION TECHNOLOGIES

3

DESCRIBE SIX SELECTED INFORMATION MANAGEMENT TECHNOLOGIES

Computer-based information technologies are developing at a breathtaking pace, rapidly becoming less expensive and ever more powerful. The most conservative forecasts claim that the cost-performance relationship for these technologies as a whole will continue to improve by 15 to 25 percent annually into the foreseeable future.[16]

In this section, we review six interrelated information technologies being used to support a wide range of managerial functions. These technologies include the Internet, extranet, intranet, decision support systems, expert systems, and group decision support systems.

INTERNET

In Chapter 16, we defined the *Internet* as a loosely configured, rapidly growing web of 25,000 corporate, educational, and research computer networks around the world. In essence, it is a network of networks and is often referred to as the information superhighway. The Internet is available to anyone with a computer and a modem, and by now you should be very familiar with it. Internet access usually provides four primary capabilities.

- **Electronic mail** (e-mail) enables users to send, forward, and receive messages from people all over the world. Users can then reply to, save, file, and categorize received messages. E-mail makes participation in electronic conferences and discussions possible.

- **Telnet** enables users to log in to remote computers and to interact with them. Users' computers are remotely connected to computers at other locations but act as if they were directly connected.

- **File Transfer Protocol** (FTP) enables users to move files and data from one computer to another. Users can download magazines, books, documents, software, music, graphics, and much more.

The Sports Authority's mission is to establish the firm as the number one choice for sports, leisure, and recreational customers. As of 1998, this rapidly growing retailer, headquartered in Fort Lauderdale, Florida, had more than 170 outlets, ranging in size from about 9,000 to 40,000 square feet.

E-mail was the first piece of Lotus Notes to be implemented, to allow employees to get comfortable with Notes. According to Dietta Slayton, business planner at the Sports Authority, being at ease with the software boosted productivity when cross-functional teams began tapping Notes' more significant capabilities. According to Slayton, "E-mail just wasn't enough. E-mail tackles communication. But you also have to look at collaboration, coordination, and systems integration. It's not enough to have one outfit that fits. You need to have a whole wardrobe."

The Sports Authority's groupware "wardrobe" now includes replication and bulletin board functions. Those functions allow individuals from different departments to update a shared database continually as an interdepartmental project progresses. When someone in one department makes changes to a Notes database, those changes are available throughout the firm. Whoever accesses the database next will be aware of those changes and can be assured of working with the most current information. Slayton believes that "replication is an important facet of Lotus Notes' messaging abilities: This allows us to communicate with our remote users. When our executives are on the road, we can still get the information they need to them. They can call in and be up to date at any time. We track things like vendor negotiations from the starting point of, 'do we want to buy a product,' right through to 'yes we want to buy it and this is how many we want.' "

Notes allows the company to keep track of the information and decisions involved in opening new stores, too. The availability and easy accessibility of information in one place associated with the leasing or construction of a new store allowed the chain to manage its breakneck expansion with relatively few problems.

Notes is allowing The Sports Authority to manage the flow of projects in a logical manner. Slayton states, "Once you have all this information out there, you have to coordinate it. We use workflow applications to coordinate business processes like tracking, routing and approvals. No one has to worry whether they are getting the right information at the right time. The database environment ensures that we are all up to date."[17]

* * *

To learn more about The Sports Authority, visit its home page at

www.sportsauthority.com

- **World Wide Web** (the Web) enables users to access and contribute text, documents, images, video, and sound. It is a set of standards and protocols used to access data and information on the Internet. The Web is nonlinear by design and permits users to jump from topic to topic, document to document, and site to site. The World Wide Web requires the use of "browsers" to view Web documents and navigate through the intricate link protocols. Of the some forty different Web browsers, the two major ones are Netscape Navigator and Microsoft Internet Explorer.[18] The World Wide Web is quite young—the first Web browser was introduced in 1993.

Tim Berner-Lee is the Web's inventor and currently serves as director of the World Wide Web Consortium at Massachusetts Institute of Technology. He comments:

I developed the Web with three purposes in mind. The first was to give people up-to-date information at their fingertips by giving them the personal power to hypertext. The second goal was the realization of an information space that everyone could share and contribute their ideas and solutions to. Part three was the creation of agents to integrate the information that is out there with real life. Enormous amounts of information would no longer be lost.[19] [Note: Hypertext generally refers to any text that contains links to other documents—words or phrases (often in a different color) that can be selected (clicked on) and then results in another document being retrieved and displayed.]

The capabilities of the Internet may be thought of as the building blocks for the explosion in information technology applications at any time and any place. Throughout this book, we have presented examples of how organizations and individuals are developing new strategic applications through the Internet.[20] The ability of United Airlines' customers to make plane reservations through the Internet is one such example.

EXTRANETS

EXTRANETS

Dynamic wide area networks that link a company's employees, suppliers, customers, and other key business partners in an electronic online environment for business communication.

Extranets are dynamic wide area networks that link a company's employees, suppliers, customers, and other key business partners in an electronic online environment for business communications.[21] Unlike the Internet, the general public doesn't have access to an extranet. Extranets are intended to provide fast, reliable, secure, and low-cost computer-to-computer communication for a wide range of applications—everything from sales, marketing, online publishing, and customer service, to product development, directory and database services, employee communications, workgroup projects, and electronic commerce.

By setting up an extranet, a company can allow customers to connect via the Web to certain information stored on the company's internal computer-based system—while maintaining security of the sensitive information within a firewall.[22] A *firewall* is a combination of computer hardware and software that controls access to and transmission of particular sets of data and information, often referred to as a *private network*. Network identification numbers and passwords are elementary components of firewalls.

FIREWALL

A combination of computer hardware and software that controls access to and transmission of particular sets of data and information, often referred to as a *private network*.

Extranets rely on four other technologies: the World Wide Web, the Internet, groupware applications (e.g., Lotus Notes), and firewalls. Security is a major issue. Richard Rebh, vice president of marketing for Web Flow Corp—a software applications firm in Santa Clara, California—comments, "Our security is a function of several things. The various servers you could get to from our Web server can be protected by name. But even if you could find the server, it's password protected. If you managed to hack your way in, you could see only what your hacked account would let you see. And finally, if you could get past that, we use encryption to hide the information inside a safe stream."[23]

The following Strategic Action Competency account describes the extranet launched by Charles Schwab & Company to meet customer needs and to stay abreast of its top competitors—Merrill Lynch, FMR, and Quick & Reilly. Schwab's main business is discount brokerage: making trades for clients who make their own investment decisions by buying and selling stocks and bonds.

INTRANETS

INTRANETS

Private or semiprivate internally focused networks that use the infrastructure and standards of the Internet and the Web.

Intranets are private or semiprivate, internally focused networks that use the infrastructure and standards of the Internet and the Web. They are normally limited to access by an organization's employees, through firewalls. Access to sensitive data and information can similarly be restricted to authorized employees. An intranet enables employees to communicate with each other and access internal information and databases through their desktop or laptop computers.[24] The intranet can be used to link employees at a single site and at diverse geographic locations,

Charles Schwab & Company launched an extranet net application in 1997. It lets 150 mutual fund companies use the Web to download decision-support data collected by the San Francisco brokerage. Schwab is among the companies at the forefront of a move to link Internet and data warehousing technologies. The idea is to give analysis-minded external users, ranging from suppliers to customers, access to online vaults of historical data.

For Schwab, the extranet project was a way to avoid printing and mailing monthly reports on stock trading activity and asset holdings to mutual fund companies that use Schwab as a sales channel. But more important, Schwab hopes that providing the ability to customize reports and then directly download the information via the Web will help endear it to mutual fund managers. The goal is to make it harder for rival discount fund brokerages to take business away from

Schwab. "The driving force for this was that the fund companies wanted to receive the information electronically," said Linda Coffey, a vice president in Schwab's fund relations department. "We want to be perceived as providing more services than our competitors, and we're trying to stay out ahead of the curve."

For Jim Robillard, chief investment relations liaison at Baron Capital, Inc.'s Baron Funds in New York, Schwab's extranet is cutting two to three weeks off the time it took to plow through the monthly printed reports and manually enter data into an Excel spreadsheet. Robillard states, "It's a tremendous amount of material, and in paper form it was unsortable. There was no automation at all. And because the reports usually didn't arrive until nearly two weeks into the next month, the analysis that finally got done was a little retrospective."

Users can download reports directly into Excel spreadsheets. To keep data from falling into the wrong hands, the server is located behind Schwab's firewall and holds a database of passwords and IDs for each user.[25]

* * *

To learn more about Charles Schwab & Company, visit its home page at

www.schwab.com

sometimes throughout the world. The use of intranets is growing rapidly. The following are four common applications.

- Organizations have volumes of policies and procedures that they would like their employees to be aware of and actually use when appropriate. Unfortunately, most of the time, a set of policies and procedures sits on a shelf somewhere and collects dust. Employees may not even know that the policies and procedures exist or how to find a current version. With an intranet, the organization merely sets up a Web server (identical to the Web servers used for the Internet), places the linked policies and procedures on it, and provides an address of the now online policies and procedures to the employees.

- A variety of human resources management uses exist for intranets. For example, an increasing number of organizations want to help employees understand their fringe benefits packages, including their 401(k) retirement plan options. The intranet often includes a program that allows employees to consider "what if" scenarios regarding their retirement investments and other benefits.

- Employees sometimes feel that they're the last to know about a company's accomplishments or activities (frequently finding out from the local newspaper that the company won an award or hired someone important). With an intranet, information such as announcements can be made available internally first (allowing employees to know about an event before it becomes public knowledge). Such information can also be linked to related documents so that employees can relate a specific news item to the larger context of the event if they so desire (by pursuing the links).

- Intranets may be used to review issues, problems, and solutions. Such postings can be linked to an internal problem management system that keeps track of employee requests and resolution of their requests. By combining the intranet with the e-mail system used by the organization, employees can send and receive e-mail to support staff and/or use the intranet for online problem solving.[26]

Headquartered in Federal Way, Washington, Weyerhaeuser is one of the world's largest lumber, pulp, and paper manufacturers. Its intranet, called Roots, serves 20,000 computers at 128 locations. Roots provides all the applications previously described. Also, Weyerhaeuser's divisions are developing their own intranets, which are then linked to Roots. Consider the following divisional application. Weyerhaeuser's Grande Prairie pulp mill, located in northern Alberta, Canada, produces 300,000 air-dried metric tons annually of bleached Kraft pulp used in tissue and towel paper and specialty applications. Recently, the information services department was looking at Web site development as a way to put documents online. At the same time, the quality assurance team was trying to improve its document management. Along with others, Sandi Ellert, project manager at the site, decided to merge the two technologies. The result was an intranet dubbed Honeycomb, which contains online versions of process manuals.

In the past, with the old manual-based procedures, an employee might have used outdated guidelines to test the moisture content of pulp. Today, current testing guidelines are readily accessible. Quality control managers can always be sure that they are performing the right tests before products are approved for shipment to customers. In addition to reducing the number of three-ring binders, Honeycomb enables those employees who use the documents to suggest changes via e-mail to a central procedures administrator. In the past, the printed documents provided little incentive for offering suggestions because they couldn't be modified quickly.[27]

DECISION SUPPORT SYSTEMS

DECISION SUPPORT SYSTEM (DSS)

A complex set of computer hardware and software that allows end users—usually managers and professionals—to analyze, manipulate, format, display, and output data in different ways.

A *decision support system* (DSS) is a complex set of computer hardware and software that allows end users—usually managers and professionals—to analyze, manipulate, format, display, and output data in different ways. Such a system aids decision making because the user can pull together data from different sources, view them in ways that may differ from the original formats, and create information from them. The system allows data and information to be printed out or to be presented in the form of charts or graphs.

A DSS enables decision makers to represent features of the environment (e.g., customer purchasing practices) and business activities (e.g., changes in prices and inflation) and quickly evaluate many alternatives and assumptions within models. Actually, you may be familiar with DSS and not even know it. If you've used an electronic spreadsheet, such as Lotus 1-2-3, Multiplan, Javelin, EXCEL, or QUATRO, you've used one form of DSS software. These electronic spreadsheets will automatically recalculate a quantity when you change the value of one of the variables in a formula.

The following DSS capabilities give the decision maker flexibility and the ability to explore various alternatives easily and quickly.

DATABASE

An organized collection of facts, figures, documents, and the like that have been stored for easy, efficient access and use.

- **Data collection and organization capabilities.** Current DSSs often have links to external databases and intranets, enabling rapid creation of a specialized internal database. A *database* is an organized collection of facts, figures, documents, and the like that have been stored for easy access and efficient use. The computerized card catalog at a library is a database. Another type of database consists of the files describing customers' buying behavior, which are kept by many retailers and credit card companies. The term *data warehouse* rather than *database* is now being used by some.

- **"What-is?" capabilities.** The current status of projects and developments can be obtained from the DSS, external databases, or other internal databases.

- **"What-if?" capabilities.** The decision maker can propose alternative actions (by means of a model) and test their likely consequences.

- **Goal-seeking capabilities.** Actions to be taken to achieve a goal specified by the decision maker can be provided.

- **Presentation and report generation capabilities.** The user can create various types of tables, graphs, text, pictures, art, audio, and video displays.

The following Communication Competency account explains how the DSS installed by Pizzeria Uno, a rapidly growing chain of pizza restaurants headquartered in Boston, improved its system of formal communication. Executives and other key personnel now have real-time information on relevant developments that enable them to make more timely and better decisions.

EXPERT SYSTEMS

Recall that an *expert system* (ES) is a computer program based on the decision-making process of human experts that stores, retrieves, and manipulates data, diagnoses problems, and makes limited decisions based on detailed information about a specific problem. These systems have problem-solving capabilities within a specific area of knowledge. If requested, the system can explain its path of reasoning to the user. The expert system is an application of artificial intelligence (AI)—the ability of computers to simulate some thought processes of human beings.[28]

Expert systems vary in complexity, both in terms of knowledge and technology. An example of the simplest type of system is a personal budgeting system running on a PC. The purpose of low-level expert systems is to improve personal decision making and thereby increase productivity. In contrast, strategic impact expert systems involve high levels of knowledge and technological complexity. Lincoln National's life underwriting system is an example. The process of underwriting an individual's life insurance application requires complex medical, financial, and insurance knowledge. Lincoln National also requires that an applicant's hobbies (e.g., mountain climbing) and vocation (e.g., possibly requiring frequent travel to politically unstable countries) be factored into policy evaluation and pricing. The information that an underwriter receives often needs to be clarified and interpreted. Lincoln National's four best senior underwriters spent much of their time for several years as consulting experts helping develop this expert system.[29]

GROUP DECISION SUPPORT SYSTEMS

GROUP DECISION SUPPORT SYSTEM (GDSS)

A set of software, hardware, and language components that support a team of people engaged in decision making.

A *group decision support system* (GDSS) is a set of software, hardware, and language components that supports a team of people engaged in decision making.[31] A GDSS aims to improve the process of team decision making by removing common communication barriers, providing techniques for guiding the decision process, and systematically directing the pattern, timing, or content of the discussion. Facilitators play a crucial role, allowing the participants to concentrate on issues rather than struggling to learn how to use the technology themselves.

Pizzeria Uno's DSS

Pizzeria Uno installed a decision support system (DSS) that enables its top executives and regional managers to manage the company's labor and materials costs more effectively. With more detailed cost information about cheese and wine on a daily basis, Pizzeria Uno executives can react faster than previously to changing conditions. The system helps executives control and improve profits from stores because they can monitor performance better than they can by reading monthly profit-and-loss statements, according to Alan LaBatte, vice president of information systems.

The firm installed Pilot Analysis Server, a software package. The online analytical processing system replaced a manual system used to track and report restaurant performance, costs, and labor information. Prior to using Pilot, each evening restaurant managers would leave voice messages about daily sales figures for their regional managers. The following day, regional managers would spend up to ninety minutes pulling those figures off voice mail and compiling the results.

Sales figures are now sent each night to a server and disseminated via Pilot software the next morning. Regional managers can dial into the system with laptop PCs and access daily sales figures immediately. Key to the success of the project is Pizzeria Uno's use of Pilot's multidimensional database system. It allows management to analyze sales and cost data in a variety of ways—such as by region and by which restaurants have been open for at least a year.[30]

* * *

To learn more about Pizzeria Uno, visit a restaurant home page at **www.unos.com**

Most executives and many managers aren't highly proficient on a computer and lack keyboard skills, which must be taken into account in designing and implementing such systems. A requirement that all parties be fully computer proficient to use support systems, such as GDSS, is likely to minimize their use. Slowness in manipulating data and the resulting frustration may even lead to disinterest and lack of support. Even computer-literate users need time to become familiar with the GDSS. A typical GDSS room might contain a series of terminals or workstations linked by some form of computer-based network, a large main screen visible to everyone and controlled by the facilitator, a photocopying whiteboard on which to record the options as they emerge, and a three-color video projector or large monitor.

Seven managers from one of Marriott's large Washington-area hotels participated in their first electronic meeting using VisionQuest, a type of GDSS software. Their challenge was to find new ways of improving quest satisfaction. They generated 139 ideas in only twenty-five minutes. Then they rated each idea twice on a scale of 1 to 5, first according to its likely effect on guests and second according to its probable cost. The Marriott managerial team emerged with a consensus on the specific types of additional training needed by hotel employees.[32]

DESIGNING INFORMATION SYSTEMS

4

STATE THE PRIMARY FACTORS INVOLVED IN THE DESIGN OF INFORMATION SYSTEMS

Four primary interrelated factors affect the design of information systems: (1) information needs, (2) system constraints, (3) goals, and (4) development stages.

INFORMATION NEEDS

Far too often organizations develop information systems without an adequate understanding of their true needs or the costs involved. An organization wouldn't construct a new manufacturing plant unless it was essential. Information system development should be approached in the same way. Any proposed information system needs to fit the organization's overall mission and strategy. In other words, the information system should make sense in terms of organizational plans, financial and technical resources, customers, competitors, and desired return on investment. Questions that need to be asked include: Is the organization planning to change or add to its customer base or its goods and services? What are the current financial constraints? Do competitors use such technology? What type, quality, relevance, quantity, and timeliness of data and information do employees currently use?

Figure 20.2 illustrates the transformation of raw data into information and then into decisions. Note that knowledge of the environment progresses from disorganized data to refined and sharply focused information.

Information needs vary by organizational level, function, and individual employee—and according to the type of decision to be made. Decision-making activities occur at three levels: strategic, tactical, and operational. The characteristics of information most used by employees and managers at these levels are summarized in Table 20.2: focus, scope, aggregation level, time horizon, currency, frequency of use, and type. Strategic decisions require information from external sources, such as customers, suppliers, and competitors. The information must be broad in scope, composite (highly aggregated), future-oriented, and both qualitative and quantitative. In contrast, information needs for operational decisions are substantially different. Operational decisions basically require internal information (e.g., inventory levels) that is well defined, detailed, reported daily or weekly, precise, and quantitative. Tactical decisions, which are of most concern to middle managers and professionals, represent the middle ground between strategic and operational decisions.[33]

SYSTEM CONSTRAINTS

Constraints are the limitations on the discretion available to decision makers and may be internally or externally imposed. External constraints vary from organization

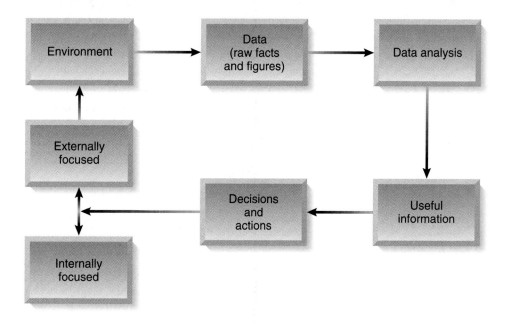

Figure 20.2 **Evolution in Information Needs**

Information Characteristic	Requirement		
	At Operational Level	At Tactical Level	At Strategic Level
Scope	Narrow, well defined		Broad
Aggregation level	Detailed		Composite
Time horizon	Historical		Future-oriented
Currency	Recent		Long term
Frequency of use	Continuous		Periodic
Type	Quantitative		Qualitative and quantitative

Source: Developed from G. A. Gorry and M. S. Morton. A framework for management information systems. *Sloan Management Review.* Fall 1971, pp. 59–62; and M. L. Markus and M. Keil. If we build it, they will come: Designing information systems that people want to use. *Sloan Management Review.* Summer 1994, pp. 11–26.

to organization and may include government regulations, supplier requirements, technological progress, and customer demands. For example, government regulations require automobile manufacturers to produce cars with safety features such as seatbelts, exhaust systems that emit limited amounts of certain chemicals, and engines that meet fuel efficiency standards.

Internal constraints are created by the organization itself. Probably the most common internal constraint on the development of an information system is cost. The best available information technology may be very costly. That's true even though the price–performance relationships for information technologies continue to improve dramatically year-by-year. Another internal constraint is lack of support from employees and top management. Without their support, or with only their limited support, an information system isn't likely to be successful.[34]

GOALS

General and operational goals should focus on the purposes that the information will serve, who will use it, and how it will be used. One goal of most expert systems is to serve as an investigative tool; that is, for answering "what if" questions such as: What would happen if Pizzeria Uno relied on more overtime to meet an increase in demand rather than adding more employees? Goals also should be established for the number and type of operating personnel and the system's cost. Setting goals provides the direction for developing and implementing the information system.

DEVELOPMENT STAGES

An information system may be created in various ways. However, the basic underlying development process generally is the same.[35] Figure 20.3 shows the four stages of information systems development. The dashed arrows indicate feedback loops, illustrating that the process is never cut and dried.

Preliminary Problem Definition. A team of information users, with technical support personnel, may be given the tasks of determining information needs, rough cost estimates, constraints, and goals.

Figure 20.3 **Stages in Information Systems Development**

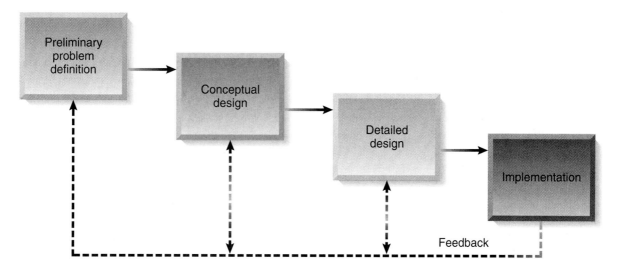

Conceptual Design. The conceptual-design stage should be primarily user led, although system development experts should act as resource people. During this stage, information generated in the preliminary problem definition stage is used to develop alternative designs. They are evaluated in terms of how well they satisfy organizational needs and goals. More accurate cost estimates are obtained at this stage. This evaluation usually leads to a preliminary selection of specific system characteristics for further review. However, it also may lead back to the problem definition stage.

Detailed Design. During the detailed-design stage, performance specifications are established. The team selects or develops hardware and software components. Information system experts are heavily involved, mapping information flows, preparing specialized programs, and defining databases. They also create a prototype of the information system and evaluate, test, refine, and reevaluate it until the stated requirements are satisfied. Users are still involved, but their role is primarily advisory at this stage. If problems arise, returning to the conceptual-design stage or even to a reanalysis of the problem definition may be necessary.

Implementation. During the final stage, models of information systems are connected and users begin testing the system. As operational problems are identified and corrected, one module after another is added. Eventually, the entire system is assembled and tested for all conceivable types of errors. Corrections continue to be made until the information system's performance satisfies all the performance criteria. At that point, the information system is ready to be phased into the organization for full-time use.

The following Teamwork Competency piece demonstrates what can happen when the design of information systems isn't coupled with teamwork involving system designers and users. It also clearly demonstrates the benefits of applying teamwork competency in solving the problems originally created by the lack of teamwork.

Hughes Space and Communications Company, a division of Hughes Electronics Corporation, is headquartered in Los Angeles, California. This division is the world's largest producer of satellites.

Hughes had a good problem and a bad problem. The good problem was that it needed to build more

satellites faster than ever before. The bad problem was poor production scheduling; some work groups were overloaded while others sat idle. Nobody seemed to have accurate scheduling information.

Hughes's information technology (IT) professionals decided that a new common scheduling system was necessary. They installed an expensive system, but no one used it. Assuming that the problem was the difficult-to-use mainframe interface, they trashed the first system and built another one at great expense. Initially, it was not used either.

After detailed analysis, the project manager realized that the problem was information behavior—how people approach and handle information. At Hughes, for example, work group managers were penalized when the schedule showed that they would

be late. Thus they kept quiet about delays. They saw scheduling information as a powerful tool to use in the organization's internal negotiations that affected people in their departments.

The situation changed when the IT people dealt with the sources of resistance head-on. They sat down with work group managers to discuss what information they'd be willing to share. Senior management was convinced to stop punishing those who admitted to being late. The second system is now being used. The company continues its record of never missing a launch date.[36]

* * *

To learn more about Hughes Space and Communications Company, visit this division's home page at

www.hughespace.com

INFORMATION SYSTEM IMPLEMENTATION

5

IDENTIFY THE CHARACTERISTICS OF EFFECTIVE INFORMATION SYSTEM IMPLEMENTATION

Although each information system has unique characteristics, seven main factors commonly influence the effective implementation of information systems. Figure 20.4 shows these system building blocks, which emerge during the initial stages of system design and development, continue through implementation, and then become important to everyday operations.[37]

USER INVOLVEMENT

Information system users should be involved in the design process. Their input gives system designers an accurate picture of current work flows, costs, and time requirements for various functions. This input helps in the identification of current operational inefficiencies that the new system should correct. Users typically know how information affects decision making, but designers often do not. For example, employees in an accounting department at Enron understand the flow of financial information and how financial reports are prepared and distributed. By working with the accounting staff, systems experts can tailor the system to the accounting department's needs.

User participation during the implementation stage is crucial because those who are to use it can often spot problems or deficiencies before the new system becomes fully operational. The costs of not involving Hughes work group managers early on in the development of the scheduling system were substantial. Taking part in implementation also helps users understand the reasons for the new system and prepares them for the necessary changes in the way that tasks are performed.

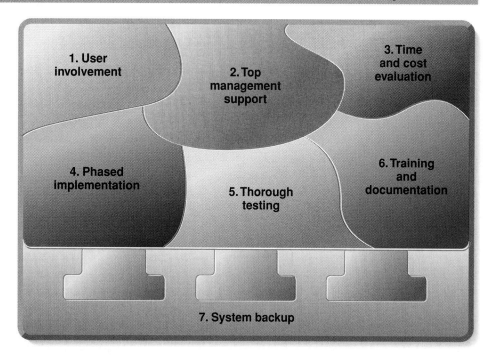

MANAGEMENT SUPPORT

The effective implementation of new information systems usually requires strong, visible support from management. Like any major organizational change effort, information technology applications must involve managers in order to succeed.[38] Without their support, information technology is less likely to be integrated into the organization. Strategic information systems planning involving top management is essential to foster a positive attitude toward system development from the beginning.

TIME AND COST EVALUATION

A thorough evaluation of time and cost requirements is necessary. The development of new information systems usually requires more time and costs more than anticipated. During the initial development stages, predicting these requirements accurately is difficult. However, management initially should have some idea of the cost of not improving the organization's information system.

To keep the development process on schedule and within budget, systems designers should project time and cost in detail. The projected schedule should include project benchmarks and perhaps even a PERT network (see Chapter 9), as is common for many construction projects. Justification of the design, installation, and projected maintenance costs help prevent cost overruns and guide decision making.

PHASED IMPLEMENTATION

Any significant new technology normally should be introduced in phases. A new information system shouldn't be turned on one day and the old system abandoned at the same time. Too many things can and will go wrong: The new system doesn't work as expected, it generates bad information, no one knows how to use it, and so on. By implementing the system in phases, problems owing to design glitches and unforeseen events can be managed. Software problems can be resolved before employees become too dependent on the system. Technical support staff can train users to work with the new system before their jobs depend on it. Gradual implementation gives employees time to adjust, thus reducing resistance to change.

THOROUGH TESTING

Testing of both hardware and software is needed. Testing should be performed on individual modules, on sets of modules as the system is assembled, and then on the entire system before it becomes fully operational. The testing process should anticipate probable errors as well as those that aren't likely to occur. The effects of incorrect commands, improper data, poor environmental conditions, and other possible problems all should be checked. The biggest problems with new technologies arise from events that system designers claim are not expected to occur or could not occur—but do. Users should be fully involved in this testing and debugging process.

TRAINING AND DOCUMENTATION

The introduction of new technologies requires training of users and adequate documentation of operational procedures. An information system is of little value if no one knows how to use it properly. At times, those in charge of the information system gain power because many others in the organization are overly dependent on them. As a result, a power struggle may develop between managers and employees who formerly controlled the flow of information and the system development staff. Organizations can avoid this sort of interdepartmental conflict by fostering cooperation. Users don't have to know how to program computers, but they should understand the capabilities and limitations of their information system. And systems development personnel must understand the capabilities and information needs of the users.

SYSTEM BACKUP

Computer systems are notorious for developing problems, especially software problems, at the wrong time. If users are too dependent on a single information system, they may believe that the quicker the fix, the better. Quick system fixes may overlook real problems that lead to other problems. A backup procedure—or even access to a backup computer system—will give analysts time to track down such problems, carefully evaluate them, and properly correct them. This approach can't ensure a problem-free future, but it does encourage solutions that are less likely to create additional problems.

Perhaps the most extreme example of system backup is the computer-based *voting* system developed for NASA's space shuttle program. Four identical computers run IBM software. A fifth computer runs software designed by Rockwell International. If the first four computers disagree, they decide what to do by a majority vote. In the event of an even split, the Rockwell system steps in to break the tie. Should some subtle software bug common to all the IBM machines cause them to stop in their tracks at once, the Rockwell backup stands ready to take over crucial functions. The use of independently designed systems is known as *dissimilar redundancy*. "We've never had to use that backup computer in flight," states Ted W. Keller, IBM's manager for the shuttle's onboard software. He claims that statistical models predict less than 3.6 bugs per million lines for the software. Thus the normal 500,000-line program should have at most 2 bugs, but nobody knows for sure.[39]

In global firms, system implementation needs to account for cultural and political, as suggested in the following Global Awareness Competency account. It demonstrates the cultural awareness and sensitivity of DHL Worldwide Express's management in the development and implementation of its intranet.

DHL's Global Intranet

DHL is a leading international document and package delivery company. Its mission states: "DHL will represent the *superior choice* in international expedited transportation and distribution services." It operates in 226 countries, including Israel and much of the Arab Middle East. "Some of the countries don't recognize Israel—don't even want them on the map," noted Alan Boehme, director of customer access and logistics marketing at the company's U.S. subsidiary, DHL Airways, Inc., in Redwood City, California. The process of developing an international intranet for the exchange of information among its autonomous country groups raised the question of whether to include Israel, which DHL did.

Cultural differences can turn seemingly routine technology-building chores into difficult decisions, Boehme noted. For instance, there's choosing icons for your Web pages. The "A OK" sign in one culture is tantamount to an obscene gesture in oth-

ers. And color schemes can prove offensive if not tailored to a country because in various cultures blue, white, red, and yellow are regarded as colors of death and mourning.

On DHL's Internet site, shippers can check Web pages that present an array of relevant information on all countries being shipped to. As a gesture of DHL's efforts to be sensitive to various cultures, the firm shows a *Cultural Tip* about a specific country on various Web pages. The country featured on a particular page changes from time to time. For example, on February 26, 1998, the Web page that informs shippers about Who is DHL? had a *Cultural Tip* in the corner that stated:

> In Turkey, when addressing a man, always use his last name followed by "bey," and with a woman, use her last name followed by "hanim." If someone raises his chin, shuts his eyes, and tilts his head back, he's not

taking a nap—this is the Turkish gesture for saying "no." Don't plan a business trip to Turkey during June, July or August, since most business people vacation during these months.[40]

Many of their other opening pages for Web sites have such tips. To learn more about DHL Worldwide Express, visit the firm's home page at **www.dhl.com**

COMPUTER ETHICS
The analysis of the nature and social impact of computer technology and the corresponding formulation and justification of policies for its appropriate use.

One closing word of caution about implementation: Even if all of the interrelated building blocks of information systems implementation are addressed (see Figure 20.4), no one can guarantee that a new system will work exactly as it's supposed to. Moreover, as with any major organizational change, the development and implementation of information technologies may meet with resistance. However, the risks and uncertainties inherent in installing such a system can be better understood and minimized if those factors are considered thoroughly. Also, recognition of those risks and uncertainties should motivate decision makers to invest in system backup. And, involvement of system users from the beginning can reduce the amount of resistance to the changes made.

ETHICS AND INFORMATION TECHNOLOGIES

6

EXPLAIN SEVERAL ETHICAL ISSUES IN THE APPLICATION OF INFORMATION TECHNOLOGIES

As computer-based information technologies become pervasive, concern with their ethical—and unethical or criminal—use has deepened in the United States, Canada, and other countries characterized as information societies.

COMPUTER ETHICS

Computer ethics is the analysis of the nature and social impact of computer technology and the formulation and justification of policies for its appropriate use.[41] An increasing number of individuals and organizations are concerned with computer ethics. The ethical issues surrounding computers arise from their unique technological characteristics, including the following.

- Computers make mistakes that no human being would make.

- Computers communicate over great distances at high speed and low cost.

- Computers have huge capacities to store, copy, erase, retrieve, transmit, and manipulate information quickly and economically.

- Computers have the effect of radically distancing (depersonalizing) originators, users, and subjects of programs and data from each other.

- Computers may collect and store data for one purpose that can easily be used for another purpose and be kept for long periods of time.[42]

The Computer Ethics Institute, a professional association headquartered in Washington, DC, was formed because of the growing concerns in this area. It has issued a "ten commandments" of computer ethics, which are listed in Table 20.3. The commandments provide an ethical code of conduct for guidance in situations that may not be covered by law.

The following Self-Management Competency feature gives you an opportunity to assess and further develop your own understanding of computer ethics. Recall that self-management competency includes (1) acceptance of responsibility for continuous self-development and learning; (2) willingness to learn and relearn continually, as changed situations call for new skills and perspectives; and (3) application of clear personal standards of integrity and ethical conduct.

PRIVACY ISSUES

The amount and types of information available about most individuals in the United States and Canada to just about any business (or individual in that business) or government agency is astounding. Most of this information originates with individuals

Table 20.3	Ten Commandments of Computer Ethics

1. Thou shall not use a computer to harm other people.

2. Thou shall not interfere with other people's computer work.

3. Thou shall not snoop around in other people's computer files.

4. Thou shall not use a computer to steal.

5. Thou shall not use a computer to bear false witness.

6. Thou shall not copy or use proprietary software for which you have not paid.

7. Thou shall not use other people's computer resources without authorization or proper compensation.

8. Thou shall not use other people's intellectual output.

9. Thou shall think about the social consequences of the program you are writing or the system you are designing.

10. Thou shall always use a computer in ways that demonstrate consideration and respect for your fellow humans.

Source: Computer Ethics Institute, Washington, DC, February 25, 1998.

SELF-MANAGEMENT COMPETENCY
Computer Ethics Survey

Instructions

Twenty statements appear in this survey. You should evaluate each statement in terms of the following 5-point scale.

1	2	3	4	5
True	**Somewhat True**	**Neither True nor False**	**Somewhat False**	**False**

If you think that a statement is *true,* record a 1 next to it. If you think a statement is *neither true nor false,* place a 3 next to it, and so on. Don't skip any statement.

_____ 1. The courts have provided clear guidance on who should have access to electronic mail at work.

_____ 2. Employees are usually informed by employers if their voice mail is going to be monitored.

_____ 3. Medical records are not available to employers.

_____ 4. Most organizations have clear written policies and procedures regarding the use of electronic mail.

_____ 5. The confidentiality of faxes is generally well maintained.

_____ 6. Nothing inherent in computer technology raises unique ethical questions.

_____ 7. Public perceptions of computers and computer professionals generally have been good.

_____ 8. Computer professionals have a level of influence that is matched by equivalent levels of organizational controls and professional association guidance.

_____ 9. The best way to deter unethical behavior in the use of computers is through legal deterrents and remedies.

_____ 10. The best way to deter unethical behavior in the use of computers is through professional codes of conduct.

_____ 11. The majority of computer science graduates have had at least one course in computer ethics by the time they graduate.

_____ 12. There are many controls over what information is kept on private citizens, who keeps it, and who can access it.

_____ 13. The majority of businesses in the United States have well-documented policies regarding what employee information is kept in personnel databases and who has access to it.

_____ 14. Computerized medical records pose no greater danger to privacy and potential for misuse than do paper records.

_____ 15. Electronic bulletin boards are fairly well "policed" and do not contain potentially harmful information.

_____ 16. The majority of computer crimes are reported, and the perpetrators are successfully prosecuted.

_____ 17. Computer abuse, such as gaining unauthorized access to a system or placing a virus or other potentially damaging program into a computer, is a minor problem.

_____ 18. Software theft, including unauthorized copying of software, is clearly a problem, but monetary losses are not yet significant.

_____ 19. Although failures of computer systems have been reported in the media, none have resulted in serious injury or significant property loss.

_____ 20. Because computer ethics is a relatively new application of older ethical concepts to new technology, there is little understanding about what can and should be done.

Scoring

Sum the point values for statements 1–20. The total points may range from 100 to 20. Most experts on computer ethics would consider a perfect score as 100; that is, all statements are considered to be *false.*[43]

* * *

To learn more about computer ethics, visit the home page of the Computer Ethics Institute at

www.brooks.edu/ITS/CEI/CEI_HP

when they borrow money, participate in a government program, or purchase goods. Consumers and borrowers routinely give information voluntarily to retailers and creditors so that they can purchase goods on credit. At least once a month, banks, retailers, credit card companies, and mail-order houses send computer tapes or other electronic files detailing their customers' purchases and payment activities to credit bureaus.[44]

The three large credit rating companies—TRW, Trans Union, and Equifax—maintain credit information on more than 160 million people in the United States. This information is accessible in a matter of seconds to merchants, clerks, and, in essence, just about anyone. A group of newspaper journalists, who acquired and published the credit rating of a U.S. vice president, demonstrated this situation. In addition to credit ratings, a large amount of information on nearly everyone in the United States—ranging from medical histories and insurance information to buying habits—is stored in computer-readable form and widely disseminated among credit bureaus, resellers of data purchased from bureaus, and many businesses.[45]

Recent studies indicate that information that used to be inaccessible or very difficult to obtain is now instantly available for use by almost anyone. Protection of privacy through the legal system, organizational and managerial policies and practices, self-regulation through professional and trade associations, and consumer groups hasn't caught up with technological developments.[46]

Kraft General Foods has computer-based information on more than 30 million customers, including their ages and how often they shop. The marketing and research staff can figure out (1) whether the company's customers fill the grocery cart in one trip or grab a few items several times a week, (2) whether they spend afternoons clipping coupons and how many children they have, (3) whether they eat out or entertain friends at home, and (4) whether they earn their living behind a desk or on a factory floor. The information on Kraft's customers comes from returned coupons, other promotions, surveys, and scanners used at most supermarket checkout counters. Every time a clerk passes a bar-coded container over a scanner it electronically records what was bought, who made it, the size, and the price. Those data are then merged with information derived from returned coupons and surveys of what shoppers watch on television, the type of neighborhood they live in, and their shopping patterns.[47]

CHAPTER SUMMARY

In this chapter, we surveyed a wide range of issues related to the development, use, and management of information technologies (ITs), which cut across all levels and functions of an organization. Through extranets and the Internet, ITs are having a profound impact on providing "any time/any place" links among employees, suppliers, customers, government agencies, and the public. Some suggest that new information technologies are having as dramatic an impact on employees and organizations as the industrial revolution more than a hundred years ago had on transforming agriculturally based economies and

cultures to industrial and urban economies and cultures.

1. **EXPLAIN SEVERAL DRAMATIC IMPACTS OF INFORMATION TECHNOLOGIES ON EMPLOYEES AND ORGANIZATIONS.**
Information technologies have major effects on the design of organizations, the roles of managers, and how employees perform their jobs. The numbers of organizational levels and middle managers have been reduced, top managers have gained strategic influence over crucial decisions, information technologies

are being used as a strategic asset necessary to compete in the marketplace, more knowledge workers are employed by organizations, knowledge workers are taking on temporary managerial roles as team leaders of special projects, information float (e.g., delay) among positions and organizational levels has been sharply cut, and real-time information networks enable knowledge workers to perform their tasks any place at any time.

2. COMMENT ON THE ROLE OF INFORMATION AS A VALUED RESOURCE.

Organizations are developing information systems as a strategic asset for use by employees. Information is a value-added resource derived from data that have been transformed to make them useful. Knowledge is used by individuals to create, store, share, and apply information. Four interrelated criteria may be used to assess the value of information: quality, relevance, quantity, and timeliness.

3. DESCRIBE SIX SELECTED INFORMATION MANAGEMENT TECHNOLOGIES.

Information management technologies continue to become less expensive and more powerful. Through real-time communications networks, the basic managerial functions of planning, organizing, leading, and controlling are dramatically changing, rapidly improving, and quickly becoming more closely linked. Six important, interrelated information technologies are the Internet, extranets, intranets, decision support systems, expert systems, and group decision support systems.

4. STATE THE PRIMARY FACTORS INVOLVED IN THE DESIGN OF INFORMATION SYSTEMS.

Information systems design should begin with a determination of information needs. This assessment should be linked to the organization's market-related goals, strategies, and plans. System constraints, which are the internal and external limitations on decision-making discretion, must be identified and evaluated. The general and operational goals for the information system should then be developed. Finally, the development stages for the system should be clearly specified. These stages includes preliminary problem definition (which normally reflects the information needs, system constraints, and system goals), conceptual design, detailed design, and implementation.

5. IDENTIFY THE CHARACTERISTICS OF EFFECTIVE INFORMATION SYSTEM IMPLEMENTATION.

Seven interrelated characteristics contribute to effective information system implementation: (1) user involvement, (2) top management support, (3) evaluation of time and cost, (4) phased implementation, (5) thorough testing, (6) training and documentation, and (7) system backup.

6. EXPLAIN SEVERAL ETHICAL ISSUES IN THE APPLICATION OF INFORMATION TECHNOLOGIES.

The unethical and criminal uses of information technologies are of increasing concern in the United States, Canada, and other information-dependent societies. Ethical issues arise from the unique technological characteristics of computers. The ten commandments of computer ethics state that radically different attitudes and actions are needed by many individuals and the media toward computer crime and the unethical use of computer-based technologies. Privacy issues also are central to computer ethics. The private and government sectors haven't yet come up with sufficient controls on the current wide-open access and use of all types of data and information about individuals.

QUESTIONS FOR DISCUSSION

1. Recall the discussion of United Airlines in the Preview feature. Assume that you have been a flight attendant for United over the past twenty years. How have the new information technologies likely changed your job during that time?

2. Why are computer-based information technologies reducing the number of management levels in many organizations?

3. Why is information increasingly viewed as a strategic asset and value-added resource?

4. Evaluate the degree of effectiveness of your college's student registration system in terms of quality, relevance, quantity, and timeliness.

5. Identify three ways that your life has been affected by one or more of the information technologies described in this chapter.

6. Identify a decision—either personal or organizational—that you (or your superior or a friend) have recently made (or are making). What information technologies were used or might have been used to make this decision?

7. What are two similarities and two differences between extranets and intranets?

8. Why should new or major changes in information systems normally be implemented in phases?

9. Has your right to privacy and sense of individualism ever been violated by a computer-based information technology? Explain.

EXERCISES TO DEVELOP YOUR MANAGERIAL COMPETENCIES

1. **Teamwork Competency.** Cambridge Technology Partners is a systems consulting and development company that generates annual revenues of $240 million. Founded in 1991 and based in Cambridge, Massachusetts, this firm employs 2,500 workers from all backgrounds in forty-one offices around the world. Its electronic commerce projects include building a Web-based automatic inventory control system for Office Depot and enhancing the customer-services Web site for Sun Microsystems.

The firm takes a unique multidisciplinary team approach to Web site development. The teams comprise diverse groups of individuals, including artists, writers, project managers, business process experts, psychologists, and, naturally, software engineers. The basic idea behind the teams is that the firm's Internet projects are too complex and too important for a purely technical approach. The database and C programmers build the fundamental program. The "creative" team members will do hands-on graphic design and multimedia development, building the entertainment and engagement aspects of the application. The entire team cooperates intimately with the customer in all stages of design.[48]

What key benefits can the firm offer its clients through multidisciplinary teams? Think about the ways in which the use of creative members can affect the final outcome of a new product or service. How is this approach different from the traditional technology-centered approach to software design? To help you answer these questions and learn more about Cambridge Technology Partners, visit its home page at

www.ctp.com.

2. **Communications Competency.** Polaroid Corporation designs, manufactures, and markets worldwide a variety of products in instant image recording fields. These include more than 50 different types of film and 100 types of photographic equipment, including cameras, camera backs, film holders, and specialized equipment used in photography. The company's products are used in amateur and professional photography, industry, graphic arts, sciences, medicine, government, and education.

By using a complex grid of Internet networks, Polaroid supports its technologically demanding users and creates paths to its main customers and suppliers. Polaroid also is developing a vast extranet to give suppliers limited access to its databases. The company already makes 40 percent of its U.S. sales over an electronic data interchange (EDI) service. "We use the extranet to build new or better relationships with some business partners and suppliers by providing them access to our inventory control database," says George Deyett, telecommunications operations manager at Polaroid. "It gives them access to information they need without opening up our entire network to them."

Since 1996, Polaroid has used EDI and maintains connections to several major customers, including Wal-Mart. Deyett said that he is considering running the EDI over the Internet in the future to simplify electronic connections. In addition to its extranet, Polaroid has developed an extensive home page that is accessible by any potential or current customer. It provides a vast amount of information to anyone interested in photography and instant imaging.[49]

What percentage of Polaroid's global sales, not just U.S. sales, are likely to be made through its extranet by 2005? What is the basis of your forecast? What three potential cost reduction efficiencies can Polaroid achieve with its extranet? What three improvements in the quality of services to Polaroid's customers can result from use of its extranet? To help you answer these questions and learn more about Polaroid, visit the company's home page at

www.polaroid.com

3. **Strategic Action Competency.** The world's largest bookstore opened for business on the World Wide Web in 1995. Amazon.com, an early pioneer of electronic shopping, now offers more than 2.5 million titles, both in print and out of print. This quantity is more than fourteen times as many books as the largest physical superstore offers! Amazon.com maintains only a small inventory—mostly bestsellers. It operates through a system of powerful computers and networking equipment, an enormous and lightning-quick database, and a Web address. This virtual discount bookstore takes your order and relays it to book distributors and publishing houses, serving as a middleman. Amazon.com offers prompt response to customer service e-mail inquiries. It also provides personal e-mail notification to keep customers up to date on newly released books in their favorite subjects. Says Jeff Bezos, Amazon.com founder and CEO, "We are changing the way people buy books."

To reduce customers' discomfort with giving their credit card numbers online, Amazon.com provides a limited financial guarantee. The server software encrypts the credit card information, presumably ensuring that Internet transactions stay private and protected. If any unauthorized use of a credit card occurs as a result of a such a purchase from Amazon.com, the customer notifies the credit card provider. If, through no fault of the customer, the credit card company finds credit card fraud but doesn't waive the customer's entire liability for unauthorized charges, Amazon.com will reimburse the customer up to fifty dollars.[50]

Why do you think that this company has been so successful? What are two key threats to its continued success? Suggest three advantages and three disadvantages for customers that Amazon.com appears to have in relation to traditional book retailers. To help you answer these questions and learn more about Amazon.com, visit its home page at

www.amazon.com

4. **Planning and Administrative Competency.** The ProShop.com is a pioneering direct marketer of fine golf products on the Internet. It provides a wide range of name-brand golf equipment, including golf clubs, balls, and apparel. In addition, it offers golf tips, tricks, and golf jokes.

Its site began going down intermittently during its busiest time—weekends. Says founder Will Pringle, "Basically, it meant we were closed for business." As with any Internet retail site, there is no backup channel in the form of a storefront, catalog, or call-in center. The ProShop.com developed a contingency plan to minimize future downtime. After its Internet service provider (ISP) inadvertently took The ProShop.com off-line, its parent company, Brainstormers, Inc., moved the Web site in-house in order to exert more control over server reliability. Even if an ISP is down less than 1 percent of the time, that may translate into the loss of millions of dollars to the company. Next, the golf retailer switched its Internet links to a large, well-known provider. Large companies such as IBM Global Network and Aegis provide disaster recovery services that include backup Web sites and constant monitoring to ensure that sites such as that of The ProShop.com are always open for business.[51]

What other problems could an online retailer encounter (e.g., shipping, handling, and exchanges)? Examine the company's Web site at

www.theproshop.com

From a consultant's point-of-view, highlight its strengths, and make recommendations for improvement.

REAL-TIME CASE ANALYSIS

LIZ CLAIBORNE, INC.

Liz Claiborne, Inc., the global apparel firm, is linking its Hong Kong mills with U.S. designers through information technology. Recently, the U.S.-based apparel and accessories company with annual sales of some $2 billion faced a strategic problem: Its designs originate in the United States, but its apparel and accessories are produced in other countries. Executives at Liz Claiborne found monitoring product timing and quality to be challenging, as the mills and factories are several time zones away from its headquarters. In addition, these great distances made reducing cycle times more difficult, which is imperative to cutting excess inventory and reducing lead time.

Facing declining profits and high inventories, Claiborne's executives concluded that the company had stagnated both in terms of the design and business aspects of its operations. To turn the firm around, management implemented LizFirst. This radical project was conceived to transform Liz Claiborne into a company that provides superior response, service, and overall value. LizFirst required a substantial investment in information technology. According to John Thompson, the firm's chief information officer, the project's main goals were to reduce excess inventory by 50 percent, reduce cycle time by 25 percent, increase responsiveness to customers, and ensure timeliness and accuracy in shipping. By 1998, the company had achieved about 70 percent of its overall goal of reducing operating costs by $100 million.

The LizFirst project was intended to streamline production and standardize garment patterns. Prior to this project, most of the design process was done manually. Liz Claiborne designers operate on a tight schedule, creating fashion collections four times a year by working in three-month time periods. Kathryn Shipman, director of corporate computer-aided design (CAD), says, "There are many processes that are being broken down into shorter cycles, so we have more time to research better designs. We are reallocating our time."

Now, Liz Claiborne designers on the East Coast are networked with manufacturing representatives throughout Asia. The company installed a CAD package in all its divisions last year in order to standardize textile design. Currently, the CAD images are shipped to the offices in Asia, with the ultimate goal of transmitting them directly to the factory floor.

Information technology (IT) has revolutionized the way Liz Claiborne does business. Designers used to write detailed instructions on alterations and sizing for its manufacturers. Designers can now take a digital photo of the garment, use the CAD program to add any comments to it, and send the image to an office abroad. In addition, the company has started using a drawing software package and a database that stores pattern designs. The designs are accessible to its design/production liaison people. Tim Loftus, data communications manager at Liz Claiborne, says, "We're trying to work more closely with our factories, and we're trying to create this collaboration of efforts within Liz Claiborne."[52]

To learn more about Liz Claiborne, Inc., visit the company's home page at

www.lizclaiborne.com

QUESTIONS

1. What role should Information Technology play in Liz Claiborne's future strategies?

2. What are two of the hurdles that the company faces in conducting business with its Far East manufacturers?

3. What are two threats that may develop as a result of networking with overseas production liaison people?

VIDEO CASE

ARCHWAY: HOW THE COOKIE COMPUTES

Archway Cookies is automating its production processes. By taking scattered information about its operations and interconnecting and broadening them, it is gaining real-time knowledge about how the business is running.

Expectations (perhaps, apprehensions) at Archway could lessen the positive effects of introducing new information technologies. For example, the attitude that "the system shouldn't change us, but support us," can be a double-edged sword. Interpreting that statement to mean that Archway is in the business of making cookies, not running computer systems, gives it positive meaning. However, far too many companies have adopted designed by computer specialists without inputs from the experts in the businesses that were being automated. When that happens, the statement takes on a negative meaning.

Introduction of new IT may permit a company to leap in entirely new directions, rather than to pursue continuous, marginal improvement (e.g., cookies two hours fresher, or 5 percent cheaper). Harvard Business School professor Shoshana Zuboff described such a case. A bank had heavily automated. The new information systems that it deployed made its traditional functions (borrowing and loaning money) more efficient. Moreover, on the strength of the analyses made possible with better data management, it opened up entire new service areas (e.g., investment market forecasting).

A firm such as Archway is unlikely to create new information service offerings, but the information technologies change *enables consideration of alternatives* that might be worth pursuing. For example, the new systems may indicate that Archway has schedulable slack in production lines that could be better utilized or actually sold to other companies. Before installation of the new information systems, that slack might have been overlooked or unusable because of limited analyses.

Archway's success or failure in the transition from its past to greater reliance on IT will also depend on how management interprets that cautionary attitude—that the system is to support the employees, not the other way around. Archway managers recognize that employees will have to record data here and observe the start of a process there for the first time. Unless doing so is easier than *not* doing so, management may face an uphill battle and eventual loss of the automation war. Whenever possible, data collection should be automated (e.g., by having a sensor note when the oven door is closed, by requiring that a worker flip an additional switch). Or the reward to the employee should be clear (e.g., using a hand-held computer to scan inventory means not having to transcribe hand-printed sheets).

Integrating new information systems into a business can be extremely challenging to management, stretching most of their six managerial competencies. Many middle and senior managers don't have information systems education or training in their backgrounds. Some of the most senior managers may not even have a computer in their offices and have never used e-mail. In taking IT to the factory floor, Archway managers will need to communicate clearly the goals to be achieved and to listen for signs of confusion, concern, or resistance. Employees may fear that increased automation will threaten their jobs (*Desk Set,* a Spencer Tracy/Katherine Hepburn film, is a wonderful treatment of this issue, as a 1950s research library receives its first room-sized computer).

Archway has focused on its production processes, but it could also be a candidate, as many other companies have been, for systems to manage employee information, human resources files, and other functions, possibly in the form of an intranet.

Beyond its internal systems Archway could consider an extranet to mesh its information systems with those of upstream suppliers or downstream distributors. The availability of the Internet has dramatically cut the price of implementing electronic data interchange (EDI) between organizations. In some industries (e.g., among the major automakers and their parts suppliers), fullscale extranet projects are being pursued.

ON THE WEB

Archway Cookies is on the Web (***www.archway-cookies.com***). Its Web site targets its customers with recipes and nutritional information. SAP is an enterprise automation provider with a significant share of the market for delivering information systems such as Archway's (***www.sap.com***), as is Oracle (***www. oracle.com***).

QUESTIONS

1. How might answering the question "What if we wanted to double the raisins in our oatmeal cookies?" differ before and after full automation of Archway's production system?

2. Why does bringing in extensive IT control make sense at Archway, but wouldn't at Tom's of Maine (Chapter 19)?

3. How might Archway utilize e-mail to improve its operations?

To help you answer these questions and learn more about Archway Cookies, visit the company's home page at

www.archwaycookies.com

Case contributed by Ross Stapleton-Gray, President, TeleDiplomacy, Inc., a technology and policy consultancy, and Adjunct Professor in Georgetown University's Communication, Culture, and Technology Program.

Chapter

21

Operations Management

LEARNING OBJECTIVES

AFTER STUDYING THIS CHAPTER, YOU SHOULD BE ABLE TO:

1. DISCUSS FOUR BASIC ISSUES IN OPERATIONS MANAGEMENT.
2. EXPLAIN FOUR POSITIONING STRATEGIES.
3. PROVIDE EXAMPLES OF DEVELOPMENTS IN OFFICE, SERVICE, AND MANUFACTURING TECHNOLOGIES.
4. STATE THE ESSENTIALS OF QUALITY MANAGEMENT AND CONTROL.
5. EXPLAIN THE BASICS OF INVENTORY MANAGEMENT AND CONTROL.

Outline

Toyota's Production System

The Toyota production system (TPS) is used at its Georgetown, Kentucky, complex and throughout the world. It applies not only to manufacturing but to almost everything Toyota does, from product development to supplier relations and distribution. Toyota sets the standard in efficiency, productivity, and quality. GM officials say that Toyota is the benchmark in manufacturing and product development.

Michael Cusumano, a professor at MIT's Sloan School and a member of its international motor vehicle program, has written extensively about Toyota. He states, "I don't know of a company that better combines superior skills in all the critical areas: manufacturing, engineering, and perhaps marketing. If they wanted to blow away GM, they could."

Inside the plant, TPS's success depends on highly experienced managers working with a motivated, well-trained workforce. Outside the plant, TPS requires a network of capable suppliers that can synchronize their operations completely with Toyota's. Mike DaPrile, who runs Toyota's Camry assembly facilities in Kentucky, describes it as having three levels: techniques, systems, and philosophy. He comments, "Many plants have put in an *andon* cord that you pull to stop the assembly line if there is a problem. A five-year-old can pull the cord. But it takes a lot of effort to drive the right philosophies down to the plant floor. A lot of people don't want to give the needed authority to the people on the line who deserve it."

Thus TPS requires a different mindset. In most plants, for instance, workers try to overproduce because, once they have filled their quotas, they can take it easy. As a result, the flow of work proceeds in fits and starts. At Toyota, overproduction is considered one of the worst forms of waste. The company designs the work to flow from process to process without peaks or valleys and still arrive in just the right quantity for the customer. That results in a more smoothly running plant, and it keeps everybody busy.

In a Toyota assembly plant, every movement has a purpose, and there is no slack. The workers experience a smooth flow: retrieving parts, installing them, checking quality, and doing it all in immaculate surroundings. Says DaPrile: "We believe in the four S's: sweeping, sorting, sifting, spick-and-span." TPS requires a big leap of faith for any manufacturer. Because there is no stockpile of parts, suppliers and workers are under tremendous pressure to perform their jobs as scheduled and even to work overtime if they fall behind. A single weak link will hamstring an entire operation.

Toyota is always tinkering with its own system. In the early 1990s it introduced more automation in its factories, only to back away when the machinery proved too costly and inflexible. More recently, Toyota has been trying to make jobs easier for its workers in the face of persistent labor shortages. It now breaks the assembly line into segments and allows workers to stockpile small buffers of unfinished parts at the end of each segment in case of an interruption.

The capacity to adapt is a fundamental ingredient in Toyota's success. Takahiro Fujimoto, a Harvard Business School graduate who teaches at Tokyo University and has studied the company, says that "Toyota's real strength resides in its ability to learn. Its employees are problem-conscious and customer-oriented, and this preparedness is the source of the company's dynamic capability. The company's practices are constantly changing, even though its basic principles are unchanged."[1]

* * *

To learn more about Toyota, visit the company's home page at

www.toyota.com

INTRODUCTION TO OPERATIONS MANAGEMENT

DISCUSS FOUR BASIC ISSUES IN OPERATIONS MANAGEMENT

Every company makes mistakes, including Toyota. But Toyota has a unique ability to study its mistakes, learn from them, and improve itself. The process has become an essential part of its culture, so much so that anecdotes about failures are a big part of the company's heritage. Moreover, TPS principles are applied to other parts of the auto firm, not just its manufacturing plants. For example, Toyota's product development process includes creativity and freedom to develop innovative designs, but it also requires discipline and control in scheduling, resource use, and product quality. Toyota treats a drawing for a change order on an engineer's desk (or its electronic equivalent) the way it would an unfinished component. As long as it sits there, it's an impediment to completion of the job.

Eliminate it or move it along, and you have improved the process.[2] More than most firms, Toyota sees every activity and function—not just manufacturing—as relevant to operations management. **_Operations management_** (OM) is the systematic direction, control, and evaluation of the entire range of processes that transform inputs into finished goods or services.[3]

In this chapter we describe operations management and its importance to quality and productivity in the manufacturing and service sectors. We present nine key areas of operations management decision making. We then discuss four of them in some detail: positioning strategies, technological options, quality management and control, and inventory management and control.

RELATION OF OM TO THE SYSTEMS VIEW

From a systems view of organizations, OM involves four primary components: environmental factors, inputs, transformations, and outputs. Figure 21.1 depicts these components and illustrates their interactions.

Environmental factors, which we have discussed in several previous chapters, influence operations management in numerous ways. Recall that such factors can be grouped into cultural, political, and market influences, examples of which are group norms (cultural), health and safety legislation and standards (political), and customer preferences (market). Toyota is especially astute in adapting itself to changes in customer preferences.

Inputs include human resources (managers and workers), capital (equipment, facilities, and money), materials, land, energy, and information. Examples are assembly workers and dentists (human resources), a factory and zero-coupon bonds (capital), seed corn (materials), a farm (land), electric power (energy), and market analyses (information).

Figure 21.1   _Operations Management as a System_

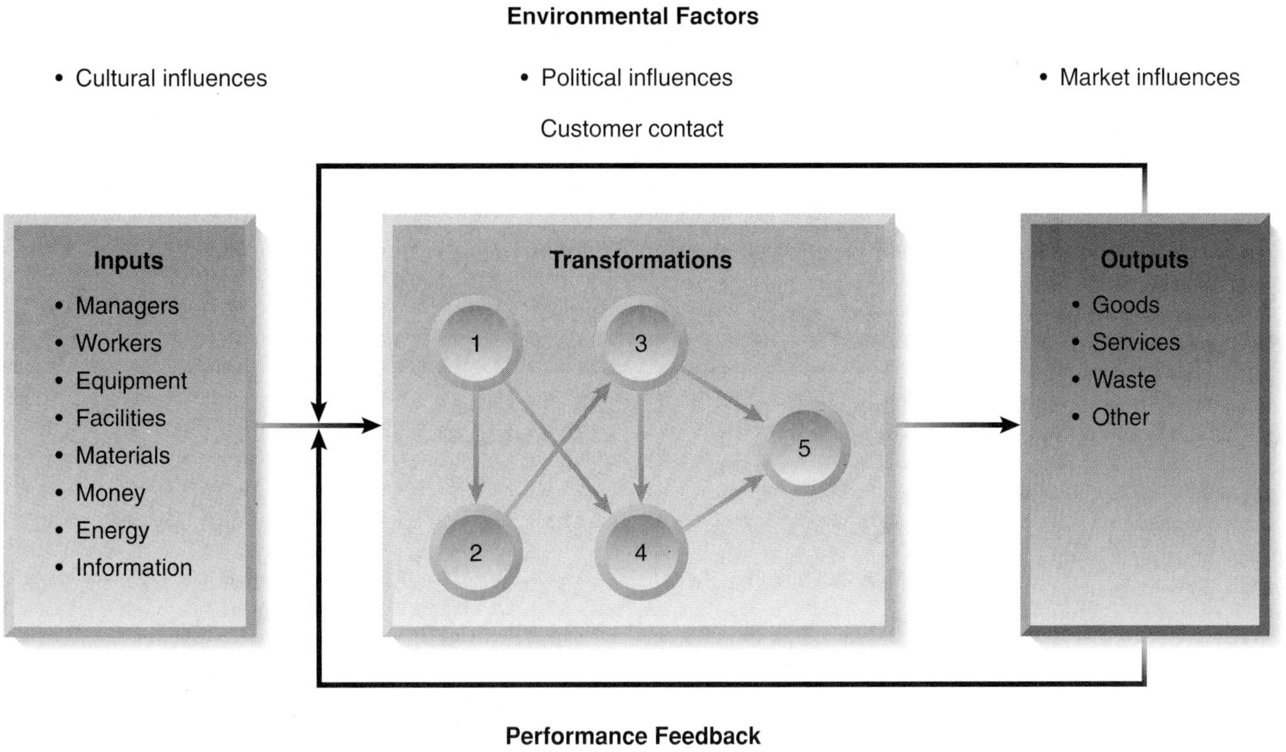

Environmental Factors

- Cultural influences   • Political influences   • Market influences

Customer contact

Inputs	**Transformations**	**Outputs**
• Managers	1 3	• Goods
• Workers		• Services
• Equipment	5	• Waste
• Facilities	2 4	• Other
• Materials		
• Money		
• Energy		
• Information		

Performance Feedback

Transformations are the operations that convert inputs into outputs. Examples are turning plastics, steel, glass, and other materials into Toyota Camry autos; saltwater into freshwater through desalinization; and filling cavities through dental skills (use of a drill) and materials (metal or porcelain). The five numbered circles in the transformations box in Figure 21.1 indicate that production of a good or service often requires several operations. An operation can be manufacturing a part (windshields for Camrys) or assembling parts manufactured elsewhere (such as assembling Camrys at the Georgetown, Kentucky, complex), combining fresh vegetables into a salad at a salad bar, or entering a code number and transaction information in an automated teller machine.[4]

Outputs are the goods (Camry autos), services (Toyota dealerships), and waste products (auto emissions) created through transformations. Other examples are government Social Security checks, garbage, and water pollution.

Customer contact often occurs in OM. Customers actively participate in the transformation process in self-service operations, as when they fill their cars' gas tanks at service stations or their soft drink cups at dispensers and take them to their tables. Customers also provide essential feedback by expressing satisfaction or dissatisfaction with purchased goods and services. *Performance feedback* (e.g., records of the frequency of Toyota Camry repairs), much of which is provided by customers, closes the system loop. This information helps organizations decide whether to make changes in the goods or services provided, the transformation processes used, and/or the inputs utilized. As noted in the Preview feature, Toyota is continuously considering the need for such changes.

DIFFERENCES BETWEEN GOODS AND SERVICES PROVIDERS

The application of OM concepts must recognize differences in the production of goods and the provision of services. Table 21.1 summarizes five such differences. These distinctions often are a matter of degree, as suggested by the continuum of characteristics. For example, Toyota may be considered a goods provider, yet it also provides services to suppliers and customers—such as its bumper to bumper warranty.

The ability of goods producers to hold items in inventory gives them flexibility in scheduling flows in the transformation process. They can partially offset peaks and valleys in demand by drawing down or adding to inventories. However, one of the special attributes of Toyota's production system is to keep inventories at a bare minimum. Recall from the Preview feature that Toyota now allows small buffers of inventory between major assembly segments to make the jobs of production employees a little easier. Service providers are more at the mercy of day-

Table 21.1	**Typical Characteristics of Services and Goods Producers**	
Primarily Services Producers	**Continuum of Characteristics**	**Primarily Goods Producers**
	Mixed	
Intangible, nondurable		Tangible, durable
Output can't be inventoried		Output can be inventoried
High customer contact		Low customer contact
Short response time		Long response time
Labor intensive		Capital intensive

to-day and even hour-by-hour fluctuations in customer demand. The peak periods of breakfast, lunch, and dinner at restaurants are common examples.

Customers themselves often are inputs to the transformation process for service providers (e.g., doctors or hairdressers). In contrast, most customers for manufactured goods have little or no direct contact with the transformation process. Customer contact is left to the marketing department, distributors, and retailers.

Service providers often must respond quickly—within seconds, minutes or hours—to customer demand. Examples are checkout lines at supermarkets, service at fast-food restaurants, and auto repairs. Thus the matching of short-term transformation capacity (especially the number of employees) to customer demand can be much more difficult for service providers than for manufacturers. Customers for many tangible, durable goods (e.g., cars, furniture, computers, and buildings) know that they may have to wait days, weeks, or even months for those products.

Goods producers generally are capital intensive (i.e., require relatively more investment in building and equipment for their operations). Services producers generally are labor intensive (i.e., require relatively more employees for their operations). The need for larger plants and more and better equipment runs up the cost of many manufacturing operations. For example, Toyota's manufacturing complex in Georgetown, Kentucky, contains more than 7 million square feet, but a bank branch in a supermarket often has less than 150 square feet.

IMPACT ON PRODUCTIVITY

In recent years, productivity has increased at about 2.5 percent annually in the United States.[5] Critics claim that government statistics understate productivity gains, especially in services. For example, telephone service has greatly improved and its price has dropped. But the productivity increase is understated because the price decrease usually doesn't fully reflect product improvements. Quality increases—such as variety, reliability, service, and timeliness—often are unrecognized or underrecognized because they are hard to quantify.[6]

The continuous increase in productivity is a key to maintaining the competitive positions of U.S. and Canadian firms internationally in the manufacture of automobiles, electronic equipment, bicycles, motorcycles, cameras, small appliances, and steel. International differences in rates of productivity growth influence exports, standards of living, and choice of jobs.

Operations management can greatly improve productivity, a primary concern of both goods and services producers. In particular, three applications of operations management principles have resulted in improved productivity.[7] First, the investment of capital in new technology and carefully managing its introduction are essential to long-term productivity growth in both sectors. Second, the reduction of waste, rejects, and returns through improved quality control pays off immediately in both sectors. Third, the reduction in work-in-progress (WIP) materials in the manufacturing sector reduces the amount of money tied up in inventories and physical space requirements.

No standard measures of productivity apply to all organizations. The most commonly used general measure is **total-factor productivity,** which is the ratio of total outputs (amount of goods and services produced) to total inputs (quantities of labor, capital, and materials used). This indicator of economic efficiency is normally expressed in monetary terms. In contrast, **partial-factor productivity** is the ratio of total outputs to a single input. Examples of partial productivity ratios are (1) units produced per day divided by labor hours of production employees per day, and (2) store sales per month divided by labor hours of sales personnel per month.[8] These and other measures are meaningful only if the outputs produced are sold.

TOTAL-FACTOR PRODUCTIVITY
The ratio of total outputs to total inputs.

PARTIAL-FACTOR PRODUCTIVITY
The ratio of total outputs to a single input.

The assessment and improvement of productivity with service operations and technologies is often challenging.[9] The following Planning and Administration competency feature reveals how a management/employee team at Texaco substantially improved its productivity in handling employee benefits questions and issues. It demonstrates the application of skills and abilities in (1) developing plans and schedules to achieve specific goals efficiently; (2) determining the need for, obtaining, and organizing necessary resources; and (3) taking calculated risks.

OM DECISION CATEGORIES

Operations management involves a number of categories of decisions. An effective OM system will link all of them, some of which you will recognize as strategic. Nine of the most important categories are:

1. **Product plans.** What products (goods or services) should be offered?

2. **Competitive priorities.** Should low price, high quality, fast delivery time, or product choice be emphasized?

3. **Positioning strategy.** Should resources be organized around products or processes?

4. **Location.** Should facilities be expanded on-site, at a new site abroad, or in a relocated existing facility?

5. **Technological choices.** What transformation operations should be automated to improve productivity?

6. **Quality management and control.** How can the quality levels necessary to maintain or better the organization's competitive position be achieved?

7. **Inventory management and control.** What are the best methods of determining and maintaining the proper inventory levels?

8. **Materials management.** How should suppliers be selected and evaluated?

9. **Master production scheduling.** Should the organization make to inventory or make to order?[10]

POSITIONING STRATEGIES

2

EXPLAIN FOUR POSITION-
ING STRATEGIES

POSITIONING STRATEGY
The approach selected for arranging resource flows in the transformation process.

Positioning strategy is the approach selected for arranging resource flows in the transformation process. Figure 21.2 provides a framework for comparing three core positioning strategies. The vertical axis indicates that resource flows can range from sporadic (unstable and unpredictable) to continuous (stable and predictable). The horizontal axis indicates that product type and volume can range from low-volume custom products to high-volume standard products. The three boxes indicate the likely range of three core positioning strategies: process focus, intermediate, and product focus.[11]

CORE POSITIONING STRATEGIES

PROCESS-FOCUS STRATEGY
Organizes the physical layout of equipment and the workforce around each operation in the transformation process.

A *process-focus strategy* organizes the physical layout of equipment and the workforce around each operation in the transformation process. This strategy meets the requirements of custom-made products and low-volume production. Scheduling is crucial because a variety of products share each resource and routines for different products vary. The resource flow pattern is unstable, changing from one order to the next. Similar equipment and operations (e.g., drill presses, welding sta-

Technological and organizational changes have allowed Texaco to improve the way it handles personnel questions from employees. Each business unit used to have its own benefit counselors that handled questions about employee benefits and payroll processing, according to Gary Morgan, manager of Texaco's administrative services center. In Texaco's downtown Houston headquarters office alone, some ten people fielded benefit questions. Recently, the function was centralized and computerized. These changes reduced the number of errors, speeded up the process, and saved the company millions of dollars a year. Only ten first-line counselors are needed, replacing the equivalent of about thirty full-time workers.

Helen Beabey, one of the ten first-line employee benefit counselors, sits in a big, airy room answering questions from employees throughout the United States about their benefits plans. With the help of a sophisticated computer program, Beabey can determine whether the company received a particular insurance form, help an employee sign up for a new health insurance plan, or answer questions about the company's retirement plan. The system uses Social Security numbers to access data, and a counselor can immediately determine whether an employee is represented by a union, which benefit plans apply to the employee, and the employee's length of service. If there are special circumstances—such as an employee is hard of hearing—it's noted at the top of the file.

If one of the first-line counselors can't answer a question, it's referred to a supervisor. And if a question is "hot"—such as an employee trying to get into the hospital and having trouble getting admitted—it's handled immediately.

Finances weren't the only driving force behind the new system—Morgan indicated that Texaco wanted to improve how it handled its benefits programs. But, without question, the company also has saved money. Texaco invested $2 million and is saving about $4 million a year—it recouped its initial investment in just six months.

Although the relatively new system is quick and efficient, it is about to become even speedier. Texaco is looking into letting people change their benefit plans, addresses, and income tax withholding from their own computers.[12]

* * *

To learn more about Texaco, visit the company's home page at

www.texaco.com

tions, and painting stations) usually are grouped in separate areas of the facility. For example, one department may perform welding operations for all products passing through the transformation process. Similarly, in a general medical practice, each patient is unique and treatment (product) is based on an individualized diagnosis of symptoms (unstable flow pattern).

Flexibility is at the heart of the process focus. The following are three common types of flexibility for manufacturing operations.

- **Product flexibility** is (1) the speed with which new products are created, designed, manufactured, and introduced; (2) the ability to design a product to a particular customer's specifications; and (3) the ability to modify existing products for special needs.

- **Volume flexibility** is (1) the ability to respond to sudden changes in market demand for a particular product; and (2) the speed with which new manufacturing processes can go from small volumes to full-scale production.

- **Process flexibility** is (1) the ability to manufacture a variety of products over a short period of time, without modifying existing facilities; (2) the ability to

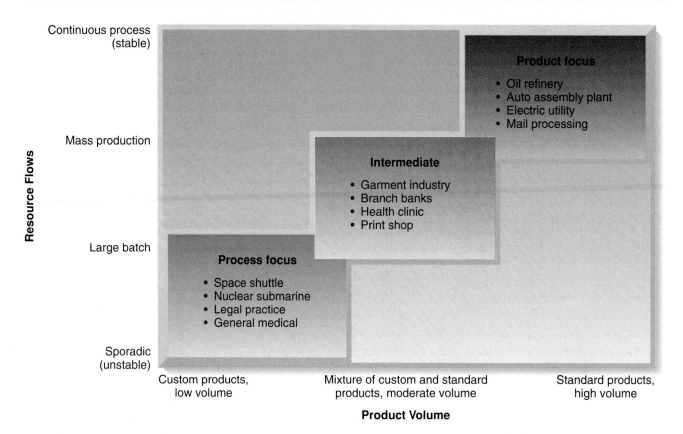

Sources: Adapted from H. K. Brown, K. B. Clark, C. A. Holloway and S. C. Wheelwright. *The Perpetual Enterprise Machine: Seven Keys to Corporate Renewal Through Successful Product and Process Development.* New York: Oxford University Press, 1994; and O. M. Upton. The management of manufacturing flexibility. *California Management Review,* Winter 1994, pp. 72–89.

adjust smoothly to changes in product mix over the long term; and (3) the ability to accommodate variations in raw materials and raw materials substitutions.[13]

PRODUCT-FOCUS STRATEGY

Arranges the physical layout of equipment and the workforce around a few outputs.

A ***product-focus strategy*** arranges the physical layout of equipment and the workforce around a few outputs. As indicated in Figure 21.2, this strategy is designed to fit high-volume, highly automated production of a few standard products with a continuous process or mass-production flow of resources. The transformation process is linear, with various operations arranged in a fixed sequence. This organization is typical of cafeterias, oil refineries, and assembly lines. In a traditional automobile assembly plant, welding machines are stationed along several different assembly lines to perform the same operation on different products. A service example is the automated teller machine (ATM), which provides a limited set of standard financial services (products) continuously by using a well-defined (stable) process.

INTERMEDIATE STRATEGY

Arranges the physical layout of equipment and the workforce so that they reflect some features of both the process focus and product focus.

An ***intermediate strategy*** arranges the physical layout of equipment and the workforce so that they reflect some features of both the process focus and product focus. Some batching can be done by merging and handling several similar orders at the same time. Some standard products or standard component parts might be made in advance and put in inventory. Kinko's and other print shops adjacent to universities and colleges use an intermediate strategy. They often run off batches of course supplements in advance for later purchase by students, but they also provide immediate customer service in response to a variety of customer orders.

AGILE STRATEGY

AGILE STRATEGY

A flexible arrangement that allows the mass customization of goods by means of advanced fabrication, information, and delivery technologies that are utilized by skilled and empowered individuals and teams.

The **agile strategy** is a flexible arrangement that allows mass customization of goods by means of advanced fabrication, information, and delivery technologies utilized by skilled and empowered individuals and teams.[14] This strategy represents a *paradigm shift* (i.e., a fundamental change in thinking) from the three core positioning strategies. The agile strategy integrates key features of the process focus (especially customization and flexibility) with the product focus (especially continuous processes and low costs). In the past, these features were, for the most part, considered inconsistent and mutually exclusive, as suggested in Figure 21.2.

This positioning strategy allows switching from rapid product development to low-cost production quickly and with minimal resources. It rejects (or at least minimizes) the view that the choices have to be one or another from among the conflicting priorities of low cost, high quality, and flexibility.[15] With an agile strategy, *flexibility* takes on special meaning: the ability to change or react with little or no adverse consequences in terms of the amount of time required and effort expended, the cost of resources, or the quality and quantity of performance.

Some experts forecast that many goods (e.g., autos, computers, and clothes) will be tailored to each customer's specifications (taste and budget) within the next five to ten years. Companies moving toward the agile strategy are being forced to cut cycle times—the period between receiving orders and delivering goods. For that reason some of the production work that left the United States and Canada in the 1980s is beginning to return. In addition, one of the goals of the agile strategy is to create real-time links between the manufacturer and its customers and suppliers. Advanced information technologies allow networked retailers or manufacturers to send their orders electronically to their suppliers' computers. These computers, in turn, relay the suppliers' needs to their own suppliers. Ultimately, the computer-based real-time communications web will extend to individual machines on the shop floor. Robert Nagel, deputy director of Lehigh University's Iacocca Institute (the think tank where the concept of the agile strategy was born in 1992), states, "If ever the term *paradigm shift* was appropriate, this is it."[16] The following Strategic Action Competency account reveals how Custom Foot, which started up in 1995, is pegging its future on the agile strategy. Jim Metscher, its president and CEO, recognized the evolving market niche of customers who want greater choice and better fit in their selection of shoes. As of 1998, the firm, which is headquartered in Westport, Connecticut, had five retail locations, with a goal of fifteen to twenty outlets by 1999. Its major threat for long-term survival is the ability and interest of other premium retail shoe chains in imitating Custom Foot's agile strategy.

THE REENGINEERING LINK TO AGILE STRATEGY

The creation of an agile service or manufacturing process usually calls for organizational reengineering. As we discussed in Chapter 13, *reengineering* is the fundamental redesign of an organization's processes (e.g., product development, logistics, distribution, customer service, and manufacturing) to lower costs, improve quality, and increase speed.[17] Reengineering focuses on selected activities that can be improved to yield benefits quickly.

The purpose of reengineering is to do things right the first time: improving quality, eliminating repeated work, spending less time on bureaucratic rules and procedures by doing away with them, tearing down barriers between departments, empowering employees and teams, substituting information technologies for paper

Custom Foot is the first shoe store to embrace the concept of mass customization through technology for all its products. It also is the first shoe retailer to dedicate an entire "inventoryless" store to mass-customized products. Thus the first thing that customers notice when arriving at Custom Foot is that there are no shoes to take home. But it does have

160 sample shoes on display for customers to choose from. Customers have their feet measured by an electronic scanner, which captures differences in size and width that typically distinguish the right foot from the left. Through this process, digital measurements of each foot are taken, one at a time, to select a size. Since size isn't the same as fit, the customer is given an actual shoe to try on to ascertain the ideal fit. The data are then transmitted to factories in Italy, where the shoes are made to order and delivered in about three to four weeks. Until now, consumers have had to sacrifice comfort for style or style for comfort.

How customized can Custom Foot get? To blend mass production and customization, the company has had to set limits. "Otherwise all we'd be doing are exceptions, and we

couldn't make any money," says CEO Jim Metscher. Custom Foot does not, for example, make prescription orthopedic footwear. But the company does allow for 10,000 variations in women's shoes and 7,800 in men's. Because computers replace middlemen and costly inventories are unnecessary, customers are able to receive custom-made footwear for $128 to $280. With a digital record of the measurements kept by Custom Foot, customers may shop from home in the future if they choose to do so.

Metscher sees all kinds of possible leather goods—line extensions. "Who knows?" he says. "Maybe we'll go into custom-made gloves."[18]

* * *

To learn more about Custom Foot, visit the company's home page at **www.thecustomfoot.com**

---

handling, and organizing processes to serve internal customers (which a human resources department or payroll department often does) or external stakeholders (especially customers). Some reengineering efforts have achieved dramatic results; others have had disappointing outcomes or have failed entirely. The essential ingredient lacking in the disappointing cases and failures often was inadequate management in terms of (1) poor goal development, (2) not creating a motivating environment, (3) inadequate empowerment at lower levels, (4) lack of meaningful measures of performance, and (5) failure to communicate with employees throughout the reengineering effort.[19]

TECHNOLOGICAL OPTIONS

3

PROVIDE EXAMPLES OF DEVELOPMENTS IN OFFICE, SERVICE, AND MANUFACTURING TECHNOLOGIES

The number and types of technologies available for improving productivity and quality continue to increase. Here, we review several of these developments in office, service, and manufacturing technologies. Recall that in Chapter 20, we covered various computer-based technological options.

OFFICE TECHNOLOGIES

Information technologies continue to change the office environment, with personal computers (PCs) being the dominant force. Today's most powerful PCs have more capabilities (because of software and hardware developments) than a 1970s mainframe that cost several million dollars. Managers and professionals in virtually all leading organizations use PCs to communicate with each other, subordinates, customers and suppliers, and large computers. The following are several other uses of computer-based office technologies.

- PCs are now the workstation of choice in most organizations for accessing databases. They also are capable of inputting to fax machines or acting as telex/TWX terminals.

- Pioneering users are now applying video imaging to their use of optical disks, graphics workstations, and new control software to merge video images with text and data.

- Numerous organizations utilize voice communication systems as part of their office automation. In certain applications—in credit and collections, for instance—telephone signals interface with computer files.

- Organizations are using information technologies to exchange data and documents—everything from memos and price lists to orders and inventory status—electronically. These systems cut internal costs and create real-time networks for communication anytime and anyplace.[20]

PERSONAL COMMUNICATION SERVICES (PCS)
An emerging set of capabilities based on wireless equipment that will enable users to stay in touch with almost anyone, anytime, anywhere.

Personal communication services (PCSs) represent an emerging set of capabilities based on wireless equipment that will enable users to stay in touch with almost anyone, anytime, anywhere. At present, PCSs extend the capabilities of cellular phones, which allowed development of mobile offices. Cellular phone technology permits oral or electronic airborne transmissions to be "handed off" automatically over special frequencies from one geographic area (cell) to another.

With PCSs, a single phone number can seamlessly follow a user, and some cellular phone providers are already moving toward this capability. Personal communication services are expected to include wireless e-mail messages, faxes, access to information services, and even video images. They operate at higher frequencies than do cellular phones, with transceiver towers twice as close together. Thus the equipment doesn't require as much battery power and can be smaller and lighter.

SERVICE TECHNOLOGIES

Airlines' computerized reservation systems, banks' ATMs, and credit card companies' billing and customer service systems are only three of the many consumer-oriented service technologies.[21] Other computer-based service technologies used by organizations are bar coding, integrated computer order systems, and voice recognition systems.

BAR CODE
A series of black lines of varying widths alternating with spaces that represent information and can be read by an optical scanner into a computer.

INTEGRATED ORDER SYSTEMS
Connection of a customer's computer to suppliers' computers to permit orders to be placed at any time.

A *bar code* is a series of black lines of varying widths alternating with spaces that represent information and can be read by an optical scanner into a computer.[22] Information contained in a bar code may include product name, lot number, manufacturing location, shelf location, and price. Bar coding has greatly increased productivity in supermarkets since the early 1980s. It speeds up the checkout process, reduces checkout errors, and makes inventory control more effective. Many new applications of bar coding are being developed, including some for goods producers. For example, some goods, such as appliances, are being tracked in inventories through the use of bar codes.

Integrated order systems involve connecting a customer's computers to suppliers' computers, allowing orders to be placed at any time. Such systems eliminate telephoned orders, mailed hard-copy order forms, and hard-copy invoices. Beamscope Canada, Inc., distributes stereos, computer gear, software, and other items to mass retailers such as Wal-Mart, Sears, and 6,000 independent camera shops and small retailers. In late 1997, it went online through the Internet with a new electronic commerce (e-commerce) integrated system that provides the following features for retailers that handle Beamscope's items.

- Online ordering, inventory availability, and price check system computers.

- Real-time access to specific pricing, inventory availability, back order status, product specifications, and marketing specials.

- Full-color literature that retailers can download and print.

- Seven days a week, twenty-four hours a day accessibility.

- No retailer training required, just point and click. Improves order accuracy and eliminates pricing errors.

Retailers can track their shipments at the Beamscope Web site because of a live data feed from United Parcel Service (UPS), which handles Beamscope's shipments. The server handles up to 200 customers at once, and response times usually are less than a second. Retailers can view color photos and video clips of most of the 6,500 products that Beamscope stocks. Direct costs have fallen from just over $5 to process a phone and fax order to about 50 cents online.[23]

VOICE RECOGNITION SYSTEMS

Methods of analyzing and classifying speech or vocal tract patterns and converting them into digital codes for entry and retrieval through computer software.

Voice recognition systems analyze and classify speech or vocal tract patterns and convert them into digital codes for entry and retrieval through computer software.[24] The plummeting cost of computing is aiding their adoption and use. Machine comprehension of human conversation may never be perfect, but, in late 1997, new powerful speech-recognition technology came on the market. These new systems can recognize what people say with more than 95 percent accuracy. In a recent special report, *Business Week* reported: "Speech technology is the next big thing in computing. Will it put a PC in every home?"[25] The following are a few of the emerging applications of computer-based voice recognition systems.

- Employees at the Boston Globe can dial colleagues just by speaking their names into the telephone.

- Customers at Charles Schwab, the discount broker, can obtain price quotes and other information.

- Users of Bell South's voice Yellow Pages can check auto ads and get stock quotes.

- Flyers on United Airlines can get seat reservations.

- Automobile drivers can retrieve e-mail and faxes while speaking into their cellular phones. This capability is achieved through text-to-speech software, which turns digital text into synthesized speech.

- Voice-based browsing enables users to scan the Web by speaking hyperlinked words into a microphone, although some use of a mouse is still required.[26]

Voice recognition systems are having profound impacts as aids for those with disabilities. Computer keyboard disabilities, such as carpal tunnel syndrome, are increasing rapidly. In 1997, IBM and Dragon Systems entered the market with major advances in their voice recognition systems. The following Self-Management Competency piece reveals how Brae Landon took advantage of this technology. She demonstrated (1) a sense of responsibility and willingness to innovate, (2) ambition and motivation to achieve objectives, (3) perseverance in the face of obstacles, and (4) a willingness to unlearn and relearn as her changed situation called for new skills.

SELF-MANAGEMENT COMPETENCY
Brae Landon Adapts

Brae Landon suffers from radial tunnel syndrome (similar to carpal tunnel syndrome, though rarer). Her injury affects the radial nerves in the forearm, making it painful for her to extend her arms toward the mouse or keyboard, or to move her hands and fingers. Landon designed interactive computer games at California-based NTN Communications. Intensive and prolonged use of the mouse and keyboard caused this painful affliction. Landon said, "I continued to work, injuring myself to the point of not being able to work at all. I left work on partial disability to see if the injury would improve."

Landon learned about voice recognition technology. She credits her company with being very supportive of her need to explore the alternative avenues of speech-input devices.

Landon stated, "NTN is very interested and involved in new technology. And they were very curious about what Dragon had to offer." Shortly after deciding to use DragonDictate, Landon became a training specialist for the company. She found that the system's multitasking capability increased her efficiency in producing the training manuals she creates. For example, she can print out ten different segments of the manual by speaking, rather than pulling down the menus for "open document, print document, and close document" each time for ten segments. During all the stages of the process, Landon is able to perform other tasks at her desk while dictating commands directly to DragonDictate. She calls voice recognition "inevitable technology."[27]

* * *

To learn more about Dragon Systems, visit the company's home page at

www.dragonsys.com

MANUFACTURING TECHNOLOGIES

As we noted in the discussion of positioning strategies and reengineering, there are numerous manufacturing technologies. In this section, we describe two of the new-generation technologies: robots and computer-aided manufacturing.

Robots are reprogrammable, multifunctional machines. A robot's frame often is a substitute for the human arm, and its microprocessor (computer) takes the place of the human brain by providing instructions for routine and standardized tasks. Robots have been programmed to perform numerous tasks in materials handling, welding, spray painting and other finishing operations, assembling, inspection and testing, materials removal, and water-jet cutting. Robots perform repetitive tasks without tiring or complaining about poor working conditions.

A robot can be programmed to move in various ways, depending on the task to be performed. Tactile (feel) and optical (sight) sensing and hand-to-hand coordination systems represent major aspects of robot development.[28] In the Matsushita Electric factory that makes Panasonic VCRs, a robot winds wire thinner than a human hair through a pinhole in the video head sixteen times and then solders it. The 530 robots in the factory wind wire twenty-four hours a day. They do this job five times faster and much more reliably than the 3,000 Japanese homemakers who used microscopes to do the work on a subcontract basis in their homes. The robots can even inspect their own work.[29]

In the service sector, robots have been used for years in nuclear power plants to avoid employee exposure to radiation and in the ocean to replace divers who require cumbersome and costly life-support systems. Anticipated and evolving applications of robots include assisting with the care of the handicapped and

ROBOTS
Reprogrammable, multifunctional machines. A robot's frame often is a substitute for the human arm, and its microprocessor (computer) takes the place of the human brain by providing instructions for routine and standardized tasks.

elderly, picking oranges, cleaning office buildings and hotel rooms, guarding buildings, and even helping surgeons.[30] For example, in early 1998, the first surgical robot cleared by the Food & Drug Administration (FDA) was introduced to assist with minimally invasive heart surgery procedures. The AESOP 3000 (an acronym for automated endoscopic system for optimal positioning) contains voice recognition technology, allowing surgeons to use spoken English to control precisely the endoscope. This specially designed optical tube, when connected to a medical video camera and light source, is inserted into the body to allow the surgeon to view the operation on a video monitor. Dr. Wayne Mayfield, a cardiac surgeon in Atlanta, helped test the surgical robot. He commented, "The AESOP 3000 effectively acts as a third arm that works in synchrony with my verbal commands, allowing me to have direct control of the endoscope, and provides a motionless image from which to operate, no matter how long the procedure. The robotic arm automates the tedious and often tiresome task of holding the endoscope, freeing nurse resources to perform other important tasks."[31]

COMPUTER-AIDED MANUFACTURING (CAM)

An array of computer-based technologies used to produce goods.

COMPUTER-AIDED DESIGN (CAD)

Uses special software to instruct a computer to draw specified configurations, including dimensions and details, on a display screen.

Computer-aided manufacturing (CAM) represents an array of computer-based technologies used to produce goods.[32] The complete CAM process begins with *computer-aided design* (CAD), which uses special software to instruct a computer to draw specified configurations, including dimensions and details, on a display screen. This method reduces the time spent in the design process and simplifies the exploration of alternative designs. The database resulting from CAD is used to help generate the instructions needed to guide the CAM process, including sequentially routing components to various machines, operating instructions for each machine, and providing for testing components against specifications. It also reports the unit cost of each operation, combines design information with materials specifications, and estimates waste and scrap rates that may affect purchasing requirements.

CAM is beginning to have an even greater impact on many activities in the manufacturing sector. They include process planning, production scheduling and control, machining instructions, matching performance, parts testing, assembly operations, shipping, cost accounting, personnel assignments, finished goods inventories, work in progress inventories, and procurement. The technology has become an important part of the competitive strategy of Xerox, Texas Instruments, and Hewlett-Packard, among others.

Computer-aided manufacturing is compatible with the product variety and flexibility associated with a process-focus strategy and the low per unit costs associated with a product-focus strategy (see Figure 21.2). Its most direct effects are reduction of the cost versus variety trade-off for goods producers and removal of rigid plant setups as a barrier to rapid product innovation. The demand for CAM has grown rapidly because flexibility is needed to meet ever-changing competition and customer demand.[33] Thus CAM is an important aspect of implementation of the agile manufacturing strategy. Moreover, shorter product life cycles mean that manufacturing plants long outlive the goods they originally were designed to produce. The lives of many products now are so short that 50 percent of their sales often occur in less than three years after they are introduced. In addition, technological advances have accelerated to the point that new goods, materials, and processes are being introduced almost daily.[34]

Cinnabar California, Inc., based in Burbank, is working to cut set-design times by applying the same three-dimensional CAD/CAM technology that has helped many manufacturers become world-class competitors by cutting costs and new-product time to market. The company creates sets, special effects, props, and environments for film, television, theme parks, and retail stores. For example, it designed sets for a television commercial depicting a battle between the Energizer Bunny and Darth Vader.

Cinnabar calls its extensive 3-D digital database Art-to-Part. This database was created because product image and superior visual perception are key focuses in the entertainment industry, just as they are in engineering departments at manufacturers. As a result, directors of photography are demanding immediate turnaround of the physical models of complex characters so that they can be subjected to a "believability test" under strict lighting requirements. Doug Morris, president of Cinnabar, stated that "in the entertainment industry, time is of the essence."

The database enables Cinnabar to digitize the intricacy of a foam model in real time and use CAD data to produce physical replicas quickly, with reduced tooling and design costs. Morris went on to say that "our ultimate goal is to create a vast compilation of 3-D digital models and provide 'on-demand' access for graphic applications such as animation, retail merchandising, virtual reality, and television and motion-picture special effects."[35]

QUALITY MANAGEMENT AND CONTROL

4

STATE THE ESSENTIALS OF QUALITY MANAGEMENT AND CONTROL

Quality management and control are generally viewed as key components of competitive strategy.[36] *Fortune's* annual ranking of America's most admired corporations has always included "quality of products or services" as one of the eight key attributes of reputation. For 1997, three of the most-admired corporations that ranked highest on quality were Toyota Motor Sales U.S.A. (motor vehicles and parts), Coca-Cola (beverages), and Gillette (cosmetics, soaps).[37] The other attributes of reputation used in *Fortune's* most admired companies survey include innovativeness, quality of management, employee talent, long-term investment value, financial soundness, and use of corporate assets. Many managers, professionals, and other employees recognize the organizational benefits of offering superior quality (as perceived by customers). These benefits include strong customer loyalty (more repeat purchases), lower vulnerability to price wars, ability to command a higher relative price without losing customers, and lower warranty costs.

COMPETITIVE STRATEGY AND QUALITY

VALUE

The relationship between quality and price.

From a competitive perspective, **value** is the relationship between quality and price. Figure 21.3 presents a competitiveness value map on which an organization can determine its price versus quality position relative to competitors. Customers who perceive superior quality at a lower relative price receive outstanding value. Organizations that provide such value are likely to grow and prosper. In contrast, the provision of inferior quality at a higher relative price results in poor value for the customer. This situation is likely to invite new competitors. If organizations continue to offer poor value, they will wither and die. Figure 21.3 also indicates a premium value, or high price and superior quality. Competitive pressures continue to challenge organizations to provide greater relative quality at the same or lower price as competitors.[38]

The interpretation of customer satisfaction—and how those perceptions translate into loyalty to the firm and its products—is no simple matter. For example, Xerox found that, if satisfaction is ranked on a 1 to 5 scale, from completely dissatisfied to completely satisfied, the 4's—though satisfied—are six times more likely to defect than the 5's. Often the assumption is made that satisfaction and loyalty move in tandem. Think of a graph with the degree of customer satisfaction on the horizontal and the degree of customer loyalty on the vertical axis. Customer reten-

Figure 21.3 **Competitiveness Value Map**

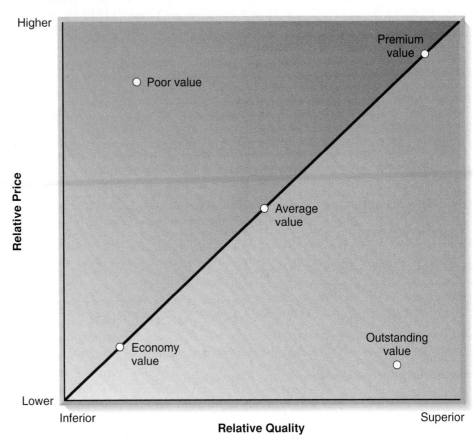

Source: Adapted from B. T. Gale and R. D. Buzzell. Market perceived quality: Key strategic concept. *Planning Review,* March–April, 1989, p. 10.

tion doesn't rise diagonally (proportionality) on the graph. Rather, loyalty rises in small increments as satisfaction increases and then rises dramatically as the highest levels of customer satisfaction are reached. Researchers have found a general correlation between delighted customers and above-average stock market returns in their industries over the long term. Related research has suggested that loyal customers—those who repeat purchases regularly—can substantially increase an organization's profits because they cost less to attract than new customers.[39]

As discussed in the Preview feature, Toyota is renowned for the quality of its products. However, it isn't known for quality customer service—except for its Lexus dealerships. As of 1997, consumers ranked Toyota dealers just average, citing everything from indifferent or shabby treatment to repeated trips to the service department to fix simple problems. Only 42 percent of Toyota buyers go back for another one, whereas General Motors manages to keep 62 percent of its buyers. In 1997, Toyota embarked on a program to woo its U.S. buyers. It changed incentives to reward dealers for quality customer service, increased training of technicians on how to diagnose mechanical problems swiftly over the phone, and speeded up vehicle delivery time. Toyota even sells over the Internet to those who hate walking into a dealer showroom.[40]

Heightened global competition has been a major force behind management's sharpened interest in quality management and control. North American manufacturers and service providers used to focus solely on the costs of maintaining or increasing quality. Now, product quality and costs increasingly are being viewed as inversely related—at least up to a point. That is, the costs of improving quality are often less than the resulting savings in reworking, scrap, warranty expenses, and product liability.[41]

Total costs for quality management and control typically include expenditures for prevention (quality planning, worker training, and supplier education), appraisal (product inspection and testing), internal failures (reworking and scrap), and external failures (warranty and product liability). These categories of costs suggest that improving quality can lead to increased productivity. This attitude is widely held among exceptional companies—such as General Electric, Hewlett Packard, and Toyota—and explains much of their dedication to improving product quality and ultimately attaining the goal of zero defects. This attitude is increasingly shared by managers and employees of more and more organizations.[42]

MEANING OF QUALITY

In Chapter 2 we briefly defined quality as how well a product (good or service) does what it is supposed to do—how closely and reliably it satisfies the specifications to which it is built. However, there are two underlying views of quality: internal and external. The internal view is that quality is achieved by meeting the organization's established specifications and standards. This view is rather limited because it ignores customers and actions by competitors. As suggested previously, the external view is that quality means achieving or exceeding the results that customers value and expect. Organizations such as Toyota, Coca-Cola, and Gillette, among others, emphasize the external view and consider it to be the starting point in defining acceptable quality.

The quality of goods and services can't be effectively represented as a single dimension. Nine of the most common dimensions of quality are performance, features, conformance, reliability, durability, serviceability, responsiveness, aesthetics, and reputation.[43] Table 21.2 provides a brief definition of each dimension, along with an example of how each one is reflected in goods (e.g., for a Toyota Camry) and services (e.g., for a VISA credit card). These dimensions indicate that customers' expectations and perceptions, as well as competitors' products and services, must be monitored and assessed continuously to ensure effective quality management and control.

Table 21.2 doesn't provide a comprehensive definition of quality. For example, we could develop indicators of service quality for a specific task or process, such as ordering and delivering goods. The following four dimensions illustrate this idea.

- **Accuracy:** whether the correct products were delivered in the ordered quantities.

- **Speed:** the elapsed time between placing the order and delivery of the product to the customer and how well that matches the customer's expectations.

- **Information accessibility:** the degree to which information is available about a shipment when the customer requests it.

- **Ease of ordering:** the degree to which customer expectations are met or exceeded with respect to order preparation assistance, ability to receive orders electronically, or notifying customers immediately when items are out of stock.[44]

TRADITIONAL VERSUS TOTAL QUALITY

In Chapter 2, we discussed the *quality viewpoint* as a major development in the history of management thought. We defined *total quality management* (TQM) as the continuous process of ensuring that every aspect of production builds in product

Quality Dimension	Definition	Examples	
		Toyota Camry	**VISA Card**
Performance	Primary good or service characteristics	Miles per gallon, acceleration	Number of merchants who accept the card
Features	Added touches, secondary characteristics	Level of road noise	Credit provisions, interest rates
Conformance	Fulfillment of specifications, documentation, or industry standards	Workmanship, emissions level	Accuracy of monthly account statements
Reliability	Consistency of performance over time	Mean miles to failure of parts	Processing of lost card reports
Durability	Useful life	Miles of useful life (with repair)	Timeliness of automatic card renewals
Serviceability	Resolution of problems and complaints	Ease of repair	Resolution of errors
Responsiveness	Person-to-person contact, including timeliness, courtesy, and professionalism	Courtesy of auto dealer, repairs completed as scheduled	Courtesy of account agents in resolving problems
Aesthetics	Sensory effects, such as sound, feel, and look	Styling, interior finish	Enclosures with monthly statements
Reputation	Past performance and other	Consumer Reports ranking, owners' reviews	Advice of friends, *Kiplinger Magazine* ranking

Sources: Based on D. A. Garvin. *Managing Quality: the Strategic and Competitive Edge.* New York: Free Press, 1988; L. F. Pitt, R. T. Walson, and C. B. Kavan. Measuring information systems service quality: concerns for a complete canvas. *MIS Quarterly,* 21, 1997, pp. 209–221; and M. Mooney and M. Hessel, *Quality Dimensions of Operations Management.* Cambridge, Mass.: Blackwell, 1998.

quality. In addition, TQM is an organizational philosophy and strategy that make quality a responsibility of *all* employees. Organizations pursue TQM through various methods of preventive and corrective control, which are intended to ensure high levels of customer satisfaction. Total quality management involves building in quality from product planning to design to evaluation to preproduction to purchasing to production to sales and service. The TQM strategy gives quality, rather than short-term profits, top priority. The only constraints are economic feasibility and competitiveness.[45]

TRADITIONAL QUALITY CONTROL

Product inspection during or at the end of the transformation process.

In comparison to total quality management, **traditional quality control** relies mainly on product inspection during or at the end of the transformation process. A particular department, such as a quality control department or a relatively small group of inspectors and lab technicians, often is given the responsibility for ensuring quality. The focus is on corrective controls, that is, fixing mistakes after the fact rather than making the product right the first time. Table 21.3 highlights the primary differences between TQM and traditional quality control. Let's now consider some of the specific things that managers and employees do to implement total quality management.

Table 21.3 **Total Versus Traditional Quality**

Total Quality Management	Traditional Quality Control
Quality is a strategic issue.	Quality is a tactical issue.
Plan for quality.	Screen for quality.
Quality is everybody's responsibility.	Quality is the responsibility of the quality control department.
Strive for zero defects.	Some mistakes are inevitable.
Quality means conformance to requirements that meet or exceed customers' expectations.	Quality means inspection.
Scrap and reworking are only a small part of the costs of nonconformance.	Scrap and reworking are the major costs of poor quality.

DEMING'S PRESCRIPTIONS

In Chapter 2, we noted that W. Edwards Deming (1900–1993) is often considered the godfather of the quality movement. We expand upon and reinforce his ideas and prescriptions that we highlighted there.

Until his death, Deming taught the Japanese about quality control. He designed a four-day seminar for Japanese executives in 1950 and subsequently became almost a guru to Japanese industry. To honor his contributions, the Japanese created the Deming Prize in 1951. Highly esteemed in Japan, this annual prize recognizes organizations that have met the qualifications for applying companywide quality control (CWQC). Ten major categories of criteria (e.g., policies and objectives, analysis, and quality assurance) are used to judge applicants for the prize, and each category is divided into subcategories. Only a small number of awards are made each year because the standards are high. The Deming Prize is awarded to several classes of applicants, including individuals, factories, and divisions or small companies.[46]

Until 1980, Deming's work received relatively little notice from top management in North American industry. Then, NBC television broadcast a documentary contrasting Japanese and U.S. product quality. Prominently featured on the program as the world's leading authority on quality control, Deming soon was in great demand and he signed a long-term consulting contract with Ford. Deming asserted, "We in America will have to be more protectionist or more competitive. The choice is very simple. If we are to become more competitive, then we have to begin with quality."[47]

Deming considered poor quality to be 85 percent a management problem and 15 percent an employee problem. His perspective on total quality and prescriptions for achieving it are deceptively simple.[48] They are interrelated elements in a total system, which he came to identify, just before his death, as *the Deming system of profound knowledge*. These interrelated ideas include the following.

- Quality is a management philosophy that has to be accepted as a way of life, as well as a way of doing business. Unless top management can adopt this philosophy and make it part of the organization's culture, the effectiveness of specific quality assurance tools will be limited at best.

- The common goal is for everybody to gain in the long run—customers, shareholders, employees, suppliers, community, and the environment. Managing a system requires knowing the interrelationships among all its components and the people that work in the system.

- A system perspective emphasizes the need for cooperation and coordination among departments, teams, suppliers, and others. A lack of cooperation, such as intense competition for monetary rewards, can destroy the system.

- Everyone must operate on the view that poor quality is flatly unacceptable. Defective materials, workmanship, products, and service will *not* be tolerated. Improve constantly and forever the system of production and service, to improve quality and productivity and thus decrease costs.

- Train and educate employees to use statistical methods in their jobs and to develop other competencies.

- Encourage employees to report any conditions that hurt quality. Drive out fear so that everyone may work effectively. Remove barriers to pride of workmanship.

- Although knowledge of variation is essential, it begins with the recognition that there is always some variance in any process—between people, in output, in service, in the product. Discovering the reasons for variability and quantifying them is crucial.

- Strict deadlines, even when based on estimated averages, are not consistent with an understanding of variation. Neither are numerical goals or quotas. It is better to work on methods for improving the process, thus reducing the variation from identifiable causes and producing the desired results.

- Use statistical evidence of quality problems (unwanted variation) before (e.g., from suppliers) and on a real-time basis as they occur during the process, not at the end of the process. The earlier errors and defects are caught, the less costly is their correction.

- Don't depend on inspection to achieve quality. Eliminate mass inspection by building quality into the product in the first place.

- Use suppliers that have historically provided quality, not on sampling inspections to determine the quality of each delivery. Select and stay with a few suppliers that furnish consistent quality. Establish long-term relationships with suppliers. Don't award contracts to suppliers merely on the basis of price.[49]

BALDRIGE FRAMEWORK AND AWARD

The Malcolm Baldrige National Quality Award annually recognizes U.S. companies that excel in quality achievement and management. The award, a gold-plated medal encased in a crystal column, was created by Congress in 1987. The award receipts for 1997—presented in early 1998—included two manufacturing and two service firms:

- **3M Dental Products Division,** which manufactures and markets a variety of products used by dentists around the world—including restorative, crown, and bridge materials—as well as dental adhesive and infection control products (manufacturing);

- **Solectron Corporation,** which offers a broad range of design, manufacturing, and support solutions to original equipment manufacturers—including product design and development and materials management (manufacturing);

- **Merrill Lynch Credit Corporation,** a subsidiary of Merrill Lynch & Company, which provides a variety of liability management services—including home financing, personal credit, and investment and business financing (service); and

- **Xerox Business Services,** a division of Xerox Corporation, which provides document outsourcing services and consulting—including on-site management of documents (service).[50]

Companies participating in the award process submit applications and complete an examination. This examination is reviewed by a team of U.S. quality experts, who also visit the companies that pass the initial screening. The 1998 application guidelines and related information fill a forty-eight page booklet. A summary of the seven interrelated examination categories for 1998, along with their maximum point values (totaling 1,000 points), follows.

- **Leadership** (110 points): This category examines the company's leadership system and senior leaders' personal leadership. It examines how senior leaders and the leadership system address values, company directions, performance expectations, a focus on customers and other stakeholders, learning, and innovation. Also examined is how the company addresses its societal responsibilities and provides support to key communities.

- **Strategic Planning** (80 points): This category examines how the company sets strategic directions and develops the critical strategies and action plans to support those directions. Also examined are how plans are deployed and performance is tracked.

- **Customer and Market Focus** (80 points): This category examines how the company determines requirements, expectations, and preferences of customers and markets. Also examined is how the company builds relationships with customers and determines their satisfaction.

- **Information and Analysis** (80 points): This category examines the selection, management, and effectiveness of information and data used to support key company processes and action plans and the company's performance management system.

- **Human Resource Focus** (100 points): This category examines how the company enables employees to develop and utilize their full potential, aligned with the company's goals. Also examined are the company's efforts to build and maintain a work environment and work climate conducive to performance excellence, full participation, and personal and organizational growth.

- **Process Management** (100 points): This category examines the key aspects of process management, including customer-focused design, product and service delivery, support, and supplier and partnering processes involving all work units. It evaluates how key processes are designed, implemented, managed, and improved to achieve better performance.

- **Business Results** (450 points): This category examines the company's performance and improvement in key business areas—customer satisfaction, financial and marketplace performance, human resource results, supplier and partner performance, and operational performance. Also examined are performance levels relative to competitors.[51]

As suggested in Figure 21.4, the criteria for 1998 further strengthened the systems view of performance management. They placed a greater emphasis on the alignment of company strategy, customer and market knowledge, a high-performance workforce, key company processes, and business results. Increased focus was given to all aspects of organizational and employee learning.[52] Most of Deming's prescriptions are included in the Baldrige categories, and both emphasize a total systems approach.

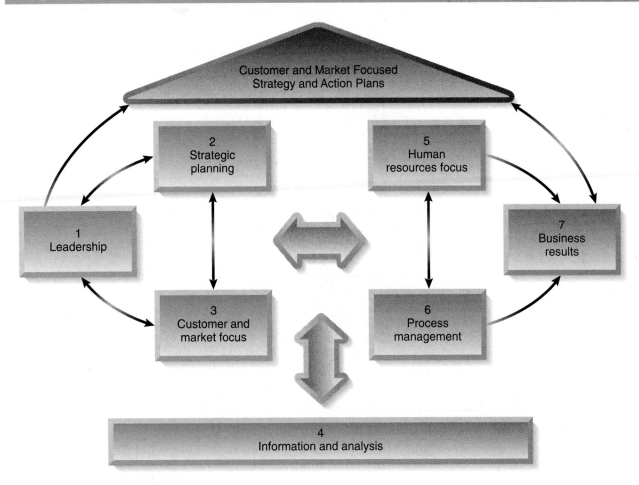

Source: National Institute of Standards and Technology. *Malcolm Baldrige National Quality Award: 1998 Criteria for Performance Excellence.* Gaithersberg, Md.: U.S. Department of Commerce, 1998, p. 43.

Communication processes—both internally with employees and externally with customers—are embedded in various Baldrige criteria. The following Communication Competency account reveals how the management of Solectron Corporation—one of the 1997 Baldrige Award winners—makes effective use of informal and formal communication processes to achieve high levels of performance. Solectron has received more than 140 quality and service awards from its customers, in addition to the 1997 and 1991 Baldrige Awards. Solectron is the first company in the history of the program to win the Baldrige Award for manufacturing twice.

THE QUALITY CONTROL PROCESS

The quality control process generally focuses on measuring inputs (including customer expectations and requirements), transformation operations, and outputs. The results of these measurements enable managers and employees to make decisions about product or service quality at each stage of the transformation process.

Inputs. Quality control generally begins with inputs, especially the raw materials and parts used in the transformation process. Recall that Toyota emphasizes quality control by its suppliers. For almost all parts, Toyota uses only one or two sup-

Solectron Corporation

As we noted previously, Solectron Corporation is a worldwide provider of premanufacturing, manufacturing, and postmanufacturing services to leading electronics original equipment manufacturers (OEMs). Solectron employs more than 20,000 people at eighteen manufacturing facilities around the world.

Solectron tracks customer satisfaction weekly by means of surveys, with an 80 percent to 90 percent response rate. Scores for delivery, quality, and service are at or near the 90 percent satisfaction level. This level of satisfaction is particularly noteworthy because of the company's stringent rating scale in which a C receives a score of 0 and a D receives a score of *minus* 100. Grades of B– or lower trigger Solectron's customer complaint resolution process. Within twenty-four hours, the account's program manager contacts the customer to acknowledge the complaint and visits the company to gain additional information. Within seventy-two hours, a corrective action plan is submitted to the customer.

Customer-satisfaction report cards are reviewed weekly by managers and employees at each site.

Solectron employees communicate with customers and suppliers at the earliest stages of a product's design cycle. The company bases its selection and regular reviews of its suppliers on several factors—including financial strength, technology leadership, TQM system, and compatibility with Solectron's beliefs. By building a strong partnership with its suppliers on a foundation of full and open communication, Solectron provides customers with excellent time-to-market and time-to-cost products and services.

Solectron aims to create a work environment in which employees can maximize their potential "by working both hard and smart, and doing what it takes to satisfy the customer." Solectron University, established in 1990, provides managers and employees with opportunities to develop their skills and competencies. This effort supports Solectron's philosophy to "hire for traits—train for

skills." The company's variable compensation plan extends to all members of the workforce. Employee pay is based on individual, team, site, and corporate performance in terms of revenue, profit, customer satisfaction, and operational performance.[53]

* * *

To learn more about Solectron, visit the company's home page at

www.solectron.com

pliers, which is consistent with one of Deming's prescriptions. On its own, Toyota produces just 30 percent of the parts that go into its cars, compared with about 65 percent for General Motors. Jeffery Dyer, a faculty member at the Wharton School, has studied Toyota's suppliers. He comments, "Toyota realizes that its cars are only as good as the weakest link in its extended enterprise. It has consciously institutionalized a set of practices for transferring knowledge between itself and the suppliers, so that the whole group learns faster."[54]

Byron Pond is the CEO of Arvin Industries, an Indiana company, which supplies exhaust systems and suspension pieces to Toyota and other automakers. He commented, "Some manufacturers ask, 'How can I club you into submission?' Toyota asks, 'How can I help you be better?'"[55] To prepare Arvin to be a supplier, two Toyota engineers spent seven months in its Indiana plant. They helped improve processes, materials management, and quality in preparation for a Toyota contract—even though the plant was then making parts for a competitor.

Transformation operations. Quality control inspections are made during and between successive transformation stages. Work-in-progress inspection can result in the reworking or rejecting of an item before the next operation is performed on it.

The systematic and widespread use of statistical process control is one of Deming's key prescriptions. ***Statistical process control*** is the use of quantitative methods and procedures to determine whether transformation operations are being done correctly, to detect any deviations, and, if there are any, to find and eliminate their causes. Statistical process control methods have been available for decades but only in the past twenty years have they been increasingly used. They serve primarily as preventive controls.[56]

Sigma is a unit of statistical measurement, which in this context is used to illustrate the quality of a process. The sigma measurement scale (ranging from two to six) describes defects in parts per million. To simplify the concept, let's consider the application of six sigma to written text. If defects were measured in misspellings, four sigma would be equivalent to one misspelling per thirty pages of text; five sigma, one misspelling in a set of encyclopedias; and six sigma, only one misspelling in an entire small library, such as a high school library.[57]

Some organizations—such as Solectron, Toyota, and General Electric—have adopted the quality program and goal of ***six sigma,*** which means eliminating defects to the level of 1 per 3.4 per million opportunities—or a process that is 99.99966 percent defect free. Five sigma is 233 defects per million, and four sigma is 6,210 per million. Most firms operate at the four sigma level.[58] A key theme in six sigma programs is the reduction of waste. Toyota trains all employees to seek opportunities to reduce waste in seven areas—called *Toyota's Seven Wastes*. They include

- waste of overproduction (also irregular production: the end-of-month or end-of-quarter surge),

- waste of time on hand (waiting),

- waste in transportation,

- waste of processing itself,

- waste of stock on hand (inventory),

- waste of movement, and

- waste of making defective products.[59]

General Electric (GE) recently developed a quality program based on the six sigma goal. One element involves training "Black Belts" for four months in statistical and other quality enhancing measures. The Black Belts then spend full time at GE plants and set up quality improvement projects. The company plans to have 10,000 Black Belts trained by 2000. Jack Welch, GE's CEO, is giving this program his strong personal support.

The following example illustrates the difference this program has made. Customers of GE's Milwaukee-based medical division were frustrated by the short life of the tubes in GE's CT scanners. The tubes lasted for about 50,000 to 100,000 x-rays and took about four hours to replace. GE assigned a team of six-sigma Black Belts to the problem. Their job was to measure and analyze each phase of the tube manufacturing process to determine how waste could be reduced and product improvements made. They reduced by nine months the time needed to perfect new models of the x-ray tubes and increased the life of the tubes by five times. The new tubes provide sharper, more complete pictures—allowing physicians to examine images of the entire brain of a stroke victim, rather than just slices at a time. GE estimated companywide savings from the six sigma program at about $600 million.[60]

Outputs. The most traditional and familiar form of quality control is the assessment made after completion of a component or an entire product, or provision of a service. With goods, quality control tests may be made just before the items are shipped to customers. The number of items returned by customers because of shoddy workmanship or other problems is one indicator of the effectiveness of the quality control process. Service providers, such as barbers and hairdressers, usually involve their customers in checking the quality of outputs by asking if everything is okay. However, the satisfactory provision of a service often is more difficult to assess than the satisfactory quality of goods.

Determining the amount or degree of the nine dimensions of quality shown in Table 21.2 is fundamental to quality control. The more accurate the measurement, the easier comparing actual to desired results becomes. Quality dimensions generally are measured by variable or by attribute. ***Measuring by variable*** assesses product characteristics for which there are quantifiable standards (length, diameter, height, weight, or temperature).

Consider the quality control process and technology used on the Mercedes-Benz M-class sport utility vehicle at the Mercedes factory in Vance, Alabama. Carmakers have traditionally tracked their body-building accuracy by taking sample vehicles off the assembly line and physically checking a large number of their dimensions with special equipment. Mercedes still does so, running about every 100th body through a measuring machine that checks 1,062 dimensions with sensitive touch probes in a process that takes about four hours.

To spot flaws that can develop between those elaborate inspections on every 100th body, Mercedes uses a new vision system. At the end of the body-building line, a *body-in-white vehicle*—factory language for an unpainted body minus doors, hood, and liftgate—arrives at the vision station. In a process that takes just forty-five seconds, thirty-eight laser cameras mounted on a superstructure check eighty-four key measurements. Slight dimensional flaws can be identified and corrected before any out-of-tolerance bodies get built. "Before laser gauging, carmakers couldn't do 100 percent inspection. Now we do it," stated Mike Hill, leader of the measurement team.[61]

Measuring by attribute evaluates product characteristics as acceptable or unacceptable. Measuring by attribute usually is easier than measuring by variable.[62] For example, testing PCs by turning them on as a final check results in a simple yes or no answer regarding acceptable quality. However, the setting and achievement of quality standards usually isn't that simple. In the production of a new type of bus—called the flexible bus—several years ago, the trade-off between the strength needed in the bus frame and the light weight needed to improve fuel efficiency was misjudged. Several cities that purchased this "new generation" of bus experienced numerous problems, including cracked frames.

The assessment of product quality doesn't reveal what the quality level should be. Desired levels of quality are strongly influenced by an organization's strategy and culture (as at Maytag) and by its competition (as at Toyota, GM, and Chrysler). This aspect of quality assurance is a central theme in the Baldrige Award process.

QUALITY PROBLEMS

The provision of quality services and goods—constantly and from the beginning—is an ideal that isn't always attained. Therefore the responses to quality problems are crucial. The following are three specific prescriptions for recovering from quality problems.

- **Encourage customers to complain and make it easy for them to do so.**
  Comment cards in service delivery facilities and toll-free telephone numbers are

two of the more common approaches used. Fred Brown is a key partner in Ford, Mazda, and BMW dealerships in Texas. The sales associates at these dealerships don't just follow up with customers to determine whether there are any problems two weeks or so after the purchase of a car. They follow up by phone six months later and again a year after the purchase to determine whether the customer has had any problems with the car or the service being received. Fred Brown often follows up with a personal call when customers express concerns. His dealerships have won many awards for quality service from car manufacturers.

- **Make timely, personal communication with customers a key part of the strategy.** Organizations frequently make two fatal mistakes in problem resolution: They take too long to respond to customers, and they respond impersonally. Timely, personal communication with unhappy customers offers the best chance to regain the customer's favor. North Carolina's Wachovia Bank & Trust has a *sundown* rule: "Employees must establish contact with a complaining customer before sunset on the day a complaint is received."

- **Encourage employees to respond effectively to customer problems and give them the means to do so.** Managers must market the idea of problem resolution to employees. Among other things, this approach involves setting and reinforcing problem-resolution standards and giving employees the freedom to solve customer problems. Employees are less likely to try to solve customer problems if doing so creates a small mountain of paperwork for them. When American Express cardholders telephone the 800 number on their monthly statements, they talk to a highly trained customer service representative. This person has the authority to solve 85 percent of the problems on the spot and the ability to do so by means of the company's advanced information technology capabilities.[63]

As we indicated in Chapter 17, various types of teams are increasingly used to address a wide range of quality management and control issues in organizations. The following Teamwork Competency feature reveals how Lynn Mercer, a manager at one of Lucent Technologies' plants that produce digital cellular base stations, uses teams. Her approach demonstrates: (1) the benefits of empowerment and an environment in which effective teamwork and quality are expected, recognized, praised, and rewarded; (2) appropriate staffing of teams, taking into account the value of diverse perspectives, technical skills needed, and developmental goals; and (3) the use of a system for monitoring team performance.

INVENTORY MANAGEMENT AND CONTROL

5

EXPLAIN THE BASICS OF INVENTORY MANAGEMENT AND CONTROL

INVENTORY
The amount and type of raw materials, parts, supplies, and unshipped finished goods that an organization has on hand at any one time.

Inventory is the amount and type of raw materials, parts, supplies, and unshipped finished goods an organization has on hand at any one time. *Inventory control* is concerned primarily with setting and maintaining minimum, optimum, and maximum levels of inventory. In part, such control is achieved by obtaining feedback about changes in inventory levels that signal the need for action to avoid going above or below the predetermined levels. The amount of inventory may have an enormous effect on a firm's capital requirements and the productivity of its capital. If a small business firm can cut its average inventory value from $1 million to $800,000, with everything else being equal, it can operate with $200,000 less in capital or borrowed funds on which it would have to pay interest. This reduction in the amount of money tied up in inventory has the effect of increasing the productivity of the investment in inventory by 20 percent. Inventory management and con-

Lynn Mercer, one of Lucent Technologies' plant managers, provides broad goals, guidance, and measurements at her digital cellular base station manufacturing plant. The 480 employees at the plant are organized into self-directed work teams.

In two years these employees haven't missed a single delivery deadline. Total labor costs represent an exceedingly low 3 percent of product costs. Operating statistics are displayed everywhere. Where performance trails a goal, the chart hangs behind a sheet of blood-red, see-through plastic. People with a few spare minutes consult an "urgent board" listing of orders that are behind schedule, and jump in where they're needed most.

Phillip Dailey works on an assembly line. He strings cables inside a steel box the size of a refrigerator—a digital transmitting station for cellular phone systems. While studying a bottleneck along the line, Dailey realized that with 25 percent more staff his team could increase

output by 33 percent. He recruited temporary workers from other teams, proved the concept, and thereby convinced the managers.

The work is technical but teachable. What isn't as teachable is initiative, curiosity, and collegiality—necessities of the self-directed workforce. Mercer puts applicants through tests intended to weed out loners and difficult people. New employees are hired as contractors. They are appointed as regular employees only after proving that they're self-starters and team players.

Teams elect their own leaders to oversee quality assurance, training, scheduling, and communication with other teams. Richard Deming, a quality leader, claims that he has more say-so in this plant than he had in his father's electrical contracting business. "My friends and family don't believe how much people listen to me here," he says.

Assemblers know the destination of every product they touch. When a completed product rolls off the line,

the assemblers sign an inside panel. Dozens of entry-level technicians know customers personally because Mercer sends them to trade shows and installation sites. Employees conduct plant tours when customers visit.[64]

* * *

To learn more about Lucent Technologies, visit the company's home page at

www.lucent.com

INVENTORY CONTROL
Setting and maintaining minimum, optimum, and maximum levels of inventory.

trol is of interest to goods producers and service producers alike. For example, supermarkets are constantly analyzing the quantity of each good they should stock, where it should be located, and how much shelf space should be allocated to it.[65]

INVENTORY GOALS

Inventories are maintained to (1) achieve some independence in transformation operations, (2) allow flexibility in production schedules, (3) safeguard against problems caused by variations in delivery of input materials, (4) meet variations in product demand, and (5) take advantage of economic order quantities.

Input materials, components, and partially completed goods sometimes are stocked at each workstation to provide some independence of operation. Thus an equipment breakdown at one station won't delay work at any of the stations farther on.

LEAD TIME
The elapsed time between placing an order and receiving the finished goods or services.

Inventories allow flexibility in the production schedule because a stockpile of finished goods lessens the pressure to produce a certain amount by a particular date and provides for shorter lead times. **Lead time** is the elapsed time between placing an order and receiving the finished goods. Larger finished goods inventories result in shorter customer lead times. For example, some auto dealers use the availability of a large number of cars as part of their marketing strategy. They advertise that customers can get the car of their choice today.

Inventories provide a safeguard against problems caused by variations in the delivery of input materials. An operations manager can't always count on raw materials arriving on a specific date. Possible reasons for delays include labor strikes, transportation holdups, bad weather, and late shipments by suppliers. Without a backup inventory of input materials, even slight delays can shut down an entire operation.

Inventories help meet variations in market demand for the firm's outputs. A company can seldom produce or provide the number of items needed to match market demand exactly. Therefore a common practice is to maintain a safety, or buffer, inventory to meet unanticipated market demand. For example, hospitals must maintain certain quantities of surgical supplies, blood, and medicines to be ready for possible disasters requiring treatment of many patients. Inventories also are needed to meet seasonal changes in demand for items such as swimsuits. Thus retailers constantly try to forecast shifts in customer demand in setting inventory levels.

Inventories enable management to take advantage of economic order quantities. Purchasing materials and carrying those materials in inventory costs money. These costs—along with any offsetting supplier discounts for quantity ordering—are factors in determining the most economical size of an order. Inventories are also used to achieve other goals, such as stabilizing employment, hedging against inflation, reducing the risk of possible future shortages, and eliminating the need for possible future overtime.[66] However, agile manufacturing and service strategy is dramatically reducing the amount of inventory required to meet variations in demand by the use of highly responsive suppliers.

INVENTORY COSTS
The expenses associated with maintaining inventory, including ordering costs, carrying costs, shortage costs, and setup costs.

INVENTORY COSTS

Inventory costs are the expenses associated with maintaining inventory, including ordering costs, carrying costs, shortage costs, and setup costs. All must be considered in making decisions about inventory levels.

- **Ordering costs** are the expenses associated with placing the order and/or preparing the purchase order.

- **Carrying costs** are the expenses of holding goods in inventory. They include losses owing to obsolescence, insurance premiums, rent on storage facilities, depreciation, taxes, breakage, pilferage, and capital invested in inventory.

- **Shortage costs** are the losses that occur when there is no stock in inventory to fill a customer's order. The customer must either wait until the inventory is restored or not place the order. Determining the costs resulting from a customer's decision not to place an order or to place future orders elsewhere is difficult.

- **Setup costs** are the expenses of changing over to make a different product. They include the time required to get new input materials, make equipment changes, make changes in the sequence of transformation processes, and clear out inventories of other items. They also include the costs of additional administrative time, employee training, idle time, and overtime.

Evaluating specific inventory goals and costs is part of the control process for determining desirable inventory levels and the ideal size of orders to replenish inventories. How much should I order? is a practical question whose answer

Figure 21.5   *Cost Trade-Offs in Determining Inventory Levels*

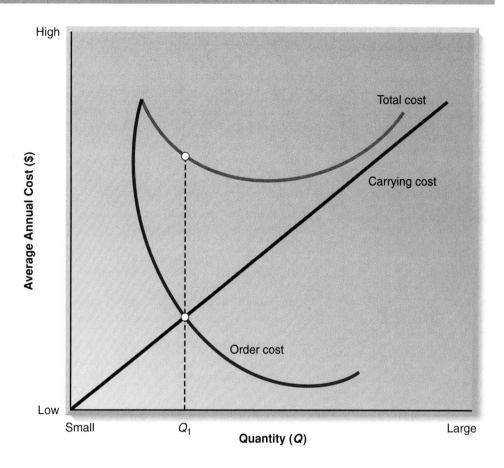

depends on cost trade-offs that every inventory manager must evaluate. Figure 21.5 identifies the typical cost trade-offs involved in determining appropriate order quantities. It shows that, as the quantity ordered increases, the cost of orders declines. The total cost also declines (but not as fast because carrying costs are accumulating), reaches a low point, and then begins to rise. Why? As order quantity and average inventory level increase, the carrying cost of the inventory also increases because more money and space are tied up in inventory. The optimum order quantity yields the lowest total inventory costs. This quantity, labeled $Q1$, is called the ***economic order quantity.*** Calculations based on inventory records, ordering practices, and costs yield the actual values of economic order quantities.

INVENTORY SYSTEMS

Two systems that have significantly affected inventory management and control are the materials resource planning system and the just-in-time system. The materials resource planning system appears to have the greatest application with process-focus and intermediate positioning strategies (see Figure 21.2). In contrast, the just-in-time system provides tighter inventory control with a product-focus strategy.

Materials Resource Planning II System. A widely used computerized information system for managing dependent demand inventories and scheduling stock replenishment orders is the ***materials resource planning II system.*** It is

ECONOMIC ORDER QUANTITY
The optimum order quantity, which yields the lowest total inventory costs.

MATERIALS RESOURCE PLANNING II SYSTEM
A widely used computerized information system for managing dependent demand inventories and scheduling stock replenishment orders.

programmed to initiate production of various components by issuing release orders to offset inventory reductions. The dependent demands for components, subassemblies, and raw materials (inputs to the transformation process) are calculated from the demand schedules of those who will use the outputs (customers) or from forecasts. Replenishment orders are time-phased relative to the date the stock is needed. For example, if a firm needs to replenish the stock of an item in week six to avoid a stockout and the lead time is four weeks, the purchase order will be issued in week two. Ideally, items arrive just before they are needed, and finished goods are produced just before they are to be shipped. Based on the assumption of uneven demand, this system attempts to minimize inventory investment while achieving zero stockouts, maximize operating efficiency, and improve customer service.

The materials resource planning II system helps meet three basic information requirements of operations management: (1) What is needed? (2) How much is needed? (3) When is it needed? The following components provide this information.

- A **master production schedule** shows which goods are to be produced, when, and in what quantities.

- A **bill of materials** describes the inputs—raw materials, parts, or subassemblies—for each finished good or component to be produced.

- An **inventory-status file** shows inventory on hand and an order for each stock item by time period (day, week, or month), including information on lead time, order size, and supplier.

Materials resource planning II also calculates gross and net financial requirements for inputs and outputs by time period. To be successful this system requires precise information, as well as extensive coordination and cooperation among individuals and departments. The intent is to get all departments to work to the same schedules and priorities. For example, the failure of sales personnel to report sales precisely and on a timely basis could throw the entire system off. Problems involving the use of this system usually occur when individuals in different departments or organizations fail to communicate and cooperate.[67]

Just-in-Time System. The delivery of finished goods just-in-time to be sold, subassemblies just-in-time to be assembled into finished goods, parts just-in-time to go into subassemblies, and purchased materials just-in-time to be transformed into parts is called, as you may surmise, the *just-in-time system,* or JIT system. At each stage of the transformation process, a JIT system delivers the smallest possible quantities at the latest possible time in order to minimize inventory costs. Toyota and Mercedes-Benz, among others, use the system.

The JIT system affects much more than just the purchasing department. It requires fundamental changes in the relationship between a manufacturer and its suppliers. The traditional use of forcing and compromise as conflict-management styles has had to shift to the use of collaboration and compromise. The JIT system has major implications for quantities purchased and produced, quality expectations, and suppliers used. The implications for quantities purchased and produced include (1) a steady output rate by the manufacturer, (2) frequent deliveries (sometimes twice or more a day) in small quantities by suppliers to the manufacturer, (3) long-term contracts and blanket orders with suppliers, (4) variable quantities from delivery to delivery but a fixed quantity for the overall contract term, and (5) little or no overage or underage acceptable in deliveries.

The implications of the JIT system for quality expectations include (1) the manufacturer helping suppliers meet quality requirements, (2) the buyer's and suppli-

JUST-IN-TIME SYSTEM (JIT)

The delivery of finished goods just-in-time to be sold, subassemblies just-in-time to be assembled into finished goods, parts just-in-time to go into subassemblies, and purchased materials just-in-time to be transformed into parts.

ers' quality control people establishing and maintaining close working relationships, and (3) the manufacturer urging suppliers to use TQM in their production processes.

The implications of the JIT system for suppliers include (1) few suppliers, who often are located near the manufacturing plant, (2) repeat business with the same suppliers and competitive bidding mostly limited to new parts, (3) suppliers encouraged to extend the JIT system to their suppliers, and (4) supplier control of shipping by using company-owned trucks or contract trucks, contract warehousing, and trailers for freight consolidation storage where possible, instead of common carriers.

As these implications suggest, JIT is a very demanding system for employees and managers. It requires high levels of communication, coordination, and cooperation. With the JIT system, buffer inventories, idle time, and other forms of slack are drastically reduced. Everyone must be constantly on their toes for it to work. Even coffee breaks must be coordinated within and between work teams.[68]

An even more demanding version of JIT is the *just-in-sequence* system. The Mercedes-Benz operation in Vance, Alabama, that started up in late 1997 uses the just-in-sequence system for some of the components that go into the M-Class sport utility vehicle. For example, once a vehicle has gone through the paint shop, a computer system sends an order to a supplier, such as Johnson Controls, Inc., to deliver a dashboard within a few hours. Just-in-sequence is risky. If an electronic data interchange system (extranet) at Johnson Controls or another supplier crashes, Mercedes-Benz could be "vulnerable to a plantwide shutdown" according to Robert Sigler, an automotive analyst at Sanford C. Bernstein & Company. However, the payoffs could be enormous. With 70 percent of its components being developed by other suppliers, Mercedes-Benz will be able to slash millions of dollars in inventory management costs.[69]

CHAPTER SUMMARY

Operations management (OM) is the systematic direction, control, and evaluation of the entire range of processes that transform inputs into goods or services. We identified nine of the principal categories of decisions in OM and discussed four of them: positioning strategies, technological options, quality management and control, and inventory management and control.

1. DISCUSS FOUR BASIC ISSUES IN OPERATIONS MANAGEMENT.

Operations management emphasizes a systems view that includes four core components: environmental factors, inputs, transformations, and outputs. Goods and services producers differ in the degree to which (1) outputs are durable and tangible, (2) outputs can be placed in inventory, (3) there is direct customer contact, (4) response time is short or long, and (5) the operations are labor intensive or capital intensive. Improvements in an OM system often are key to pro-

ductivity improvements which, in turn, affect the organization's competitiveness.

2. EXPLAIN FOUR POSITIONING STRATEGIES.

There are three traditional positioning strategies: process-focus, product-focus, and intermediate. The agile manufacturing strategy represents a relatively new approach. It provides a system and a set of capabilities that allow mass customization of goods. Reengineering is one of the methods used to assist in the implementation of an agile strategy.

3. PROVIDE EXAMPLES OF DEVELOPMENTS IN OFFICE, SERVICE, AND MANUFACTURING TECHNOLOGIES.

Technological options for improving quality and productivity in OM systems continue to increase rapidly. Innovative office technologies revolve around the personal computer and the revolution in software. Three increasingly used service technologies are bar coding, integrated order systems, and voice recognition systems. In manufacturing, two important technologies are robots and computer-aided manufacturing. Recent developments in computer-aided design and computer-aided manufacturing have made agile manufacturing strategies feasible.

4. STATE THE ESSENTIALS OF QUALITY MANAGEMENT AND CONTROL.

Total quality management and control is a strategic approach for competing effectively and efficiently. Nine basic dimensions of quality are (1) performance, (2) features, (3) conformance, (4) reliability, (5) durability, (6) serviceability, (7) responsiveness, (8) aesthetics, and (9) reputation. Under total quality management, quality is built in from product planning through sales and services. In contrast, traditional quality control focuses on inspections that take place at the end of major phases of the production process. A comprehensive quality control process is concerned with measuring inputs (including customer expectations and requirements), transformation operations, and outputs to determine whether goods or services meet or exceed acceptable quality. Deming's pre-

scriptions and the Baldrige framework provide two complementary approaches to the philosophy and strategy, processes, and methods that comprise total quality management and control.

5. EXPLAIN THE BASICS OF INVENTORY MANAGEMENT AND CONTROL.

Inventories may be maintained to (1) provide greater flexibility and reduce dependence between transformation operations, (2) increase flexibility in production schedules, (3) reduce the impact of unexpected delivery problems, (4) improve responsiveness to variations in customer demand, and (5) cut costs by taking advantage of economic order quantities. Decisions about how much inventory to keep on hand usually involve evaluation of four types of costs: ordering, carrying, shortage, and setup. The optimum inventory level (and economic order quantity) is determined by weighing certain cost trade-offs. The materials resource planning II system is a computerized system for managing inventories and scheduling orders. The just-in-time system aims to deliver the smallest possible quantities at the latest possible date at all stages of the transformation process in order to minimize inventory costs.

QUESTIONS FOR DISCUSSION

1. Give an example of each of the following for both a good (e.g., Toyota Camry) and a service (e.g., VISA card): (a) inputs, (b) transformation process, (c) outputs, and (d) feedback.

2. Choose a good (e.g., soft drink) or service (e.g., checking account) that you consume. Assume that you are a manager of the organization that provides this good or service. What measures might you use to track changes in its productivity?

3. Why is operations management important in the service sector?

4. Do positioning strategies apply to both large and small organizations? Why or why not?

5. Describe and evaluate in terms of five of the nine dimensions of quality shown in Table 21.2 an organization (nonprofit or for-profit) with which

you have had one or more transactions during the past three months.

6. Why is reengineering often a component of implementing an agile manufacturing strategy?

7. What types of problems should management anticipate because of the increasing use of robots?

8. Assume that you tried to follow Deming's prescriptions in your role as a student. How closely do your student-related activities and attitudes match his prescriptions?

9. Why is the just-in-time system not useful for all types of transformation operations?

EXERCISES TO DEVELOP YOUR MANAGERIAL COMPETENCIES

1. **Global Awareness Competency.** Amid the public outcry over foreign sweatshops, consider this manufacturer who strives to be different. Engin Altas owns and manages a company called Gon (pronounced gune) that primarily crafts fine leather purses and belts in Istanbul, Turkey. Altas could have used cheap labor to expand his growing manufacturing business, but he chose a different route.

   After three years of supplying only belts to New York-based Coach, he began investing in the labor and equipment needed to provide Coach purses—from cutting the imported leather to shipping to Coach—a premier marketer of high-quality leather goods and accessories. To learn Coach's standards, two factory engineers were trained in Coach plants in the United States. They in turn trained employees at the Istanbul factory. Also, a Coach representative regularly visits the plant in Turkey. Under Coach's supervision, Altas discontinued the use of the assembly-line approach and the work schedule that used to stretch into the evenings and over weekends. Altas instituted a team approach that involves employees working together in groups of seven or eight. This flexible approach allows quick and effective solutions to production problems "and makes a creative atmosphere," says Altas.

   Wages have risen 40 percent to nearly $3 an hour, which is far above the industry average in Turkey. Although employees are still responsible for quotas, they rarely work past their 8:00 A.M. to 6:00 P.M. shift.[70]

   Review the dimensions of the global awareness competency in Table 1.6 (page 25). What aspects of this competency does Engin Altas demonstrate? What are two explanations for Gon being able to pay much higher wages than other such foreign manufacturers? To learn more about Gon's primary customer—Coach Leatherware—visit the company's home page at

   www.coach.com

2. **Planning and Administration Competency.** If you wear jeans or khakis from The Gap or Calvin Klein, they probably came from the factory owned by Yul Ku. His company, Koos Manufacturing, makes more than 90,000 pairs of pants a week for the two companies, generating $100 million annually in sales. Ku, a Korean immigrant, employs nearly 1,000 people in his Los Angeles facility, which includes fabric storage, pattern marking and grading, sewing, laundry, finishing, and shipping. Many competitors locate cutting or laundry operations in different plants. However, Ku shaves as much as a week off the manufacturing process by having all his operations under one roof, providing evidence of his commitment to fast customer response.

   He recently installed a new conveyor system that reduces labor by 25 percent. It takes eight days for Koos to create a pair of pants from start to finish. The company can deliver a significant rush order in less than four weeks. "No one is quicker than us," Ku says.

   Two issues could potentially cloud the future of Koos Manufacturing: its limited customer base and its location. Ku produces for only the two customers, The Gap and Calvin Klein. Also, he built his current facility when many competitors were shifting production to Mexico. Ku is considering opening a facility in Mexico near the California border to gain further cost advantages without losing the time advantages of his Los Angeles location. He stated, "Personally, I'd like to stay in the U.S. because of the appeal of *made in the USA*." Many of Ku's competitors operate factories in Asia.[71]

   Review the dimensions of the planning and administration competency in Table 1.3 (page 21). What aspects of this competency are demonstrated by Yul Ku? What are two potential advantages of the current location of Koos Manufacturing? What are two potential disadvantages?

3. **Teamwork Competency.** Burley Design Cooperative may be one of the more unusual businesses in the United States. As the name suggests, its workers own the Eugene, Oregon, company. It produces $9 million worth of bicycle trailers, tandem bicycles, and rain gear a year, which it markets through independent bike shops. Bruce Creps is the general manager, but his business card bears only his name—no title. He stated, "We're not real heavy on titles around here." In this cooperative, every employee receives the same pay rate, $10.50 an hour. Creps gets paid the same as the employees at the sewing machines. When asked why he didn't just go and get a higher paying job, he replied that there were "oodles of potential here and a lot of work for a lot of people." Creps believes in the cooperative. About half the company's profits go back

into the business, with the other half being divided equally among the 95 cooperative employees. At meetings, workers raise a hand when they have something to say, utilizing a parliamentary style of group decision making.

Creps points out that the pay is enough to provide a decent living in Eugene, Oregon, but that the cooperative represents much more. Burley Design Cooperative employees earn a "second paycheck." According to Creps, "It's the involvement in work, the freedom from arbitrary dismissal."[72]

Review the dimensions of teamwork competency in Table 1.4 (page 22). What aspects of this competency are demonstrated by Bruce Creps? Consider the loose management hierarchy and team decision-making process at Burley Design Cooperative. What are two potential limitations of this organizational approach in terms of growth? What are two potential opportunities? To learn more about the Burley Design Cooperative, visit the company's home page at

www.burley.com

4. **Strategic Action Competency.** Georgia-Pacific Corporation is the second largest producer of gypsum products in North America. This highly integrated business maintains a strong market position, pursuing a low-cost leadership strategy. It operates twenty wallboard manufacturing centers and four recycled gypsum paper plants that employ about 3,000 workers in the United States and Canada.

In 1997, the company announced plans to build a $65 million gypsum wallboard facility in Wheatfield, Indiana, deciding not to reopen its Florence, Colorado, plant. It will dismantle and sell the equipment from that location. David R. Fleiner, vice president of the Gypsum Division, explains that Georgia Pacific decided to build a new efficient facility, rather than modernize existing facilities. This approach is in keeping with the firm's low-cost strategy. He explained that "the strategic location of the new facility in northern Indiana, compared to older, higher-cost plants in the region, will better position us to serve the Midwest metropolitan markets more effectively."[73]

Review the dimensions of the strategic action competency in Table 1.5 (page 24.) What aspects of this competency are demonstrated by David Fleiner and other top managers at Georgia-Pacific? To learn more about Georgia-Pacific, visit the company's home page at

www.gp.com

5. **Self-Management Competency.** The transition from working on a team to leading one is filled with challenges. Matt Scott is a software engineer and manager at Fore Systems, Inc., headquartered in Warrendale, Pennsylvania. He was placed in charge of a six-member team of engineers about a year after joining the company. He possessed little management experience, learning about team concepts and practices over a few long lunches with his manager.

For Scott, leading a team proved to be difficult and provided mixed results. He fostered an informal atmosphere and excelled in the roles of cheerleader, coach, referee, and player. Says team member David Spencer about Scott: "There aren't many jobs where I could go in and shoot the boss with a Nerf gun." However, Scott struggled with his new role as manager, growing frustrated with mounting paperwork and meetings. On top of that, he viewed himself as a peer of his team members and disliked conducting performance reviews. Scott noticed himself spending more time performing management duties instead of doing what he loves best—designing and writing computer code. He stated, "I'm sick and tired of planning. That's not what I came here for."[74]

Review the dimensions of the self-management competency in Table 1.7 (page 27). What aspects of this competency—and/or lack of—are demonstrated by Matt Scott? Imagine that you are in Scott's place. What are two things that you could do in order to become a more effective manager? How might you better balance the roles of team leader and team member? To learn more about Fore Systems, Inc., visit the company's home page at

www.fore.com

6. **Communication Competency.** At the Consumers Distribution SuperStore, a Canadian-based catalog showroom retailer, a strategic goal is no out-of-stock inventory. The company emphasizes customer service and heavily utilizes information technology to achieve that goal. For example, a customer places an order for a stereo system at the Consumers Distributing store near her home. The sales associate informs her that this particular store doesn't currently have the item in stock but uses the computer to communicate with all the company's nearby stores and distribution centers to review their inventories. Consumers Distributing then offers the customer several options, including home delivery of the item at no extra charge within seventy-two hours.

Once plagued with customer service problems, Consumers Distributing used cutting-edge technologies to build a customer-driven management process. Previously, the company's customers would have to stand in line for twenty minutes, only to be told that the product they wanted was out of stock. Perry Caicco, president and CEO, stated, "The company would antagonize 30 percent of its customers every single day and nobody outside of the counter staff and store managers seemed to care." The combination of an interstore inventory computer information system and a climate for open communication helped turn Consumers Distributing into an efficient and successful chain now known for always having goods in-stock.[75]

Review the dimensions of the communication competency in Table 1.2 (page 19). What aspects of this competency are demonstrated as companywide imperatives at Consumers Distributing? How does the integrated inventory system affect communication and create a competitive advantage for the company?

REAL-TIME CASE ANALYSIS

BOEING OVERHAULS ITS DESIGN AND MANUFACTURING PROCESS

Boeing Company is beginning to employ auto industry manufacturing techniques to drastically change the way it designs and builds aircraft and, in the process, reducing new-plane development time to twelve months. A team of 100 of the company's top personnel has been charged with devising new development techniques in a plan known within Boeing as the "cheaper-better-faster" project. Ron Woodard, president of the Boeing Commercial Airplane Group, explains that the objective is "to go from sixty-some months to twelve" months in launching new aircraft models. In addition, the company seeks cost efficiencies in the design and manufacturing processes.

Past Boeing manufacturing facilities involved assembly lines and "product-specific" manufacturing tools and equipment. However, the company intends to sustain its competitive advantage into the foreseeable future by adopting an approach that will allow rapid shifts in production in response to customer demand for different airplane models.

Boeing's production process has been less than optimal. Minor changes—such as moving the location of the emergency flashlight holder—required thousands of hours of engineering attention, hundreds of pages of detailed sketches, and could potentially cost millions of dollars to implement. Despite this cumbersome process, Boeing prospered when airlines and the Department of Defense spent heavily on planes and there were no major competitors in its market. With airline deregulation, defense cutbacks, and stiff competition from Airbus Industrie, commercial airline firms have become more price-sensitive.

Boeing continues to have two-thirds of the $65 billion global market for commercial planes with 100 or more seats. In addition, the company has experienced a string of huge orders from major airlines in Asia, Europe, and North America. For example, in late 1997, China signed a $3 billion contract to buy fifty jets for its state-owned carriers.

In 1998, Boeing more than doubled its 1996 output of 18.5 planes per month to a record 43 planes per month. To meet rising demand, Boeing managers hired more than 38,000 workers over a twenty-month period. However, because of quality problems, the company had to take a series of expensive and embarrassing actions, including stopping production on two major assembly lines for a full month.

Boeing's production reform team has developed the reengineering plan around the strategy that airlines should order airplanes the way consumers order automobiles. Previously, Boeing responded to each customer's unique demands, even offering 109 shades of white paint. Under the new plan, customers will be able to pick from a limited selection of option packages, with any special requests costing extra.

The team is replacing more than 400 computer programs currently in use. Information systems are being integrated through the use of four off-the-shelf software packages—one each for manufacturing, purchasing, inventory, and configuration management. In addition, employees meet in five-day accelerated improvement workshops where they brainstorm more efficient ways to perform their jobs. By moving machines, designing new tools, and cutting unnecessary inventory, employees at the factory that builds wings for the 747s have been able to shave production time from 56 to 28 days.[76] To learn more about Boeing, visit the company's home page at

www.boeing.com

QUESTIONS

1. What positioning strategy is Boeing moving toward? Explain.

2. What are two potential threats that Boeing could encounter by enacting this reengineering plan at a time when demand for its jets is so high?

3. What impact are Boeing's new design and manufacturing processes likely to have on quality? Explain.

4. Boeing has only one real competitor: European Airbus Industrie. What are two advantages and two disadvantages of this type of competitive environment for Boeing?

5. Investigate the Boeing home page. What other products do they offer in the aerospace industry?

VIDEO CASE

WORLD GYM: WORKING THE FAT OFF ORGANIZATIONAL PROCESSES

Management at the World Gym franchise in San Francisco applies operations management (OM) principles to optimize the gym's operation. Understanding the amount and nature of the services demanded—and the gym's capacity to meet demand—allows for minimizing slack, and maximizing customers' experiences. The gym employs a management information system to catalog and evaluate gym equipment, and to reconcile equipment and facility space with expected usage. As a midsized facility in a fairly nonautomated environment, data collection is rather rudimentary. It usually involves a visual survey of the various apparatus at the close of the working day, class rosters for all scheduled activities, and turnstile or swipe card data from the front desk.

However, opportunities for coupling information systems to customers, both to enhance operations research and to deliver services, continue to expand. In the case of World Gym, recent trends in incorporating microprocessors into gym equipment allow new means of data collection and customization. As equipment is used, a record can be obtained not just of how much it's been used, but also when and how hard. The day's reporting could include charts showing distribution of busy and idle machines for various time periods and expected times of needed replacement.

Taking data collection further, within a few years World Gym might be offering its patrons the ability to interact with the equipment themselves (digitally, that is!) by recording calories burned, miles cycled, or kilometers rowed to construct a record of activities and progress. End-user technology such as bar codes or swipe cards is already sufficiently advanced economical to make point-of-service interaction cheap and efficient. Thus the gym could collect extremely valuable information on customer preferences and

equipment use. The data could also be used to analyze customer progress and suggest other services (e.g., to recommend a personal trainer based on observed performance). Customers would find World Gym most attentive to their individual needs.

Clearly, there's a fine line between service and surveillance. Just as the video monitor that prevents employee theft from the cash register is, to be truthful, spying on employees' actions, the more that systems record customers' activities the greater cause they may have to be concerned. Invasions of customer privacy could lead to increased junk mail (e.g., if a gym sold customer weight and fitness data to a pharmaceutical company) and even to problems in securing a job, a loan, or insurance.

Unlike manufacturers of goods, World Gym's most important "raw materials" and "finished goods" are people. Expensive gym apparatus notwithstanding, people—in the form of trainers and other staff—are also the organization's most important asset.

Being human, both customers and staff are subject to human frailties (e.g., missed buses, schedule conflicts, or the flu). World Gym's management processes need to account for such potential problems. Like many service organizations, World Gym operators maintains rosters of substitute staff to ensure full coverage in the event of staff no-shows. If, despite forecasted demand, attendance is light, the gym might have to send staff home or reschedule duty hours on short notice.

ON THE WEB

World Gym is on the Web (***www.worldgym.com***). In addition to the San Francisco World Gym, gyms are franchised throughout the United States and internationally. Also on the Web is the Electronic Privacy Information Center (EPIC), a nonprofit research and advocacy organization concerned with the threats that digital information, and its collection and dissemination, might pose to citizen privacy (**www.epic.org**).

The Direct Market Association (DMA) is an industry trade association whose members make extensive use of consumer data and is on the Web (**www. the-dma.org**). It has established customer privacy standard practices to help member companies allay public concerns of invasion of consumer privacy.

QUESTIONS

1. How might service demands at World Gym change during a year?

2. Unlike a goods producer, the Gym can't put excess patrons in inventory. How might it manage to ensure a steady flow of patrons and avoid overly large crowds or lines for some gym apparatus?

3. World Gym is local, physical, and relatively low-tech. How might it make use of the Internet and World Wide Web to enhance its operations?

To help you answer these questions and learn more about World Gym, visit its home page at

www.worldgym.com

Case contributed by Ross Stapleton-Gray, President, TeleDiplomacy, Inc., a technology and policy consultancy, and Adjunct Professor in Georgetown University's Communication, Culture, and Technology Program.

Internet Appendix

3M
www.mmm.com

7-Eleven
www.7-eleven.com

84 Lumber
www.84lumber.com

AIESEC
www.aiesec.org

Allstate
www.allstate.com

AM General
www.hummer.com

Amazon.com
www.amazon.com

AMC Entertainment
www.amctheatres.com

American Airlines
www.americanair.com

American Association for Training and Development
www.astd.org

American Compensation Association
www.acaonline.org

American Express
www.americanexpress.com

American Federation of Labor-Congress of Industrial Organizations (AFL-CIO)
www.aflcio.org

American Forest Products Association
www.afandpa.org

American Greetings
www.amgreetings.com

American Honda Motor
www.honda.com

American Productivity and Quality Center
www.apqc.org

Andersen Consulting
www.ac.com

Apple Computer
www.apple.com

ARAMARK
www.aramark.com

Archer Daniel Midlands
www.admworld.com

Archway Cookies
www.archwaycookies.com

Arthur Andersen
www.arthurandersen.com

Associated Lane Emergency Response Teams
www.alertweb.org

Association for Quality
www.asq.com

AT&T
www.att.com

Au Bon Pain
www.boston.com/aubonpain

Audubon Society
www.audubon.org

Autodesk
www.autodesk.com

Avon Products
www.avon.com

Baby Jogger
www.babyjogger.com

Baskin-Robbins
www.baskinrobbbins.com

Beamscope Canada
www.beamscope.com

Ben & Jerry's
www.benjerry.com

Bindco
www.bindco.com

Birkenstock
www.gehen.com or
www.birkenstock.com

BISNIS Online
www.itaie.doc.gov/bisnis

Black and Decker
www.blackanddecker.com

BMW of North America
www.bmwusa.com

Boeing
www.boeing.com

Boston Language Institute
www.boslang.com

British Airways
www.british-airways.com

British Petroleum
www.bp.com

Bureau of the Census
www.census.gov

Burley Design Cooperative
www.burley.com

Caliber Learning network
www.caliberlearning.com

California's Public Employees' Retirement System (Calpers)
www.calpers.ca.gov

Cambridge Technology Partners
www.ctp.com

Campbell Soup
www.campbellsoup.com

Carmike Cinemas
www.carmike.com

Caterpillar
www.caterpillar.com

Caux Round Table (as described by the Minnesota Center for Corporate Responsibility, St. Thomas University)
www.Byte.stthomas.edu/www/mccr_htm

Cemex
www.cemex.com

Chargeurs
www.chargeurs.fr

Charles Schwab & Co.
www.schwab.com

Chick-Fil-A
www.chick-fil-a.com

Chrysler
www.chrysler.com

Cinnabar California
www.cinnabar.com

Cirque du Soleil
www.cirquedusoleil.com

Cisco Systems
www.cisco.com

C.I.T. Group
www.citgroup.com

Citibank
www.citibank.com

Citicorp
www.citicorp.com

Coach Leatherwear
www.coach.com

Coca-Cola
www.cocacola.com

Colgate-Palmolive
www.colgate.com

Columbia-HCA Health Care Corp.
www.columbia.net

Comair Holdings, Inc.
www.fly-comair.com

Computer Ethics Institute
www.brook.edu/ITS/CEI/CEI_HP

ConAgra
www.conagra.com

Continental Airlines
www.flycontinental.com

Cooley & Cooley Ltd.
www.copalite.com

Coopers & Lybrand
www.colybrand.com

Corning
www.corning.com

Corporate Express
www.corporate-express.com

CSX
www.csx.com

Cyrix
www.cyrix.com

Dana Corporation
www.dana.com

Dayton-Hudson's
www.shop-at.com

Dell Computer
www.dell.com

Delta Airlines
www.delta-air.com

Delta Consulting Group
www.deltacg.com

DHL Worldwide Express
www.dhl.com

Dick Clark Productions
www.dickclark.com

Digital
www.digital.com

Direct Selling Association
www.dsa.org.uk

Disaster Recovery Journal
www.drj.com

Dow Chemical Co. & Corning, Inc.
www.dow.com

Dragon Systems
www.dragonsys.com

du Pont de Nemours
www.dupont.com

Dunkin' Donuts
*www.allieddomecqplc.com/brands/
    retail/dunkindo*

Eddie Bauer
www.eddiebauer.com

EDS
www.eds.com

Eli Lilly
www.lilly.com

Encyclopedia Britannica
www.ebig.com

Ensoniq
www.ensoniq.com

Equal Employment Opportunity
    Commission
www.eeoc.gov

Etec Systems
www.etec.com

European Union's Ecology and
    Management Audit Scheme
*www.gencat.es:8000/mediamb/eng/
    a_emas1.html*

Exxon
www.exxon.com

Fast Company
www.fastcompany.com

Federal Express
www.fedex.com

Federal Mogul
www.federalmogul.com

Fel-Pro
www.fel-pro.com

Fidelity Institutional Retirement
    Services Company (FIRSCo.)
www.firsco.com

Fluor Corporation
www.fluor.com

Ford Motor Company
www.ford.com

Fore Systems, Inc.
www.fore.com

Forrester Research
www.forrester.com

Frito-Lay
www.fritolay.com

Galoob Toys
www.galoob.com

GE Capital Services
www.ge.com/gecc18/

Genentech
www.gene.com

General Electric
www.ge.com

General Mills
www.genmills.com

General Motors
www.gm.com

Georgia-Pacific
www.gp.com

Gil Gordon
www.gilgordon.com

Glass Ceiling Commission
*www.dol.gov/dol/_sec/public/media/
    reports/ceiling*

Graphic Solutions
www.graphicsolutions.com

Greyhound
www.greyhound.com

Haagen-Dazs
www.haagendazs.com

Harley-Davidson
www.harley-davidson.com

Harrah's Entertainment
www.harrahs.com

Harvey's Pro Hardware
www.harveysprohardware.com

Hay Group
www.haygroup.com

Herman Miller
www.hermanmiller.com

Hertz
www.hertz.com

Hewitt Associates
www.hewittassoc.com/rese

Hewlett-Packard
www.hp.com

Hire Quality
www.hire-quality.com

Hitachi
www.hitachi.co.jp

Hoechst-Celanese
www.hoechst.com

Home Depot
www.homedepot.com

Honda Motor
www.honda.co.jp

Hughes Space and Communications
www.hughespace.com

Human Resource Planning Society
www.hrps.org

Iams Company
www.iams.com

IBM
www.ibm.com

IBM PC Company
www.pc.ibm.com

IDEO Product Development
www.ideo.com

Intel
www.intel.com

Internal Revenue Service
www.irs.ustreas.gov.com

International Association for Human
    Resource Information Management
www.ihrim.org

International Institute for Learning
www.iil.com

International Organization for
    Standardization (ISO)
www.iso.ch

International Personnel Management Association
www.ipma-hr.org

JCPenney
www.jcpenney.com

Jian
www.jianusa.com

Jobweb
www.jobweb.org

Johnson & Johnson
www.jnj.com

Jostens
www.jostens.com

J. P. Morgan
www.jpmorgan.com

Kellogg's
www.kelloggs.com

Kimberley-Clark
www.kimberley-clark.com

Knight-Ridder
www.knight-ridder.com

Kodak
www.kodak.com

Kraft Foods
www.kraftfoods.com

Kropf Fruit Company
www.kropf-inc.com

Land's End
www.landsend.com

Levi Strauss & Co.
www.levi.com

Lexus
www.lexus.com

Life Safety Associates
www.lifesafety.com

Lincoln Electric
www.lincolnelectric.com

Liz Claiborne, Inc.
www.lizclaiborne.com

Lucent Technologies
www.lucent.com

Manugistics
www.manugistics.com

Marriott International
www.marriott.com

Marshall Industries
www.marshall.com

Marshall Space Flight Center
www.msfc.nasa.gov

Mary Ellen Guffey
www.westwords.com/guffey

Mary Kay Cosmetics
www.marykay.com

Massachusetts General Hospital
www.mgh.harvard.edu

Matsushita Electric Light Company
www.mei.jp

Maytag
www.maytag.com/index.cgi

McDonald's
www.mcdonalds.com

McKinsey & Co.
www.mckinsey.com

Mellon Bank
www.mellon.com

Mercedes Benz
www.daimler-benz.com or
www.mercedes.com

Merck
www.merck.com

Meredith
www.home-and-family.com

Merix
www.merix.com

Merrill Lynch
www.ml.com

Microsoft
www.microsoft.com

Modern of Marshfield
www.modern-of-marshfield.com

Monorail, Inc.
www.monorail.com

Monsanto
www.monsanto.com

Motorola
www.mot.com

Muratec Business Systems
www.muratec.com

NAFTA
iepnt1.itaiep.doc.gov/nafta/
nafta2.htm

NASA
www.nasa.com or *www.spacelink.nasa.gov*

National Association of Young Venture Capitalists
www.venturecapital.com

National Center for Employee Ownership
www.nceo.org

National Institute of Standards and Technology (Baldrige Quality Award)
www.quality.nist.gov

NationsBank
www.nationsbank.com.

Nationwide Insurance
www.nationwide.com

Netscape
www.netscape.com

New Balance
www.newbalance.com

Next Door Food Stores
www.nextdoor1.com

Nike
www.nike.com

Nordstrom
www.nordstrom-pta.com

Northern Telecom
www.nortel.com

Novartis
www.novartis

Novell
www.novell.com

NRUG
www.nrug.com

Nucor
www.nucorbearing.com

Oracle
www.oracle.com

Outward Bound
www.outwardbound.org

Overseas Private Investment Corporation
www.opic.gov

Palo Alto Research Center
www.parc.xerox.com

Panasonic
www.panasonic.com

Patagonia
www.patagonia.com

Pep Boys
www.pepboys.com

Pepsico
www.pepsico.com

Personal Computer Rentals
www.pcrrent.com

PETsMART
www.petsmart.com

Pharmacia & Upjohn
www.pharmacia.se

Pillsbury
www.bakeoff.com

Polaroid
www.polaroid.com

Pratt & Whitney
www.pratt-whitney.com

Price Waterhouse
www.pw.com

Printing Industry Association
www.pias.org

Procter & Gamble
www.pg.com

Project Management Forum
www.pmforum.org

Project Management Institute
www.pmi.org

PRT
www.prt.com

Prudential Insurance
www.prudential.com

Qualcomm
www.qualcomm.com

R. R. Donnelley
www.rrdonnelley.com

Radio Shack
www.radioshack.com

Rank-Xerox
www.xerox.com

Recruiters Online Network
www.ipa.com

Reebok
www.reebok.com

Ritz Carlton
www.ritzcarlton.com

Rock and Roll Hall of Fame
www.rockhall.com

Rodel
www.rodel.com

Ron Brown Award
www.Ron-Brown-Award.org

Royal Dutch Shell
www.shell.nl

Rubbermaid
www.rubbermaid.com

Rush Medical Center
www.rush.edu

Saatchi & Saatchi
www.saatchiny.com

Samsung
www.samsung.com

Saturn
www.saturn.com/index.html

Saturn Electronics and Engineering
www.cave.net/saturn

Sears, Roebuck & Company
www.sears.com

Second Chance Body Armor
www.secondchance.com

Service Corp of Retired Executives
www.score.org

Service Corporation, International
www.sci-corp.com

Shearman & Sterling
www.shearman.com

Shell Oil
www.shell.com

Shiseido
www.shiseido.co.jp

Siemens AG
www.siemens.com

Siemens Business Communications
www.siemenscom.com

Small Business Administration
www.sbaonline.sba.gov

Small Business Advancement National Center
www.sbaer.uca

Smith Barney
www.smithbarney.com

Solectron
www.solectron.com

Sony Corporation
www.sony.com

Southwest Airlines
www.iflyswa.com

Sports Authority
www.sportsauthority.com

Staples
www.staples.com

Starbucks
www.starbucks.com

State Farm Insurance
www.statefarm.com

Students for Responsible Business
www.srb.org

Sun Microsystems
www.sun.com

Swatch Watch
www.swatch.com

Tandem Computer
www.tandem.com

Tandy Corporation
www.tandy.com

Team Leadership Resources
www.team-leadership.com

Texaco
www.texaco.com.

Texas Instruments
www.ti.com

Textron
www.textron.com

The Body Shop
www.the-body-shop.com

The Custom Foot
www.thecustomfoot.com

The Evans Team
www.evans-team.com

Thermo Electron
www.thermo.com

Thinking Pictures, Inc.
www.thinkpix.com

Toastmasters International
www.toastmasters.org

Tom's of Maine
www.tomsofmaine.com

Toyota
www.toyota.com

Toys "Я" Us
www.toysrus.com

U.S. Navy Seals
www.webix.nosc.mil/seals/

U.S. Postal Service
www.usps.gov

United Airlines
www.ual.com

United Financial Mortgage
www.ufmc.com

Uno Restaurants
www.unos.com

UPS
www.ups.com

VeriFone
www.verifone.com

VISA
www.visa.com

W. Edwards Deming Institute
www.deming.org

W. H. Brady
www.whbrady.com

W. J. Hagerty & Sons
www.hagerty-polish.com

W. L. Gore
www.gorefabrics.com

Wal-Mart
www.wal-mart.com

Walt Disney Co.
www.disney.com

Web Week
www.webweek.com

Wells Fargo Bank
www.wellsfargo.com

Western Electric
www.westernelectric.com.au

Weyerhaeuser
www.weyerhaeuser.com

Whirlpool
www.whirlpool.com

Whole Foods
www.wholefoods.com

Windham World
www.windhamint.com

WorkSpace Resources
www.workspace-resources.com

World Business Network
www.worldbusiness.net

World Gym
www.worldgym.com

Xerox Business Services
www.xerox.com/XBS

Xerox
www.Xerox.com

Yahoo!
www.yahoo.com

Glossary

A

ability A person's mastery of competencies required to do a job.

acceptance theory of authority Holds that employees have free wills and thus will choose whether or not to follow management's orders.

accountability The expectation that each employee will accept credit or blame for the results of his or her work.

achievement motive The desire to succeed relative to some standard of excellence or in competitive situations.

achievement-oriented leadership Setting challenging goals and expecting followers to perform at their highest level.

activity-based costing A system that focuses on activities as the fundamental cost centers.

adaptive decisions Choices made in response to a combination of moderately unusual and only partially known problems and alternative solutions.

adjourning stage The stage of team development that involves terminating task behaviors and disengaging from relationships.

administrative management Focuses on the manager and basic managerial functions.

affiliation motive A person's desire to develop and maintain close, mutually satisfying interpersonal relationships with others.

affiliation needs The desires for friendship, love, and belonging.

affirmative action programs Efforts intended to ensure that a firm's hiring practices and procedures guarantee equal employment opportunity, as specified by law.

agile strategy A flexible arrangement that allows the mass customization of goods by means of advanced fabrication, information, and delivery technologies that are utilized by skilled and empowered individuals and teams.

alliance The uniting of two or more organizations, groups, or individuals to achieve common goals with respect to a particular issue.

alliance strategy Agreeing with other companies to pool physical, financial, and human resources to achieve common goals.

angel An individual who invests directly in firms, receiving an equity stake, and often acts as a business advisor to the founder.

authority The right to decide and act.

automation The use of devices and processes that are self-regulating and operate independently of people.

autonomy The extent to which the job provides substantial freedom, independence, and discretion to the individual in scheduling work and determining the procedures to be used in carrying out tasks.

availability bias Recall of specific instances of an event, which may overestimate how frequently the event occurs.

B

backward integration Occurs when a company enters the businesses of its suppliers, usually to control component quality, on-time delivery, or stable prices.

bar code A series of black lines of varying widths alternating with spaces that represent information and can be read by an optical scanner into a computer.

basic expectancy theory The view that people tend to choose behaviors that they believe will help them achieve desired outcomes (e.g., a promotion or job security) and avoid behaviors that they believe will lead to undesirable outcomes (e.g., a demotion or criticism).

behavioral models Leadership models that focus on differences in the actions of effective and ineffective leaders.

behavioral norms The informal rules of behavior that are widely shared and enforced by the members of a group.

behavioral viewpoint Focuses on dealing more effectively with the human aspects of organizations.

behaviorally anchored rating scale A type of performance appraisal that describes specific job behaviors along a continuum of intensity.

benchmarking The continuous process of comparing an organization's strategies, products, or processes with those of best-in-class organizations.

bonuses Lump-sum payments given for achieving a particular performance goal.

bounded rationality model An individual's tendency (1) to select less than the best goal or alternative solution (i.e., to satisfice), (2) to engage in a limited search for alternative solutions, and (3) to have inadequate information and control over external and internal environmental forces influencing the outcomes of decisions.

brainstorming An unrestrained flow of ideas in a group with all critical judgments suspended.

bribe An improper payment made to induce the recipient to do something for the payer.

budgeting The process of categorizing proposed expenditures and linking them to goals.

bureaucratic controls Extensive rules and procedures, top-down authority, tightly written job descriptions, and other formal methods for preventing and correcting deviations from desired behaviors and results.

bureaucratic culture An organization in which employees value formalization, rules, standard operating procedures, and hierarchical coordination.

bureaucratic management A system that relies on rules, a set hierarchy, a clear division of labor, and detailed rules and procedures.

business-level strategy The interconnected set of key commitments and actions intended to provide value to customers and gain a competitive advantage for an organization by using its core competencies (abilities) in specific markets.

business plan A step-by-step outline of how an entrepreneur or the owner of an enterprise expects to turn ideas into reality.

C

capital requirements The dollars needed to finance equipment, supplies, R&D, and the like.

cartel An alliance of producers engaged in the same type of business, formed to limit or eliminate competition and control production and prices.

cause and effect diagram Helps team members display, categorize, and evaluate all the possible causes of an effect, which is generally expressed as a problem.

central tendency A rating error that occurs when all employees are given an average rating, even when their performances vary.

centralization of authority The concentration of decision making at the top of an organization or department.

certainty The condition under which individuals are fully informed about a problem, alternative solutions are obvious, and the possible results of each solution are clear.

changing environment A setting that is unpredictable because of frequent shifts in products, technology, competitive forces, markets, or political forces.

channel The path that a message follows from sender to receiver.

charismatic leaders Individuals that have an unshakable belief in their mission, are supremely confident that they and their followers can succeed, and have the ability to convey these certainties to their followers.

clan culture The attributes of tradition, loyalty, personal commitment, extensive socialization, teamwork, self-management, and social influence.

closed system Limits interactions with environment.

coaching style Building confidence and motivation through supportive behavior.

coercive power The ability of a leader to obtain compliance through fear of punishment.

cognitive ability test A written test that measures general intelligence, verbal ability, numerical ability, reasoning ability, and so on.

cohesiveness The strength of members' desires to remain in the group or team and their commitment to it.

collectivism Hofstede's value dimension that measures the tendency of group members to focus on the common welfare and feel loyalty toward one another (the opposite of individualism).

commission agent A person or firm who represents businesses in foreign transactions in return for a negotiated percentage of each transaction's value (a commission).

communication competency The effective transfer and exchange of information and understanding between yourself and others.

communication The transfer of information and understanding from one person to another through meaningful symbols.

comparative financial analysis The evaluation of a firm's financial condition for two or more time periods.

competency A combination of knowledge, skills, behaviors, and attitudes that contribute to personal effectiveness.

competency-based pay Compensation that is linked to people's competencies.

competency inventory A detailed file maintained for each employee that lists level of education, training, experience, length of service, current job title and salary, and performance history. Also included are the company's assessments of the employee's competency levels.

computer-aided design (CAD) Uses special software to instruct a computer to draw specified configurations, including dimensions and details, on a display screen.

computer-aided manufacturing (CAM) An array of computer-based technologies used to produce goods.

computer ethics The analysis of the nature and social impact of computer technology and the corresponding formulation and justification of policies for its appropriate use.

computer monitoring The use of special software to collect highly detailed quantitative information on employee performance.

concentric diversification Occurs when a firm acquires or starts a business related to the organization's existing business in terms of technology, markets, or products.

concrete information bias Vivid, direct experience dominating abstract information.

Confucian dynamics Hofstede's value dimension that measures a society's tendency to value people who are persistent, observe orderly relationships between people based on status, are thrifty, and have a sense of shame.

conglomerate diversification Occurs when a firm adds unrelated goods or services to its line of businesses.

considerate leadership style Exhibiting concern for employees' well-being, status, and comfort.

contingency models Leadership models based on the idea that the situation determines the best style to use.

contingency planning Preparation for unexpected and rapid changes (positive or negative) in the environment that will have a significant impact on the organi-

zation and that will require a quick response.

contingency viewpoint Advocates using the other three management viewpoints independently or in a combination, as necessary to deal with various situations.

continuous improvement Streams of adaptive decisions made over time in an organization that result in a large number of small, incremental improvements year after year.

contrast error Basing a candidate's rating on a comparison with the preceding interviewee.

control Mechanisms used to ensure that behaviors and performance conform to an organization's rules and procedures.

controlling The process by which a person, group, or organization consciously monitors performance and takes corrective action.

co-optation Bringing new stakeholder representatives into the strategic decision-making process as a means of averting threats to an organization's stability or existence.

coordination The formal and informal procedures that integrate the activities of separate individuals, teams, and departments in an organization.

core competencies The strengths that make an organization distinctive and more competitive by providing goods or services that have unique value to its customers.

corporate-level strategy Guides the overall direction of firms having more than one line of business.

corrective control model A process for detecting and eliminating or reducing deviations from an organization's established standards.

corrective controls Mechanisms intended to reduce or eliminate unwanted behaviors and thereby achieve conformity with the organization's regulations and standards.

corridor principle Using one business to start or acquire others and then repeating the process.

cost leadership strategy Competing in the industry by providing a product at a price as low as or lower than competitors.

counter trade An arrangement in which the export sales of goods and services by a producer is linked to an import purchase of other goods and services.

creativity The ability to visualize, foresee, generate, and implement new ideas.

critical path The path with the longest elapsed time, which determines the length of the project.

critical psychological states In the Hackman–Oldham theory the identification of experienced meaningfulness, experienced responsibility, and knowledge of results as the psychological states needed to create high levels of motivation in the workplace.

cultural diversity The full mix of the cultures and subcultures to which members belong.

culture A unique pattern of shared assumptions, values, and norms that shape the socialization activities, language, symbols, rites, and ceremonies of a group of people.

customer departmentalization Organizing around the type of customer served.

customer monitoring Ongoing efforts to obtain feedback from customers concerning the quality of goods and services.

cyberspace Represents the real-time transmitting and sharing of text, voice, graphics, video, and the like over a variety of computer-based networks.

D

data Facts and figures.

database An organized collection of facts, figures, documents, and the like that have been stored for easy, efficient access and use.

decentralization of authority A high degree of delegated decision making throughout an organization or department.

decision making The process of defining problems, gathering information, generating alternatives, and choosing a course of action.

decision support system (DSS) A complex set of computer hardware and software that allows end users—usually managers and professionals—to analyze, manipulate, format, display, and output data in different ways.

decoding Translating encoded messages into a form that has meaning to the receiver.

delegating style Recognition that others are ready to accomplish a particular task and are both competent and motivated to take full responsibility for it.

delegation of authority The process by which managers assign to subordinates the right to act and make decisions in certain situations.

Delphi Technique A forecasting aid based on a consensus of a panel of experts.

Deming cycle The four stages of improving quality; planning, doing, checking, and acting.

demographic diversity The degree of mix of demographic characteristics of the people who make up an organization's workforce.

demographics The characteristics of work group, organization, specific market, or national populations.

departmentalization Subdividing work into tasks and assigning them to specialized groups within an organization.

differentiation The measure of the differences among departments with respect to structure, tasks, and goals.

differentiation strategy Competing with all other firms in the industry by offering a product that customers perceive to be unique.

digital convergence The coming together of previously distinct products that use digital technologies.

digital world The linking of people, decisions, tasks, and processes via computers and computers with other computers.

direct compensation An employee's base wage or salary and any incentive pay received.

directive behavior Reliance on one-way communication, spelling out duties, and telling followers what to do and when and how to do it.

directive leadership Letting followers know what's expected of them and telling them how to perform their tasks.

directive style Providing clear instructions and specific directions to others.

distributive justice principle A moral requirement that individuals not be treated differently because of arbitrarily defined characteristics.

diversification The variety of goods and/or services produced and the number of different markets served by the organization.

domestic instability The amount of subversion, revolution, assassinations, guerrilla warfare, and government crisis in a country.

dominant-business firm Serves various segments of a particular market.

downsizing The process of reducing the size of a firm by laying off workers or retiring workers early.

downsizing strategy Signals an organization's intent to rely on fewer resources—primarily human—to accomplish its goals.

downward channels Communication paths that managers use to send messages to employees or customers.

E

economic climate The extent of government control of markets and financial investments, as well as government support services and capabilities.

economic order quantity The optimum order quantity, which yields the lowest total inventory costs.

economics The discipline that focuses on understanding how people of a group or nation produce, distribute, purchase, and use various goods and services.

economies of scale The decreases in per unit costs as the volume of goods and/or services produced increases.

effectiveness criteria Measurements of the outcomes achieved by individual members and the team as a whole.

electronic brainstorming Use of technology to input and automatically disseminate ideas in real time over a computer network to all team members, each of whom may be stimulated to generate other ideas.

electronic commerce All types of commercial transactions via computer-based networks that involve the processing and transmission of data—including text, sound, and visual images.

electronic mail Use of computer text composition and editing to send and receive written information.

emotion A subjective reaction or feeling.

employee-centered leadership style Encouraging employees to participate in making decisions and making sure that they are satisfied with their work.

employee network groups Informal groups who organize regularly scheduled social activities that foster the establishment of informal communication channels among employees who share a common interest or concern.

employee stock ownership plans Incentive plans whereby the company funds the purchase of its stock to be held in individual employee investment accounts.

employment-at-will A traditional common-law concept holding that employers are free to discharge employees for any reason at any time and that employees are free to quit their jobs for any reason at any time.

empowerment model Sharing influence and control with followers.

encoding Translating thoughts or feelings into a medium—written, visual, or spoken—that conveys the meaning intended.

entrapment Luring an individual into committing a compromising or illegal act that the person otherwise would not commit.

entrepreneur Someone who creates a new business activity in the economy.

entrepreneurial culture Exhibits high levels of risk taking, dynamism, and creativity.

environmental uncertainty The ambiguity or unpredictability of certain factors in an organization's external environment (e.g., government regulation).

equal employment opportunity laws Laws intended to eliminate discrimination in employment. The basic principle is to ensure that job applicants and employees are judged solely on characteristics that are related to the work that they are being hired to do and on their job performance after being hired.

equity theory An approach to motivation that is concerned with individuals' beliefs about how fairly they're treated compared with their peers, based on their relative levels of inputs and outcomes.

ERG theory Alderfer's approach to motivation, which specifies a hierarchy of three needs categories: existence, relatedness, and growth.

esteem needs The desires for self-respect, a sense of personal achievement, and recognition from others.

ethics A set of rules and values that define right and wrong conduct.

exempt employees Employees who are not covered by the minimum wage and overtime provisions of the Fair Labor Standards Act.

existence needs The desires for material and physical well-being.

expectancy The belief that a given level of effort will lead to improved performance.

experienced meaningfulness The extent to which employees perceive their work to be valuable and worthwhile.

experienced responsibility The extent to which employees feel personally responsible for the quantity and quality of their work.

expert power Influence based on a leader's specialized knowledge.

export department An organizational unit that represents the interests of foreign customers to the firm's other departments and to top management, meets the increasing demand for services by foreign customers, makes special arrangements for customs clearance and international shipping, assists foreign customers in financing the goods that they are purchasing, and arranges for the collection of accounts receivable from foreign customers.

export manager An employee who actively searches out foreign markets for the firm's goods or services.

exporting strategy Maintaining facilities within a home country and transferring goods and services abroad for sale in foreign markets.

external system Organizational conditions and influences outside the team that exist before and after the team is formed, including societal and organizational culture, organization design, and the human resource management system.

extinction The absence of any reinforcement, either positive or negative, following the occurrence of a behavior. Usually, extinction occurs when the positive reinforcement that once normally resulted from the behavior is removed.

extortion A payment made to ensure that the recipient doesn't harm the payer in some way.

extranets Dynamic wide area networks that link a company's employees, suppliers, customers, and other key business partners in an electronic online environment for business communication.

extrapolation The projection of some tendency from the past or present into the future.

extrinsic rewards Outcomes supplied by the organization, such as a good salary, status, job security, and fringe benefits.

F

fairness principle A moral requirement that employees support the rules of the organization when certain conditions are met.

family business A business owned and managed mostly by people who are related by blood or marriage.

feedback (1) Information about a system's status and performance. (2) The receiver's response to the sender's message. (3) When employees receive direct and clear information about their work performance from the task itself or from others.

feelings The emotions that reflect how team members feel about each other, including anger, happiness, trust, and distrust.

femininity Hofstede's value dimension that measures the tendency to be nurturing and people oriented (the opposite of masculinity).

Fiedler's contingency model A model that suggests that successful leadership depends on matching a leader's style to a situation's demands.

financial controls A wide range of methods, techniques, and procedures intended to prevent the misallocation of financial resources.

firewall A combination of computer hardware and software that controls access to and transmission of particular sets of data and information, often referred to as a private network.

first-line managers Managers directly responsible for the production of goods or services.

focus strategy Competing in a specific industry niche to serve the unique needs of certain customers or a narrowly defined geographic market.

forecasting Predicting, projecting, or estimating future events or conditions in an organization's environment.

foreign conflict The degree of hostility one nation shows toward others.

forming stage The earliest stage of team development, at which the work team focuses on orientation to its goals and procedures.

forward integration Occurs when a company enters the businesses of its customers, moving it closer to the ultimate consumer.

framing A process whereby leaders define the purpose of their movement in highly meaningful terms for their followers.

franchise A business run by an individual (the franchisee) to whom a franchiser grants the right to market a certain good or service.

franchising strategy A parent organization (the franchiser) granting other companies or individuals (franchisees) the right to use its trademarked name and to produce and sell its goods or services.

free riding Not contributing fully to group performance because the team member can share in group rewards despite making less effort than the others.

frustration–regression hypothesis The idea that frustration in fulfilling a higher level need will result in the reemergence of the next lower level need as a motivator of behavior.

functional departmentalization The grouping of employees according to their areas of expertise and the resources they draw on to perform a common set of tasks.

functional foremanship A division of labor that assigns a set number of foremen to each work area, with each one being responsible for the workers in his line of expertise.

functional managers Managers who supervise employees having specialized skills in a single area of operation, such as accounting, personnel, payroll, finance, marketing, or production.

functional-level strategy The set of highly related commitments and actions intended to provide value and help an organization gain a competitive advantage through its operations (manufacturing), marketing, human resources, and finance.

functional work team Members from a single department or unit who jointly consider issues and solve problems common to their area of responsibility and expertise.

G

gambler's fallacy bias Believing that an unexpected number of similar chance events can lead to an event not seen.

Gantt chart A visual plan and progress report that identifies various stages of work that must be carried out in order to complete a project, sets deadlines for each stage, and documents accomplishments.

general environment External factors, such as inflation and demographics, that usually affect indirectly all or most organizations (also called the macroenvironment).

general goals Broad direction for decision making in qualitative terms.

general managers Managers responsible for the overall operations of a complex unit such as a company or a division.

generic strategies model A framework of three basic business-level strategies that can be applied to a variety of organizations in diverse industries.

global awareness competency Performing managerial work for an organization that utilizes human, financial, information, and material resources from multiple countries and serves markets that span multiple cultures.

global strategy Stressing worldwide consistency, standardization, and low relative cost.

goal-setting theory An approach to motivation that states that managers can direct the performance of their employees by assigning specific, difficult goals and providing feedback to employees about their progress in achieving those goals.

goals What an organization is committed to achieving.

grapevine An organization's informal communication system.

graphic rating method A type of performance appraisal that evaluates employees on a series of performance dimensions, usually along a 5- or 7-point scale.

grease payments Small payments—almost gratuities—used to get lower level government employees to speed up required paperwork.

green marketing Sale of products and services considered to be environmentally friendly, which makes the produc-

ing organizations environmentally responsible.

group Two or more individuals who come into personal and meaningful contact on a continuing basis.

group control The norms and values that group members share and maintain through rewards and punishments.

group decision support system (GDSS) A set of software, hardware, and language components that support a team of people engaged in decision making.

groupthink An agreement-at-any-cost mentality that results in an ineffective team decision-making process and may lead to poor solutions.

growth need strength A desire for personal challenges, a sense of accomplishment, and learning.

growth needs The desires to be creative, make useful and productive contributions, and have opportunities for personal development.

H

halo effect A rating error that occurs when knowledge of performance on one dimension colors the ratings on all others.

halo error Judging a candidate's overall potential on the basis of a single characteristic, allowing it to overshadow other characteristics.

Hawthorne effect A likely change in productivity, regardless of whether working conditions change, when employees are given special attention.

Hersey and Blanchard's situational leadership model A model that suggests that the levels of directive and supportive leader behaviors should be based on the readiness level of followers.

hierarchy of needs Maslow's approach to motivation suggests that people have a complex five-level set of needs, which they attempt to meet in sequence.

horizontal channels Communication paths that managers and employees use when communicating across departmental lines.

horizontal integration Occurs when a company acquires one or more competitors to consolidate and extend its market share.

House's path–goal model A model that indicates that effective leaders specify the task and clear roadblocks to task achievement, thereby increasing subordinates' satisfaction and job performance.

human resources management The philosophies, policies, and practices that

affect the people who work for an organization.

human resources planning Forecasting the organization's human resources needs and developing the steps to be taken to meet them.

hygiene factors Characteristics of the work environment outside the job that, when positive, maintain a reasonable level of job motivation but don't necessarily increase it.

I

impression management A leader's attempt to control the impressions that others form about the leader through practicing behaviors that make the leader more attractive and appealing to others.

incentive pay Pay that links at least a portion of pay to job performance to encourage superior performance.

incubator organization An organization that supports entrepreneurs.

indirect compensation Benefits that are required by law and those that are provided voluntarily by the employer.

individual differences The needs, values, competencies, and other personal characteristics that people bring to their jobs.

individual self-control The guiding mechanisms that operate consciously and unconsciously within each person.

individualism Hofstede's value dimension that measures the extent to which a culture expects people to take care of themselves and/or individuals believe that they are masters of their own destiny (the opposite of collectivism).

informal group A small number of people who frequently participate in activities and share feelings for the purpose of meeting their mutual needs.

information The knowledge derived from data that people have transformed to make them meaningful and useful.

information richness The information carrying capacity of a channel of communication.

information technologies (ITs) The computer-based electronic systems that help individuals and organizations assemble, store, transmit, process, and retrieve data and information.

initiating-structure leadership style Actively planning, organizing, controlling, and coordinating subordinates' activities.

innovation The process of creating and implementing a new idea.

innovative decisions Choices based on the discovery, identification, and diagnosis of unusual and ambiguous problems and the development of unique or creative alternative solutions.

inputs Physical, human, material, financial, and information resources that enter a transformation process.

instrumentality The perceived usefulness of performance as a means for obtaining desired outcomes (or avoiding undesired outcomes).

integrated order systems Connection of a customer's computer to suppliers' computers to permit orders to be placed at any time.

integration The measure of coordination among departments with respect to structure, tasks, and goals.

intermediate strategy Arranges the physical layout of equipment and the workforce so that they reflect some features of both the process focus and product focus.

internal processes The activities that enable a team to coordinate and integrate the efforts of team members, including the development of the team over time, personal feelings, and behavioral norms.

international corporation A firm having significant business interests that cut across national boundaries, often focusing on importing and exporting goods or services, and operates production and marketing units in other countries.

International Organization for Standardization (ISO) In Europe, an organization that issues certification standards for excellence in quality.

Internet A loosely configured, rapidly growing web of 25,000 corporate, educational, and research computer networks around the world.

intranets Private or semiprivate internally focused networks that use the infrastructure and standards of the Internet and the Web.

intrapreneur Someone in an existing organization who turns new ideas into profitable realities.

intrinsic rewards Personally satisfying outcomes, such as feelings of achievement and personal growth.

inventory control Setting and maintaining minimum, optimum, and maximum levels of inventory.

inventory costs The expenses associated with maintaining inventory, including ordering costs, carrying costs, shortage costs, and setup costs.

inventory The amount and type of raw materials, parts, supplies, and unshipped finished goods that an organization has on hand at any one time.

ISO 9000 A set of worldwide standards that establish requirements for the management of quality.

J

job analysis A breakdown of the tasks and responsibilities for a specific job and the personal characteristics, skills, and experience necessary for their successful performance.

job-based pay Compensation that is linked to the specific tasks a person performs.

job description An outline of a position's essential tasks and responsibilities.

job enrichment Changing job specifications to broaden and add challenge to the tasks required in order to increase productivity.

job simplification Scientific analysis of tasks performed in order to develop ways to produce the maximum output for the minimum input.

job specification A list of the personal characteristics, skills, and experience a worker needs to carry out a job's tasks and assume its responsibilities.

just-in-time system (JIT) The delivery of finished goods just-in-time to be sold, subassemblies just-in-time to be assembled into finished goods, parts just-in-time to go into subassemblies, and purchased materials just-in-time to be transformed into parts.

justice model Judging decisions and behavior by their consistency with an equitable, fair, and impartial distribution of benefits (rewards) and costs among individuals and groups.

K

key job characteristics Hackman and Oldham's view that the three critical psychological states are affected by five key job characteristics: skill variety, task identity, task significance, autonomy, and feedback.

knowledge Concepts, tools, and categories used to create, store, apply, and share information.

knowledge of results The extent to which employees receive feedback about how well they are doing.

L

language A shared system of vocal sounds, written signs, and/or gestures used to convey special meanings among members.

lateral relations An information processing strategy by which decision making is placed in the hands of those who have access to the information needed to make the decision.

law of small numbers bias Viewing a few incidents or cases as representative of a larger population (a few cases "prove the rule") even when they aren't.

laws Society's values and standards that are enforceable in the courts.

lead time The elapsed time between placing an order and receiving the finished goods or services.

leader–member exchange model Formulation by leaders of unique one-on-one relationships with followers.

leader–member relations The extent to which followers accept the leader.

leader–participation model A set of rules to determine the amount and form of participative decision making that should be encouraged in different situations.

leader position power The extent to which a leader has legitimate, coercive, and reward power.

leadership Influencing others to act toward the attainment of a goal.

leading The managerial function of communicating with and motivating others to perform the tasks necessary to achieve the organization's goals.

learned needs theory McClelland's approach to motivation, which specifies that people acquire three needs or motives—achievement, affiliation, and power—through interaction with their social environments.

learning organization Involvement of all employees in identifying and solving problems, thus enabling the organization continuously to experiment, improve, and increase its capacity to deliver new and improved goods or services to customers.

least preferred co-worker The employee with whom the manager can work least well.

legitimate power Influence based on the leader's formal position in the organization's hierarchy.

leniency A rating error that occurs when an individual rates all employees in a group higher than they deserve.

licensing strategy A firm (the licensor) in one country giving other domestic or foreign firms (licensees) the right to use a patent, trademark, technology, production process, or product in return for the payment of a royalty or fee.

lifestyle venture Often a small company designed to meet the founder's desire for independence, autonomy, and control.

line authority The right to direct and control the activities of subordinates who perform tasks essential to achieving organizational objectives.

listening Paying attention to a message, not merely hearing it.

lobbying An attempt to influence government decisions by providing officials with information on the anticipated effects of legislation or regulatory rulings.

M

machine controls The use of instruments to prevent and correct deviations from desired results.

macroculture A combination of the assumptions and values of both the society and industry in which the organization (or one of its business units) operates.

Malcolm Baldrige Quality Award The award created by the Malcolm Baldrige National Quality Improvement Act of 1987 to create standards for measuring total quality in both small and large service and manufacturing companies.

management Planning, organizing, leading, and controlling the people working in an organization and the ongoing set of tasks and activities they perform.

management by objectives A management technique whereby a manager and employee set objectives (goals) for the future. Both parties accept the objectives as appropriate, with the understanding that future performance evaluations and rewards will reflect the employee's progress in meeting the agreed-upon goals.

manager A person who allocates human, material, and information resources in pursuit of an organization's goals.

managerial competencies Clusters of knowledge, skills, behaviors, and attitudes that a manager needs to be effective in a wide range of managerial jobs and organizations.

managerial grid model A model that identifies five leadership styles, each combining different proportions of concern for production and concern for people.

market controls The use of data to monitor sales, prices, costs, and profits, to guide decisions, and to evaluate results.

market culture Values achievement of measurable and demanding goals, especially those that are financial and market-based.

market development strategy Seeking new markets for current products.

market penetration strategy Seeking growth in current markets with current products.

masculinity Hofstede's value dimension that measures the degree to which the acquisition of money and things is valued and a high quality of life for others is not (the opposite of femininity).

materials resource planning II system A widely used computerized information system for managing dependent demand inventories and scheduling stock replenishment orders.

matrix organization A design that combines the advantages of the functional and product structures to increase the ability of managers and other employees to process information.

measuring by attribute Evaluates product characteristics as acceptable or unacceptable. Measuring by attribute usually is easier than measuring by variable.

measuring by variable Assesses product characteristics for which there are quantifiable standards (length, diameter, height, weight, or temperature).

mechanistic organization An organization design in which activities are broken into specialized tasks and decision making is centralized at the top.

merit pay A permanent increase in base pay linked to an individual's performance during the preceding year.

message The verbal (spoken and written) symbols and nonverbal cues that represent the information that the sender wants to convey to the receiver.

middle managers Managers who receive broad, overall strategies and policies from top managers and translate them into specific goals and plans for first-line managers to implement.

mission An organization's current purpose or reason for existing.

modular corporation A company whose operating functions are performed by other companies.

monolithic organization Dominated by a single majority culture or subculture, and members of other cultures or subcultures are expected to adopt the norms and values of the majority.

moral principles General rules of acceptable behavior that are intended to be impartial.

moral rights model Judging decisions and behavior by their consistency with fundamental personal and group liberties and privileges.

motivation Any influence that brings out, directs, or maintains goal-directed behavior.

motivator factors Job characteristics that, when present, should create high levels of motivation.

multicultural organization An organization with a work-force that includes the full mix of cultures found in the population at large and is committed to utilizing fully their capabilities.

multidisciplinary work team Five to thirty employees from various functional areas and sometimes several organizational levels who collectively have specific goal-oriented tasks.

multidomestic strategy Adjusting products, services, and practices to individual countries or regions (for example, Pacific Rim versus Western Europe versus North America).

multinational corporation A firm that takes a worldwide approach to markets (customers), services, and products and has a global philosophy of doing business.

multiple scenarios Written descriptions of several possible futures.

N

narratives The unique stories, sagas, legends, and myths in a culture.

natural duty principle A moral requirement that decisions and behaviors be based on a variety of universal obligations.

need A strong feeling of deficiency that creates an uncomfortable tension.

negative reinforcement Engaging in behavior to avoid unpleasant consequences. Negative reinforcement causes the target behavior to be repeated.

negotiation The process by which two or more individuals or groups having both common and conflicting goals present and discuss proposals in an attempt to reach an agreement.

network form of organization A weblike structure that links several firms through strategic alliances.

network organization An organization that contracts some or all of its operating functions to other organizations and coordinates their activities through managers and other employees at its headquarters.

nonexempt employees Employees who are covered by the minimum wage and overtime provisions of the Fair Labor Standards Act.

nonroutine service technology Methods used by organizations operating in a complex and changing environment and serving customers or clients who are unaware of their needs or imprecise about their problems.

nonverbal messages The use of facial expressions, movements, body position, and physical contact (often called body language) to convey meaning.

norming stage The stage of team development at which team members become increasingly positive about the team as a whole, the other members as individuals, and what the team is doing. The rules of behavior that are widely shared and enforced by the members of the work team develop.

O

objective probability The likelihood that a specific outcome will occur, based on hard facts and numbers.

open system Interacts with the external environment.

operational goals What is to be achieved in quantitative terms, for whom, and within what time period.

operations management The systematic direction, control, and evaluation of the entire range of processes that transform inputs into finished goods or services.

organic controls Flexible authority, loose job descriptions, individual self-controls, and other informal methods of preventing and correcting deviations from desired behaviors and results.

organic organization An organization design that stresses teamwork, open communication, and decentralized decision making.

organization Any structured group of people brought together to achieve certain goals that the same individuals could not reach alone.

organization chart A diagram showing the reporting relationships of functions, departments, and individual positions within an organization.

organization culture The shared assumptions, values, and norms that characterize a particular organization.

organization design Determining the structure and authority relationships for an entire organization.

organization development A planned long-range behavioral science strategy for understanding, changing, and developing an organization's workforce in order to improve its effectiveness.

organizational change Any transformation in the design or functioning of an organization.

organizational control Formal rules and procedures for preventing and correcting deviations from plans and for pursuing goals.

organizational structure A formal system of working relationships that both separates and integrates tasks (clarifies who should do what and how efforts should be meshed).

organizing The managerial function of creating a structure of relationships to enable employees to carry out management's plans and meet its goals.

orientation A formal or informal introduction of new employees to their job responsibilities, their co-workers, and the organization's policies.

Osborn's creativity model A three-phase decision-making process that involves fact finding, idea finding, and solution finding.

outputs The original inputs (human, physical, material, information, and financial resources) as changed by a transformation process.

outsourcing Letting other organizations perform a service and/or manufacture parts or a product.

P

Pareto diagram A chart used to determine the relative priorities of issues, defects, or problems.

Pareto principle States that a small number of causes (usually 20 percent of the total) account for most of the problems (usually 80 percent of the total) in any situation.

partial-factor productivity The ratio of total outputs to a single input.

participative leadership Consulting with followers and asking for their suggestions.

perception The meaning ascribed to a message by a sender or receiver.

performance appraisal The process of systematically evaluating each employee's job-related strengths, developmental needs, and progress toward meeting goals and determining ways to improve the employee's job performance.

performance gap The difference between what the organization wants to do and what it actually does.

performance test A test that requires job candidates to perform simulated job tasks.

performing stage The stage of team development by which members usually have come to trust and accept each other, members are willing to risk presenting "wild" ideas without fear of being put down, and giving accurate feedback to each other helps focus the team on its tasks and goals.

personal communication services An emerging set of capabilities based on wireless equipment that will enable users to stay in touch with almost anyone, anytime, anywhere.

pert network A diagram showing the sequence and relationship of the activities and events needed to complete a project.

physiological needs The most basic human desires for food, clothing, and shelter.

place departmentalization The grouping of all functions for a geographic area at one location under one manager.

planning (1) Defining goals and proposing ways to reach them. (2) The formal process of choosing an organizational mission and overall goals for both the short run and long run; devising divisional, departmental, and even individual goals based on the organizational goals; formulating strategies and tactics to achieve those goals; and allocating resources (people, money, equipment, and facilities) to achieve the various goals, strategies, and tactics.

planning and administration competency Deciding the tasks that need to be done, determining how to do them, allocating resources to those tasks, and then monitoring progress to ensure that they are done.

pluralistic organization Employees are mixed in their cultural composition, but there is still a dominant culture or subculture that members of the organization are expected to adopt.

political climate The likelihood that a government will swing to the far left or far right politically.

political model A description of the decision-making process in terms of the particular interests and goals of powerful external and internal stakeholders.

political risk The probability that political decisions or events in a country will negatively affect the long-term profitability of an investment.

pooled interdependence The type of technological interdependence that involves little sharing of information or resources among individuals and departments.

positive reinforcement A pleasant consequence in the form of a reward to increase the likelihood that a behavior will be repeated.

power The ability to influence the behavior of others.

power distance Hofstede's value dimension that measures the degree to which influence and control are unequally distributed among individuals within a particular culture.

power motive An individual's desire to influence and control others and the social environment.

preventive controls Mechanisms intended to reduce errors and thereby minimize the need for corrective action.

principle of selectivity A small number of characteristics always account for a large number of effects (also known as Pareto's law).

probability The percentage of times that a specific outcome would occur if an individual were to make a particular decision a large number of times.

problem-solving work team Five to twenty employees from different areas of a department who consider how something can be done better.

product departmentalization The division of an organization into self-contained units, each capable of designing, producing, and marketing its own goods and/or services.

product development strategy Developing new or improved goods or services for current markets.

product differentiation Uniqueness in quality, price, design, brand image, or customer service that gives a product an edge over the competition.

product-focus strategy Arranges the physical layout of equipment and the workforce around a few outputs.

product life cycle model Identifies the market phases that products usually go through during their lifetimes.

production-centered leadership style Setting standards, organizing and paying close attention to employees' work, keeping production schedules, and stressing results.

productive controversy Valuing different points of view and seeking to draw them out to facilitate creative problem solving.

profit center An organizational unit that is accountable for both the revenues generated by its activities and the costs of those activities.

program evaluation and review technique (PERT) A method of scheduling the sequence of activities and events required to complete a project, estimating their costs, and controlling their progress.

project A one-time activity with a well-defined set of desired results.

project management The principles, methods, and techniques used to establish and implement a project and achieve its goals.

protectionism The mechanisms designed and used to help a home-based industry or firms avoid (or reduce) potential (or actual) competitive or political threats from abroad.

proxemics The study of ways that people use physical space to convey a message about themselves.

punishment An attempt to discourage a target behavior by the application of negative outcomes whenever it does occur. The purpose of punishment is to

reduce the likelihood that an individual will repeat the target behavior.

Q

quality How well a product does what it is supposed to do.

quality circle A group of employees from the same work area, or who perform similar tasks, who voluntarily meet regularly to identify, analyze, and propose solutions to problems in the workplace.

quality viewpoint Emphasizes achieving customer satisfaction through the provision of high-quality goods and services.

quota A restriction on the quantity of a country's imports (or sometimes, on its exports).

R

ranking method A type of performance appraisal that compares employees doing the same or similar work.

rater characteristics The personal attributes that a performance appraiser brings to the task, which often exert a subtle and indirect influence on performance appraisals.

ratio analysis Selecting two significant figures, expressing their relationship as a proportion or fraction, and comparing its value for two periods of time or with the same ratio for similar organizations.

rational model A series of steps that individuals or teams should follow to increase the likelihood that their decisions will be logical and well founded.

readiness A subordinate's ability to set high but attainable goals and a willingness to accept responsibility for reaching them.

realistic job preview A screening technique that clearly shows candidates a job's tasks or requirements.

receiver The person who receives and decodes (or interprets) the sender's message.

reciprocal interdependence The type of technological interdependence in which all individuals and departments are encouraged to work together and to share information and resources in order to complete a task.

recruitment The process of searching, both inside and outside the organization, for people to fill vacant positions.

reengineering Creating new ways to get work done, often involving redesigning the processes related to logistics, distribution, and manufacturing.

referent power Influence based on followers' personal identification with the leader.

reinforcement theory An approach to motivation that suggests that behavior is

a function of its consequences (rewards or punishments).

related-business firm Provides a variety of similar goods and/or services.

relatedness needs The desires to establish and maintain interpersonal relationships with other people.

relationship-oriented leader A person who recognizes the importance of developing strong and positive emotional ties with followers.

relevant labor market The geographic and skill areas in which an employer usually recruits to fill its positions.

replacement chart A diagram showing each position in the organization, along with the name of the person occupying the position and the names of candidates eligible to replace that person.

representation Membership in an outside organization for the purpose of furthering the interests of the member's organization.

resource allocation The earmarking of money, through budgets, for various purposes.

restructuring Reconfiguring the levels of authority, responsibility, and control in an organization.

reward power Influence stemming from a leader's ability to reward followers.

risk The condition under which individuals can define a problem, specify the probability of certain events, identify alternative solutions, and state the probability of each solution leading to the desired results.

rites and ceremonies Elaborate and formal activities designed to generate strong feelings and usually carried out as special events.

robots Reprogrammable, multifunctional machines. A robot's frame often is a substitute for the human arm, and its microprocessor (computer) takes the place of the human brain by providing instructions for routine and standardized tasks.

role perceptions Beliefs about what is required to do the job successfully, including both the specific tasks that an employee believes are part of the job and the attitudes and behaviors that an employee thinks are appropriate in terms of the organization's culture.

Ron Brown Award for Corporate Leadership A federal government award that recognizes demonstrated corporate leadership in employee and community relations.

routine decisions Standardized choices made in response to relatively well-defined and common problems and alternative solutions.

routine service technologies Methods used by organizations operating in relatively stable environments and serving customers who are relatively sure of their needs.

rules Specification of a course of action that must be followed in dealing with a particular problem.

S

satisfaction–progression hypothesis The idea that a lower level need must be reasonably satisfied before the next higher level need emerges as a motivator of behavior.

satisficing The practice of selecting an acceptable goal or alternative solution.

scalar principle The principle that states that a clear and unbroken chain of command should link every person in the organization with someone at a level higher, all the way to the top of the organization.

scapegoating The process of casting blame for problems or shortcomings on an innocent or only partially responsible individual, team, or department.

scenario A written description of a possible future.

scientific management Focuses on individual worker–machine relationships in manufacturing plants.

security needs The desires for safety and stability and the absence of pain, threat, and illness.

selective perception The process of screening out information that a person wants or needs to avoid.

selective perception bias Seeing what a person expects to see.

self-actualization needs The desires for personal growth, self-fulfillment, and the realization of the individual's full potential.

self-managed work teams Groups formed from workers and first-line managers who make decisions together to improve the way they do their jobs.

self-management competency Taking responsibility for your life at work and beyond.

self-managing work team Five to fifteen employees who work together daily to make an entire product or deliver an entire service.

semantics The study of the way words are used and the meanings they convey.

sender The source of information and initiator of the communication process.

sequential interdependence The type of technological interdependence in which the flow of information and resources between individuals and departments is serialized.

serial entrepreneur A person who founds and operates multiple companies during the course of a career.

shared assumptions Underlying thoughts and feelings that members of a culture take for granted and believe to be true.

sigma A unit of statistical measurement, which in this context is used to illustrate the quality of a process.

similarity error A bias in favor of candidates that look or act like the interviewer.

simulation A representation of a real system.

single-business firm Provides a limited number of goods or services to one segment of a particular market.

six sigma Eliminating defects to the level of 1 per 3.4 million opportunities—or a process that is 99.99966 percent defect free.

skill variety The degree to which the job involves many different work activities or requires several skills and talents.

skunkworks Islands of intrapreneurial activity within an organization.

slack resources Extra resources—materials, funds, and time—that an organization stockpiles in order to be able to respond to environmental changes.

small-business owner Someone who owns a major equity stake in a company with fewer than 500 employees.

social audit An attempt to identify, measure, evaluate, report on, and monitor the effects that an organization is having on its stakeholders and society.

socialization (1) The process by which people learn the values held by an organization or the broader society. (2) The systematic process by which new members are brought into a culture.

sociotechnical systems Consideration of the needs of both employee and organization in devising ways to satisfy customer demand.

span of control principle The principle that states that the number of people reporting directly to any one manager must be limited.

specialization The process of identifying particular tasks and assigning them to individuals or teams who have been trained to do them.

stable environment A setting characterized by few changes in products, technology, competitive forces, markets, and political forces.

staff authority The right to direct and control subordinates who support line activities through advice, recommendations, research, technical expertise, and specialized services.

staffing The process by which organizations meet their human resources needs, including forecasting future needs, recruiting and selecting candidates, and orienting new employees.

stages of moral development According to Kohlberg, people develop morally by going through six stages of moral development: obedience and punishment, instrumental, interpersonal, law and order, social contract, and universal principles.

stakeholder control Pressures from outside sources on organizations to change their behaviors.

stakeholders Individuals or groups that have interests, rights, or ownership in an organization or its activities.

standardization The uniform and consistent procedures that employees are to follow in doing their jobs.

standards Criteria against which qualitative and quantitative characteristics are evaluated.

statistical process control The use of statistical methods and procedures to determine whether transformation operations are being done correctly, to detect any deviations, and to find and eliminate their causes.

status A person's social rank in a group.

stereotyping Making assumptions about individuals solely on the basis of their belonging to a particular gender, race, age, or other group.

stock options The right given to an employee to buy the company's stock at a specified price.

storming stage The stage of team development that begins when competitive or strained behaviors emerge and may involve resistance and impatience with the lack of progress.

strategic action competency Understanding the overall mission and values of the company and ensuring that your actions and those of the people you manage are aligned with the company's mission and values.

strategic alliance Two or more firms agreeing to cooperate in a venture that is expected to benefit all the participants.

strategic business unit A division or subsidiary of a firm that provides a distinct product or service and often has its own mission and goals.

strategic planning The process of analyzing the organization's external and internal environments; developing the appropriate mission, vision, and overall goals; identifying the general strategies to be pursued; and allocating resources.

strategies The major courses of action that an organization takes to achieve its goals.

subjective probability The likelihood that a specific outcome will occur, based on personal judgment and beliefs.

subsidy A direct or indirect payment by a government to its country's firms to make selling or investing abroad cheaper for them—and thus more profitable.

substitute goods or services Goods or services that can easily replace other goods or services.

subsystem A component consisting of one or more parts of a system.

supporting style Sharing decision making when directive behavior no longer is required.

supportive behavior Reliance on two-way communication, listening, encouraging, and involving followers in decision making.

supportive leadership Being friendly and approachable and showing concern for followers' psychological well-being.

survey feedback An organization development method that allows managers and employees to provide feedback about the organization and receive feedback about their own behaviors.

sustainable development To conduct business in a way that protects the natural environment while making economic progress.

symbol Anything visible that can be used to represent an abstract shared value or something having special meaning.

system An association of interrelated and interdependent parts.

systems viewpoint Represents an approach to solving problems by diagnosing them within a framework of inputs, transformation processes, outputs, and feedback.

T

taboos Behaviors that are forbidden in a culture.

tactical planning The process of making detailed decisions about what to do, who will do it, and how to do it—with a normal time horizon of one year or less.

tariff A government tax on goods or services entering the country.

task environment External forces (e.g., customers or labor unions) that directly affect an organization's growth, success, and survival.

task identity The extent to which a job involves completing an identifiable piece of work, that is, doing a job with a visible beginning and outcome.

task-oriented leader A person who structures the job for employees and closely watches their behavior.

task significance The extent to which a job has a substantial impact on the goals or work of others in the company.

task structure The degree to which a job is routine.

team proximity The location of a team's members relative to the organization and relative to each other.

teamwork competency Accomplishing outcomes through small groups of people who are collectively responsible and whose work is interdependent.

technological interdependence The degree of coordination required between individuals and departments to transform information and raw materials into finished products and services.

technology (1) The method used to transform organizational inputs into outputs. (2) The tools, knowledge, techniques, and actions used to transform materials, information, and other inputs into finished goods and services.

tension That which causes a person to take actions to satisfy a need. Satisfying the need reduces the intensity of the motivating force.

Theory X A leadership style whereby leaders tell subordinates what's expected of them, instruct them in how to perform their jobs, insist that they meet certain standards, and make sure that everyone knows who's boss.

Theory Y A leadership style whereby leaders consult with their subordinates, seek their opinions, and encourage them to take part in planning and decision making.

360-degree appraisal system A performance review system that gathers feedback from an employee's colleagues inside the organization and from people outside the organization with whom the employee does business.

time-and-motion study Identifies and measures a worker's physical movements when performing a task and then analyzes the results.

top managers Managers who are responsible for the overall direction and operations of an organization.

total-factor productivity The ratio of total outputs to total inputs.

total quality management Organizational philosophy and strategy that makes quality a responsibility of all employees.

traditional quality control Product inspection during or at the end of the transformation process.

traditional viewpoint The oldest of the five principal viewpoints of management; stresses the manager's role in a strict hierarchy and focuses on efficient and consistent job performance.

training and development Activities aimed at helping employees overcome the limitations, current or anticipated, that are causing them to perform at less than the desired level.

traits Individual personality characteristics (e.g., the strength of various needs) that can affect a person's job performance.

traits models Leadership models based on the assumption that certain physical, social, and personal characteristics are inherent in leaders.

transformation processes The technologies used to convert inputs into outputs.

transformational leadership Leading by motivating. Key behaviors are vision, framing, and impression management.

turbulent environment An external environment that is complex, constantly changing, and both ambiguous and unpredictable.

turnkey manufacturing A process of designing, manufacturing, assembling, warehousing, and fulfilling customer orders for another organization.

two-factor theory Herzberg's approach to motivation, which states that distinct types of experiences produce job satisfaction (motivator factors) and job dissatisfaction (hygiene factors).

U

uncertainty The condition under which an individual does not have the necessary information to assign probabilities to the outcome of alternative solutions.

uncertainty avoidance Hofstede's value dimension that measures the degree to which individuals attempt to avoid the ambiguity, risk, and indefiniteness of the future.

union shop An organization whose agreement with a union stipulates that, as a condition of continued employment, all employees covered by the contract must already be or must become union members within a specified period of time.

unity of command principle The principle that states that an employee should have only one boss.

unrelated-business firm Provides diverse products (goods and/or services) to many different markets.

upward channels Communication paths that subordinates use to send information to superiors.

utilitarian model Judging the effect of decisions and behavior on others, with the primary goal of providing the greatest good for the greatest number of people.

V

valence The weight that a particular employee attaches to outcomes.

value (1) basic belief about a condition that has considerable importance and meaning to individuals and is stable over time. (2) The relationship between quality and price.

value system Multiple beliefs (values) that are compatible and supportive of one another.

vertical information system An information processing strategy that managers can use to send information efficiently up the organization.

virtual reality A surrogate environment created by communications and computer systems.

virtual team Any task-focused group that meets without all members necessarily being in the same room or even working at the same time.

virtual work team A work team that meets without everyone being physically present in the same place or even at the same time.

vision An organization's fundamental aspirations and purpose that usually appeals to its members' hearts and minds.

voice recognition systems Methods of analyzing and classifying speech or vocal tract patterns and converting them into digital codes for entry and retrieval through computer software.

W

whistle-blowers Employees who report unethical or illegal actions of their employers to management, external stakeholders, or the public.

work team A small number of identifiable, interdependent employees who are held accountable for performing tasks that contribute to the achievement of organizational goals.

workforce diversity A term that refers to the mix of people in terms of gender, age, race, and various ethnic backgrounds in today's labor force.

Z

zone of indifference responsibility An employee's obligation to perform assigned tasks.

ENDNOTES

CHAPTER 1

[1]Adapted from D. Packard. *The HP Way: How Bill Hewlett and I Built Our Company.* New York: HarperBusiness, 1995; L. Gomes. H-P to unveil digital camera and peripherals. *Wall Street Journal,* February 25, 1997, p. B6; G. C. Rogers. *Human Resources at Hewlett-Packard (A).* Harvard Business School, November 1, 1995; J. C. Collins and J. I. Porras. *Built to Last: Successful Habits of Visionary Companies.* New York: HarperBusiness, 1997; and Hewlett-Packard company Web site: www.hp.com:80/abouthp/hpway.html (May 14, 1997).

[2]Our definition of managerial competencies is adapted from definitions provided by S. B. Parry. The Quest for Competencies. *Training,* July 1996, pp. 48–56; American Society for Training and Development. *Models for HRD Practice.* Alexandria, Va.: ASTD, 1996; E. E. Lawler III and G. E. Ledford, Jr. New approaches to organizing: Competencies, capabilities, and the decline of the bureaucratic model. In C. L. Cooper and S. E. Jackson (eds.), *Creating Tomorrow's Organizations: A Handbook for Future Research in Organizational Behavior.* London: John Wiley & Sons, 1997; The American Compensation Association's Competency Research Team. The role of competencies in an integrated HR strategy. *ACA Journal,* Summer, 1996, pp. 6–20; The Hay Group. *People, Performance, & Pay.* New York: Free Press, 1996; and The Career Planning Competency Model developed by Bowling Green State University, as described at its Web site: www.bgsu. edu/offices/careers/process/competen.html (February 20, 1997).

[3]The list integrates the competencies identified in several sources: B. B. Allred, C. C. Snow, and R. E. Miles. Characteristics of managerial careers in the 21st century. *Academy of Management Executive,* 10(4), 17–27; H. Axel. *HR Executive Review: Redefining the Middle Manager.* New York: The Conference Board, 1995; Personnel Decisions, Inc. *Management Skills Profile.* Minneapolis, Minn., 1997; Personnel Decisions, Inc. *Executive Success Profile.* Minneapolis, Minn., 1997; Center for Creative Leadership. *Skillscope.* Greensboro, N.C., 1992; Center for Creative Leadership. *Benchmarks.* Greensboro, N.C., 1990; and D. T. Hall. Protean careers of the 21st century. *Academy of Management Executive,* 10, 1996, pp. 8–16.

[4]S. Elliott. Fresh from London, Saatchi & Saatchi's new chief executive in the U.S. is off to a fast start. *New York Times,* March 19, 1997, p. D6.

[5]W. M. Carley. Charging ahead: To keep GE's profits rising, Welch pushes quality control plan. *Wall Street Journal,* January 13, 1997, pp. A1, A8. Also see GE's home page at www.ge.com.

[6]Adapted from BE automobile dealer of the year. *Black Enterprise,* June 1993, pp. 123–129.

[7]J. M. Kouzes and B. Z. Posner. *The Leadership Challenge.* San Francisco: Jossey-Bass, 1995.

[8]D. Katz. *Just Do It: The Nike Spirit in the Corporate World.* New York: Random House, 1994.

[9]J. Kaufman. In name only: For Richard Thibeault, being a "manager" is a blue-collar life. *Wall Street Journal,* October 1, 1996, pp. A1, A12; H. Lancaster. New managers get little help tackling big, complex jobs, *Wall Street Journal,* February 10, 1998, p. B1.

[10]K. Serrano. Teller who climbed to top, Harding rises with PNB. *Hunterdon County* (New Jersey) Democrat, March 20, 1997, p. A23.

[11]M. Heinzl. Bre-X probe intensifies as tests find little gold. *Wall Street Journal,* May 6, 1997, p. A3.

[12]A. Taylor III. Toyota's boss stands out in a crowd. *Fortune,* November 25, 1996, pp. 116–122.

[13]John Burson does it all. *Ft. Lauderdale Sun-Sentinel,* January 24, 1994.

[14]M. A. Campion, L. Cheraskin, and M. J. Stevens. Career-related antecedents and outcomes of job rotation. *Academy of Management Journal,* 37, 1994, pp. 1518–1542.

[15]M. A. Quinones, J. K. Ford, and M. S. Teachout. The relationship between work experience and job performance: A conceptual meta-analytic review. *Personnel Psychology,* 48, 1995, pp. 887–910.

[16]For a comparison of the social networks of managers and nonmanagers, see G. R. Carroll and A. C. Teo. On the social networks of managers. *Academy of Management Journal,* 39, 1996, pp. 421–440.

[17]I. Y. M. Yeung and R. L. Tung. Achieving business success in Confucian societies: The importance of Guanxi (Connections). *Organizational Dynamics,* Autumn 1996, pp. 54–65; K. R. Xin and J. L. Pearce. Guanxi: Connections as substitutes for formal institutional support. *Academy of Management Journal,* 39, 1996, pp. 1641–1658.

[18]M. Siconolfi. Some merger bankers insist they want "relationships." *Wall Street Journal,* February 26, 1997, pp. C1, C2.

[19]R. Fisher, W. Ury, and B. Patton. *Getting to Yes: Negotiating Agreement Without Giving In,* 2d ed. New York: Penguin, 1991.

[20]C. L. Gonzalez. Desktop video interviewing brings a more diversified job market to Stern. *The Opportunity* (New York University), March 3, 1997, p. 5.

[21]S. Branch. So much work, so little time. *Fortune,* February 3, 1997, pp. 115–117.

[22]*The Hay Report: Compensation and Benefits Strategies for 1997 and Beyond.* Philadelphia: The Hay Group, 1996.

[23]An excellent source on designing teams is S. A. Mohrman and A. M. Mohrman, Jr. *Designing and Leading Team-based Organizations: A Workbook for Organizational Self-design.* San Francisco: Jossey-Bass, 1997. Also see H. Mintzberg, D. Dougherty, J. Jorgensen, and F. Westley. Some surprising things about collaboration—knowing how people connect makes it work better. *Organizational Dynamics,* Spring 1996, pp. 60–71; Outlook on teams. *Bulletin to Management,* March 20, 1997, pp. 92–94; and K. R. Xin and J. L. Pearce. Guanxi: Connections as substitutes for formal institu-

tional support. *Academy of Management Journal,* 39, 1996, pp. 1641–1658.

[24]J. M. Liedtka. Collaborating across lines of business for competitive advantage. *Academy of Management Executive,* 10, 1996, pp. 20–37.

[25]J. Vitullo-Martin. How a hot business keeps its sizzle. *Wall Street Journal,* March 24, 1997, p. A18.

[26]W. B. Wriston. The state of American management. *Harvard Business Review,* January–February 1990, pp. 78–83.

[27]For information about other factors that contribute to success in overseas assignments, see W. Arthur, Jr., and W. Bennett, Jr. The international assignee: The relative importance of factors perceived to contribute to success. *Personnel Psychology,* 48, 1995, pp. 99–114; T. Brake and D. Walker. *Doing Business Internationally.* Princeton, N.J.: Princeton Training Press; and G. M. Spreitzer, M. W. McCall, Jr., and J. D. Mahoney. Early identification of international executive potential. *Journal of Applied Psychology,* 82, 1997, 5–29.

[28]M. Waldrop. The trillion-dollar vision of Dee Hock. *Fast Company,* October/November 1996, pp. 75–86.

[29]D. Bartram, P. A. Lindley, L. Marshall, and J. Foster. The recruitment and selection of young people by small businesses. *Journal of Occupational and Organizational Psychology,* 68, 1995, pp. 339–358; and T. Teal. The human side of management. *Harvard Business Review,* November–December 1996, pp. 35–44.

[30]K. Freiberg and J. Freiberg. *Nuts! Southwest Airlines' Recipe for Business and Personal Success.* Austin, Tex.: Bard Press, 1996.

[31]S. Branch. MBAs are hot again—and they know it. *Fortune,* April 14, 1997, pp. 155–157.

[32]For an excellent description of the challenges faced by working couples with families, see B. Morris. Is your family wrecking your career? (and vice versa). *Fortune,* March 17, 1997, pp. 71–90. Also see S. Zedeck (ed.). *Work, Families, and Organizations.* San Francisco: Jossey-Bass, 1992; and Focus: Work and family. *Wall Street Journal,* March 31, 1997 (special supplement).

[33]D. T. Hall and Associates. *The Career Is Dead—Long Live the Career: A Relational Approach.* San Francisco: Jossey-Bass, 1996.

[34]R. G. Jones and M. D. Whitmore. Evaluating developmental assessment centers as interventions. *Personnel Psychology,* 48, 1995, pp. 377–388; P. Warr and D. Bunce. Trainee characteristics and the outcomes of open learning. *Personnel Psychology,* 48, 1995, pp. 347–375. Also see M. W. Daudelin. Learning from experience through reflection. *Organization Dynamics,* 24, 1997, pp. 36–48. E. Van Velsor and J. B. Leslie. Why executives derail: Perspectives across time and cultures. *Academy of Management Executive,* 9, 1995, pp. 62–72.

[35]Adapted from T. Aeppel. The favorite: Picked by her father, tough daughter runs building supply chain. *Wall Street Journal,* April 24, 1997, pp. A1, A12; M. H. Magerko. Message from the President. *84 Pro News,* April 1997

(www.84lumber.com/pres0497.html); and History of 84 Lumber (see the company home page at www.84lumber. com/history).

[36]M. V. Uzumeri. ISO 9000 and other meta-standards: Principles for management practice? *Academy of Management Executive,* 11 (1), 1997, pp. 21–36.

[37]G. H. Axel. *HR Executive Review: Redefining the Middle Manager.* New York: The Conference Board, 1995.

[38]S. A. Mohrman and A. M. Mohrman, Jr.; K. B. Evans and H. P. Sims, Jr. Mining for innovation: The conceptual underpinnings, history, and diffusion of self-directed teams. In C. L. Cooper and S. E. Jackson (eds.), *Creating Tomorrow's Organizations: A Handbook for Future Research in Organizational Behavior.* Chichester, England: John Wiley & Sons, 1997, pp. 269–292. G. M. Parker. *Cross-Functional Teams.* San Francisco: Jossey-Bass, 1994; and C. C. Manz and H. P. Sims, Jr. *Business Without Bosses.* New York: John Wiley & Sons, 1994.

[39]G. Dess, A. M. A. Rasheed, K. J. McKaughlin, and R. L. Priem. The new corporate architecture. *Academy of Management Executive,* 9 (3), 1995, pp. 7–20.

[40]Adapted from M. E. McGill and J. W. Slocum, Jr. *The Smarter Organization.* New York: John Wiley & Sons, 1994.

[41]J. S. Harrison and C. H. St. John. Managing and partnering with external stakeholders. *Academy of Management Executive,* 10, 1996, pp. 46–60.

[42]M. Brannigan and J. Cole. Delta to buy all its planes from Boeing Co. *Wall Street Journal,* March 20, 1997, p. B2.

[43]J. P. Liebeskind, A. L. Oliver, L. Zucker, and M. Brewer. Social networks, learning, and flexibility: Sourcing scientific knowledge in new biotechnology firms. *Organization Science,* 7, 1996, pp. 428–443.

[44]E. Schonfeld. Merck vs. the biotech industry: Which one is more potent? *Fortune,* March 31, 1997, pp. 161–162; and I. Sager. The new biology of big business. *Business Week,* April 15, 1996, p. 19.

[45]D. Stipp. Gene chip breakthrough. *Fortune,* March 31, 1997, pp. 56–73.

[46]L. M. Fisher. Novell selects Internet guru to lead struggling company. *New York Times,* March 1, 1997, pp. D1, D8.

[47]B. B. Buchholz. Slow gains for women who would be partners. *New York Times,* June 23, 1996, p. B1.

[48]S. Caudron. Don't make Texaco's $174 million mistake. *Workforce,* March 1997, pp. 58–66.

[49]T. Cox, Jr., and R. L. Tung. The multicultural organization revisited. In C. L. Cooper and S. E. Jackson (eds.), *Creating Tomorrow's Organizations: A Handbook for Future Research in Organizational Behavior.* London: John Wiley & Sons, 1997, pp. 7–28; and T. Cox. The multicultural organization. *Academy of Management Executive,* 5, 1991, pp. 34–47.

[50]M. J. Mandel. The new business cycle. *Business Week,* March 31, 1997, pp. 56–68.

[51]H. Lancaster. Technology raises bar for sales jobs: Know your dress code. *Wall Street Journal,* January 21, 1997, p. B1.

[52]B. Hesketh and A. Neal. Technology and performance. In D. R. Ilgen and E. D. Pullakos

(eds.), *The Changing Nature of Work Performance.* San Francisco: Jossey-Bass, 1998; and C. Hakim. *We Are All Self-Employed,* San Francisco: Berrett-Koehler, 1994.

[53]B. Vlasic. In Alabama, the soul of a new Mercedes? *Business Week,* March 31, 1997, pp. 70–71.

[54]N. Adler and S. Bartholomew. Managing globally competent people. *Academy of Management Executive,* 6, 1992, pp. 52–65.

[55]International assignments. *Bulletin to Management,* February 8, 1996, pp. 44–45.

[56]Adapted from The Microsoft Web site at www.microsoft. com (May 20, 1997); R. Stross, *The Microsoft Way.* New York: Addison-Wesley, 1996; B. Schlender. Software hardball. *Fortune,* September 30, 1996, pp. 107–116; D. Kirkpatrick. He wants all your business and he's starting to get it. *Fortune,* May 26, 1997, pp. 58–81; and K. Ballen and J. E. Davis. What Bill Gates really wants. *Fortune,* January 16, 1995, pp. 35–63.

CHAPTER 2

[1]Adapted from S. Sherman. Levi's: As ye sew, so shall ye reap. *Fortune,* May 12, 1997, pp. 104-116; R. Spevack. Levi Strauss still reinventing itself. *Daily News Record,* December 13, 1996, pp. 8–9; and Incentive plan is unveiled, linking bonuses to goals. *Wall Street Journal,* June 13, 1996, p. B4.

[2]M. Weber. *The Theory of Social and Economic Organization,* trans. by M. A. Henderson and T. Parsons. New York: Free Press, 1947. Also see D. A. Wren. Management history: Issues and ideas for teaching and research. *Journal of Management,* 13, 1987, pp. 239–250.

[3]Interview with N. L. Attaway, Human Resource Development Manager, June, 1997, Dallas,Texas.

[4]R. P. Hummel. *The Bureaucratic Experience.* New York: St. Martins, 1987.

[5]M. J. Tyre. The situated nature of adaptive learning in organizations. *Organization Science,* 8, l997, pp. 71–83; and C. Gresov and R. Drazin. Equifinality: Functional equivalence in organization design. *Academy of Management Review,* 22, 1997, pp. 403–428.

[6]F. W. Taylor. *Scientific Management.* New York: Harper & Row, 1947, pp. 66–71.

[7]Adapted from Trouble afoot. *Dallas Morning News,* February 15, 1997, p. 24A.

[8]H. Koontz. The management theory jungle revisited. *Academy of Management Review,* 5, 1980, pp. 175–188.

[9]L. J. Krajewski, and L. P. Ritzman. *Operations Management: Strategy and Analysis,* 5th ed. Reading, Mass.: Addison-Wesley, 1997.

[10]H. Fayol. *General and Industrial Management.* London: Pitman and Sons, 1949.

[11]U. M. Apte and C. C. Reynolds. Quality management at Kentucky Fried Chicken. *Interfaces,* 25(3), 1995, pp. 6–21.

[12]M. P. Follett. *Prophet of Management.* Boston: Harvard Business School Press, 1995.

[13]Adapted from J. Reed and R. Cunningham. *Team Member General Information Guidebook.* Austin, Tex.: Whole Foods Market, 1993.

[14]C. Barnard. *The Functions of the Executive.* Cambridge. Mass.: Harvard University Press,

1938.

[15]Adapted from T. B. Kinni. *America's Best: Industry Weeks' Guide to World-Class Manufacturing Plants.* New York: John Wiley & Sons, 1996, pp. 211–213.

[16]E. Mayo. *The Social Problems of an Industrial Civilization,* Boston: Harvard Business School, 1945.

[17]S. L. Robinson. Trust and breach of the psychological contract. *Administrative Science Quarterly,* 41, 1996, pp. 574–599; and E. W. Morrison and S. L. Robinson. When employees feel betrayed: A model of how psychological contract violation develops. *Academy of Management Review,* 22, 1997, pp. 226–259.

[18]R. E. Markland, S. K. Vickery, and R. A. Davis. *Operations Management Concepts in Manufacturing and Service,* 2d ed. Cincinnati: South-Western, 1998.

[19]Adapted from G. Imperato. Harley shifts gears. *Fast Company,* June-July, 1997, pp. 104–115.

[20]F. G. Hilmer and L. Donaldson. *Management Redeemed.* New York: Free Press, 1996.

[21]H. Tosi, Jr. *The Environment/Organization Person Contingency Model: A Meso Approach to the Study of Organizations.* Greenwich, Conn.: JAI Press, 1992; and K. Crowston. A coordination theory approach to organizational process design. *Organization Science,* 8(2), 1997, pp. 157–175. For an excellent review of the contingency variables that influence an organization's design, see G. P. Huber and W. H. Glick. *Organizational Change and Redesign.* New York: Oxford University Press, 1993.

[22]J. Woodward. *Industrial organization: Theory and practice.* London: Oxford University Press, 1980.

[23]F. McInerney and S. White. *The Total Quality Corporation.* New York: Penguin, 1997.

[24]C. C. Manz and G. L. Stewart. Attaining flexible stability by integrating total quality management and socio-technical systems theory. *Organization Science,* 8(1), 1997, pp. 59–70.

[25]M. Walton. *The Deming Method.* New York: Dodd Mead, 1986; J. A. Byrne. Remembering Deming, the godfather of quality. *Business Week,* January 10, 1994, p. 45; and B. A. Spencer. Models of organization and total quality management: A comparison and critical evaluation. *Academy of Management Review,* 19, 1994, pp. 446–471.

[26]J. L. Heskett, W. E. Sasser, Jr., and L. A. Schlesinger. *The Service Profit Chain.* New York: Free Press, 1997.

[27]T. Y. Choi and O. C. Behling. Top managers and TQM success: One more look after all these years. *The Academy of Management Executive,* 11, 1997, pp. 37–47.

[28]T. B. Kinni. *America's Best: Industry Week's Guide to World-Class Manufacturing Plants.* New York: John Wiley & Sons, 1996, pp. 274–276.

[29]Adapted from J. Steinhauer. Squeezing into the jeans market. *New York Times,* March 14, 1997, pp. C1ff; Guess, Inc: Labor union files unfair practices suit with National Labor Relations Board. *Wall Street Journal,* January 17, 1997, p. B7; M. Hornblower. Guess gets out? *Time,* January 27, 1997, pp. 48-49; and R. Behar. Guess: What's behind the IPO? *Fortune,* October 14, 1996, pp. 134–142.

CHAPTER 3

[1]Adapted from A. Moore. There's gold in going green. *Fortune,* April 14, 1997, 116–118. For more information, visit the EPA home page at www.epa.gov/globalwarming/home.html.

[2]W. A. McEachern. *Economics: A Contemporary Introduction.* Cincinnati: International Thomson Publishing, 1997, p. 2.

[3]M. V. Russo and P. A. Fouts. A resource-based perspective on corporate environmental performance and profitability. *Academy of Management Journal,* 40, 1997, pp. 534-559.

[4]Cairncross, F. *Costing the Earth: The Challenge for Governments, The Opportunities for Business.* Boston: Harvard Business School Press, 1992.

[5]For data on demographics, visit the home page at www.census.gov; and G. N. Powell and D. A. Butterfield. Effect of race on promotions to top management in a federal department. *Academy of Management Journal,* 40, 1997, pp. 112–128; and A. Haley, E. Fagenson-Eland, and J. Sonnenfield. Does the cream always rise to the top? *Organizational Dynamics,* Fall 1997, pp. 65–72.

[6]For additional information, visit Univision's home page at www.cisneros.com/companies/broadcast/univision.html.

[7]J. Waldrop. Career opportunities to 2005. *American Demographics,* March 1997, pp. 2ff.

[8]T. H. Cox, Jr., and R. L. Beale. *Developing Competency to Manage Diversity.* San Francisco: Berrett-Koehler, 1997.

[9]A. Harriman. *Women/Men/Management.* Westport, Conn.: Greenwood, 1996.

[10]R. J. Mockler and D. G. Dologite. *Multinational Cross-Cultural Management.* Westport, Conn.: Greenwood, 1997.

[11]N. J. Adler. *International Dimensions of Organizational Behavior,* 3d ed. Cincinnati: South-Western, 1997.

[12]R. Schuler, S. Jackson, E. F. Jackofsky, and J. W. Slocum. Managing human resources in Mexico: A cultural understanding. *Business Horizons,* May–June 1996, pp. 1–7; and C. R. Greer and G. K. Stephens. Employee relations issues for U.S. companies in Mexico. *California Management Review,* 38(3), 1996, pp. 121–145.

[13]G. Hofstede. *Culture's Consequences: International Differences in Work-Related Values.* London: Sage, 1980; and G. Hofstede and M. H. Bond. The Confucian connection: From cultural roots to economic growth. *Organizational Dynamics,* Spring, 1988, pp. 4–21.

[14]G. Hofstede. National cultures in four dimensions: A research-based theory of cultural dimensions among nations. *International Studies of Management and Organization,* 13, 1983, pp. 46–74; J. W. Slocum and D. Lei. Designing global strategic alliances: Integrating cultural and economic factors. In G. Huber and Wm. Glick (eds.), *Organizational Change and Redesign.* New York: Oxford University Press, 1993, pp. 295–322; and M. Erez and A. Somech. Is group productivity loss the rule or the exception? Effects of culture and group-based motivation. *Academy of Management Journal,* 39, 1996, pp. 1513–1537.

[15]Adapted from G. Flynn. Lilly's roots—from U.S. to foreign soil. *Personnel Journal,* September 1996, pp. 46–56.

[16]R. A. D'Aveni. *Hypercompetition: Managing the Dynamics of Strategic Maneuvering.* New York: Free Press, 1994.

[17]R. B. Duncan. What is the right organization structure: A decision tree analysis provides the answer. *Organizational Dynamics,* Winter 1979, pp. 63–69.

[18]P. Stein. Hong Kong business and labor unions, united under U.K. rule, now face rifts. *Wall Street Journal,* July 2, 1997, p. A10.

[19]www.columbia.net/consumer/datafile/boomheal.html

[20]G. Hamel and C. K. Prahalad. *Competing for the Future.* Boston: Harvard Business School Press, 1994.

[21]R. A. D'Aveni. *Hypercompetition.* New York: Free Press, 1994.

[22]N. N. Carter. Small firms adaptation: Responses of physicians' organizations to regulatory and competitive uncertainty. *Academy of Management Journal,* 33, 1990, pp. 106–128; and D. H. Maister. *Managing the Professional Service Firm.* New York: Free Press, 1993.

[23]M. E. Porter. *Competitive Strategy: Techniques for Analyzing Industries and Competitors.* New York: Free Press, 1980.

[24]B. D. Henderson. The anatomy of competition. *Journal of Marketing,* Spring 1983, pp.7–11.

[25]M. E. Porter. *Michael Porter on Competition.* Boston: Harvard Business School Press, 1998.

[26]M. Chen and D. C. Hambrick. Speed, stealth, and selective attack: How small firms differ from large firms in competitive behavior. *Academy of Management Journal,* 38, 1995, pp. 453–482; J. A. Baum and H. J. Korn. Competitive dynamics of interfirm rivalry. *Academy of Management Journal,* 39, 1996, pp. 255–291; and D. Miller and M. Chen. Sources and consequences of competitive inertia: A study of the U.S. airline industry. *Administrative Science Quarterly,* 39, 1994, pp. 1–23.

[27]To learn more about this merger, consultant Boeing's home page at www.boeing.com.

[28]W. Boeker. Strategic change: The influence of managerial characteristics and organizational growth. *Academy of Management Journal,* 40, 1997, pp. 152–170; and W. P. Barnett. The dynamics of competitive intensity. *Administrative Science Quarterly,* 42, 1997, pp. 128–160.

[29]R. N. Osborn and J. Hagedoorn. The institutionalization and evolutionary dynamics of interorganizational alliances and networks. *Academy of Management Journal,* 40, 1997, pp. 261–278.

[30]K. Singh. The impact of technological complexity and interfirm survival on business survival. *Academy of Management Journal,* 40, 1996, pp. 339–368; and B. R. Nault. Mitigating underinvestment through an IT-enabled organizational form. *Organization Science,* 8, 1997, pp. 223–234.

[31]Adapted from S. Stibbens. A sizable undertaking. *Texas Business,* January 1997, pp. 58–60; A. B. Henderson. Black funeral homes fear a gloomy future as big chains move in. *Wall Street Journal,* July 18, 1997, pp. A1ff; and E. Larson. Fight to the death. *Time,* December 6, 1996, pp. 62–67.

[32]M. Iansiti and J. West. Technology integration: Turning great research into great products. *Harvard Business Review,* May–June 1997, pp. 69–82.

[33]K. Schoenberger. Motorola bets big on China. *Fortune,* May 27, 1996, pp. 116–123.

[34]Adapted from Schoenberger.

[35]D. A. Schuler. Corporate political strategy and foreign competition: The case of the steel industry. *Academy of Management Journal,* 39, 1996, pp. 720-737.

[36]R. L. Pinkley. The impact of knowledge regarding alternatives to settlement in a dyadic negotiation: Whose knowledge counts? *Journal of Applied Psychology,* 80, 1995, pp. 403–417; and R. L. Pinkley and D. M. VandeWalle. Only the phantom knows: Impact of certain, conditional, unspecified, and zero alternatives to settlement in dyadic negotiations. *Academy of Management Journal,* 41, 1998 (in press).

[37]Adapted from J. H. Birnbaum. Tobacco's can of worms. *Fortune,* July 21, 1997, pp. 58–60; and P. Seller. Geoff Bible won't quit. *Fortune,* July 21, 1997, pp. 62–65.

[38]D. R. Dalton, M. B. Metzger, and J. W. Hill. The new corporate sentencing commission guidelines: A wakeup call for corporate America. *Academy of Management Executive,* 8, 1994, pp. 7–17.

[39]For additional information on AARP, visit its home page at www.aarp.org/index.html.

[40]D. Lei, J. W. Slocum, and R. A. Pitts. Building cooperative advantage: Managing strategic alliances to promote organizational learning. *Journal of World Business,* 32, 1997, pp. 203–223.

[41]H. G. Barkema, O. Shenkar, F. Vermeulen, and J. H. J. Bell. Working abroad, working with others: How firms learn to operate international joint ventures. *Academy of Management Journal,* 40, 1997, pp. 426–442; and C. C. Baughn, J. G. Denekamp, J. H. Stevens, and R. N. Osborn. Protecting intellectual capital in international alliances. *Journal of World Business,* 32, 1997, pp. 103–117.

[42]E. J. Zajac and J. D. Westphal. Director reputation, CEO-board power, and the dynamics of board interlocks. *Administrative Science Quarterly,* 41, 1996, pp.507–529.

[43]Personal conversation with S. Kerr, Vice President, Organizational Learning, General Electric Company, July 1997.

[44]Adapted from M. A. Hitt, R. D. Ireland, and R. E. Hoskisson. *Strategic Management: Competitiveness and Globalization,* 2d ed. Cincinnati: South-Western, 1997, pp. C105–C118; and sbweb3.med.iacnet.com/infotrac/session.

CHAPTER 4

[1]Adapted from E. W. Desmond. What's ailing Kodak? Fuji. *Fortune,* October 27, 1997, pp. 185–192; J. Flanigan. Kodak preparing for fight of its life. *Houston Chronicle,* September 22, 1997, p. C1; J. Greenwald. Kodak's bad moment. *Time.* September 29, 1997, pp. 40–41; and M. Maremont and W. M. Bulkeley. Kodak to slash 10,000 jobs, take charge. *Wall Street Journal,* November 12, 1997, pp. A3, A6.

[2]J. Hazelton. Clinton must mobilize those who will benefit from freer-trade pacts. *Bryan-Col-*

lege Station Eagle, November 2, 1997, p. E3; and D. Baron. Integrated strategy, trade policy, and global competition. *California Management Review,* Winter 1997, 145–169.

[3]T. A. Stewart. Welcome to the revolution. *Fortune,* December 13, 1993, pp. 66–77.

[4]C. Farrell. The triple revolution. *Business Week. 21st Century Capitalism,* 1997, p. 24.

[5]T. A. Stewart, pp. 16–25.

[6]Adapted from L. A. Wilson. *Eight-Step Process to Successful ISO 9000 Implementation: A Quality Management System Approach.* Milwaukee: ASQC, 1996; and R. M. Smith. ISO 9000: A value-adding process. *Quality Digest,* January 1996, pp. 31–34.

[7]D. Sullivan. Measuring the degree of internationalization of a firm. *Journal of International Business Studies,* 25, 1994, pp. 325–342.

[8]A. Farnham. Global or just globaloney? *Fortune,* June 27, 1994, pp. 97–100.

[9]J. D. Daniel and L. H. Radebaugh. *International Business: Environments and Operations,* 7th ed., rev. Reading, Mass.: Addison-Wesley, 1997.

[10]Superintendent of Documents. *A Basic Guide to Exporting.* Pittsburgh: U.S. Department of Commerce, 1997.

[11]M. Whigham-Desir. Ship it! *Black Enterprise,* May 1997, p. 10.

[12]K. Fatehi. *International Management: A Cross Cultural and Functional Perspective.* Upper Saddle River, N.J.: Prentice-Hall, 1996.

[13]D. Faulkner and S. Segal-Horn. *Principles of International Strategy.* Boston: International Thomson Press, 1997.

[14]H. Banks. Stomach share. *Forbes,* November 18, 1996, pp. 184–186; and M. L. Clifford and N. Harris. Coke pours into Asia. *Business Week,* October 28, 1996, pp. 72–75.

[15]R. D. Robinson, J. P. Dickson, and J. A. Knutsen. From multinational to transnational. *International Executive,* January–February 1997, pp. 35–54.

[16]E. W. Desmond, pp. 185–192.

[17]L. Zurawicki. *International Countertrade.* New York: Pergamon, 1994.

[18]Adapted from A. de Rouffignac. Recapturing market through export success. *Houston Business Journal,* January 3-9, 1997, pp. 15–17; and Cooley & Cooley, Ltd., home page at www.copalite.com (October 1997).

[19]A. Dunkin. Franchising: A recipe for your second career? *Business Week,* March 4, 1996, pp. 128–129.

[20]W. Doolin. Taking your business on the road abroad. *Wall Street Journal,* July 25, 1994, p. A16.

[21]P. W. Beamish and P. Killing (eds.). *Cooperative Strategies: North American Perspectives.* San Francisco: Lexington Press, 1998.

[22]N. Nohria and S. Ghoshal. *The Differentiated Network: Organizing Multinational Corporations for Value Creation.* San Francisco: Jossey-Bass, 1997.

[23]J. A. Pearce II and R. B. Robinson, Jr. *Formulation, Implementation, and Control of Competitive Strategy.* Burr Ridge, Ill.: Irwin, 1994, 328–336.

[24]G. P. Zachary. Major U.S. companies expand efforts to sell to consumers abroad. *Wall Street Journal,* June 13, 1996, pp. A1, A6.

[25]S. Caminiti. A star is born. *Fortune.* Autumn/Winter 1993, pp. 44–47.

[26]J. Edwards and T. Kelly. *Best Practices: Building Your Business with Arthur Andersen's Global Best Practices.* New York: Simon & Schuster, 1998.

[27]Adapted from M. Schifrin. Merrillizing the world. *Forbes,* February 10, 1997, pp. 145–151; and J. M. Giles. How to detect change before it arrives. *Leaders,* May–June 1997, pp. 52–53.

[28]M. A. Hitt, R. D. Ireland, and R. E. Hoskisson. *Strategic Management: Competitiveness and Globalization.* St. Paul: West, 1996.

[29]W. D. Coplin, and M. K. O'Leary. *Political Risk Yearbook.* East Syracuse, N.Y.: Political Risk Services, 1997.

[30]P. C. Roberts. A growing menace to free trade: U.S. sanctions. *Business Week,* November 24, 1997, p. 28; and B. Mintz. When national security, economies conflict. *Houston Chronicle,* August 29, 1993, pp. 1E, 7E.

[31]Adapted from D. Ivanovich. The risky business of petroleum politics. *Houston Chronicle,* July 28, 1996, pp. 1E, 2E; and D. Ivanovich. Trade sanctions: Where commerce, ethics and politics clash. *Houston Chronicle,* August 3, 1997, pp. 1E, 2E.

[32]E. A. Robinson. Ford cracks Korea's tough market. *Fortune,* October 28, 1996, p. 38.

[33]J. Barlow. A high level of welfare. *Houston Chronicle,* January 21, 1996, p. D1.

[34]E. Sasso. Financing foreign sales. *Trade & Culture,* March 1996, pp. 71–72.

[35]S. Murray. Subsidies shackle EU competitiveness. *Wall Street Journal,* October 28, 1996, p. A11.

[36]E. M. Graham and J. D. Richardson (ed.). *Global Competition Policy.* Washington, D.C.: Institute for International Economics, 1997; and M. Davis, Officials push for change in OPEC while ignoring quotas. *Houston Chronicle,* November 9, 1997, p. 13E.

[37]P. M. Barrett, R. McGough, and M. Kline. Murky Italian scandal over judicial bribery engulfs fund manager. *Wall Street Journal,* August 3, 1997, pp. A1, A8.

[38]Interviews. The Russian investment dilemma. *Harvard Business Review,* May–June 1994, pp. 35–44.

[39]Commercial corruption. *Wall Street Journal,* January 2, 1997, p. 6.

[40]C. H. Johnson. Coping with the Foreign Corrupt Practices Act. *Trade & Culture,* February/March 1997, pp. 60-61.

[41]Example provided by P. A. Golden. Florida International University, 1994.

[42]J. J. Schott. *WTO 2000: Setting the Course for the World Trading System.* Washington, D.C.: Institute for International Economics, 1997.

[42]G. Miller. *The Legal and Economic Basis of International Trade.* New York: Routledge, 1996.

[43]G. H. Anthes. Software pirates' booty topped $13B, study finds. *Computer World,* January 6, 1997, p. 24; P. Engardio. Day of the China-bashers, *Business Week,* March 17, 1997, pp. 54–55; and H. Cooper and K. Chen. China averts trade war with U.S., agrees to combat piracy on various items. *Wall Street Journal,* February 27, 1995, p. A3.

[45]This section is based substantially on T. E. Maher and Y. Y. Wong. NAFTA: Forerunner of a United States of the Americas? *Business & The Contemporary World,* 9, 1996, pp. 53–70; and P. Magnusson, NAFTA: Where's that giant sucking sound? *Business Week,* July 7, 1997, p. 45.

[46]This section is based substantially on J. A. Frankel. *Regional Trading Blocks in the World Economic System.* Washington, D.C.: Institute for International Economics, 1997; M. Bleackley and P. Williamson. The nature and extent of corporate restructuring within Europe's single market: Cutting through the hype. *European Management Journal,* 15, 1997, pp. 484-497; C. Honoré. Clouded dreams. The European Union. *Houston Chronicle,* July 1, 1997, pp. 18A–20A; and A. Baily (ed.). *The EU Directive Handbook: Understanding the European Union Compliance Process and What It Means to You.* Delray Beach, Fla.: St. Lucie Press, 1997.

[47]Adapted from D. Ivanovich. To Canada, free trade isn't trouble-free. *Houston Chronicle,* November 7, 1997, pp. 1C, 8C.

[48]This section is based substantially on A. Funakawa. *Transcultural management: A New Approach for Global Organizations.* San Francisco: Jossey-Bass, 1997; S.M. Puffer (ed.) *Management Across Cultures: Insights from Fiction and Practice.* Cambridge, Mass.: Blackwell, 1996; P. Yoynt and M. Warner (eds.). *Managing Across Cultures.* London: International Thomson Business Press, 1996; G. Hofstede. *Cultures and Organizations: Software of the Mind.* London: McGraw-Hill, 1991; and M. I. At-Twaijri and I. A. Al-Muhaiza. Hofstede's cultural dimensions in the GCC countries: An empirical investigation. *International Journal of Value-Based Management,* 9, 1996, pp. 121–131.

[49]R. Henkoff. New secrets from Japan—Really. *Fortune,* November 27, 1995, pp. 136–138.

[50]Adapted from F. Elashmawi. On trade and cultures. *Trade & Culture,* September/October 1996, pp. 15–16; F. Elashmawi and P. R. Harris. *Multicultural Management: New Skills for Global Success.* Houston: Gulf, 1995.

[51]J. Hodgson. *The Wondrous World of Japan.* Washington, D.C.: American Enterprise Institute, 1978, p. 3. Also see K. L. Newman and S. D. Nollen. Culture and congruence: The fit between management practices and national culture. *Journal of International Business Studies,* 27, 1996, pp. 753–779.

[52]R. Henkoff, pp. 136–138.

[53]Based on multiple information entries in the Esteé Lauder News On-Call Service home page at www.prenewswire.com/cnoc/EL (November 1, 1997).

CHAPTER 5

[1]E. Schine. The mountain man of office gear. *Business Week,* May 5, 1997, pp. 114–117.

[2]What biz-school undergrads see in their future. *Workforce,* June, 1997, p. 25; S. Shane. Explaining variation in rates of entrepreneurship in the United States: 1899–1988. *Journal of Management,* 22, 1996, pp. 747–781; and E. M. Friedman. The new economy almanac. *The State of Small Business,* 1997, pp. 108–121.

[3]L. Ingrassia. Dutch show neighbors some ways to attack their economic woes. *Wall Street Journal,* December 26, 1996, pp. A1, A8.

[4]S. N. Mehta. As ideas beget entrepreneurs, so does a plan. *Wall Street Journal,* February 19, 1997, pp. B1, B2.

[5]J. Chun. Search for tomorrow. *Entrepreneur,* May 1997, pp. 112–122.

[6]J. Kotkin. The best 4 small-business cities. *The State of Small Business,* 1997, pp. 58–69.

[7]Friedman, pp. 108–121.

[8]J. Hyatt. The Inc. 500: Inc.'s 15th annual list. *Inc. 500* 1996, pp. 15-25.

[9]J. A. Tannenbaum. U.S. firms owned by minority women grew by 153% in 9 years, report says. *Wall Street Journal,* June 25, 1997, p. B2.

[10]M. Weidenbaum. The Chinese family business enterprise. *California Management Review,* Summer 1996, pp. 141–156; and L. W. Busenitz and C.-M. Lau. A cross-cultural cognitive model of new venture creation. *Entrepreneurship Theory and Practice,* Summer 1996, pp. 25-40.

[11]M. Hopkins and J. L. Seglin. Americans @work. *The State of Small Business,* 1997, pp. 77–85; and J. P. Kotter. *The New Rules: How to Succeed in Today's Post-Corporate World.* New York: Free Press, 1995.

[12]D. L. Sexton and F. I. Seale. *Leading Practices of Fast Growth Entrepreneurs: Pathways for High Performance.* Kansas City, Mo.: National Center for Entrepreneurship Research, 1996.

[13]W. M. Bulkeley. Ben & Jerry's is looking for Ben's successor. *Wall Street Journal,* June 14, 1994, p. B1; J. Theroux, *Ben & Jerry's Homemade Ice Cream Inc.: Keeping the Mission(s) Alive.* Boston: Harvard Business School Press, 1991, p. 10; J. T. Broome, Jr. How to write a business plan. *Nation's Business,* February 1993, pp. 29–30; and R. L. Osborne, Second phase entrepreneurship: Breaking through the growth wall. *Business Horizons,* January–February 1994, pp. 80–87.

[14]Friedman, pp. 108–121.

[15]A. C. Cooper. Challenges in predicting new firm performance. *Journal of Business Venturing,* 8, 1993, pp. 241–154.

[16]Adapted from T. L. Prior, Tortilla flap. *Inc.,* June 1994, pp. 46–50.

[17]S. K. Kassicieh, R. Radosevich, and J. Umbarger. A comparative study of entrepreneurship incidence among inventors in national laboratories. *Entrepreneurship Theory and Practice,* Spring 1996, pp. 33–49.

[18]E. D. Branch. Career management. *Black Enterprise,* December 1997, pp. 113–122.

[19]H. Page. Like father, like son? Entrepreneurial history repeats itself. *Entrepreneur,* May 1997, p. 20.; M. Virarelli. The birth of new enterprises. *Small Business Economics,* 3(3), 1991, pp. 215–233; and M. P. Bhave. A process model of entrepreneurial venture creation. *Journal of Business Venturing,* 9, 1994, pp. 223–243.

[19]H. McLeod. Cross over. *The State of Small Business,* 1997, pp. 100–105.

[20]S. Birley and P. A. Westhead. A taxonomy of business start-up reasons and their impact on firm growth and size. *Journal of Business Venturing,* 9, 1994, pp. 7–32.

[21]S. N. Mehta. Inventor thrives on founding start-ups. *Wall Street Journal,* April 29, 1997, pp. B1, B2.

[22]D. C. McClellan. Characteristics of successful entrepreneurs. *Journal of Creative Behavior,* 21, 1987, pp. 219–233; and P. B. Robinson and E. A. Sexton. The effect of education and experience on self-employment success. *Journal of Business Venturing,* 9, 1994, pp. 141–156.

[23]C. Shaw. Sam Wyly says thank you with $10 million for new business school. *Dividend,* Winter–Spring, 1997, pp. 2–6.

[24]S. Kishkovsky and E. Williamson. Second-class comrades no more: Women stoke Russia's start-up boom. *Wall Street Journal,* January 30, 1997, A12; and J. B. Miner, The expanded horizon for achieving entrepreneurial success. *Organization Dynamics,* Winter 1997, pp. 54–67.

[25]C. Caggiano. Controlling interest. *Inc. 500,* 1996, 66.

[26]S. N. Mehta. More women quit lucrative jobs to start their own businesses. *Wall Street Journal,* November 11, 1996, A1, A5.

[27]Yahoo! History. Company home page at www.yahoo.com/docs/investor/ar96/letter.html (July 29, 1997); K. Swisher. Yahoo! finds way to top spot in '97. *Wall Street Journal,* February 26, 1998, pp. R1–2.

[28]D. L. Sexton and F. I. Seale. *Leading Practices of Fast Growth Entrepreneurs: Pathways for High Performance.* Kansas City, Mo.: National Center for Entrepreneurship Research, 1996.

[29]Adapted from L. Brokaw. Feet, don't fail me now. *Inc.,* May 1994, pp. 70–81.

[30]J. G. Longenecker, C. W. Moore, and J. W. Petty. *Small Business Management: An Entrepreneurial Emphasis.* Cincinnati: Southwestern, 1994, pp. 161–296.

[31]R. D. Hisrich. Entrepreneurship/Intrapreneurship. *American Psychologist,* 45, 1990, pp. 209–222.

[32]Letter to Shareholders. Yahoo! home page, July 29, 1997; and G. J. Castrogiovanni. Pre-startup planning and the survival of new small businesses: Theoretical linkages. *Journal of Management,* 22, 1996, pp. 801–822.

[33]Management's discussion and analysis of financial condition and results of operation: www.yahoo.com/docs/investor/ar96/discussion.html#overview (July 29, 1997).

[34]M. Warner. The new way to start up in Silicon Valley, March 2, 1998, *Fortune,* pp. 168–174.

[35]W. E. Watson, L. D. Ponthieu, and J. W. Critelli. Team interpersonal process effectiveness in venture partnerships and its connection to perceived success. *Journal of Business Venturing,* 10, 1995, pp. 393–411.

[36]M. Warner. A cut above. *Fortune,* August 4, 1997, pp. 59–60.

[37]R. C. Hill and M. Levenhagen. Metaphors and mental models: Sensemaking and sensegiving in innovative and entrepreneurial activities. *Journal of Management,* 21, 1995, pp. 1057–1074.

[38]K. Fitzsimmons. No comparison. *Wall Street Journal,* May 22, 1997, pp. R10, R18.

[39]S. D. Solomon. Growing companies hit global home runs. *Workforce,* June 1997, pp. 73–83.

[40]Adapted from J. P. Kotter, Matsushita: The world's greatest entrepreneur? *Fortune,* March 31, 1997, pp. 105–111.

[41]Adapted from J. Finegan. Pipe dreams. *Inc.,* August 1994, pp. 64–72.

[42]G. J. Castrogiovanni. Pre-startup planning and the survival of new small businesses: Theoretical linkages. *Journal of Management,* 22, 1996, pp. 801–822.

[43]W. A. Sahlma. How to write a great business plan. *Harvard Business Review,* July–August, 1997, pp. 98–108; and A. Bhide. The questions every entrepreneur must answer. *Harvard Business Review,* November–December 1996, 120–130.

[44]D. Whitford. Never too small to manage. *Inc.,* February 1997, pp. 56–61.

[45]A. C. Cooper and K. W. Artz. Determinants of satisfaction for entrepreneurs. *Journal of Business Venturing,* 10, 1995, pp. 439–457.

[46]G. Johnson and S. Christian. A litany of complaints in the booming franchise industry. *Los Angeles Times,* February 20, 1994, p. D3.

[47]E. Schonfeld. Tech report: Cool companies. *Fortune,* July 7, 1997, pp. 84–110.

[48]A. Cortese. A census in cyberspace. *Business Week,* May 5, 1997, p. 84.

[49]M. S. Malone. John Doerr's start-up manual. *Fast Company,* February–March, 1997, pp. 82–87.

[50]N. M. Carter, W. B. Gartner, and P. D. Reynolds. Exploring start-up event sequences. *Journal of Business Venturing,* 11, 1996, pp. 151–166.

[51]N. M. Carter, M. Williams, and P. D. Reynolds. Discontinuance among new firms in retail: The influence of initial resources, strategy, and gender. *Journal of Business Venturing,* 12, 1997, pp. 125–145.

[52]N. Brodskey and B. Burlingham. My life as an angel. *Inc.,* July 1997, pp. 43–48; E. P. Gunn. Would you *please* take my money? *Fortune,* March 16, 1998, p. 165.

[53]B. Javetsky. Venture capital's open pockets. *Business Week,* March 3, 1997, p. 43; and Friedman, pp. 108–121.

[54]H. J. Sapienza and M. A. Korsgaard. Procedural justice in entrepreneur-investor relations. *Academy of Management Journal,* 39, 1996, pp. 544–574; and D. M. Cable and S. Shane. A prisoner's dilemma approach to entrepreneur–venture capitalist relationships. *Academy of Management Review,* 22, 1997, pp. 142–176.

[55]B. M. Oviatt and P. Phillips McDougall. Global start-ups: Entrepreneurs on a worldwide stage. *Academy of Management Executive,* 9, 1995, pp. 30–79.

[56]H. H. Stevenson. A *Perspective on Entrepreneurship.* Boston: Harvard Business School Note 9-384-131, 1983; and H. H. Stevenson, M. J. Roberts, and H. I. Grousbeck. *New Business Ventures and the Entrepreneur.* Boston: Irwin, 1989.

[57]Adapted from K. McDermott. Going it alone. *D & B Reports,* March/April 1989, pp. 31–35; E. M. Garrett. The empire builders. *Inc.,* September 1993, pp. 115–119; and D. W. Greening, B. R. Barringer, and G. A. Macy. Qualitative study of managerial challenges facing small business geographic expansion. *Journal of Business Venturing,* 11, 1996, pp. 233–256.

[58]Garrett, pp. 115–119.

59R. L. Rose and C. Quintanilla. Tiptoeing abroad: More small U.S. firms take up exporting, with much success. *Wall Street Journal,* December 20, 1996, pp. A1, A8.

60E. O. Welles. This year's model. *Inc. 500,* 1996, pp. 28–39.

61J. M. Bloodgood, H. J. Sapienza, and J. G. Almeida. The internationalization of new high-potential U.S. ventures: Antecedents and outcomes. *Entrepreneurship Theory and Practice,* Summer 1996, pp. 61–76.

62Adapted from M. Baechler. The death of a marriage. *Inc.,* April 1994, pp. 74–78.

63S. D. Solomon. Theory of relativity. *Inc. 500,* 1996, p. 91.

64M. Selz. Caught in the crossfire. *Wall Street Journal,* May 22, 1997, p. R15.

65G. Pinchott, III. *Intrapreneurship.* New York: Harper & Row, 1985.

66The Baby Jogger Company home page: www.babyjogger.com (August 4, 1997).

67G. T. Lumpkin and G. G. Dess. Clarifying the entrepreneurial orientation construct and linking it to performance. *Academy of Management Review,* 21, 1996, pp. 135–172; S. A. Zahra. Governance, ownership, and corporate entrepreneurship: The moderating impact of industry technological opportunities. *Academy of Management Journal,* 39, 1996, pp. 1713–1735.

68J. S. Hornsby, D. W. Naffziger, D. F. Kuratko, and R. V. Montagno. An interactive model of corporate entrepreneurship. *Entrepreneurship: Theory and Practice,* Winter 1993, pp. 29–38.

69T. L. Peters and R. H. Waterman, Jr. *In Search of Excellence.* New York: Harper & Row, 1982; and Perspectives: How can big companies keep the entrepreneurial spirit alive? *Harvard Business Review,* 1995, pp. 183–192.

70M. E. McGill and J. W. Slocum, Jr. *The Smarter Organization: How to Adapt to Meet Marketplace Needs.* New York: John Wiley & Sons, 1994; Tally your chances on making it on your own. *USA Today,* May 11, 1987, p. 10E; and G. T. Lumpkin and G. G. Dess. Clarifying the entrepreneurial orientation construct and linking it to performance. *Academy of Management Review,* 21, 1996, pp. 135–172.

71H. Kahalas and K. Suchon. Managing a perpetual idea machine: Inside the creator's head. *Academy of Management Executive,* 9(2), 1995, pp. 57–66. Update based on information provided at the Thermo Electron home page (www.thermo.com).

72Adapted from D. H. Freedman. What you want before you know you want it. *Inc.,* July, 1997, pp. 59–66; Harvey's Pro Hardware home page: www.harveysprohardware.com (August 2, 1997); M. Treacy and F. Wiersema. *The Discipline of Market Leaders: Choose Your Customers, Narrow Your Focus, Dominate Your Market.* New York: Addison-Wesley, 1995.

CHAPTER 6

1Adapted from the company's home page; A. Adelson. Casual, worker-friendly, and a money-maker, too. *New York Times,* June 30, 1996, p. F8; C. Callicott. How green is your gear? *Hudson Valley Sports,* September/Octo-ber, 1996; M. Katakis and R. Chatham. *Sacred Trusts: Essays on Stewardship and Responsibility.* Mercury House, 1993; and E. O. Wells, Lost in Patagonia. *Inc.,* August 1992.

2R. H. Franke. Fraud: Bringing light to the dark side of business. *Academy of Management Executive,* 10, 1996, pp.93–95.

3J. W. Weiss. *Business Ethics: A Managerial, Stakeholder Approach.* Belmont, Calif.: Wadsworth, 1994.

4A. A. Atkinson, J. H. Waterhouse, and R. B. Wells. A stakeholder approach to strategic performance measurement. *Sloan Management Review,* Spring 1997, pp. 25–37.

5L. L. Berry. Playing fair in retailing. *Arthur Anderson Retailing Issues Letter,* March 1993, pp. 1–5.

6C. E. Harris, Jr. *Applying Moral Theories.* Belmont, Calif.: Wadsworth, 1990, pp. 7–11.

7R. R. Sims. *Ethics and Organizational Decision Making.* Westport, Conn.: Quorum Books, 1994.

8Harris poll: Is an antibusiness backlash building? *Business Week,* July 20, 1987, p. 71; and K. Gudridge and J. A. Byrne. A kinder, gentler generation of executives? *Business Week,* April 23, 1990, pp. 86–87.

9B. Z. Posner and W. H. Schmidt. Ethics in American companies: A managerial perspective. *Journal of Business Ethics,* 6, 1987, pp. 383–391.

10B. Meier. Cigarette makers in a $368 billion accord to curb lawsuits and curtail marketing. *New York Times,* June 21, 1997, pp. A1, A10; and B. Meier. White House's bottom line is reported in tobacco deal. *New York Times,* September 8, 1997, p. A3.

11Verena Dobnik. Study: Chinese workers abused while making Nike, Reebok shoes. Associated Press, *Corpus Christi Caller-Times,* September 21, 1997, p. A8; A. Chan. Boot camp at the shoe factory. *Washington Post,* November 3, 1996, pp. C1, C4.

12For a discussion of how cultural differences can affect the ethical choices of business leaders, see R. N. Kanungo and M. Mendonca. *Ethical Dimensions of Leadership.* Thousand Oaks, Calif.: Sage, 1996.

13L. Himmelstein. Going beyond city limits? *Business Week,* July 7, 1997, pp. 98–99.

14D. P. Twomey. *Labor and Employment Law: Text and Cases,* 9th ed. Cincinnati: South-Western, 1994.

15*Corporate Ethics: A Prime Business Asset.* New York: Business Roundtable, 1988.

16J. Weber. Influences upon organizational ethical subclimates: A multi-departmental analysis of a single firm. *Organization Science,* September–October, 1995, pp. 509–523.

17L. K. Trevino and K. Nelson. *Business Ethics.* New York: John Wiley & Sons, 1995.

18F. Navran. Are your employees cheating to keep up? *Workforce,* August, 1997, pp. 58–61. Other related studies are summarized in J. Krohe, Jr. Ethics are nice, but business is business. *Across the Board,* April 1997, pp. 16–22.

19L. Kohlberg. Stage and sequence: The cognitive-developmental approach to socialization. In D.A. Goslin (ed.), *Handbook of Socialization Theory and Research.* Chicago: Rand McNally, 1969, pp. 347–380.

20L. Kohlberg. The cognitive-developmental approach to moral education. In P. Scharf (ed.), *Readings in Moral Education.* Minneapolis: Winston Prisa, 1978, pp. 36–51; and G. D. Boxterand and C. A. Rarick. Education and moral development of managers: Kohlberg's stages of moral development and integrative education. *Journal of Business Ethics,* 6, 1987, pp. 243–248.

21Adapted from J. Makower, *Beyond the Bottom Line: Putting Social Responsibility to Work for Your Business and the World.* New York: Simon & Schuster.

22T. Barnett, K. Bass, and G. Brown. Ethical ideology and ethical judgment regarding ethical issues in business. *Journal of Professional Ethics,* 13, 1994, pp. 469–480.

23. G. F. Cavanagh, D. J. Moberg, and M. Velasquez. The ethics of organizational behavior. *Academy of Management Review,* 5, 1981, pp. 363–374; and F. N. Brady. *Ethical Managing: Rules and Results.* New York: Macmillan, 1990.

24J. S. Mill. *Utilitarianism.* Indianapolis: Bobbs-Merrill, 1957 (originally published 1863).

25M. A. Friedman. Friedman doctrine: The social responsibility of business is to increase its profits. *New York Times Magazine,* September 13, 1970, 32ff.

26L. Holyoke. How HR measures impact of corporate donations. *Workforce,* June 1997, p. 23.

27Friedman, p. 126.

28J. Q. Wilson. Adam Smith on business ethics. *California Management Review,* Fall 1989, pp. 59–72.

29N. D. Schwartz. The Boston Chicken problem. *Fortune,* July 7, 1997, pp. 114–116; L. Lee. Booby prize goes to Boston Chicken. *Wall Street Journal,* February 26, 1998, pp. R1–2.

30E. Schine. Kicking mud on Morgan's white shoes. *Business Week,* July 7, 1997, p. 119.

31S. M. Puffer and D. J. McCarthy. Finding the common ground in Russian and American business ethics. *California Management Review,* Winter 1995, pp. 29–46.

32J. D. Aram. *Presumed Superior: Individualism and American Business.* Englewood Cliffs, N.J.: Prentice-Hall, 1993.

33M. Velasquez, D. V. Moberg, and G. F. Cavanagh. Organizational statesmanship and dirty politics: Ethical guidelines for the organizational politician. *Organizational Dynamics,* Autumn 1983, pp. 65–80.

34G. F. Cavanagh. *American Business Values,* 2d ed. Englewood Cliffs, N.J.: Prentice-Hall, 1984.

35M. Gowen, S. Ibarreche, and C. Lackey. Doing the right things in Mexico. *Academy of Management Executive,* 10, 1996, pp. 74–81.

36C. Boisseau. Flying a route to controversy. *Houston Chronicle,* July 3, 1994, pp. 1F, 5F.

37R. E. Kidwell, Jr., and N. Bennett. Employee reactions to electronic control systems. *Group & Organization Management,* 19, 1994, pp. 203–218; F. Jossi. Eavesdroppers in cyberspace. *Business Ethics,* May/June 1994, pp. 22–25; and D. R. Comer. Crossroads: A case against workplace drug testing. *Organization Science,* 5, 1994, pp. 259–267.

[38]Adapted from H. Chura. Don't talk and chew anymore. *Houston Chronicle,* May 27, 1994, p. 2D; and Doughnut shop got a hole lot of juicy gossip. *Houston Chronicle,* May 30, 1994, p. 6A.

[39]D. Lyons. The buzz about Firefly. *New York Times Magazine,* June 29, 1997, pp. 37–40.

[40]D. W. Ewing. Your right to fire. *Harvard Business Review,* March–April 1983, pp. 32–34ff.

[41]S. B. Sitkin and R. J. Bies (eds.). T*he Legalistic Organization.* Thousand Oaks, Calif.: Sage, 1994.

[42]T. E. Weber. Mainstream sites accept ads selling x-rated. *Wall Street Journal,* January 16, 1997, p. B10.

[43]D. D. Friedman. The world according to Coase. *Law School Record,* Spring 1992, pp. 4–9.

[44]J. A. Rawls. *A Theory of Justice.* Cambridge, Mass.: Harvard University Press, 1971; J. A. Greenberg. A taxonomy of organizational justice theories. *Academy of Management Review,* 12, 1987, pp. 9–22; and J. Greenberg and K. S. Scott. Why do workers bite the hand that feeds them? Employee theft as a social exchange process. *Research in Organizational Behavior,* vol. 18, pp. 111–156.

[45]C. Goldin. *Understanding the Gender Gap: An Economic History of American Women.* New York: Oxford University Press, 1990; and B. Reskin and I. Padavic. *Women and Men at Work.* Thousand Oaks, Calif.: Pine Forge Press, 1994.

[46]J. A. Byrne. How high can CEO pay go? *Business Week,* April 22, 1996, pp. 100–106.

[47]J. S. Lublin. Bosses beware: Michael Rankin is taking notes. *Wall Street Journal,* November 14, 1996, pp. B1, B15; and J. S. Lublin. Executive pay: The great divide. *Wall Street Journal,* April 11, 1996, pp. R1, R4.

[48]J. Reingold and A. Borrus. Even executives are wincing at executive pay. *Business Week,* May 12, 1997, pp. 40–41.

[49]R. Folger and M. A. Konovsky. Effects of procedural and distributive justice on reactions to pay raise decisions. *Academy of Management Journal,* 32, 1989, pp. 115–130; and B. P. Niehoff and R. H. Moorman. Justice as a mediator of the relationship between methods of monitoring and organizational citizenship behavior. *Academy of Management Journal,* 36, 1993, pp. 527–556.

[50]B. Bemmels and J. R. Foley. Grievance procedure research: A review and theoretical recommendations. *Journal of Management,* 22, 1996, pp. 359–384; and P. Feuille and D. R. Chachere. Looking fair or being fair: Remedial voice procedures in nonunion workplaces. *Journal of Management,* 21, 1995, pp. 27–42.

[51]W. C. Kim and R. A. Mauborgne. Procedural justice and managers' in-role and extra-role behavior: The case of the multinational. *Management Science,* April 1996, pp. 499–513.

[52]L. Barton. *Ethics: The Enemy in the Workplace.* Cincinnati: South-Western, 1995.

[53]R. Florida. Lean and green: The move to environmentally conscious manufacturing. *California Management Review,* Fall 1996, pp. 80–105.

[54]For a review of this perspective, see T. Donaldson and L. E. Preston. The stakeholder theory of the corporation: Concepts, evidence, and implications. *Academy of Management Review,* 20, 1995, pp. 65–91.

[55]M. B. E. Clarkson. A stakeholder framework for analyzing and evaluating corporate social performance. *Academy of Management Review,* 20, 1995, pp. 92–117; T. Donaldson and L. E. Preston. The stakeholder theory of the corporation: Concepts, evidence, and implications. *Academy of Management Review,* 20, 1995, pp. 65–91; R. E. Freeman. *Strategic Management: A Stakeholder Approach.* Boston: Pittman/Ballinger, 1994; T. M. Jones. Instrumental stakeholder theory: A synthesis of ethics and economics. *Academy of Management Review,* 20, 1995, pp. 404–437. D. J. Wood. Social issues in management: Theory and research in corporate social performance. *Journal of Management,* 17, 1991, pp. 383–405.

[56]Quoted in R. Tetzeli. And now for Motorola's next trick. *Fortune,* April 28, 1997, p. 130. See also, Q. Hardy and J. I. Rigdon. Motorola overhauls staff structure; top management's pay dropped in '96. *Wall Street Journal,* March 24, 1997, p. B2; and P. Elstrom. Does Galvin have the right stuff? *Business Week,* March 17, 1997, pp. 102–105.

[57]Many companies have found that their incentive systems cause unwanted behaviors. This is an important topic, which we discuss in more depth in Chapters 12 and 14.

[58]America's Most Admired Companies. *Fortune,* March 4, 1997, pp. 68–76.

[59]T. Lewin. Equal pay for equal work is No. 1 goal for women. *New York Times,* September 5, 1997, p. A20.

[60]World Commission on Environment and Development. *Our Common Future.* New York: Oxford University Press, 1987. For more recent discussions see T. N. Gladwin, J. J. Kennelly, and T. Krause. Shifting paradigms for sustainable development: Implications for management theory and research. *Academy of Management Review,* 20, 1995, pp. 874–907; M. Starick and G. P. Rands. Weaving an integrated web: Multilevel and multisystem perspectives of ecologically sustainable organizations. *Academy of Management Review,* 1995, 20, pp. 908–935; and P. Shrivastava. The role of corporations in achieving ecological sustainability. *Academy of Management Review,* 20, 1995, pp. 936–960.

[61]To learn more about EMAS and the ISO 14000 standards, see D. A. Rondinelli and G. Vastag. International environmental standards and corporate policies: An integrative framework. *California Management Review,* Fall 1996, pp. 106–122, and R. Hillary. *The Eco-Management Audit Scheme: A Practical Guide.* Hillsdale, N.J.: Lawrence Erlbaum, 1993.

[62]E. A. Robinson. The ups and downs of the industry leaders. *Fortune,* March 2, 1998, pp. 86–87.

[63]N. Ulman. A new leaf: Timber industry turns to former opponents to clean up its act. *Wall Street Journal,* March 12, 1997, pp. A1, A10; L. A. Armour. Who says virtue is its own reward? *Fortune,* February 16, 1998, pp. 186–187.

[64]D. A. Rondinelli and G. Vastag. International environmental standards and corporate policies: An integrative framework. *California Management Review,* Fall 1996, pp. 106–122.

[65]P. C. Judge. Is it rainforest crunch time? *Business Week,* July 1996, pp. 70–71; and B. Cohen and J. Greenfield. *Ben & Jerry's DoubleDip: Lead With Your Values and Make Money, Too.* New York: Simon & Schuster, 1997.

[66]M. Kline. Italy's banks, mired in middle ages, face revolution: Profits before charity. *Wall Street Journal,* March 24, 1997, p. A14.

[67]M. Useem. Shareholders as a strategic asset. *California Management Review,* Fall 1996, pp. 8–27.

[68]K. H. Hammonds, W. Zellner, and R. Melcher. Writing a new social contract. *Business Week,* March 11, 1997, pp. 60–61; and M. B. E. Clarkson, pp. 92–117.

[69]J. Urquart. Wal-Mart pulls Cuban pajamas from Canada. *Wall Street Journal,* March 6, 1997, p. A3.

[70]M. Treacy and F. Wiersema. *The Discipline of Market Leaders: Choose Your Customers, Narrow Your Focus, Dominate Your Market.* Reading, Mass.: Addison-Wesley, 1997.

[71]D. Edgington. From steak holders to stakeholders. *Inc.,* March, 1997, p. 24.

[72]T. Teal. Not a fool, not a saint. *Fortune,* November 11, 1996, pp. 201–204.

[73]Smart managing: Best practices, careers, and ideas. *Fortune,* February 17, 1997, p. 127.

[74]S. Shellenberg. Investors seem attracted to firms with happy employees. *Wall Street Journal,* March, 19, 1997, p. B1; L. Grant. Happy workers, high returns. *Fortune,* January 12, 1998, p. 81; M. J. Schmit and S. P. Allscheid. Employee attitudes and customer satisfaction: Making the theoretical and empirical connections. *Personnel Psychology,* 48, 1995, pp. 521–536; C. A. Lengnick-Hall. Customer contributions to quality: A different view of the customer-oriented firm. *Academy of Management Review,* 21, 1996, pp. 791–824; and P. S. Goodman, M. Fichman, F. J. Lerch, and P. R. Snyder. Customer–firm relationships, involvement, and customer satisfaction. *Academy of Management Journal,* 38, 1995, pp. 1310–1324.

[75]A. A. Atkinson, J. H. Waterhouse, and R. B. Wells. A stakeholder approach to strategic performance measurement. *Sloan Management Review,* Spring 1997, pp. 25–37; T. M. Jones. Instrumental stakeholder theory: A synthesis of ethics and economics. *Academy of Management Review,* 20, 1995, pp. 404–437; R. D. Klassen and C. P. McLaughlin. The impact of environmental management on firm performance. *Management Science,* August, 1996, pp. 1199–1216; and D. B. Turban and D. W. Greening. Corporate social performance and organizational attractiveness to prospective employees. *Academy of Management Journal,* 40, 1997, pp. 658–672.

[76]S. P. Sethi. A conceptual framework for environmental analysis of social issues and evaluation of business response patterns. *Academy of Management Review,* 4, 1979, pp. 63-74; J. T. Mahoney, A. S. Huff, J. O. Huff. Toward a new social contract theory in organization science. *Journal of Management Inquiry,* 3, 1994, pp. 153–168.

[77]S. Greengard. Face values. *US Air Magazine,* November 1990, pp. 89–97; M. Franssen. Beyond profits: The Body Shop does. *Business Quarterly,* Autumn 1993, pp. 14–20; G. Roddick. Letter to Business Ethics subscribers. *Business Ethics,* September 22, 1994, pp. 1–10;

and J. Entine. Shattered image. *Business Ethics,* September/October 1994, pp. 23–28.

[78]M. B. E. Clarkson, pp. 92–117.

[79]E. S. Mason and P. E. Mudrack. Are individuals who agree that corporate social responsibility is a "fundamentally subversive doctrine" inherently unethical? *Applied Psychology: An International Review,* 46, 1997, pp. 135–152.

[80]J. P. Near and M. P. Miceli. Effective whistle-blowing. *Academy of Management Review,* 20, 1995, pp. 679–708.

[81]J. P. Near and M. P. Miceli. Whistle-blowing: Myth and reality. *Journal of Management,* 1996, pp. 507–526.

[82]J. P. Near, T. M. Dwarkin, and M. P. Miceli. Explaining the whistle-blowing process: Suggestions from power theory and justice theory. *Organization Science,* 4, 1993, pp. 393–411.

[83]B. J. Feder. The harder side of Sears: Safeguards didn't stop debt-collection scandal. *New York Times,* July 29, 1997, Section 3, pp. 1, 8.

[84]Adapted from J. Makower. *Beyond the Bottom Line: Putting Social Responsibility to Work for Your Business and the World.* New York: Simon & Schuster, 1994.

CHAPTER 7

[1]Adapted from Dick Clark Productions home page at www.dickclark.com/index.html (December 10, 1997); Rock and Roll Hall of Fame and Museum web site at www.rock-hall.com/induct/clarkdick.html (December 10, 1997); and Dick Clark Productions, Inc., 10-K Report available at the web site of the U.S. Securities and Exchange Commission, www.sec.gov/Archives/edgar/data/805370/00 00910680-97-000335.txt (December 1997).

[2]T. J. Galpin. *Making Strategy Work: Building Sustainable Growth Capabilities.* San Francisco: Jossey-Bass, 1997.

[3]C. W. L. Hill and G. R. Jones, *Strategic Management: An Integrated Approach,* 4th ed. Boston: Houghton Mifflin, 1998.

[4]For a critique of planning because it is frequently claimed to hinder the accomplishment of these goals, see H. Mintzberg. *The Rise and Fall of Strategic Planning.* New York: Free Press, 1994. For a contrary position on how planning can assist entrepreneurship and innovation see W. A. Sahlman. How to write a great business plan. *Harvard Business Review,* July–August 1997, pp. 98–108.

[5]A. A. Thompson, Jr. and A. J. Strickland III. *Strategic Management: Concepts and Cases,* 10th ed. Burr Ridge, Ill.: Irwin/McGraw-Hill, 1998.

[6]A. de Geus. *The Living Company.* Boston: Harvard Business School Press, 1997.

[7]M. J. Bloom and M. K. Menefee. Scenario planning and contingency planning. *Public Productivity and Management Review,* 17, 1994, pp. 223–231; and R. Bood and T. Postma. Strategic learning with scenarios. *European Management Journal,* 15, 1997, pp. 633–647.

[8]C. K. Bart. Sex, lies, and mission statements. *Business Horizons,* November–December 1997, pp. 9–18.

[9]J. C. Collins and J. I. Porras. Building your company's vision. *Harvard Business Review,* September–October 1996, pp. 65–77; D. C.

Hambrick, D. A. Nadler, and M. L. Tushman (eds.). *Navigating Change: How CEOs, Top Teams, and Boards Steer Transformation.* Boston: Harvard Business School Press, 1998.

[10]Associated Press. Chairman leads airline through flights of fancy. *Bryan–College Station Eagle,* May 26, 1996, p. C3; and C. C. Boisseau. Going long to avoid bite. *Houston Chronicle,* August 1, 1997, pp. 1C, 8C.

[11]M. E. Porter. What is strategy? *Harvard Business Review,* November–December 1996, pp. 61–78; and N. Rajagopalan and G.M. Spreitzer. Toward a theory of strategic change: A multi-lens perspective and integrative framework. *Academy of Management Review,* 22, 1997, pp. 48–79.

[12]Adapted from R. Ruggless. Dick Clark's American Bandstand Grill tests whether memorabilia-themed concept will work in smaller cities. *Nation's Restaurant News,* June 16, 1997, pp. 74–75; Dick Clark Productions, Inc., restaurants Web site at www.dickclark. com/restrl (December 10, 1997).

[13]N. J. Foss (ed.). *Resources and Strategy: A Reader.* New York: Oxford University Press, 1997.

[14]Dick Clark productions reports record profitability for fiscal 1997 at www.dickclark. com/news99 (December 10, 1997); and L. Gubernick. California dreams. *Forbes,* December 16, 1997, pp. 112–114.

[15]M. Irvine. Levi Strauss to close eleven plants. *Houston Chronicle,* November 4, 1997, pp. 1C, 7C.

[16]Adapted from K. R. Thompson, W. A. Hachwarter, and N. J. Mathys. Stretch targets: What makes them effective. *Academy of Management Executive,* August 1997, pp. 48–60.

[17]Adapted from C. C. Markides. To diversify or not to diversify. *Harvard Business Review,* November–December 1997, pp. 93–99; and J. R. Hayes. Acquisition is fine, but organic growth is better. *Forbes,* December 30, 1996, pp. 52–55.

[18]C. Adams. Cement firm paves expansionary path. *Houston Chronicle,* December 26, 1997, pp. 1C, 4C. To learn more about Cemex, visit the company's home page at www. cemex.com

[19]M. H. Lubatkin and P. J. Lane, Psst . . . The merger mavens still have it wrong! *Academy of Management Executive,* February 1996, pp. 21–39; and S. N. Chakravarty and S. Lubove. Plenty of glitter, but where's the gold. *Forbes,* March 29, 1996, pp. 106–111.

[20]Textron, Inc., home page at www.textron. com/businesses/divisions (January 3, 1998).

[21]J. L. Stempert and I. M. Duhaime. Seeing the big picture: The influence of industry, diversification, and business strategy on performance. *Academy of Management Journal,* 40, 1997, pp. 560–583.

[22]B. O'Reilly. Why Merck married the enemy. *Fortune.* September 20, 1993, pp. 60–64.

[23]A. Bianco. Virtual bookstores start to get real. *Business Week,* October 27, 1997, pp. 146–147. To learn more about Amazon.com, visit the company's home page at www.Amazon.com

[24]J. Aguayo. "We're gonna consolidate this industry." *Forbes,* August 11, 1997, pp. 65–67.

[25]C. M. Brown. The master of trades. *Black Enterprise,* June 1996, pp. 244–253.

[26]D. Whitford. Sale of the century. *Fortune,* February 17, 1997, pp. 92–104. To learn more about Boeing, visit the company's home page at www.boeing.com

[27]R. S. Dunham. Global mission. *Business Week,* May 1, 1995, pp. 132–134.

[28]M. A. Hitt, R. D. Ireland, and R. E. Hoskisson. *Strategic Management: Competitiveness and Globalization,* 3d ed. Cincinnati: South-Western, 1999.

[29]M. A. Hitt, R. D. Ireland, and R. E. Hoskisson; and R. E. Wayland and P. M. Cole. *Customer Connections: New Strategies for Growth.* Boston: Harvard Business School Press, 1998.

[30]P. B. Evans and T. S. Wurster; W. S. Mossberg; E. Gardner; and Encyclopedia Britannica home page.

[31]Adapted from P. B. Evans and T. S. Wurster. Strategy and the new economics of information. *Harvard Business Review,* September–October 1997, pp. 71–82; W. S. Mossberg. An encyclopedia that lets you stroll a Florentine plaza. *Wall Street Journal,* November 6, 1997, p. B1; E. Gardner. Britannica drops door-to-door salesmen in favor of the web. *Web Week,* May 20, 1996 (unpaginated) at www.web-week.com/96May20/comm/britannica; and Encyclopedia Britannica home page at www.ebig.com (January 15, 1998).

[32]R. E. Markland, S. Vickery, and R. Davis. *Operations Concepts in Manufacturing and Services,* 2d ed. Cincinnati: South-Western, 1998.

[33]J. Makower. Herman Miller: Setting new standards in industrial eco-efficiency. *Business Ethics,* November–December 1997, pp. 7–8. To learn more about Herman-Miller, visit the company's home page at www.herman-miller.com

[34]T. Jaffe. The corn is green. *Forbes,* December 4, 1995, pp. 86–102; the Meredith Corporation home page at www.home-and-family.com (January 5, 1998).

[35]M. E. Porter. *Competitive Strategy: Techniques for Analyzing Industries and Competitors.* New York: Free Press, 1980; M. E. Porter. *Competitive Advantage: Creating and Sustaining Superior Performance.* New York: Free Press, 1985; and R. K. Mitchell, B. R. Agle, and Donna J. Wood. Toward a theory of stakeholder identification and salience: Defining the principle of who and what really counts. *Academy of Management Review,* 22, 1997, pp. 85–886.

[36]Northern Telecom Limited. *The Anatomy of a Transformation 1985–1995.* Brampton, Ontario, Canada: Northern Telecom Limited, 1997. To learn more about Northern Telecom, visit the company's home page at www.nortel.com

[37]D. B. Yoffie. Competing in the age of digital comergence. *California Management Review,* Summer 1996, pp. 31–53; and J. Hagel III and A. G. Armstrong. *Net Gain: Expanding Markets through Virtual Communities.* Boston: Harvard Business School Press, 1997.

[38]J. Young. Digital octopus. *Forbes,* June 17, 1996, pp. 102–106; and A. Reinhardt, I. Sager, and P. Burrows. Intel: Can Andy Grove keep profits up in an era of cheap PCs? *Business Week,* December 22, 1997, pp. 70–77.

[39]Going digital. *Fortune*, Winter 1998, pp. 18–24.

[40]D. Matheson and J. Matheson. *The Smart Organization: Creating Value through Strategic R&D*. Boston: Harvard Business School Press, 1997; and M. U. Russo and P. A. Fouts. A resource-based perspective on corporate environmental performance and profitability. *Academy of Management Journal*, 40, 1997, pp. 534–559.

[41]A. Taylor III. How Toyota defies. *Fortune*, December 8, 1997, pp. 100–108. To learn more about the Toyota Corporation, visit the company's home page at www.toyota.com

[42]K. Kerwin and K. Naughton. Can Detroit make cars that baby boomers like? *Business Week*, December 1, 1997, pp. 134–148.

[43]A. Taylor III, p. 102.

[44]Adapted from J. Vijayan. Improved service top-cited outsourcing goal. *Computerworld*, December 1, 1997, p. 10; and E. Leinfus. Outsourcing: From vertical to vertical. *Business Week* (special section), December 15, 1997. Written and produced by the Outsourcing Institute, New York (www.outsourcing.com).

[45]Adapted from Citicorp's global strategy: An interview with Dennis Martin. *Leaders*, April–June 1997, pp. 66–67; and D. Setton. The king of plastic. *Forbes*, December 15, 1997, p. 172.

[46]Adapted from R. Maynard. Back to basics from the top. *Nations Business*, December 1996, pp. 38–39; and Graphic Solutions home page at www.graphicsolutions.com

[47]C. P. Zeithaml. Stage of the product life cycle, business strategy and business performance. *Academy of Management Journal*, 27, 1984, pp. 5–24; and M. H. Meyer and A. P. Lehnerd. *The Power of Product Platforms: Building Value and Cost Leadership*. New York: Free Press, 1997.

[48]P. Sellers. Sears: The turnaround is ending; the revolution has begun. *Fortune*, April 28, 1997, pp. 106–118.

[49]Adapted from C. Ryan and W. E. Riggs. Redefining the product life cycle: The five-element product wave. *Business Horizons*, September–October 1996, pp. 33–39.

[50]M. E. Porter. *Michael Porter on Competition*. Boston: Harvard Business School Press, 1998; and I. C. MacMillan and R. Gunther McGrath. Discovering new points differentiation. *Harvard Business Review*, July–August 1997, pp. 133–145.

[51]S. Lubove. Is banking different from pumping gas? *Forbes*, October 27, 1997, pp. 102–103. Wells Fargo Bank home page at www.wellsfargo.com/home (January 9, 1998).

[52]A. Ries. *Focus: The Future of Your Company Depends on It*. New York: HarperBusiness, 1997.

[53]Adapted from E. Ramstad. Defying giant rivals, many tiny PC makers are still doing well. *Wall Street Journal*, January 8, 1997, pp. A1, A8.

[54]Adapted from How to make $ with a corporate vision. *Leaders*, October–December 1996, pp. 48–50.

[55]Adapted from M. B. Brandel. Think global, act local. Computerworld, March 10, 1997, pp. 8–9.

[56]Adapted from BISNIS Bulletin, under *Russ-ian business meetings* at BISNIS online—www.itaiep.doc.gov/bisnis/bisnis (December 23, 1997).

[57]Adapted from K. Melymuka. Virtual realities. *Computerworld*. April 28, 1997, pp. 70–72; and G. J. Hofstede, A. Vermunt, M. Smits, and N. Noorderhaven. Wired international teams: Experiments in strategic decision making by multi-cultural virtual teams. Position paper available at www.info.wow.nl/people/Geert_Jan_Hofsted/wired (November 30, 1997).

[58]Adapted from S. Nelton. Going from one leader to a team of leaders means a whole new structure. *Nation's Business*, June 1996, pp. 53–55.

[59]Adapted from R. Henkoff. P&G: New and improved. *Fortune*, October 14, 1996, pp. 151–160.

[60]Adapted from R. Boettcher and M. K. Welge. Global strategies of European firms. *International Executive*, March/April 1996; and Chargeurs' home page at www.chargeurs.fr/gb/profil/profil (November 23, 1997).

CHAPTER 8

[1]Adapted from E. Ramstad. Tandy to shed Incredible Universe chain. *Wall Street Journal*, December 31, 1996, p. 3; and Tandy's Radio Shack, Computer City chains see a rebound in sales. *Wall Street Journal*, August 8, 1997, p. 158.

[2]H. Kunreuther and E. Bowman. A dynamic model of organizational decision making: Chemco revisted six years after Bhopal. *Organization Science*, 8, 1997, pp. 404–413; and J. G. March. *A Primer on Decision Making: How Decisions Happen*. New York: Free Press, 1994.

[3]E. F. Harrison. *The Managerial Decision-Making Process*, 4th ed. Boston: Houghton Mifflin, 1994.

[4]D. Bell. *Risk Management*. New York: Cambridge University Press, 1988.

[5]M. R. Kropko. Card companies re-evaluate personalized greeting cards. *Bryan–College Station Eagle*, June 9, 1996, p. 6C.

[6]M. Garcia. Fear of crime drives Florida's motorists to break laws. *Houston Chronicle*, October 2, 1993, p. 8A.

[7]A. C. Boynton, L. M. Gales, and R. S. Blackburn. Managerial search activity: The impact of perceived role uncertainty and role threat. *Journal of Management*, 19, 1993, pp. 725–747.

[8]H. L. Tosi, J. P. Katz, and L. R. Gomez-Mejia. Disaggregating the agency contract: The effects of monitoring, incentive alignment and term in office on agent decision making. *Academy of Management Journal*, 40, 1997, pp. 584–602.

[9]K. E. Boulding. Irreducible uncertainties. *Society*, November–December 1982, p. 17.

[10]G. N. Powell and D. A. Butterfield. Effect of race on promotions to top management in a federal department. *Academy of Management Journal*, 40, 1997, pp.112–128; K. S. Lyness and D. E. Thompson. Above the glass ceiling? A comparison of matched samples of female and male executives. *Journal of Applied Psychology*, 82, 1997, 359–375.

[11]Adapted from R. F. Maruca. The right way to go global: An interview with Whirlpool CEO David Whitwam. *Harvard Business Review*, March–April 1994, pp.134–145; and G. Beatty. Whirlpool's global plan. *HFN*, February 24, 1997, pp. 49–51.

[12]Adapted from B. Virgin. Firm believed gamble would pay off. *Houston Chronicle*, January 26, 1996, p. 6C.

[13]P. C. Nutt. The formulation processes and tactics used in organizational decision making. *Organization Science*, 4, 1993, pp. 226–251; and M. J. Tyre and R. VonHippel. The situated nature of adaptive learning in organizations. *Organization Science*, 8, 1997, pp. 71–83.

[14]C. C. Manz and G. L. Stewart. Attaining flexible stability by integrating total quality management and socio-technical systems theory. *Organization Science*, 8, 1997, pp.59–70; M. V. Uzumeri. ISO 9000 and other megastandards: Principles for management practice. *Academy of Management Executive*, 11, 1997, pp. 21–36; and T. Y. Choi and O. C. Behling. Top managers and TQM Success: One more look after all these years. *Academy of Management Executive*, 11, 1997, pp. 37–47.

[15]J. W. Dean, and J. R. Evans. *Total Quality: Management, Organization, and Strategy*. St. Paul: West, 1994.

[16]E. A. Robinson. America's most admired companies. *Fortune*, March 3, 1997, pp. 68–75.

[17]Adapted from A. Farnham. America's most admired company. *Fortune*, February 7, 1994, pp. 50–54; and R. Jacob. Corporation reputations: The winners' chart of constant renewal and work to sustain cultures that produce the very best products and people. *Fortune*, March 6, 1995, pp. 54–60.

[18]Muruca, p. 137.

[19]Adapted from E. A. Robinson. The plight of the Hummer. *Fortune*, April 28, 1997, pp. 58–59; and J. Keebler. Hummer revisions aimed at highway driveability. *The Business Journal—Serving Phoenix & the Valley of the Sun*, April 22, 1994, pp. 12–13.

[20]J. A. Belasco and R. C. Strayer. *The Flight of the Buffalo*. New York: Time Warner Books, 1993.

[21]D. Wallace. It's all about goals. *Success*, September 1991, pp. 39–43.

[22]E. A. Locke and G. P. Latham. *A Theory of Goal Setting and Task Performance*. Englewood Cliffs, N.J.: Prentice-Hall, 1990.

[23]Adapted from A. E. Spencer. Michael Dell turns the PC world inside out. *Fortune*, September 8, 1997, pp. 76–90; D. Kirpatrick. Now everyone in PCs wants to be like Mike. *Fortune*, September 8, 1997, pp. 91–93; and A. Goldstein. Rivals seek to mimic Dell's success at direct PC sales. *Dallas Morning News*, August 31, 1997, pp. H1–H2.

[24]M. L. Tushman and C. A. O'Reilly III. *Winning Through Innovation*. Boston: Harvard Business School Press, 1997.

[25]J. A. C. Baum and H. A. Haverman. Love thy neighbor? Differentiation and agglomeration in the Manhattan hotel industry, 1898–1990. *Administrative Science Quarterly*, 42, 1997, pp. 304–338.

[26]B. L. Rupp. Celebration of excellence: The power of communication. *Financial World*, May 20, 1997, pp. 96–98; and D. Gross. Remodeling Sears. *CIO*, December 1, 1996, pp. 70–76.

[27]M. E. Porter. What is strategy? *Harvard Business Review,* November–December 1996, pp. 61–80.

[28]S. G. Cohen and D. E. Bailey. What makes teams work: Group effectiveness research from the shop floor to the executive suite. *Journal of Management,* 23, 1997, pp. 239–290.

[29]M. Ray and R. Myers. *Creativity in Business.* Garden City, N.Y.: Doubleday, 1986, pp. 94–96.

[30]J. Pfeffer. When it comes to "Best Practices," why do smart organizations occasionally do dumb things? *Organizational Dynamics,* Summer, 1996, pp. 33–44; and C. Handy. *The Age of Paradox.* Boston: Harvard Business School Press, 1994.

[31]T. R. Kinni. *America's best: Industry Weeks Guide to World-Class Manufacturing Plants.* New York: John Wiley & Sons, 1996, pp. 306–309.

[32]H. A. Simon. *Reason in Human Affairs.* Stanford, Calif.: Stanford University Press, 1983; and H. A. Simon. Making management decisions: The role of intuition and emotion. *Academy of Management Executive,* 1, 1987, pp. 57–64; J. E. Martin, G. B. Kleindorfer, and W. R. Brashers, Jr. The theory of bounded rationality and the problem of legitimation. *Journal for the Theory of Social Behavior,* 17, 1987, pp. 63–82.

[33]Kinni, pp. 217–219.

[34]J. M. Roach. Simon says: Decision making is a "satisficing" experience. *Management Review,* January 1979, pp. 8–9.

[35]J. M. Beyer, P. Chattopadhyay, E. George, Wm. Glick, D. T. Ogilive, and D. Pugliese. The selective perceptions of managers revisited. *Academy of Management Journal,* 40, 1997, pp. 717–737.

[36]J. P. Kotter. *Matsushita Leadership.* New York: Free Press, 1997.

[37]W. A. McEachern. *Economics: A Contemporary Introduction.* Cincinnati: South-Western, 1997, pp. 662–665.

[38]E. B. Smith. Flour settles whistle-blower suit for $8.4 million. *Knight-Ridder/Tribune News,* June 23, 1997, p. 623B.

[39]A. Bernstein and P. Dwyer. This package is a heavy one for the Teamsters. *Business Week,* August 18, 1997, pp. 40–42.

[40]J. Pfeffer. *New Directions for Organization Theory.* New York: Oxford University Press, 1997.

[41]Adapted from F. Washington. Catera on a hot tin roof: It'll test GM in more ways than one. *Ward's Auto World,* October 1995, pp. 18–20; B. S. Moskal. Cadillac's quest: Find the fountain of youth. *Industry Week,* April 1, 1996, pp. 61–64; Personal conversation with C. Sewell, President, Sewell Cadillac, Dallas, March 1998; and W. Brown. The Caddy They Ducked. *Washington Post,* September 11, 1997, pp. E1–E2.

CHAPTER 9

[1]Adapted from J. A. Scansarolei and V. Eng. Interactive retailing: The threat, the opportunity. *Chain Store Age,* January 1997, pp. 2A–19A.

[2]J. A. Scansarolei and V. Eng; M. Pecenik. 2001—Some space for an Odyssey. *Journal of Internet Banking and Commerce,* July 1997, available at www.arraydev.com/commerce/JIBC/9703-01 and G. Ferné. Electronic commerce: A new economic and policy area. *Journal of Internet Banking and Commerce,* September 1997, available at www.arraydev.com/commerce/JIBC/9704-08.

[3]J. L. Webster, W. E. Relif, and J. S. Bracker. The manager's guide to strategic planning tools and techniques. *Planning Review,* November/December 1989, pp. 4–12, 47, 48.

[4]G. Celente. *Trends 2000: How to Prepare for and Profit from the Changes of the 21st Century.* New York: Warner, 1998.

[5]Adapted from J. Huber. Trend track: Experts tell you how to spot tomorrow's hottest trends. *Business Startups,* January 1995, pp. 49–51; and C. Russel. *The Official Guide to Racial and Ethnic Diversity.* Ithaca, N.Y.: New Strategist, 1996.

[6]R. Bood and T. Postma. Strategic learning with scenarios. *European Management Journal,* 15, 1997, pp. 633–647; and K. van der Heijden. *Scenarios: The Art of Strategic Conversation.* New York: John Wiley & Sons, 1996.

[7]B. B. Brown. *Delphi Process: A Methodology Used for the Elicitation of Opinions of Experts.* Columbus, Ohio: Rand, 1968.

[8]Adapted from A de Geus. *The Living Company: Habits for Survival in a Turbulent Business Environment.* Boston: Harvard Business School Press, 1997; and R. Henkoff. How to plan for 1995. *Fortune,* December 31, 1990, pp. 70–78.

[9]M. R. Kastein. Delphi, the issues of reliability: A qualitative Delphi study in primary health care in the Netherlands. *Technological Forecasting & Social Change,* 44, 1993, pp. 315–323.

[10]Adapted from L. Schultz. *Technology Foresight: The ASTEC Shipping Partnership's Experience with the Delphi Survey.* Canberra, Australia: Australian Science, Technology and Engineering Council, 1997.

[11]J. R. Evans and D. L. Olson. *Introduction to Simulation and Risk Analysis.* Upper Saddle River, N.J.: Prentice-Hall, 1998.

[12]E. Pfeiffer. Faking failure. *Forbes ASAP,* June 2, 1997, p. 94.

[13]G. A. Hansen. *Automating Business Process Reengineering: Using the Power of Visual Simulation Strategies to Improve Performance and Profit.* Upper Saddle River, N.J.: Prentice-Hall Trade, 1997.

[14]T. B. Sheridan and D. Zeltzer. Virtual reality check. *Technology Review,* October 1993, pp. 20–28.

[15]Adapted from U. Tosi. Virtual reality mountain man. *Forbes ASAP,* June 3, 1996, pp. 30–32.

[16]This section draws on A. G. Robinson and S. Stern. *Corporative Creativity: How Innovation and Improvement Actually Happen.* San Francisco: Berrett-Koehler, 1997; and T. M. Amabile. Motivating creativity in organizations: On doing what you love and loving what you do. *California Management Review,* Fall 1997, pp. 39–58.

[17]W. C. Miller. *The Creative Edge: Fostering Innovation Where You Work.* Reading, Mass.: Addison-Wesley, 1987, pp. 90–91.

[18]Adapted from G. Feigin, C. An, D. Connors, and I. Crawford. Shape up, ship out. *OR/MS Today,* April 1996, pp. 24–30.

[19]W. C. Miller, p. 7.

[20]T. M. Amabile. Entrepreneurial Creativity through motivational Synergy. *Journal of Creative Behavior,* 31, 1997, pp. 18–26.

[21]R. Lieber. Out of the box. *Fortune,* June 23, 1997, p. 76.

[22]A. F. Osborn. *Applied Imagination,* 3d rev. ed. New York: Scribner's, 1963.

[23]M. Diehl and W. Strobe. Productivity loss in brainstorming groups: Toward the solution of a riddle. *Journal of Personality and Social Psychology,* 53, 1997, pp. 497–509.

[24]A. F. Osborn, pp. 229–290.

[25]A. F. Osborn, pp. 155–158.

[26]A. F. Osborn, p. 156.

[27]Adapted from R. I. Sutton and T. A. Kelly. Creativity doesn't require isolation: Why product designers bring visitors "backstage." *California Management Review,* Fall 1997, pp. 75–91; and A. Hargadon and R. I. Sutton. Technology brokering and innovation in a product development firm. *Administrative Science Quarterly,* 42, 1997, pp. 716–749.

[28]R. B. Gallupe, L. M. Bastianutti, and W. H. Cooper. Unlocking brainstorms. *Journal of Applied Psychology,* 76, 1991, pp. 137–142.

[29]A. R. Dennis, J. S. Valacich, T. A. Carte, and M. J. Garfield. The effectiveness of multiple dialogues in electronic brainstorming. *Information Systems Research,* 8, 1997, pp. 203–211.

[30]M. M. Shepherd, R. O. Briggs, B. A. Bruce, J. Yen, and J. F. Nunamker, Jr. Invoking social comparison to improve electronic brainstorming: Beyond rationality. *Journal of Management Information Systems,* 12, 1995/1996, pp. 155–170.

[31]K. Ishikawa. *What is Total Quality Control? The Japanese Way.* Englewood Cliffs, N.J.: Prentice-Hall, 1995.

[32]Rush Medical Center's Web site at www.rush.edu/Mission/index (December 28, 1997).

[33]L. L. Berry and A. Parasuraman. Listening to the customer—The concept of a service-quality information system. *Sloan Management Review,* Spring 1997, pp. 65–76.

[34]J. A. Swift, J. E. Ross, and V. K. Omachonu. *Principles of Total Quality,* 2d ed. Delray Beach, Fla.: St. Luci Press, 1997.

[35]R. E. Camp. *Business Process Benchmarking: Finding and Implementing Best Practices.* Milwaukee: American Society for Quality Control, 1995.

[36]S. Goh and G. Edwards. Benchmarking the learning capability of organizations. *European Management Journal,* 5, 1997, pp. 575–583; and home page for the American Productivity and Quality Center International Benchmarking Clearinghouse at www.apaqc.org (January 10, 1998).

[37]Adapted from T. A. Stewart. Beat the budget and astound your CFO. *Fortune,* October 28, 1997, pp. 187–188; Rank-Xerox home page at www.xerox.com (January 10, 1998).

[38]M. L. Tushman and C. A. O'Reilly III. *Winning through Innovation: A Practical Guide to Leading Organizational Change and Renewal.* Boston: Harvard Business School Press, 1997.

[39]W. E. Deming. *The New Economics for Industry, Government, and Education.* Cambridge, Mass.: Center for Advanced Engineering Study, Massachusetts Institute of Technology, 1993.

[40]J. R. Evans and W. M. Lindsay. *The Management and Control of Total Quality,* 3d ed. St. Paul: West, 1996.

[41]Adapted and modified from G. Langley, K. Nolan, and T. Nolan. The foundation of improvement. Presented at the Sixth Annual International Deming's User's Group Conference. Cincinnati, August 1992; and J. W. Dean, Jr., and J. R. Evans. *Total Quality: Management, Organization, and Strategy.* St. Paul: West, 1994, pp. 81–82.

[42]Adapted from E. S. Fine. Pareto diagrams get to the root of process problems. *Quality,* October 1996, available at www.qualitymag.com/1096ql (January 16, 1998).

[43]D. I. Cleland. *Field Guide to Project Management.* New York: Van Nostrand Reinhold, 1997.

[44]D. Lock. *Project Management,* 6th ed. New York: John Wiley & Sons, 1996.

[45]Project Management Institute. *Code of Ethics for the Project Management Profession.* Upper Darby, Pa.: Project Management Institute, January 7, 1998, available at www.pmi.org (January 8, 1998).

[46]P. B. Williams. *Getting a Project Done on Time.* New York: Amacom, 1996.

[47]L. P. Martin. Inventory of barriers to creative thought and innovation action. Reprinted from J. William Pfeiffer (ed.), *The 1990 Annual: Developing Human Resources.* San Diego: University Associates, 1990, pp. 138–141. Used with permission.

[48]P. Ventresca and T. Flynn. PBJ Corporation: Using idea-generating tools. Reprinted from J. William, Pfeiffer (ed.), *The 1996 Annual: Volume 2, Consulting.* San Diego: Pfeiffer & Company, 1996, pp. 131–137. Used with permission.

[49]This instrument is based on the Federal Quality Institute's *Federal Total Quality Management Handbook 2: Criteria and Scoring Guidelines for the President's Award for Quality and Productivity Improvement.* Washington, D.C.: Office of Personnel Management, 1990. Adapted from G. Reagon. Total Quality Management (TQM). In J. W. Pfeiffer (ed.), *The 1992 Annual: Developing Human Resources.* San Diego: Pfeiffer & Company, 1992, pp. 149–161.

[50]Adapted from E. Leinfuss. MCI Systemhouse supports Caliber Learning Network. *Business Week* (Special section: Outsourcing: from vertical to virtual—the race to change), December 15, 1997, unpaginated; and Caliber Learning Network home page at www. caliberlearning.com/welcome (January 20, 1998).

CHAPTER 10

[1]Adapted from M. Zimmerman. PepsiCo to spin off restaurant division. *Dallas Morning News,* January 24, 1997, pp. 1D-2D; R. Gibson. Fast-food spinoff enters Pepsi-Free era. *Wall Street Journal,* October 7, 1997, pp. B1, B10; and Personal communication with R. Sorrentino, Manager, Frito-Lay, Plano, Texas, May 1998.

[2]R. L. Daft. *Organization Theory and Design,* 6th ed. Cincinnati: South-Western, 1998.

[3]G. A. Rummler and A. P. Brache. *Improving Performance: How to Manage the White Space on the Organization Chart.* San Francisco: Jossey-Bass, 1990.

[4]M. E. McGill, and J. W. Slocum, Jr. *The Smarter Organization: How to Build a Business That Learns to Adapt to Marketplace Needs.* New York: John Wiley & Sons, 1994, pp. 93–96.

[5]Personal communication with C. Dees, Alabama A&M University, Normal, Alabama, October 1997.

[6]J. Pfeffer. *New Directions for Organization Theory.* New York: Oxford University Press, 1997.

[7]Adapted from J. Reese. Starbucks. *Fortune,* December 1996, pp. 190–200; and *1997 Annual Report.* Starbucks Corporation, Seattle, Washington.

[8]Adapted from *1997 Annual Report,* Harrisons & Crosfield, London.

[9]R. McKenna. *Real Time: Preparing for the Age of the Never Satisfied Customer.* Boston: Harvard Business School Press, 1997.

[10]Adapted from *1997 Annual Report,* Fluor Corporation, Irvine, California.

[11]D. J. Ketchen, Jr., et al. Organizational configurations and performance: A meta-analysis. *Academy of Management Journal,* 40, 1997, pp. 222–240.

[12]J. C. Picken and G. G. Dess. Out of (Strategic) Control. *Organizational Dynamics,* Summer 1997, pp. 35–48.

[13]www.novartis.com (October 1997).

[14]*1997 Annual Report,* Comair Holdings, Inc. Cincinnati, Ohio, 1997.

[15]L. Kraar. Behind Samsung's high-stakes push into cars. *Fortune,* May 12, 1997, pp. 119-120; and R. M. Steers, Y. K. Shin, and G. R. Ungson. *The Chaebol.* New York: Harper & Row, 1989.

[16]L. A. Allen. *The Professional Manager's Guide.* Palo Alto, Calif.: Louis A. Allen, 1981.

[17]D. Nadler and M. K. Tushman. *Competing by Design: The Power of Organizational Architecture.* New York: Oxford University Press, 1997.

[18]C. Barnard. *The Functions of an Executive.* Cambridge, Mass.: President and Fellows of Harvard University, 1938.

[19]Personal communication with Sherry Detwiler, vice-president, human resources, Ace Cash Express, Irving, Texas, October 1997.

[20]C. R. Leana. Predictors and consequences of delegation. *Academy of Management Journal,* 29, 1986, pp. 754–774; and R. B. Nelson. *Empowering Employees Through Delegation.* Burr Ridge, Ill.: Irwin, 1994, pp. 17–38.

[21]W. A. Kahn, and K. E. Kram. Authority at work: Internal models and their organizational consequences. *Academy of Management Review,* 19, 1994, pp. 17–50.

[22]A. A. Vicere. Executive education: The leading edge. *Organizational Dynamics,* Autumn 1996, pp. 67–82.

[23]Adapted from D. Poppe. Florida sues Columbia/HCA over alleged mismanagement. *The Miami Herald,* August 19, 1997, pp. B8, B19.

[24]M. L. Tushman and C. A. O'Reilly III. The ambidextrous organization: Managing evolutionary and revolutionary change. *California Management Review,* 38(4), 1996, pp. 8–30.

[25]N. Tichy and R. Charan. Speed, simplicity, self-confidence: An interview with Jack Welch. *Harvard Business Review,* 1989, September–October, pp. 112–121.

[26]N. Brinker and D. T. Phillips. *On The Brink.* Arlington, Tex.: Summit, 1996.

[27]H. M. Trice, and J. M. Beyer. *The Cultures of Work Organizations.* Englewood Cliffs, N.J.: Prentice-Hall, 1993.

[28]P. Sellers. Pepsi opens a second front. *Fortune,* August 8, 1994, pp. 71–76.

[29]Interview with R. Hinton, president of Burgundy Group, July 1997.

[30]W. F. Joyce, V. E. McGee, and J. W. Slocum, Jr. Designing lateral organizations: An analysis of the benefits, costs, and enablers of non-hierarchical organizational forms. *Decision Sciences,* 28, 1997, pp. 1–26.

[31]Adapted from R. A. Melcher. The smudgy legacy AT&T's new prez left behind. *Business Week,* February 3, 1997, pp. 36-37; J. Case. Opening the books. *Harvard Business Review,* March/April 1997, pp. 118-127; Donnelley restructures to push down its costs. *Graphic Arts Monthly,* 68(5), 1996, p. 26; and D. A. Garvin. *R. R. Donnelley & Sons: The Digital Division.* Boston: Harvard Business School, HBS Case 9-396-154, 1996.

CHAPTER 11

[1]Adapted from L. Grant. GE's 'smart bomb' strategy. *Fortune,* July 21, 1997, pp. 109–110; and N. C. Remich, Jr. A Kentucky thoroughbred that is running strong. *Appliance Manufacturer,* July 1995, pp. GEA1-3.

[2]A. D. Chandler. *Strategy and Structure.* Cambridge, Mass.: MIT Press, 1962.

[3]D. J. Ketchen, Jr. et al. Organizational configurations and performance: A meta-analysis. *Academy of Management Journal,* 40, 1997, pp. 222–240.

[4]D. Nadler and M. Tushman. *Competing by Design: The Power of Organizational Architecture.* New York: Oxford University Press, 1997.

[5]Personal communication with Ms. K. Steinback, vice-president, franchise operations, Pizza Inn, Dallas, Texas, November 1997; *Pizza Today,* July 1997, pp. 78–88; and Total pizza sales reach new high. *Frozen Food Digest,* April-May 1996, pp. 24–25.

[6]G. Hamel and C. K. Prahalad. *Competing for the Future.* Boston: Harvard Business School Press, 1994; and P. W. Roberts and R. Greenwood. Integrating transaction cost and institutional theories: Toward a constrained-efficiency framework for understanding organizational design adoption. *Academy of Management Review,* 22, 1997, pp. 346–373.

[7]Adapted from L. Grant. Where did the snap, crackle & pop go? *Fortune,* August 4, 1997, pp. 223–224; and R. Cook. Will JWT's dedicated Kellogg's operation work? *Campaign,* May 23, 1997, pp. 20–21.

[8]Adapted from W. Pape. Group insurance. *Inc.Tech.* 2, 1997, pp. 29-31. For other examples, see S. E. Prokesch. Unleashing the power of learning: An interview with British Petroleum's John Browne. *Harvard Business*

Review, September-October 1997, pp. 146–168.

[9]T. Burns and G. M. Stalker. *The Management of Innovation.* London: Tavistock, 1961.

[10]P. R. Lawrence and J. W. Lorsch. *Organization and Environment.* Homewood, Ill.: Irwin, 1967.

[11]Adapted from J. Cosco. Black & Deckering Black & Decker. *Journal of Business Strategy,* January-February 1994, pp. 59-62; K. Holland. Retooling. *Business Week,* February 9, 1998, pp. 48–49; J. Welsh. Black & Decker to shed some lines and focus on tools. *Wall Street Journal,* January 28, 1998, p. A6.

[12]J. D. Thompson. *Organizations in Action.* New York: McGraw-Hill, 1967, pp. 51–67; and R. T. Keller. Technology-information processing fit and the performance of R & D project groups: A test of contingency theory. *Academy of Management Journal,* 37, 1994, pp. 167–179.

[13]C. Gresov and R. Drazin. Equifinality: Functional equivalence in organization design. *Academy of Management Review,* 22, 1997, pp. 403–428.

[14]E. Davies. The ins and outs of this year's 5 hundred. *Fortune,* April 28, 1997, pp. F1–F55.

[15]L. L. Berry, K. Seiders, and L. G. Gresham. The common traits of successful retailers. *Organizational Dynamics,* Autumn 1997, pp. 7–23.

[16]J. B. Quinn, P. Anderson, and S. Finkelstein. Leveraging intellect. *Academy of Management Executive,* 10(3), 1996, pp. 7–28.

[17]J. L. Heskett, W. E. Sasser, Jr., and L. A. Schlesinger. *The Service Profit Chain.* New York: Free Press, 1997.

[18]Adapted from G. Creno. Petsmart to close discovery center departments, relocate stores. *Knight-Ridder/Tribune Business News,* August 11, 1997, pp. B8–B12.

[19]S. L. Brown and K. M. Eisenhardt. The art of continuous change: Linking complexity theory and time-paced evolution in relentlessly shifting organizations. *Administrative Science Quarterly,* 42, 1997, pp. 1–34.

[20]J. R. Galbraith. *Designing Complex Organizations.* Boston: Addison-Wesley, 1973; and J. R. Galbraith. *Competing with Flexible Lateral Designs.* Boston: Addison-Wesley, 1994.

[21]Adapted from S. Booker. A case study on utilizing marketing intelligence at Harrah's Entertainment, Inc. (unpublished study). Commercial Strategic Systems Office, The Associates, Irving, Texas, December, 1997; and C. Brinkley. Harrah's builds database about patrons. *Wall Street Journal,* September 3, 1997, pp. B1, B8.

[22]L. R. Burns and D. R. Wholey. Adoptions and abandonment of matrix management programs: Effects of organizational characteristics and interorganizational networks. *Academy of Management Journal,* 36, 1993, pp. 106–138.

[23]W. F. Joyce, V. E. McGee, and J. W. Slocum, Jr. Designing lateral organizations: An analysis of the benefits, costs, and enablers of non-hierarchical organizational forms. *Decision Sciences,* 28, 1997, pp. 1–25.

[24]N. Nohria and R. Gulati. Is slack good or bad for innovation? *Academy of Management Journal,* 39, 1996, pp. 1245–1264; and J. L. C. Cheng and I. L. Kesner. Organizational slack

and response to environmental shifts: The impact of resource allocation patterns. *Journal of Management,* 23, 1997, pp. 1–18.

[25]S. E. Human and K. Provan. An emergent theory of structure and outcomes in small-firm strategic management networks. *Academy of Management Journal,* 40, 1997, pp. 368-403; and R. E. Miles, C. C. Snow, J. A. Matthews, G. Miles, and H. J. Coleman, Jr. Organizing in the knowledge age: Anticipating the cellar form. *Academy of Management Executive,* 11(4), 1997, pp. 7–24.

[26]B. Richards. Nike posts rise in profits but issues warning for year. *Wall Street Journal,* September 19, 1997, p. B13; J. Steinhauer. Nike is in a league of its own; with no big rival, it calls the shots in athletic shoes. *New York Times,* June 7, 1997, p. 21; and R. E. Miles and C. C. Snow. *Fit, Failure and the Hall of Fame.* New York: McGraw-Hill, 1994.

[27]W. Newberry and Y. Zeira. Generic differences between equity international joint ventures and international acquisitions and international greenfield investments: Implications for patent companies. *Journal of World Business,* 32, 1997, pp. 87–102.

[28]See Galoob Toys home page at www.Galoob.com

[29]C. P. Holland and A. G. Lockett. Mixed mode network structures: The strategic use of electronic communication by organizations. *Organization Science,* 8, 1997, pp. 475–488; and G. Walker, B. Kogut, and W. Shan. Social capital, structural holes and the formation of an industry network. *Organization Science,* 8, 1997, pp. 109–125.

[30]K. Crowston. A coordination theory approach to organization process design. *Organization Science,* 8, 1997, pp. 157–175.

[31]Adapted from J. B. White and E. MacDonald. At Arthur Andersen, accounts face unlikely adversary: The consulting operation they created becomes rival for power, prestige. *Wall Street Journal,* April 23, 1997, pp. 1-2; D. Whitford. Arthur, Arthur. *Fortune,* November 10, 1997, pp. 169–176; and H. Banks. House divided. *Forbes,* November 3, 1997, pp. 344–345. Also visit Arthur Andersen's home page at www.arthurandersen.com

CHAPTER 12

[1]C. Hall. Ringmasters turn a circus into an empire. *Dallas Morning News,* February 8, 1998, pp. H1–2. G. Flynn. Acrobats, Aerialists, and HR: The big top needs big HR. *Workforce,* August 1997, pp. 38–45.

[2]For a review of strategic human resources management, see S. E. Jackson and R. S. Schuler. Understanding human resource management in the context of organizations and their environments. *Annual Review of Psychology,* 46, 1995, pp. 237–264; and C. R. Greer. *Strategy and Human Resources: A General Managerial Perspective.* Upper Saddle River, N.J.: Prentice-Hall, 1995.

[3]M. A. Huselid, S. E. Jackson, and R. S. Schuler. Technical and strategic human resource management effectiveness as determinants of firm performance. *Academy of Management Journal,* 40, 1997, pp. 171–188; and B. Becker and B. Gerhart. The impact of human resource management on organiza-

tional performance: Progress and prospects. *Academy of Management Journal,* 39, 1996, pp. 779–801.

[4]B. E. Becker and M. A. Huselid. High performance work systems and firm performance: A synthesis of research and managerial implications. *Research in Personnel and Human Resources Management* (in press); and W. N. Davidson III, D. L. Worrell, and J. B. Fox. Early retirement programs and firm performance. *Academy of Management Journal,* 39, 1996, pp. 970–984. A. Davis-Blake and B. Uzzi. Determinants of employment externalization: A study of temporary workers and independent contractors. *Administrative Science Quarterly,* 38, 1993, pp. 195–223.

[5]Discussions of international issues can be found in M. J. Levine. *Worker Rights and Labor Standards in Asia's Four Tigers: A Comparative Perspective.* New York: Plenum, 1997; J. P. Begin. *Dynamic Human Resource Systems: Cross-National Systems.* Amsterdam: Walter De Gruyter, 1997; P. J. Dowling, R. S. Schuler, and D. E. Welch. *International Dimensions of Human Resource Management.* International Thomson Publishing, 1999; and J. M. Hiltrop and P. R. Sparrow. *European Human Resource Management in Transition.* Upper Saddle River, N.J.: Prentice-Hall, 1995.

[6]G. Koretz. Women storm the symphony. *Business Week,* March 17, 1997, p. 24

[7]Adapted from: More ticklish questions. *Across the Board,* May, 1996, pp. 38–43. The name of the company is fictitious, but the situation reflects a common problem.

[8]Bureau of National Affairs. Datagraph: Union membership by state. *Bulletin to Management,* July 11, 1997, p. 22.

[9]S. Greenhouse. Podiatrists to form a union, first in the nation for doctors. *New York Times,* October 25, 1996, pp. B1–B2.

[10]A. Bernstein. Look who's pushing productivity. *Business Week,* April 7, 1997, pp. 72–75.

[11]E. E. Lawler III, and G. E. Ledford, Jr. New approaches to organizing: Competencies and the decline of the bureaucratic model. In C. L. Cooper and S. E. Jackson (eds.). *Creating Tomorrow's Organizations: Handbook for Future Research in Organizations.* Chichester, England: John Wiley & Sons, 1997, pp. 231–249.

[12]D. Q. Mills. The decline and rise of IBM. *Sloan Management Review,* Summer 1996, pp. 78–82.

[13]J. Pepper. A new era for workers. *Solutions,* October 1996, pp. 24–25.

[14]S. Lublin. Rehiring former employees has its pitfalls. *Wall Street Journal,* December 30, 1996, pp. B1, B4.

[15]P. Nakache. Cisco's recruiting edge. *Fortune,* September 29, 1997, pp. 275-276.

[16]W. L. French *Human Resources Management,* 3d ed. Boston: Houghton Mifflin, 1994.

[17]A. Fisher. What labor shortage? *Fortune,* June 23, 1997, pp. 154–156; S. Baker. Forget the huddled masses: Send nerds. *Business Week,* July 21, 1997, pp. 110–116; A. Berstein. Calling all nerds. *Business Week,* March 10, 1997, pp. 36–37; and S. Gruner. Benchmark: The challenge of recruiting. *Inc.,* March 1997, p. 102.

[18]Y. Bian. Bringing strong ties back in: Indirect

ties, network bridges, and job searches in China. *American Sociological Review,* 62, 1997, pp. 366–385.

[19]J. Aley. The heart of Silicon Valley. *Fortune,* July 7, 1997, pp. 66–74.

[20]A. Fisher. The world's most admired companies. *Fortune,* October 27, 1997, pp. 220–240.

[21]T. D. Schellenhardt. Talent pool is shallow as corporations seek executives for top jobs. *Wall Street Journal,* June 26, 1997, pp. A1, A10.

[22]J. Stuller. "You'll be hearing from my lawyer." *Across the Board,* January, 1997, pp. 32–37.

[23]M. A. McDaniel, D. L. Whetzel, F. L. Schmidt, and S. D. Maurer. The validity of employment interviews: A comprehensive review and meta-analysis. *Journal of Applied Psychology,* 79, 1994, pp. 599–616.

[24]D. M. Gable and T. A. Judge. Interviewers' perceptions of person-organization fit and organizational selection decisions. *Journal of Applied Psychology,* 82, 1997, pp. 546–561; G. N. Powell. Applicant reactions to the initial employment interview: Exploring theoretical and methodological issues. *Personnel Psychology,* 44, 1991, pp. 67–83; and T. W. Dougherty, D. B. Turban, and J. C. Callender. Confirming first impressions in the employment interview: A field study of interviewer behavior. *Journal of Applied Psychology,* 79, 1994, pp. 659–665.

[25]R. C. Liden, C. R. Martin, and C. K. Parsons. Interviewer and applicant behaviors in employment interviews. *Academy of Management Journal,* 36, 1993, pp. 372–386.

[26]A. Tziner, S. Ronen, and D. A. Hacohen. A four-year study of an assessment center in a financial corporation. *Journal of Organizational Behavior,* 14, 1993, pp. 225–237.

[27]P. Carbonara. Hire for attitude. Train for skill. *Fast Company,* April–May 1996, pp. 64–71.

[28]P. Carbonara.

[29]M. K. Mount and M. R. Barrick. The big five personality dimensions: Implications for research and practice in human resources management. *Research in Personnel and Human Resources Management,* 13, 1995, pp. 153–200. See also, J. M. Crant. The proactive personality scale and objective job performance among real estate agents. *Journal of Applied Psychology,* 80, 1995, pp. 532–537; and J. R. van Scotter and S. J. Motowidlo. Interpersonal facilitation and job dedication as separate facets of contextual performance. *Journal of Applied Psychology,* 81, 1996, pp. 525–531.

[30]R. Brookler. Industry standards in workplace drug testing. *Personnel Journal,* April 1992, pp. 128–132; and B. Oliver. Fight drugs with knowledge. *Training & Development,* May 1994, pp. 105–108.

[31]S. Greengard. Theft control starts with HR strategies. *Personnel Journal,* April 1993, pp. 80–91; and H. J. Bernardin and D. K. Cooke. Validity of an honesty test in predicting theft among convenience store employees. *Academy of Management Journal,* 36, 1993, pp. 1097–1108.

[32]D. Ones, S. C. Viswesvaran, and F. L. Schmidt. Comprehensive meta-analysis of integrity test validities: Findings and implica-

tions for personnel selection and theories of job performance. *Journal of Applied Psychology Monograph,* 78, 1993, pp. 679–703.

[33]Adapted from R. Henkoff. Finding, training, and keeping the best service workers. *Fortune,* October 3, 1994, pp. 110–122.

[34]M. Moravec, O. J. Johannessen, and T. A. Hjelmas. Thumbs up for self-managed teams. *Management Review,* July/August 1997; S. E. Prokesch. Unleashing the power of learning: An interview with British Petroleum's John Browne. *Harvard Business Review,* September–October, 1997; and Moravec, O. J. Johannessen, and T. A. Hjelmas. We have seen the future and it is self-managed. *PM Network,* September 1997, pp. 20–22.

[35]S. Baker. The new factory worker. *Business Week,* September 30, 1996, pp. 59–68.

[36]M. Lombardo, M. McCall, and D. DeVries. *Looking Glass, Inc.* Greensboro, N.C.: Center for Creative Leadership, 1991.

[37]P. J. Dowling, R. S. Schuler, and D. E. Welch.

[38]Adapted from C. M. Solomon. Staff selection impacts global success. *Personnel Journal,* January 1994, pp. 88–101; and C. M. Solomon. Global operations demand that HR rethink diversity. *Personnel Journal,* July 1994, pp. 40–50.

[39]For a recent review of research, see R. D. Arvey and K. R. Murphy. Performance evaluations in work settings. *Annual Review of Psychology,* 49, 1998, pp. 141–168. For an excellent discussion of how performance standards can affect employees' satisfaction and motivation, see P. Bobko, and A. Colella. Employee reactions to performance standards: A review and research proposition. *Personnel Psychology,* 47, 1994, pp. 1–29. See also, T. E. Becker and S. L. Martin. Trying to look bad at work: Methods and motives for managing poor impressions in organizations. *Academy of Management Journal,* 38, 1995, pp. 174–199.

[40]M. H. Harris. Rater motivation in the performance appraisal context: A theoretical framework. *Journal of Management,* 20, 1994, pp. 737–756; C. E. Lance. Test of a latent structure of performance ratings derived from Wherry's (1952) theory of rating. *Journal of Management,* 20, 1994, pp. 757–771; and S. J. Wayne and R. C. Liden. Effects of impression management on performance ratings: A longitudinal study. *Academy of Management Journal,* 38, 1995, pp. 232–260.

[41]Adapted from P. R. Scholtes. Total quality or performance appraisal: Choose one. *National Productivity Review,* Summer 1993, pp. 349–363; and J. S. Bowman. At last, an alternative to performance appraisal: Total quality management. *Public Administration Review,* 54(2), 1994, pp. 129–136.

[42]Adapted from R. S. Schuler and D. L. Harris. Deming quality improvement: Implications for human resource management as illustrated in a small company. *Human Resource Planning,* 14(3), 1991, pp. 191–207; and S. Nelton. How a Pennsylvania company makes the sweet sounds of innovation. *Nation's Business,* December 1991, p. 16. See also, J. Ghorpade and M. M. Chen. Creating quality-driven performance appraisal systems. *Academy of Management Executive,* 9(1), 1995, pp. 32–41.

[43]E. E. Lawler III. *Strategic Pay: Aligning Organizational Strategies and Pay Systems.*

San Francisco: Jossey-Bass, 1990; and R. J. Greene. Person-focused pay: Should it replace job-based pay? *Compensation & Benefits Management,* 9(4), 1993, pp. 46–55.

[44]J. Greenberg and K. S. Scott. Why do workers bite the hands that feed them? Employee theft as a social exchange process. *Research in Organizational Behavior,* 18, 1996, pp. 111–156; J. Greenberg. Stealing in the name of justice: Informational and interpersonal moderators of theft reactions to underpayment inequity. *Organizational Behavior and Human Decision Processes,* 54, 1993, pp. 81–103; and J. Schaubroek, B. May, and F. W. Brown. Procedural justice explanations and employee reactions to economic hardship: A field experiment. *Journal of Applied Psychology,* 79, 1994, pp. 455–460.

[45]Adapted from Motivation the old-fashioned way. *Inc.,* November 1994, p. 134.

[46]C. D. Fisher, L. F. Schoenfeldt, and J. B. Shaw, pp. 573–577.

[47]C. D. Fisher, L. F. Schoenfeldt, and J. B. Shaw.

[48]D. J. Cherrington. *The Management of Human Resources,* 4th ed. Englewood Cliffs, N.J.: Prentice-Hall, 1995, pp. 452–453.

[49]P. J. Dowling, R. S. Schuler, and D. E. Welch.

[50]Adapted from C. M. Solomon. Staff selection impacts global success. *Personnel Journal,* January 1994, pp. 88–101; and C. M. Solomon. Global operations demand that HR rethink diversity. *Personnel Journal,* July 1994, pp. 40–50.

[51]M. Koshuta and M. K. McCuddy. Improving productivity in the health care industry: An argument and supporting evidence from one hospital. *Health Care Supervisor,* 8(1), 1989, pp. 15–30.

[52]S. C. Kumbhakar and A. E. Dunbar. The elusive ESOP-productivity link: Evidence from U. S. firm-level data. *Journal of Public Economics,* 52(2),1993, pp. 273–283.

[53]R. A. Wolfe and D. F. Parker. Employee health management: Challenges and opportunities. *Academy of Management Executive,* 8 (2), 1994, pp. 22–31.

[54]E. Matson. How to get a piece of the action. *Fast Company,* November 1997, pp. 90–100; and C. Novicki. Secrets of a superagent. *Fast Company,* November, 1997, p. 96.

[55]R. Hiebeler, T. B. Kelly, and C. Ketteman. *Best Practices: Building Your Business with Cutomer-Focused Solutions.* New York: Simon & Schuster, 1998.

CHAPTER 13

[1]Adapted from: N. Morgan. My days at Camp Lur'ning. *Fast Company,* October–November, 1996, pp. 115–124; A. W. Webber. XBS learns to grow. *Fast Company,* October–November, 1996, pp. 112–125; and Malcolm Baldrige National Quality Award 1997 Winner Services Category: Xerox Business Services. www.nist.gov/pubic-affairs/bald97 (November 7, 1997).

[2]G. Hamel. Strategy as revolution. *Harvard Business Review,* July–August 1996, pp. 69–82.

[3]E. O. Welles. Bootstrapping for billions. *Inc.,* September, 1994, pp. 78–86.

[4]R. A. Johnson. Antecedents and outcomes of

corporate refocusing. *Journal of Management,* 22, 1996, pp. 439-483.

[5]J. Martin. Give 'em exactly what they want. *Fortune,* November 10, 1997, pp. 283–284.

[6]S. Greengard. You're next! There is no escaping merger mania! *Workforce,* April, 1997, pp. 2–6; and *HR Executive Review: HR Challenges in Mergers and Acquisitions.* New York: The Conference Board, 1997.

[7]Associated Press. Kodak's hometown feels little security. *Dallas Morning News,* November 13, 1997, p. 4D.

[8]E. C. Nevis, A. J. DiBella, and J. M. Gould. Understanding organizations as learning systems. *Sloan Management Review,* Winter, 1995, pp. 73–85; P. Senge. *The Fifth Discipline: The Art and Practice of the Learning Organization.* New York: Doubleday, 1990; and G. Huber. Organizational learning: The contributing processes and literature. *Organization Science,* 2, 1991, pp. 88–115.

[9]Y-T. Cheng and A. H. Van de Ven. Learning the innovation journey: Order out of chaos. *Organization Science,* 7, 1996, pp. 593–614.

[10]T. Maxon. Southwest to go "ticketless" on all routes January 31. *Dallas Morning News,* January 11, 1995, p. 1D; M. E. McGill and J. W. Slocum, Jr. *The Smarter Organization: How to Build an Organization That Learns to Adapt to Marketplace Needs.* New York: John Wiley & Sons, 1994; and M. DePree. *Leadership Is an Art.* New York: Doubleday, 1992.

[11]C. Kim and R. Maubourgne. Fair process: Managing in the knowledge economy. *Harvard Business Review,* July–August, 1997, pp. 65–75; and R. Pascale, M. Millimann, and L. Gioja. Changing the way we change. *Harvard Business Review,* November–December, 1997, pp. 127–139.

[12]J. P. MacDuffie. The road to "Root Cause": Shop-floor problem-solving at three auto assembly plants. *Management Science,* 43, 1997, pp. 479–502.

[13]A. Kransdorrf. Fight organizational memory lapse. *Workforce,* September, 1997, pp. 34–39.

[14]N. A. Wishart, J. J. Elam, and D. Robey. Redrawing the portrait of a learning organization: Inside Knight-Ridder, Inc. *Academy of Management Executive,* 10, 1996, pp. 7–20; For an in-depth discussion of the importance of matching cultures and strategies, see A. C. Bluedorn and E. F. Lundgren. A culture-match perspective for strategic change. In R. W. Woodman and W. A. Pasmore (eds.), *Research in Organizational Change and Development,* 7, 1993, pp. 137–179.

[15]N. A. Wishart, J. J. Elam, and D. Robey.

[16]B. Laymon. Xerox chairman makes business case for "family-friendly" work culture: Allaire delivers keynote at "CEO Summit on Rethinking Life and Work." Xerox Press Release, www.xerox.com/PR/NR970915-family (September 15, 1997).

[17]Adapted from R. Jacob. Absence of management. *American Way,* February 15, 1993, pp. 38–42; S. Tully. The modular corporation. *Fortune,* February 8, 1993, pp. 106–116; and W. Kiechel III. The organization that learns. *Fortune,* May 18, 1992, pp. 93–98.

[18]D. Lei, J. W. Slocum, Jr., and R. A. Pitts. Building cooperative advantage: Managing strategic alliances to promote organizational

learning. *Journal of World Business,* 32(3), 1997, pp. 203–223; and R. C. Hill and D. Hellriegel. Critical contingencies in joint venture management: Some lessons from managers. *Organization Science,* 5, 1994, pp. 594–607.

[19]J. B. Goes and S. H. Park. Interorganizational links and innovation: The case of hospital services. *Academy of Management Journal,* 40, 1997, pp. 673–696.

[20]R. M. Grant. Prospering in dynamically-competitive environments: Organizational capability as knowledge integration. *Organization Science,* 7, 1996, pp. 357–411; and J. P. Liebeskind, A. L. Oliver, L. Zucker, and M. Brewer. Social networks, learning, and flexibility: Sourcing scientific knowledge in new biotechnology firms. *Organization Science,* 7, 1996, pp. 428–443.

[21]J. Stack. The great game of business. *Inc.,* June 1992, pp. 53–66.

[22]P. S. Goodman and E. D. Darr. Exchanging best practices through computer-aided systems. *Academy of Management Executive,* 10 (2), 1996, pp. 7–19.

[23]A. H. Van de Ven and M. S. Poole. Explaining development and change in organizations. *Academy of Management Review,* 20, 1996, pp. 510–540; P. J. Robertson, D. R. Roberts, and J. I. Porras. Dynamics of planned change: Assessing empirical support for a theoretical model. *Academy of Management Journal,* 36, 1993, 619–634; and M. L. Tushman and C. A. O'Reilly III. *A Practical Guide to Leading Organizational Change and Renewal.* Boston: Harvard Business School Press, 1997.

[24]Adapted from J. E. Ettlie and R. D. O'Keefe. Innovative attitudes, values, and intentions in organizations. *Journal of Management Studies,* 19, 1982, p. 176. Used by permission of the authors. For another description of attitudes toward change, see C.-M. Lau and R. W. Woodman. Understanding organizational change: A schematic perspective. *Academy of Management Journal,* 38, 1997, pp. 537–554.

[25]S. B. Bacharach, P. Bamberger, and W. J. Sonnenstuhl. The organizational transformation process: The micropolitics of dissonance reduction and the alignment of logics of action. *Administrative Science Quarterly,* 1996, pp. 477–506; and M. Hammer and S. A. Stanton. The power of reflection. *Fortune,* November 24, 1997, pp. 291–296.

[26]E. McColgan. How fidelity invests in service professionals. *Harvard Business Review,* January–February, 1997, pp. 137–143.

[27]G. P. Huber and W. H. Glick. *Organizational Change and Redesign.* New York: Oxford University Press, 1993. Also see A. Howard and Associates. *Diagnosis for Organizational Change: Methods and Models.* New York: Guilford, 1994.

[28]E. McColgan.

[29]R. Maurer. *Beyond the Wall of Resistance.* Austin, Texas: Bard Books, 1996.

[30]K. Skoldberg. Tales of change. *Organization Science,* 5, 1994, pp. 219–238.

[31]T. Petzinger, Jr. Georg Bauer put burden of downsizing into employees' hands. *Wall Street Journal,* May 10, 1996, p. B1.

[32]J. M. Pennings, H. Barkema, and S. Douma. Organizational learning and diversification. *Academy of Management Journal,* 37, 1994,

pp. 608–641.

[33]P. Strebel. Why do employees resist change? *Harvard Business Review,* May–June 1996, pp. 86–106.

[34]A. E. Reichers, J. P. Wanous, and J. T. Austin. Understanding and managing cynicism about organizational change. *Academy of Management Executive,* 11, 1997, p. 48.

[35]Adapted from W. M. Carley. *Wall Street Journal,* January 13, 1997, pp. A1, A8; and GE-P&W engine alliance aggressively moves forward. *PRNewswire,* September 2, 1996.

[36]Adapted from C. H. Lovelock. What language shall we put it in? *Marketing Management,* Winter, 1994, p. 41; J. Valente. British Airways sees strong gains, challenges ahead. *Wall Street Journal,* November 8, 1994, p. 4B; and P. Dwyer. British Air: Not cricket. *Business Week,* January 25, 1993, pp. 50–51.

[37]J. E. Mathieu and D. M. Zajkac. A review and meta-analysis of the antecedents, correlates, and consequences of organizational commitment. *Psychological Bulletin,* 108, 1990, pp. 171–194; J. F. Brett, W. L. Cron, and J. W. Slocum, Jr. Economic dependency on work: A moderator of the relationship between organizational commitment and performance. *Academy of Management Journal,* 38, 1995, pp. 261-271; R. E. Allen, M. A. Lucero, and K. L. Van Norman. An examination of the individual's decision to participate in an employee involvement program. *Group & Organization Management,* 22, 1997, pp. 117-143; and W. C. Kim and R. Mauborgne. Fair process: Managing the knowledge economy. *Harvard Business Review,* July–August, 1997, pp. 65–75.

[38]G. Jones, G. Oryx plan drives stock down 15%. Dallas Morning News, January 21, 1995, p. 1F; and G. James. Oryx rolls out cost-cutting plans. *Dallas Morning News,* January 20, 1995, p. 1D.

[39]T. G. Cummings and C. G. Worley. *Organizational Change and Development,* 7th ed. Cincinnati: South- Western, 1997.

[40]E. Randell. IBM's grassroots revival. The real story of how Big Blue found the future, got the net, and learned to love the People in Black. *Fast Company,* October–November, 1997, pp. 102–200.

[41]T. L. Amburgey and T. Dacin. As the left foot follows the right? The dynamics of strategic and structural change. *Academy of Management Journal,* 37, 1994, pp. 1427–1452; and E. Romanelli and M. L. Tushman. Organizational transformation as a punctuated equilibrium: An empirical test. *Academy of Management Journal,* 37, 1994, pp. 1141–1166.

[42]T. D. Ludwig and E. S. Geller. Assigned versus participative goal setting and response generalization: Managing injury control among professional pizza deliverers. *Journal of Applied Psychology,* 82, 1997, pp. 253–261.

[43]G. Flynn. A flight plan for success. *Workforce,* July, 1997, pp. 72-78.

[44]K. J. Klein and J. S. Sorra. The challenge of innovation implementation. *Academy of Management Review,* 1996, 21, pp. 1055–1080.

[45]G. Flynn. It takes values to capitalize on change. *Workforce,* April 1997, pp. 27-34.

[46]I. L. Goldstein. Training in work organizations. In M. D. Dunnette and L.M. Hough

(eds.), *Handbook of Industrial and Organizational Psychology*, 2d ed., vol. 2. Palo Alto, Calif.: Consulting Psychologists Press, 1991, pp. 507–620.

[47]For a detailed review of the effectiveness of various change programs, see B. A. Macy and H. Izumi. Organizational change, design, and work innovation: A meta-analysis of 131 North American field studies—1961–1991. In R. W. Woodman and W. A. Pasmore (eds.) *Research in Organizational Change and Development*, 7, 1993, pp. 235–313.

[48]J. Pfeffer. *Competitive Advantage Through People*. Boston: Harvard Business School Press, 1994.

[49]S. K. Parker, T. D. Wall, and P. R. Jackson. "That's not my job": Developing flexible employee work orientations. *Academy of Management Journal*, 40, 1997, pp. 899–929.

[50]L. Thach and R. W. Woodman. Organizational change and information technology: Managing on the edge of cyberspace. *Organizational Dynamics*, Summer 1994, pp. 30–46.

[51]G. Imperato. Harley shifts gears. *Fast Company*, June–July, 1997, pp. 104–113; G. Slutsker. Hog wild. *Forbes*, May 23, 1993, pp. 45–56; and K. L. Miller. The rumble heard 'round the world: Harleys. *Business Week*, May 24, 1993, pp. 58–60.

[52]C. Hymowitz. Task of managing changes in workplace takes a careful hand. *Wall Street Journal*, July 1, 1997, p. B1.

[53]E. Brynjolfsson, A. A. Renshaw, and M. V. Alstyne. The matrix of change. *Sloan Management Review*, Winter, 1997, pp. 37–54; M. Hammer and J. Champy. *Reengineering the Corporation*. New York: HarperCollins, 1993; M. Hammer. *Beyond Reengineering: How the Processs-Centered Organization Is Changing Our Lives*. New York: HarperBusinesss, 1996; and J. Champy. *Reengineering Management: The Mandate for New Leadership*. New York: HarperBusiness, 1996.

[54]A. Majchrzak and Q.Wang. Breaking the functional mind-set in process organizations. *Harvard Business Review*, September–October, 1996, pp. 93–99.

[55]J. D. Sterman, N. P. Repenning, and F. Kofman. Unanticipated side effects of successful quality programs: Exploring a paradox of organizational improvement. *Management Science*, 43, 1997, pp. 503–521.

[56]Adapted from G. Hall, J. Rosenthal, and J. Wade. How to make reengineering really work. *Harvard Business Review*, November–December 1993, pp. 124–126; and A. Nahavandi and E. Aranda. Restructuring teams for the reengineered organization. *Academy of Management Executive*, 87(4), 1994, pp. 58–68; H. Lancaster. Managing your career. *Wall Street Journal*, January 17, 1995, p. 1B. Also see D. Santos, B. L. Dos, and K. Peffers. Rewards to Investors in innovative information technology applications: First movers and early followers in ATMs. *Organization Science*, 6, 1995, p. 241.

[57]R. L. DeWitt. The structural consequences of downsizing. *Organization Science*, 4, 1993, pp. 30–40.

[58]W. F. Cascio. Financial consequences of employment-change decisions in major U. S. corporations. *Academy of Management Journal*, 40, 1997, pp. 1175–1189.

[59]P. J. Robertson, D. R. Roberts, and J. I. Porras. An evaluation of a model of planned organizational change: Evidence from a meta-analysis. In R. W. Woodman and W. A. Pasmore (eds.), *Research in Organizational Change and Development*, 1993, 7, pp. 1–39.

[60]J. I. Porras and P. J. Robertson. Organizational development: Theory, practice, and research. In M. D. Dunnette and L. M. Hough (eds.), *Handbook of Industrial and Organizational Psychology*, 2d ed., vol. 2. Palo Alto, Calif.: Consulting Psychologists Press, 1992; and T. T. Baldwin, C. Danielson, and W. Wiggenhorn. The evolution of learning strategies in organizations: From employee development to business redefinition. *Academy of Management Executive*, 11(4), pp. 47–58.

[61]A. I. Kraut. *Organizational Surveys: Tools for Assessment and Change*. San Francisco: Jossey-Bass, 1996.

[62]G. Flynn. Competing—with grace. *Workforce*, June, 1997, pp. 52–60.

[63]Adapted from P. Roberts. Kinko's: The free agent home office. *Fast Company*, January, 1998, pp. 164–179; N. Byrnes. Kinko's goes corporate. *Business Week*, August 19, 1996, pp. 58–59; and information provided on the Web sites www.kinkos.com; www.tlckinkos.com; and www.edp.com (November 10, 1997).

CHAPTER 14

[1]J. Thomas. Satisfaction in job well done is only reward for e-mail software inventor. *New York Times*, Tuesday, January 21, 1997, p. A10; S. Hamm. The education of Marc Andreesen. *Business Week*, April 13, 1998, pp. 84–92.

[2]This chapter focuses on theories that have direct implications for productivity. More detailed discussions of the causes and consequences of employees' affective reactions to their work experiences are provided in H. M. Weiss and R. Cropanzano. Affective events theory: A theoretical discussion of the structure, causes and consequences of affective experiences at work. *Research in Organizational Behavior*, 18, 1996, pp. 1–74; J. P. Meyers and N. J. Allen. *Commitment in the Workplace: Theory, Research and Application*. Thousand Oaks, Calif.: Sage, 1997; and P. E. Spector. *Job Satisfaction: Application, Assessment, Causes and Consequences*. Thousand Oaks, Calif.: Sage, 1997.

[3]For example, see P. Roussel and R. L. Heneman. Individual reward systems emerge in France. *ACA News*, Juy/August, 1997, pp. 18–19; C. C. Cheng. New trends in reward allocation preference: A Sino-American comparison. *Academy of Management Journal*, 38, 1995, pp. 408–428; R. H. Moorman and G. L. Blakely. Individualism–collectivism as an individual difference predictor of organizational citizenship behavior. *Journal of Organizational Behavior*, 16, 1995, pp. 127–142. McEvoy, J-L Farh, P. C. Earley, and S-C Lin. Impetus for action: A cultural analysis of justice and organizational citizenship behavior in Chinese society. *Administrative Science Quarterly*, 42, 1997, pp. 421–444; and D. H. B. Welsh, F. Luthans, and S. M. Sommer. Managing Russian factory workers: The impact of U.S.-based behavioral and participative techniques. *Academy of Management Journal*, 36, 1993, pp. 58–79.

[4]For reviews of the literature, see F. J. Landy and W. S. Becker. Motivation theory reconsidered. *Research in Organizational Behavior*, 9, 1987, pp. 1–38.

[5]A. H. Maslow. *Motivation and Personality*, 2d ed. New York: Harper & Row, 1970. Also see D. H. Shapiro, Jr., C. E. Schwartz, and J. A. Astin. Controlling ourselves, controlling our world. Psychology's role in understanding positive and negative consequences of seeking and gaining control. *American Psychologist*, 51, 1996, pp. 1213–1230.

[6]G. P. Zachary. The new search for meaning in meaningless work. *Wall Street Journal*, January 6, 1997, p. B1.

[7]E. L. Betz. Two tests of Maslow's theory of need fulfillment. *Journal of Vocational Behavior*, 24, 1984, pp. 204–220; and R. Hugman and R. Hadley. Involvement, motivation, and reorganization in a social services department. *Human Relations*, 46, 1993, pp. 1338–1349.

[8]C. P. Alderfer. *Existence, Relatedness and Growth: Human Needs in Organizational Settings*. New York: Free Press, 1972.

[9]This questionnaire is intended for instructional use only.

[10]C. P. Alderfer. An empirical test of a new theory of human needs. *Organizational Behavior and Human Performance*, 5, 1969, pp. 142–175; and J. P. Wanous and A. A. Zwany. A Cross-sectional test of need hierarchy theory. *Organizational Behavior and Human Performance*, 18, 1977, pp. 78–97.

[11]D. C. McClelland. *Motivational Trends in Society*. Morristown, N.J.: General Learning Press, 1971.

[12]D. C. McClelland. The two faces of power. *Journal of International Affairs*, 24, 1970, pp. 29–47.

[13]F. Herzberg, B. Mausner, and B. Snyderman. *The Motivation to Work*. New York: John Wiley & Sons, 1959.

[14]J. Brockner, B. M. Wiesenfeld, T. Reed, S. Grover, and C. Martin. Interactive effect of job content and context on the reactions of layoff survivors. *Journal of Personality and Social Psychology*, 64, 1993, pp. 187–197.

[15]M. A. Campion and C. L. McClelland. Follow-up and extension of the interdisciplinary costs and benefits of enlarged jobs. *Journal of Applied Psychology*, 78, 1993, pp. 339–351; J. R. Hackman and G. R. Oldham. *Work Redesign*, Reading, Mass.: Addison-Wesley, 1980; Y. Fried and G. R. Ferris. The validity of the Job Characteristics Model: A review and meta-analysis. *Personnel Psychology*, 40, 1987, pp. 287–322; J. B. Cunningham and T. A. Eberle. A guide to job enrichment and design. *Personnel*, February 1990, pp. 56–61; and P. E. Spector and S. M. Jex. Relations of job characteristics from multiple data sources with employee affect, absence, turnover intentions, and health. *Journal of Applied Psychology*, 76, 1991, pp. 46–53.

[16]N. G. Dodd and D. C. Ganster. The interactive effects of variety, autonomy, and feedback on attitudes and performance. *Journal of Organizational Behavior*, 17, 1996, pp. 329–347.

[17]J. R. Hackman and G. R. Oldham, pp.

72–73.; and R. W. Renn and R. J. Vandenberg. The critical psychological states: An underrepresented component in job characteristics model research. *Journal of Management,* 21, 1995, pp. 279–303.

[18]J. R. Hackman and G. R. Oldham.

[19]S. P. Brown and T. W. Leigh. A new look at psychological climate and its relationship to job involvement, effort, and performance. *Journal of Applied Psychology,* 81, 1996, pp. 358–368.

[20]R. B. Goldman. A *Work Experiment: Six Americans in a Swedish Plant.* New York: Ford Foundation, 1976.

[21]J. S. Adams. Toward an understanding of equity. *Journal of Abnormal and Social Psychology,* 67, 1963, pp. 422–436.

[22]T. Petzinger, Jr. Bread-store chain tells its franchisees: Do your own thing. *Wall Street Journal,* November 21, 1997, p. B1.

[23]A. S. Tsui, J. L. Pearce, L. W. Porter, and A. M. Tripoli. Alternative approaches to the employee–organization relationship: Does investment in employees pay off? *Academy of Management Journal,* 40, 1997, pp. 1089–1121.

[24]L. Grant. International morale watch: Unhappy in Japan. *Fortune,* January 13, 1997, p. 142.

[25]K. Aquino, R. W. Griffeth, D. G. Allen, and P. W. Hom. Integrating justice constructs into the turnover process: A test of a referent cognitions model. *Academy of Management Journal,* 40, 1997, pp. 1208–1227.

[26]R. E. Kidwell, Jr., and N. Bennett. Employee propensity to withhold effort: A conceptual model to intersect three avenues of research. *Academy of Management Review,* 18, 1993, pp. 429–456.

[27]J. Schaubroeck, D. R. May, and F. W. Brown. Procedural justice explanations and employee reactions to economic hardship: A field experiment. *Journal of Applied Psychology,* 79, 1994, pp. 455–161; M. A. Konovsky and S. D. Pugh. Citizenship behavior and social exchange. *Academy of Management Journal,* 37, 1994, pp. 656–669; J. Greenberg. Employee theft as a reaction to underpayment inequity: The hidden costs of pay cuts. *Journal of Applied Psychology,* 75, 1990, pp. 561–568; and J. Greenberg. Stealing in the name of justice: Informational and interpersonal moderators of theft reactions to underpayment inequity. *Organizational Behavior and Human Decision Processes,* 54, 1993, pp. 81–103.

[28]A common assumption is that equity perceptions may differ across cultures. However, caution is necessary when considering how culture might affect equity perceptions. For a discussion of differences between collectivistic and individualistic cultures, for example, see C. C. Chao. New trends in rewards allocation preferences: A Sino–U. S. comparison. *Academy of Management Journal,* 38, 1995, pp. 408–428.

[29]Adapted from F. K. Sonnenberg and B. Goldberg. Business integrity: An oxymoron? *Industry Week,* April 6, 1992, pp. 53–56; and F. K. Sonnenberg and B. Goldberg. New bottom lines? *Executive Excellence,* December 1992, pp. 3–4.

[30]B. F. Skinner. *Contingencies of Reinforcement,* New York: Appleton-Century-Crofts, 1969; B. F. Skinner. *Beyond Freedom and Dig-*

nity, New York: Bantam, 1971; and B. F. Skinner. *About Behaviorism,* New York: Knopf, 1974.

[31]C. Gedvilas. Recognizing and addressing international pay differences. *ACA News,* October 1996, pp. 9–10.

[32]A. D. Strajkovic and F. Luthans. A meta-analysis of the effects of organizational behavior modification on task performance, 1975–1995. *Academy of Management Journal,* 40, 1997, pp. 1122–1149; and F. Luthans and R. Kreitner. *Organizational Behavior Modification and Beyond: An Operant and Social Learning Perspective,* Glenview, Ill.: Scott, Foresman, 1985.

[33]N. Shirouzu and J. Bigness. 7-Eleven operators resist system to monitor managers. *Wall Street Journal,* June 16, 1997, p. B3.

[34]S. Kerr. Risky business: The new pay game. *Fortune,* July 22, 1996, pp. 94–96.

[35]G. A. Ball, L. K. Trevino, and H. P. Sims, Jr. Just and unjust punishment: Influences on subordinate performance and citizenship. *Academy of Management Journal,* 37, 1994, pp. 299–322.

[36]J. Macht. Pulp addiction. *Inc. Technology,* 1, 1997, pp. 43–46.

[37]Critiques of reinforcement theory are provided by R. Kreitner and F. Luthans. A social learning approach to behavioral management: Radical behaviorists mellowing out. *Organizational Dynamics,* Autumn 1984, pp. 47–65; and E. T. Higgins. Beyond pleasure and pain. *American Psychologist,* 52, 1997, pp. 1280–1300.

[38]The possible detrimental effects of external rewards have been discussed at length, but the research evidence to date indicates that rewards seldom have detrimental effects. See R. Eisenberger and J. Cameron. Detrimental effects of reward. Reality or myth? *American Psychologist,* 51, 1996, pp. 1153–1166.

[39]E. A. Locke. Toward a theory of task motivation and incentives. *Organizational Behavior and Human Performance,* 3, 1968, pp. 157–189; E. A. Locke and G. P. Latham. *A theory of goal setting and task performance.* Englewood Cliffs, N.J.: Prentice-Hall, 1990.

[40]For a study involving roofers, see Austin, M. L. Kessler, J. E. Riccobono and J. Bailey. Using feedback and reinforcement to improve the performance and safety of a roofing crew. *Journal of Organizational Behavior Management,* 16, 1996, pp. 49–75. A study of pizza deliverers is described in T. D. Ludwig and E. S. Geller. Assigned versus participative goal setting and response generalization: Managing injury control among professional pizza deliverers. *Journal of Applied Psychology,* 82, 1997, pp. 253–261.

[41]G. P. Latham and J. J. Baldes. The practical significance of Locke's theory of goal setting. *Journal of Applied Psychology,* 60, 1975, pp. 122–124.

[42]V. H. Vroom. *Work and Motivation.* New York: John Wiley & Sons, 1964.

[43]E. Matson. The discipline of high-tech leaders. *Fast Company,* April /May, 1997, pp. 34–36.

[44]J. Collins. The learning executive. *Inc.,* August, 1997, pp. 35–36.

[45]W. Van Erde and H. Thierry. Vroom's

expectancy models and work-related criteria: A meta-analysis. *Journal of Applied Psychology,* 81, 1996, pp. 575–586.

[46]J. S. Lublin. Don't count on that merit raise this year. *Wall Street Journal,* January 7, 1997, pp. B1, B2. Also see R. D. Banker, S. Lee, G. Potter, and D. Srinivasan. Contextual analysis of performance impacts of outcome-based incentive compensation. *Academy of Management Journal,* 39, 1996, pp. 920–948; and R. Edelman. Record amount of stock awards allocated for compensation plans. *ACA News,* February, 1996, pp. 5–6.

[47]R. S. Schuler and S. E. Jackson. *Human Resource Management: Positioning for the 21st Century.* St. Paul: West, 1996.

[48]G. Blau. Operationalizing direction and level of effort and testing their relationships to individual job performance. *Organizational Behavior and Human Decision Processes,* 55, 1993, pp. 152–170; M. E. Tubbs, D. M. Boehne, and J. B. Dahl. Expectancy, valence, and motivational force functions in goal-setting research: An empirical test. *Journal of Applied Psychology,* 78, 1993, pp. 361–373; and J. N. Farrell, R. G. Lord, R. A. Alexander, and W. C. Gradwohl. The measurement of performance valence: An examination of construct-related evidence. *Organizational Behavior and Human Decision Processes,* 60, 1994, pp. 157–178.

[49]L. W. Porter and E. E. Lawler III. *Managerial Attitudes and Performance,* Homewood, Ill.: Irwin, 1968.

[50]A. M. Healey. Grabbing attention for total compensation plans. *ACA News,* October, 1996, pp. 11–13.

[51]D. H. Lindsley, D J. Brass, and J. B. Thomas. Efficacy-performance spirals: A multilevel perspective. *Academy of Management Review,* 20, 1995, pp. 645–678; and R. W. Griffeth and P. W. Hom. The employee turnover process. *Research in Personnel and Human Resources Management,* 13, 1995, pp. 245–293. Note, however, that the link between satisfaction and turnover may be weaker for employees with high financial requirements. See J. F. Brett, W. L. Cron, and J. W. Slocum, Jr. Economic dependency on work: A moderator of the relationship between organizational commitment and performance. *Academy of Management Journal,* 38, 1995, pp. 261–271.

[52]C. Seltz. Compensation: Performance management boosts financial results. *ACA News,* November/December, 1996, pp. 1–2.

[53]P. Murphy and S. E. Jackson. Managing work role performance: Challenges for 21st century organizations and their employees. In D. R. Ilgen and E. Pulakos (eds.), *The Changing Nature of Work Performance: Implications for Staffing, Performance Management and Development.* San Francisco: Jossey-Bass, 1998; and L. Van Dyne and L. L. Cummings. Extra-role behaviors: In pursuit of construct and definitional clarity (a bridge over muddied waters). *Research in Organizational Behavior,* 17, 1995, pp. 215–285.

[54]J. B. White. How a creaky factory got off the hit list, won respect at last. *Wall Street Journal,* December 26, 1996, pp. A1–A2.

[55]For a discussion of this and other common pitfalls, see S. Kerr. An academy classic: On the folly of rewarding A, while hoping for B.

Academy of Management Executive, 9, 1995, pp. 7–16.

[56]S. Shellenbarger. Work and Family—Enter the 'new hero': A boss who knows you have a life. *Wall Street Journal,* May 8, 1996, p. B1; and S. Shellenbarger. Work and Family: Family-friendly jobs are the first step to efficient workplace. *Wall Street Journal,* May 15, 1996, p. B1.

[57]A. N. Kluger and A. DeNisi. The effects of feedback interventions on performance: A historical review, a meta-analysis, and a preliminary feedback intervention theory. *Psychological Bulletin,* 119, 1996, pp. 254–284.

[58]Adapted from Faught, L. At Eddie Bauer you can work and have a life. *Workforce,* April, 1997, pp. 83–90; L. Moriwaki. Eddie Bauer praised as family-friendly firm. *Seattle Times,* September 10, 1996; Company press release. Eddie Bauer dedicates new customer service satisfaction center. July 31, 1997, PRNewswire; and information provided at the Eddie Bauer company home page.

CHAPTER 15

[1]Adapted from *Industry Week.* A looser culture. September 1, 1997, pp. 1–3; and *APICS Online Edition.* Trust—The key to value enhancement: An interview with Katherine M. Hudson, President and CEO of W. H. Brady Co., 7(6), 1997, pp. 1–6.

[2]T. R. Hinkin and C. A. Schriesheim. Relationship between subordinate perceptions of supervisory influence and attributed power bases. *Human Relations,* 43, 1990, pp. 221–238; and T. R. Hinkin and C. A. Schriesheim. An examination of subordinate-perceived relationships between leader reward and punishment behavior and leader bases of power. *Human Relations,* 47, 1994, pp. 779–801.

[3]J. R. P. French and B. H. Raven. The bases of social power. In D. Cartwright and A. Zander (eds.), *Group Dynamics: Research and Theory,* 2d. ed. New York: Harper & Row, 1960, pp. 607–623.

[4]K. D. Butterfield, L. K. Trevino, and G.A. Ball. Punishment from the manager's perspective: A grounded investigation and inductive model. *Academy of Management Journal,* 39(6), 1996, pp. 1479–1512.

[5]J. Finegan. Ready, aim, focus. *Inc.,* March, 1997, pp. 44–55.

[6]J. C. Ramo. A survivor's tale: Andy Grove. *Time,* January 5, 1998, pp. 1–12.

[7]J. A. Gastil. A definition and illustration of democratic leadership. *Human Relations,* 47, 1994, pp. 953–976; and J. Pfeffer. *Managing with Power.* Boston: Harvard Business School Press, 1994.

[8]Adapted from R. B. Lieber. Why employees love these companies. *Fortune,* January 12, 1998, pp. 72–74; M. K. Ash. *Mary Kay You Can Have It All: Lifetime Wisdom from America's Foremost Woman Entrepreneur.* Prima, 1995; G. Gross and the editors of Forbes magazine. *Forbes Greatest Business Stories of All Time.* New York: John Wiley & Sons, 1996; and the company home page for Mary Kay Cosmetics, Inc., at www.marykay.com (January 1998).

[9]B. M. Bass. *Bass and Stodgill's Handbook of Leadership.* New York: Free Press, 1990.

[10]F. Fiedler. Research on leadership selection and training: One view of the future. *Administrative Science Quarterly,* 41, 1996, p. 241–250.

[11]R. Mondosa. One happy CEO. *Hispanic Business,* Online ed., December 1997.

[12]For an argument in defense of trait models, see E. Locke. Prime movers: The traits of great business leaders. In C. L. Cooper and S. E. Jackson (eds.), *Creating Tomorrow's Organizations: A Handbook for Future Research in Organizational Behavior,* 1997, pp. 75–96.

[13]D. McGregor. *The Human Side of the Enterprise.* New York: McGraw-Hill, 1960, pp. 33–58.

[14]See Note 1.

[15]R. M. Stogdill. *Handbook of Leadership: A Survey of the Literature.* New York: Free Press, 1974.

[16]E. Matson. Congratulations you're promoted. *Fast Company,* June–July 1997, pp. 116–128.

[17]C. A. Schriesheim and B. J. Bird. Contributions of the Ohio State studies to the field of leadership. *Journal of Management,* 5, 1979, pp. 135–145; and J. J. Rotemberg and G. Saloner. Leadership style and incentives. *Management Science,* 39, 1993, pp. 1299–1319.

[18]R. Likert. From production-and-employee centeredness to systems 1–4. *Journal of Management,* 5, 1979, pp. 147–156.

[19]A. H. Eagly and S. H. Karau. Gender and the emergence of leaders: A meta-analysis. *Journal of Personality and Social Psychology,* 60, 1991, pp. 685–710.

[20]R. R. Blake and J. S. Mouton. *The Managerial Grid.* Houston: Gulf, 1985; and C. T. Lewis and S. M. Jobs. Conflict management: The essence of leadership. *Journal of Leadership Studies,* November 1993, pp. 47–60.

[21]K. Thomas and B. Velthouse. Cognitive elements of empowerment. An "interpretive" model of intrinsic task motivation. *Academy of Management Review,* 15, 1990, pp. 666–681; and G. M. Spreitzer, M. A. Kizilos, and S. W. Nason. A dimensional analysis of the relationship between psychological empowerment and effectiveness, satisfaction, and strain. *Journal of Management,* 23, 1997, pp. 679–704.

[22]Adapted from S. Moffett. Jump starter with both leadership and a golden marketing touch, visionary President Nobuhiko Kawamoto has pumped new life into Honda Motors. *Time,* July 21, 1997 (accessed online at www.pathfinder.com/time/magazine/1997); and A. Taylor III and S. Purli. The man who put Honda back on track. *Fortune,* September 9, 1996 (accessed online at www.pathfinder.com/fortune/magazine/1996).

[23]G. M. Spreitzer. Social structural characteristics of psychological empowerment. *Academy of Management Journal,* 39, 1996, pp. 483–504; and S. G. Cohen, L. Chang, and G. E. Ledford, Jr. A hierarchical construct of self-management leadership and its relationship to quality of work life and perceived work group effectiveness. *Personnel Psychology,* 50, 1997, pp. 275–291.

[24]R. C. Ford and M. D. Fottle. Empowerment: A matter of degree. *Academy of Management Executive,* 9(3), 1995, pp. 21–30; and J. Martin. So, you want to work for the best. . . . *Fortune,* January 12, 1996, pp. 77–78.

[25]H. P. Sims, Jr. and C. C. Manz. *Company of Heros.* New York: John Wiley & Sons, 1996.

[26]F. Dansereau, G. Graen, and W. J. Haga. A vertical dyad linkage approach to leadership within formal organizations: A longitudinal investigation of role making processes. *Organizational Behavior and Human Performance,* 13, 1975, pp. 46–78; G. B. Graen and M. Uhl-Bien. Development of leader–member exchange (LMX) theory of leadership over 25 years: Applying a multi-level-multi-domain perspective. *Leadership Quarterly,* 6, 1995, pp. 219–247; and S. J. Wayne, L. M. Shore, and R. C. Liden. Perceived organizational support and leader–member exchange: A social exchange perspective. *Academy of Management Journal,* 40, 1997, pp. 82–111.

[27]For a study demonstrating that leaders form a unique relationship with each follower, see F. J. Yammarino, A. J. Dubinsky, L. B. Comer, and M. A. Jolson. Women and transformational and contingent reward leadership: A multiple levels-of-analysis perspective. *Academy of Management Journal,* 40, 1997, pp. 205–222.

[28]C. R. Gerstner and D. V. Day. Meta-analytic review of leader–member exchange theory: Correlates and construct issues. *Journal of Applied Psychology,* 82, 1997, pp. 827–844; R. P. Settoon, N. Bennett, and R. C. Liden. Social exchange in organizations: Perceived organizational support, leader–member exchange, and employee reciprocity. *Journal of Applied Psychology,* 81, 1996, pp. 219–227; and G. B. Graen and T. A. Scandura. Toward a psychology of dyadic organizing. In L. L. Cummings and B. M. Staw (eds.), *Research in Organizational Behavior,* 9, 1987, pp. 175–208.

[29]T. N. Bauer and S. G. Green. Development of leader–member exchange: A longitudinal test. *Academy of Management Journal,* 39, 1996, pp. 1538–1567; and R. T. Sparrow and R. C. Liden. Process and structure in leader–member exchange. *Academy of Management Review,* 22, 1997, pp. 522–552.

[30]G. A. Yukl. *Leadership in Organizations,* 2d ed. Englewood Cliffs, N.J.: Prentice-Hall, 1989.

[31]F. E. Fiedler. *A Theory of Leadership.* New York: McGraw-Hill, 1967.

[32]C. A. Schriesheim, B. J. Tepper, and L. A. Tetrault. Least preferred co-worker score, situational control, and leadership effectiveness: A meta-analysis of contingency model performance predictions. *Journal of Applied Psychology,* 79, 1994, pp. 561–574.

[33]P. E. Potter III and F. E. Fiedler. Selecting leaders: Making the most of previous experience. *Journal of Leadership Studies,* November 1993, pp. 61–70.

[34]P. Hersey and K. H. Blanchard. *Management of Organizational Behavior: Utilizing Human Resources,* 6th ed. Englewood Cliffs, N.J.: Prentice-Hall, 1993.

[35]J. Web. Mr. Nice Guy with a Mission. *Business Week,* November 25, 1996, pp. 132–137.

[36]K. H. Blanchard, D. Zigarmi, and R. B. Nelson. Situational leadership after 25 years: A retrospective. *Journal of Leadership Studies,* November 1993, pp. 21–36.

[37]W. E. Norris and R. P. Vecchio. Situational

leadership theory: A replication. *Group & Organization Management,* 17, 1992, pp. 331–343.

[38]R. J. House and T. R. Mitchell. Path–goal theories of leadership. *Journal of Contemporary Business,* 3, 1974, pp. 81–97.

[39]J. C. Wofford and L. Z. Liska. Path–goal theories of leadership: A meta-analysis. *Journal of Management,* 19, 1993, pp. 857–876.

[40]V. H. Vroom and A. G. Jago. *The New Leadership.* Englewood Cliffs, N.J.: Prentice-Hall, 1988.

[41]R. H. G. Field and R. J. House. A test of the Vroom–Yetton model using manager and subordinate reports. *Journal of Applied Psychology,* 75, 1990, pp. 362–366; W. E. Pasewark and J. R. Strawser. Subordinate participation in auditing budgeting decisions: A comparison of decisions influenced by organizational factors to decisions conforming with the Vroom–Jago model. *Decision Sciences,* 25, 1994, pp. 281–300; and M. A. Korsgard, D. M. Schweiger, and H. J. Sapienza. Building commitment, attachment, and trust in strategic decision-making teams: The role of procedural justice. *Academy of Management Journal,* 38, 1995, pp. 60–84; S. R. Kahai, J. S. Sosick, and B. J. Avolio. Effects of leadership style and problem structure on group process and outcomes in an electronic meeting system environment. *Personnel Psychology,* 1997, 50, pp. 121–146.

[42]A. H. Eagly and B. T. Johnson. Gender and leadership style: A meta-analysis. *Psychological Bulletin,* 108, 1990, pp. 233–256.

[43]R. Hooijberg. A multidirectional approach toward leadership: An extension of the concept of behavioral complexity. *Human Relations,* 49, 1996, pp. 917–946. For extensive reviews of situational moderators of leadership, see P. M. Podsakoff, S. B. MacKenzie, M. Ahearne, and W. H. Bommer. Searching for a needle in a haystack: Trying to identify the illusive moderators of leadership behavior. *Journal of Management,* 21, 1995, pp. 422–470; and P. M. Podsakoff, S. B. MacKenzie, and W. H. Bommer. Meta-analysis of the relationships between Kerr and Jermier's substitutes for leadership and employee job attitudes, role perceptions, and performance. *Journal of Applied Psychology,* 81, 1996, pp. 380–399.

[44]B. Shamir, R. J. House, and M. B. Arthur. The motivational effects of charismatic leadership: A self-based theory. *Organization Science,* 4, 1993, pp. 577–594; N. H. Snyder and M. Graves. Leadership and vision. *Business Horizons,* January–February 1994, pp. 1–7; and T. A. Scandura and C. A. Schriesheim. Leader–member exchange and supervisor career mentoring as complementary constructs in leadership research. *Academy of Management Journal,* 37, 1994, pp. 1588–1602.

[45]J. M. Howell and B. J. Avolio. Transformational leadership, transactional leadership, locus of control, and support for innovations: Key predictors of consolidated-business-unit performance. *Journal of American Psychology,* 78, 1993, pp. 545–568; and B. J. Avolio. The "natural": Some antecedents to transformational leadership. *International Journal of Public Administration,* 17, 1994, pp. 1559–1581.

[46]R. J. House, W. D. Spangler, and J. Woycke. Personality and charisma in the U.S. presidency: A psychological theory of leader effectiveness. *Administrative Science Quarterly,* 36, 1991, pp. 364–395; M. F. R. Kets de Vries. The leadership mystique. *Academy of Management Executive,* 8(3), 1994, pp. 73–93; and P. M. Podsakoff, S. B. Mackenzie, and W. H. Bommer. Meta-analysis of the relationships between Kerr and Jermier's substitutes for leadership and employee job attitudes, role perceptions, and performance. *Journal of Applied Psychology,* 81, 1996, pp. 380–399.

[47]L. Larwood, C. M. Falke, M. P. Kriger, and P. Miesing. Structure and meaning of organizational vision. *Academy of Management Journal,* 39, 1995, pp. 740–769.

[48]J. J. Sosick, B. J. Avolio, and S. S. Kahai. Effects of leadership style and anonymity on group potency and effectiveness in a group decision support system environment. *Journal of Applied Psychology,* 82, 1997, pp. 89–103; F. Fiedler and R. J. House. Leadership theory and research: A report on progress. In C. L. Cooper and I. T. Robertson (eds.), *Key Reviews in Managerial Psychology,* Chichester, U.K.: John Wiley & Sons, 1994, pp. 97–116; O. Behling and J. M. McFillen. A syncretical model of charismatic/transformational leadership. *Group and Organization Management,* 21, 1996, pp. 163–191; and M. L. Nathan. What is organizational vision? Ask chief executives. *Academy of Management Executive,* 10(1), 1996, pp. 82–83.

[49]J. C. Collins and J. I. Porras. Building your company's vision. *Harvard Business Review,* September–October, 1996, pp. 65–77; and R. B. Lieber. Why employees love these companies. *Fortune,* January 12, 1998, pp. 72–74.

[50]W. L. Gardner and B. J. Avolio. The charismatic relationship: A dramaturgical perspective. *Academy of Management Review,* 23, 1998, pp. 32–58. H. Gardner. *Leading Minds: An Anatomy of Leadership.* New York: Basic Books, 1995.

[51]B. S. Pawar and K. K. Eastman. The nature and implications of contextual influences on transformational leadership: A conceptual examination. *Academy of Management Review,* 22, 1997, pp. 80–109.

[52]J. M. Howell and B. J. Avolio. The ethics of charismatic leadership: Submission or liberation? *Academy of Management Executive,* 6, 1992, pp. 43–55. Also see B. M. Bass and B. J. Avolio. The implications of transactional and transformational leadership for individual, team, and organizational development. In W. A. Pasmore and R. W. Woodman (eds.), *Research in Organizational Change and Development,* vol. 4. Greenwich, Conn.: JAI Press, 1990, pp. 231–272.

[53]M. A. Berman. Sweating the soft stuff. *Across the Board,* January 1998, pp. 39–43.

[54]E. Pierce. Anthony Mark Hankins: He's the Calvin Klein of cut-rate fashion. *Texas Monthly,* January 4, 1998 (accessed on line at www.texasmonthly.com); Designer Spotlight. *Fashion Video Magazine,* Winter 1997 (accessed on line at www.fashionvideo.com/design); Business Week Editors. The best entrepreneurs. *Business Week,* January 12, 1998, p. 70; and S. A. Forest. He's one determined sew-and-sew. *Business Week,* Novem-

ber 17, 1997, pp. 30–41.

[55]R. M. Fulmer. The evolving paradigm of leadership development. *Organizational Dynamics,* 25 (Spring), 1997, pp. 59–72; D. P. Young and N. M. Dixon. *Helping Leaders Take Effective Action: A Program Evaluation.* Greensboro, N.C.: Center for Creative Leadership, 1996; D. H. Born and J. E. Mathieu. Differential effects of survey-guided feedback: The rich get rich and the poor get poorer. *Group and Organization Management,* 21, 1996, pp. 388–403; F. J. Yammarino and L. E. Atwater. Do managers see themselves as others see them? Implications of self–other rating agreement for human resources management. *Organizational Dynamics,* 25(Spring), 1997, pp. 35–44; M. W. McCall, Jr. *High Flyers: Developing the Next Generation of Leaders.* Boston: Harvard Business School Press, 1997; and F. H. Freeman, K. B. Knott, and M. K. Schwartz. *Leadership Education: A Source Book, Volumes 1 and 2.* Greensboro, N.C.: Center for Creative Leadership, 1997.

[56]H. Row. Is management for me? That is the question. *Fast Company.* February–March, 1998, pp. 50–52.

[57]J. Hyatt. The zero-defect CEO. *Inc.,* June 1997, pp. 46–57.

[58]Marshall Sashkin. George Washington University, Washington, D.C., 1998.

[59]M. W. McCall, Jr. *High Flyers: Developing the Next Generation of Leaders.* Boston: Harvard Business School, 1997; C. D. McCauley, R. Moxley, and E. Van Velsor. *The Center for Creative Leadership's Handbook of Leadership Development.* San Francisco: Jossey-Bass, 1998; and A. M. Morrison. *The New Leaders: Guidelines on Leadership Diversity in America.* San Francisco: Jossey-Bass, 1992.

[60]M. Hopkins. The antihero's guide to the new economy. *Inc.,* January, 1998, pp. 36–48.

[61]R. A. Kustin and R. A. Jones. An investigation of Japanese/American managers' leadership style in U.S. corporations. *Journal of International Management,* 2, 1996, pp. 111–126.

[62]The opinions of fifty European managers are described in R. Calori and B. Dufour. Management European style. *Academy of Management Executive,* 9(3), pp. 61–77.

[63]M. Ndiaye, M. Lubatkin, and R. Vengroff. Assessing managerial work in Senegal: Do Western models apply? *International Management,* 1(1), 1997, pp. 67–76.

[64]B. M. Bass. Does the transactional-transformational leadership transcend organizational and national boundaries? *American Psychologist,* 52, 1997, pp. 130-139.

[65]R. J. House et al., In W. Mobley (ed.), *Advances in Global Leadership,* vol. 1. Greenwich, Conn.: JAI Press, 1998.

[66]Adapted from R. Levering and M. Moskowitz. The 100 best companies to work for in America. *Fortune,* January 12, 1998, pp. 84–95; R. B. Lieber. Bob Crandall's Boo-Boos. *Fortune,* April 28, 1997, pp. 365–368; C. A. O'Reilly III, and J. Pfeffer. *Southwest Airlines* (undated case). Palo Alto, Calif.: Stanford Graduate School of Business; and F. E. Whittlesey. CEO Herb Kelleher discusses Southwest Airlines' people culture: How the company achieved competitive advantage from

the ground up. *ACA Journal,* Winter 1995, pp. 8–18. Two other charismatic leaders are described in M. F. R. Kets de Vries. Charisma in action: the transformational abilities of Virgin's Richard Branson and ABB's Percy Barnevik. *Organizational Dynamics,* Winter, 1998, pp. 7–21.

CHAPTER 16

[1]J. Steinhauer. Time to call a Sears repairman: A turnaround is sidetracked by its own over-sell. *New York Times,* January 15, 1998, pp. D1, D3; G. Buck. Revitalized Sears sings happy tune yet again. *Chicago Tribune,* January 24, 1997 (online edition at www.chicago.tribune.com); and G. Crawford. Credit woes are Sears' big Q4 questionmark. *Reuters Limited,* January 16, 1998 (accessed online at biz.yahoo.com/finance/980116/credit_woe_1).

[2]G. Caplan and M. Teese. *Survivors: How to Keep Your Best People on Board After Downsizing.* Palo Alto, Calif.: Davies-Black, 1997; and M. Besack. Making moviegoers the real stars. *Workforce,* October, 1997, pp. 27–28.

[3]E. M. Eisenbereg and H. L. Goodall, Jr. *Organizational Communication: Balancing Creativity and Constraint.* New York: St. Martin's Press, 1993.

[4]J. Martin. So, you want to work for the best. *Fortune,* January 12, 1998, pp. 77–78.

[5]C. Budoff. Shake hands with a corporate recruiter. *New York Times,* December 21, 1997, p. NJ4.

[6]Workplace Potpourri. Strict etiquette in Japanese firms lives on. *Manpower Argus,* August 1996, p. 11.

[7]A. Rafaeli, J. E. Dutton, C. V. Harquail, and S. Mackie-Lewis. Navigating by attire: The use of dress by female administrative employees. *Academy of Management Journal,* 40, 1997, pp. 9–45.

[8]P. C. Morrow. Physical attractiveness and selection in decision making. *Journal of Management,* 16, 1990, pp. 45–60; and R. C. Liden, C. L. Martin and C. K. Parsons. Interviewer and applicant behaviors in employment interviews. *Academy of Management Journal,* 36, 1993, pp. 372–386.

[9]E. Calonius. Tables of power. *Fortune,* April 28, 1997, pp. 146–153.

[10]N. Shirouzu. How one woman is shaking up Shiseido. *Wall Street Journal,* May 19, 1997, pp. B1, B8.

[11]*Fortune* editor's interview. How you speak shows where you rank. *Fortune,* February 2, 1998, p. 156.

[12]L. Berry and A. Parasuraman. Listening to the customer—The concept of a service-quality information system. *Sloan Management Review,* Spring 1997, pp. 65–76.

[13]J. Main. How to steal the best ideas around. *Fortune,* October 19, 1992, pp. 102–106.

[14]G. Flynn. Acrobats, aerialists, and HR: The big top needs big HR. *Workforce,* August, 1997, pp. 38–45.

[15]T. Petzinger, Jr. Two executives cook up a way to make Pillsbury listen. *Wall Street Journal,* September 27, 1996, p. B1.

[16]J. S. Lubin. Dear Boss: I'd rather not tell you my name, but . . . . *Wall Street Journal,* June 18, 1997, p. B1.

[17]D. Krackhardt and J. R. Hanson. Informal networks: The company behind the chart. *Harvard Business Review,* July–August 1993, pp. 104–113.

[18]J. S. Brown and S. Gray. The people are the company. *Fast Company,* October 10, 1996 (accessed online at www.fastcompany.com/fastco/issues/first/People.html). Also see D. J. Brass. A social network perspective on HRM. In J. Ferris and K. Rowland (eds.), *Research in Personnel and Human Resources Management,* vol. 13, 1995, pp. 39–79.

[19]R. A. Friedman. Defining the scope and logic of minority and female network groups: Can separation enhance integration? In J. Ferris and K. Rowland (eds.), *Research in Personnel and Human Resources Management,* vol. 14, 1996, pp. 307–349.

[20]The Exchange: Success by association: The breakfast club. *Black Enterprise,* Fall 1997 (accessed online at www.blackenterprise.com/docs/ex5.html).

[21]For an extensive review of research on work-related feedback, see M. London. *Job Feedback: Giving, Seeking, and Using Feedback for Performance Improvement.* Mahwah, N.J.: Lawrence Erlbaum Associates, 1997.

[22]K. M. Sutcliffe. What executives notice: Accurate perceptions in top management teams. *Academy of Management Journal,* 37, 1994, pp. 1360–1378.

[23]P. M. Barrett. Legal separation: Prestigious law firm courts black lawyers, but diversity is illusive. *Wall Street Journal,* July 8, 1997, pp. A1, A9.

[24]Adapted from *Intel Corporation 1997 Annual Report.* Santa Clara, Calif.: Intel Corporation, 1997; and L. M. Fisher. Sharing sights and sounds with your PC correspondents. *New York Times,* May 15, 1994, p. 12F.

[25]L. Grensing-Pophal. Employing the best people—from afar. *Workforce,* March 1997, pp. 30–38.

[26]Adapted from J. F. Veiga and K. Dechant. Wired world woes: www.help. *Academy of Management Executive,* 11(3), 1997, pp. 73–79.

[27]S. P. Weisband, S. K. Schneider, and T. Connolly. Computer-mediated communication and social information: Status salience and status differences. *Academy of Management Journal,* 38, 1995, pp. 1124–1151; and M. H. Zack and J. L. McKenny. Social context and interaction in ongoing computer-supported management groups. *Organization Science,* 6, 1995, pp. 394–404.

[28]D. Nye. Not made in heaven. *Across the Board,* October 1996, pp. 41–46.

[29]D. Tjosvold. Networking by professionals to manage change: Dentists' cooperation and competition to develop their business. *Journal of Organizational Behavior,* 5, 1997, pp. 745–752.

[30]B. Mesquita and N. H. Frijda. Cultural variations in emotions: A review. *Psychological Bulletin,* 2, 1992, pp. 179–204.

[31]Adapted from P. A. Herbig. *Handbook of Cross-Cultural Marketing.* New York: International Business Press, 1998.

[32]E. M. Rodgers. *A History of Communication Study.* New York: Free Press, 1994.

[33]M. Prensky. Twitch speed. *Across the Board,* January 1998, pp. 14–19.

[34]G. Flynn. A pioneer program nurtures a harassment free workplace. *Workforce,* October 1997, pp. 38–24.

[35]Based on Training Systems International's Personal Listening Profile, as described at www.managementmethods.com/Catalog2/sx120001.html

[36]These guidelines are abridged from *Ten Commandments for Good Communications.* New York: American Management Association, 1955; and C. Argyris. Good communication that blocks learning. *Harvard Business Review,* July–August 1994, pp. 77–86.

[37]Adapted from www.siemens.com and www.siemenscom.com

CHAPTER 17

[1]Adapted from Quick tips. *Advisor & Staff,* Fall 1996; Managing a yearbook staff. Article from Jostens "Y Club" curriculum, reproduced at www.jostens.com/yearbook/advisors/organization/stmgmt1.html (January, 1998); and D. E. Yeatts, M. Hipskind, and D. Barnes. Lessons learned from self-managed work teams. *Business Horizons,* July–August 1994, pp. 11–18.

[2]*The Hay Report: Compensation and Benefits Strategies for 1997 and Beyond.* New York: Hay Group, 1997.

[3]M. A. Cusumano. How Microsoft makes large teams work like small teams. *Sloan Management Review,* Fall 1997, pp. 9–20.

[4]H. Axel. Teaming in the global arena. *Across the Board,* February 1997, p. 56. R. D. Banker, J. M. Field, R. G. Schroeder and K. K. Sinha. Impact of work teams on manufacturing performance: A longitudinal field study. *Academy of Management Journal,* 36, 1996, pp. 867–890; and S. A. Mohrman and A. M. Mohrman, Jr. *Designing and Leading Team-based Organizations: A Workbook for Organizational Self-design.* San Francisco: Jossey-Bass, 1997.

[5]L. Hirschhorn. *Managing in the New Team Environment: Skills, Tools, and Methods.* Reading, Mass.: Addison-Wesley, 1991; N. Steckler and N. Fondas. Building team leader effectiveness: A diagnostic tool. *Organizational Dynamics,* Winter 1995, pp. 20–35.

[6]I. D. Steiner. *Group Process and Productivity.* New York: Academic Press, 1972; and D. Gigone and R. Hastie. Proper analysis of the accuracy of group judgments. *Psychological Bulletin,* 121, 1997, pp. 149–167.

[7]B. Nagler. Recasting employees into teams. *Workforce,* January, 1998, pp. 101–106.

[8]E. J. Lawler and B. Markovsky (eds.). *Social Psychology of Groups: A Reader.* Greenwich, Conn.: JAI Press, 1995.

[9]E. Trist and H. Murray (eds.). *The Social Engagement of Social Science. Volume II: The Socio-Technical Perspective.* Philadelphia: University of Pennsylvania Press, 1993.

[10]R. A. Guzzo. Fundamental considerations about work groups. In M. A. West (ed.), *Handbook of Work Group Psychology.* New York: John Wiley & Sons, 1996; and M. A. West, C. S. Borrill, and K. L. Unsworth. Team effectiveness in organizations. In C. L. Cooper

and I. T. Robertson (eds.), *International Review of Industrial-Organizational Psychology.* Chichester, U.K.: John Wiley & Sons, 1998.

[11]J. R. Galbraith. *Competing with Flexible Lateral Organizations.* Reading, Mass.: Addison-Wesley, 1994.

[12]A. J. Rucci, S. P. Kirn, and R. T. Quinn. The employee–customer profit chain at Sears. *Harvard Business Review,* January-February 1998, pp. 83–97.

[13]G. M. Parker. *Cross-Functional Teams: Working with Allies, Enemies, and Other Strangers.* San Francisco: Jossey-Bass, 1994; and P. Mears. *Team Building: A Structured Learning Approach.* Delray Beach, Fla.: St. Lucie Press, 1994.

[14]E. Carberry. Employee ownership case studies: Western Contract Furnishers. The National Center for Employee Ownership home page (www.nceo.org/colmuns/ec3.html), February 10, 1998.

[15]R. S. Wellins, W. C. Byham, and G. R. Dixon. *Inside Teams: How 20 World-Class Organizations Are Winning Through Teamwork.* San Francisco: Jossey-Bass, 1994; and E. M. Van Aken, D. J. Monetta, and D. S. Sink. Affinity groups: The missing link is employee involvement. *Organizational Dynamics,* Spring 1994, pp. 38–54.

[16]Teams such as these are described in depth in D. Mankin, S. G. Cohen, and T. K. Bikson. *Teams and Technology.* Boston: Harvard Business School, 1996.

[17]G. M. Parker, K. B. Clark, and S. C. Wheelwright. *The Product Development Challenge: Competing Through Speed, Quality, and Creativity.* Boston: Harvard Business School Press, 1995.

[18]J. McCalman. Lateral hierarchy: The case of cross-cultural management teams. *European Management Journal,* 14, 1996, pp. 509–517.

[19]Business Wire. Intercargo subsidiary announces Flexible Account Service Teams— "FAST." *Today's News on the Net* (www.businesswire.com) January 21, 1998.

[20]G. Dumaine. The trouble with teams. *Fortune,* September 5, 1994, pp. 86–92; and R. S. Wellins, W. C. Byham, and G. R. Dixon.

[21]R. S. Wellins, W. C. Byham, and J. M. Wilson. *Empowered Teams: Creating Self-directed Work Groups that Improve Quality, Productivity, and Participation.* San Francisco: Jossey-Bass, 1991.

[22]K. B. Evans and H. P. Sims, Jr. Mining for innovation: The conceptual underpinnings, history, and diffusion of self-directed work teams. In. C. L. Cooper and S. E. Jackson (eds.), *Creating Tomorrow's Organizations: Handbook for Future Research in Organizational Behavior.* New York: John Wiley & Sons, 1997.

[23]S. A. Mohrman, S. G. Cohen, and A. M. Mohrman, Jr. *Designing Team-Based Organizations.* Jossey-Bass, 1995; and S. G. Cohen and G. E. Ledford, The effectiveness of self-managing teams. *Human Relations,* 47, 1994, pp. 13–43.

[24]K. Labich. High performance teams. *Fortune,* February 16, 1996, pp. 88–99.

[25]K. Labich; and H. Constance and R. Fuerst. *Good to Go: The Life and Times of a Decorated Member of the U.S. Navy's Elite Seal Team Two.*

William Morrow, 1997

[26]S. A. Mohrman, S. G. Cohen, and A. M. Mohrman, Jr.

[27]Adapted from A. B. Cheney, H. P. Sims, Jr., and C. C. Manz. Teams and TQM. *Business Horizons,* September– October, 1994, pp. 16–25; C. C. Manz and H. P. Sims, Jr. *Business Without Bosses: How Self-Managing Teams Are Building High Performance Companies.* New York: John Wiley & Sons, 1993; L. C. Nielson. The only unique resource. *Across the Board,* July/August 1994, pp. 56–57; and J. R. Junkins. Confessions of a Baldrige winner. *Management Review,* July 1994, p. 58.

[28]B. D. Janz, J. A. Colquitt, and R. A. Noe. Knowledge worker team effectiveness: The role of autonomy, interdependence, team development, and contextual support variables. *Personnel Psychology,* 50, 1997, pp. 877–904. For extensive descriptions of research relevant to each of the four components, see M. West. *Handbook of Work Group Psychology.*

[29]M. C. Gentile (ed.). *Differences That Work: Organizational Excellence Through Diversity.* Boston: Harvard Business School Press, 1994. For a discussion of the consequences of mixing employees from different cultures within a single team, see E. Elron. Top management teams within multinational corporations: Effects of cultural heterogeneity. *Leadership Quarterly,* 8(4), 1997, pp. 393–412; and J. A. Wagner III. Studies of individualism–collectivism: Effects on cooperation in groups. *Academy of Management Journal,* 38, 1995, pp. 152–172.

[30]A. Sagie. Participative decision making and performance. A moderator analysis. *Journal of Applied Behavioral Science,* 30, 1994, pp. 227–246; and W. A. Kahn and K. E. Kram. Authority at work: Internal models and their organizational consequences. *Academy of Management Review,* 19, 1994, pp. 17–50.

[31]The relative importance of general cognitive ability and personality are examined in J. A. LePine, J. R. Hollenbeck, D. R. Ilgen, and J. Hedlund. Effects of individual differences on the performance of hierarchical decision-making teams: Much more than g. *Journal of Applied Psychology,* 82, 1997, pp. 803–811.

[32]J. Martin. Mercedes: Made in Alabama. *Fortune,* July 7, 1997, pp. 150–158.

[33]D. C. Ganster and D. J. Dwyer. The effects of understaffing on individual and group performance in professional and trade occupations. *Journal of Management,* 21, 1995, pp. 175–190.

[34]A. P. Hare. Group size. *American Behavioral Scientist,* 24, 1981, pp. 695–708; R. Albanese and D. D. Van Fleet. Rational behavior in groups: The free-riding tendency. *Academy of Management Review,* 10, 1985, pp. 244–255.

[35]E. Sundstrom, K. P. DeMeuse, and D. Futrell, D. Work teams: Applications and effectiveness. *American Psychologist,* 45, 1990, pp. 120–133; and K. G. Smith et al. Top management team demography and process: The role of social integration and communication. *Administrative Science Quarterly,* 39, 1994, pp. 412–438.

[36]W. R. Pape. Group insurance: Virtual teams can quickly gather knowledge even from far-

flung staff. *Inc. Tech,* no. 2, 1997, pp. 29–31. An interesting study showing how computer-mediated group decision making differs from face-to-face influence is P. L. McLeod, R. S. Baron, M. W. Marti, and K. Yoon. The eyes have it: Minority influence in face-to-face and computer-mediated group discussion. *Journal of Applied Psychology,* 82, 1997, pp. 706–718.

[37]M. D. Zalezny, E. Salas, and C. Prince. Conceptual and measurement issues in coordination: Implications for team behavior and performance. In K. Rowland and G. Ferris (eds.), *Research in Personnel and Human Resource Management,* 13, 1995, pp. 81–115.

[38]A. R. Montebello. *Work Teams That Work: Skills for Managing Across the Organization.* Minneapolis: Best Sellers, 1994, pp. 33–39; S. Worchel. You can go home again: Returning group research to the group context with an eye on developmental issues. *Small Group Research,* 25, 1994, pp. 205–223; and C. J. G. Gersick. Marking time: Predictable transitions in task groups. *Academy of Management Journal,* 32, 1989, pp. 274–309.

[39]Adapted from M. E. Kossler and S. Prestridge. Geographically dispersed teams. *Center for Creative Leadership Issues & Observations,* 16(2/3), 1996, pp. 9–11; W. R. Pape. A meeting of the minds. *Inc. Tech,* no. 2, 1997, pp. 29–31; W. R. Pape. Group insurance; and B. Geber. Virtual teams. *Training.* April 1995, pp. 36–40.

[40]S. Worchel, W. Wood, and J. A. Simpson (eds.). *Group Process and Productivity.* Newbury Park, Calif.: Sage, 1992; and R. Klimoski and S. Mohammed. Team mental model: Construct or metaphor. *Journal of Management,* 20, 1994, pp. 403–437.

[41]Adapted from L. M. Sixel. Bag manufacturing growing up fast. *Houston Chronicle,* October 16, 1994, pp. 1E, 4E.

[42]M. J. Stevens and M. A. Campion. The knowledge, skill, and ability requirements for teamwork: Implications for human resource management. *Journal of Management,* 20, 1994, pp. 503–530; and A. M. O'Leary, J. J. Martocchio, and D. D. Frink. A review of the influence of group goals on group performance. *Academy of Management Journal,* 37, 1994, pp. 1285–1301.

[43]C. W. Mueller, E. M. Boyer, J. L. Price, and R. D. Iverson. Employee attachment and non-coercive conditions of work. *Work and Occupations,* 21, 1994, pp. 179–212.

[44]J. M. Rabbie. Determinants of ingroup cohesion and outgroup hostility. *International Journal of Group Tensions,* 23, 1993, pp. 309–328.

[45]J. R. Hackman. Group influences on individuals in organizations. In M. D. Dunnette and L. M. Hough (eds.), *Handbook of Industrial and Organizational Psychology,* 2d ed., vol. 3. Palo Alto, Calif.: Consulting Psychologists Press, 1992, pp. 199–267.

[46]A. Zander. *Making Groups Effective,* 2d ed. San Francisco: Jossey-Bass, 1994.

[47]P. C. Early. Self or group? Cultural effects of training on self-efficacy and performance. *Administrative Science Quarterly,* 39, 1994, pp. 89–117.

[48]R. E. Kidwell, Jr., and N. Bennett. Employee propensity to withhold effort: A conceptual

model to intersect three avenues of research. *Academy of Management Review,* 18, 1993, pp. 429–456.

[49]D. C. Feldman. The development and enforcement of group norms. *Academy of Management Review,* 9, 1984, pp. 47–53.

[50]M. E. Burkhardt. Social interaction effects following a technological change: A longitudinal investigation. *Academy of Management Journal,* 37, 1994, pp. 869–898.

[51]R. A. Cooke and J. L. Szumal. The impact of group interaction styles on problem-solving effectiveness. *Journal of Applied Behavioral Science,* 30, 1994, pp. 415–437.

[52]K. M. Eisenhardt, J. L. Kahwajy, and L. J. Bourgeois III. Conflict and strategic choice: How top management teams disagree. *California Management Review,* 39, Winter 1997, pp. 42–62.

[53]B. Mullen, T. Anthony, E. Salas, and J. E. Driskell. Group cohesiveness and quality of decision making: An integration of tests of the groupthink hypothesis. *Small Group Research,* 25, 1994, pp. 189–204; and S. M. Miranda. Avoidance of groupthink: Meeting management using group support systems. *Small Group Research,* 25, 1994, pp. 105–136.

[54]A. Nahavandi and E. Aranda. Restructuring teams for the re-engineered organization. *Academy of Management Executive,* 8, 1994, pp. 58–68; and K. M. Eisenhardt, J. L. Kahwajy, and L. J. Bourgeois III. How management teams can have a good fight. *Harvard Business Review,* July–August 1997, pp. 77–85.

[55]Adapted from S. E. Jackson, K. E. May, and K. Whitney. Understanding the dynamics of diversity in decision making teams. In R. A. Guzzo, E. Salas, and Associates (eds.). *Team Effectiveness and Decision Making in Organizations.* San Francisco: Jossey-Bass, 1995, pp. 204–261; A seven-step model to develop team measures. *ACA News,* November–December 1996, pp. 15–16; D. C. Borwhat, Jr. How do you know if your work teams work? *Workforce,* May 1997 (suppl.), p. 7; D. R. Denison, S. L. Hart, and J. A. Kahn. From chimneys to cross-functional teams: Developing and validating a diagnostic model. *Academy of Management Journal,* 39, 1996, 1005–1023; and M. Cianni and D. Wnuck. Individual growth and team enhancement: Moving toward a new model of career development. *Academy of Management Executive,* 11, 1997, pp. 105–113.

[56]M. Walton. *Car: A Drama of the American Workplace.* New York: W. W. Norton, 1997.

[57]S. Caminiti. What team leaders need to know. *Fortune,* February 20, 1995, pp. 93–100.

[58]E. Matson. Congratulations, you're promoted. (Now what?). *Fast Company,* June–July, 1997, pp. 116–130; and A. M. O'Leary-Kelly, J. J. Martocchio, and D. D. Frink. A review of the influence of group goals on group performance. *Academy of Management Journal,* 37, 1994, pp. 1285–1301.

[59]K. A. Guinn. Performance management for evolving self-directed work teams. *ACA Journal,* Winter 1995, pp. 74–81.

[60]R. S. Wellins, W. C. Byham, and J. M. Wilson; G. E. Prussia and A. J. Kinicki. A motivational investigation of group effectiveness using social-cognitive theory. *Journal of Applied Psychology,* 81, 1996, pp. 187–198; S. G.

Cohen, G. E. Ledford, Jr., and G. Spreitzer. A predictive model of self-managing work team effectiveness. *Human Relations,* 49, 1996, pp. 643–676; and M. A. Campion, E. M. Papper, and G. J. Medsker. Relations between work team characteristics and effectiveness: A replication and extension. *Personnel Psychology,* 49, 1996, pp. 429–452.

[61]S. Caminiti. Also see A. McCauley. "Team doctors, report to ER!" *Fast Company,* February–March, 1998, pp. 170–174.

[62]S. Wetlaufer. The team that wasn't. *Harvard Business Review.* November–December, 1994, pp. 22–38; P. Reagan-Cirincione. Improving the accuracy of group judgment: A process intervention combining group facilitation, social judgment analysis, and information technology. *Organizational Behavior and Human Decision Processes,* 58, 1994, pp. 246–270.

[63]S. Cauldron. Teamwork takes work. *Personnel Journal,* February, 1994, pp. 41–49.

[64]H. Campbell. Adventures in teamland: Experiential training makes the lesson fun. *Personnel Journal,* May, 1996, pp. 56–62.

[65]J. W. Dean, Jr., and M. P. Sharfman. Does decision process matter? A study of strategic decision making effectiveness. *Academy of Management Journal,* 39, 1996, pp. 368–396; P. W. Mulvey, J. F. Veiga, and P. M. Elsass. When teammates raise a white flag. *Academy of Management Executive,* 10, 1996, pp. 40–49; and R. L. Priem, D. A. Harrison, and N. K. Muir. Structured conflict and consensus outcomes in group decision making. *Journal of Management,* 21, 1995, pp. 691–710.

[66]For a discussion of how team design and reward design combine to affect team performance, see R. Wageman. Interdependencies and group effectiveness. *Administrative Science Quarterly,* 40, 1995, pp. 145–180.

CHAPTER 18

[1]J. Case. Corporate culture. *Inc.,* November, 1996, pp. 42–52.

[2]Adapted from H. M. Trice and J. M. Beyer. *The Culture of Work Organizations.* Englewood Cliffs, N.J.: Prentice-Hall, pp. 1–32; D. R. Denison. What is the difference between organizational culture and organizational climate? A native's point of view on a decade of paradigm wars. *Academy of Management Review,* 21, 1996, pp. 619–654; and C. A. O'Reilly and J. A. Chatman. Culture as social control: Corporations, cults, and commitments. In B. M. Staw and L. L. Cummings (eds.), *Research in Organizational Behavior.* Greenwich, Conn.: JAI, pp. 157–200.

[3]T. G. Powell. Total Quality Management as competitive advantage: A review and empirical study. *Strategic Management Journal,* 16, 1995, pp. 15–37.

[4]Adapted from C. A. O'Reilly III, J. Chatman, and D. F. Caldwell. People and organizational culture: A profile comparison approach to assessing person–organization fit. *Academy of Management Journal,* 34, 1991, pp. 487–516; and J. E. Sheridan Organizational culture and employee retention. *Academy of Management Journal,* 35, 1992, pp. 1036–1056.

[5]B. Kabanoff, R. Waldersee, and M. Cohen. Espoused values and organizational change

themes. *Academy of Management Journal,* 38, 1995, pp. 1075–1104; and B. Kabanoff and J. P. Daley. Values espoused by Australian and U.S. Organizations. Unpublished manuscript. Sydney: Australian Graduate School of Management, 1998.

[6]N. J. Allen and J. P. Meyer. Organizational socialization tactics: A longitudinal analysis of links to newcomers' commitment and role orientation. *Academy of Management Journal,* 33, 1990, pp. 847–858.

[7]H. M. Trice and J. M. Beyer. *The Culture of Work Organizations.*

[8]N. Difonzo, P. Bardia, and R. L. Rosnow. Reining in rumors. *Organizational Dynamics,* Summer, 1994, pp. 47–62; and M. Noon and R. Delridge. News from behind my hand: Gossip in organizations. *Organization Studies,* 14, 1993, pp. 23–36.

[9]G. Colvin. The changing art of becoming unbeatable. *Fortune,* November 24, 1997, pp. 299–300.

[10]H. M. Trice and J. M. Beyer. *The Culture of Work Organizations.*

[11]H. M. Trice and J. M. Beyer. Cultural leadership in organizations. *Organization Science,* 2, 1991, pp. 149–169.

[12]L. S. Csoka, B. Hackett, R. J. Kramer, K. Troy, and M. L. Wheeler. *Global Management Teams: A Perspective.* New York: The Conference Board, 1996; and K. J. Fedor and W. B. Werther, Jr. The fourth dimension: Creating culturally responsive international alliances. *Organizational Dynamics,* Autumn 1996, pp. 39–52.

[13]Adapted from A. Friedman. A case of corporate culture shock in the global arena. *International Herald Tribune* (Zurich ed.), April 23, 1997, pp. 1, 11; R. Frank and T. M. Burton. Cross-border merger results in headaches for a drug company. *Wall Street Journal,* May 1, 1997, pp. A1, A13; D. Stamps. Welcome to America. Watch out for culture shock. *Training,* November 1996, pp. 22–30; and R. Calori and B. Dufour. Management European Style. *Academy of Management Executive,* 9(3), 1995, pp. 61–73.

[14]B. Schlender. Microsoft: First America, now the world. *Fortune,* August 18, 1997, pp. 214–217.

[15]R. Tung and V. Worm. East meets west: Northern European expatriates in China. *Business and the Contemporary World,* 9, 1997, pp. 137–148; and N. Rogovsky and R. S. Schuler. Managing human resources across cultures. *Business and the Contemporary World,* 9, 1997, pp. 63–75.

[16]D. A. Ralston, R. Kai-Cheng, X. Wang, R. H. Terpstra, and H. Wei. The cosmopolitan Chinese manager: Findings of a study on managerial values across the six regions of China. *Journal of International Management,* 2, 1996, pp. 79–109.

[17]Based on results reported in M. E. Phillips. Industry mindsets: Exploring the cultures of two macro-organizational settings. *Organization Science,* 3, 1994, pp. 384–402.

[18]S. C. Schneider and J.-L. Barsoux. *Managing Across Cultures.* New York: Prentice-Hall, 1997.

[19]Adapted from G. Hofstede. *Cultures and Organizations: Software of the Mind.* New York: McGraw Hill, 1995; and G. Hofstede, B. Neuijen, D. D. Ohayv, and G. Sanders. Mea-

suring organizational cultures: A qualitative and quantitative study of twenty cases. *Administrative Science Quarterly,* 35, 1990, pp. 286–316.

[20]P. Plitch. Morgan Stanley merger has rough spot. *Wall Street Journal,* February 6, 1998, p. B6C; and A. Raghavan and S. Lipin. Morgan Stanley Group and Dean Witter plan $8.8 billion merger. *Wall Street Journal,* February 5, 1997, pp. A1; A4.

[21]S. Cartwright and C. L. Cooper. The role of culture in successful organizational marriage. *Academy of Management Executive,* 7, 1993, pp. 57–71; and R. Royston, C. R. Hinings, and J. Brown. Merging professional service firms. *Organization Science,* 5, 1994, pp. 239–257.

[22]R. N. Ashkenas, L. J. DeMonaco, and S. C. Francis. Making the deal real: How GE Capital Integrates Acquisitions. *Harvard Business Review,* January–February 1998, pp. 165–178.

[23]E. H. Schein. What is culture? In P. J. Frost, L. F. Moore, M. R. Louis, C. C. Lundberg, and J. Martin (eds.), *Reframing Organizational Culture.* Newbury Park, Calif.: Sage, 1991, pp. 243–253.

[24]M. Schultz. *On Studying Organizational Cultures.* New York: deGruyter, 1994.

[25]H. M. Trice and J. M. Beyer. *The Culture of Work Organizations,* 175–253.; and R. Goffee and G. Jones. What holds the modern company together? *Harvard Business Review,* November–December 1996, pp. 133–148.

[26]A. Majchrzak and Q. Wang. Breaking the functional mindset in process organizations. *Harvard Business Review,* September–October 1996, pp. 93–99.

[27]R. Hooijberg and F. Petrock. On cultural change: Using the competing values framework to help leaders execute a transformational strategy. *Human Resource Management,* 32, 1993, pp. 29–50.

[28]S. G. Harris and K. W. Mossholder. The affective implications of perceived congruence with culture dimensions during organizational transformation. *Journal of Management,* 22, 1996, pp. 527–547.

[29]*Wall Street Journal,* February 26, 1998, p. A9; A. Bryant. The Andersen family feud: Two units split on new leadership. *New York Times,* June 28, 1997, pp. B35, B37; and D. Whitford. Arthur, Arthur. . . . *Fortune,* November 10, 1997, pp. 169–178.

[30]D. A. Morand. The role of behavioral formality and informality in the enactment of bureaucratic versus organic organizations. *Academy of Management Review,* 20, 1995, pp. 831–872.

[31]Adapted from *National Performance Review.* Washington, D.C.: U.S. Government Printing Office, 1993; and G. C. Church. Gorezilla zaps the system. *Time,* September 13, 1993, pp. 25–29.

[32]R. A. Melcher. Warm and fuzzy, meet rough and tumble. *Business Week,* January 26, 1998, p. 38.

[33]P. Spector and P. D. McCarthy. *The Nordstrom Way: The Inside Story of America's #1 Customer Service Company.* New York: John Wiley & Sons, 1995.

[34]G. Grant. Outmarketing P&G. *Fortune,* January 12, 1998, pp. 150–152; and T. Parker-Pope. Colgate's Total grabs big share in early

sales. *Wall Street Journal,* March 6, 1998, p. B6.

[35]M. J. Morgan. How corporate culture drives strategy. *Long Range Planning,* 26(2), 1993, pp. 110–118; and D. R. Denison and A. K. Mishra. Toward a theory of organizational culture and effectiveness. *Organization Science,* 6, 1995, pp. 204–222.

[36]L. E. Wynter. Rare black firm on Wall Street learns how to make its way. *Wall Street Journal,* March 4, 1998, p. B1; G. N. Powell. Reinforcing and extending today's organizations: The simultaneous pursuit of person–organization fit and diversity. *Organizational Dynamics,* Winter 1998, pp. 50–61. For a description of what it is like for gay men to work in the monolithic culture of an American automobile company, see A. Gilmore. Revelations: My life as a gay executive. *Fortune,* September 8, 1997, pp. 106–110. For the results of a study of how culture affects gay and lesbian workers, see N. E. Day and P. Schoenrade. Staying in the closet versus coming out: Relationships between communication about sexual orientation and work attitudes. *Personnel Psychology,* 50, 1997, pp. 147–163. For insights into the experiences of employees with disabilities, see A. Colella. Organizational socialization of newcomers with disabilities: A framework for future research. *Research in Personnel and Human Resource Management,* 14, 1996, pp. 351–417; D. L. Stone and A. Colella. A model of factors affecting the treatment of disabled individuals in organizations. *Academy of Management Review,* 21, 1996, 352–401.

[37]J. Messina. A gift of tongues: New immigrants drive high-tech in NY. *Crain's New York Business,* April 6, 1996, pp. 1, 41.

[38]A. M. Konrad and F. Linnehan. Formalized HRM structures: Coordinating equal employment opportunity or concealing organizational practices? *Academy of Management Journal,* 38, 1995, pp. 787–820.

[39]T. Cox, Jr., and R. L. Tung. The multicultural organization revisited. In C. L. Cooper and S. E. Jackson. *Creating Tomorrow's Organizations: Handbook for Future Research in Organizational Behavior.* New York: John Wiley & Sons, 1997; A. J. Vogel and M. Budman. "Do they get it?" *Across the Board,* March, 1998, pp. 26–33; and P. Wright, S. P. Ferris, J. S. Hiller, and M. Kroll. Competitiveness through management of diversity: Effects on stock price valuation. *Academy of Management Journal,* 38, 1995, pp. 272–287.

[40]M. L. Wheeler. *Corporate Practices in Diversity Measurement: A Research Report.* New York: Conference Board, 1996. For detailed discussions of affirmative action, see the *Journal of Social Issues,* Winter 1996.

[41]K. Eichenwald. The two faces of Texaco: The right policies are on the books, but not always on the job. *New York Times,* November 10, 1996, pp. A1–3; and A. Bryant. How much has Texaco changed? A mixed report card on anti-bias efforts. *New York Times,* November 2, 1997, pp. 3-1, 3-16, 3-17.

[42]A. Muoio. Women and men, work and power. *Fast Company,* February–March 1998, pp. 71–82; and J. R. Gordon and K. S. Whelan. Successful professional women in midlife: How organizations can effectively understand and respond to the challenges. *Academy of*

Management Executive, 12(1), 1998, pp. 8–27.

[43]R. J. Ely. The power of demography: Women's social constructions of gender identity at work. *Academy of Management Journal,* 38, 1995, pp. 589–634; and J. I. Sanchez and P. Brock. Outcomes of perceived discrimination among Hispanic employees: Is diversity management a luxury or a necessity? *Academy of Management Journal,* 39, 1996, pp. 704–719.

[44]Microsoft's diversity home page at www.microsoft.com/jobs/diversity/sergio.html (February 22, 1998).

[45]A. Markels. How one hotel manages staff's diversity. *Wall Street Journal,* November 20, 1996, pp. B1, B2.

[46]G. Robinson and K. Dechant. Building a business case for diversity. *Academy of Management Executive,* 11(3), 1997, pp. 21–31.

[47]Microsoft's diversity home; M. Barone. How Hispanics are Americanizing. *Wall Street Journal,* February 6, 1998, p. A22. A list of companies that have positive organizational cultures for Hispanic employees can be found in *Hispanic Magazine* on the the Internet at www.hisp.com (March 1998).

[48]F. Rice. Denny's changes its spots. *Fortune,* May 13, 1996, pp. 133–142.

[49]F. Rice.

[50]M. L. Wheeler, p. 17; and R. V. Hayles. *Diversity in Corporate America.* Minneapolis: Institute for Corporate Diversity, 1994–1995.

[51]A profile of Santiago Rodriguez is available in the online archives of *Hispanic Magazine* at www.hsip.com/oct96/santiago.html (March 3, 1998).

[52]Numerous books describe the options available. Recent additions to the growing list include the following: L. B. Lewis and L. Louw. (eds.). *Valuing Diversity: New Tools for a New Reality.* New York: McGraw-Hill, 1995; N. Carr-Ruffino. *Managing Diversity: People Skills for a Multicultural Workplace.* Thomson, 1996; M. C. Gentile. *Managing Excellence Through Diversity.* Chicago: Irwin, 1996; and E. E. Kossek and S. Lobel. *Managing Diversity: Human Resource Strategies for Transforming the Workplace.* Malden, Mass.: Blackwell, 1996.

[53]L. N. Spiro. Smith Barney's woman problem. *Business Week,* June 3, 1996, pp. 102–103.

[54]*Manpower Argus,* March 1996, p. 5; and P. Dwyer, M. Johnson, and K. L. Miller. Out of the typing pool, into career limbo. *Business Week,* April 15, 1996, pp. 92–94.

[55]V. Valian. Running in place. *The Sciences,* January/February 1998, pp. 18–23; Race, gender, and opportunity: A study of compensation attainment and the establishment of mentoring relationships. *Journal of Applied Psychology,* 81, 1996, pp. 297–308; K. S. Lyness and D. E. Thompson. Above the Glass Ceiling? A comparison of matched samples of female and male executives. *Journal of Applied Psychology,* 82, 1997, pp. 359–375; P. Barnum, R. C. Liden, and N. DiTomaso. Double jeopardy for women and minorities: Pay differences with age. *Academy of Management Journal,* 38, 1995, pp. 863–880; and B. R. Ragins and M. Mattis. Gender gap in the executive suite: CEOs and female executives report on breaking the Glass Ceiling. *Academy of*

[56]J. R. W. Joplin and C. S. Daus. Challenges of leading a diverse workforce. *Academy of Management Executive,* 11(3), 1997, pp. 32–47.

[57]C. M. Riordan and L. M. Shore. Demographic diversity and employee attitudes: An empirical examination of relational demography within work units. *Journal of Applied Psychology,* 82, 1997, pp. 342–358; C. Kirchmeyer. Demographic similarity to the work group: A longitudinal study of managers at the early career stage. *Journal of Organizational Behavior,* 16, 1995, pp. 67–83; B. Lawrence. The black box of organizational demography. *Organization Science,* 8, 1997, pp. 1–22; and L. H. Pelled. Demographic diversity, conflict, and work group outcomes: An intervening process theory. *Organization Science,* 7, 1996, pp. 615–631.

[58]S. Rynes and B. Rosen. A field survey of factors affecting the adoption and perceived success of diversity training. *Personnel Psychology,* 48, 1995, pp. 247–270.

[59]L. Himelstein and S. A. Forest. Breaking through. *Business Week,* February 17, 1997, pp. 64–70.

[60]A. Markels. A diversity program can prove divisive. *Wall Street Journal,* January 30, 1997, pp. B1, B5.

[61]D. A. Thomas and R. J. Ely. Making differences matter: A new paradigm for managing diversity. *Harvard Business Review,* September–October 1996, pp. 79–90; M. E. Heilman, C. J. Block, and P. Stathatos. The affirmative action stigma of incompetence: Effects of performance information ambiguity. *Academy of Management Journal,* 40, 1997, pp. 603–625. When organizations introduce initiatives intended to improve their organizational cultures, they should be prepared to detect and address concerns such as the ones described in the following articles. K. M. Thomas, K. L. Williams, and L. A. Barroso. *Affirmative Action Attitudes: Looking Beyond Race and Gender Effects.* Unpublished manuscript, University of Georgia, April 1997; and R. A. Friedman. Defining the scope and logic of minority and female network groups: Can separation enhance integration? *Research in Personnel and Human Resource Management,* 14, 1996, pp. 307–349.

[62]I. J. Dugan. Why Avon called a 'nonwoman.' *Business Week,* March 16, 1998, pp. 57–60; L. Wayne and K. N. Gilpin. Avon calls on a man to lead it: Female cosmetics executives passed over for the top post. *New York Times,* December 12, 1997, pp. C1, C7; T. Parker-Pope. Ding Dong! Avon calls up 6 executives, putting them in line for top positions. *Wall Street Journal,* March 26, 1997, p. B7; B. Morris. If women ran the world, it would look a lot like Avon. *Fortune,* July 21, 1997, pp. 74–79; and R. R. Thomas, Jr. *Beyond Race and Gender.* New York: Amacon, 1991.

CHAPTER 19

[1]Adapted from L. Grant. Why FedEx is flying high. *Fortune,* November 10, 1997, pp. 155–160; D. M. Halbfinger. Cabinet factory is being converted by Federal Express. *New York Times,* November 13, 1997, p. B6; K. Holland. FedEx's great big package. *Business Week,* October 20, 1997, pp. 48–49; and R. O. Mason, J. L. McKenney, W. Carlson, and D. Copeland. Absolutely, positively operations research: The Federal Express story. *Interfaces,* 27(2), 1997, pp. 17–36.

[2]R. Simons. Control in an age of empowerment. *Harvard Business Review,* March–April, 1995, pp. 80–88.

[3]R. Simons. *Levers of control: How managers use innovative control systems to drive strategic renewal.* Boston: Harvard University Press, 1995.

[4]J. A. Ottman. *Green Marketing.* Chicago: NTC Publishing Group, 1993; T. F. P. Sullivan. *The Greening of American Business.* Rockville, Md.: Government Institutes, Inc., 1992; and S. L. Hart. Beyond greening: Strategies for a sustainable world. *Harvard Business Review,* January–February 1997, pp. 66–77.

[5]J. L. Heskett and L. A. Schlesinger. Leading the high-capability organization: Challenges for the twenty-first century. *Human Resource Management,* Spring 1997, pp. 105–114; and K. D. Godsey. Slow climb to new heights: Combine strict discipline with goofy antics and make billions. *Success,* October 1996, pp. 4–5.

[6]Adapted from F. F. Reichheld. *The Loyalty Effect: The Hidden Force Behind Growth, Profits, and Lasting Value.* Boston: Harvard Business School, 1996.

[7]J. C. Eurfurt, A. Foote, and M. A. Heirich. The cost effectiveness of worksite wellness programs for hypertension control, weight loss, smoking cessation, and exercise. *Personnel Psychology,* 45(1), 1992, pp. 5–29.

[8]S. R. Curry. Big brother wants a close look at your hair. *Fortune,* June 23, 1997, p. 163.

[9]S. K. Parker, T. D. Wall, and P. R. Jackson. "That's not my job": Developing flexible employee work orientations. *Academy of Management Journal,* 40, 1997, pp. 899–929.

[10]T. Lowe and J. L. Machin. *New Perspectives on Management Control.* New York: Macmillan, 1987.

[11]Adapted from H. Row. This "virtual" company is for real. *Fast Company,* December–January 1998, pp. 48–49.

[12]G. Miles. Tailoring a global product. *International Business,* March 1995, pp. 50–52; and R. Leifer and P. K. Mills. An information processing approach for deciding upon control strategies and reducing control loss in emerging organizations. *Journal of Management,* 22(1), 1996, pp. 113–138.

[13]Adapted from R. Semler. Managing without managers. *Harvard Business Review,* September–October 1989, pp. 76–84.

[14]M. V. Makhija and U. Ganesh. The relationship between control and partner learning in learning-related joint ventures. *Organization Science,* 8, 1997, pp. 508–527.

[15]Adapted from K. Chandler. Master Lock, Smith actions concern non profits. *The Business Journal—Milwaukee,* March 7, 1997, pp. 26–28; T. Keenan. Tower takes a strategic leap. *Ward's Auto World,* March 1997, pp. 125–126; and J. Hoerr. The cultural revolution at A. O. Smith. *Business Week,* May 29, 1989, pp. 66–68.

[16]M. J. Tyre and E. VonHippel. The situated nature of adaptive learning in organizations. *Organization Science,* 8, 1997, pp. 71–83.

[17]D. I. Levine. Reinventing workplace regulation. *California Management Review,* 39(4), 1997, pp. 98–117.

[18]V. Vishwanath and J. Mark. Your brand's best strategy. *Harvard Business Review,* May–June 1997, pp. 123–131.

[19]Personal conversation with Carl Sewell, President, Sewell Lexus, Dallas, Texas, December, 1997.

[20]R. N. Anthony and J. S. Reece. *Accounting Principles.* Burr Ridge, Ill.: Irwin, 1995.

[21]C. P. Stickney and R. L. Weil. *Financial Accounting.* Fort Worth, Tex.: Dryden, 1997.

[22]R. N. Anthony and J. S. Reece, pp. 559–562, 574–575; C. T. Horngren and G. Foster. *Cost Accounting: A Managerial Emphasis.* Englewood Cliffs, N.J.: Prentice-Hall, 1994.

[23]S. S. Rao. ABCs of cost control. *Inc.Tech.,* 2, 1997, pp. 79–81.

[24]G. Cokins. If activity based costing is the answer, what is the question? *IIE Solutions,* 29(8), 1997, pp. 38–43; and S. Hronec. *The Effects of Manufacturing Productivity on Cost Accounting and Management Reporting. Cost Accounting for the '90s.* Montvale, N.J.: National Association of Accountants, 1986.

[25]Adapted from T. P. Pare. A new tool for managing costs. *Fortune,* June 14, 1993, pp. 124–129.

[26]D. G. Uyemura. EVA: A top down approach to risk management. *Journal of Lending and Credit Risk Management,* 79(6), 1997, pp. 40–48; and R. A. Stiles and S. S. Mick. What is the cost of controlling quality? Activity-based cost accounting offers an answer. *Hospital & Health Services Administration,* 42(2), 1997, pp. 193–205.

[27]D. R. Anderson, D. J. Sweeney, and T. A. Williams. *Quantitative Methods for Business,* 7th ed. Cincinnati: South-Western, 1997.

[28]K. J. Conlon. Privacy in the workplace. *Labor Law Journal,* August 1997, pp. 444–448; and B. Kainen and S. D. Myers. Turning off the power on employees: Using surreptitious tape-recordings and e-mail intrusions by employees in pursuit of employer rights. *Labor Law Journal,* April 1997, pp. 199–213.

[29]Adapted from B. Murray. A very smart Swatch. *U.S. News & World Report,* September 22, 1997, pp. 54–55; and J. Levine. Swatchout! *Forbes,* June 5, 1995, pp. 150–152.

[30]P. S. Greenlaw and C. Prundeanu. The impact of federal legislation to limit electronic monitoring. *Public Personnel Management,* 26(2), 1997, pp. 227–245.

[31]J. F. George. Computer-based monitoring: Common perceptions and empirical results. *MIS Quarterly,* 20, 1996, pp. 459–481.

[32]M. Abu-Hamdan and A. El-Gizaway. Computer-aided monitoring system for flexible assembly operations. *Computers in Industry,* October 1997, 34(1), pp. 1–10.

[33]D. Armbruster. On-site drug testing: On the rise and growing strong. *Medical Laboratory Observer,* 29(4), 1997, pp. 40–45.

[34]W. Arthur, Jr. Employment-related drug testing: Idiosyncratic characteristics and issues. *Public Personnel Management,* 26(1), 1997, pp. 77–88.

[35]F. D. Miller. Rising employee theft wringing out more profits. *Nation's Restaurant News,*

July 28, 1997, pp. 36–38; B. A. Jacobs. Contingent ties: Undercover drug officers' use of informants. *British Journal of Sociology,* 48(1), 1997, pp. 35–54; and S.Crock. Corporate spies feel a sting. *Business Week,* July 14, 1997, pp. 76–78.

[36]Adapted from L. R. Jaunch, S. A. Coltrin, A. G. Bedeian, and W. F. Glueck. *The Management Experience: Cases, Exercises, and Readings,* 4th ed. Chicago: Dryden, 1986, pp. 254–255.

[37]Adapted from T. P. Pope. For you, my pet: Why the veterinarian really recommends that designer chow. *Wall Street Journal,* November 3, 1997, pp. A1ff; L. Haran. Iams unleashes efforts in shelters: Public service ads, adopt-athon attempt to reach new pet owners. *Advertising Age,* 67(14), 1996, pp. 42–43; and Iams of Dayton builds loyalty database of loving pet owners. *Direct Marketing,* 58(7), 1995, pp. 15–17.

CHAPTER 20

[1]Adapted from N. Wreden. Business intelligence: Turning on success. *Beyond Computing,* September 1997, pp. 19–24; and V. Jailumar. Airline routes arriving data to one terminal. *Computerworld,* September 8, 1997, pp. 39, 42.

[2]P. Gilster. *Digital Literacy.* New York: John Wiley & Sons, 1997.

[3]H. J. Leavitt and T. L. Whisler. Management in the 1980's. *Harvard Business Review,* November–December 1958, pp. 41–48.

[4]F. Cairncross. *The Death of Distance.* Boston: Harvard Business School Press, 1997.

[5]O. Port. Dueling Brainscapes. *Business Week,* June 23, 1997, pp. 88–90.

[6]M. Casson. *Information and Organization: A New Perspective on the Theory of the Firm.* Oxford, England: Clarendon Press, 1997.

[7]T. H. Davenport and L. Prusak. *Information Ecology: Mastering the Information and Knowledge Environment.* New York: Oxford University Press, 1997.

[8]J. Pfeffer. *The Human Equation: Building Profits by Putting People First.* Boston: Harvard Business School Press, 1998.

[9]J. F. Veiga and K. Dechant. Wired world woes: www.help. *Academy of Management Executive,* August 1997, pp. 73–79.

[10]L. B. Eliot. Correcting Year 2000 (Y2K) false assumptions. *Decision Line,* December/January 1998, pp. 15–16.

[11]T. H. Davenport and L. Prusak. *Working Knowledge: How Organizations Manage What They Know.* Boston: Harvard Business School Press, 1997.

[12]J. W. Cortada. *Best Practices in Information Technology: How Corporations Get the Most Value from Exploiting Their Digital Investments.* Upper Saddle River, N.J.: Prentice-Hall, 1997.

[13]C. J. Bodenstab. *Information Breakthrough: How to Turn Mountains of Confusing Data into Gems of Useful Information.* Grants Pass, Ore.: Oasis Press, 1997.

[14]L. Kohaner. *Competitive Intelligence: How to Gather, Analyze, and Use Information to Move Your Business to the Top.* New York: Touchstone Books, 1998.

[15]G. P. Zachary. It's a mail thing: Electronic messaging gets a rating—Ex. *Wall Street Journal,* June 22, 1994, pp. A1, A10; and Computer Associates home page at www.cai.com (February 23, 1998).

[16]G. Gilder. Hot piping. *Forbes ASAP,* February 23, 1998, pp. 110–120.

[17]Adapted from Groupware enhances teamwork at The Sports Authority. *Chain Store Age,* November 1996, pp. 73–76; and The Sports Authority home page at www.sportsauthority.com (February 23, 1998).

[18]Adapted from C. B. Leshin. *Management on the World Wide Web.* Upper Saddle River, N.J.: Prentice-Hall, 1997; and G. W. Keen, W. Mougayar, and T. Torregrossa. *The Business Internet and Intranets: A Manager's Guide to Key Terms and Concepts.* Boston: Harvard Business School Press, 1998.

[19]The Founder's message. *Forbes ASAP,* December 1, 1997, p. 65.

[20]N. McBride. Business use of the Internet: Strategic decisions or another bandwagon? *European Management Journal,* February 1997, pp. 58–67.

[21]R. H. Baker. *Extranets: The Complete Sourcebook.* New York: McGraw-Hill, 1997.

[22]P. Lashin. *Extranet Design and Implementation.* Alameda, Calif.: Sybex, 1997.

[23]C. F. Franklin, Jr. Enter the extranet. *CIO Magazine,* May 15, 1997. Available at www.cio.com/archive/archive/051597_et_content

[24]J. Stone Gonzalez. *The 21st Century Intranet.* Upper Saddle River, N.J.: Prentice-Hall, 1998.

[25]Adapted from C. Stedman. Extranet brokers access to funds data. *Computerworld,* October 27, pp. 49, 54; P. Gillin. Schwab impresses. *Computerworld,* October 20, 1997, pp. 49, 51; and Charles Schwab & Co. home page at www.schwab.com (February 2, 1998).

[26]Adapted from L. Eliot. There's an intranet in your future. *Decision Line,* May 1996, pp. 13–14; and T. Greer. *Understanding Intranets.* La Vergne, Tenn.: Microsoft Press, 1998.

[27]Adapted from A. Frankel. New growth. *CIO Magazine,* November 1, 1997. Available at www.cio.com/archive/webbusiness/110197 (February 20, 1998); B. Richards. Inside story. *Wall Street Journal,* June 17, 1996, p. R23; and Weyerhaeuser's home page at www.weyerhaeuser.com (February 25, 1998).

[28]V. Dhar and R. Stein. *Intelligent Decision Support Methods: The Science of Knowledge Work.* Upper Saddle River, N.J.: Prentice-Hall, 1997.

[29]M. H. Meyer and K. F. Curley. Putting expert systems to work, *Sloan Management Review,* Winter 1991, pp. 21–31; and A. H. Ashton and M. N. Davis. White-collar robotics: Levering managerial decision making. *California Management Review,* Fall 1994, pp. 83–109.

[30]Adapted from T. Hoffman. Pizzeria Uno cuts slice from cost pie. *Computerworld,* September 15, 1997, pp. 41–42.

[31]H. J. Watson, G. Houdeshel, and R. K. Rainer, Jr. *Building Executive Information Systems and Other Support Applications.* New York: John Wiley & Sons, 1997.

[32]G. Beekman. *Computer Currents: Navigating Tomorrow's Technology.* Reading, Mass.: Addison-Wesley, 1994.

[33]S. J. Gaston. *Getting the Right Systems at the Right Price: Strategies for Successful Management.* New York: John Wiley & Sons, 1997.

[34]J. E. Hallows. *Information Systems Project Management: How to Deliver Function and Value in Information Technology Projects.* New York: AMACOM, 1997.

[35]D. Remenyi, M. Sherwood-Smith, and T. White. *Achieving Maximum Value from Information Systems: A Process Approach.* New York: John Wiley & Sons, 1997.

[36]Adapted from T. H. Davenport. Information behavior: Why we build systems that users won't use. *Computerworld: Leadership Series,* September 15, 1997, pp. 2–11.

[37]G. B. Davis (ed.). *The Blackwell Encyclopedic Dictionary of Management Information Systems.* Cambridge, Mass.: Blackwell, 1997.

[38]B. Reimus. The IT system that couldn't deliver. *Harvard Business Review,* May–June 1997, pp. 22–35.

[39]P. E. Ross. The day the software crashed. *Forbes,* April 25, 1994, pp. 142–156; and R. X. Cringely. When disaster strikes IS. *Forbes ASAP,* August 29, 1994, pp. 60–64.

[40]Adapted from M. Halper. Everyone in the knowledge pool. *Computerworld: Global Innovation Series,* December 8, 1997, pp. 8-13; and DHL Worldwide Express web site USA page on "Who is DHL?" at www.dhl-usa.com/about-dhl/index (February 26, 1998).

[41]J. Weckert and D. Adeney. *Computer and Information Ethics.* Westport, Conn.: Greenwood, 1997.

[42]Adapted from J. Sandberg. Immorality play: Acclaiming hackers as heroes. *Wall Street Journal,* February 27, 1995, pp. B1, B6; and J. Migga Kizza. *Ethical and Social Issues in the Information Age.* Secaucus, N.Y.: Springer-Verlag, 1997.

[43]Adapted from D. Kelsey. Computer ethics: An overview of the issues. *Ethics: Easier Said Than Done,* 1991 (15), pp. 30–33; and T. E. Weber. Does anything go? *Wall Street Journal,* December 8, 1997, pp. R29, R31.

[44]F. H. Cate. *Privacy in the Information Age.* Washington, DC: Brookings Institute Press, 1997.

[45]R. A. Spinello. *Case Studies in Information and Computer Ethics.* Upper Saddle River, N.J.: Prentice-Hall, 1997.

[46]G. S. Adler and P. K. Tompkins. Electronic performance monitoring: An organizational justice and concertive control perspective. *Management Communication Quarterly,* 10, 1997, pp. 259–288.

[47]J. A. Berry. A potent new tool for selling: Database marketing. *Business Week,* September 5, 1994, pp. 56–62; and M. Nannery. Shy and sometimes awkward, data warehousing comes of age. *Chain Store Age,* January 1997, pp. 3B–15B.

[48]A. LaPlante. Teamwork is good work. *Computerworld: Internet Careers.* December 8, 1997, pp. 8-9; and Cambridge Technology Partners home page at www.ctp.com (February 9, 1998).

[49]Adapted from B. Wallace. Polaroid net strengthens Business Links. *Computerworld.*

October 13, 1997. p. 56; Polaroid, Corporation home page at www.polaroid.com (February 9, 1998); and Citizens Trust home page at www.efund.com/Polaroid (February 9, 1998).

[50]Adapted from the Amazon.com home page at www.amazon.com (February 9, 1998).

[51]Adapted from E. Horwitt. When Things go Wrong . . . *Computerworld:E-Commerce.* December 15, 1997, pp. 18–21; and The ProShop.com home page at www.theproshop. com (February 12, 1998).

[52]Adapted from S. Kalin. Global Net Knits East to West at Liz Claiborne. *Computerworld: Global Innovators,* June 9, 1997, pp. 4–6; and Liz Claiborne, Inc., home page at www.lizclai-borne.com (February 10, 1998).

CHAPTER 21

[1]Adapted from A. Taylor III. How Toyota defies go. *Fortune,* December 8, 1997, pp. 100–108; T. L. Besser. Team *Toyota: Transplanting the Toyota Culture to the Camry Plant in Kentucky.* Albany, N.Y.: State University of New York Press, 1977; and Y. Monden. *Toyota Production System: An Integrated Approach.* Narcross, Ga.: Institute of Industrial Engineers, 1998.

[2]See note 1.

[3]N. Slack (ed.). *The Blackwell Encyclopedia of Operations Management.* Cambridge, Mass.: Blackwell, 1997.

[4]J. Bickens and B. B. Elliott. *Operations Management: An Active Learning Approach.* Cambridge, Mass.: Blackwell, 1997.

[5]C. Sparks and M. Greiner. U.S. and foreign productivity and unit labor costs. *Monthly Labor Review,* February 1997, pp. 26–35.

[6]W. J. Kettinger and C. C. Choong. Pragmatic perspectives on the measurement of information systems service quality. *MIS Quarterly,* 21, 1997, pp. 223–240.

[7]M. McClellan. *Applying Manufacturing Execution Systems.* Boca Raton, Fla.: St. Lucie Press, 1998.

[8]P. V. Kern and T. M. Muth III. Multifactor productivity in the metal stampings industry. *Monthly Labor Review,* May 1997, pp. 48–58; and W. Kaydos. *Measuring Performance for Total Productivity.* Boca Raton, Fla.: St. Lucie Press, 1998.

[9]L. Willcocks and S. Lester. Beyond the IT productivity paradox. *European Management Journal,* 14, 1996, pp. 279–290.

[10]L. L. Krajewski and L. R. Ritzman. *Operations Management: Strategy and Analysis,* 5th ed. Reading, Mass.: Addison Wesley Longman, 1999.

[11]L. L. Krajewski and L. R. Ritzman.

[12]Adapted from L. M. Sixel. More, better, faster. *Houston Chronicle,* June 22, 1997, pp. 1E, 2E.

[13]J. G. Monks. *Operations Management: Theory and Problems.* Riverside, N.J.: Macmillan/McGraw-Hill, 1998.

[14]J. Dong (ed.). *Rapid Response Manufacturing: Contemporary Methodologies, Tools and Technologies.* Florence, Ky.: Van Nostrand Reinhold, 1998.

[15]J. H. Gilmore and B. J. Pine III. The four faces of mass customization. *Harvard Business Review,* January–February 1997, pp. 91–101; and J. D. Kasarda and D. A. Rondinelli. Innovative infrastructure for agile manufacturers. *Sloan Management Review,* Winter 1998, pp. 73–82.

[16]R. N. Nagel. *Agile Manufacturing: The 21st Century Vision.* Paper presented at the Iacocca Institute, Lehigh University, Bethlehem, Pa., 1993; and R. E. Markland, S. K. Vickery, and R. A. Davis. *Operations Management: Concepts in Manufacturing and Service,* 2d ed. Cincinnati: South-Western, 1998.

[17]A. Braganza and A. Myers. *Business Process Redesign: A View from the Inside.* Boston: International Thomson Business Press, 1998.

[18]Adapted from The Custom Foot home page at www.thecustomfoot.com (March 6, 1998); and J. Martin. Give 'em exactly what they want. *Fortune,* November 10, 1997, pp. 283–285.

[19]P. G. Keen. *The Process Edge: Creating Value Where It Counts.* Boston: Harvard Business School Press, 1997.

[20]M. Iansiti. *Technology Integration: Making Critical Choices in a Dynamic World.* Boston: Harvard Business School Press, 1997.

[21]C. Hope, A. Muhlemann, and C. Witt. *Service Operations Management: Strategy, Design and Delivery.* Upper Saddle River, N.J.: Prentice-Hall, 1997.

[22]D. Hazel. Completing the transportation triangle: The future of barcoding. *Chain Store Age,* January 1997, pp. 3C–11C.

[23]Adapted from J. Verity. No smoke, no mirrors. *Computerworld: E-mmerce.* December 15, 1997, pp. 8–9; and Beamscope Canada, Inc., home page at www.beamscope.com (March 6, 1998).

[24]R. L. Klevans and R. D. Rodman. *Voice Recognition.* Fitchburgh, Mass.: Artech House Telecommunications Library, 1998.

[25]N. Gross, P. C. Judge, O. Part, and S. H. Wildstrom. Let's talk. *Business Week.* February 23, 1998, pp. 61–72.

[26]N. Gross, P. C. Judge, O. Part, and S. H. Wildstrom; and N. Ole Bernsen, H. Dybkjr, and L. Dybkjr. *Designing Interactive Speech Systems: From First Ideas to User Testing.* Secaucus, N.J.: Springer-Verlag, 1998.

[27]Adapted from the Dragon System Web site at www.dragonsys.com/products/profile-brae-landon (March 7, 1998).

[28]I. Wickelgren. *Ramblin Robots: Building a Breed of Mechanical Beasts.* Danbury, Conn.: Franklin Watts, 1996.

[29]B. Bowonder and T. Miyake. Creating and sustaining competitiveness: An analysis of the Japanese robotics industry. *International Journal of Technology Management,* 9, 1994, pp. 575–611.

[30]F. Martin. *The Art of Robotics: An Introduction to Engineering.* Reading, Mass.: Addison-Wesley, 1998.

[31]Computer Motion ships new surgical robots. *Business Wire,* January 27, 1998, p. 1270014.

[32]P. E. Moody. *Leading Manufacturing Excellence: A Guide to State-of-the Art Manufacturing.* New York: John Wiley & Sons, 1997.

[33]G. Bylinsky. Industry's amazing instant prototypes. *Fortune,* January 12, 1998, pp. 120(b)–120(c).

[34]S. Ashley. Rapid-response design. *Mechanical Engineering,* December 1997, pp. 72–76.

[35]Adapted from M. Valenti. CAD/CAM comes to tinsel town. *Mechanical Engineering,* October 1997, pp. 168–170; and Cinnabar home page at www.cinnabar.com (March 12, 1998).

[36]R. M. Hodgetts. *Measuring of Quality and High Performance: Simple Tools and Lessons Learned from America's Most Successful Corporations.* New York: AMACOM, 1998.

[37]E. A. Robinson. Most admired: The ups and downs of the industry leaders. *Fortune,* March 2, 1998, pp. 86–87, F1–F7.

[38]J. W. Spechler (ed.). *Managing Quality in America's Most Admired Companies.* San Francisco: Berrett-Koehler, 1996.

[39]R. B. Lieber. Now are you satisfied?. *Fortune,* February 16, 1998, pp. 161–164; L. Grant. Your customers are telling the truth. February 16, 1998, pp. 164–166; and T. A. Stewart. A satisfied customer is not enough. *Fortune,* July 21, 1997, pp. 112–113.

[40]B. Bremmer, L. Armstrong, K. Kerwin, and K. Naughton. Toyota's crusade. *Business Week,* April 7, 1997, pp. 104–114.

[41]J. Butman. *Juran: A Lifetime of Influence.* New York: John Wiley & Sons, 1997.

[42]C. Burns. *Building Your Organization's TQM System: The Unified Total Quality Model.* Milwaukee: Quality Press, 1997.

[43]D. A. Garvin. *Managing Quality: The Strategic and Competitive Edge.* New York: Free Press, 1988.

[44]J. W. Cortada and J. A. Woods. *The Quality Yearbook 1998.* Riverside, N.J.: McGraw-Hill, 1998.

[45]D. L. Goetsch and S. B. Davis. *Introduction to Total Quality: Quality Management for Production, Processing, and Services.* Upper Saddle River, N.J.: Prentice-Hall, 1998.

[46]D. Bush and K. Dooley. The Deming Prize and Baldrige Award: How they compare. *Quality Progress,* January 1989, pp. 28–30; and J. A. Swift, J. E. Ross, and V. K. Omachonu. *Principles of Total Quality,* 2d ed. Boca Raton, Fla.: St. Lucie Press, 1998.

[47]D. Halberstam. Yes we can. *Parade Magazine,* July 8, 1984, p. 5.

[48]K R. Thompson. Confronting the paradoxes in a total quality environment. *Organization Dynamics,* Winter 1998, pp. 62–74.

[49]W. E. Deming. *The New Economics.* Cambridge, Mass.: MIT Center for Advanced Engineering Studies, 1994; W. E. Deming. *Out of the Crisis.* Cambridge, Mass.: MIT Center for Advanced Engineering Study, 1982; M. R. Yilmanz and S. Chatterjee. Deming and the quality of software development. *Business Horizons.* November–December 1997, pp. 51–58; and W. Edwards Deming Institute at www.deming.org (March 15, 1998).

[50]Malcolm Baldrige National Quality Award: 1997 award winners. Association for Quality Web site at: www.asq.org/abtquality/awards/baldrige/97briefs (March 5, 1998).

[51]National Institute of Standards and Technology. *Malcolm Baldrige National Quality Award: 1998 Criteria for Performance Excellence.* Gaithersberg, Md.: U.S. Department of Commerce, 1998.

[52]National Institute of Standards and Technology, p. 33.

E–25

[53]Malcolm Baldrige National Quality Award: 1997 winners; and Solectron home page at www.Solectron.com (March 7, 1998).

[54]A. Taylor III, p. 107.

[55]A. Taylor III, pp. 107–108; and V. Reitman. Toyota's fast rebound after fire at supplier shows why it is tough. *Wall Street Journal,* May 8, 1997, pp. A1, A16.

[56]T. E. Vollmann, W. L. Berry, and D. C. Whybark. *Manufacturing Planning and Control Systems.* Burr Ridge, Ill.: Irwin, 1997.

[57]Six sigma quality discussion at www.public.iastate.edu/ ~chu_c/course/tqm/t6a (March 9, 1998).

[58]R. J. Schonberger. *World Class Manufacturing: The Next Decade.* New York: Free Press, 1996.

[59]M. J. Harry and M. Harry. *The Nature of Six Sigma Quality.* New York: Soho Press, 1998.

[60]Adapted from M. Conlin. Revealed at last: the secret of Jack Welch's success. *Forbes,* January 26, 1998; R. J. Bowman. Best practices: The joy of six (Sigma). *Distribution,* August 1997, pp. 62–67; W. M. Carley. To keep GE's profits rising, Welch pushes quality-control plan. *Wall Street Journal,* January 13, 1997, pp. A1, A8; and General Electric home page at www.ge.com (March 11, 1998).

[61]S. F. Brown. Giving more jobs to electronic eyes. *Fortune,* February 16, 1998, pp. 104(B)–104(D); J. Martin. Mercedes: Made in Alabama. *Fortune,* July 7, 1997, pp. 150–158; and Mercedes-Benz division home page at www.mercedes-benz.com (March 8, 1998).

[62]R. Lawson and B. Stuart. *Measuring Six Sigma and Beyond: Continuous vs Attribute Data.* New York: Soho Press, 1997.

[63]Adapted from L. L. Berry. *On Great Service: A Framework for Action.* New York: Free Press, 1995; and R. M. Hodgetts. Quality lessons from America's Baldrige winners. *Business Horizons,* July–August 1994, pp. 74–79.

[64]Adapted from T. Petzinger, Jr. How Lynn Mercer manages a factory that manages itself. *Wall Street Journal,* March 7, 1997, p. B1; and Lucent Technologies home page at www.lucent.com (March 10, 1998).

[65]E. A. Silver, D. F. Pyke, R. Peterson, and E. Silver. *Inventory Management and Production Planning and Scheduling.* New York: John Wiley & Sons, 1998.

[66]J. D. Viale. *Inventory Management: From Warehouse to Distribution Center.* Menlo Park, Calif.: Crisp, 1997.

[67]D. V. Landvater. *World Class Production and Inventory Management.* New York: John Wiley & Sons, 1997.

[68]R. M. Monczka, R. J. Trent, and R. B. Handfield: *Purchasing and Supply Chain Management.* Cincinnati: South-Western, 1998.

[69]T. Hoffman. Mercedes-Benz tries just-in-time. *Computerworld,* December 17, 1997, pp. 47–48; and C. H. Pragman. JIT II: A purchasing concept for reducing lead times in time-based competition. *Business, Horizons,* July–August 1996, pp. 54–58.

[70]Adapted from S. Capparell. Meet Engin Altas, who sells purses to the world. *The Wall Street Journal,* August 1, 1997, p. B1; and Coach home page at www.coach.com (March 12, 1998).

[71]Adapted from M. Henricks. Koos Manufacturing's success is "Made in USA." *Apparel Industry Magazine.* January 1998, pp. 48–50.

[72]Adapted from J. Flint. The second paycheck. *Forbes.* April 22, 1996, pp. 148–150; and Burley Design Cooperative home page at www.burley.com (March 11, 1998).

[73]Adapted from Georgia-Pacific supports gypsum business strategy with construction of state-of-the-art facility, *PR Newswire.* June 25, 1997, p. 625ATW005; and Georgia-Pacific home page at www.gp.com (March 13, 1998).

[74]Adapted from M. Murray. Who's the boss? *Wall Street Journal.* May 14, 1997, pp. A1, A14.

[75]Adapted from B. Fox. Seeking atonement for past sins. *Chain Store Age.* February 1996, pp. 145–150.

[76]Adapted from A. Reinhardt and S. Browder. Boeing. . . . *Business Week.* September 30, 1996, pp. 119–125; C. Goldsmith. Boeing plans to make "drastic" changes to slash development time for aircraft. *Wall Street Journal,* February 11, 1998, p. B2; R. Henkoff. Boeing's Big Problem. *Fortune,* January 12, 1998, pp. 96–103; C. Goldsmith. After trailing Boeing for years, Airbus aims for 50% of the market. *Wall Street Journal,* March 16, 1998, pp. A1, A10; and Boeing home page at www.boeing.com (March 13, 1998).

Organization Index

Name Index

Halbfinger, D. M., 650
Haley, A., 84
Hall, C., 388
Hall, D. T., 5, 26
Hall, G., 450
Hallows, J. E., 696
Halper, M., 701
Hambrick, D. C., 95, 220
Hamel, G., 93, 359, 428
Hamm, S., 462
Hammer, M., 438, 450
Hammonds, K. H., 202
Handfield, R. B., 741
Handy, C., 272
Hankins, A. M., 523, 524
Hansen, G. A., 292
Hanson, J. R., 552
Harding, B., 15
Hardy, J. A., Sr., 28
Hardy, Q., 198
Hare, A. P., 586
Hargadon, A., 298
Harquail, C. V., 546
Harriman, A., 86
Harris, C. E., Jr., 181
Harris, D. L., 414
Harris, M. H., 412
Harris, N., 118
Harris, P. R., 135
Harris, S. G., 625
Harrison, D. A., 603
Harrison, E. F., 257
Harrison, J. S., 31
Harry, M., 734
Hart, S. L., 596, 653
Hassink, J., 547
Hastie, R., 577
Hatsopoulos, G., 172-173
Haverman, H. A., 268
Hayes, J. A., 225
Hayles, R. V., 633
Hazel, D., 721
Hazleton, J., 113
Healey, A. M., 487
Hedlund, J., 585-586
Heilman, M. E., 641
Heinzl, M., 15
Heirich, M. A., 654
Helft, B. L., 278
Hellriegel, D., 435
Henderson, A. B., 99
Henderson, B. D., 95
Henderson, M. A., 45
Heneman, R. L., 463
Henkoff, R., 134, 136, 249, 288, 407, 745
Henricks, M., 743
Herbig, P. A., 562
Herron, M., 453
Hersey, P., 511, 514, 515-516, 518, 532
Herzberg, F., 471-472
Hesketh, B., 33
Heskett, J. L., 69, 369, 653
Hessel, M., 728
Higgins, E. T., 482
Hill, A., 563
Hill, C. W. L., 219
Hill, J. W., 103
Hill, R. C., 156, 435
Hillary, R., 200
Hiller, J. S., 630
Hilmer, F. G., 64
Hilton, R., 346
Hiltrop, J. M., 390
Himmelstein, L., 184, 639
Hinings, C. R., 622
Hinkin, T. R., 500-501
Hipskind, M., 576
Hirschorn, L., 577
Hisrich, R. D., 154-155
Hitt, M. A., 108, 124, 228, 229
Hjelmas, T. A., 408
Hock, D., 26
Hodgetts, R. M., 725, 736
Hodgson, J., 136

Hodgson, M., 555
Hoerr, J., 663
Hoffman, T., 694, 741
Hofstede, G. J., 87, 133, 249, 621
Holland, C. P., 378
Holland, K., 365, 650
Hollenbeck, J. R., 585-586
Holloway, C. A., 718
Holpp, L., 600
Holyoke, L., 189
Hom, P. W., 476, 488
Honda, S., 508, 509
Honoré, C., 131
Hooijberg, R., 521, 624, 626
Hope, C., 721
Hopkins, M., 148, 529, 533
Horan, L., 78
Hornblower, M., 74
Horngren, C. T., 666
Hornsby, J. S., 170
Horwitt, E., 707
Hoskisson, R. E., 108, 124, 228, 229
Houdeshel, G., 693
Hough, L. M., 446, 452, 592
House, R. J., 511, 516-517, 518, 519-520, 521, 531
Howard, A., 439
Howell, J. M., 521, 523
Huber, G. P., 65, 87, 430, 439
Huber, J., 287
Hudson, K., 505
Huff, A. S., 205
Huff, J. O., 205
Hugman, R., 467
Huizenga, W., 280
Human, S. E., 376
Hummel, R. P., 48
Huselid, M. A., 388, 389
Hyatt, J., 146, 525
Hymowitz, C., 449

Iansiti, M., 100, 721
Ibarreche, S., 192-193
Ilgen, D. R., 33, 489, 585-586
Imperato, G., 63, 489
Ingrassia, L., 144
Ireland, R. D., 108, 124, 228, 229
Irvine, M., 222
Ishikawa, K., 299
Ivanovich, D., 126, 132
Iverson, K., 429
Iverson, R. D., 592
Izumi, H., 447

Jackofsky, E. F., 86
Jackson, P. R., 448-449, 656
Jackson, S. E., 4, 30, 33, 86, 388, 389, 486, 489, 504, 582, 596, 630
Jacob, R., 264, 434
Jacobs, B. A., 673
Jaffe, T., 232
Jago, A., 518, 519
James, G., 442
Janz, B. D., 584
Jarillo, J. C., 166
Jaunch, L. R., 676
Javetsky, B., 164
Jensen, M. A. C., 590
Jex, S. M., 472
Jobs, S. M., 507
Johannessen, O. J., 408
Johns, H. D., 658
Johnson, B. T., 520, 521
Johnson, C. H., 128
Johnson, G., 161
Johnson, M., 638
Johnson, R. A., 219, 429
Jolson, M. A., 510
Jones, G., 219, 624
Jones, Q., 228
Jones, R. A., 529
Jones, R. G., 27
Jones, R., 33
Jones, T. M., 197, 204
Joplin, J. R. W., 638

Jorgensen, J., 21
Jossi, F., 193
Joyce, W. F., 348, 374
Judge, P. C., 201, 722
Judge, T. A., 405
Junkins, J., 280, 584

Kabanoff, B., 615
Kahai, S. R., 519-520, 521
Kahalas, H., 173
Kahn, J. A., 596
Kahn, W. A., 342, 585
Kahwajy, J. L., 594
Kai-Cheng, Y., 620
Kainen, B., 671
Kalin, S., 708
Kanungo, R. N., 183
Karau, S. H., 507
Kasarda, J. D., 719
Kassicieh, S. K., 150
Kastein, M. R., 290
Katakis, M., 180
Katz, D., 11
Katz, G., 175-176
Katz, H., 175-176
Katz, J., 175-176, 259
Kaufman, J., 13
Kavan, C. B., 728
Kawamoto, N., 508, 509
Kaydos, W., 715
Keebler, J., 265
Keen, G. W., 689
Keen, P. G., 720
Keenan, T., 663
Keil, M., 696
Kelleher, H. 17, 26, 36, 432, 534-535, 560
Kelly, T. R., 298, 366
Kelly, T., 123
Kelsey, D., 703
Kennelly, J. J., 200
Kern, P. V., 715
Kerr, S., 105, 480
Kerwin, K., 236, 726
Kesner, I. L., 376
Kessler, J., 482
Ketchen, D. J., Jr., 336, 357
Kets de Vries, M. F. R., 521, 535
Kettinger, W. J., 715
Khoshabe, J., 152
Kidwell, R. E., Jr., 193, 476, 593
Kiechel, W. III, 434
Killing, P., 122
Kim, C., 432, 442
Kim, W. C., 196
King, M. L., Jr., 521
Kinicki, A. J., 598
Kinni, T. R., 59, 69. 273. 274
Kirchmeyer, C., 638
Kirkpatrick, D., 37, 267
Kirn, S. P., 580
Kishkovsky, S., 151-152
Kizilos, M. A., 508
Klassen, R. D., 204
Klein, K. J., 445
Kleindorfer, G. B., 273
Klevans, R. L., 722
Klimoski, R., 590
Kline, M., 128, 201-202
Klipfell, J., 259
Knight, P., 11, 362
Knott, K. B., 525
Knutsen, J. A., 119
Koch, K. D., 278
Kofman, F., 450
Kogut, B., 378
Kohaner, L., 687
Kohlberg, L., 186, 188-189, 192, 195
Komansky, D., 124
Konovsky, M. A., 195-196, 476
Konrad, A. M., 630
Koontz, H., 51
Koretz, G., 391
Korn, H. J., 95
Korsgaard, M. A., 164

Subject Index

administrative management, 52
behavioral viewpoint, 55
bureaucracy, 44
comparison of viewpoints, 70
contingency viewpoint, 64
early days, 40
quality viewpoint, 67
scientific management, 49
systems viewpoint, 60
traditional viewpoint, 42
Managerial competencies
Avon Products, 644
communication competency, 17, 156
defined, 4
development, 28
global awareness competency, 23
model, 5, 16
planning and administration competency, 19, 154
self-management competency, 25, 158
strategic action competency, 23, 153
team competencies, 600
teams, 586
teamwork competency, 21, 155
transfer, 17
Managerial functions
controlling, 11
leading, 11
organizing, 10
planning, 10
Managerial grid model, 507
Managers
activities, 9
communication effectiveness, 541
defined, 7
first-line managers, 12
functional managers, 8
Gates, Bill, 36
general managers, 8
information technologies, 683
middle managers, 13
small business, 15
top managers, 14
Manufacturing technologies, 723
Market controls
customer monitoring, 664
defined, 664
profit-sharing plans, 664
Market culture
defined, 627
norms, 627
values and norms, 627
Market development strategy, 238
Market forces, 627
Market penetration strategy, 237
Market research
Barnyard Babies, 165
for new ventures, 162
Marketing, 85
Masculinity, 88
Maslow's hierarchy of needs, 465
Master production schedules, 741
Materials resource planning
II system, 739
Matrix organization, 373
McClelland's learned needs
theory, 470
Mechanistic organization, 362
Meetings, 556
Mentoring, 525, 534
Mergers and acquisitions
industry cultures, 620
Merit pay, 417
Message
defined, 544
nonverbal, 544
simplification, 564
Mexico, 130, 134
Middle managers, 13
Mission, 212, 220, 232
Modular corporation, 30
Monolithic organization, 630
Moral development
instrumental, 187
interpersonal, 187

law and order, 188
obedience and punishment, 186
social contract, 188
stages, 186
universal principles, 188
Moral principles, 181
Moral rights model, 192
Motivation
ability, 487
achievement motive, 470
affiliation motive, 470
affiliation needs, 466
Alderfer's ERG Theory, 467
Allstate Insurance, Co., 487
approaches, 463
autonomy, 474
behavioral view, 55
critical psychological states, 472
defined, 462
Eddie Bauer, 494
effort, 485
enhancement, 489
equity theory, 474
esteem needs, 466
Etec Systems, 484
Eudora, 462
existence needs, 466
expectancy, 484
expectancy theory, 483
experienced meaningfulness, 472
experienced responsibility, 472
extinction, 480
extrinsic rewards, 488
feedback, 474
frustration-regression hypothesis, 467
goal-setting theory, 482
growth need strength, 474
Hackman-Oldham job characteristics model, 473
Herzberg's two-factor theory, 471
hierarchy of needs, 466
hygiene factors, 471
incentives, 59
independence, 152
individual differences, 464
inequity, 476
initiative, 54
instrumentality, 485
integrated model, 464, 483
intrinsic rewards, 488
job characteristics, 473
job context, 464
job design, 489
job enrichment, 472
knowledge of results, 472
Lanier Office Products, 495
Learned Needs Theory, 470
lifestyle venture, 160
management by objectives, 483
managers' behaviors, 464, 477
Maslow's Hierarchy of Needs, 465
motivator factors, 471
need, 465
need for achievement, 151
negative reinforcement, 480
Nortel, 478
organization context, 464, 471
performance management, 488
personality traits, 487
physiological needs, 466
positive reinforcement, 479
power motive, 470
punishment, 480
quality view, 67
reinforcement theory, 477
relatedness needs, 467
remuneration, 54
rewards, 474
role perceptions, 488
satisfaction-progression hypothesis, 467
security needs, 466
self-actualization needs, 466
self-confidence, 152
skill variety, 473
task identity, 473

teams, 59
valence, 486
Valassis Communications, 495
Work Motivation Questionnaire, 468
Motivator factors, 471
Multiculturalism
(see also Workforce diversity)
Avon Products, 644
Multicultural organization, 33
Multidisciplinary work team, 581
Multidomestic strategy, 122
Multinational corporation, 117
Multiple scenarios, 288

Narratives, 617
Natural duty principle, 196
Needs
achievement motive, 470
affiliation, 466, 470
Bronx Business Breakfast Club, 553
defined, 465
network groups, 641
Networks
employee, 552
esteem, 466
existence, 467
growth, 467
growth need strength, 474
physiological, 466
power motive, 470
relatedness, 467
security, 466
self-actualization, 466
Negative reinforcement, 480
Negotiations, 102
bargaining power, 234
bartering, 119
collective bargaining, 393
communication, 19
compensation, 419
customers, 234
Hankins, Anthony Mark, 524
organizational change, 442
suppliers, 234
Network organization, 376
defined, 31
spin-off strategy, 172
Thermo-Electron, 172
New ventures
failure, 148
finance, 163
global, 164
growth, 165
lifestyle ventures, 160
market research, 161
National Association of Young Venture
Capitalists, 174
small ventures, 159
starting, 159
Nigeria, 127
Nonexempt employees, 393
Nonroutine service technologies, 368
Nonverbal messages, 544
Norms
cultural, 617
ethics, 205
free riding, 593
teams, 591
North American Free Trade Agreement
defined, 130
Body Shop, 212
Wal-Mart, 202

Objective probability, 258
Occupational Safety and Health Act, 192
Office technologies, 720
Open system, 61
Operations management
agile strategy, 719
automation, 671
Baldrige framework, 730
bar code, 721
benchmarking, 301
Boeing, 745
Cinnabar, California, 724

Photo Credits